The History of the Silk Road

The Land & Maritime Routes

Liu Yingsheng

translated by Hu Caohan

CANUT INTERNATIONAL PUBLISHERS

Istanbul - Berlin - London - Santiago

The publication is authorized by Jiangsu People's Publishing House Ltd., China.
The publication is funded by

B&R Book Program

The History of the Silk Road. The Land & Maritime Routes
Written by Liu Yingsheng
Translated by Hu Caohan
Original Title: 丝绸之路 / ISBN: 9787214139511
Copyright © Jiangsu People's Publishing House Ltd., October, 2014.

Canut International Publishers
Canut Intl. Turkey, Teraziler Cad. No.29. Sancaktepe, Istanbul, Turkey
Canut Intl. Germany, Heerstr. 266, D-47053, Duisburg, Germany
Canut Intl. United Kingdom, 12a Guernsay Road, London E11 4BJ, UK
Copyright © Canut International Publishers, 2018
ISBN: 978-605-9914-75-8
Printed in UK
Lightning Source Ltd. UK
Chapterhouse, Pitfield Kiln Farm
MK11 3LW
United Kingdom
www.canutbooks.com

About the Author

Professor Liu Yingsheng, 1947. He received Master's degree in history from Nanjing University in 1981 and a doctoral degree in history from the Chinese Academy of Social Sciences in 1985. Liu Yingsheng has served as the president of China Yuan Dynasty History Research Institute, vice-president of China Mongolian History Study Institute and the deputy director of China Maritime Studies Institute and China Mongolian Studies Institute.

He represented China to participate the UNESCO-organized expeditions of The Marine Silk Road, the Prairie Silk Road and The Nomadic/Altay Road, leaving footprints in the countries of Italy, Greece, Turkey, Egypt, Oman, Pakistan, India, Sri Lanka, Malaysia, Indonesia, Thailand, Brunei, Philippines, Russia, Turkmenistan, Uzbekistan, Tajikistan, Kyrgyzstan, Kazakhstan and Mongolia.

He specializes in the research on the history of Mongolia and Yuan dynasty, continental Asia, nationalities in Northwest China, Islamic culture in China and Sino-foreign relationships, and he is versed in several languages. His representative works include Study of the History of Chagatai Khanate, The Silk Road Culture-The Marine Silk Road Volume, The Silk Road Culture-The Prairie Silk Road Volume, New Twenty-Five Dynastic Histories-Yuan History, A Study of Hui Hui Guan Za Zi and Hui Hui Guan Yi Yu and The Sea Route and the land Route: a study of exchanges between the East and the West in the Middle Ages. His representative translated works include Sammlungen historischer Nachrichten ber die mongolischen Völkerschaften (co-translator) and Civilizations History of Central Asia (Vol. IV: The Age of Achievement: AD 750 to the End of the 15th century: The Achievements).

Publisher's Note

This book is a meticulous work by renowned scholar, Liu Yingsheng who has spent years in the research of history of the Silk Road. The book consists of two parts as: the land Silk Road and the maritime Silk Road, which includes 14 chapters, totally. With the following words Liu Yingsheng offers a clear view of communications among civilizations when studying the history of the Silk Road: "Civilization centers of the world have both developed separately and connected with each other directly and indirectly. A number of ancient human communities are dotted among the aforesaid civilization centers and linked with each other like a chain. Geographically speaking, China was an isolated territory in Eurasia. But ancient Chinese knew that there were brilliant cultures in the remote West. The fairy tale on Xiwangmu (Queen Mother of the West) reflects ancient Chinese people's desire to other civilizations. Hence, despite of the remoteness and distance, humankind had travelled an arduous and long way for communications. Nomadic peoples living in the Eurasia Steppes had maintained a natural economic and cultural link with their neighboring Southern agricultural peoples, and meanwhile, relying on their fast steeds, played as a liaison the for East-West civilization communications for several thousand years."

In this book, Liu Yingsheng has reviewed the original valuable historical materials preserved, in China, also those historical materials written by close neighbours of China in the old history, like Hui, Uyghur, Mongols, Arabs, Persia and utilized many other researches made by Western scholars. The book includes, more than 1,400 direct and indirect references given by world famous scholars.

The book with high academic value, not only comprehensively reflects the current research level of researches on the history of Silk Road in the Chinese academy, but also promotes academic exchanges among the world's scholars who study the magnificent heritage of civilization. We hope the book can further promote the academic dialogue and exchange among the scholars of history across the world. Lastly, we present our cordial thanks to the leaders and editors of the Jiangsu People's Publishing, especially to editors, Wang Baoding, Peng Xiaolu, Wang Tian, Li Hongyun, who have greatly contributed to the realization of the English version of the book.

Daivja Jindal,
April, 2018
London, UK

Contents

PART ONE

THE LAND SILK ROAD

Introduction

The Silk Road originates from the mutual attraction of the civilization centers of humankind. China is situated in the East of the Eurasia, with its cultural center in the basins of the Yellow River and the Yangtze River. Eurasia and Africa, collectively called the old world, are the birthplaces and cradles of human civilization. In addition to Chinese civilization, during the period from about 4999 BC to 3000 BC, several civilization centers developed separately at different sites of the old continents, i.e. the ancient Egyptian civilization at the middle and lower reaches of the Nile in Northern Africa, the Mesopotamia civilization by the Euphrates and the Tigris rivers in Western Asia, and the ancient civilization at the middle reach of the Indus in current Pakistan. To the East and South of China is the Pacific Ocean. The limited acreage and population of Japan and the islands in Western Pacific and Southeast Asia determine that they cannot evolve into civilization centers having major influence to humankind's history.

The geographical layout of the said civilization centers have determines the inter-civilizational communications in the ancient times mainly the cultural exchanges between the East and the West. These ancient civilization centers were detached by mountains, deserts, rivers and seas. The Yellow River and the Yangtze River originate from the Bayan Har Mountains, a branch of the Kunlun Mountains in the Qinghai-Tibet Plateau which is the natural border of China and India. Then, crossing the Yellow River Westward you will meet the Gansu Corridor, a narrow channel between the Qilian Mountains at the Northern border of the Qinghai-Tibet Plateau and the grand deserts. At the end of the Gansu Corridor is the lofty Tianshan Mountains, measuring several thousand km. in length. Moving Northward from the Central Plainss, you will see the Mongolian Plateau soon after overpassing the Yinshan Mountains. Stretching from the

North of the Mongolian Plateau and the Tianshan Mountains Westward is the vast Eurasia Steppes. In the South of the Tianshan Mountains and the Eurasia Steppes are the oases, extending from Gansu and Xinjiang of China Westward to the East coast of the Mediterranean sea and North Africa.

The civilization centers both developed separately and connected with each other directly and indirectly. A number of ancient human communities are dotted among the aforesaid civilization centers and linked with each other like a chain. Geographically speaking, China is an isolated territory in Eurasia. But ancient Chinese knew that there were brilliant cultures in the remote West. The fairy tale on Xiwangmu (Queen Mother of the West) reflects ancient Chinese people's desire to other civilizations. Hence, despite of the remoteness and distance, humankind had travelled an arduous and long way for communications. Nomadic peoples living in the Eurasia Steppes had maintained a natural economic and cultural link with their neighboring Southern agricultural peoples, and meanwhile, relying on their fast steeds, played as a liaison for East-West civilization communications for several thousand years.

Moving Westward from the Yellow River basin along the land route, you can see several Westward routes at the end of the Gansu Corridor. One route, moving towards Southwest of the Lop Nur and along the Southern border of the Taklimakan Desert, extends westward to the Pamirs. The other route, moving towards Northeast of the Lop Nur and along the southern slope of the Tianshan Mountains Westward via the Southeast end of the mountains, also reaches the Pamirs. These two routes, and the route from current Hongqilafu Mountain to Kashmir and South Asia, or from the Pamirs to the Fergana Valley (at the boundary of current Tajikistan, Uzbekistan and Kyrgyzstan) and then Westward to the oases between the Syr Darya and the Amu Darya, are all the routes along the oases in the desert.

Another route started from the Gansu Corridor extended Westward via Hami, then extended Northwestward to the Steppes in the North of the Tianshan Mountains. Along the North slope of the Tianshan Mountains, the route crossed the basins of the Ili River, the Chui River and the Talas (Taraz) River. Then the route extended Westward and crossing over the Syr Darya river, reaching the arable region in the North bank of the Amu Darya, or turned to Southward extend to South Asia via current Afghanistan, or turned Westward to the Mediterranean region via current Turkmenistan, Iran and Iraq. The route could also turn Northwestward proceeded downwards along the Syr Darya river to the Eurasia Steppes then Westward to the Eastern Europe.

Several routes Northward from the Central Plains lead to the Mongolian Steppes. Northward crossing the desert, the route comes to the Mongolian Plateau. The route further leads to current Lake Baikal, if Northward, or to East Europe and if Westward along the forest regions by current Trans-Siberian Railway, or Westward overpasses the Mount Hangayn, then goes Westward along the Altay Mountains, turns to South to the Steppes in the North of the

Tianshan Mountains, moves the Ili River along the north slope of the Tianshan Mountains, then crosses the Chui River, the Talas River to the Syr Darya, then downward to the Aral Sea, along its Northern coast Westward, and crosses the Ural River the Volga River and arrives at the north coast of the Black Sea.

1. The long march along the land Silk Road

In 1988, UNESCO initiated the "World Cultural Development Decade" program including the major project "Silk Road: A Comprehensive Study on the Road of Communications" to be implemented till 1997. The purpose of the initiative was to enable people to learn the importance of international communications in the history, help them review the history of Silk Road and encourage scholars of various countries to study this trade and cultural road which had benefited people from different civilizations and boosted mutual understandings and exchanges among them. To sum up, it aimed to promote the world peace. The program also aimed to encourage and support the countries along the Silk Road to further cherish and strive to protect the national cultural heritages of their own. Official organizations from more than 30 countries, and many renowned cultural institutions including the British Museum, the State Hermitage Museum, the Metropolitan Museum of Art and the State Museum, Berlin, have participated in this project.

In the late Spring and early Summer, 1991, entrusted by China UNESCO National Committee, I attended the world-known Central Asia land Silk Road Expedition. The journey covered 13,000 km. and was completed in two months. We traveled across the ancient civilization centers, such as, Khorasan, Khwarezmia, Sogdiana, Bactria, Khuttal, Suduishana, Ferghana (Dayuan), Shāsh, Edala, Talas (Taraz), Tokmok, Bishkek, Burana, Suyab, Nevaket, Rehai, which are located in the five Central Asian republics, namely, Turkmenistan, Uzbekistan, Tajikistan, Kyrgyzstan and Kazakhstan. Scholars and news media from more than 20 countries including Afghanistan, China, Egypt, France, Germany, India, Iran, Israel, Italy, Japan, Korea, Mongolia, Pakistan, Philippines, Poland, Switzerland, Turkey, Thailand, the Netherland, the UK, the USA, Canada and the former Soviet Union, have participated this expedition. Scholars, mainly archeologists, also included historians, art history experts, Buddhism scholars, Zoroastrianism scholars, agricultural history experts, geographers, cartographic experts, experts on Turkic studies, Mongolian studies, Arab and Iranian studies as well as anthropologists. Specific routes of the Land Silk Road Expedition are as following.

Phase I, starting point: Turkmenistan capital Ashgabat → Merv (capital of the Merv State) → Charyn (capital of Charyn state) → Char (Charyn state) → Charyn → Dashoguz (capital of Dashoguz) → The Republic of Uzbekistan→ Nukus (capital of The Autonomous Republic of Karakalpakstan) → Urgench (capital of Khorezm Province) → Khorezm (Khorezm Province) → Bukhara (capital of Bukhara Province) → Shakhrisabz (Qashqadaryo Province) → Termez (Surkhandarya Province) → The Republic of Tajikistan

→ Kurgan-tube (capital of Kurgan-tube Province) → Kulyab (the captial of Kulyab Province) → Dushanbe (capital of The Republic of Tajikistan) → The Republic of Uzbekistan → Surkhan (Surkhandarya Province) → Termez → Shakhrisabz → Samarqand (capital of Samarqand Province) → The Republic of Tajikistan → Panjikand (Khujand (Leninabad) Province) → go back to The Republic of Uzbekistan → Samarqand→ The Republic of Tajikistan → Ura-tyube (Khujand Province) → Khujand (capital of Khujand Province) → pass Fergana Province of The Republic of Uzbekistan → the Republic of Kyrgyzstan → Osh (capital of Osh Province) → Uzgen (Osh Province) →Osh → The Republic of Uzbekistan → Andizhan (the capital of Andizhan Province) → Namagan (capital of Namagan Province) → The Republic of Tajikistan→ Khujand Province → The Republic of Uzbekistan → Syrdaria → Tashkent (capital of The Republic of Uzbekistan).

Phase II, start pointing: Tashkent → enter into The Republic of Kazakhstan → Shimkent (capital of Shimkent Province) → Otrar (Shimkent Province) → Turkestan (Shimkent Province) → Shimkent (Shimkent Province) →Shimkent → Zhambyl (capital of Zhambyl Province) → Melkite (Zhambyl Province) → enter into The Republic of Kyrgyzstan → Bishkek (capital of The Republic of Kyrgyzstan whose old name is Frunze) → Burana (Balasagun region, Bishkek) → Ak-Beshim (Tokmok, Bishkek) → Krasnoyarsk (Bishkek) → Milyanfan (Bishkek) → Bishkek → Cholponata (Issyk-Kul Province) → enter into The Republic of Kazakhstan → Kegen (Almaty) → Panfilov (Taldyqorghan) → Khorgos (Taldyqorghan)→Almaty (capital of The Republic of Kazakhstan)→ Issykqorghan (Almaty) → Almaty → Mount Athos (Zhambyl Province) → Almaty.

From July 10th to August 5th of 1992, I was entrusted by China UNESCO National Commitee once again to attend the Altay-Nomadic Silk Road Expedition, which was jointly held by UNESCO and the Mongolian government. The start point of is Khovd, an important city in the Western Mongolia and the end point is the capital of Mogolia, Ulan Bator. The Expedition took about one month, and the distance of travel was about 4,000 km., surpassing 7 provinces of Mongolia including Khovd Province in the Western and middle Mogolia, Altay Province in the Gobi, Zavkhan Province, Arkhangai Province, Övörkhangai Province, Buergen Province and Central Province.

UNESCO proposed the expedition plan of Altay when making decision about the name of Silk Road Expedition and the purpose of the expedition was to explore the relation between different peoples of which people speak Altaic language. The reason for proposing the Expedition is that the language used by the peoples in Northern Asia and Northeast Asia is classified as the Altaic language family by Finnish scholar, Ramstedt, Russian American scholar, Poppe and other linguists. Altaic language family includes Turkic language group, Mongolian language group and Manchu-Tungusic language group, even some scholars classify Korean and Japanese into Altaic language family. The so-called Altaic language family is just a hypothesis developed from the last century and there are a few linguists doubt it and they believe that basic vocabulary of various languages in Altaic language family have different sources and long-term mutual effect and borrowing lead to the common features and contents of these languages. Even so, the Expedition is named as Altay-Nomadic Silk Road Expedition.

Totally, except 10 scholars from Mongolia, there were 44 foreign scholars from more than 20 countries attending the Expedition including Azerbaijan, China, Egypt, Finland, France, Germany, India, Iran, Israel, Japan, The Republic of Kyrgyzstan, Korea, Norway, Pakistan, Poland, Romania, Russia, Switzerland, Turkey, the UK and the USA. Experts of different subjects attended the Expedition, including history, archaeology, linguistics, geography, anthropology, economics, sociology, medical history, art history, weapon history and museology. News reporter, photo reporter, newspaper reporter, radio reporter and TV reporter from worldwide and Mongolia followed the group of this Expedition. Reporters from Xinhua News Agency, China Pictorial and CCTV also followed the group. Staff of UNESCO, Mongolian organizers, interpreters, security guard, service staff and drivers attended this Expedition, totally the number is more than 100.

The route of the Expedition is: Ulan Bator → Khovd → Khar Us Noor → Khovd → Mankhan Sum Tsenkher → Chandmani → Dorgon Noor → Khukhmorit → Bayan Uul → Jargalan Sum → Taishir Khunkher → Zabkhan → West slope of Mount Hangayn, Zavkhan Province → Uliasutai→ Chingeltai → Tosonchegel → Ider → Ih Uul → Arkhangai Province → Khorgo Sum Terkhin Tchagan Noor → Tariat Sum → Ih Tamir → Tsetserleg → Khotont → Övörkhangai Province → Ordu Baliq → Kharkhorin → Arkhangai Province → Khushuu Tsaidam[1] → southward to Uhaa Hudag → Erdene Sant → Khugenkhan → Eastward into the Central Province → arrival at the end point, Ulan Bator.

5

2. Nomadic Peoples in Chinese and Asian histories

(1) Steppes peoples and Chinese history

Talking about China and ancient history of China,what kind of image will come to your mind? Someone will think about the Yellow River, Central Plains, Homo erectus lantianensis, Homo erectus pekinensis, Upper Ages Cave Man, Yangshao Culture, Longshan Culture, Xia-shang-zhou Dynasties and so on. This kind of answer is right; however, it is not a complete answer. It is known that Homo erectus yuanmouensis which boosts longer history than Homo erectus lantianensis and Homo erectus pekinensis was found in Yunnan Province, the southwestern border region of China, rather than Central Plains. But there is no doubt about Homo erectus yuanmouensis in Chinese history. In

---

1 Khushuu Tsaidam is the sacred memorial complex dedicated to Bilge khan of Turkic empire, which flourished during the 6th-8th century, and his younger brother Kul-tegin is situated 40km Northeast from Karakorum and 20km East from Ordubalik in Khashaat Soum, Arkhangai province.

other words, we cannot just focus on the Yellow River Basin and the Central Plains when talking about history of China. We should recognize the diversity of Chinese cultural origin.

After we entered into an era of recording the history by script writing, it has been easier to find the contribution made by ethnic minority peoples who have different ancestors with the Han nationality to the history of China. Till now, people of Han nationality live in an region which is less than half of the national territory region while ethnic minorities lived in the vast regions of current China. History of China does not only include the history of Han nationality (currently majority in China), but also history of ethnic minorities and people who lived in the border regions, which are all component parts of Chinese history. Although, there were changes in China's territories, people from the Han nationality have taken the Central Plains as the base region for their dynasties. Relations between dynasties which were established by the Han nationality and kingdoms of minority nationalities have kept changing, sometimes rulers of Han nationality have extended their rule to neighbouring regions and created the great unity of Chinese people. However, minority nationalities have maintained their kingdoms in the Central Plains. Thus, it is impossible to narrate history of China without mentioning the history of ethnic minorities and people living in the border regions.

Historians recognized the significance and status of the history of ethnic minorities when ethnic peoples in the border regions had frequent interactions with the people of Han nationality. But sometimes things become complex when rulers of Han nationality were as powerful as the governors of ethnic minorities in the border region and rulers of Han nationality only were in charge of the mainland while governors of ethnic groups established local separatist powers in neighouring regions. Territories of ethnic peoples in border regions had even passed the borders of Current China. People of ethnic minorities living in the border regions interacted with the people in the neighbouring countries and also people who lived in the mainland of China. Consequently, how to treat the relationship between history of minorities and history of China has been an important theoretical and practical issue. China, as a multi-ethnic and multi-national country, enjoys a long history of thousands of years. Its mutual interactions with numerous ethnic peoples has started since the ancient times. As a great power in the world, exchanges between China and other neighbouring countries and other ethnic minorities in Europe and Asia have a long history. Looking from the perspective of the development of ethnic minorities, the great family of nationalities and the study of development history of Silk Road, the history of kingdoms established minority nationalities in the border regions is a component part of history of China and it is also the study object of Chinese history, what's more, it is the study object of world history and Asian history.

Descendants of the Yan and Yellow emperors together with descendants of the Dragon (metaphor for the Chinese nation) are the two other names of Chinese people. However, it is not suitable to refer to all the members of the great family of nationalities in China. Some historians admitted that ethnic minorities in the border region were descendants of Yellow Emperor and Xia Yu (an emperor of ancient China). While it seems that ethnic minorities in neighbouring region immigrated from the Central Plains. By conducting further study on ethnology and linguistics, we found that this kind of proposal is groundless. Ethnic and blood origin of ethnic minorities in China are different. The reason why various ethnic peoples treated each other as a family of nationalities is that they were born on the same land, interacting with each other and jointly creating the history of China.

Ethnic peoples of Southern China were scattered regionally and their forces were limited, therefore they had fewer effect on the overall course of Chinese history due to the influence of geographical and other factors. On the contrary, those ethnic peoples which dwelled in the steppes of Northern China were different, they were quite powerful and effective, which made them influential on the Central Plains region and all China in the history.

Totally, there were seven powerful dynasties in the long history of China since when the Qin dynasty was established in 221 AD till the Revolution of 1911, against the rule of Qing dynasty. The Qin Dynasty was the first imperial dynasty of China, lasting from 221 to 206 BC. Conquering the six other states, Yingzheng became the First Emperor of Qin. Qin Dynasty was the first unified, multi-national and power-centralized state in the Chinese history.

The seven successive dynasties included the Qin, Eastern and Western Dynasties, Tang Dynasty, Yuan Dynasty, Ming Dynasty and Qing Dynasty. Among these seven dynasties, Yuan and Qing were established and ruled respectively by the Mongol nationality and Manchu nationality which were both Northern ethnic peoples. Yuan Dynasty existed for 162 years after its establishment by Genghis Khan in 1206 which was overthrown by the Ming Dynasty in 1368. And the Qing Dynasty, established by Manchu nationality lasted for 267 years, from 1644 to 1911. Duration of these two dynasties were 429 years, accounting more than one fifth of the history of 2,110 years from the unity realized by by the Qin Dynasty (221 BC) to the collapse of the Qing Dynasty (1911).

Northern ethnic peoples once played an important role in the two stand-offs in Chinese history. The Western Jin Dynasty collapsed after short-term unification of China when the Sima family put an end to the situation of the Three Kingdoms warring among them. Consequently, China once fell into the situation of division for more than 270 years, beginning with the year 316 AD. The majority of the "Sixteen Kingdoms" which were hostile to the Eastern Jin Dynasty and the Northern Dynasties—including the Northern Wei Dynasty, the Eastern Wei Dynasty, the Western Wei Dynasty, the Northern Qi Dynasty and the Northern Zhou Dynasty—and the Northern Dynasties which fought against the Southern Dynasties were both established by Northern ethnic peoples. However, during the period since the collapse of Tang Dynasty in 907 to the unification of China by Yuan Dynasty in 1276, China again fell into a situation of division for more than 370 years.

Five generations of the Late Tang Dynasty and the Late Han Dynasty were established by the Shatuo tribe of the Western Turkic people. According to historical records in historical materials, the rulers of Late Jin Dynasty, were also the offsprings of Northern ethnic peoples. The Five Dynasties period, from the perishment of the Tang Dynasty to the founding of the Northern Song, took 53 years. The total existence time of the Later Tang, Later Jin and Later Han—these three of the Five Dynasties—was more than 26 years.

Although the two Song dynasties including the Northern and Southern Song dynasties claimed to have prosperous economic and cultural periods in Chinese history, they were always under the oppression of the strong neighbors of Liao, Jin, Xixia and Mongol peoples in the Northern China and could not breathe freely.

From the above narration, it is easy to find that the Northern ethnic peoples have ruled the Northern China and the whole mainland China for more than 650 years during the two eras of standoffs between the Northern China and Southern China.

We discussed the dynasties established by Northern ethnic peoples and the period of time during which all over China or Northern China was controlled by Northern ethnic peoples. In this way, we have aimed demonstrate the impact of Northern ethnic peoples on the history of China. Also we can explain this issue from another perspective: the Twenty-Four Histories are a series of comprehensive history books written in a biographical style, which are regarded as the Chinese official historical books covering a period from 3000 BC to the Ming Dynasty in the 17th century. Regional and nationwide dynasties established by Northern ethnic peoples are recorded in various history books: the Twenty-Four Histories including History of Wei, History of the Northern Dynasties, History of Northern Qi, History of Zhou, Old History of the Five Dynasties, New History of the Five Dynasties, History of Liao, History of Jin and History of Yuan. The books and histories recording history of Northern ethnic peoples take more than one third of the Twenty-Four Histories, which also reflects the impact of these Northern ethnic peoples on the history of China.

The impact of Northern ethnic peoples on the history of China is not limited to the fact that Northern ethnic peoples extended their territory to the regions where people of Han nationality lived and established nationwide and regional dynasties. Northern ethnic peoples played a significant role in the historical development of China even when rulers of Han nationality established their dynasties, taking manpower and material resources of Han people as backup and incorporating neighboring ethnic peoples.

Qin Shihuang, the First Emperor of the Qin Dynasty, ordered the building the Great Wall to defend against Xiongnu, which run out of manpower at that time and which caused a severe social crisis. People of Han Dynasty defeated the Hun and set up the Duhufu (Protectorate of the Western Regions), a military garrison in the border region to supervise and check the neighboring ethnic peoples. Anxi Duhufu, which was set up in Tang Dynasty period, is regarded as the symbol indicating the most prosperous and powerful social situation at that time, also it is regarded as the turning point after which social development entered a stagnant period. Government of the Tang Dynasty expanded its territory into the hinterland of Eurasia Steppes after defeating the Western Turkic Khanate and Eastern Turkic Khanate at the beginning of the Tang Dynasty. Development of agricultural economy was limited at that time since modern industry was not yet there. Hence, feudal dynasties established by people of the Han nationality on the basis of manpower and material resources of Han nationality could not maintain its dominant position when faced by the Northern ethnic peoples in terms of comprehensive strength which included economic and military strength. However, those nomadic peoples who became the ruling forces of the vast Steppes, besides they learnt agricultural production technology from Han nationality and from other agricultural peoples in the neighborhood and also occupied some agricultural regions. They become as strong as those people who lived in the Central Plains and even became more powerful.

When the Tang Dynasty entered into an era of rapid development, Tubo, the Tibetan regime in ancient China and Dashi, ethnic group in Western Asia gradually became strong. Confrontation among three different regimes was established then. Three khanates were established on the Mongolian Plateau respectively by the people of Turkic, Uyghur and Xiajiesi[2], i.e., the three ethnic peoples. People of nomadic tribes who spoke Turkic played an intermediary role between ethnic peoples in Eastern Mongolian Plateau and Western Central Asia steppes.

Complex inland Asian-international relationship between the Tang Dynasty and other dynasties was established due to the co-existence of several powers, which gave birth to Westward Turkification and Eastward Islamization in Central Asia.

An Shi Rebellion in the Tang Dynasty period has been the turning point after which it began to encounter a fall from its zenith of strength. And An Shi Rebellion indicated the change of comprehensive strength comparison between Northern ethnic peoples and the Han nationality in the Tang Dynasty. Government of the Tang Dynasty lost its control over the Central Asia and suppressed the An Shi Rebellion with the help of Uyghur troops. Strength comparison between Northern ethnic peoples and the Han nationality kept

---

2   Xiajiesi people, the Yenisei Kyrgyz people, Yenisei Kyrgyz may perhaps be correlated to the Tashtyk culture. They were known as Jiegu or Xiajiasi in Chinese historical texts, by the fall of the Gokturk empire in the 8th century CE, the Yenisei Kirghiz had established their own thriving state based on the Gokturk model.

continuing after the An Shi Rebellion. Ancient China was divided into several parts due to political and economic improvement of Northern ethnic peoples. There were Five Dynasties in the north and Ten States in the South. When the Song Dynasty was established, China was divided into several parts. Qidan and Jurchen were in charge of the North and the South respectively. Regimes were established by ethnic peoples in the Northwest including Western Xia, Tubo, Gaochang Uyghur, Yutian, Hala and Western Liao. The foundation of the Mongolian Empire which stretched over the Eurasia is the first culmination indicating the fact that strength of northern ethnic peoples is more powerful than that of the Han nationality.

Mongolian rulers were expelled from the Central Plains after the downfall of the Yuan Dynasty, but regimes in the North still posed great threat and challenge to the Ming Dynasty. The Government of Ming Dynasty moved its capital to Beijing to defend against those regimes in the North. However, the Tumu Crisis indicated that moving political center to the North could restrict the development of Oirats, an ethnic group in the North. In the late Ming Dynasty, Manchu became stronger and powerful outside the Shanhaiguan Pass and then controlled over the mainland of China. It can be seen that Northern ethnic peoples maintained a more favorable position than the Han nationality in terms of comprehensive strength. There were two nationwide dynasties established by northern ethnic peoples in the pre-modern times, a time period from the Song Dynasty to the Opium War[3]. Nevertheless, these facts were inevitable, rather than being accidental.

Part of the regions where Northern ethnic peoples in ancient China used to live were included in the map of People's Republic of China and currently, Northern ethnic peoples still live in the Northeast, Inner Mongolia, Ningxia, Gansu, Qinghai, Tibet and Xinjiang. People of Northern ethnic peoples are the major developers of the border regions in the North and Northwest. We enjoy and boast vast land and abundant natural resources nowadays since those Northern ethnic peoples people joined the big family of all ethnic peoples of China. The same as people of the Han nationality, Nomadic peoples in the North are also the creators of the history of China.

(2) Nomadic culture and the agricultural culture

Relationship between nomadic peoples and Han nationality is typical, the former live in Northern China and neighboring region and the latter live in Central Plains. Historical relationship between nomadic peoples and settled nationalities can be also found in other regions. Nomadic peoples including many Northern ethnic peoples in China interacted and communicated with settled peoples in Central Asia which is to the West of China. Thus it can be concluded that Northern ethnic peoples once played an important role in Asian history and the world history.

---

3   The Opium Wars were the two wars in the mid-19th century involving Anglo-Chinese disputes which targeted China's sovereignty. The disputes included the First Opium War (1839–1842) and the Second Opium War (1856-1860).

Landform of Asia had changed tens of millions of years ago due to orogenic movement of the Himalaya Mountains after which Qinghai-Tibet Plateau, Hindukush Mountains and Iranian Plateau were formed. Vast desert region was created in the middle of Asian continent since warm and wet airflows from the Indian Ocean were blocked by the plateaus and mountains. Inland rivers were formed by melting snow from high mountains due to long distance from the ocean. These inland rivers include Tarim River in Xinjiang Province, Syr Darya and Amu Darya in Central Asia and Morghab River which flows through Afghanistan and Turkmenistan. Oases are formed in the regions where these inland rivers flow through and sandbanks penetrate. Oases inside Asia are distributed in the middle of Eurasia in the bead-like pattern, stretching from the Hexi Corridor in the East to the desert near the Mediterranean. People in the ancient times irrigated by water diversion and took cereal as food, making clothes by weaving, burning soil for pottery and developing handicraft industry. Thus agricultural regions and villages are formed, together with those plains near the basins of rivers, being regarded as the cradle of agricultural culture. These oases are densely-populated as a result of stable environment. The size of oases varies with the abudancy of water source, however, even the largest oasis is not self-sufficient and people needed to trade materials for living necessities. People who lived in the oases inside Asia formed a habit of trading and they acted as the communicator between the East and the West in the past thousands of years.

Eurasia Steppes is located to the North of desert wherein lies the oasis regions, stretching from the Greater Khingan Mountains to the Black Sea. High latitude and few natural rainfall make Eurasia Steppes unsuitable for planting agriculture. Although there are mountains, nomadic people can migrate. Living environment is life-threatening due to hot summer and cold winter, however, nomadic people have adapted to this natural environment, making a living by hunting, herding and capturing. They domesticated wild herbivores and migrated along the water sources, by considering seasonal changes. Their livestock included cows, sheep, horses and camel. There were sheep and goats, the former originated from wild argalis and the former originated from wild goats. Camels consist of single-hump camels and two-humped camels. Single-hump camels live in the Near East where it is hot while two-humped camels can live in the Eurasia Steppes where it is cold in winter. Nomadic people took dairy products and meat as food and made clothes by animal fur. They used fermented milk to make various food and drinks, making fur warm and slight by tanning, making sheep and camel wool into threads, carpets and all kinds of other textiles by spinning or making them into felt blankets by rolling and pulling. In addition, they used felt blankets to establish yurts for residence. It is easy to disassemble and install the yurts, which makes it convenient to move. They made vehicles by lumbering and used these wooden vehicles to carry living necessities when migrate. They made weapons by forging iron and made their bows from wood.

Han nationality coexisted with nomadic peoples in the Mongolian Steppes on the base of contradictory relations. Relations between nomadic people in Eurasia Steppes and residents in the desert oases has been the same, relying on each other and being in mutual opposition. On the one hand, residents living in the oases needed fur and woolen knitwear to protect from cold, and they preferred to eat needed the meat like beef and mutton and dairy products to feed themselves also they needed war horses for battle. On the other hand, nomadic people needed food, textile and other handicrafts to make a living. People did not have the idea of equality after entering into the age of civilization. Tribes in the oases would extend their power to the neighboring oases when they were strong and powerful, thus forced the nomadic peoples in the North to submit to themselves. Nomadic people would invade the oasis regions when they got strong. These two parties exchange products by trading in peacetime while they grabbed each other's belongings by force in wartime. Residents in the oases and nomadic peoples used to exchange the materials they got with other ethnic peoples through their own transportation and marketing channels. They acted as the intermediaries of exchanges of material civilization and culture between the East and the West.

Nomadic peoples have kept moving. Not only nomadic peoples in inner Asia had impact on oases, but nomadic peoples living at the border region in China migrated to Central Asia and settled there and established their regimes, living and multiplying. Migration of ethnic peoples took place several times in the history. People often talk about how China affects the history of Asia and the world, however, the activity and mobility of nomadic peoples from Northern Steppes is an indication of China's effect on the history of Asia and the world.

Chapter 1. Origin of the Land Silk Road

1. Emergence of the textile industry

Natural silk industry was exclusive to ancient China. Silk products made in China were popular and attractive to people all over the world for a long time. When I was on the trip of Land Silk Road expedition which was launched by UNESCO in Uzbekistan in 1991, Askarov, an archaeologist and academician from Uzbekistan Academy of Sciences proclaimed that they discovered silk products of the 16th century BC in Uzbekistan and he has argued that silk had originated from Central Asia. But Askarov did not show samples of the silk products to us and also could not provide evidence of his conclusion about the creation time of the mentioned silk products. His argument was contradictory with our documented records and archaeological findings. It is recorded in the Great Tang Records on the Western Regions, a famous geographical book, that silkworm industry was introduced to western regions from inland China of Central Plains regions.

People in ancient China were the first ones to domesticate silkworm. According to the folklore, Leizu whose family name was Xiling, wife of the Yellow Emperor, was the first person to teach people silkworm breeding and silk making for clothing. People used to accredit great creation and innovation to certain sage until they understand their history scientifically. Nevertheless, silk industry was not developed by a certain person, it was the outcome of productive activities of ancestors of Chinese people in the past thousands of years and it was developed on the base of accumulated experience of such productive activities. Such legend indicates that silkworm industry started from China in ancient times.

Archaeological achievements of the 20th century make us re-recognize the beginning period of the sericulture—silkworm—industry. Archaeologists have discovered a half silkworm cocoon which was cut by a knife in the Xinyincun Site of the Neolithic Age in Shanxi province. The cocoon is 15.2 mm in length and 7.1 mm in width.[1]

Such discovery indicates that ancestors of Chinese nation began to domesticate wild silkworm 5,000 years ago. The silkworm cocoon which was unearthed in Xiyincun Site was once regarded as the material evidence of the beginning of silkworm industry of China.

In 1958, a batch of silk cloth produced about 4,700 years ago were unearthed in Qianshanyang Site of the Neolithic Age which existed about 5,000 years ago in Wuxing County of Zhejiang province. They were proved by scientific identification methods that the raw materials for these silk cloth pieces were domesticated silkworm silk and their weaving technology had reached certain level of development.[2]

These archaeological discoveries make us understand that local residents in everywhere of ancient China had already developed silkworm industry and used the silk of cocoon to do silk weaving.

Some chapters of Xiaxiaozheng [Explanation of the Lesser Annuary of the Xia dynasty], an agricultural almanac, are about the records of silkworm breeding. Those chapters describe that females and housewives had started to do silkworm breeding. Huangkan, a Counfucian priest in the Liang State of the Southern Dynasties interpreted the word gongshi (means daily work done by women at home) for the silkworm nurturing. It can be concluded that silkworm industry at that time was developed to a certain scale since silkworm breeding was treated as an important means of livelihood. Mulberries are necessary for silkworm breeding and there are sentences in Xiaxiaozheng and The History of Songs to describe branches pruning of mulberry.

There is pictographic script of weaving machine in oracle bone inscriptions in the Shang Dynasty and such weaving machine is the original one. Nowadays, such weaving machines are still used in some remote regions in China, for example, women of Li nationality who live in the autonomous prefecture of Li nationality and Miao nationality in Hainan province still use this old weaving machine to produce the brocade cloth of Li nationality. They sit on the ground, keeping their upper parts of the body upright, putting their feet on the crosspiece in front of the machine, holding the cloth between the crosspiece and their belts on their waists and knitting and weaving different patterns according to the images in their minds by cross-knife. The tools they use are simple but the products they made are beautiful and attractive.

1   See Historical Remains of Xiyiincun authored by Li Ji and the 3rd Edition of Research Institue of Tsinghua University published in 1927.
2   A Brief Report on Excavation in Qianshanyang, Journal of Acta Archaeologica Sinica, 1960/2, First and Second excavation reports of Qianshanyang ruins in Wuxing, Zhejiang province; Journal of Acta Archaeologica Sinica, 1960/3.

Archaeologists found pieces of silk cloth remnants on the bronze wares which were unearthed from Yinxu in Anyang, Henan province in 1950. Those silk remnants on the bronze wares survived due to the verdigris on it. The oldest silk found in China comes from the Chinese Neolithic period and is dated to about 3,630 BC, found in Henan province. After scientific analysis and examinations, it was concluded that these silk cloth pieces were produced by shadow stitch in diamond-shaped patterns and contained advanced weaving skills.[3]

This discovery indicates that weaving machines were remarkably improved and jacquard cloth could be produced. During the Shang and Zhou dynasties, some governmental departments and positions which were responsible for weaving industry issues were set up. There are written records of such governmental positions in The Rites of Zhou.

Types of silk products kept increasing and several types of silk products are recorded in historical books. Different weaving skills were created such as gum silk weaving, degummed silk weaving, simple weaving and yarn-dyed weaving. In addition, brocade silk, a kind of colorful fabric had appeared. Silk remains was found on the bronze wares which were unearthed from a tomb of the Shang Dynasty in Taixicun, Gaocheng of Hebei Province. Five kinds of silk fabric were identified from these silk remains which included fine silk fabrics, raw silk, yarn, silk gauze and crepe. Weaving techniques became more delicate, except tabby, there were twill, diversified twill, double warp, double weft and jacquard weave. There was a Qingtongyue, a battle-axe used in ancient China displaying in Swedish Far East Museum. We can find jacquard weave in diamond-shaped pattern with tabby on the residual silk on it. Silk products can be found on the bronze ware and jade ware which are displayed in the Palace Museum. On one of these wares, twill and fretwork pictures are found on the tabby and each of fretwork consists of 25 warp threads and 28 weft threads. The periphery of fretwork has thick threads which form a framework. Pictures on the fretwork are symmetrical and coordinated, well arranged and elegant. So it can be concluded that jacquard machine with multiple heddles was used in manufacturing to produce beautiful jacquard weaves. Jacquard technique is a great innovation made by people in ancient China and it is a fantastic contribution made by Chinese people to the weaving skills in the world.

15

Silk products was dyed in the Zhou Dynasty period. According to the records in the History of Diverse Crafts, a classic work on science and technology in ancient China, people used to pre-treat raw silk before dyeing. The raw silk was submerged in the limewater which was produced by calcinating shells to clear away the dirt and pectin since the limewater contained alkaline. In the daytime, the raw silk was exposed to the sun for bleaching and it was submerged into the well in the night to dissolve sericin. Such process should be repeated for several times it was important to improve the dyeing quality. Color fixing method was used to dyeing raw silk which meant submerging the raw silk into different containers with one or various dyestuff thus making the

3   Acta Archaeologica Sinica, Year 1951, Vol. 5, p. 19.

raw silk into certain colors with different color depths or various colors. If the silk was dark red then it was submerged into red dyestuff for three times. If it was submerged into black dyestuff for another two times, it would become light black with red. Finally it became dark black after being submerged into black dyestuff for two times. The silk product of the Warring States Period, tabby brocade with dragon and phoenix in shadow stitch, which was unearthed in Changsha in 1974, indicated that a sticky thickener was used to make the figures clearer and which enabled clearly contoured figures without mixing of colors.[4] Silk products were known by ethnic peoples in the neighborhood regions of China and became more and more popular. It is treated as a kind of precious treasure by people from other countries.

2. Original Primitive Cultures along the Land Silk Road

The Eurasian Steppes and its adjacent regions, these continental bridge regions linking the East with the West, were never been no man's land since the uncivilized ages of men. If we look from historical and geographical perspectives, we can comfortably say that the men's cultural sites of the Bronze Age in the Central Asian regions, adjacent to the Northwest of China, were not isolated regions, instead they were always in close interactions.

(1) Anau Culture and primitive nomadic peoples of North Asia

The representative of the early agricultural culture of Bronze Age in the Southern part of Central Asia is Anau culture, also known as Dejtun culture. Anau is a small village in Turkmenistan, located in an oasis on the side of Turkmenistan (the junction of Kopet-Dag Range and Iran). This village is 12 km to Ashgabat (current capital of Turkmenistan) in the West. In the second half of the 20th century, Russian scholars had discovered human cultural sites which could be traced back to 3000 BC, especially pottery, so they used Anau to name the same or similar primitive cultural relics in this region. Anau Culture was a kind of culture which ranged from Chalcolithic Age to Bronze Age. In the early Anau era, the locals did not know how to use potter's wheel. Although the greenwares were made by hand, they were carefully polished and colored. In 1991, I visited this site and saw the fragments of painted pottery everywhere.

After that, scholars also discovered painted pottery in China's Yangshao Cultural Site and found out that there existed some resemblances between Yangshao's painted pottery and that of Anau. Consequently, Swedish scholar Anderson put forward that Yangshao's painted pottery was influenced by the painted pottery in Central Asia, which was the famous theory of "Chinese Culture originates from the West". After the liberation in 1949, with the development of Chinese archaeology, Chinese scholars had proved that Yangshao culture was more ancient than Anau culture and even discovered Dadiwan culture appearing in 5000 BC in Gansu province, thus having showed that Chinese painted pottery developed independently.

---

4   History of China's Science and Technology, Vol. 1, ed, 1982, pp. 21-55, 60-62-115.

Having compared carefully the painted pottery in China with that in Anau, it could be found that although they were both painted with geometric forms, the prints' motifs and every unit were completely different, so were the shapes of the potteries. What's more, the expedition conditions in the ancient times were far less convenient than today. Therefore, even if the painted pottery was originated in Anau, it was impossible to cross 4,000 km. of deserts and mountains to the Northwest of China in a short time. Moreover, Chinese painted pottery was earlier than Anau pottery in terms of chronology, which showed that they developed independently and theory "Anau culture has great influence on Yangshao culture" was not reliable. However, the similarity between Yangshao pottery and Anu pottery also had proved that it was possible to develop similar culture in different regions because of similar historical conditions. Although Anderson's theory still has some influence abroad, nobody in Chinese academia believed in such a theory.

In the unearthed housing rammed earth layer of Anau excavation Phase I, people found grain (barley and wheat), while in the layer of Anau Phase II, the bones of cattle, sheep, horses, camels, dogs and other livestock were discovered, indicating that people at that time also raised livestock besides agriculture. What's more, people in Anau hunted some animals to supplement agriculture and husbandry; such as wild horses, wild boars, foxes, deer, antelopes, wolves and so on. The locals did not know how to fire bricks, so all the houses were made of dry adobes, which were slightly similar to China's Gaochang and Jiaohe Ancient Towns in Turpan, Xinjiang. It was not until the late Anau era that they learned how to use potter's wheel to make pottery.

The cultures similar to Anau culture was widely distributed and they were discovered in two regions. One was Namagan region in Fergana Valley, and the other was the expedition road station in Kath, Khwarezmia which was located in the lower reaches of Amu Darya, the latter was found by Bertold Spuler.[5]

Karasuk Culture arose in the late Bronze Age (1200 BC-700 BC), which was originally discovered in the Karasuk River of Minosinsk in Russia. Karasuk Culture was widely distributed and its ruins were found around Lake Baikal, Altai, and Semipalatinsk and Lake Zaysan in Kazakhstan. Its general feature was the thin accumulation of culture, reflecting people's high mobility due to their engagement in nomadic herding. People mainly raised sheep, which was proved by a great many sheep bones found in the tombs. They even regarded sheep as god and put them on the top of the pillars. The differences between Karasuk Culture and Andronovo Culture were mainly based on two facets: one was that nomadic economy had occupied an important part in Karasuk, and the other was that the residents here were from the Mongolian race. The bones and bronze wares were consistent with those in the Shang Dynasty, showing that they were obviously influenced by the culture of Shang Dynasty. The bronze crank knives discovered there was the same as those of the Shang Dynasty. And other daggers, spears and axes were also consistent with those discoveries

---

5   Bertold Spuler, Geschichte von Mittelasiens, Handbuch der Orientalistik, (Fünfter Band (5th Volume), Leiden-Köln, 1966, pp. 1517.

in the north China. Moreover, the pottery shapes and patterns were different from those of Andronovo culture, but similar to those found in Northern China. Therefore, scholars believed that a large number of tribes in Northern China came to South Siberia and Yenisei River between 1200 BC and 700 BC and started to interact with the Steppes culture in the Central Asia.

(2) Homeland of the Aryans

There was only little achievement in regard to linguistics across the world between 18th and 19th century except the discovery of "Indo-European Language Family". The British colonists arrived in India and established the colonial rule. In order to facilitate their rule, some British people began to learn the culture of India and study classical Indian language, namely, Sanskrit. They found that Sanskrit and European classical literature languages (Greek and Latin) had obvious similarities and regularity. The only theory that could explain the phenomenon was that Sanskrit had a close relationship with most European languages. Later Sanskrit mentioned above and the mother language which most European languages originated from was named "Proto Indo-European Language". And all the languages associated with them were classified into a language group called "Indo-European Language Family".

According to researches, those peoples who spoke original Indo-European language were divided into two branches and they spoke different dialects. Aryans and Slavs, who spoke Indo-Iranian, belonged to the East branch, while Germans, Greeks and Latin people were the West branch. Later Aryans were separated from Slavs and other peoples that belonged to the Eastern branch of Indo-European Languages. Before the l great geographical discoveries, the peoples who spoke Indo-European language lived in the region from the Arctic Ocean in the North to the Indian Ocean in the South, from the Atlantic in the West to China's Northwest region, being the world's most widely distributed language group. People who spoke Indo-European language in the Bronze Age gradually approached the Eurasian continent from its original place, which had great influence on the development of the Eastern history. Some scholars have offered different views on where people speaking original Indo-European language dwelled, and where the original Indo-European languages were born. Most scholars considered that it was in the region from the Central Europe and Balkans in the West to the Eurasian Steppes in the East. In recent years, certain scholars had believed that the region from Western Gansu to Xinjiang should be the hometown of the Indo-European people.[6]

There was a close relationship between Aryans who entered India and Iran. The branch that spoke Iranian later developed into a large family. The inscriptions from the Persian Empire times proved that people who spoke Iranian lived in almost the entire Western region of Central Asia in the 7th century BC, namely, Sogdians,

6   A.K.Narain from the University of Wisconsin, On the First Indo-Europeans: The Tokharian—Yuezhi and their Chinese Homeland, in Papers on Inner Asia, No.2, Indiana University, Research Institute of Inner Asian Studies, Bloomington, Indiana, 1987, pp.15-16.

Bactrians, Maru people, Khwarezmia people, Arsacid people and Saka tribes. Since the end of the 19th century, scholars have found various literatures belonging to Iranian language system in all parts of Central Asia including China's Xinjiang, such as Barkerian, Sogdian, Chorasmian, Khotan Saka and so on.

The Arsacid (Parthian) language belonged to Western Iranian, but it was deeply influenced by Eastern Iranian. In the first half of the period from 1 BC to 1000 BC, Iranian dialect prevailing in the Western region of Central Asia was the basic language of the Zoroastrian holy book Avesta.

The comparison among inscriptions of ancient Persian empire, Avesta and Veda, and Sanskrit and Pali, proved that Iranian had close relations with India. And they had shared a common grammatical structure and basic vocabulary. Iranian as well as Indian languages form Indo-Iranian or Aryan languages, which was a branch of Indo-European language.

The following is a vocabulary table of ancient Persian and Sanskrit, from which you can clearly see the close relationship between them.

	Ancient Persian	Vedic and Sanskrit (India)
water	ap	ap
land	dumi	dhumi
wind	vata	vata
object	tanu	tanu
hand	zasta (or dasta)	khasta
voice	vachakh	vachas
name	naman	naman
clothes	vastra	vastra
father	pitar	pitar
brother	bratar	bhratar
inside	antar	antar
two	dvadv	dvadva
four	chatvar	chatvar
five	pancha	pancha
seven	khanta	santa
eight	ashta	ashta
ten	dasa	dasha
eleven	dvadasa	dvadasha
one hundred	sata	shata

The close relationship within the Indo-Iranian language family not only shows in the common vocabulary, but also in the common grammatical structure. Take "the noun's case change" as an example:

Word: Body nominative case objective case instrumental case

Ancient Persian: tanu tanu shtanum tanva

Vedic, Sanskrit: tanu tanu shtanum tanva

In addition to the commonness in vocabulary and grammar, findings of comparative studies on religious concepts, myths, and epics of ancient Indian and ancient Iranian also show similarities in rhyme structure, mythology and epic heritage. What's more, the names of heroes and gods honored in Avesta and Veda, which are the ancient Persian Zoroastrian classic and the ancient Indian classic respectively, are also very similar.

From the 19th century, international academic have argued on questions as follows: where did the Indo-Iranian tribes live before they were separated from other Indo-European people? when did they move away from their homeland and what was the migration route? Most historians and linguists believe that the ancestors of the Indo-Iranian tribes lived in the region near the Caspian Sea initially, and later they moved to Central Asia and its neighboring regions, thus the Indo-Aryan tribe entered India, and the dialect of this Indo-Aryan tribe afterwards developed into the Vedic dialect. The Aryans, who remained in Central Asia, became the tribes speaking Iranian, while those who moved Eastward into the west of Iran later became the ancestors of Medes[7], Persians, and Arsacid people. The dialects of the latter tribes were later developed into Western Iran's tribal language, however, afterwards the Iranian-speaking tribes in Central Asia were divided into various branches.

Most of the people who speak contemporary Iranian language, such as Persians, Kurds, Baloch people and Pashtuns, lived in the Iranian plateau and its Eastern and Western neighborhoods. However from 1001 BC to 2000 BC, Iran was occupied by tribes and nationalities that spoke other languages, such as the Eminans and so on. In the first half of the period from the 1 BC to 1,000 BC, the Iranian tribes moving into Iran gradually squeezed out the local inhabitants and assimilated them.

Ancient tribes speaking Iranian lived in the regions with its West to Southeastern Europe, East to Xinjiang China, North across Ural and Southern Siberia, and South to Southern Iran, which have occupied a vast region much larger than in the Middle Ages and in modern times. The historical documents recorded the migration of the tribes speaking Iranian, namely the Scythians, from South-Eastern Europe to the Northern region of the current Kazakhstan

7 The Medes were an ancient Iranian people who lived in an area known as Media (north-western Iran) and who spoke the Median language. At around 1100 to 1000 BC, they inhabited the mountainous area of northwestern Iran and the northeastern and eastern region of Mesopotamia and located in the Hamadan.

Steppes and the Black Sea. It is possible that the following cultures are related to the Aryans, they are the Andronov Culture in Northern Central Asia, the Timber-chambered Tomb Culture in the lower reaches of the Volga River, the Tazha Baga Alpine Culture in the Caspian Sea-Aral Sea region, and the Kayrak-kum Culture in the Fergana region in the Bronze Age. At the transitional period of the 7th and 8th century BC, some of the Scythians crossed the Caucasus Mountains into the Middle East, and later the Sarmat-Alanis also migrated along the same route. According to historical records, the Sarmatians have occupied the vast regions from the Caspian Sea and the Aral Sea to the Ural and the Southern Siberia forest. They had close contact with the regional people who spoke Finno-Ugric[8] languages.

The Ossetians, currently living in the Caucasus region, are the descendants of the ancient Iranian tribes that had migrated to the Southeast.

In the Yutian region of the southern part of Xinjiang, there were people who spoke Khotan Saka until the 10th century. It can be seen from the study of contemporary scholars that Khotan Saka people belongs to the East Iranian branch, and it has a close relationship with the Sogdian language and the Chorasmian, so this Indo-European-speaking people can only be moved from Tajikistan or its northern region. According to records in Chinese historical materials, a considerable part of Xinjiang region was occupied by Saka tribe peoples since after the 3rd century BC to the 2nd century BC, but later Saka people were marginalized and assimilated by the Turkic peoples.

The writing of the Zoroastrian holy book Avesta was completed around the beginning of the period from 1 BC to 1000 BC, in which many place names of Central Asia, such as Sogd, Merv, and Khwarezm were mentioned. What's more, the Aryans' legendary homeland Aryiaham Vaichakh (meaning "the Aryan's vast land") were also mentioned in the Avesta, which some scholars have argued that it was referred to Khwarezmia, but it probably refers to the entire western regions of Central Asia.

(3) Beautiful Deer Stone–Primitive Cultural Heritage of the Mongolian Steppes

There is plenty of rain in the coastal regions of the East Asian continent due to the influence of Southeast monsoon rains. Its natural vegetation is distributed based on the latitudes, which from South to North is tropical rain forest, evergreen broad-leaf forest, deciduous forest, and coniferous forest. With the high temperature in Southeast Asia and Southern part of China, the crops grow fast, so it is suitable for human beings to live, but the mountainous geographical environment causes inconvenient transport and slower information communication. As a result, there was no regimes in Southeastern Asia or South China that were powerful enough to influence humankind's history, and the economic

---

8   Finno-Ugric is a traditional grouping of all languages in the Uralic language family except the Samoyedic languages.

development of the region was nascent for a quite long period of time. With the Yangtze River and the Yellow River as the center, China's central region boasts four distinct seasons, pleasant climate, abundant precipitation, as well as fertile land, which is beneficial to agricultural development and human settlement. Moreover, as the vast plain is easy for information dissemination, this region was densely populated since ancient times, and variety of powerful regimes were born here. In the past thousands of years, it can be said to be motive force and power source of East Asia's political, economic and cultural development.

In the north and west of the Central Plains, due to the increase of the distance from the coast, the influence of the Southeast monsoon is generally weaker and the precipitation is reduced so the original natural vegetation is determined by the climate of the Steppes and coniferous forests. Mongolian Steppes is divided into two parts, namely the Southern region and the Northern region of the Gobi desert, between which is the barren Gobi desert region. Although this place is not suitable for agricultural development, the milk, meat, hide and fur of large herbivores, such as horses, camels, cattle, and sheep do provide food and clothing for people who live there. They have created a nomadic culture that is different from the agricultural culture through long-time battle against the harsh natural environment. Nomadic production is not as stable as agricultural because they have to migrate to wherever water and grass are abundant. As a result, nomads generally do not build permanent residence, and towns in Steppes also appear quite late. Countries established by nomads were often called "moving states" in ancient China. The earliest "moving state" in the Mongolian Steppes was established by Hun (Xiongnu), an ancient nationality in China. As for other nationalities that had ruled the Mongolian Steppes before Hun, although there are records in Chinese literature, details are lacked.

The oldest representative cultural relic of the Mongolian plateau is deer stone. Deer stone is the valuable cultural heritage left by ancient Mongolian Steppes people. It is a stone column of which the section is generally rectangle. With different heights, some of them are long strips. Its four sides are engraved with the image of deer whose mouth is protrudent and long to highlight the beautiful antlers. In addition to deer, the stone surface is often engraved with knives, daggers, bows, arrows and other patterns. Deer stone is a kind of stone carving which has a meaning beyond the material life of people and it shows the spiritual life of the people living on the Steppes. It's carving requires high chiseling and carving technology, and takes a long time and needs abundant labor. Only when certain craftsmen could maintain subsistence through other means instead of nomadic activities in a long period of time, it is possible for them to master and develop this technology.

Deer stones usually stand at a specially selected place, generally related to tombs or monumental buildings. Deer stones were discovered in Tuva, South of the Baikal, the Russia's Altai region, Mongolia and Xinjiang regions of China. The deer stones found so far, in all the above regions add up to around 500, but 450 of which were discovered in Mongolia, mainly in the West of

Mongolia. In addition, stone carvings similar to the deer stones were found in the other regions of Kazakhstan and Central Asia, the Orenburg Governorate of Russia, the Caucasus, the Black Sea, Bulgaria and around the Elbe river in Germany. Scholars of the former Soviet Union and Mongolia usually regard deer stones as relics remaining from the 1500 BC to 800 BC. The question whether, which people set up the deer stones is still not confirmed, but some scholars believe that deer stones were erected by people speaking ancient Indo-European language.

Deers mainly live in forests. Unlike cattle and sheep, they are not easy to be domesticated because they run very fast. The ancient Northern nationalities that worshiped deer cannot be simply dependent on nomadic activities. Hunting plays an important role in their lives. Among the Eurasian Steppes nationalities, Turkic people have worshiped wolves as their ancestors. Scholars always pay great attention to the legends of wolf of the nomadic people in the North Asia, but little attention on researching the legend of deer. In fact, records related to the Northern nomadic people in the ancient Chinese literature expose the nomadic people's worship towards deer.

For instance, in the book You Yang Za Cu (Youyang Miscellany) Volume IV written by Duan Chengshi in the Tang Dynasty period, it mentions the ancestor of the Turkic people was the sea god named She Mo She Li, who lived in the West in a place called "A Shi De Ku". There was a sea-goddess who allured She Mo She Li to live with her in the sea by a white deer every evening, and sent him back in the next morning. After several decades, one day, as She Mo She Li's tribe was going to hunting, the sea-Goddess said to him: "tomorrow there would be a white deer with gold antlers running out of 'A Shi De Ku', and if you could shoot it, we could stay together forever, but if not, our relationship would be over". The next day, the deer really appeared and She Mo She Li ordered people to surround it. The deer jumped around till a tribe chief killed it. She Mo She Li was furious and executed the chief. However the relationship between him and the sea-goddess was over. According to this legend, the woman who married the ancestor of Turkic people She Mo She Li should be from a tribe that worshiped deer as totem. At the beginning of the book "Secret History of the Yuan Dynasty" based on the imperial family of the Yuan Dynasty in the 13th century, it is written: "The ancestors of the Yuan Dynasty were a grey wolf and a white deer. After getting married, they crossed the river named Teng Ji Si and lived besides the source of a river called Yu Wo Nan and in front of the mountain called Bu Er Han." This is to say that the paternal ancestors of the Mongolians worshiped the wolves while the maternal ancestors worshiped the deers.

The two legends have one thing in common, that is the ancestors of the Turks people in the early days once got married with tribes that worshiped deer, and Mongolian maternal ancestors once took deer as the totem. Almost all the heavy physical labour in nomadic activities was undertaken by men, so after coming to the ages of civilization, all the Steppes nomadic ethnic peoples took male as the center of family without exception. In the legends of ancestors of the Turkic people and the Mongols, tribes that worshiped deer were put into the maternal position, which indirectly shows that from the middle of the period from 1000 BC to 2000 BC to the time before the middle of the period from 1 BC to 1000 BC, the deer culture that was prevalent in the Eurasian Steppes and the Western Mongolian Plateau had lost its position before the rise of the Turkic Khanate. Today we can only look for them from the beautiful patterns of deer stones and related literature.

(4) Silk Road–Jade in the Pre-Qin Period

Rare documents and evidence about the Central Plains residents' understanding of the Western Regions in the Pre-Qin Period (2100s BC-221 BC) were discovered but they need to be confirmed with the results of archeological studies.

Documents in the Pre-Qin Period have descriptions in regard to the Northwest landscape. For example, the Classic of Mountains and Rivers refers that the Kunlun Mountains are located in the Northwest (of China). It is near to a quicksand region, stretches for more than four hundred km. and shows the nature of high lands. It also refers to "You Ze", that is the Lop Nur region. It is formed by the water of "Dun Hong" (namely water of the Tarim River) gathering with the Peacock River of Lop Nur. This statement was written by the indigenous people of the Western Regions, then was witnessed by the Persian travelers and documented in the Persian geographic book Hudud al-Alam which was completed in the 10th century.

As early as the remote times, inhabitants of the Chinese Central Plains had material and cultural communication with inhabitants of the Western Regions. In recent decades, many of the artifacts produced in coastal regions were unearthed in Northwestern China and overseas tombs. The fine stone culture discovered in the town of Qijiaojing in Hami city of Xinjiang was identified by experts as a culture which belongs to a period of nearly ten thousand years ago. Archaeologists collected a red coral bead there, which probably were from the coastal regions. It is the evidence of communication between the East and West at that time.

The Five Fort Cemeteries in Hami are tombs of primitive society about three thousand years ago, where unearthed a lot of seashells and ornaments in wool scarves and clothes. In the tombs of Warring States Period (475 BC-221BC) in Western Turpan, shellfishes exchanged from the coastal regions were found in mouths of the deceased.

Between 1976 and 1978, a large number of ancient tombs were explored in East of Alagou and Yuergou station in the Western edge of the Turpan Basin because of the construction of the Southern Xinjiang Railway. Among which, tomb No. 28 was measured by carbon 14 with a history of 2,620 years, that is the Spring and Autumn Period. The tomb unearthed had a phoenix bird pattern embroidery made by using green silk upon a plain silk with 20 centimeters length and width. As the original embroidery was damaged, the complere image was difficult to identify, but the remains could still display the body, slightly curved legs, and claws of phoenix birds which were no doubt living in the Central Plains. This cultural relic is displayed in the Xinjiang Museum. In addition, the tomb No.18 had lacquer ware from the Central Plains from the Warring States Period.[9]

Bazerek ancient tombs in Gorno Altai Wulagan District in Russia also had the Silk Road-related cultural relics unearthed. It is the place where the ancient Saka people lived. Scholars claim these tombs were built in the middle period of the 1st millennium which was during the late Spring and Autumn period and the early Warring States period. A lot of silk fabrics from the Central Plains were unearthed here. In some huge tombs, there were large or small ordinary woven fabrics plain-weaved by the Central Plains produced twist silk, with the density of 34x50 pcs/square centimetre, covered on the leather clothes. One of the most prominent pattern and production technology was a piece of patterned fabric unearthed in the Bazerek tomb No.3, with the density of 18x24pcs/square centimetre. The weaving method is "one thread in longitude by two threads in latitude" and pattern "twill of three threads down by one thread up" or "twill of three threads ups by one thread down". A piece of exquisite cocoon silk was unearthed in Baszerek tomb No.5. It is a piece of saddle mattress, plain twill, with the density of 50x52pcs/square centimetre, and 43 centimetres wide. It was embroidered by colourful silk with theme of "the male phoenix resting in a tree and the female phoenix flying between the trees". Russian archaeologists have unearthed bronze mirrors in the Altai region, and Kazakhstan, from the Warring States. These data prove that the Central Plains of China contacted with the residents of the West, i.e., the Altai people since the early 1000 BC.[10]

25

Chinese archaeologists believe that embroidery techniques and patterns of the phoenix discovered in tomb No.28 in Alagou of the Southern Turpan Basin are the same with the phoenix pattern in Baszerek tomb. Alagou and Baszerek were not ancient thoroughfares, nor the ancient economic or political centres formed by the oases which were common in the Western Regions. However, plain pattern and phoenix pattern embroidery from the Central Plains can be found in such a remote place, which explains that there was a large-scale silk trade between the Northwest and the Central Plains during the Spring and Autumn Period and the Warring States Period. The economic and cultural communication between the Central Plains and the Western Regions in the Pre-Qin Period is the prerequisite for Zhang Qian's visits to the Western Regions.

9   Wang Binghua, Historical Relations between Xinjiang and Central Plains before the Western Han Dynasty Period, Journal of Xinjiang University, 1984/4.
10   Lu Kejin, On the Ancient Relations between China and the Altai Tribe, The Journal Archaeology, 1957/2.

Artifacts from the ancient Western Regions were also found in the Central Plains. In 1976, Institute of Archeology of Chinese Academy of Social Sciences excavated an imperial tomb of the Shang Dynasty in Anyang, Henan. It was identified as the tomb of Fuhao, a spouse of the emperor Wuding from the Shang Dynasty period, dating back to more than 3,200 years ago. Among the 1,928 objects buried with Fuhao, there were 756 pieces of jade wares, accounting for 39.2% of the total. Archaeologists sent more than 300 pieces of various specimens to the Beijing Jade Factory, and to Anyang City Jade Carvings Factory and the Chinese Academy of Sciences Institute of Geology and other institutions to identify them. The conclusion was that all except the three pieces were made of Xinjiang jade.

In the Pre-Qin period literature, such as Guan Zi, the Classic of Mountains and Rivers, Biography of Mu Tianzi and other books, record that jade in the ancient Central Plains region was from Hetian (Khotan) and Kunlun prefectures. For example, Biography of Mu Tianzi mentioned that Emperor Mu of the Western Zhou Dynasty had travelled to the West. He said: "Chongshan Mountain is the highest mountain in the world" when he travelled to the Kunlun Mountains and Chongshan Mountain. Later the Emperor Mu travelled to the "Mountains of Jade". Although most researchers believe that "Chongshan Mountain" should be the Pamir Plateau.[11]

But, few people totally believe these records. Only after jade ware unearthed in the Yin Ruins being identified as the Xinjiang source, the above records in the Pre-Qin history have gained some evidence. During the Pre-Qin Period, people from Western Regions obtained silk from the Central Plains, and to form a trade, the people from Central Plains took jade from them. At that time, Western Regions' people who immigrated to the Central Plains to give the jade stone tribute- to the emperor- travelled along the Khotan River down to the Tarim River, Peacock River (Dun River water), You Ze (Lop Nur), Yumen and then reached the Hexi Corridor. This should be the origin of the Yumen County set up in the Han Dynasty period and the reason behind why they captured Loulan (also called Krorän) first in history on their expedition to the Western Regions.

3. The Persian Empire

Between 4000 BC to 3000 BC, the development of human society suddenly accelerated in several different regions of the old regions of civilizations, such as the Nile River Basin in Northeast Africa, the two river basins in West Asia, the Indus River Basin of South Asian subcontinent, the basins of the Yellow River and the Yangtze River of China. They quickly developed into the ages of civilization and were far more developed than in other regions. These regions had one thing in common, that is, they were warm and humid regions, which were suitable for human beings to live. Fertile land and the geographical

---

11   Gu Shi, Lectures on Emperor Mu's Travel to the West, Ed 1990, The Chinese Bookstore.

locations being adjacent to rivers and seas contributed to the development of the initial agricultural civilization. Compared with other regions, with lesser human labour it was possible to have more stable harvest frequency in these regions.

Among the above-mentioned civilizations, the Nile Valley civilization in Northeastern Africa and the Mesopotamian civilization in the West Asia later developed into the Mediterranean civilization: ancient Greece, Rome (including Byzantium), and the Islamic cultures were peaks in its history; Judaism, Christianity and Islam were its religious representatives. The civilization center has had a lasting impact on the history of all mankind for thousands of years. The Indus culture was the pioneer of later Buddhist civilization. Buddhist civilization spread from the subcontinent, to the Central Asia, East Asia and Southeast Asia which were extremely vast regions, and became one of the typical representatives of Asian civilizations. The main culture of the Yellow River and the Yangtze River's basins merged into the main body of the Chinese civilization, which had a great influence on the East Asia, and formed the Han culture circle from Japan and Korea to the East, Tianshan Mountains to the West, Siberia to the North and Vietnam to the South.

In the prehistoric times, there was indirect communications between these civilizations. Central Asia and Persia, located between these civilizations, were the natural bridge connecting the East and the West. The rise of the Persian Empire connected the Central Asia to the East with the Mediterranean to the West, which greatly facilitated the trade expeditions, and played an epoch-making role in the history of the Silk Road.

(1) The Rise of the Persian Empire

In the east, north and west of Iranian Plateau are mountains and it faces the Persian Gulf in the south. It is a relatively closed region. Coming into the age of civilization, the earliest local residents were Elam people who spoke Hamito-Semitic languages. They were of kinship with West Asian and North African people who created the ancient Egypt and the Mesopotamian civilizations and they were also close with the Jews and the Arabs. Elam people established a powerful country at the end of 2000 BC. In the 7th century BC, Elam was defeated by the Assyrian, and gradually declined. In the second half of the 7th century BC, Medes people who spoke some kind of Persian language established a slavery country in the Western part of the Iranian Plateau. Less than a century later, the Persians, the close relative of Medes rose. In 553 BC, Kurush, the leader of the Hakhamanesh clan of Persia, led the people against the rule of Medes, and conquered Ecbatana (current Hamadan Province in Southwest of Teheran), the capital of Med (Medes) Empire in 550 BC. Medes were terminated and we see the rapid and vigorous rise of the Persians.

The rise of the Persians caused the uneasiness of the Lydians (Lydia, in the western part of current Turkey). They formed an alliance with the Greeks and attacked Persia. Kurush asked Saka in Central Asia for help, and terminated

Lydia in 546 BC. The battle of Lydia connected the Persian Empire and Central Asia directly. Queen Tomyris of the Masagatai tribe ruled Sogdiana at that time. In 529 BC, after Tomyris rejected Kurush's proposal, Kurush attacked Eastward with his army. Persians were defeated under Sogdian's strong resistance. Kurush was killed in 529 BC.

When Kurush died, the Eastern territory of the Persian Empire included Bactria (also called "Balkh" and "Tochari" in the Chinese documents) and Khwarezm region on both sides of the Amu Darya, which were ruled by Kurush's brother Bardiya. After Kurush's son succeeded his father's reign, he continued to pursue the expansion policy and conquered Egypt in 525 BC. From then on, the Persian emperors repeatedly launched invasions toward the East. Its border was far to the Amu Darya and its influence had extended to Syr Darya. The Persian government divided the country into 20 provinces, each of which contributed a certain amount of tribute to the central government each year. There were 7 provinces in Central Asia, such as the 7th province governing the Gandarii region in the South of Hindu Kush Mountains, the 12th province governing the Balkh, the 16th province governing Parthia (Arsacid), Khorazm and Sogdiana. The Eastmost stronghold of the Persian Empire was the Falkan Basin which was adjacent to Xinjiang of China. The Persian people established Cyropolis at the Western end of the basin, wherein the ruins of the Ula Tiupe remains, about 64 km west of the Khujand city of Uzbekistan.

The Persian Empire was the first great empire with a vast territory in human history. The Persian Empire reached its culmination in the period under the reign of King Darius and its territory included the Indus to the East, Asia Minor (Anotolia) Peninsula and the Balkans region of the Europe to the West, and Egypt in the south, and it had four capital cities. For the control of the whole country, the Persian Empire established a perfect mail distribution route network, with a distribution artery which started from Asia Minor Peninsula in the west to Susa currently Shushan (one of the four capitals) in the east, which was 2,400 km. long in total.

The Silk Road is the ancient trade route which started from China in the East to North Africa and Europe in the West. The section from Central Asia to the Mediterranean was the route's middle part. Archaeologists have discovered Celestite (also known as lapis lazuli) in the ancient ruins of Western Asia at the end of the 3000 BC. It was estimated that it was a quasi-precious stone produced in the mountains of Afghanistan, which proved the existence of commercial route from Central Asia to West Asia. The establishment of the centralized system of the Persian Empire and the improvement of the mail route system had facilitated the transport from Mediterranean to Central Asia. This provided conditions for the formation of the Silk Road. Simultaneous with the rise of Persia, the Greek empire also rose in the Balkan Peninsula of Europe. The two empires had long-term conflicts in the Aegean region, and at last, Persians were defeated. The Greco-Persian Wars greatly exhausted the national strength of Persia. Persia was fast falling into decay in the 4th century BC. Persia's outward expansion had greatly enhanced the influence of Persian culture in the world. Persian's centralization system was later inherited by the Macedonian-Greek Empire and influenced the later Roman Empire. The Romanesque post-roads network[12], the fortification and siege weapons were originated from Persia. The Persian Empire's state religion Zoroastrianism was a religion that believed in a dualistic philosophy, which was introduced into China during the Northern and Southern Dynasties (420-589 AC) and also influenced the Christianity formed during the Roman Empire period.

(2) Alexander the Great

Native Greek people have resisted just after Kurush conquered the Greek cities in the Asia Minor Peninsula. And Ionia was one of the cities in ancient Greece. Traditionally, Persians called the Greek people as "Yunan" and Greece were known as "yauna" which originated from the name for Greek people, written in the Buddhist sutras. Greek was called as "Yunanidimian" in the Uyghur Yaofang (Islamic scripts) of the Ming Dynasty's transcript preserved in Beijing Library on account of these names. During the struggle against the Persians, Athens once provided support. Darius the Great dispatched forces across Thrace to expand towards Europe in 492 BC for the sake of the punishing Athenians and invading Athenian lands. From then on, the 43-year-long Persian Wars had started. Three Persian emperors including Darius and King Xerxes had led the Persian Wars and they had to finally conclude a peace treaty with Athens.

The cities in Greek had seen prosperous development after the end of Persian Wars. Influenced by the Greek culture, Macedonia, which was located in the north of Greek, had developed rapidly into a power center. Many cities in Greek were subordinated to Macedonian rule and Macedonian rulers started a expedition military in 337 BC to Persia which had led to several collisions. Alexander, the Great the king of Macedonia (his rule 336-323 BC) defeated the Darius III forces of Persia in 331 BC. Not long after, Alexander led Macedonian troops to further east to conquer Khorasan in the East of Iran and built the Alexander City in current Herat, Afghanistan. After Greek forces captured Baluchistan (at the border of current Iran and Pakistan) and Sistan (in the Southeast of Iran), thus the Persian Empire fell apart.

After Greek troops conquered Persia, the Greek forces continued to attack the cities in Central Asia. Alexander conquered Bactria in 329 BC and later captured Kandahar and Kabul in current Afghanistan. Having captured three cities successfully, Greek troops followed up the victory and sailed for Sogdiana after crossing the Amu Darya Northward. In the summer of that year, Alexander conquered the Maracanda (the capital of Sogdiana), current Samarkand in the Uzbekistan. And in Usrusana (between current Khujand and

---

12   These networks included predefined routes known as Post-roads complete with distance markers and waypoints. Unlike other forms of mounted courier, post riders collected and delivered mail over the course of their route, meeting with other riders at scheduled times and scheduled places to exchange forwarded items.

Samarkand), Sogdiana troops stoutly resisted against the invasion of Greek troops although they killed more than 20,000 native people. Greek forces soon reached Syr Darya river, the natural boundary between Northern Steppes and Southern agricultural region in Central Asia. Consequently, the agricultural peoples in the South of Syr Darya and nomadic peoples in the North of Syr Darya rebelled against Greek forces. Alexander himself was also seriously wounded hurt during the Cyrus War, meanwhile over eighty thousand Central Asian people were killed. Greeks had captured seven cities along the bank of Syr Darya after hard battles. In order to defend the aggression launched by the Saka nomadic peoples in the North of Syr Darya, Greeks established a city named Alexandria Eschate in Khujand which was located in the Fergana Valley adjacent to Xinjiang. Alexander left a large number of troops for establishing a regional garrison city, i.e, the Alexandria Eschate which can be translated as "the farthest Alexander City". In addition, Greek forces invaded the northern regions of the Amu Darya river and moved deep into the desert regions to fight against the Sakas.[13]

When Alexander the Great passed away in 323 BC, Macedonian Empire was torn apart. Seleucus, the former chief executive in Babylon, declared independence and occupied the regions in Asia which originally belonged to Macedonia, known as the Seleucid Dynasty in history. Seleucus and his son Antiochus I, had built up numerous fortified castles in Central Asia and populated it with Greeks and Macedonians, most of which had gradually developed into towns. Greek was the official language for the upper class. Shortly afterwards, Seleucid Dynasty was also dismembered. During the middle period of the 3rd Century BC, Diodotus, a Greek leader and the chief executive in Tochari and Sogdiana also proclaimed independence. Several years later, the chief executive of Parthia rebelled against the Seleucid Dynasty.

The strongholds built by Greeks were mostly located along the main expedition routes, most of which were later developed into trade centers. Persia conquered these cities in Central Asia, which guaranteed secure trade throughout the middle section of Silk Road (from Central Asia to Eastern Mediterranean). Thus, Persian forces have established direct trade relations between Europe and Central Asia, inheriting the situation after Alexander's expansive conquest of the eastern regions. So far, around the 3rd century BC, middle section and western section of the Silk Road trade routes were smoothed. As the founder of the Greek empire, on vast territories, Alexander the Great was has been alive in the memories of Eastern peoples. In the long years of history, the deeds of Alexander the Great was introduced to China's various nationalities through variety of channels. In the Northern Song Dynasty, M. Kashghari, the great scholar of the Turkic people, once wrote legends about Alexander the Great when he described the origin of Qara-hoja (Karahoca) and the tribes wih Turkic origin in his masterpiece Dictionary of Turkic language (Lügat ül Türk).

---

13   Arrian, translated by Li Zhou, Alexandria Expedition, Commercial Press, 1979, pp. 109-146; W.W. Tarn, Alexander the Great, Cambridge, 1951, pp. 50-181.

The book Zhu Fan Zhi (the records of foreign countries) by Zhao Rushi in the Southern Song Dynasty indicates: "It was said that Alexander established the lighthouse on the coast which consisted of two cellars. One was used to store harvest, the other was provided for weapons. The height of lighthouse was about 660 meters and could hold about 20,000 people. There existed a well connecting with the sea in the center of lighthouse so as to defend the country against attack. If other countries were ready to invade Alexander City, the people of the city would defeat the enemies by taking the advantages of the lighthouse. Some soldiers inside the city walls would be in charge of guarding the lighthouse, and others would go to the front. The machine like telescope was established on the top of the lighthouse so that the approaching enemies could be detected earlier and the defense plans could be made in time.[14] Some contemporary Islam scholars have suggested that the Qur'anic figure of Dhul-Qarnayn is Cyrus the Great (Alexander the Great.). This theory was proposed by Sunni scholar Abul Kalam Azad and endorsed by Shi'a scholars Allameh Tabatabaei, in his Tafsir al-Mizan and Makarem Shirazi. Also a text was found which included Dhul-Qarnayn when narrating about the famous Alexander Lighthouse. Möngkö Khan, the Emperor Xianzong of the Yuan Dynasty, sought advice from his ministers after he ascended to the throne. Yalavach, one of the ministers belonging to the Hui ethnic group, told Möngkö Khan about the deeds of Alexander the Great.

The chapter three in the Uyghur Yaofang, Ming Dynasty's transcript and preserved in Beijing Library, was created by Arastatalis for Iskandar. (In Persian language Alexander the Great (356 BC-323 BC) was called as Iskandar. Arastatalis refers to Aristotle (384 BC-322 BC), a scholar and philosopher in the ancient Greece and the teacher of Alexander the Great) Greece (Hellens) was a small nation, which did not leave persistent influence on the politics and economy of the Western Regions of China. When Seleucid Dynasty fell apart, a fully Hellenized regime was established in Central Asia. Greek civilization in Central Asia soon entered into an age when the local civilization absorbed the Greek civilization. Between 140 BC and 130 BC, Darouzhi passed through Amu Darya and moved to southwards, further conquered the Hellenized Bactria. When Zhang Qiang arrived in the South of Amu Darya in 120 BC, Darouzhi was enslaving the Bactrian people. Almost all territories belonging to Bactria were under the control of Darouzhi so that the remaining imperial families were forced to quit to the south banks of Kabul River and South Asia.

Greeks capturing Central Asia were referred as "yauna" in the Buddhist sutras, namely, Ionia. The remained forces of Bactria Kingdom entrenched in the South of Xia Dynasty and the North of India were always in pursuit of Greek culture and regarded Sialkot in Pakistan as the capital. Milinda, a Greek and the general under Demetrius (an emperor of Cyrene Empire) later become the king and he converted to Buddhism due to the influence of Indian

---

14 Feng Chengjun, Zhu Fan Zhi (Description of Various Countries) Checking and Annotating, Zhonghua Book Company, 1956, p. 69.

Culture on him. The Milinda-Panha includes an account of the Nagasena's life (a monk coming from Kashmir) and the story where ask-answer dialogues were established between Nagasena and Milinda in the Bactria Kingdom for persuading King Milinda into believing in Buddhism. King Milinda had not believed in Buddhism before, but he had a passion for something wonderful and classics including various thoughts. Later he asked Nagasena something about Buddhism and discussed further a series of questions with Nagasena, such as people's spirit, body, good and evil and so on. Finally, King Milinda became a convert to Buddhism. In addition to historical documents, some facts and practices referring to Greek Buddhist believers were engraved on the stone tablets. For instance, Greeks worshipped Buddhist relics, donated doors, stone pillars, pools and goods to the temples, etc. In accordance with these facts, the Darouzhi Buddhism was inherited from the North-west of India and Bactria Kingdom.

The Greek culture and Buddhist culture were inseparable, which was reflected by the silver coins and copper coins issued by Milinda. A large variety of inscriptions remained on these unearthed coins, such as the symbols like Sofer and Dikios, Dhramaka (Sanskrit but displayed by Greek letters) and the pictures of Falun. According to the old Buddhist sutras, Milinda retired from politics after he appointed his son as the king. As the Macedonian empire invaded Eastwards regions, many nations such as Greeks, Macedonians and Persians have migrated to the Eastern countries. At the same time, Greek religions and cultures also entered Central Asia, especially the engraving, which exerted important influence on the development of Buddhism statues. Under the influence of Greek art, Buddhism statues has expanded everywhere and became a new art in which Greek style was combined with the Indian style, known as Gandhara Art. The Gandhara style statue-carving was later introduced to China through the Darouzhi (Kushan) people.

(3) Greeks and Romans Have Greatly Affected East and China

Alexander the Great's Eastward expedition was an epoch-making event in the history of Sino-Western relations which, for the first time, linked the Europeans with the inland Asians. Greek conquerors of Central Asia and their descendants learned more about the Orient than their predecessors. They took back the message of the East to Europe, fanning the interest of their compatriots. The Greeks had touched the light beauty of silk. They called silk "Ser" which is the transliteration of Chinese characters "丝," and they knew that it was produced in the East of the conquered territory of Alexandria. That is the East of Hellenistic central Asian countries. They called the silk producing country Cyrus (Seres), meaning "the country of silk." Because the fabric was shipped to Europe through different intermediaries, the Greeks did not know its origin. Europeans were accustomed to clothes made of wool, so they initially guessed silk to be a special kind of wool. However, no wool in Europe could be woven into such beautiful textiles which led great interest to silk among the Greeks.

After long years of persistent inquiries, they finally concluded that silk was a kind of wool harvested from the trees. Pline L'Ancien, a writer on the Roman empire, in his book Natural History in AD 77, said: "the Serene people are known for their wool which they gathered from their forests. They sprayed the trees with white fluff that is washed off, which was then used by their wives to spin and weave."[15] After inquiring for centuries through various ways, the Europeans failed to reach the right answer. They still referred to silk as wool and thought that it was long, white fluff harvested from trees. In fact, silk is an animal protein fiber and not plant fiber. But in comparison to previous attempts, they were nearing the truth, because the silkworm's preferred food is white mulberry leaves, though they eat other mulberry species and even osage orange.

Until the 2nd century of King Anduin era, when Greek traveler and geographer Pausanias wrote in the Greek Chronicles, he had learnt that the Chinese silk was produced by an insect known as Ser, the silkworm. He wrote, " The land of Elis is fertile, and is especially adapted to the growth of fine flax. Now, whereas hemp and flax (both the common and the fine kind) are sown where the soil is suitable, the threads of which the Seres make their garments are produced, not from a bark, but in the following manner. In the country of the Seres there is an inset which the Greeks call a ser (silk-worm), but to which the Seres themselves probably give a different name. In size it is twice as big as the biggest beetle; but in all other respects it resembles the spiders that spin under the trees, and in particular it has, like the spider, eight feet. The Seres rear these creatures and build houses for them adapted both for winter and summer. The product of these insects is found in the shape of a fine clue wound about thir feet. The people keep the insects four years, feeding them on millet; but in the fifth year, knowing that they will not live longer, they give them a green reed to eat. This is the food that the insect likes best of all, and it crams itself with it till it bursts with repletion; and when it is dead they find the bulk of the thread in its inside. The island of Seria is known to be situated in a recess of the Red Sea."[16]

Along with the development of other natural sciences the ancient Greek cartography, had also advanced greatly. Unlike the Chinese cartography technique, Greek technique was based on spherical surfaces. About in 70-80 AD (Eastern Han Dynasty period), the Macedonian merchant, Maes Titianos, sent his men to trade along the land route to Seres (China). At the end of the first century, the geographer Marinus de Tyr used people's travelogue to author a geographical book, in which Seres was also mentioned, but currently, the great work no longer exists. In the middle of the second century, the Greek scholar Ptolemy (120-170) pushed classical cartography to its peak. In his eight volumes of Geography, there are six volumes which include latitude and longitude

15   Coedès, George, Texts of Greek and Latin Authors on the Far East From the 4th C. BCE. to the 14th C. C.E. Geng Sheng, Chinese version of Far East Ancient Literature Series of Greek, Latin Writers. Zhonghua Book Company, 1987, p.10.
16   Ibid., p.54.

values, and their level of precision had reached 1/12°. Ptolemy took advantage of the "Chinese Travelogue" written by Maes Titianos' men. Meanwhile he also extracted and revised the works of Marinus de Tyr, so he finally described the general situation of the Tarim Basin. His descriptions of Scythians outside the so-called Irmaos mountain described the four seasons of the regions as follows: The west of Scythia included the Imaos mountain as well as the Sakas region and were connected by the bend along the North mountain range; the north was a piece of unknown land; the Eastern part was Seres, and it was divided along a straight line, which the edge's latitude and longitude was roughly 150° and 63°, 160° and 35°; the southern lands was part of the Indo-Ganges region of India, bounded by the latitudes of the above marginal lines. According to scholars von Richthofen, Aurel Stein and George Coedes, Imaeus was the equivalent of Pamir. Described here is the Scythians in Congling region. In its North side, the Ely River and Du Laishui (Talas River) Grassland occupied by the Wusun and Kangju people was the "unknown land" for the Greeks. Its East was Seres. To be exact, it referred to the Western regions under the control of the Eastern Han Dynasty.

For researchers, the most interesting part of Ptolemy's description of Seres (China) is his records on Seres' (current Tarim Basin) and its Southern rivers. He said that there were two rivers running through most regions of Seres: Oikhardes (referring to the Tarim River), as it was already mentioned above, had a source in the vicinity of Ozarkia mountain (referring to Tianshan); while Asmira mountain (a part of the Kunlun Mountains) was another source, which was located at 174°, 47° 30 minutes ; there was a bend in Mount Cascia (also part of the Kunlun Mountains), which was located at 160 ° and 49 ° 30 minutes; there was the third source in the same mountain range, which was located at 161° and 44° 15 minutes. There was a river called Bautisos, which was the source of Mount Cascia, located at 176° and 39°; in the vicinity of the Mount Everest (referring to Himalayas), which was located at 168° and 39 ° degrees, on a bend; there was a source in the same mountains located at 160 ° and 39°.[17] The above-mentioned three tributaries of the Oyhardes River are similar to the three sources of the Tarim River, the Kashgar River, the Yarkand River and the Yutan River. Originating from the Ozarkia mountain is the Kashgar River, or the Aksu River; from Asmi Raya Hill is the Yutan River; the third tributary from Asmira mountain is the Yarkant River. However, Ptolemy did not mention where the three rivers drainafter their convergence downstream.

Maps of Ptolemy era are no longer available. People in the Renaissance age have speculated that there were some similarities between Cladius Ptolemy's original drawings and the restored ones by Venetian (Venice) geographer Vincenzo Valgrisi in 1561. Currently, scholars use the restored map. It is noteworthy that the Aya Sofya library in Istanbul, Turkey, has a copy of Ptolemy's

---

17 Coedès, George, Texts of Greek and Latin Authors on the Far East From the 4th C. BCE. to the 14th C. C.E. Geng Sheng, Chinese version of Far East Ancient Literature Series of Greek, Latin writers . Zhonghua Book Company, 1987, pp.30-33.

Arabic map sealed by Ottoman King Bayezid II (Mohammedian calendar 886-918, Gregorian calendar 1,481-1,512), Arabic (Collection No. 2160).

This map is similar to that of the Vincenzo Valgrisi's restored map, except that it describes the opposite direction. In the Northeastern part of Asia, these two maps clearly marked out the three upper sources and confluences of Ouhildos River. But unlike the textual descriptions of Ptolemy, it did not draw out the downstream after convergence of the three rivers.

4. The Hun Empire: An Empire on the Horseback

Since the Shang and Zhou dynasties to the Spring and Autumn Period of the Eastern Zhou Dynasty, inhabitants of Northern China were the "Hunzhou" (sound "xūn yù"), "Yun" (sound "xiǎn yǔn") and other tribes. The historian, Sima Qian of Western Han Dynasty, had argued: The ancestor of the Huns was a descendant of the House of Hya-heu-shy (Xia, 2100-1600 BC), by the name Shun-wei (Chun-wei, "Chun tribes"). Still before the times of the sovereigns Than (Tang, Taotang-Shi, 2357 BC) and Yui (Yu, 2597 BC) existed Shan-Jun, Hyanyun and Hunyui generations. But this argument does not seem credible.

The Huns never spoke Sino-Tibetan language, so they cannot be descendants of Xiahoushi tribe. Their clans however, are unclear. To expand and deepen their family history, the Mongolian scholars insisted that the Huns were their ancestors. Historical records indicate that the Huns were closer to ethnic peoples speaking Turkic language. During the Warring States Period, the Huns were centrally located in Monan Hetao and Touman city (current Wuyuan county, Inner Mongolia) of Yinshan (currently Langshan and Daqingshan, Inner Mongolia) posing a major threat to the Yuan, Zhongshan, Zhao, and Qin dynasties. During the Qin and Han Dynasties, the Huns ruled the Western Regions and controlled the key expedition routes between China and the West.

(1) The Story of Modu Chanyu

After the unification of China under the Qin Dynasty, Qin Shi Huang sent general Meng Tian with 100,000 troops Northward to eliminate the threat by the Huns on the Central Plains. The defeat of the Huns by the Qin army which set up from 44 counties in South Hetao Plateau (the Ordo plateau and Shanbei region) forced people to remote regions and settled criminals from the mainland. Tumen was the official title of the first leader of the Huns according to the historical records and scholars generally believe that the name was originated from the Turkic, which meant "ten thousand", or "ten thousand households". The leader of the Huns was called Chanyu. Unfortunately, Tumen Chanyu was defeated by the powerful army of Qin, and he therefore had no alternative but led his troops to North. After Meng Tian's death, there was chaos in the Qin Dynasty which led to rebellion of the vassal states. Soldiers guarding the frontiers abandoned their posts and fled opening room for Tumen Chanyu to invade South and recaptured the South of Hetao Plateau.

One of Chanyu's spouses was called "Yan Zhi." His son, named Modu, was established as the crown prince. But it was later put into doubt when a second son was born leading to Chanyu's plans to rescind the original decision and establishing the second son as the crown prince. Perhaps this was against the traditions and so Tumen could not accomplish it in a flagrant way. Instead, he was shrewd. Surrounded by strong peoples, East Hu in the East and Rouzhi in the West, Tumen formed an alliance with his western neighbor Rouzhi by sending his son, Modu, as a hostage to guarantee the reliability of alliance. Violating the agreement by the Huns would lead Rouzhi to kill the hostage. Shortly after handing over his son Modu to Rouzhi, Tumen ordered his troops to attack who furiously decided to kill the hostage. But knowing his plight, Modu fled back home after stealing a strong horse. Tumen praised his son's courage and even gave him 10,000 soldiers to command. Interestingly, Modu decided to kill his father and take the power of the state. To achieve this goal, the army had to submit to his command. Modu created a whistling arrow, which he ordered his men to follow during riding and shooting practice. The soldiers had to shoot the whistling arrow and those who defied this order would be killed. While hunting birds and animals, Modu often used the whistling arrow and those who slackened, despite their prowess in riding and shooting would be executed without any hesitation by Modu. To test their compliance, he tested his soldiers by suddenly shooting his whistling arrow to his beloved fine horse. Knowing his fondness to the horse, some of his followers have hesitated and guessed that

such order was mistakenly given. To uphold and demonstrate his strict military discipline, Modu killed those who did not shoot the horse. He later arranged another test, i.e., shooting his whistling arrow to his wife. Knowing that they had to shoot the target and some of them followed the order by considering the previous lesson. But this was the wife of the leader and some again failed to release their arrows. Modu ordered their execution.

After the inhumane and rather strict training, Modu's soldiers finally understood that it did not matter who the target was, the whistling arrow was a commanding signal. There was no exception and doubters would be killed. After some time, Modu aimed his whistling arrow again to his beloved horse and his soldiers immediately released their arrows and killed it. The response satisfied Modu and he knew his soldiers had absolute obedience to him and were truly loyal. He therefore waited for an opportunity.

In addition to grazing, the Huns often went hunting. This was both a means of livelihood and an opportunity to hone their riding and shooting skills. The desire to murder his father was deeply buried in him and Modu kept a tight lid on it. Tumen, on the other hand, was ignorant of these treasonous plans. When Tumen invited Modu to join him in hunting, the son saw this as an opportunity. He suddenly released his whistling arrow towards his father, and his men swiftly responded unconcerned that the target was the highest leader of the Huns. Tumen Chanyu died under the barrage of arrows. After killing his father, Modu immediately took over the leadership and exiled Tumen Chanyu's beloved wife and son to avoid a rebellion. Ministers who did not follow his orders were also killed. Donghu heard the news of that Modu killing his father and acclaiming himself as the King, he therefore sent messengers and demanded that Tumen Chanyu's fastest horse as a present. Modu called his ministers for deliberations on the issue and the ministers have argued that the horses should not be surrendered since it was a treasure. They preferred to break off their relations with Donghu but Modu thought that maintaining good-neighborly relations with Donghu was more important than a queen horse. So he gave the horse to Donghu. After receiving the horse from the Huns, Donghu considered it as a sign of fear and asked for Chanyu's wife. Deliberations with his ministers revealed their anger to these demands and rebuked them as unreasonable. Modu, however, still believed that a woman could not be important than peace and thus gave his wife to Donghu.

This move crystallized Donghu's ideas that the Huns were weak and therefore dispatched his troops to the west. The location boasted of large tracts of open land—about a thousand miles between Donghu and the Huns and the ruler Donghu asked the Huns to recognize his sovereignty over this territory. Modu consulted his ministers who dismissed the land as valueless and who held that the control of region would bring no fundamental strategic interests for the Huns. On the contrary, Modu believed that the land was quite valuable for the country and was furious against his ministers. He questioned why they could easily give a region to others and commanded the execution of the ministers who had proposed to abandon the land. He immediately sent his troops to targeting Donghu for catching him off guard since he had underestimated the strength Huns. The victors captured a large number of people and livestock and gradually became stronger.

Modu took advantage of the chaos plaguing the Central Plains in the Qin and Han Dynasties periods to centralize his strength by defeating the Rouzhi kingdom forces, and then annexed Loufan in the South and reoccupied "Henandi"—a county set up by general Meng Tian. Eventually, the Hun kingdom with 300,000 strong troops became a powerful state which threatened Northern China. The detailed story of Modu Chanyu is described in Sima Qian's "Records of the Historian: the Huns", which depicts various customs of the Huns. Tumen Chanyu was merciless when planning the murder of his son Modu, and in return, Modu did not hesitate to carry out his revenge against his father. To train his soldiers, Modu Chanyu used his wife as a target. This shows that in the noble family of the Hun, compared with the kingship, kinship or blood relations were not highly regarded, despite loving horses and their beauty; the Hun aristocrats attached far more importance on the foundation of the country—land and ranch. Hun nobles controlled and determined the lives of their men, and the Hun generals commanded the army on the battlefield by unique means such as using a whistling arrow.

(2) The Great Wall of China

The rise of the Huns in the north during the Warring States Period of China seriously threatened the stability and development of the agrarian society. At that time, among the top seven countries in the Central Plains: Qi, Chu, Yan, Han, Zhao, Wei, Qin, there were three which bordered the Huns: Yan, Zhao, Qin, and all these three countries were worried about the Hun's invasion. The main traditional strike force of Central Plains' army was the chariots and each was dragged by a number of horses. It took a number of armed personnel to hold weapons such as dagger-axe and bow among others. Preceding the chariots was the infantry. The chariots lined up in a coordinated fashion ramping up the enemy infantry. As the chariot was a formidable weapon, the countries in Central Plains invested heavily on producing them so that the strength of a country in Eastern Zhou dynasty in the spring and autumn period was measured by the number of chariot. A big state was called the "the country of a million chariots," referring to those great countries who could dispatch more than 10,000 chariots at a time; while the weak ones were known as the "the country of a thousand chariots," due to owning more than 1,000 chariots at a time.

Thus chariot equipment was developed in the process of fighting for the annexation between the countries of Central Plains. With the growing insecurity caused by the growing invasion from the northern nomadic people, chariot battle formation which was the traditional combat method of Central Plains, was

challenged. Hun forces relied mainly on cavalry. Several battles with the Huns later, the Zhao state found the chariots which were used by the Central Plains countries, were extremely clumsy when confronting Huns' flexible cavalry. The Hun soldiers dressed in short, fitting clothes, making them agile during riding and shooting, while the Central Plains' traditional wide and long-sleeved shirts restrained their movement abilities. So at the end of the 4th century BC, Emperor Zhao Wuling ordered rescinding the decision to use Central Plains' traditional battlefield over garment and chariot and instead use cavalry, which became the famous "Shooting on Horse in Hu Dress" in Chinese history. During the Warring States Period of China, there were seven powers who were very strong in the size and power, and had strength to mobilize a large number of migrant workers to build a large-scale defense force. In the face of the Hun's repeated invasions in the South, their neighboring countries devised strategies of building the Great Wall spontaneously. Qin state built the Great Wall in Longxi, the North, and Shang county. And Zhao Wuling Wang, the reformer Emperor began to build the Great Wall. The Zhao Great Wall was stretched from the Daibei (today Hebei Yuxian), moving down along Yin Shan, and ended in the Gaoque (today the northwest of Linhe County, Inner Mongolia). Along the Great Wall, he set up Yanmen, Yunzhong and Daichu counties Later Yan State began to build the Great Wall from Zaoyang to Xiangping, and he set up Shanggu, Yuyang, You Beiping, Liaoxi, Liaodong counties along the Great Wall. The countries' aim in building the Great Wall was to protect from invasions. But disputes among Warring States still gave the Hun opportunities to constantly invade borders states. Until the first emperor of Qin unified China, the Central Plains acted as unison against the Huns. Qin Shi Huang sent Meng Tian with 100,000 soldiers to hit them in the North, and along the mountain, he connected and extended the Great Wall. It stretched thousands of miles from East of Liaodong (today the border between China and Korea, Yalu River) to Lintao (Gansu Minxian) in the West. After Emperor Han Wu defeated the Huns, he extended the Great Wall Westward to Hexi Corridor-Yang Guan, which connected Loulan in the Western Regions. Thus, China's reputation for the Great Wall spread faraway to the distant West. In the 4th century, the Roman historian Ammianus Marcellinus[18] wrote in his book "The Chronicles of Events" that "Seres[19] people had a wall to protect them from enemies", in fact he was talking about Chinese people and the Great Wall.

China's Great Wall was not only a fortification against the nomadic offensives and invasions, and to protect the Han people, but also the boundary between agricultural cultural regions and the nomadic cultural regions. Researches show that inside and outside the Great Wall were two different worlds. According to the agreement with the Hun in the early Han Dynasty, "In the north of the Great Wall is the country of bow, which followed the orders of Chanyu. Inside the Great Wall was a highly developed culture, which was governed by the Han Dynasty." Historically, many peoples have constructed walls for defense purposes, but the Great Wall was the longest and the one which had the longest history. This history also includes the period of confrontation between agricultural and nomadic cultures in the North of China. In the early Western Han Dynasty period, Han and Hun reconciled and initiated friendly exchanges. Historical records show credentials exchanged through the envoys from Han dynasty emperor and Hun Chanyu, which not only recorded their diplomatic intercourse but also portrayed their exchange of national consciousness. Hun Chanyu in its diplomatic documents proclaimed themselves as "emperor designated by God" or "Hun Chanyu created by heaven and earth". However, Han Dynasty only called them "Hun Chanyu," because Chinese believed that the emperors were only designated by the destiny.

Generally, Hun's gifts to the Han Dynasty emperor were: a camel, two riding horses and four harnessing horses. In exchange, the Han Dynasty gave gifts them ranging from silk clothes, gold harness, belt and dozens of colored brocade. Central Plains' silk was far more exquisite than Huns' coarse fur clothing,

---

18   Ammianus's history, Rerum gestarum libri ("The Chronicles of Events"), consisted of 31 books, of which only the last 18, covering the years 353-378, survive. The first 13 books were already unavailable to scholars in the 6th century. (In light of the need for 18 books to cover 26 years, the first 13 must have been relatively sparse in their account of the period from 98 through 352.) The surviving books give a clear, comprehensive account of events by a writer of soldierly qualities, independent judgment, and wide reading.

19   The Seres, were the people who lived in the land of Serica, as the Easternmost countries of Asia known to the Ancient Greek and Roman geographers. It is generally taken as referring to North China during its Zhou, Qin, and Han dynasties, as it was reached via the overland Silk Road in contrast to the Sinae, who were reached via the maritime routes.

so most Hun nobles liked silk. The contacts also increased the worries of Huns about that their population was only a fraction of a county in Han Dynasty, and self-sufficiency made Hun a threat to the border of Han. By continuing to pursue gorgeous silk, the Huns began to think the likelihood of becoming partners by the Han Dynasty. Moreover, they thought that the silk clothes were not suitable for riding horses in the thorns, and the food and subsistence given by the Han Dynasty was not as sweet as Hun's dairy products. Two thousand years ago, the combined productive forces possessed by Hans and Huns could hardly produce enough food and clothing for the whole society. In addition, principles upheld by the nobility varied widely in the distribution of food and clothing for the Hans and the Huns. Han was a agricultural society, so their food production was more stable. The basic unit of the society was the clan whose residence remained unchanged for a long time. The Han people attached great importance to the worship for ancestors and respect for the elders, so their Ministers ridiculed the Huns' habits of respecting the young and neglecting the old. The Hun messengers retorted that their top priority was fighting in the battle with the young people who strengthened its main force, so they deserved food for protecting the old and the weak. At the same time, the Hun envoys pointed out that when their government enlisted the young to defend the frontiers, their elders at home sent them food, which also showed that the Hans needed to respect the elders. Han could not understand these customs. For example, father and son in the Hun community could lay in the same room; when ones father died, the son was allowed to marry his stepmother; when ones brother died, the younger could marry his deceased brother's wife; people had no crown and band decoration, while the state had no courtesy in the court. The Huns messengers argued that by implementing marriage succession, it guaranteed caste preservation. Whereas, when a husband died in the Han, his children and brothers could not marry his wife, which estranged them from their relatives. Hun did not care for official ceremonies too much due to their belief that it would be easier for them to handle matters without much restraint. The Han people placed too much emphasis on etiquette and official rules which resulted enmity in the court. Experiences have shown that between the Han and Hun people there was no distinction of superiority and inferiority in regard to their ethnic customs, the differences were the results of environmental and geographical diversity.. And the most powerful defense for the Huns was achieved by the envoy which had once escorted the Han Emperor's princess who was married a Hun ruler.

According to the records of South Hun in the History of Eastern Han Dynasty, the Hun people had "no documents, they only cared words as bindingt." The lawsuits were handled by the Hun nobility, and dictated in words to Chanyu (leaders) without official documentations. Although the Hun had no written language, they had assigned some Han scholars to work for them. "These Han scholars taught the ir population and animals," as recorded in the book "Huns in Historical Records". They taught them the Chinese characters. The Hun and

Han often corresponded with each other, and these letters were preserved in historical records, which were all written in Chinese. It also showed that the Hun and the Han communicated with each other in Chinese. According to the records of Western Regions in History of Han, with Chanyu's letter, the Huns could get food and living supplies from the countries in the vast territory stretching from Wusun in the East to the Parthia in the West. It an indicates that there was written orderly communication between the Huns and other countries in the Western Regions. They also exchanged musical instruments. Historical materials omitted mentioning what characters were used in writing these scripts. The Hun people generally used Sogdian language when communicating with the Western Regions. In the era of Eastern Han Dynasty, South Hun leaders sent Guo Heng, a Han man to present a Hun map before its surrender. Although it was probably painted by a Han figure living among the Hun people, the map was drawn by the help of Hun people. The constant interactions with the Han Dynasty has made the Hun people gradually appreciate the former's civilization. The Western Han government gave the Huns living in the Central Plains valuable musical instruments which the Hun aristocrats cherished and treated them as valuable presents to be passed from generation to generation. In the period of Eastern Han Emperor Guangwu, North Huns requested new musical instruments since those previously given to them by Western Han Dynasty had broken due to years of use. In the Eastern Han Dynasty, the Han court also gave musical instruments to South Hun. The national music of Huns was "Hu jia" and "Pi Drum". In the the period of Eastern Han Dynasty, famous musician Cai Wen Ji was captured by South Hun Emperor Zuoxian, and lived there for 18 years. She brought back these Hun instruments and Hun music to the Central Plains region.[20]

The southern regions of Eurasia was generally warm and rainy, so it was suitable for human survival. It was occupied by the settled agricultural nation; while the North, with harsh environment, was cold and arid, a place where nomadic people ran wild. The settled nation had a stable harvest and lived a comfortable life. They were densely populated and never lacked labor to develop handicrafts and various skills. Therefore, their culture was more developed; while the nomadic people, with sparse population and unstable harvest, was relatively underdeveloped in the handicraft industry. The inequity in resources made the nomadic people treasure the land. In times of peace, they would use animal products to exchange for agricultural products from the farmer peoples and in wartime, they seized wealth from the settled people. This was the root cause of continuous invasion attempts by the nomad people for decades.

An uprising by the peasants during the late Qin Dynasty gave birth to the Western Han Dynasty. At the beginning, its national strength was weak. The emperor did not have a set of identical horses while the generals and ministers of state traveled on cattle carts. At the time, the Hun state took advantage of wars in the Central Plains to restore its national strength, and constantly harassed the

---

20   See the book, Wang Zhaojun; Going Out of the Frontiers of China.

frontiers of the Chinese Han empire which has greatly damaged their agricultural production. Strengthening their security became the highest priority for the Han government. There were two ways to solve this problem: one, through forceful means and the other, through peaceful means. At that time, there were great disparities in strength between the Han and Hun. Han Gaozu (Liu Bang), once tried to combat the Huns, but was surrounded in Pingcheng. He was freed after offering a generous gift to the Queen of the Huns. The Han empire could not protect themselves from the Huns, so it adopted a "roll with the punches" attitude. Marriage became the most preferred means and so they sent a woman to marry the Hun leader while generously offering property to end their invasion attempts. The initial Han-Hun "marriage" treaty was signed by the initiative of Han leader Gaozu and Modu Chanyu in the Pingcheng city.

Agreeing "political marriages" was humiliating for the Han Dynasty, but it brought peace and stopped bloodshed and property loss of Han people living along the borders. The treaty was a negligible one compared to sending an army to combat the Hun people. The "marriage" policy was also in line with the interests of the Hun. On the other side, the Hun nobles could thus get Han's property without going wars, which was risky. The Hun people profited from trading with the Han people, because many street markets were opened.

Emperor Gaozu of the Han Dynasty ordered Liu Jing to send a princess to marry Modu Chanyu, and became brothers. In 176 BC, Modu Chanyu, in his letter to the Han Dynasty, expressed his willingness to make a ceasefire in the interest of developing the economy, help people to settle down at the frontier, and hoped that "the country prospers and peace prevails among the people." His desire was to restore peace with the Han dynasty. In order to achieve this purpose, Chanyu launched a war. With the blessing of the holy Heaven, brave soldiers as well as strong horses, the Hun state had conquered 26 countries, including Loulan, Wusun and others. In the meantime, Modu Chanyu, threatened the Han Dynasty with invasion if they stopped the Huns from living in the frontier and pushing back the Han people from the border. Thus for a long time, "military marriage" became an important means for the Han Dynasty to maintain peace with the Huns. During the reign of Emperor Wendi of the Han Dynasty, Hun Laoshang Chanzi ascended to the throne and he sent a royal concubine to become the queen of the Hun.

During the reign of Emperor Wu of the Han Dynasty, its strength grew and it launched several battles against the Hun forces. "Marriage" was too humiliating for them and they were determined to defeat the Huns. In the consecutive years, the Dynasty sent troops to crusade against Hun and finally defeated them. In the middle of the first century BC, the Huns were weakened by civil conflicts. Huhanye Chanyu finally surrendered, and the Hun kingdom became a colony of the Han Dynasty. In 33 BC, Huhanye came to Chang'an to seek audience with the Han emperor and expressed their pride in marrying Han Chinese women. He therefore asked the emperor to continue approving this arrangement. The living conditions in Hun's region were very difficult and the women belonging to the royal family were unwilling for such marriages. When Han Gaozu approved his daughter's marriage to Modu Chanyu, Empress Lü strongly opposed it, asking why they were abandoning their daughter. Wang Zhaojun had became a famous woman for her marriage with the Hun leaders. She was born in a decent family at Zigui county (today in the Hubei province), whose other name was Qiang. She was the maid for Emperor Hanyuan after entering the palace. The emperor had numerous concubines, and a hierarchical harem, Zhaojun had slept with the emperor even once during her years of stay in the palace. Therefore, grievances and grudges had grown in her mind. After she heard that the Huns were asking for a marriage, she begged the management officials of the harem to allow marry her marry to a Hun leader, eventually she got the approval of the Han emperor.

After an audience with the Han emperor, The Hun leader Huhanye left Chang'an with Zhaojun and 5 other palace maids. In the parting ceremony, people looked at the young and beautiful Zhaojun, dressed in gorgeous clothing. She made the Han palace more colorful, she earned respect and affection from everyone present there. It was the first time the Han Emperor saw Zhaojun, and he was greatly affected by her beauty. He wished her to stay, but was afraid of losing the trust of the Huns. He therefore released her to marry Huhanye Chanyu. After the Han met the Hun's marriage demand, Huhanye Chanyu requested the removal of the border defense forces. Huhanye Chanyu pledged willingness to maintain peace with the Han Dynasty to allow peaceful development. After discussions, the Han government agreed to cement peace with the Huns although they did not agree to remove their border defense. In 1954, some potteries were unearthed in Maotou village near Baotou city, with themes such as the "marriage with Chanyu," "Long Live" and "Endless Happiness" in the late Western Han Dynasty tombs. Following her marriage to the Hun leader, Zhaojun was known as "Ninghu Yanzhi" (Hu-Pacifying Chief-Consort) for the peace she brought to the two peoples. She gave birth to a son for Huhanye Chanyu and this son Yu Ti Zhiyashi, and he was became called by the king on the right (Zuoxian), among the Huns ranking second only to the khan in importance.

After Huhanye died, Ninghu Yanzhi's (Zhaojun) eldest son Wushulei (Dia Tao Mo Gao) reigned in his stead. According to Hun custom of "marrying mothers upon father's death," normally Wushulei had to marry Zhaojun. Despite her marriage house was far from home, the widow Zhaojun refused to accept this Hun custom and, she presented a memorial to the empire of the Han dynasty to return home (China). Zhaojun's marriage was not a personal affair but was instead a peace treaty between the Han and the Hun. The Han emperor responded by ordering her to obey the customs of the Hun people, thus she married to the young Chanyu. Zhaojun and Wu Shulei had two daughters, their older daughter was called Yun, and she got married to the South Hun Chanyu after she grew up. She was hence known as the "Princess Xubu." After she married the Hun nobleman Xubu Dang, Princess Xubu and her husband belonged to the pro-Hun faction of the Hun court. The younger daughter later married a man surnamed Dangyu, so she was called "Princess Dangyu". Zhaojun and Huhanye Chanyu's son gradually rose to a leadership status in the South Hun. Initially, he was known as "Youglu Liwang," according to Hun customs he should assume the title of the Golden Horde, which referred to the crown prince in the hierarchy of the Hun empire. But, the extremely ambitious Wu Shulei, soon became tired of waiting for the father to pass power to him, eventually killed Zhaojun and his father, Huhanye Chanyu's another son, which meant he killed his half brother.

The relationship between the Han and the Hun changed after Zhaojun had made a brave decision to surpass borders, thus she played a key role in the establishment of a peaceful relation between the two states.. At the beginning of the Han Dynasty, a large number of its people's property had passed to the Huns through such political marriages. And it was also a great honor for Hun Chanyu to marry daughters of the Han leaders. Therefore, after the Huns surrendered the Han, they continued to established marriage ties between the two peoples. This way, Wang Zhaojun, an ordinary folk girl, married to the Hun under the identity of a maid of Han Dynasty, and she became the ambassador of peace. In order to promote peace and harmony between the two peoples, after the death of Huhanye Chanyu, Zhaojun gave up her original Han custom and habit and had followed the Hun customs by marrying Huhanye's son. Her daughters and son-in-laws together with their offsprings became the representatives of Han Dynasty who always felt good and loyal feelings towards the Han, they always advocated peace with the Han Dynasty. While negotiating with the Huns during Wang Mang's reign (9-23 CE), the Han also chose a girl from a relative of Zhaojun family. Zhaojun's nephew Wang Xi was made the "Duke of political marriage."

The narration about Zhaojun's ambition to surpass the frontiers has a history of more than 2000 years. However, her name has remained in people's hearts dwelling in the grasslands and mainland. Zhaojun's Tomb is currently located in Daheihe in the Southern suburbs of the capital of Hohhot, Inner Mongolia, which was mentioned in the "Tong Dian" of Duyou in Tang Dynasty. According to volume 38 of "Geographical Records of Taiping" of Song Dynasty, the grass on Zhaojun's tomb has been ever green, therefore the tomb was known as the "Green Tomb." And there were also records in the "Liao History" written in the Yuan Dynasty period, which implied that people commemorated Zhaojun as a friendly ambassador between the Hun and Han people.

Another well-known Han woman who had married to the Hun leaders was Cai Wenji. There was great worldwide disorder at the end of the Eastern Han Dynasty (194-195). Dong Zhuo's army had many Hun cavalrymen, and they plundered everywhere leading to abduction of Cai Wenji. So she lived with the Huns for 12 years. Although she became a princess consort, she was sad for she was captured at the border. She wrote poems describing her miserable life in the Hun and sighed when recollecting her parents. She was however happy to meet people coming from Han. Later, Cao Cao redeemed her from the Southern Hun with a large sum of money. Wen Ji had two sons living in the Hun and when she was about to leave the Huns, her children were sad. There were many Chinese people who were abducted and who lived among the Hun people and so Wen Ji bade them farewell before leaving. They all burst into tears. The people from the Han who were unable to return back home finally merged with the Hun people. "Sixteen Kingdoms" in the Northern Dynasties, Southern Hun periods as a nation had gradually disappeared, but again they were all integrated into the Han people later on.

(4) Northern Huns Moving Westward

With the decline of the military strength of the Huns, they encountered a split in 57 BC. Five Hun nobles competed for the Chanyu title which had led to splits and conflicts among them and Huhanye Chanyu's tribe in the south Monan region and Zhi Zhi Chanyu's tribe in the Mobei. Huhanye Chanyu's forces were weaker than Zhi Zhi Chanyu, so he decided to seek refuge with the Han Dynasty. Zhi Zhi Chanyu was unable to counter the pressure from both Huhanye and Han Dynasty, so he also sought Han protection and received government's preferential treatment. But soon Huhanye and Zhi Zhi Chanyu fell into another round of battles, Zhi Zhi Chanyu could no longer control consequently the Mobei tribe moved Westward. Zhi Zhi Chanyu attempted to unite with the Wusun tribe, which has become a vassal of the Han Dynasty, at that time. Therefore they did not want to ally the Huns. Kunmi, the governor of Wusun kingdom, on one hand reported to the Western Regions Frontier Command of the Han Dynasty, while on the other, mobilized the Wusun army to attack Northern Hun regions in the name of Zhi Zhi Chanyu. But, Zhi Zhi Chanyu wisely discovered the attack plans of Wusun and were ableto defeat Wusun troops. Zhi Zhi Chanyu occupied upper and middle reaches of the current Erqisi River and the Jiankun region in the North of Mount Tangnu, thus intensified contradictions with the Han Dynasty.

Under the joint threat of Huhanye and the Han Dynasty, Zhi Zhi Chanyu moved further westward. Kangju kingdom in the west (the eastern part of Kazakhstan) was not affiliated to the Western Regions Frontier Command of the Han Dynasty, and it was hostile to the Wusun kindom. Therefore, Zhi Zhi Chanyu, took the eastern part of Kangju as his foothold. The king of Kangju kingdom and Wang Zhi (Han dynasty) formed a political marriage alliance, and agreed to deal with Wusun in an alliance. The allied forces of Zhi Zhi Chanyu led Kangju forces repeatedly attacked against Wusun territory, and finally forced them to surrender their western ranch.

Zhi Zhi Chanyu's forces were greatly motivated after defeating the Wusun forces. Zhi Zhi Chanyu began to believe that he had gained a solid foothold in the Western Regions and thus broke his relationships with the Kangju kingdom. Zhi Zhi killed the daughter of Kangju king (also his queen) and other nobles. Their corpses were thrown into Taras River that flowed through Kyrgyzstan and Kazakhstan. He also recruited the local residents to fortify his force, which lasted for two years. The city built by Zhi Zhi Chanyu was known later as Talas (Taraz) city (in Kazakhstan). Zhi Zhi also considered himself as the new ruler of Eurasian grasslands and demanded that the Dawan and other tribes pay tribute to him.

Zhi Zhi Chanyu's activities in the Western Regions had aroused great concern in the Frontier Command. The distance between the Western Regions and the Chinese mainland was wide and this delayed consultations on military conscription. In order to seize the opportunity to subdue Zhi Zhi Chanyu, the officials of Western Regions Frontier Command Gan Yanshou, Chen Tang, and others recruited four million soldiers under the false command of the Han emperor. They also dispatched Han soldiers to the wasteland in the Western Regions, compiled them into six teams, three of which marched from the South Road and trekked through Cong ridge and attacked Zhi Zhi Chanyu forces from South to North after entering into Dawan. The other 3 teams marched through Tianshan Mountains and entered Kangju territories passing through the Wusun territories.

In 36 BC, the fortress of Zhi Zhi Chanyu was sieged by troops of Western Regions Frontier Command. The troops in the city were not enough, thus even the queens joined the fight for defense. The war was intense insomuch that some queens were killed. Zhi Zhi was shot in the nose. Shortly after, the Han soldiers captured the fortress, and successfully repelled Kangju's reinforcements. After fierce fighting, Han troops captured the city of Zhicheng. They captured more than 1,500 people, including Zhiyi Chanyu, the Prince, queens and about 1,000 people after completely destroying Zhi Zhi Chanyu's forces. Wars broke out in the Central Plains region at the turn of two Han dynasties which gave opportunity to the Huns to regain their power. Eastern Han Dynasty rejuvenated itself after its establishment. In 48 BC, Hun agains split into the North and South part. The South part was led by the Huhanye Chanyu Sunbi who cooperated with the Han Dynasty. On the other hand, the North Hun were initially against the Han Dynasty, however, under the joint oppression of South Hun, the Han and Wuhuan, it was forced to reconcile with the Eastern Han Dynasty in 51 BC. On the one side, the Han dynasty maintained good contacts with the North Huns, on the other hand, they sent Banchao to the Western Regions to mobilize the troops and the South Huns cavalry to fight against the North Huns. During 89 years, the Eastern Han's army penetrated deep into the Western Mongolian Steppes and defeated the North Huns, killed more than 10,000 troops which consequently led to the surrender of the North Hun leaders together with a total number of more than 200,000 people.. Thus North Hun Chanyu with remnants of their defeated troops were forced to march towards the Golden Hill and sought the protection of the Wusun kingdom.

Part of the North Hun troops marched southwards to Pulei Sea (currently the Barkol Lake in the east of Xinjiang) from the north desert, and became the vassal of the Han Dynasty. But they soon rebelled again, and were eliminated by the Han forces. The remaining troops that fled together with North Hun Chanyu found protection of the Wusun (later known as Yueban). The Wusun kingdom was located along the Yili River, Chu River Steppes, and the Wusun kingdom had no natural barriers between Talas (Taraz) River which was then controlled by the Kangju kingdom grasslands in the downstream of Syr Darya River as well as the Euroasia Steppes. North Hun tribe soon expanded Westward and occupied Kangju. But part of the Northern Huns still lingered behind in the North of Qiuci, and that was Yule Dusi River in the upper reaches of Ili River, which extended for long miles. Later Liangzhou in Hezhou was always referred to as the leader Chanyu Wang. The Hun people moved Westward to Kangju region in the early 4th century and invaded the Sogdian people living between the Amu Darya River and the Syr Darya rivers. They killed the king. The Huns moved Westwards and lived far from the Han region. Due to communication barriers, they faded from being mentioned in the Han nationality. In European history, it was mentioned that the second half of the 4th century saw a nomadic tribe called the Huns invade from the East, and defeated the Alans in the Don River in 374. Many scholars believed that these were the North Huns who moved Westward from Mobei. After entering Eastern Europe, the Huns seized the territory of Ostrogoths and Visigoths, and chased them away from their homeland, which triggered a series of national migration. Thus the Huns were seen as the promoters of the great migration movement that caused the fall of the Roman Empire.

(5) Huns and the Land Silk Road

The Hun tribes, inhabiting the Northern desert, were mainly engaged in animal husbandry with fishing, hunting and fruit collecting as auxiliary production means. Its handicraft industry, despite of development to a certain degree, was not self-sufficient in production and living. The Hun-controlled Southern Desert neighbored the Central Plains and the nomadic pastoral people on the Mongolian Plateau had traded animals, hides and fur products for the farm and handicraft products from the Central Plains. The Hun aristocrats' demands for deluxe goods of the Central Plains were also urgent. From the Warring States Period, the Huns had paid attention to the mutual trade with the Central Plains people. Even during the warring period between the Central Plains and the Hun regimes, the Hun people would still carry out the border trade. The demand for mutual trade between the Han and the Hun peoples was the essential reason for the inclusion desert regions into the Chinese territories.

Mongolian scholars excavated the Hun tombs in the North of the desert and discovered lots of materials from the Central Plains. The findings, including both living utensils and production tools made in the Central Plains, such as iron ware, copper ware, potteries, wooden ware, lacquer ware, stone ware, tools, harness, gold, garments and silk products, proved the considerable and frequent material exchanges between the Hans and the Huns. The Huns had the capacity to cast cooper ware but relied on the Central Plains for the supply of composition brass, ores and other materials. Jia Xi suggested Emperor Wendi of the Han Dynasty to resist the Hun through controlling the metal sales to the nation. In 1940, an ancient cultural layer was discovered when the Strength Collective Farm was building a road in the 8km to the South of Abakan, capital of Khakasiya state to the North of Tannu Uriankhai in the upper stream of the Yenisei River of the former Soviet Union. Upon scholars' confirmation, there were many tiles and eave tiles from the Han. On the tiles were Chinese characters "Tian Zi Qian Qiu Wan Sui" (means Long Live the Emperor!) "Chang Le Wei Yang" (means Long happiness and endless joy). Archeologists from the Russian Academy of Sciences, Khakasiya Museum and Minusinsk Museum jointly excavated the site in 1941, 1945 and 1946 respectively. They found that it was a square Han-style building with four slopes, double-eve and tile roof and 16 rooms. According to the research of scholars of the former Soviet Union, it was the residence of Li Ling after he surrendered to the Huns.[21]

In 1924, Soviet archeologist Kozlov excavated the ancient Hun tombs in the Nuoyan Mountain, about 100 km North of Ulan Bator, the capital of Mongolia. Three valuable embroideries with the same background of deep brown wool fabrics were unearthed in No. 6 tomb. The first and second embroideries were of the same size and nailed on the exterior wall of the coffin. The pattern was embroidered mainly with white crewel as well as crewel of other colors. On one embroidery, there were the figures of a coco-like tree and a tiger-like winged beast running forward with a stretched neck and an upward tail. On the other embroidery was a blossomy tree with a bird perching in it. The bird held a shield in its left talon, a fork in its right talon and a snake in its beak. The third work, besides the said two ones, was embroidered with red, yellow, white, green, brown and other colorful crewels. Despite the damages in the left, right and upper parts, we can see a horse rider in the middle part of the embroidery. On a white horse, the rider had a hat with earflaps, an embroidered gown with a leather edge, and a pair of soft-sole leather shoes with horizontal line patterns on them. The rein and gag bit were quite distinct though the iron ring of the gag bit was invisible. Round patterned nails were used to decorate the horse breast. The first figure to the left of the white horse rider was incomplete in the head, and the second one looked forward. On the right part of the embroidery were two black horses, one horse's head upward and the other's downward. The horse with an upward head cast its white eyes on the white horse in the central part.

The pattern on the above-mentioned embroideries unearthed in the No. 6 tomb of the Nuoyan Mountain was the same with those on the gold and silver articles and pottery ware of the Scythians inhabiting the northern bank of the Black Sea. These embroideries should originate from the regions and peoples related with the Scythians. Greek style silk products were also discovered in the No. 6 tomb, and they should come from the regions which had communications with Greeks.

---

21   S.V. Kiselev: Ancient History of Southern Siberia (Volume B), the Chinese Version of Institute of Ethnic Nationalities of Xinjiang Academy of Social Sciences.

Also, many silk products were excavated from the No. 12 tomb found around the Nuoyan Mountain. One of them was probably named as Mountains and Clouds, which is 1.92 meters high, and 38 cm. in width. The brown satin bottom material has become deep gray due to fading. This satin pattern was embroidered with red, yellow and brown crewel. Three mountains with three clouds floating by each mountain were embroidered. On the central mountain there was an exuberant tree, and on both the left and right mountains, there was a fledged bird heading outward. Another was probably called the Western Dragon Flies which was embroidered on satin bottom material. It is a flying Western style dragon with its head backward and tail upward. The dragon, having four claws, a vagarious shape and two quite small wings on its shoulder, was quite different from the snake-shaped Chinese dragon. Besides the dragon were angled patterns. On the peripheral of the embroidery were pattern of triangles and circles.[22]

The pattern of these two embroideries displays an obvious Greek style. Mongolian Steppes has communicated with the West via the Eurasian Steppes since ancient times. According to the Biography of the Western Regions, History of the Han Dynasty, all peoples, from Wusun Westward to Parthia, had revered Hun. Although its political center was in the desert, Hun had an extensive influence to the Eurasian Steppes. These embroideries were the proofs of the trade route in the Steppes during the Han Dynasty period or the period before the Han Dynasty.

The communications between the Huns and the Central Plains has begun quite early. Between 1955 and 1957, archaeologists excavated tombs of the Zhou Dynasty at Kexing Village, Fengxi Township, Chang'an County, Shaanxi. The No. 140 tomb was confirmed to be a Hun tomb and its owner might be a messenger or a delegation member of Hun to the Central Plains. Many products of the Huns products were unearthed from the tomb. Two rectangular cooper ornaments with openwork carving were extremely eye-catching. The pattern of the openwork carving was two horses with brides and saddles respectively tied on two exuberant trees, and two persons were wrestling with their long hair disheveled to their necks.[23]

The folk songs of Hun were moving and fair-sounding. The Qilian Mountains and Yanzhi Mountains to the West of the Yellow River boasted flourishing trees, lush pastures, warm winter and cool summer and moderate climate for animal husbandry. In the 2nd year of the Yuanshou Period under the reign of Emperor Wudi of the Han Dynasty (121 BC), the Western Han defeated Hun and captured the Qilian Mountains and Yanzhi Mountains. The Huns were quite sad and sighed out the lyrics as follows:

---

22 See Lin Gan: The Comprehensive History of the Huns, the People's Publishing House, 1986, pp. 146-148.
23 Refer to Report on the Excavation Works in Fengxi, compiled by the Institute of Archaeology, Chinese Academy of Sciences, published in 1963 by Cultural Relics Press

"Losing my Yanzhi Mountain, Our women turn pale. Losing my Qilian Mountain, The livestock could not live."[24]

The pronunciation of Yanzhi in the lyrics was the same as both the "rouge" in Chinese language and the title of the wife of the Hun's chief. This homophony created a punny effect. Rouge was a cosmetic for beauties. Hun's loss of Yanzhi Mountains was similar to the beauties' loss of rouge, and both could not dress up beautifully. The exquisite folksongs were widely spread by the scholars throughout the past dynasties.

The Hun melody Eighteen Stanzas in Nomadic Reed Pipe (Hu Jia Shi Ba Pai) has made a profound effect to the Central Plains. Nomadic reed Pipe[25] (Hujia) was a traditional instrument of Hun. According to Biography of Dou Xian, History of the Latter-Period Han Dynasty, Dou Xian wrote: "Han leaders dispatched troops to the Jinshan Mountains and listened to the Hujia melody in the enemy's imperial court". At the end of the Eastern Han Dynasty, Cai Wenji was captured by the Southern Hun. Cai Wenji (a beautiful woman) described the music in the lines "Frontier horses neighed when they heard Hujia; lonely gooses danced with the Pipe's sound".

Nomadic reed Pipe (Hujia) was a traditional wind instrument (flute) and often accompanied by drums (Pigu). Cai Wenji in her song said that the drums of the Huns often sounded noisily at night till the dawn. Cai Wenji was a perfect talent and good at music. She had given attention to the music when she was in the Hun region and introduced the music to the Central Plains after she returned back.

"The 18 Songs of a Nomad Flute", composed by Cai Wenji of the Eastern Han Dynasty (25-220), was based on "Miss Wenji," composed by the Huns. Cai, who was fond of music, was captured by the Tatars during war, and was later redeemed by Cao Cao, a general of the Three Kingdoms Period (220-280). She expressed her sadness for being torn away from her family in the song, which has been famous for thousands of years. The nomadic music and lyrics was favored by the scholars of the Central Plains. Liu Chou and Liu Jin of the Jin Dynasty were good at playing the nomadic reed Pipe and comparable with the "frontier region melodies" played by the Huns. Their performance even made the Huns "homesick".[26]

---

24 Quotes from Story of the West of the Yellow River, Biography of Hun People, Records of the Historian.

25 Hujia was a reed Pipe used by the Northern tribes in ancient China; Hu jia was a kind of reed Pipe made of reed or wood. Blown vertically, the three-holed instrument produced a gloomy, sad timbre deeply loved by the Huns.

26 Supplements in regard to Biography of Liu Wei, History of the Jin Dynasty; Biography of Liu Kun, History of the Jin Dynasty.

5. A Through Land Silk Road from the East to the West

(1) The Nomads Who Moved to the Western Regions:

a) Rouzhi people and Tocharian

Rouzhi, also known as Darouzhi (Great Rouzhi), was neither separately recorded in the records of the Rouzhi nor in the History records of the Han Dynasty. However, some documentation on the early history of Rouzhi were found in the Biography of Wusun, Biography of Dayuan and Biography of Zhang Qian in the book "Records of the Historian". Rouzhi was a nomadic clan and "roved around with domestic animals and shared customs with the Hun".[27]

After moving Westward, Rouzhi set up the Kushan Dynasty in Central Asia. But Chinese historical books generally called it as Rouzhi. According to literature records, Rouzhi dwelled in Northwestern China in the Shang Dynasty (Yi Yin's Statement to the Shang Court). Some literatures prior to the Qin Dynasty mentioned some names similar to Rouzhi, such as Ouzhi (禺支) in the Meeting of Kings of History of Zhou Dynasty, and Ouzhi (禺知) in the first volume of Biography of Emperor Muwang of Zhou, "jade comes from Ouzhi (禺氏)" in the Country Resources of Guan Zi, and "Ouzhi (禺氏) does not come to our imperial court. Can we regard their jade as currency? Then Ouzhi will come, and the extensive Kunlun region will also send envoys to us." in the Light and Heavy Armors of Guan Zi. All the said names were argued to be the translation differences of Darouzhi. According to the Biography of Zhang Qian in the Records of the Historian, Rouzhi originally dwelled in the region between Dunhuang and Qilian Mountains. The Biography of Xiqiang, History of the Latter-Han Dynasty also said that the Huangzhong Rouzhi Hu, an ethnic group of Darouzhi, once inhabited Zhangye and Jiuquan.

In the early years of the Western Han period, the news on Rouzhi came from the capitulationists and envoys of Hun. Since the ruling of Emperor Wudi, accurate messages on the ethnic group mainly came from the reports of Envoy Zhang Qian after he returned from the Western Regions. The Rouzhi's place names Dunhuang and Qilian in Zhang's reports were not Chinese. Dunhuang, referring to the region near the Qilian Mountain, should be another transliteration of Dunhong in Legends of Mountains and Seas or of Tokhar possibly. At the end of last century, an unknown language spelled in Brahmi letters of India was found in Yanqi and Kuche, South of Xinjiang. After scholars' research, it was found that the language did not belong to the Indo-European's Indian-Iranian language but the Indo-European's Western branch. The language speakers called it Tocharian. Based on this, some linguists assumed that the language was used by Rouzhi and its kin clans.

At the end of the 3000 BC, a nation called Guit, with Gutium as its nominative, was recorded in the historical data of Babylon. The nation attacked Babylon from the mountainous region in the West of Persia. In the inscriptions

---

27　See Biography of Dayuan, Records of the Historian.

of Hammurabi, Babylon's neighboring peoples were also mentioned, such as Gutium and Tukris. According to German scholar Walter Bruno Henning, these two peoples gradually moved Eastward and settled down in Northwest China, and the Guti people inhabited Hexi (the West of the Yellow River) and evolved into the Rouzhi clan while the Tukri people inhabited Yanqi and Kuche, current South regions of Xinjiang, and were called Tocharian later on.[28] The first theory, developed by W.B. Henning in his 1965 paper, "the first Indo-Europeans in history," is discussed at some length in Mallory and Mair (2000), pp. 281-282. They explore Henning's suggestion that the ancient pronunciation of 'Yuezhi" could be approximately reconstructed as *Gu(t)-t'i and related it to the 'Guti' people who began harassing the western borders of Babylon from c. 2100 BCE.

Apparently, Henning believed that Guti in the 'Kuchean-Agnean' or 'KA' language "would have been rendered Kuči, and hence be equivalent to Kuchean. As for the toχri mentioned in the Uighur colophon, Henning believed one need look no further than the name of the Tukriš who had been neighbours of the Guti in western Persia and hence had given their name both to the toχri of the northern Tarim and the Tocharians of Bactria." Unfortunately, in regard to this argument, Mallory and Mair have found their support on the basis of similar tablets unconvincing but, "Of greater detriment to such a theory is that Henning accepted a reconstructed Chinese pronunciation of Yuezhi as *Gu(t)-t'i when, in fact, it is commonly reconstructed now as *ng-wāt-t-ĕg which makes it a far less transparent correspondence." Qilian was clearly defined by the ancient people as a region in Hexi inhabited by Darouzhi before the Han Dynasty.. In Biography of Er Zhurong, History of Wei, it is said that "Xiurong has three deep lakes located on the high mountains. They are known as Qilian Lake, or the Heavenly Lake by the Wei people." In the notes to Records on Emperor Wudi of History of the Han Dynasty written by Yan Shigu, it was written: "Tian Shan (Tianshan Mountain) is actually the Qilian Shan (Qilian Moutain) as the Huns call Tian as Qilian and Serbi do the same."[29]

Qilian was also the transliteration of word "tengri" in Turkic and Mongolian language later on. So Rouzhi was possibly related with the said two peoples, especially the peoples that had spoke the Turkic language.

Linguistic research provides a new avenue for researching the migration history of the Central Asian Steppes peoples in ancient times. But linguistic research alone is not sufficient for unveiling the said secrets. Since the beginning of this century, anthropologists have made analysis on the human skeletons discovered in the ancient tombs before the Han Dynasty in Eastern regions of Gansu and Xinjiang. Their work offers another view of angle for us in examining the issue. In the 1920s, Western scholar Davidson Black had made

28   Refer to The Earliest Indo-European People in History written by Walter Bruno Henning, translated by Xu Wenkan and published on Northwestern Journal of Ethnology Vol.2, 1992.
29   See Records on Emperor Han Wudi, in the book History of the Han Dynasty, noted on the 2nd year of the reign of Emperor Tianhan written by Yan Shigu in Tianshan Mountains region.

detailed research on the 84 skeletons of pre-historical human beings collected by Johan Gunnar Andersson from the cultural sites of Shajing, Siwa, Xindian and Machang in Gansu and Yangshao in Henan, and concluded that the pre-historical residents in Gansu had general natures of oriental race and many physical similarities with contemporary Northern China man. The Neolithic Gansu pre-historical residents had greater physical similarities with the contemporary people of North China. The skull shapes of Gansu pre-historical residents, similar to those of Xikang, are between those of contemporary people of North China people and those of Tibetan people.[30]

In the 1950s, Chinese scholars made researches on the skulls of two men unearthed from the Qi Family Tombs in Gansu and believed that they belonged to the Mongolian race and had similar skulls with the local residents of the late Neolithic period and the contemporary residents of North China.[31] In recent years, tombs of early bronze era were discovered at the Huoshaogou Site, Yumen in Hexi prefecture of Gansu. Gansu Provincial Museum collected over 100 skeletons from the tombs. Based on further study, the archeologists thought that the tomb owners belonged to the East Asian race of the Mongolian race without any mixture of Caucasoid elements, and they were possibly the ancient Qiang people instead of the Rouzhi or Wusun people. To sum up, human skeletons of the Neolithic era, Bronze era and the pre-Qin period unearthed from the ancient tombs in Gansu were all similar to those of the Eastern Asian Mongolian race, and no influence of the Caucasoid race to the residents in the region before the Qin and Han dynasties.[32]

Such conclusion is contradictory with Western linguists' point of view that Rouzhi was a branch of the primitive Indo-Europeans. Rouzhi was the first nation recorded in China's ancient historical books that moved Westward and founded a country in the remote West. Rouzhi people had close contact with Hun when they inhabited Hexi region. When Hun was under the reign of Chief Touman (about 209 BC), Maodun, son of the Chief, was sent to Rouzhi as a hostage. Soon after that, Hun attacked Rouzhi, and Maodun stole a strong horse and rode back to Hun. Rouzhi was quite powerful and had about 100,000 to 200,000 archers. After enthronement, Maodun dispatched troops led by Duke Youxian to attack Rouzhi. Rouzhi was defeated and its ruler was executed and his skull was made into a drinking utensil. After the failure, Rouzhi was dispersed and most of its people fled to the basins of the current Yili River and Chuhe River. These newcomers suppressed the native Sek people, forcing the Sek ruler to go into exile and used the Sek captives as servants. Based on the ancient pronunciation system, scholars believed that Sek was actually Saka in Western historical books. After Rouzhi moved westward, the Hexi prefecture

---

30   Han Kangxin, Pan Qifeng: About the Ethnic Classification of Wusun and Rouzhi people, published on Treatise on History of Western Regions, Vol. 3, 1990.
31   Preliminary Research on Skulls in the Qi Family Tombs of Gansu, Acta Archaeologica Sinica, Vol. 9, 1955, pp 193-197.
32   Ibid.

once inhabited by Rouzhi was occupied by the clans of Chief Hunye and Chief Xiutu of Hun people.

Some Rouzhi people who did not move Westward fled into the Qilian Mountains and lived together with the Qiang people there. They were called Xiaorouzhi (Small Rouzhi) then. In the 2nd year of the Yuanshou Period under the reign of Emperor Wudi (121 BC), General Huo Qubing defeated Hun and captured Hexi and Huangzhong (current region along both banks of the Huangshui River, Qinghai). Xiaorouzhi submitted to the Han Dynasty and moved to Zhangye for residence. Xiaorouzhi was called Yiconghu and lived in Zhangye for a long time till the first year of the Zhongping Period under the reign of Emperor Lingdi of Eastern Han (184 AD) according to the historical records.[33] Although establishing a country in the basins of the Yili River and the Chuhe River, Rouzhi was still quite near to the West border of Hun. Darouzhi neighbored Wusun when it was in Hexi. Between 174 BC and 161 BC, Hun's chief Laoshang assisted Wusun to attack Rouzhi and killed its king. Rouzhi could not have a foothold there and had to move westward again along the Saka people's routes. Striding across the Tianshan Mountains and the western Pamirs and arriving at Oxus (i.e. Amu Darya, current border river between Uzbekistan, Tajikistan and Afghanistan), Rouzhi conquered the local Daxia people (Bactrians) and finally settled down.

In the early period of the Western Han dynasty, many Saka clans traversed the Tianshan Mountains and escaped towards current Pamirs region due to the pressures by the Rouzhi. And some Saka people could not flee and became the subjects of Rouzhi. Later on, Rouzhi was beaten by the Wusun tribe. These Saka people became the subordinates of the Wusun tribe. So, today, the blood of many ethnic peoples living in the Xinjiang region contains the genes of Saka people. The ancient residents in Northern Xinjiang were somewhat consanguineous with the offspring of the Saka people in the Tianshan region of Kazakhstan and the Andronovo Culture of the Caucasian race. Also, the ancient dwellers of the Southern Xinjiang were related with the Levantine race—a branch of the Caucasian race. Contemporary scholars called the languages used before the 10th century in Khotan prefecture of Xinjiang as the Khotan Saka language. Over the past decades, many Saka gold wares were unearthed in Kazakhstan and Northern Xinjiang. These gold wares were normally hammered from gold foils and have animal shapes. Based on the examination of the forging process, we can see that Saka people had enjoyed a remarkably developed civilization.

b) Wusun kingdom of central Asia (c. 300 BC-300 AD)

Wusun was one of the most important peoples that mediated the East-west Steppes communications in the Han Dynasty period. Records on Wusun can be found in Biography of Dayuan, Records of the Historian. The contents are

---

33 See Biography of Xiqiang and Biography of Emperor Lingdi, History of the Later Period of the Han Dynasty.

generally the same with and complementary to the Biography of Zhang Qian, History of the Han Dynasty. In addition, historical records about the Wusun people can also be found in the History of the Han Dynasty. Wusun was a nomadic nation between Dunhuang and Qilian and were neighbored with Rouzhi people. In those days, it was a small race and often oppressed by the Rouzhi tribes.

The chiefs of Wusun were called Kunmo or Kunmi. The earliest Wusun ruler was called Nandoumi. According to the Biography of Zhang Qian, History of the Han Dynasty, in the 3rd year of the Qianyuan Period under the reign of Emperor Wendi (177 BC), Wusun was beaten by Rouzhi and its ruler Nandoumi was killed. But, in the Biography of Dayuan, Records of the Historian, it said that Nandoumi was killed by the Huns. Liejiaomi, son of Nandoumi, was still a baby when Wusun was defeated. The senior official Bujiu took Liejiaomi with him and fled. Bujiu put Liejiaomi in a dense clump of grass and went to search for food. When he came back, Bujiu saw a wolf lactating the baby and a raven bringing meat to the baby. Bujiu thought it was a supernatural being. Bujiu, carrying the baby, surrendered himself to Hun. Hun's Chief Maodun also believed it was miraculous and adopted the baby. According to Chief Maodun's letter to the Han Dynasty, the adoption took place in the 4th year under the reign of Emperor Wendi (176 BC).

The Hun's Chief handed over the Wusun clans to Liejiaomi after he grew up. Later on, Liejiaomi became the Kunmo (chief) of Wusun. In order to seek his revenge on Rouzhi, the Kunmo collaborated with Hun's Youxian Duke to attack the Rouzhi which had moved Westward to the basin of Yili River. Rouzhi could not resist and had to move further Westwards. Under the leadership of Liejiaomi, Wusun rapidly developed into a strong power with dozens of thousand archers. For the purpose of development, Wusun occupied the regions near currentYili River and Chuhe River in 125 BC or so. The Rouzhi people who did not escape and the Saka people under the control of Rouzhi became the subjects of Wusun. Then, Wusun neighbored Hun with the Jinshan Mountain in between, Kangju at the lower reaches of the current Talas River and Syr Darya in its Northwest, and Dayuan in its West with the oasis countries near the Tarim Basin and and the Tianshan Mountains as the border. After the settlement in the West Regions, Wusun has greatly increased its power and did not subject to Hun any more. According to the historical records, Wusun had 120,000 households with 630,000 residents including 180,000 troops and established its capital in Chigu which were frequently visited by the Han's envoys and governors of Western Regions later on. The Biography of Western Regions of the History of the Han Dynasty said that Chigu was 305 km North of the Wensu State, current Wushi, to the West of Aksu in Southern Xinjiang. Chigu, in the upper stream of current Issyk Kul Lake and Naryn River in Kyrgyzstan, featured vast and smooth land, rainy and cold climate and mountains covered with pines. Wusun people were engaged in nomad and hunting work. They lived in tents with meat and milk as the major food and followed the same customs with Hun. They did not do agricultural work. Horses were their main domestic animals. The rich even raised 4,000 to 5,000 horses. The Han's envoys believed that they were fiery, atrocious and trustless and often looted and stole.

The racial information on Wusun people was not clear. Documents on the race morphology of Wusun were rather limited. In Jiaoshi Yilin, the Han literature, it described the "Wusun women were deep-eyed people with black skin and desires different from the Han people". In one of his notes to The Biography of Western Regions of the History of the Han Dynasty, Yan Shigu wrote: "Wusun has the oddest appearance of all Western states. It should originate from the monkey-like Westerners with red hair and blue eyes". According to Yan, Wusun people should be the European race with red hair, blue eyes and light-colored skin. Despite of the differences of the two views, it is argued that Wusun was another race different from Han by both.

Wusun people had lived in Hexi before the Westward migration. But, so far, the anthropologic materials unearthed in the Hexi Corridor region had shown characteristics of the branch of Mongolian races. It indicated that it was the Mongolian race communities who inhabited the Hexi prefecture before Wusun's Westward migration. This was contradictory to the anthropologic characteristics of Wusun people recorded in historical books. Human skeletons of the period between the 10th century BC and the 5th century BC discovered in Hami, East of Xinjiang neighboring Gansu, were verified skeletons of European race through researches. The reasonable explanation can be that Wusun peoplewas probably related with ancient European race in the East of Xinjiang who had migrated to Hexi across Xinjiang.

After comparing the anthropological materials of the Wusun period from the Central Asia and the North of Tianshan Mountains, it is argued that the main racial basis for the Wusun clans was European race with slight mixture of Mongolian race. Anthropological findings also indicated that Wusun people had many branch types. Wusun and the Saka which dwelled in the regions near Tianshan Mountains were seemingly from the same ethnic group.[34]

After the Wei and Jin dynasties, during the mixture with Tiele and Turkic clans, Wusun produced consanguinity with the nomadic peoples like Kazakhs and Kirghiz peoplesetc. So, Wusun cannot be simply deemed as a specific ethnic group today. Some publications said that Kazakhstan was the offspring of Wusun because there was a "Wusun Clan" in the ethnic group. Actually, the "Wusun Clan" had originated from the Mongolian Xuwushen Clan, and had no relations with the Wusun tribe.

Many Wusun names were passed down, but today only few could be traced. Noteworthily, the 2nd Kunmi (chief of Wusun), the son of Kunmi Wujiutu, was named Fuli which was quite similar to Bori, meaning wolf in Turki, in pronunciation. In the historical books of the Tang Dynasty, the titles Fulin Khan or

---

34 Han Kangxin, Anthropological Characteristics of the People of Saka, Wusun, Hun and Turkic peoples, The Western Regions Studies, 2nd Issue, 1992, pp. 9-12.

Buli Khan borrowed the concept of wolf. Even the guards of Khan were called Fuli, also referring to wolf regarding its meaning.[35]

The Dutch scholar A.F.P. Hulsewe also notified that the word Fuli is related with Bori in his notes on the historical materials of Western Regions in the History of the Han Dynasty.[36]

The aristocrats of Wusun were often called with the rank title of Xihou, identical with those of Darouzhi. Experts believed that the official word for Xihou was the same with the latter Turkic rank Yapghu. The imperial offsprings of Wusun often added a suffix "mi" to their names. Paul Pelliot and some scholars believed that the suffix was the same with the latter Turkic rank Beg (fu, bieqi, beke), which should originate from Chinese word Bo and was probably transformed into Beg in Turkic and then came back to Chinese historical books as fu, bieqi, böke and bayi.

Wusun and Darouzhi people had lived between Dunhuang and Qilian. Qilian was the transliteration of tengri (heaven) in Turki. And also the legend of Liejiaomi fed by the wolf obviously continued the record in Biography of Turkic of History of the Zhou Dynasty, which said Ashina[37] (Asena), the ancestor of Turkic people, had dwelled in grassland and fed by the milk of a female wolf. Wusun people seems to be a tribe speaking Turkic language.

---

35   Tong Dian (Comprehensive Collection of Statutes), written by Du You, Vol. 177.

36   See China in Central Asia, Leiden Press, 1979, p. 474.

37   In Chinese texts ancient Turkic people are called the Tujue or Türks, Chinese scholars use the term Türk to differentiate it with Ottoman Turks. The totem of the early Türks was a wolf (like later that of the Mongols), and their organisation consisted of ten tribes of which the tribe or family Ashina was the mightiest and would eventually produce the khans The Ashina intermarried with the A-shi-de family. Their legendary area of origin was the Qian-si-chu-zhe-shi Mountain (unknown place, somewhere in what is today Xinjiang, according to some sources, even more to the west, or in the upper Yenissej region), some sources say, in the region of the city of Pingliang, Gansu. Later on, under the pressure of the Northern Wei empire (386-534), they moved to the area north of Gaochang (north of current Xinjiang province), where they adopted the technology of processing iron tools from the Dingling, likewise a Turkic-speaking people.

In that area, the Türks were surrounded by the "nine tribes" of the Tölös, but were subjects of the steppe tribe federation of the Rouran. The Rouran called the Türks duan-nu, which meant "ironsmith slaves". At the beginning of the 6th century, when the Rouran empire began to disintegrate, the Türks again moved south, and under the chieftain Tu-men, they started to develop trade relations with the Chinese border regions. From 545 on, North China and the Türks had regular relations. These trade relations perhaps contributed to their economical and then also political rise.

The name Tujue is first mentioned in a document dated 542 found in the history Zhoushu (biography of Yuwen Ce). In 545, the Counsellor-in-chief of the Western Wei dynasty (535-556), Yuwen Tai (507-556), sent the Soghdian; see Zhaowu Jiuxing, An-nuo-pan-tuo to the Türks, which in turn sent an envoy a year later.

(2) Zhang Qian Was Sent to Western Regions

Zhang Qian was born in Chenggu (the present Chenggu County of Shaanxi Province) during the Western Han Dynasty period (206 BC-24 AD). He was an outstanding diplomatic envoy and explorer in the Chinese history, opening up the ancient Silk Road and bringing reliable information about the Western Regions.

During the reign of the Emperor Wudi of the Han Dynasty (206 BC-220 AD), the Huns (Xiongnu) often intruded into the northern borders of the Han Empire, so the emperor was making preparations to fight against the Huns. When he knew Da Rouzhi (an ancient state in Amu Darya) had a feud with the Huns, because its ruler was killed by the Huns' Chanyu (the chief of Hun tribes) and the head made into a goblet, he decided to unite with this state to combat their common enemy. Therefore, Zhang Qian was sent as a diplomatic envoy to the Western Regions.

In 139 BC, with about 100 people, Zhang Qian departed from Longxi (currently in Gansu Province). Unfortunately, he and his attendants were captured by the Huns when they reached the Hexi Corridor and detained for ten years as hostage. Finally, they found a chance to flee. They crossed deserts including the Gobi desert, and marched through the snow-covered Pamirs. After about ten days, they arrived in Dawan (in Fergana Basin). With Dawan's guidance, they marched through Kangju (between Balkhash Lake and the Aral Sea) and reached to the region where Da Rouzhi dwelled.

To Zhang's surprise, satisfied with their life, the Da Rouzhi people refused to make an alliance against the Huns. Besides, they thought it was impossible to resist the Huns in alliance because they were far away from the Han Dynasty. Zhang Qian made an on-the-spot investigation in Daxia (Balkh) and other countries for more than one year. In 128 BC, He decided to return to Chang'an (the ancient name of Xian). On their return journey, they were captured by the Huns again and detained for more than one year. In 126 BC, Zhang seized the opportunity provided by internal disorder among the Huns. He escaped and reached Chang'an. Although he failed to finish the mission to make a military alliance with Da Rouzhi, he obtained a great deal of knowledge about the people, geography, culture and customs of 36 states in the Western Regions.

In 119 BC, Zhang Qian set off on his second journey to the Western Regions, in order to ally with Wusun (in Ili) Valley against the Huns. At that time, the Huns were expelled from the Hexi Corridor, so Zhang Qian had reached Wusun easily. Then he sent other envoys to Dawan, Kangju, Da Rouzhi, Anxi (Parthia, current Iran),Juandu (current India), Yutian (Hetian) and other countries. In 115 BC, the ruler of Wusun assigned an interpreter and a guide for Zhang Qian's disposal. Moreover, Wusun's ten envoys escorted Zhang Qian to the Chang'an city, but Zhang Qian died there in 114 BC. Then the diplomatic envoys which he sent came back in droves. Finally, the Han Dynasty was able to build good relationships with the kingdoms of the Western Regions. During the transition period from the Qin to the Han Dynasty, the Central Plains suffered many wars and the Huns have increased theirpower, greatly. The Han Dynasty, after a century-long recovery, intensified its strength greatly, compared to its initial days. When questioning the Hun captives, Emperor Wudi of the Han Dynasty learned of that Rouzhi kingdom was the bitter enemy of the Huns and hated Huns after being beaten by the latter and were forced to move Westward. Emperor Wudi thought helpers were needed to deal with the Huns and decided to send Zhang Qian to Western Regions to arrange an alliance with Rouzhi kingdom to attack the Huns. In the 3rd year of the Jianyuan Period of the Western Han Dynasty (138 BC), Zhang Qian departed from Chang'an with the Hun Ganfu and more than 100 attendants. They were captured by the Huns in Hexi Prefecture and sent to the chief of the Huns in the north regions of the desert. "Hun lies in between of Rouzhi and Han. Why does Han send an envoy to Rouzhi?" questioned the Chief, "If Hun sends an envoy to Nanyue which lies inthe south border of the Han dynasty, will Han permit that?" Hun detained Zhang Qian without any maltreatment. Zhang Qian got married and had kids in Hun. Even being captured, Zhang did not forget his mission. Ten years later, when the custody was loosened, Zhang escaped from Hun to Dayuan (Fergana Valley). Dayuan sent Zhang to Kangju (the Sogdiana to the north of Amu Darya) who sent him to Rouzhi. Ruozhi, after the settlement in Daxia, was contented with the fertile land and plentiful products there. Although Zhang persuaded them to jointly attack the Huns, Rouzhi people did not want to be enemy of the Huns. Zhang had to return back due to the failure in his mission. On his way back, Zhang was recaptured by the Huns and then escaped again and fled back to Chang'an. It took Zhang Qian 14 years in total to complete the given mission.

Although he failed to persuade Rouzhis to ally with Hans, Zhang Qian brought reliable messages in regard to Western Regions to the Central Plains for the first time. In 119 BC, Emperor Wudi sent Zhang to Western Regions again. The Han Court attached great importance to the mission which consisted of 300 members with two horses for each, brought tens of thousands sheeps and cattles, and lots of money and silk. Zhang himself directly went to Wusun and sent some vice envoys to visit the Kangju, Dayuan and Darouzhi, i.e, the tribal states.

Emperor Wudi's purpose for the mission was to ask Zhang to persuade Wusuns to move back to their previous dwelling region, i.e., the Hexi Prefecture and ally with the Han dynasty against the Huns. Liejiaomi was too old to control his clans then, and the clan chiefs did not agree to move back. However, Wusun kingdom agreed to send envoys to Han dynasty with Zhang and gifted horses to Han dynasty. In the cold weapon era, horses were the main means for the expedition of troops. Mongolian horses were largely used in the Central Plains. Mongolian horses were hardworking and enduring animals, but they were dwarfish and slow. Central Asian horses were world-famous and thoroughbred, they were long, handsome, fast and enduring. Wusun horses were quite popular in Han and honored Heavenly Horses. Latter on, after the import of more competitive Dayuan horses, Wusun horses were renamed Xiji (westernmost) Horses. From then on, the silk versus horse trade relationship between the Central Asia and Central Plains was formally established. Vice envoys sent by Zhang to Kangju and other small states also successively led envoys from those states back to Han, and established unprecedented close relationships between the Central Plains and Western Regions.

Thanks to his success in his mission and contribution to the dynasty, Zhang Qian was granted a noble rank. Many low-level attendant officials regarded this mission a shortcut for promotion and actively submitted reports to introduce exotic news. Since few people would go to the Western Regions due to the long and arduous journey, Emperor Wudi approved all applications to the court and offered attendants and equipment for them. The small states on the expedition routes to Western Regions even could not bear the hosting and accommodation costs of those many people missioned by Emperor Wudi. Zhang Jian was one of the great explorers in China's history. After Zhang's exploration, close communications were established between Western Regions and Central Plains, the history of Western Regions became a part of China's history and the Central Asian Steppes became a bridge linking Chinese civilization with Western civilization. If it is argued that the founding of Persian Empire in the 6th century BC opened the commercial route from the Mediterranean Sea to Central Asia and the Macedonian Empire' s eastward expedition extended the trade expedition route to the European continent, the Westward migration of Rouzhi and Wusun and the Westward expedition of Zhang Qian further extended the route Eastward to the Central Plains, thus the whole route of the Silk Road was thoroughly completed.

(3) Ode to Xiji (Westernmost) Heavenly Horses

Zhang Qian passed by Dayuan on his way to Rouzhi. Dayuan, the name of the Fergana Valley neighboring Kashgar prefecture of Xinjiang during the Han Dynasty period, had boasted fertile land suitable for agriculture and dense population since ancient times. It had more than 70 cities with 60,000 households and hundreds of thousands residents. Dayuan neighbored Kangju to the North, Rouzhi to the West, Daxia to the Southwest and Wusun to the Northeast. Dayuan produced grape wine which could be stored for several decades without quality deterioration. The rich even stored wine up to hundreds of thousand kilograms.

Despite the long distance, Dayuan had learned of the prosperity of Han and intended to establish relationship. The chief was quite glad to see Zhang Qian's arrival. Zhang said he was an envoy of Han to Rouzhi and needed Dayuan's help for the mission and would reward Dayuan with considerable money and valuable goods after returning. The chief of Dayuan sent interpreters to accompany Zhang to the center of Kangju (current Zeravshan River Basin in Uzbekistan). Then Kangju sent people to escort them to Rouzhi. Horses were the most famous products of Dayuan. Fergana horses, boasting tall body, high speed, great endurance stamina and outstanding performance in long-distance gallop, were extremely excellent steeds. Han envoys was surprised at the horse's blood-like sweat and called it "Bloody Sweat Horse" which was believed the offspring of heavenly horses. In a sacrifice song of the Han Dynasty, the heavenly horse "has red sweat and froth". Later on, Bloody Sweat Horse or Heavenly Horse became another name for the steeds of Western Regions. Today, scholars still make studies on the living Bloody Sweat horses in Central Asia. After researches, they discovered their secret: these horses bled due to the bites of tiny parasites living on their bodies.

After Zhang Qian came back, the Han Court sent numerous envoys to those states in Western Regions. Some envoys en route learned about the Dayuan steeds and reported to Emperor Wudi that Dayuan hid their steeds in Ershi City to avoid exposure to them after returning back. Having learned of this report, Emperor Wudi sent Envoy Che Ling with a great amount of money and a golden horse to Dayuan for horse trade. However, Dayuan had plentiful products from the Central Plains and did not value the envoys' gifts greatly. After discussion, the ruler and ministers of Dayuan thought that the heavenly horses were their treasure and should not be presented to the Han court easily. Moreover, the distance between the Han and Dayuan was quite long. The North of Tianshan Mountains was controlled by the Huns. The South of Tianshan Mountains lacked water and grass. The several-hundred-member mission of the Han often suffered severe casualties due to food shortage and arduous expedition. So, the Han would not send troops to Dayuan. Che Ling was angry at the situation, broke the golden horse and left them. The ruler of Dayuan thought that he was despised by the Han envoy and ordered the border guards chief named Yucheng who guarded the eastern border to intercept and kill the envoy and loot their properties.

Emperor Wudi became very angry by the news coming from Chang'an. Some high-officers who visited Dayuan suggested that a 3,000-archer troop could easily beat the weak Dayuan. Han had the experience of defeating Loulan with 700 cavalrymen. So, Emperor Wudi sent his beloved Concubine Li's brother General Li Guangli with dozens of thousand troops to crusade against Dayuan. Emperor Wudi granted General Li the title of General Ershi and ordered him to capture Ershi City and grab the steeds. After entering the Western Regions, all en route states in the oasis tightly closed their city gates and would not supply grains to the Han troops. The Han troops forcefully attacked the cities. The captured cities had to surrender the grains, and the troops had to give up siege and leave in case of hard ones. The arduous march caused severe depletion of numbers. When arriving at Yucheng, the eastern borders of Dayuan, General Li's army had only several thousand whacked troops left. The exhausted troops could not capture Yucheng and suffered high casualties. General Li realized that the victory was impossible and withdrew his troops. General Li had only 10-20% of the original troops left when arriving in Dunhuang two years after departing Chan'an. He submitted a letter to Emperor Wudi to describe the expedition, the depletion of numbers caused by hunger and the failure due to shortage of troops, and request ceasing the attack and preparing for another expedition.

Emperor Wudi was raged at Li's failure and ordered to close the Yumen Pass and keep the troops outside. If Han could not conquer the small state like Dayuan, not only the steeds could be obtained but also Daxia and other Western Region states would look down on the Han and embarrass the Han's envoys, thought Emperor Wudi. So he decided to send troops to attack Dayuan again. More than 60,000 troops, excluding non-official ones with self-supplied food, were maneuvered together with 100,000 cattle, 30,000 horses and over 10,000 donkeys, camels and other animals for carrying the goods. The Han troops spied that Dayuan's cities had no well and relied on water supply from rivers outside. So, they planned to arrange water engineers to reroute the rivers and pass the wall for capturing the city. Han's great army started the westward expedition for the second time. Most of the Western states en route were afraid at this action and actively presented grains to the troops. Only Luntai (tCurrent Buguer to the East of Kurla) closed the city wall and resisted the Han troops. Several days later, Luntai was captured. General Li Guangli's army arrived at the Eastern border of Dayuan and defeated the enemy troops. Li Guangli's army steered clear of Yucheng and reached the capital of Dayuan. According to the plan, Li would cut the water supply of the city and lay siege the city for over 40 days, consequently the morale of Dayuan's soldiers was shaken. Some aristocrats plotted and murdered the Dayuan ruler Wugua, and attempted to negotiate with the Han army leadership. Then, the Han troops had broken the gates of the outer city and captured the brave general Jianmi. The remaining Dayuan troops withdrew to the imperial city, the Han forces sent an envoy to persuade the enemy for surrender also requested the head of Wugua. The envoy demanded the Han troops to cease their offensive, and in turn offered to present steeds and grains to the Han troops. If the Han troops would not stop the offensive, Dayuan would kill all steeds and wait for relief troops from the Kangju kingdom to fight against the Han troops to the last drop of blood. The support forces from Kangju were near Dayuan but they and feared to fight against the powerful Han troops. General Li Guangli knew that some person from the Central Plains helped the sieged city in digging water wells. The water supply was not a problem anymore, and the food supply was also fairly sufficient in the besieged city. It was disadvantageous for the Han troops to have a long battle. So, Li agreed with the envoy. The Han troops selected dozens of first-level steeds and more than 3,000 male and female steeds of middle level or below, crowned Meicai, a Han-friendly aristocrat, as the king of Dayuan and concluded a pact with him. Finally, the troops marched back without conquering the imperial city of Dayuan. When departing from Dunhuang, Li Guangli ordered his troops to march along different routes due to the food supply difficulties. Li's main forces had approached near Dayuan for over 100 km. and besieged its capital when a 1,000-troop Han brigade arrived at Yucheng. The brigade asked the Yucheng forces to supply food for them but Yucheng forces refused. The arrogant brigade chief rashly ordered to attack, which exposed the weakness and limited number of the Han troops. Then the defense forces of Yucheng marched out of the city and attacked the Han troops. Most of the 1,000 troops were annihilated, and only few could escape and join the main force of General Li Guangli. After conquering the capital of Dayuan, General Li sent an army to capture the General of Yucheng. The General of the Yucheng forces escaped to Kangju for protection, consequently Han attacked the Kangju state, forced Kangju to surrender the General and then killed him. After the Han troops left, Meicai, the Han-friendly ruler of Dayuan crowned by General Li, was killed by other resentful aristocrats. The brother of the deceased Dayuan ruler was enthroned, and maintained a friendly relationship with the Han court.

The Han Dynasty possessed excellent horse species Xiji (westernmost) Horse and Heavenly Horse from the conquest of Dayuan and submission of Wusun.

Soon later, emperor Wudi composed an ode to Xiji titled as : Westernmost Heavenly Horses to Celebrate, which said:

Heavenly horses come from the Westernmost regions
They return to the Han after a journey thousands of miles
With the divine mighty, they will obstruct foreign peoples with ease
All peoples will be faced down due to their reputation across the deserts

The Han's expedition to Dayuan made the bonds between the Western Regions and the Central Plains unprecedentedly close. The input of Bloody Sweat Horse improved the horse species of China. Archeologists discovered that China's steeds were obviously different from those before the Han Dynasty. The Han people also introduced good forage clover and grapes from Dayuan to the Central Plains. The Han's encirclement to Dayuan's capital forced the people to learn well-drilling skills from the people of Central Plains.[38]

(4) Han People Allowed Their Daughters To Marry Leaders from Faraway Neighbors

Wusun and Han people had no direct contact at the beginning. After returning from the Western Regions, Zhang Qian reported Wusun kingdom's strength to Emperor Wudi and suggested to invite Wusun and try to persuade them to move back to their original dwelling region Hexi to cope with the Huns since Darouzhi kingdom would not move back to eastward regions. In the 4th year of Yuanshou reign (119 BC), Emperor Wudi sent Zhang Qian to the Western Regions for the second time to ally with Wusun tribe and planned a joint attack against the Huns. As a neighbor of Huns, Wusun knew a lot about Huns' powerful points, but knew little about Han's strengths, and could not dare to

---

38   See Biography of Dayuan in Records of the Historian, Biography of Li Guangli in History of the Han Dynasty.

ally with Han rashly. In the 1st year of Yunding Period (116 BC), a Wusun envoy came to the Han Empire led by Zhang Qian and Zhang Qian saw the vast land, great strength and prosperity of Han himself. The envoy reported his experience to the Wusun leader Liejiaomi, which changed his attitude toward the Han Dynasty. After learning of Wusun's contacts with Han, Hun was irritated and sent troops to attack Wusun. The ruler Liejiaomi sent an envoy with 1,000 steeds as an engagement gift to Han for a marriage. In the 3rd year of the Yuanfeng Period (108 BC), Emperor Wudi married Princess Xijun (also known as Princess Jiangdu), daughter of Jingdu Duke Liu Jian, to Liejiaomi as the Wusun chief's Right Wife, and allied with the chief as brothers. Hun also sent a daughter to Lijiaomi as his Left Wife. Princess Xijun did not know the Wusun language and wasn't unaccustomed to their native life. Living in agony with innermost pain, she sighed as follows:

"Since marrying the ruler of Wusun far from my hometown,

Living in tents with felt-made walls,
Eating meat and drinking milk,
Missing my hometown with a broken heart,
Wishing to be a swan to fly back."

But, Liejiaomi was senile and asked Xijun to marry his grandson Junxumi. Princess Xijun refused due to the incompliance with the Han custom and submitted a letter to Emperor Wudi. However, Emperor Wudi demanded her to obey the Wusun customs and maintain the marriage with Wusun to resist Hun. Xijun obeyed the decree and married Junxumi. After Liejiaomi passed away, his grand-son Junxumi succeeded to the throne, and Princess Xijun gave birth to a daughter and named her Shaofu. When Xijun was married to Wusun, the Han Dynasty sent garrison troops to open up wasteland and grow grains in Xuanlei, North to Wusun (current West of Mongolia to the north of Altai Mountains) in order to back up her. After Xijun passed away, the Han Dynasty married Princess Jieyou, granddaughter of Chu Duke Liu Wu, with Junxumi. Besides the wives from the Han, Junxumi also had a Hun wife. After Junxumi's death, his uncle Wengguimi succeeded to the throne and was known as Feiwang. Then Princess Jieyou was married off to Wenguimi according to the Wusun custom, and had three sons and two daughters who all grew up to influential aristocrats in Wusun. The eldest son was named Yuanguimi, the second son named Wannian and became Shache Duke later, and the third son Dayue became Left General. The first daughter named Dishi was married to Qiuci ruler Jiangbin, and the second daughter Suguang was married out to Wusun aristocrat named Ruohuxi. Feng Liao, a maid of Princess Jieyou, was married to Wusun's Right General and known as Madam Feng. Madam Feng was sent by Princess Jieyou to grant awards across Western Regions on behalf of the princess and won the respects of the locals.

Despite the marriage with Han, Wusun people would not offend the Huns and kept a balance between the Hans and the Huns all along. At the end of the year under the reign of Emperor Zhaodi of the Han Dynasty (74 BC), the Huns invaded Wusun and demanded Wusun to present Princess Jieyou. Princess Jieyou and Wusun ruler Wengguimi reported to the Han court to request military reinforcement and jointly attack Hun. Emperor Xundi sent 150,000 troops to attack Hun from five directions, and dispatched General Chang Hui to lead Wusun troops for the collaborative fight against the Hun. In the 3rd year of Benshi Period (71 BC), the troops led by five Han generals killed more than 7,000 Huns in total. Ruler Wenguimi dispatched 50,000 troops to attack the headquarters of the Hun Chief Youguli, killed more than 40,000 Huns including the Hun chief's uncles, sister-in-laws, princesses, dukes and soldiers, captured 700,000 livestock including horses, cattle, sheep and camels, and gained a great victory. After the battle, the Han Dynasty established the Protectorate of the Western Regions (Xi Yu Du Hu Fu), a military administrative institution, to control the vast Northwestern regions. Han generals Chang Hui, Xin Qingji and others had their garrison troops; they opened up wasteland and grew grain in Chigu, capital of Wusun.

In the 2nd year of Shenjue reign (60 BC), Wenguimi died. Nimi, the son of Junxumi and his Hun wife, was crowned as Kuangwang and married Princess Jieyou according to the customs of Wusun. The Han Dynasty was disappointed at the news as Han hoped that Yuanguimi, son of Princess Jieyou, to be crowned. Thus contradictions occurred between Han and Wusun. Princess Jieyou bored a son Chimi for Nimi, but she had an inharmonious relation with Nimi. From the end of Shenjue Period to Wufeng Period under the reign of Emperor Xuandi, during the visit of Han envoys Wei Heyi and Hou Renchang, Princess Jieyou and the envoys plotted to kill Kuangwang (Nimi). The Han envoys invited Kuangwang to attend a banquet in Chigu, capital of Wusun and intended to assassinate him at the banquet and grab Wusun's state power. But Kuangwang was only injured and fled away. Kuangwang's son Xishenshou led troops to besiege Chigu. At the news, Protectorate of the Western Regions Commander Zheng Ji, the highest official of Han in the Western Regions, immediately dispatched troops to save the envoys. In order to maintain relationship with Wusun, the Han Court sent other envoys and doctors to comfort Kuangwang. The envoys Wei Heyi and Hou Renchang were escorted back to Chang'an in prisoner carts, and then were executed for their unauthorized assassination of Wusun's chief and due to the damage they gave to Han-Wusun relationships.

When Kuangwang was injured, Wujiutu, the son born by Kangwang's Hun wife, also escaped from the banquet and hid in the Tianshan Mountains with some aristocrats and attendants. They claimed that Hun would send troops to protect Wusun and gathered many Wusun people. Later, Wujiutu attacked and killed Kuangwang and crowned himself. Wusun's Right General, husband of Madame Feng, was a janissary of Wujiutu. In order to stabilize the relationship with Wusun, Commander Zheng Ji sent Madame Feng to communicate with

Wujiutu through her husband. The Han Court hoped to enthrone Yuanguimi, son of Princess Jieyou and Wenguimi, to establish Wusun's policy of being friendly to Han. After discussion, Wusun and Madame Feng reached an agreement: Wusun decided to maintain the relationship with Han, and Han safeguarded Wujiutu's vested interest. So, Han sent Madame Feng as an envoy to Chigu and call in Wujiutu to announce the division of Wusun into a big territory and a small territory with defined boundaries. Actually, the signs of separation appeared during the reign of Liejiaomi when Liejiaomi's 2nd son Dalu boasted the greatest strength and high reputation in the army and lived separately from the main community with more than 10,000 followers.

Yuanguimi, son of Princess Jieyou and Wenguimi, was granted the title of Big Chief with 60,000 households and Wujiutu the Small Chief with 40,000 followers. Both chiefs were under the governance of the Han Court. When Wujiutu died, a civil strife occurred against the chief of the Small Wusun. The Han Court conferred Wujiutu's grandson as the Small Chief. In those days, the Wusun kingdom was reigned by two chiefs, a big one and a small one, in parallel. The throne of the Big Chief had passed down to the offsprings of Princess Jieyou for four generations till the end of the Western Han Dynasty, and the throne of the Small Chief to the offspring of Wujiutu for five generations till the end of the Western Han Dynasty. At the end of the 1st century, when Ban Chao of the Eastern Han Dynasty governed the Western Regions, Wusun people was still under the governance of the Big Chief and Small Chief namely, divided into two parts. It was more than 100 years since the conferment of Big Chief and Small Chief by "Madam Feng" on behalf of the Han Court.

Princess Jieyou and "Madam Feng" established families and feats in the Central Asian Steppes and made great contribution to the friendship between the Central Plains and the Northwestern border regions. They were outstanding women worthy of commemoration in the history of the Land Silk Road. In 1954, Ginzburg, anthropologist from the former Soviet Union, published articles in regard to Skeletons of the Wusun People in the 4th Century BC to the 2nd Century BC in the Region of Middle of the Tianshan Mountains and Alai Prefecture.[39] According to the thesis, the only female skull discovered indicated that the woman was from a typical Mongolian race. Based on the historical fact that the Han princesses were allowed to marry the Wusun chiefs as political marriages, the author of this book inferred that the owner of the skull should be a Han woman.[40]

According to records in the written literature, Cheshi (also known as Gushi) people lived in the East of the Tianshan Mountains in the Qin and Han dynasties. Some dwelled in the Turpan region and lived on irrigated agricultural in oases.

---

39 Anthropologic Documents on Ancient Residents in Eastern and Central Regions of The Kazakh Soviet Socialist Republic, published in Collection of Soviet Union's Ethnological Research Reports, Vol. 33, 1956, Russian Version.
40 Article by Han Kangxin, "Anthropologic Characteristics of the People of Saka, Wusun, Hun and Turks," The Western Regions Studies, 1992/2, p. 9.

Others lived on animal husbandry in the mountainous grasslands in the East of the Tianshan Mountains. During the Han Dynasty period, Cheshi was split into several kingdoms, namely Cheshi Border State (with Turpan as the center), Cheshi Back State (north of the East section of the Tianshan Mountains), Cheshi Duwei State and Cheshi Houcheng Long State. The total population of Cheshi was about 12,000. A number of ancient stone tombs were found near the joint of the Alagou and Yu'ergou when building the Yu'ergou Station of the Nanjiang Railway from Turpan to Korle in 1976. After a three-year-long excavation in the region, scholars identified that it was a tomb region of Cheshi people lived in the period from 800 BC to the beginning of the Christian era based on the characteristics of the cultural relics and the carbon-14 isotope dating. Tools for drilling wood to make fire were found in nearly all these tombs. They were bar-shaped wooden boards, measuring 10-20 cm in length, 2-3 cm in width and about 2 cm in thickness. Drilling holes with a diameter of about 1 cm and burning vestiges were found in the boards. The fire-making mode was nearly the same with that of the Li ethnic group in Hainan and Wa ethnic group in Yunnan still extant not long ago. The Han people also have the legend of Suirenshi who made fire this way in ancient times. So, there were cultural connections between Chinese Central Plains and the Central Asian Steppes in the ancient times.

In the tombs of Cheshi people, archeologists discovered quite a few sea-shells which were used in costumes and as body ornaments for the deceased and favored by them. According to the identifications of biologists, the sea-shells were not rare ones, but the ordinary cowries or ring-patterned cowries which were not produced in the hinterland of Asia. So, the Cheshi people must obtain these shells through trade with the coastal residents of the Bohai Sea, East Sea and South Sea in East Asia, the Arabian Sea and Persian Gulf adjacent to the Indian Ocean. Cheshi people also used the copper mirror with a diameter of over 10cm. and a wooden handle which was similar to Greek cooper mirror. Lacquer work was also seen in some tombs. The lacquer work had a layer of bright and black paint based on a wooden blank and then the scarlet clouds delineated on the superficial layer. In addition, silk products were also discovered. It was a kind of tabby carbaso with flowers and birds embroidered with dark green, reddish purple and bright red thread on white background. The lacquer work and carbaso could only originate from the Central Plains. These facts indicated that the Cheshi who dwelled in the Tianshan Mountains was not an introverted close-door people. They had close economic and cultural ties with neighboring peoples and played an intermediate role for the cultural exchanges between the people in the Eastern Central Plains and the peoples in the West.[41]

41 See Wang Binghua: Ancient Civilizations of Turpan, Xinjiang People's Publishing House, 1989, pp. 36-47.

6. Parthia (Arsacid) Dynasty and the Central Plains

(1) Anxi (Arshak): Nomadic tribe of the Parni under the leadership of Arsaces overthrew Andragoras and laid the foundations of the Parthian kingdom.

During the collapse of the Seleucid Empire, Andragoras, the Greek ruler of Northern Persia, declared independence. A nomadic tribe which came from Central Asia and spoke a Persian dialect entered Parthia (current North of Turkmenistan and Iran) and overturned the reign of Greece and founded their own state in 250 BC under the leadership of their chief Arshak. It was often called Parthian (Arsacid) Empire by Western scholars. Parth and Pars had the same linguistic origin. Parthian and Persian people had quite close blood kinship. These two languages were also fairly similar.

In China's historical books, this Arsacid empire was called Anxi, the Han's transliteration of its founder Arshak. Arsacid kingdom's position in the Persian history can be compared to those of Han and Tang dynasties in the Chinese history. In its culmination period, Arsacid kingdom confronted the Roman Empire in its Western border Euphrates river (Fırat), and covered the Amu Darya (River), Gaofu (current Kabul, capital of Afghanistan) and Daxia in its East. Geographical Record of the History of the Han Dynasty described Arsacid state as follows: "it is the biggest state which rules several hundred cities and controls vast regions under its jurisdiction."

When Emperor Wudi sent Zhang Qian to the Western Regions for the 2nd time, Zhang himself visited Wusun and sent high level envoys to visit other states including one to Arsacid. The king of Arsacid empire ordered its general to send 20,000 troops to cross dozens of cities and welcome the envoy at the bank of its eastern border river Amu Darya, several thousand miles away from its capital.

In the middle of the 1st century BC, the Roman Empire expanded Eastward and collided with the Arsacid kingdom. In 53 BC, Marcus Licinius Crassus, one of the three Praetorians of Roman Empire, led seven legions to cross the Euphrates river. An intense war occurred between the troops of the Arsacid and Roman empire. During the throat-cutting war, the Arsacid troops suddenly rolled out their dazzling standard, which shocked the debilitated Roman troops greatly. Consequently, the Roman troops were beaten, Crassus was killed and his son committed suicide. Among the renowned and valiant Roman troops, 20,000 lay in the dust and 10,000 were captured. The head of Crassus was sent to the Arsacid court and the captives was sent to the rear regions of Arsacid empire.

French historian Vallon believed that it was the silk-made flags with Arsacid technology that hit the morale and caused the defeat of Roman troops at the critical moment of war. Silk was brilliant than any other fabrics at that time. It was the first time that Romans had seen the silk.[42] Through wars against and

---

42   La Route de la Soie (The Silk Road), written by Luce Boulnois, translated by Geng

peaceful exchanges with Arsacid empire, Romans obtained the silk soon after. When celebrating his victory in Rome, Gaius Julius Caesar showed off its silk products and received the audience's surprising acclamation. The crazy interest and purchases of silk by Romans made money flow to the merchants of other countries. When Gaius Octavius Augustus was dead in the 14 AD, the Senate issued a decree to forbid the male citizens wearing silk and also restricted the use of silk dresses by the females. The people of Arsacid, as they lived in the region which was the communications center for the East-west trade route, were good in trading since the ancient times. Arsacid kingdom, had lasted for 500 years, and was replaced by Sassanian (Sassanid) Empire in 225 AD. Arsacid kingdom roughly co-existed with China's Qin and Han dynasties. The stable relationship between Han dynasty and the Arsacid kingdom played extremely important roles in the development of East-west trade. The silk trade between China and Europe was controlled by Arsacid traders. In addition to the land trade, Arsacid traders also centered on the Persian Gulf and traded with India in the East and Rome in the West. No matter via the land route or maritime route, Chinese silk always needed the Arsacid state traders for shipping goods to the Mediterranean Sea. In 97, Ban Chao sent Envoy Gan Ying to Arsacid state. When reaching the Persian Gulf, Gan Ying intended to visit the Roman Empire. However, Arsacid state, became worried that it would lose its monopoly over silk trade, it didn't want to allow direct contacts between the Han Chinese and the Roman Empire. So, the Arsacid leaders overstated the expedition risks and persuaded Gan Ying to return back due to expedition difficulties.

69

The origin of Arsacid was on the region (current Nissa, Turkmenistan), Baghir (Bagir) Village, 15 km to the West of Ashgabad, the capital of Turkmenistan. The Nysa site consisted of the old part and the new part with a 1.5 km distance in between. The Nissa (Old Nysa) was the residence of Arsacid royal family. The New Nissa (Nysa) was the administrative center of Arsacid. The old town existed in the period from the 3rd century BC to the 3rd century AD. When attending the Land Silk Road investigation held by UNESCO in 1991, the author of this book visited the Old Nissa (Nysa). The magnificent and high city walls still exist with towers built along the walls. The inner city had an area of 14 hectares and only 2 hectares was excavated. The archeological research started in the 1930s under the leadership of prestigious scholar Ma Song. The excavation was suspended during WWII and was restarted after the war. Today, Italian scholars are also participating the archeological works there. The researches had preliminarily unveiled the overview of the old Nissa (Nysa). The Arsacid buildings, built with adobes mainly and they rarely have bricks, are somehow similar to those in the Gaochang and Jiaohe ancient cities in Turpan, China. Many valuable cultural relics were unearthed in Nissa (Nysa), including a Greek-style marble statue of a nude goddess which is calm, graceful and comparable to the Venus statue and viewed as the masterpiece of Arsacid sculpture. Dozens of 50cm-long ivory-carved utensils were excavated from the

Sheng, Xinjiang People's Publishing House, 1982, p. 3.

Old Nissa. The ends of the utensils were carved into animals or figures, featuring beautiful Greek style. According to the Records of the Historian, Arsacid, the most powerful country in the Western Regions, governed several hundred big and small towns across several thousand li. Zhang Qian sent deputy envoys to the capital of Arsacid after crossing dozens of its cities. Later on, Arsacid's ruler dispatched envoys to visit China. They presented ostrich eggs and vaude-villians which they had captured from the Roman Empire to Emperor Wudi. Arsacid kingdom had changed its capital for several times. We have no idea if the capital visited by Zhang Qian's envoys was the Old Nissa. But, we are sure that the envoys had passed or heard of this place at least.

According to the History of the Western Regions, and according to History of the Latter-Han Dynasty, Arsacid's "eastern border of Merv is called small Arsacid". The location of Merv is near currentMary oasis in the South of Turkmenistan. The oasis, situated in the lower reach of the Murghab River, is one of the centers of the ancient Khorasan region and an important relay station on the Land Silk Road. The original location of Merv city was in the sites of ancient Maroons, 30 km East from the new town of Mary. The Murghab River was the water source of ancient Mary Oasis. Due to the continuous change of water courses, the political and economic centers often changed accordingly even the distance between them was not far. Today, the whole site was on a saline under governmental protection. The site of Merv was called Eric Kara in the period of the Persian Empire (in China's Spring and Autumn Period). Merv was built during the 5th to the 4th centuries BC in the center of Marv Oasis. It had a downtown area of 20 hectares, great surrounding walls with extant height of 25 meters and the foundation height of 15 meters for the majestic palaces.

Erk Kala (Kale)
Gyaur Kala
Sultan Kala
Abdullah Khan Kala
Bairam Ali Khan Kala
Murgab delta and oasis (circled) in the south of Turkmenistan
Here the Murgab river sources and takes a long journey of 850 km out and disappears in the Kara Kum desert in the North
Location
As with Gonur, Merv lies in the Murgab river delta, in the current researches this region is generally considered as the the ancient land of Mouru, the third Vendidad nationality. The ancient city of Merv (Persian Marv), lies 30 km East of the city of Mary (a changed form of Merv) capital of the province, or vilayet / welayatlar, of the same name located in South-eastern Turkmenistan bordering Afghanistan. The province has an area of 87,000 km². and a population of 1,146,800 in 1995.[43]

---

43   The ruins of Merv are comprised of five walled cities dating from the 6th century BC to the 18th century, known as Erk Kala, Gyaur Kala, Sultan Kala, Abdullah Khan Kala and Bairam Ali Khan Kala, grouped into three settlements corresponding to three periods, the

It is argued that in medieval times, Merv was the largest city in the world.

From the Seleucid to the Islamic times (from Eastern Han to Tang dynasty in China), the center of Merv was in the site of Gyaur-Kala. Gyaur was a mistaken form of the Arabic word "Kafir" (means "heathen") in Turkmen. "Kala" means "palace" in Arabic. The site of Gyaur-Kala was more than 360 hectares in total. A number of Greek-style building ruins were unearthed in the biggest city of Arsacid kingdom.

In 751, when the Tang Dynasty's army was defeated by Arabic army in Talas (Taraz), a Chinese official Du Huan was captured. Du Huan traveled to the Abbasid kingdom via Merv city. According to Du Huan's records, Merv had city walls of 15 li with an iron-made gate. Inside the city there were a salt pond and two Buddhist temples. Merv city, measuring 140 li (70 km) in East-west length and 80 li (40 km) in South-north distance, had continuous villages, exuberant trees and developed irrigation agriculture. The oasis was surrounded by quicksand. The Merv that Du saw twelve and a half centuries ago was current site of Gyaur-Kala. Scholars of former Soviet Union had made long-term archaeological research there. Ancient buildings excavated so far include the two Buddhist temples mentioned by Du Huan in his Travel Journal (Jing Xing Ji). We visited one of the excavation sites. Sakyamuni's head sculpture and Sanskrit inscription were unearthed from the site. Based on the size of the head sculpture, the Buddha statue was probably more than 10 meters high. According to the researches of scholars of the former Soviet Union, the temple was built between the 3rd and 4th centuries, and there was a salt pond in the city as described by Du Huan. In this location, Nestorian and Manichean monasteries of the period between the 3rd and 4th centuries were also discovered.

(2) Arsacid (Parthian) Language Written on Leather from Left to Right

According to the Geographical Record, History of the Latter-Han Dynasty, the Han envoys found that Arsacid kingdom used silver coins with the king's image on the front side and the queen's on the back side, and cast new coins when the throne was changed. It also stated that Arsacid people "wrote on leather from left to right", which was different from Chinese up-down writing habit. Historical documents alone cannot give us a clear understanding of the Arsacid language. Berlin Anthropological Museum had sent 4 investigation teams to Xinjiang in the years of 1902-1903, 1904-1905, 1905-1906 and 1913-1914 respectively to make excavations in Turpan. They discovered abundant scriptures in the site of the Turpan temples. It should be a rallying point of Manichaeism. Later on, archeologists of Russia, Japan and China also discovered some scriptures in the Gaochang ancient city.

These scriptures were moved back to Berlin and attracted great attention of European linguists. Researches indicated that quite a few scriptures were written in medieval Western Iranian which roughly consisted of the Southern

ancient, medieval and post-medieval Merv.

branch Parsik, generally called as Pahlavi by Iranian scholars, and the Northern branch Arsacid called as the Northern Pahlavi by Iranian scholars. The two branches were quite similar. Experts found that some Manichean scriptures unearthed in Turpan were written in Arsacid language. The language used in the scriptures was called Pahlavanik by the writer, which should be a name given by the Arsacid people themselves. So, the most detailed materials on Arsacid language are the scriptures describing the belief of Manichaeism and his followers unearthed in Turpan, Xinjiang, China. Researchers also found that the vocabulary, syntax and diction some of the Pahlavanik scriptures were influenced by other dialects and supposed that the scriptures were translated from southern Pahlavi by Manichean monks. The time of these scriptures is still unidentified. According to some scriptures with ambigious records, these Pahlavanik literature were roughly from two periods which at least had an interval of 2 centuries in between. Some works in the first period were on the lives of Manichean monks and his followers and possibly completed at the end of the 4th century. There were no works during the 5th and 6th centuries. Thus, scholars supposed that use of Pahlavanik had ceased in the period while Parsik, the official language of the Sassanid Empire, became widepread in the East. Iranian scholars thought that it was due to the Ephthalites invasion from Northeast, and the Sassanid troops set up military points in the East to resist the invasion.

During the 2nd period, Western Turks reigned over Sogdiana. Religious works compiled in Pahlavanik came into shape. Although Pahlavanik was used in the region, some changes had taken place unconsciously and gradually entered the stage of Persian. This characteristic, i.e., the split of oral and written languages, was obvious in the scholarly and literature works of this period. The writers had striven hard to write in ancient words but vocabulary and syntax of Farsi (old Persain) still often appeared in their works.

(3) Arsacid Monks in China

When Zhang Qian visited the Western Regions for the second time, Arsacid kingdom also sent envoys to the Central Plains to establish direct connections. The envoys presented "eggs of big birds" and "Alexandria's vaudevillians" to Emperor Wudi. The "eggs of big birds" should be ostrich eggs, and Alexandria, the famous Egyptian city, referred to Roman Empire. As early as under the reign of Asoka, Buddhist monks had visited the Arsacid empire to promote Buddhism. In the early days, the the Eastern border of Empire of Arsacid had extended to current Hindu Kush mountains. During the reign of Mithradates (123 BC-88 BC), Arsacid empire invaded India Southward and seized Taxila between the Indus River and the Chenag River in Northwestern India. Around the period when the Kushan Empire was founded, Buddhism started to spread in Arsacid empire. In the History of the Western Regions, History of the Han Dynasty, it said: "Arsacid kingdom boasted plentiful resources and had customs similar to Alexandria Prophthasia and Kophen". Buddhism was dominant in Kophen, which is located in Kashmir, Northwest of India.

In the region under the control of Arsacid empire and current Garlarbat Basin, near Gandhara in West of Afghanistan, remnants of some Buddhist pagodas built in the 1st and 2nd century were discovered. Buddhist statues were engraved on the unearthed gold vessels for Buddhist relics. Hinayana was popular in Arsacid empire for a long period. The spread of Buddhism in Arsacid can be clearly seen from the experience and scripture translation work of An Shih-kao who arrived in China in the 2nd year of the Jianhe Period under the reign of Emperor Huandi of the Eastern Han Dynasty (148) and An Xuan had traveled to China in end of the period of the Eastern Han Dynasty which was under the reign of Emperor Lingdi (end of the 2nd century). An Shih-kao's experience was recorded in the Vol. 13 of A Compilation of Notes on the Translation of the Tripitaka (Chu San Zang Ji Ji) by Liang Sengyou (Monk You of the Liang Dynasty). According to this book, An Shih-kao had embraced Buddhism for cultivation before he arrived in China and "was good at Abhidhrama study and grasped the subtleness of Buddhist sutra". He was a noble prince and gave up the throne to become a monk after his father passed away. This indicates the prevalence of Buddhism in Arsacid empire. Probably, there were many Dukes and aristocrats who had believed in Buddhism. Abhidhrama was a Sanskrit word which means "great law". It is a generic term for thesis or theory. The initial Abhidhrama was a theoretical work of the sect discussing "all existing things in the world". The sect paid special attention to "Zen meditation", i.e. mastering the fundamental theories of initial Buddhism through Zen meditation. Another Arsacid person An Xuan translated the Mahayana classics Fajing Sutra and Meeting of Yujia Seniors of Dabaoji Sutra based on An Shih-kao's oral instructions and Yan Fotiao's records. An Xuan was a travelling businessman and a lay Buddhist. It indicated that there were quite a few Buddhists among merchants in Arsacid empire. Many of the early monks from the Western Regions to China were Arsacid people. The aforesaid An Shih-kao was the most influential one. An Shih-kao was also known as An Qing. But both were his Chinese names, and his original name was still unknown.

Mi, the contemporary of An Shih-kao, wrote: "An Shi-kao gave up the throne and lived contentedly as a Buddhist" in his Notes to Yinchiru Sutra. According to the Preface to Anbanshouyi Sutra by Kang Zenghui of the Wu State in the Three Kingdom Period, An Shih-kao was "the trueborn son of the Arsacid king, left the state to his uncle and also left his hometown". These records indicated that An Shih-kao was from the royal family of Arsacid. Chinese scholar Feng Chengjun has made researches on the origin of An Shih-kao in the 1930s, and believed he was Parthamasiris, the son of Pacorus II, the King of Arsacid in the late period of the 1st century. In 97 AD, Pacorus II passed away and his brother Cosroes succeeded the throne. Parthamasiris receded to become the King of Armenia, and finally gave up the throne and dedicated himself to religious work due to political reasons. The Arsacid royal lineage was generally defined based on the records of Roman and Latin writers and the ancient coins and inscriptions. According to History of the Western Regions, History of the Latter-Han Dynasty and the quotes in Vol.92 of Birds of Classified Excerpts from Ancient Writers from Visiting Han Eastward (Dongguan Hanji), in the 13th year of the Yongyuan Period of Emperor Hedi of the Eastern Han Dynasty (101), Arsacid ruler Manqu presented lions and big birds to the Han Dynasty court. The ruler Manqu should be Pacorus, or Pankar in Persian, he had lived in the same period with the Buddhist missionary An Shih-kao (An Shigao).[44]

In recent years, Chinese scholar Ma Yong also made some researches and argued that An Shih-kao was not the son of Pacorus II, but the son of Cosroes. An Shi-kao's uncle, the throne successor, was Cosroes's successor Volagases II. And Cosroes should be Khusru (Kusahe in Chinese) in Persian, and Volagases is Bulash in Persian. In other word, the King Manqu who presented big birds and lions to the Han Dynasty should be the elder uncle of An Shih-kao. After the ruler Manqu died, his brother Khusru succeeded the throne. Khusru was the father of An Shih-kao. After Khusru died, his brother Bulash II grabbed the throne. An Shih-kao had to departure and leave for otherregions. (Researches on Visitors to China from Central Asia in the Late Period of the Eastern Han from Textual Researches on History, Geography and Cultural Relics of the Western Regions, Cultural Relics Publishing House, 1990, pages 46-50) Although Ma Yong's points had more details than Feng Chengjun's, it is still difficult to confirm An Shih-kao's origin because the only proof for his royal origin was the several sentences contained in the Buddhist classics.[45] According to the Biographies of Eminent Monks, An Shih-kao had travelled many countries after his father passed away. During the years between 230 and 240, he travelled in Central Asia and India and arrived in China in the first year under the reign of Emperor Huandi of the Eastern Han. In his Sutra Records (Jing Lu), Shi Dao'an said that An Shih-kao started sutra translation in the 2nd year of the Jianhe Period of Emperor Huandi (148). So, the time when An Shih-kao arrived in China should be around the first year of the Jianhe Period (147). But it is not clear how he arrived in China.

The greatest achievement of An Shih-kao was his translation of major Buddhist classics. Although it was said that Kashyapamatang and Gobharana were the earliest monks who came to China to translate sutras in Buddhism history, no sutra translation was proved to be done by them so far. From the aspect of the sutra communication history in China, An Shih-kao was the first translator that presided over the work in China and enjoyed a fairly high position in China's translation history. Buddhist sutras was not written in Chinese, and Chinese did not understand it without translation. At the beginning of sutra translation, foreign monks played a very important role. When An Shih-kao

---

44 An Shih-kao, An Shigao (fl. c. 148-180 CE) was an early Buddhist missionary to China, and the earliest known translator of Indian Buddhist texts into Chinese. According to legend, he was a prince of Parthia, nicknamed the "Parthian Marquess", who renounced his claim to the royal throne of Parthia in order to serve as a Buddhist missionary monk in China.
45 Wang Bangwei, Arshak Monks and Initial Buddhism in China, Iranian Studies in China, Peking University Press, 1993, p. 85.

arrived in China, Chinese Buddhists were in urgent need of learning the contents of sutras. So his major task was sutra translation. Yan Fudiao said that the sutras interpreted or translated by him counted "several million words". A Compilation of Notes on the Translation of the Tripitaka by Sengyou said that he translated 35 sets and 41 volumes of sutras. Three Treasures of History (Li Dai San Bao Ji) by Fei Changfang of the Sui Dynasty listed 176 sutras translated by An Shih-kao. Records on Buddhism in the Kaiyuan Period (Kai Yuan Shi Jiao Lu) said he translated 95 sutras. To sum up, An Shih-kao was renowned for abundant sutra translations in the Buddhism history. An Shih-kao's contribution to sutra translations was not only in its abundance, but also its high quality. Shi Dao'an said, "Shih-kao's translation focuses on the essence and has no ornate diction, which conforms with the plain and fluent style of ancient Indian". In the Biography of An Shih-kao by Sengyou, he said that the sutra translated by An Shih-kao featured "clear argumentation, fair diction, prudent dialectics and plain style". Dignitaries in history had highly praised An Shih-kao's translations and praised him as the best translator in early Buddhism translations.

According to the Biographies of Eminent Monks, An Shih-kao, besides transalting Buddhist sutras, was "versed in foreign classics, astronomy, geography, medicine, sorcery and zoology". He was a highly-educated scholar involved in several disciplines and had read abundant books related to the Western Regions. Thanks to his high reputation, there were many legends on him which spread among Chinese Buddhists. When Huijiao collected materials to write Biographies of Eminent Monks, he received various versions on the deeds of An Shih-kao. An Xuan, who had lived in the period a little later than An Shi-kao's era, was a lay Buddhist and made self-cultivation at home. He was also engaged in sutra translation and cooperated with Yan Fudiao, the Chinese disciple of An Shih-kao, to translate Fajing Sutra. An Xuan made the interpretation and Yan Fudiao had recorded it. An Xuan's biography was collected in vol. 13 of A Compilation of Notes on the Translation of the Tripitaka and Vol. 1 of Biographies of Eminent Monks. In the Three Kingdoms Period, Tandi, also called Tanwudi, a Sramana of Arsacid, came to the north of China. According to Biography of Tankeluo in Volume. 1 of Biographies of Eminent Monks, he arrived in Luoyang in the first year of the Zhengyuan Period of the Wei Dynasty (254 AD). He was adept in religious disciplines and translated sutras in the famous White Horse Temple. He translated a volume of Tan Wu De Jie Mo, the disciplines of the Law Section in the book. It was one of the earliest religious teachings which were translated into Chinese.

Another Arsacid scholar An Faxian translated Luomojia Sutra and Mahaparinirvana Sutra. An Faqin, another Sramana of Arsacid, translated Daoshenwu Infinite Change Sutra, Biography of Asoka and other three classics during the 2nd year of the Taikang Period of Emperor Wudi of the Jin Dynasty (281) to the 1st year of the Guangxi Period of Emperor Huidi of the Jin Dynasty (306). An Shih-kao and these monks of Arsacid did not know Chinese when they just arrived in China. Chinese monks' assistance was necessary when they were spreading and translating Buddhist classics in China's temples. The deeds and names of some of his disciples were recorded in Chinese historical books. Yan Fudiao, alias Yan Fodiao, was the most renowned one of his disciples. He was from Linhuai and the direct disciple of An Shih-kao. In addition to assisting An Shih-kao, An Xuan and other Arsacid monks to translate sutras, Yan Fudiao also wrote Ten Smart Tenets of Sramana (Sha Mi Shi Hui Zhang Ju), the earliest Buddhist work authored by a Chinese so far. An Shih-kao's disciples also included Han Lin, Pi Ye and Chen Hui. They inherited An Shih-kao's doctrines and taught others. Renowned Kangju monk Kang Senghui was their disciple and the third-generation disciple of An Shih-kao.

Chapter 2. The Great Migration Movement of Peoples along the Land Silk Road

1. Eastward Spread of the Kushan (Rouzhi) Culture

In around 125 BC, not long before Zhang Qian's arrival to Rouzhi, the Rouzhi troops crossed the Amu Darya River and defeated the Daxia which was founded by Greek migrants. Daxia, covering the land between current Gory Baysuntau Ranges in the South of Uzbekistan and Hindu Kush Mountains in the North of Afghanistan with the Amu Darya River flowing through it, was also called Bactria. Before Rouzhi's invasion, Daxia was declining though it was under the reign of the Bactrian Dynasty established by Greek migrants. As it is stated in the Biography of Dayuan in the Records of the Historian, Daxia was a residential agricultural society with townships and villages similar to Dayuan. The country did not have a highest ruler while each city had its own chief. Its troops were weak and unskilled militarily. The residents were good traders. After beaten by Rouzhi, more than one million Daxia people were enslaved by the Rouzhi.[1]

(1) The Kushan Dynasty

According to the Biography of Dayuan in the Records of the Historian, Daxia's capital was in Lanshi City before the invasion of Rouzhi. At the beginning of the conquest, Darouzhi (Great Rouzhi) was contented with tribute and

---

[1] Kushan dynasty, Kushan also spelled Kusana, ruling line descended from the Yuezhi, a people that ruled over most of the northern Indian subcontinent, Afghanistan, and parts of Central Asia during the first three centuries of the Common Era. The Yuezhi conquered Bactria in the 2nd century BC and divided the country into five chiefdoms, one of which was that of the Kushans (Guishuang). A hundred years later the Kushan chief Kujula Kadphises (Qiu Jiuque) secured the political unification of the Yuezhi kingdom under himself.

tax collection. Later on, Darouzhi moved its political center to the Daxia's previous territory to the South of the Amu Darya and chose Daxia's former capital Lanshi City as its own capital. The book titled History of the Han Dynasty had the record of these incidents as "Darouzhi established its capital in Jianshi City". The same city was called Lanshi in the Records of the Historian and Jianshi in the History of the Han Dynasty. The characters of Lan and Jian are similar in shape but different in pronunciation. So, where was the capital of Great Rouzhi? Which one is right; Lan or Jian? All scholars interested in Kushan history have raised such questions. In the early years of the 20th century, French scholar Edouard Chavannes pointed out that Lanshi refers to current Badhakhshan in the East of Tajikistan. W.W. Tarn, the scholar engaged in research on the history of Great Alexander's Empire, thought that Lanshi referred to Alexandria (in Egypt today) built by the Greeks. And the Chinese scholar Yu Taishan has argued that it referred to Balkh city, capital of Bactria.[2]

Lan and Jian should have the same or similar pronunciation due to their same phonogram based on the structure of Chinese characters in ancient times. Their difference with the current pronunciation was caused by the changes of Chinese over the past 2,000 years. Scholars studying ancient Chinese phonetics believed that words Lan and Jian should be pronounced as "glam" before the Han Dynasty due to the law of compound consonantism in ancient China. To the East of current Balkh of Afghanistan, there is a site on the thoroughfare from the North of the Amu Darya to the Hindu Kush Mountains which was identified by archeologists as the site of Klum in the Tang Dynasty. Klum, Lanshi and Jianshi should be the different transliterations for the same city.[3] After Rouzhi moved southward and settled down, it was divided into five branches during the period from 95 BC to 70 BC with each branch led by a Yavugasa. Yavugasa, a title from the orient, means "chief" just a rank only next to the king. Wusun and Kangju also had the title Yavugasa which was the same word with Turkic official rank Yapqu.

According to the records in the Biography of the Western Regions in History of the Han Dynasty, the five branches of Darouzhi were: Xiumi established the capital in Hemo, 2,841 li away from Protectorate of the Western Regions; Shuanmi had the capital in Shuangmi City, 3,741 li away from Protectorate of the Western Regions; Kushan with its capital in Huzao City, 5,940 li away from Protectorate of the Western Regions; Xidun with its capital in Bomao City, 5,962 li and Gaofu with its capital in Gaofu City, 6,041 li away from Protectorate of the Western Regions. The title of Gaofu Yavugasa disappeared in the Biography of the Western Regions, History of the Latter-Han Dynasty, and was replaced by Dumi Yavugasa in the book. These five branches should be five regional states, which existed before Darouzhi's invasion of Daxia. According to the records in the Biography of the Western Regions, History of the Latter-Han Dynasty, in around the year of 50, Kushan Yavugasa Jiuque

---

2   Research on the Sacaraucae Race, China Social Sciences Press, 1992, p. 62.
3   Hu Siwei, China in Central Asia, Leiden Press, 1979, p. 119.

became powerful, eliminated other four branches and established the Kushan Empire with himself as the king. Chinese historical books used both names of Rouzhi and Kushan.

Kushan forces marched westward to Arsacid territory and captured its eastern city Merv. In the middle of the 1st century, Kushan's territories extended to the Amu Darya River northward and the upper reach of the Indus River Southward. In its golden era, the Kushan territories reached the Aral Sea and Kangju in the north, the Ganges river in the south and extended beyond the Pamirs to the south region of China's Xinjiang. Kushan was an important power in the Western Regions then. After Darouzhi (Kushan kingdom) moved westward and conquered Daxia, its people shifted from nomadic lifestyle to the agricultural lifestyle, and rapidly absorbed the local ancient cultures of Persia, Greece and India. Kushan boasted vast land and various economic forms. Its Southern part was mainly engaged in agricultural and had the same customs with India. Its central part was the dwelling region of the Rouzhi migrants who had come from the north for a long time ago, who made living by agriculture and animal husbandry, a mixed economy. According to the narration in the Biography of the Western Regions, History of the Han Dynasty, "the regions of the Kushan kingdom had similar climate, resources, customs and money with those of Arsacid." And the nomadic economy was the economic pillar in its northern part which was plentiful in horse breeding. Buddhism was introduced to Northwestern India and its peripheral states in around 3rd century BC. In the 2nd century BC, Milindapanha, the ruler of Indian Sheji kingdom founded by the Bactrian Greeks, had converted to Buddhism. Thus, Darouzhi kingdom started to contact Buddhism not later than the 1st century BC based on the time line.

During this period, the Hinduism stemming from Brahmanism, the Persian Zoroastrianism, the Greek culture and the Buddhism influenced each other. During the reign of Kanishka, some coins had the pattern of Sakyamuni in a Greek costume and surrounded by the word Buddha which was written in Greek letters. Despite the long distance between Kushan and the Central Plains, there were indirect connections between the both many years ago. Zhang Qian saw the Qiong Bamboo Stick and Sichuan Cloth produced in South China when he was in Daxia. Zhang asked about the source. The Daxia people said that they were bought from India. Thus Zhang learned that Chinese products were well favored by the Daxia people. During the period of the Kushan Empire, the expeditions from the Central Plains to Rouzhi were mainly through the Southern route which passed Southern Xinjiang and crossed the Pamirs. When starting building the China-Pakistan Karakorum Highway linking Kashgar of Xinjiang and the Northwestern border province of Pakistan in the 1960s, many historical sites on the Silk Road were discovered. China's silk, lacquer ware was sold to Arsacid and Rome faraway via Kushan. Glass and gems of Rome, spices and ivories of India were transported via Kushan and sold in China.

(2) Gandara Art and Karosthi Script

Gandara, referring to the northwestern region of ancient India, measured more than 200 km from its East to west with its center at current Peshawar, Pakistan and the neighboring region, its northwest border was located in current Hadda in the southeast of Afghanistan and southeast border at current east bank of the Indus River. Gandara, once a province of the Persian Empire, had high mountains in its Northwest regions and the Indus Valley in its Southeast. After the Alexander's invasion, Gandara had become a part of the Macedonian Empire. After the collapse of Great Alexander's Empire, numerous offsprings of Greek migrants lived there. Then these Greek migrants founded the Bactria state. During the Indian Maurya Dynasty, Asoka sent envoys to Gandara to spread Buddhism. Numerous political vicissitudes made Gandara a convergence region of various cultures.

Kanishka, the most famous ruler of Kushan kingdom, energetically promoted Buddhism. After the capital was moved to Fulousa (current Peshawar, Pakistan), Gandara became the center of Buddhism in the Northwestern India and encountered a boom in regard to Buddhist art. Under the influence of Greek culture, the artists broke the old convention, of ban to express the image of Buddha in the artistic works and created lots of Buddhist images featured with the styles of Greek and Roman art, which imitated the Greek god and Goddess images. Based on the findings in the excavation site of these art works, contemporary Buddhist history scholars and archeologists called it Gandara Art. Gandara Art originated from the Daxia Art of the 2nd century BC. On the coins issued during the reign of King Milindapanha there was the Buddhism symbol—the dharma wheel, but they didn't include Buddha's image. Some Greek people—who remained from the expedition of Alexander the Great have settled down in Daxia and have brought the Greek art to Central Asia. Archeologists discovered that the cultural relics and buildings of Daxia had characteristics of Greek culture, and some remains were even the imitations of Greek articles. In the Kushan kingdom period, the Roman empire was the major power in Europe. Roman art had influenced the art in the Central Asia through the offsprings of Greeks.

Gandara art has emerged after the 1st century and declined after the 5th and 6th centuries when the Ephthalites invaded their land. It was a new Buddhist art form that took shape based on the Central Asia's local Daxia art with the influences coming from Greek, Roman and Persian arts. The core of Gandara art was the Buddha statue sculpture. Scholars have generally suggested that Buddha statues first appeared in Gandara in the Kushan kingdom period, i.e., the 1st century. The reason for the appearance of Buddha statues in Gandara was that European migrants brought the Greek and Roman tradition of god statue production to the region and influenced the local culture with the European art.

Extant Buddhist pagodas, buildings, sculptures and fine arts in Gandara showed the combination of Greek culture and Central Asian culture. The main characteristics included the Buddha statues were in Greek-style woolen mantle with thick pleats, the figures were calm and had apparently European faces featuring high and straight noses, plump foreheads, curled hair, plain ornaments and solemn expressions. Gandara Buddhist statues were divided into plastic statues and engraved statues based on difference in process and material used. Plastic statues were also divided into gesso statues and clay blank statues. Gesso statues were made of lime, gypsum and fine sand and had colors of white with slight yellow. Gesso statues, appeared in the 1st century, were the earliest statues of Buddha statues and are mainly kept in the east of Afghanistan today. During the rejuvenation of Kushan kingdom under the reign of ruler Gupta, i.e. from the end of the 4th century to the 5th century, gesso statues were still made extensively. Gesso statuses were also built during the Ephthalites period and continued till the Turkic period. Clay blank statues were also further classified into clay-blank white-surface statues and clay statues based on the processes and materials. Clay-blank white-surface statues had color-sketched shapes and ornaments on the lime surface of clay blanks. Clay statues had color-sketched pattern on the clay blanks. Clay blank statues, appeared quite later, in the period between the 6th century and the 8th century, gradually transformed to the local styles of the Western Regions and was later introduced to the peripheral regions. In China's Buddhist temples, there were mainly the clay blank statues.

Engraved statues, also appeared in the 1st century, was a little later than the appearance of gesso statues. Gandara's local greenish grey or grayish green limestone was the sculpture materials. The limestone was rough and contained mica crystals. The statue would have a rough surface if no grinding works. In the 2nd and 3rd century, engraved statues developed rapidly and became dominant in Gandra's Buddha status and had a different style with plastic statues. The stone-carving art quickly declined in the 4th century, and disappeared in the 5th century. Pagodas in Gandara's temples often had square based buildings, Greek-style corner columns and walls with relief sculptures which narrated on Buddhist stories. With the spread of Buddhism, Gandara Art had produced deep influences to the grotto statues and paintings in China's Xinjiang and northwestern regions. Karosthi script, originating from Western Asia's Aramic letters, was introduced from Persia. Karosthi, literally meaning Donkey Lip, was also called Donkey Lip Language and written from right to left. The spelling it used was the vulgarism of northwestern India. The northwestern regions of ancient India (current border regions of Pakistan and Afghanistan), Afghanistan, the Central Asian countries and China's Xinjiang were the core regions for the use of Karosthi. The language was popular between the 3rd century BC and the 4th-5th centuries.

At the end of the 19th century, Western explorers found documents written in Karosthi in the territory of the ancient Yutian State and the Lop Nur-based Shanshan State, especially in the latter. Most of the documents discovered in

China were worldly literatures, such as the decrees of kings, the governmental or private letters, the bonds and accounting books etc. These are valuable materials for researching the history, culture, society, economy, law, military affairs and transport of Shanshan State. Most notably, in the documents discovered in China, there appeared the names of five kings of the Shanshan State. All of them had ruled the state for about 80-100 years, which took three to four centuries. Some of the Karosthi historical records can be used to collate the records in Chinese. Ancient residents of Xinjiang were mainly the ethnic peoples speaking Indo-European languages. In the period after Western Han's power was extended to the Western Regions, many aristocrats living there have learned the Chinese language. Some wooden slips of the Eastern Han proved that Chinese was popular among the peoples of Shanshan and Qiemo. The discovery of Karosthi historical records (Karosthi script) indicated that the ancient residents of the Western Regions were influenced by the oriental Eastern Han's culture and the Indo-European culture.[4] Yutian of Xinjiang had issued coins with Chinese and Karosthi on them, which are called Yutian Maqian currently. The coins caught the eyes of ancient coin collectors upon their appearance and were grabbed by foreign Western "explorers". Nearly 300 Yutian Maqian coins were registered and mostly exhibited in the Western museums, but China has few of them in its museums.

(3) Kushan People in China

Ancient Buddhists believed that the world had only 4 countries, i.e. China, India, Rouzhi and Huguo (Persia and the countries to its West). China was in the East and famous for its great population, India in the South for its elephants, Huguo in the West for its treasures and Rouzhi, i.e. Kushan, was noted for its horses. Of the four countries, Kushan, as an important transfer station for the East-west exchanges, was a pool of goods from China in the East, India in the South and Rome in the West. In the 1930s, archeologists discovered ivory and bone scriptures from India, lacquer ware from China, glasses ware, gesso and bronze statues from Western Asia in the collection sanctum of the era of Kushan. The gold coins of Kushan in the period under the reign of Vima Kadphises were cast according to the specifications of the Roman coins. Statistics indicate that the coins of Kushan in the period under the reign of Kaniska had 6 kinds of images of Greek and Roman gods, 5 kinds of images of Indian gods and 17 kinds of images of Iranian gods.

---

4   Kharosthi inscriptions dated from the 3rd Century CE have also been found in Sogdiana and Bactria during the time of the Kushan empire (1st to 4th Century CE). There are also Kharosthi examples located further east in Luoyang, China, dated to the Han dynasty during the reign of emperor Ling (CE 168-189). The oldest examples of Kharosthi found in Gandhara are displayed on the Ashokan edicts, carved on rock pillars dated to the mid-3rd century BCE. During the following century, Kharosthi was widely used on coin inscriptions when a currency system was introduced in Gandhara after the establishment of the short-lived Indo-Greek kingdom. The coins issued had bilingual inscriptions in both Greek and Prakrit, which was sometimes written with either Brahmi or Kharosthi characters.

Kushan, as a neighbor of the Western Regions, had close contacts with China. In the early years of the Eastern Han when Ban Chao and his son Ban Yong were governing the Western Regions, Kushan and China had some peace negotiations and wars with each other. Then, Kushan was under the reign of Soter Megas and Kaniska, the kings earlier than Vima Kadphises. Kushan also offered help when Ban Chao suppressed the rebellion of Cheshi and Shule. In 90, after a marriage proposal to the Eastern Han was refused, Kushan sent his vice leader Xie to lead 70,000 troops to surmount the Pamirs and invade the Western Regions governed by the Eastern Han. Bans Chao fortified the defense works in Shule and left nothing usable to the invading enemy. Finally, the food supply of Kushan's army was insufficient, and both sides reached a peace agreement. In the period under the reign of Kaniska, Kushan's troops crossed the Pamirs again and arrived in the Tarim Basin of China. According to the Biography of the Western Regions, History of the Latter-Han Dynasty, in the early years under the reign of Emperor Andi (114-120), Shule Chief's uncle was sent to Kushan as a hostage, and later escorted back by Kushan troops to succeed the throne. In the Great Tang Records on the Western Regions, quite a few countries in the region feared Kushan's power and sent sons there as hostages. Vasudeva II and Kitara were famous kings of Kusan after Kaniska. According to the Records on Emperor Mingdi, History of Wei in the History of Three Kingdoms, Emperor Mingdi of Wei conferred the title of Wei dynasty-friendly ruler of Darouzhi to Vasudeva II. Kushan kingdom played a fairly important role in the eastward spread of Buddhism. The Notes to the Biography of Western Foreign Countries, Brief History of Wei and Biography of Eastern Foreign Countries, History of Wei in the History of Three Kingdoms written by Yu Huan, a scholar in the Three Kingdoms Period, said: "In the first year of the Yuanshou Period under the reign of Emperor Aidi from the Western Han, court academician Jinglu (or Qin Jingxian, in the Records on Buddhists and Taoists, History of Wei) learned Buddhist Sutras by the oral teaching instructions given by Yicun, who was the envoy sent by the ruler of Darouzhi kingdom. It was called Fuli (Budha). According to the narrations in Buddhist Sutras, Linpusai, Sangmen, Bowen, Shumen, Baishuxian, Biqiu, Chenmen all refer to the names of disciples."

The phrase "It was called Fuli" in the above quote is difficult to understand. The spread of sutras by Darouzhi religious missionary envoys was also recorded in the book titled as: Languages, A New Account of the Tales of the World as "It was called Fudou". This record made the inexplicable word "Fuli" clearer. The correct version should be Fudou, referring to Buddha. In Western Han, Buddhist Sutra was also called Fudou Sutra. In Fudou Sutra, the "Linpusai" meant "upasaka" (male laymen), and Sangmen, Shumen and Chenmen were similar to Sramana. The inconsistent translations were frequent in the early days. Fudou Sutra was possibly a classic Buddha text similar to Benqi Sutra, Benxing Sutra and other sutras narrating the life of the Buddha. It is the earliest record which narrated about the spread of Buddhism into the Central Plains in historical books.

The oral instruction (teaching) of Buddhist Sutras by Yicun,i.e, the envoy of King of Darouzhi, was in conformity with the prevalent methods for teaching Indian Buddhism. Oral teaching was the traditional method in the Buddhism teaching. China's early sutra translations during the Eastern Han dynasty period was also made through oral instructions. Kushan kingdom was an important transfer point for the eastward spread of Buddhism. After Yicun, quite a few Kushan monks came to the Central Plains to introduce Buddhist sutras in the Eastern Han dynasty and Three Kingdoms Period. They were called Rouzhi people in Chinese historical narrations. Later, Buddhism was further spread eastward to Korea and Japan and became one of the most important religions in the East Asia.

In the Han and Wei dynasties, people of the Central Plains often added the nationality abbreviation as a surname to the name of foreign monk, such as Zhu for India, An for Anxi, Kang for Kangju and Zhi for Kushan. Zhi Loujiachen, alias Zhi Chen, was from Kushan. According to the Records on Heshou Yanleng Sutra in Vol. 7 of Compilation of Notes on the Translation of the Tripitaka, he came to China during the reign of Emperor Huandi and Emperor Lingdi of the Eastern Han dynasty period (147-188). Some of the visitor foreign monks could speak Chinese, but most of them, including Zhi Chen, could not write. He interpreted the sutras in a temple in Luoyang, and Chinese monks, including Meng Fu and Zhang Lian, had written them down. During the reign of Emperor Lingdi and Emperor Xiandi during the Eastern Han period (168-220), another Kushan sramana Zhi Yao also had a high reputation in Luoyang. According to the book Biographies of Kang Monks in Vol. 1 of Biographies of Eminent Monks, Zhi Chen had a Kushan disciple Zhi Liang who was a Rouzhi man who was deeply influenced by Chinese culture. Another Rouzhi people Zhi Qian, living in the Wu State period, was also recorded in the same book. He initially travelled across China and then learned languages of six countries from Zhi Liang. Most of the Kushan people in China were engaged in religious sutra text translations.

2. Climax Period of Integration of Peoples along the Land Silk Road

The period of Wei and Jin dynasties witnessed severe changes in the relationships among China's ethnic peoples. Northern nomadic people continuously moved into the Central Plains to settle down and communicate with the Han people closely. Then they set up separatist regimes with long or short existence forcefully, and they were finally merged into the Han people. In the Western and Eastern Han dynasties, the Northern nomads migrated to the Central Plains were mainly the capitulated people from Hun and its troops. The migration of Northern peoples then was considerable in scale then. In the Wei and Jin dynasties, the Southward migration of nomads was more intense due to the wars in the Central Plains. According to the Records on Emperor Wendi, History of the Jin Dynasty, the migrated population was more than 8.7 million. Upon the estimation in On Migration of Western Ethnic Nationalities (Xi Rong Lun) by Jiang Tong during the reign of Emperor Huidi—the Jin Dynasty, there were more than a million people living in the Guanzhong Plain and the nomadic migrants accounted for half of the population. Migrants generally lived scattered and gathered to live in small communities among the Han people.

The nomadic migrants lived as small communities and maintained their tradition of valiancy. They became new troop sources for the regional warlords of the Chinese Han. According to the writings in the Records on Han in the Biography of Zheng Hun, History of Wei, History of the Three Kingdoms, Dong Zhuo's troops had soldiers from Huns, Tuge (Tuge, a noble race of Hun, was recorded as Xiutu and Xiutuge in the Records of the Historian and in the History of the Han Dynasty), Huangzhongyi and in other five sources. Cao Cao's troops also had soldiers from the people of Dingling, Tuge and the "world-famous" Wuhuan cavalries. After living for a long period in the Central Plains, the Northern nomad people gradually gave up nomad life and were used to agriculture and thus settled permanently. The government recorded them in the household registers and forced them to do forced labor and pay taxes. Many of them became the exploitation objects of the Han landlords. According to the records in the Biography of Imperial Relative Wang Xun, History of the Jin Dynasty, Wang Xun, a prestigious family leader in Taiyuan of the Western Jin Dynasty, "had several thousand of farmhands from Hun and the Western Regions". Many high officials also had servants and maids from Xianbei. Even the lower-level tribe chiefs of some ethnic peoples could not avoid such slavish treatment. According to the Records of Shi Le, History of the Jin Dynasty, Shi Le, the founder of the latter period of the Zhao Dynasty*, originally was a small tribe chief and military commander from the Jie ethnic group and a tenant peasants in a Han landlord's family, he finally rebelled against the Jin Dynasty. Then he was captured and sold to Shandong, and cruelly exploited. Such suppression upon the peoples was the fundamental reason for the severe turmoil in the Central Plains at the end of the Western Jin Dynasty. Shi Le, sacked the city of Luoyang. From 312 on he resided in Xiangyang and was the most powerful potentate of the whole region. With the conquest of Pingyang (contemporary Linfen, Shanxi) in 318 on he controlled the whole region north of the Yellow River. In 319 Liu Yao proclaimed himself Emperor of the Zhao empire, yet Shi Le was not willing to submit to his rule and adopted the title of Great Khan (da shanyu) and King of Zhao. Shi Le undertook military campaigns to weep out the Xianbei tribe of the Duan and came into the possession of what is today Henan and northern Anhui. In 329 he attacked Chang'an (contemporary Xi'an, Shaanxi), the capital of the Former Zhao empire, and so also was lord of these western regions and thus of a large part of northern China. It was during this time that the River Huai became the border between northern and southern China. In 330 Shi Li adopted the title of emperor (Emperor Ming).[5]

---

5   The long history of the Zhou Dynasty is normally divided in two different periods.

Despite of the civilization differences between the Han and the Western Regions, the difference gaps were gradually narrowed and the immigrants were merged into the Han nation finally, thanks to the integration of the nomad peoples in the Han territory and their offspring's long-term settlement and co-existence with the Han commoners in the Central Plains. This was the intrinsic momentum that ended the 300-year split from the end of the Eastern Han to the Southern and Northern Dynasties and China became a re-united country.

(1) States Built by Hun's Offsprings and Xianbei People

In the 24th year of the Jianwu Period of the Eastern Han (48 AD), the Hun state split into two parts. The Southern part surrendered itself to the Han and moved to inside of the Great Wall. The Northern part stayed in the Northern desert and then moved westward. Eastern Han treated the chief of Southern Hun as a duke and often gave cattle, sheep and grain to his tribes. The surrender of Southern Hun produced great importance to the history of Northern China, greatly weakened Hun's power and released the Northern people from wars. The Southern Hun inhabited the South of the desert, becoming a northern border barrier of the Han Dynasty, having more contacts with North China's residents and boosting the merge of peoples. The impairment of Hun also freed Wuhuan, Xianbei and other ethnic peoples from its rule. Later on, Xianbei tribe encountered a gradual rise. Consequently, the conditions for the separation of South and North China were created. During the periods of the coexistence of 16 states and the Southern and Northern Dynasties, the Hun migrants founded regional kingdoms in the Central Plains and Northwestern regions, mainly the Early Han and the Early Zhao founded by the Tuge people of Southern Hun, the Northern Liang by the Juqu family in Hexi prefecture, the Daxia by Tiefu Hun in the Gansu and Shaanxi regions. The Yuwen tribe of Hun was merged into Eastern Xianbei and established the Northern Zhou kingdom later on.

During the Wei Dynasty period, the Southern Hun was divided into five tribes with more than 30,000 households led by independent chiefs. The Left Tribe's Tuge family grew powerful later on. In the early period of Western Jin dynasty, Liu Yuan, chief of the Tuge family, strongly obeyed the Jin Court and controlled the 5 tribes. The rebellions by the Eight Princes in the Western Jin dynasty triggered an intense turmoil in the Central Plains. The Chengdu Chief Sima Ying ordered Liu Yuan to conscribe the cavalries of Southern Hun's five tribes to help him. According to the Records of Liu Yuanhai, History of the Jin Dynasty, aristocrats of Southern Hun thought their power declined, "the chiefs had only a futile title without any territory to control" and "the peerage downgrade to the commoners". The cruel suppression of the landlords and farmers belonging to Han people made the Hun migrants feel that "the Jin Dyansty court was tyrannical and treated them as slaves". The internal chaos of the Jin's Sima aristocrats was a good opportunity for the rejuvenation and strengthening of the Huns.

As an ambitious Hun aristocrat with deep understanding of the Han culture, Liu Yuan said: "there were no permanent emperors. Dayu was born in the West, and Emperor Wenwang in the East". They were respected as the emperor, thanks to their virtues. Hun state, before the nephew of Han dynasty, now became a brother nation of the Han. It was also reasonable for Hun to continue nurturing the people-to-people brotherhood with the Hans. The Former Hun Kingdom implemented a complex bureaucracy organization system. Many Xianbei customs were inherited, such as the emperor was called Dachanyu (great chief) and came from the Tuge family only. The relatives of Dachanyu were assigned to 16 senior ranks including the left and right xianwang, the left and righ yiliwang (i.e., guliwang). Other Hun aristocratic families, Huyan, Xubu, Lan and Qiao took the positions of ministers. The Han positions like prime minister, grand tutor, war minister and commander were also established. The Han and Hun people were ruled with different governance systems. The Chinese Han people were governed based on households. Left and Right Population Officer titles were established by the Empire to govern 200,000 households each. One sub-officer was assigned to govern 10,000 households, and there were altogether 43 sub-officers. On the other side, the Hun people were governed in communities, there were two deputies of the Hun Emperor (Khan) which had the titles as follows: the king on the right and left (2 Zuoxian), ranking second only to the Khan in importance. One Duwei (sub-general) was assigned per 10,000 community members. And a population of 200,000 people formed a community. In the chronicle of "Shi Ji" the historical recorder Sima Qian has given the following brief description of the political structure of Hun (Xiongnu) society:

"Under Maodun the Xiongnu (Huns) had the unprecedented increased power, they conquered all Northern barbarians, and in the South formed a state as powerful as the Middle Kingdom (Han Dynasty), so the delegation of power from one ruler to another, and the names of government officials [from that period], we can clarify and explain. There were 6 functional divisions as follows: (1) left and right xien-wangs (wise van); (2) left and right lu-li- wang; (3) left and right great military leaders; (4) left and right great du-wei; (5) left and right great dang-hu; (6) left and right gu-du-hou. The Huns call a wise "tu-qi", so the eldest son of [shanyu] is called the left tu-qi-wang. From the left and right xien-wangs up to a dang-hu, the strong ones having ten thousand horsemen, and the weak ones with a few thousand [horsemen], there are only twenty-four chief officers, for 24 of them a rank–wan-ci was introduced. All the dignitaries take offices by inheritance. Left and right gu-du-hou help [shan-yu] in governing. Each of the twenty-four chiefs also personally appoints thousand-men chiefs, hundred-men chiefs, ten-men chiefs, petty princes, principal assistants, du-weis, dang-hu and qie-ju"(MIS, 1:39-40, MIS, 2:11-12).

Since the Yongjia turmoil in the Western Jin dynasty, some scholars of the Central Plains moved to the Hexi prefecture and received courteous reception there. Hexi became a pool of the Han scholars then. Juqu Mengxun and the Xianbei aristocrats of the Northern Liang paid great attention to the Han scholars and assigned them to important positions. The scholar Kan Yindian had more than 30 assistants in classic collation there and collated more than 3,000 volumes of classics. Another scholar Zong Qin authored Biography of Mengxun, the history of Northern Liang. After, controlling and pacifying the Central Plains, the Northern Wei attacked the Northern Liang. After capturing Guzang, the Northern Wei placed the Han scholars in key positions of research. The Northern Wei used the Jingchu Calendar, a calendar of the Wei Dynasty, at the beginning of its ruling in the Central Plains. After conquering the Northern Liang, the Northern Wei discovered that the Xuanshi Calendar used by the Juqu Mengxun regime was more accurate. In the 1st year of the Xing'an Period of Emperor Wenchengdi of the Northern Wei (452), the Jingchu Calendar was abolished upon the imperial decree and the Xuanshi Calendar was used.

According to the Records on Music, History of the Sui Dynasty, Emperor Daowudi of the Northern Wei defeated Murong Bao in the 1st year of the Huangshi Period (396) and obtained the instruments of the Jin Dynasty collected by the Latter Yan regime. But Emperor Daowudi knew nothing about the instruments and had to throw them away. After Emperor Taiwudi of the Northern Wei captured Hexi prefecture and the local scholars, the Northern Wei had the idea on rites and music. Later, in case of important ceremonies, the Northern Wei played the music of the Jin Dynasty learned from the scholars of the former Northern Liang. One of the popular music genres during the Northern Wei reign was called Xiliang Music which appeared at the end of the early Qin dynasty established by the Fu family of the Di people. During the period of Lu Guang and Juqu Mengxun's occupation of Hexi, the music was recomposed with Qiuci music of the Western Regions and named Qinhanji Performance. After Emperor Taiwudi of the Northern Wei captured Hexi, the music was introduced to the Central Plains and renamed as Xiliang Music. According to the book "Records on Music, History of the Northern Wei Dynasty", the Northern Wei also obtained a set of "Performer's Instrument and Costume" from the Northern Liang.

According to the book Records about Helian Bobo, History of the Jin Dynasty, after establishing the Xia kingdom, Tiefu Huns often attacked the latter Qin dynasty. Helian Bobo was suggested to reside permanently in a "high and smooth and strategic" place. Helian Bobo, had replied that such a dwelling place would be prone to enemy attacks and cause great losses for them. He said: relying on our "quick cavalry and sudden attacks" we will make the enemy constantly on the run, thus it will lose its control, when it concentrates on one thing, it will lose its concentration on the whole." While we are "accustomed to nomadic life", we can capture the lands to the North of the Qinling Mountains and the East of the Yellow River, Helian Bobo added: Consequently, we as the Tiefu Huns should still adhere to the nomadic lifestyle after establishing the Xia State. Xianbei people, originating from Northeast China, were the offspring of the Donghu ethnic people of the Qin and Han dynasties. Most of the scholars believe that Xianbei was a tribe who spoke ancient Mongolian. Donghu was split into Xianbei in the North and Wuhuan in the South after being defeated by Hun chief Maodun.

Xianbei rose after the decline of Hun. After the Northern Hun moved Westward, the grassland which extended to the Northern desert was free of political control. The 100,000 troops of Hun were subordinated to Xianbei, Liaodong, and called themselves Xianbei. During the reign under Emperor Huandi of the Eastern Han (147-167), Xianbei chief Tan Shihuai unified the tribes and built his strong troops in the Southern desert. Tan Shihuai was a celebrity in the history of Xianbei. Xianbei was under the control of the Huns. Touluhou, father of Tanshihuai, had served in Hun for three years. In his childhood, other tribes grabbed his mother's animals. Tan Shihuai pursued the enemy himself and got back the animals. Tan was praised by his tribes and elected as the marshal. Then, he led the troops to defeat the Dingling in the North, Fuyu in the East and Wusun in the West and established the union of Xianbei tribes measuring 7,000km from East to West with its center on the Mongolian grasslands. For the convenience of reign, Tan Shihuai divided the vast country into three parts under the governance of their chiefs respectively: the Eastern part consisting of 20-odd tribes inhabiting the region from current Beijing Eastward to Liaohai, the central part consisting of 10-odd tribes inhabiting the region from current Beijing to the border between Shanxi and Hebei, and the Western part from the Shanxi-Hebei border to Wusun. During the reign of emperor Lingdi of the Eastern Han (168-189), Tan Shihuai passed away and the federation of Xianbei tribes collapsed. The Ke Bineng and his clique, from the Xiaozhong Xianbei in the Eastern part, gradually rose and unified the tribes in the Southern desert during the Wei Dynasty. When the chieftain Ke Bineng died in 235, the federation of Xianbei tribes collapsed again. The tribes of Yuwen, Duan and Murong of the Eastern part were the most important ones among them.

During the Wei and Jin dynasties, there were many other Xianbei tribes, such as the Tuoba (or Tufa) tribe and Qifu tribe in the Western part. In the period of Wei, Jin, Southern and Northern dynasties period, Xianbei had set up quite a few independent regimes by force of arms.

(2) Song for A'gan

Among all the states founded by Xianbei people, Tuyuhun established by the Murong Tribe of Xianbei in Liaodong had the longest duration. Originally, Tuyuhun was the name of the eldest son born by the concubine of Murong Shegui, chief of the Murong Tribe. Tuyuhun also had a brother Murong Wei. In the fourth year of the Taikang Period of the Western Jin (283), Murong Shedui passed away. Tuyuhun, as the eldest son, could not succeed the throne and only got 1,700 households (or 700 households according to the Biography of Tuyuhun in the History of Song or the History of Wei) because he was borne by the concubine of Murong Shegui. While his brother Murong Wei succeeded the throne as the son born by the wife of Murong Shegui. The pastures of the two brothers were neighboring with each other. Contradictions occurred due to the situation of increasing animals and limited pastures. Pasture disputes between the tribes of Tuyuhun and Murong Wei urged Tuyuhun to migrate faraway from

Liaodong. The migration took place between the 4th year and the 10th year of the Taikang Period of the Western Jin dynasty (283-289 AD).

Tuyuhun left Liaodong and led his tribes Westward. At that time, the Duan, Murong and Yuwen tribes struggled intensely with each other in Liaodong. The departure of Tuyuhun weakened the power of Murong tribe. Murong Wei felt regretful and sent envoys to persuade Tuyuhun to come back. Tuyuhun insisted on westward migration and would not return. Murong Wei missed his brother and composed the Song for A'gan. A'gan means "elder brother" in Xianbei language. So, it was a song to express Murong Wei's yearning for his brother. Firstly, Tuyuhun's tribes lived a nomadic life in the Yinshan Mountain to the North of the Great Wall. And then, when the Upheaval of the Eight Princes took place, they moved Southward, crossed the Longshan Mountain to the border of Gansu and Qinghai. Later on, Tuyuhun further expanded westward and southward. When Tuyan, the second chief of the tribe, came into throne in 329, the state was founded in the Northwestern region with the name of Tuyuhun. The state had existed for more than 330 years till it was terminated by Tubo in the 3rd year of the Longsuo Period of the Tang Dynasty (663). Due to the changes in pronunciation, Tuyuhun was also written as "tuihun", "tuhun" or others in historical books. Moreover, as Tuyuhun was in the south of the Yellow River, it was also called Henan or Henan State (literally means the country in the south of the river) by the states of the Song, Qi, Liang and other states of the Southern dynasties. Achai, another name of Tuyuhun, was not only used by the Han people but also found in Tibetan historical literature.

90

During the period when Tuyuhun and his son Tuyan were on the throne, the Xianbei tribes conquered the Qing tribes which dwelled in the border region of current Gansu, Qinghai and Sichuan, and occupied the regions which are in the current Qaidam Basin and Northwestern Sichuan. At its culmination, Tuyuhun had the territory from Southern Gansu and north Sichuan in the East to Ruoqiang and Qimo in the Southwest of Xinjiang's Tarim Basin in the West, from the Qilian Mountains in the North to Southern Qinghai in the South. At the beginning, Tuyuhun lived a nomadic life, and only built some small towns to shelter the dukes and aristocrats, which were not the capital. In its late period, Tuyuhun set up Fusi City as its capital. The site of Fuci was found in Gonghe County of Qinghai province, 7 km away from the Qinghai Lake, after the liberation. Situated in the Northeast, Tuyuhun was still under the influence of the Han culture. The Biography of Tuyuhun in the History of Jin said that Tuyuhun was "quite familiar with Chinese characters", had the official rank of Zhangshi (adjutant), Sima (minister of war) and Jiangjun (general) which were the borrowed from the Han court, and added the ranks of Pushe (prime minister), Shangshu and Langzhong in the period of the Han'sTang Dynasty. Tong Dian (General Codes) said that Tuyuhun "imitated China to establish its bureaucracy". Later on, the titles Zhangshi (adjutant), Jiangjun (general) and others were widely used in the Turkic and Mongolian tribes.

According to the Biography of Tuyuhun in the History of Wei, Tuyuhun's men were the same with the Han men of the Northern Dynasties in dress and personal adornments; its women also similar with the Han women in the Central Plains, but different in hairstyle. Tuyuhun women braided their hair and believed the more braids they had the more beautiful they would be. This hairstyle is still popular among the Tibetan women of Gansu and Qinghai and possibly a custom heritage of Tuyuhun. Tuyuhun music was introduced to the Central Plains via communications with the Han people. In the Sui and Tang dynasties, the music of Tuyuhun, Xinbei and Buluoji were collectively called Beidi Music. According to the Records of Music, the Old History of Tang, Beidi Music was "the music played on horses to encourage the troops" and under the management of the Guchuishu (Music Administration). A total of 53 movements of Beidi Music were still kept till the Tang Dynasty, including Murong Khan, Tuyuhun and Buluoji with lyrics in minority languages.

Tuyuhun's culture produced deep influence to the Northern nomadic peoples. The Biography of Tuyuhun in the History of Wei recorded such a story: in the 5th century, Tuyuhun Khan A'chai had 20 sons. He was worrisome about that his sons would quarrel and struggle with each other and jeopardize the nation after his death. Then, he assembled them all, and gave each one an arrow and asked them to break it. After that, he asked them to try a bundle of arrows. The sons could break one easily but neither could break a bundle. So, A'chai edified them, "Don't you know the truth? An arrow can be easily broken, but not a bundle. If you team up and make concerted effort, our nation will stay stable and long." This is the famous story "Teaching with Arrows" widely narrated among the nomadic peoples dwelling in the grasslands for successive generations. The narration was still popular among the Mongolians dwelling in the Northern desert till the Liao dynasty period. In Chapter 22 of the Secret History of the Yuan Dynasty, there is a story on the deeds of Alan Hu'a, the historical grandma of Genghis Khan. Alan Hu'a said the following to her five sons: a single arrow can be easily broken, but a bundle of them not. You were all from my womb. So you should join hands together like a bundle of arrows, and no one can defeat you. Obviously the two stories were from the same source. The story narrated by Alan Hu'a is still widely narrated among the Mongolian ethnic group and even among the Han people today. The foundation of the Tuyuhun state took place in the era when China was split into the Northern and Southern parts and the Southern people could not cross the Hexi Corridor to communicate with the Western states. The people of the Southern Dynasties entered Tuyuhun via Northern Sichuan, then marched Northwest along the roads near Qinghai to enter Southern Xinjiang and kept in touch with the Western regions.

3. From Steppes to Central Plains

(1) The Footprints of the Tuoba Tribe

As one of the tribes of the Xiebei nationality, Tuoba tribe played a significant role in the Chinese history. They moved to the Central Plains from their homeland and established the Northern Wei Dynasty, which had later estranged them from their homeland. It was said that there was a Xiebai Mountain in the boundless deserts of the Northern China. The local uncivilized people lived a very simple life, depending on animal husbandry and hunting for their livelihood. Their ancestors that they knew was called the Tuoba Mao. According to research, prior to Mao, there were 37 generations, but the details of about them unknown. Tuoba Mao, as a tribal chief, unified 36 tribes, which included 99 big clans, but these numbers cannot be accurately verified.

Among the 5th generation of Tuoba Mao, a man called Tui Yin became the tribal chief. "Tui Yin" in the Chinese character describes a person who loves studying. It was that under the lead of Tui Yin that the local people moved South from the Xianbei Mountain to "Daze", which referred to the Hulun Lake and Beier Lake. Later, a man called Ling became the tribal chief through two generations, also known as the "Tui Yin". His son called Jie Fen led the people to move Southward. Finally, although they have encountered many difficulties and reached at the Xiongnu's old haunt under the guidance of a kind of mythical beast with the shape of horse and the sound of cattle. (Xiongnu was a powerful nomadic people which controlled the Central Plains in the later period of Qin Dynasty and early Han Dynasty). After the Tuoba people established their own country in Central Plain, which was far away their homeland, they relationship with their homeland became gradually not close. But they still remembered the ancestor temple which was chiseled in the Xiebei Mountain, located in the Northwest of the Woluohou tribe. In the 4th year under the rule of emperor Taiwu in the Wei Dynasty (443), the envoys from the Woluohou tribe paid tribute to the imperial court and said that the ancestors' temple of Tuba was still preserved. Some people often visited it, and it was efficacious. Therefore, the imperial court sent envoys to go back to the ancestor's temple in a bid to engrave inscription and worship the earth and god. In 1980, archaeologists discovered the Tuoba ancestor's temple in the East side of the Northern Great Xingan Mountains, about 10 km to the Northwest away from the Alihe town, Oroqen Autonomous Banner, Inner Mongolia Autonomous Region. In fact, the temple was a cave with the height of 12m high and the width of 18 meters. The mouth of it, facing the South, was 92 meters long and 27-28 meters wide. It could be found inscriptions engraved in the wall, the content of which was same with that of the Wei Dynasty Book. The information of it can be found in the book titled Tuoba People's Homeland and Migration.[6]

---

6   The original book was written in German, titled as: Zur Urheimat und Umsiedlung der Toba. (Wiesbaden, Central Asiatic Journal, Issue 1-3, p. 86-107, 1989).

It was researched that the temple was a natural cave. According to historical books, the ancestor of Tuoba once cleaned the cave, so the cave was engraved as temple. After the Tuoba people controlled the Central Plains, they were assimilated by the Han people, and their original nomadic consciousness had a sharp contradiction with the settled life. In order to establish themselves in the Central Plains, they had to adopt to the situation. Therefore, during the reign of Emperor Wei Yuan (471-499), a series of significant reforms, were made, the most important measures of which were as follows:

The first measure was to move to Luoyang (located in Western Henan province as well as middle and lower reaches of the Yellow River). Since the reign of Tuoba Gui, known as the Emperor Daowu, the capital of Western Wei Dynasty was in Pingcheng (Datong, Shanxi province), which was a militarily strategic location, so as to prevent the invasion of the Northern nomadic peoples. It combined the customs of Hu people and Han people, which was also suitable for Tuoba people. But, located in the Northern China, the Western Wei Dynasty could not be self-sufficient in food. In addition, the economic and cultural center of Northern Wei Dynasty moved to the Yellow River basin. Therefore, in the 17th year of Taihe (493 AD), the Emperor Xiaowen led the army to march towards Luoyang with the purpose of waging war against the regions in the South. After repeated deliberations and considerations, Emperor Xiaowen decided to establish the capital here. The troops in the army who originated from Northern regions were required to be buried here after death, instead of their homeland. Secondly, it has changed official system. At the beginning of Western Wei Dynasty, their official organization and systems were quite simple and most of them still followed the old system instead of learning from the Han systems. The official ranks were named after birds. For example, "Zhu Cao Zou Shi" (Teal), describing the official taking quick actions, "Bailu" (Egret), describing the investigator carefully examined and analyzed the situation.[7]

In addition, the book, Southern Qi Dynasty Book Wei Dynasty, recorded 13 official rank names of the Tuoba tribe and these names all had a suffixes "chi" just as the Mongolian people. Some of these names could be found among Mongolians of the 13th century, such as Bitekchi, Kelemechi, Khapakhchi, Jamchi and Ba urchi. The stem of these names were originated in the Turkic language, which showed there were many Turkic words in their language. It was because Mongolians had had absorbed a larger number of people who spoke the Turkic language. When establishing the new capital in Luoyang, emperor Xiaowen declared that they would follow the official system of the Wei and Jin Dynasty and set up some official ranks in central and local government. Prior to moving the capital, emperor Xiamwen had change the old way of determining the salaries of the officials. The old ways meant that the officials could select their awards from the spoils of the war or gain money by squeezing other people.

---

7   See Wei Dynasty Book· Official Biography.

Thirdly, was Xilin the ban on speaking the Hu language. Their original language was an ancient Mongolian dialect. When they settled down in the Central Plains, they were gradually assimilated by Han people, but the Xianbei people in the army and the imperial court still spoke the Tuoba language. Therefore, if Han people wanted to serve as an official, they had to learn Xianbei language. In the 19th year of the Taihe (495), Emperor Xiaowen issued a law which banned speaking of the Xianbei language. The officials under the age of 30 would be demoted if they continued to speak Xianbei language. Only officials over the age of 30 were allowed to speak their own language. The ban on Hu language accelerated the assimilation of Tuoba people by the Han people.

As the book History of Sui Dynasty Classics Biography said: "as Tuoba people established their capital in the central Plains, they firstly still used their own language to manage their army, but later, some people were assimilated by Han people and started to speak the Han language. So some people decided to teach people to learn their own language, which is called "Native Language". In the Northern Wei Dynasty, Xianbei people had no words, so they recorded their language in Chinese. By the end of the Northern Wei Dynasty, there were a few people who knew Xianbei language due to former Han-ization. The book Classics Biography said that there were 13 books that included records about the Xianbei language, which included the following: Native Language 15 volumes, Native Language 10 volumes, Goods in Native Language 4 volumes (written by Ke Xilin, an official in the late period of the Wei Dynasty), Songs in Native Language 10 volumes, Various Kinds of Goods in Native Language 3 Volume (written by Ke Xilin), Native Language 18 Biography 1 volume, Royal Songs in Native Language 11 volumes, Command in Native Language 4 volumes, Essay in Native Language 15 volumes, Mastering the Xianbei Language Volume I (written by Zhou Wudi) and Miscellaneous Command volume I. It is a pity that these books on the Xianbei language could not be preserved.

Fourthly, the fourth measure was to promote the use of surnames used by the Han people. It was said that there were 99 surnames, namely clan names. After they settled in Luoyang, the emperor ordered people to use Han surnames, instead of Hu surnames for the purpose of establishing close relationships with the Han nationality. The Emperor Xiaowen changed their royal surname into Yuan, other nobility and Northern people also changed their names into Han surnames. Several methods of changing surnames were as follows; one method was based on the syllable abbreviation, that was to change the syllables for mono-syllabic, such as Qiumuling was changed to Mu, Buliugu to Lu, Helai to He. Another method was to adopt transliteration, such as Chounv was changed to Lang (wolf). The original word of Chounv should be Cino, meaning wolf in the Tuoba-Mongolian language. Xiaowen also imitated the method that was used to determine the rank of officials used by the Han nationality to define the grades of surnames. In order to quickly merge with the Han people, Emperor Xiaowen encouraged people to intermarry with Han people. Due to the acceleration of Han-ization, the difference between the North nationality and the

Han nationality in the Central Plains diminished, and the Northern peoples rapidly adopted to the Central Plains. In the late period of the North Wei Dynasty, the only way to recognize an ethnic origin was through their surnames. In other words, the original North-South division was largely diminished, which created the conditions for China's reunification.

(2) China Recognized as Tabqaci and Taohuashi

The "Tuoba" was the transliteration of Chinese characters, and another nationality of Tuoba tribe was called "Tufa". "Tuoba" and "Tufa" were derived from entering tone syllables (syllables ending on a plosive). In the Wei and Jin Dynasties, the pronunciation of "Tuoba" in Chinese was "tak bat", while "Tuofa" was "tuk bat". Many people in the neighboring regions of Tuoba used Turkic language, so they called "Tuoba people" Tabqaci because of the phonetic habit. The information of it can be found in the book Tuoba People's Homeland and Migration. The original book was written in German, called Zur Urheimat und Umsiedlung der Toba,(Wiesbaden, Central Asiatic Journal, Issue 1-2, p. 91-92, 1989).The Tuoba people ruled Northern China for over 1 and a half centuries, so Tabqaci (Tuoba) in the ancient Turkic language represented China.

During the 900-year period from the 4th century to 15th century, many neighboring peoples called China "Tabqaci ". The name "Tabqaci" was spread across the Steppes to many regions of Asia and Europe. At that time, the Byzantine Empire was collecting information about China through envoys and merchants who had visited China. In the first half of 7th century, i.e., the early Tang Dynasty period, Theophylacte Simocatta, a Greek scholar, once said that the people in the rule of the emperor Maurice in the Eastern Roman Empire (582-602) described Chinese history as follows; "Many defeated Abaroi people in the Northern Steppes fled to Taugaste city. It has been a very famous, city which was about a 1,000 miles distance from the border of Turkic land. Their leader was called Taisan, meaning 'The Son of Heaven'. There was a river which divided the country into two parts, one part's people wearing red clothes and other wearing black clothes. Not long ago, the people wearing black clothes have subordinated the red-clothed people across the river, and established Taugaste state. There is also has a big city called Khubdan."[8] The Abaroi people mentioned above were probably the Rouran Khanate in our historical data. A French scholar named Deguignes has firstly pointed out that Taugaste referred to China. Later, a British scholar named Gibbon and a French scholar named Klaproth have agreed the opinions of Deguignes.[9]

---

8   Coedes, George: Textes d'autres Grecs et Latins relatifs a l'extreme—Orient depuis le IVe siecles AV.J—C. jusqueau XIVe siecles, Paris, 1910) (Ge Daisi: Far East of the Ancient Literature Written by Greek, Latin Author from Fourth Century BC to 14th century, Translated by Geng Sheng into Far East of the Ancient Literature Written by Greek, Latin Author, Zhonghua Book Company, pp. 104-105, 1987.
9   Zhang Xinglang: Chinese and Western Expedition Historical Materials, Volume 1, Zhonghua Book Company, pp. 89-90, 1977.

Since then, China was called as Taugaste. As for the etymology of Taugaste, Deguignes considered that it referred to the Chinese characters "Da Wei". Later the scholar corrected his explanation and thought it should be the transliteration of "Tabqaci", while Taugaste city referred to the Luoyang, the capital of Northern Wei Dynasty. The river mentioned above by the Greek scholar should be the Yangtze River which divides the Southern and Northern China. The Northern China refered to the Sui State, namely the country wherein black suits were worn, while Southern China was the Chen State, namely the country wherein red clothes were worn. The war between the black-suits country and red-suits country referred to the war between Sui State and Chen State in the year of 589. Later,, this information about China's North-South re-unification was spread to Europe by the travelling people in a few years. Khubdan, the other city of the Tuoba, was the ancient transliteration of Xianyang, then always referred to as the Chang'an city. After the unification of China in the Sui Dynasty, the Turkic people continued to use the Tabqaci to address the people of the Central Plains. In Turkic inscriptions of the Tang Dynasty, the wars between Turkic and Tang Dynasty was called as wars between Turkic and Tabqaci. Some scholars who research the Turkic inscriptions in China translated Tabqaci into "Tang", and did not know that for the Turkic people, the Tabqaci meant China. In the late Sui Dynasty and early Tang Dynasty, the territory of Turkic Khanates extended from Mongolian Steppes to Eurasian Steppes. In the 7th century, the people from Dashi country came to Central Asia, and they were also influenced by the Turkic people and call China "Tabqaci". Biruni, a geographer of the Dashi Empire, said that the Faghfur of China (Faghfur refers to the emperor) was Tamghaj Khan, namely "Tuoba Khan". Abulfida, another Arab geographer, said that the Chinese emperor was also called Tanghaj Khan, namely "Tuoba Khan".

96

The name "Tabqaci" to refer China, was used by the tribes of the Central Asia who spoke Turkic languages for a long time. At the beginning of 13th century, Qiu Chuji, a Taoist priests, at the Genghis Khan's behest to the Western Regions. During the journey, he saw the local people in Alima City (currently Ili River basin in Xinjiang), transport water with bottle. It was people from the Central Plains that introduced the container of water to the Western Regions. The local people happily said: "the people of Taohuashi are very smart". Later, Li Zhichang, the student of Qiu Chuji often explained in his record, "Taohuashi" referred to as Han people. Hong Jun, a scholar in the late Qing Dynasty thought "Taohuashi" was another kind of transliteration of "Da He" tribe which belonged to Khitan, but Palladius, the Russian ambassador to Beijing pointed out that the original word of "Taohuashi" referred to "Tamgaj" (Tabqaci).[10]

Li Zhichang did not know that Tamgaj was originated from Tabqaci, so he translated it into Taohuashi. Mahmud al-Kashghari, a Turkic scholar in the 11th century, wrote a famous dictionary, Lughat al-Turk, which included the term

10   Zhang Xinglang: Historical Materials Related to Chinese and Western Expedition, 1977, Volume 1, Zhonghua Book Company, pp. 89-90.

"Tabqaci -Taohuashi". The dictionary recorded: "Taohuashi refers to as Macin, namely the Southern China, and it is about 4 months distance from Khitan. Çin, known as China, which was originally divided into three parts. Upper Çin (Southern China) in the East is Taohuashi, and Middle Çin (Northern China) refers to Khitan, and Lower Çin is the Kashghari (current Kashi in Xinjiang)." In an age when Mahmud al-Kashgari wrote his books, "Taohuashi" and "Maçin" were synonymous, and "Khitan" and "Çin" were synonymous.[11]

"Tabqaci-Taohuashi" in the Western Regions referred to as China, which was a kind of glorious salutation, so some minority leaders liked to add "Taohuashi" to their titles. In the Song Dynasty period, Qara Khanids, a Turkic kingdom, was established in the Western Regions, and his leader, Ali Tiginhad determined his own title as "Taohuashi·Bogra Khan" on the newly issued coins. Another khan called Bulajin-Bu-Nasulu, also was known as "Taohuashi Bogra Khan". The famous literary masterpiece of the Kara Khanidsthe Dynasty mentioned, "in the 11th century, Asan Bu Shiliemen, the ruler of Kashghari also called himself "Taohuashi Bogra Khan".[12] In 1218, when a caravan of Genghis Khan came to the Boukhara Khwarezmia (current Bukhara, Uzbekistan), he met a local man who inquired about the plans of Genghis Khan in regard to attacking the Jin Dynasty. This men called Jin Dynasty as Taughaj, that was, Taohuashi. Even though at the beginning of 14th century, when Ruy González de Clavijo, the envoy of Spain visited the Timurid Dynasty, he also mentioned that the local Mongolian people in the Chagatai Khanate called the Chinese emperor as Tangus, namely "Tabqaci-Taohuashi".

(3) Northern Folk Songs

The Sixteen Kingdoms Period and Northern Dynasties created the history of the migration of Northern minority peoples to the Central Plains. The nomadic people entering the Central Plains were gradually assimilated by the Han nationality, but they also used their own culture to influence the Han people. The poems of the Northern nationalities appeared in the form of folk songs, and they were distinct from the folk songs of their contemporaries such as those from the Eastern Jin Dynasty and Southern Dynasty, which were characterized by rough and unconstrained, impassioned, simple and smooth. So far the most famous folk song of the 16 Kingdoms Period and Northern Dynasties was the "Chile Song". The song was sung by Hu Lujin, a general of Chile tribe in the Northen Qi state. Its lyrics were originally in the Xianbei language, and now we have the Chinese translation. It was a popular pastoral, describing the beautiful Steppes scenery of the South and North Yinshan Mountain: "the vast Steppes is seemly connected with the sky, and the sky like the herdsmen's tent shrouds the Steppes. In other words, the sky and the Steppes are boundless. The dense grass hides the cattle, and when the wind blows, the grass, the cows and the sheep

11   Zhang Guangda: Mahmud al-Kashghari's Lughat al-Turk, Including the Circular Map (First Volume), The Journal of the Central College of Nationalities, 1978/2.
12   Wei Tao: Manuscripts Related to the History of the Qara Khanidsthe Dynasty, 1986, Xinjiang People's Press, pp. 53, 109-112.

can be seen." The plain lyrics depicted the magnificence of the Steppes as well as the seasonal movements of nomadic people loving their homeland and their life. Although the poem was composed of only 27 words, it had a very strong appeal. This northern folk song was greatly appreciated and enjoyed received the praise and love of people in China, and put into the textbooks of the PRC.

Another masterpiece of minority literature in North Dynasties was Mulan's Glory, which was a widely popular folk song. It described the heroine Mulan who disguised herself as a male soldier to take her father's place in the conscription army. Later, when she won the battle and made great contribution to her nation, she chose to return to her hometown to live as an ordinary girl instead of being a heroine who pursued money and fame. Although there is no reliable information to show where Mulan was from, but from the lyrics of the "Invaders are attacking, Last night, Khan has called for troops", it could be found that Mulan was not a member of Han people, but was a Xianbei girl who migrated to the Central Plains. As it can be seen from the lyrics, Mulan's family was deeply assimilated by the Han people. She was like other Han girls who weaved cloth. When she learned that the country was in trouble and called for soldiers, since her father was old and could no longer join the army, she resolutely decided to fight for the country on behalf of her father. The lyrics "She thinks she hears her mother calling her name. But it is only the sound of the river crying." and "in the darkness she longs to hear her father's voice but hears only the neighing of enemy horses faraway." expressed a just young-adult girl who was loved by their parents at home and she also missed the parents after leaving home.

The lyrics said: "when father and mother heard their daughter was coming, they walked outside the wall to meet her, leaning on each other. When elder sister heard younger sister was coming, she fixed her rouge, facing the door." The parallelism showed the whole family was very happy when they heard the news that Mulan was returning. Further, the lyrics also said: when Mulan put on the women's dress, she deliberately walked ahead of the male partners, which was a great surprise for everyone. It vividly embodied the naughty and lively character of Mulan. In the end of the lyrics, it said that ordinary people can distinguish between male and female from running rabbit, showcasing Mulan, the Xianbei girl who was as brave as men.

Mulan Glory not only embodied the martial spirit of the people in the Northern China, but also showed the feeling of people loving peace. It is an outstanding masterpiece of the Northern folk songs. Mulan, as a heroine, was long praised by the Chinese people.

4. The New Masters of the Grassland Silk Road

After Xianbei (Inner Mongolian) nomad people in the inland China established a large number of separatist small states, they became a group of people that enjoyed the privileges in the Central Plains, stimulating more Xianbei tribes to move to inland China. The vacant Steppes regions caused by the migration of Xianbei people was soon occupied by other peoples. After the establishment of Northern Wei Dynasty, the situation between Mongolian plateau and Eurasian Steppes changed greatly. A new nomadic power, called RouranKhanate sprung up in the North of the Gobi desert (Outer Mongolia). RouranKhanate was bordered by Chile, known as "Gaoche state" which located at the Northern and Southern part of the Tianshan Mountains, to the West. In addition, there was a tribe, called Da, which borders Chile to the East. These three nationalities formed and controlled the trade expedition route of the Steppes in this period, connecting the trades of the Wei Dynasty in the central Plains in the East, Persia in the West and India in the South.

(1) The Gaoche State (Kingdom)

Many of Chile tribes in the Eastern Han, Three Kingdoms, and Western Jin Dynasty together with other tribes in the North of the Gobi desert (Outer Mongolia), migrated to the South. But their migration was not uniform. For example, some of them moved to the south of the Gobi desert (Inner Mongolia) to join the Xianbei tribal, while some moved Southward into the Hexi Corridor and Central Plains. In the Sixteen Kingdoms Period, although the Chile tribe (Tiele) did not like the Huns, Xianbei, Jie, Di and Qiang—namely the so-called "five Hu"—the five ancient ethnic peoples in China—they have established a federal type of a dynasty, which controlled vast territories and also played an important role in the history of China. In the historical records, the peoples who have moved to inland were called the "Dingling". After the collapse of the Northern Wei Dynasty, the Chile (Tiele) people were gradually merged into the Han nationality.

In the 4th century, the Chile tribes had scattered on the North of the Gobi desert. By 5th century, these tribes were under the control of the Rouran Khanate. Later, in the frequent war with the Northern Wei dynasty, Rouran Khanate asked the Chile people to join the army, which caused frustration among the Chile people. In 478, Afuzhiluo, the leader of Chile, with his brother, Qiongqi led more than 100,000 people in their migration to the region in the Southern Tianshan Mountains (current Turpan, Xinjiang region) since he couldn't bear the oppression of the Rouran Khanate, and established the Gaoche state. The Chile people called Afuzhiluo "hulug bir", meaning "Emperor or the Son of the Heaaven", and called Qiongqi as the "houbei", meaning "the successor to the throne." At the end of 5th century, the territory controlled by this state was quite vast: its Northeast extended to the central Mongolian plateau including Selenga, Orhon River and Tuul River as in, North to Altai Mountains, West to Chuban of the Ili River basin, South to the Eastern part of Tianshan Mountain, East to Northern Wei Dynasty. Later, this Gaoche state controlled the Gaochang region, the important artery of the East-west expedition, which caused the opposition of many neighboring tribes. Due to the intervention of Tuyuhun, Gaochang, Northern Wei and Rouran Khanate, lost its control over Gaochang. At that time, another tribe, called Da, attacked and killed the

Qiongqi, the successor to the throne. In addition, the Gaoche state encountered a civil strife and faced a decline. Under these conditions, the Gaoche state chose to cooperate with Northern Wei Dynasty to hinder the development of Rouran Khanate. In 541, Rouran Khanate had collapsed.[13]

The most of trades between Gaoche state and Central Plains was in the form of "tributary" and "reward". Gaoche state was located in the North and South of Tianshan Mountain, so its main product was livestock products. In addition, the Altai Mountain region had been home to gold reserves since the ancient times. At that time, the nobles in the Gaoche state were fond of the silk in the Central Plains, in turn, the people in the Central Plains demanded the products from Gaoche state. Therefore, the commodities of the Gaoche state including livestock, fur, gold and silver were transported to the Central Plains, while Northern Wei Dynasty mainly gave them silk and handicrafts produced in the Central Plains. For example, in the 1st year of the Yongping in the North Wei Dynasty (508), Mietu, the son of Qiongqi, suddenly sent envoys with tributes consisting of gold, silver, two gold scepters, 7 horses and 10 camels to the emperor of the Northern Wei Dynasty, and in return, the Northern Wei Dynasty gave them 60 bolt of mixed-color silks. In the same year, Mietu offered tributes, such as five horses, gold, silver, mink and the other things to the Northern Wei Dynasty, while the dynasty sent envoys with gifts including 10 bolts of red silks and 60 bolts of mixed-color silks. When Yifu, the brother of Mietu, was in the rule of Gaoche (Tiele transliterated as Chile) state, he with the excuse of offering tributes to the emperor of Northern Wei Dynasty, asked the Wei emperor to give him a famous painting, a silk Longpao, a fan-shaped umbrella and five red lacquer umbrellas as well as ten drums and horns (used in the army similar to contemporary bugle).[14]

During the late Northern Wei Dynasty period, with the increasingly close relationship between Gaoche state and the Central Plains, the local music of Gaoche was also introduced into the Central Plains. When the palace in the Northern Wei Dynasty held feasts and festivals, the Tiele (Chile) dance was often seen. (The Northern Song Dynasty, Erzhurong Biography). In addition, the people of the Gaoche state were also interested in the music of Central Plains. In 508, as the Northern Wei Dynasty sent envoys to give gifts to the Gaoche state, the envoy also presented them several musical instruments and 80 musicians.[15]

(2) The Rouran Khaganate and the Rouran People

The period of the Wei, Jin and Southern and Northern Dynasties (220 AD-589 AD) was a period of the large-scale mergers among the ethnic peoples of China, witnessing frequent ethnic migrations across the land of China, and also the period which witnessed migrations to the Xinjiang region by many ancient

13   Zhou Weizhou: Chile (Tiele) and RouranKhanate. Shanghai People Press, 1983 and Duan Lianqin: Dingling people, Gaoche and Chile (Tiele), Shanghai People Press, 1986.
14   History of Wei Dynasty Historiography of Gaoche.
15   Ibid.

ethnic peoples, such as the Rouran (Jorjan), Gaoche, Yeda and Tuyuhun. The Rouran tribe were the descendants of the Donghu, an ancient people rising in the Northern Steppes in the early 5th century. After establishing a powerful state in the Mongolian Steppes in 402 AD, they fought against the Northern Wei dynasty (386-534) for the domination on the Western Regions. The nomadic Gaoche, also called the Tolos or Teli, first appeared around Lake Baikal and the basins of the Orkhon and Tura rivers. In 487, Avochilo, chief of the Puwurgur tribe of the Gaoche, and his brother Qunqi led more than 100,000 families to migrate Westward, and founded the state of Gaoche to the Northwest of Anterior Cheshi (the ancient city of Jiaohe near contemporary Turpan). The Yeda, rising in the region North of the Great Wall, moved Eastward to the Tarim Basin, attacked the Rouzhi in the South and set up a state in the late 5th century. They crossed the Pamir desert, and once controlled part of Southern Xinjiang. The Tuyuhun, originating from the ancient Xianbei people, moved Westward from Liaodong (the region East of the Liaohe River in Northeast China) in the early fourth century, and set up their own regime after conquering the ancient Di and Qiang peoples in the region of Southern Gansu, Sichuan and Qinghai.

Although a large number of Xianbei people had moved into the Central Plains in the period of Wei Jin Northern and Southern Dynasties, there were still many Xianbei tribes who remained in North of the Gobi desert. These tribes formed a Xianbei Group, and fought against the Tabqaci in the Central Plains. In fact, the group was Rouran Khaganate recorded in the history books. The regime of the Rouran Khaganate existed for about 150 years in the Mongolian Steppes, and it was another power behind of Xiongnu and Xianbei in the Mongolian Steppes.

In the Western Jin Dynasty, that was at the end of the rule of Liwei in the Tabqaci Xianbei (Liwei died in 277), Tabquci people snatched a young slave. The child gradually forgot his real name, and his owner did not pay attention to his real names. At first, because he was baldheaded, hence he was called "Mugulv", meaning "bald". Later, the child was due to his strong body, and promoted to be a knight from a slave. During the reign of Yilu (304-316), he delayed a military action, so he was sentenced to death in accordance to the Tabqaci Xianbei's law. But he escaped and hid himself between vast desert and valley. Since then, he started to gather fugitive slaves together to be attached to the Hetulin tribe, and later to from his own tribe. Their descendants read "Mugulv" into "Yujiulv" because of inaccurate pronunciation, and regarded the "Yujiulv" as the surname of Rouran Khaganate. Therefore, Rouran Khaganate was a tribal group mainly consisting of slaves of the Xiebei. At the end of the 16 Kingdoms Period, Rouran Khaganate had extended to some regions of the North and South of the Gobi desert. At the beginning of the 5th century, in the era of the Shelun Khan, Rouran Khaganate defeated various tribes in the North of the Gobi desert, and became strong. Later, the territory occupied by it extended to Korea to the North, Northern Wei Dynasty to the South, and Jinshan Mountain to the West as well as Lake Baikal to the north. In short, it was flourishing at that time.

Rouran Khaganate had close relations with the Sixteen Kingdoms in the North of the Gobi desert and the Central Plains in the Northern Dynasty, In the beginning of the 5th century, in the rule of Hulv, the brother of Shelun, it once cooperated with Northern Yan to hamper the Northern Wei Dynasty, and married the Northern Yan's princess Lelang with 3,000 horses as betrothal gifts. Although there were many wars between the Northern Wei Dynasty, and the Rouran Khaganate they still had communications. Tuoba Tao, the emperor of the Northern Wei Dynasty, not only betrothed princess Xihai to Wuti Khan in the Rouran Khaganate, but also married the sister of Wuti Khan. Wuti Khan specially sent his brother together with hundreds of people carrying 2000 horses to escort his sister to the Northern Wei Dynasty. These escorts received warmly welcome and were entertained by the court of the Northern Wei Dynasty. After the Northern Wei Dynasty moved to the south, its political center also moved Southward, so Rouran Khaganate and the Northern Wei Dynasty was at peace and had less wars. During f half a century from eleven years of the rule of emperor Wendi in the Wei Dynasty (487) to the death of Northern Wei Dynasty (534), Rouran Khaganate invaded the Northern Wei Dynasty four times, and Northern Wei Dynasty once attacked Rouran Khaganate twice, but the numbers of sending envoys between them was up to 22 times.

After the Northern Wei Dynasty was destroyed, the Western Wei Dynasty and the Eastern Wei Dynasty competed to pull Rouran Khaganate over to their own side, and intermarried with the upper nobility of Rouran Khaganate. For example, the emperor Wendi, called Yuan Baoju, in the Western Wei Dynasty (535-551) betrothed the princess Huazheng, the daughter of royal clan to Tahan, the brother of the Anagui Khan, and himself married the eldest daughter of the Anagui Khan. Later, the emperor abolished his original empress and rose up the eldest daughter of the Anagui Khan as the new empress, who was known as empress Diao in the Wei Dynasty. In addition, Anagui Khan sent 700 carriages to escort his daughter and prepared a lager dowry including ten thousands of horses and thousands of camels.

At the same time, in order to hinder the Western Wei Dynasty, Rouran Khaganate also was connected with Western Wei Dynasty through marriage. The emperor of the Eastern Wei Dynasty changed the name of Le'an princess into Lanlingjun elder princess. Rouran Khaganate with a thousand of horses as dowry married the princess of the Western Wei Dynasty. In 542, Anagui Khan betrothed his granddaughter, Linghe princess, to Gaozhan, the fifth son of the emperor Guanhuan in the Eastern Wei Dynasty. In 545, Anagui Khan also betrothed his daughter who was known as "Ruoruo Princess" to Gaohuan. It was recorder in the Western Wei Dynasty Empresses Biography that Anagui sent his brother to escort his daughter "Ruoruo Princess" to Central Plains and his brother had remained here till the Princess gave birth to a child.

Rouran Khaganate, settled the in Central Plains, and was strongly influenced by the culture of Central Plains. In the early days of Rouran Khaanate, it implemented regional rule in the North of the Gobi desert, which was the same as the former generation. After Shekun Khan conquered the Gaoche state and its tribes in 402, he started and carried out an important reform in the military system through setting up the "Jun commander" (commanding general) to rule a thousand people as well as "Zhang commander" (commander) to rule a hundred people, which replaced the original regional rule system. The new military system was actually created by the Tabqaci people. In the 1st year of the rule of Emperor Daowu in the Northern Wei Dynasty (386), "Zhang commander" unit was set up, who had the right to lead 500 sergeants. In addition, the higher level of the commanders was "Jun commander", who could lead a thousand of sergeants. "Zhang commander", as a kind of military unit, was also found in the rule of Beiliang (Beiliang was one of kingdoms in the Sixteen Kingdoms period) in the Hexi reign. It was obvious that the military system of Rouran Khaganate, such as "Jun commander", "Zhang commander" was learnt from the Tabic people. Wei Dynasty Book ·Ruoruo Biography quoted historical data and said: the Rouran Khaganate people learned to establish laws from Central Plains region, and after the war they learned the army building methods and military tactics. In addition, Rouran Khaganate had already known the way of numbering the years and imitated the Central Plains to set up the title of an emperor's reign. The historical data mentioned in the five titles of emperors' reign as follows: Yongkang, Taiping, Taian, Shiping and Jianchang. Later, Rouran Khaganate also set up official ranks such as Shizhong and Huangmen.

Rouran Khaganate in the North of the Gobi desert faced the threat of the Northern Wei Dynasty, so it had sought contacts and alliance with the Southern Dynasties, the enemies of the Northern Dynasty. Due to the barrier posed by the Northern Wei, Rouran Khaganate generally communicated with the Southern Dynasties through Western Regions, Tuyuhun and Northwest Sichuan. During more than 30 years from 442 to the end of the Chinese Kingdom of Song, Rouran Khaanate sent 10 missions to Jiankang, the capital of the Kingdom of Song, and sometimes sent two missions once a year. Wang Honggui, the general of the Song Dynasty also reached Rouran Khaganate in 479, intending to combine with Rouran Khaganate to attack the Northern Wei Dynasty. After Qi Dynasty replaced the Song Dynasty, Rouran Khaganate continued to associate with Qi Dynasty. In addition to the jointly hinder the Northern Wei Dynasty, Rouran Khaganate also asked the Southern Dynasties for doctors and weavers. (Qi Dynasty Book·Rouran Khaganate Biography.) In the late of the Rouran Khaganate, the Ling Dynasty ruled the regions of the south of the Yangtze River. According to historical records, in this period, Rouran Khaganate sent envoys to visit the Liang Dynasty five times.[16]

The commodities exported by the Rouran Khaganate to the Central Plains were mainly livestock and livestock products. During the reign of the Datan Khan, he once exported 3,000 horses and 10,000 sheep to North Yan Dynasty. Likewise, he also mainly exported fur, livestock and gold to the Southern Dynasties. At that time, Rouran Khaganate conquered some countries and

---

16   Zhou Weizhou: Chile (Tiele) and RouranKhanate, Ed, 1983, Shanghai People Press.

controlled the trade route between Central Plains and Western regions. It was not until Gaoche state rose that Rouran Khaganate lost the control the trade route. Nevertheless, Rouran Khaganate still played an important role in the economic and cultural exchanges between the Central Plains and the Western Regions. In the rule of Qi Dynasty, the route from Tuyuhun to Central Plains was often through Rouran Khaganate. There were many Hu people among the Tuyuhun caravan who traveled to the Central Plain. These Hu people have made money by trading with the Central Plains and the Western Regions.

(3) Da People (Ephthalites)

Da people who were originated from the South of Jinshan Mountain, was a nomadic tribe, which were also known as "Hua people". Originally they were subordinated to Rouran Khaganate, later in order to escape the oppression of Rouran Khaganate, they had migrated Westward. In the 370s, they arrived at Sogdiana. Shortly thereafter, they headed South through Tianshan Mountain, and defeated some kingdoms occupying almost the entire Tarim Basin and its surrounding regions. It was not until the 420s that the regions remained Rouran Khaanate. In the 420s, they moved southwards across the Amu Darya to conquer the kingdom named as Kidara Kushan which controlled the Tokharoi region and drove its king to Gandhara. Later, they invaded the Sassanian Persian regions, which had occurred in the first year of the rule of the Sassanid ruler Yezdgerd II (438-457). The war lasted for more than one century. Since then, Hephthalites (Chinese name Yeda) people followed Yueshi, nomadic people living in Central Asia, marched southwards across Hindu Kush Mountains to attack the Indian Gupta Dynasty. In 490s, they marched through the Tianshan Mountain and fought with Gaoche kingdom, killing Qiong-qi, the next emperor of the Gaoche kingdom and captured Mietu, the son of Qiong-qi and the prospective emperor of the Gaoche. By the beginning of the 6th century, Hephthalites became the most powerful kingdom in Central Asia, and its territories well surpassed the old Kushan Empire. After the rise of the Turkic Khanate, the Sassanian Persian dynasty allied with with it to fight against the Hephthalite empire. In 560s, Da Empire perished under the attack of the two hostile states, and its territory was divided among the victor kingdoms.

Located between China and Persia, Hephthalite empire controlled the East-West land trade. It greatly benefited from the trade between China and Persia and used its trade gains to buy Chinese products produced in the Northern Wei Dynasty of China. Among the Persian silver coins found in the Ding county, Hebei province, there was also a coin which was engraved together with "Hephthalite" scripts.[17] The Wei Dynasty Book mentioned about the Da (Hephthalite) envoys that visited the Central Plains besides other envoys from Byzantium and Persia several times. Gao Wei, the envoy of the Western Wei Dynasty, has visited Da twice in 512-515 years and 518-520 years respectively. In this period, Song Yu, the monk of the Northern Wei Dynasty also visited the

---

17   Xia Nai: Summarizing the Persian silver coins unearthed in China, The Journal of Archaeology, 1974/1.

Da kingdom. While keeping in touch with Northern Dynasties, Da Kingdom also sent envoys to the Southern Dynasties. At the same time, the small kingdoms under the control of Da Kingdom also sent merchants to Central Plains.[18]

(4) The Turkic Empire

From the 5th century onwards, the history of Asia has undergone tremendous changes, one of its main features was the continuous migration waves from East to West. From the East, the Hexi Corridor, in Central Asia to the vast regions that extended to the west of Persia, were occupied by peoples who spoke Iran language or other Indo-European languages since the beginning of the recorded human history. From the 5th century, the Turkic tribes, which were formerly following nomadic life in the Mongolian Steppes and Jinshan regions, they had migrated gradually to the West, and quickly assimilated those peoples who spoke Iranian and other Indo-European languages. This process had almost lasted until the time of Mongol empire.

In contrast to massive Turkic migration waves from East to West, there occurred the Islamization movement from West to East. In history, Western Asia's culture had a great influence on the settlement of the oasis dwellings in the Western regions and the nomadic peoples of the Eurasian Steppes. Northwest Indian dwellers have long used the Alama alphabet to spell the local saying, which is Kharosthi. It was later introduced to Southern Xinjiang, where it was popular for quite a long time. The Turks were influenced by Western culture in the creation of Turkic scripts, and Uyghurs were inspired by Sogdian to create Uyghur texts. After the establishment of the Dashi Empire, with the forceful expansion outward, the Islam religion had spread widely. The Turkification and Islamization Movement has fundamentally changed the history of the region along the Silk Road, and their consequences still effect our contemporary times. Today, there are many Turkic-speaking peoples in the vast range of Northern Eurasia, East to the Heilongjiang River, West to the Balkans, South to Iran and North to Arctic. The Turkic ethnic profile in the Eastern Europe is similar to that of Eastern European Caucasian, the Turkic ethnic peoples in Northern Asia resemble those of the Mongols, while the Turkic peoples distributed in Central Asia are, in appearance, between India, China and Iran. This is because they are married and mixed with the dwellers residents in their regions.

Although the physical appearances of these nationalities are different, and their geographical distribution is far apart, but the languages used have many similarities. In the world historical literature, this language is called Turkic language. In fact, the Turkic tribe originally refers to Ashina tribe which was a small tribe with the core of its close relatives clan staying and grazing in the Jinshan region, because they established a great empire across the Northern part of Asia during the Sui and Tang dynasties, conquering many regions and dominated the peoples of the Mongolian plateau and the Eurasian Steppes, their name became the common name of the nomadic peoples under their rule.

18   Yu Taishan: The Research on Da History, Qilu Press, 1986.

The earliest accurate data refers to the Turkic name of the historical data is "Zhoushu Yuwen Ce Biography," it said in this record that before 542, the Turkic people have entered the Chinese Western Wei's frontier fortress to plunder them. Later the Turkic Khanate leader Tumen decided and asked to trade with the Western Wei dynasty. In the 11th year of Datong (545), the Western Wei sent a Hunni Annopantuo to the Turkic people from Anguo (current Uzbekistan Bukhara) of Jiuquan, and the next year the Tumen merchants made their way to mainland China.

Tumen (originally Bumin Khan) was a prominent figure in the history of the Turkic kingdoms, when he ascended to the throne, the Turkic people were forcefully enslaved by the Rouran kingdom. The word "Tumen" in the Turkic language means "Wanhu (10.000 households)", when the Turkic tribes had quite strong fighting forces. In 546, the tribe of Gaoche planned to attack Rouran, and was defeated by Tumen Khan forces on their way to attack Rouran. Tumen asked a political marriage to Rouran to ally with them, while Rouran kingdom did not agree since they thought Turkic people were slaves with lower status. Tumen was unbearable to the insult, turned to request a marriage from Western Wei, and Western Wei married Changle Princess to him. In 552, Tumen Khan defeated Rouran (Cücen), after these victories he self-titled himself as "Yili Khan" (Illig Khan), and established the Göktürk Khanate kingdom. Tumen Khan ordered his brother Istami to lead "10 surname" tribes to move to the Western Regions. After the death of Tumen Khan in 553, the throne was given to his son Muqan Khan, who expanded the territories greatly. At that time, the most powerful nomadic country in the Western regions was Da (哒, ephthalites), Istami Khan married his daughter to Khosru Anushirwan, the ruler of Persian Sassanid Empire, and the two sides joined forces in 563-567, defeated Hephthalites empire forces and partitioned its territories. At the same time, Muqan Khan defeated Khitan in the East; annexed the Qigu (Kirgiz) in the North. Its territory was East from the Liao Sea, West to "Western Sea" (current Caspian Sea), West sea (current Caspian Sea), with the distance of more than thousands of miles; South to the desert, North to the "North Sea" (current Lake Baikal), with the distance of five or six thousand miles. Its central state court was located in the Otgontenger uul region in upper reaches of Orkhon River. In the Western region it was Istami governing the Turkic tribes, he dispatched an envoy to Byzantium empire in 567, this envoy was received by the King Justinian. Byzantium allowed Turkic traders to sell silk in its territories.

At the end of the Sui Dynasty, Han region was in chaos, using this as an opportunity many tyrannical figures have established separatist small kingdoms such as Xue Ju, Liu Wuzhou, Liang Shidu, Li Gui, Gao Kaidao, Wang Shicong and Li Yuan and others, in order to consolidate their status, all submitted to Eastern Turkic Khanate, and some even accepted the Turkic titles and ranks. In the early Tang Dynasty period, under the reign of Sheguy Khan and his brother Tung Yabgu Khan of Western Turkic leadership, they conquered Xue Yantuo who occupied the current Junggar Basin, extended the territory to the Northeast to Jinshan, Southeast to Yumen Pass, Southwest to Hindu Kush Mountain, and crossing Amu Darya to occupy the land of Tukhara. Its Khan camp was often in the Yuleduos Valley, upstream of Yili River, North of the current Xinjiang Tianshan Mountains, and West of the Suyab, near Talas and Qianquan. In the 1st year of Zhenguan (627 AD), Xueyantuo and other Tiele tribes rebelled again, the Xi (奚), Xi (霫) and Khitan tribes in the east of the Mongolian plateau betrayed the Turkic Khanate, and collided with the Tang Dynasty. Emperor Tang Taizong took this opportunity and sent troops to attack the Eastern Turkic Khanate forces. Jiali Khan betrayed the country and fled, and then was captured on the way and was sent to Chang'an (current Xian). Thus the Eastern Turkic Khanate state had perished.

The origins of the Western Turkic people was the "On oq" (Ten oqs) left by Istami Khan. "On oq" was divided into two parts as East and West bordered by the Suyab River, East of the river was "Five Dulo" clan, and West of the river was "Five Nushibi" clan. In the winter of Zhenguan the 2nd year (628 AD), Tung Yabgu Qaghanof Western Turkic state died in a civil war, and the Western Turkic state split into two parts, each chose its aristocrat as Khan, and contested between themselves. Emperor Taizong of the Tang Dynasty (Tang Taizong) used the time of the decline of the Western Turkic Khanate to extend his influence to the Western regions, and in the 4th year of Zhenguan (630 AD), he occupied the gateway of the Western region, Yiwu (currently, Hami in Xinjiang).Ten years later, Tang captured the Gaochang (today, Turpan Gaochang Gucheng) to establish Xizhou and Anxi Frontier Command; also took Pagoda Khan city (current Jimsar County, Xinjiang), set Tingzhou. In the 22nd year of Zhenguan (AD 648 AD), Tang Dynasty forces captured Qiuzi (today, Kuqa in Xinjiang), and moved the Anxi Frontier Garrison Command headquarter there. In the following years, the Tang army in the Western region gradually occupied the north of Tianshan Mountains. In the 2nd year of Xianqing (657 AD), the Tang army defeated the Western Turkic army led by Ishbara Qaghan. Two years later, the entire Western Turkic Khanate territories were occupied by the Tang Dynasty. After the demise of the East Turkic Khanate, Xue Yantuo established a regime in Mobei. The rest of the Eastern Turkic people founded a state in the South of the desert under the protection of Tang Dynasty. There were a number of Turkic aristocrats moved to Chang'an, plus the people included attached, the total population was more than 10,000. More than 100 of them were above the fifth rank, accounting for nearly half of the total officers in the court. After the Western Turkic Khanate was subordinated to the Tang Dynasty, the Tang government divided the Khanate land into two Duhu (Protectorate) governments, the five Dolu clans to the East of Suyab River was the Kunling Frontier Command, and the Five Nushibi clan to the West of Suyab River was the Mengci Frontier.

After the Turkic people migrated into the Western regions, some part of the Avar people who were hostile towards the Turkic people (Many scholars believe that the Avars were associated with Rouran) moved westward, into the Byzantine territories. In order to recover the enemy Avars, Istami Khan had sent an envoy to negotiate with the Byzantine empire. Byzantium was the main rival of Persia in the west. After the deterioration of relations between the Turkic people and Persia, the Sogdian merchant Mannah, who served in the court of the Western Turkic Khanate, advocated an alliance with Byzantine. He was sent by Istami (İstemi) Khan, arrived in Constantinople (current Istanbul) in 568 and formed a alliance with the King Justinian II against Sassanid empire (Persia), after this alliance Byzantine empire allowed Turkic merchants to directly trade in the the Byzantine territories. Byzantium empire also sent envoys led by Zemarchus and Sogdian merchant Mannah to the Turkic Khanate to pay a return visit. Zemarchus arrived in the Western Turkic Khanate's leadership tent which was located in the "White Mountain" of Yin Suo Chuan (current Yili River tributary Yuludu Si Valley in the North of Tianshan Mountains in Xinjiang). The mission led by Zemarchus established close relations between Western Turkic Khanate and Byzantium, and the two sides jointly attacked Persia repeatedly, and exchanged envoys.

The Turkic leader had always used the term "Rome" (as Rum) for Byzantine in the Roman Empire times. Many nationalities along the Silk Road did not have the vocabulary with the first consonant "r". They often have to attach some kind of phoneme when they encounter a foreign loan word with the first consonant of "r". For example, "Rome" was called Hrom or Horom in the language of Al-Mani (Armenian), and Hrom in the medieval Posbalevi language (Pahlavi), "Rome" in Khwarezmian and Sogdian language was thus turned into Hrom. The Turkic people were informed of "Rome" through the intermediary of the Sogdian or the Khwarezmian. The Turkic language has no consonant form read as Porom. According to the Turkic "Kultigin Inscription", after the death of Domon Khan, there was an emissary from Porom in the foreign envoys who came to pay tribute to the emperor, should be the envoy of Byzantium. The name of the Byzantine Empire of the Roman Empire in Chinese historical materials "Flynn" should come from Sogdian merchants or Turkic people.

The friendship between the Turkic people and Byzantium did not last long. Later, Byzantium hosted the defector ministry of the Turkic, which caused the discontent of the Turks, causing the two countries to communicate coldly. Soon after the demise of the Turkic Khanate state, the Dashi Empire appeared in Western Asia, in the Mongolian Steppes and the Eurasian Steppes region there also appeared many nomadic regimes, such as Turgesh, Ge Luo Lu, the Uyghurs, Kyirgizs and so on, the exchanges between the East and the West through the Grassland Silk Road, ushered in a new era.

(5) The Jimi Policy: The Frontier Prefecture System

In order to appease and control the Eastern Turkic tribes, the in 4th year of Zhenguan (630), Tang government established two Dudufu(s)[19] of Yunzhong Dudufu and Dingxiang Dudufu in the South of the desert, and divided the

---

19   Dudufu was a command center, which assumed surveillance and geo-strategic military tasks, and administered client state affairs.

South-migrated Eastern Turkic Khanate into 6 sub-states (client states). 23rd year of Zhenguan (649), Tang dynasty government again adjusted the client states which were under the jurisdiction of the 2 Dudufu(s) mentioned above, of which, Yunzhong Dudufu administered five states such as Sheli state, Ashina state, Chao state, Helu state and Ge Luolu state. And the Dingxiang Dudufu controlled six client states, such as Sounon state, Aster state, Zhishi state, Beishi state, Yushe state and Yishi state.[20]

In the 1st year of Diaolu (679), Tang dynasty also established 6 client prefectures in Hequ for the Hu people in the Turkic territory. In the 3rd year of Longshuo (663), the former client state of Yanran, which was originally located in the South of the desert South, was given to the control of the Hanhai Dudufu, later Yanran's control was transferred to Mobei, Yunzhong Dudufu was established in the old territories of Yunzhong city of Han Dynasty (today, the Togtoh county of inner Mongolia). All these Southern Turkic client states and prefectures were under their jurisdiction. In the next year, the government changed Yunzhong Dudufu's status as the Grand Chanyu Frontier Command. After the demise of the Eastern Turkic, the replaced Xue Yantuo Khan country existed for 19 years, also destroyed by in the 2nd year of Zhenguan (646) by the Tang dynasty. In the following year, Emperor Tang Taizong established six prefectures and seven states in the nomadic Mongolian Steppes region wherein the Tiele tribes dwelled, and all of them were put under the jurisdiction of Chanyu Tai Yanlan Frontier Command, which was located between the two states of Xia and Sheng in the South of the desert. The six prefectures and seven states were as follows:

Hanhai Prefecture in Uyghur
Jinhui Prefecture in Pugu
Yanlan Prefecture in Duolange
Youling Prefecture in Bayegu
Guiling Prefecture in Tongluo
Lushan Prefecture in Sijie
Gaolan State in Qun
Gaoque State in Huxue
Jilu State in Xijie
Jitian State in Yan-ti
Yuxi State in Qibi
Ling State in Sijiebie
Zhiyan State in Baixi.

Tang Dynasty determined the governors in the above prefectures, Cishi (provincial governors) in the states. All the Governors and Cishis were assumed by local chiefs. In the same year, Xuanque State and Jiankun Prefecture were set up in Quriqan and Jiegu (Kirguises) in the North of the Mongolian plateau, both were located in rhe current Tuva Republic and the Republic of Kazakhstan

---

20   The meaning of Jimi policy was a system of vassal (client) state to govern the tribes so as to maintain unification.

in Russian Federation. Tang Dynasty also set up Xitan state and Qilian state for the remnants of Xue Yanto. Later, in the 3rd year of Longshuo (663), Yanran Dudufu was changed to Hanhai Dudufu and its center was moved to Mobei. In the 2nd year of Longshuo (669), the name of Hanhai Supervision Office was changed as the Anbei Supervision Office.

After settling of the Western Turkic kingdom, Tang Gaozong added nine Dudufu (s), 76 states, 110 counties, 126 military garrisons in the Western Regions, which were controlled by the of Anxi Supervision Office, such as:

Rouzhi Dudufu, located in the Ehuan city of Tukhara region (current Kunduz in Northeast of Afghanistan);

Tianma Dudufu, located in Suman city in Jiesu (near current Dushanbe, Tajikistan);

Gaofu Dudufu, located in Wosha city in Guduoshi (currently in the drainage basin of Vakhsh River, tributary of Amu Darya in the South of Tajikistan);

Yuepan Dudufu, located in Yan city in Shihanna (current Sulhan River Basin in the south of Uzbekistan);

Persian Dudufu, located in the Jiling city in Persia (current Zereng, Sistan province in Iran);

Heme State, located in Damo city in Damo (current Termez city, adjacent to Afghanistan, the North bank of Amu Darya river in the South of Uzbekistan).

In addition, it also included the 9 imperial government offices under the administration of Qunling Supervision Office and Mengchi Supervision Office, which were located in the West and East of Suyab River, wherein Western Turkic people dwelled.

The prefectures and client states mentioned above in the Northwest frontier region were quite different from the prefectures and county governance system practiced in the mainland China, the former ones carried the features of Jimi policy (appeasement and control). The government gave the Central Plains's title to the hereditary native leaders of the neighboring ethnic peoples in the Tang Dynasty period, in order to maintain their vassal status.. This was the first time in history that the Han dynasty had set up administrative organs in the North of the desert and West of Cong Long ridges. This administrative system had great significance for promoting the exchanges between the Central Plains and the border regions and its surrounding regions.

(6) Silk-Horse Exchange Trade

After the demise of the Turkic Khanate, the Uyghur Khanate replaced it. During the Sui Dynasty, Uyghur people had lived on the banks of current Mongolian Selenga River and Orkhon River region, then became a part of the Turkic region due to the rise of Turkic Khanate. The Uyghur was a member of Sogdian Tiele tribe, which is the ancestor of current Uyghur ethnic nationality. In the 4th year of Zhen Yuan (788), Uyghur Khan submitted a memorial asking that they should renamed as Uyghurs. The Uyghurs were originally composed of nine tribes, of which the Yuoluoge clan was the leading clan. The Uyghurs have different origins from the Turkic people. According to the legend of the Uyghurs recorded in the Persian history of the 13th century, there was a mountain called the Qut Tagh in the mountains of Mobei Halaheling, and in the mountains there were nine rivers in one place and ten rivers in another place, people lived in the place of nine rivers was called as "Tughuz (Dokuz) Uyghur", and lived in the place of ten rivers was called as called "Ten Uyghur (On Uyghur)". There were two trees of pine and cypress grew between the Tola River (current Tuul River in Mongolia) and Xueliangge River (current Selenga River), close to each other, between the two trees emerged a large hill, every night the light from the sky fell on it, and later the large hill open a door, inside the door it was divided into five rooms, every room sat a boy, who sucked a nutrition tube. The five children could speak soon after they got out of the large hill. When they ask people about their parents, they learnt that their parents were the two trees, and they saluted them. Later, people found that the last of the five children was the most intelligent, so he was elected as the Khan.[21]

Uyghur Khanate maintained long-term friendly relations with the Tang Dynasty, and all the Khans of the past dynasties in the Western Regions were conferred Khan titles by the Tang Dynasty leaders. During the An Shi Rebellion, the Central Plains was in chaos, the army of Tang Dynasty was completely routed, and it was forced to borrow some troops to recover the two capitals of Changan and Luoyang. In the third year of Zide (758), Tang Shuzong married the young princess of Ningguo to Gele Khan, who had led the army into the Central Plains war. In the 4th year of Dali (769), Tang Daizong conferred the title to the Minister Bu Gu Huaien's young daughter as Conghui princess, to marry Mu Yu Khan. In the 4th year of Zhen (788) Tang Dezong again married his daughter Xianan Princess to the Uyghur Khan Dayton Mohe. In the first year of Changqing (821) Tang Muzong conferred the title to his sister as Princess Taihe, to marry the Uyghur Zonta Khan. The Uyghurs, like other nomadic originated peoples in the history of Mobei, have maintained a long-term exchange with the Central Plains of livestock products and agriculture and handicraft product. Uyghur people love the Central Plains's silk, Tang Dynasty promised to give the Uyghur silk 20,000 pieces each year because of the Uyghur's meritorious of helping Tang counter-insurgency. When the princess was married, Tang government escorted the Zeng color 20,000 pieces for one time. The most famous trade of Han region and Steppes in Tang Dynasty was "Silk-horse exchange trade". Tang dynasty was very generous in dealing with the Uyghurs, and from the middle of the 8th century on, 1 Uyghur horse was exchanged for 40 pieces of silk for a long time, and sometimes even up to

---

21 See Juvayni's (Atâ-Malek Juvayni (1226-1283) work from Persia, He Gaoji's translation: "Biography of World Conquerors", Volume 1, Inner Mongolia People's Publishing Press, 1980, p. 62-64; Lashiduddin: "Historical Collection" Chinese translation, Volume 1, Book 1, pp. 239-241. The Chinese Zhiwen "Gaochang Wang Shixun monument" written according to Uyghur Gaochang Wang family's oral accounts, by Yuan Dynasty literati Yu Ji, has also recorded a similar legend.

50 pieces of silk for 1 Uyghur horse. Not only the price ratio of silk-horse was great disparity, and the amount of exchanges was extremely large, often tens of thousands horses per year. The silk-horse exchange trade was initially possessed the nature of rewarding the Uyghur that they would become obedient, but it had laid a heavy burden on the Central Plains people over the long-term.

Those who used and enjoyed the Han silk was certainly not ordinary Uyghur people, but the upper nobility. It was unprecedented in history that Uyghur traders had continued to buy such a large number of silk from the Central Plains. In the Steppes region, under the circumstances without a fundamental change of economic and social life, these silk could not be consumed normally among the Steppes people. The Uyghur's foreign trade activity was controlled by the Sogdian merchants from Central Asia. They had earned the trust of the Uyghur nobility, and traded the silk flowing into the Steppes from the Central Plains to the distant West countries, which had become an important channel for the Chinese silk to flow to the West. After the 820s, in the Uyghur Khanate kingdom there appeared a civil strifes, and leaders changed frequently. In the 4th year of Kaicheng (839) the Western Turkic Shada, which was a vassal of the Uyghur Khanate kingdom, colluded with domestic rebel forces in Uyghur, overthrew the Uyghur rulers, rebels killed Zhangxin Khan. Soon after the new Khan had ascended to the throne, Kirgiz again colluded with Uyghur internal rebel forces, attacked the Uyghur capital, consequently the Uyghur Khanate kingdom had finally perished. The Uyghur people scattered in Mobei, in addition a small number of them in the South subordinated to the Tang dynasty and some of the Uyghurs living in the East had subordinated to Shiwei, a small group of them moved to Ganzhou and a small group moved to Al-Mu'miniya, to settle down. Those Uyghurs who moved to Ganzhou merged together with the residents in Hexi region and those moved to Beiting merged with the peoples in the other regions of the current Xinjiang, and gradually became part of the current Uyghur society.

5. The Land Silk Road during the Western Liao and Jin dynasties

(1) The Westward Migration and the Land Silk Road

At the time of the 11th century, Maweiji, from Maru in current Turkmenistan, mentioned in his work "Animal Properties" in Chapter 9 titled as the "Turks", and gave a series of reasons for the migration movement occurred in the North Asian Steppes, he said: "there was a Turkic tribe named Qun, who believed in the Nestorianism, which migrated Westward due to fear of the Khitan, and due to the lack of grassland areas. They were tracked by a Qay tribe who has driven the Qun people out. The Qun people migrated to the land of Shari, while the Shari was forced to move to the land of Turkman. In turn, Turkman entered the Eastern part of the country of Ghuzz (Oghuz or Oğuz in current Turkish). The Ghuzz (Oğuz) Turkic people migrated to Bajanak (Peçenek), near the coast of the Alimani (current Armenia)".

The Qun people mentioned here should be the Qun tribe of the Tiele federation which was composed of 15 tribes. The name "Hun" was first mentioned in the "History of Sui Beidi Tiele Biography": "The ancestors of Tiele, was Xiongnu's offsprings, most of them coming, from the East of the Western sea, and who lived along the valleys, for a long period, there were Pugu, Tongluo,... and were called as Irkin, Monchen, Sijie, Hun, Huxue spit and so on surnames lived at the North to Le River, stronger than 20,000 soldiers." The New and Old "Tang Records" listed 15 kinds of Tiele tribes scattered around Qibei, also referred to Hun, it shows that it was an ancient nomadic tribe which dwelled near the deserts of North of China. In the 20th year of Zhen Guan of the Tang dynasty (646), after the Xueyantuo perished, the Chiefs of Tiele tribes came to Tang to honor the Emperor, the next year Tang Taizong set up 6 prefectures 7 states in other regions, where the Qun lived in Gaolan state (today Mongolia Tura River watershed), then was divided into two states of East and West. After the rise of the Turkic Khanate kingdom, the old land of Tiele was occupied by Mochuo Khan, the 4 tribes of Qun and Uyghur, Qiebi and Sijie were forced to move to desert South, migrated and lived between Gan (current Zhangye) and Liang (current Wuwei), soon returned to Qibei. Although the Hun tribe was closely related to Uyghurs, they did not belong to Uyghur. There were families of nine surnames within Uyghur, and then added Geloulu and Baximi, a total of 11 surnames, were "equal Yi (Foreigners)" with 6 tribes of Pugu, Hun, etc. which were not among the surnames of Uyghur.

After the collapse of Uyghur Khanate in 840, the Qun did not seem to migrate with the Uyghurs. From February, of the 3rd year of Tongguang (925) of the Later Period of the Tang Dynasty, there is still a historical record about the "Turkic Hunjielou" which said: Turkic Hunjielou sent official envoys to pay tribute to Tang dynasty"[22]. At this time the Huns were probably together with the remnants of Turkic people. Liao Dynasty Tai Tsu Yeh-lu A-pao-chi began to expand westward after controlling and pacifizing the neighboring tribes. In Autumn July, the 1st year of the History of God (916 AD), he began the West-conquest, defeated the Turkic people, Dangxiang, Tuyuhun, small Tibet, including the Shatuo tribes, all of them were pacified, including their leadership structures. Among them, the Turkic peoples refer to the Qun and Tiele (Tele) and Turkic tribes related to the Qun. In the 3rd year of Tianzhang (924), troops made of Qidan (Kitan/Khitan) tribe people again "crossed the drifted sand, captured the Futu City, to control all the tribes in the West." Futu City was in the vicinity of Al-Mu'miniya, and the Hun's western migration probably began after this event.

In addition to describing the migration of the Qun (Qungrat/Onggirat) people, Ma Wei Ji also recorded that Akinchi, a former Khwarezm Shah which served the Seljuk Sultan, was a Hun. His father was named Qochqar. It is not

113

22   See the book written by Ce Fu and Yuan Gui "The Ministers of Foreign States Paying Tribute"; "History of Old Five Dynasties", Volume 32; "The New Five Dynasties History" Vol. 5.

hearsay that Akinchi was a Khwarezm Shah, and it is true that Akinchi was among the Shahs of Khwarezm. Akinchi was a slave of Seljuk Sultan, then was appointed as the Khwarezm Shah.There was a part of the Qun people who remained in the West of the desert with the neighbors of Najman and Uyghur and so on. At the turn of the 12th and 13th centuries, Mongol Empire rose rapidly, the tribes in Mobei both united, merged and fought each other, and the Steppes regions were chaotic. Genghis Khan unified various tribes, Kuchlug led remainder of the Najmans migrate to the West Liao dynasty territory, there were also some residuals of the Najman people, Qun and other tribes who moved to the Central Plains, was accepted by the Jin dynasty government, and utilized as "loyal and filial troops". As it is mentioned in the "Jin Dynasty History Annals, Biography of Wanyan Chen Monk": "Loyal and filial troops are formed by people of Uyghur, Najman, Qiang, Qun and those people from the Central Plains who are captured as prisoners, and they are cruel, ruthless and were in great numbers who are very difficult to control." Until the Yuan Dynasty, there were still Hun people scattered around the Hexi region. "Yuan History: Biography of Yuan Yu" recorded: "In Xixia, the Qiang people and the Hun people lived together, it was very hard to distinguish the good from the bad."

Abu Said Gardizi, a Persian geographer, wrote in his book "Zeyn al-akh-bâr" around 1050, referring to the story about a part of the Tatars migrating Westward, into the Rocky River valley of Yeer, and established the Kimek[23] tribe federation (7 tribes). Gardizi wrote: The head of the Tartars left two sons after he died. The elder son had ascended the throne, the younger one who was named Shad, attempted to kill his brother due to envy, but he could not and became worried about himself. Then Shad took a slave girl (Kanizak) and fled from his brother's tent court. Shad went to the bank of the Rocky River of Yeer (current Irtysh River), where he settled down. Later, the heads of seven Tatar tribes moved to this region due to lack of grasslands in their original dwelling region. They grazed on the banks of Yeer's Shi River. After the spring of the following year, they sent a person to the dwelling region of Tatar tribes but found that some enemy forces had killed many Tartar people when they were leaving the region, therefore their native land was empty, so they made Se as their leader. Later, other tribes learned about this fact and went to join them, 700 people had gathered. As time went on, their population increased and they spread out of the Rocky Mountains, forming the seven tribes.

The Kīmek tribe had appeared long ago, which was already mentioned in the book "Hudud al-Alam", a Persian Anonymous geography work written in the 10th century, said that the east of it was the Kirgiz land, the South was Yeer's Rock River, the West was Kipchak, and their kings were as called Khan, his

23   The Kimek or Kimaek were one of the Tungusic tribes known from Arab and Persian medieval geographers as one of the seven tribes in the Kimek Khanate in the period of 850-1050 AD. The other six constituent tribes, according to Abu Said Gardizi (d. 1061), were the Yemaek, Kipchaks, Tatars, Bayandur, Lanikaz, and Ajlad. Ancestors of the modern Korean ethnic group.

men were 11 amīr. There should be a true historical basis behind Gardizi's legend about the Kīmek that they originated from the Tartars. A small group of Tartars had probably moved to the Rocky River basin in the year of 840 before or after the Uyghur moved westward. They had also maintained some kind of connection with the Tatar tribe, which was then cut off by some other reasons, such as the remoteness of the region, or because of the war, the scourge of God, so that the Kīmek only kept the legend of that they were from the Tartar. By 11th century, the Turkic scholar Mahmoud Keshgeri wrote as he was explaining the word "Yu du Jin", he wrote: It is "a place's name of a Tatar desert near the Uyghur". From this, it can be seen that the Tatars and Mongolian tribes had occupied the central region of the Turkic and Uyghur Khanate kingdoms at that time.

Mahmoud Keshgeri's suggestion is similar to Ma Weiji's records about the Qun's travelling thousands of miles to the West, as well as the Chinese historical records of the deeds that a nomadic tribe had originated from Turtuha, who was a general of Yuan Dynasty, who moved Westwards to Kipchak land. According to historical records, Turtuha was a "Kipchak, his ancestors were from the tribe in Zelianchuan Andahan Mountains in the North of Wuping, who had afterwards migrated to the Northwest region." "There was a mountain called El-borili (Yu Li Bury) with two rivers, the river on the left was called Yayi, the river on the right was called Yedili, then settled down, and named themselves as Kipchak".[24] After the relocation of the ancestors of Turtuha, they settled in a region called Yu Li Bury between two famous rivers, this region was the left of the "Yayi", namely the Zhaya Black Water (current Ural River), the right of "Yedili" was the Turkic name of the Volga River. The ancestors of general Turtuha had succumbed to the El-Borili (Yu Li Bury) clan attached to Kipchak tribe of El-Borili and became its new ruler. During 1215-1217, when General Subedei (Sabutay) launched a punitive expedition to attack to El-Borili clan who hosted and protected the remnants of Mieerqi (Merkit) clan with the order of Genghis Khan, the chief of the clan state was Yinasi, Turtuha's great-grandfather. In the early period of the 13th century, the Boyuewu clan had subordinated the El-Borili (Yu Li Bury) at least for three generations. The grandson of Turtuha, Yan Tamerlane was a powerful minister in the late Yuan Dynasty period, his daughter was the Queen of Yuan Shundi, who was called the Boyawu Queen, and the Turtuha family was a Boyuewu surname a tribe of Kipchak. The "Yuan Shi" vol. 134 mentioned a monk with Kipchak's name, was "surname of Boyuewu Dai from the El-Borili clan, whose grandfather was Khorachar, who led his tribe to Taizu of Yuan Dynasty." As Khorachar was both from El-Borili and Boyuewu clans, he was the clansman of Turtuha clan.

Located between the Ural River and the Volga River, wherein the ancestors of Turtuha dwelled, has been an important place. The founding clan of the Sultan state in Delhi, Northern India, were the El-Borili people. The founder

24   See "Jurong Wu Yi King", contained in the "Biographical Sketch of Famous Officials of Yuan Dynasty", Volume 3-3, Zhonghua Book Company.

of the Suanduan kingdom in Delhi, was Iltutmish's father, the Il Khan of the El-Borili clan. We know that he had a lot of relatives, clansmen and followers. When Iltutmish was less than 10 years old, his relatives due to jealousy sold him to merchants, after several twists and turns, he was finally brought to Delhi, India, then the general of Ghazni (Gazne) dynasty, Kutb al-Din Ay Beg[25] bought him, and put him in charge of the royal stables.. This had happened roughly in the 1180s. Mongolian general, Subedei went on a punitive expedition to Mieerqi (Merkits), and attacked the El-Borili tribe many El-Borilipeople were forced to leave their land. According to the Tizanidine records, among the descendants of the Abar Khan, who had ruled 10,000 families of the El-Borili, some of them forced to immigrate to Central Asia, and were later enslaved by Iltutmish in above-mentioned Delhi Sultan country, and lived as slaves.

Boyuewu was a clan that aroused the attention of many historians of the Yuan Dynasty, because it was not only a branch of the Mongolian tribe, but also seen in Kuri, Yemek, and Kimek. And the Kipchak. The word Boyuewu has other kind of writings such as Boyawute, Boyaodai, Bayawut (Bayads), etc., which are the inconsistent translation of identical items of Bayawut, the complex of "rich" bayan (Bo Yan) in the Mongolian language. The surname of Boyuewu can be seen among the various ethnic peoples, which can a good study subject when studying the history of migration and differentiation of Mongol and Tatar tribes which has been ignored in the current researches. In accordance with the 13th century Persian historian Rashid-al-Din Hamadani's division, Boyuewu tribe belonged to the Dielelejin Mongols who dwelled on the both sides of the Xueliangge Water. In the book "The Secret History of Yuan Dynasty" it is written that: the 13th level ancestor of Genghis Khan, (in early Liao dynasty period), Maalihe of Boyuewu took his son to exchange him for some deer meat because of poverty. Thus the Boyuewu people had since become the servants of the Mongolian nobility. There were also Bayawut (Bayads) branch in the Yemaek tribe. The dwelling region of the Yemaek tribe was in the Rocky River Basin of Yeer and the West. In the "Athar ul-Baqiyah" written by Al-Biruni, from Chorasmia (Khwarazm) in 13th century recorded, in the era of Genghis Khan, the mother of Khwarazm leader Ala' al-Din Mohammed II, Terken (Türkan) Hatun and Ala' al-Din Mohammad II's imperial concubine, all were from Yemie (Yemek) Bayawut (Bayads) tribes.

There was also Bayawut (Bayads) branch among the Kangli (Qangli tribe). At present, we have noticed among the Yuan Dynasty historical materials that in the Yuan Dynasty period, there were two Bayawut (Bayads) in the Kangli who entered and lived in the Chinese land, one was the Yiesudaer tribe, the other was the Woluosi tribe, there were some records for these two tribes in the "Yuan History". "Yiesuer Biography" said: "Yiesuer, born in Kangli, whose surname is Boyawut [Shi], led the people in the period of Emperor of Taizu."[26]

---

25 Qu-b al-Dīn Aibak, Aibak also spelled Aybak, (born 1150–died 1210), a founder of Islam rule in India and was an able general of Mu-izz al-Dīn Mu-ammad ibn Sām of Ghūr.
26 The above-mentioned records are according to Cheng Jufu's "Boyawut Cemetery

The text further added: "Hangli, from the old capital of Mobei, with sur-name of Boyawu, the noble family in the country. After Genghis Khan, i.e., the Shengwu Emperor of Taizu initially settled down all sides, Hangli was subordi-nated and Boyawu tribe also migrated into this land. There were many Boyawu people who enjoyed to live in Jiyin". "Yuan History: The History of Woluosi" also said: "Woluosi people, the Kangli, great -grandfather of Hashi, Boyao, all merged together." Sorghoqtani Beki (Saruk Hatun) became the wife of Tuolei, who was the fourth prince born from Queen Zhuangsheng (Börte Hatun) and Genghis Khan. It can be seen that Woluosi tribe was also part of the Kangli Boyuewu tribe. The origins of the Boyuewu tribe should be in the East, and their integration into the history of the Turkic tribes was a few fragments of the process of Mongol and Tartar migration to the West. The West migration move-ment of Turkic people, Mongolian tribes, occurred continuously throughout a very long historical period and covered a fairly wide region. Their forced or spontaneous migration, although scattered, did not have a fixed destination and a clear route, but there was generally a general trend, that is, from East to West.

What were the reasons for this wave of westward migration? By a brief analysis, we can find that in the eastern regions of the Asian continent, the South was a large region of arable agriculture, the adjacent North was the vast Mongolian Steppes. The Han Chinese civilization has developed in the agricul-tural regions, and was a stable entity. The excellent conditions of livestock in Mongolian Steppes combined with Han's long-term of huge political, cultural impact has made the Mongolian Steppes become the cradle of strong nomadic features, for long period of centuries. In the West of East Asia, for a long time, there occurred an absence of a strong political and economic center, whether in agricultural regions or grasslands. For the Mongolian Steppes, the result was that, for quite a long period of time, the pressures from the East and the West had been uneven, which caused that the nomadic people have constantly migrated Westward in waves. The Mongolian part of Genghis Khan's origina-tion, which lived by the Wangjian River (current Eguna River) during the Tang Dynasty, moved towards the source of Sanhe, which was just one link in the chain of many nomadic tribes, similar to the migration waves we have outlined above. The westward movement of these nomadic peoples was a prelude to the western-conquest led by Genghis Khan and his descendants.

(2) Gaochang Uyghur Kingdom and Its Culture

Before the beginning of 9th century, the Khan position of the Uyghur Khan state was occupied by the Yaorogge clan (Yaghlaqar) of the Uyghurs. At the end of Uyghur Khan kingdom, there was a civil unrest in its territories, and the Khan's clan, i.e., the Yaorogge (Yaghlaqar) clan was overthrown, Adie clan (Ediz), one of the Tiele tribes had ascended to the throne, but the kingdom still maintained its name as Uyghur. Kirgiz which lived in the northern part

---

Monument "Snow House Collection", Vol. 17, Rare Book Collections on Yuan Dynasty, Taiwan.

of Donnu (current Tuva Republic of the Russian Federation) in 840, could not endure the oppression of the Uyghur, revolted with 100,000 solders, allied with the opposition forces of the Uyghur Khan's domestic tribes and scored into Woerduo Bali, the capital of Khan. After the demise of the Uyghur Khanate, the tribes fled, part of them crossed the Jinshan to the South, moved to the territory of original Tang's Anxi Frontier Command. Uyghur moved from Mobei to the Western Regions, although their leader had changed frequently, probably since the main of the kingdom was the Uyghur people, the word "Uyghur" as the title of kingdom was always maintained as the Gaochang Uyghur, in the era of the Yuan and Ming Dynasty. After Uyghur kingdom moved westwards, it was often called "nine surnames" (Toquz oghuz) by the Islam historians. The Uyghurs who moved westward experienced a complex domestic change, and soon Khan rank was captured by the Pugu branch of the Tiele tribes.

At the beginning of Gaochang Uyghur kingdom's founding, this state was quite prosperous, and controlled a vast territory. The literature which recorded Gaochang Uyghur's territories in this era was inconsistently described, such as the "Records on Wang Yande's Travel to Gao chang" recorded about the Gaochang controlled regions as follows: "Gaochang is a Western state. The land from the south of Khotan, southwest the Dashi, Persia, and the West Bulushe, the Snow Mountains, Pamir, are thousands of miles...... there live all the Southern Turks, the Northern Turkic people, the Dazhongyun, Xiaozhongyun, Yagma, Guolu, Kirgiz, Moman, Gechizu, Yulongzu and so on." The word Dasjo here should refer to the Samanid Dynasty (one of the first Iranian Islamic states), and the Bulushe region is current Peshawar in the north of Pakistan. According to this record, Gaochang Uyghur controlled regions had extended from the North of Jinshan, south of Lop Nur, southwest beyond the Kashi (Kashgar). At the beginning of this century, the wooden pestle inscription found by a German academic research expedition team among the ancient ruins of Gaochang said: "On February 3rd, the fire sheep year (year of Dingwei)", Gaochang Uyghur kingdom ruled the vast majority of the land between East of Sachiu (Dunhuang, Gansu Province of China) and West of Nuch Barsxan, "Nuch Barsxan" is located at the coast of the Issyk Kul lake).[27]

The above mentioned "Nuch Barsxan" is located in the coast of the Issyk Kul lake (Atami) in currentthe Republic of Kyrgyzstan. According to this description, the territories of Gaochang Uyghur Kingdom extended from the West of the Issyk Kul lake (Atami), to the East Shazhou (Dunhuang). In Xianping the 4th year (1001 AD) of Song Zhenzong, the envoy Cao Wantong from Qiuci who visited the Song Dynasty, said: "Our country is from the East to the Yellow River, the West to the Snow Mountains, which includes hundreds

---

27 See German research document: "Abhandlungen der Preussischen Akademie Wissenschaften zu Berlin", 1915, No. 3, Category of language, history, F.W.K Mueller, "Two wooden pestle inscriptions unearthed in Turpan" (Zwei Pfalinschriften aus den Turfan funden), and see appendix "The third pestle was unearthed in Huozhou."

of small towns."[28] Until the Mongolian era, the descendants of Uyghur still remembered the events when their ancestors moved from the North of desert to Jiaozhou, "Governing the Beshbaliq, North to Aju River, South to Jiuquan, East to Wudun, Jiashiha, dwelling in the west of western Barbarians."[29] The Uyghurs used the direction terminology of the Turkic people, and generally counterclockwise 90 degrees difference when compared with the direction concept of the Chinese people, the so-called South should be the East, and the so-called East should be the North. So "Wudun" should be the different writing way of "Woduan"; and "Jiashiha" should be the other translation word for "Kazakh".[30]

In the early days of Gaochang Uyghur kingdom, the land was vast, but later, its national power gradually declined due to the limitations of the desert and oasis environment. Although its territories were expanded and contracted, its central space has always covered the north and south of current Tianshan mountain. There are five central cities: Beshbaliq (Turkic, meaning "five cities", today in the territory of Jimsar, Xinjiang), Yangi Baliq (in Turkic language, means "new city"), Jan Baliq, Gaochang (Qocho, current Turpan) and Solmi (today Yanqi, Xinjiang). Most of theseregions are the traditional oasis irrigated agricultural regions in the ancient Western regions, where Uyghurs have gradually changed their lifestyles and have become half-agriculture involved and half nomad type grassland peoples.

The top leader of the Gaochang (Ganzhou) Uyghur kingdom was called as Khan or "Assaran Khan" for a long period of time. "Assaran" for the Turkic language "Arslan", meaning "lion", so the translation into Chinese means "Lion King". Later, it also adopted the title of "Iduq Qut", which was originally resident in the vicinity of Al-Mu'miniya, meaning "The Lord of Happiness". Uyghur people moved to the Western Regions, gradually using the scripts created by the Turgesh during the Tang Dynasty period, that was, the Turkic spelled by using Sogdian scripts (letters), and later this Sogdian scripts were widely used in various regions, known as the "Uyghur" script, was aslo used till the end period of Ming Dynasty. During the Mongolian era Genghis Khan ordered the Uyghur scholar Tata-tonga to create Mongolian script on the basis of Uyghur scripts, and then Manchu created the Manchu script according to Mongolian script in the later period of Ming Dynasty.

---

28 See The Compilation of Song's Regulations by Fan Yi, IV, 13. Volume 197, p. 7720.
29 See Yu Ji: "Records of Daoyuan Xuegu", Vol. 24, "The Monument of Gaochang Wang Shixun", Vision of series of the four categories, p. 218; and also refer to "History of Yuan Dynasty Biography of Baerju Aerte Dijin", and Huang Wenbi: "Records of Yi Du Hu Gaochang Wang Shixun Monument Restoration and Proofreading", contained in the Journal of Cultural Relics, 1964/2.
30 See article by Yiling Zheng: "Ethnic Origin of Northern China and Mongolians", contained in the Journal of Inner Mongolia University, 1979, No. 3-4 (Double issue), p. 17, Note 1.

Gaochang Uyghur Kingdom and the Central Plains had maintained close political, economic and cultural ties. In 924, Liao Dynasty, the King Yelü Abaoji (temple name Taizu) carried out a large-scale Western-conquest expedition, Gaochang Uyghur kingdom was subordinated to Khitan. After the demise of Liao Dynasty in 1130, Yelu Dashi, the noble of Khitan, led the tribe in their migration to the west. Later, Gaochang Uyghur kingdom became a vassal of West Liao. The civilization degree of the Uyghur people was the highest in the Northwest of the Liao Dynasty, this received the attention of the Qidan nobility in Western Liao, they asked Uyghurs to teach the West Liao nobles and court. The Naiman people that neighbored Uyghur Kingdom at Northwest was also strongly influenced by the Uyghur civilization. The court of Naiman asked Uyghur experts to be in charge of gold seals, management of treasury and grain collecting issues for them. Western Liao dynasty attached great importance to the reign of the Uyghur region, the last emperor of Western Liao Dynasty Zhilugu sent a Taishi monk Shaojian to the Uyghur region to strengthen control, who had unruly used his ruling power, extravagance and self-encouragement, causing the strong dissatisfaction among the Uyghur nobility. In 1208, Genghis Khan crushed the remnants of Naiman tribes, then occupied the Rock River basin of Yieer, and hit a heavy blow to the Uyghurs. At that time, the ruler of the kingdom, Baerju Aertedi Jin Idiqut decided to be a vassal state of Mongolia. In 1209, they "mobilized to beleaguer the monk Shaojian who escaped to a building, they ran upstaira to kill him, and threw his head downstairs".[31]

Later, the Mongol forces defeated the remnants of Naimans and drove them out of their territories. In 1211, Baerju Aertedi Jin Idiqut personally visited the Kelun River to see Genghis Khan. Genghis Khan praised him and promised to marry him with his daughter, Yieli Anton, and promised Uyghur leader to enjoy the treatment of "fifth child". The land of Uyghur was annexed by the Mongols, and put under the rule of the Mongol Khan.

(3) Western Liao (Mongol) Kingdom[32]

At the beginning of the 12th century, the Nuzhen tribe (the predecessor of the Manchu nationality) dwelling in northeastern regions under the rule of Khitan were severely frustrated under the brutal oppression of the Khitan aristocracy, they organized a rebel army to fight against Liao under the leadership of Wanyanaguda, established a state called the Jin Dynasty. The Khitan's central government forces could not suppress the rebel army which was quite strong and ambitious, consequently central government forces were defeated and the Khitan rule fell apart. In 1125, the emperor Yelü Yanxi from the Liao dynasty was captured in Yingzhou, rhus Liao Dynasty (907-1125) had perished. On the eve of the demise of Liao Dynasty, the Khitan noble Yelü Dashi—the 8th son of Baighū—led the Khitan remnants and made various efforts to save the Khitan court at this critical juncture, for example, he enthroned Wei Wang Chun, and supported Tian Zuo of the Liao dynasty, in his fight dynasty, but Yelü Dashi

---

31   See "Biography of Gaochang Xie Family", contained in "Guizhai Collection", Volume 11.
32   Western Liao is also called the Qara Khitai state.

still could not save the situation. Then in July, the 4th year of Baoda (1124), Yelü Dashi resolutely decided to lead the people for a rebellion against the emperor Tian Zuo of Liao dynasty, and declared himself as the ruler, and later went to see Chen Dezhi who lived by the Blackwater (current Ebiha River in Maoming Union Flag, currently Inner Mongolia Autonomous Region).[33]

With the assistance of the chief of Ongut tribes, Chuangguer, went to the North of the desert and founded his military base, developed his troops to tens of thousands of people. As it was temporarily hopeless to restore the state by attacking Jin forces, Yelü Dashi decided an expedition to conquest the West, through the road in Qianzhou, north of Tangnu Mountain in the Northwest of Mongolia, and then to the Southwest to Yemili River Basin, and there his troops united with the Qidan people who originally lived in the Western region, to threaten the Qara Khanid (Western Liao dynasty). The Qara Khanid's original ruling center was around the Suyab River. In 1134 year or so, Yelü Dashi took the chance of that the ruler of East Qara Khanids Dynasty came to ask for assistance due to the harassing attacks by Kangli and Hakaru tribes, led his army to conquer the capital of Pei Luo Jiangjun City (that is, General Pei Luo City or Husi Ordu city).

Since then Yelu Dashi had tried hard to annex the lands in the east, but failed to defeat the Jurchen kingdom forces. Consequently, Yelu Dashi decided to expand westward, thus attacked the West Qara Khanids which dwelled in the Northern region of Amu Darya, Yelu Dashi used the local Halalu (Qarluk) tribes continuously to harass, and defeated the Thaler Zhu Sultan Jiaer's army which had come to help the Qara Khanid dynasty forces, then Yelü Dashientered into the Saqianqian (that is, Samarkand), where he established the Hezhong government. Since then, the Western Liao army continued to march down along the Amu Darya, defeated the Chorasmia forces (Harzem), the tribe of Thaler of the Zhu Dynasty, forced them to submission.

When Yelu Dashi died in 1143, the Western Liao was controlling vast regions in the East to the Kerait tribe at Tula River, West to Amu Darya, North to Qianzhou and Aral Sea, South to Hindu Kush (Hindukush) and Khotan. Its capital was Husi Ordu, which was the original capital of Qara Khanids. Western Liao was also called the Qara Khitay, meaning the black Qidan, this was the name how the Qidan people called themselves, and Western Liao dynasty has continued to use this name after the demise of the Liao Dynasty. Western Liao, as the Mainland dynasty, used Chinese to mark their reign title, dynastic title, their rulers were called as "Gur Khan" by the tribes of the Northwest, meaning "Pukhan", or "Khan who ruled all the tribes".

After the death of Yelu Dashi, his queen Shanta Buyan acted as an emperor, then changed the title of reign as "Xianqing", claimed herself as the "Gantian Queen", she led the kingdom for 7 years. In 1150, the Gantian Queen

121

---

33   See Chen Dezhi: "Miscellaneous Research on Yelu Dashi North-Related History and Geography", contained in the Journal of History & Geography, 1982/2.

transferred her powers to Yelü Dashi's son, Yelü Yilie, and changed the title of the reign as "Shaoxing." At that time, the residents register files included 84,500 households. Yelü Yilie led the kingdom for 13 years, died in 1163, his dynastic title was "Ren Zong". The emperor Ren Zong's posthumous edict ordered that his sister Yelü Pusuwan should succeed the throne as the new emperor, and changed the title of reign as "Chongfu era, or era of "Empress Dowager of Chengtian". Soon an internal court strife happened, an exterior relative Xiao Wolichi launched a coup, killed the Empress, made the second son of Yi Lie, (Yelü Zhilugu) as the emperor, and changed the era title of the reign as "Tianxi". In the end period of the reign of Yelü Zhilugu, the strenghth of Western Liao Dyansty declined. In 1206, the Chorasmia (Kharezm) kingdom refused to pay tribute, and betrayed the Western Liao Dynasty. Superficially looking, the Western Liao dynasty was still a powerful state, and had deterrent power against the surrounding states. In the same year, after the army of Genghis Khan defeated the Naiman tribe, then Kuchlug—the son of Tayang Khan—the leader of Naimans, Kuchlug fled to the Southeast to the Beshbaliq in the north of Uyghur region, and then crossed the Tianshan Mountain to the south reaching Kuuzhu (currently Kuqa in Xinjiang), in 1208, marched to Husi Woerduuo to attack the Western Liao dynasty. Yelü Zhilugu, accepted Kuchlug, and married him to a princess, so Kuchlug became the emperor's son-in-law supported by the Western Liao dynasty.

Utilizing the crisis of the Western Liao Dynasty as an opportunity and gaining the trust of the last emperor Zhilugu, Kuchlug gathered the remnants of the Naiman, and the Mieerqi (Merkits) scattered in the Haiyali, Yemili and Beshbaliq, secretly enhanced his forces againgt the Western Liao. After gaining a full-fledged power, he colluded with the ambitious Chorasmia Shah (Şah), who was planning to usurp the throne. The two allies agreed to attack the Western Liao from the East and West, and agreed to partition the Western Liao territory after the victory. If the Chorasmia Shah would succeed earlier, then his forces could extend their land to the region of Almaliq, Keshi Haer and Woduan, and Naiman could keep the region of Beshbaliq, Zhizi Yemili and Haiyali. If Kuchlug would win the victory earlier, then the land of Western Liao and Benakat (current Southwest of Tashkent, the Uzbekistan's capital) by the side of Huchan River, were all controlled by Naiman people. In 1991, as I and my team participated in the "Grassland Silk Road" research expedition organized by the United Nations Educational, Scientific and Cultural Organization (UNESCO), we have visited the Benaket ruins in the Southwest of Tashkent, about 50 km from the city center. The Benakat ruins are located on the banks of Syrdaria River, which was the hometown of Ahmmad, the famous official of Hui-Hui Dynasty (end period of Chines Yuan Dynasty) at the beginning of the Yuan Dynasty. During the Ming Dynasty period, Tamerlane (Timur-Timurlenk, Aksak Timur) had established the Shakhruhiya (Sharkiya) city here, Chen Cheng had visited this city, during his western expedition. Safety of the architectural constructions of site of ancient settlement of Shahruhiya allows transforming after preservation it into unique city—museum on the

Great Silk Road—the most valuable tourist object. Site of ancient settlement of Shahruhiya in many respects is original. In comparison with other similar monuments discovered an affinity to such largest monuments like Otrar (Kazakhstan) and Ahsiket in Namangan Region (Ferghana Valley, Uzbekistan). Shahruhiya is one of the very large archaeological sites in Central Asia. It consisted of citadel, two cities' territories and wide tradecraft suburb-rabad, in total area—400 hectares. Fortress walls with towers have surrounded by citadel, Shakhristan and Rabad. Shahruhuya was destroyed by Mongols, later has reconstructed by Amir Temur, and named as Shahruhiya. Since that time, it became an important economical and cultural center in the state of Temurids and Sheybanids. Here was functioned own mint. The city connected with the names of outstanding scientists, poets, penmen and artists lived here. The current archaeological excavations focus on the suburbs of the handicraft workshop ruins. The existing ruin research area is 260 hectares, and due to Syrdaria River's flowing bed, a large number ruin units were flooded by the river, the area has contracted and is gradually mitigated.

In 1210, Kuchlug led his troops towards the West at the occasion when Zhilugu sent his army for an expedition to Ho-chung fu (Samarkand), looting the treasury of Western Liao dynasty in Ejikan City located in the lower reaches of the Syrdaria River, they succeeded and then marched Eastward to the river basin of Suyab River, raided the Western Liao's capital Husi Woerduo (Quz Ordo meaning strong army), but were defeated by the Western Liao troops. Later, Chorasmia allied with Kuchlug, took the chance that Zhilugu's troops withdrew from Ho-chung fu, sent troops to occupy the land, and thus went East into the Syrdaria River, attacked the Western Liao general Tayanggu who was guarding the Talas city, finally the Western Liao's main force were defeated by Chorasmia's army, the remnants of the defeated troops returned back to the capital, but the guards and the people of Husi Woerduo (Quz Ordo meaning strong army) closed the city doors and refused their entrance.. The troops of Western Liao had stormed for 16 days, and after they entered the city, wantonly killed many people and looted people's property. The King Zhilugu ordered them to stop, and ordered the army to return the looted property, causing the army to mutiny. Kuchlug took advantage of this opportunity to win the rebels to his side, thus his strength rapidly increased. He took the chance that Western Liao Dynasty court lost the command of the army, and in an occasion when Zhilugu went hunting, launched a sudden attack and seized him. On the surface, however, Zhilugu was still respected as the retired emperor, and the state title of the Western Liao was taken over. At this time the Qarluq people of Almaliq were subordinated to Genghis Khan. In order to consolidate his own rule on the territories of Western Liao, Kuchlug seized the Qarluq people's Wozhaer Khan of Almaliq, and attacked Almaliq. After Wozhaer was killed, the Mongolian Khan court scouted the whereabouts of Kuchlug, and sent troops to subjugate them.

After Kuchlug subordinated the Western Liao dynasty, sent troops to the Kazakhstan and the Woduan, where the army implemented excessive taxes and levies. As Kuchlug was a believer of Nestorianism, and his Princess was a Buddhist, then they forced the local people to give up Islam. In 1218, Genghis Khan sent his general Jebie (Jebe) to take the revenge of Wozhaer. Jebie (Jebe) led the army towards Almaliq and met the troops of Kuchlug, the forces of Kushlug were forced to retreat, then the general Jebie (Jebe) continued to march the Westward to the Fergana basin, and there met the Western Liao's Hala Lu army led by the generals Huosimaili and Wosijiancheng in the city of Keshan, Western Liao surrendered military East bound to Kashgar (Kesi Haer) (today in Xinjiang). When Kuchlug heard the news, the Uyghur in the Northeast of Kashgar (Kesi Haer) was subordinated to Mongol forces led by Jebie, and the escape route through the Hunbasheng crossing the Tian Mountains to the Steppes in the North of Hushan River was cut off by the troops of Halalu of Almaliq, the road to Arti Basheng, the Nalin Valley into Bahanna was controlled by the General Jebie (Jebe) led forces, and the East of Kashgar (Kesi Haer)—a barren land—which had no conditions for founding a state. All in all, after learning about these important facts, Kuchlug Khan then had to flee from Kashgar to the West, came to the borders of Badakshan region, here Kuchlug Khan was captured by the local people, and was handed to the Mongolian army, and was killed, the Western Liao dynasty (Qara Khitai empire) perished. At this time the western territories of the Mongolian empire were entirely surrounded by the Khwarezmia kingdom.

Chapter 3. New Era of Communications between the Hu and the Han peoples

1. Exchanges between the Persian Sassanian Dynasty and China

Persian Sassanian (Sasanid) Dynasty (226-642) was founded by Persians. After the fall of the Persia, the control of Persia was taken over by Parthians, its Northern neighbor. Persians always lived in the Southwest of Persia. During the reign of the 5th Ardavan (Ardavan-i Panjunl, 216-224), the end period of the Parthian Dynasty, Persians enhanced their strength again. Led by Ardashir (226-240), the grandson of Sanan, Persians defeated the Parthian army and seized the power, thus established the new dynasty that was named the Sassanian (Sasanid) Dynasty. Ardashir was a famous emperor in the Persian history, whose many sayings were well known and was disseminated from generations to generations, which are still quoted by Persians, currently.For example, "There can be no government without men; no men without money; no money without prosperity; and no prosperity without justice and good government." It was before long that Shah Ardashir and Shah Shapur started on expedition to Central Asia, which occupied Khwarism (Harzem), Sute, Bactria, defeated the Kusana Dynasty, and became the strongest country in West Asia. In West, the long war was made between Sassanian Dynasty and Roman Empire. After the fall of Roman Empire, in order to struggle for the control rights for East and West trade, Sassanian Dynasty declared a battle against the Byzantine Empire. After the 5th century, Ephthalites from Altai Mountains started to transfer to Central Asia, occupy Sute region, and constantly invaded the South of Amu Darya River and Khorasan region. After the rise of Turkic empire, Ephthalites began to suffer the combined attack by Sassanian Dynasty and Turkic from the 560s, finally Ephthalites were eliminated. In the early 7th century, we see the rise of the Arabs. In 637, Arabs invaded and occupied the capital of Sassanian Dynasty while its ruler Yazdegerd fled. After the fall of Sassanian Dynasty, Peroz, son of King Yazdegerd fled to Chang'an (current Xia'an) to seek help. The culture of Sassanian Dynasty has considerable influences on China. Zoroastrianism and Manichaeism of Persia were introduced into our country, China's architecture and paintings arts were also influenced by Sassanian art.

(1) The Discovery of the Ancestral Tablets in the Tumen Village of Xi'an City

In the winter of 1955, the epitaph of Mrs Su Liang, Nee Ma, of the Tang Dynasty (simply named the Epitaph of Mrs Ma) was discovered by Shaanxi Cultural Relics Management Committee at Tumen Village, Xi'an. This epitaph is currently preserved in Xi'an City Steles Museum. The front upper half of the epitaph stone is carved with a certain foreign script, with six transverse lines; the front lower half of the epitaph stone is carved with Chinese, with seven lines. It was confirmed by Prof. Ito from Kyoto University in Japan that this foreign script was a kind of Medieval Persian—Pahlavi language. The number of carved stones preserved till today is no more than 20 pieces, the majority of which are preserved in Iran and the minority of which are preserved in Western big museums. The bilingual Chinese-Pahlavi language stele discovered by Xi'an, through the publication of Ito (Japan), rapidly attracted the attention of specialists in "Iranistic" (Persian) at home and abroad. Because fewer steles carved with Pahlavi language are preserved till now, nearly each discovery of a new carved stele causes an academic sensation. The Inscription Dictionary of Pahlavi and Parthia written by the French linguist and which was published in 1972, had named the inscription of "the epitaph of Mrs Ma" as SN inscription (the abbreviation of "Xi'an") and included a vocabulary into this dictionary with a definite reading method.

Some parts of the Chinese inscription of the "epitaph of Mrs Ma" are preserved relatively well that it can be basically identified and read. It was reported by the Shaanxi Cultural Relics Management Committee that the Chinese inscription includes 7 lines, and 44 words in total. The Chinese inscription includes the following:

Ms. Ma (Mashi), wife of Su Liang (Suren), the the commander of the left wing Army of Divine Strategy (Sizinsay), was born in the Jisi year and died at the age of 26. She died between 15:00 and 17:00 on the 2nd day of 2nd month of the 15th year of the Xiantong period. It is hereby to erect the tablet for remembrance."Compared with the Chinese inscription part, the Pahlavi inscription part is longer but preserved worse. The Pahlavi (The middle Persian) version of the inscription can be translated as follows which is different than: this was the passed royal, Ms. Ma, who was born in the Su Liang family, the daughter of the commander of the left wing Army of Divine Strategy Sizinsay, and died in Yazdkat 240, 260 of Tang Dynasty period, Xiantong 15th year of

Xiantöng (Chonggao), on December 5th (Persian calendar). She passed away when 26 years old. "May her place be with Ohrmazd (Ahura Mazda) and with the Amahraspands (angels) live in a beautiful paradise of light! Wish Health!" According to the Pahlavi inscriptions, the original word "Su Liang" is Suren which was the name for one prominent family in Parthia Dynasty and Sassanian Dynasty and the surnames are from royal families of Sassanian Dynasty. Thus, it can be known that the death persons were the descendants of Persian royal families.

There are some important differences between Chinese language inscription and Pahlavi language inscription. For example, it was written in the Chinese inscription that Mrs Ma was the wife of Su Liang, the commander of the left wing Army of Divine Strategy (Sizinsay); while it was written in Pahlavi inscription that Mrs Ma was the daughter of the late Farrroxzad (son) of Dadweh, from the Suren (Su Liang) family Here, Farrroxzad means commander of cavalry. Here Dadweh means Army of Divine Strategy (Sizinsay). Besides, about the year on which Mrs Ma died, it was recorded in the Pahlavi inscription that it is the 240 of Yazdkart corresponding to the March 17,872, which is about two years different from the March 19,874 recorded in the Chinese inscription. There are not yet reasonable explanations on these issues.

The above referred Dadweh (Army of Divine Strategy (Sizinsay) in the "epitaph of Mrs Ma" was the military official titles granted by the Tang government and these commanders were sent to different countries of the Western regions, who had stayed in Chang'an city of China for a long time. According to the New History of the Tang Dynasty Wang E Legend, in the end of Tianbao, there were thousands of army commanders, from Jiaoshi of Anxi and Beiting in the Western regions. The Longyou region was briefly occupied by Tubo army troops of the time, though the army wanted to return back, but it could not. Their foods were provided by Tang government, which continued for nearly 40 years. Till the reign of Tang Dezong, Tang government stopped to provide foods for these people, and over 4,000 people led by the Emperor Ming were granted with the Sizinsay (commander) title (Qarib). The book Zi Zhi Tong Jian (History as a Mirror) recorded this in the 7th year of Zhenyuan (787), whose narations were roughly same with New History of the Tang Dynasty, while the narration here was more detailed which said as follows: "The Hu guests, namely the prince ambassadors of the West region, no one wanted to return back, the Tang government had no choice but to split them into two groups. "Prince ambassadors are both commanders of army and ambassadors, and all have remained in the regions where they were sent to", which can refer to the Epilog of the Epitaph of Liang Ma's Wife of the Tang, in the Archeology in 1964, p. 460. It can be seen that the Sizinsay whom Su Liang had served for was the army consisting of foreign royals of Tang Dynasty. There are more than 100 years between this page of epitaph and Tianbao wars, and there are also nearly 80 years that prince ambassadors from West region are compiled in the Sizinsay by Tang government in the 3rd year of Zhenyuan. Thus, Su Liang should be the 3rd generation or the 4th generation of descendant of prince am-bassadors to Persia by the Tang dynasty. Su Liang and his partner Mrs Ma had probably learned Pahlavi language in China. Far away from home for many years, they were still able to use their mother language and write epitaph, which can explain that there were education activities of Pahlavi and Parthia among those Persians and Parthians who believed in Zoroastrianism.

(2) Sassanian Literature Discovered in China

The so-called Pahlavi language refers to a kind of Middle Persian written by the Aramaic alphabet. The word "Pahlavi" has been the Middle form of Parthava language, which is a noun seen in the Old Persian cuneiform scripts. Parthava was under the jurisdication of the ancient Parthian Empire (An Xi), and Parthava is generally known as Parthia in the current Chinese world history books, while it is named as Buai-tiuk in China's History of Han—History of Han/Biography of the Western Regions/An Xi (Arsacid), which is currently in the border region of Iran with Afghanistan and Turkmenistan. The Pahlavi orig-inally refers to a dialect in East Iran, but this word's (Pahlavi) original mean-ing is different from latter's usage. In the current Iran's domestic academia, Pahlavi typically refers to the written language of Middle Persians spelt by various alphabets; while according to Western expert scholars of Iran, Pahlavi typically refers to a written language of Middle Persians spelt by Aramaic al-phabet. The Middle Persian spelt by this kind of alphabet, if looking from the grammar level, is quite similar with the new Persian grammar. The ancient Persian culture was strongly influenced by the West Asian civilization, there-fore Pahlavi alphabet not only directly originated from the West Asian Aramaic scripts, but also Pahlavi language had also absorbed considerable number of Semitic vocabularies that were used as phonogramic and written according to original Aramaic language scripts. These ideograms were written according to original texts, whose meanings keep unchanged (Semitic language), while the pronunciation was according to the corresponding Persian language. This can be compared to Chinese's exegetic pronunciation in the Japanese language.

The discovery of the Epitaph of Su Liang's Wife, Nee Ma, the combination of Chinese—Pahlavi, has important significance for the studies on ancient cul-tural exchanges history between China and foreign countries. In ancient East, except for the Indian civilization, Han civilization and Iran civilization respec-tively formed two highly-developed cultural circles which mutually influenced their neighboring geographic ranges. Since the last 19th century, along with the expansion of Western powers into Central Asia, the cultural relics of China's northwest regions wherein ethnic peoples dwelled were chased by expeditors from UK, Russia, Sweden, Prussia (Germany), France, Japan, etc. From 1902 to 1914, an expedition team from Kingdom of Prussia, led by Grunwedel and Von le Coq, had made 4 "expeditions" to Turfan, Xinjiang and ancient relics in Turfan were illegally unearthed, and a large number of literatures were plun-dered by them. After these foundings and literature arrived in Berlin, by the studies of scholars as F.W.K. Muller, Lentz, Henning, etc. which were divided into three ancient Iran literatures, including Middle Persian and Parthian language spelt by Manichean scripts belonged to Western Iran, and Sogdian language belonged to Eastern Iran languages. They all belong to the 8th century to 10th century. These Middle Persian literatures discovered in Turfan have stimulated the development of European Oriental researches, and led to the emergence of an academic branch similar to "Dunhuangn-ology"—"Turpan-ology".

After the compilation and study of Turfan literatures by scholars, they discovered that, in Turfan regions of Tang Dynasty, centered on Manichaeism temple, there was one consistent migrant group speaking Iranian. The majority of them were Manicheans who used alphabets that were called Manichaean scripts by contemporary scholars to spell their languages, who had lived in Turfan for nearly 100 years. This migrant groups who spoke Iranian language can be roughly divided into three races. One was the Persians, whose language was known as Parsig in Turfan literature, who were called the "Manichaean Middle Persian" by the contemporary scholars, which shared the same language with Pahlavi, the southwestern dialect of Middle Persian language, they were the direct ancestors of contemporary Dari people. The second was the Parthia people, who were also called the Parthians whose language was called as Pahlavanig in scriptures and literature unearthed in Turfan city, and also called as "Mani Anxi" by the contemporary scholars. This language belonged to the northern dialect of Middle Persian language, which was quite similar with the above the "Manichaean Middle Persian" language, and they were also the direct ancestors of contemporary Dari people.

The third was the Sogdians group who were the Eastern Iranians. Although their language belonged to the Middle Iranian category, together with the Parthia and Pahlavi languages, it was quite different from the former two languages and had similarities with the Khotan Saka language discovered by Chinese scholars, this language of Sogdians was also similar to the Khwarezmian language (Chorasmian language). According to the language character used in the literatures, Sogdians who believed in Manichaeism in Turfan, and other Sogdians who believed in Buddhism and Zoroastrianism had dwelled in China's Northwestern regions, they belong to different dialects groups. Their script is called "Manichaean- Sogdian" by the current scholars. The number of Middle Iranian literatures which were plundered from Turfan by the expedition team of Kingdom of Prussia, have caught the attention of many researchers. Mary Boyce, a British scholar, spent numerous years to compile these literatures and published the book titled as "A Catalogue of the Iranian Manuscripts in Manichean Script in the Prussian German Turfan Collection, Akademie-Verlag, Berlin, 1960".

We know that there are thousands of Manicheaism Middle Iranian literatures discovered in Turfan by Prussian German archaeologists. We can guess that the Parthian literature can be much than those discovered literatures (including Iran) till today, which can be evaluated as a big fortune. For a long time, the majority of these literatures were preserved in the Department of Archaeology of Eastern Berlin German Academy of Science. In the winter of 1988, when I paid a visit to East Berlin, W. Sundermann showed some remaining fragments to me. These literatures are currently preserved in the Berlin National Library. After studying and reading these remaining fragments of Manicheaen Middle Persian and Manicheaen Parthian in detail, it can be found that these literatures can be classified into two categories. The first category in the text is about purity and heavenly forces. People can comfortably guess that these literatures are original Manichaeism literatures or its copies brought by migrants to China of the time, or works created by migrants who could skillfully use Manicheaen Parthian language as their mother tongue.

The others are some literatures that can be roughly included into Manicheaen Middle Persian or Manicheaen Parthia literatures, while after careful studying, it can be discovered that there are some Parthia vocabularies mixed with Manicheaen Middle Persian literatures, or appearing some grammar phenomena only existing in Parthian literature and vice versa. Even, there appears Dari Persian in some literatures. It can be imagined for people that this kind of literatures are created by descendants of Iranians who live in Turfan for a long time. That is to say, compared with the former scriptures, these scripts were written in the later years. As the times passed, the racial distinctions between Persian and Parthian immigrants were marginalized, consequently they increasingly communicate with each other. And this communication has enabled the mixture of their former languages. For a period they probably used two languages, simultaneously, whose language has evolved into the phase of new Persian and their spoken language has approached to the Dari Persian language. However, in written language they still used Manichaean scripts. And during their language education, they learned to use the relevant old Middle Persian language. This separation between the spoken language and written language, could make it inevitable to understand the author's original dialect. We are faced with this problem in the written texts found in Turfan excavation sites.

With the fall of Sassanian Dynasty, Middle Persian language was increasingly replaced by the New Persian one. There are only few document from the early phase which are available today. V.F. Minorsky, a Russian-British scholar has mentioned that, among the preserved New Persian books before the early 12th century, half of them were discovered in the city ancient city of Khotan, Turfan of Xinjiang. Among them were the New Persian secular literature written with the scripts of Hebrew, Syrian and Aramaic by the followers of Judaism, Nestorian Christians and Islam, respectively, who lived in the northwestern regions of ancient China.[1]

(3) Sweet Hu Pies in Chang'an (Xi'an)

Chang'an was the political, economical and cultural center of Han Dynasty and Tang Dynasty, which had inherited the past development of the Xianyang city—the capital city of Qin dynasty. In literatures of Persia and other ancient

1   See V.F. Minorsky, Some Early Documents in Persian (1), in JRAS, 1942, pp. 181-184; and his collected papers Medieval Iran and Its Neighbours, London, 1982.

West Regions, in a relatively large historical period, Chang'an was called Kumdam. According to the studies of contemporary scholars, this is the pronunciation of "Xianyang" of Han and before the Han period.

Chang'an city achieved its peak prosperity in the Tang Dynasty period, with 35 km. city surrounding, nearly 1 million people, neat streets, and abundant shops. People from the Western regions and Northern peoples immigrated to Chang'an city, which made Chang'an become international. The wine shops opened by Hu[2] people mainly centralized in the region of West District, Chunming Door, and Qujiang Pool, and usually made girls from Western Regions as maids filled with exotic features, which was called "Huji wine shops".

They were favored by the educated refined people of the time, and many scholars and authors have patronized these wine shops and left some poems to describe these wine shops. Hu foods were popular in Chang'an of the Tang Dynasty, thus after the Kaiyuan, "Foods of royals and Emperor are all Hu foods" recorded in Official Garments Zhi of Old History of the Tang Dynasty, and in Wang Zihui's book.[3]

The development of exchanges between China and foreign countries has enabled considerable exotic foods entering into the mainland China. In Northern Dynasties, many exotic foods and their preparing methods were recorded in Qi Min Yao Shu (Important Arts for the People's Welfare), such as cucumber method, Hu-rice method, Hu-soup method, etc. The most well-known is the Hu-pie which is made by roasting fermented flour inside furnace. In contemporary Xinjiang, and countries in Central Asia, and Pakistan, Bangladesh, Persian Gulf Region of South Asia believing in Islam, it is called Nan (Persian), and written as "馕" (nang). After Han passed the Western Regions, Hu-pie settled down in inland China with Hu people. Shaobing, popular in China, is one kind of it. According to Tai Ping Yu Lan (Imperial Readings of the Taiping Era), quoted from Xu History of Han (Continuation of History of the Han Dynasty), Emperor Lingdi in the late Eastern Han Dynasty liked eating Hu-pies, and all imperial relatives demanded Hu-pies. The book also quoted the record of Wei Zhi, Zhao Qi of the late Han Dynasty fled to Hejian, and transferred to "North Sea", and "often sold Hu-pies in street". When the army of Lyu Bu lacked food, people had made thousands of Hu-pies for his troops.

During the Tang Dynasty period, Hu-pie became more popular. Recorded by an Anecdote of the Sui and Tang Dynasties, Liu Yan got up at dawn to go to court, still felt very cold, thus, he bought Hu-pie during the journey to the court and felt a strange pleasure. Recorded in Travel Notes in Tang Dynasty for

2   Hu was a general term for non-Chinese peoples living north and northwest of China. It was used mainly between the Warring States (5th Cent.-221 BCE) and the Southern and Northern Dynasties period (300-600). The mighty steppe federation of the Xiongnu was also often referred to as Hu.
3   See Wang Zihui, Huji Wine Shops at Chang'an of Tang Dynasty, in Historic Talk of Cooking, book series of Chinese Cooking, 1986, China Commercial Press, pp. 105-107.

Learning Buddhism by Yuan Ren, he referred that, in Chang'an, "He received Hu-pie, porridge. And Hu-pie was popular, all the officers were satisfied." Hu-pie was also called "Hu sesame pie". Bai Juyi, in his poem titled as Sending Hu Sesame Pies to Yang Wanzhou, wrote that, "Learning Hu Mabing in capital, with crisp skin and fragrant oil. Sending it to hungry Yang, tasting the Fuxing?" Today in China, Hu sesame pie bought and experienced by Bai Juyi is the current Crispy Sesame Cake in China.[4] There are various kinds of Hu-pies, and some are served as part of meals. For example, the "Shaobing cooking method" was recorded in Qi Min Yao Shu (Qi-People Essential), "one bushel of flour, a kilo of mutton, 20ml of onion white, bitter melon and salt, then baking". This is a kind of mutton cake baked without sesame.

2. Nine States (Tribes) in the Oases of Zhaowu

The name of "Nine states in the oases of Zhaowu" was firstly recorded in the Legend of Western Regions of History of Northern Dynasties, which was the general term for some countries in Amu Darya, Syr Darya basin in the Sui and Tang dynasties period. According to records in the History of Northern Dynasties, the origin of "Nine states in the oases of Zhaowu" was narrated as in the following: The King was surnamed Wen, and was born in a Rouzhi (Yuezhi) family, who originally lived in Zhaowu, the North of Qilian Mountains, Hexi Prefecture. Because his country was invaded by Xiongnu, he crossed Congling from West and invaded Sogdiana. Then he divided his country into branches named with Zhaowu to show its origin. Probably, this legend was produced after the Westward migration of the Rouzhi people, whose main theme was the Rouzhi's Westward migration. The Nine Tribes of Zhaowu (Zhaowu jiuxing), also called the "nine barbarian families" (jiuxing hu) founded several smaller or greater states in the region of Soghdia (also called the Sogdiana, by the Greeks known as Transoxania). These were known as the "many states of the Zhaowu [tribes]" (Zhaowu zhuguo). It was traditionally believed that the nine tribes had migrated Westwards after leaving their home city Zhaowu at the foot of Mt. Qilian (current Linze close to Zhangye, Gansu). Their home place was thus located in the Western parts of the Han empire (206 BCE-220 CE). They evaded this place after being defeated by the steppe federation of theXiongnu.

132

Arrived in the plain of the rivers Amu Darya and Syr Darya, they founded the cities or states of Kangguo,Anguo, Caoguo, Miguo, Heguo, Shiguo, Shiguo, Wudi, and Huoxun. The last two were quite unimportant during the 6th and 7th centuries, but Huoxun (i.e. Khwarezmia) emerged as a dominant state in Central Asia in the 11th century. The political heads ("kings") of these states bore the family name Zhaowu. There are different ideas on which countries the "Nine states in the oases of Zhaowu" refer to in the history books. It generally includes "Kang", the Samarqand of current Uzbekistan, "Kang" should

---

4 Huang Yongnian: Talks on Life in the Ancient Capital; Wang Zihui, Brief Study on Hu Sesame Pies, in Historic Talk of Cooking, book series of Chinese Cooking, China Commercial Press, 1986, pp. 108-109, 471-472.

be the transliteration of Kand (Sogdian Persian language); "An", the Bukhara of Uzbekistan; "Cao" refers Khebud of the Northwest Samarqand; "Shi" (Chach) refers to Tashkent, the capital of Uzbekistan; "Mi", also translated into Maimargh, situated near Samarqand and the South of Zela Fushan River; "He" (Koshana), located between Samarqand and Bukhara; Khwaresm, located in the downstream region of Amu, the boundary of Uzbekistan and Turkmenistan; Betik, located in the Southwest of current Uzbekistan; Kesh, located in Shahr-i Sabz, the South Uzbekistan. Han people usually surnamed Hu traders from the name of theirregions. "Kang" was the most important one among these "nine states", which was mainly dated back to the Kangju of Han and Wei Dynasties. In fact, Kangju was different from "Kang State". Buddhism was transferred to Kang State from Bactria. At the end of the 2nd century, after they spread Buddhism in Rouzhi, Tianzhu, Parthia, the Kangju monks also came to China to teach Buddhism. The famous monks who translated Buddhist scriptures were Kang Mengxiang, Kang Senghui, etc. they have mainly translated many Mahayanan Buddhism classics.

"Nine states in the oases of Zhaowu", all had dwelled in the oases of Central Asia. Generally, the region of these states were not big, and all were equal to the area Sogdiana. The distance among these oases were different, the distance was no more than one-day by riding a camel, for example, between the Kang State and Mi State; the distance was more than 10 days by a camel ride, for example, An state and Khwaresm. For the limited lands of the oases and less population, people's survival relied on the exchanges with other regions, which made peoples of "Nine states in the oases of Zhaowu" have the tradition of trading. Their footprints cover the Central Plains in East, Mongolian Steppes and Steppes grasslands in North, India in South, and Dashi kingdom in West. Due to the limited material resources and human resources in these regions, still there couldn't survive powerful dynasties, and the kingdoms established in this region were successively subordinated to Persian Empire, Macedonian Empire of Alexander, Rouzhi (the Empire of Kushan, Ephthalites (the Gupta empire), Turkic empire. In the middle of the 7th century, after the defeat of the Western Turkic Khanate by the Tang dyansty, Tang government promoted the establishment of many small kingdoms in Sogdiana. After the rise of the Dashi Empire (Arabs), it expanded towards the East, the Sogdiana land was again invaded by Dashi Empire.

(1) The Sogdian Civilization

Sogdian was the branch of Eastern Iranian people, who had close blood relationship with Saka of Yutian, Xinjiang and Khwarezmian near Aral Sea. Sogdians are ancient dwellers of Central Asia, who were called Suxda, referred in Avesta, the Zoroastrianism classic. And it is also referred in the inscriptions of Persia and Greek literatures. There are many translation names in Han literature, which can be roughly divided into two systems. It was called Suyi in the book "history of the Later Han", was called Shuyao in the book Weilüe; called Suli in Great Tang Records on the Western Regions; called Suli in the book Travel Notes in Tang Dynasty for Learning Buddhism; called Sunling in Yijing's Thousand Sanskrit Words; called Suli in Tang Liyan's Miscellaneous Names in Sanskrit. All these words have been the transliterations of Sūlika, i.e., Sogdiana in the Middle Persian language. It was also called Sogdiana in the book "History of Northern Dynasties", which was probably translated from Sogd, and meant to refer to Sogdians. As for settling down in different oases of Sogdians, the geographical division made them have no unified language. Sogdians which dwelled in the banks of Zela Fushan river used Aramaic alphabet to write their own language which was called the Sogdian language. On the other hand, Sogdians who believed in Manichaeism used Manicheaen alphabet to write religious Manichaeism classics which was called the Manicheaen in the Sogdian language. Sogdians who believed in Zoroastrianism used another Aramaic alphabet, namely Syriac alphabet to write Zoroastrianism classics. It is discovered by experts after researches that Sogdians believed in different religions and spoke different dialects.

Among Sogdian people the most popular language had been the Sogdian language. There were totally 22 letters in the Aramaic alphabet, 17 of which are from Sogdian script. Basically, Sogdians write from right to left, but after the influence of Han culture, some Sogdians wrote from up to down. The early Sogdian alphabets were written separately; latter they were increasingly connected. The earliest person who refered to the Sogdian language was Bian Ji, the student of Xuan Zang. He wrote in the Great Tang Records on the Western Regions: "Sogdian script has over 20 letters which can be transformed into different words. It was very popular and was read vertically". In 1932, Soviet Union scholars discovered documents written with Sogdian language in Kuh-i Mugh of Tajikistan, 140 km, in the east of Samarqand (Uzbekistan). Through the unearthing work, 94 documents and some coins were discovered in total. Two were Arabic documents, which were written on the sheep leather; and 5 Han documents which were written on the back of Sogdian documents. These documents were the first historical materials discovered, which recorded the relations among the early Tang, Sogdiana, Dashi, and Turkic dynasties in the 8th century, which have attracted many scholars' interests.

Sogdian merchants assumed trade functions of the nine states, and developed trade relations with China. Marc Aurel Stein, a British "explorer", has discovered the 6 letters written with Sogdian scripts in the beacon tower, the West of Dunhuang. These 6 letters were written by Hu merchants from "Nine States" who traded in China, to their families. The letter, with 63-line length, narrated about Chinese Emperor's fleeing from Luoyang, and Luoyang's invasion by Xiongnu kingdom, etc. which was the earliest Sogdian literature in the world which could be preserved till currently. Among the Dunhuang literature, there are Sogdian Buddhism literatures; in Turfan literature, there are Manichaeism scriptures written by local Sogdians believing Manichaeism. And in the inscriptions of Turkic, Mobei in the Tang Dynasty, there are also some inscriptions carved with the Sogdian script. During the Tang Dynasty period, Turgesh people, who dwelled in Suyab were the first to express their own language by Sogdian alphabets. Later, this method was adopted by westward migrating Uyghurs and was widely used, and later named as the Uyghur script. In the 12th century, this kind of language was introduced into the west of Mongolian Steppes by Uyghurs. In the 13th century, after Genghis Khan unified the Mobei, he learned from Uyghurs to express Mongolian tongue with the Sogdian scripts. Later, at the end period of the Ming Dynasty, Manchus learned this script from the Mongolians, who created the Manchu script.

Sogdians are a nation with high culture. Wall paintings are major parts for Sogdian culture. Till now, in the discovered Sogdian relics, like Afrasiyab Relic, the Kang Relic discovered in suburb of Samarqand; Paikent Relic near Bukhara; Bunjkend relic in Tajikistan, etc., there are exquisite wall paintings founded in all these paintings. Among them, the most well-known is the wall paintings discovered in Kang Relics of Samarqand city, whose Southern wall included a drawing and paint of a big white elephant, and several warriors riding horses and camels, some warriors wore protective masks and armors. The Western wall included the drawing and paint of three warriors wearing colorful clothes with traditional Sogdian patterns, and many men wearing yellow clothes, three of whom seem to be the peoples from the Central Plains region. And the Northern wall included the drawing and paint of a man riding a flying horse, and handing on spear to pierce one leopard, and this man was dressed in typical Central Plains clothes.

Sogdians had the tradition of trading and commerce. It is written in the History of the Old Tang: Biography of Western Regions as follows: "Sogdians are good in trading, and they like struggling for one-fen profit". They "like benefits", as long as benefits, they would be there. If they give birth to sons, sons would be fed with candy, and their palms would be glued. They hope their sons that were good at saying sweet words, and hands could gather money like glue. When the man was 20 years old, he had to leave home to trade for benefits. It is also written in the Great Tang Records on the Western Regions: Sogdians were cunning, "generally greedy for high profits, and also even greedily calculated benefits between fathers and sons". It also refers that "Sogdians appreciated those people possessing considerable money and material wealth as the criterion for noblity, despite good or bad". Although some powerful figures had much money, they still did "not eat well". Many Sogdians had separated from agricultural work, and "few Sogdians sought to benefit from agricultural work".

In the Northern and Southern Dynasties period, Sogdian traders moved between the Central Plains and Western regions. After the traders' movement has increased on the Silk Road, generally cities and towns were established on the main expedition routes. After leaving the Sogdiana and oases, the first eastward station for the traders of the "Nine states" was in the Steppes located in the northern part of Syr Darya river. Sogdians established many small towns in Suyab, etc. which made Suyab become a densely populated region of the Steppes. In the first half of the 4th century, there were more than 100

Hu people in the Dunhuang region, and whose subordinate population could be about 1000. It is written in History of Northern Dynasties: Biography of the Western Regions: Sogdians that, there were many Hu people of 9 states in Liangzhou in the period of 16 Kingdoms, most of who were Sogdian traders who traded in Liangzhou. After the Northern Wei Dynasty controlled Hexi, there Sogdian traders were all detained. Till the reign of emperor Wencheng (452), the Sogdian ruler sent his ambassadors to beg for the freedom of these Sogdians, which was affirmed by the court of the Northern Wei Dynasty. Sogdians did well in the trade of jewels, consequently there are many stories about their (Hu traders) expertise in regard to jewels which are still narrated among the Chinese people. Tai Ping Guang Ji referred to a Hu man who was good in identifying jade stones.[5]

During the era of the Sui and Tang dynasties, the immigration regions of Sogdians were distributed more widely in the East of Congling. In Western regions and Hexi regions, there were Shule (Kashgar), Yutian, near Pu Changhai (Lob Nor), Boxian town (current Xinjiang Qie Mo), Shicheng, Xizhou (Ancient City of Gaochang, current Turfan city), Yizhou (current Hami), Dunhuang, Suzhou (current Jiuquan), Ganzhou (current Wuwei), Liangzhou (current Zhangye), Ling, Xia, etc.. In Guanzhong region, there were the cities of Chang'an, Lantian, Luoyang; in North China, there were Fanyang, Yingzhou, in the Monan grasslands, and there was the Liu Huzhou located in Hetao region of Inner Mongolia, also in Mobei grassland, there was the Orhon, etc. The people of Sogdiana were also famous for their music and their expertise in astronomy. The religious spectrum was remarkable. It included Buddhism, Zoroastrianism, and Manichaeism, and also Islam since the 8th century. Outside of the cities, Sogdians engaged in agriculture, and some were engaged in pastoral nomad production mode. In some regions, these people bred horses.

(2) Playing the Neck-bending Pipa (qujing Pipa): Greatly Popular among the Sogdians

Sogdiana (currently Tajikistan) was the cradle region of songs and dances.[6] It is written in the Old History of the Tang Dynasty: Biography of the Western Regions that people of "Nine States dwelling in the oases of Zhaowu, specifically enjoy singing and dancing. The songs and dances of Sogdians are beautiful and moving, which are very impressive." During the Sixteen Kingdoms and Northern Dynasties period, many songs from the Western Regions were introduced into the Central Plains. During this period, the spread and development of songs in of the Western Regions have roughly experienced two stages. The first stage was the period of Sixteenth Kingdoms, Lu Guang of the Later Liang conquered the Qiuci (current Kuqa in Xinjiang) of the Western Regions,

5   See Wen Tingjun's Qianzi, Book243, published by the Zhonghua Book Company, 1961, Volume V, p 1877.
6   A rigorous, twirling dance, the Sogdian Whirl Dance was usually performed on a colorful felt carpet.

and captured musicians. After the Northern Wei Dynasty got the control of the Hexi region, Qiuci music was also introduced into China. The second stage was the period which started after the reign of Emperor Xuan Wu (500-515) of the Northern Wei Dynasty. Since the nobles of the court loved the musical instruments such as "husheng", "Pipa", "Banjo", "Konghou", "Hugu", and "Cymbal", and dance of Western regions had become increasingly popular in the Central Plains. It was not until the fall of the Northern Wei Dynasty that Hu music was still popular among the people. The rulers of the Northern Qi Dynasty and the Northern Zhou Dynasty also loved and enjoyed Hu dances and Hu music.[7]

Traditionally, different musics of Western regions was named according to the place of their origin. For example, the music of Kang and An, the culture center of Western regions, are named as the Kang music and the An music. Kang music was introduced into China when Emperor Zhou Wu married the Turkic queen, whose songs included Ji Dian Nong He Zheng, dancing music pieces included He Lan Bo Bi Shi, Mo Xi Bo Di, Nong Hui Bo Bi Shi, Qian Ba Di Hui Di, etc; the songs of An music pieces included Fu Sa Dan Shi, dancing music pieces included Mo Xi, and the composed music pieces included Ju and Di. The words "Kang" and "An" were theregions wherein Sogdians gathered, thus the music piece names above should be the transliteration of Sogdian language. The towns in the southern Tianshan were closer to the Central Plains. During the Northern Dynasties period, the most well-known southern music of Western regions was the Qiuci music and the Shule music. Later, Lu Guang successfully invaded Qiuci that he got the Qiuci music. The Qiuci music sounded sad and plaintive. The famous songs among Qiuci music were the song of Shan Shan Mani, a composed music of Pojiaer, dancing music of Xiaotian, Shule Yan, etc.[8]

The musical instruments were introduced into the Central Plains with exotic dance and music. According to scholars' studies, Konghou originates from Western Asia which spread into the Central Plains in the Eastern Han Dynasty, was generally used in Xiliang music, Qiuci music, and An music, and had become the beloved instrumenta among the Chinese people. In Cao Zhi's Yuefu poems, Konghou Yin was mentioned. It is described in the book Southeast the Peacock Flies of the Southern Dynasties that, Liu Lanzhi, of Jiao Zhongqing's wife, could play the Konghou instrument at the age of 15. The earliest introduced instrument into China, i.e, the Konghou was vertical, and later it was improved and developed by our country's musicians, and the lying Konghou

7 See Zhou Jingbao's Musical Culture across on the Silk Road, Xinjiang People's Publishing House, 1987, pp.169-170.
8 See records in the Book of Sui: Music Zhi, under the general name of Shule music, there were songs of Keng Li Si Rang Le, dancing music of Yuan Fu, composed music of Yan Music. The Book of Sui) is the official history of the Sui dynasty. It ranks among the official Twenty-Four Histories of imperial China. It was commissioned by Emperor Taizong of the Tang dynasty, and written by a team of prominent scholars, including Yan Shigu, Kong Yingda, and Zhangsun Wuji, with Wei Zheng as the lead author. It was completed in 636 AD.

was created. Hujia, the Nomad flute—is well known and generally appreciated by the people, which is a kind of wind instrument. It was made by animal horns, and possessed holes to arrange sounds. Cai Yan described: "playing the Hujia, horses are cry; the lonely geese come back, sounds are plaintive", which makes people feel sorrow.

As Recorded in the Book of Sui: Music Zhi, the Pipa was also not an instrument which belonged to Huaxia, but was introduced to Huaxia from the Western Regions. As for the Pipa, a foreign musical instrument, there was no no consistent translation of it. In the Han Dynasty, it was called "Piba". In the Northern Dynasties, Pipa was quite popular in the Central Plains that it could be seen on Dunhuang wall paintings and Datong Yungang Grottoes. After the emergence of this kind of instrument, through it was improved, Shuangfeng Pipa, Longjing Pipa, Da Hulei, Xiao Hulei, etc. were created. Currently, Pipa is regarded as a national instrument of China. Cao people a branch of the the Sogdian people were usually surnamed Cao in the Central Plains. In the Northern Dynasties period, musicians of Cao were very talented, especially were good in playing the Pipa. The earliest well-known person was a Cao Brahmin believer who bought Pipa from the Qiuci traders. Later, there was one Cao monk who lived in the last Northern Wei and early Northern Qi, and was good at playing the Pipa. His son, Cao Miaoda was very qualified in playing the Pipa. When, Cao Miaoda played in front of the court of Northern Qi dynasty, Emperor Wenxuan could beat the Hu drum by himself, thus Cao Miaoda was granted a special title for this reason. The whole family of Cao Miaoda was good at playing the Pipa, and were highly appreciated by the Emperor. His younger sister entered into the imperial harem; his younger brother was titled as prince; the elder sister had a high talent of playing several musical instruments, and Cao Miaoda had become well-known by many people and many regions. After the fall of Northern Qi by Northern Zhou, Cao Miaoda has served the Northern Zhou; after the fall of Northern Zhou dynasty, Cao Miaoda was protected and promoted by the Sui Dynasty.

On the wall paintings of Bunjkend Relic, there is a lady harpist who is contemplatively playing a harp. In the same Relic, an exquisite wooden statue was discovered, who was a statue of a dancer. The statue is shaped gracefully, with necklace, bells, and beautiful clothes, which are consistent with the slim figure. Probably, this should be the image of a famous "Hu-xuan dancer". On the wall paintings discovered in 1958, there was one wall painting with 4 dancers who wore high-waist dresses, and among them, one was playing a Pipa. A large number of Sogdians had migrated into China during the Tang Dynasty period, who brought their dances and songs into the Central Plains. And this kind of song and dance was quickly well received by the Central people. In the 15th year of Kaiyuan (727 AD), Kesh presented these dancers to Tang Dynasty; in the 17th year of Kaiyuan (729), Maimargh presented Hu-xuan dancers to the Tang Dynasty court.

The Cao people of the "Nine states in the oases of Zhaowu" were good at playing Pipa, who had been well-known by the Central Plains in Northern Wei Dynasty and Sui Dynasty. During the period of Zhenyuan, Cao Gang's Pipa playing techniques were famous among all neighboring regions. Liu Yuxi wrote a poem: "The bold strings are noisy while fine strings are bright, meanings with snow and winds. Once hearing Cao Gang's Baomei, was going out Jiangcheng, when life is unsmooth." Cao Gang used "plectrum" when playing the Pipa, so that his music was more powerful. It is written in the Yuefu Zalu that the sound is "like wind or like rain". At that time, Pei Xingnu was also quite good at playing the Pipa, and directly used his fingers to pluck the strings, consequently it is written in the Yuefu Zalu that "his fingers have become slightly softer". Cao Gang was not only proficient in playing the Pipa, he had taught his performing techniques to Han people. Lian Jiao, the well-known Pipa performer of the Tang Dynasty, was his student. And another female Pipa performer Cao Gongfeng, also had students to train. In order to demonstrate gratitude, her student asked the renowned Bai Juyi to write a poem for her teacher, Cao Gongfeng.

He (Koshana/Koshan) people were proficient in singing who were also known and appreciated by the people of Central Plains. It is narrated in the History of the Northern Dynasties: Legend of Enxing that, He Hongzhen, a singer from Koshana, and his father were titled as king and queens of singers. The best known singer in Han region of Tang Dynasty was He Manzi who was born from Kaiyuan and Tianbao, who lived in Cangzhou. A poem of Yuan Zhen, mentioned about He Manzi, said "He Manzi can sing, can weep, it is quite rare in Tianbao". Yuan Zhen also described her expression when she was singing, Yuan Zhen said: "Concentrating on singing, nothing with clouds' stopping and dust's down, sound flies far."And some lines of Bai Juyi also eulogized her, by saying that: "One song and four tones sing eight levels, it is heartbroken sound from beginning." He Manzi was later sentenced to death, before dying, she made a song of He Manzi to beg for a mercy and avoid the death sentence, but her demand was not accepted. After her death, the song of He Manzi was widely spread. He Yi of the reign of Emperor Zhongzong, and another Hu person were good at singing "Hesheng", namely a kind of double singing, which was very popular.

Mi (Maimargh) people were also good at singing. In the period of Yuanhe (806-821), Mi Jiarong's fame overwhelmed all the singers in the Central Plains. His songs, "the momentum originated from mouth and heart, generously spit out voiceless sound", the sound was sonorous that "broke through the clouds into the sky". Liu Yuxi deeply interacted with him that he made a poem, "Leaving back Jiarong for 30 years, it is still good when I suddenly hear the old songs". He also wrote another poem titled as: To Singer Mi Jiarong, which said: "To say person singing the unexpected sound of Liangzhou, it is only Mi Jiarong." Shi (Chach) people, had dwelled between the grasslands of North of Syr Darya river and agricultural regions in oases, were well-known for their dances. The Volume 64 of Classified Collection of Tang Poems collected Liu

Yanshi's Zhongcheng Wang Observes Huteng Dance, which said the following: "only few Shi (Chach) people can be seen, but like bird faced with dancing". Huteng Dance is a kind of dance with sprightly movements, the dancers wear pinged cap and Hu clothes with narrow sleeves.[9]

Due to trade with the Central Plains people, Sogdians have often used Chinese coins, and greatly favored the form of Chinese coins, circle form, with a square hole in the middle, and this form was convenient for holding and saving them. Later, they copied the form of Han coins in Sogdiana, forged the Sogdian coins with inner holes which were smaller than Han coins. During the process of archaeological excavation in various relics sites of Central Asia, this kind of coins were discovered. On the wall paintings of Kang Relic site of Samarqand, there was one painted with several ambassadors to East from Sogdiana, among who there was one wearing cap with two pointed decorations. It was the same as the Korean ambassadors on Tang wall paintings of Xian. Thus, this was the image of Koreans.

3. Scientific-technological and Cultural Exchanges between the Hu and Han peoples

(1) The Westward Introduction of the Silk Industry

There was no silk production in the Western regions. According to Sima Qian's record, in the the west of Dawan, "there is no silk."[10] For a long time after Buddhism was introduced into China, there was still no silk in the Western Regions. The Volume IV of Fayuan Zhulin recorded that, "Hu people do not believe that worms eat trees to spin silk when they saw the silk."[11] Although, people of Western Regions have known the silk products, they still didn't know how to produce the silk.

Before the development of silk industry, the silk demand of nobles dwelling in the ancient Western Regions was mainly depended on trade exchanges with the inland China. Since the ancient times, silk products were the main export products to Northern Western Regions from the Central Plains of China. The Han silk was unearthed in the ancient tombs of middle of the 1st century BC in Pazyryk. China, Kazakhstan, Altai region of the Russian Federation also unearthed the copper mirror belonging to the Warring States period. These materials discovered show that the dwellers of Chinese mainland and the West of Altai region interacted with each other in the early and middle period of the 1st century BC.[12] For a long time after the silk was introduced into Western

---

9   See Zhou Jingbao's Musical Culture on the Silk Road, Xinjiang People's Press, 1987, pp. 153-164.
10   See The Historical Records: Dawan Commentary Section.
11   Recorded in Taisho Tripitaka, Volume 53, p. 296. Taishō Tripitaka is a definitive edition of the Chinese Buddhist canon and its Japanese commentaries used by scholars in the 20th century. It was edited by Takakusu Junjiro and others.
12   See Lu Kejin's On Ancient Relations between China and Altai Tribes, Acta Archaeologica Sinica, No. 2, 1957.

regions, some countries of the Western Regions still did not know to weave silk, and considered raw silk as a ready material. According to the records by Huichao, a Silla monk, Kings of Kashmir regions often ordered two or three hundred people to plunder and rob. "Let people rob silk, keeping in warehouse, let them decomposed, but not make clothes".[13] Till the 13th century when Mongols dominated the "Western Regions" the promotion of sericulture industry in the Western Regions was limited. Yelü Chucai noted his observation in Samarqand as follows: "there are many white mulberries in this region, but people can rarely feed silkworms, that hinders to produce raw silk".

The early weaving of silk had occurred in Gaochang and Yutian. It is recorded in the Sui Book: Notes on Western Regions that, Gaochang was very convenient for breeding silkworms. Great Tang Records on the Western Regions, Tibetan classic of History of Yutian, and New Book: Notes on Western Regions, all refer that the seeds of silkworms of Yutian were introduced from China's mainland.

The volume 12 of the Great Tang Records on the Western Regions records that the process of silk industry was spread into Yutian. More specifically, long before, Yutian did not know silkworms. Later, they heard from that there were silkworms in the Central Plains. Thus, they sent ambassadors to ask for seeds of silkworms. But Emperor of the Central Plains did not want the seeds of silkworms to be spread to other regions, thus ordered strict measures and controls in the frontiers. Then, Emperor of Yutian came up with idea which humbly advocated realizing marriage political diplomacy with the Han dynasty. The Emperor of the Central Plains had always been arrogant, when he saw that Yutian state from the Western regions advocated marriage political diplomacy would like to marry with the Central Plains, the Emperor of the Central Plains agreed to allow a princess to marry a Yutian leader. After Emperor of Yutian got the message, he sent ambassadors in the name of welcoming the princess to the Central Plains, who quietly sent messages to the princess that there was no silk and silkworms in Yutian, if the princess wanted have silk clothes after marrying, she must bring the seeds of silkworms to conveniently make silk by oneself. After receiving this message, the princess secretly prepared the seeds of silkworms, hiding them in the phoenix crown. When the teams arrived at the frontiers, officials still examined the whole baggage, except the princess crown. Thus, the seeds of silkworms could finally safely arrive in Yutian. The princess for a while lived in the place of Ma-Za, and then moved to the imperial palace. Before leaving, the princess left the seeds of silkworms here. Till the March spring, all things began to grow, and people began to feed silkworms. At beginning, people did not understand that silkworms were fed by Mulberry Leaves, so that they tried to a variety of leaves. Later, they discovered that only Mulberries were most useful. Then, they planted many Mulberries. And the princess ordered to protect the mulberries that made silk industry develop in Yutian. Later, in order to remember this, people established the Temple of Seeds of Silkworms in the place of Ma-Za. Till the Tang Dynasty period, there

---

13 See Taisho Tripitaka, Volume 53, p. 979.

were several withered kinds of Mulberries. The Tibetan History of Yutian also said, there was a king named Vijaya-jaya who married a princess from the Central Plains. The princess secretly brought the seeds of silkworms fed in the place of Ma-Za. In the early days of the 20th century, a wall painting was discovered in Dandan Oilik Relic in the east of Yutian, on which the story of Han princess bringing the seeds of silkworms to Yutian was painted.[14]

The time that seeds of silkworms were introduced into Yutian was about the period of Sixteen Kingdoms to the Northern Dynasties. The territories of the Western Regions were convenient to plant mulberries. Thus, the sericulture industry was quickly introduced there, not only introduced into various regions of Western regions including the West of Congling. But also the Western regions had become the junction region for the further westward spread of sericulture.

(2) The Silkworms Were Introduced into Eastern Rome and India

It's quite difficult to confirm when the sericulture industry was introduced into Europe. In History of Later Han: Legend of Western Region: Da Qin, this book has recorded that people do farm work, most of whom planted mulberries in Da Qin (namely Roman Empire). However, within a considerably long time, the silk of Roman Empire mainly relied on China. Though, there was some sericulture industry in country, whose materials were also imported from the East. The Chinese imported silk was unwoven by Roman silk workshops, and newly dyed and finished. Due to the silk that was more elaborate than other weaving products, the demand of silk was large in Rome. A considerable Chinese silk entered into Roman market through Persia, which cost great and state treasury could not meet the needs of its expenditure. Thus, in order to control the import of silk, Roman Empire reached an agreement with Persian Sassanian Dynasty in 297, which prescribed that the silk was monopolized by the state. The monopoly for European silk trade brought huge benefit for Persia. This forced European people to find other origins within the whole Byzantine Empire, try to get rid of relying on Persian people in sericulture industry, which caused the unhappiness of Persians. Persians did not expect that Byzantine established direct contact with China, and also were unwilling to let Europeans understand the manufacturing process of silk.

According to the record of Procopius of Caesarea, the famous historian of Eastern Rome, nearly 550, several Indian monks in Byzantine knew that the Emperor of Eastern Rome (Justin) was trying to decrease the deficit of silk trade, and the rely on Persians, then they asked to meet the Emperor, claimed to be able to manufacture silk and could help Byzantine dissolve this problem. They told Justin that they lived in the North of India called Serinda that they not only understood the manufacturing process of silk, but also imagined to manufacture silk in Byzantine; they told Justin that the silk was produced by a kind of worms that were born to produce silk. But for the short manufacturing cycle of silk worms and the feeding problem of silkworms, it was difficult to get

---

14　See Ji Xianlin, et al.: Annotation on Great Tang Records on the Western Regions records, Zhonghua Book Company, 1985, pp. 1021-1023.

this kind of living silkworms. However, it was easy to reproduce because silkworms were hatched from the eggs. They also introduced incubating process, namely using manure to cover the eggs, letting them produce heat, later young silkworms would drill out from eggs. The writer Theophile de Byzance, of the turn of the 8th century and the 9th century, said that it was a Persian monk who brought the silkworms into Byzantine.[15] The place where these monks get the seeds of silkworms, Serinda, was constituted by Ser and Inda. Ser was Seres which means silk country, namely China; Inda was India. Serinda refers to the place between China and India, which corresponds to the Western regions in Chinese historical materials. The sericulture industry was introduced into Western regions through Yutian of the time, so the seeds of silkworms were introduced into Byzantine by these Indian monks from Yutian or from its near regions. These Indian monks not only brought seeds of silkworms to Eastern Rome, but also successfully incubated eggs of silkworms, and imparted the means of planting mulberries and feeding silkworms. Thus, the sericulture industry originating from ancient China, from materials manufacturing to silk products, completely settled down on the soil of Eastern Roman Empire.[16]

The climate of Mediterranean region was good for the planting of mulberries, which made sericulture industry rapidly develop there. During the 6th century, Byzantine established contacts with Western Turkic Khanate. At that time, Turkic Khanates controlled the vast Steppes, in the East from Liaohai and in the West to Caspian Sea, and controlled the silk trade between the East and West. Emperor Justin introduced the manufacturing process of silk to the visiting Turkic people, which made Turkic people astonished and do not know how Eastern Romans knew this secret. As we have mentioned above, in the p. 116 of the History of Northern Dynasties: Legend of Western Regions, it is recorded that the soil of Da Qin (Rome) was convenient for planting rice, mulberries, and for people to do silkworms fields. After the rise of the Arab Empire, the sericulture industry spread into the West along North Africa, and crossed over the Strait of Gibraltar to enter into the Spain controlled by the Arab Empire. In 1146, the King of Sicilia (current Sicily in Italia) employed the captive Byzantine Greek craftsmen who knew the techniques of silkworm breeding, and started to produce silk in Sicilia. Later, sericulture industry was introduced into Italy and other European regions from Sicilia. In the early ancient times of India, people knew to make silk and weave clothes by using wild silkworms, this silk was called the Kauseya. Later, India began to import silkworms and silk from China. In the Arthashastra written in the 4th century BC, there is the word "cinapatta" which means bundles of Chinese silk. It can be seen that, since the early times the Chinese silk was exported to India.[17]

143

---

15   See Ge Daisi, Geng Sheng: Far Eastern Chinese Ancient Literaturanzeiger of Greek and Latin Writers, The Chinese Publishing House, 1987, p. 116.
16   Ibid., p. 96-97.
17   See Ji Xianlin: The Preliminary Study on the Issues about Chinese Silk's Export to India, in Papers on Cultural Relationship between China and India, Sanlian Bookstore, 1982.

However, within a considerably long period, Indian people did not know the technique of breeding silkworms. When Hui Chao, the Silla monk of Tang Dynasty, was in India, he saw that Indians could not manufacture silkworms. But, soon after the sericulture industry was introduced into India and developed soon. Till 1220s, when a the Nuzhen man Wugu Sun Zhongduan visited Central and South Asia, he discovered that there was abundant silk production in India.

(2) The Spread of Papermaking

Papermaking has been one of the greatest contributions that Chinese people made to the world's civilization. China has been one of the world's ancient civilizations, but not the earliest civilized and modernized country of the world. Many peoples created excellent languages and scripts during their development process of civilization, among which some peoples used languages and scripts earlier than before China. Before the invention and spread of papermaking, the world's civilization centers respectively developed their own written carrier materials suited to their countries. Among these carrier materials, some were same as stone, pottery and others, some carrier materials were unique to regional civilizations. The original creation of the Central Plains people included bamboo slips, wood slips, oracle bones, silken like soft sheets and others; the original specific creation in the of region of the two rivers and Nile region included clay-tablets, leathers and others; the original creation of ancient India included bhurja, patra and others. According to historical literature, papermaking was invented by Cai Lun in the first year of Yuan Xing during the reign of Emperor Han He in the Eastern Han Dynasty.[18]

In fact, papermaking existed before the Eastern Han Dynasty. In 1957, ancient papers of the Western Han Dynasty were unearthed in Baqiao, Xi'an; in 1974, hemp papers of the Western Han Dynasty were unearthed in Juyan, Gansu; in 1978, ancient papers of the Western Han Dynasty were unearthed in Taibai village of Fufeng county, Shaanxi. These papers of the Western Han Dynasty which were discovered during the process of archaeological excavations, prove Cai Lun's invention. Besides bhurja and patra, Indians originally considered cotton fabrics, leathers, and metal plates as materials to write on. After the Western Han Dynasty opened the expedition routes to western regions, Han paper gradually introduced to western regions. Before the 7th century, Indians began to use papers and Yi Jing referred to this. And also in Sanskrit, there appeared several different "papers", one of which was called "shaya". Indian scholars have argued that "shaya" was the translation of Han "paper" into the Sanskrit language.[19] Although, the South China could create papers at least in Jin Dynasty, Linsi, Jiaozhi (Vietnam), Chenia located adjacent did not know how to make paper till the age of Song, Yuan, Ming Dynasty.

18　Notes on History of the Late Han Dynasty Era (Dong Guan Han Ji), The Legend of Cai.
19　See Ji Xianlin: Issues on Chinese Papers, Time and Place that Papermaking Entered into India, Articles on Cultural Relationship History of Paper between China and India, Ed, 1982, Sanlian Bookstore, pp. 11-39.

Meanwhile, Borneo, Jawa, Malacca did not use paper till the age of Zheng He. It be noted that Chinese paper was introduced into India through overland not sea-route.[20]

Still, it remains unclear when the papermaking was introduced into India. However, when Zhen He sailed to the West ocean in the 15th century, the follower Ma Huan saw local people using white papers made from bark in Bengal, which was smooth and creamy and similar to buckskin.[21] Generally, people would think papermaking was introduced to Abbasid (Dashi) by the captured craftsmen after Tang troops were defeated by the Abbasid (Dashi) troops in Talas in 751. This idea is still largely accepted by most scholars. However, this does not mean that people of Western regions had not Han paper before this battle. Researcher Stein discovered several Sogdian letters written in Chinese paper in Dunhuang, which were confirmed to be written between 312-313 AD. This gives us some new ideas. These documents were letters that Hu traders from inland China, had written to their relatives in the Central Asia. Probably, due to some reasons, these letters could not be delivered to their homes, but be left to Dunhuang. We can estimate that many traders of that time have carried letters of relatives and friends, to Dunhuang region, many letters from inland China were delivered to their destinations, by them. Thus, people of Central Asia not only heard of, but also saw and used Chinese paper in the early times. This kind of writing material that was light and soft, cheap, and easy to be massively produced, had caught the attention ofpeople in the Western regions, in the ancient times. This should be the historical background of papermaking's Westward spread.

After general Gao Xianzhi of the Tang dynasty was defeated in Talas (Taraz) in 751, many of the captured Tang soldiers were sent to Dashi. A Military officer, Du Huan was also captured in the battle of Talas, whose Stories on Journey (Jing Xing Ji) referred to some Chinese craftsmen of painting and weaving, no about papermaking. But according to the historical material of Arab, there were papermaking craftsmen among the captured Chinese soldiers, so that Dashi people employed Han craftsmen to make paper in Samarqand. Then, they spread the papermaking to the Central Asia, later to Damascus and Baghdad. The vast territory of Dashi Empire crossed over the Eurasian Continent, which provided the extremely favorable conditions for papermaking spreading to the distant West, rapidly. Before 1109, papermaking was introduced from Cairo to Sicilia, then to Italy. Besides, papermaking continued to spread Westwards to the Northern Africa, from Cairo through Mediterranean coast. Since then, "Samarqand paper" had become the formal name for Han paper. Still today, Chinese Xuan paper is called as the "Samarqand paper" in the Persian language. After the entering of Chinese papermaking, in Eastern and Southern Mediterranean coast, "Samarqand paper" coexisted with the local traditional

20 Ibid., pp. 44-50.
21 See Overseas Wonders That Was Narrated by Feng Chengjun, Commercial Press Beijing, p. 61.

papyrus paper and parchment paper for a certain period. Later, the papyrus paper was gradually replaced; parchment paper constantly withdrew from the historical stage. Until the early 20th Century, Egyptian papyrus paper had been lost. The currently available papyrus paper in the Western markets is manufactured by contemporary experts after examining the traditional papyrus paper-making in ancient times. In the 16th Century, the papermaking workshops had spread everywhere in the European continent.

Books are the carriers of human's scientific knowledge. Moreover, the invention of paper have enabledthat books get out of the house of nobles, enter the homes of common people. The rapid spread of Han Chinese papermaking across the world was the proof of its superiority. Later, the paper industry has laid the foundations for the emergence of printing technologies. Thus, Chinese papermaking has been one of the greatest inventions in the history of human civilization. Since the 14th century, development had accelerated in Europe, the Renaissance and Reformation thought trends appeared, and the society progressed rapidly. Actually, this was the basic element behind Europe's disseminating of Chinese papermaking.

(3) The Eastward Spread of Species Origination from Western Regions

(1) Crops

Medicago

Medicago is a kind of perennial leguminous caudex, and also a kind of green fodder which possesses extremely high nutrient qualities. When Zhang Qian was in the Western Regions, he found that the main forage for good horses in Dayuan was Medicago, and then he reported this to the Han court. The value of this discovery at that time was similar to current discoveries of new-type of autos without oil, which shocked the whole country. Good horses were the basic foundation for strengthening the armies, therefore, many Han ambassadors came back with Medicago seeds when travelled West. Emperor Wu of Han Dynasty even planted Medicago in his mansions. Thus, Medicago quickly spread. Yan Shigu[22] from the Tang dynasty period noted in the Han Shu[22], as follows: "There are Medicago in provinces in North route, the old Anding, northland. All are planted in Han Dynasty." For the good nitrogen fixation of Medicago, farmers quickly found that it could improve the fertility of soil. Thus, it became an important method to plant rotating crops and to enhance agricultural production, and has playes an important role in the prosperity of inland China's agriculture and animal husbandry.

22　Yan Shigu (581–645), formal name Yan Zhou a famous Chinese author and linguist of the Tang Dynasty. Han Shu, the Book of Han or History of the Former Han is a history of China finished in 111, covering the Western, or Former Han dynasty from the first emperor in 206 BCE to the fall of Wang Mang in 23 CE. It is also called the Book of Early Han Dynasty Period.

The Grape and the Wine Production

In China, there were always wild grapes, but the ancient Chinese people did not plant it. The grape was initially planted by ancient Egyptians. When Zhang Qian of Han paid a visit to Western Regions, he saw the popular grape wine in Dawan, and the preserved wine of rich people sometime was up to 10, 000 dan. The alcohol content of wine made by ancient China was not high, and could easily get sour and go bad, but the wine made by the Dawan people could be preserved for ten years, which astonished the Han ambassadors. And ambassadors also saw many grapes in Kangju, and they took with them the grapes into the Central Plains, after they went back and accepted by Emperor Wu of Han, Emperor Wu ordered to plant grapes into his other mansions. The Northwest territories of ancient China was connected with Dawan, Kangju and other regions, wherein the climate has been similar to theseregions. Therefore, grapes were first planted in these regions since the early times. The Volume 97 in Imperial Readings of the Taiping Era quoted sentences from Records of Later Liang said, "When Lyu Guang of Later Liang in the period of "the 16 Kingdoms" conquered Qiuci (current Kuqa, Xinjiang Kuqa), he found that lo-cal people loved to drink grape wine, the preserved wine of some rich families were even up to 1,000 hu. Sogdians played an important role in the aspect of spreading grape planting. Kang Yandian, the chieftain of Kang in Tang Dynasty period, established some migrant settlements in the south of current Lob Nor, one of which was called the 'grape city'."

Previously, Zhang Qian called the grape "putao". The ancient Iranians called the grape wine buda, while the Greeks called grape botrvs. The name "putao" that Zhang Qian heard in the Western Regions, possibly originates from Iranian or Greek language. It is still uncertain.

(2) Livestock and Lapis lazuli

Improvement of the Horse-Breeds

In the ancient times due to the regional neighbourhood and expedition routes, nomadic people living in the Central Plains have always kept contact with the main residents in Mongolian steppes. The military horses in the Central Plains were mainly the Mongolian horses. The Mongolian horse is one of the ancient world's famous good horse-breeds, which can endure hardships, and is easy to be raised, with bigger head and belly, shorter limbs, and short type. Although, the Mongolian horse has many advantageous features, it lacks endurance during long journey and has slower speed during short journeys. When Zhang Qian paid a visit to the West Regions, especially after Li Guangli overcame Dawan, the good horse-breeds of Fergana Valley began to be introduced into Han land, but there were a few good horse-breeds. Hybridizing good horses of Western Regions with native horses of Mongolia had improve its descendants' traits, therefore intro-ducing the hybrid horses of the Western Regions were extremely stressed by every Chinese ruler and excellent horses of Dawan and Wusun were constantly introduced into the Central Plains (China). Horse industry played an important role in Tuyuhun's economy. The most famous horses of Tuyuhun can be divided into two kinds, with "dragon type" and "Qinghai cong" included. According to History of Northern Dynasties: Legend of Tuyuhun, "dragon type" was a kind of horse that was freely raised in small islands within the Qinghai Lake.

"Qinghai cong" is the descendant of "Persian grass horse". The so-called "Persian grass horse" which is in fact the Dawan horse. By introducing Persian horses, Tuyuhun cultivated the new "Qinghai cong" to fit for the nature in Qinghai and Hexi. In 1969, archaeologists discovered one copper horse stepping on the flying swallow in a tomb of the Eastern Han Dynasty in Leitai, Wuwei, Gansu province, which was named as "Horse Stepping on Flying Swallow", and later became the emblem of China's tourism. This cultural relic is not only a rare art treasure, but also highly valuable in understanding the history of animal husbandry. According to domestic studies by animal husbandry experts, the most important trait of the copper horse found in Leitai, Wuwei, i.e, the "Horse Stepping on Flying Swallow", is its footwork of "amble". The horse-breeds in the south and north of Qilian Mountains and around Qinghai Lake, not its type, appearance, and body size are consistent with this copper horse, but also can walk "amble". The current researches show that, the descendants that foreign horse-breeds cross with the local horse can also walk "amble", which can prove horses in Qinghai and Hexi with strong heredity of "amble", and also confirms that this is an ancient horse-breed.

148   The breeding and cultivation of one kind of good horse-breed needs much time, thus, Tuyuhun people needed to breed the "Qinghai cong race" based on the experience of former Northern West people. The discovery of copper horse shows that, since Han Dynasty, nomads in the Northwest regions have constantly made local horses hybridized with Dawan horses of Central Asia. The biological prototype of Han copper horse should be one of the important segments during the cultivating process of "Qinghai cong reace". Specialists have argued that "Qinghai Cong race" probably had some blood relationships with current"Haomen horse race" which is bred in Qinghai. Currently, by examining the prototype of copper horse, China's animal husbandry specialists are searching and filtering the heretic traits of "Haomen horse", and planning to cultivate a new generation of "Qinghai Cong race".[23] In the 20th year of the reign of Emperor Taizong, the nomad Quriqan tribe, which dwelled in the north of current Altai Mountains, tributed 100 horses to the emperor, among which 10 were quite appreciated by him, and he named them as the "Ten Horses". Therefore, in the book the New History of the Tang Dynasty: Bing Zhi wrote: "Longyou had hybridized the Hu-breeds so that the horses could become stronger". The appearance of good horses in wall paintings, sculptures, carved stones, terra cottas of Tang should improve its breeds based on this.[24]

---

23   See Zhou Weizhou: The History of Tuyuhun, Ningxia People's Publishing House, 1984, pp.109-110.
24   See Zhang Zhongge: Historical Narrative of Livestock, in Zhang Zhongge, Zhu Xianhuang: Historical Materials for Chinese Livestock, ed 1986, Science Press, pp. 16-30.

Besides good horse-breeding, the sheep and horse breeding experience of nomads in the Northern regions also entered into the Central Plain region. After Jin Ri, son of the ruler Xiu Tu from the Xiongnu tribe federation[25] entered the Han dynasty territories, he mastered the horse breeding. Due to the healthiness and fatness of his sheep and horses, Jin Ri was repeatedly rewarded. When Emperor Han Wu was seriously ill, Jin Ri and Huo Gunag were granted and entrusted the citizenship.

Camel Husbandry

Camels live in arid deserts. According to the historian Sima Qian, before the Tangyao-Yushun times, the Northern nomadic people have raised many horses, cows and sheep, but they treated camels as exotic animals.[26] It can be seen that camels were a kind of rare livestock at that time. In the Shang and Zhou dynasties period, camels became one of the main livestock that neighboring peoples of the Northwest regions had exchanged with Central Plains people. According to Yi Zhou Shu, among the tributed objects by Dasha, Shache, Xiongnu, Loufan and Rouzhi, there were camels. In the period of Warring States, camels were raised in Yan and Dai, the border region of Central Plains and Northern Steppes. It was recorded in The Warring States Stratagems: Su Qin's Persuasion to Emperor Wei of Chu that, "Camels and good horses of Yan and Dai must fulfill provincial stables". It describes this kind of scene. In the early Han period, the Han government had turned its attention to domestic issues for a while, the hybrid livestock which were bred in cooperation between the Northern Han people and nomads developed fast. Along with the frequent communications between Xiongnu and Western Regions, camels became the important logistic transport animal for Han army and government. Han had inherited the Qin's system, which established the "Taipu" department in the central government. And raising camels was one of its main duties.[27]

Han government also established "six pastors" at the rim of Northwestern regions, and established 36 ranches to raise horses and camels during the reign of Emperor Jing. (History of Han: Record of Emperor Jing) Besides the Northwestern regions, people in the Central Plains gradually became similar to camels. In Discourses on Salt and Iron, it referred to "horse, donkey and camel respectively came into the land." There were more and more artistic images of camels. According to Temples and Monasteries in Luoyang, there were three copper camels in Luoyang, with 10-feet tall and long. Five or six miles away from the ancient Suiyang in the north direction, the tomb of Qiao Xuan, Han official was found. In front of the tomb, there were two stone camels. Meanwhile, many other camel sculptures were found in this region, for example, camel relief in the third level of stone sculptures in Xiaotang Mountain, the Southwest of Feicheng, Shandong; the image of two-humped camel in the upper level of the 16th stone, Xicheng, Shandong; the image of riding camel,

25   The Xiongnu were a nomad people living north and northwest of China during the Qin (221-206 BC) and Han (206 BCE-220 CE) periods.
26   See Records of the Historian Sima Qian: Biography of Huns.
27   History of Han: Records of Emperor Jing.

unearthed in Qizhou, Shandong and preserved in Tokyo museum now. On the lacquer ware unearthed in Hunan in 1976, there were camel images that were described by gold foil printing.

In the period of the Northern Wei dynasty, nomads have migrated to the Central Plains. The camel breeding and trade achieved unprecedented development. The government bred millions of camels in Hexi. (History of Wei: Monograph on Food and Currency) Camel was the main transport means of the East-West trade route. The huge camel stocks in the period of Northern Dynasties has laid a favorable foundation for Sui and Tang's activities in the Western Regions. Camels in three-colored art style are the true reflection for the important role of camel breeding industry.

Donkeys and Sheeps

Donkeys originated from the Northern Africa, about 7500 BC to 5000 BC, people there had begun to breed and train donkeys. About the 4th millennium before our era, domestic donkeys emerged in currentXinjiang. Donkeys feature all common characteristics of animals from tropical or subtropical regions. They can stand the cold not the hot; some can eat nothing for several days; they drink little, with strong ability to resist water escaping. So, they are suitable for laboring under the dry and hot climate conditions, and become the main livestock of Hexi in Western Regions. Till the late the Spring and Autumn Period, few donkeys and its bastard mule came into the Central Plains, and became the rare and exotic beats bred by the high-level people. According to the Lyu's Spring and Autumn Annals (Lyu Shi Chun Qiu), "Son of Zhao Jian has a white mule, and loves it too much". Till the early Han, Lu Jia still put the donkey with amber, coral, jade, pearl as treasure, which could prove its high value. The main reason that high-level people raised donkeys of the time was to entertain. In the Eastern Han Dynasty, families of some officials favored the sound of donkeys, and often learned its sound to entertain; while Emperor Lingdi of the Han Dynasty rode four donkeys and allowed them to wander free in the palace gardens for entertainment. The Han Dynasty opened the expedition roads to Western Regions, which caused massive donkey population entering the Central Plains. When Zu Ti waged the Northern expedition, he achieved more than one thousand donkeys for transporting food. From here, we can see that donkeys were popular in the Central Plains of the time, and later donkeys have become one of our nation's main livestock.[28] Sheep originated from the wild pan which lived sheep the in Eurasian Steppes. The wild sheep was bred in Western Asia and Central Asia, and was introduced into Chinese mainland through the Silk Road. The large-tailed Han sheep which was widespread in Huaihai Plain was originated from fat-tailed sheep in the eastern Mediterranean coast.[29]

28 See Yang Zai: Historical Narrative of Raising Donkeys in China, in the Journal of Yuxi Agriculture Science, 1982/2; also See Book by Zhang Zhongge, Zhu Xianhuang: Historical Materials for China's Livestock Breeding, Social Science Press, 1986, pp. 123-125.
29 See Shan Naiquan: Ancient Studies on the Han Sheep, in Zhang Zhongge, Zhu Xianhuang: Historical Materials for Chinese Livestock, Science Press, 1986, pp 160-167.

Lapis Lazuli

Lapis Lazuli was called Lajurd by the Persians, while people of Western Regions have called it as Lapis Lazuli. It was produced in Faizabad, the East of Afghanistan, whose main chemical components are siliceous, alumina, sodium and so on, its hardness is 5 to 5.5. Lapis Lazuli generates within limestone with crystal and lump styles. It was considered as a jewel in ancient times because of its beautiful color, cyan and translucent. Since the 3rd millennium BC, Lapis Lazuli was traded to Iran, Western Asia, Egypt and India. Lapis Lazuli was introduced into China mainland at least in the 2nd century. In 1969, the tomb of Liu Gong, Emperor Jing of Eastern Han Dynasty was discovered in Xuzhou, in which an animal-shaped gold-plated bronze ink stone box was unearthed, with particles of Lapis Lazuli. This was the earliest object that was found until now. After the Eastern Dynasty period, with the spread of Lapis Lazuli across China, it was enjoyed greatly by the noble and the rich, therefore it was often discovered in numerous archaeological excavations.

In 1975, one golden ring inlaid with Lapis Lazuli was discovered in the tomb of Li Xizong of Eastern Wei in Zanhuang, Hebei province. This Lapis Lazuli, was carved with reindeer stripes, parts of curb were carved with combined pearl motifs. The golden ringprobably belonged to Cuishi, wife of Li Xizong from Northern Qi dynasty (550-577 AD). There also square golden accessories inlaid with two pieces of Lapis Lazuli discovered in the golden necklace that was unearthed in the tomb of Li Jingxun (608) from the Sui Dyansty in suburb of Xi'an. The above Lapis Lazuli unearthed in the tombs of Cuishi and Li Jingxun was both made in Central Asia, which were probably brought to the Central Plains by the Sogdian traders. From the Northern Dynasties to the early Sui, Lapis Lazuli was grounded into powder, and then used it as paint of wall paintings. The paint with blue mineral on Dunhuang 285 cells, Xinjiang Kizil Grottoes was confirmed to be the powder of Lapis Lazuli. Lapis Lazuli was introduced into Japan from China in the Tang Dynasty. The square and semicircle plaques in "gan yu dai" preserved in the central Shosoin were all Lapis Lazuli. Both the ruyi in the South Shosoin and the sunflower mirror in the North Shosoin had particles of Lapis Lazuli.[30] After the blue-and-white Ming porcelain was exported to different countries, people from the Central Asia and Persia called this kind of china porcelain as "Kasa-i lajurdi", which meant Lapis Lazuli bowls; they called blue-and-white porcelain as "Kuza-i lajurdi", which was extremely important. Ambassadors from Western Regions often asked the Ming government to reward this kind of "Kasa-i lajurdi" and "Kuza-i lajurdi", namely the blue-and-white porcelain.[31]

151

---

30 See Su Zhe: Lapis Lazuli, the Ancient Cultural Exchanges between East and West, see also the People's Daily (overseas edition, 30.3. 1993), in China Cultural Heritage News column, Vol. 344.
31 See Minobu Honda: On the Hui-Hui-Kuan I-Yu (Chinese Persian Vocabulary), Documents of the Literature Department of Hokkaido University, Vol. 11, 1963, pp. 149-157, 1, 13, 17, 26.

(4) The Bianwen (Pianwen) Art: Lyrics and Narratives

Many collections of writings found in Dunhuang Grottoes (Caves) are related to literature, and most of which include lyrics and narrative works similar to later Tanci (a script for a lyrics). Some included proses that could be narrated without singing, some of them included verses that could be either narrated or be sang as a song. The written materials of these lyrics and narrative works are mainly rooted from Buddhist scriptures, while some are from folk legends and historical tales. In the previous researches, these lyrics and narrative works found in Dunhuang were evaluated as Buddhist melodies, for example, Luo Zhenyu made such an evaluation in the book "Dunhuang Lingshi", which was printed in 1924. Names of some Bianwen(s) as Mu Lian Bian, Ba Xiang Bian, were preserved in their original scrolls, thus, this kind of works were considered as "Bianwen" type of literature.

Bianwen, was a kind of literary genre which was popular during the Tang dynasty period (618-907). It is a type of literature that was influenced by the Buddhist changdao (lit. "guidance [to enlightenment] by [publicly performed] singing") which inherited and advanced the literary tradition of the songs of the Music Bureau (yuefu shi) they were vernacular and prosimetric narratives and tales of strange events and rhapsodies that were very popular during the Han (208 BCE-220 CE), Wei (220-265) and Southern Dynasties (420-589) periods.

152

According to the monk Huijiao (497-554), Buddhist missionaries urgently needed a kind of vernacular literature that could be understood by everyone. Such lyrics and verses would help to entertain the audience and easily help to express even those complicated matters. The genre of Bianwen literature includes Buddhist stories as well as tales which includes anecdotes from the Chinese history. Pienwen exerted considerable influence on subsequent Chinese literature.... The reasons for this influence lie first and foremost in its fundamentally new form.... [There are] certain other peculiarities which stipulate the influence of Pienwen .... All subsequent genres of Chinese literature in which, to one degree or another, these features are found (the drama, the short story, the early novel, and the sung-narrative genres) show either direct or indirect links to Pienwen.

The meaning of the word "Bianwen" is approximately the same as that of yanyi "演義" (literally: "extended meaning/morale [of an episode]"), a term often used for historical novels. This means that a historical event is narrated in a new form that will sound more attractive than in the historical records. Thus, "Bian" either means that a historical content is "transformed" into a popular form (hence the common translation used is "Transformation Texts"), or that a plot is created within an ordinary historical narration. Bianwen is a literature genre that was long forgotten and only came into attention with the discovery of manuscript novellas found in the famous Dunhuang Grottoes (Caves). Since then, according to Yue Fu Za Lu and Lu Shi Za Shuo by Duan Anjie, and in the

Travel Notes in Tang Dynasty for Learning Buddhism written by Yuan Ren, scholars knew that there was one kind of folk talk which was popular in monasteries in the Tang dynasty period. There were words such words "Ceremony of Folk Talk" written in a document which is currently reserved in Paris Museum (Code nr. 3894) So we can say that the so-called "Bianwen" was the scripts about "folk talk". What was "Bianwen" on earth? In the academic circles, there have been many opinions which have tried to answer this question. As V. Henry Mair, an American scholar once said: "When I first saw a Bianwen, I surprisingly found that Bianwen was extremely important, but there existed deep disagreement on several aspects of Bianwen Wen." Regarding the number of the existing Bianwen texts, and about the relations among Bianwenand other literature genres, meanings of Bianwen itself, and others, scholars hold different opinions.[32]

The word "Bian" of Bianwen means transformation, which has no deep meanings.[33] Zhou Shaoniang is an expert who works on History of Chinese Literature in the Literature Research Institute attached to the Chinese Academy of Social Sciences. The word "Bian" means adaptation, and the word "Bianwen" means an adapted work. According to historical records, in those days an adaptation from one genre to another genre, such as adapting religious Buddhist storytelling scriptures to secular Bianwen narratives and secular lyrics works, or adapting a narrative work to a lyrics work, were all called as Bianwen. There were different genres of Bianwen, some were sang with a tune; some were as long poems.

153

According to "Travel Notes" of Yuan Ren who lived in the Tang Dynasty period, he wrote about Learning Buddhism, he had explained: "in the first half of the 9th century, there existed some prominent masters of sujiang (folk talks). They were Hai Yan, Ti Xu, Qi Gao and Guang Ying from the left street, and Wen Xu and other two masters from the right street. Among them, Wen Xu was especially prominent, who was claimed as the first influential person of Jing. These people were called masters of sujiang (folk talks)." However, today we do not have their scripts in our hand. Among the existing works, only the Bianwen as follows was preserved which was written by Bao Xuan: "Pin Po Suo Luo Wang Hou Gong Cai Nu Gong De Yi Gong Yang Ta Sheng Tian Yin Yuan Bian" And the, the author's name—Bao Xuan—was written at the end of the script.

Besides, in the end of two Bianwen (s) there is one passage for dedication, which was the self-introduction of the author. The first one: Po Mo is preserved in Paris (Code: Bozi 2187), the second one: Ba Xiang is presereved in Beijing (Code: Fangzi 24). There are two others which were preserved in Paris

---

32   See article by Victor H. Mair, "My Study on Bianwen Texts Found in Dunhuang", in the Journal of Chinese Literature and History, Issue,1988/8.

33   See V. H. Mair, in his academic works called Bianwen as "Transformation Texts" and See Zhou Shaoniang, "On Folk Literature of Tang Dynasty after Reading Bianwen Texts" published, in the Journal of New Cultural Construction, 1963/1.

Museum: The first one: Chang Xing Si Nian Zhong Xing Dian Ying Sheng Jie Jiang Jing (Code: Wen of Bozi 3908), the second one: Fu Mu En Zhong Jiang Jing (Code: Wen of Bozi 2418). They were also written by masters of Sujiang (folk talk), however, except Bao Xuan, we don't have the names of these masters.[34] The scripts of Bianwen (s) from the Tang dynasty period were not limited to monasteries, but also popular among the secular people in the society, and were greatly enjoyed by people of the time. The Bianwen called "Xiang Mo" which,s preserved in Paris Museum (Code nr. 4524), tells about "Raudraksa's magical battle against Sariputra" (a religious Sutra otiginally). In this story, in Sariputra subjugates the six representatives of other religions.

On the back of this scroll, there are pictures which described the story of "Raudraksa's magical battle against Sariputra". And thispictures corresponded to Bianwen, which described the story. Besides Bianwen, there was the "Bianxiang(s)"[35] which referred to the transformation of a story a pictorial representation, namely Hua, found in Luoyang Longmen Grotten (stone cave). There is the "Niepan Bian" which was made during the reign of Empress Wu of Tang dynasty, which is the earliest among the known "Bianxiang(s) from the time of Tang dynasty". Therefore, it can be said that, till the end of the 7th century, Bianwen was quite popular. In the early half of the 9th century, there was eminent master of "Sujiang" named Wen Xu. Although, he attacked high officers and Kings of dynasties and was sent to exile for 20 years for such behaviour, his reputation remained intact and he was not forgotten.. No matter kings, or common people, he could affect and fascinate people from all walks, his power and influence was unprecedented. According to writings of Wen Xu and after studying his (Sujiang) folk talk, we can say that this folk talk was too superficial, it was not complex, refined, consequently, they were not appreciated by the educated people. Due to their superficial nature, it was popular among the common people, whose listeners built monasteries, and believed in it, called monks. And music groups transformed their verses s to lyrics. Thus, the "folk talk" became a kind of new literary genre that was well received by the people. This folk talk has played a pioneering role in the gradual formation of talkers, scripts and folk literature since after the Song dynasty.

Sujiang (folk talk) literature has opened a broad avenue. The contents of them were adapted from tales and lyrics which were included in Buddhist scriptures, folk legends, and also history stories. Certainly, Buddhist stories aimed to promote Buddhism. For example, the scroll 1 of Tai Zi Cheng Dao Jing and Ba Xiang Bian, whose stories were adapted from Fo Ben Xing Ji Jing. Another example is the Xiang Mo Bianwen and Zhi Yuan Yin You Ji, whose stories were in the scroll 10 titled as Xian Yu Jing (The Sutra on the Wise and Foolish). Their vivid form of narrating and lyrics, made them unforgettable among the

---

34   See http://sino-platonic.org/complete/spp012_tang_transformation_texts.pdf.
35   Bianxiang refers to the transformation of a Buddhist sutra into a pictorial representation. That bianwen is extricably linked to bianxiang is not disputed, but the precise nature of the relationship remains undetermined.

people. For example, Xiang Mo Bian, was one of them which included a narrative and lyrics, telling about the story of "Sariputra subjugating the six representatives of other religions". Another example is the Wei Mo Bian, which included a narrative and lyrics, telling about the story of "Manjushri inquiring about the illness of a rich lay man named Vimalakirti"[36] And this Wei Mo Bian was extremely complex and interesting, and the meaning of religion was almost intertwined with humanity.

(5) The Frontier Regions Poetry

The Tang Dynasty has been the peak of poetry creation in the Chinese history. There are many styles of Chinese ancient poetry. For example, pastoral poetry, love poetry, praise poetry, and frontier poetry. Frontier poetry has a long history, and becomes an important component of Chinese ancient poetry. Different from other poetry styles, frontier poetry expresses the political life of the individuals, the political relations and actions of the countries and political groups. In addition, frontier poetry has an obvious frontier region characteristic as it takes frontier as the main object. Xu Zong writes in The History of Tang Poems: Frontier Poetry is the outcome of the culture of a special region. As a result, from the perspective of reflecting lives, frontier poetry is an irreplaceable poetry style. On the other hand, frontier poetry has rich national culture elements. It shows how nomad people's culture conflicts and mixes with farming culture while expressing the civilization process of different nationalities and different times. Hence, frontier poetry bears strong national feelings, foreign customs, and grand aesthetical pictures. These illustrate that frontier poetry is a unique poetry style and hence occupies important position in Chinese ancient poems and has a significant value.

155

The Tang dynasty in its early periods was strong and powerful, and the empire expanded its influence outwards forcefully with military means. Thus, the Central Plains and the border regions had maintained unprecedentedly close relations with each other. In regard to poetry creation, frontier-style poetries

---

36   The original story was as follows: Manjushri, with this throng of bodhisattvas, major disciples, and heavenly beings reverently surrounding and accompanying him, proceeded to enter the city of Vaishali. At that time the rich man Vimalakirti thought to himself, "Now Manjushri is coming with that great assembly!" At once he employed his supernatural powers to empty the room, clearing it of all its contents and his attendants, leaving only a single bed on which he lay in sickness. When Manjushri entered the house, he saw that the room was bare of contents, with just one bed, Vimalakirti lying alone on it. Vimalakirti said, "Welcome, Manjushri! You come without the marks of coming, you see me without the marks of seeing me."Manjushri said, "Just so, layman. What has already come can hardly be coming. And what has already departed can hardly be departing. What do I mean? What comes has nowhere it comes from, what departs has nowhere it goes, and what is seen cannot be further seen. l But let us put that aside for the moment. "Layman, this illness of yours-can you endure it? Is the treatment perhaps not making it worse rather than better? The World-Honored One countless times has made solicitous inquiries concerning you. Layman, what is the cause of this illness? Has it been with you long? And how can it be cured?" See Xiang Da: Preface of Dunhuang Bianwen Collections, Dunhuang Bianwen Collections, People's Literature Publishing House, 1957.

spawn, which eulogized patriotism of people, the giant frontier scenes and the pain of frontier soldiers. Wang Changling, in his Army Life (Cong Jun Xing), used beautiful lines, "The dessert was with strong wind and dust that makes sky seems gloom, swiftly depart after accepting war communiqué. The vanguard soldiers have launched fierce battles in the Northern bank of Tao River at last night, however, quickly received the victory to defeat Tuyuhun". Also, Cen Shen, in his Waiting Feng Dafu in Beiting, described the scenes of Tang army officers accepting and applauding the surrender ceremonies of local tribes in the North of Tianshan, with his brilliant sentences as follows: "Medicago is beautiful in the border regions, and the battling horses are very fat in Luntai. Feng Dafu fought against Hu people, and continued his Western expedition. Before warring, the enemy troops surrendered left arms and went back to their homes. With continuous camel troops and yurt tents in the region of Yinshan, the beacon-fire disappeared since then, and even with rare alarming documents in region of Jianshui."

Wang Wei, in his Seeing off Judge Ping Zhanran, he just employed two poem verses to reflect the strength of the early Tang empire. Cen Shen was the prominent frontier poet, whose poem Seeing off Judge Liu Dan to Anxi in Wuwei vividly reflected the spectacular conditions after Tang official entered into Western Regions, with sentences as "Duhu started expedition, just dispatching military uniforms in May. Thousands of soldiers continued on their expedition, armors and swords sparkled! Army flags fluttered over Kunlun, sounds of war drums shook Puchang. The Venus led the army, power of the king lighted the wild. The mist of army troops was like snake looking from the West, imaging that must be changed or defeated. The soldiers chased good horses of Dawan and the army officers captured the King of Loulan." Many educated men have eulogized the spirit of frontier soldiers in their poetries and promoted the patrioric literature. Cen Shen was one of them, who wrote the following poem: "Blaring horned within Luntai at night, and the maoxing was falling in the north of Luntai. The army letter was sent off Quli, Chanyu had invaded from the West Jinshan......The war drums were like waves, three troops produced a great resonance with Yinshan. The gloomily murderous look of enemy camp rose into the sky, bones in battle fields were weaved with grass roots. Cold wind with broad snow in Jianhe, cold stone with horseshoes frozenly tore......There were many eminent people remembered by descendants, now officer surpassed over ancient people."

This vast border regions were defended by millions of troops. After a war victory, the army officers received awards from the imperial court, while the ordinary soldiers who have lost their lives in the war, would be forgotten by the people. As it was described in Chang Jian's Sai Xia Qu (Under a Border-fortress), "seeing the home place on Zhao Jun Ci, backbones of soldiers spread over the city wall". Many poets have evaluated Kings' ambitions to expand frontiers, while the ordinary soldiers left their homes and made great sacrifices. Li Bai wrote in Guan Shan Yue (Moon over Guanshan Mountains), "Kings like to conquer battlefields, while few soldiers come back from battles; people on frontiers see the scenes and miss their hometowns." Cen Shen, a frontier poet, described this kind of "sadness of conquers" in his many poetries. In his Sending Judge of Liu Dan to Anxi in Wuwei, he wrote "The night is quiet, the ghosts cry on streets. There are many backbones on the floor, they are all ancient battlefields". In Sending Yan Zhenqing to Helong by Hujia, he wrote "Jun feels sad to not hear Hujia, Hu people plays the Hujia……"

The frequent frontier activities made people to have chance to visit and see different aspect of inner land regions. When people read poetry verses of Guan Shan Yue by Li Bai, they could feel the grandness of the Northwest. However, Cen Shen's poetry is different from Li Bai, his Westward Conquer similarly takes us into the endless desert. In the verses of Cong Jun Xing by Wang Changling, it similarly takes the readers into the fall of the far Suyab. Sometimes, a kind of sad atmosphere was reflected in this frontier poetry. For example, the Seeing off Judge of Liu Dan to Anxi in Wuwei by Cen Shen we can see this sad feeling. Letters of men in frontier were deeply sad when they saw other soldiers which were called back to inland regions. In Seeing off Wu Judge back to Jing with White Snow Song, Cen Shen described the earlier snow which reflected the sad feeling of seeing off friends in his first three verses. Many frontier poets have reflected the grand occasions of cultural exchanges between Inland China and the frontier regions. In the poet "Listening to Yue from An Wanshan" authored by Li Xin, he wrote: "Using Nanshan Jiezhu to make Zhujia, this music is from Qiuci. The music became magical after it spread into Han people, Hu people of Liangzhou play it to me." There were poetry verses in the "Farewell to Du Gu" authored by Chen Shen, "Huamen Jiangjun is good at Huge, while the Yehe King masters Han language." Huamen refers to "Uyghur Khaganate", the "Huamen Jiangjun is good at Huge" refers that Huamen Jiangjun from the Uyghur Khaganate is good at singing folk songs; Yehe refers to the Suyab kingdom whose ruler knew the Han Chinese language. Only these two poetry verses, can perfectly reflect the scene of Han and Fan cultural exchanges.

(6) Merger of the Central Plains Culture and the Steppes Culture

Turkic people and many Tiele (Chile) tribes spoke Turkic language. With the closer communications between Turkic peoples and the Central Plains, Turkic peoples were greatly influenced by the Han culture. Many Han words were adopted into Turkic language and entered the daily language of the Turkic— Uyghur people. The German scholar, Annemarie von Gabain, in her book Grammar of Ancient Turkic, listed all her collected Chinese-borrowings in ancient Turki, as bir (bi), ciq (chi), xua (hua), la (luo), long (long), mir (mi), sangun (jiang jun), tan—si (tian zi), tutuq (du du).[37]

What impressed scholars most in the above Chinese words that was adopted into the Turkic language was the names of offices and ranks. Since the ancient times, Turkic people had dwelled in the Northern desert regions, thus

---

37   See Xue Zongzheng: History of Turkic Peoples, China Social Sciences Press, 1992, p. 719.

they had formed their own system of office/ranks names. For example, the supreme chieftain was called the qaghan, namely khan, which was inherited from the Tuoba people, founder of Northern Wei Dynasties. The tribal chieftain of Turkic people was called the irkin, translated as "yi jin", which was also from Tuoba people; disciple of the khan was called "tegin", transliterated as "te qin", which was typically misspelled as "te le" in the ancient Han records; the great official of Turkic people was called the Yapqu, transliterated as "ye hu", which was also used by Rouzhi people, Wusun people, and Xiongnu people in the ages before the Jesus was born. The officers of other tribes were called called the shad, translated as "she" or "sha" or "cha", etc.; the noble men was called beg, transliterated as "fu", which probably came from ancient Indo-European language "bege", or from "bo" of archaic Chinese; the leader was called buiruq, transliterated as "mei lu"; leader of one tribe was called chur, transliterated as "chuo"; supervisory officer was called tudun, transliterated as "tu tun"; hero was called isbara, which was transliterated as "shi bo luo" or "sha bo lue"; the old was called "qari", transliterated as "ge li", thus there was "ge li da guan".[38]

After assimilating the the Han Chinese culture, some new official ranks appeared among the Northern minority peoples. According to New History of the Tang Dynasty: in the Kirgiz Turkic administration, there were 3 dudu, 10 chigshi among Kirgiz's officers, all were officers of military; there were 15 changshi, and unlimited jiangjun. These officers are all from Chinese. Chigshi was transliterated as from chishi in ancient Turkic inscription, which should be the cishi. When officer in Tang recorded officers of Kirgiz, without judgment, he arbitrarily chose Chinese-transliterating words, thus translated cishi into chigshi.

In the end of 19th century, Finnish scholars discovered many Turkic inscriptions of Tang relics in the North of Mongolia and upper basin of Yenisei River, some were distributed over regions of Kirgiz. Many of these inscriptions referred to titles and ranks of officers, besides among those referred by Annemarie von Gabain, were the "chigshi", "changshi", "qunchu", etc. These documents greatly prove the realistic nature of the records in the existing literature. Later, "changshi" rank was accepted by other minorities speaking Turki language, and had been used for several centuries, and was introduced into Khitan, Mongolia and other minorities. The title of "tian zi" in the Central Plains was also brought into Central Asia by Hu traders. Within the remnant papers of Sogdian language, scholars found that Sogdians called their ruler as "bagfur" which means "tian zi". Sogdian traders not only made trading exchanges with the Central Plains, but also traded in the other parts of the Western Regions. They brought the word "bagfur" to the minority peoples who spoke the Persian language. Contemporary scholars have discovered this word "bagfur" in the Parthian language, too.

---

38   See Han Rulin: Researches on the titles of Turkic officers, in: Collected Works of Han Rulin, Jiangsu Classics Publishing House, pp. 503-524.

The civilization and culture of the Central Plains were widely influenced by the Turkic civilization. The Northern nomads lived on livestock, thus they knew less about seasons change than agricultural peoples. Before interacting with the Han civilization and culture, their system was simple and they had little understanding about the numbering years. According to the Zhou Book: The Legend of Turk (Tujue), "Turkic people did not know the year, they only could mark time by grass". The tradition of Han people considered 60 years as one cycle. Alongside with the developing exchanges between Turkic people and Central Plains people, this method of numbering years was also introduced into the Northern dessert regions. Roughly, there were 12 phases in the motion of the moon and 12 months, so that it was easy to remember. Thus, Turkic people initially accepted the Earthy Branches of 12, and 12 years as one cycle. In the 4th year of the Kaihuang reign of the Sui Dynasty (AD 584), Shabolue Khan, of the Turkic Khanate sent ambassadors with books to Sui Dynasty, and in them there was a note as "September 14th...... to Sui Emperor"[39].

This was the first time to refer Earthy Branches of 12 to record a year's number in historical materials. Turkic people had constantly learned from Central Plains people. In the Sui Book: by Gao Zu the event about Turkic scholars learning the numbering of the years, was recorded, the event had occurred in the 6th year of the Kaihuang reign, Sui Dynasty, (AD 586) Although, Turkic people accepted the Earthy Branches to number and mark the years, they were initially not used to using terms of Han Earthy Branches of 12, while they were accustomed to use the Chinese zodiac which was easy to remember and which enabled vivid description. The Mongolian Wong Jin Inscription, was the earliest existing cultural relic about how the Turkic people used the Chinese zodiac to number the years, whose Turkic inscription said that the owner had died in the "dragon year", namely AD 692. This kind of methodology to number years was often seen on various ancient Turkic inscriptions, such as the famous Kultigin Inscriptions, Bilge Khan Inscription of post-Turkic, Bilge Khan Inscription of Uyghur, etc. It was also recorded in the "Kirgiz" entry of Volume 199 of Geographical Records of the Taiping reign, and the New History of the Tang Dynasty, as follows: "Kirgiz people used zodiac to number the years. Besides, the Uyghur people also used it in the period of the Uyghur Khanate. Later, Mongolians also employed this kind of method to count the years."

When communicating with the Han nationality, minorities that spoke the Turkic language discovered that using zodiac to number years was much easier to remember, and also easy to repeat, while Han nationality's Heavenly Stems and Earthy Branches was quite complex, but with low repeat rate. Therefore, Heavenly Stems and Earthy Branches was superior to the zodiac method. Through long-term observation and consideration, they found that Heavenly Stems and Earthy Branches were actually ranking of least common multiple. The least common multiple of Heavenly Stems of 10 and Earthy Branches of 12 was 60, which was the reason that Heavenly Stems and Earthy Branches

---

39   See The Book of Sui: Turkic Khanate.

did not repeat within 60 years. However, Heavenly Stems of 10 and Earthy Branches of 12 were even, thus when Heavenly Stems of 10 reduced it by half to correspond with Earthy Branches, it would not repeat within 60 years. This was because the least common multiple of 12 and 5 was also 60. After they learned about this secret, they found that Jiazi of Han was not so complicated, thus they simplified Heavenly Stems of 10 to 5, respectively represented by metal, water, wood, fire and earth. Scholars discovered this kind of way in literatures after the Westward migration of Uyghurs, as fire sheep year, earth rabbit year, etc. And this kind of calendar way was later claimed as "Turkic calendar" by Islam historians.

(7) Visional Origin of the Yellow River

Ancient Chinese always thought that they lived in the center of the world, thus they called where they lived as "China". Ancient Chinese emperors called their country as "tian xia", namely the so-called "all regions belong to emperors". The Qin's Central Plains people's activity range was limited, and knew little about the world. But with the entrance of Buddhism, the vision that Chinese civilization swept the world was broken; the idea that China was the center of the world was shocked. Indians called where people lived as "shan bu zho"u, also "shan fu zhou" or "yan fu ti zhou", all these were all transliterations of "Jambudvipa". Indians thought that there was Jambu in the center. With the spread of Buddhism, the geographical knowledge of Indians had developed greatly. They started to learn about the many regions of the Asian continent, and thought that there were four big countries of the world (Jambudvipa) and were respectively led by four masters. This kind of geographical opinion was also introduced into China with the Eastern spread of Buddhism. Kalodaka, an Indian of sutra translator of Eastern Jin, translated Buddha's Twelve Sutras and said, "There were four "tian zi" in "Jambudvip"a: "Jin tian zi" in the East, with many people included; "Indian tian zi" in the South, with many elephants on the earth; "Qin tian zi" in the West, with much treasure on the earth; "Rouzhi tian zi" in the Northwest, with many good horses on the earth."[40]

In the eyes of monks which accepted Buddhism, Chinese emperor was no longer the supreme and exclusive "Tian Zi", there were at least other three other emperors: "Qin tian zi" in the West, "Rouzhi tian zi" in the Northwest, "Indian tian zi" in the South. Chinese emperor was the monarch who only ruled the East. During the Eastern Jin and Tang Dynasty periods, throughout about 300 years, the content of "four masters" ruling "tian xia" in Buddhist ideas had encountered some changes. Dao Xuan's Record of Shakya has argued that the first master of Jambudvipa was the master of elephants, i.e, the king of India; the second master was treasure's master, the king of Hu. The fourth master was master of men, the king of China. Only the third master was changed to the master of the horses, the king of the Turkic Khanate, the so-called the rulers

---

40   See Taisho Shinshu Daizokyo, Volume IV, No.195, p. 147. About this issue the readers can refer to Bo Xi and Legend about Four Tian Zi, translated by Feng Yongjun, among the Translations of Studies on Nanhai Sea in the Western Regions, 3rd, pp. 83-103.

of the "The North of snowy mountains to the Northern sea, with cold earth, a region good for horses.[41]

Indians put Jambudvipa, namely the center where human lived, on the snowy mountains—the Pamir mountains. They thought that the snowy mountains, namely the Pamir mountains, were the watersheds of the river system in the whole Asian continent. They thought that there was the so-called Anavatapta. Rivers originating from this watershed became the eminent rivers in the world. In opinion of Indians, there were 4rivers in the world, namely the Ganges River, it discharged into the East Sea (current Bengal Bay); Indus River, it discharged into the South Sea (current Arabian Sea); Oxus River (Amu-Daria), it discharged into the West Sea (current Caspian Sea), while Amu-Daria currently discharges into Aral Sea, but had discharged into the Caspian Sea many times in the history; the last was Sita River (Syr Darya River), which discharged into the North Sea (current Aral Sea). Among the Han literature from the Tang dynasty, records about above "four rivers" have encountered interesting and thought provoking changes, especially the records about the Sita River. When Travel Notes in Tang Dynasty for Learning Buddhism described the above "four rivers", it not only rotated the flow direction of rivers Eastward 45 degrees, but also referred Sita River as current Tarim River and became the origin of Yellow River, etc. Thus, it contacted the Sita River with Tarim River, further contacting with the Yellow River. Therefore, these two rivers: Sita River and Yellow River, without any relations, even with difference of 90 degrees of flow direction and with distance of 1,000 miles, were seen as the upper stream and lower stream. Datang Daci'ensi Sanzang Fashi Zhuan (Biography of the Tripitaka[42]-master of the Great Ci'en Monastery) also repeated some records in Travel Notes in Tang Dynasty for Learning Buddhism, which said: after the water of Dalong chi joined with the Sita River, "it entered Yangtze Eastward, flew down the earth, and outflew the stone mountain. Thus, it was the origin place of country's rivers."[43]

161

The reason why Xuan Zang considered the Sita River as the Tarim River, further thought it as the origin of Yellow River, was his two world outlooks in his mind. Xuan Zang was from the Central Plains, and grew up in currentYanshi of Henan, thus he was deeply influenced by the saying that Yellow River was originated from Kunlun. And he was also a Buddhist, and he traveled to Western world to seek the truth, thus he believed that four rivers separately had discharged into the same sea. This was the mixed result of different geographical arguments raised by China and India. After Tang Dynasty, few people had called the Tarim River as the Sita River.

41 The regions ruled by the master of horses. The blood sweating horse was Turkic. See Records of Shakya, revised edition, Zhonghua Book Company, pp. 11-12.
42 Taishō Tripitaka is a definitive edition of the Chinese Buddhist canon and its Japanese commentaries used by scholars in the 20th century. It was edited by Takakusu Junjiro and others.
43 See the Legend of Ci'ensi Monastery, collated edition of Zhonghua Book Company, pp. 117-118.

4. Travelers from the Orient

(1) Fa Xian's Westward Journey

Fa Xian was one of the eminent monks who traveled to West to search for the dharma in ancient times, but also was one of the least so-called world's famous travelers. Fa Xian was born in the Sixteen States Period. He was sur-named as Gong, and became a monk when he was three years old. During the process of learning dharma, he deeply felt the lack of Vinaya books, thus he could not meet his appetite for knowledge. Then, he gathered with and monk Hui Jing, Dao Zheng and other monks to go to India for the dharma.

Fa Xian and other monks left for Chang'an in the 2nd year of Hongshi (400). Started off from Chang'an, they climbed the Long Mountains to enter the Western Qin that was established and led by Qifu Qiangui, the chieftain of Xianbei, and remained there during the summer. In autumn, they marched through the East of Qinghai, and climbed the Yanglou Mountain (Qilian Mountains) to Zhangye of Hexi Corridor, which was controlled by Southern Liang State established by Tufa of Xianbei tribe. When they were in Zhangye, Juqu Mengxun of Xiongnu rebelled to kill Duan Ye, the Taizong of Zhangye. Then, Juqu Mengxun acclaimed himself as Zhangye Gong. Temporarily, Zhangye was in disorder, and the Westward expedition route was blocked. Under the retention of Juqu Mengxun, Fa Xian temporarily stayed in Zhangye, and spent a summer there. Meanwhile, he persuaded a lot of monks who con-tributed to studying dharma, and gathered strength to go to West.

In the fall of the same year, Fa Xian traveled Westwards to Dunhuang. From Dunhuang, he marched through the Yangguan Pass, Bailongdui Desert, where-in no birds or no animals could survive. Fa Xian could find any clues to find the dharma, what he only considers as the clue was the bone of dead people. Fa Xian crossed the Lop Nur region, walking for 17 days, and arrived in Shanshan (current Ruoqiang of Xinjiang). Although, this country was too small, all coun-try believed in Buddhism that there were over 4,000 monks who believed in Hinayana. In the period of Fa Xian's Westward era, not only Central Plains, but also Hexi were in disorder, meanwhile the situation of the Western Regions was unstable. Initially, Fa Xian could directly go to Yutian from Shanshan. Given for the security, he had to take the long process than the short process, going along the Che erchen River and Peacock River Basin, crossing over the Western bank of Lop Nur. Fa Xian started off from Yanqi, firstly going along the South of Tianshan Mountains, then crossing over the Tarim River and Taklamakan, finally arrived in Yutian. Totally, it took them one month and five days. According to Fa Xian, Yutian believed in Mahayana and had thousands of believers. Only in monastery where Fa Xian lived, there were 3,000 monks. At that time, there were 14 big monasteries in Yutian, and numerous small monasteries. Then, Fa Xian traveled Westward from Yutian, through Jiecha Country (current Kashi of Xinjiang) to Pamirs, then through Xintou River (Indian River) to the Northern India. Then, he arrived India, and entered the basin of Ganges River. Later, he sailed to Indian sea, i.e. to Shizi Country (current Sri Lanka), finally returned to his own country. Fa Xian had traveled for 14 years, and wrote a book after returning back, which was named Biography of Fa Xian, or A Buddhist's Journey to India or Journey to the Buddhist Country.

(2) Song Yun's Pursuit of Dharma

Song Yun was born in Dunhuang, and an officer who managed monks during the reign of Emperor Xiaoming of the Northern Wei Dynasty. Buddhism was widely spread due to the promotion of the Northern Wei rulers. Only in Luoyang, there were 500 monasteries. Meanwhile, there were several sects of Buddhism who interpreted the classics differently. Therefore, Empress Hu (Dogawer) sent Song Yun, Hui Sheng and others to India for the truth.[44] At the end of the 1st year of the Shengui reign in Northern Wei Dynasty (518), Song Yun started off from Luoyang. Before leaving, Empress Hu ordered her officers to give him lots of money and gift objects which he could give to people throughout his journey, meanwhile he conveyed state documents to other countries.

Song Yun crossed over the Longshan Mountains and continued to walk for 40 days, and arrived in Chiling, the western border of Northern Wei Dyansty. And he entered into Tuyuhun from here, through Qinghai Lake and Qaidam Basin, crossing over Altun Mountains, marching Northwestward for over 1,750km, finally arrived in Shanshan Country. Then, Song Yun traveled along the North of Kunlun Mountains for 637km to Zuomo City (current Qiemo of Xinjiang). Continuing to go Westward to Yutian, through Zhujubo (current Yecheng of Xinjiang), Hanpantuo (current Tashkurghan of Xinjiang), Song Yun arrived in the Congling Mountains (the Pamirs).

In the 9th month of the 2nd year of Shengui Period (519), Song Yun visited the Bohe state (situated in Wakhan in the East of the border between current Tajikistan and Afghanistan in the Congling Mountains (current Pamirs region), then arrived in Da (Ephthalites kingdom) the next month. The Ephthalites people had no "cities" and lived a nomadic life. In summer, they climbed to the cool meadows; when the winter approached, they moved to the warm grassland regions. Song Yun also narrated that Ephthalites kingdom bordered the Tiele tribe in the North, and they bordered Yutian in the East, and bordered Persia in the west. Also, Song Yun saw ambassadors of about 40 countries paying their respects, which could prove that Ephthalites people had the highest status among the minorities. And, he also noticed that Ephthalites kingdom did not believe in dharma religion, but "worshipped foreign gods". It was possibly the Zoroastrianism that Da people believed in.

44　The Empress Dowager was a devotee to Buddhism, and spend huge amounts to built the lavishly decorated Yongning Monastery 永寧寺 in Luoyang 洛陽, with a Buddha statue eight paces high and a nine-storey high pagoda, and the Buddhist stone caves of Yique 伊闕 (currently known as the Longmen Grottoes).

Some months later, they arrived in Wu Kingdom Capital[45] (current Swat River in the north of Pakistan). The King called the Northern Wei as "Da Wei". When he met Song Yun, he received the official state document with respect. And when he heard of Empress Hu's faith in Buddhism, he was deeply impressed. There were some people in Wuchang Country who knew Chinese, who were sent by the ruler to learn about China, and wanted to learn whether China had saints or not. Song Yun introduced the virtues and wisdom of Zhou Gong, Confucious, Zhuang Zi and Lao Zi, the immortals in the Penglai Island, and told about the famous doctor Hua Tuo and others. The king was deeply moved by all these, and said: "if China was truly like what Song Yun said, China must be a dharma country. He would like to die and have a rebirth in China in his next life. Song Yun and his attendant Hui Sheng took the saved traveling money to build one stupa in the mountain outside Wuchang, and carved inscription in the li-style calligraphy to eulogize the virtue of Northern Wei Dynasty. However, this stele hasn't been discovered till today.

In the 4th year of the reign of Emperor Zhengguang (520 AD), Song Yun came to Gandhara which was conquered by Da in the end of the 4th century and enthroned a new king. When Song Yun handed on the state document, the King sat on the chair and accepted the document. Initially, given the hierarchical differences among the countries, he had to agree. Later, through several exchanges, he thought they could exchange ideas. Thus, Song Yun blamed, "Wei was a big and strong country, the master of thousands of countries, thus, the minorities, including Gandhara, must respect it", and "mountains and waters have different levels. Thus, there is a hierarchy among the countries of the world." And he also said that King of Ephthalites and King of Wuchang both knelt on their knees when accepting the Wei Dynasty's state documents, the King of Gandhara should learn from them. The King of Gandhara said that he might kneel to the Emperor of Wei himself but not to the document. When people received letters from parents, they sat to read. Even Wei was his parents, it was reasonable to sit to read the document. Song Yun could not persuade him. Song Yun had not seen the true lions. When he saw the 2 lions that the Bati Country sent to Gandhara, he was so surprised that he felt there were great differences between the lions in pictures he saw in the Central Plains and the true ones.

Later on, Song Yun traveled to India, and returned back to China in the 3rd year of the Zhenguang reign (522) with 170 classics of Mahayana. And he wrote Song Yun's Records. Meanwhile, Hui Sheng wrote the Travel Notes. The

45 The Wu Kingdom Capital site was the capital city of the Kingdom of Wu during the Three Kingdoms period. In AD 221, Sun Quan went to Hubei province from Gong'an. Soon afterwards, he accepted the title of King of Wu, conferred by Cao Pi, Emperor Wendi of the Wei Dynasty. In August that year, he started to construct the capital city of Wu Kingdom. Sun Quan renamed Exian county as Wuchang in the hope of "flourishing by force of arms." In lunar April of AD 229, Sun Quan proclaimed himself Emperor of Wuchang, also known as the great capital city of Emperor Wu. In September, Sun Quan moved the capital to Jianye (current Nanjing in Jiangsu province). He assigned senior general Lu Xun to assist Prince Sun Deng to guard Wuchang.

above two books were scattered and had disappeared. Yang Xuanzhi who was a contemporary of Song Yun, wrote Record of Buddhist Temples in Luoyang to introduce the journey of Song Yun according to some records.Besides Song Yun and others, the Northern Wei dynasty sent many other envoys to the Western Regions several times. During the Taiyan Period under the reign of Tuoba Tao (435-439), Wang Ensheng, Xu Gang and others were sent to Western Regions. Not long after that, Dong Wan and Gao Ming were sent to Western Regions, and they arrived in Poluona (tCurrent Ferghana Basin out of Xinjiang). During the Taiping Zhenjun Period (440-450), Han Yangpi was sent to Persia.

(3) The Tang Monk's Pilgrimage for Buddhist Scriptures

Among those monks who devoted themselves to collect Buddhist scriptures, Xuan Zang was the most famous one. Xuan Zang was surnamed Chen, he was from Luoyang, Henan. He became a monk when he was young, and studied Buddhist classics. Later, he travelled around to study, and arrived in Chang'an in 627. Because he felt the contradictions among Buddhist classics, and could not get answers in many problems, then he decided to go to India for scriptures. He submitted to the court, and demanded to go out. However, the West of Dunhuang was controlled by Western Turkic Khantae. Tang dynasty and the Turkic kingdoms were enemies, thus his demand was not approved. In the 3rd year of Zhengun Period (629), he started off from Chang'an (Xian), through Liangzhou to Guazhou (current Anxi of Gansu). Despite of the prohibition, he sneaked into Guanyi, through Mohe Yanqi to Yiwu (current Hami). Next year in January, he arrived in Gaochang and traveled Westwards to Turpan Basin, and then turned to the South of Tianshan, traveled Westwards to Balujia (current Aksu). Then walked Westwards for 150km, and crossed over the branch of Tianshan mountain to Daqing Chi (namely Atami, current Issyk Kul of Kyrgyzstan).

Xuan Zang traveled further Northwestwards for over 250 km, crossing over Tianshan mountain to Suyab which was the important artery of land expedition route between East and West, wherein there were many people and many towns here. Further going West was Talas River, and then Syr Darya. The Steppes from Suyab to Syr Darya was the richest grassland regions, and also the cradle wherein the powerful nomadic states were built. At that time, this region was controlled by the Western Turkic Khanate. Xuan Zang traveled 100 km Westwards to Baishui City (current Shymkent of Kazakhstan), later went to Chach (capital Tashkent of current Uzbekistan) from Syr Darya, and later went to Southwestwards to Sogdian agricultural region. The most important city here was the Samarqand. According to the Great Tang Records on the Western Regions, over 10 km far from Samarqand was extremely dangerous, since Sogdians often went out to trade in this city, there were many exotic good things gathering here. This city was located by the Zelafushan (Nami or Zeravshan) River, and was the most famous city in Central Asia and here the soil was fertile that was good to plant. Besides, agriculture, it was convenient for horse breeding. At the same time, the handicraft industry was also prosperous.

Xuan Zang, traveled Westwards from here to another important city Buhe (current Bukhara of Uzbekistan), then turned Southwards to Baixuntao Mountain of the West of Tianshan, later crossed over the territories of Sogdiana and Tocharians, he finally entered Tocharians. Tocharians strode across the banks of Amu Darya, with over 1,500 km, neighbored Congling (Pamir) in the East, Persia in the West, the Daxue Mountains (Hindukush Mountains) in the south, the Tiemen in the North. At that time, the whole region was divided into 27 prefectures and under the control of Turkic Khanate. Xuan Zang noticed that language of Tocharians was a little different from other countries, and similar to Sogdian language. The words were made from 25 letters. Tocharians did better in writing than Sogdians. Its writing wrote from left to right. Dami (current Termez of Uzbekistan), in the Northern bank of Amu Darya, was the most important city of Tocharians. When Xuan Zang arrived here, the city's circumference was up to 10 km, and there were over ten Buddhist monasteries and thousands of monks.

Xuan Zang continued to cross over the Daxue Mountains, through Bamian (current Bamyan of Afghanistan), then travelled Southwards to India. In total Xuan Zang had travelled for 17 years, and started off to go back in 641. Trekking through the Pamirs and the Southern border of Tarim Basin, he returned back to Chang'an via Yutian and Qiemo. Under the orders of Emperor Taizong of the Tang Dynasty, with the help of his disciple Bian Ji, he wrote Great Tang Records on the Western Regions which recorded his experiences of seeking dharma. His records included valuable materials about geography, history, agriculture, handicraft industry, economy, culture, religion and others.

(4) Hui Chao, Monk of Silla

Hui Chao was a monk from Silla in the Korean Peninsula, and entered China when he was young. He sailed to India from China, and later came back China via the Western Regions. He arrived in Anxi (current Kuche, Xinjiang) in the 15th year of the Kaiyuan Period (727). Hui Chao saw the great changes of political situation in the Western Regions in the early 8th century. He described the confrontation between the Tang Dynasty and Tubo. And he said, Kasmira (current Kashmir), big Bruzha in the Northwest (current Gilgit Region in the Northwest of Pakistan), Yangtong belonged to Tubo, while the neighboring small Bruzha, though as same as Big Bruzha in aspect of "clothes, folk custom, food and voice", was administrated by Tang Dynasty. The big Bruzha was originally part of the small Bruzha, and the garrison of small Bruzha, later the small Bruzha had to give up the big Bruzha under the great pressure of Tubo, and escaped to the small Bruzha, however its residents in big Bruzha were controlled by Tubo (Tibetan empire).

Walking northwestward for one month from Kasmira to Gandhara, Hui Chao recorded the process that Western Turkic Khanate conquered the country, and said: "horses and soldiers were controlled by Turks, and the locals were the Hu people." After Turkic aristocrats conquered this region, they were influenced by the local culture, became Buddhists and believed in "three Buddhist treasures". At that time, there were many countries with Turkic horses and soldiers. Khuttal (current Kulob of the South of Tajikistan), the North of Panj River in the upstream of Amu Darya, whose king was a Turkic man. The country's language was the "mixing of Tocharians, Turkic, and local languages". Although, it was conquered by Dashi people, the king, chieftains and common people believed in "three Buddhist treasures" and there were monasteries and monks, and Hinayana was popular here. Hui Chao also traced experiences that Persia was ruined by Dashi. He said, "Dashi was originally the camel-feeding tribe of Persia, later betrayed Persia and killed the king of Persia, and ruled the country." Hui Chao has noticed that Persians did well in trade, many Hu traders traveled from Western Sea (current Arabian Sea) via the Southern Sea South region of India) by ships. They bought valuable goods to the Lion Country (current Sri Lanka) and gold from Kunlun Country (current Southeast Asia), and also sailed to Han (China), for trading.

The agricultural region in the West of Congling (the Pamirs), namely "Nine states in the oases of Zhaowu", were controlled by the Dashi people. Although, there were many Kingdoms here, they generally were controlled by the Dashi rulers. Many of these oases believed in Zoroastrianism and did not know the dharma (Buddhism). Only Kang Country (current Samarqand) had "one monastery and one monk", but did not seriously obey doctrines. Bahena Country, the East of Kang Country (current Fergana Valley), was the interaction of Western Turkic and Dashi. Hu Country, namely the North of Sogdiana, "north to the Northern Sea (current Aral Sea), West to the Western Sea (current Caspian Sea), East to the Han (mainland of Tang)", were all territories of Turkic people. Through a 7-day journey to Tocharians, Hui Chao met a Tang ambassador in Humi. Although they walked towards different directions, they both felt the difficulties of the long and arduous expedition. Hui Chao wrote poetic lines to express his feelings, "You hate the remote Western Regions, while I sighed over the Eastward journey" and "I seldom shed tears in my whole life, but my tears pour today". When he returned back home, Hui wrote the book "The Journey to India" which was similar to Tang Lin's The Sound and Meaning of the Tripitaka, but it was scattered by his descendants. After the scripts of Dunhuang (written on paper) were discovered in the early 20th century, "explorers" from Western countries crowded here and robbed abundant historical materials, including those scripts. According ro scholars' identification, there was one fragmentary transcript without the beginning and end parts but which with Hui Chao's "The Journey to India" among the Dunhuang fragmentary transcripts, later scholars have agreed that this fragmentary transcript written by Hui Chao.

(5) The Experiences of Du Huan

Du Huan was the nephew of Du You, the Prime Minister during the reign of Emperor Dezong of the Tang Dynasty and the writer of Tong Dian (A Comprehensive Study of History). In the 7th year of the Tianbao Period under the reign of Emperor Xuanzong of the Tang Dynasty (748), Du Huan, together with Gao Xianzhi, the Gaoli-minority General and the Western Military Officer of the Tang Dynasty, led troops to attack the Shi kingdom (current capital of Uzbekistan). Shi kingdom was subordinated to the Tang dynasty. But due to Tocharians' mischief, Gao Xianzhi conquered the capital of Shi Country, captured King Chebishi and his concubines and sent them to Chang'an, and looted their treasures. However, the Prince of Shi kingdom escaped from the arrest of Tang army, who hated the cruelty of Tang army and complained this cruelty the the countries in the Western Regions. Thus, some countries as Sogdiana betrayed the Tang Dynasty and considered Tang as its enemy, also allied with the Dashi army to deal with the Tang Dynasty. After hearing about this, Gao Xianzhi recruited soldiers from the Northwestern tribes and fought against the Dashi forces. In 751, Gao Xianzhi encountered with the Dashi (Arab) army in Talas (Taraz) (current Jaunpur in Kazakhstan), in the riverside of Talas River and the Northern grassland region of Tianshan. They fought for several days. During the battle, the Geluo Lu led troops of the Tang dynasty army betrayed and helped the Dashi forces to fight against Gao Xianzhi, finally Tang dynasty army was defeated. Du Huan and many Tang army officers were captured, while Gao Xianzhi had escaped to the Central Plains.

Dashi forces took with them Du Huan and other Tang troops, who were forced travel through Shi Country, Kang Country (current Samarqand), Yamei (current Cha'er of Turkmenistan), to Molu (current Mali of Turkmenistan). Du Huan knew that in Bahanna (Kokand) (current Fergana Valley), there were about 10 cities there, wherein people lived in earthenware rooms, with clothes made from leather and cotton. Their women were not like the Han women who used make-up powders, but loved to use to paint their eyes.Du Huan was the first person who had exactly introduced knowledge about Islam to China. He wrote: in the Dashi country, "women must cover their faces when going out." There was no difference among Dashi people, they worshiped the god at five o'clock. He also called the Islam mosques as the "hall" that provided worshipping and gathering place for thousands of people. Every week, the King had to go to the temple to worship, and make a speech to the people. His speeches were about teachings stipulated in the holy Koran. Du Huan also saw many Chinese people in Dashi country, among whom there were the prominent painters like Fan Shu, Liu Ci; weavers from Hedong, like Lue He and Lyu Li. He also noticed the famous excellent Arab horses. The Arab horses have "a small belly, long ankles, and can gallop 500km per day. 12years later, Du Huan returned back by a commercial ship in 762, the 1st year of Baoying Period under the reign of Emperor Daizong of the Tang Dynasty.

5. Network of the Grassland Silk Road

The prosperity of China during the Sui and Tang dynasties caught rhe attention of many neighboring countries. And the vast territory of Sui and Tang dynasties made unprecedented close communications between Central Plains and Northwestern frontier regions. In the later period the Tang dynasty administration was extended to Mobei (desert area in North China) region, and opened post-roads from Mobei to the Central Plains. After Tang government defeated the Western Turkic people, expedition routes were built in someregions around the North of Tianshan. And post expedition routes were opened, that could be used from Yizhou (current Hami) to Beiting. Also, there were many post expedition routes from Beiting to Gaochang, which were separately called "Tadi road", "Wugu road", "Xinkai road", "Huagu road", "Yimo road", "Sahan road", "Tubo road", etc. Going Westwards from Beiting, there were post expedition roads to Yili River basin, then going Westwards to Suiyechuan and could continue further to west. Going Northwards could arrive in Yudujin Mountain where living tents of Uyghur Khanate of Mobei situated. Network of grassland silk road became the bond which connected nomadic people s Central Plains people, and the important route of exchanges between East and the West.

(1) Expedition Road to Worship the Heavenly Khan

In the 4th year of the Zhenguan Period under the reign of the Tang Dynasty (630), Eastern Turkic Khaganate was terminated by the Tang Dynasty. Chieftains of tribes of the Mobei region were subordinated to the Tang court one after the other, and paid respect to Emperor Taizong of the Tang Dynasty (Tang Taizong) as "Heavenly Khan". Xueyan Tuo Khanate, rising by replacing the Eastern Turkic, was ruined by the Tang dynasty in 646. Tang Taizong established Jimi Prefectures in departments of Mobei Tiele, which were led by chieftains of tribes, and established head of Yanran Duhufu. Soon, in line with requirements of departments, he opened the "Road to Worshipping the Heavenly Khan", also established 68 expedition posts and road marks, and made it became the main route from Mobei region to the Central Plains.The North of Tang territory greatly surpassed the vast Mongolian Plateau, and reached into the Northern Asian region; in the West, it reached to the grasslands of the North of Aral Sea. Tang was an unprecedentedly prosperous dynasty, which made close relations between the Central Plains people. During this period various works about nomads were created. For example, Dai Dou's Zhu Fan Ji, Li Fan's Long Record about Northern People, Gao Shaoyi's Four Barbarians' Tribute to Court, Lu Shu's Kirgiz's Tribute to Court and Travel to the Western Regions revised by Tang Gaozong. Jia Dan was the most important scholar, who wrote 10 volumes of Maps, 10 volumes of Huang Hua Si Da, Four Barbarians' Talk about Ancient County Roads, etc, but these books were lost.

Jia Dan learned history and geography when he was young, and held the post of director of the court forstate ceremony affairs. In 784, he was ordered by Tang Dezong to revise Guo Lu, and took about ten years to ask for origins. In 801, Hainei Huayi Map (Jia Dan's Map) was drawn with 1 inch to 100 miles. This picture was with width of 3.3 zhang and length of 3 zhang. It was lost, but Wei Qi had finely carved it on stone, which could show the general idea of the picture, and was preserved in Xi'an Forest of Steles[46] (Beilin). Seven "roads and routes to neighbor countries" in New History of the Tang Dynasty: Geography were written according to what Jia Dan mainly wrote and which included the following information:

Route from Yingzhou to Andong,
The shipping route from Dengzhou to Koryo,
Route from outer of Xiazhou to Datong, Yunzhong,
Route from the Central Shouxiang City to Uyghur Khaganate,
Route from Anxi to Uyghur Khaganate,
Route from Annan to India,
The shipping route from Guangzhou.

Among the above seven routes, there were four or five routes which went deep into the lands of Northern nomadic nationalities, which were part of the grassland silk roads that the Central Plains of Tang dynasty exchanged with the North and Northwest. The fourth one, "the Route from the Central Shouxiang City to Uyghur Khaganate" should be the "Road to Worship the Heavenly Khan" of Northern nomad peoples during the reign of Tang Taizong. This route roughly started from the Central Shouxiang City (currently west of Baotou where the Kundulun River joins the Yellow River), extended northwards through Huyangu, Guitangshan, Pitiquan to Gobi, later passing through the Lu'er Mountain, Cuojia Mountain, and another 400 km. to Yangzijing, then was extended went to Northwest direction to Mishu Mountain, Dadanpo, Yemapo, Khan Qan, Hengling, Mian Quan, Jing Po, and finally another 350 km of march to the tents[47] of Uyghur Khaganate, namely the Eer Hun basin of Yudujin Mountain.

There was another route to Mobei (northern part of the Gobi desert) from Pitiquan, namely through Gongzhu City, Meijian City, Talas Mountain, Chiya, etc. and then returned back to the tents of the Uyghur Khaganate (744-840). After the Sui Dynasty reunified China, its economic strength arose dramatically by having great influence on the neighboring regions and minorities. Emperor Yangdi of the Sui Dynasty sent Wei Jie, Du Xingman to the Western Regions. After returning back, Wei Jie wrote Xi Fan Ji (Records on the Western States), while this book was lost. At that time, Hu traders, from Western Regions countries, often made exchanges in Zhangye. Emperor Yangdi of the Sui Dynasty sent vice minister Pei Ju to Zhangye for the governance. Pei Ju was a bright person. He collected local books and interviewed Hu people in Hexi to learn

---

46   The Stele Forest or Beilin Museum is a museum for steles and stone sculptures in Xi'an, China. The museum, which is housed in a former Confucian Temple, has housed a growing collection of Steles since 1087. Since 1944 it was the principal museum for the Shaanxi province.

47   Despite the urban court space that the Uyghur rulers established, they themselves maintained a symbolic "nomadic" life in a magnificent golden tent, noted in Chinese accounts as well as that of Tamīm ibn Bahr, which became an important marker (historian) of royal power.

the geography, culture and local products of the Western Regions. He titled what he collected as the Picture Collection of Western Regions, tributed it to Emperor Yangdi and got the appreciation of the court and was granted with a special official title to deal with the foreign affairs. What Pei Ju did was to promote the communications between the Western Regions and the Central Plains. There were over 30 Western Regions countries that often paid tributes to Sui at that time. More and more Hu people came to Chang'an, Luoyang, etc. And Sui government established "Sifang Guan" in Chang'an to receive traders from foreign countries and handle trading business.

There were three volumes in Picture Collection of Western Regions in total, which recorded 44 countries' affairs, with maps and pictures. However, only the preface was preserved in History of the Sui Dynasty: Biography of Pei Ju. Picture Collection of Western Regions recorded three main expedition routes of the communication between the East and the West in the Sui Dynasty. The first was the "Northern Route". It started from Yiwu, crossing over Tiele tribe Northwestwards near Pulei Sea (current Barkol Lake in Xinjiang), then going through camps of Turkic Khan Northwestwards, later going Westwards and crossing over Yenisey River, Ob River and other Northward-flowing rivers. Finally, it arrived at the Fulin Country (Byzantine Empire) on the shore of the West Sea (Mediterranean Sea). The second was the "Central Route". It started from Gaochang, going along Qiuci in the South of Tianshan Mountains to Shule, then crossing over Congling (currentPamirs region) to Bohan (current Fergana Valley at the border of Uzbekistan, Tajikistan, and Kyrgyzstan), and going Westwards to Sogdiana, next through cities of Sogdiana as Kang Country (current Samarqand), An Country (current Bukhara), crossing over Amu Darya to Persia, finally arriving at the West Sea (Mediterranean Sea).

The third was the "Southern Route". It proceeded Westwards from Dunhuang, through Yangguan to Shanshan, and extended Westwards along the South of Tarim Basin to Yutian, then crossing over Congling, extended Westwards to Tocharians, finally entered Persia and from Persia extended to Westwards and reached the West Sea (Mediterranean Sea). Among the above 3 expedition routes, the first "Northern Route" was the route that European-Asian Steppes and Northern-Asian nomads used two advantages: fast horses and the giant natural block of Mongolian Steppes and European-Asian Steppes, to make communications between the East and the West. The other two routes, namely the "Central Route" and the "Southern Route" were traditional routes which passed by the desert oases.

The routes which passed through the European-Asian Steppes in the Tang Dynasty were smoother. Starting from Anxi (current Kuche of Xinjiang), going Westwards and crossing over Badaling (currently a branch of Tianshan), through Dunduo city of the original Wusun and Atami (current Issyk Kul of Kyrgyzstan), and crossing over Tianshan to Suiye Chuan, namely the Eastern border of Kazakhstan and Kyrgyzstan, then going 40 km Westwards to Peiluo (Balasaghun), next furher marched 10 km Westwards to Suyab, 5km to Miguo city, another 15 km to Xincheng, then 30 km to Dunjian city, and 25 km to Barskhan, then 35 km to Kulan, 5 km to Shuijian city, and 25 km to Talas (Taraz). There were many small cities to the West of Suiyab, among which the most important was Talas.

After the Battle of Talas, Dashi people increasingly entered into Central Asian Steppes. The woks of Dashi (Arab) geographers also recorded the route that extended to the East through Central Asian Steppes. Some sections of the route from the West to the East recorded by these Islam scholars could be compared with what Han materials recorded. For example, Ebn Kordādbeh, a Dashi geographer, described in his Masālek (Mamālek), as follows: "3 Farsakh from Talas (Taraz) to Barskhan, then 4 Farsakh to Kulan, 4 Farsakh to Mirch, 4 Farsakh to Asbarah, 8 Farsakh to Nuzhicheng, 4 Farsakh to Ak-tepe, 4 Farsakh to Zhule, 7 Farsakh[48] to Salick, 4 Farsakh to Turgesh, 4 Farsakh to Xincheng, 3 Farsakh to Copar, finally to Barskhan which was the frontier of China." Although, Suyab was not referred in this text, Copar was Suyab according to Ibn Qudamah, a Dashi scholar from Jeruselam.[49] The routes referred by these Dashi scholars were the routes that Dashi merchants and ambassadors traveled to China after the establishment of Dashi (Arab) Empire.

(2) Towns and Cities alongside the Grassland Silk Road

Between the 8th century to the 11th century, the North of Asian Steppes had encountered complex political changes. In 750, the control of Tang dynasty in the Western Regions was its peak period, and Tang armies destroyed the Shi kingdom (Suyab). In the following year, Tang army and Dashi army met and fought in Talas (Taraz), Tang army was defeated. And the consequent "An Shi Rebellion" had greatly weakened the Tang's power. In the end of the 8th century, the Eastern part of Central Asia was controlled by Tubo Kingdom (Tibet originated) which fought against Uyghur Khaganate. In the early 9th century, the north of current Mobei and Tianshan belonged to Uyghur Khaganate. In 840, Uyghur Khaganate was defeated by Kirgiz. Thus, part of Uyghur Khaganate people escaped from Mobei to the East of Tianshan, who were historically called "Gaochang Uyghurs". After the Westward migration of Uyghur Khaganate people, many peoples converted to agricultural nations. This part of Uyghur Khaganate people was called "Weiu'er" (Uyghur) in Yuan and Ming Dynasty. While the Eastern grassland regions of Central Asia (including Mongolia) was controlled by Kirgiz, Khitan, Nüzhen, and Kara-Khitan Khanate kingdoms after the migration of the Uyghur Khaganate people. Towns in the grassland Silk Road quickly developed in this period. Here, below we will briefly introduce some important ones as follows:

---

48   Farsakh (Fersah) is a measure of 12.000 footsteps, 4 hours in time.
49   See Zhuang Guangda: Current Research on the Geography of Suyab, in the Journal of Peking University, 1979/5.

(1) Beiting

Beiting city was "bes baliq" which was the transliteration of Turkic language and meant "five cities". The place "five cities" first appeared in Stele of Kul-tegin (The Kul Tigin Stele of the Turkic people). In the Grand Dictionary of Turkic Language, bes baliq (Beş Balık) was listed as one of the five cities in Weiwu'er, and the biggest city in Weiwu'er. The name of "five cities" was extremely ancient, which was first discovered in Han literature of Old History of the Tang Dynasty: Geography: Jinman, "The old Hu court had five cities, which was vulgarly called 'the place of five cities'". And the city existed before long Tang Dynasty. Besides Han and Turkic literatures, other peoples also knew the place of "five cities". In 760, Bes Baliq (Beş Balık) was controlled by the Tubo kingdom. After 840, Bes Baliq became the capital and political center of Weiwu'er. In the end of the 10th century, Wang Yande, ambassador of the Northern Song referred in his journey diary that there were Gaotai Temple, Yingyun Taining Temple and others in Beiting. And he referred that the local people did well in crafts, weapons and jades.[50]

Otherwise, Qiu Chuji knew that there was Longxingxi Temple in Beiting, referring to The West Journey of Changchun Zhenren, reversion of Wang Guowei, and suicide note of Jing An. After the Westward of Uyghur Khaganate, Uyghurs lived in the North still kept the nomadic life. When Wang Yande came to Beiting, he saw that there were many horses in Beiting, King, Queen and Prince respectively bred horses. The Beiting ancient site is an ancient city ruins located in current Jimusar, Xinjiang, whose relic consists of five parts: the outer city, the north of outer city, the western extension of the city, inner city and small city in the inner city. The outer city is an irregular rectangle which extends long from south to north and a narrower street which extends from east to west, with a circumference of about 4,430 meters. The city walls were made by original clay. Each wall had city gates and horse faces; the four corners had turret-platforms. The Northern city wall was constructed with Weng city. The outside of the Weng city was with Guan city, whose city wall opened on East. The Western wall of outer city was built with Yan city from its west, with about 690 meters which extends from south to north, and about 310 meters which extends from east to west. There lies the inner city in the north of middle outer city, and with trenches around it. There is the small city in the east part of the inner city. Among them, the outer city, Bei Guan city of the outer city and inner city were all built by the Tang architecture; while the inner city and small city located in the inner city were built by the architecture style of the Gaochang Uyghur Khaganate.[51]

---

50   See Wang Yande's Journey to Gaochang.
51   See Meng Fanren: The Historical Research on Beiting, Xinjiang People's Press, 1985, pp. 190-196.

(2) Suyab (Ak-beshim)

Suyab Chuan region, the plain formed by the alluviation accumulation of the Suyab River, contains the richest soil in the north of Tianshan Mountains, accordingly has been the region with numerous densely-populated towns and cities. The Suyab River is the Chüy River in the border of current Kazakhstan and Kyrgyzstan. The length of Suyab River is about 500 km, whose west is Talas River basin which belonged to the Shi kingdom. According to Du Huan, here dwelled numerous Turkic and Mongol tribes with different names. Each had thousands of troops and horses and constantly fought against others. However, many farmers lived in cities and towns, and they provided armors and troops for the fighting tribes, these farmers raped and exploited their neighbors as slaves, for this purpose. In the New Book: Geography, it referred to cities and towns along the route from East to West, as Balasaghun, Suyab, Mi Country city, New city, Dunjian city, etc.

When Xuan Zang marched to west, he passed through Suyab and narrated: "the city's periphery is about 3-3.5 km. and merchants from various countries live there together". He also observed the agriculture around Suyab and found that "the soil was very convenient for millet, wheat and grapes". And there were few trees. The local people dressed „felt-made clothes". In 679, the Tang Dyansty government made adjustments in regard to „four towns of Anxi", replaced Yanqi (Karasahr) with Suyab and determined Suyab to be one of the "four towns of Anxi". Wang Fangyi and Pei Xingjian, governors of Anxi, built the Suyab city with "12 gates in its four directions" in a period of only "50 days". After the completion, the Hu people of Western Regions came to visit the city.[52] In 692, Tang forces re-captured Suyab again. In 719, Tang government agreed the demands of the Western Turkic Khanate, and allowed Turkic kingdom to control Suyab. Thus, Suyab was no longer considered as one of the „four towns of Anxi". In 748, the Beiting Governor of Tang attacked Suyab, thus it was heavily destroyed. Du Huan saw the "city walls were all destroyed and only few houses remained complete."

174

The Suyab site includes the relics of Ak Beshim[53], which locates in the East of capital of current Kyrgyzstan, Bishkek and on the southern bank of the Chuy River. Current Suyab relic site consists of outer and inner parts, whose outer part has 16 km. in total and is longer than what Great Tang Records narrated in the records about Western Regions. Probably, what Great Tang Records on the Western Regions wrote was about the circumference of the inner city. The dense residential area covers 2.25 square km, which can date back to the 5th century to 12th century. However, probably there were some people living in

---

52   See The Old History Book of the Tang Dynasty: Biography of Wang Fangyi, and Vol. 73 of Tang Huiyao by Wang Pu and Vol. 967 of Cefu Yuangui. Tang Huiyao literally: "Institutional History of Tang") is an institutional history of Tang dynasty compiled by Wang Pu and presented it to Emperor Taizu of Song in 961. The book contains 100 volumes and 514 sections. Cefu Yuangui is the largest leishu (encyclopedia) compiled during the Chinese Song Dynasty (AD 960–1279). It was the last of the Four Great Books of Song, the previous three encyclopedias published in the 10th century.
53   Ak-Beshim which is in the region of Chüy is located in Kyrgyzstan, about 53 km, far from Bishkek, the capital of Kyrgyzstan.

some certain place in the 15th century. There was also a relic of a residential area 600-700 meters away from the city walls. Gardizi, a Persian scholar, referred that there were 3 villages near Suyab in his book called "The Ornament of Histories: A History of the Eastern Islamic Lands AD 650-1041. These residential areas which Gardizi talked about should be related to it.

In 1938, Bernstein, a Soviet archeologist, began an excavation and found a Buddhist temple which dated back to the 8th -9th centuries. But, Bernstein only made a general description and did not give comprehensive details. Later, another Soviet archeologist I.I Kyzlasov continued the unearthing work, thus he found that this Buddhist temple covered an area of 704 square meters. About 100 meters Southwestern from the outside of the city walls, there was a long mound which was covered with weeds, and without architectural relics. In 1957-1958, Soviet scholars found the second Buddhist temple which dated back to the 6th-7th centuries and was in the same period with Niesicong temple discovered in the place. The scale of the Buddhist temple was larger than the original discovered Buddhist temple. The wall of temple was a rectangular, with length of 80 meters and width of 25 meters, whose gate faced East. The city wall was constructed by earth, and wall of houses was made of mud bricks; the roof was an arch made of mud bricks. In the entrance of the Buddhist temple there was the monk's dormitory, latter's front hall and the final main hall. The main hall was flat roof with eight columns. Two sides of the entrance were Buddhist images: in the left was Buddha, and in the right was Maitreya. There were statue platforms outside of hall and copper Buddha images inside. The layout of the whole Buddhism temple was similar to that found in Turpan (Turfan) and Karasahr. This kind of stele decoration was affected by Chinese the Central Plains.[54]

This Buddhist templecan be the Dayun Temple where where Princess Jiaohe, daughter of Ashina Huaidao, used to dwell (today near the Turfan city).This temple still existed when the Chinese traveller Du Huan travelled Westward. Suyab was the place where Li Bai's grandfather and father lived and was also the birthplace of Li Bai. Tang court stationed troops and a garrison there to control the grassland regions. Suyab was the principal capital of the Western Turkic Khanate, and also thic city was the necessary strategic place to cross over the Mongolian Steppes and Central Asia Steppes to the far West. On June 4, 1991, I participated the UNESCO expedition team of „Grassland Silk Road", through Bishkek, the capital of Kyrgyzstan to some ancient relics in Chu River basin such as the Balasaghun and Suyab sites. And, when I looked down from northwest of the Suyab relics, I could clearly see the Islamic Minaret the Burana Tower of Balasaghun[55] (Burana).

54   See Zhao Huashan: Buddhist Temples and Buddhas in India and Central Asia, Cultural Relics Publishing House, 1993, pp. 308-311; Zhang Guangda: Current Research on Suyab, in the Journal of Peking University, 1979/5.
55   The Islamic Burana Tower (Minaret) is a large minaret in the Chuy Valley in northern Kyrgyzstan. The tower, along with grave markers, some earthworks and the remnants of a castle and three mausoleums, is all that remains of the ancient city of Balasagun, which was established by the Karakhanids at the end of the 9th century. The Burana minaret became a prototype of the basic type of Islamic minarets of Central Asia, e.g. the Uzgen Minaret.

(3) Balasaghun (Burana)

Around 1134, Yelü Dashi occupied the Balasaghun city. Yelü Dashi was the founder of the Qara Khitai state, also known as the Western Liao dynasty, In 1131 or 1132, Yelü Dashi was proclaimed Gurkhan by his followers, the new Central Asian title implying that he was adapting to his new homeland, he established his authority over Almaliq and Qayaliq. To the west was the disorganized Kara-Khanid Khanate, the Karakanid ruler of Balasaghun, Ibrāhīm II b. Ahmad, asked for help against the Karluks and Kankalis; in 1134 Dashi dethroned him and controlled Balasaghun. Currently, there is the Burana relic, which is 18 km. to Tokmax. Soviet archaeologists started the unearthin work in this old city in the 1970s. And about 1 km. west from here was the famous graveyard of ancient Nestorians. The whole relic is currently protected by the local government, whose entrance was established in the front of Islam Minaret of Turkic Qara Khitai Dynasty. This tower (minaret) was established in the 11th century to 12th century, with original height of 44 meters. However, it was destroyed by the earthquakes in the 15th-16th centuries, thus the height of the preserved part is only 24 meters. And it covered a base of 100 square meters. The wall around relic still exists. Balasaghun was probably covered a larger area which included Suyab city, and even the Nevakat (the New City).

According to a Tang Dynasty officer called Jia Yu (his book Huang Hua Si Da), here was the first station of route from Suyab to the Central Plains, which was 10 km. far from in total. According to current measurement units, there were 6 km. from the wall of Burana relic to Suyab relic. There was an open relic collection center in regard to Turkic Shi people, which gathered the remnants from the main Turkic Shi people of 6th century to 10th century discovered in Chu River basin, and they were completely preserved. And there is also a museum in the site, where locally unearthed ancient pieces were exhibited. Among those collections, there were Zoroastrianism carved-stone quartets, on which there were crosses and Syriac inscriptions; and also seven square copper coins are exhibited, of which four were Kaiyuan tongbao, one was similar to Han coins, but the scripts on the coin was not Han letters, and probably they were created between 8-9th centuries.

(4) Navekat (The New Town)

According to New History of the Tang Dynasty: Geography, 10 miles West of Suyab was the Mi Country, further 30 miles towards West was the „Navekat" (the New Town). On June 4th, 1991, I have participated the expedition team which visited the relics site of Krasnaya Rechka (Red River) or called the Upper Chu Valley in Kyrgyzstan) which is located in 20 miles northwest of Suyab. According to Soviet scholars' researches, here was the Navekat which is also confirmed in the book called "Huang Hua Si Da" written by a Tang officer named Jia Yu. A single Tang dynasty „Dali tong bao" coin and a Turgesh coin were unearthed here. The whole relic site covered about 10-12 square kms. and dated to the 5th century to later 12th century. And the buildings covered

11,000 square meters, which were built in the 7th century and was from Tang dynasty period. Two Buddhist temples were discovered among the relics, one of which was discovered in 1931, and probably built between 8-9th centuries. There were also clay Buddhist statues discovered here, and length of the Buddhist statue was concluded to be 12 meters according to the fragment part of neck and chest. Within the city, there were also Zoroastrianism temples. Among the relics in the regions of Suyab, „the small red streak" was the best preserved one.

(5) Talas city (Taraz)

In the west part of the Suyab city was the Talas river basin. Xun Zang said: "the city had a wall measured 4-4.5km and was inhabited by abundant foreign merchants. And Talas (Taraz) was the most important town here. In 751, Gao Xianzhi of Tang met Dashi army, and was defeated by Dashi army. And the battle of Talas became the famous battle in the history of China and Western countries. In the South of Talas, there was a „small lonely town" with over 300 households. Xuan Zang discovered that they were all Chinese people who were plundered by the Turkic people, later they gathered here and formed a town of Chinese emigrants. They built city to protect themselves and established houses in the city, whose clothes were similar to Turkic people, and they still preserved the language and etiquette of the Central Plains.

(6) Towns in the Mongolian Plateau

Towns in Mongolian Plateau have emerged in quite early periods of history. During the Tang Dynasty period, Mobei Uyghur Khaganate had established Ordu Baliq (city of Uyghur Khaganate) in Orkhon river basin. In New History of the Tang Dynasty: Geography, it referred that there were plains in the East of Uyghur's camps, and were next to Wudejian Mount (branch of Hang'ai mount) in the West, near Wakun River in the South. Here was the activity center of Northern nomads from the period of Xiongnu. In the period of Liao, more towns appeared here. In the summer of 1991, I arrived here to attend the study on „nomads or Altai silk road" in Mongolia held by UNESCO. The main relics were Khar Balghas here. This city was abandoned in the early Liao dynasty period, while was completely preserved till now. The height of the city was about 6meters, and there were sub-cities and extended cities around it, and inscription fragments written in Sogdian script. And also Stele of Bilge Khan and Stele of Kul-tegin, 60km. North of Qurum, are the world's famous relics of civilization. Stele of Bilge Khan was damaged and broken into several pieces, while the Stele of Kul-tegin is basically complete.

Qurum relic, in the capital of Mongolia was the most important relic in Orkhon river basin. The complete name of Qurum was Qara Qurum (Karakorum) located in the current Mongolian Övörkhangai Province. The region that Qurum city located was originally summer base of the Kerait tribe, and there were monasteries there in the Liao dynasty period. During the Tang dynasty, there appeared towns in Kemkemjik, the Northwest of Mongolian Plateau. Kemkemjik, which was also called Qianzhou, lies in the North of Tangnu Mount and was built by the Kirgiz people. The center located in Ilan, which was one of the regions good for agriculture in the Mobei region. In the period of Kara-Khitan Khanate, it was also an important military garrison.

Chapter 4. Western Religions Entering China

As a nation good at learning from other peoples, the Chinese people have absorbed the thoughts of many other peoples through a variety of channels in history. The large-scale enlightenment from foreign thoughts began by the Eastward spread of Buddhism. In China, Buddhism gradually became a part of Chinese culture after being introduced into China. Besides some of the religions, mainly Manichaeism, Zoroastrianism, Nestorianism, Judaism and Islam, originated in West Asia spread towards Eastern China as a result of the development of East-West exchanges since the "Sixteen Kingdoms" era.

1. Manichaeism

(1) Introduction of Manichaeism (Mingjiao) to China

Mani (also known as Manes and Manichaeus), founder of Manichaeism was born in South Babylonia (Mesopotamia, part of the Empire of Arsak) in April 14, 216 AD. He preached actively throughout the Persian empire until the Sasanian Great King Bahrain I had him fettered and thrown into prison early in 276 AD. According to Manichaean sources, Mani died there within a month of his imprisonment.

His father Patek was not a native, and his ancestors were the people from the central part of the Empire of Arsak. Patek moved from his hometown Hamadan to Mesopotamia at the end of the Arsak Dynasty. His mother Maryam came from the clan Kamsarakan, a famous noble family often mentioned by Armenian historians who lived in the 4th century of Armenia. The family claimed its origin was the imperial family of Arsak. Therefore, A Brief Introduction to Teachings and Rites of Manichaeism said: "Mani was born in the imperial palace of Suristan, Babylon and his mother was Maryam, the Kamsarakan wife of Patek."

At the beginning of the 3rd century, Persia was still under the rule of the Empire of Arsak established by the Parthians. It was replaced by the Sassanid Dynasty in 226, but the social status of the country was not changed. Mani saw the pains of the people since his childhood and felt the evils in the social life.. According to him, the angel had told his mother before his birth in a dream that he would shoulder great responsibilities. At the age of 12, the angel instructed him for the first time to leave the baptismal sect, which of course was groundless. But, undoubtedly, he studied theology, Zoroastrianism, Christianity and other religions when he was young.

At the age of 24, Mani claimed that he was instructed by the angel for the 2nd time. He was required to establish and spread a new religion. From then on, he regarded himself as the embodiment of the holy spirit and knowledge, and the "messenger of light" sent by the god to the world. He began to preach to the people around him. At the beginning, it was not successful and only his father and two others believed in him. He believed that the teachings of the prophets of the past were imperfect and were even distorted, and he said that only the revelation which he preached was the complete truth. He also believed that the previous religions only played a role in some regions, for example, Zoroastrianism in Persia, Buddhism in the East, Christianity in the West, and only Manichaeism was the universal and solid truth. Mani preached that Manichaeism was to replace other religions and save the humankind before the destruction of the world. The religion founded by Mani borrowed the thoughts of Zoroastrianism (Zerdüşt), Christianity, Buddhism, Sol Invictus and Gnosticism[1], but it was not the simple mixture of them.

In 241, the founder of Sassanid Dynasty, King Shahanshahi yi Ardashir passed away and his son Shapur (242-271) succeeded the throne. Mani the founder of the Manichean religion was introduced to the new King Shapur by the King's brother Firuz, and Mani got support and protection for his missionary work. Mani had argued that the former prophets could not write books, but he was able to write by himself. He included a large number of illustrations in his books and enjoyed great popularity. So his ideas could compete against Zoroastrianism in a very short period. He wrote a book Shapuragan which was dedicated to King Shapur. Shapuragan, literally means "Shapur's", elaborated on the tenets of Manichaeism. In 243, King Shapur formally accepted the book which Mani had written for him.Manichaeism is a dualistic religion whose core is "two sources" and "three stages".

---

1   Gnosticism a prominent heretical movement of the 2nd-century Christian Church, partly of pre-Christian origin. Gnostic doctrine taught that the world was created and ruled by a lesser divinity, the demiurge, and that Christ was an emissary of the remote supreme divine being, esoteric knowledge (gnosis) of whom enabled the redemption of the human spirit.

"Two sources" are the light and the dark, which are the beginning of the world, meaning all things contain goodness and evilness. The prophet Mani said that the light and the dark are two adjacent countries, and the country of the "Light" occupied the North, East, and West while the country of the "Dark" the South part. The country of the "Light" is a beautiful world ruled by Zawan and filled with tranquility and joy without any worry and sorrow. On the contrary, the country of the "Dark" is a country full of filth. Mani used two trees to represent these two sources, i.e., the "tree of life" for the light and the "five-poison dead tree" for the dark.

"Three stages" refer to the phases of world development, namely, the initial, the middle, and the later. In the initial stage, there was neither the universe nor the things, but the contradiction between the light and the dark was contained. In the middle stage, the dark intruded into the light and caused great chaos. Mani thought that the real world was in the middle stage and in this world the good and the evil were mixed, and people should help the good and remove the evil. In the later stage, the world would once again split into two, i.e, the light and the dark to distinguish the good and the evil.

The difference between Manichaeism and other religions is that it does not promote that the good will defeat the evil, instead, that there is always the good-evil contradiction, while the good and the evil should be separated.

Manichaeism in China is known as the Mingjiao or Mingzunjiao or transliteration as moni, mouni, momoni, mamani and so on. Volume 39 of "History of the Religious Ancestors" wrote that in the year of 694, the Persian Fuduodan[2] brought Manicheaism religious books to the Tang Dynasty.

This was the first time when Manichaeism was mentioned in China's historical records. In fact, the time that Manichaeism spread into China was probably earlier than 694.[3] According to Vol. 971 of Ce Fu Yuan Gui, in the 6th month of the 7th year of Kaiyuan Period of the Tang Dynasty (719), "The king of Tukhara recommended Muzhe to the Tang dynasty for consulting Tang dynasty in the sphere of astronomy. Muzhe possessed great wisdom and profound knowledge who could answer all questions. Thus, he was recommended to the Tang dynasty for his expertise. The king demanded from the Tang court to build a hall to enshrine the talented Muzhe for the religious teachings."[4]

In order to double check the reliability we can look into other literature, in regard to spread of Manichaeism to China, the introducers led by Fuduodan during the reign of Dowager Wu Zetiang and Muzhe during the reign of

2   Fuduodan is not a personal name but the title for a Manichaean bishop in Sogdian form ('βt'δ'n), literally 'seventieth', namely 'is one of seventy-two bishops', which was supposed to have been created by Mani to give the impression of apostolic succession.
3   Lin Wushu: Questions on the Time of Manichaeism Spreading into China, from Manichaeism and Its Eastward Spread, Zhonghua Book Company, 1987, pp. 46 -63.
4   See Vol. 186 of the Taiping Huanyu Ji ("Universal Geography of the Taiping Era, 976-983).

Emperor Xuanzong. Muzhe held a higher rank than Fuduodan according to the hierarchical ranks of Manichaeism. After being introduced into China, Manichaeism further spread to the Northwestern border regions. Chinese historical documents had a "decree on building Dayun Guangming Temple for the Manichaeism believers of Uyghur" in the 3rd year of the Dali Period (768).[5]

In the 20th year of the reign of Emperor Kaiyuan (732), the Tang government banned Manichaeism saying that "Manichaeism is an evil religion that cheats the common people. It should be strictly prohibited." Soon after that, Manichaeism became popular again due to the occurrence of the An Shi Rebellion. The Chinese inscription on the stele of Uyghur Pijia Khan recorded how Manichaeism was introduced to Uyghurs when the Uyghurs played a major role in the suppression of the An Shi (An Lushan) Rebellion in 763. The inscription said: When Mouyu Khan stationed the troops in Luoyang, a dignitary visited him with four Manichaeism monks to preach their doctrines of the two sources and three stages. They were talented, good at propagating and also proficient in the grasp of seven classics of Manichaeism. Thus, the Uyghur aristocrats were all persuaded. All the ministers and officials expressed their wish to "correct their wrongdoings, sins and believe in this orthodox religion". After the conversion to Manichaeism, the Uyghurs have burned the previous "devil pictures ". The inscription also said: "after the conversion, the Uyghurs' customs were greatly changed: "they give up meat and eat vegetables, from a warlike nation to a benevolent one". Uyghur's faith in Manichaeism played a significant role in promoting the East-west grassland Silk Road. "Since then, Muzhe had many disciples who shuttled between the West and the East to promote Manichaeism".[6]

182

The remaining scripts of the Uyghur language-written Mouyu Khan's Conversion to Manichaeism also recorded that Mouyu Khan's acceptance of Manichaeism, saying: "The heavenly king—i.e, Mouyu Khan and the selected people—i.e., Manichaeism believers—discussed for two days and two nights. On the third day, the heavenly king fasted, suffered greatly and then was moved at his innermost... Later, Mouyu Khan held a meeting and knelt before the selected people for their forgiveness."[7] The Jiuxing Hu (Hu among the nine surnames) played an important role in the Uyghur's conversion to Manichaeism. Many of the Hu merchants who shuttled between the Uyghur, the Western Regions and the Central Plains had believed in Manichaeism. They controlled the foreign trade of Uyghur, and greatly influenced the Uyghur aristocrats. The Tang Dynasty has preferentially treated the Uyghur due to the contribution it had made in the An Shi Rebellion. The Tang government's preferential treatment to the Uyghur also extended to Manichaeism. Consequently, the Uyghur

---

5   See History of Religious Ancestors Vol. 41.
6   See Helin Jin Shi Lu (Helin Inscriptions) collated by Luo Zhenyu.
7   See the newly-discovered incomplete script of MouyuKhan's Conversion to Manichaeism Religion , pp. 7-9 of Vol. 2 Turkische Turfan-Texte by W. Bang und A. von Gabain. It is based on the records in the page 38 of the Uyghur Historical Materials Compendium.

kingdom had become the supporter of Manichaeism religion in the Central Plains.

After the collapse of the Uyghur Khanate in 840, Emperor Wuzong of the Tang Dynasty issued a decree to ban Buddhism and Manichaeism. Although Manichean was officially banned, it was still popular among the people in the basins of Yangtze River and Huaihe River. Today we have several well-documented materials about the monasteries of Manicheaen temples built and operated during the the Song and Yuan Dynasties: Chongshougong in Siming (current Ningbo, Zhejiang), Qianguangyuan in Pingyang of Wenzhou, Manicheaen temple at Shidao Mountain in Quanzhou of Fujian, Manicheaen Thatched Hut in the Huabiao Mountain of Quanzhou. The private secret religious organizations during the Five Dynasties, Song, Yuan, Ming and Qing, such as Mingjiao, Bailianjiao, etc., were all related with Manichaeism. Between 920 and 1120, the Manichaeism believers launched the Mu Yi and Fang La uprisings. The existing Manichaeism sites include the murals in Dunhuang, the monastery in Turpan and the thatched hut in Quanzhou. these facts demonstrate that Manichaeism was widely embraced by the Uyghur people in Ganzhou and Xizhou.In the 1950s, archaeologists found a stele with inscriptions in Chinese and Nestorian Turkic language in Quanzhou. The script said that a person named "Malishilimen Abisiguba Malihaxiya" was authorized to lead theMingjiao, Qinjiao and other religions in the South of Yangtze River. Mingjiao was in fact the Chinese of Manichaeism, and Qinjiao was Nestorianism. The inscriptions has indicated that Manichaeism was an officially recognized religion in the Yuan Dynasty.

(2) Monasteries and Monks of Manichaeism

Among the scripts found in Dunhuang at the beginning of the 20th century there is an incomplete Manichaean sutra titled as A Brief Introduction to Teachings and Rites of Manichaeism, which was composed by Manichaean monks in Chang'an (current Xian) according to a decree in the 19th year of the Kainyuan reign (731). The chapter "On Temples" introduced the form of Manichaean temples. A Manichaean temple generally included a hall which was used as a place to store scriptures and pictures, similar to the Sutra Storage. Manichaeism was good at preaching by using pictures. So in addition to the sutra texts there were pictures. Apart from the hall that stored scriptures, there were also halls for lectures, confessions, teaching and healthcare. The hall for healthcare for the monks was specially designed for the treatment of monks suffering from diseases. This was probably the embryonic form of China's ancient hospital system. Monks in the monastery lived a collective life. Chanting the sutra and "cultivating the goodness" were their routine work. No one was allowed to set up their private kitchen nor to raise any animals or hire servants. The monk's life was very humble and hard. They kept on vegetarian diet. Their economic source was mainly from the support of alms giver. The Manichaeism rules required the monks to accept the donation in a decent mode. In case that the donations were insufficient, the monks were allowed to beg according to the rules. The Manichaeism monument sutra also indicated that the monks had new clothes only once a year and ate only one meal per day. During traveling, the monks lived very plain,simple lives and praised facing hard conditions and hardships, which clearly indicates the strong ascetic character of Manichaeism. At the same time, many Manichean monasteries had agricultural farms under their control. According to the Uyghur records in regard to Manichean monasteries discovered in Xinjiang, the monasteries also had workers for cooking, making pies, sewing, chopping firewood, pasturing animals, raising geese, woodwork, felt work and even doctors etc. in addition to fields. The monasteries also raised horses and cattle.[8]

There were three kinds of monks in the upper hierarchy levels of the monastery. The first was called "A Fo Yin Sa" who was responsible for the learning of laws. The word A Fo Yin Sa came from the mid-ancient Persian and it was the transliteration for "afwrynst", meaning eulogy. His job was to read the classics, and only people who mastered high level of knowledge could assume this post. The second was called "Hu Lu Huana" who was responsible for awards. The third was called "E Sai Jian Bo Sai ", who was in charge of almsgiving. Although, on the surface, Manichaeism promoted both asceticism and equality, but there were strict hierarchy among its monks. And all followers were classified into five classes in the A Brief Introduction to Teachings and Rites of Manichaeism:

Class I, the 12 muzhe, i.e. those pass on the religion and preach the teachings;
Class II, the 72 samusai or foduodan, i.e. those support the teachings;
Class III, the 360 moxixide, i.e. the chiefs of sub branches;
Class IV, aluohuan, i.e. all pure kind-hearted persons;
Class V, ruoshayan, i.e. all pure believers.

Of the said five classes, "special plain suits" were required for the first four classes and no special garment suit was required for those who belonged to Class V.

2. Zoroastrianism

(1) The founding of Zoroastrianism

In the history of China, Zoroastrianism was also known as the Persian Religion, Fire Zoroastrianism and Parseeism etc. Currently, it is also called the religion of Zoroastrianism, which is named after the name of the religion's chief. The creator of Zoroasterism was Zoroaster, this name was how the Greeks called him. In the ancient holy book of Avesta[9], written in Persian, he was called Zarathustra, which was composed of Zarath and Ustra, meaning "yellow camel". In the ancient Chinese literature, it was transliterated as "Suluzhi".

---

8 Geng Shimi, Preliminary Explanation to Uyghur Documents of Manichean Monasteries, Journal of Archaeology, Issue, 1978/4, pp. 497-516.
9 Avesta was the holy book, which included the sacred texts of Zoroastrianism

The teaching of Zoroastrianism had originated from the Aryan faith. Herodotus said that the Sakas "only worshiped the sun amid all the gods, and they sacrificed horses to the sun.. The reason why they sacrificed horses to Gods was that only the fastest horses in the earth were worthy of a son, the fastest among all creatures.". This belief of the Sakas was also reflected in the ancient names of the Western Regions, such as Khwarezm, which means "the land of the sun" in the Persian language, and Sogd means "the fire land".In addition to the Aryans who later moved into Central Asia, the indigenous peoples of Persia included those people speaking Semitic, such as the Assyrians, who also appreciated light and fire. Therefore it can be said that the Zoroastrianism is the product of the original beliefs of the Aryans and the indigenous peoples of Iran, Central Asia and Persia.Zoroastrianism worshipped fire, but this practice cannot summarize all the teachings of this religion. The doctrine of Zoroastrianism can be concluded as believing in the duality of good and evil, which is a typical dualistic religion. The good end was called Niki in Zoroastrianism worshipping the fire, the light, the creation, and the life. The supreme god of this religion was Ahura Mazda, who was the god of wisdom and the master of the goodness in the world. The evil end in the Zoroastrianism (Badi) was darkness, filthiness, damage and death, its representative being Angra Mainyu. Although Angra Mainyu was very powerful, Angra Mainyu was not a god in the Zoroastrianism, instead he was the creator of all evils, but his power could not be compared to Ahura Mazda.

According to the doctrine of Zoroastrianism, Ahura Mazda sent a prophet to guide the mortals because they were ignorant, and too vulnerable to be deceived, and could not tell the right from the wrong. In the 8th century, a book named Zaspari chronicled the legend of Ahura Mazda and Angra Mainyu in Persia: Zurvan (translated as "damingzun" and "mingfu" in Manichaeism), the Lord of the world, had no child, and failed to get one despite praying for thousands of years. Zurvan doubted the heaven when offered sacrifice. Later, Zurvan had two babies: one was the representative of good, Ahura Mazda, the other was the representative of evil, Angra Mainyu. Zurvan had wished that the elder one of the twins to rule the world, but Ahura Mazda learned about this wish and tried to be the first one to be born. Zurvan had to keep the promise and let Ahura Mazda rule the world for 9,000 years, and with the rest of the ruling years kept for Ahura Mazda. The basic moral principles that guide the life of a Zoroastrian are three:

Humata, "Good Thoughts" the intention or moral resolution to abide by Asha, the right order of things.

Hukhata, "Good Words" the communication of the above intention.

Havarashta, "Good Deeds" the realization in action of that intention.

The Persian Empire set Zoroastrianism as the state religion. After Greece ruined the Achaemenian Empire, Zoroastrianism seemed disappeared, but in fact it was still disseminated among the Persians. At the beginning of the 3rd century, when the Persians overthrew the Arsak kingdom and established their own Sassanian dynasty, the Zoroastrianism had rapidly rejuvenated.

(2) Spread of Zoroastrianism in China

The Zoroastrianism was first introduced into the Chinese mainland in the Northern Dynasties period. At that time the Chinese people already knew that Saskatchewan believed in Zoroastrianism. The book, History of Wei Boshi wrote: "Persian country...... vulgar fire gods, gods......" Wei received the Original History of Wei Western Biography, and later generations of the Tang Dynasty repaired it based on the Northern History of the Western Regions. The History of Zhou Dynasty Volume 50 wrote: "Persian country had a fire Buddha God." People in Northern Central region knew that the Western region of the Amur River also pursued Zoroastrianism. In the Kang book, Kang Guo Zhuan said: "Kangguo...... there were the Hu laws, which were placed in the Zoroastrian Temple." Kangguo is currently in the region of Uzbekistan Republic, i.e., in the suburbs of Samarkand city Afrasiab settlement ruins. The "Hu law" here referred towas probably the Avesta[10] compiled in the Sassanid dynasty period.

The Zoroastrianism word which we see in the book titled as "History of Wei Kang Guo Zhuan" can not prove that the North had already had known this word. History of Wei Western Biography was originated from the Northern History of the Western Biography, and Northern History of the Western Regions Biography was all collected from the ancient book called "Sui Shu" (History of Sui). Therefore, the word "Zoroastrian" which was firstly seen in the book "History of Wei" should be first mentioned in the Sui Shu(History of Sui).. Sui Shu book was first repaired in the early Tang Dynasty period, therefore the word "Zoroastrian" should be the new word used in the early Tang Dynasty period. Tang people used the word "Zoroastrian" and God at the same time to refer to Zoroastrianism. Zoroastrianism was introduced into the Northern regions and peoples of China a long before. The Volume 101 of The History of Wei Dynasty recorded the national customs of the gods in Gaochang nation. Duan Chengshi of the Tang Dynasty recorded worship of Gods by the Turkic people, in the book Youyang Zazu: "the Turkic people worshiped the Xian God, but they set no shrines and carved the felt into the shape of Xian God in order to put it in their leather bags, and they put grease on it while they were moving around; or they tied the felt on the top of a rod and worshiped it in every season."

Some people of the Tuoba (Tibet people) ruling group, who established the Northern Wei Dynasty, also believed in Zoroastrianism. The Biography of the Ling Empress Dowager from the History of Wei Dynasty once recorded: "Ling Empress Dowager visited the Song Mountain with hundreds of followers, and she abolished all worship ceremonies except the Hu Tian God." The History of Sui Dynasty once recorded: "in the last years of Emperor Qi, he himself held the worship ceremony of Hu Tian God and established several worship customs which lasted till now." The book also said that the later Zhou Dynasty

---

10   Avesta was the holy book, which included the sacred texts of Zoroastrianism.

came to the Western regions and worshiped the Hu Tian God by the Emperor himself, and the Emperor followed the Barbarian customs which indicated that, in the Northern Dynasty, the followers of Xian God worshiped in a way which was practiced by the Persian and Western regions.

The Zoroastrianism of the Tang Dynasty further continued to spread in the mainland China. The History of Chang'an (Xi'an city) once cited The New History of the Two Capitals that there were four Xian God temples in Chang'an. Chinese materials were named by the mainland leaders of Zoroastrianism Sabao, Xianzheng, Xianzhu, Muhu and so on. The Tang Dynasty followed the Northern Dynasty and Sui Dynasty in grading the Xian monks. The Civilian Officials Records of Tong Dian recorded that, Sabao was ranked as the 5th grade Secretary within the imperial court hierarchy and was ranked as the 4th grade Secretary outside the imperial court. The Wuwei City Museum has a collection of Zoroastrian epitaphs made in the beginning of the Tang Dynasty with ten lines carved on it. The name of the tomb was Ada, a person lived in Kang nation. His grandfather's name was Da Liang, who was closely related to the Tang Dynasty, and he served the military of the Liang, Gan and Gua states. He was in charge of the religious affairs of Zoroastrianism and he was honored as the prefecture chief of Wuwei after his death.

The Volume 193 of Tong Dian cited the records about the Kang nation of West Barbarians and mentioned the burial custom of Zoroastrianism belief: "the people there thought highly of the customs and they wore black suits but no shoes for the dead, and they cried loudly with tears bursting out from their eyes. About three hundred or five hundred men and women wondered around the field and begged God for seven days. Another two hundred citizens outside the village would also join in the event. The body of the dead would be sent in a yard with dogs living there, and the dogs would eat the meat of the corpse. Till all the meat was eaten up, the bones of the dead would be buried without a coffin."

Such celestial burial, namely feeding the dead body dogs, was exclusively owned by the Zoroastrianism. Zoroastrianism thought dogs were sacred animals, and the body of the dead shall be watched by dogs. This custom was introduced in China together with Zoroastrianism. The Biography of Li Hao in the Early History of Tang Dynasty recorded: "In the Tang Dynasty period, a monk in Taiyuan followed the old customs and sent the dead body to the suburbs in order to let the birds and animals eat the meat of the corpse, and after several years, people called the place as 'Huang Keng' wherein there would be hundreds of starving dogs who would eat the corpse, but many people living nearby were disturbed by such customs, but officials could not call a stop of such events. After Hao ascended to throne, he strictly banned such events and ordered soldiers to hunt and kill those dogs, since then such customs had perished."

The New History of Tang Dynasty also contained such a record, but it changed the word "monk" into "Fu Tu Fa Zhe" while other words remained almost the same. Chinese scholar Lin Wushu pointed that both "monks" and "Fu Tu Fa Zhe" meant they did not come from ordinary families. There was no custom like celestial burial in the Buddhism of Tang Dynasty or in ancient China, let alone abandoning the dead body in wild field for dogs to eat. These monks should be the followers of Zoroastrianism, because their burial customs was the same as that of the Zoroastrianism believers of Kang nation as recorded in the West Barbarians. Since, the local Zoroastrianism had great influence in those days, the officials could not forbid such customs for a long time.

There were also examples of the Zoroastrians who have changed their funeral custom when they moved to China. Covered by the atmosphere of Confucian culture, some of Zoroastrian's upper class accepted the traditional Chinese funeral way, since their ways of funeral was humiliated by other peoples. Mr. Xiang Da cited two monuments in the Book Chang'an and Western Civilization during Tang Dynasty period, in which the first monument was the Sui Zhai Tu Po Epitaph of Yuanyang Qi Zhi Zhai. It is written as follows: "My name is Tu Po, and Bo He Biduo is my nickname; my hometown is Taiyuan in Bing Zhou. My father is Po Mohe who served as Da Sabao. Bo He Biduo lived for 70 years and got sick on January 18th in the 10th year of Daye reign and died in Jia Shanli, Chongye Town, Junyang County, Henan Province and buried in the south of Zhai Village and the North of Mang Mount." The father of Zhai Tupo was Mr. Po Mohe, who served as Da Sabao, was the leader of Fire Zoroastrian. Mr. Zhai Tupo died at the age of 70, so we could image his father was leading the team during Northern Qi and Northern Zhou Dynasty. Mr. Zhai Tupo, born in Taiyuan, was a native of China's Zoroastrians, but then left Taiyuan. Just as the Zoroastrians in Taiyuan still kept their celestial burial customs, he buried his father underground according to the funeral custom of Han nationality which might be forced by surrounding pressures.

The other inscription cited by Mr. Xiang Da was the No.2 Mi Sabao Epitaph collected in the 6th Volume of Peking Library Journal. The tomb owner was Zhaowu people whose surname was nine of the Mi Dynasty. Inscription recorded the funeral like this: "He died at the age of 65. This day was the January 26th of the third year of Tianbao." His "Bian" was set in Gao Lingyuan...." "Bian" meant the coffin. As mentioned before, Mr. A Da, from Kang Dynasty, also buried his father underground. According to the Chapter 3 of Vendidad which was the first part of Avesta mentioned that if someone buried dog or person under ground for sixth months, he would be punished to suffer 1,000 caning; if buried for 1 year, he would be punished to endure 2,000 caning, and if buried for 2 years, his penalty could not be avoided, and the relavent punishment can be seen in the Section 15 Chapter 3 of the Introduction of Sacred History of the East Series, vol. IV, The Zend Avesta. If these Zoroastrians did not live under the Chinese culture, their funeral customs would be punished severely by the Zoroastrian religious community.

We can see from the current researches that the Zoroastrians of the Chinese mainland were almost Western region people and and their descendants. Their activities were mostly centered in Hexi, Guanzhong and Central plains besides the Western regions and the Northern nationalities. In the year 845 of Tang Dynasty, as the Uyghur Khanate was dissolved, the Tang emperor Wu Zong declared the dismissal of Dharma and suppressed foreign religions, among which the Zoroastrianism was excluded. Zoroastrian monks were called "mughin" in the Iranian language, and in Chinese transliterated as "Ma Ge" or "Mu Hu."[11]

3. Nestorianism[12]

(1) Christian Churches of the East

As was written in the ancient Persian documents, in China the word Qin Jiao (qinjao), etc., refered to the Christian Nestorian religion in the Tang Dynasty period, and it was called Nestorianism until the Yuan Dynasty period. Nestorianism as an ancient branch of Christian religion almost no longer exists today in China, but it had a considerable impact in the ancient East and was introduced to Central Asia and China.

Christianity whose leader is Jesus was born out of Judaism. Jesus' disciples believed that he was the "great man" (Messiah/Mesih) whom the Jewish people aspire to, therefore they called him the Christ, meaning the anointed one. After Jesus' death, his disciples spread the truth of his creeds to the East and West. The emperor Constantine of the Roman Empire issued an order for the protection of the Christianity in 313 and summoned all the bishops of Rome in the Asian city of Nicaea in 325, establishing the famous Naxia Code in the history of Christianity. The meeting affirmed the "trinity" creed of Christianity, claiming that Jesus was both "God" and "man", combining both "divinity" and "human" natures in himself. However a different understanding in regard to the unity of "divinity" and "human" natures of Jesus was created. Some people have argued for the merger of both natures of Jesus, but some people have argued the separation of the two natures, these two different views have regarded each other as "heretical" views and contested with each other.

189

---

11   In the historical records The Ruin of Temples in Tang Dynasty wrote that about three thousand Zoroastrian monks were forced to return to lay life, which also can be seen in the Volume 113 of Tang Da Zhao Edict; Volume 20, Li Deyu: Huichang Yi Pin Collection; Historical Records On Food and Grocery; Volume 248, Zizhitongjian. We can observe that there were thousands of people who worshiped Zoroastrianism at the end period of the Tang Dynasty in the Central Plains of China. Although Zoroastrianism was banned during the reign of Tang Wuzong (840-846), there were still some Zoroastrian temples in China in the time between the Tang and Song Dynasty. See the article by are Chen Yuan: The Introducton of Fire Zoroastrianism into China, Chen Yuan Academic Essays Episode 1; and article by Wang Su: Wei Jin Southern Fire Zoroastrianism, Chinese Literature and History 1985, No. 2, pp. 225-233; article by Gong Fang Zhen: Western Religions, Zoroastrianism in Mongolia, Zoroastrianism in Tibet, The Journal of Chinese Literature and History, 1986/2.
12   Nestorianism is a Christological doctrine that emphasizes a distinction between the human and divine natures of the divine person, the Jesus.

Nestorius, who served as Archbishop of Constantinople (Istanbul), between 428-431held a unique view on this question. At that time, it was generally believed that the mother of Jesus Mary was not only called as "mother of God" in the Constantine Church, but also known as "the mother of man." Nestorius did not regard Mary as God and that she gave birth to the physical body of Jesus, as a sacred container of his spirit. He had argued that "God Mother" theory was not consistent with the apostolic teachings in regard to Jesus, nor authorized by the church and carried with the meaning of "multiple Gods". Nestorius,advocated the use of his Mesopotamian priest Dioudu's (Theodore's) eclectic saying. "Mary isthe mother of Christ".Nestorius said "I have separated the divinity of Jesus from human nature, but they are joined as a unity in worship." Nestorius taught that Jesus had two natures, which were, in a sense, switched on and off at different periods of his life. According to Nestorius it was impossible that the Logos, the divine son of God, suffered in the passion; hence, only Jesus' humanity suffered in the passion. Likewise, Nestorius claimed that the Logos (that is, the pre-existent second person of the Trinity) had not been born of a woman; only Jesus' humanity was born of a woman. He refused to use the title Mother of God (Theotokos) – the most beloved title the East could give the virgin mother – for Mary. He said, "Mary is not the mother of God, but the Mother only of Christ and not of God." Egypt, Alexander city's archbishop Cyril (the Christian leader hostile to Nestorius) held a fierce opposition against the arguments of Nestorius, and finally the emperor of the Roman Empire arrested both sides. Nestorius was sent back to Syria, and later was exiled to Arabia, and ultimately died in the desert of Egypt. While Cyril was soon released and resumed the Archbishop post, and finally the "Mother of God" argument had won.

190

Although Nestorius was dead, his believers have gradually spread their beliefs to the eastern world and reached to almost all the eastern churches. They mostly lived on the banks of Tigris and Euphrates rivers. In 498, Nestorius decided to cut off his relarions with the Roman Church at a meeting held in the capital of Salsan Dynasty Cyprus. They elected the independent archbishop of the Orient Church; formally accepted the Nestorianism faith; and gave up the clergy of the celibacy system. They also promoted vegetarianism and opposed the worship of the Virgin Mary.The Archbishop of Nestorianism was stationed in Seleucia-Ctesiphon, and they moved their headquarters to Bagdad after the Arab conquest in the 7th century. Islam was tolerant against the Nestorianism preaching, so the missionary activities of the Eastern Church were very active. The missionaries they sent had jurisdiction of the 25 bishop parishes from the Mesopotamia to the vast territory of China's coast, but it was disintegrated by troops led by Timur in 1370. The heyday of the ancient oriental church in Central Asia and the Far East lasted at least 600 years.

(2) The Nestorianism in Chinese Tablets

People did not know that Christianity was introduced into China in the Tang dynasty until the 17th century. The Nestorian tablets in China was not found in the Western suburbs of Xi'an City until the year 1625[13] of the Ming Dynasty, when people knew that Nestorians had sent missionaries to China in the Tang Dynasty period.

The Nestorian monument was built in 781 during the Tang Dynasty period with black stone hewn. It was about 3 meters high, a meter wide, 30 centimeters thick, weighing about 2 tons. There was cross pattern at the upper part of the tablet and 32 lines of Monument inscriptions on the front, each line of 62 characters, and less than 2,000 words in total. No words were on the back of the tablet. 70 names and titles of the Nestorian monks were engraved at the end of both sides of the stele (monument) in Syriac letters. Twenty-one names were on the left, while forty-one names were on the right side. These names all had Chinese translations except for 8 names. This world famous monument is currently exhibited in the Xi'an Beilin museum.

The contents of the inscription can be divided into two parts as the following:

The first part is the preface, which is a longer text. Firstly, brief introduction to the basic beliefs of Nestorian was graved on the stele, and then detailed description of the Nestorian monk Arropp, who traveled to Chang'an (Xian) city of China and received preferential treatment by Emperor Taizong and later five emperors. There is also the development of the Nestorianism in China in the 150 years. The second part is the eulogy, which is shorter than the preface and written in a verse form.

According to the inscriptions, Daqin (Nestorian) bishop of Arroyo came to Chang'an and was welcomed by emperor Tang Taizong to court in 635. Taizong not only sent the prime minister Fang Xuanling to the western suburbs of Chang'an for grand reception, but also let Aroben and other people translate Bible in the emperor's library and discuss the meaning of Bible in the emperor's palace. Three years later in the year of 638 (The 12th year of Zhen Guan), Taizong issued a decree to allow preaching of Nestorianism, and built the "Daqin Temple" funded by the government in Chang'an Yining Square. At that time, Nestorianism was called "Persian Scripture (Bible)". "Scripture" meant "the Bible". This is also seen in the Volume 49 of Historical Records of Tang written in the Northern Song Dynasty by Wang Pu, which recorded the emperor Taizong's decree: "The establishment of religions was to serve the people. The Persian bishop took a very long distance to bring us the religious teachings. Those teachings should be introduced to the whole nation. "A town was built with 21 monks in it. From this moment on, there were about 20 monks in the Daqin temple of the Chang'an city.

13   In 1625, about 377 years before, in the temple of Zongren of Zhouzhi county in the West of Xi'an city, a famous Sino-Syriac bilingual Nestorian Inscription of Xi-an-fu (or Si-Ngan-fou) which was erected in 781, was found. The finding shocked the whole country and the world. Nestorianism, as a branch of Christianity in the Middle Ages, also was called Ärkägün in Turkic and Mongolian language (Christian Nestorianism was also called Yelikewen in Chinese sources), entered China via Persia and Central Asia on Silk Road in the 7th century AD.

Later, during Gao Zong's reign, Nestorianism had spread to regions outside the Chang'an city. The inscription said: "Different states all had Nestorian temples. There were temples in hundreds of cities." Here was described how the Nestorianism was spread during Tang Gaozong's reign. There may be some exaggeration, but at that time there was probably considerable development in regard to Nestorianism. Emperor Tang Gaozong had named him "Da Fa Zhu". While during the time of the female emperor Wu Zetian, Nestorianism probably encountered a low ebb.

Emperor Tang Xuanzong had helped the development of Nestorianism in China. Emperor Tang Xuanzong had ordered his five brothers and relatives to establish altars in the Daqin Temple and repaired this building. He also ordered Gao Shili to send five pieces of emperors' portraits, Tang Gaozong, Taizong, Zhongzong, Rui Zong in 742 and ordered that portrait should be placed in the temples, and also gave them hundreds of silk packs. Also, at that time a Persian missionary Heji (George) arrived here to assume the position of Bishop. Xuanzong had asked the missionary Luo Han, Pu Lun Paul, "Paul" as its transliteration and other 17 people and the new bishop Heji to repair the Qingxing Palace, to enable worshipping, and Xuanzong also personally wrote the name plaque of the temple.

The Nestor's tablet said that the monastery built in Chang'an by Tang Taizong was called the "Daqin Temple". According to other historical materials, this monastery was called "Persian Temple" at the time of its early construction, and was called "Persian Hu Temple" by the local people. The first volume of Song Ming's Chang'an History Records wrote that there was a Persian Hu Temple in the North of the Yi Ning Fang Street. In 745, Xuan Zong released an order saying: "The Persian teachings came from Daqin, and people need to learn from the Bible. Two Jings (here Chang'an and Luoyang) Persian Temple should be changed to Daqin Temple. If it was needed to establish a government, they would have to follow The Historical Records of Tang Dynasty Volume 49. Some of the emperors after the reign of Xuan Zong also supported the development of Nestorianism. In the inscriptions it was mentioned that Suzong Temple was built in Lingwu and other five counties; on the day of emperors' birthday, royal food would be given to monks; Dezong was giving new life to the Nestorians, meaning that Nestorian believers would access to a new life.

The monastery of Nestorians was sponsored by "Wang Shecheng", namely the Afghanistan Barih (Balkh) priest Yisi (Yazedbuzid), whose father was the Nestorian Monk Min Li (Milis). Yisi later became a Ziguanglu official, Shuofangjieguo official, and vice-deputy on the hall, having received the purple robe given by the emperor. The Nestorian monument which was found later, praised him for being kind and willing to charity, that he knew the deep truth, and worked hard. Yisi began to work for Su Zongting and wrote his name in emperor's Mu Fu Book. As Guo Ziyi's troops stationed in Shuofang, Yisi was with him. He gave out his salaries as gift, including the Du Li (glass) and money given to him by the emperor, and used all these funds to repair the Daqin (Nestorian) Temples. He also invested in erecting stele (stone monument) of The Nestorians in China, the inscription on this stele was also written by his son Jingjing.

It was mentioned in the tablet that it was built during Tang Dezong's reign on the 7th day of the first lunar month in 781, which was the "Da Yao Sen Wen" day. The words "Yao Sen Wen" mentioned here should be the transliteration of the ancient Persian "yak shanba" (Sunday). At that time the Orient Church Archbishop was Ningshu (Hanan Yeshu). In fact, Ningshu was dead in 778, that was three years before the establishment of the monument, but the time of his death could be 779 or 780 AD. As Baghdad was far from the China, the news of his death did not spread to China until the monument was set up, so in the Tang Dynasty, Nestorianism was also the main religion.

Christianity was originally called "Scripture" in the imperial edict of the Tang Dynasty in the 12th year under Tang Taizong's reign, meaning "the teachings of the Bible". Tang Xuanzong's order in September of the year 745 was called the "Persian classics". In addition to being found in this monument, the word Nestorian is also found in other documents, such as the Daqin Nestorian Xuan Yuan Ben Jing from 2th October of 717 AD, and Daqin Nestorian Great Truth on 20th May, 720. The Daqin Nestorian Three Wei Mengdu Zan discovered in Dunhuang was written in the year of 700, so the name of "Nestorian"has probablyappeared in the late 7th century. When, talking about the name "Nestorian", the inscription said: "It is nearly too hard to name this religion, which can be called Nestor." That is to say, at that time, it was difficult for people to find a suitable Chinese translation. The word Nestorian was probablythe homophobia of "Jingjiao". Besides a large part of Chinese inscriptions, there were also a few paragraphs in Syric writing were inserted in them. The first paragraph was the introduction of the inscription writer Jingjing, who was to be the godfather of China (Chinistan), district bishop and the elder and whose Syriac name was Adam (Adan in Judaism). From the Chinese inscription and the Syriac inscriptions, Jingjing seemed also to be called Lingbao.

At the end of another Syriac text, it was said: "The son of the elder of Milis in Balkh, namely the Khumdan Jingdu district the bishop Yezdduzid set up the monument in 1092 according to the Greek calendar..." The monument covered many names of the Nestorian monks, such as the bishop of Iohanan, the Chinese translation was Yaolun; the elder Ephrem, Folin; the elder Moses, Huilong, etc.. There were about 70 names of monks listed in the inscriptions, indicating the number of monks in Chang'an, but in fact its development cannot be compared with that of the Buddhism. Shu Yuanyu wrote in the Heavy Rock Temple Monument Order that there were other religions in the temple, such as Mani, Daqin, Yaoshen and so on. The number of the three religions was less than that of a temple in a small town, recorded in the Volume 727 of The Complete Works of Tang Dynasty.

After the collapse of the Uyghur Khanate in 840, the court of Tang Dynasty began to forbid the spread of Buddhism, and the Nestorianism was also implicated. In July of the 5th year of Huichang, two departments of the Tang's court reported to the emperor that Daqin (also the Nestorianism) was also an "evil" religion and should be forbidden together with Buddhism and Manichaeism. The Chinese followers of them should be sent to their homes while the foreign believers should be kept under strict supervision and control. After Tang Wuzong's order to eliminate Buddhism in 844 AD, According to the New History of Tang: "around 4,600 temples were destroyed together with some smaller ones. The number of monks and nuns who were forced to resumed secular life reached 260,000, and about 150,000 maids were set free, and all these people were made tax payers." The edict of the emperor gave Nestorianism a heavy blow in the mainland China, but it was not swept away." After that, there were still activities of Manichaeism across China. At the beginning of the 20th century, 7kinds of literature about the Chinese Nestorianism in the Tang Dynasty period was discovered in the Dunhuang stone chamber. These documents are Daqin Nestorian San Wei Meng Du Zan, Zun Jing, Daqing Nestorian Xuan Yuan [Zhi] Ben Jing, Zhi Xuan An Le Jing, Xu Ting Su Shi Suo Jing, Yi Shen Lun, Daqin Nestorian Da Sheng Tong Zhen Gui Fa Zan and so on.

The Nestorian Stele (upright stone) is also referred to as the Nestorian Monument, Nestorian Stone, Nestorian Inscription, or in its original Chinese title Daqinjfngjiao liiaing Zhongguobei literally meaning "Memorial of the Propagation in China of the Luminous Religion from Daqin." For monograph-length treatments of the Nestorian Stele, see also, Holm, Carus, and Wylie, The Nestorian Monument; Saeki, Nestorian Monument; P'an, Nestorian Tablet; Feng, Nestorian Stele; Pelliot, L'inscription nestorienne.[14] These ancient remnants, like the stele of The Nestorians in China, are important sources for studying the activities of the Nestorianism in China in the Tang Dynasty period.

(3) The Spread of Nestorianism in the Northern Grasslands

At the end of the Tang Dynasty, Nestorianism disappeared from the Central Plains, but it was widely disseminated in the Northern grasslands. The name of Nestorianism was first seen in Ma Shi Shi Pu Xu, Volume 43 of Jin Hua Collection by Huang Jin in the Yuan Dynasty. It recorded the history of the Wang ancient family of Ma in the Liao Jin Dynasty (AD 1115-1234): "The ancestors of the Ma family was the Nestorian nobles of Western regions..." Nestorianism was also known as the Qin Jiao in the Yuan Dynasty, namely the abbreviation of "Daqin" or "Daqin Nestorians".

In the Liao and Jin Dynasties period, people who had faith in Nestorianism were the Kerait (Kelie) tribe living in the middle of the Mongolian Plateau, Wanggu tribe living near the Golden Great Wall, the Hun Tribe moving from the Western Khitan border to the Central Asia, Naiman tribe living in Shihe

---

14 See also various essays in Drake, "Nestorian Literature," 609-14; Saeki, Nestorian Documents, pp. 7, 11, 27-31, 360-62; Kung, Christian Religion, pp. 16-23.

region between the Altai Mountain and Yarkent river, some of the Uyghurs who settled in the Eastern part of the Tianshan mountain regions after the Westward movement, and the tribe of the Hakaru people who occupied the regions around the Yi Lie River, Chui River, and Ta Ji Si River.

The family of Ma mentioned in the Ma Shi Shi Pu Xu was the people from the Wanggu tribe. Living in the South of the desert, Wanggu Tribe was a people speaking Turkic and writing Turkic by using Syriac letters, and it was a famous tribe preaching the doctrines of Nestorianism. Since the 1930s, archaeologists have found monuments (stele) of Nestorianism in the dwelling regions of the Wang ancient tribes. The Ye Lv Gong Shen Dao Zhi Bei found by the Scientific Mission of Southwest China in current southwestern Wulanhua, the city of Siziwang, Inner Mongolia said: "The ancestors of Yelü … Tie Li Xue in the Western Regions". Here the "Tie Li Xue" should possibly be "tersa", that is the "Die Xie" mentioned in the Changchun Live Journey to the West, also the followers of Nestorianism in the Persian language were called as "tersa".

The Wanggu tribe became the most famous tribe in the East that preached Nestorianism after entering the Yuan Dynasty period. Therefore, Odoric regarded the Wanggu region as the country of the elders, and Marco Polo also considered Kuolijisi (the founder of Nestorianism in China9 as the grandson of Onggut tribe chief A La Hu Si Ti Ji Hu Li, Kuolijisi became the prince of Wanggu tribe. Kuolijisi was descendant of the elder John. In the site of ruins of Tucheng in Yuan De Ning Lu Zhi, the remains, which narrate Nestorianism was discovered. The main inscription found there summarizes mainly, the Nestorian doctrine, mythology and rituals.

Another base of Nestorianism was the dwelling region of the Wanggu or Ongud Tribe. One of the two priests Mogusi who traveled for pilgrimage to the West was the son of Da Fu Jiao (Bayniel) in the Dongsheng Region. Junbuhua, the uncle of Kuolijisi and his father "Aibuhua" have settled in a county near the Dongsheng region, and they had tried to keep the two Western priests in this region. Many a believers of Nestorianism, dwelling in the east the Wanggu tribe region have moved to inland China regions. Guillaume de Roubruck, had mentioned that there was a Nestorian Bishop in Xijing, referring to the Xijing in Jin Dynasty period, which is the Datong county in Shan'xi province today. In the southern districts of the city of Datong lived a number of Nestorianism believers.

Another important tribe who believed in Nestorianism was Kerait (Kelie) tribe. Living in the center of Hang Ai Shan region of the original Turkic Khanate and Uyghur Khan kingdom during the Liao Jin Dynasty, the Kelie (Kerait) tribe was the most powerful nomadic tribe in the Mongolian Plateau. It was in the early 11th century that Kelie (Kerait) tribe believed in Nestorianism. According to the Syriac scripts and literature, the Metropolitan bishop Merv city sent a letter to the Patriarch bishop or Catholicus of Baghdad in 1009 CE, in which it was mentioned the following: "the leader of Kerait (Kelie) Tribe once got lost on his way back home from hunting, and but later he found his way after being guided by a saint, consequrntly he became a follower of Jesus Christ." Soon later, this leader, called on the local Christian merchants to learn Nestorian Christian teachings, saying that the 200,000 people in his tribe were willing to be Christian and asked the priest to baptize them.[15]

The Naiman Tribe living in the Shihe region between the Jinshan and Ye Er region was also a tribe believing in Nestorianism, because they were influenced by the Uyghurs. In addition, according to the Arab historical records, the Hun Tribe which originally lived in the North of the desert of believed in Nestorianism. After the rise of the Khitan people, they were forced to move to the West of Central Asia to the Aral Sea region.

(4) The Christian Nestorianism (Ye Li Ke Wen) in Western Regions

From the existing literature and cultural relics, the Nestorianism in the Northwest Region of the Yuan Dynasty were mainly spread and active in the following six regions.

The Uyghur Region

The time of the Nestorianism to be introduced in to the Uyghur region cannot be approved. In the era of Mongolian, the followers of Nestorianism were sometimes named "Die Xie" or "Tie Li Xue" by the Han nationality. This is the transliteration of the Persian "tersa", which means "fear"i.e, obedience to God, and it was also the Persian's unique way of calling the Nestorians. The word Nestorian in the monument of Nestorians in China was translated as "Da Suo", which refers to the word "monks". It was probably because there were many Nestorian people in the Uyghur region, some people confused the "Die Xie" with Uyghur people, for example, the historians of Armani (Armenia) called the land of Uyghurs as "the country of Die Xie". As Qiu Chuji (a Taoist scholar) went to see Cheng Ji Si Han (Genghis Khan) in the court, his journey passed through the Uyghur land This event was recorded as: "In the East of Su Lun Tai (current north of Urumchi), we were welcomed by the leader of Die Xie" in the Suicide Note by Hai Ning Wang Jing An Xian Sheng, in the first part of Chang Chun Zhen Ren Xi You Ji Zhu, Volume 39, page 28.

The "leader of Die Xie" talked about the existence of organized Nestorian missionary teams. In the last century, located in the Zhetysu or Semirechye region of Russia, located at the junction of the Republic of Kyrgyzstan and the Republic of Kazakhstan, together with the ruins of the Tang Dynasty, several Nestorian tombstones with inscriptions in Uyghur language were also found which belonged to Uyghur Zuo Bo Hao Lang: Also, Uyghur translation of the

196

15 In the 13th century, Syrian historians Bar Hebraeus quoted the letter in The Yearbook of Shengjiao, see Feng Chengjun's translation of Duo Sang History of Mongolia, Volume 1, Chapter 2, page 4, the Commercial Press, 1936. However Bo Xihe doubted the credibility of this narration of Bar Hebraeus, see the Sheng Wu Qin Zheng Lu Jiao Zhu by Guowei Wang, p. 208.

wretched "Christ Gospel" remnants were found in Turpan (Xinjiang) at the beginning of this century.[16] In the end period of Xi Western Liao Dynasty period, Uyghur had had a prime minister Zhi Lu Pu Er, one of whose grandson named Sargis (Sa Ji Si). His name was commonly used by the Nestorians, which was the transliteration of Sarghis in Syriac texts. Due to the role of the vowel and harmony, the name in the Mongolian and Turkic languages was read as Sergis or Sirgis, and in the Yuan Dynasty Chinse used the following words Xi Er Ji Si or Xi Li Ji Si.

From the travel notes of the Westerners at that time, we could see that the Uyghur Nestorians lived together with other various religions together. For example, as the Guillaume of Rubrock, the Franciscan envoy sent by King Louis IX of France, travelled to see Möngke Khan, the 4th Great Khan of Mongols, and his journey passed through the Uyghur region, and he saw the Uyghur Nestorian monks. He said that they lived together with the Saracens, and there were always fights between the two:[17]

In the description of the Uyghur land, Marco Polo said: "In addition to the Ou Xiang followers (or Buddhists) of the Huo Zhou Zhi Di, there were many Nestorian Saracen people. Christians were often intermarried with Buddhists, as written in Marco Polo Travels, by Muller and Beth, English translation, pp. 155-160. In fact, Marco Polo did not travel to the Uyghur region, the above was what he had heard about.

Almaliq Region

Almaliq region was the dwelling place of Qarluk (Halalu) tribe in the Jin and Yuan Dynasty periods, and a Nestorian religious center in the Northwest Region. (the modern name of Almaliq region is Huocheng), Among the Nestorian tomb inscriptions unearthed in the Semirechie or Seven River Region collected by Zuo Bo Hao Lang, only 10 owners of the tombs could be be traced, and 7 of them were people from Almaliq Tribe. The time of their death (only those can be identified) ranged from 1287 to 1300, both women and men, and some of them were scholars.[18]

China's archaeologists also found several stones in the Almaliq site, on which Syriac words and scripts were carved and some also contained the Christian cross. Xinjiang Museum also found several Huang Wenbi.[19] Among those Nestorian Bishops who travelled to preach religion in 1349, the place names such as Hanbaliq (current Beijing) and Al Falik (probably Almaliq) region were listed. The Al Falik should be the Almaliq city. At the end of the 14th

---

16 See Nestorian Studies", p. 840, No. 83, The Nestorian tombstones.
17 The English version of Travel Notes of Guillaume of Rubrock, pp. 143-144, translated by Lv Pu Han, p. 155.
18 See the Nestorian Studies, p. 792, No.8 Tombstone; page 804, No.11 Tombstone; p. 854, No. 135 Tombstone; p. 486, No. 461 Tombstone; p. 883, No. 500 Tombstone.
19 See the Yuan Almaliq Ancient City Archaeological Studies, Archaeology Volume 10 in 1963, p. 577.

century, the Italian catholic traveler Giovanni de Marignolli (Bartholomen) mentioned in his writings that Almaliq was a city of Khitans or Tatars. It is generally believed that Nestorian Bishop in charge of spreading Nestorianism in other regions was located in Almaliq, which was the northern capital of the Chagatai Khanate the vassal of Yuan dynasty at that time. In addition to the Nestorianism religion, Islam religion was also popular among the Almaliq people.

There was a very close relationship between the Almaliq Nestorian community and the Qayaliq Nestorian community. In addition to religious ties between the two, there were also political relations. When Yelü Dashi[20] (the ruler of the Western Liao Dynasty) led his troops to Central Asia, the Karakanid ruler of Balasaghun, Ibrāhīm II b. Ahmad asked for the help of Yelü Dashi* against the Qarluk (Halalu) and Kankalis tribes which often assaulted the Karakanid dynasty.

The chief of Qarluk, (Halalu) Dashiman Dejin (Danişmend Tigin), whose origin was Almalliq (Elmalık) city had died in Qayaliq city, in 657[21] (Islam lunar calendar), and his corpse was carried back to Almaliq and buried there near his father—Xigenahei Dejin's (Suğnak Tigin or Suknak Tigin)— tomb. It can be seen that during the Karakanid dynasty and through the Western Liao Dynasty period to the Mongolian era, both in Almaliq and Qayaliq towns, lived the Qarluk (Halalu) people. Ibn Batuta wrote Almaliq was the proper capital of the empire of Tatar Sultan Ala-eddin Tarmashhirin. In addition to the Almaliq Nestorian community who were living near the near Maver-al-naher (Transoxiana) Region, there were also Nestorian activities in the Almaliq region.

Qayaliq Region

It was one of the dwelling regions and center of Nestorian Qarluk(s) (Halalu) tribe who had migrated to this region, led by a former Uch-Karluk bey with the title Kül-Erkin. Guillaume of Rubrouck wrote that people who worshipped the Nestorianism conducted religious activities in their own languages and words. The words should be the Turkic language spelled by Syriac script which was common among the Nestorian religious followers. Guillaume of Rubrouck described the situation when he first time met a Nestorian in the region: "He (referring to the Nestorians) had a small cross written in ink on his hand and thus I was sure that he was a Nestorian, He told me that he was a Christian. Then I asked again: "Why do you have no cross and the picture of Jesus Christ?" He replied: "Our teachings are different from those of the Christians." So I guessed that they were also the Nestorians, they were ignoring some of the Christian teachings doctrines they believed to be.wrong. Guillaume of Rubrouck also

---

20   Yelü Dashi or Yeh-Lü Ta-Shih (r. 1124–1143) was the founder of the Qara Khitai state, also known as the Western Liao dynasty. He was also known in Islam sources as Nūshī Taifū, Qushqin Taifū or Qushqīn, son of Baighū.
21   657, Islam lunar calendar, is 1259 AD, The chief leaders of Qarluq(s) was called Tigin.

mentioned that they found a village not far from the East of the sea where only lived Nestorian followers and they had their own teachings and beliefs.[22]

Semirechie (Zhetysu) Region

In the autumn of 1883, two cemeteries (one is bigger than the other) where 610 Nestorian believers were buried was discovered near the ancient capital of Western Liao, the Semirechie region, (or Seven Rivers Region) administered by Russia in 1883, and it is the Burana relics around current Tokmak city of Kyrgyzstan. One of the cemeteries is not far South of Tokmak city, and the other is about 1.5 km from Bishkek. Among the 610 tombstones, about 537 could be identified, and 37 of them could not be identified at all. There are 432 tombstones of which we can say their years of establishment, but for the 131 tombs we cannot say their years of establishment. The earliest tomb was established in the year 858, which demonstrates that it was quite early when the Nestorians had preached here.

The narrations about the Nestorians dwelling in the north of Hu Chan Bei grasslands in the 9th century, were recorded Islam literature. According to Narshaki's Bukhara History, the ruler of Samanid Dynasty (Saffarids), İsmail dispatched a war expedition to Talas (Taraz) and Otrar in 893, Samanid Dynasty made these 2 cities key military outposts in the fight against Turkic nomadic confederations and important centers of Islamic learning in the Turkic lands. After this war, local residents were suppressed and surrendered, so their main churchs were changed to mosques. As Talas (Taraz) was not far from Semirechie, the records in Bukhara History above were partly in contrast with the information we get from tombstones erected in 858 AD, which were unearthed in the Semirechie.

The traces of Nestorians can be found in the north of Hu Chan Bei grassland in the 9th century from the Islam literature. The vast majority of the tombstones that can be studied and read were erected in 1248-1342, indicating a large number of Nestorians who had lived in the era of Mongolian Kingdom reign. According to the calendars craved in these tomb stones, there was an average annual death of about 5 people from 1286 to 1347. Estimated with normal mortality, the Nestorian monks gathered here at that time can be added to more than one thousand people. The identities of the tombs were different, ranging from top officials, bishops, and archdeacons, general believers, and some of which belonged to female believers. The local Nestorian group was led by the bishop of Almaliq. The cravings on the tombstone display that the death rate of the inhabitants had decreased during the years of late 1330s and early 1340s, whichprobably was caused by terrible plagues and since the region began to decline socially and economically, and the Nestorian community in this region also greatly decreased.

---

22   Travel Narrations of Guillaume of Rubrouck, pp. 141-144; the Chinese trans. version translated by Lv Pu Han, pp. 154-155.

There were two ways of numerating the years on these gravestones. One was the Greek calendar using 310 BC as its first year, so the year on the tombstones minus 310 would be the AD year of setting up the tombstone. The other way was numbering the years by using the 12 Chinese Zodiacs calender.

Kashgar (Ke Shi Ha Er) and Yarkant (Ya Er Kan)

Today, Kashgar (Keshihaer) is in Xinjiang-Uyghur Autonomous Region. Marco Polo has visited Kashgar (Keshihaer) and he said that some of the residents there were Turkic peoplewho believed in Nestorianism, and they had their own churches and religions. They pursued the Christian Nestorian doctrines and lived along with other residents who had different beliefs.[23] In the middle of the 13th century, the Bishop of Nestorians resided in Kashgar, indicating it was an important center for this religion. The owners of the tombstones found in the last century in the Seven Rivers Region administered by Russian at that time were from Kashgar. Yarkant city (Shache), is in Xinjiang Uyghur Autonomous Region PRC. Marco Polo recorded: "Residents in Shache (Ya Er Kan/Yarkant) are mostly Islam (Mu Su Lu Mang), and only a few of them are Nestorian monks and Ya Ge Monks."[24] The time when Nestorianism was introduced to this region cannot be identified.

Samarkand City

Chinese, European and Islam literature all recorded that Samarkand was a well-known Nestorianism center in Central Asia. The Chinese records were mainly in the Daxingguo Temple by Liang Xiang of the Yuan Dynasty. The following statements of Liang Xiang and Marco Polo are probably from the same sources.Marco Polo said: The inhabitants of Samarkand were Nestorian believers and the Huis (Islam). The Mongolian Khan's brother Cha Hetai was baptized as a Christian. The Nestorianism followers in Samarkand built a church under the support of Cha Hetai to commemorate the birth of Jesus. Cha Hetai took a boulder from a house of the Huis and Nestorian Christians put this boulder in their church in order to support the marble pillar. Thus Samarkand's Huis were afraid of Cha Hetai and obeyed his orders.

After the death of Cha Hetai, the ruling power passed to Haidu. But, Haidu hated the Nestorian Christian (Ye Ke Li Wen) religion, so Samarkand's Huis demanded the boulder back. Although Nestorian Christians admitted that the boulder belonged to them, they also declared their will to buy it considering that the stone was used to hold the churchurch. However, the Huis insisted on taking back this boulder, and they got the support of Haidu. Haidu ordered Nestorian Christians to return the stone within 2 days. After they received the order, they were caught in an extreme sadness and anxiety, and did not know what to do. After the death of Cha Hetai, they lost their supporter, so they could neither calm the situation with money nor they didn't know how to remove the boulder and preserve this well-built, charming church. Therefore they prayed to Jesus Christ, asked for His mercy and demanded His help to curb the trouble.

23 Travels of Marco Polo, translated by Mu Le, Xi Bo, p. 143.
24 Travels of Marco Polo, translated by Mu Le, Xi Bo, p. 146.

Then a miracle occurred, when the time was due, to give back the boulder, as ordered by the emperor Haidu, the Nestorian believers saw that people found that the pillars standing on the demanded boulders have automatically moved upwards from their basis for by about 3 feet by the will and powers of the Lord Jesus Christ, and stood there as if the boulders were still under it. From that day on, the pillar remained hanging without any support. Consequently, the Huis were disappointed and to take away the boulder.[25]

Jesus Christ's supernatural power is of course irrational, but this story reflects the battle between Christians (Ye Ke Li Wen) and the Huis (Islam) in Samarkand of the Mongolian era. In this battle, Christians (Ye Ke Li Wen) was supported by the Mongolian rulers. The letter of Shambat (Sempad), the brother of King Hethum I of Armenia (Cilicia/Kilikya), to his own country from Samarkand on February 7th, 1248 reflected the struggles between Nestorian Christians (Ye Ke Li Wen) and the Huis (Islam). This letter also described the spread of Nestorianism among the Mongols, and said that Khan himself the Great khan Güyük, (Gui You) had recently converted to this to orthodox belief. Shambat (Sempad)also visited the local rchurch and saw an image of the Christ and read the three sages. Shambat (Sempad) also said: "The Islam people have mistreated them (the Christians) and now endured the double sufferings of their past."[26]

There ara similar records in the book of "Shu Zha Ni". The book said: A Sayyid from Samarkand, (referring to the prince, lord, leader, or master, etc., now translated as Said), came back to Delhi City in 657 according to Islam lunar (Hicri) calendar (also the year 1259). Sayyid's name was "Ashraf-ud- Din", whose family had an imam (Islam priest) in every generation and he worked in the temple of "Nur-ud-Di-A'ma" in Samarkand. He said: "that there is a Nestorian Christian (Die Xie) who converted to Islam in the Samarkand City. Also there was a Mongolian from China who did not believe in any religion, began to preach Nestorianism. The Nestorian Christians (Ye Ke Li Wen) in the city complained that the Huis (Islam) have seduced their believers. The Mongol leaders ordered that the young man who had converted to Islam would be brought to them and they have forced the young man to abandon Islam with various prsssures, but this attempt had failed. So the Mongols rulers became furious and tortured him to death. Huis in Samarkand complained these events to Kepchak Khan Berke, and Berke suppressed the Nestorian believers. Once as all the believers gathered in the church, they were all arrested, and the church was also demolished.[27]

Samarkand was the traditional center of Nestorianism in Central Asia. Until 1404, during the Spanish envoy Ruy González de Clavijo's stay in Samarkand till 1404, he said he saw the following: "In this place, besides Islam people,

25 Travels of Marco Polo , translated by Mu Le, Xi Bo, pp. 143-146.
26 Barthold: Turkestan Down to the Mongolian Invasion, Russian Complete Works, pp. 569-570.
27 The History of the Asian Muhammadan Dynasty, London, 1881, pp. 1287-1290.

there are the Armenians, the Greek Orthodox, Jacobian Christians, and the Nestorians".[28]

(5) Nestorianism (Qin Jiao) in the Chinese mainland

After entering the Yuan Dynasty, as the tribes that believed in Nestorianism in the Northwest region was suppressed by Genghis Khan, some of the Nestorian believers were forced to migrate across the country, so Nestorianism was re-introduced to the Chinese mainland.

In the Yuan Dynasty's literature, the name Yekelewen "Ye Ke Li Wen" often appeared. In Mongolian language, plural form of this word was spelled as Ba Si Ba is in fact "Erke'ud", see the 6th volume of Shi Mo Juan Hua, which was used to refer to Nestorianism and its priests and believers. In the modern times, there lived Mongolian people in the Southern Ordos, known as the Erkud tribe, who still kept the customs of smearing the body with sesame oil, and putting the corpses as crosses, etc.. As they named their tribe as "Erkud", it is likely that they were rhe adherents of Nestorianism.[29]

The government department who was in charge of Nestorian Christians in the Yuan Dynasty was Zong Fu Department in 1289, which was a high level department attached to the empire court. "It was responsible for the affairs (several religions) Ma Er HaXi, Lie Ban, Nestorian Christians (Yekeliwen), Church building and others affairs."[30]

202

The Ma Er Haxi was the transliteration of the Syriac Mar (saint) Hasia (Apostol), which was the rank for the Nestorian high bishop. In other Chinese historical data, it was sometimes translated as Mali Ha Xi Ya.[31]

"Lie Ban" was the transliteration of Rabban in Syriac, which was a title of rank for Nestorian monks. Like other religious clerics, they also enjoyed the exemption of Juan (tax). The departments that were in charge of Nestorian Christians (Yekelewen) (Ye Ke Li Wen) were distributed in all parts of the country, reaching up to 72. It is unclear whether the Chong Fu Department of the court n was authorized to govern Catholic missionary activities. Nestorianism was re-introduced to the mainland China in Yuan Dynasty period from the Northwest region, and in Yuan Dadu[32], most of the Northwest and even Yangtze River regions had its believers.

Yuan Da Du (today Beijing) was the political center of the Yuan Dynasty, thus it had become the "hot-spot" region that Christian fought for. The influence Nestorianism in Yuan Dadu was quite large, and the remains near Dadu in

---

28 Clavijo's Eastern , translated by Yang Zhanjun, Commercial Press, 1957, p. 157.
29 Tian Qingbo: Ordos, Fu Jen Catholic University Journal, Volume 9, p. 14.
30 The History of Yuan Officials.
31 See Liang Xiang: Daxingguo Temple and Shunzhen Jiang Volume 9; Xia Nai: The Yekelewen (Ye Ke Li Wen) (Nestorian) Tombstones in Quanzhou Written in Two Languages, Journal ofCultural Relics, 1981/1.
32 Dadu, Beijing (then called Dadu–Great capital or Khanbaliq)

the Fangshan San Pen Mountain was preserved till current times. In the letter written by John of Monte Corvino (1247-1328) Franciscan, it was written that : The Nestorians, a certain body who profess to bear the Christian name, but who badly deviated from the Christian religion, have grown so powerful in those parts that they will not allow a Christian of another ritual to have ever so small a church, or to publish any doctrine different from their own. To these regions there never came any of the apostles, nor their disciples. And so the aforesaid Nestorians, either directly or through others whom they bribed, have brought on me the sharpest of persecutions. For they got up stories that I was not sent by our lord the pope, but was a great spy and impostor; and after a while they produced false witnesses who declared that there was indeed an envoy sent with presents of immense value for the emperor, but that I had murdered him in India and stolen what he had in charge. And these intrigues and calumnies went on for some five years.[33]

The most important figure who spread Nestorianism in the region of Samarkand (South of the Yangtze River) was "Mar Sarghis" (Ma Xue Si Ji Si) who was mentioned by Marco Polo. He worked in an official's mansion in Zhen Jiang Fu Road in the 14th fyear of Zhi Yuan, and during his tenure he has built 7 churchs, one of which was in Hangzhou. The most famous one of the several temples in Zhenjiang was the Daxingguo Temple. The Nestorian temples in these regions had reached to 70 which were used by both the officials and common people. The Da Xing Guo which recorded Nestorianism deeds was so far the only written literature which reflects the Han people's knowledge about Nestorianism in the Yuan Dynasty period. Its full text no longer exists, and people can only find its abstract in the Zhi Shun Jiang Volume 9.

203

The text recorded: "Semiz Kent (Xue Mi Si Xian) was more than 10.000 miles in the Northwest of the Central Plains, and it was where the Nestorians (Ye Ke Li Wen) preached their doctrine." If you asked them how to preach, they would answer: "There were 12 'cross (Christian)' temples in this region, and in which there was a Buddha who was 40 chi high and made of wood. Mu Le and Ji Le were both the transliteration of Mar Elijah. They also regarded "This spirit lasted for more than a hundred years" as the Greek calendar. At the beginning of the 1500 of the Greek calendar (AD 1190), there was indeed a bishop named Mar Elijah (Elias/İlyas) who had died, when he was more than a hundred years old.[34]

This record and Marco Polo's legend of Samarkand's holy temple was clearly from the same source. The "Xuemi Sixian" referred here was the transliteration of Samaritan Turkic name "Semiz kent", meaning Li Fei Cheng, and also written as Xue Mi Si Gan, Xie Mi Si Gan, and Xun Xi Gan etc. in the Yuan Dynasty. From the 2 names of "Semiz kent" (Xuemi Sixian in Daxing Guo Temple and "Mar Sargis" (Ma Xueli Jisi), we can sense the usage of the vowel

33   See John of Monte Corvino, Serve As an Envoy to Mongolia, pp. 224-227. See also: http://www.thenagain.info/Classes/Sources/MonteCorvino.html.
34   See Christians of Zhenjiang, Jiangsu Province p. 635.

and harmony rule, which showed that "Mar Sargis" (Ma Xueli Jisi) came from a Nestorian family in Samarkand, but who used the Turkic language. As for the teachings of Nestorianism, the Daxing Guo Temple recorded: "teachings of Nestorianism are different from that of Tian Zhu."[35]

Zhenjiang was an important region where the Nestorianism people preached their doctrines. There were also a number of cross (Christian) temples built by others. According to Marco Polo's writings, there were three cross Nestorian temples in Yangzhou city which is separated with the Zhenjiang city by a river.

According to Marco Polo, there was only one Nestorian church in Hangzhou, which was undoubtedly the temple established by "Mar Sargis" (Ma Xue Li Ji Si), namely it was the Nestorian (Da Pu Xing) Temple. After the entrance into the Ming Dynasty period, the "Shi Fang Temple" relics located in the east of Jiang Qiao was changed to "San Tai Fu Hall".[36]

In the Yuan Dynasty, specialized officials were in charge of check-ing Nestorianism in the South of Yangtze Region. In the view of Mongols, there seemed to be no significant difference between the Mingjiao religion (Manichaeism) introduced from Persia and the Christian Nestorianism. So, Mongols had nominated Wanggu (a tribe in the region) aristocrats who be-lieved in Nestorianism and whose language was Turkic to manage the religious affairs in Quanzhou.[37] These officials were specifically "in charge of Mingjiao (Manichaeism) and Qinjiao (Nestorian) religions".[38]

204

In addition to the above major regions, there were other Christian sects in other regions. Such as the charge of red (current Yunnan, Kunming) urban resi-dents there were a number of Nestorian believers (Nie Si Laisi). There was considerable concentration of Nestorian believers in Liaodong region. In the rebellion led by Prince Nayan[39] the Christian cross painted on the battle flag to mobilize Nestorains.

After Nayan's failure, the local Nestorian Christians were humiliated or forced to migrate to mainland China. The discovery of the relics of Nestorian (from Yuan Dynasty period) in the ruins of the ancient city of Liaodong has proved that there were still Christians living in this region after the rebellion.

---

35 See the book, Zhishun Zhenjiang ((Local gazetteer of Zhenjiang from the Zhishun reign), Volume 9, Monk Temple.

36 See West Lake Tour written by Tian Rucheng (in shi 1526).

37 Wu Wenliang, Religious Stone in Quanzhou, Science Press, 1957 edition, p. 46.

38 The Mongolian grasslands and the forests around Lake Baikal were also home to many other tribes such as Tartar, Wongjiqa, Mierqi, Woyela, Kerait (Kelie), Naiman and Wanggu, which varied in size and economic and cultural development.

39 Nayan was a prince of the Borjigin royal family of the Mongol Empire. He raised a noteworthy and serious rebellion against the Mongolian Khagan, Kublai Khan. He was a Nestorian Christian. Much of what is known of Nayan was recorded by the Venetian travel-ler Marco Polo.

4. Judaism

(1) The Jews That Moved to China

In ancient times, the Jews were already among those foreign merchants who came to trade and live in China. As there was already an unprecedented prosperity of the expedition during the Tang Dynasty times, the Nestorianism and Manichaeism was introduced into the mainland of China. Although there was no specific record in the history of the Han Dynasty that the Jews came to China, it was no doubt the fact that at that time there were living Jews in China. According to Abu Zaid al-Hassan, during the Huang Chao rebels in the late Tang dynasty, Guangzhou was captured and about 12,000 people were executed, including Jews, the Huis, Christians and Zoroastrians.[40]

Ali Masudi, an Arab geographer, also made the same records. Those Jews who resided in Guangzhou have probably arrived in China by maritime expedition.

In 1901, Aurel Stein found a new Persian letter written by Hebrew letters near Luo Fu, Northeast of Hetian. In 1908, Bo Xihe found a remnant of Hebrew prayer in Dunhuang. This found is classified among the relics from the Tang Dynasty period. This found shows that besides sea expedition, a part of Jews have traveled to China by taking from the land route.

In the period of Song dynasty, the Jews had settled down in Kaifeng, and they built a Zhu Hu Yuan (Jewish monastery) in 1163. The monastery was later severely damaged due to long years of negligence, but fortunately there are 4 four inscriptions about it, currently. These inscriptions were respectively engraved in the 2nd year of Hongzhi reign of the Ming period (1489), the 7th year of the Zhengde reign of the Ming period (1512) and the Qing Emperor Kangxi's reign (1663-1697). These 4 inscriptions are valuable original materials for studying the history of Judaism in China, and one of the main vouchers of Chinese and foreign academic writings on this subject.

205

From the beginning of the Yuan Dynasty, there were more records of the Jews in China. In the records of Chinese historical literature of the Yuan Dynasty, the Jews were called Zhuhu, Zhu Hu, or Zhuhu Hui Hui, and they belonged to "Se Mu People"(It was a kind of social estate division in the period of Yuan Dynasty). The Jews were called Yahudi in Hebrew, and the Arabs and the Persians also accepted this name, calling the Jews Yahud as well. Probably the name of Yahud, which the Han people had heard a lot, was read by Kipchak people who spoke the Turkic language, and they pronounced "y" as "j" in the Kipchak dialects, so it was written as "Zhuhu" in Chinese. The word "Hui Hui" did not necessarily represent the Muslims (Islams) back in the Yuan Dynasty, but it was almost the synonym for "The Western Region". At the same time

---

40   François Renault: Arabs and the Persian's travels in India and China, Vol. 1, Paris, 1945, p. 64; Zhang Xingzhi, Compilation of Historical Materials on Chinese and Western Communications, Volume 2, Zhonghua Book Company, 1977, pp. 207-208.

there were many similar practices between the Judaism and Islam, thus the term "Zhuhu Hui Hui" was created.

The History of the Yuan Dynasty also recorded an event: In December of the 16th year of Zhi reign of the Yuan period (AD 1279), "The Hui Hui only ate those sheep which were butchered by them, so the local people suffered a lot. The emperor said angrily, "You are all my slaves, and how dare you not listen to me or not follow our rules?' So the emperor banned the Hui Hui People from eating sheep butchered only by themselves."[41]

Mongolian would cut open the chest when they slaughtered the sheeps, while the Huis, including Islams and Jews would cut the throat. In the opinion of the Huis, the way the Mongolian slaughtering of sheep was impure. In the Yuan Dynasty the Huis and Jewish merchants enjoyed the privilege to be provided food as they traveled through the expedition road-posts, but they did not eat the lamb meat prepared for them, claiming it was not clean and demanded sheep slaughter only to be realized by themselves, which caused dissatisfaction among the people running the road-post inn. As this fact was reported to the court, the emperor Kublai Khan released an order to prohibit the Huis' refusing to eat the offered lamb. It seemed that matter only involved the Huis, not related to the Jews according to the records of the History of Yuan Dynasty, but we still need other documents in order to verify the truth of it.

Jāmi' al-tawārīkh by the historian Rashid-al-Din of Persian Yili Khan in the 13th and 14th century also recorded a story: "A group of Hui merchants from Huoli, Barhu, and Jilijisi to pay tribute for a special sea bird and white eagle to the Hehan court. Hehan was very pleasant and bestowed them food, but they refused to eat. Hehan asked them why and they replied the food was not clean. Hehan got furious and decreed that the Huis and the Biblical (Christian) people cannot cut open the chest to kill the sheep any more, and they must cut the sheep's throat as the Mongolians did. Those who slaughter sheeps in the former way would be executed to death, and their wife would be "given" to the informer."[42]

Later, In his book Jami'al-Tarikh, Rashid-al-Din described how the Nestorian Ngai-Sie took this opportunity to attack the Huis. It is clear that what Rashid-al- Din had recorded was the same as what was mentioned in the History Collection of Yuan Dynasty. However, as things happened in China, the History of Yuan Dynasty clearly described the Huis as those people who did not eat food served by the hosts in the road-post inns, but when the news came to Persia, it was rumored as the Hui people did not eat the food which Kublai Khan had bestowed them.

However, the History of the Yuan Dynasty did not record the original text of Kublai Khan's decree. In contrast, Jāmi' al-tawārīkh had more detailed records on Kublai Khan's edicts. What was of particular importance was the fact that the edicts mentioned the so called "Biblical doctrines" besides the Huis. Here

41   See The History of the Yuan Dynasty.
42   See Jāmi' al-tawārīkh written by Rashid-al- Din, Tehran Persian edition, p. 654.

the "people who believed in doctrines" referred to the Christians and the Jews in Persian. In addition to the History of Yuan Dynasty and and the Persian version of Jāmi' al-tawārīkh, it can also be found in Decrees and Regulations of the Yuan Dynasty. The text is as follows: Ban on Cutting Open the Neck of Sheep:"On the 24th December of the 16th year of Zhi Yuan in the Yuan Dynasty, the emperor Genghis Khan was born and abundant food distributed to the tribes. However the Huis did not accept the food." The Mongolians from the court said: "you (the Huis) were ruled by us, but you did not eat Mongolian food, so you have all broken the law." "Therefore, from this day on, no matter who cut open the sheep's neck to eat would be punished. The informer would be rewarded with money."[43]

It is clear that what was recorded in the Code 57 was the original text of those recorded in History Collection. According to the records in the Code 57, the Mu Su Lu Mang Huis only refers to Shu Hu Huis, so the so called "biblical people" which only refers to the Jews, not including the Christians.

There are a few other Chinese and foreign historical materials where the Jews in the Yuan Dynasty were mentioned. According to Yang's Shan Ju Xin Hua, "The officials of the Sugar Bureau in Hangzhou were all rich Zhu Hu and Hui traders". Here the 'Zhu Hu' refers to 'Zhu Hu' (same pronunciation with different Chinese characters), namely the Jews. Probably the Jews and the Huis mastered the technology to make sugar, so they were dominant in the sugar production in Hangzhou. The Jews of the Ming Dynasty in Hangzhou were the descendants of "Zhu Hu" who had mastered the sugar technology. Ibn Tatu, a Moroccon traveler who had traveled to Hangzhou and was recorded in history, said that there were numerous Jews in Hangzhou and they had a community. In the second district of the city, there was even a gate for them, called "The Gate of the Jews". Thus, Ibn Tatu's records support the Chinese historical data.

(2) Kaifeng's Jewish Community

The earliest attention to the Chinese Jews was recorded by the Catholic Jesuit missionary Matteo Ricci in the early 17th century. He came to the south of China in the Ming Dynasty period (1582). In 1601, Matteo Ricci had arrived in Beijing. In late June 1605, hearing the news about Matteo Ricci, a Chinese Jew came to Beijing and visited him. This person was Ai Tian. According to Matteo Ricci, Ai Tian narrated the following :

There were 10 to 12 Jews in Kaifeng, Henan Provinces. There was also a Jewish temple where the Mosaic Five, which was written in the sheepskin and had five or six hundred years of history, was collected. Ai Tian also said that there were more Jewish households in Hangzhou, where there were also Jewish temples. There were also Jews in other regions, but no Jewish temples. The Jewish family in Hangzhou should be the descendants of those officials of the sugar bureau in the Yuan Dynasty.

---

43   Taiwan photocopies, Code of Yuan Dynasty, Volume XIX, Code 57.

As the Jews do not eat pork like the Huis, the common Han residents cannot tell the difference between them and the Huis. There were many Huis in Kaifeng, and the Jews did not like them, nor contacted with them. Ai Tian called himself "Yi Ci Le Ye", i.e, as the Israeli. They did not know about this naming of the Jews but only knew that "Ya A Jue Wu" (Jacob) was their ancestor. Ai Tian also told some of the stories in the Old Testament and he knew that there were 12 branches led by Moses in Israel. Ai Tian told Matteo Ricci that he came to Beijing to take the exams for an official job. The reason for the visit was not only because he was curious, but he also wanted to be recognized. He did not understand the difference between Catholicism and Judaism, so he had paid the visit without an appointment.

Three years later, in 1608, Matteo Ricci sent a Chinese Catholic to Kaifeng and confirmed what Ai Tian had said and the Chinese also brought back the transcript of certain chapters of the Pentateuch. There were no vowels in the Hebrew language used in Pentateuch kept in Kaifeng. It was the ancient version of Pentateuch, and it coincided with the Hebrew text of Torah in the 16th century of Belgian Antwerp bookseller Christopher Plantin.

Matteo Ricci himself did not know the Hebrew language, so he sent a Chinese person again to Kaifeng and sent a letter to the Haham (priest in Jews) of the Kaifeng Jewish temple. Matteo Ricci said that in Beijing he had the Old Testament and doctrines which recorded the words and behaviors of Messiah who had come to the mortal world, but the Haham in Kaifeng responded that Messiah had not yet come to earth, and he as the savior would come after one hundred thousand years has passed.

The discussion between Matteo Ricci and the Kaifeng Jews revealed the basic distinction between Judaism and the Christianity (Catholic) which was later derived from Judaism. Judaism believed that a savior Messiah would come to earth and save the Jewish people, while Christianity believed that Jesus Christ was the Messiah they expected who would save them.

Knowing that Matteo Ricci was a prestigious missionary in the Western Regions, Kaifeng's Haham expressed his willingness to let him rule the Kaifeng Jewish Temple. The only condition was that Matteo Ricci could not eat pork and had to live with the Jews. This showed that the Chinese Jews in Kaifeng did not understand the difference between Judaism and Catholicism.

After the communication between Matteo Ricci and the Kaifeng Jews, three Jews one of whom was Ai Tian's nephew came to Beijing from Kaifeng and expressed their willingness to convert to Catholicism. They told Matteo Ricci that Kaifeng's Judaism was declining rapidly, and people did not know Hebrew. What's more, the Haham had died and his son was young and he was not very familiar with Judaism. Matteo Ricci immediately reported to the Vatican that it was advisable to send missionaries to Kaifeng as soon as possible. The Jesuits wanted to pull the Chinese Jews to the Catholic Church and turned them to believe in Catholicism. In 1628, Jesuits finally set up a missionary base in Kaifeng, which was very close to the Jewish Temple.

The Western biblical scholars have questions about the accuracy of the text and have held many discussions on the issue. The European Church has suspected that the ancient Jews had removed the prophecies concerning the birth of Jesus from the Old Testament. After contacting with the Chinese Jews, Jesuits gradually produced another idea: they got the ancient Torah from the hands of the Kaifeng Jews and made comparative studies, but the Kaifeng Jewish Temple had collected this Hebrew Torah Bible of since about four hundred or five hundred years ago. Leibniz, a famous German philosopher, also attached great importance to this question. Leibniz sent several letters to the Jesuits in the early 18th century, expressing his desire to get the ancient Torah Bible from the Kaifeng Jews who were isolated from the Western world. However, the Kaifeng Jews cherished their ancient Torah Bible, but they did not accept the sale of the Bible, and regarded it as the sale of the God, but they also did not accept to give the copy of it.

The first person to conduct research on the Chinese Jews in Kaifeng has been the Italian priest Juliu Aleni, who is known as the "European Confucius" and who knew Hebrew language. In 1613, he visited Kaifeng under the Roman Curia's mission. He saw the Kaifeng Jewish Temple but the old Haham had died. The people who took him to visit the temple refused to lift the curtain on the Bible, so he did not see the Hebrew Torah Bible of Kaifeng.

The detailed report on the Kaifeng Jewish community was published by a Portuguese P. Jean-Paul Gozani, a French P. Jean Domenge, and P. Antoine Gaubil, who have visited Kaifeng for about a century later.

P. Jean-Paul Gozani was directly assigned by the Church of Rome to visit Kaifeng in 1704. He received warm reception by the Jews living there. He learned that there used to be abundant Jews in the past, but only seven surnames left, when he visited Kaifeng: Zhao, Jin, Shi, Gao, Zhang, Li, and Ai. P. Jean-Paul Gozani visited their Jewish temple and saw a variety of inscription plaques and the 13 tables kept by the Haham, above which were 13 niches covered by net mantle, and 13 volumes of scriptures were collected in them. One of those scriptures was used to commemorate Moses, and the other two six volumes were for commemorating the 12 branches of the Israelis. The volumes were all in sheep skin texture and written in Hebrew. In addition, there were some boxes where various so-called "other scriptures" were kept. P. Jean-Paul Gozani did not understand nor could read Hebrew.

Kaifeng Jews called their religion as "Yi Ci Le Ye", whose ancestors came from the Western Regions. They were led by Johua from Egypt, via the Red Sea and passed across the desert and spread to different regions. They said that there were 600,000 Jews as they started from Egypt. Their Hebrew had 27 letters, but only 22 were commonly used. This is exactly the same as what St. Jerome (about 340-420 years) pointed out, as he translated the Torah (Judaism Bible) into Latin. He said that Hebrew only had 22 letters, and there were 5 other changes in the wording. The Kaifeng Jews, when they read the Torah, they would wear a veil in order to commemorate Moses' masking as he read the Ten Commandments made by Jehovah and other laws under the mountain of Sinai.

Every Sabbath (Saturday), they would read a passage. Like the Jews of the European countries, they could read all of the 53 chapters of the book all the year. The reader put the Torah on the throne of Moses in the Jewish Temple, where a speaker was on his side. There was a Haham a few steps down to help the reader to correct mistakes. On the back of the throne of Moses stood "Long Live Card" where the name of the emperor was on it. Above the "Long Live Card" hang a silk banner with words of gold, meaning "Israel. You need to listen to us! Jehovah, you are the only Lord. Bless my name, forever in the future."

The Kaifeng Jews maintained the Sabbath rule of the Jewish religion on Saturdays. On that day they did not make fire as the food was already prepared on Friday. The Jews also did not marry people who believed in other religions. As they only ate beef and mutton without tendons, the locals called them "religious people without tendons". However, they didn't feel humiliated with this naming, so such naming was used to distinguish them from the Huis. When P. Jean-Paul Gozani referred that Messiah was prophesied in the Bible as Jesus Christ, the Kaifeng Jews were surprised and felt confused in the darkness. They did not preach nor absorbed the Han or the Huis into their church. They also respected Confucius, but there were no idols of Confucius in the temple. P. Jean-Paul Gozani received rubbings of the Ming Hong Zhi monument and Ming Zheng De monument and sent them to Rome.

In1722, the Father Meng Zhengqi lived in Kaifeng for more than 8 months. He made two line drawings of Kaifeng Jewish Temple, one for the panoramic view of the Tomb, one for the temple. This temple was severly damaged by a fire incident during the Ming Dynasty. Moreover, Li Zicheng laid siege to Kaifeng in 1643, and the Ming army fought against him in the Yellow River, and the temple was flooded as well. In 1663, a Kaifeng Jewish official named Zhao Yingsheng spent huge amount of money to rehabilitate this temple. The Jewish Temple was all demolished in the mid-19th century. If there was no these two pictures by Mengzhengqi, people today cannot imagine the size of this temple that had existed for 700 years in Kaifeng.

According to Meng Zhengqi's hand drawings, we can see Kaifeng Jewish Temple was 6 Zhangs (a unit of length, 1 Zhang equals 3.13 meters) long and 4 Zhangs wide. If added its auxiliary buildings, it was 30-40 Zhangs long and 15 Zhangs wide. In the courtyard, people walked through three doors before going into the temple. Its front door was toward the east direction, and they worshiped facing the west as that is the direction of the Holy Land Jerusalem. The Jews in Europe were facing the east direction, which also meant facing Jerusalem. There was a pair of stone lions outside the gate. The door was a 3.8 meters high archway, on which the Emperor Kangxi wrote "to respect the God and wish good luck for the country". Here the "God" of course referred to Jehovah. They also respected Confucius, so every spring and autumn they would go to the temple to participate in the memorial ceremony of Confucius. There were ancestral halls in the temple. The ritual of worshiping the ancestors had no big difference with that of the Han people. The only difference was that there was no image, nor pork sacrifice.

Walking through the second door would come into the "Yi Ci Le Ye Hall" which was about 13 meters wide and 18 meters deep, where several famous monuments were standing. Behind this hall was another hall, whose West wall was engraved with the Ten Commandments, and tables on both sides exhibited volumes of scriptures. On the two sides of the hall stood the teaching hall, the kitchen, and the ancestral temple of the ancestors to commemorate the ancestors of Israel, such as Abraham, Esau, Jacob, Mercy (also Moses), Ezekiel (Ezra) and etc.. These ancestors only had the memorial tablet but no images.. There were also ancestral temples of those whose surnames were Zhao and Li. Kaifeng Jews worship their ancestors in this temple every year in Spring and Autumn Period in traditional Chinese ways. Meng Zhengqi understood the Hebrew, and he had tried to get the scriptures from the Kaifeng Jews, but failed.

In 1723, Priest Song Junrong who was a scholar to study the Hebrew Torah Bible, came to Kaifeng. From the inscriptions on the inner walls of the temple, Song Junrong found out that Kaifeng Jews had lost the original ancient scriptures in 1462 during the Yellow River floods, and later the Jews in Ningbo and Ningxia donated to them the Torah Bible. At the end of the 16th century, Kaifeng was flooded again, and the Jews once again lost their book. Later they bought one from a Hui people in Shaanxi, but the Hui people in Shaanxi bought the volume which was said to be very old from an old Jew. In 1642, as Li Zicheng laid siege to Kaifeng, the dike was breached and Jewish temple was flooded again. About 26 volumes of scriptures were destroyed and the only remaining Moses' volume, which was particularly valuable, was stained with water.

From the records of Song Junrong and other materials we can see that the Jews in the late Ming and early Qing dynasties were distributed throughout China in the cities of Henan, Zhejiang, Ningxia, Shaanxi, Guangzhou, and Yangzhou. They kept close relationships among themselves.

Song Junrong said: "Kaifeng Jews were quite unfamiliar with the Hebrew." "Since, more than during two centuries the people from the Western Regions have greatly affected them, consequently, they now read the Hebrew with a Chinese accent." Song Junrong's research has found that the Kaifeng Jews had lost contact with the Western Regions since about the 16th century, consequently their bonds within the Jewish community was severed, thus Judaism gradually declined, which was the root cause of their demise.

According to Song Junrong's research: "in Kaifeng there are 7 surnames which had survived, which amounted to about 1,000 people. Their baby boys are still circumcised, they observe the Sabbath, the Passover, the Puer Festival, and other festivals." Kaifeng Jews allowed Song Junrong to ask people to transcribe the Pentateuch. Later, as the Emperor Yongzheng ordered the prohibition of this religion in 1724, the missionaries were deported and Song Junrong could not get the transcription.

Since the 19th century, there were constant contacts between the Western missionaries and these Kaifeng Jews. From the records of these Western visitors, we can see that no one in the Jewish community in Kaifeng knew Hebrew, and the Jewish temple was dilapidated. These Jews were later assimilated into the Huis.The Jews who came to China soon encountered a decline. All the Jewish monuments found in Chinese were written in Chinese, which was a sign that the Jewish culture began to die. There were some special Jewish vocabularies in these Jewish inscriptions, which were mainly Jewish names and names of regions, and their translations were very different from those of today.

Kaifeng's Jewish Temple was called the mosque, and the Jewish believers would wear blue cap as they went there on weekends, so the other people called them "blue capped Huis". They called the priests who can read the Hebrew Scriptures "Man La", namely mullah, which was evidently influenced by the Persian culture.

The general Hebrew Pentateuch was divided into 54 volumes, but that of Kaifeng only had 53 volumes, which was completely the same with the Persian Jews' volumes. They combined the 52nd and 53rd parts as one volume, so that they could finish reading the whole volume in a year.

The Jews in Kaifeng called teachers as "Wu Si Da" in the Song and Yuan Dynasty, which was the transliteration of Persian word "Ustad", meaning "master". Certain people in Jewish community was also named as "An Du La", which was the transliteration of the Arabic word "Abd al Allah", meaning "Slave of Allah", which is translated as "A Bo Du La" (Abdullah) today. It can be seen that these Jews were influenced by Islam. It was estimated that they had lived in Central Asia for a while before moving to China. There were many Jews in Central Asia, whose mother tongue was Persian and who were engaged in agriculture or trade and lived together with Islam believers in the history. At present, there were many Jews who spoke Tajik (a dialect of Persian language) and lived in the city of Samarkand and Bukhara. In history, many people whose surname was Hu of the Sogdiana region and the Huis of the Central Asia lived by the trading Han people's lands. They took the "silk road" and traveled between the Central Plains and the Western Regions. Some of them lived in the Central Plains for a very long period of time for various reasons. There were often some Jewish people among the merchants of the Sogdiana region and the Huis in the Western Regions. The ancestors of the Kaifeng Jews were probably the descendants of the Jewish merchants who were mixed in the merchants.

It can be seen from the Kaifeng Jewish temple inscriptions that the Kaifeng Jews were deeply influenced by the Chinese culture. They spoke Chinese, wore the Han costumes, and some intellectuals also studied the Confucius and Mencius classics, and became officials through the imperial examinations.

(2) Reasons for the Demise of Kaifeng Jews

The Huis in the mainland of China knew clearly that there were Jews in the mainland, and they were regarded as heterogeneous by the Jews until the mid-Qing Dynasty. The famous scholar Liu Zhi (about 1660–1730) in his book Heaven Ceremony volume 14 said: "There must be a mark on those who do not belong to the Hui people. We can't allow Ouruo Tang (churches), Zhuhu Yuan (the Jewish temple), the Buddhist temple, and the Taoist temple to cause confusions among the Huis." Here "Ouruo" refers to Europe, and "Ou Ruo Tang" is the Catholic churches. The "Ouruo" mentioned here is the transliteration of the Persian word Yurup, meaning Europe. "Zhuhu Yuan" is the Jewish Zhuhu Institute, which is the official name of Jewish temples called by the Huis. This name was also can be seen in the Kui Si Cun Gao, Volume 13 written by the mid-Qing Dynasty scholar Yu Zhengxie (1775-1840).

That is to say that the Hui people have drawn a clear distinction with the Christians. However in fact, later the Kaifeng Jews were willing to acknowledge the Huis and finally they converted to Huis' religion, Islam. What was the reason for this? As Kaifeng is the place where there were the most materials of the Jewish people in China, so we can know the demise of the Jews in other parts of China through discussing the reasons for the demise of the Kaifeng Jews. There were several reasons for the assimilation of the Kaifeng Jews community which had lasted for about 700 years, below are 4 main reasons for their decline and assimilation:

213

(1) They were in a helpless situation.

The situation of the Kaifeng Jews was quite different from the Jews who were scattered across Europe. Although European Jews were always discriminated by the majority nationalities where they dwelled, they had close relationship with other Jews in their neighboring regions. In Europe, the position of Haham (religious leadership) was orderly inherited. However, as there was a long distance between China and the Western Regions and the Mediterranean region, coupled with the seclusion policy followed by the late Ming Dynasty and the early Qing Dynasty, Kaifeng Jews and Jews outside China cut off their contact, so there was no successor of Hahams. Moreover, as there were only a few Jews in China, sustainable Jewish communities can't be formed. In 1722, as Meng Zhengqi visited Kaifeng, he found that the Jews at that time had little knowledge about Judaism, since it had been 100 years since the last Haham had visited Kaifeng. The reason why the Jewish communities around the world can be maintained was that Judaism played an important role in connecting Jews. The Kaifeng Jews were in a helpless situation for a very long time, so it was difficult to maintain their religious traditions, which was an important reason for the demise of Kaifeng Jews.

(2) Frequent disasters.

Located beside the Yellow River, Kaifeng was hit by flood repeatedly. In the year 1663's monument, it was said that in 1624 during Li Zicheng's uprising, Kaifeng was flooded again. "The temple thus was destroyed and the scriptures were vanished too. Only about 200 people survived." This was a magnificent loss of population, personnel, money, and culture for the Kaifeng people who were already in trouble, and a loss that can't be saved.

(3) The influence of Confucian tradition.

It was difficult for the Kaifeng Jewish communities which were in a helpless situation to resist the influence of China's strong feudal Confucian tradition. As China's feudal economy was very strong and the commodity economy was underdeveloped, it was impossible to form a usury creditor class like European Jews. Therefore, if the Kaifeng Jews were interested in improving social status, there was only one way for them which was to completely accept the Han culture, study the Four Books and Five Classics since childhood, and pass the imperial examination, and become officials. Ai Tian, who won the third place in the imperial examination, said to Matteo Ricci that he had learned Chinese characters since childhood, but did not learn Hebrew. There were quite a few Jews who knew a lot about Chinese culture in Kaifeng's Jewish Communities. For instance, Zhao Yingdou, who was a county magistrate in the Qing Dynasty, wrote a couplet as he worshiped in Kaifeng: to know heaven and earth, no matter how far they are..

Correction of righteousness and knowledge is the source of saints. It can be seen that these Jewish were deeply influenced by Confucianism. The Confucianization of the upper class of the Kaifeng Jews played an important role in the decline of the whole Jewish community, prompting it to gradually lose its national and religious characteristics.

However the influence of Confucianism to the upper class of the Kaifeng Jewish community should not be emphasized exaggeratedly, because the continuation of the existence of a nationality depends largely on the ability of the majority of the people, their ability to maintain their culture,, this cannot depend on the minority, i.e, the upper classes of the society. There were not so many Kaifeng Jews who became officials through imperial examinations of China (a few in hundreds of years of time), and their Sinicization was only one of the reasons behind the demise of the Jewish people. Moreover, most of the Kaifeng Jews were among the lower classes of the society, and they did not choose the way to take the imperial examinations for official jobs. As long as they refused to be assimilated into the Han people, the Jewish community could survive. However, among the Huis who lived in the mainland China, many of them had studied hard and took the imperial examinations of the Ming Dynasty, to assume officials posts and such Hui officials were not so little in numbers, thus the Huis have maintained their identity. Therefore, if the Confucianism was the reason for the demise of the Kaifeng Jews, it will be difficult to explain why the Jews were assimilated into the Han people, but the Huis did not.

(4) Tolerant Religious Environment of China.

Christianity, Islam, and Buddhism around the world have often combined or allied with the local ruling class to form a system of political and religious unity. Such polities often have extreme exclusionary attitudes towards pagans, resulting in strong antagonistic tendencies and cohesion within the pagan communities. After the Song Dynasty, the ruling class of China generally adopted a more tolerant policy towards various religious organizations and believers as long as they did not rebel. In this peaceful environment, the cohesion of Kaifeng Jews had gradually weakened and its practice of avoiding ethnic intermarriage was also difficult to sustain. In 1866, the United States missionary Ding Weiliang (W.A.P. Martin) visited Kaifeng and he saw that the Jews did not know Hebrew, nor went to church, and the contact between them was no longer so close, as a result of which, many people were assimilated by the Hui people. There was a Jewish who even became a monk. The gold plaque decorated on the door of the Jewish temple "Yi Ci Le Ye" was taken away by a local mosque. The Jews were no longer circumcised and they even got married with the Hui or Han people. There was a Jew who on the spot confessed that his wife was not a Jew. Most of them no longer remembered nor celebrated their traditional Jew feasts. It can be said that Kaifeng Jewish community had actually died out at that time. The demise of the Kaifeng Jews has been the result of the combined effects of several factors as we have discussed above.

5. Islam in China and Asia

The introduction of Islam from West to Eastern regions and to regions of central Asia of the world changed the entire region and the influence of this change has maintained till today. As the origin of world civilization, West Asia has cultivated cultures which spread to three continents of Europe, Asia, and Africa, changing the face of the world. The spread of Islam to the East was part of the history of the Eastern spreading of West Asia's thoughts and culture. Foreign religions of China originated in West Asia, such as Zoroastrianism, Manichaeism, Nestorianism, and Judaism were introduced to China together with merchants trading along the land Silk Road from the Northern Dynasties to the Song dynasty. The spread of Islam was significantly different from that of the above-mentioned religions of the West, but it was accompanied along with the Arab Empire's military expansion. Therefore, it was spread to many parts of Asia. In China, many ethnic peoples who believed in Islam lived in the Northwestern regions. The Islamization of those peoples was the result of the Eastern spread of Islam along the land Silk Road, which was also part of the entire process of Islam spreading in the Central Asia. Besides Buddhism, among the other foreign religious cultures, Islam has played a comparative important role in the modern society of China.

(1) The Creation and Emergence of Islam

Islam was originated in the Arab peninsula. The Arab people was a branch of nomadic Bedouin (Bedevi) tribes who dwelled in the deserts, which belonged to the Semitic people group. Before the birth of Islam, the Arabs believed in many religions. Judaism was the original native religion of West Asia, which was introduced into the Arab peninsula before the Arab principality was formed. After 129 BC, with the decay of the Seleucid empire, a predominantly ethnically Arab principality arose in Lower Iraq, based on a settlement on the lower Tigris banks named Charax of Hyspaosines. Later Christianity as an independent religion from Judaism, had partially an influenced the peoples of Arab peninsula. The Arab peninsula was controlled by the dynasty which was established by the Persians, alongside with the Persian domination Zoroastrianism and the Manichaeism of Persia was introduced to the Arabpeninsula region. In addition, the Arab tribes had their own primitive religions, consequently they worshiped nature, animals and plants, spirits, ancestors and idols.

The Arab peninsula is located between the Indian Ocean and the Mediterranean, and it is a thoroughfare station for the trade between the West and the East since ancient times. The Persian Gulf on the east side of the peninsula was the waterway leading to the Indian Ocean from the Mesopotamia region. The west side of the peninsula is the waterway that connects the Mediterranean Sea and the Red Sea. This favorable geographical location has made the Arabs skillful traders since the ancient times.

The founder of Islam was the prophet Muhammad who came from the ancient clan of Mecca. Muhammad lost his parents and grandfathers since he was a child and he was raised up by his uncle. Having served in the trade caravans, he had traveled to Palestine and Syria, which provided him the knowledge about Judaism and Christianity. These two religions had an important influence on his later creation of Islam. Later, he served a rich widow who was a few years older than him, and finally married her.

During the time in Mecca, Muhammad often recited in a cave wishing to be inspired by Allah. Finally he founded his own religion—Islam. "Islam" means "conversion" in Arabic, and the believers of Islam were called "Islams", namely those who believe in Allah and obey the prophets. Islam regards the god of the ancient tribe Allah as the only god. In order to make it easier to preach the religion, he acknowledged that there existed the prophets of Judaism and Christianity, but he claimed to be the last prophet that Allah sent to earth. At first, only his relatives believed in the religion. As a result of the fights within the clan, the Islams were persecuted. Later, a person named Umar (Ömer) from the upper class of the Quraysh also accepted Islam. Although the development of Islam in Mecca was not so well, it was comparatively successful in Medina. Muhammad then led his believers to Medina on September 24, 622, so the day was set as the beginning of the Islamic calendar. The Islamic calendar was known as the "Hajra", which means "migration" in Arabic. In January 630 Muhammad occupied Mecca, forcing the Mecca aristocrats to accept Islam. Muhammad died on June 8, 632, and his successor was called "Caliph", meaning "successor".

The holy book of Islam is the Quran. The Quran is a collection of Muhammad's mission to the believers for Allah. According to the teachings of Islam, the will of Allah is passed to Muhammad through the mouth of the archangel Jibra'il. The Quran was not an intact book when Muhammad was alive since the Quran referred to the records sporadically written on the leaves of the dates and on the white slabs or the memory of the people who were alive as Muhammad was explaining Allah's will. The Quran was not collated as an intact book until the Caliph Abu Bukel era (632-63). However, the Islams had different understandings when they read the original Quran transcripts, so Caliph Osman ordered to collate the Quran and burned the rest of others, thus producing the final version of the holy book. Therefore the final version of the book was also called the "Osman Version".

There are 114 chapters and 6211 sections in Quran. It contains Islam's teachings, rituals, codes of conduct, laws and regulations, and ethics etc.. It is not only the holy book of Islam, but also the basic material for the study of ancient Arab history. The Quran is made of classic Arab prose with a beautiful language. It has played an important role in the history of Arab literature and in the formation of Arabic written language and standard spoken language, thus becoming the basis for maintaining the unity of Arab nationalities and Islams.

Islam stipulates that the believers must perform five kinds of tasks: firstly, to express their faith through reading "Allah is the only god and Muhammad is the Messenger of Allah". Secondly, is to worship facing the direction of Mecca 5 times every day (namaz). Islams would hold ceremony in the local mosque every Friday (the Jumah day). Thirdly, during the Ramadan month, the Islam believers should perform fasting (Sawm) and should have sexual intercourse from dawn to sunset. Fourthly, the wealthy Islam families should donate certain Zakat (financial donation) as a kind of tax to the mosque community and to the poor. Fifthly, if their wealth permitted, they should make a pilgrimage to Mecca once in December of the Islamic calendar in their whole life. The Islams who visited and worshiped in Mecca is called the "hajji".

(2) The Contact of the Two Great Empires of the East and West: Arabs and China

In era of prophet Muhammad's successors, the Arabs have established an unprecedentedly colossal empire by foreign conquests. The Tang Dynasty of China called this Arab empire as Dayi. The Persians called their neighbors, the Arabic tribe of Tayyi, as Tachik. The Tang dynasty Chinese heard this name from the Persians and translated it as Dayi, which was specifically used to refer to the Arab empire. Caliph was the Islam leader who enjoted both political and religious powers. When Caliph Umar (Ömer) was on the throne (634-644), the Arab empire began to expand their land to the regions outside the Arab peninsula. Umar (Ömer) has occupied Syria and Palestine and defeated the Byzantine and Persian Sassanian dynasty successively. The Umayyad (Emevi) clan seized the dynasty power in 661 and established the Umayyad dynasty. It continued wars of foreign expansion. Umayyad dynasty invaded the north Africa and west Africa and also occupied parts of Spain in 711.

The expansion of the Dayi (Arab) Empire in the East (Asia), was quite strong. After its occupation of the whole Persia, it continued to march Eastwards. In 664, the Arabs occupied today's Kaofu in south of Hindu Kush Mountain (near current Kabul, capital of Afghanistan). In 674, it invaded the central region of Sogdiana across the Amu Darya region. In 705, Qutayba, the commander of Khorasan Province of Dayi launched an offensive and occupied Balkh, an important city in Tokharoi. The army led by Qutayba conquered Amara (Bukhara) and its surrounding regions which took about 3 years, i.e,706- 709. Between 710-711, the army marched from Amara to further East, they occupied Samarkand and Khwaresm. Till the year of 715, they marched further East to Syr Darya and occupied most of the regions attached to the Jimo Perfecture, which was established by Tang dynasty after destroying the Western Turkic Khanate which was a threat to the Tang dynasty. In the early period of the 9th century, the Dayi (Arab) Empire reached its acme, whose territory covered regions from the Atlantic Ocean to China's borders. It had controlled three continents including Europe, Asia and Africa. It was one of few colossal empires in the world history. In human history, only Persian Empire, Macedonian Alexander Empire, Tang Empire, Mongol Empire, British Empire and Russian Empire can be compared with it.

218
———
During the period of the Caliph Umar, Dayi had started to communicate with China. Both Tong Dian-Biography of Dayi by Du You and Biography of Dayi in Tang Records mentioned that in August of Yonghui 2rd year (651 AD), Dayi began to send envoys to Tang. According to the record, the king of Dayi of that time was named as Amir al-Mum'inin. The Dayi kingdom lasted 34 years and saw 3 kings in its life. "Amir al-Mum'inin" was the Arabic, which means leader of believers. It was the official appellation of the Caliph. The king on the throne at that time was the third king of the kingdom, Caliph Umar (Ömer), which is in line with the history, but the 34 years above is not accurate.

Yazdgird III, the last monarch of Persian Sassanian dynasty was fatuous. He was helpless about the expansion of Dayi empire. According to the Arab historical records, when Dayi troops approached Merw,(in the east of current Mali in Turkmenistan, in 651, Yazdgird III fled to Small Merw to ask help from the monarchs of several countries, including the emperor of Tang dynasty, King of Ferghanah, King of Kaofu (today Kabul, Afghanistan), King of Sogdiana and King of Khazar, which was a vassal state of Western Turkic Khanate at the North of Caspian Sea. According to New Book of Tang-Biography of Persia, envoy of Yazdgird III came to Chang'an (current Xi'an) with numerous difficulties and risks to ask for emergency help from the Tang dynasty. The Emperor Gaozong of Tang thought that Persia was far and it was hard to send troops, but gave a general to escort the Persian Sassanian envoy to restore the Sassinid order. so he sent this envoy back home after placating him. The Arab history book, Periods of Ages, recorded this letter of Tang dynasty to Yazdgird III. The letter shows that even though Tang dynasty sent a troop, they were beaten and driven away by Dayi (Arab) forces. So Tang dynasty advised Persian to get along with Dayi (Arabs) and not to offend them.

In the very year when Yazdgird III sent envoy to Tang dynasty for help, he was killed by Dayi troops in Khorasan. His son prince Peroz escaped to live in Zereng, Seistan, which is currently located in Iran's border with Afghanistan. This event had occurred, soon after when the Tang dynasty annihilated Western Turkic Khanate. Tang dynasty sent secretary to the Western regions and had set the Jimo Prefecture, so the Persian Prefecture was established in Zereng and the prince Peroz was appointed as its governor. In the 1st year Longshuo reign (661), Peroz sent an envoy to Tang dynasty to report the invasion of Dayi again and ask for help. But the Tang dynasty did not send troops. Shortly after the establishment of Persian Prefecture, Zereng was occupied by Dayi, Peroz was forced to move to Tokharoi. Although his land was occupied, he still associated with Tang dynasty under the title of king of Persia until the end of the reign of emperor Xianheng (reigned between 670-674).

Since Dayi empire was increasingly expanding to the East, Peroz had nowhere to hide and had to flee to the Tang dynasty territory in 4th year of the reign of Xianheng (674) and was welcomed by the Tang dynasty. Peroz died in the 3rd year of the Yifeng reign (678). Later, the Tang dynasty appointed Pei Xingjian as "Dayi conciliation envoy" and also arranged troops to escort Narsieh, the son of Peroz, to his country. Pei Xingjian's title "Dayi conciliation envoy" was just a nominal title since Tang was stuck to the forces of Tubo in the Western regions at that time and had no second plan against the Dayi empire, if things went wrong. Pei Xingjian escorted Narsieh to Tokharoi and then returned back. Narsieh stayed there for 20 years. In the 2nd year of the Jinglong reign (708), Narsieh sent an envoy to Tang dynasty and was appointed a nominal title, General Zuoweiwei. Narsieh died soon but his descendants kept good contacts with the Tang dynasty for a long period.

During the reign of emperor Xuanzong of Tang dynasty, there were four powers in Western region, namely Tang, Tubo, Turgesh and Dayi dynasties or empires. In alliance with Turgesh, Tubo planned to invade the Western regions of the Tang dynasty. In the 22nd year of the Kaiyuan reign (734), the Tang dynasty adopted the strategy of "ally with the distant countries and attack the neighboring ones" and sent the envoy, Zhang Yaoshe, to Dayi empire to strike a deal against the Tubo and Turgesh kingdoms, together. Dayi sent troops from the west while Tang dynasty sent troops from the east to attack the Tubo and Turgesh kingdoms. Although there were difficulties to perform the plan, but after all, it reflected the common interests of Tang and Dayi. From 737 to 738, Dayi used armed forces to launch a series of attacks to Turgesh in Tokharoi and Central Asia. In the 27th year of the Kaiyuan reign (739), the Tang troops attacked Turgesh in Suyab and recovered Suyab and Ferghana.[44]

---

44 See Wang Xiaofu, History of Political Relationships between Tang and Tubo and Dayi, Peking University Press, 1992, pp. 195-88.

The alliance of Tang dynasty and Dayi weakened the power of the Tuigesh. Then Tang concentrated on dealing with Tubo. In Tianbao 6th year (747), General Gao Xianzhi led the troops across Congling Ridges and won the battle with Little Burusho. Under the rule of Dayi, Khwaresm, Khuttal (currentsouth Tajikistan) and Chach (currentTashkent) had contacts wirg the Tang dynasty. In Tianbao 10th year (751), Tang and Dayi lost the battle in Talas. Soon, "An-Lushan Rebellion" occured in Tang dynasty period. Tang dynasty gradually withdrew its forces from the influence contention in the central Asia region and chose a defensive attitude in Western regions. Until Zhenyuan 8th year (792), Tang forced had retreated from the Western regions. Tubo (Tibet forces) also began to decline soon afterwards. After the decline of Tang, Tubo and Dayi, there appeared abundant kingdoms in the Western regions, among which, Qara Khanids, Gaochang Uyghurs, Seljuq Empire, Khwarezm and Western Liao dynasty had affected the Eurasian steppes greatly.

In more than a century, the Arabs have conquered vast territories in Asia, Africa and Europe. They have formed a large but loose empire which contained a vast population, many nationalities, diverse social forms and various religious. Control upon such a vast territory entirely relied on military conquest, and lacked traditional economic ties between the regions it controlled, therefore it could not maintain unity for a long time. Even in heyday of Dayi Empire, Caliph could not rule the whole country especially the outlying provinces. When the Arab-Islam empire began to decline and the central leading authority had lost its internal cohesion, many strong feudal lords expanded their spheres of influence and set up independent kingdoms, which caused the collapse of the Dayi (Arab-Islam) empire.

(3) The Islamization of the Western Grassland Regions

In the 7th century, with the expansion of Islam Empire (in Chinese Dayi), Persian speaking peoples also migrated to the East. This Sogdiana regions, which originally was occupied by East Iranian speaking peoples were soon Persianized. In the beginning of 9th century, Islamic Empire (Dayi) gradually disintegrated and in the various parts of the empire, a variety of big clans became autonomous (Tahirids,Saffarids,Samanids). In 874, Persian speaking peoples got rid of the rule of Dayi (Islamic Empire) and established Samanid dynasty in Bukhara. The Samanid Dynasty (Islam), existed for over 100 years, but perished in 999 under the joint attack of Ghazna dynasty and Qara Khanids. The center of Samanid Dynasty was located between Amu Darya and Syr Darya, where Sogdiana was located. Its territory was North to Aral Sea, South to Southeast of Afghanistan and Iran, East to upstream of Amu Darya and Syr Darya and West to Caspian Sea. The people of the Central Plains under the rule of Liao dynasty called those regions between Amu Darya and Syr Darya as Islam Empire (in Chinese Dayi). The book Liao History-Taizu Period, wrote: "in the 2nd year of Tianzan reign period of Emperor Taizu of the Liao Dynasty, in September, next year (923 AD), Dayi paid tribute to Liao". Here, the word "Dayi" should be the Samanid dynasty. The so-called "tribute" is only to trade or visit. In the 1st year, of Tianzan reign period of Emperor Taizu of the Liao Dynasty, emperor sent military forces to Mobei and invaded the ancient city of Huihe, which was located in center of Mongolian plateau and upstream of Orkhon River. Then the army marched towards West, across Jinshan Mountain and then further to South. Then the Liao army captured Beiting[45] which was once the center of Protectorate of the Tang dynasty.

Hearing these events and fighting abilities of the Liao dynasty troops, Islamic Samanid dynasty army marched into the Liao territories from central Asian grasslands, North of Jinshan Mountain and through Mongolian plateau.

After the Western Turkic Khanate declined, many Turkic speaking tribe confederations became active to utilize the opportunities that appeared. Under the rule of Samanid Dynasty Turkic speaking tribe confederations had they gradually accepted Islam and were expropriated as military powerhouse by local rulers. It caused that Turkic army generals gradually were able to master key posts of the army. After Samanid Dynasty began to decline due to internal religious divisions, some Turkic tribe leaders seized the opportunity to rebel and established local states, among which, the earliest one was Ghazna (Gazne) dynasty. It was translated as "Ghaznavid dynasty" in history works in China. Ghazna dynasty was built in 962.The founder of Ghazna was a Turkic former slave, and ex-general (Alp Tigin) in the Samanid dynasty, who was appointed as governor of Khorasan Province. After falling into disfavor, he occupied Afghanistan and declared independence. In its heyday, Ghaznavid dynasty expanded as far as to East to India, West to Northwest of Iran, North to Khwarezm. In 1186, it was destroyed by the rising Ghurid Kingdom.[46]

In his works, Sharaf al-Za'man Tahir ai-Marwazi mentioned a letter of credence from emperor Shegnzong of Liao dynasty to Ghazna dynasty. The date signed in it was the year of Mouse, i.e., the 4th year of the Taiping reign (1024). Marwazi mentioned that the the year was 1027, so it can be estimated that the letter was written in 1024 but was delivered to Ghazna dynasty by the envoy 3 years later. According to the letter, Emperor Shengzong betrothed the noble princess to the son of Qadir Khan, Chaghritqin and asked Qadir Khan to keep the expedition roads open in order to be convenient for communication of envoys. He also asked Ghazna dynasty to send envoy to Liao. He hoped a permanent friendship between the two countries and was willing to connect the two countries through marriage. This request was refused with the reason that Ghazna was a Islam country but Liao was not, thus they could not agree on the inter-marriage deal.[47]

---

45 Beiting, ancient Ting prefecture (Jimsar County); In 2014 the Beiting city ruins were designated a part of the Silk Road UNESCO World Heritage Sites.
46 Ghūrid kingdom was centred in Ghūr (modern Ghowr) in west-central Afghanistan from the mid-12th to the early 13th century. Its founder was Alā-ud-Dīn Husayn.
47 See article by Huang Shijian Liao and Dayi (Arabs), in the Journal of Modern History, 1992/1.

Qara Khanid (Kara-Khanid) was a dynasty established in central Asia on the remains of Western Turkic Khanate. It was explicitly mentioned in the Jin History-Biography of Nianghanu. According to it, it was the Uyghur tribe that set up Qara Khanid state. This tribe was likely the Chigil tribe which has been the origin of the Western Turkic Khanate. Islamic historical records have mentioned that the founder of Qara Khanid was Bilge Kul Qadir Khaghan. In the end of 9th century, Qara Khanid had intense struggles with the Samanid dynasty, which was established in Bukhara by the Persian speaking peoples. In 960 led by Satuq Bughra Khan, Qara Khanids had accepted Islam. From the end of 10th century to early 11th century, Qara Khanid conquered the Buddhist Khotan Wei Chi's regime. In 1130s, ruler of Qara Khanid, Ibrāhīm II b. Ahmad was frustrated by the invasions and harassments of Kankalis and Halalu (Karluks) and asked Chinese Western Liao dynasty for help. By using this opportunity, Yelü Dashi emperor of Western Liao dynasty led the army into the city of Balasaghun and replaced Ibrāhīm II b. Ahmad and de-throned him. According to Persian historian Ata-Malik Juvayni, Yelü Dashi "ascended a throne that had cost him nothing." Dashi took in 16,000 Khitan former mercenaries in Balasaghun, then established his authority over Kashgar, Khotan, the Kirghiz, and the Uyghur center of Beshbalik.

Then, which was a sub-tribe of Qara Khanid which occupied Keshhar had become a vassal state of the Western Liao dynasty. After Qara Khanid occupied Sogdiana, Liao Dynasty and its people still called it Dayi, the name they called Samanid dynasty. The Liao History of Shengzong Period, in October of Kaitai 9th year (1020), wrote as follows: "Dayi sent envoy to Liao to ask to connect the two countries through marriage". In March of the following year, Dayi sent an envoy again. Emperor Shengzong of Liao dynasty betrothed the daughter of Prince Banlanhusry to Chaghri. This word "Chaghri" was probably be Chaghritqin, the Prince of Qara Khanid and the one who married was his father Qadir Khan.[48]

Khwarezm was an ancient state in Central Asia, which was located in downstream of the Amu Darya. In ancient times, Khwarezm people were a branch of Eastern Iranians. They believed in Zoroastrianism and made irrigated agricultural production,for their livelihoods. In the 8th century, after the Arab kingdom conquered central Asia, Khwarezm became one of the Arab kingdom territories. Islam was introduced from Sogdiana to the Northern regions. At the same time, Turkic speaking Kankalis and Guth, nomadic tribes dwelling in Northeast of the Aral Sea, constantly migrated towards the South, too, which caused changes in ethnic composition and cultural features. By the 11th century, residents of Khwarezm were basically assimilated by nations which spoke Turkic language, but their king was also called "Shah" as in Persia.(Iran).

---

48   See article by Huang Shijian, Liao and Dayi, in the Journal of Modern History, 1992/1.

In 11th century, Khwarezm became a vassal state of the Seljuq Turkic dynasty. In 1141, after Western Liao defeated Seljuq Turkic Empire led by Sultan Sanjar consequently, Yelü Dashi sent General Erbus to attack Khwarezm along Amu Darya and also forced Khwarezm state to concede. He also forced the condition of annual payment by Khwarezm to Western Liao, which was 30 thousands of gold "Dina".

Under term of "Herat" in Biography of Countries in Western Regions by Chen Cheng & Li Xian of Ming dynasty, the big silver currency was named "Denger" while the small one "Dina". In the 1170s, nobles of Khwarezm had a domestic inner fight to grab the throne. The prince Tekesh defected to Western Liao dynasty. Ciaodolub, the emperor's son-in-law of Western Liao, used force and supported him to return back to his country and get the throne.

After Khwarezm state surrendered and affirmed allegiance to the Western Liao state, they continuously battled Western Qara Khanid state along Amu Darya. As an alternative, they attacked to Khorasan region,in the Northern part of Amu Darya, to fight against Seljuq Empire. They even attacked Iraq and threatened Baghdad and gradually became strong. Because the shift in the balance of power between Khwarezm and Western Liao dynasty and brutal oppression policied led by the Western Liao bureaucrats, aristocrats of Khwarezm started to resist against the rule of Western Liao. The Sultan Teiqish had ever killed an insolent envoy of Western Liao dynasty. Ciaodolub, the emperor's son-in-law of Western Liao, attempted to depose Teiqish Shah with military force and supported his brother, Sultan Shah, to get the throne. But he failed. So, he supported Sultan Shah to establish the kingdom in Maru, Khorasan. Although Teiqish Shah had constant conflict with Western Liao, he always avoided breaking away from it and he always paid geld. In 1200, his son Mohammed acceded to the throne. Early in his reign, he still remained the vassal relationship with Western Liao dynasty. But with the decline of the Western Liao dynasty, in the year of establishment of Mongolian by Genghis Khan in 1206, Khwarezm, the vassal state of Western Liao, betrayed it and killed the envoy who was in charge of collecting the gold and declared independence from the Western Liao dynasty.

The rise of Mongolia and Khwarezm was the decisive factor for quick collapse of Western Liao's rule. After defeated by Genghis Khan, remaining forces of Naimans, collaborated with Khwarezm forces, thus the Western Liao dynasty forces were attacked from both West and East side. The regime of Western Liao fell into the hands of Kuchlug Khan (Naiman tribe) in 1211. After Genghis Khan annihilated the remaining forces Kuchlug Khan, the two rising great powers at the same time in central Asian continent had bordered with each other in East part of Syr Darya river basin.

Chapter 5. Genghis Khan and His Descendants

The Asian history of the 12 to 14th century is known as the Mongolian era in World History. The Mongolian cavalries led by Genghis Khan and his descendants swept across almost the entire Asian continent and Eastern Europe, and the historical Sino-foreign interaction in this period was inevitably branded by the spirit of times.

1. The Mongolian Conquest of the West

(1) The Origins of Mongols

According to the scholars' research, the ethnic origin of the Mongol Nationality is as follows—Donghu→Xianbei→Shiwei→Tatar→Mongolia.[1] Xianbei was the offspring of Donghu. Tuoba Xianbei, a branch of Xianbei tribe had once established the powerful Northern Wei Dynasty in Northern China. Tuoba people, which settled in the Han Chinese regions, wrote many books, including those in Xianbei language. In the "Monograph on Literature of History of the Sui Dynasty", these book titles in Xianbei language can be found. Although these books do not exist today, some transliteration words of Xianbei language with clear interpretation were also preserved in other Chinese classics.

In "Yuanhe Maps and Records of Prefectures and Counties", the Geography Book of the Tang Dynasty, it is mentioned that there is the "Qichin Mountain", 30 li from the East of Yunzhong County (current Datong, Shanxi), and "Qichin", the Xianbei language is used, meaning 30 li in Chinese. Scholars have noticed that "Qichin" is apparently similar to "ghuchin", the cardinal numeral

---

1   Yi Linzhen, "Nationalities in North China and the Ethnic Origin of Mongol Nationality", "Journal of Inner Mongolia University", 1979/3, pp. 1-23.

in Mongolian. In "The History of Nan Qi Dynasty·Wei Lu Biography", the 13 Tuoba military officer titles were recorded, all with the Mongolian suffix "chin" which represents identities and occupations. Among the Xianbei people which dwelled in the Han Chinese region, there was the "Yujiulü Chounu" clan, and later it was changed to the Wolf's, a Chinese surname. Yao Weiyuan, "Research on Surname Hu of the Northern Dynasty". "Yujiulü Chounu" is certainly the transliteration of "Wolf", which is "chino" in Mongolian, which demonstrates that the "Yujiulü Chounu" clan was also the one which used the Mongolian language.

Initially, "Mongolia" was just a tribal name among various tribes speaking Mongolian language, of which the records can be found in Shiwei tribes of the Tang Dynasty. It is called "Mengwu Shiwei" in "Old History of the Tang Dynasty: Beidi Biography", and "Mengwa" in "New History of the Tang's History: Beidi Biography". Mengwu Shiwei lived around "Wangjian River" (the upstream of Erguna River now), which was one tribe of "Great Shiwei". According to the Mongolian legend, in the ancient times, Mongolians were defeated by other tribes, and only two men and two women were survived. They escaped into the valley of Er Er Gu Nie Kun, and formed two clans—Kiyan and Nie Gu Si.

In the dynasties of Song, Liao and Jin, the contacts between Mongolia and the outside world increased gradually, and its name appears in various literatures. In "The National Records of Khitan", Mongolia is called "Meng Gu Li". In the Chinese literatures of this age, Mongolia was mentioned by other names, such as, "Meng Gu" ("History of Liao"), "Meng Gu" ("The Sketches in Jin Dynasty" quoted from "Qidan Stories"), and "Meng Gu", and so on.

When the Mengwu Shiwei dwelled around the present-day Greater Khingan Mountains, some Mongolian-speaking tribes had moved to the Mongolian grasslands, and lived together with the local tribes speaking Turkic language. These original Mongolian tribes were often called as "Tatars", which initially refer to the "Tatar" tribes living around Ju Lun Po[2] (current Hulunbuir).

Since Tatars were once very strong, they had conquered a variety of ancient-Mongolian speaking tribes who moved into the Mongolian Steppes, these feudatory tribes attached to Tatar which called themselves Tatars. "30 Surname Tatars" and "Nine Surname Tatars" mentioned in Turkic and Uyghur inscriptions should be these Mongolian people. Later, the name "Tatars" were adopted by many of the nomadic tribes living in steppes adjacent to vast deserts.

In addition, there were some Mongolian-speaking tribes which were assimilated by the Tiele people. For example, "Ba Ye Gu", one of the 15 Tiele tribes in the dynasties of Sui and Tang, should be the later Mongolian "Ba Er Hu"

---

2 During the Han Dynasty (206 BCE-220 CE), Hulunbuir was part of the Liaodong Commandery. During the Qing Dynasty (1644-1912), Hulunbuir was part of Heilongjiang province. The 1858 Treaty of Aigun established today's approximate Sino-Russian border, at a great loss to Heilongjiang's territory.

tribe. "Ba Ye Gu played a very important role in the Uyghur people's battle to overthrow the second Turkic Khanate. Besides, a few Mongolian-speaking tribes moved to the surrounding region of present-day Lake Baikal very early, and they once used Luni Turkic scripts as their written language. One of the most famous tribes was the Kurykans, which included the coalition of three tribes, they were called "three-surname Kurykans". Later, during the Tang Dynasty period, with "4,500 after the arms' victory, and over 10,000 people", they were called the Mongolian "Qori" tribe.

In the year of 840, after Uyghur Khanate in Mobei (the Northern desert part of Mongolia) was defeated by the Mongolian-speaking tribes, who had moved into the Mongolian plateau, did not follow these escaped Uyghur people. The grassland regions wherein Uyghur tribes dwelled attracted a large number of Mongolian tribes who formerly lived in the Erguna river basin. These Mongolian tribes who left the Greater Khingan Mountains in succession, and entered the Mongolian Steppes. Among them, the Mongolian tribe which migrated to Burqan Qaldun (current Khentii Mountains in Mongolia) on the upstream of Onon River (the present-day Onon River in Mongolia) in the East. The leader of this Mongolian tribe was called Borte Chino (meaning "grey wolf"), and his wife's name was Gua Maral (Qohai Marral) (meaning "white deer"). The migration of these people have formed the federation of Mongolian-speaking tribes which became the dwellers of the Mongolian Plateau.

227

In regard to the early history of Mongolia, there was nothing to boast about. It is written in "The National Records of Khitan" that in Mongolia "there is no King to rule", and "there is no fight with Khitan". Only cattle, sheep, camels, horses, fur and other goods were exchanged or traded with Khitans. In the period of, Genghis Khan's 9th ancestor, Borjigidai Mergen, the Mongolian tribe conquered a small tribe of Wuriyayhai people. However, the Liao people were the 70-Zhang Zha La Yi Er ones defeated by Khitans.

But the Zhalayir (Jalair) beaten by the Qidan (Khitan) in the Liao Dynasty, defeated the Mongolian tribe on their way of withdrawal. Thus, the remnants of this Mongolian tribe had to throw themselves into the lap of Barhu Tribe.

Later, Khaidu, Genghis Khan's 16th ancestor, defeated a big clan of Zha La Yi Er people, consequently the Mongolian tribes gained a great strength.

Genghis Khan was born in the riverside of Onon River in 1162, and his father, named Yesugei, was from the Mongolian nobility (Khamag Mongol federation). When he was born, Yesugei won the battle against the Tartar tribe and captured its head Temujin Uge. To commemorate the victory, Genghis Khan was named Temujin.

When Genghis Khan was 9 years old, Yesugei stopped for a feast with a group of men he met, but little did he know that they were Tartars, archenemies of the Mongols. While they harmlessly feasted together, the Tartars secretly poisoned Yesugei's food. Temujin was summoned back to assume leadership of the coalition, but the other clan leaders were not impressed by his young age. The other clan leaders of the coalition abandoned Temujin's camp, and soon, even his Kiyad clansmen deserted. In the end, all that was left of Temujin's camp was his mother, his four siblings, his two stepbrothers, and a family servant.

Thus, Temujin's family declined rapidly and was in a frustrating situation. The Mongolian tribes were controlled by the Tayichigud nobility. The remaining forces of the Mongolian tribe was Jamukha (Zha Mu He) of the Jadaran[3] tribe. In the 12th century, besides the Mongolian tribes, there were several strong tribes that dwelled on the Mongolian Steppes:

Kerait tribe: Kerait people probably belong to the Turkic tribe, or to the Mongolian people strongly influenced by the Turkic culture. They believed in Nestorianism, a branch of christianity. The leader Togrul Ong (Wang Han) and Genghis Khan's father, Yesügei were peers (half-brothers, and they had a close relationship with each other. Kerait people lived in the upstream region of Tola River and Wo Er Han River.

Merkids Tribe, called as "Mei Li Ji" or "Mi Er Ji" in the Liao Dynasty period, was located in the North of the Mongolian Plateau. They fought with Kerait and Mongol tribes for many years. Tatars was the most famous tribe in the Mongolian Steppes before the rise of Mongols. After the Tang Dynasty, a number of tribes in Mobei (the North desert of Mongolia) were self-proclaimed Tatars. In the 12th century, Tatars were gathered and developed the animal husbandry in Bu Yu Er Hai Zi (the present-day Hulunbuir). Not only Mongolia was a feud to Tatars, there were also many conflicts between Tatars and Keraits.

228

Nai Man tribe, located in the West of the Mongolian Plateau, once was submitted to the Kara-Khitan Khanate. Naiman tribe was the most advanced tribe on the Mongolian plateau at that time. They absorbed the culture of Kara-Khoja Kingdom, adopted the Uyghur script for its alphabet, and learned to use stamps for cashier. They frequently fought with Kerait state, their Eastern neighbor, and fought against the Merkit state, which was their Northern neighbor. Most scholars believe that Naiman was a tribe which used Turkic-language.

During the 12th century, the Liao and Jin Dynasties constantly resorted to military forces on the North to subjugate other tribes dwelling on the Mongolian Plateau. Besides, different tribes' internal aristocrats tried to kill each other for titles of Khan, land and population, and there were constant fights among tribes. Consequently, all the ethnic peoples that dwelled on the vast grasslands have faced great hardships. It became an inevitable historical trend which unified the tribes living on the the Mongolian Plateau tribes and which determined their rivalry with the Liao and Jin Dynasties.

---

3   Jadaran, was a sub-tribe of the Khamag Mongol confederation.

Genghis KhanTemujin grew up in turbulent times; Temüjin's early life was difficult. When he became an adult, he first chose to go and seek refuge with the Khan of Kerait, and also he gathered more than 10,000 troops. With the support of the Khan of Kerait and Jamukha, (Zha Mu He), who a noble of Zha Zhi La's, he defeated the Merkits (Mie Er Qi) tribe, and was elected as the Khan by the nobility council in 1189. Tatars were subordinated to the Jin Dynasty. In the 6th year of Emperor Zhangzong of the Jin dynasty (1195), Zhi Wu Ti and He Da Jin, the two nomad Mongolian tribes, invaded the border of Jin dynasty together with Hong Ji La Tribe. The Jin dynasty dispatched troops to the current Hulunbuir and won the battle against them. On the way back, the livestock which they had gathered were robbed by the Tatars. The next year, Jin Dyanasty sent troops against the Tatars. After hearing the news, Genghis Khan Temujin believed it is a great chance to avenge the ancestors and weaken Tatar kingdom, his old enemy. Therefore, he, together with the Khan of Kerait, assisted the Jin Dyansty troops and defeated Tatars. After that, Tatars began to decline. Genghis Khan Temujin was given the title of (Wang Khan) "Zha Wu Ti Hu Li" by the Jin Dynasty in 1197, and the Khan of Kerait got the title of "King".

Genghis Khan Temujin's strength increased greatly after controlling the Eastern part of the Mongolian Steppes, which endangered the alliance basis between him and the Khan. In 1203, the Khan decided to defeat Genghis Khan before Genghis Khan became a full-fledged power. Receiving this secret report, Genghis Khan launched the battle in haste and failed. Since the Khan won the victory, the interior cohesion of Kerait tribe federation was disturbed and its strength weakened. Genghis Khan Temujin launched an offensive against the Kerait forces, and the main force of the Khan was smashed. On his escaping way to Nai Man tribe state, the Khan of Kerait was killed by the generals of Nai Man. Senggum, his son, headed the remnants to flee to Qu Xian (the present-day Kuqa of Xinjiang) on the way toTangut, and he was killed. Thus, the once mighty Urus Khan of Kerait state fell into the hands of Genghis Khan.

After the destruction of Kerait state by Genghis Khan Temujin, the sphere of influence power of the Mongolian tribe extended Westward to the border with Nai Man people. The Nai Man nobilities had always looked down upon the Mongolian people, and this victory had shocked Nai Man. Taiyang Khan of the Nai Man decided to attack the Mongolian tribe, and the messenger was dispatched to Ongud in the South of the desert for assistance in the attack. However, the head of Ongud informed Genghis Khan of this news. Genghis Khan called an assembly, and as a result, his troops were purged, and the systems of "1000 households" and "100 households" were established. The Mongolian Genghis Khan army became an ever-victorious force. In contrast, Nai Man state was divided into two parts—Taiyang Khan and Buyulu Khan, and due to numerous contradictions of each other, they were faced with the possibility of being destroyed one by one. In 1204, Genghis Khan led the army Westward and defeated the Taiyang Khan tribe. The wounded Taiyang Khan was captured and died soon. Two years later, Genghis Khan dispatched troops and conquered the Buyulu branch of the Nai Man. The son of Taiyang Khan defected to Kara Khitai Khanate for shelter, thus Naiman state was destroyed. The entire Mongolian Plateau was under the rule of Genghis Khan.

In 1206, Genghis Khan Temujin called a noble assembly in the source of Onon River. His honorific title was "Genghis Khan", and the country was called "Yeke Mongghul Ulus", namely, "Great Mongolia". Before that, all tribes on the North and South of the desert all had their own titles, and Mongolia was just one name among them. After the establishment of the Mongolian Kingdom, the tribes ruled by Mongolia all became its members, and Mongolia was adopted as the general term. A unified Mongolian national community ascended to the historical stage.

(2) Mongol Conquest of the Western Regions

In 1217, Genghis Khan decided to send troops to the Western Regions, and the Western Xia state was ordered to levy soldiers and follow Genghis Khan. Upon the refusal, Genghis Khan immediately dispatched an army against the Western Xia. The emperor of the Western Xia dynasty fled to further west and sent an envoy to Genghis Khan and begged for mercy. Genghis Khan decided not to wipe out the Western Xia for the moment and focused on the conquest of the Western regions. The Mongol troops retreated to the North of the desert. During the period of Genghis Khan's conquest of the West, the court of the Western Xia had a lot of arguments over the issue of joining Mongolia or Jin Dyansty. Genghis Khan discovered the plot of the Western Xia leaders, and ordered Beilu, the son of the Muqali, who managed the North China, to go on a punitive expedition to Yinzhou city. In the autumn of 1224, Bei-lu led the Mongolian army to invade Yinzhou city, he won the war and tens of thousands of Tangut troops who belonged to the Western Xia[4] were killed.

In 1225, Genghis Khan withdrew his troops from the Western Regions. After evaluating Western Xia's refusal of dispatching an envoy for the hostage exchange, and its secret meeting with the Jin Dynasty, in the next year, Genghis Khan decided an offensive Xia was carried out the next year. In succession, Black Water City (today's Southeast of Er Ji Na Banner), Gan Zhou (current Zhangye, Gansu), Su Zhou (current Jiuquan, Gansu), Liang Zhou, and Ling Zhou (current Lingwu, Ningxia) were all captured. After eliminating the main forces of the Western Xia army, Genghis Khan left a group of troops to besiege Zhongxing government, and he himself led the main forces to attack the territories of Jin and Song dynasties, adjacent to the Western Xia state. In the summer of 1227, Genghis Khan was seriously ill. He gave the following instructions before he died: his own funeral should be kept secret to avoid that enemies would not know about it, and strictly suggest that his successors should wait for the surrender of the Western Xia state. After the siege by the Mongol army

---

4 Western Xia was based on the Tangut tribe, out of the Qiangic people which would later evolve to Western Xia Kingdom led by the Dangxiang nomads or the Tanguts.

for half a year, Zhongxing government was out of food and had to surrender. Thus the Western Xia state perished after nearly 200 years after its foundation.

After Genghis Khan wiped out the subordinate members of Buriyuh (Bu Yi Lu Hei) Khan, including the Naiman leader, Kuschlug (Qu Chu Lv), the son of Tayang Khan—after his father was killed—Kuschlug went through Stone River of Ye'Er and sought refugee to Kara-Khitan Khanate. He gained the trust of Zhi Lu Gu, the last emperor of Kara-Khitan Khanate. When Kuschlug Khan gained full-fledged power, he began to collude with Khwarezm kingdom, which was the vassal state of Kara-Khitan Khanate, plotting to usurp the emperor power. In 1218, Genghis Khan ordered his general Jebe to subjugate Kuschlug Khan. Kuschlug Khan fled towards West from Ke Shi Ha' Er (current Kashi, Xinjiang) but he was captured and executed by the Mongol army. Kara-Khitan Khanate perished. At that time, the West side of Mongolia was adjacent to Khwarezm kingdom. The descendants of Kara-Khitan Khanate migrated Westwards to Persia and established a local separatist kingdom there.

In 1219, Genghis Khan, personally led huge armies to conquer Western Regions under the pretext of punishing Otrar Ghaiyr Khan Inalchuq, the governor of Otrar (a Khwarezmia border town) Genghis Khan demanded the extradition of Ghaiyr Khan, but the Khwarezm Shah not only refused, but ordered to kill the ambassadors. This was the reason for the war against the Khwarezm kingdom. Genghis Khan's pretext was to take the revenge of the killed Mongolian trade caravan and envoy by the Otrar governor. Genghis Khan divided the army into four forces to attack the cities of Khwarezmia. The army commanded by his eldest son Jochi, attacked lower reaches of Huzha River (Syr Darya), after conquering these regions this army decided to fight in the Northern regions of Aral Sea. The governor of Otrar, Ghaiyr Khan defended desperately. The siege of Otrar lasted almost five months. When approaching Otrar, Genghis Khan left for its siege the troops under his sons Chagatai and Ogedei. At the end of the fifth month of the heroic defense, Khwarezmian commander Karadza-Hadzhib with a ten thousand detachment surrendered to the Mongols, letting them into the city. However, Otrar still was not crushed. Ghaiyr Khan with a group of soldiers strengthened in the citadel for the taking of which the Mongols needed another month. When all the defenders perished, Otrar was taken in February 1220. Ghaiyr Khan was captured and executed.

After this victory, the Genghis Khan army marched forward and passed Qizeli Deserts (today's deserts between lower reaches of Syr Darya and Amu Darya) to attack the Urgench city, the former capital of Khwarezmia. The other army was ordered to attack those cities along middle reaches of Huzha River. Genghis Khan and Tolui, his youngest son marched into the Northern regions of Amu Darya crossing Huzha River, directly attacked and seized Samarkand (today Samarkand of Uzbekistan), the new capital of Khwarezmia and Bolara (today Bokhara/Buhara of Uzbekistan), former capital of the Sulala Samaniyya kingdom, and then attacked Southern regions of Amu Darya, Khorasan and Southern regions of the current Hindukush.

Although the national power of Khwarezmia kingdom was vigorous, its foundation period was fairly short with unstable ruling structure. Moreover, its military leaders adopted defensive strategies against the Mongol invasion, but were incapable to defend against the powerful Mongol army. When Mongolian army invaded Samarkand, Mohammed, Shah of Khwarezmia (Shah means King) abandoned his city and escaped, Genghis Khan dispatched Jebe and Subutai to press the advantage. Mohammed escaped at the island of Kuantianjisi Sea (today Caspian Sea), soon after, died of illness. In 1221, Jochi, Chagatai and Ogedei captured Urgench (today Kunya Urgench of Turkmenistan), former capital of Khwarezmia. Genghis Khan and Tolui conquered cities of Khorasan (today the regions to the South of Amu Darya, to the North of Hindukush) by dividing forces and afterwards, defeated army led by Jalal ad-Din Mingburnu, son of Mohammed at Indus riverside. Jalal ad-Din Mingburnu withdrew to India. In 1223, after Mongolian armies set officials and guardian, they returned to Mongolia.

After seizing many regions of Persia, army led by Jebe and Subutai invaded Kipchak grasslands crossing Tai Karakorumg (currently the Caucasus Mountains), in 1223, during the first Mongol invasion of Russia, an army led by Jebei and Subedei defeated an alliance of Russian princes and the Cuman tribal group along the Kalka River (probably the modern Kalchik River in southeastern Ukraine). The victory, part of a prolonged raiding campaign, devastated the Russian princes' armies and demonstrated the raw power of the Mongol cavalry, battle and seized Southern regions of Russia. Although this defeat left the Russian Kievan principality at the mercy of invaders, the Mongol forces retreated and did not reappear for 13 years, during which time the Russian princes of went on quarreling and fighting as before, until they were startled by a new and much more formidable invading force than at Kalka battle.

Later, in 1236, the vast Mongol hordes of around 35,000 mounted archers, commanded by Batu Khan and Subutai, crossed the Volga River and invaded Volga Bulgaria in the autumn of 1236. It took them a year to extinguish the resistance of the Volga Bulgarians, the Kypchaks and the Alani. In 1251, Mongke Khan, ascended the throne, he intended to strengthen his familial power. Mongke Khan ordered all senior governors and noblemen to select two twelfths people from their own administrative regions to form a branch of army in 1252. Hulegü, his brother who had the same mother with him commanded such army to conquer those peoples which had not surrendered in Western Regions and ordered Tatar Salinayan to invade Kashmir to coordinate the military expedition of Hulegü Khan. Also the army of Chormaqan, which had conquered many regions in the Caucasus region at Taizong times, was ordered to fight under the command of Hulegü. By the order of Mongke Khan, Hulegü collected riprap machinists, cannon shooter, crossbowmen, totaling 1000, and plenty of weapons for Hulegü to use [5]

5   Jami' al-tawarikh, written by Rashid-al-Din Hamadani (1247–1318) Volume 3, Chinese version, p. 30.

It was recorded in The History of Yuan Dynasty Guokan Biography, in 1252, weapons and warriors were delivered to Karakorum for Hulegü to conquer Western Regions. Army commanded by Hulegü trudged and crossed Beshbaliq, Northern regions of Amu Darya and arrived in Persia. At that time, Ismailists of Islam settled in present Mazandaran cities of Iran, they were called as "Mullahidah" by the other Islam believers, which means "heretic" in the Arabian language. The Abbasid Dynasty (Abbasids) with the history of over 500 years since its foundation had declined and the regions which were directly under its control was limited to the surrounding regions of Baghdad (current Baghdad, capital of Iraq), which was the capital of Abbasid Dynasty. In 1256, Hulegü Khan—the founder of Il Khanate—wiped out Mura'i and in 1258, his armies captured Baghdad and killed the Islam Caliph of the last generation. The Abbasid caliphs were the holders of the Islamic title of caliph who were members of the Abbasid dynasty, a branch of the Quraysh tribe descended from the uncle of the Islamic prophet Muhammad, al-Abbas ibn Abd al-Muttalib. In 1259, west-conquest armies of the Mongols were divided into three arms in order to invade present Syria regions. Various kinds of gunpowder weapons produced in the Chinese Han played tremendous role in their battles. In the spring of the following year, Mongolian diplomatic corps led by Shigi-Qutuqu came to the army garrison and reported the information about the death of Mongke Khan, after which Hulegü Khan retreated to Persia and the commander pioneer Kitbuqa continued to fight. In the September of the same year, the army of Kitbuqa was defeated by Saif ad-Din Qutuz, an Islam leader who controlled Egypt, at Ain Jarute Battle. Hereto, the Mongol's aggressive expansion and Western conquest of Mongols had ceased. After the Western conquest, Hulegü Khan continued to control Persia and did not return back to the East any more.

233

2. Frequent Interactions between the East and the West

(1) A large-scale Movement of Immigrants

When Genghis Khan took Westward conquest, there were many levied Jurchen, Khitan people, Han people, Uyghur and people from Western Xia in the army. After they came to Western Regions along with Mongolian army, some person pressed advantage of large-scale property by the military forces and powers and levied huge wealth, however, the local Hui people "have no liberty right of the land and have to subordinate to Han people and Khitan people, Hexi and etc." Travels to the West of Qiu Chang Chun, Mongolians are the nationality "on the back of a horse" which lacked agricultural technology and governing towns and cities was alien to them. After they conquered the populous and affluent and fertile lands in the North of Amu Darya, the people from Han, Qidan, and the Western Xia accompanying the army became the most reliable aides for them to governing settled residents. Father and son, Yelü Ahai and Yelü Miansige were Khitan people who guarded Samarkand. In the book Summary of Minutes on Ho-chung fu written by Yelü Chucai, Jurchen, a Pucha marshal of Bolara was mentioned for several times and his son was a "general" in the local garrison. The Persian book "Ta'rikh-i wassaf" also mentioned about a "prime minister" for several times who governed Samarkand jointly with Ma Suhu, a governor in charge of "Department of State Affairs in the region Amu Draya" later. It is obvious that the "prime minister" was an official from the Han Chinese region.

Besides, those who assumed official posts in the Mongolian state, were mostly those common people who had forcedly moved to the Northwest or who were captivated by Mongols. In the 1220s, when Qiu Chuji travelled along the north route of Mountain Tianshan Westwards, he saw people who were engaged in music and drama in the region of Beshbaliq were people of "Central Plains". At Luntai, he met a scholar from Central Plains. After 30 plus years, Changde was sent as an envoy abroad to regions controlled by Hulegü on imperial orders of Xianzong, he saw many Han people in Beshbaliq. Nearby Tianchi (current Sayram Lake in Xinjiang), "it is said that the guardians of Temur Chancha are all from Han people". In the city of Almaliq, "Uyghur and Hans live together." To the south of it, in Mohe ancient city, most residents are Shanxi Bingzhou and Fenhe people. Under the reign of Kublai Khan, supplies for military garrisons were scarce due to the frequent battles among senior armed governors in the Northwest regions. In order to relieve the transportation pressure, the most convenient way of obtaining military supplies was the direct levying from the local regions. After, the collapse of the Song Dynasty, the government of Yuan Dynasty levied a large scale of taxes and funds for the Han army, newly affiliated army and farmers, craftsmen and dispatched them to Northwest regions. The government had promoted immigration of the Han people to open up wasteland and grow food grains in Beshbaliq, current Hotan city in Xinjiang, Hamili and many other districts which belong to Western Regions, and set smelting field to cast farm implements and weapons in Beshbaliq. Chen Fushen, from Mi County of Henan, was registered in weaver lists of Pingyang, Shanxi and later was dispatched to Huozhou where he worked for 15 years.[6]

The cities and towns in Mongolian Plateau were established very early. However, the peak development in such regions was during the Mongol empire times. Ancient city's typical representative in Mongolian Plateau was Qara-Qorum. The full name of Qara-Qorum is Qara Qurum, locates at Kharkhorin, Uvurkhangai of Mongolia. The place where Karakorum originally was summer camping place of Kerait people and it had temples built by the Liao Dynasty of the Khitans.[7]

Adjacent to Qara-Qorum, Ordo was set during Genghis Khan's reign and it was once defended by empress and imperial concubines. At that time, in this region, "hundreds of carriages", "carriages and stands look dignified enough and there is no city governed by Chanyu have never been more prosperous than it",

---

6   See Epitach for Family Name Chen, Collected Works of Ju'ang Volume 7.
7   Chen Dezhi: Establishment of Temples in the Administrative Province in Yuan Dynasty (Upper Part), recorded in Collected Papers of Study on Yuan Dynasty and Northern Nationality History of Nanjing University, Issue, 1985/9.

recorded in the book Travels to the West of Qiu Chang Chun. In 1235, Ogedei, (i.e Yuan emperot Taizong posthumously), ordered to establish the Wan An Palace (Ogedei Khan Palace), and mansions for senior governor and ministers, warehouses and temples along the east bank of Orkhon River, the construction works were led by Grand Counselor-In-Chief Liu Min, a Yenching craftsman from the Han nationality.[8]

According to the records of Guillaume de Rubrouck, the France envoy, "naves of Wan An Palace or "Palace of Myriad Tranquilities" or the Ogedei Khan Palace, was structured on some 2800 square meter plots of land and was a three story edifice with very attractive, ravishing golden roofs. The palace is like a church, with a middle nave, and two sides beyond two rows of pillars, and with three doors and all of these doors look southwards. And beyond the middle door on the inside stands the tree, and the Great Khan sits in a high place to the north, so that he can be seen by all; and two rows of steps go up to him : by one he who carries his cup when he goes up, and by the other he comes down. The space which is in the middle between the tree and these steps by which they go up to him is empty; because here stands his cup-bearer, and also envoys bearing presents; and he himself sits up there like a divinity. On (his) right side, that is to the west, are the men, to the left the women. The palace extends from the north (southward). To the south, beside the pillars on the right side, are rows of seats raised like a platform, on which his son and brothers sit. On the left side it is arranged in like fashion, and there sit his wives and daughters. Only one woman sits up there beside him, though not so high as him. In the entry o(this great palace, it being unseemly to bring in there -skins of milk and other drinks, architect and goldsmith William Bouche the Parisian had made a great silver tree, and at its roots are four lions of silver, each with a conduit through it, and all belching forth white milk of mares. And four conduits are led inside the tree to its tops, which are bent downward, and on each of these is also a gilded serpent, whose tail twines round the tree. And from one of these pipes flows wine, from another caracosnios, or clarified mare's milk, from another bal, a drink made with honey, and from another rice mead, which is called terracina ; and for each liquor there is a special silver bowl at the foot of the tree to receive it. Between these four conduits in the top, William Bouche made an angel holding a trumpet, and underneath the tree he made a vault in which a man can be hid. And pipes go up through the heart of the tree to the angel."

235

The city of Qara-Qorum in the 13th century had the same size with Saint Denis. There were two districts in the city, one for the Hui people, the other one for the Han people. Merchants and handicraft men lived in a compact community in the Han Chinese people district. There were 12 Taoist (Buddhist) temples in Qara-Qorum, 2 mosques for the Hui people, 1 church. There were 4

---

8   See Gongcheng Yuan Haowen: Collected Works of Master Yi Shan, initial edition of Series of Four Categories, Volume 28, Grave Tablet of Family Name Liu, Grand Counselor-In-Chief.

gates in the city, the east gate was for the grain market, the west gate was for the sheep market, the South gate was for cow and carriage market and the North gate was for the horse market.[9] The architecture of Qara-Qorum was preserved till to the times of Mongke Khan (Mongol). The further building of the Qara-Qorum (Karakorum) continued until Mongke Kaghan's reign (1251-1259). In a place 35 km north of Qara-Qorum, a town called Sahurin and the Gegen Kaghan palace were built on the orders of Ogedey Khan; and more than 15 km south of Karakorum, Tuzqu town and another Tuzqu greeting empire palace were also built on his orders.

According to archaeological excavations, Wan An (Ögedei Khan) Palace was situated in Southwest direction of Qara-Qorum, it was encircled by a palace wall all around and some 1 kilometer. Stereobate in central palace was 3 meters high, 80 meters long and 55 meters wide. 9 rows of hall pillars from North to South, 8 rows from East to West, totaled 72 sticks. The audience hall covered an area of 2,475 square meters and it embodied the Han style architecture in its every aspect. About 6 km. around Qara-Qorum, there were two avenues in East-west and North-south direction threading the center of the city, leading to four gates. Two sides of the road, official residence, temples, dwellings and workshops distributed.[10]

In the 11th year of Dade (1307), Yuan Dynasty set Executive Secretariat in Qara-Qorum and other regions and later changed it as Lingbei Province, thus KaraKorum became the capital of this Lingbei province.

Chenghaicheng (Balaqasun) was the political, economic center in the Western Regions ruled and controlled by Mongols during the Yuan Dynasty period and its leading position ranked only second to the Qara Qorum city. It was built by a skilled captive Chinese Han craftsman who were prisoned by Genghis Khan Jinhae officer and the city was named after him, also called Tian Zhenhai Balaqasun, "balaqasun" was a Mongol name, meaning was "the city". The Han people built this city, opened up wasteland and grew food grain, and also engaged in handicraft production. Warehouses were built in the city. Later, due to its location being adjacent to Antaishan, Jingim, Balaqasun city region became the key city for the military operations of the Yuan Dynasty in defending against the regional rebellions. In the period of Temür Khan[11], the

9   The Mongol Mission, Narratives and Letters of the Franciscan Missionaries in Mongolia, edited by Christopher Dawson, London and New York, 1955, pp. 175-177, 183-184.

10   It was recorded in the Ancient Mongolian Cities, authored by S.V.Kiselev (Russian edition С. В. Киселев, ДревнемонгольскиеГорода, Москва, 1965) Mockba, 1965, pp. 138-168, 173-182. See also Huttel, Hans-George. 'Ögedei Khan Palace–Die Ausgrabungen des Deutschen Archäologischen Instituts im Palastbezirk von Karakorum [The Palace of Ögedei Khan–The Excavations of the German Archaeological Institute in the Palace District of Karakorum], in Dschingis Khan und Seine Erben, Das Weltreich der Mongolen [Genghis Khan and His Heirs, the Empire of the Mongols]. (München: Hirmer, 2005): pp. 140-146.

11   Temür Khan, Temür Öljeytü Khan, born Temür (also spelled Timur, Mongolian: 1265-1307), also known by the temple name Chengzong (Emperor Chengzong of Yuan; was the second emperor of the Yuan dynasty, ruled 1294 to 1307. Apart from Emperor of China, he

son of the Crown Prince Zhenjin and the grandson of Kublai Khan, and during the period of Qayshan Guluk / Khaisan Külüg Khan the two leaders have commanded massive forces to guard this place and the military garrison under their leadership had mainly recruited Kipchak troops. In early stage of the 14th century, the government of Yuan Dynasty established the Chenghai Pacification Superintendence and the annual cereal harvest in Chenghaicheng reached over 1,200 kilograms by opening up wastelands and growing food grain.[12]

The central town of Kemkem, which was located at Northwest of Mongolian Plateau, North of Tangnu Mountain was located in Ilan territories. Its meaning was "snake' in Turkic language. Kemkem was one of the regions suitable for agriculture in Mobei. During the Genghis Khan reign period, Kemkem was the fief of Sorghaghtani Beki, who was the legal wife of Tolui, the 4th son of Genghis Khan. Kemkem had provided large number of men for the Han troops and craftsmen.[13]

According to historical records, there were thousand households, most of them were Mongolians, Hui people, and most of Han people were craftsmen immigrated from initial stage of Mongolia foundation and most were on active service in Official Labor Department, The History of Yuan Dynasty–Geographical Annals. Silk fabrics yielded in the local place were very famous. Iron-smelting skill brought by Han craftsmen made it become an important place of manufacturing farm implements and weapons The government in Yuan Dynasty set "Kemkem Weapon Bureau" here, Journal of Chinese Historical Geography. At Kublai times, there were feudal official, warehouses and workshop and so on. Archaeology of former Soviet Union found an ancient city site of Yuan Dynasty and there were architecture relics, such as government offices, folk houses within the ruins and also some cultural relics such as weapons, farm tools, grind and etc. were found here. Itbe Ilan.[14]

The government in Yuan Dynasty set about to compile New Calendar after wiped out Song Dynasty, and it was in the charge of Wang Xun, Guo Shoujing and etc.. In the 16th year of Zhiyuan (1279), Guo Shoujing proposed to dispatch people for conducting actual measurement of day-night length and the sun, the moon and the stars from place to place, making use of the conditions of spacious territory. Kublai agreed with the opinions of Guo Shoujing, sending people to leave for 27 surveying spots for observation. Distribution of surveying spots recorded in The History of Yuan Dynasty, Astronomical Treatise as "east to Korean, west to Dian Lake, South to Zhuya, North to Tiele", among

is considered as the sixth Great Khan of the Mongol Empire or Mongols, although it was only nominal due to the division of the empire. His name means "blessed iron Khan" in the Mongolian language.

12   See Chen Dezhi: Chenghaicheng (Belasagun) Jindikao in Yuan Dynasty, recorded in Collected Papers of Study on Yuan Dynasty and History Northern Nationalities, Special Issue of Journal Nanjing University, Issue 1980/4.

13   See The History of Yuan Dynasty Biography of Jiatalahun.

14   S.V. Kiselev: Ancient Mongolian Cities, Moscow, 1965, pp. 59-119.

which 3 surveying spots in Mobei, as Qara-Qorum, Tiele and Beihai. Data from Qara-Qorum surveying spot: included angle between horizon tangential and direction of the earth's axis was 45° converted into 44°4', the length of gnomon shadows was 324''on the Summer Solstice, 64*15 minutes in daytime and 36*15 minutes in night. Calculated by it, such surveying spot was located at 45°51' Northern latitude, about two hundred miles from Qara-Qorum.

Tiele surveying spot showed, included angle between horizon tangential and direction of the earth's axis was 55°, the length of gnomon shadows was 501' on the Summer Solstice, 70*15 minutes in daytime and 30*15 minutes in night. Calculated by it, such surveying spot was located at 55°51'7''northern latitude, somewhere West of Baikal. Beihai surveying spot showed the length of gnomon shadows was 678'on the Summer Solstice, calculated by it, such surveying spot was located at 64°4'4'' Northern latitude, was close to Arctic Circle, be at the downstream of Yenisei.[15]

In the massive immigrant movement, inland immigrants brought advanced production technology, infused fresh blood into Northwest ancient culture and accelerated the production technology communication between borderland and hinterland. People in Almaliq only understood "getting water by bottle, return home when the moon appeared ", their efficiency was fairly low. After they saw the extractor used by the Han people, they have admired that greatly and could not help praising "everything that is engaged by the Han people is skillful enough", which was recorded in Travels to the West of Qiu Chang Chun, the Volume II.

"Taohuashi" was the designation of Tuoba people, who were the governing nationality of the Northern Wei Dynasty which was named by nationalities in Turkic originally, later theye were referred to as the Han people. "Everything is skillful" indicates people in the Inland regions had discovered and introduced many advanced production technologies to those people dwelling in the Western Regions.

In the 20th century, print works from the 13th century were discovered in Turpan region, among which many of them were engraved on plates with Uyghur scripts, but Han writings pages and names of Han craftsmen were added in the centre joint. It indicates the carving type of printing in Uyghur was operated or taught by craftsmen from inland China (Han Chinese people). Such hundreds of Uyghur scripts carved in wooden tablets were discovered in Dunhuang, Gansu province.[16]

They were all formed by wood carving in the hardwood with the same height and thickness. It was consistent with recordation of wooded type letters recorded in Agricultural Books by Wang Zhen. So this evidence demonstrates

15 See Geography Outline of Three Surveying Spots in Yuan Dynasty by Chen Dezhi, published in Collected Papers of Study on Yuan Dynasty and Northern Nationality History Nanjing University, 1981/5.
16 See The book "The Invention of Chinese Printing Works and Its Westward Spread", Chinese Version, pp. 126-188.

that such technology was spread from the hinterland of China to Gansu. After Mongols have conquered the Western Regions, they mobilized manpower and material resources of the Western Regions to invade the Central Plains region. Large numbers of Western region people came to Han region accompanying the Mongolian army. Among those people who came to Han region from surrounding regions of Northwest included the officers, soldiers, craftsmen, intellectuals, priests and so on. They were named as the Semu by Mongolians whose positions were secondary to that of Mongolians. It was unprecedented that such enormous scale of immigrants from foreign nationalities had migrated to the Central Plains region. After the Yuan Dynasty was wiped out, the appellation of Semu disappeared. The Hui people who were a branch of Semu people have developed into the Hui nationality. And, other Semu people who had moved to the Han region and were integrated into the Han nationality.

Exchange of production technologies was bi-directional. While people from the Han region exported their production technology to the Northwest region, in turn, they received the production technology and crop species from the northwest regions. The traditional textile raw materials of Han region were silk and hemp. The sericulture production was difficult to develop in Northern region and the texture of dressing material made of hemp was too rough. In Song and Yuan Dynasties, cotton plantation was generalized gradually in the hinterland. The introduction of cotton was via sea and land route, the land route was mainly from Western Regions.

The book "Essential Practice to Farming and Silkworm Rearing" in Yuan Dynasty, called cotton as "Ceiba". The book says: Ceiba was originated in Western Regions, since the Yuan Dynasty Ceiba was planted in the Shaanxi regions, it was thick and flourishing, as good as those planted in the mainland. Uyghur people played important role in the popularization of planting cotton in the Shaanxi regions. An Uyghur man Yanli Timur wrote: "initially, people from Xixiang County, Shaanxi did not know, the material benefits of planting cotton; since the Yuan Dynasty, the expeditors gave seeds to the local farmers and taught them the way how to plant them", thus, the people have benefited from it and their lives were somewhat greatly improved".[17]

(2) The period of great prosperity of land route transportation between the East and the West

In the period of Liao, Jin Dynasty, due to obstruction from the Western Xia regime, the interaction between Central Plains and Western regions were mostly made via Mobei. At the early years of the 13th century, after Baurchuk Art Tekin, Idiqut of Uyghur and Qarluq leaders of Almaliq, Qayaligh surrendered Genghis Khan, the transportation between China and the West via Mobei was more prosperous. In the first half of the 13th century, the routes connecting North China and the Western Regions were on the whole: from Central Plains

---

17   Pu Daoyuan: Heritage of Envoy of Yanli Timur to Xixiang, Homebound Essays during the Abstinence Breaking, Volume 16.

upwards to the North, leading to Jinshan by crossing Mobei, turn around and down South to Beshbaliq, then along the Northern slope of Yinshan Mountains (today Mount Tianshan) to Almaliq. From here, to the North, it could lead to Talas (Taraz) city; to the Northwest, which led to Europe; to the Southwest, which led to Persia. During the times of Genghis Khan's expeditions Westwards which aimed to conquer several countries westwards, several precipitous sections of the roads were renovated.

Original Jinshan zone was "with steep barranca and carriage was inaccessible to it". Ogedei, the third son of Genghis Khan "opened up the expedition road for the first time" when he led the army to conquer Westward. The surrounding terrain of Tianchi (today Sayram Lake in Xinjiang) was inaccessible with strategic advantage. When Chagatai Khan, the second son of Genghis Khan passed, "chisel stones and cleared the route for the first time, built forty-eight bridges by using timber and carriages which could move on the bridge side by side".[18] In the past, "thousand miles across the East and West, even the monkey and swan dare not to cross it", mountain pass of Mountain Tianshan became "forty-eight bridges are accessible side by side, surrounded by spectacular scene" after renovated.[19]

In the 1420s, Qiu Chuji[20] who was the founder of Quanzhen Taoism school, met and talked with Genghis Khan in Central Asia via the route. After about two decades later, Changde left for Persia on imperial orders of Xianzong also via the route, recorded in Wang Yun Qiujian Sets, Volume 94.

Establishment of a post communications system, was an important administrative mission undertaken by the Mongols. After Ogedei ascended to the throne, he ordered the establishment of post stations nationwide and he made contacts and arrangements with the Mongol imperial court, led by Chagatai Khan, Batu Khan, Tolui Khan[21] (the fourth son of Genghis Khan), to cooperate for this task, which was narrated in Compendium of Chronicles.

Although the post roads in the north of Mountain Tianshan were renovated, it was difficult for people to drive on it. Besides, from Central Plains to Westward regions via Mobei, it was not the shortcut. Especially, the regions of Mobei and North of Mount Tianshan where the route passing were high and cold with limited production. It was insufficient to maintain the frequent East-west transportation at that time. After Mongolia wiped out Western Xia and seized the Guanzhong region from the Jin Dynasty, the time was ripe for opening up the expedition road from Central Plains through Western Regions via Hexi, Uyghur again. It was the main artery of expedition road between

18   Travels to the West by Qiu Chang Chun, Volume II.
19   Yelü Chucai: Rhymed Verse of Yinshan Mountains, Collection of Zhanran Householder Vol. 2.
20   Qiu Chuji was the founder of the school called Dragon Gate Taoism. Qiu was on good terms with the Mongol monarch Genghis Khan who put him in charge of religious affairs.
21   Tolui Khan, the fourth son of Genghis Khan by his chief khatun Börte. His ulus, or territorial inheritance, after his father's death in 1227 was the homelands in Mongolia.

East and West, since the pre-Qin period to the middle period of Tang Dynasty. And the Ongud[22] people, was put in charge of recovering and maintaining such expedition road.

In 1228, he was committed to undertake a task of guarding Shandan (today Shandan in Gansu), "established post stations from Zhangye, Jiuquan to Yuguan, which could reach to Western Regions"[23].

Another important figure who contributed to the development of transport and expedition between Hexi Corridor and Uyghur region was Uyghur Yue Lin. During his visit to his parents from Central Plains to Uyghur region, he noted: "when I was travelling in the Hexi Corridor, alongside the road, I have observed that there is lack of farming and water, we should improve and celebrate ineighborhood, to dig wells for water and set fortresses."[24]

Rebellions by Arik Böke temporarily negatively affected the expeditions between Central Plains and Uyghur region as well as the surrounding region, but according to the records of Weisu, soon after the failure of Arik Böke's rebellion, Yelü Xiliang made an expedition from the region of Ulus Alghu, to Woduan under the control of Chagatai dynasty on imperial orders by the travel route of Kucha (today Kuqa in Xinjiang), and Huozhou and returned to hinterland, (which was recorded on the Gravestone of Yelü Xiliang, Sequel of Weitaipu, Volume 2). After this expedition Yelü Xiliang saw that the South route of Mountain Tianshan was accessible. This expedition route was maintained sustained for a long time in Yuan Dynasty. The 10th year of Zhiyuan (1273), Kublai Khan sent people to collect jade from Woduan and otherregions, which needed "six horses from every post station". Due to endless journey and heavy weight burden on the camels, the jade stone pieces needed to be carved from their defect parts before the delivery, for the convenience of postal transport mission.[25]

It took the journey from Woduan to Kashgar Eastwards, desert and Gobi was seen everywhere and the supplies was fairly inconvenient along the way. Tallinn (today Tarim) had abundant water yield in summer. It started from Quxian and could easily arrive at Woduan and Yarkend (today Karghalik in Xinjiang) and otherregions separately from upstream of Khotan River and Yarkant River along the South sources of the river. After opening up post-roads

22   Genghis Khan's daughter Alaga ruled the Ongud people as regent for several underage princes until the reign of Güyük Khan (1246-48). Many famous post-Genghis Mongols are of Ongud descent.
23   See Inscriptional Writings of Yonggugong Roads, by Yuan Mingshan, Yongle Canon Encyclopedia (The Great Canon of the Yongle Era) Volume 10888.
24   Ouyang Xuan, Gaochang Xie Family Biography, Guizhai Literary Collections , Volume 11.
25   Books and Records of Administrative Affairs-Post Stations, see Yongle Dadian (Encyclopedia) Canon, Volume 19417. The Yongle Encyclopedia or Yongle Dadian, literally: "Great Canon of Yongle") was a Chinese leishu encyclopedia commissioned by the Yongle Emperor of the Ming dynasty in 1403 and completed by 1408. Its sheer scope and size made it the world's largest paper-based general encyclopedia.

at the South region, the government of Yuan Dynasty discovered the beneficial natural conditions soon. In the 11th year of the reign of Zhiyuan (1274), Yuan leaders ordered to establish 13 water post stations in two cities of Khotan and Yarkend", these 13 post stations were seasonal ones.

At such times, the government in Yuan Dynasty was confronted with rebellion challenges from the Uyghur region. In order to avoid the chaos caused by battles in Uyghur, Kublai Khan ordered to set water post station and land post station in North of Shazhou. Among these post stations, the water post station was located at the water channel of Shule River via Lop Nor, it would lead to Karasahr city in the Northwest and to Khotan city in the southeast. In the 19th year of Zhiyuan (1282) and later, the government in Yuan Dynasty was constantly dedicated to improve the post road from Shazhou to West regions along Shule River. In the years of 1285-1287, the government in Yuan Dynasty successively set road-posts in Lop Nor, Dulihui (today Qarqan in Xinjiang), Qietai and etc.. The post-road passed through from Hexi-Shule River –south of Lop Nor-Tarim Basin, North of Kunlun Mountains-Congling, to Western Regions– and became a main line between the East and the West. Both the journey of Marco Polo to China and the westward travel of Rabban Sauma, famous monk of Persian Sutra Religion were realized via this route.

In the meantime, the government in the Yuan Dynasty period improved the East-west expedition conditions in the Southern region of Mount Tianshan, it undertook the mission of building post stations connecting Uyghur region and China hinterland. In the 18th year of Zhi Yuan (1218), the government in Yuan Dynasty set 30 new stations along the line from Taihe hill to Beshbaliq, recorded in the History of Yuan Dynasty Geographical Annals. Taihe hill was located in the North of cpresent Shanxi, adjacent to Yanmen, direct connected to Dadu by station road. The establishment of 30 post stations directly connected the regions of Uyghur and political center of Yuan Dynasty. Later, the government in Yuan Dynasty constantly strived to improve the conditions of those post stations. In the 22nd year of Zhi Yuan (1285), the Yuan Dynasty government added 18 more post stations.[26]

The expedition conditions from Central Plains to Mobei was improved significantly. There were two expedition routes from Qan-baliq to Qara-Qorum in Yuan Dynasty period, one route was from Shangdu (East of Zhenglan Banner, Inner Mongolia), Ying-chang (southwest of Dalinor, Hexigten Banner, Inner Mongolia) to upstream of Kerulun river towards Westward direction and turning around to Qara-Qorum in Westward direction, with total 57 stations. The other route was from Xinghe (current Zhangbei, Heibei), Fengzhou (Baita Town, East of Hohhot), across Daqing Mountain, passing via Jingzhou (Chengpuzi, Siziwang Banner, Inner Mongolia), Shajing, Damo to Ongiyn Gol towards the west direction, to Qara-Qorum in North direction, with total 38 stations, which

---

26 See Books and Records of Administrative Affairs- Post Stations, see Yongle Dadian (Encyclopedia), Volume 19418.

was called as the Mulin route. In Qara-Qorum, there was another post station on the trade expedition route leading to Jinshan, Qianzhou.

Only senior governors, lord relatives, envoys, high officers and merchants having close relationship with royal court had enjoyed numerous exclusive privileges. But the establishment of post stations on the trade expedition routes which extended to remote regions in Northwest were closely associated with relations between central government and various vassal states, Hans and Uyghurs as well as its surrounding regions, conducive to interactions among the people belonging to various ethnic races. During the chaos times, when Haidu and Duwa fought for gaining the control of Northwest region against Yuan Dynasty, the land expedition and transport between mainland China and the West were frequently cut off. After Chagatai Khanate began to govern Central Asia, the post routes that were originally set and operated by the government of Yuan Dynasty were totally controlled by Chagatai Khanate and were fully utilized. At the turn of the 20th century, Uyghur writings and letters and Mongolian official documents were discovered by the Western scholars in Turpan, among which envoy related official documents sent by Chagatai Khanate governors to Huozhou authorities.[27]

(3) Envoys and Merchants Once Seen on the Silk Road

Establishment of the Mongol Empire that spanned across Europe and Asia broke the long-standing border restrictions among distant countries. The reputation of the Mongolian Empire and improvements in expedition routes conditions helped the East attract many merchants and envoys. Meanwhile, Mongolians' gaining a foothold in the remote Western countries made the link between the East and West ever closer than any time in history. Many of the Chinese and foreign travelers along the Silk Road kept their records.

(1) Yelü Chucai

Yelü Chucai (1190-1244) was a distant descendant of Yelü Abaoji, Emperor Taizu of the Liao Dynasty, and surrendered to the Mongol army when Genghis Khan attacked the Jin Dynasty. At the end of 1218, Genghis Khan asked Yelü Chucai to escort him with the Western expedition. YelüChucai marched out of the Juyong Pass, passed through Yunzhong (Datong, Shanxi), over Tianshan Mountain (today Yinshan Mountain) and across the desert and finally arrived at the Genghis Khan's camp by the Qielvlian River (today Kherlen River). Then, Yelü Chucai moved Westward from the Northern part of the desert, and crossed the Western part of Jinshan Mountain to Shihe River, Ye'er. Next, Yelü Chucai travelled Southward to Yili River, passed Bulacheng and Almaliq and moved Westward to Suiyechuan, a former place in Western Liao, crossed Husi

27   Mongolian Official Documents Conveyed by Mounted Courier of Chagatai Khanate) Michel Weiers, recorded in Central Asian Studies, Central Asian cultural study room, University of Bonn, 1967/1, p. 7-54; Fu Haibo: Another Mongolian Official Documents Conveyed by Mounted Courier of Chagatai Khanate (14th century) recorded in the Journal of Central Asian Studies, 1968/2, p. 7-14.

Orda (City of General Peiluo, Balasaghun) and Talas River basin and reached Syr Darya river. Then, he marched upstream to Kuzhan, Bapu and Keshan in the West part of Fergana Basin, and then to Samarkand and Buhe (today Bokhara/Buhara), both important towns North of Amu Darya, before moving Southward to Bancheng (today Balkh*) across Tiemen and Amu Darya.[28] Before YelüChucai returned home, he passed through Bieshibaliq (Beiting/Beşbalıq), Hezhou (today Gaochang ruins, Turpan) and Yizhou North of the Tianshan Mountain. After he returned, he wrote the Records about the Journey to the West to record the local customs and practices of the Western regions.[29]

(2) Qiu Chuji's Travels and Travel Notes

Qiu Chuji (1148-1227) was the head of Quanzhen Taoism, a branch of Taoism; He is also known by his Taoist name Changchun zi. He was a Daoist disciple of Wang Chongyang. He was the most famous among the Seven True Daoists of the North. He was the founder of the Dragon Gate sect of Taoism attracting the largest following in the streams of traditions flowing from the sects of the disciples.

During the expedition to the Western regions, Genghis Khan heard about Qiu Chuji's superb magic power and ordered him to join his militaryexpedition. In the autumn of 1220, Qiu Chuji led his disciples and set off from Laizhou, Shandong. Crossing through Xuanhua (today Xuande, Hebei Province) and over Yehu Mountain, they travelled Northeast to Hulunbuir before moving Westward along Qielvlian River. Next, they crossed the Mongolian Plateau and Jinshan Mountain, travelled Southward through Beshibaliq, Changbaili (today Changji, Xinjiang), Almaliq, Talas River, Sailan (today Chimkent, Kazakhstan), (Syr Darya), Samarkand, Jieshi (today Shaheli Shaboci Uzbekistan) and Amu Darya, and finally met Genghis Khan on Daxue Mountain (today Hindu Kush (Hindukuş) Mountain in Afghanistan) in the early summer of 1222. They returned back in the next spring. Li Zhichang, the disciple who traveled with him, wrote the book entitled The Journey to the West by Changchun Zhenren to record what Qiu Chuji saw and heard in this journey to the West.[30]

(3) Wugusun Zhongduan, the Envoy of Nyuzhen

Wugusun Zhongduan was an envoy of Nyuzhen, who was sent to the camp of Genghis Khan for peace talks in 1220. Wugusun Zhongduan travelled Northward from the Central Plains, through the Northern part of the desert to Meiliji (Mie'erqi/Merkits) and Tuma (Tumati) in the downstream regions of Selenga River. Then, he moved Westward through Helihesi (Jilijisi), Naiman and Hangli (Kangli), crossed Jinshan Mountain, and travelled Southward through

---

28 Balkh is an ancient city, with a 2500-year long history, situated on the plain between the Hindu Kush Mountains and the river Amu Darya (historically known as the Oxus) in the north of Afghanistan. Known by Arab conquerors as Umm-al-belad, the 'mother of cities'.
29 Yelü Chucai: Records about the Journey to the West, annotated by Xiang Da, 1981, Zhonghua Book Company.
30 Li Zhichang: The Journey to the West by Changchun Zhenren, annotated by Wang Guowei, was published in the book titled as the Last Words of Mr. Wang Jing'an in Haining.

Meigu (Uyghur) and Westward through Helu (Halalu) and Yili River basin before reaching the Western regions. He met Genghis Khan at Tiemen in the next summer, and returned home in that winter. In 1222, he traveled to the Western regions again and begged for a meeting with Genghis Khan. The peace talks failed as Genghis Khan asked for territory concession from Jin (Jurchen tribe-led Jin Dynasty). After return, he wrote the book entitled The Journey to Mongolia and Western Regions as an Envoy to record his experience in exotic regions.[31]

(4) Giovanni de Plano Carpini, Envoy of the Pope

In 1241, the Mongolian army led by Batu Khan attacked the Eastern European regions, which shocked all the imperial courts and the Holy See (Vatican) in Europe. In 1245, Innocent IV sent Giovanni de Plano Carpini, the Italian that's one of the leaders of Franciscan Christian, to Mongolia as an envoy. In April, Giovanni de Plano Carpini started off from Lyon, France, and travelled through Poland and Russia to Sarai in the downstream region of Yedili River (today Volga River), where he met Batu. Then, he crossed the grasslands in the North of the Caspian Sea and Aral Sea, and moved Northward along the Syr Darya, through the former territories of Western Liao dynasty and Naiman and marched into the Mongolian Steppes. On July 22, 1246, he reached Syra Orda near Karakorum. On August 24, he attended the enthronement ceremony held for the emperor Dingzong of the Yuan Dynasty. In that winter, he met Emperor Dingzong and handed him the letter of credence from the Pope. The letter of credence condemned the Mongolian army for slaughtering Christians, sued for peace and expressed the hope that Mongolians could be converted to Christianity. Emperor Dingzong replied to Innocent IV in a letter that Mongolia's attack into other territories was directed by the God and Mongolians would never become Christians; The Pope should come in person if he sincerely hoped for peace, or they would meet on the battleground. Emperor Dingzong also refuted the saying that the God blessed Christians and considered the victory of Mongolians as the result of Tengri's blessing. Not long after that, Giovanni de Plano Carpini set off and returned to Lyon, France in November 1247. After meeting the Pope on completion of his task, he wrote his report in Latin language. This report can be seen an important document to study the history of Mongolia and Eastern countries of the early 13th century. Both the letter of credence that the Pope sent to Mongolia and the reply letter by Emperor Dingzong of the Yuan Dynasty were preserved till today. The reply letter by Emperor Dingzong was written in Uyghur and Persian languages and stamped with the imperial seal of the emperor.[32]

31　The Journey to Mongolia and Western Regions as an Envoy, published in Volume 13, Guiqianzhi, Guiqianzhi is a privetly written history of the Mongols' conquest of northern China compiled by Liu Qi, annotated by Cui Wenyin, 1983, Zhonghua Book Company.

32　Records about the Journey to Mongolia as an Envoy, translated by Lv Pu: published by China Social Sciences Press in 1983; Records of the Journey of Jean-du Plano Carpini to Mongolia, translated by Geng Sheng, published by Zhonghua Book Company in 1985; Mongolia and the Holy See written by Paul Pelliot, translated by Feng Chengjun, published by Zhonghua Book Company in 1994.

(5) Guillaume de Rubrouck

Guillaume de Rubrouck was a San Franciscan Catholic. In 1253, at the order of Louis IX, King of France, he headed for Mongolia to execute do missionary work and persuade Mongolia to ally with Christians and jointly deal with the Islamic countries in Middle East. He set off from Acre (today North of Haifa, Israel) on the Eastern bank of the Mediterranean Sea, and crossed the Black Sea to Sarai in the downstream region of Yedili River (today Volga River), where he met Batu. Batu sent him to Mongolia to meet the Great Khan of Mongolia. He travelled Eastward across Zhayahei River (today Ural River), Talas River, Uyghur River and the former territory of Naiman before entering the Mongolian Plateau. In the winter of 1253, he reached the winter camp of Mongolia by the Wangji River South of Helin. In the next July, he started back with the letter of credence that the Great Khan sent to the King of France. In 1255, he reached the Eastern bank of the Mediterranean Sea. After returning home, he wrote the Records about the Journey to the East in the Latin language, which is an important document which was utilized to study the exchanges between the East and West in the first half of the 13th century.[33]

(6) Hethum I, King of Armenia Minor

In 1243, the Mongolian General Baiju had defeated the atmy of the Seljuq Empire in Rūm country (today Asia Minor), and Hethum I, King of Armenia Minor (today Armenia), a dependent state of the Seljuq Empire in Silesia, decided to surrender. During 1247-1248, he sent his brother Sembat to Mongolia as an envoy. In 1254, at the call of Batu, Hethum I started from Xisi (today Kozan, Turkey), the capital of Armenia Minor, to Batu Orda. Then, Hethum I travelled eastward across Zhayahei River (today Ural River), through the former territory of Western Liao dyansty and Naiman tribe, across Irtysh River (today E'erqisi River) before reaching the court of the Great Khan in the north part of the desert. On September 13, he met Möngke, Emperor Xianzong of the Yuan Dynasty, who awarded him an imperial edict with the imperial stamp to protect his state and allowed the legal existence of Christianity. Hethum I stayed in the camp of Möngke for 50 days, and passed through Humushengji'er (currently Ulungur River, the upper part of Irtysh River), Bieshibali (Besbaliq), Yele, Zhangbali, Yangjibali, Yemishi, Naihu Lake (today Sayram Lake), Almaliq, Yilabali, Talas (Taraz), Miaomaerhan, Buhuala (Buhara), Malu and Tbilisi (Tiflis Georgia) before returning to his state. His attendant Kirakos Ganjakeci wrote the Hethum's travel notes in his book entitled as "the History of Armenia".[34]

---

33   See Records about the Journey to the East, translated by Lv Pu; published by China Social Sciences Press in 1983; Records about the Journey of Jean-du Plan Carpin to Mongolia, translated by Geng Sheng, published by Zhonghua Book Company in 1985; Mongolia and the Holy See written by Paul Pelliot, translated by Feng Chengjun, published by Zhonghua Book Company in 1994.
34   Records about the Journey of Hethum I, written by Kirakos Ganjakeci, translated by He Gaoji, published by Zhonghua Book Company in 1981.

(7) Changde, the Envoy to the Western Regions

Changde was an envoy sent by Emperor Xianzong of the Yuan Dynasty to West Asia. In the first lunar month of 1259, Möngke sent Changde to Mulahid and Baghdad, where Hulagu conquered. Changde started from Helin, travelled across Linhe and moved Southward to Beshibaliq, Bolod, Almaliq, Husi Orda, Talas (Taraz) and Sailan. Then, he travelled Westward across Huzhang River (today Syr Darya) and through Samarkand and across Amu Darya before finally reaching the destination. He returned to Mongolia 14 months later. His attendant Liu Yu wrote the book entitled the Journey to the West as an Envoy after the return. The records about the folk customs in the Western regions in the early Yuan Dynasty as well as the descriptions about Hulagu's Western expedition are of high historical values.[35]

(8) Rabban Sauma and Marcus

Rabban Sauma was a famous Uyghur Nestorius priest in the Yuan Dynasty. He traveled to Jerusalem for pilgrimage along with the Ongut person Marcus in the 12th year of the Yuan Dynasty (1275). They set off from the Dadu, passed through Dongsheng (today Tuoketuo County of Inner Mongolia), Ningxia (today Yinchuan), Woduan, Keshihaer, Talas and Tusi (near Meshed, today in Iran) before reaching Mielahe, Il Khanate, where he met Mar Denha, Bishop of Nestorius (Nestorian). Afterwards, he visited the Christian ruins in Persia, Armenia and Georgia. He did not go to Jerusalem because of the war, and stayed near Maozili (today Mosul, Iraq). In 1280, Mar Denha appointed Marcus as the bishop of Dadu (Beijing) and Ongut, who was renamed as Yabbh Allah, and named Rabban Sauma as the army general director and sent them back to the East. But they failed to return because of the war between Il Khanate and Chagatai Khanate. In 1281, Mar Denha died, and Marcus was elected to be the new imam and called Yabbh Allah III. In 1287, ArGun Khan of Il Khanate sent Rabban Sauma to Europe. Rabban Sauma passed through Constantinople and Naples to Rome, where the pope was absent. Then, he travelled Westward to Paris, and handed the letter of credence of Il Khanate to Philip IV, King of France. After that, he traveled to Bordeaux, a city in the South of France, and met Edward I, King of England. During his return expedition in 1288, he heard that Nicholas IV had ascended to the throne, and returned to Rome to meet the pope. The pope's reply letter to Ar Gun, the King of Il Khanate is still kept in Secret Archives of Apostolicum Vaticanum till today. The biography of Rabban Sauma was once written in the 13th century, but was lost later. As the main contents were included in the Biography about the Imam Yabbh Allah and Patrol Director Rabban Sauma, the author of which is unknown, their deeds were passed down to the later generations.[36]

---

35 Journey to the West as an Envoy, by Liu Yu, Volume 4 of the Collected Works of Mr. Qiujian, by Wang Yun; See Annotated Records of the Ancient Journey, Volume 37 of the Last Words of Mr. Wang Jing'an in Haining, by Wang Guowei.
36 See The Monks of Kubilai Khan, E.A.W. Budge, New York, 1928.

(9) The Venetian Traveler Marco Polo

Marco Polo was a famous traveler. Not long before he was born, his father and his uncle Niccolò and Maffeo—Polo brothers—traveled to the East for trading and reached as far as Sarai, the capital of Kipchak Khanate. On their way back, they marched to the East due to the war between Kipchak Khanate and Il Khanate. They met an envoy that Hulagu sent to the Central Plains in Buhuala, and traveled with him to Shangdu in 1265. Kublai met the Polo brothers, and asked them to visit the Holy See as Mongolian envoys when they returned. In 1269, brother Niccolò reached Ake'er (north of Haifa city, current Israel) on the eastern coasts of the Mediterranean Sea, but learnt that the former pope had died and no new pope was elected by then. So, they had to return to Venice. In 1271, the Polo brothers decided to take the cousin Marco Polo to the East expedition, too, and visited the new pope Gregory X in Ake'er. The pope sent an envoy along with them to the East, but the envoy returned on the way and handed the letter of credence from the pope to the Polo's. The family passed through Taolishi (today Tabriz, Iran), the capital of Il Khanate, Hormoz, Badakhshan, Keshiha'er, Woduan, Shazhou and Ningxia (Yinchuan) before reaching Shangdu in 1275.

With his smart attitudes, Marco Polo won the trust of Kublai Khan, who sent him to manyregions as an envoy. Marco Polo, The Description of the World (translated by A.C. Moule and P. Pelliot, London, 1938) recorded dozens of cities in the China, including Dadu, Jingzhao (Xi'an), Chengdu, Dali, Jinan, Yangzhou, Zhenjiang, Fuzhou, Hangzhou and Quanzhou. In 1289, Ar Gun, the King of Il Khanate sent an envoy to the court, and demanded a new concubine for himself since his concubine had died. The Yuan Dynasty chose a girl named Kuokuozhen. Marco Polo and his family were entrusted to accompany this girl to Il Khanate, consequently Marco Polo and his family had lived in China for 17 years by that time. In 1291, they left from Quanzhou for Persia via the sea route. After taking Kuokuozhen to Il Khanate, they returned to Venice from Taolishi.

Not long after Marco Polo returned home, the war broke out between Venice and Genoa. Marco Polo joined the war and was captured. In the prison, He orally described what he saw and heard in China, which was recorded by Rusticiano, the novelist who was also imprisoned, into the book entitled The Travels of Marco Polo. The book was circulated widely and quickly. Marco Polo died in 1324.

(10) Giovanni di Marignolli, an Envoy of the Pope

Giovanni di Marignolli was a Florentine and a San Franciscan. In 1336, Emperor Shundi of the Yuan Dynasty sent 15 envoys to the Holy See. Meanwhile, Fuding, a noble of Asu, Dadu, also sent a letter to the pope, requesting the Holy See to send a successor because Bishop Mengtegeweinv died eight years ago. Pope Benedict dispatched Giovanni di Marignolli to the Yuan Dynasty. At the end of 1336, Giovanni di Marignolli left from Avignon in the South of France, where the pope lived, and reached Sarai, the capital of Khanate of Kipchak, where he visited Mohammed Öz-Beg Khan. Then, he continued to travel Eastward and reached Almaliq, the capital of Chagatai Khanate. In 1342, Giovanni di Marignolli arrived in Shangdu and visited Emperor Shundi of the Yuan Dynasty. Giovanni di Marignolli handed the letter of credence from the Pope to the Chinese emperor, and presented him a fine horse. The court of the Yuan Dynasty mostly saw Mongolian horses, which were small and short. As the horse brought by Giovanni di Marignolli was strong, big and tall, both the emperor and his ministers loved it and called it the "sky horse". It was painted by the imperial painter Zhou Lang and praised by many scholars in poems, causing a sensation at that time. Giovanni di Marignolli had stayed in Dadu for about three years before going to Quanzhou, where he left via the sea route for his homeland. In 1364, he returned back to Avignon.

(11) The Exchanges between Mongolians and the Holy See (Vatican)

After taking the throne, Emperor Taizong of the Yuan Dynasty ordered Shuo'er Mahan to lead an army and attack the Taikeling region (today Caucasia). After Shuo'er Mahan died, Baizhu Nayan succeeded him as the commander in chief. Because many Christians were killed in Mongolia's Western military expeditions, the Pope sent a letter criticizing the massacre made by Mongolia. Baizhu sent Aybeg and Sargis as envoys and asked the Christian pope to choose between peace and war.

After Emperor Dingzong of the Yuan Dynasty ascended to the throne, Yeli Zhijidai, the Mongolian General sent by the emperor to West Asia, also had exchanges with the Pope through envoys. In 1248, Yeli Zhijidai sent Saifuding Muqifei Daodi and Ma'er Husi to give a letter to the Pope. The letter did not show the arrogant attitude generally seen in the letters that Mongolian nobles sent to foreign leaders, but claimed that Mongolians were the protectors of Christianity and treated each school of Christianity, such as the Latin School, Greek School, Armenian School, Nestorius School and Jacobite School, without discrimination. In 1255, on his return from Mongolia, Rubruk, an envoy of the King of France, encountered five envoys sent by the pope to Mongolian Dukes Salita and Buli and Emperor Xianzong of the Yuan Dynasty.

After Hulagu eliminated the residual force of the Arab Empire, the princes and dukes across Europe were greatly encouraged, considering the Crusades could ally with Il Khanate to tackle the growing Islam forces in the Middle and Near East. Il Khanate had maintained exchanges with the Holy See in the past. In 1268, Abaqa Khan, successor to Hulagu Kahan, wrote a letter in Latin to the Pope in Vatican. In 1274, Abaqa's envoy also sent a letter in Latin to the Lyon Church in France. Ar Gun (Argoun) Khan once sent Rabban Sauma as the envoy to visit kings of England and France as well as the Pope. In 1291, Ghazan Khan of Il Khanate also sent a letter in Mongolian to the Pope. Yabbh Allah, who left China for Persia and was assigned as the archbishop of Nestorian Church, wrote a letter to the Pope respectively in 1302 and 1304, which was in Arabic and stamped with seals in the Uyghur language.[37]

249

---
37   Mongolia and the Holy See (Vatican), written by Paul Pelliot, translated by Feng Chengjun, published by Zhonghua Book Company in 1994.

During the reign of Emperor Yanyou (1314-1320), Byzantine Empire sent an envoy to the Yuan Dynasty, who should be Andrew that joined the mission of Mengtegeweinv in Dadu (current Beijing).[38]

He reached Quanzhou in 1318 as the successor to Pelleg Green, bishop in Quanzhou who had passed away. Andrew had lived in Quanzhou for four years before his death. The inscription on the memorial tablet in his tomb is preserved in Quanzhou till today. In 1336, Emperor Shundi of the Yuan Dynasty sent 15 Europeans including Andrew to the Holy See to convey pope a letter, who also took letters from Fuding, a noble of Asu, Dadu and an official at Zhishumi, and Xiangshan, commanding official of Zuoasuwei. Learning that Mengtegeweinv was already dead for 8 years, the pope sent a 32-member team led by Giovanni di Marignolli to the court of Yuan Dynasty.

3. Religious and Cultural Exchanges between the East and West during the Yuan Dynasty Period

In the Yuan Dynasty period, thanks to the tolerant attitude of the Mongolian rulers, different kinds of religions and cultures gained development. Alien religions mainly included Buddhism, Nestorius School of Christianity and Islam, and Catholicism was introduced into China at that time. Taoism, which was popular in the Central Plains regions, and it was introduced to the Western regions with the Westward migration of the Han people.

(1) Spreading of Buddhism in the Northwestern Regions during the Tang and Yuan Dynasties

As early as the Northern Song Dynasty period, Buddhism became prevalent in the regions east of Pamirs. The book History of the Song Dynasty Kingdom of Khotan had narrated that the King of Khotan begged for the title of „Linhei Hanwang" in the 8th year of the Jiayou reign (1063). "Lin" was a Sanskrit word and meant "a bird with golden wings". That indicated that although Khotan was conquered by the Qara Khanid that believed in Islam, its royal family was heavily influenced by Buddhism.

After Yelü Dashi established the Western Liao Dynasty, the Buddhism somehow developed in Central Asia as its royal family and nobles followed the old tradition and believed in Buddhism. Naiman people used to believe in Nestorianism. After Qu Chulv became the son-in-law of the emperor of the Western Liao Dynasty, he gave up his former belief and converted to Buddhism. Then, Qu Chulv usurped the throne of the Western Liao Dynasty and attacked Keshi Ha'er and Woduan. After that, he forced local residents to give up Islam, instead choose Nestorianism and Buddhism or follow the customs of Qidan people. Moreover, he also sent soldiers to monitor and suppress local people in their houses. Under the threat of force, the people of Keshi Ha'er and Woduan

---

38   Chen Dezhi, Chinese Historical Records about the Visit by the Pope's Envoy to China during the Reign of Empeor Rengzong of the Yuan Dynasty, published in the Collection about Chinese History, Tianjin Ancient Books Publishing House, 1994.

had to obey the oppression. Working was also banned for Islams and Mosques and Islamic schools were banned.[39]

Qu Chulv's oppression had met strong opposition from local Islams. Islams held a meeting in Woduan to discuss the problems, more than 3,000 Imams had participated, in this meeting Ala al-Din Muhammad boldly spoke in favor of Islam and defended religious rights, but was imprisoned and tortured before crucified on the temple gate.

The Buddhist influence based on military force could not last long. After Qu Chulv was executed by the Mongolian army, Islam quickly gained the upper hand again in Khotan and Keshi Ha'er. Therefore, in the 1370s, when passing by, Marco Polo could not see any Buddhists in these cities. According to the Sequel to Guixin Notes by Zhou Mi, Prime Minister Boyan Chang reached Khotan, where he had a well dug and got a jade Buddha. The Buddha was about one meter tall, with the skin white and smooth and veins clearly seen inside.[40]

The story indirectly reflects the decline of Buddhism in these regions.

After the Tang Dynasty, the Buddhist centers in the Northwestern regions were concentrated in the East of the Tianshan Mountain, wherein the Uyghur people dwelled. After moving to Anxi, the Uyghur people continued to worship Manichaeism and deeply respected Buddhism as well. According to the records by Ouyang Xuan, a scholar in the Yuan Dynasty, "King of Gaochang has a stamp conferred by the Tang Dynasty. As Buddhism was respected in those days, Sanskrit scripts were used."[41]

In the early period of Northern Song Dynasty, after returning from Gaochang, Wang Yande quoted the records that Gaochang had more than 50 Buddhist temples, all with the plaques conferred by the Tang dynasty, and there were Tripitaka, Tangyun, Yupian, Jingyin and many other Buddhist sutras kept inside them.[42]

Abundant Buddhist sutras written in Uyghur scripts from the Gaochang Uyghur (Kingdom) period were recently found in Turpan, indicating the prevalence of Buddhism in this region, back then.

Among the Gaochang Uyghur people, Buddhism was strongly influenced by Manichaeism religion. For example, in the Uyghur Buddhism, many names came from the gods or evils in Manichaeism they believed in. For example, Brahma was translated as Poluoximo, Poluohemo or Polanmo in Chinese Buddhist sutras, meaning the father of all the living things. Azrur was the wrong

---

39   See Ata-Malik Juvaini, History of the Conquests in the World, Chinese version, p. 73 and p. 85.
40   Xuejin Taoyuan, pp. 17- 18; Nancun Chuogenglu, Volume 28 The Xuejin taoyuan "A plain frequented to quench the thirst for learning" is a collectanea compiled by the Qing period (1644-1911) scholar Zhang Haipeng.
41   Records of Gaochang Xieshi, Guizhai's Collected Works, Volume 11.
42   The Last Words of Mr. Wang Jing'an in Haining, Volume 37, p. 5.

translation of Zervan; Indra was translated as Yintuoluo in Chinese Buddhist sutras, meaning the emperor. Khormuzta was the wrong translation of Ormuzd, the God of Light.43 The terms from Central Asia in the Uyghur Buddhist literatures were related to the Sogdiana people. So, the Uyghur people replaced the word „naraka" with the word "tamu", which was borrowed from the Sogdiana language that had the same meaning, replaced the word "klesa" with the word „nixwan" and used the word "midik" instead of "prthgjana".

Mongolian rulers appointed officials for Buddhism administration in Uyghur. The Uyghur Yu'er Siman "served Emperor Xianzong of the Yuan Dynasty, inherited the title of his father and administered the monks".44

Yue'er Siman has administered the local Buddhist affairs between the 1350s and the 1370s. There were also records about the Buddhism in Uyghur in the literatures left by the European envoys and travelers to the Yuan Dynasty. Guillaume de Rubrouck, an envoy sent by the King of France, saw many Buddhist monks in Uyghur on his way to the East to visit Mongke Khan in 1253. He described, "Entering the temple, I saw monks. On the first day of each lunar month, they opened the gate, wore robes, burnt joss sticks and presented sacrificial offerings... Wherever they went, they were dressed in golden belted coats, and covered by cassocks from the left shoulder to the right side of the body."45

Although Marco Polo never traveled to Uyghur, he heard about the Buddhism being prevalent in Uyghur. He said, "Uyghur was a big state affiliated to the Great Khan. With the capital called Halahuozhou, it governed many villages and towns. Its residents followed Buddhism...Christians and priests often got married with followers of Buddhism"46.

Hamili, a place in the east of Uyghur, was also a center of Buddhism in the northwestern regions. According to the History of Yuan Dynasty·Biography of Sakyamuni and Laozi, the name of the state preceptor Bilan Nashili was pronounced in the same way in Mongolian, and meant wisdom and luck in Sanskrit. In the History of Yuan Dynasty Records about Emperor Wenzong, his name was also called Bilate Nashili, and he was from the Kingdom of Ganmulu (current Kumul, Xinjiang). According to the History of Yuan Dynasty, "He was originally named Zhilawa Midili. He was familiar with the books in Uyghur and the Western regions, and proficient in Buddhist languages. In the 6th year of the Dade period (1302), on an imperial order, he became a monk at the Guanghan Hall and was given the present name. During 1312-1313, he

43 Overview of the Civilization History of Western Regions, translated by Zheng Yuanfang, published by The Commercial Press in 1934, p. 81; Concise Edition of the Historical Materials about Uyghur, 1958, p. 93.
44 History of the Yuan Dynasty·Biography of Halayi Hachibeilu.
45 The Journey of Guillaume de Rubrouck to the East, 1253-1255, William W. Rockhill, pp. 147-148.
46 Marco Polo, The Description of the World, translated by A.C. Moule and P. Pelliot, pp. 155-156.

translated classic Buddhist sutras on the order of the emperor. During the reign of Emperor Yanyou (1314-1320), he was ordered to translate the words on the documents presented by foreign tribes to the imperial court. With extensive knowledge, he was admired by others. In 1323, he was honored the title of 'Shajinaihuchi' and was appointed as Yinjinshi."[47]

In 1331, he was granted a jade seal, and honored the title of State Teacher Pujueyuaming Guangzhaohongbian Sanzang... He had translated many volumes of Buddhist sutras in Chinese or the languages of Western regions. Marco Polo said, "The residents of Hamili were Buddhist followers as the residents of the said otherregions."[48]

There were records about the belief in Buddhism among the residents of Halahuozhou and Hamili till the Ming Dynasty.

According to The Journey to the West by Changchun Zhenren, there were no Buddhist monks in the regions West of Changbala, Uyghur. But according to the Journey to the West as an Envoy written by Liu Yu, "In 1259, I passed through Sailan and saw a Buddhist temple where the local people attended religious services."[49]

That indicates there were still some Buddhist sites scattered in the regions West of Uyghur of the Mongolian time and even in the Huchan River basin.

(2) Famous Buddhist Figures and Literatures in Uyghur

During the century of passage from the late Tang Dynasty to the early Yuan Dynasty, Buddhism had boomed in Gaochang Uyghur territories. In the 1320s, Qiu Chuji was welcomed by hundreds of Uyghur nobles, gentries and civilians, Buddhist monks and Taoists at Bieshibali (Besbaliq) when travelling Westward to visit Genghis Khan. He saw all the Buddhist monks dressed in reddish brown clothes. At the banquet that a Uyghur tribe leader arranged for him, the guests included Buddhist monks, Taoists and Confucians. There was Longxing Temple at Bieshibali, where Buddhist sutras were kept. He traveled further Westward to Changbala, where the Uyghur leader received him, and those who came along included Buddhist monks. Buddhist monks were also seen at the banquet arranged for him. Qiu Chuji asked the monks what sutras they read. The monks replied they read Buddhist sutras.[50]

What Qiu Chuji saw were probably the Uyghur Buddhist monks. In the period right after Mongolia was established, as Uyghur kingdom was the first kingdom that submitted to Mongolia, its head Yiduhu and the Mongolian

47   According to the annotator of the History of Yuan Dynasty, the word "Sazin ayghuchi" in Turkic language meant scripture teachers, see the Explanation to Two Uyghur Contracts, the Journal of the Central University for Nationalities, Issue, 1978/2, pp. 46-47.
48   Marco Polo, The Description of the World, tr. by A.C. Moule and P. Pelliot, p. 154.
49   Records of the Ancient Journey, Volume 37 of the Last Words of Mr. Wang Jing'an in Haining, by Wang Guowei.
50   Li Zhichang: The Journey to the West by Changchun Zhenren, the Last Words of Mr. Wang Jing'an in Haining, Volume 39, pp. 27-29.

princes called each other as brothers.[51] After that, many Uyghur monks moved to China and served Mongolian rulers. For example, according to She Lanlan, who was from Gaochang, "The people here believe in Buddhism. Male monks were called Bhiksu in Sanskrit and female ones as Bhiksuni." Haidu's rebellion caused many Uyghur people immigrate into China. At the age of 8, She Lanlan moved with her family to Dadu and served Queen Chabi, the wife of Emperor Shizu of the Yuan Dynasty. By the order of the emperor, She Lanlan took Grags Pa'odzer as her teacher. After finishing her learning course, she was respected by both princesses and princes and called Bahashi. Later, she moved to Miaoshan Temple, and "wrote a dozen of Buddhist sutras in the Tibetan language like Ashtasahasrika Prajnaparamita Sutra, as well as Avatamsaka Sutra and Surangama Sutra in Chinese and Lotus Sutra in the Uyghur language... Meanwhile, she donated funds to build or run Buddhist temples in Tibet and Gaochang, etc."[52]

Although Shelanlan moved to Dadu and became a famous Buddhist master, she did not forget her hometown Uyghur. An Zang came from Bieshibali (Besbaliq). His Courtesy name was Guobao and literary name was Longgong Laoren. All his family believed in Buddhism. An Zang had "heard his father and brothers chant sutras" since childhood, and "learnt from a teacher since the age of nine and had a good memory. He could recite Abhidharmakosa-sastra at the age of 13, fully understood Confucian and Buddhist books at the age of 15, and was called in by the emperor at the age of 19. After Emperor Shizu of the Yuan Dynasty took the throne, he presented 11 volumes of Baozanglun Xuanyanji to the emperor, who felt very happy."[53]

An Zang was also a famous translator in the Yuan Dynasty and translated many Buddhist sutras in Chinese into those in the language of minorities. Dachengdu came from a noble family in Bieshibali (Besbaliq), Uyghur. "He left home and came to visit the emperor of the Yuan Dynasty. Emperor Shizu knew about his family and extensive knowledge, and talked with him about Buddhist sutras. Little by little, they developed close relationship, and the emperor granted him nice clothes, gold and silver wares and jade Buddha sculptures, etc." His sons were called Dalidu and Dacidu.[54]

Aluhun Sali was also born in a Uyghur family that believed in Buddhism. His grandfather Atai Sali was proficient in Buddhism. After Genghis Khan returned from the Western regions, he accompanied him to Yandu. His father was Qitai Sali, "who was also proficient in Buddhist sutras. After completing scripture learning, his teacher named him 'Wanquan'. In 1275, he was elected

254

51   General History of Buddha, Vol. 22.
52   Ibid.
53   Cheng Jufu: Sacred Tablet for Wenjinggong of the Kingdom of Qin and the Collected Works of Cheng Xuelou, Vol. 9, published by the National Central University Library, Collected Works of the Yuan Dynasty.
54   Ibid.

as Shijiao Duzongtong."[55] According to the Imperial Tablet for Qitai Sali, he "learnt Buddhism from Zhiquanweili Kewupodisha". His teacher Zhiquanweili Kewupodisha was a Buddhist master who lived in Yandu. The Buddhist name of "Wanquan" indicates the teacher was probably from the Han nationality. As his father was named "Wanquan", Alunhun Sali had the family name of Quan. He "was smart when he was little and learnt from Bahasiba". Aluhun Saili's teacher Bahasiba should be Basiba, a senior Tibetan monk. Aluhun Sali was a Buddhist monk proficient in several languages. In 1283, "a monk form the Western regions claimed he could understand celestial phenomena but nobody could know what he said. The emperor asked who could interpret what he said. Tuolie replied, 'Aluhun Sali could do that!' Then, the emperor called him in, who disputed with the monk and won respect from the monk."[56]

The Imperial Tablet for Qitai Sali mentioned Qitai Sali rather than his son Aluhun Sali. During the Yuan Dynasty period, Uyghur monks played an important role in the religious activities of the Yuan court. They were often ordered to pray for the royal family. So, records about Gaochang monks holding Buddhist religious services were often seen in the "History of the Yuan Dynasty" and "the General History of Buddha".

In the Mongol Empire, Kuolijisi, the minister who governed the western Asian region, was from a place near Bieshibali (BeşNaliq). According to Ata-Malik Juvaini, he was once a Buddhist. Buddhist culture also had influence on Chagatai Khanate. In the 1430s, there were Ulus leaders named Tarmashirin in Chagatai Khanate. This name probably came from Sanskrit and meant luck.

255

Karunadaz was one of the best-known translators in the Yuan Dynasty. He was also from Uyghur, and was "proficient in the religion and language in ancient India". Recommended by An Zang, he entered the court and taught the State teacher about sutras. As the State teacher was a Tibetan, he did not know what Karunadaz said. So, Kublai (Kubilay) ordered Karunadaz to learn the Tibetan language from the State teacher, and Karunadaz became proficient in the language very soon. He "translated the Uyghur sutras into Indian and Tibetan languages, and presented them to the emperor, who had them published and distributed among ministers."[57]

The Tibetan document (No.TM14, U4759) is an incomplete Buddhist book. The preface of the book mentioned about Karunadaz. It said, "The best translation of this work was achieved by Karunadaz, who did it successfully and without omission. The translation was done in the exquisite Stupa in Dadu in the 7th month of the Year of Tiger." The literature indicated that the printed Buddhist sutras were not only distributed to the princes and ministers in China, but also to the nobles in the Uyghur regions of Chagatai Khanate. This reminds us of another Buddhist book in the Mongolian language which is unearthed in

---

55 General History of Buddha, Volume 22.

56 History of the Yuan Dynasty · Biography of Aluhun Sali.

57 History of the Yuan Dynasty · Biography of Karunadaz.

Turpan. According to the preface of the book says:, "At the order of Khan, the Buddhist book was printed for thousands of copies in the Stupa of Dadu on the 1st day of the first summer month of the Year of Rat."[58]

The Mongolian Buddhist sutra was also printed in Dadu (Khanbaliq/Beijing) before distributed by the court of the Yuan Dynasty to the nobles in Gaochang (Uyghur). According to the Informal History of the Year of Gengshen, "After Jiangnan submitted to the Yuan Dynasty in the early Yuan Dynasty, Yingguogong, the former emperor of the Song Dynasty, willingly became a monk in the Stupa." That indicates Stupa was called so in Dadu in the early Yuan Dynasty, and the site of "Stupa", where Buddhist sutras were translated and printed as mentioned above was the said place, which is the current White Stupa Temple near Xisi, Beijing.

After the middle period of the Yuan Dynasty, although Uyghur kingdom was taken over by Chagatai Khanate, Uyghur leaders still had close ties with the court of the Yuan Dynasty. Like the princes and ministers in China, the Uyghur nobles in Gaochang were also given Buddhist sutras translated into the Uyghur and Mongolian languages which were printed in Dadu (Khanbaliq/ Beijing). The court of the Yuan Dynasty also funded the daily operation of the Buddhist temples in Gaochang. Hexi, a region adjacent to Chagatai Khanate, was another hub of the Buddhist culture in the Uyghur regions during the Yuan Dynasty period. During the reign of Emperor Shizu of the Yuan Dynasty, the Yiduhu family moved from Hamili to Hexi and settled there. Among the literatures stolen by Stein from Dunhuang, China, there were a collection of poems in the Uyghur language, which is currently kept in the British Museum (No. Or 8218). With a size of 147 mm × 193 mm, the poem collection is decorated in the Chinese style with white and thin paper. It's well preserved without any page damaged. The words were written in a brush in a fine point, and are clear and easy to read. The words were also spelled in a standard way, without any change of letters except the conversions between t and d and between z and s. Following the first poem, there is an essay about Buddhist philosophy which is entitled as "About the Nature". The postscript said it was written by Vapshi Baqshi who possibly lived in Dadu.

There was another piece of Buddhist literature stolen by Stein from Dunhuang. It was translated from the Tibetan language to Uyghur language in the Yuan Dynasty. It was copied by Sarigh Tutung, a Uyghur person from Ush Lukchung, on the 4th day of the 6th month of 1350, at the order of Asutai, the son of Sulaiman, King of Xining.

(3) Islam and Other Religions

After the 10th century, the Islam culture gradually spread from the Amu Darya to the grasslands in the East of the Syr Darya river and east of the Pamirs. In the reign of Mongolian era, Islam was widely introduced to the

---

58 Heinishi: Mongolica der Berliner Turfan-Sammlung, Ein buddhististisches Bruchkfragment von Jahr 1312, ADAW, 1953/3, Berlin, July 1954.

Northwestern regions. From the late period of Chagatai Khanate to the beginning of the 13th century, regions including the north of the Amu Darya river, regions of Ghaznavid and Fergana basin were flooded with Islamic culture, but there were also the Nestorianism in these regions. The situation in the grasslands, located in the east of the Syr Darya, and oasis towns, cities located in the north of the Mount Tianshan were alike, except that among the Uyghur people Buddhism belief had gained the dominant status. The Mongolian invasion had given a big blow to the development of Islam, but it had not changed the general historical trend, i.e., the spread of Islam Eastward. At the end period of Yuan Dynasty, the Mongol originated ruler of Chagatai Khanate accepted Islam, which quickly replaced other religions and became the main religion in Xinjiang later. In the 1220s, Qiu Chuji[59] during his travel to West, had learned that Uyghur people and leaders only believed in Islam, as "No monk to the West road, Uyghur must worship towards the direction of Heaven". When Qiu Chuji arrived in Almaliq, the dwelling region of Qarluq (Karluk) people, he was greeted by the Islam ruler and by a Mongol officer (Daluhuachi[60]).

The name "Musslinal", was a kind of transliteration of Farsi dialect "Musalman" and accordingly the word "Musalman" in Farsi language (means "Islam"), and was also transliterated as "Masuki" in the Yuan Dynasty period. At that time, the ruler of Almaliq was Siqnaq Tegin, the son of the Qarluq chief Ozar Tegin who was killed by Kuchlug Khan (King of Nayman tribe federation). Kuchlug Khan later joined a westward military expedition together with Genghis Khan. This King of Musslinal who met Qiu Chuji was probably one of the family members of Wo Zha'er left to guard the hometown and homeland.

Another group living in Qayaligh was the Qarluq (Karluk) people led by Alsilanhan. In 1211, Alsilanhan, together with a Qarluq noble Mama had an audience with Genghis Khan. Later Hajj, the grandson of Mama was taken as a prisoner, and he later became the chief Huang Jin of Emperor Taizong of the Yuan Dynasty.[61]

There was no choice but to let Hajji free as the hostage to prove that he was the blood relative of Alsilanhan. The name of Mama's son was Ali. Moreover, his three generations had used Islamic Christian name. Only the pilgrims who visited to Mecca could be called Hajji, which vividly demonstrates that the upper class of Qarluq people in Qayaligh were practicing Islam.[62]

---

59 Qiu Chuji 1148-23 July 1227), also known by his Taoist name Changchun zi was a Daoist disciple of Wang Chongyang. He was the most famous among the Seven True Daoists of the North. He was the founder of the Dragon Gate sect of Taoism.
60 Daluhuachi, (overseer or supervisor) every Chinese or Jurchen official was controlled by a Mongol or Central Asian supervisor, an office called darughachi ("daluhuachi").
61 Tombstone of Xuanhuishi, Grand Guard, Dingguozhong with posthumous name Lianggong, Collection of Huang Jinhua, Volume 24.
62 See Yang Zhijiu: Several Danishmands in Yuan Dynasty, contains Three Theories of History in Yuan Dynasty, People's Publishing House, 1985, p. 220.

Traveller William of Rubruck had seen 3 Nestorius temples, and also seen a place where the Nestorians and the Islam people lived together.

According to History of Yuan Dynasty·Records of Emperor Shun, the imperial concubine of Kusala, also the mother of Emperor Shun, Michael To Di was from Qarluq tribe. Since Geng Shen called her as a Hui lady, this evidence shows that the name Micheal To Di was from a Qarluq family which had embraced Islam. In the period of Song and Yuan Dynasties, the nation, which lived in the regions between Balasagun and Sailan, was called Argyns. At the beginning of Yuan Dynasty, a part of these people basically practiced Islam.[63]

In the region of Balasagun, those Argyns (tribe) people who believed in Islam lived together with Nestorians. The oases region in the South of Mount Tianshan have largely believed in Islam before Mongol invasion. In 1270s, when Marco Polo entered into Yuan along the South road, he deeply felt that Islam was dominant in Kashgar, Khotan, Duchan and some other regions.

In addition to Nestorianism, Islam had penetrated into the center of Buddhist faith Uyghur in the Northwest region. In 1209, among the envoys sent by Duhu Baurchuk Art Tekin to be subordinated to Genghis Khan, there was Turki Omar.

In the middle of the 13th century, when traveller Rubruck went to meet Mongke Khan, he saw that: "Nestorians and Islam people dwelled in all the Uyghur towns and cities."[64]

258 According to Juwayni, in 1251, Duhu Saliandi had ever discussed with some nobles, with the intenton to sweep all Islam people out of Beshbaliq (Uygur capital) when he saw them praying in the mosque on Fridays. Afterwards, this plan was uncovered and failed to be realized. This showed that there were large numbers of Turkic people in Beshbaliq, the political capital of Uyghur.

The Mongols in Central Asia have undergone a long period before they accept Islam. The local Hui culture was wantonly destroyed at the period of the Mongol conquest Westward and the beginning of Mongolia establishment in Central Asia. Eminent scholars and Hui nobles who have rebelled against the rule of Mongolia would be killed or abused. Because Mongolian enforced its law, the custom and habit of Turkic people were suffered from groundless interference. All this aroused strong dissatisfaction among people, leaving Chagatai who was ordered to guard Western regions cursed by Turkic people.

Many Hui nobles and intellectuals had surrendered to Mongol invaders, becoming the right-hands of Mongol ruler, such as Khwa-rizmians Yalawachi (Yalavanchi) and his son Masqut Qurumsi (Mesud), Otrar Habashi Ami. The Mongolian population was too few and was surrounded by indigenous civilizations. Mongols, after living in the Western Regions for a long time, were gradually affected by the surrounding environment, and deepened their

---

63 See Yang Zhijiu: Argyns people in the Yuan Dynasty, including Three Theories of History in Yuan Dynasty, People's Publishing House, 1985, pp. 226-236.
64 William of Rubruck's Travels by William W. Rockhill, p. 141.

understanding of Islamic culture, consequently some Mongol nobles began to accept Islam. The name "Mubarak Shah", which means "King of Good Fortune" in Arabic and Persian, reflects the influence of Islamic culture. After the failure to invade the state of Yili Khan, Baraq accepted Islam and took the name of Heiyashuding. These two Chagatai Uyghur Ruth khans in the 13th century were the pioneers of the Mongols who converted to Islam.

The passage of time made the Mongols in the Western regions were gradually assimilated by the local people. By the 1320s, when Behan was the ruler, the Chagatai Khanate center was moved to oasis region where Western agricultural culture was prevalent, and the Mongols had settled to live in the Islam world. In 1331, when Tarmashirin called Khan, many of the Mongols in the Western part of Khan Country became Islams. In response to the times, Tarmashirin changed the practice of Eastern march tour and ordered the conversion to Islam, so that Islam took greater advantages than other religions among many Mongolians in the Western region.

After Khan's death, the state of the Taiwan Khan was divided. At that time, the Western Mongols had accepted Islam. In 1348, under the support of Dohelati, Taimur claimed to Khan in Eastern regions. He promoted Islam enthusiastically under the persuasion of Turkic forces, thus 160,000 Mongolians in the Eastern Khan converted to Islam. It marked the completion of Islamization process of Mongolian people living under the rule of the Chagatai Khanate, this laid the foundation for Islam becoming the main religion in Northwest regions. Since the Tang Dynasty, Islam became quite popular among Persian and Arab merchants living in China's coastal regions. But the spread of Islam was restricted in the period of Song Dynasty. During the Yuan (Mongol) dynasty period, large number of people from all nationalities in the central Asia moved to hinterland, among them were part of Islam. It was at this time that Islam had spread across China.

The word "Islam" was first seen in Chinese,be in the Jin Dynasty period, and was translated as Yixilan at that time. History of Jin Dynasty·Zhangehannu Biography: "During the period of Jin Shizong, 3 Uyghur people traveled to Southwest for trading." Naturally, this three Kara-Khitan Khanate persons were Islam. It was translated into Islam in Yixialn, and coincident with the words phonetic. Furing the Yuan Dynasty, Islam was generally written as Musliman or Musman. The Arabic Islam was the literature of Farsi Musalman. In Chinese history, they were often called Turki. Initially, the Hui was another appellation of people in Song Dynasty for Uyghur. In dynasties of Song, Liao and Jin (Jurchen), Uyghur and Hui referred to Central Asia people, it was mainly because Song Dynasty's territory was limited to mainland, so that people in Song dynasty understood worse than those in Tang Dynasty. However, Uyghur people were located in the communication center of central and Western region after the Westward migration. Thus, people in Song dynasty always regarded the Western people as Turkic people who pass Uyghur when entering mainland for trading and spoke similar language. In Yuan Dynasty, Turkic people referred to Islam, but also included other Western people, such as Nestorian Christians. Sometimes, Jews were called as "Shuhu Uyghur", while Aorsoi believing in the Orthodox Eastern Church was called as "Green eye Uyghur", the Gypsy "Luoli Uyghur". Later, even Greeks, ancient Romans were both called as "Uyghur". But in most occasions, it was referred to Islam, and Turkic people who migrated to various regions during Yuan dynasty period, and formed the current Hui nationality in China. Turkic people in the Yuan Dynasty period were mainly craftsmen or civilian captives from central Asia and Persia, soldier captives after successive wars, numerous officials and scholars in Yuan Dynasty, merchants who came to China to do business, and the descendants of Persian and cannibals that had lived in central China since previous dynasty. Hui was the majority of Semuren. As they were deeply trusted by the Mongolian rulers, many Turkic origininated officials were given key positions in the central or local government organs. They had great influence on domestic and foreign trade affairs. "Great merchants are good at trading in both mainland and maritime. Famous and big cities are always at the key points and have abundant natural resources."[65]

In 1263, there were 3,000 Hui households when making registration, and most of them were wealthy merchants. Naturally, there were large number of upper class Hui craftsmen and civilian employed to feudal official or nobles' artisan bureau to engaged in textile, construction, military machinery, paper making, sugar refining, gold and silver utensils and other industries, such as made Simali artisan bureau (Simali, Ximali, Southwest of Zhang Jiakou, Hebei province), which was built by 3,000 Hui craftsmen in Ogedei, most of the craftsmen were Samarkand people.[66]

Turki from East were pleasant to live in central China, just as the saying goes: "people all take the Central Plains as home, especially South of the Yangtze River, no longer back to homeland." Zhou Mi: Miscellaneous observations from the year of Guixin one, "Uyghur desert", resulting in the situation of "Hui was everywhere in Yuan dynasty".[67]

On the other hand, most of the Turkic people had accepted the principles of Islam, as "living in central China and accustomed to the dining there, only the custom was the same."[68]

Though used to this different region and carried on the family line, they have never attempted to migrate for generations."[69]

Coupled with these the religious compatibility policy of the Chinese Yuan government, Islam was introduced to every corner of China and the regions influenced by it, i.e., the Western Regions, Central Plains and the Border

---

65 Xu Youren: Monument Hajj, Zhizheng Collection, Vol. 53.
66 Journal of Chinese Historical Geography; History of Yuan Dynasty Hahsana Biography.
67 See History of Western Regions.
68   See Xu Youren: Monument Hajj, Zhizheng Collection, Vol. 53.
69   Wu Jian: Story of Qingjing Mosque Restoration, Religious Stone Inscriptions and Carvings at Quanzhou, pp. 22-23.

Regions. According to the rule of A New Collection of Ordinance, Yuan government has set up the government Department of Hajj led by Master Hajj, which was transliterated as Qadi (judge) in Arabic. All religious activities, legal cases regarding household, marriage, money and grain and parts of punishments should comply with the law of Hui. When emperor Renzong took his office, he canceled the Department of Hajj and founded Yamen.[70]

The Yamen organizations outside the court was a corresponding local official organization set up everywhere. These organizations were attached to the central organ of Hui Hajj Deperment. After the year of 1313, local offices attached the Hajj Department were among the list of abolishing. In these days, the Yuan government aimed to take back certain civil and public responsibilities of the Hui Hajj Deperment, thus the Yuan government wanted to limit the responsibilities of the Hui Hajj within the purely religious activities, such as taking charge of temples and chanting scriptures. During the period of emperor Wenzong, a royal edict was issued which stipulated the dismissal of the Hui Hajj Department.

Although Islam was spread all around the country in the Yuan dynasty period, it was mainly popular among Turkic peoples. Mongolians migrated to Northwest turned to Islam successively, while few kings and nobles living in Chinese region had also faith in Islam, the most famous one among them was Kublai Khan's grandson Ananda, who was the son of Mongalan (King An Xi Mongalan). The Guanglong Hexi region governed by King Anxi was a region wherein the Turkic peoples had dwelled. Astronomer of the Chinese Yuan Dynasty sent the information about the Hicri calendar and hourly times of Mecca to king Mongalan, so that the Turkic people could use it when praying. Brought up by Turkic people, Ananda inherited the throne of King Anxi in 1280, and they made most of the 150,000 soldiers in Mongolia army to believe Islam. Until the late Yuan period and the beginning of Ming Dynasty, most of the Uyghur people lived in the Gansu province.[71]

Islam was long divided into several factions. The historical materials of Yuan Dynasty on inland Islams were claiming that they were mainly out of the Han people, which seemed to pay little attention to the factions among the Islam believers. If we examine carefully, we can still find some materials that reflect the activities of several Islam factions and their mutual relations. The Arabic epigraphy in Qinjin Temple in Quanzhou in 1310-1311 said, "I wish Allah "forgive the Ali faction, forgive Mohammed and his family members." This implies that there were Shia Islam activities in Quanzhou, so it is probable that Qinjin Temple was a Shia mosque since Shia Islam follows Ali. In addition, the Islams in Quanzhou worshiped the Lingshan Holy Tomb, which coincided with the doctrine of Sufi. According to Ibn Battuta's narration, mysticism and Sufi were introduced into China since Yuan dynasty.[72]

261

---

70 Ordinance of Yuan, Vol. 53, Ministry of Penalty 15, Hajj Questions.
71 See the History of Ming and Chronicles of Western Regions.
72 See Tasaka Xindao: The Introduction of Islam and Its Development in China, Tokyo, 1964, p 773.

The common title of Islam dervishes in the Yuan Dynasty was also unique to Sufi faction of Islam.Since the 10th century, Persian has gradually become the world literature language in Eastern Islam and was widely used in Central China in the era of the rise of Mongol empire In the Mongol empire period and in the Yuan Dynasty period, most of the Uyghur people from the Northwest came from the above regions. Therefore, the documents related to Islam and Islamic cultural relics found within the territory of Yuan, demonstrates the colors of the Persian culture. The inscriptions found in the ruins of the site of Hala and Tuohui Temples were Persian. Moreover, a line of exotic words on the imperial monument of the year 1235 unearthed in Qufu was considered to be Phags-pa script, actually the Persian.[73]

Karakorum (Qara Qorum), the former capital of Mongolia also conteins a Persian monument built in 1339. The special words about Islam in the official documents of the Yuan Dynasty included a lot of words from the Farsi (Fars) langıage, such as "danishmand", "darvish", "marth" (Persian Namaz) and so on.

Mosque has been the holy place for Hui People's religious activities, the Hui people in China built their mosques in the very early times. The mosques before the Yuan Dynasty were mainly located throughout the coastal regions of China. During the Yuan Dynasty period, more and more mosques were built in the Northern regions and inland China. In 1348, Zhongshan mansion (current Ding county, Hebei province) Story of Mosque Rebuilding said: "Today, millions of temples near the capital, worship the heaven towards West."[74]

Although this narration is a bit exaggerated, it also reflects the fact that the construction of the Islam mosques during the Yuan Dynasty had spread to all over the country. Beijing, Hangzhou, Yangzhou, Dingzhou, Kaifeng and otherregions had new monasteries built by Hui people. Russian Kozlov and other researchers have also found mosques and remnant Steles written in Persian which are from 14th century period inthe East Mesozoic-Cenozoic.[75] The Persian monument which was erected in 1339 in the Mongolian capital of Qara-Qorum mentioned about the local figures such as Liu Yingsheng, Shi Weimin and Siqin Chaoketu.[76] The Persian monument shows that Hui people have built temples and promoted the Islam religion.

The Gypsies

Gypsies were originated from India. They called themselves Luri, and were called Multani by others. Multan is a Pakistani city and the headquarters of Multan District in the province of Punjab, located on the banks of the Chenab River. After

73 See Shawan: Mongolian Edict Inscriptions and Writings, the 21st, Toung Pao, 1908, pp. 307-308; Bo Hexi: The Ancient Arabic Inscriptions in China, Asia Magazine, 1913.
74 Sun Guangwen: Story of Mosque Rebuilding Memorial Colophon, Journal of Cultural Relics, Issue, 1961/8.
75 See the book Persi: Ancient Arabic Inscriptions, Asia Magazine, 1913, p. 179, note 2.
76 The Grassland Silk Road, Historical Geography of China's Borderlands, 1992, No. 3, pp. 119-140.

the 15th century, some of the people of Luri wandered through Egypt to Europe, so they were called Egyptians. The name of the Gypsy in English today came from the word Egypt. In addition, they are called Tziganes in some countries. This nationality was characterized by wandering around. In Yuan Dynasty, the Hui people from East mixed with gypsies, the Yuan called them Lyuli and Lali. They still maintain the national character of Idleness. History of Yuan Dynasty Records of Emperor Chengzong mentioned that in 1302, officials of Department of Imperial Secretariats complained to court that Lyuli people were disturbing residents, the Yuan government decided to allocate settlement field for them. In Records of the Emperor Shun, more than five hundred Hui people crossed rivers to Haizhou, Jizhou and other regions. The state system of the Yuan Dynasty had stipulated that the Mongolian, Semu people and the Southern people would not be back. At the end of Yuan Dynasty, hundreds of Lyuli people in South of the Yangtze River looted everywhere, from this looting only helpless residents could survive. Thus, official Hu Song made a banquet with wine for the Lyuli people, persuading them to stay there. There is still a village called the Luri in county Jing today.

During the Yuan Dynasty period, there were traces of Lyuli in Northwestern regions. Luri household of Hui did last in Ming Dynasty, they only married among their community. Since, their population was limited in those days, there was even intermarriages among them. When learning about this problem, the local officials did a research and discovered that Qinshui, Huaian had Luri households, solving the problem of marriage among close relatives.

263

As Lyuli had different living habits, they regarded stealing as legitimate occupation and often had disputes with the Han people. In 1559, some Lyulis had certain conflicts with the local government, and shot an official. In 1587, Ma Youzhong, the head of Luri, lead one thousand people to stir up trouble and was finally defeated, with over 20 people killed. Afterwards, they continued looting in Fengxiang region, but took in poor miners and starving people. Defeated once again, they never ascended to the stage of history. In 1640, Lyuri began to plunder Qinshui again, and were chased and killed by magistrate of a prefecture at The Hall of Avalokitesvara Buddhisatva.

A part of people in Xuan Jiawan, Bei Yongdeng County, North of Lanzhou, was called sibyl, which attracted scholars' attention before the liberation and they were linked with Gypsies. They called outsiders "Huojia", and till currently American, British and Gypsies called them Gaje or Gagio, which is very similar. According the researches of Lanzhou University, they came here 100 years ago, with 4 surnames in the village, such as: Gao, Liu, Liu and He, they intermarried within the community rather than strangers. After liberation, although they had land, they still enjoyed to implement fortune-telling, left the farm work to the employees. They believed in Duke Zhou, Taohua empress and Wuliang. They no longer embraced Islam, were not Hui people any more.[77]

---

77   See Yang Zhijiu: Gypsies in the Yuan Dynasty- Luri and Hui, published in the Journal of Historical Studies, 1991/4.

The Taoism of the Yuan dynasty also spread to the Northwest frontier regions of China. In the 1220s, Qiu Chuji traveled to Western regions to have an audience with Genghis Khan in 1222, when he passed by the Uyghur capital Beshbaliq, he was greeted by several hundreds of people, including Idiqut's family members, officials, gentry and civilians, Buddhist monks and Taoist priests. Qiu Chuji himself was a Taoist priest, so he had made a careful observation in regard to Taoist etiquette. In his view, "the local Taoist etiquette is different from that of Chinese etiquette". At the welcoming banquet on his honor by Uyghur's leader, the companions were monks, Taoists and Confucianists.[78]

In Almaliq, there was a Chinese craftsman Zhang in the East Park, "three alters, and over 400 people has participated in the ceremony and paid full attention." He once invited Qiu and let him lead a preaching.[79]

It seems that many of the followers of Taoism were Han people, and probably, Taoism was also spread among the local people.

Due to vastness of the Mongolian Steppes, Taoism was introduced to Mobei region by the Han Chinese people who were conquested by the Mongols.

Currently, at the Erdene Zuu Monastery of the Helin Relics (Karakurum city) still stands the Stele of the "Sanlinghou Temple" (Three Spirits Hou Temple—A Taoist temple) which was erected in the 9th year of the Zhizheng Period (1349). The inscription of the stele was included in the Collections of Helin's Inscriptions. However, the one in the book has some discrepancies with the actual inscription on the stele.[80]

The people that participated in building this temple included people from every nationality.

4. Colorful national cultures

(1) The Ancient Scripts on the Grassland Silk Road

During the period of the Song dynasty, Western Liao and Jin dynasties, North nationalities such as Khitan (Khitay), Jurchen and Mongol forces entered the Central Plains regions, making this period a new era of multicultural coexistence in China's history. Mongolian people used Mongolian language, and some of the Kitanyes people used Khitan scripts. Peoples, dwelling in different geographical locations and people with different religious beliefs and with different racial roots, that used the Turkic language adopted the scripts (letters) of Uyghur, Syriac, Turkic and Chagatai Khan respectively. And, the Persian-speaking people who believed in Islam used the Farsi language.

---

78   Posthumous Papers of Mr. Wang Jinan in Haining, Vol. 39.
79   Ibid.
80   See Liu Yinsheng, Shi Weimin, Siqin Chaotu; The Grassland Silk Road, contained in the Historical Study of China's Border Regions, 1992, 3rd edition, pp. 119-140.

Mongolian Scripts

Mongolians have created their own script in the Yuan dynasty period, and they used Uigarjin Mongol bichig and Phags-pa script during the period of Mongolia and Yuan dynasty. Uyghur scripts (letters) was created in the Genghis Khan period. Initially, Mongols didn't have scripts, but when Genghis Khan wiped out Naimans, he captured Tata-tonga, an official from Uyghur who was a leading officer in the Naiman kingdom, who persuaded Genghis Khan about the importance of writing. Genghis khan immediately ordered Tata-tonga to spell out Mongolian language in conformity with the letters of Uyghur, from left to right vertical writing, and taught Mongolian disciples. This kind of script was called the Mongolian Uyghur script. The earliest extant document was the Genghis Khan Stone preserved in Leningrad Museum of the Soviet Union from the year 1225. As Kublai Khan ordered Phagpa to design new Mongol scripts, the Uyghur scripts was no longer official, but was still popular among the people. After continuous reforms, Uyghur scripts are still used today.

After ascending to the throne, Kublai Khan conferred Phagpa, the title of teacher of the state to and ordered him to create Mongol scripts. The new scripts were issued in 1269, and was renamed as the Mongol Book, the next year. As the officially approved scripts, Phagpa scripts were supported by the Yuan dynasty. After the Yuan dynasty was toppled, Northern Yuan dynasty still utilized Phagpa scripts to cast chops, but later abandoned them. Restructuring by the Tibetan letters, this Phagpa script, amounting to over forty letters, had square forms, written from top to bottom, right from left. Adopting the Chinese square characters to spell Mongolian, with a square body word spelling a syllable, it resulted that words were fragmented, which was not easy to read.

In 1270, when the new Mongol alphabet was promulgated, it was explicitly provided for "translating and writing all words". Therefore, in addition to spell and express Mongol language, Phagpa scripts were also used to spell Chinese words. The alphabet was basically universal, but some of the alphabet spelling of Mongol and Chinese represented different phonetic value. Kublai Khan attempted to spell all nationality's language by one common letter, which was an unprecedented attempt in the history of Chinese language and characters, and also the first attempt to establish a Chinese phonetic alphabet.

Although few Mongols migrated to Northwest region, they have maintained their own culture for quite a long time. Until the 15th century, the descendants of the Chagatai Khanate still used the Uyghur scripts. Mongol people in the states of Chagatai Khanate and Kipchak Khanate had still used silver coins with Phagpa scripts.

(2) Khitan Scripts

Khitan people spoke the ancient Mongolian dialect. There were two types of Khitan scripts with different sizes. In the period of Emperor Liao Taizu, Tulv created Khitan large script by adding and subtracting Chinese character strokes in accordance with Chinese language. Khitan small script was created by Diela, who learned about the spelling method of Uyghur script and expressed Khitan language by a few symbols. Though some Khitan people moved to central Asia with Yelü Dashi, they still tenaciously preserved their culture. In Kara-Khitan Khanate dynasty, people used the Khitan scripts. A Khitan copper seal with 3.9 centimeters high was found in Ili, and the scripts on the seal belonged to Khitan alphabet, and around the seal were also Khitan scripts.[81] This was the proof that government offices were using Khitan scripts. Until the end of the Kara-Khitan Khanate dynasty, some Chinese officials could write Khitan texts, too. For example, when Yelü Chucai arrived at the Western regions, he had learned Khitan script from a Chinese named Li Shichang, the Chinese (or Bohai) assistant to the prime minister of the last Gürkhan. Yelü Chucai claimed that he learned a little when he was only one year old. Virtuous and good at writing, and poems, the temple master can compare favorably with Su Shi and Huang Tingjian. Drunken righteousness song, written by Khitan script, was his masterpiece. It was once translated into Chinese in the Western Liao dynasty period, but was lost after a long time. After finishing the study of Khitan language, Yelü Chucai found the Drunken righteousness song and translated it into Chinese again.[82]

Undoubtedly, after the death of Liao, Khitan people were soon assimilated by the local nationalities who spoke Turkic language. We cannot be clear whether Khitan scripts were used in Kara-Khitan Khanate dynasty was large or small.

Uyghur Scripts

There were no unified language among the Turkic peoples in the Western Regions in the Mongolian dominancy times. In this era, three kinds of Turkic texts were generally used: Uyghur scripts, Syriac scripts and Chagatai Turkic scripts. The Uyghur script was used by the Uyghur and Hamly people from the 8th century to 18th century. This script was called Uyghur script. China's academic community called it "ancient Uyghur script". It was originated from Millet letters of Arab Latin alphabet and affected by Turgesh people who lived in Sui Yechuang in theTang Dynasty period. Among the coins unearthed in Kyrgyzstan, Kazakhstan and China's Xinjiang, there was a Turgesh coin, whose form was like the Han coins, with a hole in the middle and having a circle form. The coins have Turkic words spelled in Millet letter as the script on the coin, but the coins were smaller in size compared to the Han coins. Since Uyghur moved to West from Mobei, this kind of Turkic language that spelled by Millet letters was widely introduced into China, and became the main script among Uyghur people. Therefore, it was often called Uyghur script by the scholars.

---

81   Museum of Xinjiang Uyghur Autonomous Region: Xinjiang Historical Relics, Cultural Relics Publishing House, 1978, p. 43, Picture 42.
82   Yelü Chucai: Collected Works of lay Buddhist Zhan Ran, Vol. 8, edited and compiled by Xie Fangdian, Zhonghua Book Company, 1986, p. 171.

In the era of Song, Liao and Jin dynasties, the use of Uyghur was centered in the Uyghur Gaochang (Karakhoja) city, and had gradually spread to Naiman tribe. After the rise of Mongol empire, Uyghur scripts were enormously pervasive and popular. During the period of Mongol dominance, in the region Chinese and Hui scripts were used simultaneously, but Hui scripts were dominant as. The master of Hui scripts was the court official Zhenhai, who had established a port city at the north of Jinshan. People who could write this Hui scripts could easily assume an official position and were promoted smoothly, so many people in Yanjing learned Uyghur scripts. As the Mongol forces had expanded their territories to West Asia, the Uyghur officials introduced Uyghur scripts (writing) to the West Asia and Kipchak grasslands. Besides, the migration of Idiqut tribe to the East affected the Hexi region and the popularity of Uyghur script was expanded to Hexi. The states of East Chagatai Khanate and Timur Empire kept using Uyghur scripts after the collapse of the Yuan dynasty. From the Ming to the early Qing dynasty, it was always one of the main scripts used in Ming and Qing dynasties, local authorities in the Xinjiang region, and Western Afghanistan. TillEmperor Qianlogn conquered Dzungaria, Uyghur scripts were finally abandoned in the history, and the Gaochang (Katakhoja) garrison was abolished in the Qing dynasty period.

According to the Highlights of Chinese Calligraphy history of Tao Zongyi, Uyghur script had over twenty letters, only 15 letters left except the same one, resulting in the substitution of letters. Like all the Almaliq script letter variants, each letter of Uyghur script had several different forms, five vowels and two semi-vowels. Uyghur civilization had great impact on the North of China. The Mongolian royal family invited the scholars as teachers even entering the Yuan dynasty, they continued to do so. Many Uyghur intellectuals served as officials in Kipchak Khanate, Chagatai Khanate, II Khanate and the later Ordu state of Timurid Empire. At the time of Genghis Khan, Uyghur people Tata-tonga created Mongolian. Moreover, at the end period of the Ming dynasty, Manchus have adopted several beneficial characteristics of the Mongolian letters and created the Manchu scripts. The basic letters and spelling rules of Uyghur script are currently used in Mongolian and Manchu.

Syriac and Turkic Scripts

In the era of Liao and Jin dynasties, some Turkic peoples who believed in Nestorian Christianity used Syriac letters to express the Turkic language. This kind of script was called Syriac script Turkic scripts by scholars. The centralized regions were Balasagun, Almaliq region and Ongud station, lasting until the end of 14th century. It was not clear what the original name was so far. The documents discovered in Balasagun presently were mainly epitaph. Ongud people who had immigrated into Han territory to get official positions had brought this script into mainland, including the Quanzhou city.

Chagatai Language and Scripts

Chagatai language a kind of Turkic language was the most popular language in Northwest China during the Yuan dynasty period. In the 11th century of the Chagatai Khanate state, scholars who spoke Turkic became accustomed to write with Arabic and Farsi scripts, but when writing these scholars had inevitably used a lot of Turkic words, which gradually formed the trend of writing the Turkic spoken words with Persian and Arabic alphabet. This action also appeared in the Khwarezm Turkic literature works of the 13th century and also in Persian historical documents. This trend gradually developed as Persian alphabet spelling the Turkic spoken language, which produced the Chagatai language. Due to the effect of Islam civilization, many Persian and Arabic words were mixed with Chagatai language and script. Its linguistic foundation was a central Asian dialect of Turkic language. In the middle period of the Mongolia domination era, especially after Dowa Khan, the name of Chagatai became the antonomasia of Chagatai Khanate, particularly the nomadic people in the Western region. Among the contemporary languages of Turkic, Uyghur and Uzbek languages were the closed ones with it. Though it was Chagatai, it was not widely spread in the era of Yuan (Mongolia) period. At the time of Timur Khanate, Chagatai language script became very popular and replaced Uyghur and Syriac script Turkic script, becoming the only writing language for Turkic dialect in central Asia. It also replaced Farsi and Arabic, became the common writing language of Turkic peoples in East central Asia and northwest regions in China.

Hui (Uyghur) Language and the Uyghur Scripts

Generally speaking, Hui language refers to Persian, but it has also differences. The book Hei Da Shi Lue's Short Notes on the Black Tartars (Mongols) noted that: "There is no Tartar (Tatar) script at all, but three types of scripts are still used today, the Tartar people could use small trees with three or four cun, sculpturing its four corners, people in Uyghur should use Uyghur scripts, led by Zhenhai, who was a a high official in the court and who was the master of Hui alphabet. There were mainly 21 letters in the Uyghur alphabet, as others were formed by the side of a script. The people of Han dynasty, Khitan dynasty, and Jurchen dynasty could only use Chinese characters, which was in charge of Chucai. Short Notes on the Black Tartars (Mongols) also said: before the Chinese paperwork was developed, Zhenhai the master of Hui alphabet always used the Uyghur alphabet in written correspondence. The motive behind Zhenhai's this attitude was to compete against Chucai, so Uyghur script was prevalent. A document which was not written by the Uyghur alphabet was not regarded as a genuine document".[83] The "Uyghur alphabet " in the charge of Zhenhai had only 21 letters.

---

83 Wang Guowei: Short notes on the Black Tartars (Mongols), Posthumous Papers of Mr. Wang Jinan in Haining, Vol. 39, p. 8.

Historiography and the Secret History of the Mongols

After the founding of Mongol empire, it rapidly entered the age of civilization. With the creation of Mongolian scripts, the important historical book, Tobchiyan (Secret History), which records Genghis Khan and his family deeds, appeared in the 13th century. In addition to Tobchiyan, historian officials of the Yuan Dynasty also compiled "The Actual Records" for the emperors.

Both Tobchiyan (Secret History), and The Actual Records are royal secret books. Yu Ji, famous scholar of the Yuan Dynasty was ordered to "record the stories of the Yuan in Jing Shi Da Dian like Hui Yao (a historical book recording systems, history, geography and culture) in the Tang and Song Dynasties periods. He asked the Imperial Academy to refer to the book "The Actual Records" because some stories were not recorded in other documents. An official of the Imperial Academy reported to the court and stated that anything recorded in The Actual Records was not allowed to be shown to the public. Yu Ji asked again to read Tobchiyan when he was compiling stories of Genghis Khan and was refused again. Yu Ji was a Han person, who was regarded as an outsider. So he could not read Tobchiyan or The Actual Records.

Tobchiyan was written in Mongolian. As recorded in Yuan Shi: Chagan, Chagan translated Zhenguan Zheng Yao into Mongolian which pleased Emperor Yuan Zong of the Yuan Dynasty who ordered him to translate the Tobchiyan into Chinese, which was called Shengwu Kai Tian Ji. No Han people could read Tobchiyan while Chagan could. According to the above mentioned information, the Tobchiyan is a book which recorded the events about Genghis Khan's founding of the Yuan Dynasty and his foreign conquests. During the reign Emperor Wen Zong of the Yuan Dynasty, Toghon Temür was already named as the heir of the throne. But the emperor intended to make his son, Alatenadala, as the heir. According to Toghon Temür's nurse, when the Emperor Ming Zong was in power, he thought that Toghon Temür did not share his clan's blood, and dethroned him and exiled him to the South. Therefore, Emperor Wen Zong ordered Alin Timur and Huduludu Mesh to write it down in Tobchiyan scripts and ordered Yu Ji to declare an imperial edict to the world. It is true that Tobchiyan and The Actual Records were constantly updated in the future ages.

After the disintegration of the Yuan Dynasty in 1368, Tobchiyan was inherited and supported by the Ming government. When Ming government organized to compile Yuan Shi, Tobchiyan written in Mongolian scripts could not be referenced. But the Imperial Academy of the Ming Dynasty took this book for teaching Mongolian to train translators and interpreters. To facilitate the reading of Mongolian and teach pronunciation of Mongolian language, it was written word by word with Chinese characters. In order to understand the original text, every Mongolian word was explained in Chinese. The text was divided into 282 sections, and there were Chinese transition for each section. The title The Secret History of the Mongols was equivalent to "Mongqol-un

Nihuca Tobchiyan" in Mongolian, meaning "the secret history of Mongolia". The Secret History of the Mongols was divided into 12 volumes for publication, and 15 volumes for being included into Yongle Encyclopedia.

In 1262 (the third year of Zhongtong), Kublai Khan ordered a Han, Wang E, to compile the historical book whichbe the preserved Shengwu Qin Zheng Lu. It was referred by the Yuan people in the compilation of Yuan Tai Zu Shi Lu which was the main basis of the Yuan Shi: Tai Zu. The Yuan government also sent the Mongolian historical documents to all dependent countries. At the turn of the 13th and 14th centuries, The History of the Genghis Khan, written in the Il Khanate, has a great consistency with the book Emperor Sheng Wu's Expedition and Yuan Shi: Tai Zu. From this we can see that the Mongolian historical documents of the Yuan Dynasty to the vassal countries could be from Emperor Sheng Wu's Expedition which has something similar to The Secret History of the Mongols. In addition, the Yuan people wrote the Ten Ancestral Lineage in accordance with the contents of section 1-68 of The Secret History of the Mongols.

Tobchiyan's original text in the Mongolian was lost in the Ming Dynasty and disappeared. When the Mongol royal family withdrew to the North, Tobchiyan (Secret History) was also brought to Mobei and a Tatar scholar in the Ming dynasty once copied it, regretfully there is no copy of the Mongolian text which could be preserved till today. In 1926, curator of Mongol Ancient Books Museum Zha Muyang found an ancient book named Huang Jin Shi (The Golden History) in a Yongxiebutaiji's house. It includes the sections 1-38, 40-176, 208-254, 256-266 and 268, accounts for about two-thirds of The Secret History of the Mongols. However, there is a considerable amount of missing parts and mistakes, and some individual sections are incomplete. We can comfortably say that it is the original Tobchiyan (Secret History) in the Mongolian language, which can be studied by researchers and people.

According to The Secret History of the Mongols and other historical materials, many nomadic tribes which dwelled on the grasslands had their own historical legends. Only Genghis Khan's clan history was recorded in a relatively complete way, since he has achieved the grand unification. The Secret History of the Mongols records the ancestral lineages of Genghis Khan and the deeds of Genghis Khan. It is the only extant full-length work in the Yuan Dynasty and an encyclopedia of the ancient Mongolian society from which we can see the development of the ancient Mongolian society.

In the preserved Chinese texts if we examine "The Secret History of the Mongols", we can see that the sound rules and specification of written words and phrases are very clear and orderly, at the same time, there are a series of particular words indicating grammatical forms, thus this work has a high scientific value. The Secret History of the Mongols is also well known all across the world. In 1866, a Russian named Bodie published a Russian translation of it in St. Petersburg. In 1907, Japanese Naketongshi has published the Japanese version. Later, the German, French, Turkish, the new Mongolian and Chinese versions were published. Currently, there are many scholars in different countries studying The Secret History of the Mongols. It is called "the study of the secret history".

Historical Works by the Han people in the Chagatai Khanate

At the early period of Chagatai Khanate setting down in the Western regions, the ancient customs of Mongols were still preserved, and the past things were remembered and recorded by oral language. At that time, some Han intellectuals who were captivated by Mongols and kept in the Western regions, have written down some facts they have experienced. Shi Ji (Jami'al-tawarikh) records the fact that one of the ministers of the Chagatai kingdom named Qushuq Noyan was the one who knew the past best. In one occasion, Chagatai Khan[84] asked him about the history of Genghis Khan and which countries he had conquered. He was not certain about and went back to ask his servants to give the details of the past they knew.

One of his slaves, a Khitan, was a servant of a Khitan doctor. After the doctor died, he had become a slave of Qushuq. When the slave heard Qushuq's questions outside his house, he checked the details given by the servants, and finally everyone agreed with him. Qushuq was surprised to see how the Khitan slave could remember the past so clearly. The Khitan slave took out a book wherein he wrote his diaries. Then Qushuq Noyan took this slave with him to meet Chagatai Khan who was surprised too. Then the Khitan slave became Chagatai's retinue and was highly valued by him. He was also given a name "Vazir", meaning "Vajra".[85]

It can be seen from this that there was a wise scholar in Central Plains who wrote about the early era of Chagatai kingdom. Unfortunately his writings could not be preserved.

Historical Works by the Hui People in the Western Regions

Mulhaqat al Surah is a historical book written by Jamal Qarshi in Chagatai Khanate during the Yuan Dynasty period. Jamal Qarshi was born around 1230 in Almaliq, who received education in the court of Halalu (Qarluq) kingdom, so he was also called "Qarshi", meaning "royal man" in the Turkic language. He spent most of his life in Qarshihar (current Qarshi in Uzbekistan), where he lived until the beginning of the 14th century. He was a witness to the history of the Chagatai Khanate in the 13th and 14th centuries. The book records all situations of Chagatai and Haidu family and stories of Rumasudu, a Hui from the central Asia, and describes various people towns of central Asia such as Wozhaer family of Almaliq Halalu tribe (Qarluk tribe). It is one of the most important historical documents when studying the history of Chagatai Khanate. The book has a copy in Arabic scripts.

---

84   Chagatai Khan, the second son of Genghis Khan.
85   Shi Ji, (The Records of the Grand Historian) translated version in Chinese, Vol. 2, p. 185.

Historiography of the Uyghurs

Uyghur people dwelling in the Western Regions during the reign of the Yuan Dynasty period had their own historiography. They have their own legends about origin of their ruling family, decline of Mobei Uyghur Khanate and the Uyghur people's migration from Mobei to Gaochang. In the 13th century, the Persian historian, Juvayni, recorded the legends he heard from the Uyghur people.

Uyghur people's former dwelling regions were by the rivers of Urqan, Xuelinge and Tuhula where there were two holy trees. There was an uplift mound between two trees where lived the 5 sons of Aryadeva. The 5th son was Bugudejin who was elected as the khan. After the accession, Bugudejin started the expedition to the West and the East such as Mongolia, Qirqisud, Xixia, the mainland of China, and Suiyechuan. They originally believed in shaman, and the priest was called "Gan". Subsequently, they converted to Buddhism under the propaganda of monks from the mainland of China. Later, for some reason, they moved their families to Beshbaliq where they settled down.[86]

This story could also be found in Yu Ji's book "The Monument of King of Gaochang". The monument says: "the land of Uyghur has a mountain (Heavenly Mountain-Tangri Tagh-Dağ) where the two rivers (i.e. Tuhula River and Xuelinge Rivers)[87] are originated. There are two sacred trees between the two rivers, beneath two trees, were the light-impregnated mounds in which, the Uyghur's five ancestors were born.

The youngest of them, Bügü Khan, was chosen to rule, he received each night for more than seven years, a supernatural visitation from a maiden who entered through the smoke-hole and carried him off to a mountain. This mountain is the guarding mountain for Uyghurs which was burn by Tang troops when Bugu's descendant Yulundejin Khan fought against the Tang dynasty. Then the state began to decline and was forced to move to Jiaozhou."

Both of the two similar legends are undoubtedly from the same document, which is absent today. In addition, Biography of Oghuz Khagan written by the Persian historian Lashiduding is very similar to The Legend of Oghuz Khagan written in the Uyghur language, which indicates the close relationship between them. In the Yuan dynasty period, there were also some Chinese documents about Uyghur clans which ambigiously narrated about the history of changes in regard to Uyghur Khans and power struggles among the 3 clans, i.e, the Yaoluoge clan, Adie clan and the Bugu clan.

According to the above-mentioned Chinese and Persian records, Uyghur historical materials in regard to their own ancestral history seem vague from some aspects. It is particularly noteworthy that they generally ignore that their ancestors were forced to withdraw from the history of the Mongolian plateau after they were defeated by the Kirgiz forces. This shows that Uyghur

86 See He Gaoze, The World Conqueror, Ed. 1981, Inner Mongolia People's Press, pp. 62-67.
87 These rivers were the current Selenga and Orkhun rivers.

historiography was still in its infancy before the Yuan Dynasty period. During the Yuan Dynasty period, Uyghur historiography has greatly improved. At present, the most important historical monument from Uygurs is The Monument of King of Gaochang which is preserved in the museum of Wuwei city of Gansu province. This monument is 1.82 meters high, 0.47 meters thick and 1.73 meters wide. The inscriptions in the extant part includes 61 rhymed verses by a man named "Kiki qorsa ichqu".

(3) Food Customs

Mongolia had enjoyed a vast territory, which meant that numerous peoples which dwelled in the Mongolian Steppes had enjoyed abundant cultural exchanges among themselves and with those peoples which dwelled as neighbours to Mongolian Steppes. Consequently, numerous excellent cuisines and rare items were only enjoyed by the royal family and nobles. Yin Shan Zheng Yao, a cookbook of the Yuan court edited by Husihui, contains not only traditional food of Hans living the Central Plains but also the cuisines of other peoples, most of which were from the Western Regions. The cuisines of the Western Regions and grasslands mainly included mutton and various garnish foods including vegetables and certain spices. For instance, it was recorded in this book how to make a kind of popular food and drink called Shuoluotuoyin, as follows: Firstly, knead dough and press them in the form of copper coin. Then put mutton, the tongue of sheep, Chinese yam, mushrooms, carrots, ginger, spices and other supplementary foods as garnish according to different seasons. Finally, fry them while delicious mutton soup, vinegar and onion are added into them. This meal is very similar to fried lamb slices, cooked with onions and noodles.

273

Another popular meal was called the Tutumashi, a kind of special pasta. Pu Shi Tong, a book written in Chinese and authored by Gao Li in the Yuan Dynasty period has once described how to make this food. Firstly, add some water into flour to knead dough. Secondly, press them into small pancakes with your hands after immersing them in a cold water. Then place the steamed pancakes into plates. At the last step, fry mutton slices with shortening and put some salt until they start to singe. Tutumashi making is finished by mixing fried mutton slices either with sweet and sour soup. Moreover, you can add mashed garlic and cheese, as your own taste and eat them with bamboo sticks. This is fried steamed pancakes with sweet and sour mutton slices.

Steamed lamb with willow branches is also a kind of special food, whose recipe was described as follows. First, dig a stove whose depth is 3 feet and burn it into red with fire. Then place the lamb on banana leaves and use willow branches to cover the lamb. This special food is actually quite similar to baked lamb, but no water is utilized in its cooking.

There were abundant kinds soup meals in the book. Take Masidaji soup (Masidajia was also called mastic, a substance that came from the bark of a tree and was used in making varnish) as an example, it has the functions of warming the middle energizer and smoothing qi. One way to make the soup was three ingredients including caoguo, aniseed and peas which are mashed and peeled are added into the chopped leg of lamb. Then filter out peas after stewing these ingredients. Finally, add polished round-grained rice, Masidaji, salt and barley and make them into the soup. The author Husihui suggests in his masterpiece that sweet and non-toxic peas are mainly used for wasting-thirsting (Diabetes), he also warned that peas should not be cooked with salt. Peas plant grew in the regions where Hui people lived. The sprout of pea plant is similar to bean and peas were planted in the farms.[88]

He also explained that Masidaji without toxicity would taste bitter and smell sweet, which could also used to drive away the bad luck, warm the middle energizer, guide qi downward, relieve the pain, slake thirst and help produce saliva, and freshen up your mouth.[89] The other way to make the soup was stewing the chopped leg of lamb, firstly cook the barley, add caoguo, then filter the barley and add some salt.

Baerbutang, also called Xitianchafan, had the function of invigorating qi. First of all, add the chopped leg of lamb into the cooking soup, add caoguo, peas which should be were mashed and peeled. After straining out the water, cut mutton and carrots as small cubes, then mix small pieces of cubed mutton and carrots, Zanfulan (saffron/safran), turmeric, pepper, ferulic, coriander with vinegar. It was widely eaten with Japonica rice. According to the records of Husihui, sweet and non-toxic Zanfulan (saffron) was commonly used to relieve anxiety and stress. Once people eat them, they will feel delightful.[90]

In addition, ferulic was spicy and non-toxic, which was used mainly for killing insects and driving out bad smell, removing abdominal mass, driving away bad luck and detoxifying.[91]

The method of making Shaqimouer soup was to mix the chopped leg of lamb, caoguo, peas and Shaqimouer (cabbage) and cook them thoroughly. In addition, cook into the soup about 30 or 40 clean knee joints of lamb with some water added. Filter out water, sesame oil and dregs provided that only one quarter of soup remains. This kind of soup was finished by solidifying all ingredients, which was actually equivalent to lamb bone soup.Heximitang porridge which was introduced to the Western Xia dynasty from the Central Plains could strengthen the middle energizer and nourish qi. In order to cook the Heximitang porridge, firstly the water from the soup made by the chopped lamb leg should be filtered. Then add some clean Hexi rice, fine Qima rice, onion and salt and make them into the porridge. In addition, there existed another special food called Hexifei. The ingredients of this dish are lamb lung, Chinese

274

88   Yin Shan Zheng Yao (Proper and Essential Things for the Emperor's Food and Drink), Shanghai Chinese Classics Publishing House, 1990, p. 210
89   Ibid., p. 320.
90   Ibid., p. 320.
91   Ibid., p. 320.

chive juice, mushy flour, butter, pepper and ginger juice. Hexi food and drink also belonged to the food of the Western Xia regime.

The names of meat in the court of Yuan Dynasty still shared many similarities with the names used by the Northern peoples, such as Tacibuhua (marmots), Yekeshicihun (big geese), Chulugehun (small geese), Suerqici (the geese which can't tweet), Acihun (the geese with some colored feathers), Abaerhuyu (salmon), Qilimayu (sturgeon) and so on. It is said that the fish whose length is ten feet or twenty feet which lived in the northeast ocean near the Liaoyang City.[92]

There were also various kind of beverages. A very popular beverage was called the Aciji wine, and Aciji was the transliteration of Arabic. Aciji wine was spicy and hot, which was mainly used to dispel cold. The distillation method was used to make the Aciji wine, and the concrete procedures are to steam good wine and collect the evaporated water. The distillation method has brought some radical changes in the methods of making wine. Nomad people had also called hard liquor as Aciji. In Chinese tradition, people always use rice, millet and other crops to make the wine. Although the grape wine in the Western Regions was acknowledged by Chinese for a long time, it is still regarded as a kind of beverage coming from foreign countries. However, the situation has changed in the Yuan Dynasty period. The grape wind was also produced in China, such as Taiyuan in Shanxi Province and Pingyang. Nevertheless, the best quality of grape wine was produced in Turpan, Xinjiang, which has been much famous than that of North China and Tibet.

275

A rare drink called Sherbet (a transliteration from Arabic) refers to a traditional juice drink which is still popular in Arab countries. There is a large variety of Sherbet kinds, among which the main difference is determined by the fruits used. In order to make this beverage, firstly the fruit was cooked with sugar thoroughly, then filtered out the dregs, purified and let to be cooled, after it has a delicious taste with a combination of sweet and sour and with a beautiful color. This beverage, is still called sherbet, and popular in the Central Asia and West Asia.

Maxuelisiji is well-known for making sherbet in Zhenjiang. As introduced in the volume 28 of Xu Tong Kao, Sheliba is also called Shalibie. According to Zhi Shun Zhen Jiang Zhi, sherber can also be produced by adding some honey into the fried fruits.

---

92   Ibid., p. 265.

Chapter 6. The Grassland Silk Road during the Ming and Qing dynasties

1. The Relationships between the Ming Court and the Northern Yuan, Tatar and Wala (Oirats) Kingdoms

At the end period of the Yuan Dynasty, a large-scale peasant uprising broke out, and the rule of the Yuan Dynasty has collapsed rapidly. In 1368, Zhu Yuanzhang established the Ming Dynasty in Yingtian (current Nanjing). Ming army captured most of the Central Plains and occupied Dadu (today Beijing), the Toghun Temür, Emperor Huizong of Yuan fled to the Upper capital, the Mongolia grasslands, and took this region as his foothold to continue dealing with the Ming Dynasty, which was known as the "Northern Yuan".

(1) The relationship between the Ming Court and Tatar (Tumeds) and Wala (Oirats) states

"Northern Yuan" dynasty was a continuation of the collapsed Yuan Dynasty. Yuan Dynasty moved to the North, but it still dreamed of restoring the Central Plains forcefully. While the Ming Dynasty wanted to continue its Northern Expedition and completely wipe out the remnants of the Yuan Dynasty. Conflicting interests have driven a long tug of war between the two sides. In 1370, Emperor Huizong of Yuan died in Yingchang (located in currentInner Mongolia), so his son Biligtü Khan Ayushiridara (or The Emperor Zhaozong of Yuan) ascended to the throne and he changed the era name to Xuanguang (宣光, 1371–1378) after the succession. In 1387, Naghachu, general of the Northern Yuan dynasty, took army to defend military forces of the Ming. The Ming army once again attacked Mongols, causing the power of the North Yuan suffered a great loss. Uskhal Khan (or the Last Emperor of Yuan) was attacked and defeated by Yesüder, a descendant of Ariq Böke. As the war failed, it was hopeless for the restoration of the Central Plains, so Khan's authority diminished greatly. On the other hand, the other Mongolia nobility began to grow, and the throne changes frequently. Later, Gün Temür Khan was killed by Gulichi who was not a descendant of Yuan, and the throne was usurped. Gulichi was soon killed, so Gün Temür Khan's crown was succeeded by his younger brother Öljei Temür Khan Bunyashiri, but the real power was in the hands of the minister Arughtai. After that, people in the Ming Dynasty called the descendants of the Northern Yuan "Tatar" who ruled Northern and Southern parts of Eastern Mongolia desert. The tribes of Tatar regarded descendants of the Yuan emperor as suzerain.

During the middle period of the Ming Dynasty, the most famous Tatar (Tümed) leader was Altan Khan, the Chinese transliteration of "Great Yuan". Altan Khan placed more than 100.000 Han people to Tumote Plains of Inner Mongolia who had formerly moved to Monan Mongolia, he gave them cattle, sheep and yurts (a round tent used by nomads) and designated farmlands for them. Altan Khan also invited Chinese and Tibetan craftsmen to build fortification and temple in Tumote region. Mongolia was adjacent to the Han Dynasty, and they had already exchanged livestock and agricultural products in history. Not only the upper nobility of Tatars needed Chinese luxury goods, the ordinary people of Mongolia also needed Chinese handicrafts in their daily life. For this cause, Altan Khan asked Ming Dynasty to open trade relations for dozens of times, but his request was rejected by the Ming dynasty. Besides, the Ming government had killed two envoys of Altan Khan, resulting in a severe conflict between the two sides. He conducted a raid into Ming China in which he took 200,000 prisoners and seized over two million head of livestock. His raids into China became an almost a yearly exercise.In 1550 (the 29th year of Jiajing), Altan Khan crossed the Great Wall, and his troops arrived near Beijing, demanded open passes and markets. In 1570 (the 4th year of Longqing), Altan Khan and the Ming Dynasty finally concluded a peace treaty, and Altan Khan was granted the title Shunyi Wang ("Obedient and Righteous King") from the Longqing emperor. Tartar was allowed to offer tributes to the emperor, and they also established the trade system. The Ming Dynasty set up 11 passes and markets in Shanxi, Gansu and Ningxia, which were opened one or two times a year, and 3 to 15 days for each time.

When the market opened, horses were first bought by government, and government exchanged silver for horse, cloth, pots and other objects. Such kind of market was called the "official trade" (a bazaar established by the government). So every time before the opening of market, the Ming government had to prepare a lot of food, cloth, iron and other goods and materials. Herdsmen's trade with the Han people in border regions was known as the "trader folk", mostly in the form of barter. Livestock production depends on the weather, and in the arid days, the herdsmen had to rely on grain to survive the famine, so they attached great importance to the exchange of grain with livestock products. A cow could be exchanged by more than 100 liters rice, while sheep and grain also had some price parity. For those poor Mongolians without livestock, they could exchange grain with firewood, salt and furs, etc.[1]

In addition to livestock, fur, and herdsmen also sold wood and other items. Han people sold a wide range of items, in addition to food, there are various food, textiles, paper, medicine, paint, tea and so on. In order to restrict the Tartar's production of weapons, copper, iron and other metal and weapons were strictly prohibited by the Ming government. However, the herdsmen could still buy farm implements, iron and copper pot, armor, arrow, even bronze gun and other objects. Such kind of exchange was not only beneficial to herdsmen, but also profitable for the Han merchants. Due to the backward production conditions, most of Tartar's goods were primary products, but instead, Han people had more processed products. As a result, Han traders could often exchange a cloth for a sheep, a rough wear for a leather garment, which enabled to earn as high as 100% profits through such an exchange.[2]

The beginning of trade exchanges has led to a long-term peace in the North of Ming dynasty, and thanks to trade exchanges the markets in the territories of the Ming dynasty reached unprecedented prosperity that has never existed in the periods of Han and Tang dynasties.[3]

Mongolian Steppes had its own medicines since ancient times, also the grassland nomadic people did long knew the fame of Han doctors. When the illnesses of Tatar nobles could not be cured, they often turned to Han doctors for treatment. In the early Ming Dynasty, Arughtai sent Hui merchant Hafeth to the Ming territories to pay tribute, and asked for Han medicine. Emperor Yongle (Yung-lo in Wade-Giles; 21360-12 August 1424) complied with his request and ordered Imperial Academy of Medicine to give him medicines. When Mongolian nobles were seriously ill, they also asked the Ming Dynasty for help and requested the Ming Dynasty to send doctors to make a diagnosis and give treatment. Chinese medicine was a traditional gift given by the Ming government to Tatars to thank and honor them after they presented their tributes to the court. The Mongolian aristocracy also recruited talented artisans from the Han people who secretly immigrated into its territories. Many followers of the so-called White Lotus sect who were persecuted by the Ming government fled China to join those in southern Mongolia, who eventually numbered about 50,000. The discontented leaders of these migrants played agents provocateur between Altan Khan and the Chinese, instigating Altan Khan and other Mongol rulers to invade the Ming borderland many times. Needless to say, the Ming government sought for many years to have the rebels returned to Chinese control.

---

1   See Martial arts records during the 1590s, Volume 8, The Biographies of Great Yuan (B).
2   The Biographies of Anda (B), the 8th Volume of Feats of Emperor Wanli.
3   Records of Ming and Qing Dynasties, Volume 33, pp. 15-74.

Altan Khan supported and sheltered many Han people who were the members of the White Lotus sect, among whom a man named Zhou Yuan was good at medicine preparing.[4]

Not only the Mongolian nobles used the Chinese medicines, ordinary Mongolian people also knew that Han doctors were highly skilled. When Monan Mongolian people were suffering from smallpox, they would often ask Han people for treatment. Besides, Mongolian merchants often purchased Chinese medicines from the markets.

Wala (Oirat) referred to the Mongolian Weilate tribe during the Yuan Dynasty period. Scholars have many explanations for the origin of this tribe name. The article by Dorji Balzarov, an expert of Mongolian studies, from Russian Federation, seems more convincing. He has argued that the name Weilate was made up of two words, "oyi" and "arad". In Mongolian, the former means "forest", and the latter means "people" forming the word "Forest Mongolian". Wala people were also called Oirad and Orirats during the Qing Dynasty period. The surname of chief in Durbat and Jungar tribes among the Oyirad was Choros, and they belong to the Oyirad left-wing tribe. In the Mongolian language, "left" was called "Jonqar", so sometimes the Oirat people were called as the "Junggar(s)".

Documents found describing the Oirat tribes written with Todo Mongolian Scripts recorded some legends about the origin of Junggar and Durbat people. According to the legend, the ancestor of the Junggar was the Amooney, who had 10 sons; the ancestor of Durbat was Domooney, who also had 10 sons. Later, these two tribes became populous. While they were hunting in the forest, they found a baby lying under the tree. The tree was the mother of the child, shaped like an arched chorgo, from which flowed out a juice that fed the child. There was an owl beside the tree, and he was the father of the child. People believed that the child was the offspring of God, so they brought the child back and made him the chief of both the Junggar and Durbat tribes when he grew up. The Mongolian plural form of "Chorqo" is "chorqos", then its consonant "q" was lost, so it finally became "choros". This is why Junggar and Durbat were both called Choros. There are also many similar legends, some of which are mixed with Buddhist content, but they are all about a tree feeding the baby.[5]

When we compare these legends with the "The Stele for King of Gaochang" written by Yuji based on the dictation made by the King of Uyghur's descendants and History of the World Conqueror written by Persian historian Ata-Malik Juvayni in the middle of the 13th Century, we can see the legends about the Durbat(s) and Jungar(s) legend about the origin of their ancestors, this legend has some similarities with that of the Gaochang Uyghur people' legends about their ancestors. Consequently, we can deduce that they were culturally influenced by the Uyghur culture.

4 The Biographies of Anda (B), the 8th Volume of Feats of Emperor Wanli.
5 See The Brief History of the Mongolian Oirat Tribe, Volume I, Xinjiang People's Publishing House, 1992, pp. 6-7.

Oirats (Mongol origin) as a nomad tribe dwelled in the forest region of Lake Baikal during the Liao and Jin Dynasties of China, and later they migrated to the upper reaches of the Yenisei River. After the rise of Genghis Khan (life 1162-1227), Oirat kingdom surrendered to Genghis Khan's Mongol Empire and established political marriage alliance with the Genghis Khan clan. Historically, the Oirats were composed of four major tribes: Dzungar (Choros or Olots), Torghut, Dörbet, and Khoshut. Then the four major tribes of Oirats made a strong alliance, which was called "Four Oirat" (Dorben Oirat), and lived around the Khovsgol Lake in the West of Khangai Mountains. At the end of the Yuan Dynasty, "Four Oirat" gradually moved to the west of Mongolia and the north of the Tianshan mountain, namely they dwelled between the Yuan Dynasty, the Chagatai Khanate and the Kipchak Khanate. At this time, "Four Oirat" absorbed and subordinated people from many other tribes. For example, during the Liao and Jin Dynasty periods—the Keraits, living in the central part of Mongolia plateau were defeated by Genghis Khan and, a part of them blended with the Oirat tribe, and other part of them joined the Naiman tribe (which believed Nestorianism, situated in Western Mongolia, they were later wiped out by the Yuan Dynasty).

In the period of the early Ming Dynasty, Oirat tribe (Mongol origin) was known as Wala (Oirats) by the Central Plains people, and was divided into 3 parts, and their 3 chiefs were Mahamud, Taiping and Batum Polo respectively. There was great chaos in the Central Plains at the end period of the Yuan Dynasty, Emperor of Yuan lost the control of the state, entered a long-lasting war between Northern Yuan Dynasty and Ming Dynasty, Yuan imperial heirs gradually lost their authority. Chagatai Khanate which was located in the western part of Wala had split, and the descendants of Genghis Khan also became a puppet, since the power rested in the hands of Tamurlane, a minister of non-Genghis Khan system, and the Kipchak Khanate was defeated by Tamurlane (Timur[6]/Timurlenk). The Persians and Mongolians have encountered the same fate, and Genghis Khan clan was replaced by the powerful ministers of Zhalayier.

The decline of Genghis Khan clan offered an opportunity for Wala (Oirats) to become powerful and prosperous. After the war with Chagatai Khanate and Ogadai in the middle period of the Yuan Dynasty, territories of Wala kingdom (Oirats) had no war for more than half a century. Therefore, after recuperation, strength had greatly increased, and Wala kingdom began to join the political contests in the Mongolian Steppes. Emperor Yongle took advantage of the contradiction between Wala (Oirats) and Tatars, and enfeoffed Mahmud with the title of King of Shunning (stable and loyal), and enfeoffed Bunyashiri (Eastern Mongol Tatar leader) with the title of "the King of Peace". Although Yongle at first tried to conciliate these two leaders of Tatars and Oirats but later he broke with Bunyashiri (Eastern Mongols) when Bunyashiri had ordered to kill Yongle's emissary, in 1409. Then Yongle allied with Oirats against the Eastern

---

6   Timur lived between 1336-1405, also fought with Ottomans in the Angora (Ankara) battle.

Mongols and decided to start a war campaign against them. In 1412, Emperor Yongle led the 500 thousand troops to fight in Mobei (Outer Mongolia). Bunyashiri was defeated and fled to Wala (Oirat) kingdom, but in the spring of 1412, Mahmud's Oirat Mongols found and killed Bunyashiri during his flight from the Ming armies. Delbek, the son of Bunyashiri was assigned as Khan by Mahmud (Oirats) and Delbek besieged Khara Khorum (Karakurum), the old Yuan capital.

The Chinese court attitude became more disdainful and negative towards the Oirats. The Yongle Emperor denied the Oirats chieftain Mahmud's request for the bestowal of rewards to his followers who had fought against Bunyashiri and Arughtai.

Mahmud soon became angered by the Ming court's disregard towards him. He imprisoned the Ming envoys who had arrived from China, so the Yongle Emperor sent the eunuch envoy Hai T'ung in an unsuccessful attempt to secure their release. Mahmud feared from a new alliance between Ming and the Eastern Mongols, therefore, in 1413, feeling threatened, Mahmud of the Oirat had dispatched 30,000 Mongol troops to Kerulen River against Ming China. Late 1413, Arughtai informed the Ming court that Mahmud of the Oirats had crossed the Kerulen River, which would prove to trigger an imminent war with the Ming. On 6 April 1414, the Yongle Emperor departed from Beijing to lead a military campaign against the Oirat Mongols. The Ming advanced via Xinghe

to Kerulen, to meet the Oirats in battle at the upper Tula River. The battle between the Ming army and Oirat ensued between the upper courses of the Tula and Kerulen rivers. The Oirat Mongols were overwhelmed by the heavy bombardment of the Ming cannons. They were greatly reduced and were forced to retreat. Mahmud and Delbek fled from the Ming armies. The Yongle Emperor returned to Beijing in August 1414.

Arughtai had so-called excused himself from battle on the claim that he was allegedly unable to join due to illness. Even though Mahmud sought out reconciliation with the Ming, the Yongle Emperor looked to the thought with much suspicion. In any regard, before anything could happen, Arughtai had attacked and killed Mahmud and Delbek in 1416.

The Ming emperor, enfeoffed Mahmud's son Toghon, with his father's title of Shunning Wang and tried to eatablish peace between the two Mongol factions. Toghan called himself Taishi (great ruler) and held the real power.

In the year of 1439, Esen Tayishi (the son of Toghan) succeeded his father, Wala (Oirats) forces had made great progress in his reign, controlling Eastern Mongolia and expanded westward to the Western regions. In 1449, Ming Dynasty limited the number of Esen Tayishi's envoys to China and decreased gifts and support to Esen Tayishi and refused to implement the political marriage policy, which caused Esen Tayishi to mastermind a large-scale war plan in cooperation with those tribes dwelling in the Mongolian Steppes. The three-pronged offensive began in July, with Taisun Khan leading the Easternmost forces that marched to Liaodong, the grand councillor Alag led the offensive to Ganzhou and Xuanfu (today Xuanhua, Hebei province), and Esen Tayishi himself had led the troops that sacked Datong in August. Under these conditions the nine border regions of the Ming Dynasty were forced into a difficult situation.

The Ming Dynasty was shocked by the news of Esen Tayishi led offensive war campaigns. The eunuch official Wang Zhen, who was very influential in the Ming court, encouraged the 22-year-old Emperor Zhengtong to lead his own armies into battle against Esen. In August of the same year, the Emperor arrived in Datong with 50,000 troops, then the vanguard fighters of Wala (Oirats) mongols have arrived Juyong Pass. Face with this ferocious Wala cavalry, Ming army withdrew troops but were chased all the way to the Tumu Fortress and was defeated by the Wala mongols. Therefore, Ming armies were surrounded in the Tumu Fortress by the Wala forces. At first Esen Tayishi pretended to withdraw his army and make peace with the Ming dyansty. However, when the Ming army was called out, Wala Mongols suddenly attacked it. As a result, the disheartened Ming army accepted the battle in haste but under a poor command. After the war, most of the high-ranked Ming generals and court officials were killed. The Ming army was basically in disarray and almost annihilated, and the Ming emperor was captured by the enemy.

Emperor Zhengtong sent messengers to Ming government asking them to ransom him back, the Ming government immediately complied with his request. However, Esen Tayishi did not returned the Emperor after he accepted the treasure sent by Ming dynasty, and attempted to force the Ming Dynasty to accept more concessions. However, his plan was foiled due to the steadfast leadership of the Ming commander in the capital, General Yu Qian. Emperor Zhengtong's brother (a prince referred to as Zhu Qiyu, later the Jingtai Emperor) was by then installed on the throne in order to show their determination of resisting to the end. However, the fighting spirit of Wala had enhanced greatly after the defeat of Ming army. Learning that the Ming dynasty had installed a new Emperor, Esen Tayishi sent the captive emperor back to Beijing. In fact, what Esen Tayishi really wanted to do was to move further Southward, wanted to breaking through the Zijin Pass and aimed to force Ming dynasty to moving their capital while restoring Great Capital of Yuan.

General Yu Qian mobilized all forces to guard the emperor. At the same time, he defended Beijing resolutely and finally defeated the Esen Tayishi forces. General Yu Qian also split the Wala army, negotiated separately with Tatar Khan, Taisun Khana, and the leader of right wing high officers of the Wala kingdom. Esen Tayishi finally decided to make peace, since he saw that the defense of the city was comprehensively strong, hard to crack, and the cohesion among the city people was sound. Besides, Esen Tayishi was also afraid that Ming Dynasty would cut all kind of the trade relationships with the Wala kingdom. Consequently, in the year of 1450, Wala led by Esen Tayishi and Ming Dynasty reached an agreement which included the freeing of the Emperor Zhengtong, later the two sides restored and bettered their relationships.

The Tumu Crisis had shocked the Ming Dynasty, and this crisis was also the symbol of the decline of the Ming Dynasty which was leaving back its ascent period and entered its stagnant period. From then on, Ming Dynasty could no more station its armies in the Mobei region, as it did in the reign period of emperor Hongwu and Yongle, instead the Ming Dynasty changed its strategy and assumed a posture of defense against the Tatar and Wala forces. In order to strengthen the defense of the border regions, the Ming government vigorously re-strengthened and further extended the Great Wall, so that it could reach Yalu River in the east, Jiayu Pass in the west, consequently the length of the Great Wall was increased to about 13,000 miles. This is the Great Wall left to this day.

Wala maintained official and people-to- people private trade relations with the Ming dynasty. Official trade took the form of paying tribute and giving gift in return. The tributary envoy of Wala usually entered from Gansu and arrives in Beijing via Shanxi. In Mahamud's son Toγon era, tributary envoys were more than 260 people and the number of tributary horses was more than 1,500. In the Esen Tayishi era, tributary envoys made up to thousands of people, the number of vicunas for tribute was up to more than 40 thousand. In Wala's trade with Ming Dynasty, the Hui people played an important role. For example, in 1447, to Wala tribute envoy was called Pir Muhammad who should be a Persian speaking Hui people, and it means old Muhammad. There were 2,472 men and 4,172 vicunas as well as 12,300 fur products along with his missions.[7]

The Ming Dynasty often limited the number of their gift in return: four multicolored damask and eight pieces of silk for every finest horse; two multicolored damask and two cotton yarn for the middle horse; one wire silk and eight pieces of silk and one cotton yarn for the middle-inferior horse; while only six pieces of silk and one cotton yarn for the inferior horse. Wala's fur was also very popular in Ming Dynasty, such as marten skin, ermine skin, white rabbit skin, and white fox skin.[8]

The nomads under the control of the Wala and the Hui people in their governing regions also came to trade in the frontier fortress. In the early Ming Dynasty, they did not open market for Wala, so if there were only a few cattle brought by Wala, they would trade in Gansu; while if the number was large, they would entered in Lanzhou, Ningxia to trade. In 1438, the Ming Dynasty set up horse market in Datong and traded with Wala. During the trade, Wala merchants would firstly exchange their horse for gold, silver, cloth, silk and other handicrafts. After the official trade, the folk trade would be opened, allowing Wala to exchange products with their remaining horses with Han people.

At that time, Mongolia craftsmen had already have metallurgy, but it was very difficult for the mining of copper and iron, so Mongolian craftsmen often smelted copper and iron they bought from common Han people to make tools, armor and weapons. In order to restrict the forces of Mongolia, in exchange,

7 See Volume 160 of the Records of Ming Emperor Zhengtong, November, 1447.
8 See Volume 211 of Veritable Records of Ming Emperor Zhengtong, December, 1451.

the output of copper and iron was strictly prohibited by the Ming Dynasty, while the rest goods could be freely traded.

(2) Spread of Gelug Doctrines

Tibet was included to the Chinese territory in Yuan Dynasty period, and many Tibetan monks were invited to the mainland Mongolia by Mongol aristocrats, conferred them with the titles of "State Preceptor" or "Imperial Preceptor", and in this case, Lamaism was also accepted by the Yuan Dynasty royal family. At the end of 14th Century, Qinghai Lama Tsongkhapa had opposed the corruption among the upper Lama monks, so he made a reform in Lamaism by establishing the Gelug[9] school.

The Gelug advocated observant, and its monks dressed in yellow, so they were called Gelug. After the demise of the Yuan Dynasty, although the upper nobility in Gansu, Mongolia and Wala still believed in Lamaism, most of the Tatars (Tartars) believed in Shamanism. In 1558, Altan Khan launched an expedition to Sari Uyghur, encountered with the Tubo merchants and more than 1,000 Lama monks on the way, which was his first contact with the Gelug religion. A few years later, when his grandson Huangji Kyrgyzstan and his army marched into Tubo, 3 Tubo tribes were summoned to surrender on the condition of common development of religion. Later, the 3rd Dalai Lama Sonam Gyatso sent an eminent monk to teach Buddhist scriptures to Altan Khan, so Altan Khan and his wife were converted to Gelug. Thus, as the forces of Altan Khan entered Qinghai in the latter half of the 16th Century, Gelug was introduced into Mongolia from Tibet.

285

Altan Khan has repeatedly invited Sonam Gyatso to introduce Buddhist teachings into Mongolia, and built a temple in Qinghai with the consent of the Ming government to meet him. The emperor was named "Yanghua temple". In 1578, Altan Khan and Sonam Gyatso met in the Yanghua temple, they held a ceremony, and over 10,000 Mongolian people participated. In honor of this auspicious convocation Altan bestowed upon Sonam Gyatso the title of "Dalai Lama". Dalai is a Mongolian word meaning "vast" or "oceanic"; it is also a direct Mongolian translation of the Tibetan word gyatso and thus a particularly fitting title for Sonam Gyatso. In turn, Sonam Gyatso gave Altan Khan the title "King of the Turning Wheel and Wisdom" and officially recognized him as a reincarnation of Khubilai Khan, the grandson of Chingis Khan and founder of the Yüan Dynasty in China.

Since then, Altan Khan has established many temples in his territory, in the single one city Guihua (today Hohhot), there were famous Da Zhao (Hong Ci temple), Shiretu Juu Zhao (Yan Shou temple), Qingyuan temple, Meidai Zhao (Ling Shou temple). "Zhao" means "temple" in Mongolian. Altan Khan passed away in 1581, Sonam Gyatso introduced Gelug to the tribes along the

---

9   Gelug was the newest of the schools of Tibetan Buddhism. It was founded by Je Tsongkhapa (1357-1419), a philosopher and Tibetan religious leader. The first monastery he established was named Ganden (which gives an alternative name to the Gelug school.

way to his funeral. The 3rd Dalai Lama later left his last word that he would be reincarnated in the Altan Khan family after his death. Therefore, Dayan Khan's great-grandson, Yonten Gyatso, was selected as the 4th Dalai Lama.

When the 3rd Dalai Lama attended the funeral of Altan Khan, Abag Khan of Khaki Kharky also converted to Gelug and asked him to spread Buddhist teachings. Abag Khan's ruling center was in the former sites of Yuan Dynasty and Lincheng at the middle of the Erhun River. In 1586, Abag Khan built the huge Gelug monastery Erdene Zuu (Guangxian Temple) with building materials such as masonry in the ruins of Lincheng. Later, the Khalkha people took the holy things and Buddhist sutras from Lhasa and put them in the monastery to enshrine and worship. Erdene Zuu became the most important Gelug monastery in the north of the Gobi desert, which is preserved till currently.

The 3rd Dalai Lama arranged Donkor Khutuktu as his agent to do missionary work among the Mongols. The chief of Heshuote tribe of Wala (Oirats) invited Donkor Khutuktu to spread Buddhist teachings among its people. In addition to Donkor Khutuktu, the 4th Dalai Lama also sent eminent monks to spread Gelug beliefs among the officials of Wala. Under the leadership of Baibakesi, the tribe leaders of Wala kingdom converted to Gelug religion. They rapidly established a direct connection with the Tubo (Tibet) kingdom. Wala kingdom sent Zaya Pandita to study Lamaism in Tibet via Qinghai, and he lived together with the 5th Dalai for 22 years, so he gained trust of upper Gelug people. At the age of 40, he returned to Wala and propagated Buddhism by the instructions of the 4th Dalai Lama and the 5th Panchen. After Zaya Pandita returned to Wala, he spent more than 20 years from 1638 to 1662 traveling to Qinghai in the east, Zhai River (current Ural River) in the West, Irtysh River in the north, and upper reaches of the Yili River as well as Chu River that flows through Kyrgyzstan and Kazakhstan in the south. In addition, he also introduced Gelug beliefs in the lands along the Talas River, thus enabled Lamaism spread across Mongolia in a short period.

The Ming Dynasty supported Gelug in Mongolia, and often rewarded Tubo (Tibetan) Lamas for their religious teaching. At the same time, the Ming Dynasty provided favorable conditions for the Mongolian tribes to welcome and see off Dalai Lama, allowed them to pass through the Ming territories which extended between Mongolia and Tibet. The Ming government had also printed Buddhist scriptures in Beijing, produced various musical instruments and gave them to Mongolian tribes. When the south and the north of desert regions built temples, they needed a large number of Han craftsmen, and to get building materials from Han region was also essential.

At the end of the Ming Dynasty, Torgout tribe of the Wala migrated to the West and reached the Volga River valley where they settled down. But they still kept their faith in Lamaism, and frequently sent monks to pilgrimage in Tibet. At the beginning of the Qing Dynasty during the reign of Kangxi Emperor (4 May1654-20 December 1722), Ayuka Khan of Torgout was awarded the title and seal by the Dalai Lama. The spread of Gelug has led to a more close relationship between the Mongols and Tibetans that has already existed in history, and it has had a far-reaching impact. Through the efforts of Mongolia and Tibetan people for nearly two centuries, the scope of Gelug distribution has expanded greatly. By the end of 17th Century, most of the nomads in Mongolia believed in Lamaism within a large region, stretching from the border of Nepal in the South to Siberia in the North, and from the Xing'anling in the East to the Volga River and the Don River in the West, which was unprecedented in the history of Buddhism. And this was an unprecedented prosperity for the spread of Buddhism in history.

After the Mongol tribes accepted Gelug, it was popular for Mongolian intellectuals to study Tibetan. And a large number of Tibetan scriptures were translated into Mongolian language. At the same time, the scientific culture of ancient India was also introduced into Mongolia by Tibetan. A large number of Tibetan loanwords were introduced into Mongolian language. Until today, the Mongolian ordinary people have the same respect for Tibetan medicine as the Han people's respect for Chinese medicine.

2. Timur and the Ming Court

After the middle of the 14th Century, the Mongol-Yuan Dynasty fell apart. In the four great Khanates, Chagatai Khanate dynasty in Central Asia split into two dynasties, one was the Eastern Chagatai Khanate in the east, and the other was the western part which was later toppled and replaced by the Timur empire.

(1) Timur and his empire

Timur was from the Barlas clan of the Mongols, his father Taraghay was head of the tribe of Barlas, a nomadic Turkic-speaking tribe of Mongol origin that traced its origin to the Mongol commander Qarachar Barlas. Taraghay was the great-grandson of Qarachar Noyon and, distinguished among his fellow-clansmen as the first convert to Islam.

With the establishment of the Mongolia and appointment of heroes with a title, Khorachar (ger. Halachaer) was given the title of Minggan (one thousand households), then enfeoffed the second son named Chagatai with the title of Khan, and that was how the Barlas tribe had come to settle in the Central Asia. The ancestors of Timur was servant of Chagatai Khanate, so they got the fief of Kish (Kesh) today, southern part of present Uzbekistan Shakhri Sabz (Shahr I Sabz, in Persian-Turkic language, means "green city").

In 1350s and 1360s, while Tughlugh Timur Khan and his son in Eastern Chagatai Khanate were trying to unify Chagatai Khanate with war, the Barlas Chagatai Khanate surrendered to them initially in order to maintain power and gain time to enhance and develop their own forces in the later stage.

In 1370s, Timur defeated his competitors and became the ruler of Western Chagatai Khanate khan. He made a great conquest of the surrounding region. In the north, he firstly conquered Khwarezm, making his own territory connect with the Kipchak Khanate. In 1390, he sent troops to attack Kipchak Khanate and gained a complete victory. In 1394, he once again attacked Kipchak Khanate, made his way into Don River and Crimea, and captured the capital Sarai in Kipchak Khanate. In the West, he conquered Persia and South of Hendu Kosh after years of war from 1380, and later he conquered the South of Caucasia and Mesopotamia, threatening Ottoman Empire that rose in the ruins of the Khanate of Persia and Mongolia. In 1399, he invaded Ottoman Empire. Three years later, in the battle of Ankara, he defeated Ottoman's army and captured their emperor. In the South, Timur attacked India in 1398 and once occupied the capital of Sultan, Delhi. In the East, Timur had repeatedly attacked the Eastern Chagatai Khanate Khan, and he also once attacked Turpan Prefecture in Xinjiang.

Timur had married Princess of Genghis Khan Family, so he claimed himself to be the consort prince, so the Ming dynasty had always called him Timur consort prince. Since 1387, Timur began to establish formal contact with the Ming Dynasty. In April of this year, Timur sent an envoy named Man Khaily to the Ming Dynasty, and Ming emperor Zhu Yuanzhang rewarded the ambassador generously. In 1392, Timur's envoy came to Nanjing with tribute like textile, red and green woolen knitwear as well as steel armor and sword. There were also some Hui people from Timur region trading horse in Liangzhou, so Ming emperor Yuanzhang ordered them to trade in the mainland and requesting more than 1200 people in the Gansu to return to Samarkand. In 1394, Timur sent Hui people Delibishi, which refers to priest of Sufism to the Ming Dynasty with 200 fine horses. Timur's tone was very modest in the tribute letter, saying that he had heard about Ming emperor's great ambitions of unifying the whole world although he was in a secluded place thousands of miles away. He was very satisfied with credentials and gifts of the Ming Dynasty.

Timur had a vast territory in his later years, but he still dreamed of conquering the Ming dynasty. He has dispatched his army to quarter at the Syr Darya, and prepared to march into the East. In 1405, the Ming Dynasty received information that Timur was preparing to invade the Ming Dynasty through the Eastern Chagatai Khanate Khan territory. It was the early years of Emperor Yongle's reign, and the Ming Dynasty was at its height. If there were conflict between the two big powers, Timur could not be certain about his victory. While Ming Dynasty might start Western expedition with the aim of destroying all the remnants of Yuan Dynasty, if that was the case, the two sides would pay a heavy price. However, it was in this year that Timur died in Farab, so the war ended. This was a blessing for the people both of the Central Plains and of Western regions.

(2) The Spanish Envoy Ruy González de Clavijo

After the fall of the Khanate in 1350s, Ottoman Empire appeared in Western Asia and soon clashed with the Christian forces in Europe. In 1396, Ottoman Emperor Bayezid defeated the French and Hungarian forces. Soon, Ottoman army surrounded the Constantinople (current Istanbul), leaving the remnants of the Byzantine Empire (East Rome Empire) in a state of ruin. The French sent fleet into the Dardanelles Strait and defeated Ottoman's fleet. And the French army landed in the Asia Minor Peninsula (Anotolia), which relieved the siege of Constantinople (Istanbul). But a year later, Ottoman army defeated the French army again. When the French army retreated, they brought the emperor Manuel from Eastern Rome to Europe. Manuel called for the aid of European countries, but country responded positively. Just at this point, Timur's army attacked Ottoman Empire. In the battle of Ankara (1402), the two sides mobilized nearly a million troops. In the end, the army of the Ottoman Empire suffered a defeat, and the Emperor Bayezid himself was also captured by Timur and was put in a cage. This defeat actually relieved and delayed the siege of Constantinople (Istanbul), making the Eastern Rome Empire (Byzantine) linger for further half a century.

The rise of the Timur Empire shocked European Christian princes and dukes. The king of Spain sent a mission to the Near East in 1402. The mission sailed through the Mediterranean to Aegean Sea and landed on the Little Asia Peninsula (Anotolia). The envoys returned to their country after meeting Timur in Ankara city. Later, the king of Spain once again sent diplomatic corps led by Clavijo to the East. Timur returned to the East after defeating the Ottoman army. Clavijo and and his attendants arrived in Tabriz by Constantinople (Istanbul), Trabzon and Tabriz. On the way, Clavijo met an Egyptian mission and traveled Eastward together with them. They traveled through the cities of Sultaniye, Mashhad, Balkh, Kesh and other cities and finally arrived in Samarkand. According to traveler Clavijo, when Timur met him, the officer led him to a seat on the right side of the throne. This seat was once used for the Chinese envoy who visited Samarkand to ask Timur for tribute. Timur had thought about the seats of the Spanish and Chinese envoys before receiving Clavijo. The officer had arranged the seat of Spanish envoy lower than that of Chinese envoy, but Timur disagreed and moved the seat of Clavijo forward and beyond the Chinese envoy. After Clavijo took his seat, a prince talked to the Chinese envoy, and told Timur's will as follows: Timur is friendly with the king of Spain, while Chinese envoy is the enemy of Timur." Placing Spanish envoy before Chinese envoy was to show Timur's dissatisfaction with China. But, the contradiction with China would be soon resolved, and there would be no need for China to send envoys asking for tribute in the future. Timur has transferred his grace from Chinese envoy to Spanish envoy. Clavijo also said that Timur once paid tribute to China in the past but he refused to do that in the future.

The Chinese envoy that Clavijo met in Timur court should be Fu An who was dispatched in 1395 by Ming emperor Zhu Yuanzhang. According to Biography of the Western Regions in History of the Ming Dynasty, Fu An was a Supervising Censor in Ming Dynasty, and he traveled with the vice-ambassador Guo Ji and led more than 1500 soldiers in his expedition. Fu An and his entourage arrived in Samarkand and were all imprisoned by Timur for many years. In 1397, the Ming Dynasty once again sent surveillance commissioner of Beijing Chen Dewen to the Samarkand, and Chen Dewen was also detained in Samarkand. After the emperor Yongle ascended to throne, envoys were sent again to Timur kingdom with seals, books, silk and other gifts, but envoys were again detained. It was not until the death of Timur that his successor Khalil sent these captives back to China in 1407. Fu An was also freed, after his return, Fu An said that when Timur detained him and stopped paying tribute to the Ming Dynasty and that he ordered people to took him around the country to show the vast territory of Timur kingdom. Chen Dewen had also traveled in the Western regions, and he had persuaded some tribe/kingdom leaders to pay tribute to the Ming Dynasty, but most of the small kingdoms refused to do so with the excuse of the long distance, probably Timur's obstruction was the main reason for their refusals. Clavijo heard a lot of news about China at the court of Timur. For example, Chinese emperor was called Cayis Han, which means "the great emperor of the nine states". The Tatar called China Tanguz, which means "Meat lover". Clavijo heard that the title of Chinese emperorbe the translation of "master of nine states" in Chinese. Maybe "Tauqach" was the variation of "Tanguz" (Turkic nationality's addressing for Central Plains people). And it was transliterated as "peach blossom stone" in Yuan Dynasty, which refers to Han people. The name originated from the Turkic people's addressing for the founder of the Northern Wei dynasty.

Ruy González de Clavijo also witnessed Timur's dialogue with Chinese envoys. China envoy said that Timur has not pay tribute for 7 years. Timur replied that the Emperor had the right to ask for tribute, but 7 years of tribute was a large amount, so he would send tribute to Chinese as soon he collected enough gifts. The Chinese leaders were not satisfied with the answer, saying that China did not ask for tribute in the past 7 years, because there were some changes within the country. The envoy who had the dialogue with Timur was probably the one sent by Emperor Yongle to Samarkand city.

When Timur launched the military offensive Minor Asia Peninsula (Anotolia), he has brought back a German named Johanan Schitbarga. The man served in Timur's army for many years and lived in Central Asia for a long time, and it was not until 1427 that he returned back to Germany. In his written travel notes he also referred to the exchanges between China and Timur. He said, Chinese emperor sent envoys with 400 horses to Timur for forcing him to pay tribute, since Timur did not pay tribute for five consecutive years. Timur sent an envoy to Samarkand and sent a message that he would no longer pay tribute. Instead, he would launch a military expedition targeting China and force the Chinese emperor pay tribute to him.[10]

10 See Compilation of Historical Materials on Chinese and Western Exchanges, Vol. 2, p. 140.

Although Timur Khan's capital was far from China, he was personally very concerned about China. When the Chinese envoys introduced the Chinese situation, Clavijo heard the famous story of Jingkang Incident. It was said that when Chinese emperor died, he gave an order that the three princes should lead the whole country respectively. But the eldest prince wanted to monopolize the whole country by occupying the land of his two brothers, which resulted in a battle among them. The eldest prince was defeated in the end and burned himself to death with numerous people. The so-called eldest prince was Emperor Jianwen of the Ming Dynasty. In order to consolidate the throne, Emperor Jianwen planned to remove the military powers of the seigniors, in this way the prince of Yan which controlled the North took over the power.

Clavijo also asked about the way to China, he said that the name of Chinese capital named as "Khan baliq" was Turkic, meaning "King City". It's six month's journey far from Samarkand to this city. According to him, several months before they arrived in Samarkand, there was a large Chinese caravan with 800 camels. Timur had looted this caravan. Timur attached importance to the collection of information about Chinese local conditions and customs, geography, situation, population as well as wealth. In addition, he also sent people to stay in the Chinese capital for half a year, the main task of these people would be investigation and gathering information. According to these investigators, the capital of China was not far from the sea and was 20 times larger than the Tabriz city in Persia. They also noted that China had a populous atmy, even when the emperor personally led his soldiers for big a military campaign, there remained about 400 thousand troops as reserve in the rear.

In another feast, new envoys of various countries help entertain the guest of honor. Some of them came from regions near China, which were once under the rule of China. These envoys Clavijo had met this time were probably from the Eastern Chagatai Khanate. Later Timur was seriously ill, Ruy González de Clavijo returned to Spain via Bukhara, and followed approximately the same route but for a swing up into the southern part of the Caucasus.[11]

After his return, he wrote a travelogue Journey from Cartes to Samarkand in Timur era. Not long after, the book spread widely. The Madrid Museum has a copy that was published for the first time in 1582. During the War of Resistance against Japan, Yang Zhaojun, a Chinese scholar, translated the Turkic version into Chinese, titled Ruy González de Clavijo's Journey to the East. Ruy González de Clavijo died in 1412. Although his visit to East was for nearly a century later than that of Marco Polo and although he had never traveled to inland China, we can understand the significant influence of China in the Western regions during the Ming Dynasty period from his travel accounts.

---

11 Clavijo sailed through the Mediterranean, passing Majorca, Sicily and Rhodes to Constantinople. Using modern names for the countries through which he passed, Clavijo sailed along the Black Sea coast of Anatolia to Trebizond and then overland through Armenia, Iran to Turkestan. He visited Tehran in 1404.

(3) Chen Cheng's Journey to the Western Regions

Ming emperor Zhu Yuanzhang and Emperor Yongle have sent many envoys to the Western Regions, among which the most famous one was those led by Chen Cheng. Chen Cheng was born in 1365 in Jishui of Jiangxi province. He obtained the positions of Juren when he was young. In the spring of 1396, he was sent on a mission to offer amnesty and enlistment to the rebels in Hexi and to rebelling Uyghur tribes. In the same year, he traveled to Annan to negotiate over the territorial disputes. In 1401, he was dispatched to Mongolia on a diplomatic mission. These missions made him experienced in developing exchanges with the neighboring ethnic peoples. After the emperor Yongle ascended to the throne, he wanted to develop and improve communications with the Four Barbarian kingdoms, so he selected some talented person who were familiar with the situations in the border regions, and Chen Cheng's former rich experience had made him a suitable candidate.

After the death of Timur (Temerlan), the Timurid Empire[12] was in chaos. From 1408 to 1409, the 4th son of Timur Shah Rukh, which means "the spirit of king" in Persian language, had suppressed the civil war and became the king. Shaharu abandoned Timur's plan to conquer the Ming Dynasty and adopted the good neighbor policy towards China.

In autumn of July, 1413, his diplomatic envoys arrived in Beijing from Herat (current western Afghanistan). The Ming Dynasty's long-lasting hope of establishing a normal relationship between the two major powers with Timur Empire has finally perished. Emperor Yongle was excited and sent diplomatic corps with the official Li Da to escort Shaharu's mission to return and visited their country. Chen Cheng acted as the general secretary of the mission, and before his leaving, his friend Hu Guang advised him to observe the mountains and rivers, record thee interests as well as the food and customs of peoples dwelling in the foreign countries. So after his return, he could correct the fault parts of the old records, making it an important reference for the future historical studies. Later, Chen Cheng followed his advice and recorded his expedition experiences in detail, and he wrote A Record of the Barbarian Countries in the Western Region and Travel in the Western Region.

In the next 1st month of the lunar year, the diplomatic corps started from Jiuquan, and passed through Dunhuang, Hami, Yumen, Lu Chen (currentLiucheng of Turpan),and Turpan, and they only stayed for around three to five days or only one day in these aboveregions, thus they quickly arrived at the ruins of Jiaohe in early March. Next,they planned to go via the Eastern Chagatai Khanate, so they stayed for 17 days in the ruins of Jiaohe so as to inquire about the right direction. At this time, Muhammad Khan of the Eastern Chagatai

---

12　The Timurid Empire self-designated as Gurkani (Persian: Gurkāniyān), was a Persianate Turco-Mongol empire comprising modern-day Iran, the Caucasus, Mesopotamia, Afghanistan, much of Central Asia, as well as parts of contemporary Pakistan, Syria and Turkey.

Khanate just moved Westward with his people to the Ili River due to the military pressures made by the Wala kingdom. They learned that Muhammad had moved to somewhere in "Shannan", so they divided themselves into two sub-groups after leaving the ruins of Jiaohe, one moved northwards under the leadership of Li Da; and the second group moved westwards, Chen Cheng and Li Si were in the second group. The former has passed through Beshbaliq and theough otherregions along their way northwards. While the latter group passed through Tuoxun, and crossed Botuo Mountains, climbed the Tianshan Mountains, and finally arrived at the Kunes River which is the upper reaches of the current Yili River. Wang Jiguang: Study on Chen Cheng and his Work—Travel in the Western Region and A Record of the Barbarian Countries in the Western Region, which was published in the third series of Journal of Central Asia, 1990. Then they continued to move Westbound and encountered the envoys sent by Muhammad. They stayed in its territory for 13 days and continued their journey in earlyby crossing the Yili River to move Southwards. At this point, the Northward mission has arrived at the North bank of the river, Chen Cheng sent one of the officials Hassan, who was a Hui people, to get back to Beijing with the fine horses obtaining along their way.

The Northern mission still moving along the North shore of the Yili River, while Chen Cheng and his group marched through the mountain pass and traveled upward along the Sharyn River, and then marched Southward to Shan-Tac which was in the North part of Kegen in Kazakhstan. Chen Cheng recorded that "There were a large pile of stones on the North side of road, which isjust like a hill." In 1991, I have passed here, while participating in the Grassland Silk Road project sponsored by UNESCO, and these stones were still there. After that, Chen Cheng and his group traveled Westward and crossed branch vein of Tianshan Mountain, and then marched over the Kazakhstan border into the territory of Kyrgyzstan and arrived at Isik Kul (today Issyk-Kul'Ozero in Kyrgyzstan). And the Western faction, traveled all the way Westbound along the north bank to the west bank of the lake. Then they passed North through the breach of Tianshan mountain and entered Sui Yechuan plains to arrive at Kazakhstan, Yengi Baliq (current Taraz (Talas)), Sairan (today Shymkent). Li Da's regiment had arrived this place in advance, and the two divisions had met and joined in this spot. Later, they marched Southwest from there into the current Uzbekistan. By the end of the day, they have reached the capital of Uzbekistan, Tashkent. I once passed through this spot in the opposite direction during my participation in the expedition of the Grassland Silk Road project. After that, I traveled further south to Shah Rukh Qaya, which locally means the Shah Rukh cliff, and it was located in the south of the current Tashkent city. The ancient ruins remained on the left bank of the Syr Darya river. Because the bank was made of mud, after centuries of erosion caused by the river, a considerable portion of the ancient site was included into the river bed. I have also been to this spot during my participating in the Grassland Silk Road project. The Ming's diplomatic corps arranged presents to be given to the leader of

Heicheng, diplomatic corps in order to travel to Southwest, came to the birth-place of Timur, Shahrisabz.

Moving South from Shahrisabz, the Baisuntao Mountain in the South part of Shahrisabz's old haunt was not far away. And the Iron Gate Pass in the mountain was the natural boundary of Sogdian and Bactrian since ancient times. The Ming diplomatic corps traveled all the way southwest through the Iron Gate Pass to Termez on the river bank of Amu Darya, which is the current ferry Levon Metz connecting Uzbekistan and Afghanistan. After they crossed the Amu Darya river they marched to the Khorasan region through the city (Baliq) of Mazari Sharif in the northern border of currentAfghanistan. The mission traveled along the Amherst Valley, passed through Andkhuy, the northern border of Afghanistan near Andkhvoy of Turkmenistan. Then they moved southwards through Almar, Qeysar and Chechaktu of Turkmenistan close to northern border of Afghanistan. From there they traveled West to Mari Chaq close to Turkmenistan and then to southeast, after 7 days of travel, they arrived at the station of Haru.[13]

During this mission, the diplomatic corps of Ming dynasty went through 16 countries, and were welcomed by most of the ethnic peoples dwelling in the Western regions, which had a great impact on the improvement of mutual relations. When they returned, the leaders of Herat, Shiraz, Samarkand, Huozhou of Xinjiang, Turfan and otherregions sent envoys to join the group and pay tribute to the Ming dynasty.

294

In 1415, the Ming mission and envoys for the Western regions had returned to Beijing. Chen Cheng was conferred with rewards by the emperor Yongle. In the next autumn, these envoys left Beijing for their home, and the emperor Yongle ordered Lu An and Chen Cheng to travel to the Western regions with them. There were only 8 months between the two missions. The Ming government ordered the mission to deliver gifts for Ulugh Beg who lived in Samarkand, and he was the eldest son of Shaharu. His name was a Turkic language, meaning "High-ranking official persons". And they also prepared gifts for all the leaders who had paid tribute to Ming Dynasty. The trip took various routes with the last mission. They went West along the South Tianshan, and entered Fergana Valley from Kashi of Xinjiang. After that, they went to Isfahan of present-day Iran. So the mission also carried gifts for leader of Andijan in present-day. The mission lasted for two years, and Chen Cheng returned to Beijing in April, 1418.

Chen Cheng arrived in Beijing with Timur imperial envoy Althusser. In September of the same year, Althusser departed for home, so Emperor Yongle once again sent Li Da and Chencheng to go with him to the Western regions. This time, the mission also carried gifts for Melk Temur and Uais. After completing the mission, Chen Cheng returned to Beijing in November, 1420. This mission was also recorded in the historical data of the Timur Empire.

---

13   See the first set of books in the National Library of Peiping (in Beijing)—copy of the Travel to the Western Regions.

The following spring, the Ming government again planned to send Chen Cheng to the Western regions, but because the fire incident in Ming Palace on the 8th day of April of that year, but the mission did not take place. In 1424, the Ming government was going to resume its diplomatic relations with the four barbarian tribes on the borders, so Chen Cheng was sent on a diplomatic mission to Western regions. Starting from Beijing in May, Chen Cheng arrived in Gansu after several months. And when he was ready to go through Jiayuguan Pass, it was received the news of the death of Emperor Yongle. Therefore, Chen Cheng was recalled to Beijing.

During his ten years, Chen Cheng was sent to the Western regions for three times and he had become a prominent figure due to his contribution to the peaceful exchanges between the Ming Dynasty and the Timur Empire. Travel in the Western Region was written after his return, which recorded the detailed mileage from Hexi to the Western region of present-day Afghanistan. His other work, A Record of the Barbarian Countries in the Western Region, recorded what he saw and heard in 17regions like Herat, Samarkand, ruins of Jiaohe, etc. And it is an important document from the early 15th century in regard to humanities and history studies in regard to Western Region, which caught the attention of scholars globally.

(4) Credentials of Emperor Yongle

Between 1368-1398, Timur was busy to arrange and mobilize military forces for expanding, so he asked Ming Dynasty for peace and assumed a humble attitude. In 1394, Timur presented fine horses to the Ming Dynasty, and presented to the Ming emperor a memorial expounding his greatness, since he had conqueredregions that was never conquered by other emperors. All merchants who saw Chinese cities praised their prosperity and glory. People of the tribes under the rule of Timur were all grateful to learn that Ming emperor Zhu Yuanzhang had sent a letter to show his grace.

The letter dicatated and endorsed by the Ming emperor mentioned in the above memorial no longer exists. And the original text of Timur's reply letter also does not exist among the archives. What we have in hand today is only a Chinese version for Western Biography in History of the Ming Dynasty, Samarkand. Western Biography in History of the Ming Dynasty, also mentioned about the exchange of letters between the Shah Rukh and Emperor Yongle. According History of the Ming Dynasty, after Timur died, his grandson Khalil had occupied Samarkand, and his son Shah Rukh had occupied Herat, and they did not get along well with each other and had conflicts of war now and then. What Shah Rukh did was actually an open defiance to the hierarchical relationship between China and its vassal, as advocated in Confucianism. In other words, Shah Rukh simply did not accept the kind of Timurid Kingdom–Ming relationship declared by the Ming court. For Shah Rukh, the Timurid.

Empire existed outside the perimeter of the Sinocentric order, and the relationship between the two nations were equal. According to historical records, Emperor Yongle sent a "high-handed" letter to Shah Rukh (Mirza), saying: "God created the people and assigned a king for them, so that each people would know his own proper place. I rule the world, and act fairly to all men without discrimination. I was once very satisfied with your ruling style. Once I heard you and your nephew Khalil had an internal fights, and I did not believe it. If united, the clans can resist foreign aggressors, but if divided, how can the clans coexist with those who are sparse? From now on, you should offer peace to your people and re-arrange your troops for a shared peace."

The history book of Timur Khanate Matla'al Sa' dain we Majma'al Bahrain included the credentials of the Ming emperor sent to Shah Rukh Khan. Compared with its Chinese version with the credentials of Emperor Yongle recorded in the book History of the Ming Dynasty, people will immediately see that both of them were of the same original edition. The content of History of the Ming Dynasty was relatively rough, so it might be the excerpts of Emperor Yongle's credentials, while the Persian history book recorded more detailed information, thus would be the original Persian text of Emperor Yongle's credentials. The word "gurgan" in the original Persian was the counterpart of "emperor's son-in-law" in Chinese, and it was from Turkic, but it did not use this word in the Persian version, and was transliterated into "Timur Fuma" instead. Persian version of the command paper complied with the Chinese command paper format. The words like "Daiming", "Khudawand", "Taizui Padshah A'li" were all written on the top of another line, which showed that it was directly translated from the Chinese command paper.

History of the Ming Dynasty recorded that Shah Rukh paid tribute to the Ming court after he received the command paper, and the gifts were lions, horses, the leopards, etc. But books in Ming Dynasty did not preserve tribute gift list of Shah Rukh. Thankfully, the Persian historical records included the original texts of Shah Rukh's memorial to Emperor Yongle. The first sentence of his statement was: "Great Daming Emperor, Shah Rukh wishes you a good health." Then he talked about the faith of Islam, and he said that the God once sent the almighty Adan (Adam) to the world, and his descendant Ibrahim was Abraham in Judaism and Christianity. Musa refers to Judaism and Moses in Christianity. Dawu't, namely, was Judaism and David in Christianity. Mohammed was Peighambar, meaning "seer" and "prophet". Their sacred words were observed by all nations. The descendants of Genghis Khan who lived in the Kipchak and Persia believed in Islam, so they wanted the Ming Dynasty to convert to Islam.

Later, Emperor Yongle sent Li Da as an envoy to Persia, and Shah Rukh sent envoys to visit the Ming Dynasty with lions and horses as their tribute for Emperor Yongle. Emperor Yongle then sent Li Da and Chen Cheng to the Western Regions, and once again submitted the Ming Dynasty credentials to the imperial court of Timur. The original Chinese version of these credentials is not available now, but its Persian version can be read in the history book of Timur Khanate. In credentials, Emperor Yongle expressed no positive reply to Shah Rukh for his suggestion converting to Islam, but he praised Shah Rukh as a monarch that was sent to earth by Khudawand (God-Deity) to rule the Hui people. When the ruler Shah Rukh was mentioned in the credentials, his name was written on the top of another line like "Daiming" and "Khudawand".[14] From this we can see that through its contacts with the Western Regions, the Ming government has understood the importance of the vast territory controlled by Shah Rukh and Timurid empire, consequently recognized him as the monarch of that region.

(5) Diplomatic Envoys Sent by Shah Rukh (Mirza)

Among the travel reports of Persian envoys who had visited China, the most famous work was authored by Ghiyath al Din Naqqash (Giyasettin Nakkaş), a Persian embassy to China. According to his records, Timur sent a diplomatic envoy to visit the Ming Dynasty in 1419, and this diplomatic envoy did not include the Minister of Shah Rukh, but also included the eldest son of Shah Rukh, Ulugh Beg who defended Samarkand and Shah Rukh's second son. Ghiyas-ud-din Naqqash was sent as the envoy of Shah Rukh's third son Baisunqur. The second part of Ghiyas-ud-din's name was Naqqash, which means painter in Persian, so he was also known as painter Ghiyas-ud-din. During his mission, he kept diary beginning from his first day off from Herat and recorded what he saw and heard during his whole journey. After returning back home, he wrote his journey observations across China according to this diary notes.

Ghiyas-ud-din Naqqash left Shah Rukh's capital Herat in 1419, just after Chen Cheng's third mission to the Western regions. From Herat the envoys traveled via Balkh to Samarqand. According to his records, the ruler of Samarkand Ulugh Beg sent a mission to visit China with Ming Dynasty envoys two months before. They expected to meet there with another group of envoys, sent by Shah Rukh's viceroy of Transoxania, Ulugh Beg. However, it turned out that Ulugh Beg's delegation had left already, and Shah Rukh's team had to proceed separately. They left the Samarqand city for China on February 25, 1420, along with Chinese envoys which were returning back home. They entered Eastern Chagatai Khanate via Shigan and Cylan and at this time there occurred a civil unrest, and Uwais Khan had captured the power. To avoid any risk of aggression by Wala kingdom forces, they traveled along Chen Cheng's route in the reverse direction and passed across the Kunes River (current name) on the upper reaches of Yili River and traveled Westward after crossing Tianshan mountain, via Turfan, Kumul, Jiayu Pass, Suzhou, Ganzhou and Hebei, they finally arrived in Beijing on December 14, 1420. The whole trip took 385 days. And the Persian envoys spent 5 months at the court of the Emperor Yongle. On18, 1421, the envoys left Beijing for their trip home. They passed through

14   Suǒ Lǔ Tán, the title of Shah Rukh, See Shao Xunzheng's The Relationship between the Early Ming Dynasty and the Timur Empire and Historical Proceedings of Shao Xunzheng, Peking University Press, 1985.

Pingyang of Shanxi, Ganzhou, Suzhou and Jiayu Pass. On their way home, they traveled along the Southern expedition road to Mt. Tianshan, Yutian, then Kashi Junggar, Qisar, Shuman, Suerhan River Basin and many otherregions. The Herat envoys returned to their hometown on August 29, 1422 and the trip lasted 2 years and 10 months.

The book "A Persian Embassy to China" authored by Ghiyas-ud-din quite different from other travel writings. Generally, most of the travel writings are written by travelers after the travelers' return, but Ghiyas-ud-din's travel writings was sorted out according to his daily diary notes, which makes his book "A Persian Embassy to China" a highly reliable historical material. He wrote about China's politics, military affairs, institutions as well as conditions of people, and everything which was new and interesting for him.

He also mentioned about the communication and border security warning system and wrote: "there are many beacon towers erected in the border of Ming Dynasty, and the distance between them is within the range of visibility.

Each smoke pier has 10 soldiers and they would immediately form a fire smoke once they detected an enemy." Besides, he also narrated the ways used by the Ming Dynasty when hosting foreign envoys: "when the mission arrived at the border, the border officer registered number of the people and number of the baggages. After entering the country, the mission was only allowed to carry necessary amount of baggage when entering the capital city except the baggages which contained tributes, the rest of the baggages was deposited on the border station and returned back when the envoys were leaving China. In the territories of the Ming Dynasty, the diet and the livestock of the mission were all taken care by the local administrations at all levels."

Once, the Persian mission had visited the Great Buddhist Temple in Hebei. According to Ghiyas-ud-din, there was a statue of gold gilt bronze Buddha with many hands, and there was an eye in each centre of the palm, which was known as Qianshoufo in the country. The temple formerly known as Longxing Temple and was built in 586. A large bronze statue of Buddha was cast in 965, which was 73 feet tall and has 42 arms. The temple was repaired and restored in 1301, and it was later seen by the Persian mission.

During their stay in Beijing, the Ming Palace was lit by, and the whole city was visible at night when the flames were blazing. Ghiyas-ud-din said that Emperor Yongle was so terrified that he visited the temple to pray. This was after the great fire disaster which occurred in the imperial palace in May, 1421 that was recorded in the book of "The Memoir of Ming Dynasty". As a result, this fire destroyed three newly-built great halls including Hall of Offering Heaven, Hall of Canopy and Hall of Practicing Moral Culture.

According to the records of Ghiyas-ud-din, Emperor Yongle went hunting in March 1421. During his absence, one of his princes came to Beijing from a place called Tamnai to preside over government affairs. According to The Memoir of Ming Dynasty, the prince was Zhu Gaochi (later Hongxi Emperor), and he was in Nanjing before his going to the capital. "Tamnai" was an error of Persian "Namtai". "Namtai" refers to "Namtai", and in The Huis' Collection of Words, the Persian equivalent of the place name "Nanjing" was exactly "Namtai". While "Namtai" was the name of a censor in the Yuan Dynasty, and he was located in Nanjing city. During the Yuan Dynasty period, "Nanjing" was called "Namtai" by Hui people, and this name was maintained by the Ming dynasty.

(6) Sa'id Ali Akbar Khatai and His Book Khatai Nama

In 1516, there was a man named Sa'id Ali Akbar Khatai in Istanbul, the capital of Ottoman Empire, and the Hui people wrote a book called Khatai Nama (Katay Name). However, the author was not mentioned in any other historical records. Persian people often included their native town names after their own names. From his last name "Khatai", we can tell that he or his father was probably born in China. Besides, the author used many special words used by the Eastern Turkic language, which showed that his mother tongue could be some Turkic dialect from China's Xinjiang or a region around Xinjiang. Khatai Nama described three routes from Central Asia to China, including the Kashmir road, Hetian road and Mongolian road. The first two routes were traditionally from Southern Xinjiang to the Western regions, while the Mongolia road was also known as the Chagatai Khanate road, which was a trade route from northern Xinjiang to Gansu under the control of the Eastern Chagatai Khanate.

Khatai Nama cited the two names of the Chinese emperors, "Kin Tai" and "Cin Khwar", saying that they were father and son. In fact, Cin Khwar was the nephew of Kin Tai. The book described the details of the Tumu Crisis, and said that Esen Tayishi of Wala attacked China with 60 thousand soldiers, and he captured Chinese emperor Cin Khwar. These Wala people took the emperor Cin Khwar to Qara-Qorum and allowed him to marry their daughter. However, Chinese people made a new emperor. Later, the Wala people sent Cin Khwar back to China for restoration. In fact, Akbar's narration was wrong, because it was Emperor Ming Zhengtong, the father of Cin Khwar who was captured by Wala (Oirat) people. The author also said that there were often envoys of four barbarian tribes in the Chinese imperial court. And these envoys came from the Huis, Tubo, Tatar, Uyghur as well as Jurchen etc. Khatai Nama also recorded that the Chinese called Islam as Kinke Zin.

The author has explained that in China, Baikhu refers to the officer who commanded a hundred men, and Sankhu for the officer who commanded a 1,000 men, and Gukhu for 10,000 men, Yan Samzan for 20,000 men, Samzan for 30,000 men, Yan Zunbun for 40,000 men, Zunbun for 50,000 men. These Chinese officers went out and inspected people in sedan chairs and were accompanied by attendants. He also introduced 12 Chinese provinces, including Shaanxi province which has many famous cities such as Kinjanfu, Kanju, Sukchu; Manziastan and its famous city Namtai—the Huis called Nanjing as Namtai in the Yuan Dynasty.

Qanbaliq (Beijing or Dadu), a name for the capital of Yuan Dynasty in Uyghur or Tatar language. They called the current Zhejiang province as the Jing Shi province, and Khotan city as Koryo that was rich in jade stone.

The author especially mentioned the porcelain manufacturing industry in Lamsin. Lamsin was the ancient name of Nanchang, and the place where porcelain was produced should be Jingdezhen. He described the production process of porcelain: first grind the stones and after mixing with water into a paste, then draw it into the first precipitation tank, then draw the semi-flux into the second and third tanks. Clay in the first tank was the roughest one, and could only be made into coarse porcelain, while there was the smoothest clay in the third tank and could be made into fine porcelain. These official kiln porcelains had seals in the bottom and they were as precious as gold, for they were not allowed to export to other countries.[15]

3. Rocia's (Russia's) Eastward Expansion

Mongolia was further divided at the end of Ming dynasty. Tatar, namely, the East Mongolia, was divided into South and North of the Gobi desert. However, Wala in the West of the Gobi desert was more powerful. There were three tribes in North of the Gobi desert, Tüsheet Khan, Zhasaketu Khan and Chechnya Khan. Neiman, Kalaqin and Erdos and other tribes were in the South of the Gobi desert, while Dzungaria, Dorbet, Khoshut and Torgout were in West of the Gobi Desert. At the decline of the Ming dynasty, the Jurchen people in Northeastern part became strong, and at the same time, the Russian dynasty in Europe got rid of the rule of Kipchak Khanate and became a powerful state and entered a glorious period. Thus Russia rose and began to compete with the European powers in its West, and Ottoman Empire in its South, and it controlled vast grassland and forests in its East. The expansion of Genghis Khan and its descendants had established a close connection between Russia and the Eurasian nomads. With the collapse of the Kipchak Khanate, in the vast regions, i.e, Russia in West to China in East, there were no more powerful kingdoms which could compete against or rival Russia, which created quite favorable conditions for Russia's (Rocia) Eastward expansion. Russia was called Rocia in Chinese historical texts in the early Qing Dynasty.

(1) Leagues and Banners[16] of Mongolia

South of the Gobi desert, starting from Jilin in the East to Helan Mountain in the West, was bordered by the Great Wall in the South and big desert in the North. It included Horqin, Bahrain, Zarult, Neiman, Erdos and other regions,

---

15 Akbar's work was translated by Zhang Zhishan, SDX Joint Publishing Company, 1988.
16 Banners were first used during the Qing Dynasty, which organized the Mongols into banners except those who belonged to the Eight Banners. Each banner had "sumu" as nominal subdivisions. Among Mongols, several banners made up a league. In the rest, including Outer Mongolia, northern Xinjiang and Qinghai, Aimag was the largest administrative division. While it restricted the Mongols from crossing banner borders, the Qing dynasty protected Mongolia from population pressure from China proper.

which was roughly similar to current Mongolia. By the early 17th century, the power of the Altan khan was greatly weakened, and the pattern of decentralized rule re-emerged. Small tribes within each tumen became petty realms ruled over by individual princes. Division of inheritances further weakened the overall power structure, and tumen subdivisions (battalions, referred to in later Mongol history as banners or koshuus in Mongol) were widely dispersed and therefore fragmented.

Among them, Chahar Mongols held a dominant positions and became the chiefs of many tribes. In 1636, 49 officials who were ranked below that of the Prince (according to the rank system of the Manchu nobility) from 16 ministries in South of the Gobi desert have gathered in Shengjing to support the ruler Huangtaiji, and people in the South of the Gobi desert were all subordinated to the Jurchen kingdom. Essentially nomadic in origin, the Manchus were descended from the Jurchen, who earlier had established the Jin Empire. Early in the 17th century, under their leader Nurhaci (Nu-erh-ha-ch'ih)(1559-1626), the Manchus began to press into the southern Mongolia.

The Khalkha Mongolia, the vassal state had a vast territory, starting from Heilongjiang in the East to Wala in the West, was bordered by the Gobi Desert in the South and Russia in the North. And, it roughly included currentouter Mongolia and the Mongolian tribes in the neighborhood of Lake Baikal in Russia. When the Mongolian regions in the south of the Gobi desert was dominated by the Manchu Dynasty, in turn the Khalkha tribes which dwelled in the North of the Gobi desert established contacts with the Qing Dynasty. And, Khalkha kingdom and its people had close relations with the tribes which dwelled in the certain region of Mongolia,i.e, the West of the Gobi desert. In 1640, 44 Mongolian nobility and Lamas such as Dzungaria, Khoshut as well as Khalkha have gathered and made the Mongolian-Wei Late Code, which defined the rights, obligations and borders between the tribes. Later, whenever there was civil strife in Khalkha, its leading officers would escape South to find shelter in the Qing Dynasty. In 1688, taking advantage of the civil strife in Khalkha, Dzungaria marched against Hangay Uul with his troops to conquer the kingdoms in the East, and soon they captured Qara-Qorum—the former capital of Erdene Zuu Mongoli (today Mongolian Harhorin). Then they crossed Tuul River located in Eastern region of Khalkha. Thus, Qing government had achieved suppressing these Khalkha tribes that moved Southward. In 1691, Emperor Kangxi met with Khalkha Khan and Jebtsundamba Khutughtu at the Dolon Nor and announced that he would implement the same rule as that of the South of the Gobi desert in the North of the Gobi desert. In 1696, the Qing emperor Kangxi defeated Dzungaria (Lama) and controlled the territories of Khalkha tribes. In the late Ming dynasty period, Wala in the West of the Gobi desert extended its range of control. The Torgout Department of Wala had moved to the middle and lower reaches of the Ejrich River (today the Volga River), and the Dorbet Department had moved to the upper and lower reaches of the Irtysh River. The Dzungaria Department was located in the Northern part of Mt. Tianshan, Eastern Kazakhstan. Wala's Torgout moved West to the middle and lower reaches of the Volga River, while Dorbet moved to the upper and lower reaches of the Irtysh River. And the Dzungaria was located in the Northern part of Mt. Tianshan, the Northern part of Xinjiang and the Eastern part of Kazakhstan. In 1637, led by Gushri Khan, Khoshut crossed Mt. Tianshan into Qinghai via Tarim Basin, defeating the former nomadic Mongolian tribes. In addition, there were also some Khoshut tribes, along with Torgout, which moved West to the Volga River basin, or scattered in other parts of the Western Region. During the Ming and Qing Dynasties period, the control of Wala territory stretched from Hangay Uul Mongolia in the East, Volga River in the West, the middle reaches of Ertix River in the North, and India in the South.

Dzungaria was one of the Kalmuck's four tribes, and became stronger under the rule of tribe chief Khara Khula and his son Batur in the late Ming Dynasty. During the early Qing Dynasty period, Dzungaria Khan Galdan had annexed its surrounding regions. In 1679, Galdan Khan attacked the Eastern and Southern parts of Mt.Tianshan in Xinjiang and also established his rule there. Soon he launched a war against the Kazakh tribes in the West. After the battle, he expanded territories of the kingdom to Tashkent, Fergana Valley and grasslands in the Southern part of Eastern Europe. After that, Galdan Khan took advantage of the civil strife in Khalkha and attacked north of the Gobi desert in 1688, forcing three Khanates to go south of the Gobi desert and asked Qing Dynasty for shelter. In 1690, Galdan Khan moved South across the desert, which shocked Beijing. Therefore, Chinese emperor Kangxi personally led the army and defeated Galdan in Ulan Buh. In 1696, Chinese emperor Kangxi again led the army to the North of the Gobi desert, and Galdan commited suicide after the defeat. After twenty or thirty years of recuperation, Dzungaria kingdom became powerful again, and repeatedly collided with the Qing Dynasty in Tibet and North of the Gobi desert. Dzungaria was very powerful at that time, stretching from Khalkha Mongolia in the East to Kazakhstan in the West, and from Russia in the North to India in the South. Since 1640s, civil strife has taken place within the Dzungaria kingdom. So Manchu troops took the opportunity to send troops in 1755 and controlled Northern part of Mt. Tianshan in a short term. But soon some Dzungaria nobility who had surrendered has rebelled once again, thus Emperor Qianlong dispatched the army and completely defeated the Dzungaria forces, thus included the Northern and Southern parts of Mt. Tianshan as well as the Eastern part of Central Asia into the Chinese territory.

Based on the special relationship between Mongols and Jurchens, Manchu Dynasty set up Mongol Yamen (an agency in the government of the Qing Dynasty) to take charge of affairs in the South of the Gobi desert in 1636. Two years later, the name was changed to "Lifan Yuan" in Chinese and "Tulergi golo be dasara jurgan" in Manchu. The Manchu name literally means the department for the administration of outlying regions. Its main function was administering affairs like offering official posts, registering permanent residence and other issues beyond the borders of China proper. Its status was the same as Six Ministries of medieval and early modern imperial China (Personnel, Revenue, War, Rites, Public Works, and Justice). In addition, general and commander-in-chief (military-administrative organizations of the Han nationality in the Qing Dynasty) were set up in the South of the Gobi desert, and general, ministry departments were set up in the North of the Gobi desert, in Qinghai and in the Northern and Southern parts of Mt. Tianshan to deal with the affairs of tribes in Mongol.

Before the armies of the Qing Dynasty occupied Shanhaiguan Pass, the 24 tribes in South of the Gobi desert Mongolia was already divided into 49 banners and 6 leagues. The adjacent banners have fixed time and determined places to convene. After the surrender of Mongols dwelling in the north of the Gobi desert, the Qing Dynasty has gradually divided Khalkha into many banners and leagues. Banner was the basic administrative unit of the Mongolian region in Qing Dynasty, and it was also the Mongolian nobility's free hold estate given by emperor of the Qing Dynasty. The establishment of the league and banner system helped building of a standard relations between the south of the Gobi desert, the north of the Gobi desert and the grasslands of the Western Regions and China's central government, which played a significant role in the formation of the modern Northern China and Western regions.

(2) Torgout People and Torgout Kingdom Moving Westward and Tulichen Envoys

Torgout people originated from Keraites during the Western Liao and Jin Dynasties, and regarded Wang Han as the leader of Kerait(s) and as their ancestor. At that time, all the Mongol tribes had their own escorts that were called "torqud" in the Mongolian language. The ancestors of Torgout were originally escorts with Kerait origin. At the end period of the Yuan Dynasty, these Keraites have joined Wala (Oirats) and became one of the four tribes of Kalmuck. At the end period of the Ming Dynasty, they led a nomad life in the middle and upper reaches of Ertix River with Dorbet and Dzungaria. In the early 17th century, its capital was located in present-day Yili.

Later due to defeat in the war with Eastern Mongol empire and due to internal contradictions with Kalmuck tribe which they had cooperated, Kho Orluk[17], the leader Torgout kingdom sent some people to explore the coast of the Caspian Sea and the downstream of present Volga River in 1618.

And they found it was a good place with plenty of water and lush grass as well as few inhabitants. So Torgout, led by Kho Orluk, settled there with more than 50 thousand households of Khoshut and Dorbet. According to Todo

---

17 Kho Orluk (Mongolian:; died 1644) was an Oirat prince and Tayishi of the Torghut-Oirat tribe. Kho Orluk persuaded the other Torghut princes and lesser nobility to move their tribe en masse westward through southern Siberia and southward along the Emba River to the grass steppes north of the Russian garrison at Astrakhan. During the process of securing the steppes for his people, Kho Orluk met limited resistance from the local Islam tribesman, therefore setting the foundation of what later became known as the Kalmyk Khanate

uzug (a kind of Mongolian language) historical records History of Four Oirat, Torgout moved to the West around 1628, and set their capital on the riverside of Volga, Astrakhan.

Torgout tribe, although far from home, remained in close contact with other Mongolian tribes. In 1640, Kho Orluk returned to his native place with his son Shukhur Daichin. And he attended the meeting of the feudal lords in Mongolian tribes and signed on the Mongolian-Wei Late Code. Later, Torgout ordered people to copy this code on the white ribbon with Todo uzug, and then preserved it in the Khan's tent at the Volga River Valley, making it the evidence of his rule. In 1620 his daughter married Ishim-khan (son of Kuchum, khan of Sibir). In order to maintain the relationship with Dzungaria, Kho Orluk married her daughter to the head of the Dzungaria Batur. Later, his grandson married Batur's daughter. The grandson of Batur was Ayuka Khan who grew up in Dzungaria and was brought to the Volga River valley by his grandfather Shukhur Daichin at the age of 12. Ayuka Khan arranged that his sisters marry with tribal leaders.

Despite the long distance, Torgout people still adhered to the belief of Lamaism and maintained close ties with Tibet. In 1646, Kho Orluk's son Shukhur Daichin traveled to Tibet region to offer incense and stayed there for many years, so Dalai Lama awarded him the title of Khan. During the reign of Shukhur Daichin's grandson Ayuka Khan, Torgout maintained close relationship with upper classes of Tibetan monks and laymen. In 1690, Dalai Lama awarded him the title of Khan and granted him the seal. Since then, Ayuka Khan had called himself as the Khan.

When the leader of Khoshut who occupied Qinghai and Tibet established contact with the Qing Dynasty, Shukhur Daichin also submitted tribute to the Qing government, which was recorded in the Volume 9 of A Brief History of Imperial Court and Outline of Kalmuck.

Then the Torgout leader has maintained tributary relations with Qing Dynasty although there was a great distance between the two states. However, after the deterioration of relations between the Dzungaria and Torgout, Dzungaria had repeatedly intercepted Torgout's mission to the Qing Dynasty and blocked the connection between the Torgout and Tibet. Therefore, Torgout had to give up the traditional route, and traveled to Beijing via Siberia, passed through Khalkha Mongolia and South of the Gobi desert Mongolia. In 1709, envoys of Ayuka Khan arrived in Beijing along this unconventional expedition road and received by the Emperor Kangxi. Then Kangxi sent a mission headed by Yin Zana to visit Torgout with them.

There were 32 envoys visiting Torgout, including Tulichen from China's official deperment called the Lifan Yuan.[18] After his return from the travel, Tulichen recorded his travels and experiences in the Torgout territory, which has become an important document to study the Grassland Silk Road in this period. And it has attracted the attention of Chinese and foreign scholars and was translated into a variety of languages. The mission set out from Beijing on June 23, 1712, along the route of Torgout pass, via Khalkha, Siberia, the downstream of Volga River, and arrived at the boundary of Torgout kingdom. Torgout kingdom ordered Tai Ji and Lama to receive these envoys. And after they crossed the Volga River, they finally arrived at the tent of Ayuka Khan on July 12, 1714. The envoy loudly read the imperial edict of the Chinese emperor Kangxi.

During the feast, Ayuka Khan asked the mission about his home in detail. Ayuka Khan said with emotion: "Manchuria and Mongolia are roughly similar, so the two must be homologous at first." He also said that Mongolian "style of hats and suits are slightly different from the Chinese ones, "however, Russia is not of the same, because they have different clothes and languages in Russia." These words of him expressed his deep yearning for his native homeland. In another speech, Ayuka Khan expressed his dissatisfaction with Dzungaria's hindering theirs contact with Tibet, saying that it was extremely difficult to find and get Tibetan medicine. Although they could go there via Russian Siberia, he was still afraid that Russian princes would block this expedition road and then there would be no route left for the Torgouts to pay tribute."

During their stay in Torgout, the Qing mission group was well received and entertained by many Torgout nobles. The mission stayed in Torgout for two weeks and returned home in 1714. On April 30, 1715, the mission returned to Beijing and made a report on completion of their mission to the Qing court. This mission had a profound impact on Torgout, which provoked strong surges of nostalgia of Torgout people for their hometown and motherland, making them consider China as their spiritual supporter for a long time.

In 1730, the leader of Torgout kingdom sent a mission to the Qing court. After their arrival in Beijing, they stated to the Qing government that they did not serve or obey the Russian dynasty, thus the Qing government believed that Torgout people were a branch of Mongolian people. After returning home, the mission was detained by Russia government because they denied that they were represented a vassal state of Russian dynasty. In the same year, Emperor Yong Zheng sent a mission to St. Petersburg to congratulate the enthronement of Queen Anna of Russian Dynasty. Then the mission visited Torgout, and was warmly welcomed there by the upper monks and laymen. Later, the leader of Torgout sent a mission of 37 people to Tibet to pay homage to Dalai Lama in

---

18   Lifan Yuan: Lifan Yuan, government bureau established in the 17th century by China's Qing (Manchu) dynasty to handle relations with the peoples of Inner Asia. It signified the growing interest of China in Central Asia. The office appointed governors to supervise Chinese territories in Central Asia and Tibet.

1737. In order to monitor their visit, the Russian government sent officials and interpreters in the mission. When they reached the border of Mongolia, they were refused to enter, since some Russian figures were among the mission team.

In 1753, Torgout sent a mission led by Choijinzhab to offer gifts to the emperor Qianlong, and they arrived Rehe palace after three years of travel. The bows and arrows of these gifts are still preserved in the Museum of Chinese History. Emperor Qianlong approved Choijinzhab's request to offer incense in Tibet and sent people to escort them. After coming back from Tibet, Choijinzhab and his members were received by Emperor Qianlong when they passed through Beijing. Choijinzhab told Emperor Qianlong about Torgout's helping Russia to fight against Sweden. He also added that Torgout was only attached to Russia, but it did not surrender to them, saying "How can one be willing to be a servant of another, unless he is commanded by the great emperor?" Choijinzhab asked the Qing government to order central Kazakh tribes so that they should allow Torgout envoys visit to go to China via its territory. He even presented a sketch of Torgout's territoriesto the Qing dynasty court.

(3) Trade in the "Business City"

In 1581, a number of Cossack led by the leader Yermak crossed the Ural Mountains and attacked the center of the Sibir Khanate. Yermak himself was killed in this battle, later the Moscovy Czar sent support and reinforcements and and Cossaks finally conquered Sibir Khanate. Then Russia supported Cossacks had expanded eastward, and established many colony castles alongside Irtysh River, Yenisei Tuomuer River, and Ob River basin. At the beginning of 17th century, they expanded towards the Yenisei River, the Angara River, Begall and Heilongjiang.

As Russia expanded eastward, many Russian traders also came to the East. After Russia conquered the Sibir Khanate at the end of Ming Dynasty, Russian traders soon discovered the benefits of trade with the East. In 1574, the Russian Czar ordered the Hui (Islam) merchants of Bukhara together with Wala and Kazakh merchants to trade goods with the above-mentioned Russian castles. Besides, all the trade was exempted from tax.[19]

Taras of Russia was the major trade place between Wala and Russia. In this way, Russia established indirect trade relations with the Ming Dynasty through exchanges with the Hui people, Wala and Kazakh people.

In 1618, the Cossack Ivan Petlin from Russia has visited China. Ivan Petlin arrived in Beijing via Tatar, returning home with the command paper of Emperor Wanli (Ming Dynasty). After Manchu Dynasty entered the Shanhaiguan Pass, Czar consecutively sent envoys to visit China in 1655 and 1660, and have brought credentials from Shunzhi Emperor. However, while the main forces of

---

19 See Li Sheng: Trade History of Xinjiang with Russia, 1600-1990, Xinjiang People's Press, 1993, p. 6.

Manchu Dynasty were busy entering Shanhaiguan Pass, Russia occupied some of Chinese territory, causing the long term Sino-Russian border issue.

At the beginning of Qing Dynasty period, China and Russia finally decided to establish a peaceful relationship. Therefore, they signed the Treaty of Nerchinsk in 1689, which allowed the merchants of the two countries to trade with each other. The treaty stipulated in article five that "People of the two countries with a passport can cross the border and trade with each other."[20]

In more than a century later, Russian merchants entered the Chinese territory via Nerchinsk and then headed for the Nenjiang valley. Li Fanyuan of Qing Dynasty had placed certain restrictions on the number of Russian traders, for example, the number of envoys sent by Tsar should not exceed 200, while the mission sent by the Russian border authorities should be limited to 50 persons. The Russian mission was only allowed to enter Beijing once in every three years. And they had to live in the Russian posthouse (inn) during their stay in Beijing. After the beginning of the 18th century, Russian merchants and envoys often entered Beijing from the Baikal region via Mongolia, Inner Mongolia and Zhangjiakou.

Fur was the main traditional product of trade from North Asia to the Central Plains. With its reign in the Siberia region, Russia collected a vast amount of fur from the many subordinated nationalities under its control in the East. According to statistics, the prices of black mink, squirrel skin and red fox skin in Siberia were 3 times, 5 to 7.5 times and 3.3 to 6 times than that of in Beijing. Huge price differences prompted Russia to trade these fur goods with China with lucrative profits. The Russian authorities have repeatedly sent large-scale missions to Beijing, and the number of envoys had once reached as many as 800 people, despite the restrictive provisions of the Qing government in regard to number of people and in regard to frequency of visits.

Russian people in Tuomuersike traded with China with the aid of the Huis in Bukhara who had traditional trade connections with Dzungaria. Russian trade caravans led by the Huis started from central Siberia, via Dzungaria, the upper reaches of Ertix River, Dzungaria, Jinshan, Outer Mongolia, Inner Mongolia, Zhangjiakou and finally arrived in Beijing. Three years later, they returned to Tuomuersike and sold all the goods taking from China in Moscow, at last they earned three times the profit. Later, this trade route has become one of the main routes between China and Russia.[21]

In 1727, the Qing government and Russia concluded the Treaty of Kyakhta, which delineated the boundaries of the Mongolia regions of the two countries. As the Article 4 of the treaty, except for the previous limitations on fixed number of people and years, "Merchants at the national boundaries of the two

---

20   Wang Tieya: Book 1 of Compilation of Chinese and Foreign Old Treaties, SDX Joint Publishing Company, 1982, p. 2.
21   See Li Sheng: Trade History of Xinjiang to Russia, 1600-1990, Xinjiang People's Press, 1993, pp. 25-26.

countries can build housing in Nerchinsk and Kiakhta of Selenge. People are free to go and trade there if they are willing to." There were walls and fence around the border trade market.[22]

In the same year, Russia began to develop and construct markets in Kiakhta, the border at the South side Lake Baikal, while the Qing government also built a market called "business city" in opposite side. "Business city", the Chinese geographical name, is still used by Mongolian and Russian people.

The signing of Treaty of Kiakhta had led to massive growth in the Sino–Russia trade. At the second half of the 18th century, trade volume between China and Russia in Kiakhta and "Business city" had accounted for 7% to 9% of the total foreign trade volume of Russia and 67.6% of the Russia-Asia trade volume. According to Russian statistics, in 1760 custom tax fees collected by the Qing Dynasty accounted for 20.4% of Russia's total custom tax payments, and rose to 38.5% by 1775. In response to this situation, the Russian population in Asia has also risen rapidly. The population grew even faster in the banks of Selenga river and the Irkutsk city (Siberia) that was close to the border region of Mongolia in the Qing Dynasty period.[23]

During this period, after Qing Dynasty pacified the Huis and Dzungaria, trade in Xinjiang and the Kazakh tribes submitting to Qing Dynasty has increased greatly. The Kazakh (Cossaks) merchants shipped goods purchased from Northwestern China to Siberia, and bought and re-sold goods from Russia, at the same time. Trade between Northwestern China and Russia has brought prosperity to border cities such as Urumqi and Yili.

During the Sino-Russian Nerchinsk war in the early Qing Dynasty period (1689), some Russians had surrendered to the Qing Dynasty and were placed in Beijing. The Qing government enrolled these nearly a hundred Russians (the Albazin community) under the control of the 17th division of Yellow Banner.[24]

The (Qing) Manchu dynasty also allowed them ro dwell in a Hutong (neighborhood) of Beijing with the supply of accommodation, food and clothing as well as annual wages. Russian historical records called them as "Russian Centuria". Emperor Kangxi gave these people a temple, which was changed to an Orthodox Church which was as the Nikolsky Church ("Sheng Ni Gula"; later consecrated as the Church of Hagia Sophia. In 1715, Tulichen visited Torgout at the Volga River Valley, and they returned to Beijing with Orthodox priests sent by Russia. Article 6 of the Treaty of Kyakhta stipulates that the Russian people in Beijing will be settled in Russian Posthouse. China agreed to Russia's request to build an Orthodox Church in Beijing. Before the two

22　Wang Tieya: Compilation of Chinese and Foreign Old Treaties Vol. I , SDX Joint Publishing Company, 1982, p. 2.

23　History of Russia's Aggression against China Vol. I, People's Publishing House, 1978. Published by the Institute of Modern History, CASS.

24　The Eight Banners were administrative-military divisions under the Qing dynasty into which all Manchu households were placed. Yellow Banner was one of them.

countries signed the treaty, there was a Russian Orthodox priest in Beijing, and the Qing government allowed three more Orthodox Christians to live in the church. The Russians who stayed in Beijing were allowed to go to church in accordance with the rules of worship. Since then Russia sent a group of Orthodox priests to China every ten years, and a total of 20 batches was sent till 1949.

Some of the Orthodox priests in Beijing were keen to learn Chinese, Manchu, Mongolian, Tibetan as well as Chinese of history and culture, so they became famous Sinologists and taught Chinese and Manchu in Russia after they returned home. Li Fanyuan also founded Russia language school, and sent children of the Eight Banners to learn Russian so as to cultivate negotiating talents with Russia.

4. The New Era for Cultural Exchanges

(1) Asian Institute—Ethnics House

In order to promote exchanges with the neighboring countries and ethnic minorities, the Ming Dynasty established Ethnics House (Siyi Guan) in 1407. There were altogether eight houses in the Ethnics House, such as Tatar, Jurchen, Western Barbarians, ancient India, the Huis, Bai Yi, Gaochang and Burma. The chief executive of Ethnics House was Shao Qing, in charge of translating and interpreting staff, and they were all subordinate to Hanlin Academy. Ethnic House students had a length of schooling, after completion of their studies, they needed to pass the examinations at all levels, and the qualified ones would be employed as interpreters by the country. Later, with the development of external exchanges, the original eight languages were not enough to meet the needs of government, so the Ming government added another two houses of Ba bai and Siam. In order to teach ethnic minority languages, Ethnic House has written books of Chinese and ethnic languages, namely, Bureau of Translators' Multilingual Dictionary (华夷译语, Huá-Yí yìyǔ, 'Sino-Barbarian Dictionary'). In addition, neighboring nationalities' memorials to the throne were compiled and preserved. After the demise of the Ming Dynasty, the Qing Dynasty continued to develop Ethnic House. Because Manchu was not the Han people, so the Qing government renamed Ethnic House into The Imperial Translation Training Agency of Regional Languages. The Ethnic House was the earliest Asian institute established in China.

The name Bureau of Translators' Multilingual Dictionary has two different meanings in the academia. In the narrow sense, Bureau of Translators' Multilingual Dictionary is title for a book of classified vocabulary for Mongolian and Chinese written by Huo Yuanjie in Ming Dynasty. While in the broad sense, Bureau of Translators' Multilingual Dictionary refers to a large number of classified vocabularies for Chinese–ethnic minority languages compiled by Ethnic House Department and School of Combined Learning, and some of them also includes collection of important letters and documents which were sent to the court or vice versa.

a. The Chinese Department of North Asia—Tatar House and the Jurchen House

Since the early period of the Liao Dynasty, the Northern ethnic peoples began to imitate or adopt Chinese characters to create their own scripts. Through adding and re-structuring of the components of Chinese characters, and also assimilating the merits of the Uyghur Pinyin, Khitan people have created the Khitan large and small script. After the collapse of the Liao dynasty, Jurchen people learned from Khitan people and have created the Jurchen script. After the demise of the Jin Dynasty and Yuan Dynasty, Jurchen script was still preserved. During the reign of Temür Khan[25] (1265-1307), the Mongolian scholar Chos-kyihod-zer (Lama scholar) has reformed the Uyghur scripts.

In 1269, Kublai Khan (the 5th emperor of the Yuan (Mongol) Dynasty) began to set up Mongolian schools among his tribes. Two years later, he established regular Mongolian schools—the imperial education of the Great Mongol Empire. Mongolian was the ruling class, so mastering Mongolian language has become a shortcut for pursuing an official career. Besides, Chinese-Mongolian books began to appear in the society, which helped Han people to study Mongolian, among which the most famous one was Dictionary of Yuan Dynasty (Zhi Yuan Yi Yu). It is a kind of classified dictionary, which divided Mongolian words into 22 categories according to meaning, such as astronomy, geography, personnel, grain, foods, body, clothes, utensils, vegetation, vegetable and fruit, season, color, characters, birds, animals and other treasures, etc. There was no original text of Mongolian in the dictionary, but was translated into Chinese characters with Mongolian phonetic notation.

During the Ming Dynasty period, people in Central Plains and in Northern Asia communicated with each other mainly in Mongolian and Jurchen that were taught by Tatar house and Jurchen house respectively in the Ethnic House. If Ethnic House can be evaluated as a general Asian institute, then we can say that Tatar House and Jurchen House were its attached departments for the North Asian languages.

During the Ming dynasty period, people still learned Mongolian utilizing dictionaries as the main textbook which was available in the Tatar House, which explained the meaning of the Mongolian words. The above-mentioned Bureau of Translators' Multilingual Dictionary was such kind of book, in it the Mongolian word was written first, then the meaning of the word was explained, and finally its expression with Chinese characters was added. For example, "tengri, 天, 腾吉里". This dictionary could be divided into 18 categories, such as astronomy, geography, season, flowers, birds and animals, palace, utensils, clothes, foods, treasure, character, personnel, sensual, number, body, and interpreting, etc. So it was obviously influenced by Dictionary of Yuan Dynasty (Zhi Yuan Yi Yu). Later officials in Tatar House compiled Supplement Edition of Bureau of Translators' Multilingual Dictionary and added more words in it.

---

25 Temür, also called Öljeitü, grandson and successor of the great Kublai Khan; he ruled (1295-1307) as emperor of the Yuan (Mongol) dynasty (1206-1368) of China and as great khan of the Mongol Empire. He was the last Yuan ruler to maintain firm control over China.

In addition to teaching Mongolian, Tatar House also in charge of the translation of official dispatch. The Ming Dynasty used Mongolian in communicating with Tatar and Wala. Besides, official documents for Jianzhou Jurchen in Northeast China were also written in Mongolian. Currently, some of these documents are preserved in the Gaochang House.

During the era of the Ming Dynasty, there were various official and private Mongolian-Chinese dictionaries, due to the need to interact with Tatars and the Wala kingdom, and, among them the most important ones were the Lu Long Sai Lue, Required Readings for General Officers and A Corpus of Classified Military Writings. Obviously, these materials are important materials for us to study the Mongolian culture and understand the cultural ties between the Han Dynasty and Mongolian Steppes during the Ming dynasty period.

During the Ming Dynasty period, although Mongolians had withdrawn from the Central Plains, due to frequent exchanges between Mongolian ethnic peoples and the Han nationality, a large number of Chinese vocabularies, especially the various official ranks and titles were adapted by the Mongolian poople, and used among the nobles of the Mongolian tribes. For example:

Taiji—Prince
Hong Taiji, Khong Taiji, Huang Taiji—Crown Prince
Fujin—Nobleman's wife
Ji Nong—Prince of Jin
Zai Sang—Zai Xiang (prime minister in feudal China)

Jurchen belongs to the Manchu branch of Manchu–Tungusic, and was most similar to language of Hezhe ethnic people living at the downstream region of Heilongjiang on both sides of the Sino–Russian border, and also has a close relationship with Manchu and Sibo languages. Today, there are many nationalities who speak a similar language to Jurchen and who live in the regions of Eastern Siberia attached to the Russian Federation.

There were two different Jurchen scripts: a "large script" modeled on the Khitan large script was devised in 1120 by the command of Wanyan Aguda, the first emperor of the Jin dynasty; and a "small script" that was created in 1138 by the Emperor Xizong. After the demise of Jin Dynasty, the majority of Jurchen people entering the Han's land was Sinicized, only people in the Northeast of China still used Jurchen language, in addition, some of the Choson also knew Jurchen. Because Jurchen's memorial to the throne was mostly written in Jurchen script, so Jurchen House was set up in Ethnic House in order to cultivate Jurchen translation talents. And Jurchen language that has survived so far is the Jurchen large script.

Chinese-Jurchen classified dictionary compiled by Jurchen House was called Sino-Jurchen Vocabulary of the Bureau of Interpreters (Nǚzhēn Yìyǔ, 女真馆译語). It was also like some other translation languages and is divided into two versions, one was called "Yongle script" including three parts: Jurchen,

Chinese and Chinese transliteration; while the other one was "Huitong Guan version" which only had transliteration of the Jurchen language and Chinese translation without including its Jurchen script. The two versions of Sino-Jurchen Vocabulary of the Bureau of Interpreters were prepared separately. It probably existed in some form in the Yuan Dynasty, and the text book of Jurchen dictionary probablyfollowed the style of the dictionary written in the Jin Dynasty period.

Sino-Jurchen Vocabulary of the Bureau of Interpreters divided Jurchen vocabulary into 19 categories, of which the most complete book contains 917 words. These written materials of Jurchen script are of great value in the study the relationship between Jurchen, the history of cultural exchanges between Turkic and Han people as well as other ethnic peoples (including the Manchu nationality) who speak similar languages as well as the relation between Ming Dynasty and the kingdoms in the Northeast China and North Asia.

There are 79 pieces of Laiwen recorded in Jurchen script which is archived in the Jurchen House, most of which were memorials given to Ming court from the end years of emperor Yongle to the early years of emperor Jiajing. From the perspective of studying Jurchen language, these Laiwen documents were certainly not written by native Jurchen speakers, and they embodied Chinese grammar expressed with Jurchen (script) characters, and almost none of them conform with the grammatical structure of Jurchen language. Therefore, we can comfortably argue that these Laiwen documents were originally written in Chinese and were later translated word by word into the Jurchen text. According to the rules of Ming Dynasty, a memorial should be handed when the representatives of the vassal states paid tributes to the emperor. It can be estimated that some Jurchen leaders might have bribed officials in the Ethnic House to draft these memorials, which were later archived in the Jurchen House and known as the Lanwen Documents of Jurchen.

Nevertheless, the Lanwei Documents of Jurchen are still rare documents for the study of history of the ethnic peoples in the Northeast Asia region during the Ming Dynasty period. From the distribution range of tribute ministries mentioned in the Lanwei Documents of Jurchen, Jurchen tribes that were subordinated to Ming Dynasty were mainly in the three Northeastern Provinces of China at that time. However, there were also some tributaries coming from the regions beyond the border regions. These materials reflect the close political, economic and cultural ties between the Central Plains and those numerous nationalities who dwelled in the Northeast Asia region, during the ancient times. Because of the multi-faceted contacts between the Jurchen people and the Han people, many Han Chinese words were adopted into the Jurchen language. Even many words in the Jurchen language were taken directly from the Chinese language. For example, capital, prefecture, county, palace, hall, brick, jin, liang, dukes, marquis, general, monk, Taoist (府、州、县、宫、殿、楼、堂、砖、瓦、斤、两、王、公、侯、伯、将军、指挥、尚书、侍郎、和尚、道士）and etc.

b. Department of Inland Asian Languages Teaching— Uyghur House and the Gaochang House

After Abag Khan Dynasty replaced the Umayyad dynasty, political center of Arab Empire moved Eeastwards, and the written language of inland Asia became Persian. From the beginning of Yuan Dynasty, people in the Central Plains called such kind of Persian spelled with the Arab alphabet as the Uyghur script. At the end period of the Northern Dynasties, the rise of Turkic Khanate caused the Turkic speaking people migrate Westward. During the Song, Yuan and Ming Dynasties, Uyghur was a common language used by the Turkic speaking people in Northwest China. Such kind of Islamic tide from West to East and Turkification movement from East to West made Persian and Uyghur script the main written language of the exchanges between people in the Central Plains and the inland Asian residents during the Song, Yuan and Ming Dynasties. In the Ethnic House, Uyghur House and Gaochang House departments were in charge of teaching Persian and Uyghur language, respectively. Thus we can say that the Ethnic House can be seen as an Asia studies institute, and Uyghur House and Gaochang House can be seen as its departments of studying the inland Asian languages.

Persian textbook compiled by Uyghur House was preserved in the Bureau of Translators' Multilingual Dictionary, which is called as the Collection of Words in Uyghur House and also a Multilingual Dictionary in Uyghur House. There were two versions of the Multilingual Dictionary in Uyghur House – the Yongle version and the Huitong Guan version. Yongle version consists of two parts, the Collection of Words and the Lanwei documents, while the former is in fact the book known as the Collection of Words which is archived in the Uyghur House.

Collection of Words which is preserved in the Uyghur House is a Chinese-Persian classified vocabulary text. At that time, scholars still did not know how to arrange words alphabetically, they took classified arrangement method, which was similar to other languages in the Bureau of Translators' Multilingual Dictionary. Therefore, it was equivalent to current classified dictionary. Collection of Words in the Uyghur House was compiled earlier, and the best one includes 777 words, while the supplement part to the book of Collection of Words included 333 Persian words. Therefore, altogether it had 1,110 Persian words.

The Lanwei documents constitute 26 tributary memorials to Ming dynasty from Kumul, Turfan, Samarkand, Balkh of Afghanistan, Basrah of Iran, and Egypt. There are abundant translation difficulties and errors in most of these memorials, since they were not issued by their own government. In addition, some of these memorials were not presented by the official envoys but common merchants. In order to enjoy free access to the Han Chinese territory these merchants pretended to be envoys, aiming to freely trade in the Han Chinese territory under the protection of Ming Dynasty officials. They also asked Han people (or Hui people) who knew Persian to forge such diplomatic documents and tributary memorials to raise their prestige in face of the court. There were few officials in court who knew Persian, so that they could be easily deceived. These forged documents are archived in the Uyghur House and are preserved till today. Probably, those people who wrote these documents had some background knowledge about the Persian language, but they were not fluent in Persian, so errors were inevitable. Scholars have estimated and argued that these people might have learned Persian in the Uyghur House, or they might be away from their native homeland for several generations, or they were employed as staff in the Uyghur House.

Huitong Guan version of the Multilingual Dictionary in Uyghur House had only the part of "Collection of Words" without Lanwei documents. Besides, "Collection of Words" only had main body of the text without "Supplement to Collection of Words". Since the Ethnic House and Huitong Guan compelling Collection of Words in Uyghur House and Multilingual Dictionary in Uyghur House were foreign affairs agencies established by the Ming dynasty, so most people naturally regarded them as works from the Ming Dynasty. However, in the studies related to the Bureau of Translators' Multilingual Dictionary in the recent years, domestic scholars have found a copy of Multilingual Dictionary in Hall of chastity for Yuan family in Qing dynasty. Multilingual Dictionary of Uyghur was from page 69 to 80. The dictionary was divided into 17 categories, and had included 673 Persian words. There was an official seal script with "Grand Commandant Seal" on it, and on top of it, we can see the text "Grand Commandant Seal, Made by the Ministry of Rites in Feudal China in 1371". If we consider these facts, we can say that the transcript of the Multilingual Dictionary in the Uyghur House which was based on the master copy was firstly copied in the period of Ming Dynasty, and its original edition was probably completed with the same copy of Multilingual Dictionary in Hexi Region—Personnel. Therefore, we can say that Multilingual Dictionary in Hexi Region was finally completed in the period of Ming Dynasty, but it was firstly edited in the Yuan Dynasty or its master copy had taken shape at that time.

This Multilingual Dictionary only had Chinese Pinyin and paraphrases, and Multilingual Dictionary of Gaochang was called Multilingual Dictionary of Uyghur in it, and was the same as the Bureau of Translators' Multilingual Dictionary in Huitong Guan that we mentioned above, especially in the aspect of its content. This shows that it is the original mother edition of Huitong Guan version of the Multilingual Dictionary in Uyghur House, and at the same time, it has also proved that among the different texts of Collection of Words in Uyghur House and Multilingual Dictionary in Uyghur House, Huitong version is the oldest one and were probably compiled in the Yuan Dynasty period. Probably, it was also related to the teaching materials of the Islam language teaching activities in Uyghur's Imperial Academy and Directorate of Imperial Academy.

Gaochang House was also attached to the Ethnics House, and it was in charge of the teaching and translating of Uyghur language. The current Documents of Gaochang House can be divided into two parts, Multilingual Dictionary of Gaochang Guan (or Words Collection of Gaochang Guan) and Documents of Gaochang House. Like other multilingual dictionaries, there are two versions for Multilingual Dictionary of Gaochang Guan. The first version was written with Uyghur scripts, called "Ethnic House version"; while the other has no Uyghur scripts, called the "Huitong Guan version". The dictionary which includes the Uyghur script is the same as the Multilingual Dictionary of Tatar House, since it includes the word in ethnic minority languages first, then explains its meaning, and finally gives the expression of word in Chinese characters. For example, "tengri, 天, 腾克力". The format of the second version was like Dictionary of Yuan Dynasty (Zhi Yuan Yi Yu), for it had only phonetic annotation of Chinese characters and Chinese translation, but its categories and words were also less than the first version. These two kinds of Multilingual Dictionary of Gaochang Guan were edited and compiled separately. Since the first version was prepared in the Ming dynasty, and the second one was probably some kind of revised version of the Multilingual Dictionary of Gaochang that was handed down to the Yuan Dynasty.

Turkic language was popular in many parts of Inner Asia. Ming Dynasty followed the former practices of Yuan Dynasty, and translated a considerable part of its documents with the help of Inner Asia ministries under the organization called the "Gaochang House". According to Rules of the Imperial Translation Training Agency of Regional Languages, Gaochang House was in charge of correspondence with the border fortress such as the Kumul region. Many of these transcribed documents have remained safely till currently and most of them are preserved in Documents of Gaochang House. The contents of these included paying tribute, asking for reward and official posts from chiefs of the ministries of the Northwest China and various other states. When we examine the signatures, these regions from near to far are the West region of Gansu (Province), all regions in Xinjiang like Kumul and Turfan, regions beyond the borders of China such as the Afghanistan and Tajikistan, and the farthest region was the Herat in Western Afghanistan.

Hungarian scholar L. Ligeti has studied 41 Laiwen documents, and Documents of Gaochang House published by Chinese scholars Hu Zhenhua, Huang Runhua has included 89 Laiwen documents of Gaochang House. In the winter of 1993, I have found two Lanwei documents that wasn't studied in National Library of Germany. These documents were mainly written with Chinese and Uyghur scripts, both by using the writing brush. Besides, some of the words were written on the top of another line, such as the "Imperial Court", "Great Ming" and "Imperial Decree".

Thanks to the discovery of Multilingual Dictionary of Gaochang Guan and Documents of Gaochang House, scholars have learned how to solve the meaning of these Uyghur texts so that a large number of ancient Uyghur (Uyghurn) documents from the late Tang Dynasty to the early Qing Dynasty were unknown to the world. According to the study of scholars, In fact, the Uyghur scripts in the Lanwei documents preserved in the Gaochang House are not the authentic spoken Uyghur language and it is quite impossible that they were written by a native speaker of the Turkic language. This shows that these documents were not real diplomatic documents and were probably written by the Han Chinese after these envoys have reached the Chinese border. If we examine the style of writing, we can say that the Chinese should be written first and then was translated word for word into Uyghur.

(2) The Emergence of Chagatai Khanate Alphabet

Turkic experts called the Eastern Turkic language spelled by the Persian alphabet after the 14th century as Chagatai Khanate language. In modern Turkic languages, Uyghur and Uzbek language are most closely related to it. After the 8th century, the cultural outlook of Central Asia has dramatically changed with the Islamic tide from West to East and Turkification movement from East to West. The written language such as the Sogdian, and He Tian language, which were popular in the Northwest of China during and before Tang Dynasties, were eventually replaced by Arabic and Persian language under the influence of the Islamic rise, while Turkic language became the most popular language in the Northwest of China under the influence of Turkification wave.

During the reign of Qara Khanids, Turkic literati were accustomed to write in Arabic and Persian, but their works inevitably included a large number of Turkic vocabulary, so it became popular for people to transliterate Turkic words with Persian and Arabic alphabets. In addition, a large number of Persian and Arabic alphabet spelled Turkic and Mongolian words also appeared in Khwarezm and Turkic literature works of the 13th century and the Persian historical documents of 13th and 14th centuries.

In the 15th century, Persian alphabet gradually developed to spell the Turkic language, which therefore produced Chagatai Khanate alphabet. Due to the influence of Islamic culture, Chagatai Khanate language has a large amount of Persian and Arabic words in it. Its foundation was the Central Asian dialect of Turkic language. The word Chagatai (Chagatay) derives from the name of Chengiz Khan's second son, Chagatai. When Chengiz Khan before his death (1227), divided up the Mongol empire among his sons, Chagatai. received Transoxania (except Khorazm), the Semirechye and Eastern Xinjiang. Chagatai khan had his residence in Ili Valley, since he knew best the legal code established by Chengiz Khan, he was highly respected among the Mongols. Chagatai khan dies at the turn of 1241-1242, The empire bearing his personal name—the Chagatai Ulus was established by his grandson Kara Hülagü, (1242-1246), the state was re-organized by Duwa Khan, who was a descendant of Chagatai khan.

Since the mid-1180s, especially after Duwa Khan (Dua Khan- c. 1274-1306), this state was officially called as Chagatai Khanate. Moreover, the Turkic and all nomads speaking Turkic language (Turkicized) in the Western Regions and Transoxania which formed military forces of the Chagatai Khanate were also called "Chagatai"[26].

Although it was called Chagatai Khanate language, it was not popular in the Yuan Dynasty period. It was widely circulated in the Timur Khanate era, and later it not only replaced the Uyghur and Syriac Turkic texts, but also replaced Persian and Arabic language, becoming a common written language for the Turkic people of Eastern Central Asia and the Northwest China.

After the Song Dynasty, mainland Chinese people's understanding of the language of the Western regions was not completely consistent with the cultural changes there. The imperial court of Yuan dynasty used Persian to communicate with the Khanate in Northwest China and the foreign countries, which was consistent with the fact that Persian was the prevailing written language of the Islam world at that time. A large number of Northwest people moved into the mainland, consequently Uyghur and Persian language was introduced into the mainland, and there were also public and private school teaching of Uyghur and Persian language in Yuan Dadu (capital of Yuan Dynasty).

After the demise of Yuan Dynasty, the Ming Dynasty inherited all the knowledge of the Western regions in the Yuan Dynasty, and continued to use Persian and Uyghur as their official language of communication with all parts of Western regions and countries. Gaochang House (teaching Uyghur) and Uyghur House (teaching Persian) were related to the Western Regions in Ethnic House in the capital city. The fact that Chagatai Khanate language had become the written language of the Turkic language was soon manifested in the official documents of the countries in the Western Regions. After the reign of Zhengde Emperor (1491-1521), some of the documents written by the Western regions to Ming government was written in Chagatai Khanate scripts and language. Chagatai Khanate language was called as the "Gaochang dialect, Uyghur script and regional language" by interpreters and officials in the Ming Dynasty.[27]

317

Officials of the Ming government once looked for "Gaochang dialect, Uyghur script and regional language" sent from the Western regions in 1518.[28] The so-called "Gaochang dialect, Uyghur script and regional language" refers to the Gaochang language spelled with Uyghur script. In Words Collection of

---

26   See written by Jin Guangping, Jin Qizong: Studies on Jurchen Language and Words, Cultural Relics Publishing House, 1980; Dorzh, Heague: The Sino-Jurchen Vocabulary of the Bureau of Interpreters, Supplement to Journal of Inner Mongolia University, Inner Mongolia University Press, 1983.
27   See Hu Zhenhua, Huang Runhua: Documents of Gaochang House in Ming Dynasty— Transcriptions of Latin Alphabet, Collection of Xinjiang Historical Research Materials, Xinjiang People's Publishing House, 1982.
28   The nomad people living in the eastern part of Chagatai Khanate were called as "Moghul".

Uyghur House—Geography, The Chinese word "Gaochang" corresponds to the "Turki" in Uyghur script. Rare Ancient Books in Beijing Library, Volume 6, page 470. The mainland people in the Ming Dynasty learned Turkic language through interaction with Uyghur people, so "Gaochang dialect, Uyghur script and regional language" was Central Asia Turkic language spelled in Persian alphabet. During the reign of Cin Khwar, although some Lanwei documents of the Western Region vassals were written in "Gaochang script, Uyghur script and regional language", the Chagatai script was still not taught in Ethnic House at the end of Ming Dynasty. But on the contrary, the Uyghur House and Gaochang House continued enrollment and teaching of their languages. In the eyes of the Ming government, if Persian was still very useful and practical then it was not necessary to use the Uyghur language as the official language to communicate with the Western Regions. This showed that the Ming government had ignored the fact that the written language in the Central Asian had changed from Uyghur to Chagatai language. And the literature preserved till today indicates that during nearly 100 years under the reign of the Ming dynasty, the documents written by the Ming government, which were addressed to the kingdoms of the Western Regions were written in Persian and Uyghur, despite the fact that Uyghur language has gradually left the historical stage since the 16th century.

A few remaining documents from the countries of the Western Regions to Ming Dynasty after mid Ming Dynasty period and some other documents concerning the Western regions were gathered and kept in the Documentary Archive of Uyghur Museum and Documents of Gaochang (Karahoja) Museum. These documents are generally written in Persian and Uyghur, and none of them was written in Chagatai language.

During the reign of Cin Khwar, since the Ming government could translate such kind of "Gaochang dialect, Uyghur script and regional language", then it could be concluded that some of the mainland people has understood the ChagataiKhanate language at that time. Information from the Ethnic House showed that the staff in Uyghur House was involved in the translation of documents from other nationalities. It is estimated by the scholars that after the "Gaochang dialect, Uyghur script and regional language" was adopted from the Western regions, Uyghur House and Gaochang House interpreters studied them together and discovered that such kind of documents were expressed in Gaochang dialect.

Inheriting the literature preserved in the Ethnic House, the Qing Dynasty took over the literature of the Ethnic House of the Ming Dynasty and continued teaching of the Persian and Uyghur languages that were still used in official correspondence among the rulers of the Western Regions. In the early decades of the Qing Dynasty, the letters to Western regions written by the Qing Dynasty were not written properly, which was also the case in the late Ming Dynasty period, i.e, the little-known Uyghur language was used. The reason was that before the reign of Emperor Kangxi, people knew little about the Western Regions, so they had no choice but to follow the old practices of Ming Dynasty.

During the reign of Emperor Qianlong (25 September 1711-7 February 1799), Uyghur and Persian were no longer the official language of the Qing government and the Western Regions. In the last years of Emperor Qianlong's reign, several voluminous books compiled and published by the government were all written in Chagatai Khanate language instead of Persian and Uyghur such as Wu Ti Qing Wen Jian and "A survey of Geography and Figures of the Western Region". From these facts, we can see that after the Qing dynasty's battles with the Dzungar Khanate (1687-1757) and after suppression of the rebellions by the Three Feudatories the relationships between the mainland China and the Northwest regions was greatly enhanced.[29]

In this new period, the Qing government finally realized that the Chagatai Khanate language had become the most popular language in the Western regions.

(3) Chang Zhimei and His Book Minhaj al-Talab

In the summer of 1978, Iranian scholar Abu Talib Mir Abidini collected data in Beijing in order to accomplish the work of compilation and proof reading of the "Persian Dictionary". When he attended the ceremony in the Mosque of Dongsi, he found that there were three copies of Persian works with the same content, and he said that he had never heard of these three books before. The title was Minhaj al Talaib, and its translation was the "learning approach". The author called himself as "Mohamed, the son of Zinimi, a Chinese scholar from Shandong".[30]

Old texts such as "Zashia,da-fawat and qandil namah" as well as recently printed books such as "Manasik-i kamil-i islam" which are preserved till today consist texts and interpretations of Islamic rituals in Persian. These rites and expressions were learnt and practiced by heart. Many of the terms used in these texts as well as Persian words were borrowed by and included into the Chinese language.

In traditional Islam teaching centres such as Xinjiang, Shandong and Shaanxi, Persian has been the primarily taught language. The spread and current usage of the Persian language among Chinese Islams and Non-Islams has been studied widely by Chinese researchers.

Quoted below are two quotations from two famous Islam scholars which give an insight into why Persian manuscripts were so widespread and used in China. These two well-known scholars of fiqh (Fıkıh/interpreters) who had lived in two different eras, three hundred years apart, and their statements relevant to the point in question confirm the continuity of the use of Persian language as the first and initial religious and cultural language among China's Islams. Among the first generation scholars, Muhammad ibn Hakim Zinini,

---

29   The Dzungar-Qing Wars (1687-1757) were a decades-long series of conflicts that pitted the Dzungar Khanate against the Qing dynasty of China and their Mongolian vassals.

30   Zinimi is expressed as Zeynami in the Persian language

the founder of the Shandong Centre of Islamic traditional learning, in his book "Minhaj al-talib" which he wrote in the year 1070 Islam Lunar Calender/1660 AD, said: "In China most of the texts of fiqh, tasawwuf and tafsir are written in Persian and a scholar of fiqh in order to understand the religious texts has no other choice than to learn Persian properly, because if a problem arises in connection with the religious matters which requires a fatwa-(legal opinion) how can one cope with the problem, if he does not know Persian properly?"

The other scholar, Muhammad Nur al-Haqq ibn Luqman al-Sini, a renowned scholar of fiqh of the Shanxi Islamic teaching centre in the last half of the 19th century, in his work "Kimiya" said: Since China is close to the Persian land (Iran) and since most of our ancestors are originally Persian the Persian books on fiqh,tafsir,tauhid (tevhid) and tasawwuf are numerous in China. It is inevitable that students of Islam and the beginners need to learn the Persian language."

The book "Minhaj al-Talab" was completed in January-February 1660 AD, was a Persian grammar book in terms of its content. (in the 1st month of the 17th year of emperor Shunzhi of the Qing Dynasty)

The Persian scholar Mir Abedini believed that this Persian textbook written by ancient Chinese scholars was very valuable, so he copied it and took it back to Iran. Then he sorted out the revised the old texts after examining the above three copies, and published the book in the city of Isfahan (Iran) in 1981, written by Mohamed, son of scholar Zinimi, edited by Dr. Abu Talib Mir Abedini Minhaj al-talab, (The oldest book on the grammar of Persian Language) Kuhantarin Dastur-i Zaban-i Farsi, Muhammad b. Al Hakimal Zinimi, bakushishi Duktur Muhammad Jawad Shir't, Isfahan, publishing date, (1360 Iranian Calender/1981 AD.).

After examining the related teaching books, he found that this was the oldest Persian grammar book written in Persian in the world. In fact, the book Learning Approach was widely introduced among the Hui nationality, and was kept in many mosques.

Learning Approach was actually the book titled as "Mi Nuo Ha Zhi" written by the famous scholar Chang Zhimei in the late Ming and early Qing Dynasty period, which was one of the language teaching materials in folk Islam scripture department during Ming and Qing Dynasties. But the word "Zinimi" in the following text "the son of Mohammed, Zinimi a scholar from Shandong, China" is probably an because, Zinin means Jining, Shandong, and Zinini means the Jining people. The son of Mohammed, Chang Zhimei had long presided over the Shandong mosque in Jining, so he saw himself as a member of Jining people.

The book Minhaj al-talab (Learning Approach) was divided into two chapters. The first part consists of the following sections: irregular verbs, infinitive, past tense, subordinate and negative form, future tense, imperative mood and negative imperative mood, active nouns and passive nouns, and adjectives, etc.

Its content was as follows: the author divided the Persian vocabulary into three categories, nouns, verbs, and functional words. Such classification was obviously influenced by the traditional Arabic grammatical system and did not correspond with the actual word class in Persian. In the category of verbs, the author makes a detailed description and discussion of its changing rules. He divided them into four groups according to the similarities and differences between corresponding person forms of past and future tense of the Persian verbs:

Group 1 refers to the verbs with exactly the same past and the future form, but the pronunciation was different.

Group 2 refers to the verbs that stem's number of letters in its past tense was less than that of in the future tense.

Group 3 is the opposite of Group 2, refers to the verbs that stem's number of letters in its past tense was more than that of in the future tense.

Group 4 refers to the verbs with different stems of the past and future tense, which is actually strong irregular verbs.

And then the first chapter discussed transitive verbs and intransitive verbs. The infinitive section described root verbs, derived nouns, and same-rooted adjectives, etc. It should be noted that Chang Zhimei in the use of the above grammatical terms, sometimes its meaning is not equivalent to its current meaning. For example, the infinitive in Chang Zhimei's grammar system was a very broad concept, and was not equal to the root verb. Later, the author described active past tense, passive past tense and its negative form, future tense verb, imperative mood and negative imperative mood. Chang Zhimei was influenced by the traditional Arabic grammar, so he divided the imperative mood into two categories: Hazir and ghayab, the second person and third person imperative mood. His commentary on the word "say" before the second verb was particularly noticeable. The author then introduced active nouns and passive nouns. The last chapter was on adjectives. He divided adjectives into three categories: derivational adjectives, such as "rawan", means "fluent", "guya", means "good at speech"; "muzu", that is, the so-called root adjectives; "murarkab", such as "nikkhuy", means "good temper", and "mahruy", means "looks like the moon".

The second chapter included the nouns section, verbs section, functional words section and the conclusion.

The content of noun chapter was very complicated. Chang Zhimei defined nouns as words that indicate their own meaning and have no concept of time. Noun was characterized by being able to act as subject, predicate, actor and behavior object. In subject and predicate sections, the author described personal suffix of verb, the correspondence relations between verb and subject and so on. After that, he introduced the action performer, attached parts verbs and so on. Afterwards, he also discussed the position of the object, occasion for the appearance and talked about the absence of accusative verbs' marker "ra", central words as well as modifier, etc.

The content of functional word section was also very rich, including harf-i izafa, conjunctions, pishwand, puswand and some adverbs.

The author discussed the differences between Arabic and Persian, as well as many common words, in these two languages, such as the relative pronoun "ka", pronouns "an" and "in", adverbs "chun", "ta", and "ham", "ast", the third person singular of linking verb "budan" in present tense, etc.

On the scale, the book Minhaj al Taleb has included most of the grammatical rules of the Persian written language. However, because the whole book was all about grammar, so a beginner could not learn Persian with it. This was probably one of the reasons for the poor teaching effect of Persian of Hui nationality in scripture halls.

Introduction of the Chinese Art to the West

In the 11th century, the Turkic speaking people of the Central Asia moved to the West, and a Western Turkic tribe settled in Persia and founded dynasty there. During this period the pottery industry in Persia witnessed a new development, and the Persian potters mixed sand into clay. The alteration of the pottery's raw materials has made the pottery more exquisite, and its shape mostly imitated the porcelain of Song Dynasty.

In the Yuan Dynasty, with the unprecedented political connection between the Central Plains and the Western regions, the art of the Central Plains was introduced into the Western regions on a large scale. The aesthetic view of the Han deeply influenced the Western regions, images of lotus, peony, phoenix, flying crane were generally accepted by Persian and its surrounding region, and these images were frequently used in their painting, textiles and utensils.

After the demise of the Yuan Dynasty, the Central Plains and the Western regions did not sever their relations. On the contrary, there was a new upsurge of East-West cultural and artistic exchanges. The handle of pottery, metal and gem utensils, which were decorated with the image of dragon in Central Plains, appeared in large numbers in Persia and its surrounding region.

The Ming people called Ottoman Empire in the West of Asia as "Lu Mi". The name "Lu Mi" came from Rom, namely Rome. This was the traditional name for Byzantine Empire (East Rome) called by the Turkic speaking people in Central Asia. After the replacement of Byzantium by the Ottoman Empire, people continued to call it "Lu Mi". Ottoman Empire was very fond of Ming Dynasty porcelain, and royal kings, princes as well as the nobility all collected Chinese porcelain. In1478, Ottoman Sultan Mehmed II built the Topkapi Palace in Istanbul, the most distinctive collection of this palace was Chinese porcelain. There were more than 10,000 pieces of porcelains of Song, Yuan, Ming and Qing Dynasties in the palace, including blue and white platter and big bowl at the late Yuan and early Ming Dynasties, and various celadons during Yuan and Ming Dynasties. Here was the largest collection of overseas Chinese ancient porcelain. The palace had a blue and white porcelain bowl of Ming Dynasty with the whole text of Ode of Chibi and drawing of tour in Chibi. It was note-worthy that, Ottoman craftsmen had added gold and silver trim, rabbet, bottom and handle with rich national characteristics on Chinese porcelain. Researchers found that the gold and silver wrap on Chinese porcelains was not for the pur-pose of decoration, but for the reuse of these porcelains, because these Chinese porcelains had different degrees of defects. This also proved Chinese porcelain was extremely precious at that time.

In order to meet the market demand for Chinese blue and white porce-lain, Ottoman Empire large-scale made copies of the blue and white pottery on a large scale. Iznik on the Little Asia Peninsula, which was the major city Nicaea in Byzantine Empire, has become an important producing region of blue and white pottery. In the 16th century, Ottoman Empire defeated Persia and countries on the East coast of Mediterranean, thereby reducing the barri-ers for Chinese goods entering its land and thus the Chinese porcelain demand by the upper class was eased. However, Iznik city of Byzantine still produced blue and white pottery, and the character and price of its products were conve-nient for the mass consumption. During this period, blue and white pottery in Ottoman and in Persian al-Safawiyyah developed synchronously. It was deeply influenced by Xuande porcelain, and was capable of producing large diameter plate with underglaze color technique.

Chinese arts was long introduced to the West of Asia. In 751, Tang dynas-ty was defeated by the Arabs in Central Asia, as a result, a large number of Chinese officials and soldiers were captured. These Chinese people were taken to Arab centers, including a man named Du Huan who was the nephew of Du You (author of Tong Dian). He saw a Chinese painter was drawing picture in an Arab capital. In the 10th century, Mad'udi, a famous Arab geographer, once mentioned in his writings that a Chinese was selling his drawings in the market. The drawing was painted on a silk, a bird standing on a grass. The painting was shown at the market fair for a long time, and each passing man was amazed at how lively the Chinese painting was. However, only one man strongly belittled this painting, so the Chinese painter took the man to Sultan and asked him where he did not paint well. This man pointed out that everybody knew that the birds could not live on the upright grass, because the weight of the birds would bend grass. Therefore, the Chinese painter made a second drawing. This time, the grass was straight and the bird was flying in the air. The story recorded by Mad'udi showed that Chinese painting was introduced to West Asia in the late Tang and early Song Dynasties, and was appreciated by the local people. Later, experts in art history studied the records and believed it to be reliable, because birds were one of the main themes of excellent painting works in the Song Dynasty period. Arabia was later divided, and the ruler of Egypt was the Fatima dynasty. During this period, there was a genre called "Fatima school" in the Arab painting, which was deeply influenced by Chinese painting style.[31]

31   F.R. Martin: The Miniature Painting and Painters of Persia India and Turkey from the 8th to the 18th Century, Vol. 1, London, 1912, p. 6.

The painting art of Persia and China have developed independently. Chinese paintings were not heavy in their coloring, while Persian painting art was highly colorful. After the Mongolian era, there were several new phenomena in Persian painting: the emergence of a large number of Chinese and Mongolian characters in the painting, which reflecting the historical reality that Persian Yili Khanate was once served as the vassal state of the Yuan Dynasty; the emergence of unique patterns of the Central Plains in Persian paintings, such as the imaginary animals like dragon and phoenix, which reflecting the depth and breadth of cultural exchanges between the Central Plains and the Western regions at that time; Chinese painting techniques were introduced into the Western regions, and Chinese aesthetic view of art also influenced Persian artists, so there appeared works painted by only Chinese writing brush in Persia. Persian meticulous painting was greatly influenced by that of Han painting, so art historians believed that "Chinese painting was the father of Persian meticulous painting".[32]

Both the existing Chinese and Persian materials showed that Hongwu and Yongle dynasties witnessed the closest relationship between China in the Ming Dynasty and Persia. During this period, many paintings of the Timur Dynasty were copied by Chinese paintings. These copied paintings were called "Timur School" in the history of Islam painting. Persian painters believed that the originator of Timur School was Ustadi Gung, and he was a dumb. His name was very similar to a Chinese name, but he was probably treated as dumb because he did not knew Persian. There is rare information about him, and one of his students has been Ustadi Jahangir, who was a very famous scholar in Bukhara.[33]

There was little information about the interactions between the Ming Dynasty and the Al–Safawiyyah (Safawiyah Dynasty), but the Isfahan city, ruled by the Shah (king) Abbas, the ruler of Safawiyah Dynasty, was deeply influenced by the social atmosphere of the Ming Dynasty. For example, in the aspect of clothing, women from upper class imitated the women of Ming Dynasty; while in the aspect of painting, local painters has copied works from the Song and Yuan Dynasties.[34] The themes of the book ranged from flowers and birds to scholars and maids.

Conclusion

Before the Neolithic Age, mankind was engaged for long hours just for producing the subsistence materials it needed. Every kind of foodstuff which the men could obtain from the nature, whether it was hunted or collected was just sufficient for the reproduction of men. We can say though different in their or in dwelling regions of the world, there was not much difference among them

---

32 Ibid., p. 19.
33 Ibid., p. 28.
34 E. Blochet: Musulman Painting from 12th to 17th Century. Its original was French. Cicely M. Banyon's English translation: Islam Painting, 12th to 17th Century, London, pp. 62-63.

in the aspects of their production modes and lifestyles. With the advance of the times, the mode of human production has undergone tremendous changes. Mankind developed from collection mode to agriculture in the regions with abundant rain and favorable climate, meanwhile they have surpassed hunting and embarked animal husbandry production in the grassland regions with less precipitation.

The history of the exchanges and struggles between the agricultural people and the nomadic peoples runs through the history of the major countries in Eurasia. And the nomadic people on the Eurasian grassland were not only the main participants in the history of the Eurasian continent, but also served as the intermediary actors in cultural exchanges between East and West. While Grassland Silk Road, was one of the main channels for national intercourse between East and West before the emergence of modern means of transportation and transit lines. Today, China has entered an unprecedented period of national harmony. Currently, the historically recurrent confrontation between the nomadic and settled agricultural peoples no longer exists, and grasslands nationalities from both the grasslands of Inner Mongolia and people dwelling in the Tianshan region have all become equal members of the big family of Chinese nation. Dairy product, a traditional food of grassland nomads, has become a favorable food among the urban and rural people all over the country. Leather and fur, the livestock products produced by the grassland people, have become the major raw materials used in the tailoring of the costumes dressed by the numerous ethnic peoples of China. Tea, vegetables and fruits of the Han nationality as well as industrial products from the mainland China have greatly enriched the lives of the grassland people. There were also a large number of Han people who had migrated to the Northwest border regions and built border regions with local minority nationalities.

Since 1990s, the international situation has undergone a series of radical changes. After the disintegration of the Soviet Union, some of the central Asian republics as part of the former Soviet Union have become independent countries, and their relations with China has developed rapidly. In addition, the Republic of Mongolia has also become a friendly neighbor of our country. The Inner Mongolia railway, built in 1950s, has become vibrant again, and it was also extended to the East line of the new grassland Silk Road. Besides, the westward extension project of Lanxin Railway (Lanzhou-Xinjiang Railway) has been completed, which was connected with the railway network of Kazakhstan, and has become a component part of the new Silk Road.

Grassland Silk Road has benefited Asian people in history, and it still has its meaning in today and in the future. We have entered a new century, and the world will change in the future. China will become one of the world's leading industrial powers in a few decades, and China's influence on world affairs will change dramatically. Mongolia and several Central Asian republics along the Silk Road including the former Soviet Union, Kazakhstan, Kyrgyzstan, Uzbekistan, Tajikistan and Turkmenistan have a common feature: a vast territory with a small population and abundant resources. However, these countries are all far from the center of the world's major industry, and they do not have their own sea port. In the new century, they will form a new relationship with China. That is, China will become the main supplier of their industrial products, and our country will also become the main market of their agriculture, animal husbandry and mining primary products. So the new Grassland Silk Road will become a link between our country and these neighbors, and it will continue to benefit our children and grandchildren.

PART TWO

THE MARITIME SILK ROAD

Introduction

Today, most of the learned people in the world have become familiar with the word "Silk Road". In the book launch gathering of the English version of the book titled as "The Stories of the Silk Roads (authored by Sanjiva Wijesinha, Stories of the Silk Route, Sri Lanka, 1991), a child named Vijay Sinha, asked the following question to author: "is the silk road entirely paved in silk?" To answer this seemingly simple question, we need a brief overview on the development of silk production, as well as its distribution network reaching to the West.

The earliest inhabitants of the Central Plains discovered that wild Lepidoptera could spin cocoons throughout its life. The silk extracted from these cocoon could be used as raw material for textile production. People, therefore began taming the insects, which became known as a silkworm. According to Chinese ancient literature, Leizu, the legendary ancestor of the Chinese nation, had personally started the sericulture production, and taught people the silkworm breeding methods. Emerging facts indicate that, probably people were trained about the sericulture technology, but invented and developed over time by many people. In 1926, archaeologists discovered a knife used for cutting cocoons in lime ridge Neolithic sites of West Yin Village, Xia County in Shanxi city of China, indicating that silkworm already existed. Early residents of Jiangnan had already begun sericulture production about 5,000 years ago, this can be proven by a small piece of silk cloth unearthed in the Wuxing Qianshan site near Zhejiang city.

Chinese silk products—light and colorful—were long popular abroad, and they were traded as far as to Europe. Greeks called China "Seres", which meant "the land of silk." The Roman civilization which rose after the Greek one, called the silk, as the "cloth of Seres country" or "yarn of Seres country". In the 19th Century, German historical geographer Ferdinand von Richthofen, 1833-1905) proposed to call the route extending from East to the far West as the "Silk Road" (die Seidenstrasse). The name "quickly spread and gained acceptance among the scholars and the people all over the world. It is still used currently and has gradually become synonymous with ancient cultural exchanges between the East and the West.

1. Brief Overview of the Maritime Silk Road

China is the genesis of the Silk Road. The country is located in the East of the Eurasian continent, which is connected to Africa through a narrow isthmus between the Mediterranean and the Red Sea. Eurasia and Africa are called the old continent because they are the cradle of human civilization. From 5000 BC to 3000 BC, independent civilization centers sprouted in several regions in the old continent. The ancient Egyptian civilization, in the middle and lower reaches of the Nile basin in the North of Africa, Mesopotamia civilization between the Euphrates and Tigris rivers, which is an ancient civilization found in the middle reaches of India River in Pakistan and the ancient civilization along the Yellow and Yangtze River in China. In the middle of these ancient civilizations, there were tiny spots of human communities, which had some interconnections with each other. So these centers of civilizations have developed independently, but at the same time, they have nurtured each other directly or indirectly. If we speak about the civilization in the Pacific Ocean region which lies in the East and South of China, there was no other important civilization center apart from the Chinese civilization.

The Silk Road bond has grown from mutual attraction among different civilizations. China's civilization started along the Yellow River and the Yangtze River Basin while other civilizations settled across the mountains, deserts, big rivers and the sea. The distance was wide and the expeditions among them were difficult. The distance to other civilizations was farther than the distance among the other three civilization hubs. On the contrary, the Indus civilization in Pakistan region was very close to Persian Gulf along the sea route, so it had long-cultivated contacts with ancient Mesopotamian civilization. Mesopotamia and Egypt were close, so there was a very candid connection between the two civilizations.

The Asia continent is surrounded by seas on the eastern, southern and northern directions. There has been a vast expanse of the Pacific Ocean to the east, the Indian Ocean on the south while the Arctic Ocean lies on the north. The Arctic Ocean is quite far from the Yellow River and the Yangtze River Basin, its frozen state during the most part of the year makes the maritime navigation difficult. Consequently, the Pacific and the Indian Ocean remain to be the key maritime routes for the early Asian inhabitants.

Around the eastern part of ancient China lie the supplementary seas of the Pacific Ocean: the Sea of Japan, Bohai Sea, the Yellow Sea, the East China Sea and the South China Sea. The rivers flowing to the seas from inland China, such as the Heilongjiang River, Liao River, the Yellow River, Huai River, Yangtze River, Pearl River, Lancang River and Nu River provided natural sea transport channels for the Chinese people living in inland regions to interact with their neighbors along these rivers.

Geographically China could possibly become an isolated region of Eurasia, but due to the mutual bonds between the ancient civilizations made up of small communities, indirect exchanges between East and West begun early. The Chinese already knew there existed a rich civilization in the West, the legend of the queen mother of the West denotes the yearn for other Western civilization. So despite the distance, human communities have overcome hardships and undertaken risks to communicate with each other.

There are thousands of islands near the East Asian continent along the ocean, such as Japan, Philippines, Indonesia and others. Before the middle ages, islands of Southeast Asia were seen as barbarian regions by the Chinese. Interestingly, it's the natural foothold of ancient mankind in navigation activities of Western Pacific and North Indian Ocean. Following the development of the sea navigation technology, the islands became important markers to navigate through while pinpointing the route and served as relay stations to provide expedition supplies. Thousands of Islands which lie in the West Pacific and Indian Ocean enabled humans to successfully sail with underdeveloped technology. Ancient Chinese seamen mainly used islands to navigate, making them geographical coordinates that determine routes.

In pre-historic times, China's coastal residents would reach across to offshore islands and Southeast Asia. The East coast of China runs from South to North, so Chinese navigators knew that sailing East could get you to Japan, and South to Southeast Asia. Inhabitants of Eastern China coastal regions closely mingled with the Japanese and North Koreans using the Yellow Sea. The coastal residents living in Southern China Sea also had close links to Southeast Asia

During the period around the late Tang Dynasty, the Chinese islands from Southeast Asia to Indian Ocean were divided into "eastern" and "western" by the Chinese. There are several descriptions of "eastern" and "western" in ancient history, modern scholars have also done in-depth studies on the geographical concept of "eastern" and "western", but none of them understand the division fully. There were two main routes for ancient Chinese navigator to Southeast Asia; one by departing from coastal ports of Fujian and Guangdong, cross the East China Sea towards Taiwan or Luzon (Philippines), and along Philippines to the South, to an island called Borneo. The route along the Western Pacific Islands was called the "eastern". The other one is from the China coast, along the mainland China's southern coast, across the Indochina Peninsula. The regions crossed were called "western". The dividing line between the east and the west is the South China Sea. Therefore, the "eastern" and "western" mainly refers to the South China Sea region which is not far from Chinese mainland.

One of the main islands found in Southeast Asia is "Kunlun," wherein mainly by the Malays and other indigenous peoples had dwelled. In ancient time, these peoples have perfected the art of sailing. There was cultural contact among the Malays, the subcontinent of India and East of African continent. Chinese voyage to India was realized with the help of these peoples. As mentioned before, the Indian sub-continent and the Persian Gulf had traditional maritime links, so maritime expedition between China and West Asia could have also received a boost from India and West Asia. Although there were a few long routes in ancient times, and the main form of sailing was by using the baton. With the development of navigation technology, more and more long and direct navigation were attempted.

Land routes were the primary transportation channel between China and the West. The main transportation mode was by using horses or camels. Using these livestock animals limited the load and increased the costs. In addition, natural conditions were tough and expedition security was a major problem. So when the marine navigation technology was developed, the water became a more preferred transport channel between the East and West. After the great geographical discoveries in the 15th century, the sea gradually replaced land.

The maritime Silk Road was a thoroughfare of friendly material exchange for ancient communities. Before the Tang Dynasty, silk and gold was the main export products overseas for China, namely "taking gold and other treasures to go" in "History of Han Geographica".

The fine quality and high price of Chinese silk made it difficult for people in the West to easily acquire and buy it. After years of research, the Eastern Roman Empire (Byzantine) finally learned the silk production process and initiated silk industry in the Eastern Roman Empire. Silk was one of the main tax items in the Chinese Tang Dynasty, in order to secure the treasury income, in the 1st year of the reign of Emperor Dezong of Tang, all kinds of brocade and silk trading in the market was banned.[1]

It is just at this time that Changsha's kiln porcelain, southern China's celadon, north China's Sancai porcelain, Xing Zhou white ceramic production ware had developed rapidly. These fine porcelains easily found demand in the overseas markets. Porcelain is different from silk; it is cumbersome and fragile and so sea transport was the most preferred way of trade. It soon became one of the main export commodities of China. In the recent decades, ceramic fragments from the Tang dynasty period were found by archaeologists in the following regions; east to Japan, and South to Brunei and Sarawak of Southeast Borneo, Pahang of Malaysia, blue slope of Thailand and India River of Pakistan on the Malay Peninsula, West to Fustad in Cairo, Egypt and more than 70 sites

---

1   History of Ming Dynasty, Vol. 4 B, p. 999.

in East Africa. After the arrival of Chinese porcelain in overseas ports, it was rapidly moved to other regions through various distribution channels by local merchants. This trend continued to expand with a large number of Chinese porcelain being exported after the Song Dynasty. Large quantities of porcelain were found in different overseas locations that originated from the Song, Yuan, Ming and Qing Dynasties. The worldwide sales network of Chinese porcelain existed for almost a millennium. Good quality products directly affected overseas ceramics development and the pursuit of China porcelain became a prosperous venture, so that overseas countries gradually saw these wares as setting the bar for ceramic quality standards, resulting to a large number of imitations. A "Thai celadon" was created in Thailand, similar to Chinese kiln, but it was rougher. West Asian countries struggled for years only to fail in producing porcelain. A large number of underglaze blue-and white potteries were produced, which imitated Chinese blue-and-white porcelain, in order to meet people's psychological demand for Chinese blue-and-white porcelain. Although, Germany has finally discovered the secret of porcelain production in modern times, Chinese ancient porcelain was still regarded as precious products in the foreign countries.

After the great geographical discovery, a large number of Europeans came to the East. In addition to silk and porcelain trading, the drinking culture of Chinese tea found export value. The trend of tea drinking rose rapidly in the United Kingdom, which soon became the world's largest importer of tea. To reduce the trade deficit, the British introduced tea planting in the British colony of India. Despite local tea production increasing rapidly over the years, India and Sri Lanka have become leading global exporters of the beverage.

Trade is a two-way street. With Chinese traditional export commodities marketing overseas, some goods in foreign countries came back to China and spices were the main commodities. Overseas spice input has a long history; storax was mentioned in literature during the Han Dynasty. Incense wood in Rinan County and India, tulip in Kophen, storax in Parthia, pistacia lentiscus in Daqin were carried to China by merchants around the world in Northern and Southern Dynasties. The increasing import volume of spiced made it a daily consuming product from luxurious. In the Song Dynasty, spice tax alone accounted for 10% of the total revenue. Certainly, in addition to spices, textiles, medicine, glass, gold and silver were also introduced to China.

The Peoplesin the old continent not only exchanged material culture but spiritual too through the sea Silk Road. Buddhism in India, Hinduism, Manichaeism in West Asia, Judaism and Islam, Catholicism and Christianity spread to China successively. India's linguistics and ephemeris science from India and Arab have exerted great influence in China. For over 2,000 years, Chinese culture formed a strong vitality cultural circle in East Asia, with a scope of Japan in the North and Vietnam in the South, China's compass, painting, historical knowledge, paper currency were all introduced to the countries in the old continent.

All in all, the maritime Silk Road acts as the main channel of the Eastern and Western cultural exchanges before the Western colonialism. In addition to the Crusades and the conquest of Mongolia overseas, the maritime route between East and West was basically a route of peace. The long years of exchanges in the history have proved that the Chinese and other ethnic peoples in the old continent have both benefited significantly, from these exchanges. Exploring and reviewing this history is not only beneficial in educating people about the glorious past and bright future of Chinese civilization and culture, but also conducive for enhancing mutual understanding in the global human society and for the promotion of human progress and world peace.

UNESCO has planned to implement a ten-year-plan of Silk Road Expedition from 1987 to 1997, known as the "Integral Study of the Silk Roads: Roads of Dialogue." When, its official name was being discussed in the formulation of this plan, some scholars have proposed that spice, porcelain and other objects form the bulk commodities between ancient East and West maritime trade route, thus impressing that the maritime trade route between East and West should be called "spice road" or "porcelain road".

But other scholars have argued that in addition to commodity exchanges there existed cultural exchanges that included. Buddhism, Zoroastrianism, Nestorianism (in "Cihai" region it was called Daqin, but Western historians called it as "Nestorian Christianity" and in this book we call it Nestorian." The

spread of Islam religion, and the westward dissemination of China's paper-making technology, printing, and the compass and gun-powder using weapons are also component part of cultural exchanges. If the name is changed to "spice road" or "porcelain road," it may limit the meaning of the project itself. Only the name "Silk Road" contains both the rich content of the material and cultural exchanges between the East and West, which is affirmed widely by scholars globally, consequently the name was adopted by UNESCO eventually and has become the official name of the project. This project has received positive response from the governments of many countries and non-governmental organizations.

Appointed by the Chinese government, I have participated in the maritime Silk Road investigation activities which specifically studied the route from Venice, Italy to the Guangzhou as a Chinese expert. I started from Beijing in October 20, 1990, entered Guangzhou in February 9, 1991, and then moved to Quanzhou, Fujian to participate in activities, which lasted nearly four months coupled with a voyage of more than 21,000 km.. In the second stage of the investigations, it started from Oman Muscat to Colombo. I was elected as deputy leader of the scientific communications commission, from Colombo to India Madras; I also served as the commission leader. And I have lived for more than three months with different scholars from several countries, and visited more than 10 countries.

During my researches, I have become further convinced that Chinese civilization is indeed an ancient civilization with glorious history and splendid culture. It has a prominent culture and civilization among others in the world, and has spread its influence throughout the Maritime Silk Road. There is no other country in the world like China which has preserves such wealth of cultural written cultural and civilizational material, the Chinese ancient books have recorded all the countries and regions we have passed by. This fact has impressed the peer scholars from all around the world, whether from developed countries or from the Third World countries, who have expressed their deep admiration on the splendid culture our ancestors have created. Passing Sri Lanka to the East, especially in Southeast Asia, Chinese ancient Dynasty calendar, such as the Tang Dynasty, Five Dynasties, Song Dynasty, Yuan Dynasty, Ming Dynasty and Qing Dynasty, has been praised by the scholars from all over the world. Even though many of them have little knowledge about the Chinese language, yet they are conversant in the use of reign titles like "Yongle emperor" or "Kangxi emperor" of China. Therefore, we can surmise by saying that those who do not understand Chinese history and culture cannot study the Silk Road comprehensively, nor can they study Asian history, especially the history of India and Southeast Asia.

In all the countries we have traveled through, Chinese ancient ceramics could be seen everywhere. For centuries, Chinese have advanced the porcelain technology. Chinese porcelain had become popular in the numerous countries of the world and constituted the main bulk commodity in China's exports. This has led to jokingly remarks made by some scholars: "the ancient Chinese celadon and blue-and-white porcelain had the best quality, but gained the lowest price! Its popularity in those ancient times was similar to Japan's household appliances brands such as the Sanyo and Toshiba". China has played a critical role in the ancient world, and many of the major events in Chinese history have been important factors which have influenced the world history at that time. During the research expedition, I have noticed that China has been included in all of the 16 forums which were part of the research process. Along the expedition, after we left the border of Egypt, discussions were centered on Zheng He, who is known as "admiral Zheng" in the foreign academia.

2. The Discourse of Overseas "Barbarians" in the Chinese Historical Records

China has a long history of studying overseas peoples. China has the most historical records in the world. There are abundant records about the history of the Maritime Silk Road in the Chinese historical records. It is recorded in the "Bamboo Annals" that emperor Mang of Xia Dynasty ordered Jiuyi to catch big fish in the sea. The Chinese words of "xiang shi lie lie, hai wai you jie" in the "Shang Song" part of "The History of Songs" show that the influence of the merchants of the Xia Dynasty has reached beyond the Bohai Sea or Yellow Sea. The systematic and detailed record of overseas peoples by Chinese was first seen in Han Dynasty. The ancient Chinese divided the world into several states, which was not based on the round earth theory. Traditionally, the Chinese people name the overseas nationalities by regions. The people lived in the region East of China including Korea and Japan were called "Dongyi"; the people of Southeast Asia were generally called "Nanman;" the people of India and Pakistan subcontinent were called "Tianzhu" or "Yindu"; the people of Persian Gulf, Arabia Peninsula and East Africa were called "Dashi" and the people of Mediterranean coastal regions were called "Daqin", "Xiyu", "Dashi" and "Uyghur" respectively. This ancient Chinese classification was roughly based on sea routes and lasted until the Western colonialism reached Chinese shores.

The last paragraph of "Dilizhi: Yuedi" of "History of Han," China's first biographical dynastic history book, recorded the sea route from Han Empire's Southern shores to Indian Ocean: the ships started the journey from "zhang sai" of "rinan" (current Quang Tri province of Vietnam), "Xuwen" (current Xuwen county of Guangdong province) and "Hepu" (current Hepu county of Guangxi province)through Southeast Asia waters and reached "Huangzhi" (current Madras of India), which was called "Jian zhi bu luo" in Tang Dynasty, and "ji cheng bu guo" (current Sri Lanka). This is the earliest systematic record of maritime links between China and Southeast Asia and South Asia. The Han Dynasty interpreters could handle the language translations during the voyages without problem. The traditional business languages of the regions East of Indian Ocean were the ancient Tamil (originally Dravidian) of India and Bahasa Melayu Kuno of South Asia. It is quite probable that the Han Dynasty interpreters have mastered the two languages.

The ancient Chinese called the Mediterranean eastern coastal regions of Roman Empire as the "Lixuan," "Daqin," "Haixi" and "Folin". The name "Lixuan" first appeared in the "Treatise on the Dayuan" of the "Records of the Grand Historian," which was written by Sima Qian. "Lixuan" is current Alexandria Port of Egypt. According to Sima Qian's records, envoy of the Western Han Dynasty visited "Lixuan." The acrobats of "Lixuan" entered Han through Parthia. Du You of Tang Dynasty described the looks of the people of "Lixuan" in the "Bian Fang Niu" part of his book "Tong Dian" as having frowned eyebrow, steep nose and tendrils of hair. "Alisan" is the transliteration of "Lixuan." It is narrated in the book "Milindapanha" that the King Milinda of Bactria said, he was born in "Daqin" (Roman Empire), which country's name was "Ailisan", and which is current Alexanderia of Egypt.

"Daqin" was in the west of Red Sea or Mediterranean Sea so it was also called "Haixiguo", whose literal meaning is a country adjacent to a sea and located in the West. People of the Eastern Han Dynasty already knew the sea route from Persia to Red Sea. Ban Chao, while governing the Western Regions, sent his envoy Gan Ying to "Daqin" in 97 AD Gan Ying only reached as far as "Tiaozhi" because the sailor people of Parthia strongly warned him the danger of crossing the sea, which is obviously the current Persian Gulf. There was a sea route linking the Persian Gulf and Egypt, which was at the north tip of the Red Sea. The exchanges between "Daqin" and Han Dynasty were mentioned in the "Western Regions" part of the "History of the Later Han Period." The merchants of "Daqin" hoped to directly deal with the Han Dynasty merchants, but the Persian traders as the middlemen traders were worried about the risk of losing their monopoly position on the trade of Chinese silk to Europe. The book "Biographies of the Southern and Southwestern Barbarians" mentioned that the people of "Daqin" reached Han through "Danguo", which is current Myanmar, in 120 AD. It also mentioned that Marcus Aurelius Antoninus, king of "Daqin" sent envoy to pay tributes to Han through "Rinan" in 166 AD. The historical records show the hardships experienced by the Roman merchants while they explored sea routes to China through Persia, India and Southeast Asia.

Pei Songzhi made annotations to the "Records of the Three Kingdoms" written by Chen Shou during the reign of Emperor Wen of Southern Song. More than 150 references were cited in his book, but unfortunately many of these original books are now lost. The "Weilue, Xirongzhuan" part of the "Wu Wan Xian Bei Dong Yi Zhuan" mentioned that "Daqin" traded for Chinese silk with countries like Parthia in the sea. Due to the preciousness of the Chinese silk products, the Roman merchants have often tailored the Chinese silk products into more and lighter clothes. The historical records show the silk trade was the major reason for the "Daqin" traders to explore the sea route through the Indian Ocean to China. The "Weilue, Xirongzhuan" mentioned that "Daqin" traders not only used the maritime route but also used the land route to China, which was not known by others before them. The author has also described the local conditions and customs of "Daqin". The historical records show that in those days Chinese had already knew much about the peoples of Southeast Asia and the Mediterranean.

"Folin" mentioned in the Chinese historical records is the only word that is directly originated from the word Rome. "Folin" is one of the names which referred to the regions in the Eastern part of the Roman Empire. The name "Folin" was also passed to China through the land route.

China was divided after the collapse of Tang Dynasty. The land route between China and the Western countries was blocked as a result. With the sharp rise of the dependency to overseas trade by the Song Dynasty, which ruled the south regions of China, in this period the Chinese people's knowledge about the overseas peoples had also increased dramatically. "Zhu Fan Zhi" written by Zhao Rushi already mentioned the Alexander Lighthouse, the Arab Maghreb peoples on the Southwest coast of the Mediterranean and the Sicilian volcano of Italy.

The ancient Chinese geography generally did not know much about the African continent, but this didn't mean that they were totally blank about Africa. We have already mentioned above that the ancient Chinese took the

Persian Gulf, Arabia Peninsula and Eastern coast of Africa as one geographical unit. "You Yang Za Zu" written by Duan Chengshi of Tang Dynasty gave his description of the "Ba Ba Li Guo" in the "Xi Nan Hai", which is the current Arabian Sea. "Ba Ba Li Guo" should be the transliteration of Barbary (Berberi land), which refers to current Somalia. This was the first time for a geographic name of Eastern Africa was ever recorded in the Chinese history books.

The ancient Chinese people's exchanges with the overseas peoples reached its peak in Song, Yuan and Ming Dynasties. The official envoys and private merchants frequently set sails to travel to the overseas nations. The Chinese gained more and more knowledge about the overseas nations. There were a lot of official and private records of the overseas nations' geographic data, local conditions and customs emerging. The overseas trade of the ancient Chinese was part of the trade networks located in the West Pacific and North Indian Ocean. The overseas trades of the Chinese merchants must go through the local partners, which were "Kunlun" people in Southeast Asia, Indians in South Asia and Persians and Arabs along the Arabian Sea coasts. The purpose of the expeditions by the merchants were to make fortunes. Thus, the populated and flourishing regions has become increasingly attractive. Besides, the merchants belonging to various nations which used the Maritime Silk Road expedition routes had their own exclusive market which they enviously protected, therefore except accidental drifts, the Old World countries (Europeans) didn't opt for planned expeditions in order to explore new trade routes before the end of the Middle Ages. The major overseas trade partners for the "Kunlun" merchants were Chinese in the North and Indians in the West. The Indian merchants' major overseas trade partners were the Chinese, Southeast Asian people, Persians and Arabs. The major business partners for Persians and Arabs were the people from the Mediterranean, India, Southeast Asia and China. The traditional overseas business partners for the ancient Chinese did not change for thousands of years. So the Chinese ships reached only as far as Western coasts of the Pacific and Northern coasts of the Indian Ocean. They never reached the shores of Australia, South Africa and America.

The Oriental People Recorded in the Foreign Books

In the ancient world, besides China, the European peoples carrying forward the Greek and Roman civilizations and Islam peoples carrying forward the West Asia and North Africa civilizations also have rich historical records, which also include the data about the Maritime Silk Road. Though the South Indian people played an important part in the maritime trade between the East and the West, they did not have the habit to keep historical records. The Tanjore monument was set up in 1050. Its inscription in Tamil language has high historical value. The Malays held the key place in the maritime routes between the East and the West, but their first annals, Nagarakrtagama, was written as late as in 1365. The foreign ancient people including Greeks, Romans and Islams had the most historical records on the sea routes between the East and the West.

The Europeans had long established contact with the people in the regions to the east of the Mediterranean and the Red Sea. The Persian Empire had long-time war with Greece in 5th century BC. In the 330s BC, Macedonian King Alexander defeated and ended the Persian Empire extending its empire's territories to India and Central Asia. These wars objectively boosted the trade between the ancient Europe and Asia. The Greeks first acquired silk through the middlemen of India and Persia and learned that the fabric was called "Ser", which was clearly a transliteration of Chinese silk. So the Greeks called the people producing and selling silk "Seres" referring to the Chinese and the related nationalities. The Greeks had heard a gossip that the silk's raw material was "wool" which could be obtained from a kind of tree.

After the rise of the Roman Empire, the fine silk textiles were favored by its upper classes. Curiosity made people constantly seeking the truth about its raw material. Despite the long distance and expedition inconvenience, finally in the Augustus (Octavius) era, the Europeans learned the "Seres" people were living in the region beyond India and "Daxia" (Bactria). The Roman scholar Pline LAncien wrote in his book "The Natural History," finished in 77 AD, has recorded that the trees of the "Seres" were covered by white fine hair and the "Seres" used water to flush down silk from the trees. The silk was exported to the Roman Empire and the local women made silk into textiles. Finally in 2nd century AD when Mac Aurel had reigned the Roman Empire, the Romans learned that the silk's raw material was produced by silkworms. Pausanias wrote in "Description of Greece" that the "Seres" did not make silk from trees. The silk was produced by the insect, which was called "Ser" by the Greek and was fed with reed leaves by the "Seres". The record was found in the book "Stories of Greek and Latin writers on Far East" which was compiled by Coedes and translated by Geng Sheng. The book was published by Zhonghua Book Company in 1987.

In Roman Empire, the European merchants traded for silk with the Persian and Indian merchants and resold the silk to Europe. During the trades, the Romans gained more knowledge about the world geography. The geographer Strabon drew the first map of Asia, which showed Asia's eastern part was facing the sea. The book "voyage of Eritrea" written by an unknown merchant in Alexander of Egypt at the end of the 1st Century AD is an important historical account. The author himself sailed in the Indian Ocean. He gave a rather precise description of the overall landscapes of India's East coast and Thinai (China) and wrote about the trades between the Eastern Han Dynasty and its neighboring peoples and the West. The Westerners have gained deeper understanding about China with more exchanges between China and the West. In 4th century AD, the Roman scholar Ammien Marcellin already mentioned the Great Wall of China in his book "Res Gestae".

Persia was also a traditional maritime power. Located in Western Asia, Persia's maritime merchants long played the middleman role in the trades between the East and the West in ancient times. Before 4th century BC, the

Persian Empire's navy battled in the Arabia Sea and even Eritrea. During the era of Western and Eastern Han, the Chinese envoy to Parthia already found that the Parthia's merchants bought Chinese silk from the Indian Ocean peoples and re-sold it to the Roman merchants.

In its peak time, Persia once ruled the regions in current eastern Arab nations. Some of the overseas traders of Persia and Parthia were probably the Semitic-language-speaking ancient Arabs. The Roman Empire once ruled the Near East. So, the Roman merchants doing trade in the India Ocean and Southeast Asia also included many ancient Arabs. After the rise of the Arabs, Islamization of West Asia and North Africa were quickly realized. The Persian and Arab merchants actively continued their traditional maritime trades between the East and the West during the periods of Achaemenid, Seleucid, Parthian and Sassanid Dynasties and also during the reign of the Roman Empire. The Persian and Arab personages have left a lot of cultural classics, among which their East-related writings are important historical data for the current study of Maritime Silk Road.

The Arab geography, directly inherited the Greek and Roman geographies, holds an important place in the world geography history. Though a considerable part of the East-related accounts of the Arabic geography were simply copied from the previous records, they were still much more detailed and accurate than achieved by their Latin counterparts in the Roman Empire era.

There were many Arabic geographers giving accounts of the sea routes leading to the East. Al-Biruni once visited India and his accounts of the regions to the West of India have high historical values. His accounts about the Far East were direct copies of the ancient Greek and Roman scholars. The other famous Arabic geographers including Al-Idrisi and Abu al-Fida, like the previous Greek and Roman scholars, thought the Indian Ocean was an enclosed ocean and that the African coasts were linked to China. The reason for such a mistaken concepts was not that the ancient West Asian navigators had no knowledge about the Far East, but because many geographers of those days time wanted to incorporate their new geographic knowledge into the world's pravelent framework already described in the Greek and Roman sources of the past times.

Ahmad Ibn Khurdadhbih was one the most outstanding Arabic geographers. He was born in 820s AD and passed away around 911 AD. He mentioned in his book "Kitab al-Masalik wa-l-Mamalik (History of Routes and Kingdoms)" that he once read Ptolemy's work and translated it into Arabic language. He did not let the past Greek and Roman geographic ideas limit his thinking. He gave detailed accounts about the routes from Persian Gulf port Basra through India and Southeast Asia to China listing every stop's name and respective voyage time needed. His many accounts are still worthy comparing with the Chinese historical accounts.

Another important book is "travel notes of Sulayman" ("my experiences in China and India"), which was written in mid-9th century AD. Like many other Arabic geographers, Ibn Khrudadhbah gave descriptions about the East with abundant facts and quoted written materials. On the other hand, "travel notes of Sulayman" was based on the oral accounts of the Arabic traders and sailors who had sailed to India and China, which made its accounts more detailed and persuasive.

The above mentioned Chinese, Greek, Latin, Persian and Arabic historical records constitute the major historical materials in the study of the Maritime Silk Road.

Chapter 1. The Emergence and the Initial Period of the Maritime Silk Road

1. People in East Asia and the Seas in the Ancient Times

The history of man's bonds with seas are almost as long as the history of humankind itself. In the Upper Caveman site in Zhoukoudian in Beijing, many ark shells with small holes were found. It was estimated that humans once tied these shells together to decorate themselves, which proved that the Upper Caveman was related with coastal regions. The East Asian continent, where China is located, faces the vast Pacific Ocean on the east. Between the Pacific Ocean and the East Asian continent, there is the Okhotsk Sea, the Sea of Japan, the Yellow Sea, the Bohai Sea, the East China Sea, and the South China Sea from North to South. Besides, there are the Kuril Islands, the Japanese Islands, the Ryukyu Islands, the Taiwan Island and the Philippines Island in parallel with Mainland China. The Pacific Ocean is on the east of these islands. Due to such geographical conditions, there were two kinds of maritime navigation routes in ancient East Asia, including crossing between islands and mainland from East to West and sailing parallel to the coasts on the edge of the west Pacific Ocean from south to north. This region is typically the monsoon winds zone affected by the land and sea location of East Asia. In winter, the northern wind is suitable for navigation to south and, in summer, the Southern wind is convenient for the sea navigation to north. Meanwhile, there are regular ocean currents along the inshore waters of West Pacific, mainly including the North Equatorial Current, that is, the Kuroshio or the black stream. The black stream is as wide as 180 km. and it has stable flow direction all the year round. Favorable natural conditions were of great importance for ancient Chinese people to develop nature-powered sea and river navigation.

The sea and river navigation activities began in primitive society, even before the emergence of words. From cultural relics of ancient times in coastal regions of East Asia, it can be roughly judged that the spread route of civilization is related to sea and river navigation activities. According to the Spring and Autumn Annals, in the 8th year of Lu Zhuanggong (the emperor Lu), Qi Xianggong (then emperor Qi) made a visit to Gufen and went hunting around the Shell Mound. Shell Mound here proves that people in coastal regions lived on ark shells of the Neolithic Age. People threw leftover ark shells near their houses, so a Shell Mound came into being. Still, there such kind of sites can be found in coastal regions. In 1953, Chinese archaeologists found Shell Mound in severalregions more than 30 km. away from the sea in Ninghe County of Hebei province, according to the Investigation of Pre-Qin Dynasty Sites in the Ninghe County in Hebei Province written by An Zhimin published inn Cultural Relics.

The Chinese people have realized the vastness of the surrounding seas in the early stages of time. When a boat floated away from the mainland, sailors would see the Great Ocean ing away to meet the sky and the small boat became insignificant. Liezi ever mentioned that the ancient people had noticed that water run into the ocean but the ocean did not spill over. So they thought that somewhere in the ocean was a bottomless valley. So, the sea was called "Heaven Pool" by Xu Shen in Origin of Chinese Characters. Zhang Hua in Jin dynasty ever mentioned that the Milky Way was connected with the sea in Natural Science.

Original navigation activities in East Asia were short distance drifts between coastal regions and offshore islands. Archaeologists made researches on more than 30 Neolithic sites in Zhoushan islands in Eastern China and it was proved that the culture of Zhoushan islands was deeply influenced by the Hemudu Culture in Yuyao, Zhejiang province. The Neolithic Culture exists in the Liaodong Peninsula and its neighboring islands. The sand-tempered potteries found in East Village site, Daqin Island of Miaodao Islands are similar with the unearthed relics in Baishi Village site, Yantai, Shandong Peninsula. Archaeological materials proved that, as early as six or seven thousand years ago, coastal regions in Eastern Zhejiang, Liaodong Peninsula and Shandong Peninsula were all connected with residents on offshore islands. However, there still existed differences between Liaodong Peninsula and Shandong Peninsula in culture in the Neolithic Age, which proved that people were incapable of crossing the 22.8-nautical mile-wide Laotieshan Strait between North Huangcheng Island in the Northern part of Miaodao Islands and Laotieshan in Lvshunkou in Southern part of Liaodong Peninsula.

In the late period of the Neolithic Age, the navigation ability of people in East Asia had improved greatly. The sites dating back to five or six thousand years ago found in the Korean Peninsula and Peter the Great Gulf in Vladivostok in Russia were all related with Xiaozhushan Lower Period Culture in Liaodong Peninsula. Nearly 5,000 years ago, the influence of Dawenkou

Culture in Shandong Province spread to Liaodong Peninsula and the current cultural relics in the Liaodong Peninsula are also found in Shandong Peninsula. About 4,000 years ago, Longshan Culture in Shandong Peninsula spread to coastal regions of Liaodong Peninsula. However, Dawenkou Culture and Longshan Culture in Shandong Peninsula can only be seen in the south of Liaoning Province and no trace of them was found in the other regions in the northern parts of the Bohai Sea. It indicates that residents in Liaodong Peninsula and Shandong Peninsula contacts with each other directly through Laotieshan Strait, not the west coasts of the Bohai Sea. With the representative of thin and lustrous black pottery, Longshan Culture, which originates from Shandong Province, had spread rapidly to Jiangsu Province, Zhejiang Province and Fujian Province, even to Taiwan.

The Neolithic Culture in Southeast coastal regions had two main features. One was the stamped pottery, which could also be found in Taiwan. The other one was the grassland adze.[1] According to the statistics provided by archaeologists, it was most commonly seen in Fujian, Guangdong and Jiangxi, secondly they were commonly seen in Jiangsu province, thirdly, commonly seen in Anhui and rarely seen in the eastern part of North China, and also rare in the middle and west part of Changjiang River Basin. But, it was never found n the western part of the North China. Certainly, it was mainly found in the coastal regions. Besides the Longshan Culture research sites, the grassland adze was also found in Taiwan, especially Yuanshan Shell Mound. According to several researches, the grassland adze was a tool to build canoes. Therefore, the distribution of the grassland adze is of vital importance in deepening the studies on the sea navigation activities in the southeast coast regions of China in the Neolithic Age.

343

The distribution of the grassland adze is rather wide, for example, it was found in the Philippines, North Borneo, Sulawesi in Indonesia and Polynesian Islands in the Pacific Ocean. This culture spread through several directional ocean currents in the Pacific Ocean. Archaeologists ever have examined the bones unearthed in Dawenkou and Xixiahou sites in Shandong, China. The results showed that the residents at that time were related to Polynesians.[2]

Similar conclusions were drawn from the examination of bones unearthed in the Hemudu Site which is in suburban of the Zhejiang city.[3] These historical materials show that the remote ancestors of Polynesians came from Southeast of Mainland China. In the process of out-migration, they spread the grassland

1   Adze, a tool like an axe with the blade at an angle of approximately 90° to the handle, used for cutting and shaping wood Adzes and axes made of jade and serpentine were in common use. Stone chisels were fastened into handles with sockets, in which the stone was inserted. These tools were also used for building canoes. For cutting and carving chipped-stone knives and or beaver-tooth knives were used.
2   Research Report of Dawen Site in the Neolithic Age, in the 1st edition of Acta Archaeologica Sinica in 1972).
3   Human Bones found in Hemudu Site in Yuyao, Zhejiang in the Neolithic Age on the second edition volume II of the Acta Anthropologica Sinica by Han Kangxin and Pan Qifeng.

adze to other regions. Polynesians were closely related to Malayans, and they were famous for their sea navigation in the Pacific Ocean. Their migration routes to Pacific islands were realized along the coastal regions of Southeast of China or cross-sea drift first to Taiwan, then to the Philippines, north of Borneo and Sulawesi. This was the spread routes of the grassland adze as well. And then Polynesians spread the adze to Polynesian Islands, New Zealand and other regions.

The Neolithic Culture in Liaodong and Shandong has inner relationship with Vladivostok Culture of Russia. Due to the navigation of coastal residents in East Asian Continent, the black pottery in Longshan was introduced to Taiwan and grassland adze also spread widely. There is a sentence in the History of Songs, which ways: "Xiangtu, an ancient emperor of Tang dynasty, expanded his country to coastal regions with his bravery." During Xiangtu's reign, the territory of Shang tribe had expanded to the Bohai Sea, even included certain overseas regions. According to the History of Documents and On Balance, during the period of emperor Cheng of the Zhou dynasty, China had developed bonds with Japan and Vietnam.

2. Initial Shipbuilding Industry in China

The spread of East Asian civilization through the sea indicates that the ship, an indispensable tool, must have come into being during that time. Ancient people found the buoyancy principle in their daily life. They observed that the wood can float on the water and found that the hollow wood can bear more weight when floating. That is what was written in the Hanfeizi: "With a ship, the heaviest things can be floated, without a ship, even the lightest things will sink." In ancient times, the most important floating vehicles were the rafts and canoes. There is a sentence, in the History of Changes, as follows: "Fuxi, an ancient emperor of China, took the raft" which proves the existence of raft in ancient times. In order to enhance the buoyancy and stability, ancient people gradually tied the trunk and bamboo together and the raft vehicle came into being. After the invention of raft, people also observed that a fallen leave could float on the water, so they invented the canoes. Sailing vehicles were mentioned repeatedly in the historical documents of pre-Qin period. For example, the History of Changes mentions that "ancient people made hollow wood as the canoe and flat wood as paddles to promote connection among people". In fact, the origin of shipbuilding was earlier than these inventions. The earliest sailing vehicle was the ancient canoe. Many canoes and accessory equipment originating from the end of the Neolithic Age were found in many regions in China. Between, 1973-1978, archaeologists have found 6 paddles in Hemudu Site in Zhejiang. The length of the remaining wreck paddle is 60 cm, meter, the width is 12 cm, thickness is 2 cm. and the blade part is 50 cm. There were several geometric patterns which consist horizontal and oblique lines on the hand grip part of the paddle. There is another paddle with the residue length of 92 cm. This one is flat and long with the shape of willow leaf. It is a cultural relic dating back to about 7,000 years ago. In 1979, a canoe in the Neolithic Age was found in Guojiacun Village, which is in the North of Rongchengwan Bay in Shandong. It is as long as 3.9 meters, the width of the its middle part is 0.7 meter and the width of its prow and stern is 60 cm, the depth of the cabin is 30 to 40 cm, and there were two cross girders in the canoe. Around 1958, five or six wooden paddles, which were made about 4,700 years ago, were unearthed in Qianshanyang in Wuxing and Shuitianfan in Hangzhou, Zhejiang Province. Among them, the elongated paddles with slight curvature unearthed in Qianshanyang are as long as 96 cm. and as wide as 19 cm. and the grip of the paddle is as long as 87 cm. In 1973, a canoe, which was made about 2,200 years ago, was unearthed in Lianjiang County, Fujian Province. Its length is 7.1 meters, the width of its prow is 120 cm. and the width of its stern is 1.6 meters.[4]

The shape and material used in building boats in the Neolithic Age can be seen from unearthed boat-shaped pottery. A ship-shaped pottery made about 7,000 years ago was unearthed in Hemudu Sites. There is a mooring hole on the prow and the boat is of smooth and sleek lines. In 1979, a boat-shaped pottery made about 6,000 years ago was also found in Dandong, Liaoning. In 1973, a boat-shaped pottery made about 5,700 years ago was found in Honghuatao, Hubei. In 1979, two boat-shaped potteries made about 5,000 years ago and 4,000 years ago respectively were found in Changhai County, Dalian and Lvshun in Liaoning.

In order to improve the stability and carrying ability, ancient people began to install wooden planks around the canoe. With the increasing row number of wooden planks, the canoe, as the carrier of wooden planks, did not need to be dug so deep. Therefore, original canoe turned into the keel and the V-bottom wooden boat came into being. While, the flat-bottomed wooden boat had evolved from the raft.

345

It is a difficult thing to make sure who invented shipbuilding in China. The vastness of Huaxia, an ancient name for China, in ancient time led to inconvenience in transportation and communication and the ship-building technology might develop independently at the same time or successively in regions along the seas, rivers or lakes. It was reflected in the historical materials, for example, the Shiben, The Classic of Mountains and Seas, Mozi and Lv's Spring and Autumn Annals. In the Hemudu Site of Zhejiang, people found wooden planks and mature mortise-tenon timber technology, indicating that ancient people had the technical capacity to build wooden boats. In 1979, stern remains of a wooden boat were found in Daheishan Island, Shandong Province. The thickness of the flat plank is about 5 cm. with clear mortise-tenon. Archaeologists thought that it could date back to 4,000 years ago. It proves that China had produced wooden boats with mortise-tenon structure before the end of the 3rd millennium BC.

4   These materials are recorded in the China's Ancient Ships Opening the Maritime Silk Road written by Xi Longfei on China and Maritime Silk Road published by Fujian People's Publishing House in 1991.

According to Guangzhi, a history book of China, wrote that the invention of sail was inspired by the fine of horse foot. And in the book called the Wuyuan, it is written that the rudder and paddle were invented by Diku. However, these records cannot be regarded as completely true and reliable historical evidences. Probably, sail, rudder and paddle was created and improved by those people who lived on waters and made a living and production practice from the water sources for long generations, not by certain wise man.

In the pre-Qin period of China, people in the coastal regions in ancient China had begun to utilize boat to transport. So Confucius said, "I would take raft if the land route was unavailable" in the Analects of Confucius. At that time, the navigation skills had developed and safety and comfort of sea expedition was also improved, so the emperor Qi had preferred a sea voyage happily which took minimum 6 months. Although, possibly Qi's sea route was not so far from the coast, the ships used by the nobles were certainly large and well-equipped and had certain degree of anti-wind ability, so that the sea voyage could be a pleasant thing.

In Spring and Autumn Period, the shipbuilding technology of ancient China had reached quite high level. In Southern China, navy forces which used various ships to fight were founded. In the dialog between He Lv, the emperor of Wu, and Wu Zixu, a strategist of Wu, recorded in Yuejueshu, a history book of Wu and Yue, which was possibly written in the end period of the Spring and Autumn periods or in the early Warring States period,-- mentioned about various kinds of ships and their sizes. Among the navy ships of Wu, there was a ship neamed Dayi with the length of 10 Zhang (a Chinese unite of measurement, equals to 1/3 meter) and the width of 1.52 Zhang, which was similar to combat ships with heavy military equipment. There were also a ship named Xiaoyi with the length of 9 Zhang and the width of 1.2 Zhang, which was similar to combat vehicles with light equipment; Maotu, which was similar to Chongche, an attacking vehicle; tower ship, which was similar to Louche to pry into enemy; Qiaochuang, which was a small speed boat. These were recorded in Taiping Imperial Encyclopedia, Zhaoming Princes Literary Selections, and Yuejueshu. In 485 BC, Qi state defeated Wu state in a battle.

Yue, a neighboring state of the Wu, was another power specialized in shipbuilding. It boasted spear ships and tower ships. After the Yue state conquered the Wu state, Yue moved its capital to Langya, currently the Jiaonan County in Shandong, in 468 BC. Yue used 300 spear ships which carried 8,000 troops. By the Han dynasty period, the shipbuilding skills of the Chinese craftsmen had become mature. Emperor Wu of Han dynasty established a large navy and trained it in the Kunming Lake. According to Youyang Miscellany by Duan Chengshi, the big Yuzhang ship, which belonged to Han's navy, could carry 1,000 people and a palace was built on the ship. While, Taiping Imperial Encyclopedia recorded that the huge Yuzhang ship could carry 10,000 people. It seemed that it was wrong. It can be seen that the carrying capability of these huge ships at that time had reached about 100 tons. According to Liu Xi in Han dynasty, there was a kind of tower ship with the height of more than 10 Zhangs (35.8 meters). Besides rudder, paddle and long oar, there were several rooms (called Lu in Chinese) in the second floor, another several rooms (called Fei Lu in Chinese) in the third floor, and watch rooms, named "Que Shi" in Chinese, in the fourth floor. Big ships with the carrying capability of 500 Hu (a Chinese unit of weight) also had small room used for observation, named as Chi Hou in Chinese. It is written in Hanshu that the navy ships with towers once battled in Southeast coastal regions of the Han dynasty.

3. Navigation Skills in Early Times

(1) Early Offshore Sailing and Use of Terrestrial Navigation

The basic outline of east coast of Asian Continent extends from South to North. Due to geological activities, a chain of islands were formed in the east of the continent, including the Japanese Islands, the Ryukyu Islands, Taiwan and the Philippines. On the east of these islands, lied the vast Pacific Ocean. According to these natural conditions, ancient people mainly sailed from South to North and from North to South. Only ships from the East coast to above islands or in the Indian Ocean through the South China Sea made Eastbound and Westbound voyages. The navigation skills in the ancient times were underdeveloped, so the navigation activities were carried out only in coastal regions. Even for oceangoing voyage, ships only sailed in waters between coastal regions and islands on the Pacific during the first phase of voyage after setting sail from East Asia Continent. According to above natural conditions in the East coast of Asia Continent, the navigation in East Asia in ancient times mainly used the terrestrial navigation.

Terrestrial navigation was developed in long-term navigation practice by people lived in coastal regions. In ancient times, the power for navigation was mainly wind and ocean current. Therefore, the speed and shipping line could not totally control by sailors freely. Under this circumstance, one of the most important factors that could ensure a safe navigation and chose the correct direction was to clearly determine the position/coordinates of the ship.The terrestrial navigation in ancient times mainly depended on land marks. It required the sailors to remember the position and natural land form of islands and coastal regions they passed and recognize them from any direction and in any season or climate.

Besides land marks, benthal land form recognition could also help to determine the position of the ship, including measuring water depth, examining the seabed soil properties and seawater colors through silts adhered to the bottom of plumb bobs with wax oil or grease. Therefore, for correct navigation, sailors must remember the land form of the sea and coastal regions. In order to pass on the navigation skills to their offspring, some steersmen drew maps of mountains along the routes and carefully noted and collected the land marks, water depth and seafloor soil properties. These materials were arranged and turned into Genglubu, Zhenjing (guidebooks on sailing directions) and nautical charts.

(2) Observing Stars in the Seas

There are stars and planets in the sky. In human history calculated by year, century, or millennium, the position changes of stars can be neglected. That is to say, in s certain season, people can observe that the position of stars would be relatively stable from certain observation point on the earth's surface. When the longitude and latitude of observation points would change, then the position of stars would also change. The movement trajectories of the planets in the sky had also attracted people's attention.

Using stars as the reference system, people could make clear their geographical positions in early times through measuring angular changes of stars and by observing positional deviation of planets. The navigation skills based on observation of stars and planets at nights came into being. During Han dynasty period, materials and experience of people's observation in regard to stars were mentioned in many books. According to Hanshu, they are Sea Astrology, Haizhong Wuxingjing Zashi, Haizhong Wuxing Shunni, Haizhong Ershibaxiu Guofen, Haizhong Ershibaxiu Chenfen and Haizhong Riyue Huihong Zazhan. Here, the word Wuxing refers to the five planets (Mercury, Venus, Mars, Jupiter and Saturn) and Ershibaxiu the stars. These books contain rich content on divination, which indicates the existence of marine weather forecasts. So they are called the pioneers of subsequent scientific books on celestial navigation and marine weather forecast methods. During Qin and Han dynasties, celestial navigation was only a supplementary means.

(3) Nutritional Supplements Used during the Maritime Expeditions

When people have accumulated navigation methods and used tools which helped the maritime navigation materials, the chances for sailing in the vast oceans had increased. Such oceangoing maritime expeditions depended on navigation skills and shipbuilding techniques. Advanced navigation skills and strong ships were the basic technical requirements. However, the survival ability of sailors was another constraint. The survival of sailors in the sea depended not only on their will and experience, but also required adequate nutrition. With the development of shipbuilding techniques, the ships became bigger and bigger, so they could carry enough food to feed seamen for months, even years. However, seamen one-sidedly fed with cereals have faced some illnesses. After 15th century, when the Portuguese colonists heavily pushed overseas expansion, many sailors have become ill, even died due to a lack of vitamins which are contained in fresh vegetables and fruits during long sea expeditions. So, supplement has been a decisive factor that constrained long-time survival on the sea.

In materials about Chinese oceangoing voyage in ancient times, there was nothing about the illness of sailors caused by a lack of adequate nutrition. That was not only because there were differences between Chinese and Westerners, but also because there were many islands in the Western Pacific and Indian Ocean, especially Southeast Asia, wherein mainly Chinese seafarers sailed.

These islands helped sailors recognize directions and get supplement. Trade ships were usually berthed populous and prosperous islands, where merchants loaded and unloaded goods and got supplement of fresh water, vegetables and fruits.

Even after the invention of magnetic compass in Song dynasty, land mark navigation still played an important role in oceangoing voyages in China and voyages mainly depended on a series of stops along the routes. So, to some degree, oceangoing voyages in ancient times were short-distance voyages along coastal regions guided by land marks, which was decided by natural conditions in Western Pacific and Indian Ocean.

(4) Navigation by the Help of Monsoon Winds

The navigation of ships on the sea requires manpower, natural power or mechanical power. Alongside with the industrial revolution in modern times, the mechanical power began to be used in oceangoing expeditions, which substituted the use of the manpower and natural powers. In ancient times oceangoing expeditions had mainly relied on natural power. Wind power and currents in the seas and oceans, especially wind power, were two primary natural forces.

The east part of the Asia Continent lies in typical monsoon belt, so the north winds blow in winters and south winds in summers, quite regularly. The ancestors of the Chinese nation who lived within the monsoon winds belt had long realized to recognize the directions of winds. According to the Taiping Imperial Encyclopedia, during Xia and Yu dynasty periods, people had invented Xiangfengniao, a wind direction recognition tool. According to Chinese Meteorology History by Liu Zhaomin, an oracle bone unearthed in Anyang was engraved with the name of winds blowing from four directions. The east wind in spring is warm, harmonious and melts icing which greatly promotes plants to sprout; the South wind in summer is gentle and mild, which enable plants grow; the west wind in autumn is cool, which promote plants to ripe; the north wind in winter is cold, which enable plants to save energy. There are also many materials about winds blowing from both four directions and eight directions, including the Classic of Mountains and Rivers, Lv's Spring and Autumn Annals, Huainanzi and Records of the Historian.

According to Shi Yi Ji, a Chinese mythological treatise written by Wang Zinian, Emperor Shun and Ehuang, his wife, once used wind direction recognition to forecast the wind direction in four seasons. Although it cannot be regarded as true history, it can still reflect that sailors had already begun to recognize wind direction in quite early times, even before Shang and Zhou dynasties. By using wind power, the wind sail can propelled the ships. The invention of sail was later than that of ship. Before the invention of sail, seamen had already discovered the function of wind power in sea navigation. With a favorable wind, ships could sail fast and smoothly;. while, in unfavorable wind conditions, or when encountered with strong storms ships sailed slowly. There are no reliable historical materials indicating the time of invention of sails in

China, but it is certain that the sails were utilized in the Han dynasty period. Liu Xi who lived in the East Han dynasty said: "when the sail opens, the ship moves fast around" in Shi Ming, a book which was about the origin of names of things.

At least before East Han dynasty, Chinese sailors had found the secret of monsoon. According to Qing Jia Lu, a book on customs in Suzhou and neighboring regions, Cui Shi once mentioned intermittent drizzles in the rainy season and trade winds in Peasant's Proverbs, a poem. It is indicated that the trade wind is junk wind after the rainy season, which is the southeast monsoon. During Three Kingdoms Period, Wu dynasty had a strong navy. In the history books, Wu Fan from Wu Dynasty was good at forecasting and using monsoon winds. Alongside with this period, books narrating about using trade winds for sailing has remarkably increased. For example, Monk Fa Xian in West Jin dynasty once wrote that a business ship to Southwest direction arrived in Simhala within 14 days with the help of trade winds in early winter in Record of Buddhist Countries. In the History of Song Dynasty, during Liu Song period in Han dynasty, ships sailed far distances with the help of trade winds. At that time, merchants from Southeast Asia and Indian Ocean had widely used trade winds to enable maritime expeditions.

4. Ancient Civilizations Related to the Silk Road

The Silk Road has originated from mutual attraction between world's civilizations.

The Chinese nation feels proud of ancient civilization created by their ancestors. However, if Chinese people still regard China as the center of the world as ancient people and think that ancient Chinese civilization had been the best, then we can say that this idea is untenable. During the 4th millennium BC to the third millennium BC, when ancient Chinese civilization along the Yellow River and Yangtze River gradually developed, other independent civilizations were also developing in several regions of the Old World, that is the ancient Egyptian civilization in Northeast Africa, Mesopotamia civilization in West Asia and Indus Valley Civilization. Among the centers of these civilizations, there were many races and tribes with connection with each other. Although the Yellow River and Yangtze River, the centers of ancient Chinese civilization, were far away from other civilizations, ancient Chinese people still had indirect connection with other civilizations. The legend about the Queen Mother of the West in ancient Chinese mythology reflected Chinese people's knowledge about Western civilizations.

(I) Ancient Egypt and Babylon Civilizations

Ancient Egyptian civilization originated from downstream valley of the Nile, which flows South to North to the Mediterranean. Mountains and deserts lie miles from both river banks. The most suitable place for people's survival had been regions along river valleys. The river valley along the Nile has boasted fertile land and humid climate and could get water from the Nile river conveniently. Lower Egypt, which is a swamp, is located between the mouth of the Nile and Cairo. Meanwhile, the areas between Cairo and the First Cataract of the Nile River were called Upper Egypt. A great many bones of ancient Egyptians were unearthed in numerous tombs and ancient Egyptians were also drawn into ancient wall paintings. According to these materials, ancient Egyptians with black skin and hair were high, so they must have blood relationship with races in East Africa and West Asia. Experts analyzed ancient Egyptian characters, which indicated that the language of Egyptian belonged to the Semito-Hamitic family and related to modern Arabic and Hebrew.

In the 5th millennium BC, ancient Egyptian people along the river valley of the Nile were still in the late period of the Neolithic Age, but also considerable development was achieved in agriculture and animal husbandry. In the early of the 4th millennium BC, ancient Egypt begun to use both stone implements and copper wares and there were about forty small kingdom along the river valley of the Nile. By the middle of the 4th millennium BC, these small kingdoms merged with each other and the Lower Egypt came into being in the down-stream Nile delta and the Upper Egypt was located on its South.

When Chinese people were still in the late period of primitive society, ancient Egyptians had already built the magnificent tall pyramids. The Khufu Pyramid built in the 4th dynasty during 2680 BC to 2560 BC is as high as 146.5 meters and the length of its tower footing is 230 meters. Nearly 2.3 million stones with an average weight of half a ton, were used in this building. It was the highest building globally before the establishment of Eiffel Tower in Paris. Beside, ancient Egyptians also built grand temples, among which main shrine of the Amun Temple in Thebes has been the most famous one. Covering an area of 5,000 square meters, there are 134 columns in this shrine. Among them, the highest one is 21 meters. The top of this column can hold 100 people. There are also many vivid wall paintings and embossment.

After the initial creation of hieroglyph scripts, Ancient Egyptians gradually turned some characters into syllables and ideograph, which were turned into 24 letters, making ancient Egyptian become alphabetic writing. Ancient Egyptians only wrote with consonants, without vowels, which became the spelling rules of ancient writing in West Asia. Ancient Egyptians wrote on papyrus, which was a kind of plant in Lower Egypt. People split its stalks and put them together into pieces. After flattening and drying, they turned into a kind of paper. At that time, people wrote with reeds and the ink came from the mixture of vegetable juice and carbon black in smoke.

About 6,200 years ago, Egyptians had already created a calendar. They stipulated that there were 12 months per year and 30 days in a month. There were three seasons a year with four months per season. The 12th month was five days more than the others, so there were 365 days a year. It was only 1/4 day less than a tropical year. It has been the earliest calendar in the world.

Egypt locates at coastal regions of the Red Sea and Mediterranean with the Nile flowing from South to North which crosses the whole country. Ancient Egyptian has dug a canal connecting the Nile and the Red Sea very early and this making of this water canal took long decades of digging and dredging in history. Egypt is located between the Red Sea in the Indian Ocean and Mediterranean in the Atlantic Ocean, making it a shortcut on the sea connecting the East and West. Thanks to favorable geographical conditions, the Egyptians have became good sailors. There were many sailing scenes in wall paintings in ancient Egypt. In 1954, the wreckage of Khufu ship, which can date back to 4,700 years ago, was unearthed beside Cheops Pyramid behind the Sphinx. After many years' study, Western scholars finally restored this ship. It was a kind of ship with seams. There were holes in 4 angles of the deck and cordage made of coconut fiber was used to link these decks. This kind of ship was simpler than ships with mortise-tenon structure. However, it had poor anti-wind ability and anti-seepage ability. While, this Egyptian shipbuilding skills were accepted by many Western Asian countries and were used until the Middle Ages.

The downstreams of Euphrates and Tigris rivers in Iraq was called the Mesopotamia region. The North of it was Assyria and South was Babylon. Babylon had two parts, Akkad in North and Sumer in South. Here was the birthplace of the Western Asia Civilization. In the middle of the 4th millennium BC, Sumerians of unknown origin, with round head and straight nose settled in Mesopotamia. They irrigated the farmlands and tamed sheep, goats, pigs and poultry. Several cities came into being in Sumer.

In the early of the third millennium BC, Akkadians who spoke Semitic language settled in North of Babylon. Different from Sumerians, Akkadians had long face, Roman nose and beard and hair. In 24 century BC, Akkadians unified Babylon. In the end of the third millennium BC, the Third Dynasty of Ur appeared in Mesopotamia. During the 20th to 18th century BC, Babylon conquered Mesopotamia. There were altogether four dynasties in the Babylon kingdom and the 4th dynasty ended in the 7th century BC.

In the middle of the 4th millennium BC, Sumerians had created scripts. At first, Sumerian scripts belonged to hieroglyph type, however, with gradual appearance of syllables and ideograph, the number of scripts were reduced. In the end, the number of scripts reduced to less than 600. This kind of script was not letters, but syllables consisted with consonants and vowels. Sumerians wrote with reeds and clay tablets. At that time, people engraved scripts on clay tablets with reeds. Today, this kind of scripts are called cuneiform and accepted by neighboring races.

In ancient times, society and economy in Tigris and Euphrates developed to a high level. In the middle of 18th century BC, Hammurabi, the 6th ruler of the ancient Babylon kingdom, codified laws- the Code of Hammurabi. The articles of these codes were engraved on stone stele in cunei form. This is the earliest well-preserved code of written laws discovered in 1901. Its content contains preface, main body and conclusion and the main body includes 282 articles.

In the ancient Sumer-Babylon literature, there is a legend related to a great flood and Noah's Ark. Later, this legend was adopted by Jews and became a part of the holy Old Testament. They were written into the Torah Bible and spread throughout the world.

The science and technology in the ancient Babylon was quite developed. Babylonians adopted algorism and sexagesimal system. Its sexagesimal system was adopted by all races around the world to divide sidereal revolution, circumference and time. Ancient Babylonians had understood the Pythagorean Theorem and the methods to solve quadratic equations and some special cubic equations. In the study of ephemeris, Babylonians can already tell stars and planets and define the apparent motion orbit of the sun surrounding the earth, which is ecliptic. At that time, astrologers regarded visible stars as constellations and drew pictures of zodiacal signs. Their names, including Leo, Libra and Cancer, were still used by Western astronomers. The astronomers in the 4th dynasty of Babylon can predict eclipse, lunar eclipse and planet's opposition. Babylonians had accurately observed the motion of the moon and measured its motion time, which was 29 days, 12 hours, 44 minutes, three and one-third seconds, which was only one-third second longer than modern measurement. Babylonians used lunar calendar, there were 12 months a year, seven cycles a week, and every day was named after the earth, the moon and five planets. The concept of week was accepted by races around the world. Babylonian calendar divided one day into 12 two-hour periods and one year into 354 days. The way to coordinate lunar calendar and solar year was to add leap month.

Archaeologists have found the site of Babylon city during the 4th dynasty of Babylon. Its city wall was 13.2 km. long. There are altogether more than 300 towers with the distance of 44 meters between each tower. The double north city gate with double openings is as high as 12 meters. There is a 25-meter earth mound with plants and flowers, so it is called a "Hanging Garden." It is one of the wonders of the world which we have inherited from the ancient times. Ancient Egyptians kept touch with ancient Mesopotamians.

(2) The Ancient Civilization along the Indus River

Ancient subcontinent civilization is in fact the ancient Indian civilization. Ancient India refers to the current South Asian subcontinent region, which is a relatively independent cultural geographical unit. Original inhabitants of ancient India were Dravidians and other races who spoke Austronesian languages and Malay. Ancient Indian civilization is also called Harappan Civilization along the Indus River in Pakistan. More than one hundred sites were discovered and the most famous one is the Moenjodaro site in the Sind province of India. With an area of 260 hectares, Moenjodaro has been an ancient city which had existed between 2500 BC to 1500 BC. However, we have no available historical documents. It had high city walls and brick buildings with reasonable layout. Its East-west and South-north streets was probably as wide as 10 meters and the corners were built into arc for easier transportation. There was also arched drainage system made of bricks. Citizens used well water and the well walls were made of bricks. There was a wide gap between the rich and the poor.

Citizens of Harappan Civilization (the Indus Valley Civilisation) had entered the Bronze Age and lived an agricultural life. They planted barley, wheat, cotton, flax and vegetables and fed white horses with a black mane, cattle, sheep, pigs, dogs and poultry. They had created hieroglyph for archaeologists found thousands of patterns with cattle and stamps with characters. Breakthroughs have not been made in the interpretation of these words. Citizens of Harappan Civilization kept in touch with West Asia Civilization through Indus River, Arabian Sea, Persian Gulf or Red Sea.

Harappan Culture fell from the first half of the second millennium BC and extincted in the middle of the second millennium BC. What brought this highly developed agricultural civilization to an end is not clear, yet. Even though there are no records in existing historical documents, most of the scholars explain the perishment of Harappan culture and civilization with the invasion of Aryans.

Around 1500 BC, many tribes who spoke Indo-European languages entered northwest of India from middle Asia. They called themselves Ariya, meaning the elegant. Even thought they were nomads originally, Aryans gradually adopted a agricultural lifestyle after settled along the Indus Valley. By the early periods of the first millennium BC, Aryans can be found all regions along the Indus Valley and Ganges Valley. The Aryans, together with original Indian inhabitants, created the highly advanced Indian Civilization.

Ancient Indians kept in touch with China through various channels, including land route through Myanmar and Yunnan and sea route through the Southeast Asia.

(3) Original Inhabitants of the Southeast Asia-- Kunlun People

The languages in Southeast Asia and neighboring regions are called Austric languages by linguists. The Austric languages cover regions between islands in South Pacific and Madagascar in eastern Africa. Malay had been the most important language among them. The original inhabitants here have probably migrated from Southeast Asia in quite long period of time. It is generally argued that original inhabitants who spoke Malay migrated from Malaya to Indonesian islands and the islands of the Philippines in the 2nd millennium BC. While inhabitants who spoke Malay migrated to islands on the South Pacific, the Baiyue ethnic people which originated from the southeast China have gradually moved to the Southeast Asia region. Indo-China Peninsula and Malay Peninsula in Southeast Asia and numerous islands on vast oceans enjoy a warm climate, large population and abundant resources, which is the only way to China for Chinese in India and the Indian Ocean and West Asian for East Asian merchants. Especially in ancient times, the navigation skill was underdeveloped and the fleets did not have oceangoing ability and must depend on supplement along the voyage by using terrestrial navigation methods. Therefore, numerous islands became ideal stops on the seas between the Pacific Ocean and the Indian Ocean. Many civilizations on the world spread through forceful means, while Southeast Asia in ancient times was a gathering place of merchants. The Han Civilization in the North, Indian Brahmanism and Buddhist civilization in the West, the Islamic Civilization in West Asia all spread through trade exchanges, not forceful means. The aboriginals in the Southeast Asia, who were good at sailing, were called Kunlun people in the ancient Chinese historical records. Kunluns traded with merchants on the sea coming from afar and their ships, which were called "the Kunlun ships", sailed in China, India and the Arabian Sea. So Kunlun were intermediary traders in the many kind of exchanges between the East and the West due to their rich geographic knowledge and navigation experience. Their role was gradually replaced by the Europeans during the 15th century.

5. Maritime Routes between the East and the West in Early Times

(1) Ancient Sea Route to Yichengbu Country, Current Sri Lanka

Han Shu Record (also known as The History of the Han Dynasty) kept the first complete vivid record about the marine trade and expeditions between the East and the West. It recorded sea routes to Huangzhi Country, current Kanchipuram in India and Yichengbu Country, current Sri Lanka through Indo-China Peninsula and Southeast Asia from the coastal regions in Guangdong. The starting points were generally Rinan, current Quang Tri Province in Vietnam, Xuwen, current Xuwen County on Leizhou Peninsula in Guangdong, Hepu, current Hepu County in the north Guangxi, and otherregions. Starting from theseregions, the ships could reach Duyuan Country in 5 months, Yilumo Country in another 4 months and Chenli Country in another 20 days. The fleet could reach Fugandulv Country in more than 10 days on foot from Chenli Country. In another more than two months, the ship could sail to Huangzhi Country. It had a vast territory and large population. Its customs were similar with those of Hainan Island at that time. From the Han dynasty, the ambassadors from Huangzhi Country paid tribute to Emperor Wu and other emperors for several times. Yichengbu Country was located in the north of the Huangzhi Country. The Han dynasty used its people as translators along the route. When the fleet made a return voyage, they sailed 8 months from Huangzhi Country to Pizong, and sailed another 2 months to Rinan.

Many researches were made by scholars in regard to this sea route. It is generally believed that Duyuan County is probably the Luoyue Country mentioned by Jia Dan in Tang Dynasty period. It extended along the southeast of the Malay Peninsula, next to Dungan, a river in the Singapore Strait. Dungan seems to be the origin of Duyuan. Yilumo Country, the second stop, was probably the Loujuloumi mentioned in the book Tang shu. It was called Rahmi, Rahma or Rahman by Arab geographers during the Tang Dynasty period. It was located in the region where the Sittaung River meets the Gulf of Mottama in the South Myanmar. Chenli Country, the third stop, was probably inthe Pugan, an ancient country in the midstream of Irrawaddy River in Myanmar. After reaching the Yilumo Country, the fleet of Han dynasty sailed towards the southeast to the river mouth of Irrawaddy River and then sailed upstream. The 4th stop was probably the Fugandulv Country, which is current Tagaung in Myanmar, next to the Bay of Bengal. Huangzhi Country was probably the Canjeeveram in the South of Madras, the capital of Tamilnadu province, which extends along the eastern coastal regions of South India, and Yichengbu Country, current Sri Lanka. The Pizong region in the return voyage was probably the Pidang Island in the East of Malacca. This record in the "Han Shu book" indicates that Chinese trade ships and envoys could already sail directly from China to the south region of the South Asia subcontinent.

However, some scholars have argued that the fleet crew have left the ships and taken the land route after reaching the East coast of Kra Isthmus of Kra Peninsula due to the small size of the ship, poor wind conditions and lack of ocean-going ability of the ships. The fleets have probably moved Eastward to Fugandulu Country in the current Myanmar and then sailed to Southeast India through the Bay of Bengal. It is recorded on Isthmus and Geographic Pole in the South China Sea in the Ancient Times on the Journal of the South Seas Society. Due to limitations in navigation skills, the ships at that time could not sail far away from the continent and could only sail along the coast of Southeast Asian Continent, so the voyage schedule was rather long. Besides, it was possible to abandon the ship and take the land expedition route.

In the Han dynasty period, there were officials who were familiar with foreign languages. Huangzhi Country and Yichengbu Country were home to Tamils and Chinese Han people were familiar with their language. When the ambassadors of the Han dynasty went for a mission voyage, they mainly took gold and silk with them. During the voyage, they usually traded with foreign ships and they could make big gains. However, there still existed certain risks, for example, looting and shipwreck.

Trading has been the basic motive force for the overseas expeditions and transportation. During the Western Han dynasty, overseas products continuously entered into China. According to Hanshu, "in the spring of the second year of Emperor Ping in Han dynasty, Huangzhi Country pay tribute to him with a rhinoceros." It also mentioned that "Huangzhi Country brought a rhinoceros from 30,000 miles away." In fact, the time when rhinoceros entered into China through trade was earlier than the book records. In 1955, four pottery rhinoceros horn models were unearthed in the No. 2 tomb, a tomb in South Yue Period, in Plum Blossom Village, East Hill, Guangzhou. These reddish yellow models are of the same size and the remaining length is about 10 centimeters. In 1960, 15 pottery rhinoceros horn models were unearthed in the No. 1 Tomb in Mapeng Hillock, Sanyuanli, Guangzhou. Among them, six were slate grey and hard. The other nine were reddish yellow and slightly soft. They were the same in shape and structure. The bottoms of them were hollowed out into cones. The horn tips were cut flatly. The pictures of these pottery rhinoceros horn models with the length of 17 cm. and with the width of 6 cm. were printed on page 26 of The Collection of Antiquities from Silk Road on South China Sea. A wooden box with the height of 34.2 cm. and width of 35.9 cm.. was also unearthed in the same tomb. On the both side of the box was an excellent drawing of rhinoceros painted in red. Probably, the box was painted by craftsmen according to living rhinoceros. The animal Rhinoceros lived in Southeast Asia, South Asia and Africa. It was very difficult to transport themfrom Huangzhi kingdom to China. People demanded high pay to do this task. During the reign of emperor Wen of Han dynasty, Zhao Tuo, the emperor of South Yue kingdom, subordinated himself to the rule of Han dynasty. He entrusted Lu Jia, an ambassador of Han dynasty, to offer ten rhinoceros horns to emperor Wen. We can understand that rhinoceros horns were prestigious and expensive products which were enjoyed by the upper ruling class.

In 1983, the tomb of Zhao Mei, the 2nd king of South Yue kingdom, in Xianggang Mountain in Jiefang North Road street of Guangzhou was excavated. Five big ivories unearthed in the West room overlaid on each other. These ivories are all longer than 120 cm. and the longest one is 126 cm.. There are obvious differences between these ivories and the ivories of Asian elephants, which are slender, so they should be ivories of African elephants. These materials are recorded in Water Transportation and Archaeological Discovery of Fanyu in Han Dynasty and the Eastern Birthplace of Maritime Silk Road. It can be seen that the South end of South Asia Subcontinent was not the terminal of marine Silk Road during Western Han dynasty. The products of Africa were transported to China, indicating direct or indirect connection between China and Western Indian Ocean and Africa in the pre-Qin dynasties period. The sea route from South China to Indian Ocean in Western Han dynasty had existed in pre-Qin period. But the record did not emerge until Han dynasty. The characteristics of the navigation from Pacific Ocean to Indian Ocean during this period were that ships were motivated by monsoon, ship routes were not far from coastal regions and ships needed to get logistic support during their voyages. India served as the intermediary logistic support point in the connection between South China and Western waters.

(2) Eastward Sea Routes Used by the Greeks and Romans

Since Persian Empire in the 6th century BC to the 5th century BC, Persia was in continuous connection with Greece, sometimes in war and sometimes at peace. After Alexander, the emperor of the Macedonian Empire, made the eastward military expedition, Central Asia and India were put under the control of Greeks. The empire established by Alexander had controlled Europe and Asia, which promoted their exchanges and communication into a new era. At that time, Europeans could only reach Central Asia and India. Two centuries later, emperor Wu dispatched Zhang Qian[5] to the Western Regions, thus China established direct bonds with the Western Regions.

China also got to know Great Qin Country (ancient Roman Empire) located in the Mediterranean region through the introduction of Western people. With the transportation between the East and the West, information and news of China could now spread to the West truthfully and silk fabrics were sold to Europe through Mediterranean by land route or sea route. In land route, merchants from Balkh, Sogdiana and Parthia played an important role as middlemen. In regard to the sea route, merchants of Southeast Asia, India and Parthia have played key roles.

Roman nobles lived a luxury life and they preferred silk clothes. Although silk was sold in Europe, it was rare in Roman Empire. Originally, Roman nobles can only use silk products as lace and then use them as facing. Due to scarcity of silk, Romans even reeled off silk from leftover materials. Romans liked silk products was not only because it was light and thin, but also because Romans preferred dark purplish red. At that time, craftsmen in Mediterranean region use certain kind of shell to make purplish red dye and silk was easy to be colored.

With the start of the transportation between the East and the West, silk products from China increased. Upper nobility had access to silk clothes. According to Lucanus, an expert on Roman history lived in the middle of the first century, the silk clothes possessed by Cleopatra, Queen of Egypt who ruled the throne between 48 and to 30 BC, which had caused envy of others. In fact, the raw materials of her clothes was not made of silk originally produced in China, but was re-knitted damask silk. Emperor Julius Caesar also wore this kind of clothes and used silk umbrella. Pliny, a historian, ever mentioned that Roman maidens in Chinese silk clothes were prettier and more charming. The rekintting skills of Roman craftsmen were also recorded in Chinese history. According to Du You, a historian in Tang dynasty, people in Great Qin Country reknitted Chinese thin silk into damask silk. Thick waterproof silk was made of tough and thin silk. The reason why Roman craftsmen reknitted silk raw materials was probably that the silk was inaccessible in that time and it could be made more thin silk through reknitting.

5   Zhang Qian was a Chinese official and diplomat who served as an imperial envoy to the world outside of China in the 2nd century BC, during the time of the Han dynasty. He was the first official diplomat to bring back reliable information about Central Asia to the Chinese imperial court, then under Emperor Wu of Han, and played an important pioneering role in promoting China's bonds with the Western Regions including Xinjiang.

Today Zhang Qian's travels are associated with the major route of transcontinental trade, the Silk Road. In essence, his missions opened up to China the many kingdoms and products of a part of the world then unknown to the Chinese. Zhang Qian's accounts of his explorations of Central Asia are detailed in the Early Han historical chronicles, Records of the Grand Historian, compiled by Sima Qian in the 1st century BC. The Central Asian sections of the Silk Road routes were expanded around 114 BC largely through the missions and explorations of Zhang Qian. Today asser Qian is revered for the key role he played in opening China to the world of commercial trade.

The Isthmus of Suez canal is located between European continent, Asian continent and African continent. So it was well known by the people due to its favorable geographical location. With the gradual development of shipbuilding skills and navigation skills, people found that the cost of water transport was quite lower than that of land transport. Therefore, trade between the East and the West prospered. Since ancient times, the Red Sea was the natural channel for merchants from the Indian Ocean to Mediterranean region and Western sailors traveling to Asia. In ancient Egypt, the canal between the Red Sea and the Nile connected Mediterranean in the Atlantic Ocean and the Red Sea in the Indian Ocean.

In the ancient times, the Red Sea was called Erythraean Sea. There is a long trade history between coastal regions of the Red Sea and the Indian Ocean. Egyptians had sailed out of the Red Sea very early. In the first millennium BC, seaborne trade on the Red Sea and Arabian Sea had developed rapidly. During 336 BC to 146 BC, Egypt was under the rule of Ptolemaic Dynasty of Greece and the Greeks used to sail southwards along the Red Sea. Goods from India and East Africa were unloaded from the both sides of Mandab Strait in the south of the Red Sea, which connects Djibouti (Africa) and Aden in the south of the Arabian Peninsula. Loads from Somalia and Ethiopia were transported by sea expedition along the Red Sea to the Mediterranean sea. After silk products from China arrived in India directly or through intermediaries,, they were also transported to Europe through intermediaries. After a series of transshipments, silk products became much expensive when arrived at Mediterranean regions. Romans always wanted to establish direct connections with the East to break the monopoly of Western countries on the silk trade.

When Augustus was in office, Roman Empire conquered Egypt. The port of Alexandria located at the Nile Delta was the necessary way to the East for Roman Empire. At that time, the power of Han dynasty had expanded to Central Asia. Parthia was between the Roman Empire and West Regions of Han dynasty, so the only way to avoid Parthia was to find waterway to the East. Around the first millennium BC, Hippalos, a Greek captain, once arrived in the west coast of India by chance. At the beginning of the first Century AD, Annius Plocamus, a tradesman, collected the taxes from the Red Sea controlled by the Roman Empire and he dispatched Publius, a freed slave, to the Red Sea as the tax collector. Publius encountered storm and accidentally arrive in Sri Lanka, which was called the Simhala in the Chinese history, after drifting on the sea for 15 days. He stayed there for half a year and returned back to Europe with Rachias, an ambassador from Sri Lanka to Roman. According to the records of Pliny, Publius' oceangoing voyage was happened during the rule of Claudius (between 41-54 AD). While, according to a Greek and Latin inscription on the expedition road to the Port of Berenice in 100 km. South of Koipato, the return date of Publius was on July 5, of the 6 AD. According to Natural History by Pliny, Rachias' father once arrived in Seres, which was Han dynasty of ancient China. What these two Roman sailors depended on was the monsoon winds on the Indian Ocean. Later, in quite long period of time, monsoon winds[6] in the Indian Ocean was called the Winds Of Hippalos by Europeans.

These voyages enabled Roman merchants to find the sea routes to the East. Romans began to sail into and out of the Indian Ocean frequently. According to records of Strabo, at that time, there were nearly 120 ships which sailed to India annually. Roman merchants started from Italy and arrived in India in October after a three months' voyage. They would stay there until next April and return using the monsoon winds. The author of Periplus of the Erythrean Sea, which was written in Latin at the end of the first century, was a Greek who had settled down in Port of Alexandria. He once arrived in Sri Lanka. According to his records, Chinese silk, leather goods, pepper, Chinese cinnamon, spice, metal and medicine were all uploaded at the port in India. Before, the Romans arrived in the East, they all predicted that cinnamon trees grew in the Arab Peninsula. Since Chinese cinnamon was used in cosmetics, medicine and balsam, so it was greatly demanded in the Roman Empire and therefore it was expensive. One Roman pound of high quality Chinese cinnamon was worthy of 1,500 ancient Roman silver coins, even Chinese cinnamon of poor quality was worthy of 50 ancient Roman silver coins. Latin literature once mentioned the trade between the Roman Empire and China. Pliny also described the luxurious life of the Roman nobility, who did not only enjoy wearing jewelry, but alsoenjoyed to exchanged silk. Roman nobility even traveled to Seres (China) to exchange silk for tailored clothes. What Romans exported most was the glass products. The Mediterranean region under the rule of the Roman Empire was the manufacturing center of glass products. According to Piny the Elder, about 100 million Sesterces flew into India, Seres (Chna) and to ArabPeninsula. This was the trade value between Roman Empire and the East at that time. Piny the Elder wrote: "The Seres (Chinese), are famous for the woolen substance obtained from their forests; after a soaking in water they comb off the white down of the leaves... So manifold is the labor employed, and so distant is the region of the globe drawn upon, to enable the Roman maiden to flaunt transparent clothing in public."

(3) Chinese Envoys to Marcus Aurelius Antoninus, the Emperor of Great Qin Country

After the merchants of Western Han dynasty arrived in India, they found a waterway to Great Qin Country in the Indian Ocean, so traders have traveled to Roman Empire with Indian trade envoys. According to the peace of Parthians and Coronation of Augustus (the first Roman Emperor) in Epitome of Roman History written by Florus, a historian of Roman Empire, at the end of the first century, in the BC 30s, wrote: "Even the rest of the nations of the world which were not subject to the imperial sway were sensible of its grandeur, and looked

---

6 Throughout the last few thousand years the mariners and trade routes of the Indian Ocean have moved to a unique rhythm based upon the prevailing seasonal weather patterns. These are known individually as a monsoon, derived from the Arabic mawsim (mevsim), meaning a fixed and regular period of year.

with reverence to the Roman people, the great conqueror of nations. Thus even Scythians and Sarmatians sent envoys to seek the friendship of Rome. Nay, the Seres (editor: Chinese) came likewise, and the Indians who dwelt beneath the vertical sun, bringing presents of precious stones and pearls and elephants, but thinking all of less moment than the vastness of the journey which they had undertaken, and which they said had occupied four years. In truth it needed but to look at their complexion to see that they were people of another world than ours."

Since, this visit was not available in the records of Han dynasty, so probably Chinese merchants traveled to Roman empire, as private people and pretended to be ambassador. For seeking fortunes, Roman merchants rapidly began to reach the Eastern regions after they discovered the sea route of the Indian Ocean. The gold producing center in ancient Indian Ocean was the current Indonesia region and Indo-China Peninsula, so relevant records emerged quickly in Roman literature. In the early years of the first century AD, authors wrote in Greek and they named the current Sumatra as Chryse, meaning the gold continent.

The book "History of the Later Han" mentioned that Yong You, the king of the Shan State, located in the ancient Myanmar, dispatched ambassadors to pay tribute to the Han dynasty and offered thousands of singers and magicians to perform acrobatics. These magicians said they were from Haixi, that was Great Qin country. One can reach Great Qin (Rome) country through the West of Shan State. It was indicated that Roman merchants were not satisfied after arriving in India and made every efforts to get to Seres (China). After arriving in Myanmar, they found the Shan State was connected with the Han dynasty, so they got the help of the Shan State to reach the Luoyang. At that time, a lot of Romans visited ancient China, including merchants and craftsmen. The route to China through Shan State had existed for a long time. In the second millennium BC, when Zhang Qian was dispatched to the West Regions and arrived in Bactria between the South of Baisuntau of Uzbekistan and the South bank of Amu Darya, he found that there were bamboo canes and cloth produced in Shu transported through India. These products from Shu were possibly transported through Yunnan, Shan State, Bengal Bay and India to Central Asia.

The mountain roads through Shan State to Han dynasty were too hard for expeditions, so the silk products transported through these roads were of high value. Roam merchants had to find another way Eastward. After unremitting efforts, they finally sailed to Vietnam's coast of Indo-China Peninsula. In History of the Later Han, Marcus Aurelius Antoninus, Emperor of Great Qin country, dispatched an ambassador to offer ivories and rhinoceros horns through Vietnam in the ninth year of Emperor Huan in Eastern Han dynasty. Officials also noted that it was the first communication among Han dynasty, Shan State and Great Qin Country (Rome).

However, they also thought that this ambassador's presents were not that priceless and rare. The Emperor of the Great Qin country in the History of the Late Han Period mentioned above was Marcus Aurelius Antoninus, who was on the throne between 161-180 AD. In the book History of the Late Han Period, there is no record on the names of people in these envoys, so they were probably private traders. The author of the History of the Later Han, Fan Ye wrote: "Their kings always desired to send embassies to China, but the An-hsi (Parthians) wished to carry on trade with them in Chinese silks, and it is for this reason that they were cut off from communication. This lasted till the 9th year of the Yen-hsi period during the emperor Huan-ti's reign (AD 166) when the king of Ta-ts'in, An-tun sent an embassy who, from the frontier of Jih-nan (Anam) offered ivory, rhinoceros horns, and tortoise shell. From that time dates the (direct) intercourse with this country. In AD 166 the Roman Emperor was none other than Marcus Aurelius Antoninus.

Chapter 2. Maritime Silk Road in the Indian Ocean

1. The Bustling Sea Routes in the Indian Ocean

(1) From the Far East to the Red Sea

Over three-and-a-half century, from the end of the Three Kingdoms of the Han Dynasty (230 to 280) to the national unity of Sui Dynasty (589 AD), the land contact between the South China and Western countries was blocked by the division caused by North-South wars in China. Thus, South China had to rely mainly on maritime contacts with other countries. This requirement objectively promoted the development of navigation technology, thereby enhancing the safety of maritime navigation. China and the Roman Empire had maintained maritime contacts. According to the record in the book of Liangshu—Zhong Tianzhu Zhuan, in the fifth year of Huangwu (year 226) during Sun Quan's reign in Wu country, a merchant named Qin Lun from Imperium Romanum came to Jiaozhi (currently in the north of Vietnam) and visited Sun Quan's royal court along with a messenger sent by procurator of Jiaozhi before returning home. At about the same time, Sun Quan sent a mission led by Zhu Ying and Kang Tai to visit overseas countries. After returning home, the mission members recorded what they saw abroad in two books—Funan Yiwuzhi (Tales of Funan Kingdom) and Wushi Waiguo Zhuan (Foreign Tales written in the Wu Dynasty) Unfortunately, these two books had disappeared, leaving some of their fragments in the books such as Commentary on the Waterways Classic, Yiwenleiju, Tongdian and Imperial Readings of the Taiping Era.

Although recorded contacts with overseas peoplesof the Jin dynasties are limited, books recording information of foreign countries began to appear in large numbers. According to record of Suishu Jingji Zhi II, the following books could be found at the beginning of Tang Dynasty: One volume of Youxing Waiguo Zhuan (Stories of Travelling Foreign Countries) written by Shamenshizhimeng, five volumes of Waiguo Zhuan (Stories of Foreign Countries) written by Shitan Jing, two volumes of Liguo Zhuan (Stories of Different Countries) by Shifa Sheng, five volumes of Dasui Fanjing Brahmin Fashi Waiguo Zhuan (Stories of Foreign Countries from Master Brahmin in Sui Dynasty) by an anonymous person, one volume of Jiaozhou Yinan Waiguo Zhua (Stories of Foreign Countries in the South of Jiaozhou) by an anonymous person, one volume of Yiwuzhi (Foreign Stories) and one volume of Jiaozhou Yiwuzhi by Yang Fu who was an officer in the late Han Dynasty, one volume of Rinan Zhuan by an anonymous person, one volume of Linyiguo Ji by an anonymous person, two volumes of Fanshu Fengsu Ji (Customs of Foreign Countries) by an anonymous person, 27 volumes of Zhufanguo Ji by an anonymous person and one volume of Funan Yiwu Zhi by Zhu Ying and so on.

The expedition routes development between ancient China and the Indian Ocean facilitated crowds' mobility, and the number of foreigners visiting China leapt. In the record of the eighty-five volume of a book Yiwenleiju, in the second year of Taikang in West Jin Dynasty (281), subordinate envoys from Imperium Romanum entered the ancient China from Guangzhou and paid tributes which included amazing treasures and particularly rare and precious clothes. During Three Kingdoms period (220-280), foreigners were rare in Southeast cities for a long time. In the biography of Shixie, records of Wu record of a book titled The Records of Three Kingdoms, dozens of foreigners could be seen in the street burning incense when the local officials of Guangzhou city patrolled.

After learning more about geography, maritime merchants and sailors started recording conditions of sea regions which they have navigated through. Since after the Later Han Dynasty period (20-220), China's South China Sea waters began to be recorded as "Zhanghai" in the historical records. In the book of History of the Later Han Dynasty, it was written that seven counties including Jiaozhi paid their tributes through Zhanghai. Later not only Chinese historical documents mentioned "Zhanghai" but foreign historical literatures referred to this sea name as well. At the 9th century, an Arab geographer Sulaiman recorded his route to China "Started the journey at the Kunlun Island, the fleet sailed into the waters of Zhanghai."[1]

With the progress of navigation technology, ships which sailed from the Chinese mainland to Southeast Asia no longer sailed close to the coasts and could opt to sail in open seas. Consequently, on their sailing route through the South China Sea, the sailors began to pay attention to the South China Sea

---

1   G. Ferrand quoted: the Volume I of the Oriental Travel and Geographical Literature of Arabs, Persian and Turkic People from 8th to 18th Century, Paris, 1914, The book was translated into Chinese by Geng Sheng and Mugen Lai and the Chinese version is titled as "Edition and Insertion of Orient by Arab and Persian Geographers", Ed, 1989, published by the Zhonghua Book Company, p. 41. In addition to Sulaiman, some Islam geographers also wrote about "Zhanghai".

islands. In the book of Funan Zhuan (Journeys to and from Phnom) it said when Kang Tai and other sailors embarked their sea expedition, in Zhanghai, they found, many coral reefs which grew on stones.[2]

The sea mentioned above was the current South China Sea. South China Sea islands such as the Nansha Islands, Xisha Islands are in fact formations of coral reefs. In 1957, during Guangdong Museum's archaeological activities in the Xisha Islands, six-ear pottery jars and pottery rings of Northern Dynasties were unearthed. Not only Chinese sailors, but foreign navigators communicating China to the Indian Ocean also noticed the coral reefs in South China Sea. The Arab geographer Sulaiman narrated that when the ship entered "Zhang" (Zhanghai), the ship passed through gaps between reefs as the coral reefs were swollen by the sea. So the lives and safety of sailors depended on the mercy of Allah (God).[3]

Other Islam geographers have also mentioned about the South China Sea islands, showing that the navigation technology were advanced all across the world. According to the available literature, we know that during Song and Qi dynasties—which were among the Southern Dynasties, more than 10 countries have reached to China along the coast. During Liang period in the Southern Dynasties age, many overseas vassal states were subordinated to the Southern Dynasties as their suzerains. It is said that more countries than the previous dynasties had sailed to pay their tributes to China. With the increase of communications, Chinese people had a more accurate overall understanding of the maritime routes to the West Asia and more knowledge about geographical location of the countries. "Countries around Hainan were probably located in the south of Jiaozhou and southwest of Dahaizhou. These countries were adjacent to Xiyu (the Western region) in the West. The nearest countries were only three or five thousand miles away while the farthest were twenty or thirty thousand miles away."[4]

During the Liu-song dynasty—one of the Southern Dynasties, its territories extended to the center of current Vietnam and close relationships with Southeast Asian countries and the Indian Ocean were established. Linyi, Funan (the present Cambodia) sent envoys to pay tributes to China and the Heluotuo nation located in the territories of Indonesia and other peoples asked for trade exchange with the Song dynasty. During Liu-Song dynasty period, mutual communications and expeditions between the Indian Ocean and the Western Pacific Ocean became more frequent. In the 5th year of Yuanjia (year 428), the king of the lion country (current Sri Lanka) wrote to China's Liu-song dynasty

---

2　See the Geography 34, Vol. 69 of Taiping Imperial Encyclopedia.
3　G. Ferrand quoted: the first volume of Oriental Travel and Geographical Literature of Arabs, Persian and Turkic People from 8th to 18th Century, Paris, 1914, The book was translated into Chinese by Geng Sheng and Mugen Lai and the Chinese version is titled as "Edition and Insertion of Orient by Arab and Persian Geographers", 1989, published by the Zhonghua Book Company, p. 57.
4　See Liang Shu, Introduction About Countries around Hainan.

leaders, saying: I appreciate, we two nations benignly exchange letters despite a long distance".[5]

This shows that a regular official bond between China and Ceylon Island was maintained at that time. In the 2nd year of Yongming of South Qi (year 484), Qiao Chenru, the emperor of Funan, after hearing that the Qi dynasty state was newly established, sent a Tianzhu Taoist priest Na Jiaxian to pay tributes with a statement saying that in Funan, a traitor Jiuchouluo rebelled and captured the Linyi. He asked for Qi state's military assistance against Jiuchouluo, and against other mobs, which robbed the local people. The emperor of Wudi of Qi state agreed to send his reinforcements. Qiao Chenru asked the emperor of Qi dynasty for help, because at that time, China's southern territories extended to Jiaozhou and Chinese kingdoms had a great influence in Southeast Asia. Guangzhou, with its prosperity in the field of overseas trade, rose and thrived in Southern Dynasties period and replaced two thriving cities of Xuwen and Hepu of the Eastern and Western Han Dynasties periods.

Due to support given by Emperor Liangwu to the spread of Buddhism nationwide, most trade items from Funan were Buddhism related ornamental commodities such as coral Buddha, Tianzhuzhantanrui statue and leaves of sāla tree (Aesculus Chinensis Bunge) and so on. Yunbao of Shramana was dispatched to welcome a strand of hair about 3.96 meters long from Funan (it was said that it was the hair of Sakyamuni, the founder of Buddhism) as Emperor Liangwu heard about it. Other southeastern countries also had frequent maritime communications with Liang, such as Panpan (today in the Wanlun Bay, Southern part of Thailand), Dandan (current Kelantan in Malaysia), Gantuoli (today Malaysia Kedah), Langyaxiu (today in Changwat Pattani, southern part of Thailand) and Poli (current Borneo).

The western Pacific and Northern Indian Ocean waters were connected by the Kra peninsula. Siam Bay, in the east of Kra peninsula, was included in water system of Pacific Ocean while Andaman Sea, in the west of Kra peninsula, was a branch of the water system of Indian Ocean. The narrowest land part of the Malay peninsula is called the Kra Isthmus only about 40 km. In the era wherein the wind power was the main support for the seafarers, it took quite a long time to sail around the Malay peninsula, therefore traders chose to use the Kra Isthmus land route, to save time and costs, when transporting their commodities. This kind of "sea+-and+sea" combined transportation routes were recorded and suggested in the ancient Chinese literature recordings.[6]

---

5   See Stories of Barbarian Songs during the Southern Dynasties Period.
6   See Han Zhenhua, "Research on the Silk road Maritime Route of the Wei, Jin and the Southern and Northern Dynasties and Study of Maritime Routes across South Thailand and Kra Isthmus of Malay Peninsula". included in China and the Maritime Silk Road, p. 235-245.

Since the period Wei and Jin Dynasties, many ocean-going ships from China preferred and used Siam Bay which is at the east of the Malay peninsula as their port. In the small bay around the Siam Bay, merchants from China loaded their goods to boats from Kra Isthmus and loaded local goods they purchased before the trade wind blew in the reverse direction. Sailing along the small rivers, these boats arrived at the foot of the Malay ridge, with human force or animal-drawn vehicles, goods were transported over the mountain ridge and were re-loaded on board on the other side of the ridge, then the loaded ships set sail to the Andaman Sea. Around costs of the Andaman Sea, many merchants from India, West Asia, east of Africa and the Imperium Romanum unloaded their goods and waited to purchase Chinese goods from the other side of the Malay peninsula. Their goods sold to the local merchants were taken to the other side of the Malay ridge and resold to Chinese merchants.

In the Western Han Dynasty period, Chinese ships were able to sail as far as the southern end of the South Asia Subcontinent, that is, they could reach the current Sri Lanka. In the Eastern Han Dynasty, merchants of the the Imperium Romanum began to have stand-on vessels from the Red Sea to the Far East. In the Stories of Barbarian of Song in the Southern Dynasties period it was written that "Tianzhu and Imperium Romanum were located in the West Ming (the West Sea). Envoys of the Western and Eastern Han Dynasties thought that their mission to those two countries were dangerous. But tempted by huge benefits of the trade, various merchants from different countries, after a long journey, took thousands items including treasures found in the mountain or sea, precious jade, jewels and asbestos clothes and other rare goods came to trade with the help of the trade wind."

For the Chinese seamen, the key to sail to the Western Indian Ocean was to master the route which led the ships from the current south of India and Sri Lanka to regions along the Arabian Sea coasts. In the period after the Eastern Han Dynasty, communication between China and South Asia has become more frequent. Chinese people had a new understanding and cognized that India was located between China and Western countries and they knew how to sail from India to the Arabian Sea when Chinese monks traveled to the Western Regions for religious purposes and Indian Buddhist masters came to China to spread and preach Buddhism. The History of Funan was written by a monk called Zhu Zhi in Liu-song in the Southern Dynasties on the basis of what the author saw and heard. He wrote in his book as follows: "Parthian Empire, facing the sea, is 20,000li (10,000km) away from Simhadvipa. With nearly a population of million, it is the biggest country." The "Parthian Empire" referred here was the Persian "Parthian Empire". Although Persia was ruled by Sassanid Empire at that time, Chinese people called it in its old name. "Simhadvipa" referred to the Sitiao (transliteration of Sihaladipa in Pali language), a name mentioned in book Stories of Countries in the South written by Wan Zheng during Three Kingdoms (220-280). At that time, Chinese people had learned route sailing from India to the Persian Gulf.

(2) Nanhai Buddhism Road

At the end of Han Dynasty, China was split by wars. The introduction of Buddhism on the immortal soul and reincarnation during the Western and Eastern Han Dynasties were rapidly spread across China. When Easter Jin Dynasty (317-420) was established in the South of China, financial resources were collected to build Buddhist temples to spread Buddhism as South of China was relatively stable and peaceful. Foreign monks were welcomed by local people. At that time, because the traditional route leading to the West was blocked by the Northern separatist regime, the maritime route between Sino-Indian was increasingly critical.

A monk Ying Jing of the Tang Dynasty recorded in his book, forty relay stations away from East of Nalanda, along the Ganges River, stood a Lu Yuan Temple. "Not far from this temple, there was an ancient temple, built with brick foundation, was called Zhina Temple." It said that during the King Srigupta's reign, the King ordered to build temples for more than 20 monks from Guangzhou of China so that they could rest there and gave 24 fiefs of a big village to them. Until the Tang Dynasty, villagers of three villages were still identified as residents of Lu Yuan Temple. During Tang Dynasty, the East Indian King Tipomoba decided to rebuild Lu Yuan Temple for the new arrivals of Chinese monks.[7]

On the basis of Ying Jing's narrations, the king Srigupta's reign was five hundred years earlier than of his time. Scholars found that the 1st king of India's Gupta dynasty was Srigupta, who was called Maharaja, the "king". Thus, the "king" narrated by Ying Jing probably refers to Srigupta who ruled the Gupta dynasty at the end of the 3rd.[8]

The more than 20 Chinese monks mentioned in the book have probably first travelled from Sichuan to Guangzhou and from Guangzhou sailed to East India by a ship.[9]

Among a large number of monks who studied Buddhism in the Tianzhu[10] region during this period, the most distinguished was Fa Xian. Fa Xian came from Wuyang, Pingyang (current Linfen city in Shanxi province) in the north of China.

---

7   See Ying Jing, Memoir of Eminent Monks in the West in the Tang Dynasty, annotated by Wang Bangwei, Zhonghua Book Company, published in 1988, p. 103.

8   Ibid., pp. 105-106.

9   See Yang Heshu, "On China and Foreign Cultural Exchanges from the Perspective of Buddhism Spreading in Guangzhou between 700-300 BC", included in the book Guangzhou and the Maritime Silk Road, p 114.

10   Tianzhu is the historical East Asian name for India. Originally pronounced as Hin-duk in Old Chinese, it comes from the Chinese transliteration of the Persian Hindu, which is itself derived from the Sanskrit Sindhu, the native name of the Indus River. Persians travelling in northwest India named the region after the river around the 6th century BC. Tianzhu is just one of several Chinese transliterations of Sindhu. Yuāndúappears in Sima Qian's Shiji and Tiandu is used in the Hou Hanshu (Book of the Later Han). Yintejia comes from the Kuchean Indaka, another transliteration of Hindu. A detailed account of Tianzhu is given in the "Xiyu Zhuan" (Record of the Western Regions) in the Hou Hanshu compiled by Fan Ye (398–445).

In the 1st year of emperor Hongshi in the Late Qin Dynasty period(year 399), started his journey from Changan (Xi'an), then to Tianzhu (India) along the land route and arrived in India after marching via the Hexi Korridor, Taklimakan Desert, Congling (Pamirs), Central Asia. He had studied Sanskrit and translated and transcribed Buddhist classics for 3 years in Pātaliputra, the capital city of Magadha. Then he travelled along the Ganges River, to Tāmralipti, the well-known port in the Northeast of ancient India, which is the Tamluk in the south-west of Kolkata in the current West Bengal. In the 5th year of Yixi (409), Fa Xian boarded a trading vessel sailing towards the Southwest, with the help of mansoon trade winds of early winter, arriving in The lion country (current Sri Lanka) after 14 days and nights". In was during the early winter, the vessel Fa Xian took sailed before the north wind along the east coast of India. The distance between Calcutta and Sri Lanka was about 1,200 nautical miles. Scholars have determined that, what Fa Xian boarded was a trading vessel, an Indian trade ship with an average speed of 85 nautical miles per day and night. In the autumn of the 7th year of Yixi (AD 411) autumn, Fa Xian took a merchant ship from Sri Lanka (the lion country) for returning back home by crossing the Bay of Bengal. This huge merchant ship could carry more than 200 people. After the departure, the ship sailed eastwards with the Mansoon trade wind. But the ship encountered a heavy storm after a two days-sail, since in autumn seasons, monsoons of the northern Indian Ocean were irregular, and their directions could change, unexpectedly.[11]

Fa Xian was forced to drift to an island and the Japanese scholar Adachi Kiroku has argued that this was one of islands of Nicobar Isa in the east part of the present Indian Ocean.[12]

369

When the tide ebbed, the damaged ship was repaired and resumed its journey. After a sail of a nights and day, the ship arrived at Yāva-dvīpa. In Indian epic "Ramayana", it mentioned that in the East stood a big island named Yāva-dvīpa. In Ptolemy's geography book, the same island was mentioned and Ptolemy had called it "Iabadiou". The 6th chapter and 116th chapter also mentioned Yāva-dvīpa. Historian Zhang Xun has argued that the Yāva-dvīpa has been the co-name for ancient the Java and Sumatra because they were connected since the ancient times.[13]

It was estimated that due to the storm, Fa Xian's ship sailed off its route and got to the East of Sumatra after sailing along the Southwest coast of the Sumatra islands. Fa Xian stayed there for five months, waiting for the monsoon. In the spring of the 8th year of Yixi (year 412), Fa Xian resumed his journey by taking a merchant ship which could carry 200 passengers, sailing to Guangzhou with food sufficient for 50 days. He did not disembark form the boat in Guangzhou but arrived in present Shandong coast due to the wind conditions.

---

11   See Zhang Xun, Annotations to Fa Xian's Expedition, Ed, 1985, Shanghai Ancient Book Publishing House.
12   See the book Journey of Fa Xian—to Central Asia, India and the South China Sea, p. 220.
13   See Zhang Xun, Annotations to Fa Xian's Expedition, 1985, Shanghai Ancient Book Publishing House, p. 170, note 29.

After returning home, Fa Xian wrote a book Journey of Fa Xian (also called Journey in Buddhist Countries or some other titles) about his 14 year experience abroad. In his book, he vividly portrayed customs of South Asia and Southeast Asia at that time, which was of great value for us to understand aspects of sea transportation in the ancient Indian Ocean, such as ships, navigation, routes, maritime trade of Southeast Asia and South Asia.

During this period, many monks in China and South Asia took maritime routes. It was noticed that many monks from China usually took land routes for the first time when they traveled Westward, but often returned by ship. Zhi Yan, a monk from Xiliang, traveled to Kashmir and returned home from India with a Kashmirian (today Kashmir) monk Jue Xian, and they landed in Qingzhou, Shandong just like monk Fa Xian. Later, Zhi Yan went to Tianzhu by a trading ship.[14]

During the same period, Li Yong from Youzhou also arrived at Guangzhou from the South of Tianzhu by ship after he took land routes to India and studied there.[15]

Monk Dao Pu from the Gaochang took ship from India to return home and landed in Qingzhou port in Shandong province.[16]

This illustrates that Chinese monks lacked connections with merchants engaged in overseas trade and knew little about maritime routes between China and South Asia. Thus, they preferred a land route when leaving for the West and usually took a maritime route when returning as they knew about frequent sea transportations between China and South Asia from the people who lived abroad. This was the reason why in Southern and Northern Dynasties period foreign monks took maritime route when visiting to China.

Many western foreign monks have taken the maritime routes to the East for the first time. A monk Qiunabatuoluo from Zhongtianzhu (Madhya-des) first arrived in the lion country (Sri Lanka) from which he took a ship. In the 12th year of Yuanjia, (year 435), he landed in Guangzhou.[17]

Even some of inland Kashmirian monks also chose maritime route instead of land route. Monk Jue Xian mentioned earlier decided to come to China after he met Chinese monks Zhi Yan in Kashmir. He firstly traveled to Cochin and then to Shandong by sea. Qiunabamo, prince of Kashmir, firstly traveled to the lion country (Sri Lanka) and then to Java where he was known for teaching and spreading Buddhism. Monks from Liu-song in the Southern Dynasties had also heard about him. Thus, emperor Song Wen sent an official of Cochin to invite Qiunabamo to China.[18]

---

14 Huijiao, Stories of Eminent Monks, Vol. 2, see A Collection of Stories of Eminent Monks, Shanghai Ancient Books Publishing House, 1991, p. 15; Volume 3, p. 20.

15 Huijiao, Stories of Eminent Monks, Vol. 3, see A Collection of Stories of Eminent Monks, Shanghai Ancient Books Publishing House, 1991, p. 19.

16 Huijiao, Stories of Eminent Monks, Vol. 2, see A Collection of Stories of Eminent Monks, Shanghai Ancient Books Publishing House, 1991, p. 15; Volume 3, p. 17.

17 Ibid., p. 24.

18 Huijiao, Stories of Eminent Monks, Vol. 3, see A Collection of Stories of Eminent Monks, Shanghai Ancient Books Publishing House, 1991, pp. 20-21.

In the 1st year of Datong of Liangzhong (year 546) in Southern Dynasty, monk Junatuoluo (Chinese dharma named Zhen Di) traveled across Langkasuka, Funan to Nanhai County (current Guangzhou) by sea. Later, he once intended to return Langkasuka by ship.[19]

Monk Putidamo from the South of Tianzhu also visited to China by sea, later was respected as "the ancestor of Zen". During this period, in addition to Indian monks,, many Southeast Asian monks also visited China, among which the famous ones were Sengjiapoluo (Chinese dharma name Seng Yang) from Fu Nan and Mantuoluo (Chinese dharma name Hong Ruo).[20]

These declared that maritime route became more critical in the communication between China and South Asia since after the Western and Eastern Han Dynasties.

(3) Wind from All directions for Sailing

Since the Western and Eastern Han Dynasty, the development of overseas exchanges accelerated rapid progress of navigation. The most remarkable improvement was in sail. During Three Kingdoms (between220-280), Wan Zhen, procurator of Wu described sailing of the boats on the South China Sea "foreign people set four sails in accordance with the size of the boat and combined them in the front and at the back. A piece of Lutou wood was in the shape of a fan with a ten-foot long woven sailing cloth on. The four sails did not face right ahead but were removed to take wind in a better way."[21]

It could be seen that this woven sail with Lutou wood was used for monitoring the sea navigation. It was not common to sail downwind but when encountered left or right wind in the rear, horizontal wind or front wind, right forward arrangement of sails could not effectively use the wind, instead would drive the ship off the planned course and result in great risks. Therefore, when monitoring the sail, the angle of the sail must be adjusted accordingly, and use the propulsion force generated by the wind on the sail surface and overcome horizontal drifting force with the cooperation of rudder so that the ship advances in a predetermined course. Wan Zhen also recorded that, the rear sail of the double sails set in the front and rear when encountering horizontal wind, could be adjusted to face the angle of 45 degrees to reflect the wind to the front sail to drive the boat forward. Full sails could be set if the ship needs to speed up and a half sail for slowing down. A design of small sail in the top and large one below ensured the lower area could take more wind. By lowering the center of gravity, the ship could sail steadily. Although the record described ships of foreigners sailing in the South China Sea, due to the improvement of sail usage techniques, speed of the boats was accelerated as it could sail in strong wind and huge waves.

---

19   See Dao Xuan, Sequel to Stories of Eminent Monks, Vol. 1, see A Collection of Stories of Eminent Monks, Shanghai Ancient Books Publishing House, 1991, p.111.
20   Ibid., p. 106.
21   See Wan Zhen, Stories of the Countries in the South, see the section of boats in Taiping Imperial Encyclopedia.

Generations of navigators drive ships with monsoon, which contributed to progress in sails to some extent. In the long-term practice, boatmen grasped use of the wind. Certain sailing period was set between major ports in the Indian Ocean and the Pacific Ocean. When Fa Xian left from the mouth of Ganges River for The lion country (Sri Lanka), it took him 14 days and nights sailing toward Southwest with the trade wind in the early winter. And when he started journey in Yāva-dvīpa, he took sufficient food for 50 days. It took at least a month to Imperium Romanum from Jianatiao Island with a ship set seven sails.

Another important progress of navigation in this period was the development of astronomical navigation. According to Fa Xian, "no one knows direction on the infinite sea but navigates the ship by observing the sun, the moon and stars. If it rains, navigators follow the wind." It was evident that ships were able to sail in the ocean far from the land, no longer relying geography on land as navigators did in the early ages. In the sunny days, the ships were navigated by the sun in the daytime and by stars at nights, and if it rained, they were navigated by the wind. At that time, Chinese ships sailing in the East of East Asian mainland navigated offshore, no longer relying solely on coastal landmarks. According to Ge Hong's Taiqing Jinye Shendan Jing in Taoist scriptures, it took more than ten days and nights to Funan to sail from Qinnan Pu, Rinan (Shoulengpu) Southward, if astronomical navigation method was used as sailing against the direction of the North star, towards Ji star which was one of the 28lunar mansions.

(4) Perilous Journey

Despite advances in navigation technology, sailing journey was full of uncertainties. Ancient times witnessed high-frequency shipwrecks. The main risks were storms, reefs and pirates. In the Geography of History of Han Dynasty, on the sea route to India, pirates murdered passengers and robbed good and envoys feared of drowning in the water.

According to Fa Xian, he disembarked in the lion country (Sri Lanka) for home in the year of 411. At that time boatmen already knew to tie a small boat in the rear of the ship as a backup. In the second day of his journey, the ship he took was destroyed by storm. At the extremely critical moment, passengers and sailors took the small lifeboat to escape. The cable was cut off in case too many people on the lifeboatcapsize it. People who remained on the ship had to throw goods into the sea. Fa Xian was also trapped on the ship and drifted to a desert island after floating for 13 days in the sea. Fa Xian did not mentioned destiny of those who jumped into the lifeboat. In such storm, disasters rather than blessings were impending for a leaf boat floating in the ocean. In addition to storm, Fa Xian said: "you are dead when your boat encounters reefs". Besides, "robbers and thieves were common in the sea, and you lose your life and goods when meeting them".[22]

22　See Zhang Xun, Annotation for Journey of Fa Xian, 1985, published by Shanghai Ancient Book Publishing House, p.167.

After leaving Yāva-dvīpa, Fa Xian sailed home with the help of Southeast wind. He planned to return home in 50 days, but because of the storm, the ship deviated from the route and spent more than a hundred days in the sea before arriving in Guangzhou. The food and water were exhausted and each person was allocated two-liter half fresh water and half seawater. Passengers also experienced other perils.

Another monk Zhi Yan from West Liangzhou had similar experience with Fa Xian. He invited an eminent Kashirian monk Jue Xian to spread Buddhism in China with him. On their way to the South China Sea, the ship they took berthed in an island, waiting for the wind. One day many ships set sail before the wind, solely leaving the ship Zhi Yan and Jue Xian took which continued to identify direction of the wind. But those ships were all destroyed. After the ship Jue Xian and others took set sail, the rest ships left were robbed and destroyed by pirates.[23]

Monk Qiunabatuoluo from Zhongtianzhu (Madhya-des) intended to spread Buddhism in the East so he embarked on a boat Eastward but the wind stopped in the half way. At that time, since the ships used trade winds as the main sailing power, the ship berthed in the sea when the wind was gone. Subsisting on limited food and fresh water, passengers felt panic when the fresh water was nearly exhausted. Later, the unexpectedly emerging trade wind and pouring rain ensured them to arrive in Guangzhou safely.[24]

Victims of shipwrecks included sailors, merchants, Buddhist monks, and sometimes kings and nobles from the countries of the South China Sea. The book South Qi Dynasty, Stories of Foreigners in the Southeast has narrated that, Chu Non, the king of Linyi kingdom (currently in the middle region of Vietnam), who admired Chinese culture, sailed to China personally, yet was unfortunately drowned in the sea.

2. The Climax of Cultural Exchanges between China and India

(1) Introduction of Chinese Products to India

Cultural exchange was the main trend of bonds between China and India. Silk was the most important product which was introduced to India by China. China was the first country in the world that domesticated silkworm and spun and wove silk threads. The word "cinapatta" in Zhili Ye's book Arthasastra meant "a bunch of silk made in China" and in the Sanskrit language, the word "cinamasuka" meant "Chinese clothes" and "silk clothes". These two words share same root "cina" which referred to "China", indicating that the Chinese silk was introduced to India in the pre-Qin era.

---

23   Hui Jiao, Stories of Eminent Monks, Vol. 2, see A Collection of Stories of Eminent Monks, Shanghai Ancient Books Publishing House, 1991, p. 15.
24   See ibid., p. 24.

Since they didn't have paper, Indians wrote on wood, bamboo, corypha umbraculifera, and birch bark and so on. Almost all Indian literature was passed to later generations by oral narration. During the Tang Dynasty period (618-907 AD), the book "Sadhana of Countries in India and South Asia" which was written by Yi Jing said that in India, "literature is told from mouth to mouth instead of being written on paper." Yi Jing also mentioned in the book "Memoir of Eminent Monks in the West during the Tang Dynasty", he asked Guangzhou for paper and a writing brush when he travelled to Sriboja (current Sumatra). During the Tang Dynasty period, Indians probably knew the paper. In the "Thousand-Character Classic in Sanskrit", "kakali" in Sanskrit referred to Chinese character "paper" but in Names of Sanskrit, was "kakari". These were not Sanskrit words, but were borrowed from a foreign language. In the books written by Sanskrit and Chinese languages during the Tang Dynasty, paper (zhi) was called "saya", which was possibly the transliteration of Chinese pronunciation of "zhi".

Steel was another Chinese product introduced to India. "Cinja", one of Sanskrit words that referred to "steel", meant "produced in China". This indicated that steel was introduced from China into India from some region at a certain era.[25]

(2) The introduction of Indian phonetics

Sanskrit has been an ancient Indian language, with fixed pronunciation, and did not encounter big changes throughout 2000 years. It can be compared to Latin among the Western languages, although it is dying currently. With the introduction of Buddhism to China, Sanskrit phonetics was also introduced to China, which had greatly promoted the Chinese phonology.

(1) Xitan (Siddham)

"Xitan" is transliteration of siddham in Sanskrit, which means "achievement" or title of primary school. Siddham also means 47 syllables including "moduo" (vowel) or "tiwen" (consonant). In the Sutra of Final Nirvana, siddham is called the "half word". Shortly to say, the word "siddham" means the Indian Sanskrit.

In the ancient times, Chinese monks marked Chinese characters on siddham in order to learn Sanskrit. The introduction of Indian phonetics had a tremendous impact on Chinese phonetics. Generally, Sanskrit contained 46 syllables, including 13 vowels, 33 consonants. With another long vowel "l" of some school of Buddhism, they were so-called the 47 syllables in Chinese Buddhist classics. Some Chinese monks added the auxiliary symbol "am" (Anusvara), "ah" (Visarga) into the list of vowels. Hui Lin added a compound consonant "ks" in volume 25 of the book Annotation of Siddham and increased the syllables of siddham to 50.

25 See Jixian Lin, Sino-India Wisdom Exchange, edited by Zhou Yiliang, History of Chinese and Foreign Cultural Exchange, Henan People's Publishing House, 1987, pp. 140-143.

Phonetics of Sanskrit is very special, completely different from the current vowels and consonants. For example, currently, generally speaking, vowel is pronounced by letting breath flow out without closing any part of mouth or throat. But the 13 (or 14) vowels in the Sanskrit language, including pronunciations of "r 鲁" "r 流" "l 卢" and "l 楼" which are regarded as current consonants are listed at the end of the syllable list.

It is unclear when "Siddham" (Indian Sanskrit) was introduced to China. According to research of historians who study Buddhism, more than 300 Buddhist classics were translated into Chinese in the late Eastern Han Dynasty period. In that climate, many monks were supposed to study "siddham". During the Western Jin and Eastern Jin and Song Dynasties, Buddhism became extremely popular and even the famous literati Xieling Yun had studied siddham. In Journey of Hui Rui, Stories of Eminent Monks, Song Shi said that Xie Lingyun from Chenjun enjoyed studying Buddhism. He consulted Hui Rui about some syllables he did not understand and some siddham words with multiple meanings. He then wrote a book Annotation of Fourteen Syllables which was well-organized and clear and provided reference for studying siddham. It is difficult to verify whether this book was preserved among the Chinese ancient books but his comments on siddham can be seen in the Japanese Buddhist classics. In the 5th volume of Scriptures of Siddham written by An Ran from Japan noted that in the History of Xuanyi, it recorded that Xie Lingyun of Song said 50 letters in the Mahaparinirvana Sutra were the roots form which different siddham words was created, among which 12 letters including "a" "a" "i" "i" "u" "u" "e" "ai" "o" "au" "am" "ah" sound similar to the neighboring one and couldeasily cause misunderstandings. The first four alphabets has shorter pronunciation in the front than that in the rear while the last six letters had no difference. But the last two letters added "-m" and "-h" to "a" and "a" respectively in pronunciation. And four letters "r" "r" "l" "l" are listed at the end because they are barely used. Among the 34 consonants, 25 were consonants and 9 were semi-vowels. In a five-syllable siddham word, if the 3th and the 4th letter are the same, then their stresses should be different. Small words are called half word. As shown above, 12 letters can make 34 siddham words by combining vowels and consonants. If a siddham word is made by two letters, it is called "full word". A combination of vowels and consonants have formed the Hu language which was in fact siddham.

A "Hu word" referred to siddham letters: (a), 阿 (a), 亿 (i), 伊 (i), 郁 (u), 优 (u), (e), 野(ai), 乌 (o), 炮 (au). In the ancient times, people wrote from top to bottom, and from right to left. Each siddham letter sounded similar to the neighboring letter. 庵 (am) and 痾 (ah) were lingering sound of 嗯 (a) and 阿 (a). But one letter could not represent a complete word so two letters were combined to create new words. The above letters could form 12 siddham words.

迦(ka), 呿(kha), 伽(ga), 恒(gha), 俄(na), guttural sound

遮(ca), 车(cha), 阇(ja), (jha), 若(na), palatal sound

吒(ta), 呬(tha), 茶(da), 袒(dha), 孥(na), velar sound

多(ta), 他(tha), 陀(da), 弹(tha), 那(na), dental sound

波(pa), 颇(pha), 婆(ba), 滼(bha), 摩(ma) labial sound

The following four siddham words, 虵 (ya, palatal sound), 啰 (ra, velar sound), 罗 (la, dental sound), 啝 (va, labial sound) were semi-vowels whose points of articulation varied from inside to outside. Three siddham words 奢 (sa, palatal sound), 沙 (sa, velar sound), 娑 (sa, dental sound) were sibilating sounds whose points of articulation also varied from inside to outside. With 呵 (ha, aspirated and guttural and voiced sound), 茶 (ks, compound consonant), the above nine siddham words were pronounced with lips to the tongue. There were 34 siddham words altogether that articulated in such a way. The 4 siddham words 鲁 (r), 流 (r), 卢 (l), 楼 (l) were barely used and they could form 50 words.

History of Sui, A collection of Books and Classics included one volume of Brahmanas (note: and one volume of Funan Book written by Liang You) and four volumes of Foreign Books. In the bibliography, A collection of Books and Classics wrote "Since the Eastern Han Dynasty period, Buddhism has been popular in China, with books written in Siddham language, 14 Chinese characters could annotate all the Siddham syllables. The content of the holy Brahmanas is concise and meaningful."

(2) The Source of the Fanqie Method of China

Fanqie method has been a traditional method of indicating the pronunciation of a Chinese character by using two other Chinese characters, the first having the same consonant as the given character and the second having the same vowel. When debating the origin of Fanqie method, Chinese scholars can be divided into two groups: some of them believe that the Fanqie method was influenced by Sanskrit language while the some other scholars hold that it was invented by the Chinese people. Ancient Chinese people did not have the concept of syllables. Zheng Qiao said in his book On Discussion of Chinese and Sanskrit, "Indians are good at using syllables as they create them on the basis of what they hear while Chinese are good at using hieroglyphics as they create them on the basis of what they see." This illustrates the fundamental difference between alphabets and hieroglyphics.

In the ancient times, the Chinese characters were created by the method of "Xiesheng" (pictograms) and "Jiajie" (borrowing), i.e. they have the nature of hieroglyphics. Firstly, the characters such as "工" "可" "公" "白" were created and then "江" "河" "松" "柏" were created. Onomatopoeia and borrowing method were essentially similar because for creating a Chinese character, adding radicals had meant employing the method of onomatopoeia, otherwise it was the usage of the borrowing method. Some characters are difficult for even knowledgeable scholars to pronounce and understand. In ancient times, Chinese people used Chinese characters for annotation of phonetics instead of syllables. In the book Origin of Chinese Characters written by Xu Shen during Han Dynasty period, it said: "a character reads as "some character" which means they have same pronunciation." For example, in Shijing (History of Odes), the character "掇" in the phrase "薄言掇之"was explained in Study of History of Odes as ""掇 is the synonym of"拾"". Besides, Lu Mingde explained that "拾 is pronounced as 十"", that is to say, these two characters have same meaning. This method of annotating phonetics was called the Zhiyin method. The method of Zhiyin has a lot of limitations as sometimes it is quite difficult to find a homonym. For example, in the Mandarin Chinese, you can't find the exact homophone for character "丢". Sometimes some uncommon homophones make no sense if they are used for annotating phonetics, since it violates the rules of helping people learn new characters.

To solve the problem of annotating phonetics, another way is to firstly indicate a homonym with different tones and then tones, however, although this method has been improved, still it cannot guarantee solutions to all phonetic problems of Chinese. Consequently, since the Eastern Han Dynasty period, the Fanqie method came into being, which was called as the "Fan" method before the Southern Dynasties period. Specifically, Fanqie method refered to the pronunciation of a Chinese character by using two other Chinese characters, the first one having the same consonant with the given character and the second character having the same vowel the given character.

During the Northern and Southern Dynasties period, gradual development of prosody demanded study of Chinese. Some of Chinese literati, through the translation of Buddhist scriptures, identified Indian phonetics and found 4 tones of classical Chinese phonetics. They realized disadvantages of Chinese method of annotation phonetic and popularized the Fanqie method. Before the introduction of Sanskrit to China, a concept of "combining consonants with vowels" had existed in China, with the impact of Indian phonetics, Chinese consciously used it as an academic language. Therefore, the Fanqie method was co-created by Buddhist monks and the Chinese literati, who would not erase greatness of our ancestors, on the contrary, indicating that Chinese nation, favored embracing excellent foreign culture. Since Fanqie method became popular, same characters under Fanqie method were collected to be "rhyme" which was widely introduced after Wei and Jin Dynasty periods.

(3) Thirty-six Chinese Phonetic Alphabets

In Chinese phonology, the so-called alphabet refers to "Niu", Chinese character representatives for consonants. In ancient study book of phonology, Chinese characters with same consonants commonly used different characters, but later on ancient Chinese phonologists summarized those characters and chose one word from them as a representative. Although it seemed that the work those phonologists did was similar to summarizing rhyme, but it progressed slowly. Although during Six Dynasties, Xie Lingyun was proficient in using "Siddha" phonetic system, it took a long period for Sanskrit to be embraced by scholars rather than monks at the end of Tang Dynasty. Fanqie method and summary work made significant progress. The so-called "thirty-six Chinese phonetic alphabets" In Chinese phonology referred to thirty-six character representatives, which provided consonants for indicating characters. In the Song and Yuan Dynasties (960-1368 AD), the following character representatives were agreed by people:

对应梵文字母 equivalent Sanskrit phonetic

见溪群疑 k, kh, g, gh,

端透定泥 c, ch, j, jh, n

知彻澄娘 t, th, d, dh, n

帮滂并明 p, ph, b, bh, m

非敷奉微

精清从心邪

照穿床审禅 s, s, s

晓匣 h

影喻

来日 l, r

If you look carefully, you shall find that the thirty-six alphabets originated from Sanskrit and their arrangement was influenced by Sanskrit. They were used for many years as character representatives of consonants. In the History of Yuhai, it was written that Shou Wen had one volume of Table of Thirty-six Chinese Phonetic Alphabets which is lost. A damaged paper of Dunhuang currently preserved in the National Library in Paris is divided into three parts writes eight characters "南梁汉比丘守温述" without a title. It also writes the following characters:

唇音：不芳并明. labial sound

舌音：端透定泥是舌头音. lingual sound

知彻澄娘是舌头音. lingual sound

牙音：见君溪群疑等字是也. velar sound

齿音：精清从是齿头音. tip-dental sound

审穿禅照是正齿音. right-dental sound

喉音：心邪晓是喉中音，清. medium-guttural sound, unvoiced

匣喻影亦是喉中音，浊. medium-guttural sound, voiced26

---

26   See "Appendix of study of Shou Wen's Thirty-six Chinese Phonetic Alphabets arrangement", included in Guoxue jikan ((National Studies Quarterly, 1923-1952), Vol. 1, the third section, p. 460.

In the paper, 30 alphabets were recorded. Character representative started at the end of Tang Dynasty. This method was a milestone in the history of Chinese phonology. With other six alphabets added in Song Dynasty, those alphabets became the thirty-six Chinese phonetic alphabets representing consonants in Tang and Song dynasties.

Phonologists of Yuan and Ming dynasties respected Shou Wen as "Shouzuo of Liangshan." According to Zhao Yintang's research, Shou Wen, from South Liangzhou (currentHunan Baoqing county), became "Shouzuo" after he entered Liangshan Temple in the Wuling county as a monk. His life was not recorded in the holy Buddhist books since the "Shouzuo" rank was not as high as that of a Buddhist abbot. Possibly, he was born at the late years of the Tang Dynasty period and died in the early Song Dynasty.

In the preface of appendix of the book "Views" written by Zhu Mi (year 1241) which is preserved in Four Branches of Literature, it said: "from study books of Chinese phonology such as Yupian written by Gu Yewang and Guangyun by Lu Fayan, people could identify how to pronounce phonetics. As for rhyme and sound, at present no one could understand the book Jiunonfanniu Luowenceniu written by Shamenshengong. Only Thirty-six Chinese Phonetic Alphabets written by Husengliaoyi was spread. And this was the earliest book that described Husengliaoyi's contribution. On the basis of this preface, in the book Huangjijijing Shengyintu written by Shangguan Wanli, it said that "since Husengliaoyi, people knew thirty-six Chinese phonetic alphabets." Thus, it seemed that more than one monk contributing to summary of Chinese character representatives.

(3) Blending of the Sino-India Literature and Art

(1) Translation of Buddhist Classics

China's large-scale acceptance of foreign culture started from translation of Buddhist classics. Buddhist translation was neither organized by official departments, nor by Chinese literati but developed among public, thus it had a lasting impact on Chinese culture. The translation of Buddhist scriptures was an activity about religious classics and philosophical theories and also about literature because it translated some literary stories and language translation itself was also a literary activity. As a kind of literature, Buddhist translation gradually melted into Chinese literature and became part of it, however, translation theories that developed with the translation of Buddhist scriptures were mostly discussed from the literature perspective. Translation of Buddhist classics had a close relationship with Chinese literature and aesthetic theory and itself was also a part of literature and aesthetic theory in medieval times.

The translation of Buddhist scriptures, till Sui Dynasty (581-618 AD), became mature. According to statistics, until Sui Dynasty, the number of Buddhist scriptures translated in Chinese was 1950 items (6198 volumes) in total including Buddhist vehicles, precepts, theories and records, among which were

617 Mahayana Sutras items (2076 volumes), 487 Theravada Sutras items (852 volumes), 380 mixed-content scripts (716 volumes), 172 mixed-and-question-content scripts (336 volumes); 52 Mahayana Sutras precepts (91 volumes), 80 Theravada Sutras items (472 volumes), 27 mixed precepts (46 volumes); 35 Mahayana Sutras theories (141 volumes), 41 Theravada Sutras theories (567 volumes), 51 mixed-content scripts (437 volumes) and 20 records (464 volumes).[27]

Many foreign Buddhist masters came to China by sea and translated Buddhist scriptures in Buddhist temples. As early as Sun Hao's reign of Wu Kingdom (year 270), a foreigner Lou Zhi (Zhen Xi) from Shamenqiangliang (current Borneo) arrived in Guangzhou and translated one volume of Twelve Buddhist Stories. In the second year of Taikang of Jinwu Emperor, (year 281), another monk Jiamoluo arrived in Guangzhou, establishing Buddhist temples and preaching Buddhism. A Kashmirian named Dhramayasa (Fa Ming), in the year of Jinlonganzhong (year 397-401 AD), arrived in Guangzhou after travelling many countries and settled in Baisha Temple. He earned his name "big Piposha" as he was good at chanting "Piposhalv". He had left the South for Changan where he continued translation work and later returned to the South. His independent or cooperative translation classics were a volume of Chaimojing, Shelifo and Apitan and so on. In the middle of the year of Yuanjia in Liu-song in the Southern Dynasties, he returned his home in the West also by sea (not sure).

Actually, translation was a cultural transformation. It was pretty difficult for translating in the early time due to language barriers and Sino-India cultural differences. In order to find common points between two different cultures, translators selected traditional Chinese words in translating Buddhist terminologies, such as "Xingkong" or "Zhenru" for "emptiness", "Wuwei" for "Nirvana" and Taoist Tuna (inspiration and expiration) for Buddhist "Anapana" and so on.

There was no definite version of Buddhist doctrine in the early spreading period in ancient India and West countries as "Buddhism was passed from mouth to mouth without any recordings." This was recorded in the book Extraordinary Stories about Buddhist Monks. Fa Xian also mentioned that "in Northern India and other countries, Buddhism was passed on through oral communication.[28]

At early days of Buddhist translation, firstly original Buddhist classics were recited by foreign monks and then were translated to Chinese and written down by Chinese monks who understood foreign languages. This was the reason why translated Buddhist scripts were plain.

---

27   See Bibliography of South Asia written by Geng Yinceng, 1990, Peking University Press, p. 97.
28   Zhang Xun, Annotations from the Journey of Fa Xian, 1985, published by Shanghai Ancient Book Publishing House, p. 41.

The key to studying Buddhist translation theory was a debate over literal translation or liberal translation. Famous monks such as Dao An, Jiumoluoshi, Seng Zhao, Hui Yuan and so on discussed on this issue. Fundamentally, this debate was focused on the form or content of translation. There were three different opinions on this issue: Dao An argued for literal translation, Jiuluomoshi argued for free translation and Hui Yuan argued for the combination of the both.

From the history of Buddhist translation, basically literal translation method was used. At the beginning of translation, it was difficult for many foreign monks as they did not quite understand Chinese. For example, when Wei Zhinan translated Buddhist scripts in the Wu, he invited Zhu Jiangyan to co-translate due to his poor Chinese but found that Zhu Jiangyan was not very good at Chinese. Therefore, their translation version was "plain and unnatural."[29]

During the Eastern and Western Jin Dynasty, Language barriers were reduced and the translation text was more fluent and expressive because most translators were familiar with Sanskrit and Chinese. Chinese mainland monks and literati's participation in translation built a closer tie between translation literature and Chinese translation and a tie between Chinese literature theory and translation literature theory. During the Liang dynasty, more importance was attached to literati's participation in Buddhist translation, accordingly Emperor Liangwu (464-549) set up an official position called as the doctor of Buddhist translation. Chinese monks and literati, on the one hand, brought Chinese study style and literature style into translation and on the other hand, absorbed diction and literary description style of Indian literature from the Buddhist translation.

381

(2) Mystery Novels

Since the Southern and Northern Dynasties, Indian fables, fairy tales and novels swarm to China. Since Liuchao to Sui, mystery novels, a special literature form which themed telling supernatural stories came into being in China. The rise of mystery novels was a new trend in Chinese medieval literature, among which the most renowned were Bowuzhi (Ancient Encyclopedia) written by Zhang Hua, Shiyiji written by Wang Jia, Soushenji (Stories of Immortals) by Ganbao, Soushenhouji (Sequel of Stories of Immortals) by Tao Qian, Yiyuan by Liu Jingshu, Youminglu by Liu Yiqing and Qixieji by Dongyang Wuyi, Sequel of Qixieji by Wujun and so on. The content of mystery novels, from the late Eastern Jin Dynasty, have begun to involve more Buddhist stories such as Xunshi's book Ghost, Buddhist stories and the traditional Chinese ghost stories were mixed up. Xie Fu's's Stories of Avalokitesvara Bodhisattva was also a good example. In the book Soushenhouji (Sequel of Stories of Immortals), immortals, ghosts and Buddhist stories were blended together. Since then, a large number of books which spread Buddhist thought of karma appeared.

---

29   Wei Zhinan Stories of Eminent Monks.

The forms in which mystery novels were adopted from Buddhist stories can be summarized as follows:

(1) The first way was the use of basic structure of Buddhist stories which expounded in two cases: the one was duplicating and imitation without citation and gradually localizing the story characters and the environment and second way was localizing the introduction part of Buddhist stories without changing story structures.

(2) The second way was collating some events of Buddhist stories into the Chinese stories.

(3) The third way was transplantation of Buddhist story mode which meant creating a seemly native Chinese story by combining Indian story mode with local Chinese environment and Chinese story characters.

Mystery novels, in the stimulation of foreign culture, paved way for legendary literature in the Tang Dynasty in terms of progress in artistic thinking, character description and narrative style.

Indian stories have penetrated deeply into all sectors of the Chinese society, which was reflected in works of Chinese literati. The story that described two people Guo Xian and Fan Ying put out fire by wine in Fan Weizong's History of Later Han was almost the same story of Fo Tucheng. The famous story of a man Cao Chong weighed an elephant in Chen Shou's book Warriors of Fate was also born out of an Indian story. Historical records in the Northern and Southern Dynasties always described the appearance of the monarch of the country. For example, in the Biography of Emperor Ming of Wei in Warriors Of Fate, Pei Zhu cited Sun Sheng's description that emperor Ming's hair was so long that it reached down to the ground; Biography of the Emperor Xianzu of Wei in Warriors Of Fate said that Liu Bei's arms were quite long to knee and his eyes could see his own ears. Similar descriptions could be found in Chen Book, Biography of the Emperor Gaozu, Chen Book, Biography of Xuandi, Wei Book, Biography of Emperor Taizu, Beiqi Book, Biography of Wushen, Zhou Book, Biography of Wendi and so on. A comparison of these descriptions to those of Sakya-muni in Buddhist classics, big ear, long hair and arms to knee, it was concluded that these Chinese depictions were influenced by Indian culture.[30]

(3) Concave-Convex Painting Method

After the Northern and Southern Dynasties, Buddhist statues were spread throughout China. The development of Buddhist statues was due to Indian painting techniques. The book Sequel History of Comments on Painters written in the year of Tianzheng of Liang (551) by Yao Zui from Liang gave comments on more than 20 painters of Liang including three foreign painting monks.

---

30 See Ji Xianlin Sino-India Wisdom Exchange, see History of Chinese and Foreign Cultural Exchange edited by Zhou Yiliang, Henan People's Publishing House, 1987, pp. 144-145.

According to Xu Song's book Records of Jiankang, it said that during Liang, a painter Zhang Sengyao tried India concave-convex painting method in a temple. This mural was painted in red and green. "From a distance, it looked concave and convex but seemed smooth when you came closer. The temple earned its name 'concave and convex temple' because of this painting." This mural was produced of modeling Indian concave and convex method, with shades of shadows and a mix of dark and light color, looked three-dimensional. Zhang Sengyao was a renowned painter at his time. Yao Zui highly praised that Zhang Sengyao was "an extraordinary master of painting towers and temples. He could depict foreign-looking figures vividly in different clothes." This indicated that Zhang Sengyao absorbed elements of Indian art into traditional Chinese painting style. In the book Painting Experience of Yuntai written by Gu Kaizhi, a painter in the Eastern Jin Dynasty (317-420) said that "shades of shadows depicted a mountain" which illustrated that shadow painting method, the concave and convex method, were used in the landscape painting.

Although modern scholars were divided on the connection between Indian "Sadaga" and "Six Techniques" put forward in the preface of a book A Catalogue of Ancient Paintings by painter Xie He of South Qi, they all agreed that ancient China and India had exchanged on painting theories.

Magic, which was acrobatics, was also introduced to China from India. It was recorded in many ancient books as it interested Chinese people. In the book General Musicology, in the second century during Emperor An in the Eastern Han Dynasty (107-125 AD), it said that "Tianzhu performers, in different dynasties, could perform cutting off their own hands and feet, ripping their intestines out." The item "Tianzhu people" in the second volume of Soushenji (Stories of Immortals) written by Ganbao in Jin Dynasty recorded that during the year of Yongjia in Jin Dynasty (year 307-313), Indian performers performed repairing a broken tongue and breathed fire. In the seventh volume "spells" of the book called Fayuanzhulin, it also quoted descriptions from the book Ghost that foreign Taoists could swallow knife and breathe fire and spew jewels, jade, gold and silver.

(4) Sino-India Exchanges of Science and Technology

According to Buddhist historical records, among eminent monks from Tianzhu, some famous Buddhist monks were masters in science and technology. For example, monk An Shigao was "knowledgeable, skillful in fengshui, astronomy (Siven Zheng), prediction, natural disaster study, acupuncture, medical treatment, animal language and musical instruments".[31] The so-called "Siven zheng" referred to the sun, the moon, Venus, Jupiter, Mercury, Mars and Saturn which indicated that he knew astronomy. In addition, he was also skilled in medical treatment as the Journey of Eminent Monks said that An Shigao was a master of "foreign classics, astronomy, the five elements (metal, wood, water,

---

31 Preface of the 6th Vol. of Anban shouyi jing ((Scripture on the ānāpānasmṛti, hereafter ABSYJ), translated during the Later Han dynasty by An Shigao), Records by Chusanzang.

fire and earth) and medicine". The main knowledge hebrought to China was science and technology.

In addition, Hui Jiao's Stories of Eminent Monks has narrated that monk Kang was a comprehensive disciple who "mastered Buddhist classics, six channels and astronomy". Besides the monk Ketanjialuo "was a master of Buddhist classics, medical treatment, prediction and other regions; a foreign monk Qiunabatuoluo was proficient in "astronomy, mathematics, medical treatment and spells."

(1) Four Emperors in the Yanfuti State

Chinese people thought that they lived in the center of the world, thus they called the place where they lived as "China", i.e., the central country, despising their surroundings asthe regions of barbarians. In the pre-Qin era, residents in heartland of the Central Plains knew little about the world because of their limited range of mobility, however, with the introduction of Buddhism, established illusions maintained by the Chinese civilization was broken and Chinese fantasy of China being the center of the world was greatly shaken.

The land wherein all people of the known world lived was called the Jambu (Jambudvīpa) state or Shanfu state or Yanfuti state (Yanfuti is a transliteration of Jambu) since the ancient Indians have believed that in the central region stood the Jambu. With the spread of Buddhism, their geographical knowledge was enhanced and included the many regions of the Asian continent. They believed that the regions of the Jambu was governed by four monarchs. An Indian Buddhist translator Kalodaka quoted from the translated book Twelve Buddhist Classics that the Yanfuti state (Jambudvīpa), included sixteen countries, eighty-four thousand cities, eight kings and four Sons of Heaven in the land of Jambudvīpa. Emperor of the Jin land with a large number of population controlled the east; emperor of Tianzhu (India) controlled the southern regions where the elephants were common; the emperor of Imperium Romanum controlled the western regions with abundant land and sufficient gold and silver; finally emperor of Rouzhi controlled the Northwest regions with excellent horses. In the eyes of Buddhist monks, the Chinese emperor was no longer the supreme nor unique emperor but just one among other three emperors of Imperium Romanum in the West, Rouzhi in the Northwest and Tianzhu in the South. The emperor of China was only the ruler of the eastern regions.

The author Bian Ji—a Buddhist monk—from the Tang Dynasty period, added: "the emperor in the South had numerous elephants due to hot and moist weather, the emperor in the West possessed plenty of treasures as the land faced the sea, the emperor of the north fed quality horses owing to the cold weather and the emperor of the East was mild with a large number of residents.[32]

32　See Great Tang Records on the Western Regions compiled by Bian Ji , Vol. I.

Three hundred years passed away from the Eastern Jin Dynasty to the Tang Dynasty, the Indian "four emperors" recordings also undergone some changes. Local Chronicles of Sakya-muni written by Dao Xuan held that Jambu state was ruled by "four emperors". The first was the "elephant emperor", the king of India who held the South of the snow-capped mountains adjacent to the South Sea. In his land, elephants were common due to hot and humid weather and the king drove elephant troops. His people were fierce and firm, favoring study and perfume. This was the kingdom of India. The second emperor was the king of Hu who controlled the west of snow-capped mountains to West Sea. In this fertile land, courtesy was ignored while commodities were worshipped. This was the kingdom of Hu. The third kingdom was the "emperor of horses" the khan of a Turkic tribe who controlled the north of snow-capped mountains to the North Sea. Due to cold weather, quality horses were fed there. In his land, people, were violent and cruel, and wore thick clothes. This was the Turkic kingdom." The fourth kingdom, the king of Zhina (China), controlled lands which extended from the east of the snow-capped mountains to the East Sea. In this land, peaceful and moderate manner was upheld and kindness and righteousness were promoted. Besides, people were loyal to their native land. Zhina (China) was the so-called "kingdom of Zhendan." The above four emperors ruled their kingdoms respectively, separated by borders.

To implement this new concept of geography, the Indian people moved their beloved capital from Jambu to the snow-capped mountains, Pamirs. The Indian people noticed that the snow-capped mountains, which were the mountains surrounding Pamirs, were the watersheds of river systems and mountains of the Asian continent today. Consequently, they have assumed that on the snow-capped mountains was the Anouda water source, origin of many world-renowned rivers. The Indian people believed that there were four great rivers in the world—the Ganges, the Indus, the Amu and the Sita River. Some Buddhist scriptures have argued that there were 5 rivers in the world, yet the first four were still the above 4 rivers.

Commentary on the Waterways Classic, a book written by Li Daoyuan from Northern Wei Dynasty (AD 386-534) period is an excellent book that reflected the progress in Chinese understanding of the world's geography. In this book, China's water systems and geographical conditions in and out of China's borders, especially conditions of the South Asian sub-continent and the Indo-China Peninsula, was narrated in detail. Li Daoyuan's descriptions in this book about the South Asia had focused to the 2 largest rivers in the region—the Indus and the Ganges. The map drawn by Chinese in Tang Dynasty included the whole Central Asia (including Northwest of China, starting from the Yumen pass in the East, to the Tokmok in the North, to the Khorazm in the West, and to Tibet in the South), subcontinent, the West Sea (The Arabian Sea), the lion country (Sri Lanka), Southeast Asia (Sriboja (current Sumatra) Linyi (current middle region of Vietnam)) and the Southwest of China.

(2) Miraculous Cure by Brahmin

A climax of the first round of cultural exchanges in China's and foreign history had occurred when Indian Buddhism was introduced into China. A large number of Indian medical books were brought into China by the Buddhists. In the book Sui Shu Jing Ji Zhi (Books Catalogue in Sui Shu), such medical books were listed among which the following were related to Indian medicine: one volume book of Shi Dao Hong Fang, one volume book of Acupuncture of Shi Seng Kuang, four volumes of Remdey of Nāgārjuna Bodhisattva, 23 volumes of Western Immortals (one volume of catalogue and content list, plus 25 volumes as the content), 10 volumes of Remdey of Xiangshan Immortals, 3 volumes of Remedy of Western Boluo Immortals, four volumes of Remedy of Western Doctors (12 volumes of content), 20 volumes of Remedy of Brahmin Immortals, five volumes of Remedy of Brahmin, two volumes of Remedy of Immortals Told by Jivaka (one catalogue content list, plus 3 volumes as the content), ten volumes of Remedy of Qiantuoli, four volumes of New Remedy of Qiantuoli, two volumes of Nāgārjuna Bodhisattva's Method of Making Incense, one volume of Nāgārjuna Bodhisattva's Method of Mental Cultivation.

Some monks were proficient in Buddhist scriptures and medical treatment. During the emperor Xianwen in Northern Wei Dynasty, the imperial head doctor Li Xiu, who learnt acupuncture from a Shramana monk Tan, presided over writing and reorganizing remedies. Teng Yongwen, a procurator of Hengyang in the late Zho, when he temporarily lived in Man Shui Temple in Luoyang, Indian monks healed his years-long sickness. Monk Fa Kai learnt medical treatment from Jivaka and had a good command of medicines. Once he helped a woman of dystocia in the host family a safe delivery with acupuncture and mutton soap when he begged for accommodation. In the year of Shengping in Eastern Jin (year 361), Fa Kai treated royal patients.

With a long history, Indian medical treatment was self-contained. Medical records were found in In the Atharvaveda and Arthasastra. In the book Classics of Wuwang, theories of pathophysiology were discussed as human's health is controlled by four points. If one of the four points was dysfunctional, man will catch and illness and could catch hundreds of illnesses, if all of the four points dysfunctional. Fokaifanzhia Jing said that "the universe, earth, human and object was all controlled by the four qi (materials): the earth, the water, the fire and the wind." In other words, human was composed of four points whose dysfunction caused sickness. Indian medical theory was absorbed by the Chinese medical scientists since it was introduced to China. In the Tao Hongjing's preface to Bu Que Zhou Hou Bai Yi Fang, it mentioned that "a human's health is controlled by four points. If one point was dysfunctional, a man shall get one illness or more."

The book title as the Precious Remedy written by the renowned doctor Sun Simiao of the late Sui dynasty period and the beginning of the Tang Dynasty period has duplicated the Indian medical health theory of the "four points". Sun

Simiao wrote that "a man is a combination of earth, water, fire and wind. If the fire was dysfunctional, a man's body would steam; if the wind was dysfunctional, a man's body was stiff with pores closed; if the water was dysfunctional, a man's body would be swollen with asthma; if the earth was dysfunctional, a man feels tired and hard to voice… If the four points was functional, a man is healthy while one dysfunction causes one sickness and four dysfunctions led to all illnesses."

Inspired by the Indian medical theories, Sun Simiao included the Indian remedies in his book Valuable Remedy, such as the "Chang Pu remedy" and "a remedy for weak and cold" in chapter of mental cultivation in the 12th volume; the "sulfur boiling for weak and cold" in the stroke of 17th volume, "honey boiling for thirsty", "sheep bone marrow boiling for thirsty and dryness", "honey boiling for mouth dryness" in the chapter of various sickness of 19th volume; "Ajiatuo medicine for all sickness", "Aweilei pill remedy", "Panax ginseng C.A. Mey. Remedy", "white medicine remedy", "black medicine remedy", "soap remedy", "native pill", "ten remedies for pellagra", "remedy for epilepsy" in the chapter of sickness in 21st volume and "Jivaka's remedy for sickness in internal organs and for longevity in the chapter of chains in 22nd volume.

At the end of the "Chang Pu remedy", it was mentioned that it was translated by Master Sanzang, Bamomidi of Yituo Temple of Shecheng city, king of Mojietuo, Tianzhu (India), along with an envoy of the kingdom of Turkic Khanate, from the 8th year of Dayeto the July 23th to the 6th year of Wude, for Dade, Buddhist master in the Jingtu temple in Luozhou. At the end of "Panax Ginseng C.A. Mey. Remedy", it said that it was included in History of Jivaka's Remedy. The ancient Indian people, like the Chinese, sought the help of witchcraft in addition to medical treatment when they were sick. Witchcraft spells, were regarded as a method of curing disease, were introduced to China along with Buddhism due to common psychology shared by the Indian and Chinese people. Sun Simiao's books included Indian spells as well as remedies. In the driving ghost spell of the Pigu, the 13th volume of Valuable Remedy, it recorded the spell "然摩然摩，波悉谛苏若摩竭状阗提" which meant the disease could be cured if you were smart and if you desired health. In the Jivaka's Remedy of same book, also spells for longevity was mentioned.

According to Mr. Chen Yinke's opinion, Qi Bo mentioned in the ancient Chinese medical books might be the transliteration of "Jivaka"[33], a medical scientist in ancient Indian legends.

Stories recorded in Wei, Warriors Of Fate about Hua Tuo, a distinguished Chinese doctor was quite similar to stories about Qi Yu in the book A Female Qi Yu's Story, indicating that the Chinese surgeon technology was probably influenced by that of India.

---

33 Jivaka referred to "耆域" in the translated book A Female, Qi Yu's Story.

(3) Foreign Species

The development of overseas trade and foreign merchants' coming to China have expanded Chinese people's knowledge of overseas medicine and species. In the book Flora of South East Asia written by Ji Han of Jin dynasty in the second year of Yongxing (year 305), it recorded four species of grass, tree, fruit and bamboo in ancient Linyi (current middle of Vietnam), Jiuzhen in South of Vietnam, Cochin and otherregions. Besides, it mentioned that jasmine was transplanted from the West to the South China.

China had its own calendar and dates. Many people know that West Asia, North Africa have also produced a kind of "date" which was called the "Iraqi jujube". Actually this kind of date was known by the Chinese scholars for a long time. In the books of History of Wei and History of Sui, it mentioned that a "thousand-year jujube" was produced in Persia. Du Huan from Tang Dynasty mentioned in his book "Story of My Journey to Molin" and Laobosa" (the present Somalia region) of Tazi (Arab Empire), jujube was people's principle food. Duan Chengshi of Tang Dynasty named this kind of plant as the "Persian jujube" and called it "Kumang" in Persian. "Kumang" was the transliteration of Persian "khurma", that was, jujube. Duan Chengshi described the shape of the plant as follows: "the tree was thirty to forty feet long with width of five to six feet. Its leaves looked like vine yet it did not wither. It blossomed in February, like banana flowers, had two hard petals. Gradually the flower opened, more than ten pistils stood inside and two-inch long fruit in yellow and white within which was a stone of the flower. When the fruit was mature, it looked like a dried date with sweet taste and the stone became black."[34]

Chinese people knew this plant and before or in the Tang Dynasty had introduced it in Southern China. According to the Products of Lingnan written by Liu Xun of Tang Dynasty, "in Guangzhou there was a Persian date palm whose trunk was three to four feet high with no branches. Until the top of the palm, about ten branches were spreading with palm-shaped leaves. This kind of palm was called "the sea palm tree". Each three or five years, the tree yielded fruit that similar to the "northern green date", but smaller than the Chinese date. The same kind of fruit that foreign merchants brought to China was bigger and was as red as brown sugar. "It tasted soft and sweet, like jujube in the north but its stone, different from that of jujube, was round-end like a piece of amethyst."

Duan Chengshi also described a foreign plant "Qi Dun fruit" as "Qidun tree came from Persia and Byzantine Empire. It was called "qi" by people from Byzantine Empire. The tree was green, two to three feet high. Its white flowers, like grapefruit blossoms, smelt fragrant. Its fruit, like a carambola, was ripe in May." The oil plant that Duan Chengshi depicted was oil olives grown in the Mediterranean region.

---

34 Youyang Zazu (A Tang Miscellany: An Introduction to Asian Thought and Culture), Volume 18, contained in Four Treasure Notebook Series, Shanghai Ancient Books Press, 1991, p. 756.

In the book titled Materia Medica Supplements, Chen Cangqi of Tang Dynasty described a foreign plant in the 31st volume as "Abole was a plant from Byzantine Empire, shaped like Chinese honey locust fruit, tasted sweet and delicious." Duan Chengshi also mentioned this plant as the Persian honey locust" and he said that it was called "Huyeyanmo" in Persia and "Aliqufa" in Byzantine Empire. The tree was three or four feet high, four to five feet wide, and its leaves were short and small. It did not wither in cold and it grew fruits without blossoming. The pod, two feet long, was separated in the middle. Each side of the pod had a fruit which was as large as fingertip. It was dark red and black in the middle, tasted sweet and could be used as a kind of medicine". Obviously, the "Alebo" was mistakenly understood as "Abole" by Chen Cangqi. "Alebo" was transliteration of Sanskrit "aragbadha", referring to the Cassia mimosoides L. "Aliqufa" mentioned by Duan Chengshi was another transliteration of Sanskrit aragbadha rather than another name in Byzantine Empire. The term "Huyeyanmo" in Persia should be transliteration of the ancient Persian "xiyar-chambar".

The common narcissus in China today was introduced from overseas. Duan Chengshi recorded a plant "zhi" as "it originated from Byzantine Empire, with a three to four feet long flower seedling. Its root was as big as chicken eggs and its leaves looked like garlic. Its center stem was long, with six red and white blossoms bursting at the stem end. The pistil, yellow and red, yielded no fruits. This plant grew in summer and died in winter. "Zhi" was the transliteration of the ancient Persian "nargi", the narcissus. It could be inferred that it was introduced to China through foreign merchants who spoke Persian. Narcissuswas probably firstly brought to China's coastal regions of Fujian, if we consider the reputation of narcissus in Zhangzhou, Fujian today. Duan Chengshi also recorded a plant "Abosen" as "it, produced in the Byzantine Empire, was ten feet high. It was green and white with narrow leaves each in two pairs. Its fruit was red like pepper. The branches run juice like oil if they were chopped." The oil could be used to cure scabies but its price was high. The "Abosen" was actually a transliteration of "afursama" (olive ointment) in the Aramaic language.

(4) Calendar of Seven Planets

Indian astronomy and calendar, along with Buddhism, were introduced into China. Certainly, the Indian astronomy influenced Chinese people through Buddhist classics. Ancient Chinese people had different theories about the origin of the universe. The most heated discussion among the scholars during the Three Kingdoms period to the Jin Dynasty was that at the beginning, the universe, similar to an egg, was surrounded by waters. In fact, this theory had some similarities with Brahman's hiranyangarbha from India.[35]

Astronomy and calendar also attracted Chinese monks apart from Buddhist scriptures. He Chengtian from Liu-song in the Southern Dynasties asked Shi Huiyan, a monk from Dongan temple in the capital city about Indian calendar

389

---

35   See Rao Zongyi, Anda and Wu and Jin's View on universe, see History, Selected Works.

and Shi Huiyan introduced the length of shadow cast by sun, calendar, weights and measures of India to him. He Chengtian also checked the information with monks from Bali.

A large number of works of Indian astronomy and calendar were brought by Chinese monks who studied Buddhism in India on their journey home and by foreign monks who came to China. In the book Sui Shu Jing Ji Zhi (Books Catalogue in Sui Shu), some works related to astronomy and calendar were listed, such as 21 volumes of "Astronomy of Brahman", 30 volumes of "Astronomy of Jiejia Immortals", a volume of "Brahman Astronomy", 3 volumes of "Qiyaobenqi" (qi yao: seven planets; written by Zhen Shuzun of late Wei), a volume of "Qiyaoxiaojiazi calendar", a volume of "Tuiqiyao calendar" (four volumes of Qiyao calendar of Liang), a volume of "Qiyaoyaoshu", a volume of "Qiyaolifa", a volume of "Tuiqiyaoli", 4 volumes of "Qiyaolijing" (written by Zhang Bao), a volume of "Qiyaolishusuanjing" (written by Zhao), a volume of "Qiyaolishu" (written by Li Yexing), a volume of "Qiyaoyishu", 2 volumes of "Qiyaosuanshu" (written by Zhen Luan), five volumes of "Qiyaolishu") (written by an official Zhang Zhouxuan), 3 volumes of "Brahman Suanfa", a volume of "Brahman Yinyangsuanli" and 3 volumes of "Brahman Suanjing" and so on.

Shi Daoan, Shi Sengfan and Seng Hua were all proficient in astronomy, seven Yao (seven planets) and Shi Tanying, Xiao Ji, Wei Yuansong, Ru Ruke and others were masters of shu (yin and yang). The book Biography of Northern Dynasties recorded that Yin Shao, a high-rank official who mastered astronomy and shu during the Emperor Wu of the Northern Wei Dynasty reported to the emperor that he studied astronomy and shu from Shi Tanying and Dao Mu.

Counting method of India was different from that of China. Centesimal system and thousand-system were the two main counting systems in India. Centesimal system was recorded in the 12th volume of the Buddhist Classics, for example, 10 million was called "one hundred-hundred-thousand" and the unit was translated to "juzhi"; one billion was called "a hundred juzhi" and the unit was translated to "ayouduo"; hundred billion was "hundred ayouduo" and its unit was translated to "ayouta"; ten trillion was "hundred nayouta" and the unit was translated to "boluoyouta"; thousand trillion was "hundred boluoyouta" and its unit was translated to "jialuo" and so on.

In addition, times of counting method was also used in India, for example, in the 45th and 46th volume of Dafangguangfohuayan Classic, it said that "one hundred thousand was called "luocha", a hundred luocha was one "juzhi" which was the same "juzhi" in the paragraph above; square on "juzhi" was called "ayuduo", equal to a hundred trillion which was the same "ayouduo" in the paragraph above but expanding in large number; square of "ayuduo" was called "nayouta", square of a hundred trillion, expanding in large number than "nayouduo." These two kinds of counting method could be found in ancient Chinese mathematic books such as Shushujiyi, Wujingsuanshu written by Zhen Luan in the North Zhou and Sunzisuanjing.

Twenty-eight xiu (lunar mansions)

Ancient Chinese people divided the sphere near the equator into 28 segments and each segment was one mansion. They marked one constellation near the equator when setting the 28 xiu (mansions) and used one among the 28 mansions to measure distances. "Xiu" meant "night". At the beginning, 28 xiu was used to mark the movement route of the moon in each stellar month and it changed for 27 or 28 positions each month, thus was called "28 xiu." In ancient times, the orbit discussed was equator instead of zodiac and the two met in vernal equinox and autumnal equinox.

In addition to China, ancient India (including India, Pakistan, Bangladesh), Arab, Iran, Egypt and other countries had the concept of 28 lunar mansions, among which China and India were the earliest. The twenty-eight lunar mansions appeared in Egypt after the 3rd century and during the Coptic Era, 500 year in Iran and not before the writing of holy Koran was finished in Arab land. It was reasonable that the idea of 28 lunar mansion was introduced to those countries from India. Chinese scholars Zhu Kezhen, after studying similarities and differences of the concept in China and that of India, concluded that the two were homologous. China was the home to 28 lunar mansions and introduced the concept to India which was adapted and localized in India.[36]

The following are reasons why Zhu Kezhen, believed 28 lunar mansions had originated in China:

Firstly, Chinese name of the 28 lunar mansions could date back to a long time ago and most of the name source could be found. And the development process could be traced back. But in India, the source of names of 28 lunar mansions required a reasonable explanation and the development process was not clear.

Secondly, the ancient Chinese attached great importance to the North celestial pole because in China more circumpolar stars could be observed as the latitude of Yellow River where ancient Chinese lived was higher than that in Babylon and India. Traditionally, ancient Chinese knew the season by observing the handle point of the Big Dipper—the observation center among circumpolar stars. Some stars of the 28 lunar mansions could be found when people prolonged the direction to which the Polaris pointed towards these circumpolar stars. Apart from four mansions, a middle mansion of 28 lunar mansions was at the core. All these proved that the concept of 28 lunar mansions and circumpolar stars were originated in China. But in ancient India, only stars around the zodiac were observed and circumpolar stars such as the Big Dipper were not highlighted. The seasons were determined in relation with position of the sun, the moon and the 5 famous stars. Besides, in India, it had no idea that the Polaris pointed directions for 28 lunar mansions through circumpolar stars. Although the 4 mansions were discussed, middle mansion was not discussed. These showed that the 28 lunar mansions were introduced to India.

36　Zhu Kezhen, "Time and Place Origins of Twenty-eight Lunar Mansions", published in the Journal of Thought and Times, 1944/34, pp. 10-13.

Thirdly, China's 28 stars were not the brightest, nor the brightest near the equator. Among the 28 stars including the distance-measuring star, only one first-rank star and one second-rank star and generally third-rank or fourth-rank stars, and even four five-rank stars and a six-rank star could be found. The distance between the stars were not the same, thus the distance-measuring stars were to observe distance between the adjacent stars. This showed that the ancient Chinese astronomy focused on measurement and observation. The 28 stars were chosen on the basis of appropriate distance and coupling. While in India, like ancient Babylon and Greece, theories were emphasized and observation was neglected. The distance between 28 stars was similar, 13 degrees 20 points between each and the stars were scattered with no obvious coupling arrangement. India also had the concept of distance-measuring star—generally the brightest among the stars unlike the star that had measuring function in China. This illustrated that Indians did not understand the principle of how 28 lunar mansions were chosen in China. Besides, the Indians did not attach importance to the astronomical observation but modified the Chinese 24 lunar mansions to meet the Indian astronomy traditions.

Fourthly, Chinese 28 stars were divided into "Four lu" on the basis of four seasons. China's four seasons were set in accordance with the climate of the Yellow River Valley, which conformed to "Four lu" of 28 lunar mansions. Though ancient Indians divided the year into six seasons, it had "Four lu" like the division of Chinese 28 stars. The Four lu in India was a season-independent and nonfunctional factor, indicating that theory was introduced from China which Indians did not fully understand.

Fifthly, the ancient Chinese did not focus on zodiac until the Eastern Han Dynasty, and before Han they took the equator as the benchmark for the celestial sphere while India, Babylon and Greece chose equator as the benchmark. This was the fundamental difference between Eastern and Western astronomy. But India's 28 stars (or 27 stars) took equator as the standard like China, indicating that it was a foreign factor in Indian astronomy.

In summary, it could be conclude that the 28 lunar mansions were originated from and developed in China, by comparing the ancient astronomical system between China and India. The concept conformed to ancient astronomical traditions in China while going against that of India. The introduction route remained unclear. Xia Nai, "discussion on the 28 lunar mansions on the basis of a star map found in tomb of Liao in Xuanhua."[37]

Twelve sui and twelve signs of the zodiac

"Twelve sui" was recorded in 2 ancient books Master Lv's Spring and Autumn Annals and Huai Nan Zi. The names of "twelve sui" were strange, for example, the "taisui" was called "kundun" in the Huai Nan Zi. No equivalence could be found in Chinese and it might be transliteration of Sanskrit, in other

---

37   See Ancient Chinese Astronomical Relics, Heritage Publishing House 1989, pp. 287-312.

words, the concept of "12 sui" was likely imported from India, but the introduction time was probably not earlier than Qin or early Western Han Dynasty. Zhu Kezhen, "origin time and place of twenty-eight lunar mansions".[38]

The zodiac was an imaginary band in the heavens centered on the ecliptic that encompassed the apparent routes. Region of eight degree within both sides of zodiac was called zodiac band, with 16 degree width. The sun, the moon and main planets traveled within this band. The ancient Chinese divided the zodiac band into twelve parts, known as the twelve signs of the zodiac each ranged 30 degrees and signed with a constellation across the zodiac band.

The 12 signs of the zodiac were divided on the basis of the zodiac rather than the equator. The "number twelve" referred to 12 months in a year. Each sign of zodiac ranged 30 degree, consistent to twelve equal parts of 360 degree in Western astronomy, required no distance-measuring star like 28 lunar mansions did. Thus, it can be seen that the 12 signs of the zodiac and the 28 lunar mansions belonged to different astronomical systems.

The concept of the 12 signs of the zodiac originated in the Babylon as there were traces of zodiac on the cuneiform script of 2100 BC and it was brought to Greece 800 years later. After the Eastern Expedition of Alexander the Great around the second century BC, the twelve signs of the zodiac came into India. Twelve signs of the zodiac in India had two sets of names from Greece: one was transliteration version with some errors and the other was liberal translation version.

The concept of 12 signs of the zodiac was introduced to China with the translation of Buddhist scriptures. Early in the Sui Dynasty (581-619 AD), this concept appeared in the book Da Cheng Da Fang Deng Ri Cang Jing translated by Ye Lian Ti Ye She who started translation work as early as Qi. Da Cheng Da Fang Deng Ri Cang Jing was a part of Da Fang Deng Da Ji Jing which was translated in the early Sui Dynasty, the second half of 6th century. From the early Sui to the Song Dynasty, the twelve signs of the zodiac appeared frequently in different Buddhist scriptures in different names. At the end of the Tang Dynasty and the Five Dynasties, the concept of twelve signs of the zodiac was discussed in books written by Chinese when they mentioned "shu" and prediction. At that time, the name of 12 signs of the zodiac translated was gradually unified.

The image of the twelve signs of the zodiac was introduced into China around the Tang Dynasty. The earliest one was remains of astrology, unearthed in Turpan, Xinjiang, with a map, seven mansions among the 28 lunar mansions and three signs of the zodiac among the 12 and some Chinese characters. The map of stars was already localized. Another was the Buddhist painting on both sides of the corridor wall in the cave number 61 among the Dunhuang Thousand Buddha Cave. In the background sky of the mural, it painted twelve

---

38   See Journal of Thought and Times, 1944/34, pp. 8-9.

signs of the zodiac both in the North and the South. The shape and painting skill clearly seem as the Chinese style. Murals in the cave were painted in the early Song Dynasty while those in the corridor were painted during Kingdom of Xia (1038-1227 AD). In 1974, a colored painting map was found in the dome center of a Tomb of Liao in Xiabali village in Xuanhua district, Zhangjiakou, Hebei province. On the map 28 lunar mansions, the Big Dipper and 12 signs of the zodiac were drawn and the zodiac painting was in completely Chinese style. Xia Nai, "discussion on the twenty-eight lunar mansions on the basis of a star map found in tomb of Liao in Xuanhua".[39]

Since, the 12 signs of the zodiac repeated the concept of original 28 lunar mansions and twelve star ranks introduced in Qin and Han dynasties to some degree in the astronomical observation, they were not used in Chinese calendar study. In the Jin Dynasty (1115-1234 AD) and Yuan Dynasty (1271-1368 AD), numerous Uyghur people came to China with Mongols, bringing their Uyghur calendar. The measurement method of Uyghur calendar originated from ancient Greek astronomy with zodiac as the observation benchmark. Rulers in the Yuan Dynasty attached great importance to Uyghur astronomy by setting up a special astronomical secretary to make calendar on the basis of Uyghur calendar. The Uyghur calendar was used among people from the Western regions in the Yuan Dynasty period and acted as a reference calendar for the verification of Chinese traditional calendars. Since overthrow of Yuan Dynasty, Uyghur people had lost their political power, they had previously enjoyed in the Yuan Dynasty period but their culture was maintained and developed. In the Ming Dynasty (1368-1644 AD) before Western missionaries' coming, Uyghur astronomers has worked in the special department of astronomy, they have studied on calendars, examined the foreign calendars and translated Uyghur astronomical books in which the most detailed information about 12 zodiac signs in ancient China was recorded.

(5) Vegetarianism

Vegetarianism has existed in China for long. In the pre-Qin Dynasty, the rich and powerful often ate meat while the poor people basically ate grain for food, thus phrases like "the meat eaters despised it" were recorded in the book of Spring and Autumn Annals. In the book "Zhuangzi", it was recorded: "since Yanhui, one of the disciples of Confucius, was poor, he did not drink alcohol nor ate meat for months". In the book Biography of Wang Mang, History of Han Dynasty, it recorded that in the late Western Han, Wang Mang ate no meat when natural disasters of flood or drought happened. On hearing it, the empress dowager sent someone to tell him that she knew he was so sorrow that he ate only vegetables and fruits. Obviously, the main food of the the poor people was fruit and vegetables. The Buddhism advocated that animals should be set free rather than being people's food. Later on, Devadatta, a disciple of Sakyamuni, held that Buddhists should practice Buddhist rules and drink no milk and

---

39 See Ancient Chinese Astronomical Relics, Heritage Publishing House 1989, pp. 287-312.

ate no eggs, fish and meat. In addition to animal meat, the Buddhist took no pungent ingredient such as garlic, ferula sinkiangensis, brassica campestris and coriander and so on.

Mahayana Buddhism was mainly introduced to Chinese mainland. It held that alcohol, meat and five pungent ingredients should be banned for monks as it believed that "alcohol spoiled people". It listed ten misbehaviors, thirty-five misbehaviors and thirty-six errors of drinking alcohol. It believed that eating meat opposed mercy because eating meat meant killing, which violated five precepts of Buddhism and so on. Thus, after the introduction of Buddhism into China, the "vegetarian food", a new diet branch appeared as it combined vegetables the poor used to eat with the doctrine of Buddhism. The "vegetarian food", inheriting the mercy of Buddhism and vegetarianism of school of Devadatta with China's Taoist rules, cooked food in Chinese way. Even the leeks were in the "meat" dish list. But in fact, common folks ate vegetables in the "meat" dish list. During the emperor Liangwu in Southern Dynasties, the vegetarianism greatly progressed, for instance, a monk cook of Jianye temple in Nanjing could make a dozen of dishes out of a cucumber in a dozen of flavors. In the independent chapter of "vegetarian food" in "Qi Min Yao Shu", it listed dishes such as "onion leeks soup", "gourd soup", "oiled laver" and so on; ingredients such as wax gourd, gourd, leeks, celery, mushroom, eggplants and so on; spicy sauce like onions, ginger, cinnamon, pepper, tempeh, salt, oleum sesami and honey.

395

Vegetarian food was gradually optimized even before the Yuan Dynasty, as a result, a branch of pictographic vegetarian food developed. In the book A Collection of Household Stuff written in Yuan Dynasty, it recorded that some vegetarian dish was named after meat in the pursuit of the shape of the meat. For example, the dish "vegetarian lungs" was named due to the lung-shape of the food and "double fish" was named on the basis of fish-shape of the hand-making food. Some dish named after eel was colored so that it looked like the color of eels. After the Ming and Qing Dynasties, vegetarian food was mainly developed in the temple. The Chinese "Laba porridge", also known as "Buddhist porridge", was a kind of vegetarian food. Besides, vegetarian steamed stuffed bun was called "suanjian".

(6) The Indian Ocean Rim Recorded in the Ancient Chinese Books

The cultural traditions of China and India were different. Chinese paid attention to science and practice while the Indians were full of fantasy. Ancient Indians gave full play to their imagination, thus, fables and myths were extremely developed but valuable historical works were few. The Chinese were just the opposite. Records on the Indian and South Asian subcontinent were consistently preserved in official and individual documents or in Buddhist works in different dynasties for 2,000 years.

Some other countries, apart from China, also preserved bibliographies of Indian history. For example, in the book Indian Chronicles written by Arian from ancient Rome and Geography Chronicles written by Strabo, some descriptions about India in Maurya dynasty in the 4th century BC in ancient Greece were retained. But these materials, could not rival the Indian recordings in ancient Chinese books, in terms of richness and authenticity. So it could be said that the history of India was preserved in Chinese historical writings without which the study of Indian history was almost impossible.

Chinese historical records on Indian Ocean rim before the Tang Dynasty was extensive, including the relationship between China and Southeast Asian countries and that between China and the Indian Ocean countries, the local history, customs, species and specialties, commercial trade, geographical transportation, spread of Buddhism and other religions, culture and art and other information. From the classification, the recordings covered both official and unofficial historical books and other materials.

In the official historical books, the most distinguished content was the recorded route from South China to South Asia in Geography of History of Han Dynasty, which was quoted in the previous chapter. Geography of History of Han Dynasty, written by Fan Ye in the 22nd year of Yuanjia during the period of the Song dynasty of the Southern Dynasties, recorded that Guishuang dynasty communicated with Imperium Romanum after conquering the north of India. When the transportation was blocked to the the Western Regions, it frequently visited China from Rinan (currentmiddle region of Vietnam). In the History of Song, Biography of Foreigners written by Shen Yue in the 6th year of Yongming (488 AD), two translated diplomatic letters from the period of Later Han, which were addressed to Chinese dynasties were given: one of them was a credential written by the lion country (Sri Lanka) to emperor Wen of the Liu Song dynasty and the other was a credential written by king Yue Ai of Kapilavatthu, Tianzhu (India) to emperor Wen of the Liu Song dynasty. In the book History of South Qi, Biography of Southeast Asia written by Xiao Zixian, a story was narrated about a Tianzhu (India) Taoist Najiaxian's experiences in Funan city of Linyi region (currentmiddle of Vietnam) and South Qi, but Taoist Najiaxian was robbed in the Linyi city on his journey back home from Guangzhou to Funan while travelling on the sea.

There were many records about the Indian Ocean rim in unofficial works, among which Wei Lue written by Yu Huan from Jingzhao, Wei, during the Three Kingdoms was a critical one. The book described the West Asia, the Eastern Mediterranean region and the Indian Ocean region. For example, the book referred to the birthplace of Sakya-muni "lin er nation" which was luomingda in current Nepal, "che li nation", more than three thousand km. away from Tianzhu (India), "Panyue Kingdom" in the East of India where merchants of Shu used to trade. Yu Huan also wrote: "if you sail Southward, going through seven counties of Cochin, you can reach the Imperium Romanum. Besides, there are waterways accessible from Imperium Romanum to Yizhou and Yongchang, which are used as trade transportation from Yunnan to over-seas through Myanmar". However, Yu Huan's whole work was lost, but there are some extant texts of him in the Annotation of Warriors of Fate written by Pei Songzhi in the 6th year of Yuanjia (429 AD).

Buddhist works such as Journey in Buddhist Countries, also known as Fa Xian Zhuan, Fa Xian Xing Zhuan, Fo You Tianzhu Ji and Li You Tianzhu Jizhuan and so on, written by Fa Xian in Jin Dynasty and Stories of Eminent Monks written by Hui Jiao of Liang were also remarkable historic records. Fa Xian, set out from Changan, crossed rivers and climbed mountains and finally arrived in North Tianzhu. In the year of 408, he reached East Tianzhu, taking a ship to the lion country (the present Sri Lanka) and returned in the year of 412. Fa Xian's autobiographical work was recognized as the most important historical material for studying the history and culture of countries along the maritime Silk Road at that time. Hui Jiao's Stories of Eminent Monks was a collection of biography of eminent monks from the Eastern Han Dynasty to the beginning of the Liang. Many biography books of monks appeared during Jin and Liang such as Recordings of Renowned Monks written by Bao Chang. The book Stories of Eminent Monks was written on the basis of Hui Jiao's absorb-ing essences of the previous works. The book, recording a lot of stories about monks who came to China or Chinese monks who studied Buddhism abroad, was highlighted by scholars who studied the spreading history of Buddhism.

There were some critical mystery novels during this time, such as Bowuzhi (Ancient Encyclopedia) written by Zhang Hua, Flora of South East Asia writ-ten by Ji Han, Stories of Countries in the South written by Wan Zhen, geo-graphic work Commentary on the Waterways Classic written by Li Daoyuan. The content of Bowuzhi was extensive, including mountains and geography, exotic flowers and trees, beasts and insects, myths and legends. Commentary on the Waterways Classic provided annotation for Waterway Classic written during the Three Kingdoms. Commentary on the Waterways Classic preserved immeasurable valuable and rare information about India and Southeast Asia. Books that Li Daoyuan quoted in describing rivers out of China such as Funan Zhuan written by Wu Kangtai, Guangyi written by Guo Guangyi in the Jin Dynasty period, Waiguoshi written by Zhisengzai, Shishi Xiyu Ji and the Fo Diao Chuan written by Shi Daoan, History of Funan by Song Zhuzhi were lost, leaving fragments preserved in Li Daoyuan's annotation in his work. Since the 20th century, it has been a hot academic trend to study the pre-Tang Dynasty history of communications between China and foreign countries on the basis of Chinese historical recordings.

Chapter 3. Unprecedented Development of Cultural Exchanges between China and Foreign Countries

1. Chinese and Foreign Currencies

When we studied the ancient economic exchanges between China and foreign countries, it can be found there exits such a phenomenon: Chinese coins get into circulation in the foreign countries and the foreign precious metal coins flowed into China. Since there were trades between countries, there was a problem of payment. The trades between ancient China and overseas countries were mainly through barter, which inevitably encountered the imbalance in trades. Once the value of the barter was not balanced, the deficit party must be paid by currency. There were two ways of currency payments: one was to use precious metals, and the other was to use their own currency that gained the international recognition in purchasing power. Generally speaking, the currencies of weaker countries were hard to be accepted by other countries, so they were required to pay the barter deficit with precious metals, while countries with stronger economies could pay in their own currencies because we accepted their currencies circulating in their own countries as international ones.

Comparing with the countries along the Maritime Silk Road, China was strong and rich. Therefore, the foreign demands for Chinese currencies were gradually increasing, which made the Chinese coins more valuable than overseas goods. However, foreign people found that Chinese currencies were mainly copper coins, a kind of inferior metal coin; on the contrary, their currencies that flowed into China were mostly gold, silver and other precious metals.

The ancient Southeast Asia had been at a lower development stage in production and exchange for long ages, so they had little or no local coins, and had allowed the flow Chinese into their countries as a generally accepted currency. Therefore, Chinese copper coins and precious metals which flowed into Southeast Asia were used as their local currencies rather than flowing back to China as local merchants purchased the Chinese goods. It was for this reason that the demand for Chinese coins had grown in the past thousands of years.

The Southeast Asia traded not only with China, but also with South Asia and West Asia, so with the passage of time and the development of trades, the coins of South Asia and West Asia also flowed into Southeast Asia, and were as recognized by the local people as the Chinese copper coins. That was to say, it was possible to find the Chinese, Indian and Western Asian ancient coins in Southeast Asia. In short, the Western precious metal coins and the Chinese copper coins had played the function of large denominated banknotes and less valued coins respectively in the history of the Southeast Asia.

(1) The Outflow of Copper Coins from China

Before the Qin Dynasty, the Chinese currency had flowed to the Northeast Asia, such as Korea and Japan.[1]

We do not have enough evidence about when Chinese coins were introduced into the Southeast Asia and the Indian Ocean. It is argued that many people had used the sea shells as currency in the Southeastern China and the Sulu Islands of the Philippines and in the northern regions of Borneo, indicating that China and islanders of the Southeast Asian had trade relations in the period d before the Han Dynasty.

Before the Westerners came to the East, in addition to the inflow of currencies of India and the Western Asian, the Southeast Asia had used Chinese coins for more than 1500 years and this phenomenon had lasted till the modern times. The earliest Chinese currency found in the Southeast Asia was casted in the Western Han Dynasty. And in Brunei (ancient Borneo) and Indonesia also some coins of the Tang Dynasty was unearthed which were, called "Kaiyuan Tongbao". Since the Tang Dynasty, the Chinese coins started to flow to Vietnam, Kampuchea, Thailand and Malaysia. The court in the Song Dynast banned the outflow of the Chinese coins, but this had failed in vain. According to the book, The Introductions of Foreign Countries written by the Zhso Rush, "the merchants in the Song Dynasty often secretly carry copper coins to trade pepper in Java. In addition, Ma Huan in the Ming Dynasty wrote a book, The Overall Survey of the Ocean's Shores, and said, "the most of foreign people are rich and they use Chinese ancient coins, in trading".

---

1 Wang Guichen and Wang Dawwen, See the Maritime Silk Road in Guangzhou from the Ancient Chinese and Foreign Currency Exchanges, Guangzhou and the Maritime Silk Road, p. 93.

After the Song Dynasty, the outflow of Chinese copper coins was more serious. According to reports in Brunei, they have found there were various kind of Chinese coins of the Song Dynasty, such as "Xianping Yuanbao" (998-1003), "Xining Yuanbao" (1068-1077), "Yuanfeng Tongbao" (1078-1085) and "Kaixi Tong bao" (1205-1207).[2]

Large quantities of Chinese coins were often found in ancient Chinese shipwrecks in Java and Southeast Asia. At the end of January 1991, when I participated the activity of investigating the Maritime Silk Road sponsored by UNESCO, I have seen that there were many Chinese coins of the Song Dynasty in the Brunei National Museum, such as, "Shengsong Yuanbao", "Huangsong Tongbao", "Yuanfeng Tongbao" and "Shaoding Tongbao" (1228-1233). The Chinese copper coins found in Java and Bali, Indonesia, were mainly from the dynasties after the Northern Song Dynasty. In the middle of January, only a small part of coins, "Kaiyuan Tongbao", were from the Tang Dynasty. In addition, in the middle of 1991, the author also saw some the Song Dynasty coins including "Daguan Tongbao" (1107-1110) and "Xuanhe Tongbao" (1119-1125) at the Majapahit Museum site of East Java Province. The fundamental reason that Chinese copper coins had occupied a dominant position in Southeast Asia was that Chinese ancient coins were technologically advanced, abundant in quantity, stable in color and lower in cost. So after the Tang Dynasty, the Chinese currencies were used not only in Southeast Asia and the Eastern Indian Ocean region, but also in the Western Indian Ocean. At the end of November 1990, I have also witnessed the Song Dynasty coins at the opening ceremony of the Cultural Center of the capital of the Dhofar Province, i.e., the Oman.

With the development of trade and the increase of the demand for coins in Southeast Asia, the influx of Chinese ancient coins could not meet their needs, so they began to cast their own coins. Their early coins often imitated the style of the Han Dynasty period casting in order to promote their popularity and acceptance, since the Chinese coins were recognized and popular among the Southeast Asian peoples. After 9th century, some regions in Java began to use Chinese or Japanese raw materials to cast the Hang Dynasty copper and tin coins with the shape of a circular form with a square hole in the middle. However, the Chinese characters on coins were replaced with the patterns of the Buddhism and Indian Shaivism. The earliest local minted copper coin in Vietnam, "Taiping Xingbao", also narrated about the style of the Tang Dynasty and the Song Dynasty copper coins. In the 13th century, Java had casted native coins imitating the style of Northern Song Dynasty, and these coins were also cut the Chinese characters, such as "Xianping Yuanbao", "Jingde Yuanbao", "Xiangfu Tongbao" and "Tiansheng Yuanbao". Some old coins can be still found today, their shape is a circle form with a square hole in the center and the Chinese characters, "Xiangfu Tongbao" on them can still be clearly read.

---

2   William L.S. Barrett, Brunei and Nusantara History in Coinage, Bandar Seri Begawan, Pusat Sejarah Brunei, p. 98, 1988.

It was not until modern times that the Bali of Indonesia ceased using Chinese copper coins. It is written that the number of Chinese copper coins hidden by the people in the Lombok, Bali and other islands roughly reached 1,000 tones. Taiwan and Japan sometimes bought dozens of tons of copper coins from these places and then selected the best coins. After the issuance of Yuan Dynasty banknotes, Chinese banknotes had also begun to circulate in the Southeast Asia. Due to widespread use of Chinese currency in Southeast Asia, so gradually the rate of exchange between the Chinese currency and the foreign currency was formed. According to Wang Dayuan in the book Daoyi Zhilue (a book which introduced the foreign countries) records, "a country called Jiaozhi in the Yuan Dynasty (located in the Northern Vietnam today) uses copper coins in circulation. The ordinary people exchange 67 copper coins for one banknote while officials exchange 70 copper coins for one banknote." Therefore, such conclusion can be drawn: there were two kinds of exchange rate between officials and ordinary people, and the exchange rate of the ordinary people was lower than that of officials. At the same time, the book said "in the Lopburi kingdom (located in the regions Ochoa Phraya River, Thailand), the local people use seashells as currency. The rate of exchange between seashells and banknote is 100,000:24. In the Wudi (located in Burma today), the local currency could exchange 11 banknotes or more than 15,020 seashells. "

(2) The Gold and Silverware Served as Currencies in Jiaozhou and Guangzhou

The ancient China had a vast territory, but due to restrictions of expedition conditions, there were many local markets. Even in the unification period, although the national decree was unified, the economic development still had strong regional features. What's worse, the imbalances in economic development were more obvious in the period of the country's disintegration. The book, The History of Sui Dynasty Food and Currencies Record said, in the Liang Dynasty the most regions of inland in ancient China traded with copper coins or through barter system, only in the Jiaozhou and Guangzhou (located in the Lingnan region) used silver and gold as currencies. Why did the Jiaozhou and Guangzhou implement the gold and silver standard system? The book of The History of Sui Dynasty ·Food and currency Record said, in the early Zhou Dynasty, many counties in the Hexi region (in the Gansu Province)used gold and silver as currencies in their trade and the official did not take many measures to stop this behavior. As the throat of the ancient land Silk Road, Hexi region was flourishing in foreign trade, so the people here used the Han Dynasty's coins as well as silver and gold in the transaction. It can be deluded that the reason of silver and gold serving as currencies in the Jiaozhou and Guangzhou was that it was a gathering place for the merchants from the Hexi region. The truth of the silver and gold serving as currencies in the Lingnan region was recorded by many poets. For example, Zhang Ji in the Tang Dynasty Zhang said: "the countries along the sea fight with elephant and the people in the Lingnan region use silver as a currency." Yuan Zhen wrote a poem and also mentioned: "from the south of the Lingnan region, gold and silver served as currencies. Han Yu, who was demoted to Chaozhou, also said: "Lingnan region uses silver in all trade transactions."

Some ancient Chinese scholars have noticed the spread of foreign coins in China long ago. Since the Historical Records written by Sima Qian, a historian in Han Dynasty, the Chinese history books began to record the shape of foreign coins. As a branch of ancient artifacts, ancient coins was first issued and promoted in the ancient China, and some staff who were responsible to keep the record of the issued coins appeared in the Han Dynasty period, yet it is not clear when these staff began to record the foreign coins. Hong Zun (1120-1174), a scholar in the Southern Song Dynasty period, wrote a book named Currencies. It was said this book was not the first to record foreign coins in China. This book introduced 348 coins, 85 of which were foreign coins, accounting for nearly a quarter of the whole coins. Hong did not witness all the coins in this book, so the records about some coins were inaccurate. In addition, some records were too brief because of lacking related information. But Hong said, he witnessed some coins in this book in Guangzhou, such as the coin of the Dashi country (refers to the Arab Empire as well as the Muslim people who belong to those races which spoke the Persian languages) A book titled as the Guangzhou Records said: "Dashi country is rich in gold, and does deals with gold." Meanwhile, a book, the Important Events in courts of all Dynasties wrote, "the Dashi country offers the emperor silver coins and gold coins as tributes. These coins with hieroglyphics that were mainly made of gold were very small, which could be seen in the South Sea."In short, the emergence of a variety of foreign coins in China reflected the ever increasing frequency of maritime exchanges between Chinese and foreign countries.

In recent years, numerous ancient foreign currencies were discovered in the archaeological excavations made in the Lingnan region. As data display, the outflow of Chinese coins have been mainly inferior metal coins including copper ones, but on the contrary, the foreign currencies that flowed into China were mostly made of precious metal coins.

According to the statistics, silver coins of the Persian Sassanid Empire were discovered in the Lingnan region between 1915 to 1974, twice. Firstly, on July 1960, when the Guangdong Relic Management Committee together with history Department of the South China Normal University conducted an archaeological excavation targeting the tomb of Southern Qi Dynasty at the turning of the 5-6 century, and discovered three silver coins of the Sassanid Empire, two of which were mutilated and one was intact. There are two holes in the middle of the intact coin which was used for jade rope or meant to imitate the shape of the Chinese copper coins, with a hole in the middle of it.[3]

---

3 The South China Sea Silk Road Cultural Relic Atlas, p. 44.

In addition, in the one face of this silver coin was the head of the king with his crown and the other face of the coin contained a Zoroastrianism fire altar with burning fire and cut the sun and the moon on the top. The 2 mutilated coins were probably broken into 2 parts during their use in circulation. According to Prof. Xia Nai's research these three silver coins were issued during the reign of the Luz Emperor—Peroz, who ruled the Sassanid Empire from 459 to 484. Secondly, experts found 9 silver coins from the Sassanid Empire in Shaoguan, located in the northern Guangdong province.[4]

These 9 mutilated silver coins were found in the tomb of the Southern Dynasty, in March 1973, located in the southeast hillside of the Nanhua temple, Qujiang County, Guangdong Province. These mutilated coins cannot be pieced together. Probably, there coins were also damaged during circulation.

On September 29, 1984, when a common man was leveling the foundation for building his house, he discovered a covered pot, which was full of gold and silver utensils in the Bianwan village, Fucheng district, Suixi County, Guangdong Province. This pot was filled with about 100-200 silver coins, but the government only took back 20 silver coins. In addition, the government also nationalized 3.55 kg damaged silver, two gold rings, two gold cups. It was an unprecedented discovery. These silver coins can be classified into 4 designs, but they had some common nature: on the obverse of these coins was the head of a king wearing the crown and the on the reverse of them were the Zoroastrian fire altar with burning fire and the sun and the moon was engraved on the top. The experts have estimated that 3 silver coins were issued during the reign of the Shabre III (383-388 AD) because the crown of the king was decorated with a sphere and a ribbon; 5 silver coins were issued during the reign of the Yazdgerd II (438-457) because the front of the king's crown had a new moon and the king was surrounded by pattern of a string of beads. The rest 12 silver coins were two different kinds of Peruz silver coins, many of which were perforated to be used as hole for threading the string of adornment or a string of coins like the Chinese pepper coins. Therefore, it could be deluded that these coins in the affluent homes not only were used in circulation, but also served as adornments. These silver coins as change were often cut into many pieces. From 1 kilometer to the East of the Suixi where Persian silver coins were found, there was a West Xihe River and its estuary to the sea was away about 10 km. Possibly the Persian silver coins were related to the sea merchants.

The Persian coins that circulated in the Lingnan region were undoubtedly brought by the traders from the Western Asian through maritime trade. According to records, in the Southern Dynasty, the number of the foreign vessels arrived in Guangzhou everyday was at least three or five, sometimes more than ten.[5]

4   Xia Nai: Silver Coins of Persian Sassanid Empire Unearthed in China, Journal of Archaeology, 1974/1.
5   The History of Southern Dynasty, Biographies of Wuping hou Jing and Zili.

In other words, the numbers of foreign vessels arrived in Hong Kong, were at least one on average per quarter, and at most reached one ship per month. The majority of overseas precious metal coins circulating in Lingnan flowed into China through this channel. The purpose of the Persian merchants to visit Guangzhou was to buy silk material. A Tang Dynasty monk, Xin Luo, once mentioned, that the Persian people liked trade and business, "they often cross the West Sea (refer to as Persian Gulf) by ships into the South Seas (refer to as the India ocean) and assume treasures of the lion country (current Sri Lanka) so that they are rich in treasures. Sometimes, they go to the Kunlun country (refer to as Southeast Asia) to purchase gold and on the way, they also stop in Guangzhou to purchase silk. The Persian traders have sailed eastwards for several important purposes: firstly, assess to the treasures of the Sri Lanka (the lion country), which is located in the south end of South Asia Sub-continent, which abounds in gem; secondly, purchase gold from the Kunlun country, which was rich in gold, and finally, buy silk from China."

In the world trade at that time, China's relationship with overseas countries was similar to current relations between developed and developing Ed countries: China was a society with relatively higher productive forces and its products were appreciated by the people in many countries, so its markets was wide and a numerous kind of manufactured goods were exported to foreign countries. On the contrary, the foreign goods, with the exception of incenses and herbs, were unpopular in China. Therefore, the foreign traders exchanged Chinese goods for gold and silver. This was the reason why overseas gold and silver poured into the Lingnan region since after the Southern Dynasty to the Tang Dynasty. In the Tang Dynasty, the circulation of gold and silver in Lingnan region was known as "South Gold". The poet Wang Jian wrote a poem to show the foreign traders came to the Chinese seaport to purchase goods with a larger amount of gold, which affected the price of the gold in the Lingnan region. When the domestic people heard that the price of the gold went downwards, they could guess that foreign ships had arrived in the port. Only when the excessive inflow of gold and silver in the Lingnan region would flow to inland China, the price of the gold in Guangzhou would return to the normal levels. But as the next foreign ship arrived, the price of the gold and silver would firstly fall and then rise again.

(3) The Currency Flow into the Southeast Asia Region

The precious metal coins of the Western Regions (a Han Dynasty term for the region in the West of Yumenguan including the current Xinjiang and parts of Central Asia) flowed into not only the China's Southeast coast, but also Southeast Asia. In the 20th century, many coins were discovered in the Southeast Asia which originated from the West countries before the Song Dynasty, including Indian coins. For example, the Indian coins in the reign of the Kumaragupta I (414-455) of the Gupta Dynasty, was found among the foreign currency in Thailand.

The Persian silver coins which were discovered in Borneo included the silver coins made by the Khusraw II (591-628), the kingdom of the Sassanid Dynasty in Ctesiphon (in the following year after he ascends the throne) and in Sirjan (he ascends the throne in 33 years). In addition, a variety of silver coins of the White Tazi (Umayyad Caliphate) were found here, including the silver coins forged in the Basr of Iraq in 679 during the reign of the Ummayadallah B. Ziyad. These silver coins forged by the early Arab still retained the features of that of the Sassanid Dynasty: the one side of the coins was a crowned king, and the other side included a Zoroastrian flaming fire altar. But the silver coins forged by Abd al-Malik (who ruled between 65-86, according to the Islam calendar) in the Basra city had no longer imitated the style of the Sassanid Dynasty coins. The coins casted by the Umar II (Islam calendar 99-101) in the Damascus city, Shan country (Syria), the coins forged by Hi Sharm (Islam calendar 105-125) in the Wasit, Irakvasit in the Islam calendar 121. The various silver coins in the period of the Black Tazi (Abbasids) found in Borneo include: the coins casted by the Al Mansur(Islam calenda36-158) in the Baghdad, Iraqi in the Islam calendar (year 155), the coins casted by the Harun al-Rashid (Islam calendar 170-193) in the Salam in the Islam calendar 189.[6]

After the Song Dynasty, in the Southeast Asia region, foreign coins including the Western precious metal coins and China's copper coins had increased abundantly. At the same time, the native coins of Southeast Asia also began to become popular. The Chinese and foreign currencies that converged in Southeast Asia witnessed the flourishing of East-West trade in this period.

2. Foreign Goods Flood China's Markets

Since the Sui Dynasty replaced the Chen Dynasty, the territory as extended to the South of China and the Chinese reverted to reunification. During the Tang Dynasty, the Chinese feudal society entered its heyday, and overseas trade developed to a new stage. According to the Japanese monk records, "in the period of the Kaiyuan in the Tang Dynasty, there are many ships with various incense and medicines and treasures from the Brahman, Persia, Kunlun countries and from several other countries in the Pearl River, Guangzhou."[7]

In the period of the emperor of the Daizong in the Tang Dynasty, the number of ships arriving in Guangzhou each year was minimum four or five, and more than 40 but it was more than that of the Southern Dynasty period.[8]

Han Yu in the preface of his book "Send Zheng" described the prosperity of overseas trade in Guangzhou and said: "as long as the foreign ship arrive in Guangzhou, the pearl incense, elephant rhinoceros, tortoise shell and other exotic objects will widespread in China."Liu Yuxi also wrote a poem to describe the flourishing scene of foreign trades in Guangzhou.[9]

6   Brunei and Nusantara History In Coinage by William L. S. Barrett; published by the Brunei History Center, Brunei Darussalam in 1988, pp. 99-101.
7   Zhenren Kaiyuan: The History of the Monks Traveling to the West during the Tang Dynasty Period, quoted by the Wang Xiangrong, Zhonghua Book Company, p. 74, 1979.
8   The History of New Tang Dynasty·Li Mian Biography.
9   Poetry of Liu Yuxi, Vol.4.

After the Tang Dynasty, the overseas trades continued to develop, and the coastal ports and cities maintained their prosperity. Many documents recorded this boom in Guangzhou. For example, Li Tao said: "all the treasures of the foreign countries are gathered here."[10]

The History of the Song Dynasty History recorded: "Guangzhou is full of treasures."[11]

A poet, Cheng Shimeng from the Song Dynasty period said: "there are many pearls in Guangzhou, the city is very prosperous."[12]

In 1153, the foreign ships arrived in Guangzhou across the Zhanchen (ancient Indochina), Zhenla (current Cambodia), Sanfuji (Sumatra), Dupo (Java) and brought many popular goods such as the Rhinoceros, elephants, beads and various incenses.[13]

(1) The Golden and Silver Products As Well As Glassware

Because China and the West were far away from each other, they have developed their own metallurgy and metal technology respectively. Since the ancient times, there were great difference in the manufacture process of metal products. The Chinese people liked to cast metal products while the Western people loved to hammer metal and then made products. The Western Region's silver and gold wares made by the hammer technology gained the favor of the Chinese people for the long time and were the treasures of the royal kings, princes and rich people. In the early ancient China, the technology of making gold and silver wares was not yet advanced, currently we have only some dozens of gold and silver wares from the Tang Dynasty period, but many of them were imported from the foreign countries through both land and sea.

In 1983, the archaeologists excavated the tomb of Zhao Mei, the second generation king of the Nanyue kingdom—Western Han Dynasty, located in the Xianggang Mountain of the Jiefang North Road, Guangzhou found a total of more than 1000 relics, including a flat spherical Persian silver round box with lid. With a height of 12.1 cm, abdominal diameter 14.8 cm and weighed 272.6 grams, it was a treasure from the early Western Han Dynasty period. Its cover and body were decorated with the main stripe of the garlic-shaped, which was a typical Persian pattern. In addition, the edges of the cover and body were decorated with a spike-like narrow strip and plated with a thin layer of gold. Later, this silver box flowed into China and then was engraved with the ancient

10   The continuation of the Zi Zhi Tong Jian, Vol. 6, The Zizhi Tongjian is a pioneering reference work in Chinese historiography, published in 1084 , in the form of a chronicle, by Sima Guang.
11   The History of the Song Dynasty·Cai Jing Biography Cai Jing (1047-1126), courtesy name Yuanchang, was a government official and calligrapher who lived in the Northern Song Dynasty.
12   Wang Xiangzhi, Yu Di Ji Shen, Vol. 99, (Yudi jisheng is an imperial geography of the Southern Song period compiled by Wang Xiangzhi).
13   Shi Wu Tang Ji of Panzhou Anthology, Vol. 30.

Chinese characters. It was said that this was the ware that placed the medicine of the King Zhao Mei. The silver box was similar to the wares of carving the Xerxes in the Ahemenide Dynasty in 5 BC, which were unearthed in Susa of Iran. It was probably the artifacts of the ancient Empire era. The excavation of it suggested that maritime trades between China and Persia had started in the pre-Qin era.

In 1984, a group of exquisite gold and silver wares made by hammer technology were unearthed in the Bianwan village, Suixi County, where the Sassanid Dynasty's silver coins in the Southern Dynasty were discovered.[14]

These exquisite gold and silver wares included the following:

Two round bell-shaped gold cup with a height of 7.2 cm and 8.3 cm in diameter. These gold-plated both inside and outside were engraved with fish, birds, phoenix, honeysuckle pattern, lotus petals pattern in the surface. Another was a silver bowl with the Sassanid type. Its height was 18 cm and its maximum width caliber 18 cm. It was known as the "12 silver Bowl" because its body was decorated with 12 petal–shaped patterns. There were the medieval Iranian writing words with the Aramaic letters on the surface of the bowl. Some scholars believed that this silver was not produced in Persia, but in Central Asia. It was a wave made by the people of the Sugda.[15]

Since after the 1970's, various foreign scholars had distinguished the East Iranian or Sogdian silverwares from the Iranian silverwares.

Sogdian people were also known as "Sogdian Hu people". The "Hu" people were well known as the trader peoples of Central Asia and their traces are easy to be found along the Land Silk Road connecting the East and the West. They traveled deep into the grasslands of Central Asia and North Asia to trade furs with local nomadic tribes, and traveled to the East to purchase the Chinese silk. But less attention is paid to the activities of Sogdian people in the Maritime Silk Road. In fact, considerable part of the Sogdian people believed in Buddhism, and they had maintained close ties with India For example, Kang Senghui, the famous monk spreading Buddhist religion and culture in China, was born in Kang Ju (the Kang country in the North and South Dynasty, refers to the well known historic city, Samarkand, which is currently in Uzbekistan). Initially, his family moved to the Tianzhu (India) and was engaged in trade and business, later Kang's father moved to Jiaozhi for trade. Being a monk, Kang Senghui had been learning from a famous monk Zhi Liang, and read many books and mastered six languages (native language, plus the Chinese

14   Suixi Museum: The Gold and Silver Wares in the Southern Dynasty Discovered in the Suixi County, Journal of Archaeology, 1986/3), (Guangdong Museum and Hong Kong Chinese University's Heritage Museum: The Relics Unearthed during the Jin Dynasty to the Tang Dynasty in Guangdong, Hong Kong, 1985).
15   Jiang Boqin: Iranians between Guangzhou and the Maritime Silk Road and the New Archaeological Discoveries in the Suixi County, Guangzhou and the Maritime Silk Road, pp. 22-23.

language, the Jiaozhi language, the Northwestern Indian proverb, the Sanskrit language and Pali languages. Later, he acted as a monk and engaged in translating Buddhist scriptures in the Wu country.[16]

There were also some Sogdian people among the foreign traders who did business with the Chinese traders along the coastal regions in Tang Dynasty. Zhang Zhuo, in his book Long Jin Feng Sui Pan mentioned the "Anxi states", which included Sogdian kingdom. In addition, Liu Zongyuan also said that there were hundreds of countries and regions that traded with Guangzhou reached at Liuqiu (Taiwan), the great Ling country, Dato country and Kangju country.[17]

Here, the "Kangju country" refers to the Sogdian controlled Samarkand city. The monk, Jian Zhen, in the Tang Dynasty was afflicted with an eye disease, but Hu people had treated it.[18]

"Hu" in the Tang Dynasty often referred to Sogdian people, so Hu people who treated the Jian Zhen's eye disease was a Sogdian man who had come to China through the sea.

In the Suixi cellar, there was also a silver box with height 1.5 cm and diameter 5.5 cm. its patterns features peacock and lotus stripes, so apparently it was from South Asia. In addition, there were some gold and silver bracelets among the gold and silver wares found in Suixi. The gold diameter was 5.8 cm and thickness 0.4 cm. while the 13 silver bracelets can be divided into two categories: one was that they were 8 cm in diameter and 0.9 cm in thickness, 145 grams in weight. And there were no patterns in the surface of them. There were a total of 14 such silver bracelets; another category was only one. Its diameter was 1, 8.5 cm, thickness 1.5 cm and weight 295 grams. Meanwhile, it was engraved with four-petal cross pattern. In addition, several silver hairpins with a length of 3,5-4 cm were unearthed here. The head end of them was petal-shaped and the lower end was broken, as well as the body was adorned with some writing words and cultural relic picture with circle pattern.[19]

The Persian silver unearthed in China was of great significance to the study of Persian culture. The number of the existing Persian silver was quite a few, even though the Persian silverwares, which were hidden in various parts of the world, were also passed by the former generation and their unearthed sites or the age of manufacture were unclear. However, most of the Persian silver wares found in China had clear unearthed sites location, and many of which came from tombs with definite years. Although some tombs did not have a definite year, but there were other artifacts, so it was not difficult to determine its corresponding year according to the Chinese archaeological age genealogy

---

16 See Three Kingdoms period of the Chinese history.
17 Liu Zongyuan Poetry, Volume 26, Jiedu Shi (an official) in Lingnan Reign Give a Banquet in the Army Auditorium.
18 The Chronicles of the Monks Traveling to the West during the Tang Dynasty Period, p. 74.
19 South China Sea Silk Road Cultural Relic Atlas, pp. 445-447.

framework built based on a large number of archaeological data. That was to say, the artifacts unearthed in China were particularly important in the study of Persian silverwares and even can be used as a dating standard for Persian silverware. During the Tang Dynasty period, China continued to import Persian silverware by the maritime trade. The foreign merchants often sailed northwards along the Grand Canal to China and Yangzhou was the most important commercial port of the Grand Canal.[20]

The book, The History Old Tang Dynasty·Tian Shengong Biography has mentioned: "in the years 760-761, thousands of Hu merchants living in Yangzhou were killed". In the March of 768, Tian Shenggong has traveled to China and visited the Chinese emperor, offering 50 pieces of gold and silver goods. We can thus comfortably say that many gold and silver artifacts exhibited in the museums were brought to China in the Tang Dynasty period.

Compared with the Southern and Northern Dynasties, the number of gold and silver wares found in the Tang Dynasty had greatly increased, and thousands of the unearthed and collected wares had been publicly displayed, including imitations and imports. The long cup in the Tang Dynasty was an imitation of that in the Sassanid Dynasty, because the most important feature of this long cup was almost the same as that of the Sassanid Dynasty, especially the wares before 8th century imitating the style the Sassanid Dynasty. (Han Wei: The pictures of the gold and silver wares in the Tang Dynasty at home and abroad, figure 83-84, Three Qin Publishing house, 1989). It was only after comparing them with all Sassanid long cups that could their uniqueness was found, such as for the Chinese long cup, the elaborate fine plant patterns appeared, the upper body of the cup deeper and the lip of the cup wider. These subtle differences showed the craftsmen of the Tang Dynasty imitated the appearance of foreign objects, but they did not blindly follow the imitation and began to transform them into Chinese artifacts. In the evolution of China's long Cup, it has some unique characteristics, such as the deep cup body, high bottom and wide the lip of the cup. Later, the subsequent long cups developed into two directions: firstly, change the octagon into eight-petal shape. Secondly, maintain the basic features of the octagon, but the body of the cup was deeper, almost the shape of the bottom of the round bowl, and the bottom of the cup was higher, long like horn-shaped, in addition, the edge connecting the body and the bottom had disappeared. The long cup was decorated with the China's popular lotus leaf pattern and form. As the innovation of the Tang Dynasty, the long cup in China was developed into two branches, and then serviced as two different utensils.

410

---

20 The Grand Canal, known to the Chinese as the Beijing-Hangzhou Grand Canal (Jīng-Háng Dà Yùnhé), a UNESCO World Heritage Site, is the longest as well as one of the oldest canal or artificial river in the world and a famous tourist destination. Starting at Beijing, it passes through Tianjin and the provinces of Hebei, Shandong, Jiangsu and Zhejiang to the city of Hangzhou, linking the Yellow River and Yangtze River.

The History of Old Tang Dynasty· Xuanzong Emperor Biography, in December 714 said "Zhou Qinggong, an official that controls the foreign traders in Annan city, often talks with the Persian monk and imports their treasures" It showed from the Southern and Northern Dynasty to the middle of the Tang Dynasty, China imported not only the gold and silver artifacts with the style of the Sassanid Dynasty, but also Persian gold and silver products made by the local craftsman. The Persian hammer technology and the plastic arts had the great influence on the production of the gold and silver wares in the ancient China.

In addition to gold and silver products, the glass was another kind of foreign commodity which was popular in ancient China. The Southeast coast of the Mediterranean was one of the main origins of the glass. The glass produced by this technique was called sodium-calcium glass because of its high content of sodium and calcium. China was also one of the origins of glass, and its production process was developed independently from the Warring States period. However, the raw materials between the Chinese native glass and the foreign glass were different, so the modern chemical analysis technique could evidently judge these two kinds of the glasses. The Chinese native glass with high content of lead and barium was called lead barium glass. In addition to the above two kinds of glass, there was also a potassium glass with high potassium, which was produced in Southeast Asia.

In the book, History of the Former Han Dynasty, the foreign glass was called as "Bi Liuli". Later, it was known as "Bili" or "Liulu", "Luli". Still today, the glass is still called the "Liuli" in Japanese. In fact, the pronunciations of these words were the homophony of the Sanskrit "vaidurya" and Indian slang "veluiya". This showed that, during the Han Dynasty period foreign glass was introduced to China by the Indian intermediary traders, not directly by the Mediterranean merchants. In addition, Yang Fu, in the Eastern Han Dynasty, mentioned in the book The Introduction of the Foreign Things, there was an article, named "Huo Qi". Its shape looked like mica and its color was the same as the gold. This "Huo Qi" was obviously the glass, but it was not clear whether it was the potassium glass the above mentioned.

The glass industry in ancient West Asia was far more developed than that of China, and making glass was a traditional technology for people in the Mediterranean. The Egyptians had begun to produce glass in the 2500 BC. Later the Phoenicians, Romans and Syrians mastered the exquisite glass-making technology, and their products were not only brightly colored, transparent and cold, but also superior to our native glass. While China's domestic glass was produced by low-temperature firing. Chen Dachang, a figure living in the Song Dynasty period, said "China's domestic glass with poor quality is quite fragile, it cannot be used to boil wine." This kind of glass is often decomposed when it was unearthed. It is due to difference in quality between the domestic glass and the imported glass. And before the Wei Dynasty and Jin Dynasty periods, the imported glass was considered as precious as gemstones, consequently the trade of overseas glassware was profitable. Over the past dozens of years, in many parts of China's Southeast coasts imported glass commodities were unearthed.

During the pre-Qin era, the foreign glass were imported to China. A blue glass bead was unearthed in the Chu tomb from the Warring States Period in Changsha (Xi'an), Hunan province, and later it was identified as the potassium glass.[21]

The experts conducted some research and reported that among the 13 glass wares of the Han Dynasty period which was unearthed in Guangxu, only 2 glass wares which belonged to the lead barium glass produced in China, and the rest were potassium glass. While the one milky-white glass beads in the Western Han Dynasty tomb No. 3019 and 3 glass beads of the early period of the Eastern Han Dynasty, unearthed in Guangzhou, all belonged to the potassium type of glass. Therefore, the potassium glass had emerged in the Chinese market for a long time.

In 1954, three glass bowls were unearthed in Hengzhigang, Guangzhou, which had the same shape as that of the Western Han Dynasty. With flat bottom, these bowls were purplish blue and translucent. Their inner wall was smooth, and their outer wall and rim were polished to the shape of the ground-glass. According to the isotope X-ray fluorescence analysis, they were calcium silicate glass, like the products made by the Roman Empire's glass production center on the southern coasts of the Mediterranean sea.[22]

(2) The Places Where the Foreign Merchants Lived

During the Western Han Dynasty period, with the development of overseas trade, more foreigners came to China. The Lingnan region unearthed some lamp holders, one kind of which was the lampholder with terracotta figures. The terracotta figures were mainly male. Some of them were similar to Western Asian race with deeper eyes and high nose, and some terracotta figures were short headed, wide nose and thick lips. In addition, some terracotta figures with dense body hair were naked who hunkered down and lifted the lamp plate with their head or kneeled down with their one knee and lifted the lamp plate with a hand. These foreign terracotta figures refers to thise men who came into China with merchants, and later were reduced to the servants of the rich families.

There were also many treasures among the foreign terracotta figures discovered in China. Such as: in 1955, Dayuangang, Guangzhou unearthed a terracotta lamp of the late Western Han Dynasty with 25.7 cm high. The foreign terracottas with dense body hairs kneeled down with their one knee, lifted the lamp plate with 10.4 cm in diameter with his left hand, supported the right hand on their legs to balance themselves, looking straight ahead and with open months tucking out their tongues. In 1956, the tomb in the Sanyu road,

21 Gao Zhishan: On the Glass and Related Issues in the Spring and Autumn Period. Journal of Cultural Relics, 1985/12.
22 See Photos and Descriptions of South China Maritime Silk Road Heritage Atlas, p. 24.

Guangzhou unearthed a terracotta lamp of the Eastern Han Dynasty with 28.5 cm high. It was a muddy gray pottery with the high nose and deep eyes. The terracotta fighter figure was naked and muscular covered with the dense hair. The fighter hunkered down and placed hands on the knees respectively, and slightly opened his mouth. In addition, there was a lamp on his head wrapped with tower; in 1984, the tomb in the Xiling Mountain, Chen village, Shunde County unearthed a 14.5 cm terracotta lamp of the Eastern Han Dynasty. With high nose and punctured ears, the naked terracotta figure sat down and lifted a plate on the head. In 1988, another 18.5cm unearthed from the tomb in the Zhusigang, Sanshui County. The naked figure with dense hair placed the lamp on the head.[23]

The people in the Han Dynasty had started to pay attention to the foreign people who came into China. Yang Fu wrote a book, The Introduction of the Foreign Things, and mentioned a kind of people, called "Wen people". Their teeth and eye were white, and skin was black, looking like shining. In addition, they were muscular and served as servants. Although "Wen people" had some differences with the above terracotta figures, they resembled Dravidian people and East African people. They should be the slavers that were sold into China by the foreign merchants.

At first, the foreign traders who came into china to do business lived in China temporarily due to various reasons, including bad weather and lacking goods. Gradually, they settled down in China and starred to building house along the ports. Many foreign merchants from Dashi country, Persia, Tianzhu and other countries settled down in China in the Tang Dynasty, so the people in the Song Dynasty said "in the Hang Dynasty, the people in Guangzhou live together with the foreign traders."[24]

It was said that some foreign traders had been living in China for ten years.

This residential region of the foreign merchants was called the Fanfang. The first appearance of term "Fanfang" was in the book Tao Huang Za Lu written by Fang Qianli during the rule of the emperor Tang Wenzong (827-835 years). For example, "when I visited the Fanfang in Guangzhou, I have seen that the food is plentiful including molasses, musk deer, fish and so on."[25]

The Fanfang in Guangzhou during the Tang Dynasty period is located in the current Guangta Road of Guangzhou.

According to book The Law of the Tang Dynasty, "if the foreign people have conflicts among themselves, they can settle them with their own laws, but if they have conflicts with foreign people, they are required to follow the Chinese law.[26]

---

23   South China Maritime Silk Road Heritage Atlas, pp. 35-36.
24   The Introduction of the Lingnan Region, Vol. 5, Zhang Wangzhi, Repair of the Temple of God in the South Sea.
25   Merits and Drawbacks of the Provinces and Counties in China, Volume 140.
26   The Law of the Tang Dynasty, Vol. 6.

In such cases where the foreigners were involved, the Tang government appointed some foreign people as a minister to deal with civil disputes and these ministers could enjoy some degree of autonomy. Such ministers were called "Fan Zhang" and this was first mentioned by Li Zhao in 806-820 AD, he wrote the following: "the Fan Zhang controls all the foreign affairs such as trading and foreigners visiting China, and the Fan Zhang has been preserver in the Song Dynasty period."[27]

If the foreign merchants who lived in China died, their heritage was managed by the officials in the Tang Dynasty for three months, till their relatives applied for the heritage. After three months, the heritage that was not claimed by anyone was confiscated. But since a three months time was not enough for a distant family, so the duration term for claiming the heritage was further extended. In addition, a number of foreign people who lived and traded in China married Chinese people, and formed have a family.[28]

At the end of the Tang Dynasty, Guangzhou had developed into an international metropolis city, with foreigners occupying a large proportion among its inhabitants. A geographer from the Dashi country wrote: "there are 120,000 foreign merchants and 200,000 Islam people.[29]

When the Huang Cao led his rebel troops to attack the foreigners in Guangzhou, they killed tens of thousands of them. However, with the development of overseas trade and the increasing relationship between China and foreign countries, the districts where the foreigners lived had quickly recovered. During the Song Dynasty period, still many foreign people dwelled in Guangzhou.. A poem from the Hundreds of Poems of the South China Sea written by Fang Xingru mentioned: "there are many tombs of foreign people in Guangzhou". So, we could draw a conclusion that the population of the foreign merchants was large and they had been living here for generations. Most of them were the Islam people from West Asia because in their tombs, their heads and feet were toward South and North respectively, as well they faced West, showing they wanted to go to the Holy Mecca.

(3) The Tributary and the Overseas Trade Systems

During the ancient trades between the China and foreign counties, the tributary trade was the most noteworthy part. The so-called "tributary" was actually equivalent to current official barter trade. For quite a long time, ancient China in economy was obviously more than the surrounding countries, and the neighborhood rulers and people loved Chinese goods. Therefore, some rulers and even some private traders who wanted to obtain China's fine products often

---

27 Ping Zhou Ke Tan, Volume 2 Between 1111 and 1117 AD, Zhu Yu wrote the book Pingzhou Ketan (Pingzhou Table Talks), published in 1119 AD. It covered a wide variety of maritime subjects and issues in China at the time.
28 The History of Old Tang Dynasty ·Lu Jun Biography.
29 The Introduction of the China and India, Zhong Hua Book Company, p. 96, 1983. and see Ibid, p. 140, Golden Prairie.

introduced their local treasures into China through tributary, such as beads, ivory, rhinoceros horn and gemstones, and then obtained the right to Chinese goods. Chinese rulers often gave them more generous goods in order to country' richness and power. This was actually an unequal exchange. In order to control the financial expenditure, there were strict restrictions on the objects of tributary trade in successive dynasties, so not all countries could do tributary trade with China. The concrete procedure of tributary exchange during the Tang Dynasty period was as follows: firstly, after the foreign ships entered the Chinese port, their goods were needed to be checked and registered. Secondly, they chose a leader and two other fellows to visit the emperor and their tributaries were given to the designated court officials. Thirdly, according to the value of tribute goods, the court donated them certain Chinese goods and were offered some favors.[30]

In order to adapt to the change of overseas trade, the Tang Dynasty (around 661) began to set up a new rank called the Shi Bo director, in Guangzhou, directly attached to the imperial court, to manage the foreign cargos and foreign trade. This was the initial step by China to regulate overseas trade and customs tax system. The reason of establishing the overseas trade system was mainly that through the Rebellion of the Tang Dynasty, it was in economic depression, which caused the greatly reduction of the tributary trade. The core of the system was the sale's monopoly system. The government levied taxes for the foreign ships to increase the national income.

The taxes included "Bojiao" tax. Han Yu said that "when the foreign ship stop in the port, they should pay parking tax, which was called "Bojiao tax" or "Xiaddian tax".[31] The meaning of sale's monopoly system was that the court monopolized some goods among the imported goods to earn fabulous benefits. The Tang Government understood the importance of reducing tax rate to flourish the overseas business. In the reign of the emperor, Tang Wenzong (in 834), the government announced such a policy that "they will not increase the taxes for the foreign traders and allow them to exchange freely, aiming to foster the development on the foreign business. In addition, sometimes they also care for the foreign merchants".[32]

At the early period of the Song Dynasty, the emperor inherited the Tang system and set up the various institutions including the Shi Bo Shi rank to administer the foreign trade in many regions, especially in Guangzhou. The book, Ping Zhou Ke Tan, mentioned that in the North Song Dynasty (1102-1106), three regions set up Shi Bo Si. If compared with the other two regions, Guanzhou was developed and its revenues were much higher. During the reign of emperor, Gangzong, an official of the Song Dynasty said: "the two kinds of incomes of the Shi Bo department reached 2 million stings of silver coins".[33]

---

30   The New History of the Tang Dynasty· The Official History Records.
31   The Poetry of the Mrs. Changli, Vol. 33, The Epitaph of the Official Kong Fu.
32   Quan Tang wen, Volume 75, Ji Yu De Yin in 834 AD. (The whole prose writings of Tang were compiled in the late Qing work Quan Tang wen).
33   The Main Events Related to the Song Dynasty Officials.

After the establishment of the Southern Song Dynasty, due to its severe and tense relationships with the surrounding countries and shortage of the national treasure, they attached great importance to overseas trade and reduced the taxes on them in order to raise money. The emperor of Gaozong once said: "The benefits of the Shi Bo are fabulous as long as we can manage it properly."34

Under the guidance of this kind of thinking, the overseas trade in the Southern Song Dynasty had developed greatly.

3. Progress in the Seamanship

During the 1200 years from the end of the Eastern Han Dynasty in the late 2nd century to before reunification again in the Yuan Dynasty in the 1270s, the ancient Chinese history had encountered ruptures for several times. In this case, the land transport connecting the trade and business of the East and West were blocked, and the overseas trade of China had rapidly and continuously developed. China started to increasingly rely on the maritime transports to do business with the people living in the Persian Gulf and the Mediterranean region. It was during these periods that the seamanship was greatly improved.

(1) Navigation Technologies

The Chinese navigation technology in the Tang and Song dynasties had been developed in the world. In addition to the development of the traditional navigation technology, such as overseas geography, geographical navigation, astronomical surveying star and ship handling technology, the emergence of the ocean astronomy positioning technology which used the celestial rulers as measuring methods and the use of all-weather magnetic compass navigation were the basic symbols of the advanced Chinese navigation in this period, and also the most important material foundation that made the Chinese navigation advanced and ahead of other countries in the world.. The compass could be used to determine the direction of the ship, and the astrology could be determined the latitude of the ship in the sea, so the combination of these two technology had the ability to determine the position of the ships in the vast seas.

(1) Astronomical positioning technology

The generation of astronomical navigation was preceded by the compass centered navigation. After the invention of the compass, astronomical navigation was still one of the most important method used in the ocean navigation, often these two methods were used together. The coastline of East Asia basically extends towards north or south, which made the astronomy supported navigation easily play a role in the sailing of the ancient East Asian seafarers. Chinese ships sailed, whether coastal navigation or offshore navigation, generally along the north-south direction, and astronomy supported navigation had mainly depended on the North Star. Ge Hong in the Jin Dynasty wrote a book, Bao Pu Zi Wai Pian and said, "the North Star and compass is vital for the ships sailing in the seas."

---

34   Ibid.

When the ships sailed in the Southeast Asian seas and in the Indian Ocean, it was far from enough to only rely on the North Star to determine the location and direction because the geographical conditions could change dramatically and depending on the coastline was nearly impossible. For example, Indo-China Peninsula and Malaya Peninsula was separated by the Gulf of Siam, the Malay Peninsula and India by the Gulf of the Bengal, as well as India and East Africa by the Arabian Sea. Since the pre-Qin era, the traditional way of sailing in Southeast Asia and the Indian Ocean was along the tortuous coastline of Southeast Asia continent and South Asia continent. Although it was safer, the expeditions took much longer time.

The development of navigation technology made it possible that ship did not need to sail along the coastline. The ship began sailing across the ocean. In the case of far away from the coast, the traditional method of physiographic positioning had no effect, and a new track-reckoning method was needed to calculate the ship's location and direction. The emergence and development of astronomical navigation was in order to meet this demand. A monk expert in astronomical navigation, named Fa Xian, once went to India and Sri Lanka by land and then returned by sea. In his travel diary, he wrote: "The sea is boundless, the ships sail by observing the location of the sun, the moon and the stars," indicating that his ship sailed from Sri Lanka directly eastwards to Sumatra. That was to say, in the Southern Dynasties, the boats that sailed across the Indian Ocean had mastered the astronomical positioning technology, which was a major breakthrough in the history of maritime expeditions.

The development of the astronomical positioning technology in the Tang Dynasty period focused on the geodetic survey that determined the variation of North-South distance by using the height difference of the Northern Star in the tworegions. The famous astronomer Seng Yi Xing (his common name Zhang Sui, 673-727, led some people to carry out a large-scale geodetic survey on the Tang Dynasty's territories to measure distance bwrween latitudes across China. Seng Yixing also created a simple instrument to measure the height from the North Star to the horizon. He was the first to describe proper stellar motion, or the apparent motion of stars across the plane of the sky relative to more distant stars. He was the first to successfully measure the length of the meridian line: he made the first estimation of the length of a degree on the meridian. Yi Xing measured it as 351.27 li or 129.22 kilometers.[35]

It had a certain error when compared with the modern astronomical geodetic value of 111.2 km, but his calculation had once played an important role in the maritime navigation.

In 1973, a trade ship's wreck from the Song Dynasty period was unearthed in Quanzhou, Fujian. The primary cargo of the ship was incense wood; around 2,400 kilograms of it was found in 12 out of the 13 compartments of the ship. The ship was divided by 12 bulkheads into 13 compartments.

35   The New History of the Tang Dynasty · Astronomy Annals.

There were also small amounts of various valuable commodities: five "Chinese liters" (sheng) of black peppers, ambergris (which, according to chemical testing, must have ultimately come from Somalia), 6.3 grams of frankincense (possibly from the Arab lands), almost 4 kilograms of mercury, a small amount of "dragon's blood" and haematite, and one turtle shell.

The Quanzhou Ship or Quanzhou wreck, was a 13th-century Chinese sea-going sailing junk that sank near the city of Quanzhou in Fujian Province. It remains one of the most important marine archaeology finds in China, and is an important piece of physical evidence about the shipbuilding techniques of the Song China and the international maritime trade of the period.

Also, a bamboo ruler with 20.7 cm long and 2.3 cm wide, was found, simultaneously. The first half of the ruler had scales on it and was divided into five divisions with 2.6 cm, each. Probably, the measurer held the send half of the rule that no any scale to measure the height of the stars in the sky. When measuring the distance, the man who measured should stretch his arm, hold the ruler vertically, make the lower end of the ruler tangent to the sea water, and then observe the value of the intersection between the ruler and the measured object. It was very easy to use this ruler to measure celestial bodies in the sky, such as measuring the position of the Northern Star, you could determine the geographical latitude of a ocean-going ship in accordance with value determined by this ruler.

(2) The Compass

The key to astronomical navigation was to observe the sun and the moon and to determine the height of the star, with the aim of determining the ship's latitude and direction. However, astronomical navigation was affected by the weather, for example, if it was rainy, we could not determine the location of the ship according to the direction of the moon and the height of the star. The invention and usage of the compass made navigation no longer be dependent upon climate. It was a major invention in the history of global navigation industry.

The compass was originally invented to determine the geomantic omen and came out at the beginning of 11th century. It was known that the first reference to the compass was in a book, Ying Yuan Zong Lu (a book of introducing the geomantic omen) written by Xiang Mu in 1041. The book mentioned that if you wanted to judge direction, you must use the magnetic declination of the compass. This indicated that magnetic declination had been used by people, so the invention of the compass should be long before that.

According to a book Meng Xi Bi Tan (the encyclopedia written by Shen Kuo in the Song Dynasty in China], there were 4 ways to place a compass: "(1) the magnetic needle crosses over the wick, floating the water surface, (2) the magnetic needle is placed on the nail, (3) magnetic needle is lied in lip of the bowl (4) the middle of magnetic needle is tied by a thin thread and hang it on the place without wind." In addition, a book, Wu Jin Zong Yao (an official military study during the Song Dynasty period) written by Zeng Gongling, also documented a guide fish, which was made of a fish-shaped and magnetized thin iron. The guide fish floating in the water could point to the north and south direction. During the Southern Song Dynasty period, Chen Yuanliang in the book Shi Lin Guang Ji*also narrated about another kind of guide fish made of wood. The people firstly carved the wood into a fish-shaped model, and then placed a magnet into this wooden body and let it float in the water.[36]

Around the second half of 11th Century, the compass became a sea navigation instrument. Zhu Yu wrote a book, Ping Zhou Ke Tan (Introduction to Various Developments in the Song Dynasty period, Including Trades, Technology, Customs and so on), and said: "I with my father have been in Guangzhou from 1098 to 1102. When we observed the navigation activities in Guangzhou, we have found that the captain of the ships depended on to the sun, during daytimes, and the on the moon during night times, in order to determine the direction, when sailing. But if the weather is bad, the captains relied on the compass instrument."

In 1124 Xu Jing, wrote a book, titled as: Xuan He Feng Shi Gao Li Tu Jing (An Introduction Book on the Situations of the Gaoli Dynasty). The author narrated similar facts, as in Zhu Yu's book. But, the compass at that time was the floating compass which could float on the sea surface which was called the floating water compass. This compass was used for navigation, by the experienced persons in the Song Dynasty period.

419

Compass navigation technology rapidly spread abroad and was learned by the foreign seamen. In the Song Dynasty, this advanced technology was spread to Europe. According to the research of Needham, the earliest record of the compass navigation in Europe was in 1190 as mentioned by the British Alexander Neckam (1157-1217).

The usage of the compass in Arab regions was earlier than the European regions, but the written records of the former about the use of compass was later than the latter. The Europeans learned to use the compass by the help of the Dashi (Arab) inventions. In a book "Merchant Is How to Identify Treasure" written in 1282, by Bailak al-Qabajaqi, a mineralogist from the Dashi country, said he had sailed from Terry to Alexander City. In his voyage he saw the crew used the magnetic needle that placed the wood chip or the reed and floated on the water, to determine the direction. This showed that Dashi seafarers also used the compass floating on the water, which had close related with the China's compass. In addition, the above book also mentioned that the ships sailing in the Indian Ocean also relied on the fish-shaped magnet floating water to identify the South and North direction. This guide fish should also have a relationship with the China's guide fish mentioned in the book titled as "Wu Jing Zong Yao".

---

36   An Encyclopedia of Ancient Chinese Folk Studies, Vol. 10.

After the compass was introduced to Europe, its device method was improved and a new compass with a fixed fulcrum was invented. This new compass called land compass because it did not need to float on the water, and could be used in the land. The Portuguese arrived in Japan in the first half of the 16th century, and Japanese navigators introduced this land compass to their countries. In the Ming Dynasty, Li Yuheng wrote a book Tui Peng Wu Yu (an introduction to the Chinese traditional medical) and said "China has been used the water floating compass, but later when Japanese invades China's Southeast coast in the second half of the century, we found they used the land compass."Since then, the traditional water compass was gradually replaced by the land compass in China.

The famous British scholar, Dr. Joseph Needham, highly appraised the invention of the compass in the chapter 29 of his masterpiece, The History of Chinese Science and Technology. The usage of compass was a great change in the navigation technology, which symbolized the end of the original sailing era and the beginning of the new era of navigation. Only after mastering the compass, was ocean no longer an insurmountable obstacle for mankind.

Zhou Qufei, a man in the Song Dynasty in his book, Ling Wei Dai Da (a work of geography in the Song Dynasty), said according to the report of the Dashi country, if the boats set off in mid-winter from Guangzhou by the North wind, it could arrive at the Lanli (refer to Bandazia in the Northwest of Pulau Sumatera) in 40 days. The boats started to set off in the approaching of the Northeast wind, and then boats departed once again and reached the Maboli (refer to Mribat in the East of the Salale, the capital of Dhofar, Sultanate of Oman. That was to say, the ships that could achieve such a long voyage from South China to the southern end of the Arab Peninsula which took 2,500 nautical miles was enabled by magnetic compass and astronomical positioning navigation method.

(3) The Progress in Mathematics

The knowledge on the navigation guide had appeared and developed in the Tang Dynasty period. Jia Dan, a prime minister of the Tang Dynasty said, "the Asian ships have already assumed relatively fixed routes from the Western Pacific to the North Indian Ocean and also the navigators have a more accurate understanding and knowledge about major routes."

The key for geographical navigation was to correctly identify the geographical coordinates along the route. It was particularly noteworthy that alongside with the progress of mathematics, the navigators were able to measure the land by using some mathematical principles, such as the Pythagorean Theorem and the similarity proportional relation. This scientific progress had led to rapid development of coastal surveying. Li Chunfeng, a mathematician of the Tang Dynasty wrote a book, titled as Hai Dao Suan Jing (The earliest mathematics book in China). It was the book that helped the ancient people measure the distance from the Wanghai Island to the astronomical table besides it.

(Astronomical table was an ancient calendar that was invented to simplify the calculation of the motion of the sun, the moon and other stars). This clearly proves that the Chinese seafarers during the Tang Dynasty period had achieved important progress.

During the Southern Song Dynasty period, Zhou Qufei once described the situation of captains when they used geographical features when determining their direction: "the ship masters use the coastal islands and the towering peaks of the land as markers, which is geography navigation. When there is a mountain in the sea, they try to identify it and figure out the location of this mountain. Before setting off, the ship masters have already had a rough understanding of the moment the ship arrives somewhere as well as change the direction. In case when the ship sailed before the wind, even though it is not the time for the ship to take a turn, the sailors also decisively change the direction when they see the predetermined geographical marks".[37]

The description mentioned above shows that the ancient Chinese seafarers have inherited countless practical experiences of the former many generations. This experience was passed orally by the experienced captains. On the long route, because the geographical indications and the direction of changing course wee different, so a little carelessness of the captains have caused the errors of judgment and deviation in the ship's route, leading to many tragedies. So the people who knew the words would write down the route and the signs along the way. The navigation guides and maps came into being in this case.

Chinese navigation maps have appeared at least in the Song Dynasty period. In the 6th year of the rule of the emperor Xianfeng of the Northern Song Dynasty in 1003, the Guangzhou magistrate once handed over Overseas Country Map to the imperial court.[38]

In the 5th year of the reign of Emperor Xuanhe during the Northern Song Dynasty Xuan (1123), when Xu Jing visited to the Gaoli country, he drew a map which explained the sea route to Gaoli.[39]

Zhao Rushi, the author of the book "The Introduction of Foreign Countries", mentioned in the preface of his book: "when I examine the foreign maps, I can well determine the location of the islands in the South China Sea."[40]

---

37   See Author Zhou Qufei, the book title Ling Wai Dai Da(Lingwai Daida variously translated as Representative Answers from the Region beyond the Mountains, Notes Answering [Curious Questions] from the land.

38   The Continuation of the Zi Zhi Tong Jian, Vol. 54 The Zizhi Tongjian (Chinese: 資治通鑑; literally: "Comprehensive Mirror in Aid of Governance") is a pioneering reference work in Chinese historiography, published in 1084, in the form of a chronicle. In 1065 AD, Emperor Yingzong of Song ordered the great historian Sima Guang (1019-1086 AD) to lead with other scholars such as his chief assistants Liu Shu, Liu Ban and Fan Zuyu, the compilation of a universal history of China.

39   The Map of Xuanhe visiting the Gaoli, Volume 34.

40   Feng Chengjun: The Annotation of the Introduction of the Foreign Countries, Zhonghua Book Company, p. 5, 1956.

It could be seen that the map should be the navigation map. Unfortunately, most of these early navigation maps could not be preserved.

(2) The Foreign Ships and Chinese Ships

(1) The Foreign Ships in the South China Sea

At that time, the boats plying among China's Southeast coast, Southeast Asia and the Indian Ocean, involved in both foreign ships and Chinese ships. The various kinds of foreign ships were also from different countries, for example, Yuan Kai in the book The Autobiography of the Jianzhen Monk visiting the East mentioned the Pearl River in Guangzhou moored Brahman ship (South Asian ship), Kunlun ship (Southeast Asian ship) and Persian ship (Western Asian ship) in the Tang Dynasty. These foreign ships were mostly from the South China Sea, also known as the "South China Sea Ships". In the book The Supplement to the History of Tang Dynasty (the second half volume) said: "the so-called South China Sea ships refer to the foreign ships and these ships arrive in Annan and Guangzhou every year".

Among the Brahman ships, there was a kind of ship, called "lion country ship" (Sri Lankan ship). The Supplement to the History of Tang Dynasty (the second half volume) said that this ship was largest among the foreign ships. While Kunlun ship (Southeast Asian ship) played an important role in the Southeast Asian and the Indian Ocean sailing. When Yi Jing of the Tang Dynasty left Guangzhou for India, he took the Persian ship (Persia was located in Southeast Asia, referring to the Pathein, Myanmar).[41]

When Yi Jing arrived at Srivijaya, he visited Luoyu (the Southern end of the Malaysia) by a Srivijaya ship, and then he stopped in many regions and finally arrived at India. During the journey, the ships that he used were mainly Southeast Asian ships, which showed that Southeast Asia ships had higher quality in those days. Therefore, the book The New Introduction of the Tang Dynasty written by Wang Fangqing recorded as follows: "there are many Kunlun ships with treasures that do business with the people in Guangzhou."

Among the Western Asian ships, the big ones were called as the "Dashi Gaint Ship", the biggest of which was the "Mulanpi" boat. The homophonic of the "Mulanpi" was the Maghreb in Arabic. Today, the Maghreb is translated as "Mahelibu", which means "the Westernmost land". The book "The Introduction of the Foreign Countries" narrated as follows: "Mulanpi boat can carry thousands of people as well as trade commodities plus many other objects such as food, wine and tools."[42]

Zhou Qufei called this ship Mulan boat instead of Mulanpi boat. He said that this ship was larger than ship of the South Sea (current Southeast Asia), which could carry thousands of people and many equipment. The people living in the

41 The Introduction of Monks, Note by Wang Bangwei, 1988, Zhonghua Book Company, p. 159, Note 3.
42 The Annotation from the book The Introduction of the Foreign Countries, 1956, published by Zhuang Hua Book Company, p. 67.

coastal cities of the Song Dynasty named foreign ships not only after the place names, but also according to their transport capacity (weight).

A book titled The History of the Song Dynasty: Goods and Currencies Record, narrated: "the largest foreign ship is Duqiang Ship which carried 1000 polan (polan is a weight unit used in foreign countries whose ton equivalent is unclear yet); the second largest boat is the Niutou Ship which could carry the 1/3 weight of the largest ship, and the next is the Sanmu Ship carrying the 1/3 weight of the second largest ship". Zhou Qufei also wrote: The ships sailing in the South China Sea, looked like tall buildings, which could travel tens of thousands of li(s), and carry thousands of people. In addition, the carrying capacity of some ships reached 600 tons, which were called "Wanhu boat" ("wan" means "ten thousands of", "hu" is a weight unit in ancient China, 1 hu=60kg)

These "Wanhu" ships" could carry about 1,000-2,000 tons. In the era when the wood timber was the basic shipbuilding material, this was probably the largest ship with maximum carrying capacity. It was difficult to build such a huge boat by using timber and wood of a single place, because only for its rudder, the general normal wood could not carry such a large ship body. So a special wood was imported from the foreign countries which was, called the Wulan wood, produced in Qingzhou, in the South China of Guangxi province), which was so sturdy and could not be broken up in the bad weather such as strong wind and heavy storm and rain. It was said that this wood was cheap in this local place, but the price of it would greatly rise, 10 times higher than the previous price.[43]

In short, the large boats were built with the cooperation of the Sino-foreign countries.

The manufacturing process of the ship in Indian Ocean was vastly different from that of the China. Liu Xun of the Tang Dynasty said in the book, Ling Biao Yi Lu, (introduce the products of the Lingnan region, including food and customs) that at that time, the foreign ships were built without iron nails, instead olive sugar was used as cohesive mud. This mud had very strong cohesive effect, but was sticky such as paint once it met with water. The Buddhist monk, Hui Lin also wrote that Kunlun ships were stuck together with olive sugar rather than iron nails. Wang Dayuan had mentioned this kind of ship. In addition, Marco Polo also mentioned that the ship was ubiquitous in the Indian Ocean. But, Wang Dayuan pointed out the weakness of this ship, which was, the hull of it was weaker and could not resist the strong wind and waves, and was easy to leak.[44]

43 Zhou, Qufei, book name Ling Wai Dai Da, Vol. 6, (Lingwai Daida variously translated as Representative Answers from the Region beyond the Mountains, Notes Answering [Curious Questions] from the land).
44 Yi Dao Zhi Lue, Zhonghua Book Company, pp. 365-366; Yi Dao Zhi Lue narrates the transportations between China and foreign countries in the Yuan Dynasty.

(2) The Chinese Ships

By contrast, the Chinese shipbuilding in the Tang Dynasty had not used this primitive and crude technology of the India Ocean, and started to use nail, mortise and tenon to join the wooden parts of the ship together. The archaeologists in China discovered wooden boats of the Tang Dynasty in the ruins of Shiqiao Town, Yangzhou of Jiangsu province and Rugao country of Jiangsu province respectively in1960 and 1973. Their types of two ships were different, but they joined together with nails and tenons. In addition, the ship discovered in Rugao country also built 9 watertight compartments, which greatly enhanced the ship's lateral strength and the ability to withstand waves and sinking. There was another ship called "Falcon ", because ship's sides were placed two floating plates in order to prevent leaking, which looked like the falcon's wings. In fact, the floating plate was a broadside breakwater.

During the Tang Dynasty period, China was able to build huge ocean-going vessels. According to what Hui Lin said in his book, Yi Qie Jing Yin Yi (the annotation of the Buddhist scripture), "there is a kind of vessel known as "Cang vessel" with 20 Zhang length ("Zhang is a unit of length, 1 Zhang = 3.3 meters"), carrying 600-700 people." Meanwhile, many Arab travelers once described the ships sailing through the Indian Ocean in the Tang Dynasty: "under the effect of the Euphrates and Tigris Rivers, Persian Gulf boasts a lot of shoals, but the Chinese vessels have big breadth and deep draft so it is difficult for the Chinese vessels to pass the bay." Therefore, Suleiman, an Arab traveler, said that the ships that sailed among the ports of the Persian Gulf were mainly the local smaller ones. These ships transported local commodities to the Siraf port, and then the goods were transferred to Chinese vessels which sailed to the East. At that time, all the ships from various countries provided fresh water from a port in the Southwestern India, where the Chinese ships got charged 1000 Dirkhan (Dirkhan is an unit of currency) while the ships belonging to other countries charged only 10-20 Dirkhan.[45]

Apart from imposing different tax rates on vessels in different regions, the difference in fees was clearly because the Chinese ships were larger than other countries' ships..

In the Song Dynasty, the craft and technology of the vessels made remarkable progress. Based on the relics of ships in the Song Dynasty unearthed in Quanzhou, Fujian province in 1974, and the ship of the Yuan Dynasty discovered in Xinan, Korea in 1976, the basic characteristics of the Chinese ocean-going ships built during the Song Dynasty period were as follows:

Firstly, they could carry heavy loads. According to records of the Meng Lianglu (a book that introduces the capital of the Southern Song Dynasty), written by Wu Zimu, said: the big ships load can reach to 5,000 Liao (1 Liao = 60 kg), which can also carry about 500-600 people." At that time, the

---

45   Suleiman Travels, see Mu Genglai, the Chinese Translation, The Introduction of the China and India, pp. 9-10.

medium-sized ship loaded the goods from 1,000 to 3,000Liao and carry two hundred or three hundred people. In fact, the most common medium-sized ship was called "Kezhou" ship, which more than 10 Zhang lengths and 3 Zhang widths, loading 2000 Liao. While there was a kind of ship called "Shenzhou" ship, and its length and width were three times of that of the "Kezhou" ship.[46]

The "Shenzhou" ship was three times bigger in length and width, so its loading volume was 20 times bigger. Based on this calculation, the "Shenzhou" ship loaded more than 50,000, Liao, which was equivalent to 3,000 tons. It was a very impressive ship. Zhou Qufei once described a giant ship which was built during the Song Dynasty period which sailed in the South China Sea: "the ship is so large that it can carry hundreds of people and abundant food could be stored which could be sufficient for a year. The people on the boats can breed pig and make wine. This giant ship what Zhou Qufei described was possibly the "Shenzhou" ship. The giant ship can resist huge waves, during its expeditions, but it is easily stranded in the shallow waters."[47]

Secondly, the ships had study hull and versatile structure. The hull "is folded with a huge wood".[48]

When we examine the ancient ship which was unearthed in Quanzhou, it was found that the ship's keels were joined by two pines, which increased the longitudinal strength of the ship. The hull and bottom of the ship were folded with double plates, and the side was folded with a triple plates. From keel to side plate, there were 14 lines, 1-10 lines of which were folded with two plates and 11-13 lines with triple pates, using lap and splicing technology with dowel as the main components. The upper and lower plates of the inner hull were jointed with dowels. The sharp bottom shape required a high demand on the hull curved arc. In this case, the usage of the multiplex plate craft could make the material, construction and maintenance easier, and reinforced side plate and the hull plat with double or triple plates strengthened the structure and improved resistant to waves, conducive to long voyage.[49]

The vessels of the Quanzhou Bay used many extremely long and large nails, and used Tung oil, hemp wire and lime plug the cracks in order to prevent leakage and rust of the nails' head. Although China's neighboring countries in East Asia have greatly learned from the Chinese shipbuilding technology, there still remained an obvious gap technological gap with China. According to records, The Sedual to the Xuan Lan Tang Cong Shu (an introduction the history of the Ming Dynasty), the Japanese ships were connected without iron nails and Japan carpenters did not plug the cracks to prevent leakage. In a word,

425

46   Xu Jing, The Map of Xuanhe Visiting the Gaoli, Volume 34, pp. 116-117.
47   Zhou, Qufei, book name Ling Wai Dai Da, Vol. 6 (Lingwai Daida variously translated as Representative Answers from the Region beyond the Mountains, Notes Answering [Curious Questions] from the land).
48   Xu Jing: The Map of Xuanhe Visiting the Gaoli, Vol. 34, p. 117.
49   Overseas Expedition History Museum in Quanzhou, Fujian Province: The Excavation and Research of Vessels of the Song Dynasty Period, The Marine Press, 1987.

the advanced shipbuilding technology that was developed during the Tang and Song dynasties in China are still widely used in the construction of wooden vessels today, such as reinforcing the ship plates by tenon-joint and iron nails, and plugging the creaks with the Tung oil.

When we examine shipbuilding, during the Song Dynasty, we can see that the hulls of the Chinese ships usually contained more than 10 watertight compartments. The ships of the Quanzhou Bay used 12 partitions to divide the hull into 13 watertight compartments with high water density, due to such watertight compartments, even if one or two of them would be, the ships could carry on sailing and shipwreck events could be avoided. This 13-cabin (13 watertight compartments) wooden vessels are still used by the coastal people of Fujian in current times. According to experts, ships which include such 13 cabins had specific names and purposes.[50]

Xu Jing narrated in his book, The Map of Xuanhe Visiting the Gaoli that: "the ship hulls built during the Song Dynasty period are very versatile, the lower side of the hulls are like a blade." In addition, the book, Song Hui Yao Ji Gao, also mentioned the upper side of the hulls built during the Southern Song Dynasty were about three Zhang width, and their bottoms three Chi width (1 Zhang = 3.58 m.)" As mentioned above, the ships built during the late Song Dynasty period had similar characteristics with the ship which was unearthed in the Houzhu port in the eastern suburbs of Quanzhou in 1974, which can be summarized as follows: tip bottom, flat and larger hull as well as a small ratio of width to length of the ship, looking like the ellipse. The V-hull structure of China ships not only enhanced the stability but also reduced the resistance of the underwater, which enabled sailing in the strong wind and waves. In order to reduce the rocking of the ships, the seafarers of the Song Dynasty periods have attached thick bamboo sticks on both sides of the ship's abdomen to resist the waves."[51]

Ibn Tuta, a Moroccan traveler at the end of the Yuan Dynasty, once described Chinese ships in the Indian Ocean and said: "that China's ships can be divided into small-sized, medium-sized and lager- sized ships. Among them, the larger-sized ship boasts thousands of crews, including 600 sailors, 400 guards. At the same time, with 3 to 12 sails made of bamboo, the larger-sized ship was followed by various sizes of ships that were smaller than the leading ship. The larger-sized ships were only produced in Guangzhou and Quanzhou. In the bottom of such ships were placed three plates which were jointed with giant nails, and the cabin part had four floors which included numerous public and private rooms. The crew often grew vegetables in the tubs. Its oar attaching two chains was huge and needed 10 to 15 people standing along the oar sides to row it. Marco Polo also gave a detailed description of such ships in his travel notes."

50   See Article by Zhang Jinghui: The Historical Analysis of the Structure of Ships during the Song Dynasty in Quanzhou, The Journal of Xiamen University (Philosophy and Social Sciences edition), 1977/4.
51   Xu Jing, The Map and Route of Xuanhe Visiting the Gaoli, Vol. 34, p. 117.

(3) The Ships of the Dashi (Arab-Islam) Empire

After the demise of the Roman Empire and the Sassanid Dynasty, the Dashi Empire encountered a vigorous rise. The Dashi Empire had boasted due to its favorable geographical location between Europe and the Far East, which made it the center of navigation. The Chinese literature recorded the sea expedition routes from the southeastern coasts of China to the West while the Dashi Empire literature gave a detailed description of the sea expedition routes from their country to the East.

Ibn Khrudadhbah (life 820 or 825- 911), the earliest geographer of the Dashi Empire, wrote a work called The Book of Routes and Provinces (846-847). Jia Dan who lived in the Tang Dynasty period, has described the route from Guangzhou to the Basra of the Persian Gulf, while Ibn Khrudadhbah recorded the course of the opposite direction—from the Basra of the Persian Gulf to China, which was comparable in detail to the Jia Dan's record. According to the Ibn Khrudadhbah's book, the sea routes leading to China was divided into three sections:

Record a route from Basra to China: Basra - Hulunmus (now Hormuz Strait) - The mouth of the Milky Way - along the west coast of the Indian Peninsula (Sri Lanka) - Crossing the Bay of Bengal to Borus (now Nicobar Islands) - Miluo (Malay).

The first section, from the end of the Moluo (today refers to as Basra of the Iraq) to Xilan (today refers to Ceylon): the ship sets sail from Basra passes through the Moluoto Hulumosi (today refers to as the Strait of Hormuz.), and from Fars coastal region to Daibul with a total of 8 days sail, and then to the estuary of the Milan river (today refers to as Xintou River or Indian River) through 2 Cheng (1 Cheng is equivalent to 6.24 km). Later, the ship continued to sail and arrived at Mulay (current Malay) in 17 days and then reached at Bullin with 2 days (refers to as the Daan of the Southern Tianzhu (India) country as narrated by Jia Dan). Finally, the ship spent a days to arrive in Xilan.

The second section was that the ship sailed from the Bullin to East sailing for 10-15 days. During this period, the ship crossed the Bengal Bay and reached at Langabalus (current Nicobar Islands). The ship continued to sail to the East and arrived at Kalah (current Kedah in the Malay Peninsula, Thailand) in 6 days. Later, it stopped in the Balus (today refers to as the Great Deer Cave, the West coast of the Northern Indonesian Sumatera), and then sailed through the Salahit and arrived in Harang.

The third section, the ship set off from Mayd, where was close to the Western of the Sumatera to the Tiyuma (today located in the Southeast of Pahang, Malaysia). Later, it took 5 days to arrive Qimar and 3 days to Sanf. Finally, the ships arrived in China. Ibn Khrudadhbah even mentioned about the Silla port, which was located on the Korean peninsula, and which was rich in gold.[52]

52　See the book written by Hua Tao: Ibn Khrudadhbah's Record of China's Maritime Silk Road and Its Position in the Arab-Islamic Geographical Literature, China and the Matitime Slik Road. pp. 131-135.

Suleiman, an Arab traveler who had visited China during the late period of the Tang Dynasty, besides describing the sea routes from the Persian Gulf to Southeast Asia, also introduced the route from Muscat to China. He said: "the ship sailing before the wind takes one month from Muscat to Kalah, and then to Guluo. Later, it arrives to the Tiyuma in more than 10 days and Panduranga in another 10 days. Finally, it took10 days to arrive at Sanf, and then stopped in Guangzhou across Zhanghai Sea (current South China Sea)".[53]

4. Advances in the Geographical Knowledge

(1) The Maritime Routes from Guangzhou to Foreign Countries

(a) Guangzhou Tonghai Route

After the Sui Dynasty realized the great unification of China, China became stronger and stronger. At the beginning of the Sui Dynasty (605-606), Yangguang, the second emperor sent troops to pacify Jiaozhou. At that time, the navy forces sailed to South along the East coast of Indochina Peninsula and arrived at Linyi where defeated certain Indian troops, called Elephant Troop. Since then, Sui Dynasty established close relationship with the Southeast Asia. According to the record of "The History of the Sui Dynasty"· in the winter of the October in 607, the emperor sent some people including Chang Jun to visit Shitu country (refers to as Cham Islands of current Vietnam). Their fleet set off from Guangzhou, and then stopped in the Swallow Cape in the North of the Tropic of Cancer across the Jiaoshanshi (today refers to as Shan Islands of Vietnam) in two days. Later, the ship sailed to the South and reached the Shizishi (today refers to as Kunlun Island of the Vietnam), and then further sailed to the West to Langkasuka, of the Malay Peninsula (today refers to as Pattani, a town in the far south of Thailand) finally, the ship sailed southwards and arrived in Shitu country. The king of the Shitu kingdom sent 30 boats to greet the Chinese fleet and held a grand welcome ceremony. And their prince who accompanied the Chinese fleet came to China to offer tributes to the Chinese emperor.

During the Tang Dynasty period, more and more people traveled to India by sea. According to the record of the monk Yi Jing, the number of monks who traveled to the West to seek Sutra scriptures was 56, and 34 of them sailed there by trading ships, and returned back via the South China Sea. Yi Jing, also mentioned about 4 other monks who had traveled to the West by sea. There were various sea routes to India, and their starting points were various. Some of the Chinese monks departed from Guangzhou while some from Jiaozhou, even from the Sanf region. In addition, the ports they stopped on the way were also different, including Srivijaya, Harang of the Indonesia, Malay Peninsula, numerous ports in South Asia and India.

---

53 See Travels of Suleiman, Chinese trans. by Mu Genglai, The Introduction of China and India, pp. 8-9.

If we take monk Yi Jing'a narrations as an example, he set off from Guangzhou with a Persian ship and arrived at Srivijaya (a huge port of Sumatra, Indonesia) toward the South in more than 20 days where he stayed for half a year. In the next year, he took the local king's ship to Malayu (located the South end of the Malay Peninsula) and stayed there for two months. Later, he sailed towards North with another ship and arrived at Kedah of the Malay Peninsula. At the same time, in December that year, he set off to his planned destination and passed through the Andaman Sea and Bay of Bengal.[54]

The Red Sea-Indian Ocean route, pioneered by the Roman Empire, was later inherited by Arabs. Muhammad realized the unity of clans dwelling in the Arab Peninsula in 629 and his successors founded the Dashi (Arab) Empire, which spanned the Eurasian and African continents. Muhammad himself had participated in the business trip many times, and knew something about China. He told his believers, "We should learn from China, even though we live far apart." According to Chinese historical records, in the 2nd year of the reign of Emperor, Gaozong during the Tang Dynasty period (651), the emperor of the Dashi firstly sent an emissary to visit the Tang Dynasty. In this period about in 50 years the, Dashi Empire had sent emissaries to China for 39 times. However, the Tang Dynasty and the Dashi Empire have started a war due to their competition upon several regions of Central Asia, and the army of the Tang Dynasty was defeated. Consequently, Dashi troops captured a number of Chinese people including Du Huan who had to stay there for 12 years and then returned back to Guangzhou by a trading ship.

429

The book in the History of New Tang Dynasty Geographical Records, gave a detailed description on the sea routes which started from Guangzhou and led to the Western Regions. In addition, Jia Dang also wrote a book, called Huang Hua Si Da Ji, which introduced many sea routes from Guangzhou to several foreign Countries. In this book there are parts where sea expedition from the West Pacific Ocean to the Indian Ocean was narrated. In this book, the sea expedition routes from Guangzhou city to the Dashi ports were described as follows:

The ships set sail from Guangzhou and when it arrived at Pearl River estuary, it sailed towards Southwest and sailed along the East coast of Hainan Island with several days to Bulaoshan (currently Shan Islands in the East of Vietnam). Later, it sailed Southwards across the Jinglingshan (today refers to as the Swallow Cape in the Tropic of Cancer), Mendu (Quy Nhon), and then turned to the Southwest and crossed the Bentulang (today refers to as Phan Rang of Vietnam) and Juntunongshan (today refers to as the island of Kunlun, Vietnam). Later, it took 5 days to arrive the Strait of Malacca and then sailed toward the Northwest along the Strait to the Nicobar Islands of the India. Finally, it passed through the Isthmus of Lan (current Nico Islands of India), westward through the Bengal Bay and arrived in the Shizi country. If the ship continued to sail, two routes would lead to the Dashi country ports as in the following:

54   See book by Wang Bangwei, Collation and Annotation of Biographies of Eminent Monks Seeking for Buddha dharma in West Regions in Tang Dynasty, written by (Tang) Yi Jing, collated and annotated by Wang Bangwei, published by Zhonghua Book Press, pp. 152-153.

In the first route the ships sailed westwards along the western coast of India, and when they reached the mouth of the Milan River (today refers as to the Indian River), it turned to the Northwest and sailed along the Persian Gulf to the mouth of the Foley River (currently the Euphrates river).

In the second route the ships set off from the Shizi country to Sanlan (current Aden, Yemen), and then sailed to the Northeast along the northeastern coasts of the Arab Peninsula and arrived at the mouth of the Persian Gulf (current Sohar, northeast of Oman). Finally, the ships sailed along the east coast of the Persian Gulf to the mouth of the Foley River, where these ships met with those ships which took the first route, which is mentioned above.[55]

According to the narrations about the sea expedition routes made by Jia Dan, it was particularly noteworthy that China's ocean-going shipping capacity had reached to unprecedented levels during the Tang Dynasty period. For example, during the Wei and Jin Dynasties, when the monk Fa Xian returned back to China, the trade ship he took sailed across the Bengal Bay and directly arrived at Indonesian Sumatra, next the ship sailed to Shizi country (current Sri Lanka). During the Sui Dynasty period, when Chang Jun traveled to the Chitu country, he also departed from the South end of Vietnam and reached the Malay Peninsula next his ship passed across the Gulf of Siam. In short, according to what Jia Dan narrated, in those days, Chinese ocean-going ships not only inherited the seafaring skills of the previous sailors that could cross the Siam Bay and Bengal Bay, but also had the ability to sail across the Arabian Sea after setting off from the Shizi country (current Sri Lanka). Therefore, it can be said that in the period of Tang Dynasty the Chinese ships sailed all adjacent Oceans including the Western Pacific and northern Indian ocean waters.

(b) Two Unique Books about the Foreign Countries

The two most important books of the Song dynasty that introduced information about the foreign countries were Lingwai Daida (Notes for the Land beyond the Passes or Representative Answers from the Region beyond the Mountains) and Yongle Dadian (The Introduction of the Foreign Countries), which demonstrated the achievements of the Song people in regard to overseas geography, this second book was written by Zhao Ruoshi).

The book Lingwai Daida was written by Zhou Qufei who was born in Yongjia during the Southern Dynasty period. He had once served as an official in Guilin of the Southern China and loved the facts and events. After he retired, he lived in Lingnan and started to write this book to introduce the foreign countries to Chinese people, which he finished in 1178.[56]

---

55 The New History of the Tang Dynasty Geographical Records Vol. VII.
56 The original book was lost, so currently what we can examine is from another book, titled as the Yongle Dadian (The encyclopedia, covering numerous facts before the 14th century (written by Zhao Ruoshi).

Zhao Ruoshi's book, has introduced many facts about foreign countries and various regions as part of the overseas countries, the book also described the Song people's views on the world geography. The book classified the western Pacific Ocean, the northern Indian Ocean and the Mediterranean Sea that belonged to the Atlantic Ocean into a number of seas, and then recorded a number of "metropolitan" regions which have played key roles in the overseas sea trade as in the following:

Dupo (current Java, Indonesia) was regarded as a metropolis among the South Sea nations. Its Eastern ocean, the Western Pacific, was called as the "East Ocean Sea". However, the author has argued that Western Pacific only referred to the Indonesian Islands and Luzon (Philippines) Islands, in fact, it included all the islands in the South Pacific. While Sanfuqi (today refers as to the regions among the Sumatra, Indonesia and its left regions) was the metropolis of the foreign countries besides outsides South Sea. Its South ocean, the South Pacific and South Indian Ocean, was known as the "South Ocean Sea", including Indonesia, the South Pacific islands and Australia. However, Zhou Qufei had believed that Australia was the southernmost place in the world, so he did not know the existence of the Antarctica continent.

Zhao Qufei had argued that the Southwest China Sea was boundless, and there were two metropolises near China, Zhancheng (current southern Vietnam) and Zhenla (current Cambodia). He named the Bengal Bay as the "Xilan Sea", which was named after Xilan country (current Sri Lanka). He named the Arabian Sea as the "East Dashi Sea". Besideshe evaluated, the west of Tianzhu (India), and the Daqin country far away from China as two important metropolises. If the ships sailed across the East Dashi Sea, they would arrive at the Dashi Country. He also narrated about another metropolis, called Maboli (currently Mirbat of the East of Salai, the capital of Dhofar, Oman). Its West had a huge sea, called the West Dashi Sea, namely the Mediterranean Sea. The sea was bordered by the Mulanpi country in the West, which was a metropolis (Mulanpi country, current Maghreb, a country in the north of Africa, the regions of the south coasts of the Mediterranean Sea). The west of the West Dashi Sea (Arabian Sea) was the Atlantic Ocean. Zhou Qufei had not a deep understanding about the Atlantic Ocean. Zhou Qufei has also described some other countries in the Southeast Asia region including Zhancheng, Zhenla, Pugan, Sanfuqi and Dupo. South Asian countries consisted of Gulin, Zhunian and many states of the Xitian. The countries of western Asia included Daqin, Dashi empire such as, the Malipa, Bada (current Baghdad, the capital of Iraq), Jizini (current Afghanistan), Wusili (current Mosul in Iraq), Persia and Mulanpi. In addition, he also narrated about the countries in and around the Southeast Sea (the Kunlun Cenqi country in the Indian Ocean). "Kunlun" means "black people". Cenqi refers to the Zanzibar region of Tanzania.

The book, Yongle Dadian (The Introduction of Foreign Countries), was written by Zhao Ruoshi. He was an official that administrated the ships of the Fujian province during the Sothern Song Dynasty period. He had rich knowledge about the overseas geography, he had examined many foreign maps, discussed about them with many domestic and foreign scholars. He selected many useful knowledge from many other books, especially from the book of Zhou Qufei, i.e, the Lingwai Daidawhich was written by Zhou Qufei, and started to write his own book. He completed his 2 volume book in 1225, the first volume included facts about numerous foreign countries and the second narrated about the foreign goods. Regretfully, the original books were lost, so what we can examine today is another relevant book, titled as the Yongle Dadian. Zhao Ruoshi narrated about countries according to their distance from China and the book's content is more detailed than the book titled: Lingwai Daida.

Numerous countries were recorded in Zhao Ruoshi's book. Zhao Ruoshi narrated about the countries, which are located in Southern Asia, i.e., the Jiaozhi, Zhancheng, Bintonglong (current Southern Vietnam), Zhenla, Dengliumai (Nakhon Si Thammarat, located in the Malay Peninsula), Samfiqi, Lingya Sijia (currently located between the southern Thailand and the north part of the Malay Peninsula), Fuluoan (currently located in Malay Peninsula), Xintuo, (current Eastern Java), Jianbi (current Kampar on the east coast of Sumatra), Lanwuli (today in the Northwest corner of Sumatra), Dupo, Sujidan, Yantuoman (Bay of Bengal and the Andaman Islands in Eastern India), Shahuagong, Borneo (current Brunei), Mayi (current Mindanao in the Philippines), Sanyu and so on. In his book, Zhao Ruoshi wrote about the countries that are located in the South Asia such as: Xilan, Nanbi (Ma'abar which was a vassal of the Yuan Dynasty in the southeast coast of India.), Gulin, Huchasong (Guzerat, Gujaratin in India), Maluohua (the north region of Malwa in Narbuda of India), Zhunian, Pengjialuo (Bengal), south Nihualuo in Tianzhu (India).

The Major States in the West Asia were the Daqin and the Dashi Empires

During the Song Dynasty period, China did not make any distinction between the West Asia and North Africa, consequently Chinese people called these two regions as the Dashi country—the Islam countries attached to the rule of the Dashi Empire or Arab Empire-. The book also recorded more than 20 major regions which were attached to the Dashi Empire, such as the "Misr" (current Egypt), Luoshimei (currently in the middle and lower reaches of the Amu Darya between Turkmenistan and Uzbekistan) and Mujulan (refers to current Makran on the border between Pakistan and Iran).In addition, the author also narrated an event about the lighthouse of Alexander, i.e., the Byzantine Empire had made planned an offensive to destroy this famous lighthouse. The author cited numerous facts about the foreign countries, indicating that the sea merchants of Fujian during the Song Dynasty period had already had a good understanding of the Islam states, and mentioned about the prosperity of trade between the Islam countries and the Southern Song Dynasty. Moreover, the author also mentioned about a country, which he called "Jialisiye country". "There is a deep cave wherein a fire kept burning all through the year. The fire is so strong that it can crumble huge stones weighing 500 or 1,000 kg. In addition, the huge stone hill which delivered fire from its top once every five years, and the fire violently burn the surrounding woods and also turned the stones into ash."[57]

In fact, the "Jialisiye country" that derived from Arabic pronunciation, referred to the Italian island of Sicily, where the Etna Volcano is located. The author Zhai Rushi gave a detailed description of the Etna Volcano: "in the morning, the people can see its smoke and dust, and at the noon time, the Volcano starts to deliver a violent fire which melts the rocks. The melting rocks are so hot that no one can approach them.If one throws a huge stone into it, the stone will crumble into many fragments. He wrote: The Etna Volcano erupts in every several years, the lava it delivers looks like a "flowing fire river", it burns everything around it and flows into the Mediterranean sea like other ordinary rivers. Zhai Rushi's book was the first book to mention the name of the Sicily island in Chinese historical literature.

(c) East Ocean and the West Ocean

Chinese people were already familiar with the regions of the Western Pacific Ocean- India ocean-the Mediterranean Sea (the Atlantic), but the ocean name of the region in the different historical literatures was quite inconsistent. Sometimes the same sea was named differently in various books, for example, the Arabian Sea was called as the "West Sea" or "East Dashi Sea". Sometimes the same name referred to different seas, such as the "South Sea" referred to the China South Seas or the sea around the Sri Lanka. In short, the names of the seas was quite confusing. It was not until the end of Tang Dynasty that the two concepts of "West Ocean" and "East Ocean" emerged. Later, the name of the region of the Southeast Asian-the India Ocean was gradually unified in the literature and had been used in the Qing Dynasty in the folk. Of course, in different times, the meaning of "West Ocean" and "East Ocean" was also different. Later, the name "South Ocean" also appeared. At the end of the Ming Dynasty, with the introduction of the Western knowledge of modern geography, Chinese gradually learned that the world was spherical, and gradually began to use the Western ways to classify and name the world continents and oceans, consequently gave up the traditional Chinese ways.

The Foreign Coordinate System of the Overseas Place Names

That the the ancient Chinese people named the West Pacific Ocean- Indian Ocean- Mediterranean Sea region with different names was due to inconsistencies in geographical coordinates. The overseas geographical information knowledge in ancient China had originated from different sources. Some of the knowledge was accumulated through individual records and observations made by Chinese travelers and navigators, there were two groups among them, the first group according to their conception thought that the center of geographical coordinates in the world was China, but the second group were keen to learn from foreign countries, consequently for them the center of geographical

---

57 Feng Chengjun, The Introduction of Foreign Countries, pp. 75-76.

coordinates was the foreign countries. During the Qin and Han dynasties periods, the sea names that originated in China were the coastal waters around China, while the geographical knowledge and names about the Southeast Asian-Indian Ocean-West Asia regions in China mainly originated from foreign countries. Such, geographical knowledge came from South Asia (India) and West Asia respectively. Therefore, the geographical names of the Southeast Asia-Indian Ocean-Mediterranean sea and Mediterranean regions differed greatly due to two reference points, i.e., the domestic geographical coordinate ystem and the foreign geographical coordinate system. South Asian system and Western Asia system evaluated the geographical coordinates as themselves being its centers, respectively.

South Asian geographical coordinate system

Let us first describe how the names of the seas in South-East Asia were determined by taking South Asia as the center of geographical coordinate system.

The subcontinent of South Asia is a huge peninsula which extends deep into the Indian Ocean, which is located between the Bay of Bengal and the Arabian Sea. Dynasty recorded, the origin of sea name was to put the South Asia as a geographical observation center. When South Asia (India) was regarded as the center geographical coordinate system, they had to evaluate the adjacent Bengal Bay in the east and the Arabian Sea in the west. Therefore, they have nemed the Bengal Bay as the East Sea or Southeast Sea, while they have named the Arabian Sea as the West Sea or Southwest Sea. The Indian Buddhists have often mentioned about the Ganges River flowing into the East Sea (or the Southeast Sea), and the Indus River flowing into the West Sea (or the Southwest Sea).However, the South Sea referred to the Indian Ocean waters in the South of India. This geographical concept of ancient South Asia also entered into the East Asia regions with the introduction of Buddhism. Besides, Dunhuang Shi Shi Yi Shu (Lost Books from a Stone Chamber at Dunhuang", which is a collection of rare Dunhuang texts compiled by Luo Zhenyu and published in Beijing at the end of 1909 (cf. Luo, 1909, introduces the Diary: Memoir of the Pilgrimage to the Five Regions of India (Religions of Asia Series), which narrated the experiences of the monk Hui Chao. The monk Hui Chao also wrote about West Sea and South Sea, where they referred to the Arabian Sea and he waters around Sri Lanka respectively. In a word, the India-centric geographical coordinates were found in many Chinese historical records, as in the following:

The book titled as the "East Sea", a geographical masterpiece book which was written by Li Daoyuan, during the Northern Wei Dynasty period, wrote as follows: "the Ganges River flows into the East Sea".

"West Sea": in the Post-Han Dynasty Book· Western Regions, mentioned about India and said: "the region that from the west of the Yueshi and Gaofu country to the South Sea belongs to India. In addition, in the volume 44 of the book Fu Zu Tong Ji (an introduction of the scriptures) also used the term "West Sea", and there was such a phrase in the book: "West Sea refers to the waters in the west of India". In the book, "South Sea" written by the Buddhist monk Yi Jing also mentioned about the "North Sky" and "South Sea" and he also referred to the northern Tianzhu (India) and current Sri Lanka. In the volume 44 of the Fu Zu Tong Ji, here the "South Sea" meant the waters around the Southern India. But the ancient Chinese people did not abuse the sea names of the Indian system. It was only when Chinese people narrated about the Indian geography that did they used the geographical concepts of India.

West Asia as the juncture region

In the early Chinese historical records, the people named West Sea with the Western Asia as the juncture region. In fact, it was with West Sea as center. In the Western Han period, Si Maqian had described West Sea (near the Tiaozhi country, current West Asia). In the Historical Records as Dawan Country. Since then, the term "West Sea" used in the Chinese history books adopted the above approach and this approach was also followed by the later historians. Ban Gu also used West Sea to refer to the waters near the Tiaozhi country.[58]

When Ban Gu mentioned about the Daqin country, he said: "Daqin country, called Liqian, is located in the west of the West Sea." Liqian refers to the Alexander City in Egypt. Literally, the "West Sea" here refers to the Mediterranean sea. The Mediterranean sea is located in the west of Western Asia, so it was called as the West Sea. At the same time, Alexander City which had bonds with the Western Asia across the Mediterranean sea, was known and called as the "West Sea city". But, through carefully reading the Post-Han Dynasty Book· Western Regions, we can see that when Ban Gu sent Gan Ying to the Daqin country, the West Sea he mentioned was the Persian Gulf. In the book, "Wei Dynasty and the Western Countries" it was written as follows: the reason that Daqin country was called as the West Sea country was that, this country was located in the West of the "sea"" Here, the "sea" refers to the domestic river of Daqin, the Nile River in Egypt. Therefore, a conclusion can be drawn that the West Seas mentioned together with the Western Asia as the juncture region were in fact the waters between the Persian Gulf, the north of the Arabian Sea and the Red Sea, which regarded the Western Asia as the juncture region. This approach is different from the above West Sea conception which regards the north of Indian Ocean as the West Sea.

In the later period, the concept of "West Sea" gradually changed which not only referred to the north of Indian Ocean, the waters of the Persian Gulf-Arabian Sea-Red Sea, but also sometimes included the Mediterranean Sea and the Black Sea. For example, The History of Sui Dynasty· Pei Ju Biography described the 3 expedition routes which could lead to "West Seas", the Persian Gulf and Arabian Sea.

---

58 Han Dynasty Book·Western Regions.

Start from Dunhuang, cross the Congling (Pamirs), Suduishana and Persia and arrive at the destination. Secondly, start from Dunhuang, cross Congling and North Brahmin and arrive at the destination.

The third route started from Yiwu (currently Hami) passed through the South Siberian and Eurasian grasslands to reach Fulin country, from Fulin country as the last step arrived at the West Sea. Here, Fulin country refers to the Byzantine Empire, and obviously here the West Seas refers to the Black Sea or the Mediterranean Sea.

In 751, the Tang Dynasty and the Dashi kingdom had a but Tang army was defeated. Consequently, many defeated troops were captured and taken to Dashi. Du Huan was also taken to Dashi country and stayed there for 12 years, and when he returned back to China, he wrote a book, called the Jing Xing Ji (which included his travel during the return journey). He wrote in his book: "Fulin state often fights against Dashi state, which is located in the west of the West Sea and the south of the South Sea. The "West Sea" here refers to Mediterranean Sea, and the "South Sea" refers to the Red Sea."

After the rise of the Dashi Empire, the name of the western Indian Ocean-Mediterranean Sea region in Chinese historical records had also changed, but the name of the seas which was related with the Western Asia as the geographical juncture center still remained. The most obvious example was the naming of the "East Dashi Sea" and the "West Dashi Sea" mentioned in the "Ling Wai Dai Da" written by Zhou Qufei. Du Huan, said that the west of the East Dashi Sea was the Dashi country. The so-called "East Dashi Sea" was the Arabian Sea. Besides, Jia Dan also said that the ships sailed along the East shore of the sea from the Nanjing, Brahman to Wucui country, Persia. The west shore of the sea was the Dashi country. By comparison, we can assume that the East Dashi (Arab) Sea what Zhou Qufei talked about and the sea what Jia Dan talked about was the Arabian Sea.

As for the so-called "West Dashi Sea", Zhou Qufei wrote the following: "the territories of the Dashi state is vast, and it also controls many other smaller states. It borders the West Dashi Sea in the West. If you go westwards, you can arrive at Mulanpi country and its surrounding countries, but if you continue to go toward the West, no one knows what the place it is." It is clear that the "West Sea" mentioned here is the Mediterranean Sea and the adjacent north Atlantic. "Mulanoi" was the transliteration of Arabic "Maghrib", meaning "West". The "the surrounding countries around the Murampi "were the countries of the Arabian Maghreb region in North Africa. At the time, the farthest place in West that Chinese people knew was the Mediterranean Sea, and they had no idea of the situation in the West seas of the Mediterranean Sea From a geographical point of view, the principle of naming the so-called "East Dashi Sea" and was based on the Arab Empire (the south of the Western Asia). Zhou Qufei wrote: "if the ship sails to the West along the West Sea, it can arrive the Mulanpi country and its surrounding countries", meaning East Dashi Sea and

West Dashi Sea were not only the with Western Asian as center, but also their names themselves were originated from foreign regions.

In the 12th century, Edrisi, a geographer from Sijiaye country (current Sicilia, Italy) in 1153-1154 wrote a book, Geography Book, the map of which noted the sea, called as the "Bahr al-Muzlim al", meaning "West Islam Sea". In addition, Umari, an Arab historian of the Yuan Dynasty, also mentioned the sea in his book Yan Li Zhu Guo Xing Ji (introduce his experiences of traveling in foreign countries) and called the sea Bahr-al Gharbi, meaning "West Sea". In the second half of the 10th century, an anonymous Persian book, The World's Realms, described the scope of the West Sea, which was from the ends of the Sudan and the surrounding countries of the Mulanmpi to the Lumei (Asia Minor-Anotolia) Strait.

Obviously, the sea, whether called as the "West Islam Sea" or the "West Sea", was the source of the "West Dashi (Arab) Sea". The Arab geography literature also recorded "Mulampi Sea" (Bahr al-Maghrib) or "Lumei Sea", referring to the Mediterranean Sea (Bahr al-Rum).[59]

The East Dashi Sea mentioned by Zhou Qufei also was found in the historical books recording Western Region. If you research the records about the India Ocean in the Islamic geography writings, you can see that the anonymous Persian geography book (Hudud al-alem)[60] which was translated by Minorsky which says that there was an ocean, called as the Bahr al'Azam in them (meaning the Great Ocean)[61] which was connected to China and included five big gulfs.

The first gulf was the Barbari Bay, that was, the Gulf of Aden at the southern end of the Red Sea and the Arabian Sea. It started from Abyssinia and extended to the west.

The second gulf was connected to the first gulf, known as the Arabian Sea. It extended to the Egyptian on Northwards as well as it border was narrower, and the narrowest part of the Northern end was only a mile wide. It was the Red Sea. The third gulf began at the coast of Fars (Persia), which extended to the northwest. The Arab land was situated between the sea and the Arabian Gulf, and it was the Persian Gulf.

The fourth gulf, known as the Pars (Persian) Sea, began at the border of Persia, where it was narrow and extended to the boundary of Xindu. This sea should be the Gulf of Oman.

---

59   E. J. Brill, Encyclopaedia of Islam, New Edition, Volume 1, pp. 933-936.
60   See the English translation by Minorsky, Vladimir Fed'orovich's book titled as Hudud al-'alem, or "The regions of the world"- London, revised. 1970, pp. 52-53, and Note 3, pp. 179-180 Professor Minorsky's magnum opus translation book appeared in the Gibb Memorial Series in 1937—a critical translation of the anonymous Persian geography book entitled Hudud al-'alem, or "The regions of the world", written in the year 372/982; the translation of Minorsky contained 12 maps, together with an English translation of V.V. Barthold's original Russian preface.
61   Ibid.

The fifth gulf, which started from the border of Hindustan, extended north-wards and formed a gulf, known as the "Xindu" bay. This sea was probably the Bengal Bay.

The scope of the seas that mentioned by the above Persian anonymous book—"Hudud- al-alem", or "The regions of the world"—was almost same with that of the East Dashi Sea which was narrated by Zhou Qufei, except the four gulfs mentioned above.

(2) Overseas Geographical Names Given to Chinese Native Land

The names of the Northern Indian Ocean-the Mediterranean Sea region mentioned above were originated from the foreign countries. In the pre-Qin period, the Chinese had limited knowledge of overseas geography. But they realized that China was a vast land, but it was only a part of the world, and the world was not as vast as the sea. In the Warring States period, Qi Yan of the Qi Dynasty said that many countries were surrounded by small seas, and the continents in the world were also surrounded by big seas.

The "South Sea" and the "Southeast Sea"

Since the Qin and Han dynasties, Chinese seamen and merchants had more un-derstanding on the sea in generations of nautical activities. Thus the sea naming system with China as the coordinated center was established. Among them, "South Sea" had close trades with Southeast Asia - Indian Ocean waters. The Chinese coast extends to north and south, so if we want go to the Southeast Asia-Indian Ocean waters, we must sail in a Southward direction. In the pre-Qin period, the Chinese people already had the concept of "South Sea", which referred to the sea in the Southern China, including the East China Sea. After the Han Dynasty, "South Sea" only referred to the South China Sea. Therefore, the concept of "South Sea" in China was different from India and Western Asia. In the era of insufficient devel-opment of nautical and extraterritorial knowledge, the geographical concept of the "South Sea" covered a wide range of regions, which not only referred to the South China Sea, but also the sea of the Southeast Asia and the East India. In the Tang Dynasty, the book recorded that "Guangzhou was near to the South Sea, where the ships from Kunlun country exchanged treasures with China every year."[62]

Here the "Kunlun" refers to the regions of the Southeast Asia and the East Indian Ocean. In 663, "in the Tang Dynasty period, the Zhenla country (locat-ed in the Southern Asia) invited the monk named, Natwasangzang, to Zhenla. Natidsanzang visited Zhenla on the grounds of health and remained there and did not return back home."[63]

In the volume 222 of the New Tang Dynasty Book, it was said that: "Panpan Country was located Nanhaiqu (current Malay Peninsula in the West coast of Siam Bay). The people of the Tang Dynasty used to call overseas ship as the "South Sea ship", meaning those ships from the South Sea.

62 The Old Tang Dynasty Book, Wang Fangqing.
63 Shi Daoxuan: The Monk Biography, Volume 5 of Natwasanzang Biography.

It is noteworthy that in the navigation field, before the Tang Dynasty period, Chinese sailors have paid much attention to identify the sea entrance of the rivers, which was the sign of destination port and transfer port. For example, when The Liang Dynasty Book described the sea route from Funan (current Cambodia) to India, he mentioned two estuaries rather than the sea name that the ship crossed." The two estuaries refer to the Juli estuary and Tianzhujing estuary (Ganges River estuary). When Jia Dan in his book The Route of Foreign Ships Sailing to Guangzhou mentioned the route of the West coast of the India, he said that the Milan River (Xintou River) in the Western Tianzhu flowed into the sea from here, which was Indian River Estuary. When Jia Dan wrote the boundary route between Iraq and Iran, he said the ship sailed to the West from here and could arrive in Wula country in one day, where there was a Fulila river of the Dshi Country and it flowed into sea. In fact, the Fulila river estuary was the Arab Sea estuary, the meeting of the Tigris River and Euphrates River. It showed that other than the sea in the South of the Hainan Province that was called the Zhanghai Sea, and all the other foreign seas were all called the South Sea. Gradually, the Chinese navigators became more and more abundant in the overseas geographic knowledge and orientation concept. In the Tang dynasty, the new concept of "Southwest Sea" appeared which referred to the Northern Indian Ocean. According to the New Tang Dynasty Book· Western Region, the Shizi country (current Sri Lanka) was in the "Southwest Sea", but in the volume193 of the Tong Dian, it was narrated said that the Shizi country was located in the "West Sea". The "Southwest Sea" here refers to the sea around the Southern part of the Indo-Pakistan subcontinent. At the end of the Tang dynasty, another man, called Duan Chengshi, described the Baboli country (the coastal regions of Somalia in the eastern coast of the African continent), which was located in "Southwest Sea".[64]

The "Southwest Sea" here refers to the current Arabian Sea. If we compare the similarities and differences between "South Sea" and "Southwest Sea", we can evaluate that their concepts took China as the center of observation, but scope of the "Southwest Sea" was more accurate than the "South Sea".

The concept of "Southwest Sea" adopted during the Tang Dynasty period has continued to be used by the Chinese people during the Song Dynasty period. Zhou Qufei wrote: "the Persia is located adjacent to the Southwest Sea."[65]

Zhao Rushi also said: "Kunlun Cenqi country (The Zanzibar Island of Tanzania) lies in the Southwest Sea".[66] Liu Yu wrote: "the Persian Shiluozi country (current Shiraz in Iran) is also located adjacent to the Southwest Sea."[67]

---

64   Volume 4 of Xiyang (Miscellaneous from Xiyang).
65   Lingwai Daida, Volume III, (Lingwai Daida variously translated as Representative Answers from the Region beyond the Mountains, Notes Answering [Curious Questions] from the land beyond the Pass or other similar titles, is a 12th century geographical treatise written by Zhou Qufei.
66   The Introduction of the Foreign Country, Volume: the overseas countries.
67   Liu Yu: The Journey to the West Regions, Zhonghua Book Company.

Therefore, the "Southwest Sea" mentioned above have generally followed the conception used during the Tang Dynasty, consequently refers to the Northern Indian Ocean Sea. We can see the concepts of "South Sea" and "Southwest Sea" which were used in the ancient books written by Chinese seafarers and scholars have contained different connotations and meant different geographical coordinates.

China's overseas geographical cognition has made a rapid development in the Five Dynasties and the Song Dynasty periods. Zhou Qufie, a geographer of the Song Dynasty period, who created the geographical naming system for China has mainly based himself on the Islam geographers of the Western Asia, so he named East Dashi Sea and West Dashi Sea to refer to the Northwestern Indian Ocean and the Mediterranean Sea. In addition, he used the Southwest Sea to refer to the Northern Indian Ocean. Moreover, he also mentioned a series of new geographical names to refer to the different waters of the Western Pacific and the Indian Ocean. For example, the "Eastern Ocean Sea" refers to the ocean of the South Eastern China (current Western Pacific, the ocean of the East of Indonesian Java). The concept of "South Sea" was used to refer to the Southern ocean of Sanfuji (refers to the sea waters between the South Pacific of the northern Australia and the Southern Indian Ocean).

In the Song Dynasty period the Bengal Bay was called the "Xilan Sea", named after "Xilan country" (Sri Lanka). Later, in the Yuan Dynasty, the people began to called the Southern Bengal Bay between Sumatera in Indonesia and Sri Lanka "Nanwuliyang". These were things that the previous generation did not know about.

"Eastern Ocean" and "Western Ocean"

Another significant advance in regard to nautical geography was made in the Five Dynasties and Song dynasties period, and the concept of the "Eastern Ocean" and "Western Ocean" put forward. According to records of the Xwashan Magazine, Pu Youliang and Pujia, the member of the Pu family in the Quanzhou served as an official in Zhanchen who managed the things of the Western Ocean respectively in the Five Dynasties and in the late period of the Song Dynasty.[68]

It shows that the geographical concept of the "Western Ocean" was used in the Song Dynasty period. In addition to the "Western Ocean", the Song Dynasty and Yuan Dynasty also acknowledged the geographical concept of "Small Western Ocean". This name can be found in the South Sea Biography written by Chen Dazhen of the Yuan Dynasty. The so-called "Small Western Ocean" was almost the same as the "Western Ocean" mentioned above, which the number of the Pu Family managed. In general, the "Small Western Ocean" referred to the wares around the Malay Peninsula and the Indonesian Sumatra,

440

---

68 Cai Yongjian, Xwashan Magazine, Volume 1. Based on the Zhuan Weiji, The Research on the Pu Family's Private Ship among the Song Dynasty ships in Quanzhou, See China and Maritime Silk Road, p. 347.

which was slightly smaller than the "Western Ocean" recorded in the Research on the Eastern Ocean and Western Ocean in the Ming Dynasty. However, when the book South China Sea Biography which mentioned the "Small Western Ocean" was published, the Song Dynasty was in its declining period and was overthrown in about 20 years later. Therefore, the term "Small Western Ocean" was only used in the Song Dynasty period.

The term the "Western Ocean" had been widely used in the Song Dynasty and Yuan Dynasty. From the present literature data, the "Western Ocean "has been used in the Song and Yuan Dynasties as well as in the Five Dynasties, but its geographical scope was greatly changed. Yuan Liumin in the Bu Ali's Tombstone of the Zhong An Ji (the Encyclopedia of Ancient China) said: "the ancestors of Bu Ali moved from the Western Regions to Western Ocean and settled down there". By conducting research on the book, history of Yuan Dynasty· Ma'abar (Malabar) Biography, the "Western Ocean" referred to the Ma'abar in the Southeast coast of India.[69]

When China was under the rule of the Shizong in the Yuan Dynasty, Bu Ali served as prime minister of his country and accommodated many envoys from China. This demonstrates that it was in the Song Dynasty period that Bu Ali's ancestors had moved to the "Western Ocean".

Wang Dayuan in his book Dao Yi Zhi Lue also mentioned: "Western Ocean", which refers to the Ma' abar (Malabar) country and its surrounding regions. In addition, the "Western Ocean's cloth "and "Western Ocean's silk "were mentioned in the book, later, "The Zhenla Feng Tu Ji" (literal meaning The Natural Conditions and Social Customs of the Zhenla Kingdom) also said the cloth from the Western Ocean. All the cloth mentioned above were probably be the textiles from the Ma abar. The "Eastern Ocean" was related with the "Eastern Sea". The concept of the "Eastern Ocean" was found for the first time in the South Sea Biography where it was divided into "Small Eastern Ocean" and "Big Eastern Ocean".

If we evaluate the place names, the "Eastern Ocean" in the early and middle of the Yuan Dynasty mainly referred to the Western Pacific Ocean including the East of the Philippine Islands, Kalimantan Island and Java. While the "Small Eastern Ocean" mainly referred to the Philippine Islands and Kalimantan Island, which led by Funi the Buddha Ni State (that was, the Marco Mud, this Brunei) tube collar. And "Big Toyo" mainly referred to the Kalimantan, Pulau in the seas of South of Australia. "Big Toyo" was divided into two parts. East of Indonesia, including current Kepulauan Maluku in the East of the land, in the west were mainly Bali and Java Islands in Indonesia.[70]

---

69   Chen Gaohau, Bo Hali, The Prince of the Ma'abar (Malabar), India, Visits China, Journal of Nankai University, 1980/4.

70   Chenlianqing: "The Great South China Sea in the South China Sea". See the Western Region of the Southern Ocean of the Country, Journal of Literature and History, 1986/27; pp. 145-164.

Wang Dayuan also mentioned about the "Eastern Ocean". He said that Java belonged to the Eastern Ocean. Later, he also said that the people of the Eastern Ocean all were afraid of the Posheye. In addition, he mentioned: "the Zwashan extends in the Small Eastern Ocean, although he did not mention the name of Big Eastern Ocean, although he probably knew it. The South Sea Biography gave a detailed description the exchanges between Guangdong city and foreign countries, while the Dao Yi Zhi Lue described the connection between Fujian and oversea countries. The name of the "Eastern Ocean" has firstly appeared in the South Sea Biography, so it was conclude that the name was originated from Yuan Dynasty and it was familiar with merchants in Guangdong and Fujian over the ten years. In short, the names of the "Eastern Ocean ", "Big Eastern Ocean" and "Small Eastern Ocean" used in the Yuang Dynasty only followed names in the Song Dynasty.

After Yuan Dynasty, the people continued to use the name "Eastern Ocean" and "Western Ocean ". Zhang Xie from the Ming Dynasty wrote a book, The Research on the Eastern Ocean and Western Ocean. There was only the name of the "Eastern Ocean "without the "Small or Big Eastern Ocean". But the "Eastern Ocean" recorded in this book mainly referred to the "Small Eastern Ocean" in the Song and Yuan Dynasties, which was current Ma'abar (Malabar) of the Southeast coast of the India. Meanwhile, it was called "Western Ocean Suoli" in the era of admiral Zheng He.

<u>442</u>   In the book of The Research on the Eastern Ocean and Western Ocean, it was written: "Brunei was the division between the Eastern Ocean and the Western Ocean." Therefore, it could be sure that the geographical scope of these two oceans had been changed, which brought a big challenge for the following research. It was difficult to explain the change of their geographical scope through seeing the place names. Luckily, Zhang Xie recorded the routes to the Western Ocean and Eastern Ocean in his book, The Research on the Boatmen. The division between the "Western Ocean" and "Eastern Ocean" were based on the different sea courses.

There were two sea routes which the ships used when they sailed to the regions of the Southeast Asia during the Tang Dynasty and Five Dynasties periods. The first route started from Fujian or Guangdong, sailed Southwards along the continent of the Eastern Asian with the various topographies along the way as marks. All the foreign regions here were called as the "Western Ocean ". When the member of the Pu family served as the official who managed the things of the "Western Ocean ", he was in charge of the trades in the route. In the Song Dynasty and Yuan Dynasty, the foreign regions along the route were called "Small Western Ocean ". Probably the route was defined as the "Continental Route". If the ship had sailed across the "Small Western Ocean", it would arrive at India if sailing to the West, and was also called "Western Ocean" in the Song Dynasty and Yuan Dynasty periods.

Another route was that the ships that started from the Fujian port arrived at Liuqiu (Taiwan) across the Taiwan Strait or the ships starting from the Gongdong arrived Luzon (Philippines) Island across the North of the South China Sea. Later, the ship sailed to the South along the Philippines archipelagos with the islands in the South of the Western Pacific Ocean. The foreign regions along the way were called "Eastern Ocean", namely the "Island Course". The Philippine Islands and the waters near the Southern Kalimantan Island in the "Eastern Ocean" were known as "Small Eastern Ocean". The sea in the South of Kalimantan Island was called "Big Eastern Ocean ". There were two routes from the "Small Eastern Ocean" to the "Big Eastern Ocean". One route was the ship set off from the West coast of the Kalimantan Island to Western "Big Eastern Ocean", which was the Java Sea and Bali Sea. Another was the ship firstly arrived at the Sulu Sea across the strait between Kalimantan Island and the Palawan archipelago in the Philippines, and then sailed to the South along the East coast of Kalimantan Island and reached the Eastern "Big Eastern Ocean", namely regions in the Sulawesi Sea, Molucca Sea, Banda Sea and Flores Sea. In a word, the geographical scope of the Eastern Ocean generally referred to the East of the South Sea, while the geographical scope of the Western Ocean generally referred to the West of the South China Sea. They were divided by the South Sea,

5. Introduction of Exotic Religions to China

(1) The Introduction of Islam

The scholars studying the history of Hui nationality have long been concerned about the time of Islam's introduction to China. According to Chinese literature before the Ming Dynasty, the times that Islam was introduced to China was various, for example, in the period of Kaihuang or Daye in the Sui Dynasty, and in the period of the Wude, Zhenguang or Yonghui in the Tang Dynasty. Among them, it was impossible that the China in the period of Kaihung of the Sui Dynasty, because at that time, Islam was not created. In addition, the opinion that Islam was introduced into China in the period of Daye of the Sui Dynasty was not trusted because Islam was still in its infancy. Other points of view, from the perspective of the development of Islam itself, are worth further research. By further exploring the accurate period that Islam spreading to China in the Tang Dynasty, it can be found that the opinions about Islam entering to China has originated from the Ming Book written by He Qianyuan. The book recorded that prophet Mohammed had four outstanding missionaries in Medina, and four missionaries came to China in the period when Wude reigned the Tang Dynasty. Two of them visited Guangzhou and Yangzhou respectively. The rest went to Quanzhou and were dead in the way and were buried in the Linshan mountain of Quanzhou. Although the Arabic words on the tomb belonged to the Yuan Dynasty, the tomb itself was probably from the Song Dynasty period.

In addition, based on the tomb of Wo Gesi in Guangzhou, the people have argued that Islam had spread to China in the period of Zhenguan of the Tang Dynasty. In fact, Wo Gesi was a missionary who had to Guangzhou. It can be said that this opinion is dubious because Wo Gesi was his Chinese name, "Wo Gesi" was a transliteration in the Yuan Dynasty, which was different from the transliterations made during the Tang Dynasty and Song Dynasty periods. Therefore, a conclusion can be drawn that the statements about the Wo Gesi and his tomb were made in the Yuan Dynasty period. The view that Islam had spread to China during the reign of Huizong of the Tang Dynasty was based on the records of the Old Tang Dynasty Book·Dashi Biography. It narrated that in the 2nd year of Yonghui, the Dashi country sent envoys to visit China. Therefore, some researchers have confused the time of establishing relationship between Tang Dynasty and Dashi country with that of Islam spreading to China. As the Arab geography works have often referred to the Huang Chao Uprising, they wrote that the rebel army broke into Guangzhou and killed 120,000 foreign people, including a large number of Islams. Therefore, it is certain that Islam was introduced to China during the Tang Dynasty period. But there are still different views about the specific date when Islam had entered into China. In fact, it is a difficult problem to determine the accurate time of Islam entering China in the Tang Dynasty period. Scholars who have studied the history of maritime communication between China and foreign countries acknowledge that the direct maritime connection between China and Western Asia was established during the Han Dynasty period. After the Eastern Han Dynasty, the Chinese merchant ships set off from the Southern China and docked along the way, and directly reached to the coast of the Arabian Sea. The ship of Roman Empire also departed directly from the Red Sea to the Southeast coast of China. During the hundreds of years from the Han Dynasty to the Tang Dynasty, China and West Asia had maintained maritime connection. The foreign merchants lived or settled in China's coastal and inland regions because of monsoon winds or other reasons. After the establishment of the Islam communities in China, the maritime intercourse between them was more frequent, deducing that there must be some Islams among the foreign merchants from Western Asia. But it was unclear when the first tradessman who believed in Islam had traveled to China. Moreover, the concepts that Islamic merchants arrived to China, and Islam was introduced to China are different and can not to be confused. For example, the Chinese merchant ship arrived in India in the Han Dynasty, which was not equipment to the introduction of Confucianism into India.

When Islam reigned in Western Asia, there were numerous Islam merchants among the foreign merchants who originated the West Asian countries. Foreigners who come to China's coastal regions generally lived in the specific region called Fanfang, where foreigners kept their customs. So the original Islamists in the Tang Dynasty were mainly from the Western Asian merchants and their family who settled down in China. It took some time before their religious beliefs were paid attention by the Chinese people, let alone, it needed some time for the Islam religion to take root in China.

The Hui people who came to China by land route and sea route in the Yuan Dynasty were obviously different. Since the Tang and Song Dynasties, many merchants from Persian and Dashi country came to China by boat from the South Sea, and lived in the foreign trade port of Southern China. Since the Yuan Dynasty, Hui people still went to China by sea route and settled in the port cities. For example, a Hui who once repaired the Shengyou Temple (an Islam Mosque) in Quanzhou was from Jerusalem. Compared with the Hui people who came to China by land, these people were greatly affected by the Arabian culture. In the 20th century, people have found abundant Islamic cultural relics of the Yuan Dynasty in Quanzhou, such as Hui people's tombstones, inscriptions on the temples, and a considerable part of the Arabic language.[71]

Islamic cultural relics of the Yuan Dynasty in Arabic language was also be found in otherregions, such as the Arabic inscriptions on the tombstones from the end of Yuan Dynasty found in Shensi Temple of Guangzhou, and the Arabic inscriptions on the tombstone in the Yuan Dynasty found in Yangzhou and in the Niujie mosque of Beijing. In the period of Zhennian, Repair the Inscription on the Qingjin Temple in Quanzhou mentioned four kinds of posts, which were served by Shaikh Al-Islam, Imam, Mutawalli, and Muazzin.[72]

These names were Arabic transliteration, which was distinctly different from the idiomatic Persian language of the Hui people who had entered China.

(2) The Early Islam Mosques

Mosques were not only the house of religious activities in the eyes of the Islam Hui people, but also reflected their economic and cultural lives. The Islam Hui people in China began to build mosques very early. The mosques before the Yuan Dynasty period was mainly distributed in China's coastal regions. But since the Yuan Dynast, more and more mosques were built in the Northern China and the inland China. At present, the most ancient mosques in China were the Huawasheng Mosque in Guangzhou. When Suleiman from Dashi country arrived in Guangzhou in the middle of 9th century, he had seen several mosques there. When Yu Ke of Southern Song Dynasty moved to Guangzhou in the late 12th century, he also saw the Huawasheng Mosque located in the Pearl River. The Reconstruction the Inscription on the Huawasheng Temple also mentioned the temple was built in the Tang Dynasty. Quanzhou also boasted a lot of Islamic ancient temples, according to the Arabic words on the stone wall of the Northern street near the door of the Shenyou Temple, the temple was built in the Hi calendar 400 years, that was, in the second year of Xiangfu of the Northern Song Dynasty (1009). Based on the record of Reconstruction the Inscription on the Qingjing Temple in Quanzhou, Qingjing temple was built in the 1st year of the reign of Emperor Shaoxing during the Southern Song Dynasty period (1131 AD).

---

71   Quanzhou Religious Stone Inscription, pp. 1-26.
72   Ibid., pp. 22-24.

There were many mosques built by the Islam Hui people in Yuan Dynasty. The Reconstruction of Inscription on the Libai Temple in Zhongshanfu (Ding County, Hebei) in the eight years of Zhizhen in the Yuan Dynasty said: "There are millions of temples around the Beijing. If you go to the west, along the way you can immediately encounter a temple to worship."[73]

Although the number he narrated in the book was a little exaggerated, it reflected the vigorous efforts by Islam believers to build mosques all across China during the Yuan Dynasty period. Shenghuai Mosque in Guangzhou, Shengyou Mosque and Qingjing Mosque in Quanzhou Mosque mentioned above were all preserved and protected by the rulers of the Yuan Dynasty.

At the end of Yuan Dynasty, Wu Jian's The Restoration of Qingjing Temple Monument mentioned, "another six or seven Libai Temples were built in Quanzhou...". The relics of the Mosque found in Quanzhou, included not only the above-mentioned Shengyou Temple and Qingjing Temple, but also Yemen Temple of the Song Dynasty as well as Mohammed Temple, Nakhid Chongxiu Temple and Wuming Temple of the Yuan Dynasty.74 In addition, temples built by Hui people could be seen in Daduo (Beijing), Hangzhou, Yangzhou, Dingzhou, Kaifeng and other regions. Kozlov and other people from Russia also found the 14th-century temple site and the remnant monument with Persian words in the Yijinailu, a city of the Yuan Dynasty. (Today refers to as Halahetuo, the East of Ejin Banner in the Inner Mongolia).[75]

The 1339 dated Persian inscription which was found in Helin, the capital of the Mongolia, referred to the local economics college. These proved that in the Yuan Dynasty, Hui people had been widely building temple in China to promote Islam. Among the many early mosques, Shengyou Temple in Quanzhou built in 1009 had the most characteristic architectures. Because it was designed and built by foreign people, so it was Damascus style, totally different from the mosques with Han style.

(3) Indian Shaivism

There were no records about Shaivism among the literatures of the Yuan Dynasty period. Since 1930s, in Quanzhou, about more than 200 carved stone relics related to Shaivism which belonged to the Yuan Dynasty period were found. In the recent years, the scholars have made new achievements on Shaivism of India in the ancient Chinese territories. In the late days of 1984, scholars found a stone carving of Shaivism about 1 km. near the wall around the Tonghuai gate in the Quanzhou city.

73　Sun Guanwen: The Reconstruction of Inscriptions on the Libai Temple, The Journal of Cultural Relics, 1961/8.

74　Zhung Weiji, Chen Dasheng: New Research on the Relics of the Mosque in Quanzhou, The Journal of World Religion Studies, 1981/3.

75　Bo Xihe: Chinese Ancient Inscriptions in Arabic words, Asia Magazine, p. 179, Note 2, 1913.

With 47cm x 57cm x 22cm in volume, this stone is rectangular and made of diabase. Its main part was carved into a house-shaped square niche and the top of it was a bell-shaped decoration. In addition, the roof was decorated with a lion head and the ends of the eaves were engraved with a multi-layer column of Lotus. The middle of the ache was carved with a tower-shaped millstone, supported by the blooming lotus. There were two statues of god on the left and right of the millstone. The statues wore crowns, rosary beads and bracelet rings on their heads, necks and wrists, as well as they sat in the same posture. The statue here should be Siva, the destroyer of the Hinduism or his followers, while the tower-shaped millstone in the niche should be the most basic incarnation of Siva. Siva believed that after destructing the old things, new thing must be created, proving that Siva was the God of destruction, but had the ability to create new thing. This stone carving belonged to the ornaments of the Shaivism's architectures, and was often embedded in the top of the inner floor of the building. In the early 1950s, Wu Wenliang also collected a similar niche as that above mentioned.[76]

Many statues of Shaivism have been found in Quanzhou.

After 1985, Quanzhou also collected a number of Shaivism's stone carvings. Among them, there were two flower-type heads of the column. One with 25x98x98 cm in volume was carved with lotus petals and cross-shaped flowers on the anterior and frontier sides, and it was flanked by flowers symmetrical to droop. The other with 26x86x86 cm in volume, had the same shape with the one mentioned above. Quanzhou unearthed a lot of flower-style heads of the column, most of which were the style of the Southern Tianzhu, namely Gandhara's art styles. The Greek-style stigma stone was found near the South gate of Quanzhou in 1985, and a gourd-like headboard was found near the Lingshan of Deer Garden in 1989. In addition, in the road construction works, stone transverse beam technique was used, two sides of which were carved with pattern. The left side of it was a deformation pattern that cobras coil together, and the right was a rectangular box, the middle and edge of which were carved with begonia flowers and oblique lotus petals. It was the transverse beam between the eaves of the column head. In 1956, Wu Wenliang once found the inscription written by foreign words in the Douya county, Wubao Street, Quanzhou.[77]

447

Later, Indian scholars and Japanese scholars believed these foreign words was Tamil. These stone carvings about Hinduwasm in Quanzhou proved that in the Yuan Dynasty, there were once Shaivism temples in Quanzhou.[78] The believers of the Shaivism in Quanzhou were mainly merchants who come to China across the Ma'abar Sea in the South India. Ma'abar, also known as Nanpi country, had close maritime relationship with Quzhou in the Song, Yuan

76   Quanzhou Religious Stone Carving and Figures pp. 111-114.
77   The Religious Stone Carving of Quanzhou, Supplemented Figure 1 and 2.
78   Yang Qinzhang: The New Certificate of the Relationship between Quanzhou in the Yuan Dynasty and South India, China and Maritime Silk Road, Fujian Press, 1991.

and Ming Dynasties. According to the record of Zhao Rushi, at the end of the Song Dynasty a man with his son, called Luoba Zhiligan, lived in the Southern Quanzhou from Nanpi country, while a large number of Shaivism stone carving and Tamil inscription that mentioned above were also unearthed here. It can be imagined that the man and his son was the member of the Shaivist community in Quanzhou.

The close exchanges between South India and China were both two-way because when the Saiva came into China, Chinese people also come to India. Based on the record of Wang Dayuan, "South India boasted a tall tower, called Tu Tower. The tower, located in the Badan plain, was surrounded by the wooden stone, on which Chinese characters were engraved as follows: "Xian Chun San Nian Wan Gong", meaning the tower was finished in the 3rd year of Xianchun rule. It was said that the Chinese characters were engraved by the Chinese people who came to here in that year, and which still can be seen to-day.[79] Fujita Toyohachi pointed out that the "Tu Tower" should be the Chinese Tower, which was about 1 mile to the Northwest apart from the Negapatam of the South India in the book, Marco Polo Travels noted by Tu Ershi. The tower still had three floors in 1847 and was destroyed in 1859. This tower was located in Badan plain, the "Badan" of which should be the transliteration of Tamil language "Pattinam", meaning the town was surrounded by the wall.[80] The tower was constructed in the third year of the reign of Xianchun (1267) of the late of the Song Dynasty period.

6. Transplanting of the Overseas Crops

(1) Overseas Herbal (medicine) Materials

The trade of overseas herbal materials (medicine materials) played an important role in the Chinese and foreign sea trades. Throughout the nearly 1000 years from the Han Dynasty to the end of the Tang Dynasty, the knowledge on overseas herbal materials or medicines became deeper and many overseas medicines were incorporated into medicine making. However, the focus of herbal works in the past were to introduce the domestic medicines, while the foreign imported drugs were rarely mentioned in these books, so it is difficult to find information about them. In addition, due to the limitation of the historical conditions, Chinese drug scientists had no clear understanding on the specific characteristics of foreign drugs, such as origin, shape, efficacy, taste, purpose, taboo and other aspects. Moreover, some information on foreign herds was recorded based on what other people said instead of the truth, so there were many errors. Later, with the development of Chinese trade in the Tang Dynasty, the number of imported oversea medicines greatly increased, which made Chinese drug scientists gain a new understanding of overseas medicines and have more experience in using foreign medicines. At the same time, Chinese

79   The Introduction of Foreign Things, Zhonghua Book Company, p. 285.
80   Xin Daosheng: Trade Relations between South India and China during the 13th and 14th centuries, Journal of East and West Maritime Relations, Volume 1, pp. 59-81, 1989.

drug scientists also found that some overseas medicines were produced in different countries and even in China, but their effects varied from the production. In this case, a book Overseas Material Herbs appeared. In Chinese ancient medicines, there were many herbs, so call the book Overseas Material

The writer of Overseas Herbal Materials was Li Xun. He was a native Persian descendant, but had been lived in Sichuan province in the Southern China. He had never assumed an official post in his life, and was born in a family which traded overseas incense drugs. He himself received good education in China as well as was able to recite or write various Chinese poems, in other words, he was almost educated like a Chinese native. Therefore, it was his family background that had made him a suitable person who could introduce overseas medicines to the Chinese people. Overseas Herbal material were incorporated into the National History: Classics Biography in the period of Wanli of the Ming Dynasty. However, the book was lost, consequently contemporary people cannot examine the original book. Fortunately, many parts of the book was quoted in Tang Zhenwei's book[81]—who lived in the Song Dynasty period., Classified Material Herds and Li Shizhen of the Ming Dynasty when he wrote The Compendium of Medical Herbal Materials, thus current scholars can have quite an idea by examining his book the Overseas Herbal Materials.

After the introduction of the overseas medicine into China, medical scientists and drug scientists, in accordance to the long-term clinical use, had a new understanding on their taste, efficacy of the treatment. In addition, they combined the domestic medicines with overseas medicines to form a new medicine, and then to find the efficacy and taboo of the new medicine. For example, Li Xun pointed out that the combination of fructus piper longi (a pepper kind) and ferula asafetida had a very good effect, but the combination of Shihuo and erula asafetida had a bad effect. In addition, he also said: pistachio barkcan combine with radix aucklandiae or fructus corni, and the combination of rhizoma

449

---

81 The book Overseas Herbal Materials. mainly included medicines and plants imported by the sea. Scholars conducted research and collected more than 100 kinds of medicines mentioned by Li Xun. Many of medicines were firstly appeared in this book, such as, jinqian ore (fibro ferrite ore) in the mineral, rhizoma corydalis, cubeb, Shiluo (cumin), curculigo orchioides gaertn, tanarius major, cortex erythrinae, circassian bean, Barbados aloe, gamboges, commiphora myrrha, geranium, Borneo, Korean pine seed from the plant, and animal-related giant clam and pearls. Some of these drugs are still commonly used in modern Chinese medicines. As one of the national higher medical college textbooks, Chinese Medicine published in 1984 introduced 493 kinds of traditional Chinese medicine that commonly used in most regions of China, 9 kinds of medicines of which were rhizoma corydalis, cubeb, Shiluo (cumin), curculigo orchioides gaertn, tanarius major, cortex erythrinae, Barbados aloe, commiphora myrrha were widely understood and used in the contemporary pharmacy l industry after being found in the Overseas Herbal Materials. Currently, the 9 kinds of medicines has become an important part of contemporary Chinese medicine science and their original names are not changed and used as official names. In addition, the characteristics of medicines recorded in the book written by Li Xun, including taste, efficacy, procession, usage are similar with that summed up in the contemporary Chinese medicine science.

corydalis, sanleng, turtle shell, rhubarb was a good medicine. Although previous medical works have mentioned many overseas medicines, they only mentioned the name of drugs rather than the effects. In the book, Overseas Herbal Materials, the efficacy of the medicines that were used in the process of treatment were recorded. Even though some previous books mentioned some efficacy of overseas medicines, the book also added their new efficacy that discovered by the Chinese medical scientists in the long-term practice. For example, Collective Notes to the Canon of Materia Medica said: agila wood was inappropriate to be included among the medicine materials. Supplement to Materia Medica also mentioned the only efficacy of the agila wood was used to remove the odor of the cloth. However, Overseas Herbal Materials recorded agila wood can be boiled with alcohol, which can be used in the treatment of heart pain, cholera and instantly fatal illnesses. In addition, it can be made into adhesive plaster to treat sores and swelling.

Overseas Herbal Materials laid the role of sea medicines in Chinese medicine industry and made valuable contributions on enriching the knowledge of Chinese medicine, so that Chinese medicine in the continuous learning of overseas scientific knowledge gained rapid development. Later, many important herbal experts such as Tang Shenwei, Li Shizhen in his books also quoted some related information from the Overseas Herbal Materials.

(2) Cotton

450

There was no cotton in ancient China, so the Chinese character "mian" (cotton) did not exist. Latter, with the introduction of cotton, the people used the another Chinese character "miao" (silk floss) to refer to cotton, and called cotton as "mu mian". In the Song Dynasty, the Chinese character that referred to cotton appeared. "Mian" (cotton) and "mian" (silk floss) had the same pronunciation, but their radicals were different. The radical of "mian" (cotton) was to refer to wood or plant while the radical of "mian" (silk floss) meant silk. Yuan Wen of the Southern Dynasty in his book Weng You Xian Tan (introduce the ancient things in all respects) mentioned, "now, a new Chinese character (word) was created to refer the cotton. "The textile in the ancient the Central Plains and Jiangnan region was mainly silk or remie. The people who were born in rich and noble family can wear the clothes made of silk, while civilian people wore the clothes made of ramie. This situation had not been changed until the late of the Tang Dynasty and the early of the Song Dynasty. After the emergence of cotton in the Song Dynasty, the structure of Chinese fiber fabric began to change.

Although China did not produce cotton in ancient times, people found that the material of foreign people's clothes different with them. The book, Yu Gong (an introduction to the Chinese geographical features) said: "the cloth of foreign merchants was made of hui and zhibei. The foreign merchant refers to the islanders of the Southeast Asian. "hui" means grass or plants such as cotton and "zhibei" later also known as "jibei", was the Sanskrit "karpasi", which was the transliteration of the word "cotton". However, some scholars still have doubts on the meaning of the "zhibei" and were uncertain whether it refers to cotton.[82] The cotton in the ancient Southeast Asia was from India, today it is commonly known as the "Asian Cotton" (Gossypium arboreum).

The cotton of the Southeast Asia was very early introduced to the Southeast and Southwest China through different channels. The ancestors living in the Zhuya region and Western Yunnan in the Han Dynasty period had already planted cotton and woven cloth. The cotton was clearly mentioned was in the book, "The Post-Han Dynasty Book, Southwestern Foreign Countries Biography", this book said that the people in the Western Yunnan have woven "miandie", the transliteration of for Sanskrit language "bhardvji". The cotton planting industry slowly expanded to the surrounding regions after the Han Dynasty and was introduced to the Sizhou province in the period of Western Jin Dynasty. In the Tang Dynasty period, the cotton-woven boutique produced in Guangxi was called "gui cloth" and Jiangnanregion hadal so produced cotton. Bai Juyi in his poem, The New Cloth, described: "gui cloth was white like snow and Wu silk floss was soft as cloud. The cloth made of the thick cloth and cotton kept people quite warm." The South-north route from India, through Southeast Asia, to China's Southeast coast and Southwest region was used to transport cotton in the history, which was called "South route."

In addition to the South route, cotton was also imported from the Northwestern China to the mainland. In 1959, in the Eastern Han Dynasty's tombs in the Minfeng County, Xinjiang, a group of textiles including cotton materials were unearthed, such as two pieces of blue and white calico cloth covered in the sheep bone, the bowl of the iron knife, the cloth trousers of the male owner and the handkerchief of the female owner.[83]

The book, Liang Dynasty Book· Northwestern Foreigners Biography recorded: "Gaochang country was rich in vegetation. The grass was like a cocoon, and the silk in the cocoon was fine, called white Diezi. So the people weaved it into cloth. The cloth was very soft and white, and can sell in the market."White Diezi was the transliteration of Sanskrit bhardvji, and it called "Miao Die", meaning the wild cotton in the book, The Post-Han Dynasty: Southwestern Foreign Countries Biography. The wild cotton was the Gossypium herbaceum. The cotton in the Tang Dynasty unearthed in the Bachu, Xinjiang, was identifies as Gossypium herbaceum.

The origin of the Gossypium herbaceum was in the Western Asia or Africa, it was introduced into the Northwestern China across Persia and India. The West-east routes that are used to transport cotton were known as "North Line" in the history. Compared with the Gossypium arboretum, the Gossypium herbaceum was smaller in size and lower in yield, but its maturity was earlier, suitable for

---

82   Chen Zugui, Cotton, Chinese Agricultural Heritage Anthology, Category A, the Fifth Variety, the First Half Volume, 1957, Zhonghua Book Company, p. 3.
83   Sa Biti: From the Archaeological Excavation Data to See the Ancient Xinjiang's Cotton Planting and Textile, The Journal of Cultural Relics, 1982/10.

growing in Xinjiang and Northwestern China. During the hundreds years from the late Tang Dynasty to the early Yuan Dynasty, China had been divided, so the spread of cotton was basically spontaneous. After the reunification of China in the Yuan Dynasty, the exchange of goods was cheaper and had a radically change. The government considered the issue of livelihood from a broader perspective and began to promote the cultivation of cotton in an organized manner. Wang Zhen, an agronomist of the Yuan Dynasty, in the Agriculture Book· Agricultural Device Atlas, wrote: "the people in China only know that the silk spun by silkworm can be used to make cloth, and don not know the usage of the cotton. The cotton firstly was only planted in Haina, later it was planted widely in the Southern China such as the region of Yangtze River, Uyghur River, Sichuan and the people here find it was profitable to plant cotton. It was not until the unification of China that merchants start to do business around the country and the cloth made of cotton had spread nation-wide." He also described many advantages of cotton as follows: "compared with sericulture, planting cotton was easier and more profitable". In addition, the cotton was no high requirement on the natural condition, so it could be planted in all regions of the China and whether the rich and the poor all need cotton. Therefore, the Yangtze River Valley and Jiannan region he came the home of producing cotton in the early of the Yuan Dynasty. Hu Bilie, the emperor of the Yuan Dynasty set up some offices to be in charge of things related with cotton in the East of Zhejiang, Jiangnan, Jiangxi, Hunan, Guangzhou and Fujian in 1289, as well as ordered people to hand 100 thousand Pi of silk cotton (Pi was a measurement unit).[84] A woman, called Huang Daopo in the Songjian River had an important role on promoting cotton's textile technology in the ethnic minorities in South China. At the same time, the cotton that originated in the Western Region was planted in Shanxi and it grew as luxuriant as the original cotton.[85]

The new fine cotton seeds were introduced into China in the Ming Dynasty period. At the end period of the Ming Dynasty, Xu Guangqi once introduced numerous types of cotton. Among them, four of them, i.e., "Huangdi", "Qinghe", "Heihe" and "Kuandyi" were extremely good. The ratio of lint yield to lint was 20:9, more than 45%, which was far more than any variety of the Gossypium arboretum and the Gossypium herbaceous. In the end of the Qing Dynasty, the cotton varieties mentioned above were still planted in Jiangnan. Huang Zongjian, a scholar of the Qing Dynasty, in the Experiment on Planting Cotton certificated the above facts as follows: "for the Heihe cotton, the ratio of lint yield to lint was 20:9." Xu Guangqi also saw "Banggeci" cotton. The core of cotton was superfine and its cotton was also soft, which was different from the varieties of the Chinese cotton". But no one knew whether this kind of cotton existed or not.[86]

84   The History of Yuan Dynasty· Emperor Shizu Biography.
85   Mengqi, Chang Shiwen and Miao Haoqian: Compilation of Essentials of Agriculture and Sericulture · Ramie and Silk Cotton).
86   Li Changnian: The Story of Agriculture, Ed. 1981, Shanghai Science and Technology Press, pp. 170-179.

(3) Incenses

There were no incense-burning customs in China, but the incenses that were produced in foreign countries were imported to China. Historical Records and Han Dynasty Book, mentioned among commodities from overseas, a commodity was called "Gubu", namely "Gubu Polv", which should be the transliteration of Kapar barus, it was a kind of incense that was abundant in Sumatra, Peninsular Malaysia, Borneo and other regions. It belonged to luxury consumer goods in those days, and could be burnt to reverse the unpleasant odor in the clothes. After the Han Dynasty, the habit of burning incense gradually spread from Southern China to Northern China. The incense was found in the relics unearthed from the Western Han Dynasty mausoleum of the Nanyue King in Xianggang Mountain, Guangzhou in 1983. According to the statistics, there were a total of more than 200 incensories in the relics of the Han tombs unearthed in Guangzhou. Among them, a piece of Siamese copper incensory container, 14.7 cm high was unearthed in 1983. Its cover and body were separately casted, and then the four parts and the square seat was fixed together. In 1955, another incensory container that was made of glazed pottery was found in Huaquaixin village of Guangzhou. It was 16.5 cm in height and 11 cm in abdomen diameter, which was made into raised hollow out geometry. Its top had a bird-shaped button and body resembled bean decorated with carved lines. In addition, its surface was decorated with black glaze. The photos and description of the cultural relics can be seen in the page 25 of the Silk Road Cultural Relic Atlas of the South China Sea.

453

The styles of incensory containers were different between the South and North of China. For example, the appearance of the bean-type incensory container in Nanyue was earlier than the incensory container that looked like Boshan mountain in Central Plains, which proves that the incensory from the overseas firstly arrived at Panyu, Guangzhou and was later introduced to Central Plains.

(1) Storax

The storax was the transliteration of Greek "sturaz", and its oil was called storax oil which was the extraction of the gum from a kind of maple branches, called Gao Ada. The Chinese knew this incense long ago. The Liang Dynasty Book: Central Tianzhu Biography mentioned "China do business with these countries that lied West to China, such as Daqin and Anxi", so there were many treasures including storax from Daqin in China. It also mentioned, "the storax was made by boiling its juice and it needed to be processed. Before the incenses was sold to the other countries, the people of the Daqin had extracted its juice to make ointment, in other words, the incense that they sold belonged to dreg, so it not too fragrant". In the Tang Dynasty, storax was introduced into China by sea and land, so Tang Materia Medica said: "it was from Western Regions and Kunlun, which resembles purple sandalwood to smell extremely fragrant. In addition, it was heavy like stone, and if its ash was gray, it was the top grade incense."The storax could be served as liniment."The people of Fanyu often smear it on their bodies, later, the people in Fjian suffered from leprosy due to the influence of the damp weather, so they also smear storax on their body.[87]

(2) Myrrh

Myrrh was the transliteration of Arabic "murr", which was kind of incense with strong odor and which could be used for treating trauma and activating blood. It was early mentioned in the book, Nan Zhou Ji, written by Xu Biao in 5th century, but the book was lost, so some ancient naturalist and scholars did not know the origin of myrrh. Duan Chengshi of the Tang Dynasty once mentioned, "myrrh was born in Persia, called "ashan". The myrrh tree was tall, up to 1 Zhang height (Zhang was a unit of length), and its bark was bluish white and its leaves was as long as the leaves of the Japanese pagoda tree. As well as its flower was as big as orange's. In addition, its seed was black and as big as cornel, and taste sour and sweet." The so-called "Ashan" should be Aramaic "ass" (this Arabic "as"), referring to Myrtus communis, but Duan Chengshi mistook it for myrrh.[88]

The purpose of China's myrrh import was to make medicine, so many medical related books have mentioned the myrrh. In the book Kai Bao Ben Zao (a medical book), it recorded myrrh produced in Persia, and its size was various and its color was black, looking like benzoin. Another medical book, called Tu Jing Ben Zao, said that: myrrh was transported into China by sea, so it was easy to find it in Hainan and Guangzhou. Its root was as dense as olive. The sap of old tree was rich and could drop in the ground and could condense into different shapes of block. It resembled the benzoin and could be collected at any time. In the book, The Introduction of Foreign Countries, it said that the "myrrh produces in Maluobo state of Dashi country, referring to Mirbat, about 10 km apart from the Salalah, the capital of Dhofar province, Oman. It was as tall as China's pine and bark was thick, up to one or two Cun (Cun was a unit of length). The way to collect it was: "firstly dig tree, and then cut its bark with the axe and make its sap flow into tree pit, finally take the rap in about 10 days."[89]

(3) Styrax benzoin

Anxi incense referred to as styrax benzoin. "Anxi" was the transliteration of the name of the Persian Dynasty "Arsak", which was built by the Parthian nationality, a close relative of the Eastern Persian. The incense was solidified from the resin flowing from the wound of its tree. China originally bought this incense from Persian merchants. Tang Materia Medica said: it came from Xirong, called "the Anxi (Arsacid-Parthian) country", so the incense was named as the Anxi incense. Later, China imported it from the Southeastern Asia, so the book Overseas Herbal Materials said it was produced in the Persian states,

454

---

87 Annotation of the Introduction of the Foreign Things, pp. 98-99.
88 See The book Nan Zhou Ji, p. 95. (Records of Extraordinary Things from the Southern Rivers).
89 See the book "The Introduction of Foreign Countries", p. 95.

while The Introduction of Foreign Countries said it was produced in the Sanfuji country. In short, styrax benzoin was an imported product from overseas in Chinese history.

Duan Chengshi from the Tang Dynasty specifically described this incense and mentioned: "its tree was out of Persia, where it was regarded as talisman. The tree was 3 Zhang long, and its bark was yellow and dark, as well as its leaves with quadrangle cannot fade all the year around. It blooms in February. Its flower was yellow, but flower core was green and not strong. If its bark was cut, it will be find its gum was very sweet. In fact, the gum was styrax benzoin. The gum can be solidified and taken in June or July. The people think that firing the tree can drive the evil."[90] From the plant morphology, the styrax benzoin tree was deciduous tree and leaf with ovate or elliptic alternates, on the one side of which was no hair, but the other side white stellate hairs as well as the vein of which was rust-colored. It bloomed in summer and the flower with red smells fragrant and was terminal or auxiliary cyme. The shape of the resin was like turpentine that was yellow-black, blocky and translucent. Although the resin was without fragrance and unsuitable for burning, many resins that put together could give off a nice smell. Therefore, Zhao Rushi said: "the people put many resin together to gain their fragrance. The resin, namely styrax benzoin, was a common medicine in the traditional Chinese medicine and was used for the resuscitation of blood as well as treating hearth strokes, faint and postpartum anemic faint.

455

(4) Frankincense

Frankincense oil Ruxiang incense (frankincense) in China was called Luban in Arabic, which is the resin secreted by the trees of the genus Boswellia in the family Burseraceae, particularly Boswellia sacra. Frankincense that was imported by China, was combined with other incenses to make new incense that was used for burning, and it was in great demand. It was also known as "Xunluxiang incense", which was the transliteration of the Arabic "Kundur", or the Sanskrit "kunduru". When it was burnt, it gave off sweet fragrance. The frankincense was mainly from the Maluoba, Shihe and Nufa. Marober, where was regarded as a traditional product. Malubo means Mirbat, a province of Oman in the southern end of the Arab peninsula. Shihe was Shehr, which was near to the Maluobo. Nufa refers to the current Zufar province of Oman.

Besides the Dashi territories, the other countries including India and Persia were also the home of the frankincense. Tang Materia Medica said: "the incense resembles white gum in shape. The incense from Tianzhu and Chanyu was white and green respectively. "Journey from Great Tang to Western Regions mentioned the leaves of the incense that came from Azhengli of Indian were like pear.[91]

---

90   Youyang Zazu, Vol. 18 (The Miscellaneous Morsels from Youyang is a miscellany of Chinese and foreign legends and ... Miscellaneous Morsels from Youyang).
91   Ji Xianlin: The Annotation of Journey from Great Tang to Western Regions, Ed. 1985, Zhonghua Book Company, p. 907.

Overseas Herbal Materials by Guang Zhi (a book that introduces the material in Southern China) said: "the incense was the resin of pine in Persia, which was as violet red as cherry and if it was transparent, it could be concluded that it was high quality."[92]

The frankincense was divided into different grades according to the quality. The top grade was called "Jianxiang incense", which was as round and big as finger, and its common name was "drip milk". The second grade was called "bottle milk", and its color was not as good as that of the top grade. The third grade referred to the "bottle incense", which was still a good quality among all kinds of frank incense. The reason that was called "bottle incense" was that it was stored in the bottle. In addition, the "bottle incense" can also be divided into three grades; upper grade, middle grade and lower grade. The incense that was inferior to the "bottle incense" in quality was called "bag incense" because it was stored in the bag. Like "bottle incense", the "bag incense" also consisted of upper grade, middle grade and lower grade. Among them, a kind of incense that was inferior to the "bag incense" was called "black couch" due to its color was darker. The incense was under the "black couch" in quality was called "water wet", which was the damp "black couch" in transit. There was a kind of incense behind "water wet" in quality, called "hack cut", which was mixed with sand and gravel. The lowest grades were the powder of the frankincense with worst quality, known as "lowest incense".[93]

According to the record of Zhao Rushi, he gave a detail description on the production and transportation of the frankincense "the frankincense trees were like Banyan tree. The aborigines with axe cut the bark, which makes the resin outflow, and then form knots. After collecting these knots, the local people ship them to the seaside with the elephant, and then the merchants from Dashi country transported them to Sanfuqi (Srivijaya) in a bid to exchange their distribution of goods. Finally, the frankincense was shipped to the Chinese port by Southeast Asian merchants.

Frankincense oil was bulk commodity among the imported incenses, which was mainly transported to China by sea. Only in the 10th year of the Xining in Northern Song Dynasty (1077), the Shi Bo Shi[94] of three major ports in the Southern China bought more than 175,000 kilograms of frankincense, Guangzhou accounting for more than 90%.[95] Although the port in Quanzhou started to rise at the beginning of the Southern Song Dynasty, the trade and custom volume of frankincense oil here had reached nearly 70,000 kilograms in the 4th year of Jianyan (1130).[96]

---

92 Feng Chengjun: The Annotation of The Introduction of Foreign Countries, Note 1, p. 94
93 Ibid., pp. 93-94.
94 Shi Bo Si's Oceangoing and Marketing Department, was set up in each port to administrate foreign economy-related affairs by sea during the dynasties of Tang, Song and Yuan, and the early part of the Ming Dynasty.
95 Liang Tingnan: Guangdong Customs Records, Facts from Former Generations, Vol. 3.
96 The History of the Song Dynasty, Commodity Exchange Records - The Incense.

The merchants also directly transported frankincense oil from their country to China, which did not cross the Southeastern Asia. In the 6th year of Shaoxing (1136), the Shi Bosi in Fujian handed out a report to the court officers of the Song Dynast, this report said that: Pu Luoxin, a merchant from the Dashi country, traded frankincense oil to Quanzhou, and Shi Bosi gained benefit of 300,000 Guang (Guang was a unit of currency in ancient China). Therefore, the emperor conferred on him an official position, and urged him to encourage more merchants from Dashi country to trade frankincense to China.[97] It can be seen that the demand for frankincense oil in the Chinese market was huge. A large amount of incense barrels, including frankincense oil, were also found in a ships' cabins, which was unearthed at the Quanzhou of the Southeastern suburb of Fujian, this ship was used at the end of the Song Dynasty.

The earliest records of the Chinese doctors using frankincense oil were found in the book, Famous Doctors' Records, written by Tao Hongjing of the Southern Liang Dynasty. Chinese Traditional Medicine (CTM) said: "frankincense oil was available for the treatment of the wind edema, eczema and Itchy rash". Chen Cangqi, a man in the Tang Dynasty wrote a book, Materia Medica Supplements. The book recorded, frankincense cure deafness, apoplexy, mute, women "blood gas, diarrhea, all kinds of sores, subsiding swelling and cold". In the Song Dynasty, the efficacy of frankincense was further understood by the doctors. Li Shizhen in the Ming Dynasty quoted the content of Rihua Materia Medica and said: "frankincense oil has been efficient for curing cholera, and abdominal pain. It can be made into ointment to relieve pain and promote tissue regeneration". This means that frankincense in the treatment of surgical diseases was of the efficacy of relieving pain and promoting tissue regeneration. After liberation, most of the imported drugs were incorporated into the Pharmacopoeia of the People's Republic of China that were promulgated in 1963 and 1977, and clinical research and pharmacological analyses have been carried out. According to the information, frankincense oil can increase white cells in the blood system, and relieve the pains in the nervous system. In addition, it also has the role of anti-vaginal trichomonas.[98]

---

97 Song Hui Yao Ji Gao (Draft collection of fragments of Collected documents of the Song dynasty) Exchanges with Foreign Countries.
98 Wang Huifang: The Effect of Imported Drugs in the Song Dynasty Sea Ships Unearthed in Quanzhou Bays and the book on the History of Chinese Medicine, The Journal of Maritime Exchange Researches, 1982/4.

Chapter 4. The Era of Marco Polo

1. The Overseas Expansion of the Yuan dynasty

(1) Expansion to the East

During the Northern Song Dynasty, Fujiwara ruled Japan and implemented the closed-door policy. Therefore, the Japanese private traders were strictly prohibited to sail. On the contrary, Chinese navigation to Japan was very active under the encouragement of the Northern Song Dynasty. From 978 (the 3rd year of Taipingxingguo Period under the reign of Emperor Taizong of Song) to 1116 (the 6th year of the reign of Emperor Zhenghe under the reign of Emperor Huizong of Song), there were more than 70 documented cases of sea navigation to Japan in the Song Dynasty period, many of which were directly related with China-Japan trade. Besides, countless cases that occurred were not recorded. At that time, most ships of the Song dynasty which sailed between China and Japan could carry only sixty or seventy people. As in the Tang and the Five Dynasties, ships of Song dynasty mostly departed from the Chinese ports at Zhejiang province of the South of the Yangtze River, mainly Mingzhou (current Ningbo city). After crossing the East China Sea, they would firstly reach Hizen, then sail to the Hakata Bay (current Fukuoka of North Kyushu) of Chikuzen. At the end period of the Northern Song Dynasty, some ships of Song passed by the Hakata bay, went deep into the Japan Sea, and directly arrived at Tung region near the capital. Ships of Song dynasty when sailing to Japan generally made use of the Northeast monsoon and chose the summer or early autumn for sailing, they carefully avoided being hit by typhoons which occurred in the late autumn or in winter. When the sailing was smooth, the journey to Japan would take about a week.

When merchants of Song arrived on Hakata, the Japanese authorities generally sent a supervisor and interpreter to check the official documents, the personnel and cargo list. When the Japanese court allowed to trade, then the merchants would be placed in Honglu inn. First, the official trade was allowed, then private trade followed it. The goods exported by China were mainly brocade, ghatpot, the spices and perfumes, porcelain, bamboo and wood, stationery, etc. Then they brought things back from Japan such as the sand gold, mercury, pearls, sulphur, brocade, tough silk, cloth and sword, folding hand fan, screen and so on. Ouyang Xiu of the Northern Song Dynasty had a poem Song of Japanese Sword which says "A treasure sword comes from Japan, the merchant gets it at the East of the sea".[1]

Chinese people of the Song dynasty period loved the Japanese swords. Merchants who travelled between China and Japan sometimes carried the letters of Chinese and Japanese officials. In 1072 (the 5th year of Xining Period of the Northern Song Dynasty), Japanese monk Cheng Xun, together with his disciples Lai Yuan and others, took the merchant Sun Zhong's ship to pray for the Buddha in China. Later they were summoned by Emperor Shenzong of Song Dynasty. In 1073 (the 6th year of Xining period), they went back to Japan by Sun Zhong's ship and carried an imperial letter, Lotus Sutra, and brocade. Sun Zhong was also received by the Japanese court. In 1078 (the 1st year of the Yuanfeng period), an interpreter, monk Zhong, sent by Japan, took a keepsake to Mingzhou also by Sun Zhong's ship. In addition, local officials of Mingzhou asked the merchants to send official documents inscribed with the seal of the Song dyansty, and Dazaifu took charge of replying those letters.

After Song moved its capital to the South, economy of the South developed rapidly while Japan has experienced Hogen Rebellion (1156) and Heiji Rebellion (1159). Then Tairano Kiyomori established the warrior regime in the noble, abandoned the policy of seclusion, and encouraged the official and private trade with China. In Fukuhara of Settsu (currently near Kobe of Japan), Tairano Kiyomori built a pavilion to attract the people of Song, and built the port of Hyogo, which allowed the ships of Song dynasty to enter the inland sea of Seto and visit a port near Kyoto. Therefore, Maritime interrelations between China and Japan had resurged. The number of ships of Japan bound for China increased greatly. "Japanese people run the risk of whales and waves to take goods for sale by ships after ships." Trade ports related with Japan in the Southern Song Dynasty period had still focused on Mingzhou and there were also other ports like Huating of Xiuzhou (current Songjiang county of Shanghai), Hangzhou, Wenzhou, Jiangyin, Quanzhou, etc. Japan's trade port to Song was controlled by Hakata, and the Hirado Island of Hizen has become a common intermediate port. In the Southern Song Dynasty period, Chinese copper coins began to flow into Japan. After the first emperor of the Yuan Dynasty, Kublai Khan had ascended to the throne in 1260, he ordered Heidi and others to attack Japan from Korea in 1266 (the 3rd year of Yuan). They were forced

---

1   Wenzhong Ouyang's Collection, Vol. 15.

to come back in fear of the gale when they arrived at the Geoje Island. Kublai was eager to see Japan's surrender and sent Heidi to Japan again in the next year. Korean government was ordered to help Heidi. Consequently, a Korean envoy and Heidi visited Japan with the royal letter written in Mongol scripts and this envoy remained in Dazaifu for five months. The Kamakura shogun, which ruled Japan, and the imperial court sent the envoy back without any reply. In 1268 (the 5th year of Yuan), Kublai sent Heidi and others to Japan for the third time. They were refused in the Tsushima Island and captured two Japanese men and took them to China. Kublai said to the two Japanese: "I did not force your people to come to China, I just want my name to be carved in the history". It fully showed that Kublai was ambitious to be known in theoverseas countries and gain admiration for the thoughts of the emperors who were ruling the flourishing Han and Tang Dynasties. Kublai asked them to visit Yanjing, and ordered them to carry the loyal letter written by the Central Secretariat to Japan. At the end of the 7th year of Yuan, Zhao Liangbi was sent to Japan. He was not allowed to enter the capital of Japan and retained in the city of Dazaifu. In 9th year (1272), Liangbi was sent back by 12 Japanese men and he asked these Japanese people to pretend to be the Japanese envoys. Zhao Liangbi went to Japan and retained in the Dazaifu again in the same year. He did not arrive in Kyoto and returned back in the following year.

In seven years, Kublai sent envoys to Japan for five times, but the shogun of Kamakura refused to reply. Therefore, Kublai had planned to attack Japan. In 1270 (the 7th year of Yuan), garrison troops were set in Korea, "Storage provisions and money for troops to attack Japan, was also provided".[2] In 1274 (the 11th year of Yuan), he ordered Korea (Koryö) to build ships and recruit troops. He also set up a military command of the east with Xin Du as the commander and Hong Chaqiu as the vice-commander. In October the same year, Xin Du recruited 25,000 troops from Mongols, Hans, and Koreans to occupy Tsushima, Iki, and landed on Hizen and Hakata (near Fukuoka). Chinese Yuan forces won the first battle but failed to go further. Soon after a typhoon, the Yuan ships were destroyed, and the first invasion attempt had thus failed. The battle took place in the 11th year of Bun'ei period under the reign of the Japanese Emperor Akihito, which is known in Japanese history as the "Battle of Bun'ei".

After the first war to the east failed, government of Yuan dynasty sent Du Shizhong, the Ministry of Rites, to persuade Japan for surrender in 1275 (the 12th year). At the same time, he ordered Korea again to build new ships and weapons for the next war. After the destruction of the Song Dynasty, a large number of Song troops had surrendered to Yuan Dynasty, known as the new-added troops. Kublai ordered the former general of the Song troops Fan Wenhu to prepare for and lead the war against Japan. General Fan Wenhu also sent envoys to Japan, led by Du Shizhong, however, as soon as Du Shizhong arrived in Japan, he and his attendants were executed by the Japanese shoguns. Kublai reinforced his plan administratively by establishing a new governmental organ,

---

2   History of Yuan: The Army.

the Ministry for Conquering Japan. The official order to attack came in the summer of 1281.

Therefore, general Fan Wenhu, decided to attack Japan once again. In the summer of the 18th year of Yuan, Yuan army, divided into two arms, began to cross the sea from Korea and South of the Yangtze River. In May, the Korean troops led by Xin Du and Hong Chaqiu attacked Tsushima, Iki, and Hizen with 40.000 troops and 900 ships. The Japan forces resisted bravely, so Korean forces had to retreat to Shiga Island in failure. As the second arm, 10.000 troops and 3500 ships led by Ala Khan, Fan Wenhu and Li Ting started the attack from Qingyuan (current Ningbo of Zhejiang) to Hirado Island in June. After the confluence of the two armies, there was a divided opinion among the generals, so they stayed in the Eagle Island and Hirado Island for a month. On August 11st, many ships were destroyed by hard typhoons and huge Ocean waves and many soldiers drowned in the sea. The generals Xin Du and Fan Wenhu left their army and took the safest ship back to China. The remaining soldiers were heavily destroyed by the Japanese forces. Only one fifth of the 140,000 troops had survived. The second war with Japan was also a defeat, which took place in the 4th year of Hong'an period under the reign of the Japanese emperor, Hirohito, which is known in Japanese history as the "the battle of Hong'an". After two failed attempts of conquering Japan, in 5 years between 1283-1288, Kublai established the Eastward Crusade Headquarters for three times, ordered to build new ships, recruited massive military forces and made plans for another attack. But the attack was not made. Further plans for an advance against Japan were complicated as the Yuan dynasty became increasingly embroiled in domestic rebellions. Kublai's death in 1294 ended further expeditionary attempts. Nevertheless, Japan did not abandon its defense measures until the end of the Kamakura era.

(2) Expansion to the South by the Yuan Dynasty

Champa kingdom was in the South of Annan. It only took one day from Qiongzhou of Hainan to the Champa kingdom by ship. For long, Kublai Khan had felt ambitious to control and subdue the Champa kingdom. A general of Yuan Dyansty Ma Chengeang boasted: I only need 3000 troops and 300 to conquer Champa. After the Song dynasty had collapsed, Pu Shougeng, from the Pu family, who was specialized in maritime trade in the port city of Quanzhou acted loyally to the Yuan Dynasty. Kublai ordered Pu Shougeng to be in charge of leading relations with Champa and Java kingdoms. In 1278 (the 15th year of Yuan), Sogetu, a general of Yuan sent an envoy to Champa to tell the news of the destruction of Song dynasty. The envoy returned with a letter from the king of the Champa, [Shrijaya Simha Varmaha (ri) Deva] that Champa would like to be subordinated to Yuan dynasty. The Yuan dynasty soon awarded him as "Rongludaifu" (an official rank) and the king of the Champa county. In 1279 (the 16th year of Yuan), Kublai dispatched the Ministry of War Jiaohuadi and Sogetu to Champa, and asked the king of the Champa (Malay) to visit the Yuan court. The next year, the king of Champa sent tributary gifts to Yuan dynasty to show his allegiance.

Kublai was not content to mutual visits and trade, instead he aimed to expand the Yuan territories forcefully and plunder more wealth. In the 19th year of Yuan, he sent Sogetu to Champa and set up the Yuan province of Champa. Then, Liu Shen and Ike Mese were ordered to lead an army with 10.000 men and a hundred ships to prepare for the expedition to overseas in the 19th year of Yuan. Kublai had thought Champa as the springboard for expansion in the South-east Asia regions and ordered the city to supply the army. Nobles of Champa were discontent with Kublai's overseas expansion policy. Champa's prince Bu Di detained He Zizhi and YouYongxian and other envoys of Yuan to Siam and Malabar. All these events became excuses for the Yuan to start a war.

At the end of the 19th year of Yuan, Kublai sent Sogetu to take the army to depart from Guangzhou, through the South China Sea and to the port of Champa (current the Binh Dinh Province of Vietnam) and stationed along the coast. Champa people had built a wooden town with more than one hundred cannons in the West of the port in order to prepare to fight against the Yuan army. The Champa army also built a palace in the 5km West of the city for the backup troops. The Yuan army had sent several envoys one after the other to ask for surrender, however, Champa rejected and chose to fight to the death for independence. At the beginning of the 20th year of Yuan, Yuan court deployed several navy ships to attack the wooden town, but due to the unexpected bad sea conditions many ships were seriously damaged. At the time, Champa opened the gate and sent 10.000 troops to attack the Yuan forces. The Yuan forces fought bravely and captured the wooden town. As a retaliation, the king of Champa killed the prisoned envoys, You Yongxian, and others, and then retreated to the deep forests with the rest of his army. After the defeat in this battle, the king of Champa did not give in. Since the Yuan army occupied the kingdom, the king sent an envoy to show his will to surrender so as to avoid being wiped out. The Yuan army demanded that the king himself should surrender, but the king only sent his uncle to the Yuan garrison, and said that he was wounded in the battle. In order to verify the injury of the king, Sogetu sent his envoys to visit the king's camp, and was not allowed to enter. The Champa king also killed He Zizhi.

The King's uncle claimed that he was coveted to the throne to have Sogetu's trust. Thus the King of Champa could gather troops in the mountains and waited for help that could possibly come from his allies. In order to keep the secret, the king planned to kill all Chinese in the region, but some Chinese fled to the Yuan camp to report the truth. Sogetu did not believe in the tipster, and fell into the trap of the King. Sogetu sent a group of troops with the king's uncle to capture the king, but the king's uncle escaped to the Champa army camp on the way. In the meantime, Yuan army learned that the king had gathered over 20,000 people, and had borrowed troops from Cochin, Zhenla, Java and Panduranga. Under these severe conditions, Sogetu still decided to take the risk and attack the Champa forces. Although Sogetu won smaller battles, Champa army constantly and effectively attacked the Yuan army from the forests, although the

Yuan army had fought bravely, it had to retreat to its garrison. Next year, this time Sogetu was ordered to attack Annam from the North of Champa, thus the battle of Champa was ended. In the end, Sogetu was killed in the battles of Annam (current central Vietnam).

(3) Yuan Expansion to the Southeast

Kublai said: "among all the wars we fought overseas, the war with Java was the greatest one".[3] Wang Dayuan narrated: "In Java kingdom, there is a magnificent palace, vast land but a small population, and is more beautiful than any country in the East......It also has flat and fertile lands which is convenient for grain planting and much beautiful and rich when compared with other countries."[4] At that time, Java was quite strong kingdom when compared to other South Asia countries. Kublai thought that as long as he could conquer Java, other weaker countries would all surrender. Consequently, Kublai sent envoys to overseas countries to tell the news of the destruction of the Southern Song Dynasty. In 1279 (the 16th year of the Yuan), Sogetu sent Zhao Yu to Java. Next year the Yuan Dynasty sent envoys to Java again. In the same year, Haji Krtangara, the King of the Tumapel of Java, had sent envoys to express his friendly attitude. In 1281 (the 18th year of the Yuan), Kublai Khan asked the King himself to come to the court. Then he sent Meng Qingyuan and Sun Shengfu to Java next year and sent Bila Man in 1286. Although Haji Krtangara sent envoys to the Yuan dynasty again in 1286, Kublai decided to start a war because the king did not visit the Chinese empire court when Kublai had called him. In the 29th year of the Zhiyuan reign, (1292), the King of Java, Haji Krtangara, decided to send back the Yuan envoys Meng Qi and Qing Mian which become the reason for Kublai to start the war. Before departing, Kublai addressed the army: "You will go to Java and tell the people that we were friendly with Java before the King sent our envoys back. So we will start this war".[5] In fact, it was only the direct reason. Two years ago, in the winter of 1289 (the 26th year of Yuan), Shi Bi entered the court "when Kublai Khan wanted to put levies to the Java Kingdom. Kublai Khan said to Bi: "I don't trust other ministers, and I want you to lead the army to Java". He answered, "Your majesty, I will do whatever you want me to do."[6]

Kublai Khan was planning a war against Java for a long time. At the beginning of 1293 (December of the 29th year of the Zhiyuan reign), generals of Yuan, Shi Bi, Ike Mese, and Gao Xing led 5,000 naval troops which set sail from Quanzhou, through the Qizhou Ocean (currently the north waters of the South China Sea), Wanli Shitang (current Paracel Islands), Cochin and Champa. During the next January, they reached to Dong Dong Mountain and Xi Dong Mountain (current Natuna Islands of Indonesia), then to the ocean of

3   History of Yuan : History of Java
4   Wang Dayuan, A Brief History of Foreign Islands, revised ed. 1981, published by the Chinese Book Compilation and Revision Bureau, p. 159.
5   History of Yuan Dynasty: Java History.
6   History of Yuan Dynasty: The Leader Shibi.

Hundun (currently South waters of the South China Sea), the Olive Island (currently an island in the west Kalimantan), Kalimantan, Goulan Mountain (currently near the southwest Kalimantan) and then to approach to Java. Since the waters of the Java Sea were shallow, it was easy for the ships to land, therefore the Yuan army built and used small boats to land Java successfully.

While preparing for the conquest of Java, Ike Mese led a squad with 10 ships to ask Java to surrender. knee. In February, the Yuan forces arrived at Karimon (currently Bawean in the north of Java), then sailed to the port of Tuban. Here, the Yuan troops were divided into two arms: one was led by Ike Mese and Gao Xing to the land and another led by Shi Bi sailed to the port of Janggala (current Surabaya, the capital of East Java) then to the South of Surabaya where the two troops had agreed to meet. At that time, Java was in civil war. Haji Krtangara was attacked by Haji Ghaldeh of Galuh Kingdom in Kediri and Haji Krtangara had fled to the Majapahit Empire.

Yuan navy reached to Majapahit and built a floating bridge to march forward. Yuan army was far more powerful than the Tuhanbizheye's force stationed at Majapahit. Once Tuhanbizheye heard Yuan's army landed, he sent an envoy to offer their mountains and rivers, registered permanent residence and the map of Galuh, and demonstrated his will to surrender. According to Wang Daoyuan, Yuan's conditions of surrender were: to pay tributse, set the government, make the law, send soldiers, and sign the contract.[7] It seems that they accepted these conditions. On March 1st, after the two troops met, the the army led by Shibi, defeated the army of Galuh. At that time, the main force of the Galuh was fighting against the Tuhanbizheye's army. On March 8th,the Yuan army decided to help the Tuhanbizheye's forces army and, on March 15th, armies of Yuan and Tuhanbizheye jointly attacked the Hada city of the Galuh kingdom and defeated the enemy which led 10,000 troops. Haji Ghaldeh was forced to surrender.

465

Later, Yuan army decided to take Tuhanbizheye back to the Imperial palace in April, 1293. But, Tuhanbizheye was a very tactful Javanese noble who had allied with the Yuan forces when he was weak. During the days when he jointly fought with Yuan army, he had learned the fact that only thousands of men had crossed the sea. He thought that, as long as he could recruit enough fighters, he could be able to defeat the Yuan army. He presented an official declaration of surrender and requested to sail back home with the excuse of taking some treasure. Since Gao Xing and Ike Mese totally believed in Tuhanbizheye's deeds of surrender, they ordered 200 troops led by Wan Hoo and Gan Zhou to escort Tuhanbizheye in his journey back home. On the way, Tuhanbizheye escaped, and killed Wan Hoo, gathered enough troops and attacked against the Yuan troops. Shi Bi's army in Java fought bravely but had to retreat for 150 km. to reach the Yuan ships. Thus, the military expedition to Java had failed with a casualty of more than 3,000 troops. After returning to the Imperial court, Shi

---

7   A Brief History of Foreign Islands, p. 159.

Bi and Ike Mese were punished for the defeat. As in the case of Japan, Kublai Khan was determined to realize his Java conquest dream. He attempted to recruit about 100,000 troops to attack and conquer Java again, but failed to send a single soldier.

2. The Unprecedented Development of Communications with China and Foreign Countries

The Yuan Dynasty had established an empire with an unprecedented scale, its territories extended from the Pacific Ocean to the East, the Mediterranean Sea to the West, the Arctic Ocean to the North, and India and Southeast Asia to the South. The territories of the Yuan Dynasty was not only far larger than the Han and Tang Dynasties, but also greater than any empire in human history before the geographical discoveries of the 15th century. In such a vast land, there lived numerous nationalities, some of whom had no direct communication in the past, due to distance barriers. The Mongolian conquest made them suddenly feel that the boundaries of the long-term confinement were almost broken overnight, and various peoples with different racial origins ethics were enslaved and subordinated to the Mongolian aristocracy. It seemed like that the particular historical conditions had shortened the geographic distances. Consequently, the prosperity of overseas trade during the Yuan Dynasty period was far greater that in the Han and Tang periods.. When observing Zheng He's maritime voyages in the early Ming Dynasty, all the world powers were envious of the Chinese maritime and navigation technology. Zheng He's voyages can be seen as the prelude to the prosperous maritime and trade exchanges that were realized in the Yuan Dynasty period. Researchers and people from different quarters hold e different views on the evaluation of the Yuan (Mongolian) dynasty era, but they generally agree that this era has been the unprecedentedly prosperous in regard to communications and exchanges between the East and the West.

(1) Historical Records in Regard to Overseas Countries and Regions

(1) Dade Nan Hai Zhi

Dade Nan Hai Zhi (literally translated as Records of the South China Sea during the Period of Dade), also known as Nan Hai Zhi can be literally translated as the Treatise on the South China Sea—was authored by Chen Dazhen in 1304 (the 8th year of Dade reign in the period Yuan Dynasty).[8]

It was no more than 70 years since Zhu Fan Zhi (also translated as Records of Foreign People) was published in 1225 and half a century since Dao Yi Zhi Lue (also translated as "A Brief Account of Island Barbarians") the writing of which was finished in 1349 and it was better than the above 2 books to some extent. Nan Hai Zhi describes the foreign trade situation in Guangzhou during the Yuan Dynasty period. Guangzhou city was one of the gates of south China,

---

8   The fragment of Da De Nan Hai Zhi is kept in Beijing Library.

and together with Quanzhou, are the most important foreign trade ports and collecting and distributing centers in the middle ages of China. Nan Hai Zhi includes valuable records about the trade goods and foreign countries which traded with Guangzhou and has reflected the realistic situation of trade between South China and the Asian and Africa countries in the early period of the Yuan Dynasty.

The original version of Nan Hai Zhi consisted of 20 volumes but most of them are non-existent except for the Volume 6 to Volume 10 which are preserved in the Beijing Library. Among which, the Volume 7 "The Products" gives lists of many goods and countries which are generally well known. But there are also large amount of specific regions which are very helpful for the current researches. Besides, Yongle Encyclopedia which can be classified as one of the Ming Dynasty period records includes valuable information about 147 countries or regions. Through the remaining part of the book, we can see that the overseas trade in the Yuan Dynasty period has made great improvements when compared with the Song Dynasty period. During the Yuan Dynasty period, the Guangzhou foreign trade department has classified the overseas countries into several regions as follows:

1) From the west coasts of the South China Sea to Siam bay, which includes the Hizen, Champa, Zhenla, and Siam. 2) Xiao Dong Yang (literally the Small East Ocean), which refers to the Philippine islands and the Northern part of Kalimantan, which was led by the kingdom of Po-ni (current Brunei). 3) Da Dong Yang (literally the Great East Ocean), which was divided into the two parts. The Eastern part refers to the islands of the Philippines and the Southeast sea of Kalimantan, especially the kingdom of Chan Zhong Bu Luo and the Western part includes Java and Lesser Sunda Islands 4) Xiao Xi Yang (literally the Small West Ocean), which refers to the top of Malay Peninsula and the Sumatra Island; 5) The Western countries, which includes India, Sri Lanka, the Arabian Sea, the Persian Gulf, the Red Sea, and the Mediterranean Sea. The classification principle was as follows: the first 4 parts were the regions which were geographically located on the route of sailing, and the fifth was far too wide. During the early Yuan Dynasty period, Guangzhou's trading business included vast regions from Malilu (current Philippines) in the east to Jabulsa (namely the furthermost region in the west which was then controlled by the Arab empire, which includes the Maghreb, current Morocco), which also included some regions in Spain, Southeast Asia, South Asia, East Africa, North Africa and part of Europe such as Italy and Byzantine Empire.

There were no important descriptions about the communications in the books of Ling Wai Dai Da and Zhu Fan Zhi which were also written in period of Song Dynasty, while the book Nan Hai Zhi has summarized early Yuan Dynasty's communication with other countries in Guangzhou, which is more credible than the two above mentioned books written during the Song Dynasty period. Nan Hai Zhi is an important historical treasure for the study of the history of maritime Silk Road, which provides convincing historical records about the

Song Dynasty period and valuable on Zheng He's expeditions during the Ming Dynasty period. It gives an overview of the cultural communication between the East and the West during the Song Dynasty and Yuan Dynasty periods.

(2) Dao Yi Zhi Lue

The "Dao Yi Zhi Lue", which can be translated as A Brief Account of Island Barbarians, is a book written by Wang Dayuan—who was a Yuan Dynasty period Chinese traveler. Wang Dayuan, wrote his travel accounts when he visited different countries and regions. It was attached in the book Qing Yuan Xu Zhi compiled by Wu Jian in 1349 (the 9th year of Zhi Zheng). In 1350, Wang Dayuan republished the book named as Dao Yi Zhi in his hometown Nanchang, Jiangxi province. He invited the well-known scholar Zhang Zhu to write the preface for the publication. Wang Dayuan, a native of Nanchang, was born in 1311. When he was 20 years old, he first went to sea from Quanzhou in 1330 and sailed along the Western route to the Indian Ocean. He said that he was in the Dafoshan (current Sri Lanka) in 1330 and went West to the Arabian Sea. The voyage took about five years. After returning home, he wrote a journey. Soon he began his second trip from Quanzhou to the Southeast Asia. This time he sailed along the Eastern route. He started from Quanzhou, crossed the sea to Taiwan first, then to Xiao Dong Yang, namely today islands in the Philippines, Brunei, and Kalimantan Island, and then he turned into Da Dong Yang, namely Java and Timor. According to Wang Dayuan, he passed Quanzhou in 1349 when Wu Jian was compiling Qing Yuan Xu Zhi. Wu Jian asked him to write Dao Yi Zhi Lue as an appendix of Qing Yuan Xu Zhi because he knew foreign countries. Wang Dayuan's Dao Yi Zhi Lue was based on his two travel experiences, so it was quite different from what he wrote the first time.

Wang Dayuan wrote in the preface: "The language and culture of the Yuan Dynasty have influenced countries all around the world. Thousands of foreign states, as vassals compete among them to present the best jade to China. They travelled long distances to trade with China and Chinese merchants also frequently travelled to their regions." Wu Jian also wrote: "Chinese emperor leads the social order and judicial systems in the vast regions of both China and overseas countries around it. There are tens of thousands of countries overseas, but it is very difficult to sail through the "North sea" due to strong winds and huge waves. For those countries of the east, west and the north, they should sail thousands of miles to get there (North Sea)."[9]

That is to say, people had a cognition that China was located in a continent surrounded by seas. The "north sea" in the north of Korea, namely, the Sea of Japan, the Sea of Okhotsk and the Northern Pacific, was desolate and blowing hard. Chinese seafarers seldom sailed in the Northern Pacific. There are many countries in the East, South and West where Chinese has managed to reach by ships. The Mongol forces created a great empire across Asia and Europe, which created favorable conditions for the communications between the East

---

9   Wu Jian, preface of Dao Yi Zhi Lue, i.e, A Brief Account of Island Barbarians .

and the West. Traders travelled to foreign countries like travelling in their home country.

Wang Dayuan narrated that what he wrote about the foreign countries, local customs, the sceneries, and the product were all things he had seen by his own eyes and listened by his own ears. He never recorded any tales. There are 99 entries in the book, which Wang Dayuan visited, and the last entry describes the old anecdotes which have nothing to do with his travels. Dao Yi Zhi Lue recorded Wang Dayuan's travels to over two hundred regions of Asia, Africa and Europe which is well-reserved till today. This literature is very valuable for the research of maritime activities during the Yuan Dynasty periods. Wu Jian commented: "What he said must be true".

Before that, there were Ling Wai Dai Da written by Zhou Qufei (variously translated as Representative Answers from the Region beyond the Mountains, Notes Answering [Curious Questions] from the land beyond the Pass or other similar titles) and secondly Zhu Fan Zhi written by Zhao Rushi (variously translated as A Description of Barbarian Nations, Records of Foreign People, or other similar title) during the Song Dynasty period, and after these 2 books, there were travel books like Ying Ya Sheng Lan by Ma Huan and Xing Cha Sheng Lan by Fei Xin written during the Ming Dynasty period. However, they were just stories that the authors heard about or heard of. But, Wang Dayuan's book is mainly based on his direct individual experiences. The writing style of Dao Yi Zhi was greatly influenced by Zhou Qufei and Zhao Rushi, but Wang Dayuan's travelling experience had been far richer than theirs. He travelled in the seas when he was just 20 years old, and travelled in the East and West oceans twice during his lifetime. Just as the book, Si Ku Quan Shu Zong Lu (can be translated as Complete Series Books of the Four Storehouses) has puts it as follows: "most of the authors which wrote historical books about foreign countries, in fact didn't travel abroad, namely, Zhao Rushi's Zhu Fan Zhi was based on gossips of merchants, but Wang Dayuan has written this book by his own individual experiences. This is why his book is so valuable".

The Ma Huan from the Ming Dynasty period was also greatly influenced by Wang Dayuan, he said in the preface of his book Ying Ya Sheng Lan (a book about the countries visited by him over the course of Zheng He's treasure voyages): "I have read the book Dao Yi Zhi Lue (A Brief Account of Island Barbarians) which recorded different weathers and climates and various geography and people. How different the world is!...... I have also read many translated works but none of them have records like this. Then I followed his steps and went to theregions and countries he travelled. I have been to the vast ocean thousands of miles away from home and seen the weather, climate, geography and people there. Consequently, I know that he has told the truth...... So I collected facts about various peoples, their native customs, crops, grains and regimes of different countries, in my book". This proves that Ma Huan had read Dao Yi Zhi Lue before he travelled with Zheng He. He verified Wang Dayuan's records with his own observations and decided to write the book

Ying Ya Sheng Lan. Although he has described the details of more than 20 countries and regions, it includes far less regions than the Dao Yi Zhi Lue.

(3) Zhenla Feng Tu Ji

Zhenla Feng Tu Ji, which can be literally translated as the Nature and Culture of Zhenla— was authored by Zhou Daguan, who was from the Yongjia county, Wenzhou city, in Zhejiang province. In 1295 or the 1st year of the Yuan emperor Yuanzheng (also called Cheng Zong or Temür Khan (Mongol origin), Zhou Daguan was ordered to go to Zhenla country together with an envoy. He arrived at Zhenla in the next year and stayed there for more than a year. After he returned to China, he made this book according to his personal experiences. But surprisingly, there is no record of this official mission in the diplomatic archives of the Yuan dynasty. The scholars and people of the world only know about this journey from the records in the book written by Zhou Daguan, which was directly experienced by him.

The 10th-13th century was the most splendid era of the Cambodian civilization, also known as the era of Angkor. The book reflects the situation of Angkor. It records the various aspects of Cambodia during the late 13th century, which is both informative and vivid in its narrations. Many buildings and carvings in Angkor recorded in the book are the cultural relics of this era. In addition, the economic activities of the native peoples, including their agricultural activities, handicraft industry, trade, etc., have been extensively described. The daily life of the native people, such as their clothing, food, shelter, and their life styles and religions, was introduced. The book with about 8500 words, is divided into more than 40 chapters as follows: the walls, palace, clothing, subordinate, three religions, character, delivery, handmaiden, language, savages, text, time, litigation, infection, disease, death, farming, mountains and rivers, produce, trade, goods of the Tang Dynasty, plants, birds, animals, vegetables, fishes, ferments, salt, vinegar and sauce, silkworm, equipment, carriage, ship, village, anecdote, bath, outlander, army and horses, the king's routine, etc. Zhou Daguan's records are the only historical material about the ancient Angkor culture.

(2) The Merchants of the East Merchants and the Mongolians

(1) Pu family and Quanzhou Merchants

Pu Shougeng, a Hui originated family leader who had monopolized Fujian's overseas trade during the Southern Song Dynasty, and helped Yuan to destroy Song. According to Xin Shi in the Yuan Dynasty and Min Shu in the Ming Dynasty, Pu Shougeng's ancestors had migrated to Guangzhou from the Western region at the end of the Tang Dynasty. Then they had moved to Quanzhou and lived there. The Pu family was specialized in the overseas trade, which was known by the rulers and was ordered to lead overseas trade affairs.

During the period of Five Dynasties and Ten Kingdoms, Pu Youliang was ordered to sail to Champa as the transshipment official of the Atlantic. The Pu family was gradually assimilated into the Song, the Pu family's tradition of overseas trade in the Southeast Asia has been passed down from generations to generations. During the Shaoding period under the reign of Emperor Li Zong (1228-1233), Pu Zongmin who belonged to the Pu family was enrolled in the Civil Palace Examination, served as an official in the court of Wenling and then was ordered to travel overseas for many times. In 1236 (the third year of Duan Ping under the reign of the Emperor Li Zong of the Song Dynasty), Pu Zongmin was sent to Annam, and two years later Champa. In 1247 (the 7th year of the reign of Emperor Chunyou), he was sent to Bo Ni (current Brunei), and died there. His gravestone is still in Brunei, which was discovered by the German Sinologist W. Franke. In the early 1991, I saw his grave and tombstone in Brunei when I participated at the "Maritime Silk Road" expedition event. It wrote: "This is the tomb of Master Pu, supervisor in the court of Quanzhou during the Song Dynasty period, erected by his son Yingjia in the Jiazi[10] year of Jing Ding".

"Master Pu in the court of Quanzhou in the Song Dynasty" referred to Pu Zongmin and it says the gravestone was erected in "the Jiazi year of Jing Ding" (1264) whichwas probably not the same year with Pu Zongmin's death. Pu Zongmin died overseas. The gravestone was probably erected some years after his death. "Yingjia", according to the Xi Shan Za Zhi, is his two sons Pu Ying and Pu Jia. Then Pu Ying was sent to Brunei and Pu Jia succeeded the Chinese official post in Champa and made good trade contacts and friendships with Dashi (Arab Empire), Persia, and Shizi (Sri Lanka). After the death of Pu Zongmin, his eldest son Pu Ying once again visited Brunei and the second son visited Champa which was near to Brunei. The gravestone was probably set up by his son in Brunei. It is not clear whether Pu Ying and Pu Jia have later gone to Brunei and Champa or returned to Quanzhou. But judging from the Pu Jia's monopoly on overseas trade, the family had probably lived abroad and not in Mainland China. Under the favorable conditions in the Southeast coast of China, Champa and Brunei, Pu family kept in touch with Dashi (Islamic-Arabia), Persia and South Asia.

471

Circa in 1st year of the reign of Shao Xi during the Southern Song Dynasty period (1190), Pu Kaizong family has moved from Guangzhou to Quanzhou. After more than 10 years, Pu Kaizong baceame a junior official in the Anxi County, and was also involved with overseas trade. The family had accumulated a great deal of wealth with overseas trade. They were good at overseas trade and gradually grown up in Quanzhou. The family owned many ships and

10   Jiazi year is according to ancient Chinese calendar, with a 60-year cycle, Chinese 60-year calendar cycle is based on the combinations of a cycle of ten heavenly stems and twelve earthly branches. Each year is named by a pair of one stem and one branch. The Year of Jia Zi (Jia from the heavenly stems and Zi from the earthly branches) is the beginning of the sexagenary cycle. The next Jia Zi Year will come 60 years later.

even armed forces. According to the records in the book Chong Zuan Fujian Tong Zhi: "officials, pirates attacked Quanzhou in the late Song Dynasty period (1274) and was defeated by Pu Shougeng, son of Pu Kaizong. Soon Pu Shougeng was promoted. He controlled the local financial authority and owned a private navy."

After the Yuan army captured Lin'an, the remaining forces of the Southern Song Dynasty fled to Quanzhou. Although they were weak at that time, they still did not know how not solve all internal contradictions and ignored the force of Pu family. In order to strengthen the fight against the Yuan Dynasty, Zhang Shijie, a Song general arrested the private trade ships of Pu family, and grabbed their property to put them into the military funds. This act had provoked the Pu family. Consequently, Pu Shougeng began to attack against the Song court, their imperial members, high officials and soldiers with the help of Yuan general Sogetu. Then the weak court of the Southern Song Dynasty was forced to retreat to Guangdong. At the same time, the naval forces controlled by Pu Shougeng joined the Yuan army which enabled it to be much stronger in naval battles. In the following year, together with the armed forces of Pu Shougeng, Yuan army marched southwards Fujian province which accelerated the collapse of the small state led by the Southern Song Dynasty.

The Pu family was still powerful in Quanzhou. According to Zhou Mi's book titled as: Kui Xin Za Zhi, "there is a very rich Hui tycoon in the south of Quanzhou, who is named as Fo Lian, son-in-law of the Pu Family. The family owns the properties of more than one hundred pearls and eighty ships".

In addition to people of the Western Regions and Hui, there were also many merchants of Han in the Quanzhou city. Wang Dayuan, author of the book "Dao Yi Zhi Lue" (A Brief Account of Island Barbarians), had travelled twice to foreign countries. Wang Yi's book Qang Chang Zong Ji in the late Song Dynasty recorded "Biography of the Two Brothers". It mentioned that Sun Tianfu and Chen Baosheng regarded each other as brothers. They have established partnership "to seek fortunes by overseas trading". Chen's father Chen Sigong was a merchant in Quanzhou who had died in the sea. Chen Baosheng followed his father's businesses and traded with Korea, Java, and Luohu (current Thailand). Wang Yi wrote: "In those regions which are hundreds of thousands of km.km. away from China, their families, customs, men and women, clothes, food, living style, and hobbies are all different from China. The two brothers saw numerous ships from different countries which visited China for trade or in order to pay tribute, but the ships from China to foreign countries were few.

(2) Chinese envoys

During the Yuan Dynasty period, Chinese travellers had achieved a new record in foreign contacts. According to Jingshi Encyclopedia, Zhanchi, in 1301 (the 5th year of the reign of Emperor Dade), the Yuan Dynasty government sent a Hui envoy Mai Shuding to Mugudushu (current Mogadishu, the capital city of Somali) to purchase lions, leopards, etc. He was given funds which could support him for two years. In the same year, the government sent another 37 envoys to Diaojier to purchase several foreign commodities, gave them rations and funds which could support them for three years. In terms of the number of rations allocated and utilized by the envoys, Diaojier should be far more distant than Mogadishu, possibly this region was the current city of Tangier in Morocco. The Moroccan traveler Ibn Battuta, must have heard of China before he came to China.

Ike Mese

Ike Mese came from Uiher. Before conquering the Song Dynasty, Kublai Khan had supported overseas exploration and journeys. Kublai Khan sent Ike Mese to Baluobei Kingdom (currently Malabar region between the Western Ghats and the Arabian Sea in the Southwest of India) in 1272 (the 9th year of Zhiyuan). This was the first he went overseas and it took two years to return with Baluobei's envoy and tributes in 1274. Kublai was very satisfied with Ike Mese's mission and gave him the golden Hufu (a tiger-shaped tally).In the following year, Ike Mese started his second voyage to Baluobei Kingdom, and this time returned back with the "national master" and "famous medicines". Hence he was awarded as Bing Bu Shi Lang (vice commander of the Ministry of War). At the time of the two travels, the South of China had not yet achieved unity. Consequently, Ike Mese's ships had to set sailing from the ports of the Shandong province orfrom the ports located in the North of Jiangsu and sailors were also from the North. Through the two travels to the South of India, he accumulated a lot in navigation to Southeast Asia and the Indian Ocean, and mastered many overseas knowledge. After the Song Dynasty was destroyed, the Yuan government ordered him to join in the deliberations about the overseas conquests. In 1281 (the 18th year of Zhiyuan), it was the third time that Ike Mese was ordered to start a maritime expedition. Yuan dynasty attempted to turn the Champa kingdom to a vassal state and a military base for the conquest of Southeast Asia, but it was rejected by Champa. Ike Mese, together with Sogetu's army invaded Champa. After years of war, the Yuan army occupied the coastal regions of Champa but the Champa's army retreated to the inner regions of the mainland. It fought bravely and was determined to break the endurance of theYuan army. During the fierce battles the commander of the Yuan army had lost his life. Ike Mese was among the troops of Zhen Nan Wang who was very cautious. They did not have too much casuality and finally returned back.

During the military expedition to Champa, Ike Mese was recalled back from the front by Kublai in 1284 (the 21th year of Zhiyuan). He was ordered to go to the "overseas kingdom of Seng Jia La" (current Sri Lanka) to visit the holy Sarira of Sakyamuni. "Seng Jia Ji" in Singhalese means "lion". Sarira of Sakyamuni in Sri Lanka has been was the world famous tooth relic of the Buddha (Buddha's Tooth). Ming Yuan, a monk of the Tang Dynasty, had visited this Temple of the Tooth. He admired the Buddha's Tooth and wanted to

473

take it back home, certainly the Buddha's tooth[11] was a local treasure which the native people would not agree, this demand.

So the monk Ming Yuan tried to steal it. He almost got it, but caught by the native by people, consequently, he was humiliated by the locals, and had to leave for South India. According to historical records, the local people believed that if they lost the Buddha's Tooth, they would be swallowed by the devil. So they protected Buddha's Tooth very well and enshrined it in tall buildings and behind several locked doors. All of them were sealed with mud and five people were in charge as guardians. When one of the doors was opened, the whole city would hear it. People of the Kingdom of Seng Jia La worshiped the Buddha's Tooth orderly and offered flowers every day. It is said and believed that "if you wish deep heartedly, the Buddha's Tooth will be on flowers". Some people even claimed that they have seen different lights in it."[12]

Buddhism was also popular in Ike Mese's hometown, and he was probably a Buddhist.[13]

Ike Mese had heard of the Buddha's Tooth when he visited the Southern India and told about it to Kublai. That's why Kublai recalled him from the front line of Champa and ordered him to visit the Buddha's Tooth. In 1990, I have witnessed Buddha's Tooth in Sri Lanka when I participated in the research expedition of the "Maritime Silk Road" organized by the UNESCO. In 1287 (the 24th year of the Zhiyuan, the reign of Kublai Khan), Ike Mese was ordered for the fourth time to sail overseas. This time he was sent to the Malabar Kingdom in the southeast coast of the Southern India. It took him a year to get the destination because of the wind on the sea. He found good doctor and medicine and purchased narra. Finally he went back with Malabar's tributes and then he was ordered to stay in Quanzhou. In 1292 (the 29th year of Zhiyuan), Ike Mese was ordered to go North to participate in the discussion of Java. Emperor Shizu (Kublai Khan) established Fujian province and ordered him, Shi Bi and Gao Xing as the Pingzhang (local officials). Shi and Gao were in charge of military affairs and Ike Mese led the sea navigation. Kublai ordered that they would not return to their homeland after the conquest of Java, but remained there and sent envoys to other countries for tributes. It was the fifth time that Ike Mese sailed to the sea. When the Yuan army arrived at Champa on the sea route to

---

11   Located in the appropriately-named-to-Western-ears town of Kandy in Sri Lanka, the Temple of the Tooth offers some sweet Eastern architecture surrounding a religious relic. As the legend goes, the Buddha's tooth was given to the Sri Lankan monarchy in ancient times, and was passed around through various kings and holy men who hid, moved, and relocated the tooth a number of times across the centuries. Now the tooth is housed in a dedicated temple where worshipers can visit the relic, which is held in a golden stupa inside the two-story shrine. Although parts of the shrine were destroyed and rebuilt over the years in various bombings and acts of war, the building still retains its opulent style of gold and moonstone, surrounded by Buddhist carvings and offerings.

12   See Yi Jing: Biography of Eminent Monks to Western Religion in the Tang Dynasty, revised by Wang Bangwei, pp. 67-68.

13   See Bei Cungao: Ike Mese's Buddhist Activities in the Yuan Dynasty Period.

Java, Ike Mese sent an envoy to Nan Wu Li (currently North of Sumatra Island in Indonesia), Su Mu Du La (also in north Sumatra), and Bu Lu Bu Du which should be the place "Mo Li Pi Pa Du" in Sumatra mentioned in the volume 7 of Dade Nan Hai Zhi or the Pulau Buton in the East of Sumatra,[14] and Ba La La which should be the transliteration of Perlark (currently Peureulak) in the Northeast of Sumatra.[15]

In 1293, Yuan army defeated the King of Ge Lang. Then Ike Mese sent envoys to Mu Lai You (Malayu of Sumatra) and other countries to persuade them to surrender. But, soon later the Yuan army was defeated by the Java army which had rebelled, so the Yuan forces had to retreat, and when retreating, it took with the envoys of vassal countries of the South Asia, to China. According to the Yuan Shi: Shi Zu, envoys of these countries weren't allowed to return back home till October 1294 (the 31st year of Zhiyuan). Ike Mese was active in overseas affairs for more than 20 years, and had participated in 5 the sea voyages, and paid 4 visits to India and Sri Lanka. He was an outstanding Chinese seaman and navigator in the early Yuan Dynasty period who had greatly contributed to the communications between China and foreign countries.

Yang Tingbi

Yang Tingbi was one of Sogetu's fellows in the Mongol military expedition to the South. He was then Zhao Tao Si of Guangdong after the collapse of the Song Dynasty. When Sogetuo was the minister of the of Fujian province, he was ordered to send an envoy abroad. As a result, Champa, Malabar and other countries all accepted to be vassal states except the Kaulam kingdom (today's South of India). In 1279, Kublai Khan sent Yang Tingbi to Kaulam. They departed in the December and arrived there in the following March. King Binade ordered his brother Kenaquebulamuxing to write a loyalty letter in Persian language and promised to pay tribute to China, in the coming year. Then Yang Tingbi went back to China with the King Binade's brother.

In October 1280 (the 17th year of Zhi yuan), Qasar Qaya (Hasaer Haiya) was awarded as Xuan Wei Shi of the Kaulam Kingdom and made the second trip to Kaulam with Yang Tingbi. In the next January, Yang Tingbi departed from Quanzhou and arrived on Seng Jia Ye Shan (current Sri Lanka) after three months sailing. By this time the North wind had stopped, they were waiting for the monsoon winds and gradually ran out of provisions. The sailor Zheng Zhen explained the truth of insufficient supply and suggested to take advantage of the South wind to Malabar and then travel to Kaulam Kingdom by the land route. Yang Tingbi arrived at Malabar in the next month and was welcomed by Mahema, the prime minister of Malabar. Mahematold Yang Tingbi that the merchants of Malabar were treated well by the Chinese government in Quanzhou and that Malabar kingdom was willing to respond in a best manner.

14   Chen Jiarong, Xie Fang, Lu Junling: Interpretation of the Names of Places in the Ancient South China Sea, Zhonghua Book Company, 1986, pp. 182, 449.
15   Ibid, p. 117

However, when Yang Tingbi and his attendants told Mahema about their request, Mahema rejected and explained that the expedition route from Malabar (Ma'bar) to Kaulam was blocked, which was just a fake excuse. Then, Yang Tingbi and his attendants met another Malabar (Ma'bar) minister Buali and were rejected similarly. Yang Tingbi and others had to stay in a guest house in Malabar and waited for a positive response.

On an early morning of May, Mahema and Buali arrived at the guest house and told the truth to Yuan envoys. First they told the truth of sending envoys to the Yuan Dynasty in the past that the envoy was sent by them privately. But, later this secret plan was acknowledged by the Malabar leaders and the king. The king was angry about what they had done and ordered to confiscate Mahema and Buali's properties, wives and children. They finally avoided the death by sophistry. The two ministers also told him that the relations between Malabar (Ma'bar) and Kaulam was very tense. The king and his princes gathered soldiers in Jia Yi and had declared a war against Kaulam kingdom, still there was no agreement between the two kingdoms. They also complained that the country became poorer when the Yuan army was there. As a matter of fact, the gold and jewels accumulated in the Islam countries were all from this region, and other European countries had also begun to plunder this region. All the South Indian kingdoms had the intention to surrender to the Yuan Dynasty, and if Malabar surrendered to the Yuan, the two ministers could send envoys to carry the letter to neighboring countries. Finally, Yang Tingbi had to decide returning back to Quanzhou (China).

476

When the north winds began to blow in 1281, following Qasar Qaya's recommendation, the court ordered Yang Tingbi to set sail for the third time. This time he went to Kaulam alone and arrived at Kaulam in February 1282 after three months of sailing. He met with the king and the prime minister and gave them the submission letter sent by the Yuan Dynasty. Yang Tingbi spent a month in Kaulam. In Kualam Yang Tingbi also met the leader of Yelikewen (Christian) Tuzaner Smali. Tha latter had heard about the visit of Yuan envoys and met with Yang Tingbi and talked about his visit plan to China with a precious plate and two bottles of special medicine. In those days the leader of Sumuda kingdom (Somnath-currently Gujarat) (an Islam kingdom) Mahemashi was in Kaulam, he expressed his will to send a messenger and gifts to the great Khan (Kublai Khan). At that time, there was another envoy from Sumuda Kingdom (in current India) which was visiting the Kaulam kingdom. When he heard Yang Tingbi had planned to come back to China, he represented his King Daguer to send an envoy to come to the Yuan court with Yang Tingbi with tributes. Yang Tingbi accepted their requests.

In March 1282, when the South winds had started (the 19th year of Zhiyuan), Yang Tingbi planned to return back home. Kaulam envoy Zhu'ali shamanglibadi traveled to China together with Yang Tingbi, they were carrying some treasures and a black ape. On the way to China they arrived at Nawang Kingdom (currently Nicobar Islands in South of Andaman Sea) after one month of sailing which was one of the most prosperous countries of the region. Yang Tingbi persuaded King Mang'ang to send an envoy to China which could accompany him. No one could read in the Nawang Kingdom, so they only sent four people but without sending a submission letter. Yang Tingbi continued to sail to the East and arrived at Sumudula Kingdom (current Northern Sumatra), where the King Tuhanbade, personally welcomed him. Yang Tingbi has bragged about China's strength and Yuan intention of expanding to overseas by force. King Tuhanbade indicated immediately that they would accept the vassal status and pay tribute to Yuan. Sumudula Kingdom ordered its envoys led by Hasan and Suleiman to travel to China with Yang Tingbi's ships. In September of the same year, all the envoys which joined Yang Tingbi arrived at Dadu (Beijing) and met Kublai in the court.

In January 1283 (the 20th year of Zhiyuan), Kublai ordered Yang Tingbi to go to Kaulam Kingdom for the fourth time. Yang Tingbi was successful, and till 1286 (the 23th year of Zhiyuan), 10 countries has positively responded to the requirements of Yang Tingbi and successively came to pay tributes. Among them were the Malabar, Xunamen (Sumuda), Singili (currently Cranganore in the west coast of the southern India), Nanwuli (current Northern Sumatra), Malandan, Nawang, Dingheer (current Kuala Terengganu of Malaysia), Lala (current Gujarat of India), Jilanyidai (currently Kelantan of Malaysia), and Sumudula.[16]

Rabban Sauma

Rabban Sauma was the first Chinese traveler who visited Western Europe and wrote his travel records. He was from Dadu (Beijing), born of a rich family who believed in Nestorianism, and his native tongue was Turkic language. His father, Xiban, was a monk of the Nestorian church. Rabban means "teacher" in Syriac script. When he was in his early 20s, he practiced in a Christian temple in the vicinity of his home, and later became a famous priest. Ma Husi from the state of Dongsheng (current Togtoh in Inner Mongolia) came to him. About the 12th year of Zhiyuan, Rabban and Ma Huisi decided to go to pilgrimage to Jerusalem and received an imperial edict. They departed from Dadu and went West with a group of merchants. When they arrived at Il Khanate's capital Mielahe (current Azerbaijan of Iran), they met the Mar Denha, the bishop of the church of Nestorius.

Mar Denha awarded Ma Husi as the bishop of Dadu and Wang Gu Du, and gave him a new name: Yahbh Allah. He also awarded Sauma as the chief inspector of the church, and was sent back to the East. He did not make it home because of the war between the Il Khanate and the Chagatai Khanate in Amu River and died in 1281. Then Ma Husi was elected as the new archbishop, named Yahbh-Allah III.

---

16   See The History of Yuan Dynasty: Kublai Khan and also The History of Yuan Dynasty: Mala'bar.

In 1287, Arghun, the Khan of Il khanate, intended to gather the crusaders to fight and capture Jerusalem and Syria, and sent Rabban bar Sauma (diplomat) to Roman Curia, British and French kings. Sauma went to Rome via Constantine and met the newly elected Pope. He left Rome and traveled to Paris, staying a month at the court of King Philip IV, and to Bordeaux, where he met Edward I of England. They were treated well by the French government for a month and then went to Bordeaux of French to meet King Edward of British. Both the British king and the French king agreed to establish an alliance with the Il khanate. In 1288, Sauma—on his way home—heard the news that Nicholas IV was assigned as the Pope. Then he sent the loyality letter to Rome again. After the new Pope read the letter from the king of Il Khanate, he wrote two letters back to Arghun (Ar Gun). The first letter demonstrated his thanks for Arghun's kindness to Christians and the second letter agreed Arghun's plan to get baptized there after capturing the Jerusalem city. He also gave many gifts when Sauma made his second visit.

After completing the mission, Arghun (Ar Gun). praised him and allowed him to build and lead a temple near Taoli Tenple (current Tabriz in Azerbaijan-Iran). Later, he moved to Mielahe and built another magnificent church. In 1293, Sauma went to Baoda (current Baghdad, the capital of Iraq) to help Yahbh-Allah III to manage the church affairs until he died. Rabban Sauma's visit to Rome convinced Rome Curia that the emperor of the Yuan Dynasty and the ruler of the Mongol were both Christian. It pushed Rome to send missionaries to the East. When Sauma reached Persia, he wrote his journey down in Persian, but the manuscripts were lost. For Sauma's experience, there is a detailed narration in the following book which also includes parts of Sauma's manuscripts.[17]

Yang Shu and Bolod

So-far mentioned Chinese navigators, such as Ike Mese and Yang Tingbi, have sailed to the sea for many times and the Western coast in the Southern India was the most distant place they have reached. Actually voyages were far beyond this in the Yuan Dynasty. Among the three Mongol Khanates-Chagatai Khanates, Il Khanate, and Kipchak Khanate, Emperor of Yuan and Il Khanate were sons of Tolui, Genghis Khan's fourth son. They were related in blood. After Hulagu Khan and his descendants established a country in Persia, he served the Yuan Dynasty loyally. Initially they mainly relied on the relation through lands, and then sailing became more and more important after the rebellion of Haidou. The ministers of Malabar have offered to provide supplies to the envoys of Kublai and Il Khanate, who had been travelling between East and West. Il Khanate's envoys had taken the family of Marco Polo on their way back home. They set sail from Quanzhou in the winter, and sailed for more than two years before arriving in Persia. In addition to the official envoys from the Persian Gulf to Quanzhou, Chinese and Western merchants of Guangdong and

---

17   E.A.W. Budge: The Monks of Kublai Khan. Religious Tract Society, London 1928.

Fujian often sailed through here too. Persian Gulf was in the lists of merchant countries in Dade Nan Hai Zhi. At the end of the Yuan Dynasty, Buluhanding, the abbot of Quanzhou Qingyuan Temple, was a scholar who came to China by ship from Persia. There are not many voyagers to the Persian Gulf recorded in the history, and the most famous of which are the two official envoys: Yang Shu and the Bolod.

Yang Shu was an intermediate level marine official during the Yuan Dynasty period. When he was at the age of 19, he "took official ships" to "Xi Yang" in 1301 (the 5th year of the reign of Emperor Dade). Some scholars believe that the "Xi Yang region" which Yang Shu visited was the Persian Gulf region.[18] The word "Xi Yang" used in the Yuan Dynasty period was different from that used during the Ming Dynasty period. "Xi Yang" used during the Yuan Dynasty period was a name a specific place, which referred to Malabar on the southeast coast of India. There he met Na Huai, the envoy of Il Khanate who was on a mission to the Yuan Dynasty. Consequently, they traveled together from Malabar.

Yang Shu and Na Huai have established a close friendship in Malabar and during their journey to China. After Na Huai completed his mission, he was ready to return to Persia. Before the return voyage, he asked Emperor Cheng Zong of the Yuan Dynasty to allow Yang Shu to go with him. The emperor agreed and named Yang Shu as "General of Qianhu". In the winter of the 8th year of Dade (1304), Yang Shu sailed again with Na Huai to Persia. The trip took 3 years and he arrived at the Hormuz port in 1307. Yang Shu bought native white horses, black dogs, amber, wine and so on in Persia and it took him 5 years to return to China. Apart from this arduous journey, preparation before departure is also a meticulous work. Yang Shu went to the sea twice, but he did not rely solely on the government when he prepared to ships, food, navigation equipment and other debris. He did all the stuff by himself. He knew that sailing was a risky business and he knew how to deal with it. Without thorough preparations, it would be helpless if there's an accident. He also understood that sailing was a climate dependent activity. From the moment of his being appointed to the time the Northwest wind came, all preparations should be made, or the season would pass, and it will not be able to sail. His own preparations for the work showed that he was an experienced navigator. Yang Shu was later promoted to a rank as the "Sea Transportation Qianhu of Jiading."[19]

Bolod was a Mongol aristocrat, and a Mongolian bureaucrat who was highly influential during the reign of Kublai. In 1283 (the 20th year of Zhiyuan), he was sent to Il Khanate with his deputy Ngai-Sie, a Syrian Nestorian who served in the Yuan court. At that time, there occurred the rebellion of Haidou, and the apostole cut off the land from the East to the West. Consequently, Bolod had to take the maritime expedition although it was the winter time and arrived in

18   See Sun Guangqi, History of Navigation in Ancient China, p. 422.
19   Huang Jin, the Sea Transportation Qianhu–Yang Shu's Epitaph, collected in volume 35 of Huang Jin Hua Ji.

Hormuz in the next year, along with Aersilan of the Aorsoi. They landed on Farsi of Persian and traveled to North regions. They finally arrived in Alan (current Azerbaijan and met with Arghun of the Il Khanate in October 1284. The brilliant talent of Bolod was praised by Arghun, so he kept him in Persia and sent Ngai-Sie back to China. Ngai-Sie reached the Yuan Dynasty and told Kublai Khan about it in 1285. Kublai had protected Bolod since he was a child and supported him for years. Kublai was sad when he knew that Bolod had migrated to Persia and he said: "Bolod born in my land ate in my table and now settled down in another country".[20]

Bolod was also highly appreciated by Il Khanate and become the 4th powerful official in the court. He had helped Arghun, Gaykhatu, Baydu, Ghazan and Khodabandeh. He became a prominent person in the cultural communication between China and Persia. He narrated the detailed history of Mongols to the Il Khanate royal family, and was appointed to compile world-famous historical book Jāmi al-tawārīkh on the charge of the minister Rashid al-Din. He introduced many advanced Chinese systems to Il Khanate. Under his advice, Gaykhatu has followed the steps of the Yuan Dynasty and issued the first paper money which was printed in Chinese, and which included quotes from the holy Koran and Gaykhatu's Lama religious name "Rinchindorj". However, it was rejected by merchants because the Persian economy had not yet reached the stage of using paper money.

480 (3) Buali, the Prince of Malabar

Buali, also named Syed whose ancestor was Halahadi in the Western region (currently the site of Qalhat), which had a traditional trade relationship with India. Syed's ancestor was a Hui merchant in the Persian Gulf and south India. His family moved from the homeland in the Song Dynasty to the Western country, which was Malabar in the East coast of Southern where he traded for living. His father's name was not Ali, and he was trusted by the king of Malabar. The king had five brothers and Buali was "the sixth brother". Soon he was appointed as the general and so he accumulated a great deal of wealth. After his death, Syed inherited his father's path and continued to maintain the trust of the king. The king was accustomed to call him by his father's name, and did not use Syed's own name. The Southern part of India lies between the East China and the West Persian Gulf. It touches great importance in the trade of local Hui merchants between the East and the West. In the age of Buali, the situation in Asia changed dramatically, and Mongol army first swept West Asia and established the Yili Khanate in Persia. Then it conquered the Southern Song Dynasty. Both the Song Dynasty and the Arab Caliphate in the West Asia were powerful regimes that had quickly disintegrated. From regions of sunrise toregions of sunset, the vast lands from China to West Asia were ruled by the Mongols. The Hui merchants of India, whether trade to the East or to the West, must deal with the Mongolian authorities.

---

20   Cheng Jufu: The Sacred Monument of the King Zhongxian of Rome, Vol. 5.

When Buali heard that the Song Dynasty was toppled by the Yuan dynasty, he said: "Chinese people are all around the world and the whole world is peaceful. I will surrender to it". So he made a decision to send Jamal ol Din to pay the tribute to the Yuan Dynasty. In addition, he sent envoys to the princes Albaha and Hashan who were the descendants of Hulagu Khan. All the envoys from the Yuan Dynasty or Il Khanate who were sailing by Malabar would receive ships and supplies from Buali. He did this because the Mongol army had a great influence on the Hui merchants overseas, and he hoped to maintain a good relationship with the Mongolians to protect his business interests. Buali's behavior discontented rulers of Malabar. They confiscated his land and even intended to execute him. Buali's protected him from execution through tricks. On Yang Tingbi's second trip via Malabar, he was told by Buali about these things. Kublai heard Buali's behavior of protecting Mongolian regime overseas from envoys of Il Khanate and the Yuan Dynasty. In 1291 (the 28th year of the reign of Zhiyuan), he sent Bie Tiemuer, Iliashikin, and Alibo to Malabar to call Buali to the Yuan court. Due to the disagreement with the king, he abandoned his own estate and moved to China with a hundred of men. Buali's father was so-called brother of the king, thus he called himself the prince of Malabar after he came to China. Kublai gave him a great deal of money and awarded him as a high official of Zhong Shu. Later, Buali emigrated from Quanzhou to Dadu (current Beijing) and married a Chinese woman. After the Prime Minister Sengge was executed, his wife Cai from Korea was married to Buali. After Cai died, Buali married another Chinese woman. In 1299 (the 3rd year of Dade), he died in Dadu, and his body was buried in Quanzhou where many Islam people lived. Buali who was born to an Arab family had moved from the Persian Gulf to Malabar in the southern India. He lived in Malabar and kept good relationship with the Yuan Dynasty and Il Khanate. Then he moved to China and married a Korean woman. His life line reflects the skillful activities of the Hui merchants in the seas between the East and the West.

481

(4) Emperor of Siam–Rama Khamheng

Before the late 13th century, Thailand was divided into two countries: one was Siam in the north and the other is Lopburi in the south. Siam kingdom was a small kingdom founded by the Thai people, and its capital city was the Sangkhalok, around the upper banks of the Menam River. After Yuan army took the control of the south regions in China, the Yuan Dynasty sent He Zizhi to Siam kingdom who was arrested by the king of Champa. Later the Yuan Dynasty invaded Champa, with the pretext that He Zizhi were arrested and executed by Champa. In 1292, the King of Siam sent envoys with the gold album to Guangdong. Guangdong's officials delivered the gold album to Dadu. Kublai Khan sent envoys to Siam in the next year. In 1294, "Rama Khamheng of the Perchaburi sent envoys to pay tributes". The Yuan emperor Cheng Zong treated Siam as a vassal state. Soon "he wrote a letter to call the king of Siam to the court. If he could not do it, he could send his children and courtiers".[21]

---

21 Emperor Cheng Zong

In 1295 (the 1st year of Yuanzhen period under the reign of Emperor Cheng Zong), Siam's envoys took gold presents to Dadu (Khanbaliq/later Baijing) and asked Yuan's court to send envoys to Siam. At that time, the envoys of Yuan Dynasty to Siam had left the Dadu (Beijing) city. The Yuan Dynasty gave envoys of Siam the Gold Symbol of Dadu, and ordered him to go to the South as soon as possible to meet with the Yuan envoys.[22] In a word, the envoys to Siam were not able to complete the mission of calling the king of Siam to the Yuan dynasty court. According to the History of Ancient Siam by the Siamese historian prince Damaron, Rama Khamheng was twice in China in the years 1294 and 1300. However, there was no record about these visits in Yuanshi. Whether he visited the Yuan Dynasty has become an interesting question among the Chinese scholars. Gong Shitai Wan Zhai Ji collected Siming Ciji Temple Monument in Volume 9 which mentioned that Yin Yangxiu from Dehua County of Quanzhou was a trade official of the Song Dynasty. After Yin Yangxiu had surrendered to Yuan forces, he was sent on a diplomatic mission to Siam to ask the king of Siam to visit the Yuan court. Although the inscription did not mention the accurate time of Yin Yangxiu's trip, itwas probably the 1st year of Yuanzhen according to the above listed records of the envoys of the Yuan Dynasty and Siam over the years. And the king who came with him was probably Rama Khamheng and the time he came to the Yuan Dynasty should be after the 1st year of Yuanzhen. According to Yuanshi, the Yuan court gave "the person coming to the court" precious clothes as gifts. If "the person coming to the court" of Siam was Rama Khamheng, then the first time he entered the Yuan Dynasty was not in 1294, but in 1297. According to Gong Shitai's records, Yangxiu and the king of Siam experienced the sudden furious storms and many ships were destroyed on their way to the Yuan Dynasty. According to the book Yuan shi (History of Yuan Dynasty), the new king of Siam said in 1299 (the 3rd year of Dade), that his father had been given harness, white horses and golden clothes.[23]

The new king was probably the son of Rama Khamheng, Loetai. In the 3rd year of Dade, Siam, Mok-la-yu, and Lophuri came to pay the tributes. "The eldest son of the king of Siam" came and was awarded with a tiger-shaped tally. He should be the new king Loetai who visited the Yuan Dynasty to ask for gifts in the same year mentioned in Yuanshi: Siami. There was confusion in regard to the new King's name in the Chinese literature. From this, the Thai historian mentioned the second time of Rama Khamheng coming to the Yuan Dynasty was his son Loetai. Loetai demanded that he should be awarded with a saddle, a white horse and a golden cloth like his father. When the Yuan court discussed the matter, the prime minister said that Siam was a small kingdom. If they gave him the horse, saddle and golden clothes, powerful kingdoms like India would disagree. The Yuan court adopted his proposal, and only gave Loetai golden clothes.

482

---

22 In the book History of Yuan Dynasty: History of Siam.
23 Ibid.

There was a poem written by Wang Dong in the late Yuan Dynasty which was recorded in Huang Yuan Feng Ya Volume 22, entitled as the "Song of the Hui Envoys of Siam". It said in the preface of the book that Siam had sent envoys to the Yuan Dynasty in the early Tian Li period; After the Emperor Shun accended to the throne, Siam again presented "a golden emblem, a turtle, and two elephants, two peacocks, and two parrots" to the Yuan Dynasty and the Yuan responded the Siam king ten beautiful and strong horses, and awarded Siam's envoy as an official and general. In fact, the envoy was a Chinese who settled in Siam and was sent to China as an envoy.

(5) Maps and Atlas works of Hui People

Before the Song Dynasty, the mainland Han people knew very little about the Western regions and the map of China was only painted to central Asia and India. After conquering the Western countries, the Mongolians greatly broadened the horizon of the Chinese people and enriched their knowledge of geography. According to people of the Yuan Dynasty, "The language and culture of the Yuan Dynasty have influenced countries all around the world. Thousands of foreign countries compete to present the best jade to China as vassal states. They travelled a long way to trade in China and Chinese merchants also travelled to their regions frequently".[24]

After the Mongols built the great empire across Eurasia, the work of drawing the full picture of the empire was on the agenda. The first step of completing this work was to collect maps of China and foreign countries. In the era of Song and Yuan, the most developed graphics technology was from China and the Islam world. Therefore, the main work of collecting the map of China and foreign countries were to collect the map of the Han and the Hui, and then we could talk about the position, proportion and place name of the various maps, and combine and redraw them. The vast territory of the Yuan Dynasty created excellent conditions for the collection of foreign maps. In 1285 (the 22nd year of the reign of Zhiyuan), the Yuan court commanded to "combine all maps into one to show the unprecedentedly vast territory of the Yuan Dynasty". That is to say, the scholars gathered by the government have collected the atlas of the world, and compiled a map of the great Yuan Empire.

People who was ordered to be responsible for drawing the map of the Yuan Empire was Jamaladin, an Islam official, famous Hui astronomer and geographer. His mother tongue was Persian and he did not know any Chinese. So the government arranged Wang Shidian as a translator to him.[25]

It was the Central Secretariat's (Zhongshu Sheng) responsibility to collect maps for the Ministry of War. But its collection work was not perfect. After the establishment of the Mongol empire, the administrative divisions had changed a lot, and the Mishu Jian ordered local officials to hand in their maps. Jamaladin

---

24 Wang Dayuan, Dao Yi Zhi Lue (A Brief Account of Island Barbarians), p. 385.
25 Islam People during the Yuan Dynasty, revised by Gao Rongsheng, Zhejiang Ancient Books Publisher, 1992, p. 28.

asked Kublai Khan to collect all the maps and geographic works and order all governments to offer relevant local administrative divisions, wild land, mountains, forests, paths and hills. The work of collecting maps was slow at first. The Yuan government has repeatedly informed the local authorities to report about it promptly. The geographer Jamaladin intended to draw a picture of the whole Yuan Dynasty, including the crown of the Yuan Dynasty (i.e. mainland China ruled by the Yuan Dynasty), Chagatai Khanate, Il Khanate and Kipchak Khanate. He needed not only documents of Chinese Han maps but also atlas drawings made by the vassal kingdoms. Therefore, when the Yuan government gave orders to all regions, it also gave a special order to authorities of "border regions" to send the documents as soon as possible.

After collecting all the maps and documents he needed, Jamaladin reported to Kublai Khan about the latest situation of his study. He and his colleagues had collected 40 or 50 Han's maps, some maps of the remote regions, namely about central Asia and the Western Asia. He asked to splice the maps of the Han to the maps of Hui to complete a map from the "sunrise" (east) to the "sunset" (western). This unprecedented work was granted by Kublai. Traditionally, Han dynasty drew maps in grid and Hui drew maps in circular which accepted the ancient Greek idea of "the earth is spherical". It was a difficult work to put the two different maps into one, especially into the Chinese traditional grid system. Regretfully, Jamaladin's map could not reserved. Judging from maps in Jingshi Encyclopaedia published in 1330 and place names of Chagatai Khanate, Il Khanate and Kipchak Khanate recorded in the book "History of the Yuan Dynasty: Geography of the Northwest Regions", map and the Yuan history, Jingshi Encyclopedia have praised Jamaladin's work and his map. The meticulous efforts by Jamaladin and his colleagues had produced a great scientific achievement and left a valuable document for later generations.

Jingshi Encyclopedia of Map was prepared in 1330 (the 1st year of the reign of Emperor Zhishun). You can also see the image of this map in the Classified Edition of the Yuanshi. Jingshi Encyclopedia of Map is a kind of grid map based on the Chinese traditional style of counting mile into grid. Its directions are different from current maps. The northwest in the current maps is the south direction in it. The Southeast in the current maps is the North direction in it. In other words, compared with current maps, its direction goes counterclockwise around 135°. The east of the map starts from Shazhou Jie. Tashibali in the West Shazhou (i.e., Tashi of the Yuan Dynasty) and Qamul (current Hami of Xinjiang province) was drawn in the map, which was called "Fief of Temur" by Chagatai Khanate, "Fief of Abu Sa'id" by Il Khanate, and "Fief of Uzbekistan, later generation of Genghis Khan's first son Jochi" by Kipchak Khanate.

The east of the map starts from Shazhou Jie of Hexi Corridor; in the north of the map is Zhande which is located in the lower reaches of the Syr Darya tiver and Bulghar which is located in the middle and lower reaches of the Volga River; the Northwest is Aluosi (current Russia); the West is Mishiji (Damascus), and Misier (current Egypt); the Southwest is Bahalayin) (current

Bahrain in the Persian Gulf); the South is Tianzhu. The map includes current northwest China, the five central Asian countries of CIS, namely, Kazakhstan, Kyrgyzstan, Tajikistan, Uzbekistan and Turkmenistan. The map also includes Russia, the Caucasus countries, Iran, Iraq, Egypt, countries in the Persian Gulf, Afghanistan, Pakistan, India, etc. The picture covers an unprecedented extent of land, and has played an important role in the history of ancient Chinese cartography, and reflects the communications between the West and the East in the Yuan Dynasty in the time when Chinese geography had developed quickly. Yuan shi (the book History of Yuan Dynasty): Geography of the Northwest also records the names of three vassal states in the Northwest of the Yuan Dynasty. There are 37 names of Chagatai Khanate recorded after Temur, 10 names of Kipchak Khanate attached to the name of Uzbekistan, and 45 related to Il Khanate, which is after Abu Sa'id. Most of them are only names without any description and some have brief explanations about the history of the Yuan Dynasty. When compared with the Geography of the Northwest with Jingshi Encyclopedia Map, we can see that the former one has referred to the latter one when it was compiled during the Ming Dynasty period. The Map includes 37 place names of Chagatai Khanate, 45 place names of Il Khanate, and 10 place names of the Kipchak Khanate. The Hui atlas that Yuanshi: Geography of the Northwest has talked about should be the map of the West Asia and Northwest China drawn by Islam scholars. Probably, Islam scholars couldn't have the map information of the Kipchak Khanate.

When drawing the map on the grand unity of the Yuan Dynasty, Jamaladin also paid special attention to the collection of Hui's map of the sea. At that time, Hui people who engaged in overseas trade were living in coast of Fujian. Mishi Jian of the Yuan government issued a special report to the administrative authorities of Fujian province to investigate if someone in the Hui ships knew any Rah Nama (directions and maps).[26] It was requested to report the investigation to the Central Secretariat. Arabs had established an unprecedented great empire in the 8th century. So in the Abbasids era, Hui's geography developed greatly. There were countless geographical works which recorded the Atlantic to the West, Japan to the East, and equator to the South. The geographical knowledge accumulated by the Hui astronomers and geographers is the precious scientific wealth of mankind. Although, this knowledge was transmitted to China by sailors and merchants before the Song Dynasty period, it had not attracted the attention of Chinese geographers. It was only during the Yuan Dynasty period that the works by Hui geographers were valued highly. These Hui maps have provided great help for the future cultural communications between the East and the West. People who study the history of navigation often ignore the historical background of Zheng He's voyages during the Ming dynasty period. Zheng He and many important people in his expedition team,

---

26   Chen Dezhi, "Overseas Transport in the Yuan Dynasty and Zheng He's Voyage in the Early Ming Dynasty", published in the Memoirs of Zheng He's Voyage, Nanjing University Press, 1985, p. 199.

were all Hui people, whose ancestors came from the distant Western regions. It was because of Jamaladin's introduction of Hui's geography and sea maps to the geography of China that Zheng He was able to sail during the reign of Ming dynasty. In the navigation information used by Zheng He in his voyages, there was probably a navigation map drawn by the Hui People.

3. World's Famous Explorers

The Mongols have established the great Mongol empire across Europe and Asia, breaking the boundaries among various nations, and greatly facilitated the expeditions and trading among many nations. Thus, the Yuan Dynasty encountered an unprecedented era of cultural exchanges between the East and West in the world history. Although there were already some Europeans who came to East before the Yuan Dynasty, but their understanding of the East had been quite superficial. More and more Europeans came to the East since the Yuan Dynasty by land or by sea and among them were many world famous travelers. The records they left were excellent materials for studying the cultural exchanges between the East and the West in that era.

(1) Marco Polo

Marco Polo has been one of the most famous travelers who had visited the Yuan Dynasty. He was born in 1254, his father Nicole Polo was an Italian businessman in Venice. Shortly before the birth of Marco Polo, Marco Polo's uncle Niccolo and his uncle Maffeo Polo left for Salai (currently near Astrakhan in Russia), the capital of Kipchak Khanate for trade and business. However there was a war between Kipchak Khanate and Il Khanate when they planned to return back home. So they had to go to the Eastbound line for safety and lived in Chagatai Khanate (current Bukhara in Uzbekistan) for three years. Then Niccole and Maffeo Polo met the envoy assigned by Il Khanate which would visit Kublai (the Chinese emperor), so they traveled with this envoy and came to Shangdu (Kaiping) about in 1265, and hosted by Kublai. Kublai asked them about the situation in Europe, and sent an envoy to the Holy See with Niccolo and Maffeo Polo as deputy-envoy. The envoy was frustrated on the way because of a disease and its credentials were delivered Polo brothers. They continued to travel by land and reached Acre (today's North of Haifa in Israel) in 1269, intending to meet the Pope. But the Pope Clement IV died and the new Pope has not yet ascended the throne, consequently they had to return to Venice.

Marco Polo was 15 years old when his father returned back from China. In 1271, Polo brothers together with son Marco Polo, visited the new Pope Gregoire X in Acre. The Pope ordered them—Marco Polo and his elders—to return to Yuan Dynasty together with two priests who were conveyed the credentials and letters to Kublai. Due to fear from difficulty, the priests returned back from Armani (Armenia) in the half-way and delivered the credentials and letters to the family of Marco Polo. Then Marco Polo family traveled via Il Khanate to the Persian Gulf, planning to go to Yuan Dynasty by sea. They changed their minds later and went to the East by land. They drove along the ancient Silk Road, through Samarkand in Uzbekistan, the Pamirs, and Badakhshan in Tajikistan, finally arrived in Kashi (Kashgar) region of Xinjiang, which was under the Yuan Dynasty. At that time the trade routes in Southern foot of the Tianshan were cut off by the rebels, they had to be Westbound by Kashi, along the Taklimakan desert, passed Yecheng, Khotan (current Hotan), Ruoqiang, reached Shangdu in 1275.

According to the travel notes of Marco Polo, he was well-received by Kublai, and became an official in Yuan Dynasty. He had been ordered to travel around the country, and went to manyregions in China. Many Chinese cities were mentioned in, such as Dadu, Shangdu, Jingzhao (current Xi'an), Chengdu, Dali, Jinan, Yangzhou, Zhenjiang, Hangzhou, Fuzhou, Quanzhou, and the customs of these regions. Some of the major political events in Yuan Dynasty were recorded, such as the rebellion of Haidu and Naiyan, Acmat incident and so on. Most of them were generally consistent with the records of other literature. On the other hand, there are abundant versions and is many parts with hyping in his narrative.

The Family of Marco Polo lived in China for a long time and missed their hometown. In 1289, Arghun, the Khan of Il Khanate, sent envoys to Yuan Dynasty asking for marriage because of the death of his princess. Kublai ordered Cocacin to marry Arghun, and the Marco Polo family could go with the envoys via Persian to Italy. So they left Quanzhou at the beginning of 1291 sailing on the sea for two years and two months, traveled through Sumatra and India, and reached Hormuz. Arghun had died at that time and his brother Gaykhatu ascended to the throne. Gaykhatu married Cocacin in 1293. The Marco Polo family left the capital of Il Khanate, through Constantinople (Istanbul) by boat, finally arrived in Venice in 1295.

In 1296, Marco Polo was captured in the naval battles between Venice and Genoa. While imprisoned in Genoa, Marco Polo has told the story of his travels to a fellow prisoner named Rusticiano, a man from Pisa, Italy, who wrote in the romantic style of 13th Century literature in 1298. A combination of Marco Polo's gift of observation and the magnificent writing style of Rusticiano was apparent in the final version, i.e., the book "Travels of Marco Polo". The book included Polo's personal remembrances as well as stories related to him by others. In the summer of the same year, Marco Polo's book was published in Italy. He died in 1324 and was buried in St. Lauren church.

The original manuscript of The Travels of Marco Polo was written in medieval French–Italian, but it has been lost after making private copies repeatedly and being translated into various European languages. There are about 140 kinds of publications of it in different languages. Among them, the (Zelada) Latin transcripts collected in Spain is the earliest and most complete among others, and its handwritten manuscripts version of Paris B.N.F. (Bibliotheque

National de France). collected in the National Library of Paris is closest to the original manuscripts. Today, the book's existing versions and its translations to different languages are more than 120, among which the English translation published by Pelliot and Muller in 1938 is the best. In China there are four Chinese versions of the "Travels of Marco Polo".

The Travels of Marco Polo has made a great influence in Italy. In the early 14h century, the ruler of Verona in Northern Italy called himself Can Grande. This title means Khan which has been obviously influenced by The Travels of Marco Polo. Many Europeans thought the pasta popular in Italy were introduced by Marco Polo. Before the end of the middle ages, Marco Polo's travels had always been one of the main sources of Europeans' understanding about the East. Many famous navigators had read the book before the great geographical discovery. Because of the record of Marco Polo, Columbus sailed Eastward attempting to reach Japan, and finally discovered America.

Due to the rapid development of exchanges between the East and West, it was not accidental that Macro Polo came to China. At that time, the Italians who came to China were not only Marco Polo. He was only one of the world's travelers who had the honor to leave their names in history. For example, the Latin epitaph of the Genoese, Kadlin (female) and Antonio in Yuan Dynasty was found in Yangzhou in the 1950s.

(2) Missionary work of Odoric

Odoric von Pordenone was born around 1286 in Northern Italy. He was a Franciscan missionary and lived a poor life as a Islam dervish in his early years. He lived only on water and bread, traveled with bare feet, refused to ascend in the church, and was willing to live in seclusion. This dervish kind of life has greatly helped him in his later long and arduous travel. He and Marco Polo, Ibn Battuta, Nicolo Conti together, are praised by the Westerners as "the Four Major Travelers in the Middle Ages". His influence trails only that of Marco Polo.

He insisted his journey even when he was unhealthy, and written by Friar William in plain Latin, consequently some parts of the text are out of order. According to current researches, his Eastern journey was as follows: from Constantinople to Trebizond (Trabzon), and then to the Il Khanate, Baghdad and Ormuz. Later, he sailed through Malabar, Chola, Sri Lanka, then took another ship to sail cross the Bay of Bengal, through Sumatra, Java, Zhancheng, arrived in Censcalan (current Guangzhou in China). When he reached Guangzhou, he marched northwards to Quanzhou, Fuzhou, Hangzhou, and Nanjing, finally arrived at Dadu (Beijing). He lived in Dadu for three years. In those days, Giovanni di Monte Corvino was the bishop in Dadu. Three years later, Odoric left Dadu, traveled through Shanxi, Shaanxi, Gansu, Tibet, Central Asia, and Persia, returned to Italy. Odoric had died in 1331.[27]

---

27 East Tour of Odoric, He Gaoji translation, Zhonghua Book Company, 1981.

Odoric von Pordenone has narrated that there were Nestorians and the Jews around Kaulam, which are in consonance with the literature of Yuan Dynasty. He also mentioned that the Mongol army had lost the battle against the Java kingdom.

Many his descriptions of China are quite consistent and trustworthy, such as the snake dishes in Guandong, Catholic monastery in Quanzhou, lots of bridges and Catholics who were called Frank Rabban in Hangzhou, luxurious life of the great landlord in Jiangnan, domesticated osprey for fishing in Eastern China, the walls and the Yangtze River in Nanjing, Qionghua Island in Dadu, the sea of liquor in Yuan Court, the status of different churches in Yuan Dynasty, the celestial burial in Tibet, the dresses of Mongolian women, the customs of Shangdu, the imperial bodyguard and the Chinese duct of Yuan Dynasty and so on. There are many transcripts about Odoric's travels. Guo Dongchen, who studied in Italy, translated these into a Chinese book in 1879 then published it in Wuchang Zongzheng academy. Later, one weekly publication in Hongkong reprinted the book, but deleted the notes. The activities of Odoric had certain influence on missionary work in China during the Qing Dynasty.

(3) Giovanni da Montecorvino and Catholicism

Giovanni da Montecorvino was born in Salerno province, which located in Southern Italy. Later he attended Franciscan and became a priest. He participated in the Franciscan mission in Armenia and Persia around 1280. In 1289, he returned to the Vatican and reported the news that Arghun gave the Christians preferential treatment. At that time Pope Nicholas IV had received Arghun's envoy Rabban Sauma, so Nicholas IV also believed this news. Therefore the Pope ordered Giovanni da Montecorvino as the envoy to do missionary work in China with credentials. Giovanni de Montecarvino first came to Tabriz and India, then sailed to China. In 1294, he arrived in Dadu accompanied by Italian Peter and presented the credentials to the emperor of Yuan Dynasty. They stayed in Dadu later.

Giovanni da Montecorvino wrote 2 letters to his uppers and colleagues in January 1305 and February 1306 respectively, which included his missionary achievements and which narrated about the customs of Yuan Dynasty. The envoy has carried his first letter to Franciscan Catholics in Crimea, and then the latter was delivered to Holy See (center of world Catholicism in Vatican) a. The second letter was conveyed to Rome by Italian Thomas who had been to China, before. He described the progress of his, i.e., the Roman mission in the Far East. In spite of Nestorian opposition; alluding to the Roman Catholic community he had founded in India, and to an appeal he had received to preach in "Ethiopia" and dealing with overland and oversea routes to "Cathay," from the Black Sea and the Persian Gulf respectively.

It is 12 years since I have had any news of the papal court, or of our order, or of the state of affairs generally in the West. Two years ago indeed there came hither a certain Lombard...surgeon, who spread abroad in these parts the most incredible blasphemies about the court of Rome and our order and the state of things in the West, and on this account I exceedingly desire to obtain true intelligence. I pray the brethren whom this letter may reach to do their possible to bring its contents to the knowledge of our lord the pope and the cardinals, and the agents of the order at the court of Rome...

I have myself grown old and gray, more with toil and trouble than with years; for I am not more than fifty-eight. I have got a competent knowledge of the language and character which is most generally used by the Tatars. And I have already translated into that language and character the New Testament and the Psalter, and have caused them to be written out in the fairest penmanship they have; and so by writing, reading, and preaching, I bear open and public testimony to the Law of Christ."

According to Giovanni da Montecorvino, the rulers of the Yuan Dynasty had received him well, and given him a special room and seat in the palace. He enjoyed the right to enter the palace since he was the envoy sent by the Pope in Vatican. The emperor of the Yuan Dynasty had already heard about the Holy See (center of world Catholicism in Vatican) and the European countries and was affirmative to receive such religious missionary envoys. The main obstacle to his missionary work was the Nestorian Church and its believers. In the first five years of his arrival, Nestorian Church actively resisted missionary work. He was not allowed to enter into his own church and preach the Catholic doctrine. But, Giovanni da Montecorvino removed all the difficulties to build the first Catholic Church, and later built a bell tower with three bells. Armenians in Dadu[28] also established a church, which was possibly an Orthodox Church.

Later, Italian businessman Lucalongo purchased a piece of land nearby the Chinese imperial palace, Giovanni de Montecorvino received the land in the early August 1305 and built the second church with the money raised from benefactors. This church had walls, houses and a church with a red cross which could host 200 people. The two churches were about 4 km away from each other. According to the location of the imperial palace, this temple should be located in Fuchengmen street a neighborhood of Beijing. From the letter we can see that the missionaries could not build Gothic-style stone houses, so the churches should be the Chinese style building with brick- wood construction. Giovanni da Montecorvino learned Mongolian, and then translated the New Testament and the psalms of prayer. He bought 40 boys and taught them to pray. These boys were divided into the two churches, and he went to one church every other week. He was baptized for about 6,000 believers, mainly the Onguds and the Alans. The Khan of Ongud tribe who was named as Korguz (George) who originally believed in Nestorianism had also converted to Catholicism, and Korguz's son was named as John after Saint John, which is the original name of Giovanni da Montecorvino. In addition, Korguz Khan also built the Catholic

---

28   Khanbaliq or Dadu was the capital of the Yuan dynasty, the main center of the Mongol Empire founded by Kublai Khan in what is now Beijing.

Church in his own fief. By his call, the people of Onguds tribe confederation had converted to Catholicism. But some Ongud nobles opposed converting to Catholicism, and after the death of Korguz, the Onguds had converted to Nestorianism. As we know, the name of Korguz's son was Shu An, which is the pronunciation of the word "John" in the Turkic language.

In the first 11 years of his stay in China, no envoys came from the Holy See till 1305. Then Arnold, a Catholic, came to Dadu (Beijing) to help him. In 1307 the Pope Clement V. appointed him as the archbishop and sent 7 priests to help him in China. Unfortunately, only three of them came to Dadu: Gerardo Albuini, Peregrino de Castello and Andreas de Perusio. The livelihood of these missionaries was maintained by the government. In 1328, Giovanni di Monte Corvino died in Dadu (Beijing).

Giovanni da Montecorvino set up a diocese in the Quanzhou city and appoint-ed Geraldo as the first bishop of it. A wealthy Armenian woman in Quanzhou donated a church land and funds to Geraldo. After the death of Geraldo, Palegelino succeeded the bishop of Quanzhou, where he had three Catholics from the Western Regions. Palegelino died in Quanzhou in 1322, so Andreas succeeded. Andreas built a new church in the outskirts of Quanzhou. There were 4 rooms of this new church and 20 priests could live in its living quarter. Andreas was buried in Quanzhou after his death, and his epitaph written in Latin was found in 1945. Although remains of his writing are vague, part of the text is still readable: "here is buried Andreas... 1xx2 years." The date of seal cutting has fallen off, but it also could be estimated for 1332, because Andreas once wrote a letter to his friends in 1326. The letters of Giovanni di Monte Corvino, Palegelino and Andreas are still in existence, which are important documents to study Chinese and foreign cultural exchanges. From their letter, we learned about the activities of many Europeans and Xiyu People in China during the Yuan Dynasty.

(4) Ibn Battuta

Ibn Battuta (1304-1377) was born in Tangier, Morocco. He left his home-town and made a pilgrimage journey to holy Mecca in 1325. Then he travelled to various countries and visited the holy Mecca three times. He once travelled through Persia, the Arabian Peninsula and North Africa. In 1332, Ibn Battuta started from Mecca, via Egypt, Syria, Little Asia, Black Sea, Crimea, into Kipchak Khanate. In the same year, he accompanied the princess of Kipchak Khanate to visit the parents of the princess in Constantinople. When he re-turned to the capital of Kipchak Khanate, Ibn Battuta continued Eastward to the Kipchak grasslands, Bolara (Bukhara) and other cities in Chagatai Khanate, then arrived in Delhi in 1333. He stayed in Delhi for 8 years and was called "Master of Ha Di" (the Judge). In 1342 emperor of Yuan Dynasty sent the en-voys to Delhi, and Ibn Battuta was ordered to pay a return visit to China with these envoys.They started from Calicut port and fell into distress shortly after the sailing began. The envoys of Yuan Dynasty fled to Kaulam and returned to China by boat. Ibn Battuta survived and did not leave the ship, but he lost many of his attendants and gifts and was unable to return to Delhi. Hence he traveled to the Maldives islands, Ceylon, Malabar and other regions. Later, he traveled by a ship from Bengal (current Bangladesh) to Java, and then sailed to Quanzhou, China. Ibn Battuta was lucky enough to meet the envoys of Yuan Dynasty in Quanzhou. These envoys help him report to the court through the local officials. When he was waiting for the orders, he traveled to Guangzhou. After returning to Quanzhou, he was ordered to the North. After his arrival in Hangzhou, Ibn Battuta turned back to Quanzhou again and took the boat back to his hometown. In the "Travels of Ibn Battuta", he mentioned the use of silver ingots and banknotes, government agency which was responsible for the rearrangement of banknotes, concentrated regions of Hui people in Chinese cities, handing portraits of prisoners for searching, inspection system of sea boat going out to sea and coming back. He also indicated that the Chinese people used coal as fuel. What's more, he mentioned the leader of Hui people in Quanzhou, which has been confirmed by Pure Temple in the late Yuan Dynasty. There were also some false descriptions of China in Travels of Ibn Battuta. For example, he said that he has been to Dadu, but from his description we can understand that he had never been there.

After he left Quanzhou, Ibn Battuta travelled to Java and Samalanga, and then arrived in India in 1347. Later he went back to his hometown via the east coast of the Arab peninsula, the Persian Gulf, Syria and other regions. On his way home he went for a pilgrimage to Mecca again, and in 1349 he returned to Fez, the capital of Morocco. Since then, Ibn Battuta traveled to Spain and to central Africa. In 1354, the King of Morocco ordered him to come back to Fez to dictate his travel records, and then chronicled his travels for a book in Arabic with the help of a court officer.[29]

His travel notes include important materials for studying the history and culture of the Eastern countries in the first half of the 14th century.

4. Cultural Exchanges and Overseas Trade

The advanced Sino-foreign transportation systems in the Yuan Dynasty period created excellent conditions for cultural and trade exchanges between the East and the West. Many Chinese traveled abroad with the expeditions launched by the Yuan Dynasty, and they have delivered the Chinese culture to distant lands. The highly developed navigation technology has caused the rapid growth of Sino-foreign trade. Many people in Western Regions entered into Yuan Dynasty territory for official, business, missionary and travel reasons. Many of them settled down in China, bringing exotic objects and civilizations. A distinct feature of Yuan Empire different other dynasties was that it has been a global empire. And cultural and trade exchanges between the East and the West during this period also demonstrate global characteristics.

---

29   Ma Jinpeng, trans., Travels of Ibn Battuta, Ningxia People's Publishing House, 1985.

(1) Jami al-tawarikh and the Chinese History

The Mongol empire had expanded to the vast Western Regions and settled there, establishing Il Khanate, Kipchak Khanate and Chagatai Khanate. Ilkhanate ruled the land of Persia, whose rulers had similar kinship with the rulers of the Yuan Dynasty. Their father was Thore (Tolui Khan), the 4th son of Genghis Khan. Therefore, the relationship between Yuan government and the Il khanate was much closer compared to other bilateral relation in that period. Abundant envoys from the both sides had traveled by land and sea.

The founder of Il Khanate, Hulagu Khan, was the brother of Kublai. His descendants would still have to be conferred by the Yuan Dynasty when they inherited the throne. When Ghazan Khan Mahmud ruled Il Khanate, the Mongols who settled in Persia gradually became more Islamic and Turkic. So Hulagu Khan organized the compilation of Jami al-tawarikh for the preservation of their own history. Jami al-tawarikh was a Persian literature, the literal translation of its title is "The Collection of Histories". It is an unprecedented masterpiece which consists of three parts. Each of the part includes a number of chapters. The content of the books is as follows:

History of Mongolia
Tribal Chronicles (history of Mongolia before Genghis Khan).
Chronicles of Genghis Khan (history of Genghis Khan's ancestors and his own deeds)
Genghis Khan's successors (described the descendants of Genghis Khan, including the Kipchak Khanate, Chagatai Khanate, Ogedei Khanate and the history of Yuan Dynasty before early years of Emperor Yuan Chengzong.

History of Il Khanate (history of the Mongolians in Persia before the rule of Ghazan Khan Mahmud)
World History
History of Israel (the story of Genesis in the Bible).
Turkic history (the history of Ugu Khan and the Turkic speaking tribes).
History of Frank (Frenk European History)
Indian History
Chinese History

1. Five lineages (the lineage of Mongols and other important nationalities)

We can see from above that Jami al-tawarikh has been the greatest comprehensive historical encyclopedia in the world before modern times.

Chinese history written by Rashid al-Din is the first Persian book to describe Chinese history in detail. He introduced the history of Qidan (Liao) and the Song Dynasty, earlier than History of Liao and History of Song presided by Tuotuo during the Yuan Dynasty. Later, he introduced ancient lineage of Chinese emperors until his time, including Liao, Jin and Southern Song Dynasty.

"The 1st dynasty", included the 1st Emperor Pangu and his descendants, such as the Heavenly Sovereign, Earthly Sovereign and Human Sovereign, totaling 10 people;

"The 2nd dynasty", included the 11th Emperor Fu Xi, his sister Nuwa, and their descendants, totaling 16 people;

"The 3rd dynasty", included the 27th Emperor Shennong and his descendants, totaling 16 people;

"The 4th dynasty", included the 33th Emperor Huang Di and his descendants, totaling 18 people;

"The 5th dynasty", included the 53rd Emperor Shao Hao and his descendants, totaling 10 people;

"The 6th dynasty", included the 63rd Emperor Gao Yang and his descendants, totaling 10 people;

"The 7th dynasty", included the 73rd Emperor Gao Xin and his descendants, totaling 10 people;

"The 8th dynasty", included the 82nd Emperor Yao;

"The 9th dynasty", included the 83rd Emperor Shun;

"The 10th dynasty", included the 84th Emperor Yu and his descendants, totaling 17 people, this is the Xia Dynasty.

"The 11th dynasty", included the 101st Emperor Tang and his descendant, totaling 30 people, this is the Shang Dynasty;

"The 12th dynasties", included the 130th King Wu of Zhou and his descendants, totaling 37 people, this is the Zhou Dynasty;

"The 13th dynasty", that is, the Warring States period;

"The 14th dynasty", included the 133rd emperor Qin Shi Huang and his descendants, totaling 3 people, that was the Qin Dynasty;

"The 15th dynasty", included the 136th emperor- the Conqueror, this is Xiang Yu;

"The 16th dynasties", included the 137th Emperor Gaozu of Han and his descendants, totaling a 13 people, this is the Western Han Dynasty;

"The 17th dynasty", about Wang Mang;

"The 18th dynasty", included the 151st Emperor Gengshi and his descendants, totaling 2 people;

"The 19th dynasty", included the 152nd Emperor Guangwu of Han and his descendant, totaling 14 people, this is the Eastern Han Dynasty;

"The 20th dynasty", that is the Three Kingdoms;

"The 21st dynasty", included the 171st Emperor Wu of Jin and his descendants, totaling 3 people, this is the Western Jin Dynasty;

"The 22nd dynasty", included the 174th Emperor Yuan of Jin and his descendants, totaling 11 people, this is the Eastern Jin Dynasty;

"The 23rd dynasty", included the 185th Emperor Wu of Song and his descendants, totaling 8 people, this is the Liu Song Dynasty;

"The 24th dynasty", included the 193rd Emperor Xiao Daocheng and his descendants, totaling 7 people, this is the Southern Qi Dynasty;

"The 25th dynasty", included the 200th Emperor Wu of Liang and his descendants, totaling 4 people, this is the Southern Liang Dynasty;

"The 26th dynasty", included the 204th Emperor Xuan of Liang and his descendants, totaling 4 people, this is the Late Liang Dynasty period;

"The 27th dynasty", included the 207th Emperor Wu of Chen and his descendants, totaling 5 people, this is the Chen Dynasty;

Chinese history of Rashid al-Din regards the South Dynasty as orthodox. After the Western Jin Dynasty, the Northern history is not narrated consistently. He divided it into several parts: the 1st group of Sixteen Kingdoms, the 2nd group of Northern Wei Dynasty, the 3rd group of Eastern Wei Dynasty and Western Wei Dynasty, the 4th group of Northern Zhou Dynasty and the 5th group of Northern Qi Dynasty. The details are as follows:

The 1st group of Sixteen Kingdoms: In the North, the first occupied region was "Liang", containing five kings-Zhang Gui, Wu Gu, Li Gao, Meng Xun and Lu Guang. The second was "Yan" in Cambaliech, containing 4 kings-Murong people like Murong De, Feng Ba and another king. The third is "Qin" in Jing Zhao (Shaanxi), containing three kings-Fu Jian, Yao Chang and Qi Fu. The fourth is "Zhao" in Ahe Bali (Hebei, Zhen Ding), containing two kings-Liu Yuan, Shi Le. The 5th king is Helian Bobo in Xia Dynasty in Tibetan region. The 6th king is Li Te in Shu Dynasty in the land of barbarians (namely the South regions of China);

The 2nd group of Northern Wei Dynasty: Emperor Daowu of Northern Wei and his descendants, totaling 13 people;

The 3rd group of Eastern Wei Dynasty and Western Wei Dynasty: Emperor Xiaojing of Eastern Wei and Emperor Wen of Western Wei;

The 4th group of Northern Zhou Dynasty: Emperor Xiaomin of Northern Qi and his descendants, totaling 5 people;

The 5th group of Northern Qi Dynasty: Emperor Wenxuan of Northern Zhou and his descendants, totaling 5 people.

After the introduction of the Sixteen Kingdoms and the Northern Dynasties, Rashid al-Din resumed the dynasty order. Chen Dynasty ranked 27th dynasty, so the Sui Dynasty became the 28th dynasty:

"The 28th dynasty", included the 212nd Emperor Gaozu of Sui and his descendants, totaling 3 people, this is the Sui Dynasty;

"The 29th dynasty", included the 215th Emperor Gaozu of Tang and his descendants, totaling 22 people, this is Tang Dynasty;

"The 30th dynasty", included the 237th Emperor Taizu of Liang and his descendants, totaling 3 people, this is Later Liang Dynasty;

"The 31st dynasty", included the 240th Emperor Zhuangzong of Tang and his descendants, totaling 4 people, this is the later Tang Dynasty;

"The 32nd dynasty", included the 244th Emperor Gaozu of Jin and his son, totaling 2 people, this is Later Jin Dynasty period;

"The 33rd dynasty": Yelu De Guang in Qidan usurped the throne of the Later Jin Dynasty;

"The 34th dynasty", included Emperor Gaozu of Han and his son, this is the Later Han Dynasty;

"The 35th dynasty", included Emperor Taizu of Zhou and his descendants, this is Later Zhou dynasty;

"The 36th dynasty", included Emperor Taizong of Song and his descendants, totaling 16 people, this is Song Dynasty.

After Song Dynasty, Rashid al-Din described the history of Jin Dynasty: Emperor Taizong of Jin and his descendants, totaling 9 people.

From the above content, it can be seen that the Chinese history is a rare book. It reflects the truth of Chinese culture spreading Westward with the establishment of Mongolian Empire. Although there are some mistakes about the name of the Chinese emperors and their historical chronology, it still reflects the extent to which Persian and Western intellectuals knew about Chinese history. It is really a brilliant flower during the cultural exchanges between China and foreign countries in Yuan Dynasty.

(2) The Spread of Gunpowder

Before the invention of gunpowder, the main components of Chinese incendiary weapons for war were rosin, mugwort, oil, sulfur and so on. The firearms have already appeared during the Zhou Dynasty period. Around the 4th Century BC, the Greeks began to use fire weapons. Later this technology was delivered to the Arabs by Romans and Byzantines. The Arabs called it "Greek fire", which contained petroleum and naphtha. During the Five Dynasties period, the "Greek Fire" spread into China and was translated as the "fire oil". Chinese people have noticed the violent fiery nature of such a firearm in water. Before the invention of gunpowder, none of the fire weapons had nitrate in them. The so-called "Greek fire" was a sticky liquid, and had no resemblance with the modern gunpowder. Gunpowder was first invented by Taoist alchemists. In the 9th century, an alchemy book, a Taoist book, Zhen yuan miao Dao yao lue (Classified Essentials of the Mysterious Tao) of around 850 CE, warned "not to mix certain ingredients, including sulfur, saltpeter, and other ingredients, because the mixture had been known to flame up, can burn hands and houses". The book warned that nitrite must not be burned with sulfur, realgar and orpiment. Or else "it would be a curse". During the end period of the Tang Dynasty, the gunpowder which was used in military and the artillery was yet a powder bag launched by trebuchets[30].

During Song Dynasty period, the formula of the black powder recorded in the book of Wu Jing was very close to the modern one. In those days, the explosive firearm "bang fireballs" appeared, including addition of porcelain chips in powder, which greatly increased its lethality. During the Jin Dynasty period, the power of explosive firearm has been enhanced, which can penetrate cowhide and armor. At the end of Jin Dynasty, there were also tubular emission firearms. The gunpowder of China has spread overseas at a very early time. In Yuan

---

30 Trebuchets were machines of war that were deadly in sieges of castles and other battles. They grew and evolved to fit their environment as time passed, and they traveled all over Asia and Europe. They were extremely popular for sieges and defense of castles. The trebuchet traveled throughout the cultures of Eurasia. It was first made by the Chinese to help with military strength and strategy.

Dynasty, Zhou Daguan paid a visit to Zhenla (current Cambodia), and saw people there set off fireworks. Chinese exports to Zhenla were sulphur, nitrate and other raw materials which could be used to make gunpowder. The Gunpowder did not only spread into Southeast Asia, but also reached the Western world. The Western countries have not only imported Chinese gunpowder products, but also learned to make gunpowder according to the formula. In the middle of 13th century, Arabs began to make gunpowder. From 13th century to 14th century, a book called Burn Enemies and Fire Attack written in Arabic contains how to make gunpowder and firearms. The nitrate used in producing gunpowder had been an important export commodity of ancient China. In 1240, the book Synopsis of Single Drug written by a Tajik doctor Ibnal Baytar mentioned saltpeter, and called it "Chinese snow" (Thaij Sini). While Persians called it "Chinese Salt (namak Chini). This shows that although Persians and Arabs could produce gunpowder, yet one of the main raw material-nitrate was originally imported from China.

(3) Exports of Ceramics

The hard pottery or proto-porcelain of the Pre-Qin Period was painted with ash glaze by using iron as the colorant. During the middle period of the Eastern Han Dynasty, greenish-brown potteries painted with lead glaze appeared. Copper or iron was used as colorant in the production of this new kind of pottery about which we cannot trace its roots in ancient China. However it was similar to the greenish-brown potteries of Roman Empire which had once controlled the regions in the east of Mediterranean sea. China's ceramics industry probably learned this coloring technique in its exchanges with the Roman Empire and accepted its aesthetic view.[31] After the Tang Dynasty, with the rapid development of maritime exchanges between the East and the West, China's exports also increased rapidly. Many Chinese goods found vast markets in overseas. Porcelain was the new rising exported bulk products in the 8th century. Ceramics of Tang Dynasty was known as "Southern Green and Northern White", both the green porcelains and white porcelains were highly developed. The green porcelain of Yue Zhou, Changsha and other regions poured into the international market. According to the archaeological discoveries, large amount of porcelains in Guangdong Province were exported to other regions, which made Guangdong a significant base to manufacture porcelains for export trade, thus forming the export-oriented ceramics industry in Guangdong. Of the 22 ceramics kiln sites of Tang Dynasty found in modern times, 8 were used to produce porcelains for export trade, accounting for 36% of the total number of the kilns. Built in coastal regions, 2 of them were in Eastern Guangdong (one in the North of Chaozhou and the other in Shuiche of Meixian district), 4 in the central regions of Guangdong (Nanhan district, Guanchong in Xinhui district, Sanshui district, and Xicun of Guangzhou), and 2 in the West of Guangdong (Liangjiang city and Suixi county).[32]

---

31 Mikami Tsugio, Ceramics Road, ed. 1984, Cultural Relics Press, p. 12.
32 Ceramic Unearthed from Kiln Sites of Tang and Song Dynasty in Guangdong, Hangkong Feng Pingshan Museum, 1985, p. 11.

According to archaeological findings in foreign countries, pot with crest spout made in the kiln of Guangzhou Xicun in the Tang Dynasty was unearthed in Southeast Asia and the Philippines. Zhang Weichi, Hu Xianman: On Ancient Sino-Philippines Relations from Unearthed Ceramic, in Papers on Ceramics of Jingdezhen, Volume 1. Archaeologists in Bangkok Thailand also excavated products of Shuiche kiln in Meixian district.[33] As I was on the "Maritime Silk Road" investigation tour in Thailand at the end of 1990, I have seen many porcelain shards in the coastal region of Laem Pho (Chaiya)—Gulf of Thailand). These porcelain shards were produced by Changsha Tongguan Kiln Site during the Tang Dynasty period. I have seen them in Changwat Surat Thani town (Changwat province) in the Siam Bay that is in the south of Thailand and this town is six miles away from Laem Pho (Chaiya). On the other hand, numerous Islamic style potteries were discovered at the river mouth where the Takuapa River in Phang Nga Province pours into the Andaman Sea. It is can be seen from the map that the Malay Peninsula extends southward from the south of Thailand to the two oceans. It is still a natural boundary of the two oceans, the Pacific Ocean and the Indian Ocean. The Siam Bay, in the east of the Malay Peninsula is the sub-sea of the Western Pacific- and the Andaman Sea is the sub-sea of the eastern Indian Ocean. The straight-line bird-fly distance between Andaman Sea and Siam Bay is short, but the maritime expedition is not so short, because ships have to sail around the long peninsula to go from the one place to the other, thus increases the distance, risks, and cost. The narrowest part of Malay peninsula is less than 40 km., so a route trade which depended on the water-and-land coordinated journey emerged, i.e., Siam Bay, Malay Peninsula, and Andaman Sea. Laem Pho port and Takupa river mouth ports were ports of transshipment at the two sides of the peninsula.

It can be inferred from the two sites that the Pacific-Indian Ocean trades at that time were not all direct ones, but a considerable part were indirect trade. At the end of Tang Dynasty many Chinese maritime merchants sold potteries and porcelains to overseas countries, but they did not sail their merchant ships directly to India and Western Asia, instead they anchored their ships at port like Laem Pho which is in the Siam Bay. Chinese merchants loaded their ships with Indian goods brought by the local merchants who had sailed around the Malay peninsula before they returned to China. In the same way, merchants from India and Western Asia would unload their ships at port like Takuapa after crossing the Bay of Bengal, and loaded the Chinese goods which had traveled around the Malay peninsula down the edge of Siam Bay into their ships and returned back to China.

Other ports which acted as the transshipment ports of the East-west sea route in the west of Malay peninsula were Sri Lanka and Southern India. There were several important trading ports in Sri Lanka, such as Mantai in the northwest, Sambalturai in the North, Trincomalee in the Northeast, Godavaya in the south,

33 Guangdong Museum: Report on Research and Excavation o Ancient Tombs and Ancient Kilns in Guangdong, Journal of Archaeology, Issue 1987/3.

Sinigama in the Southwest, and Colombo in the West in the late Medieval Ages, etc. The Mantai peninsula which was located in the Northeast of Sri Lanka and near the South Asian Subcontinent was the most significant one among all the ports. A large amount of Chinese and Islamic style potteries and porcelains around the 11th century were discovered in Mantai. The earliest ceramics among them were produced in the Tang Dynasty, such as tri-colored glazed pottery of the Tang Dynasty, celadon of Yue ware, Changsha Tongguan kiln's hard pottery and black-glazed porcelain, while among them the brownish-blue ceramic with white bottom was the earliest. The shapes of bowls found in Mantai were similar to those unearthed in the Tomb of Princess Yongtai. There were also many celadon shards in Mantai, which might be made in the middle of the Tang Dynasty.[34]

Malabar in the South of India and Sri Lanka were separated by the sea. Due to its geographical position, it was an important port of transshipment of the East-west sea route and a place where the Chinese potteries and porcelains were sold. Before the Medieval Ages, Chinese ceramics were seldom exported to India as Indian Saiva did not use plates or bowls. Instead they ate in a very simple way by putting food on a piece of leaf of Japanese banana on the ground and eating with hands other than tableware. As Islam was spread to India, many Indians changed their living habits. They began to use tables when they ate and put pottery and porcelain which were filled with food on the table. Therefore after the Song Dynasty, more and more Chinese ceramics were exported to India.[35]

499

According to the navigator Wang Dayuan, another place named "Da Ba Dan" was discovered after "Xi Yang" and merchants in Yuan Dynasty had traded in "Da Ba Dan". After the discovery of "Xi Yang", the Chinese regarded China as the center to name other regions that were to be discovered, so the navigation must have started from China and arrived in "Xi Yang" before "Da Ba Dan" was discovered. It can be inferred that "Da Ba Dan" was probably located in the coastal region near the West of "Xi Yang". It has been mentioned that "Xi Yang" was the Chinese name of the country Mabalar which was located in current Tamil Nadu state of India. Since "Da Ba Dan" was discovered after "Xi Yang", it should be also located near Tamil Nadu state of India. A professor of archaeology named Y. Subbarayalu in India's University of Madras found some Chinese Longquan celadon shards of the 13th-14th centuries and Jingdezhen's blue and white porcelain shards of the 14th century in a small village called Pariyapattinam in the coastal region of Southern India which faced the Mantai peninsula of Sri Lanka around the 1980s. Xin Daosheng, a professor in the University of Tokyo thought the village Pariyapattinam was "Da Ba Dan" as

34   P. L. Prematileke: Chinese Ceramics Discovered in Sri Lanka an Overview, in Papers on Sri Lanka and the Silk Road of the Sea, ed. by Senake Bandaranayake et. al., Colombo, 1990, pp. 233-237.
35   Xin Daosheng: Trade Relations between Southern India and China in the 13th-14th Centuries, recorded in East-west Sea Route Transportation, Ed 1989, Volume I, p. 61.

"pariya" meant "Da" (big) in Tamil and "Ba Dan" was the transliteration of "pattinam" which meant "port city". In 1987, Indian archaeologists excavated this village and found more than 1,000 shards of Chinese ceramics. Of these shards, the celadon accounted 60% (Longquan celadon 35%, Fujian celadon 25%), white ware 15% (Dehua white ware 10%, Jingdezhen white ware 5%), Jingdezhen blue and white porcelain 10%, brown-glazed porcelain 10%, and other ceramics 5%. The earliest shard was probably produced in Xingzhou in the 9th-10th centuries. In the middle period of Tang Dynasty, Chinese ceramics were exported to Western Asia and North Africa. The al Fustat (meaning "tent"), which sited in Egypt's capital Cairo, was a famous overseas place of discovering ancient potteries and porcelains. In the center of the site, more than 600,000-700,000 shards of ceramics were piled up like a mountain. Japanese archaeologists began to excavate this place since 1912 as Egypt government entrusted Japanese scholars to investigate the unearthed shards. The Japanese scholars not only differentiated shards of the Far East with those of Syria, Iran, Italy, and Spain from the imported shards, they also found shards that imitated the Chinese ones from the local shards in Egypt.

According to statistics by Japanese scholars Koyama Fujio and Mikami Tsugio, except for Egyptian pottery shards, the around 12,000 shards of Chinese ceramics were the most, accounting for 1/50-1/60 of all the shards discovered. There were also products from Thailand, Vietnam, and Imari of Japan among the ceramic shards of the Far East. The time of the Chinese shards ranged from the Tang Dynasty in the 8th -9th centuries to the Qing Dynasty, among which shards of tri-colored glazed pottery of the Tang Dynasty were the earliest. Moreover, there was also Xingzhou white ware, celadon of Yue ware, yellowish-brown-glazed porcelains, porcelains of Changsha Tongguan kiln, etc., while products of the Yue ware were the most. As for porcelains of the Song Dynasty, most of the porcelains discovered were shadowy blue ware and Longquan kiln porcelains. Most of the Chinese ceramics found in this place were made in Southern China while only a few were products of Northern China. For example, white ware of the Western Liao Dynasty (which were ptoduced in the North of China in history) indicated that China traded with the Red Sea (today Kuwait) region mainly via the ports located in southern China. Al Fustat was not the only place in Cairo-Egypt, where Chinese shards were discovered, but an example was Ba Darbal Mahruq Mountain where many Chinese shards were scattered around, including Longquan celadon of the Southern Song Dynasty, the Yuan Dynasty, and the Ming Dynasty and Jingdezhen bluish white porcelains, and blue and white porcelains of the Yuan, Ming, and Qing Dynasty.

The Chinese ceramics found in al Fustat were well-made, which impressed Japanese scholars who involved in the investigation. Of the celadon of Yue ware and yellowish-brown-glazed porcelains unearthed in al Fustat, those that were made in the same time were decorated with different patterns on the inner side, and there were a few pieced porcelains, all of which were elaborated products. A large number of shards of Yue ware were also discovered in the Peaceful Poolroom Site in the Hakata Kitakyushu of Japan, namely the Kōrokan in Japan during the end of Tang Dynasty and the Five Dynasties. These wares were probably precious tableware for foreign guests, but they were all stoneware without any patterns. Even the ornamental porcelains of Yue ware collected by Japanese collectors could seldom be compared with those unearthed in al Fustat. Moreover, products of Yue ware discovered in Nishapur Site of Eastern Iran, the coastal region of the Persian Gulf, and East Africa were mostly stoneware. Although the blue and white porcelain became popular at the end of Yuan Dynasty, its output was not high at that time. It was estimated by Japanese scholar Koyama Fujio that there were only 200 pieces of intact blue and white porcelains of the Yuan Dynasty worldwide, but hundreds of their shards were found in al Fustat, which the Japanese scholars believed showed that the economic development and imports in Egypt at that time greatly exceeded Japan and other regions.[36]

The Chinese ceramics in Fustat were resold to Alexandria at the mouth river of the Nile by merchants from Tazi, then to Maghrib (North Africa),regions along the Eastern coast of Mediterranean, and Europe. Iraq, the center of Abbasid Dynasty, was the main sales target regions of the Chinese potteries and porcelains in Western Asia. In the Song and Yuan Dynasty, Chinese porcelains were constantly exported to this region. In this century, several large-scale investigations and excavations had been conducted in Samarra (the capital city of Abbasid Dynasty from 836 to 892) which was 120 miles North of Baghdad. The Chinese shards discovered were bowls and plates of the tri-colored glazed pottery of the Tang Dynasty, green-glazed and yellow-glazed porcelain pots, and white ware and celadon, most of which belonged to late Tang Dynasty, the Five Dynasties, and the Song Dynasty and were products of Yue ware in 9th -10th century. In Southeastern Baghdad, archaeologists also found shards of brown porcelains of Yue ware and white ware of Southern China. Mikami Tsugio, The Ceramics Road, Cultural Relics Press, 1984, p. 82. Longquan celadon shards of the 12th-13th centuries were also discovered in the Ctesiphon site which was 35 miles South of Baghdad. In Wasit, 70 miles Southeast of Kut in Iraq, celadon shards of the Southern Song Dynasty with edges on the outside and Longquan celadon shards of the Yuan Dynasty with patterns in the inside and center were unearthed.

501

In the other regions of Abbasid Dynasty and Il Khanate and its neighboring regions in Mongolia times, traces of Chinese ceramic could also be found. In Syria, the investigation team from National Museum of Denmark excavated shards of white ware of the Yuan Dynasty, blue and white porcelain, and celadon from 1931 to 1938. Archaeologists regarded some of them as white ware shards of Dehua kiln in the Song Dynasty, shards of celadon with peony raised pattern of the Guan kilns of the Southern Song Dynasty, and shards of celadon with patterns in the inside and center produced in Longquan kiln of the Yuan

---

36   Mikami Tsugio, The Ceramics Road, Cultural Relics Press, 1984, pp. 14-16.

Dynasty. In Baalbek of the Beqaa Valley in Lebanon, researchers found shards of celadon with patterns of lotus petal in the Song Dynasty's Longquan kiln and shards of celadon with patterns of flowers and grass made in the Yuan Dynasty. Wang Dayuan mentioned in his "A Short Account on the Islands of the Barbarians" that blue and white porcelains were Chinese commodities that the Arabic countries needed. The archaeological discoveries in Persian region and the South of Arabic Peninsula verified Wang Dayuan's records. In Bahrain, researches have collected 28 fragments of celadon and 58 fragments of blue and white porcelain in the mosque site and the coastal region. Besides, Chinese shards were unearthed in many regions of Yemen and Oman in the South of Arabic Peninsula.

The Khorasan region, located in the East of Iran, had a close relationship with China since the ancient times. The Metropolitan Museum of Art in New York excavated the ancient city Nishapur three times, respectively in the year 1936, 1937, and 1939. A number of porcelains and broken ceramics were discovered, among which were white ware earthen bowls and broken bowls of the Tang Dynasty.[37] Moreover, Chinese copper currency (coin) of the Song Dynasty period were also unearthed in the Persian Gulf region. Located on the other side of Bahrain, Dhahran was near Qatif where copper coins were discovered, which were "Xianping Tongbao" (998-1003) and "Shaosheng Yuanbao" (1094-1097) of the Northern Song Dynasty and "Shaoding Yuanbao" (1228-1233) of the Southern Song Dynasty.

502

Pottery and porcelain were the most popular commodities among Western Asia and North Africa. Chinese ceramics were of high heat, hard texture, various kinds, beautiful shapes, and soft colors. However as it was difficult to transport for such a long distance, only a few wealthy families could afford Chinese ceramics. Appealed by the huge market, skillful craftsmen in Western Asia endeavored to study and imitate the popular Chinese ceramics. In the year 1936 and 1938, green-glazed, tri-colored glazed and yellowish-brown-glazed potteries were unearthed in Samarra of the Abbasid Dynasty in the 9th century. These were all imitated potteries made by local craftsmen according to Chinese pottery's styles and patterns, but they were not as hard as the Chinese potteries since the firing temperature was not high. Although they could not be compared to Chinese products, they were very welcome by families who could not afford the real ones.

In the Fatimid Caliphate, a craftsman named Sayyid finally succeeded in imitating after porcelains in the Song Dynasty. He formed his own school after training many disciples. They paid very attention to the changes in Chinese porcelains and constantly updated their imitations by making celadon and white ware at first, then blue and white porcelains after the Yuan Dynasty. The shapes and patterns of their porcelains were all made according to those of

---

37   Shen Weifu, History of Sino-Western Culture Exchanges, ed. 1985, Shanghai People's Publishing House, p. 208.

Chinese ones. Based on records by a Persian named Nasir Khusraw, these imitations were "so elaborated and transparent that people could see their hands through the porcelain".[38] From the ceramics found by archaeologists, we can understand that the imitation works produced after the 11th century were indeed quite similar to the genuine ones. Although the craftsmen in the Western Asia and North Africa left no stone unturned to imitate Chinese ceramics, their imitations were potteries rather than porcelains as the production of porcelains required two necessary conditions, one was the raw material porcelain clay which was a special kind of clay called kaolin clay. The other was the technique of firing kiln, since the heat needed for making porcelain is much higher than that of pottery. It was much more difficult to learn how to make Chinese porcelains than what it was seen from surface. These foreign craftsmen at that time were only intended to make what superficially looked like the Chinese porcelains, but they were not true porcelains, but potteries. China's blue and white porcelain used underglaze color technique which was painting blue pigment of cobaltous oxide before furnacing it in the kiln, then glazing it and mixing it into kiln once again. The color of products made under this procedure would never be washed off as the color was under the glaze. At first sight, the imitated celadon, bluish white porcelain, and blue and white porcelain made in Egypt were very similar to those of China in shape, color, and pattern, but their body was pottery which was softer than Chinese ones and the glaze was much thicker, like a layer of glass on the surface, and its quality could not be compared with Chinese ones. Despite that, the common people in Western Asia were satisfied with imitations as they loved Chinese porcelains but could not afford the genuine ones.

503

In the al-Fustat site of Egypt where shards were piled up like a mountain, 70%-80% were imitation shards. After coming to the Ming Dynasty, the Asia Minor of Ottoman Empire (1290-1922) became the new center of imitating Chinese blue and white porcelains. Products of this region were discovered in many regions in Western Asia and North Africa. The intact and precious ones were collected by many famous big museums, indicating an important stage of development of ceramics in the Islamic world. Discoveries in al-Fustat and the large amounts of Chinese porcelains imitations unearthed in Western Asia and North Africa showed the export of large quantities of Chinese porcelains changed the social aesthetic standard in Western Asia and North Africa as they regarded Chinese porcelains as their standard for porcelain making. Since then from the end of Tang Dynasty, imitating Chinese pottery became a tendency and a profitable industry in Western Asia and North Africa, and lasted for centuries. We have mentioned before that al-Fustat in Cairo Egypt was a famous ceramic collecting and distributing center in North Africa in 9th-12th centuries. A considerable amount of the Chinese ceramics in this place should have come from Aydhad which was located in current Red Sea coast of the Republic of Sudan in East Africa. According to records by traveler Ibn Jubayr

---

38   Philip K Hitti, History of the Arabs, Ed. 1979, The Commercial Press, p. 756.

in the latter half of 12th century, since the 10th century commercial ships from India to Egypt would have arrived in Aydhad first and most of the goods on the ships were Chinese porcelains. So far along the 2-mile stretching coastline of Aydhad, Chinese shards can be found everywhere. The earliest of these ceramics were in the late Tang Dynasty, and others were shards of celadon of Yue ware, Longquan celadon, white ware, bluish white porcelain, blue and white porcelain, and blackish-brown-glazed porcelain from the late Tang Dynasty to the early Ming Dynasty. Some shards of the simple and un-adorned blackish-brown-glazed pot were stamped with the following characters "Kou Qing Xiang" (meaning fragrance in your mouth), which confirms the reliability of the records. When the Chinese porcelains arrived in Aydhad, they were transported to Kusiti and Aswan in the middle reaches of the Nile. Ships from Kusiti kingdom could sail reverse upstream in the Nile river to Ethiopia; and from Aswan they could sail downward with the Nile to al-Fustat and the mouth of the Nile. Another important port of loading and unloading Chinese porcelains along Red Sea coast was Kusel in the South of Egypt which was 650 miles away from the mouth of Gulf of Suez. A large number of shards of porcelains of Yue ware in the late Tang and early Song Dynasty, Longquan celadon in the Song Dynasty, Jingdezhen bluish white porcelain, and blue and white porcelain can still be found up to now.

After the Tang and Song Dynasty periods, the Eastern African regions in the South of Cape Guardafui (current Somali) also became an important market place for selling Chinese ceramics. In many sites along the East Africa coast, there were so many Chinese shards piled up that they could even be excavated with a forklift. B. Davidson: Old Africa Rediscovered, London, 1960. These Chinese shards' discovery, collection, classification, and identification provided valuable materials for the study of Sino-Africa economy and culture history and history of East Africa's economic development. Some scholars even believed that "the history of East Africa was written by Chinese porcelains".[39]

504

There were numerous transshipment ports used for the export of Chinese ceramics in the coastal regions of East Africa in the medieval times. In Somalia, there were Berbera, Mogadishu, Kismayo, and some other islands. In Kenya, there were Manda Island, Lamu, Malindi, Kilifi, Mauna Lani, and Mombasa, etc. In one of these regions elaborated porcelain whose color was red copper was discovered and scholars believed it was a diplomatic gift.

In the coastal region of Tanzania, 46 sites of Chinese shards were discovered, mainly the Pemba Island, Mafia Island, and Kilwa, etc. In Kilwa, there were various porcelains including porcelains of Yue ware in the late Tang and early Song Dynasty. Beyond these, white ware bowl, blue and white porcelain with phoenix and creeping weed patterns, white ware with carving patterns, and many celadon in 14th-15th centuries were also discovered in Kilwa. What's more, blackish-brown-glazed pottery of Vietnam, Thailand Song Jialu celadon, and one fragment of Imari blue and white porcelain in 14th-15th centuries were

39   G.S. Freeman Grenville: The Medieval History of the Coast of Tanganika, Berlin, 1962.

also excavated in the coastal region of Tanzania.[40] Another vase was also discovered, which was of the same kind as that was discovered in Kenya, and its color were red copper and blue and white.[41]

Chinese porcelains were not only commodities, they were also architectural decorations. For example, in many ancient mosque sites of the coastal region in Kenya, there were Chinese porcelain bowls or plates on the wall at certain distance. In some mosques, the Chinese porcelains were decorated on the mosque dome of the hall. Even in Gondar which was far away from Ethiopia, the wall of Palace was also decorated with Chinese porcelains. It proved that there was a trend among the upper class in East Africa to use Chinese porcelains as building decorations in the Medieval Ages, and the trend was not only in the coastal region, but it was also spread to the inland of East Africa. Moreover, many tombstones in East Asia were decorated with Chinese porcelains of which the patterns were flowers, trees, fruits, fish, and birds and beasts. On the top of some of the tombstones was a Chinese porcelain pot, indicating that the dead can also be associated with the Chinese porcelain in another world was the greatest wish of their relatives.

(4) The Technological Exchanges of Refining Sugar

China has been the country where the sugar canes originated. In the course of long history, Chinese people had continuously compared native sugar canes with the foreign one, thus introducing new kinds of sweet sugar canes from Jiaozhi (northern Vietnam), Funan Kingdom and India. In the early times, Chinese people planted sugar canes to extract the juice. In the Three Kingdoms period (220-228 AD) of China, Sun Quan ordered his craftsmen to imitate the Jiaozhi's way to make the cane sugar. In that time, people directly boiled the juice of sugar canes into solid sugar form. Later, the way of refining sugar by using lime as clarifier in India entered China by the sea trade. Since about the 5th to 6th century, China had begun to make the granulated sugar. In fact, the name of the granulated sugar is originated from Sanskrit "gula" or "guda", which means "ball" and was mentioned as sugar or granulated sugar in the Buddhist scriptures.

During the Eastern Han Dynasty period, the jaggery of India and Persia entered China. In the 21th year of Zhenguan Period (647), Emperor Taizong of the Tang dynasty dispatched some people to Magadha, India (current Patna in India) to learn the way of making jaggery. According to Xin Xiu Bencao, the jaggery was made of granulated sugar (solid sugar), water, milk and rice flour. Mixing these materials and then boiling them into some kind of solid thing. When these people learned this technique and came back from India, Emperor Taizong ordered Yangzhou to devote the sugar canes. Then these people made better jiggery than that in Western Regions.

40   Mikami Tsugio: the Ceramics Road, Ed. 1984, Cultural Relics Press, p. 32.
41   He Fangchuan: Long-standing and Promising Sino-Africa Cultural Exchanges, in Papers on History of Sino-foreign Cultural Exchanges, p. 815.

505

Chinese people learned how to make granulated sugar in the Three Kingdoms period, but what they learned was brown granulated sugar not the white. The white granulated sugar was rare imported goods. According to The Biography of Tazi in the History of the Song Dynasty, the Tazi People offered a lot of tributes, the white granulated sugar included, in the first year of Yongxi (985 AD) and Zhidao (995 AD). And Song Dynasty Manuscript Compendium also recorded that the Tazi people offered the white granulated sugar in the second year of Xianping (999 AD). At the end of Song Dynasty, it was said that Dupo (current Island of Java, Indonesia) produced brown and white cane sugar according to Representative Answers from the Region beyond the Mountains. It was thus clear that Southeast Asians mastered the technology of making white granulated sugar before Chinese people. And Chinese people knew that the white granulated sugar was better than the brown, which drove Chinese people to introduce the technology of making white granulated sugar. The process was as follows: The foreigners made living by making sugar and then this method gradually spread, which was gradually well known by the Chinese craftsmen.

Introducing the technology of making white granulated sugar into China can be traced back to Yuan Dynasty. In Yuan Dynasty, Bureau of Sugar was established in Hangzhou; people who worked in Bureau of Sugar were "Zhugu", i.e., the rich Islam people.[42]

506

"Zhugu" is the transliteration of "Juhud" in the Arabic language, which was also translated as "Shuhu", meaning Jews in Yuan Dynasty period. That is to say, Jews were in charge of making sugar in Hangzhou during the Yuan Dynasty period. The author, Yang Yu explained that the Jews were some rich Islam people and they were probably the Western merchants who knew the technology of making sugar. Consequently, the Mongolian aristocrats trusted the Jews greatly. In the Yuan Dynasty period, Unguen county in Quanzhou, Fuzhou province was the most important place where sugar was produced. According to Marco Polo, people in Yongchun did not know how to refine the white sugar so they just produced the brown sugar before Yongchun becoming a part of Yuan Dynasty. Then craftsmen of West Asia taught how to de-colorize sugar by using wood ash, which made Yongchun becoming the main place of making cane sugar as well as providing sugar for Mongolian aristocrats in Dadu (Beijing). The technology of making the white granulated sugar gradually spread. Ibn Battuta, a Moroccan traveler, came to China in 1340s. He found that China produced a lot of cane sugar, whose quality was even better than cane sugar in Egypt.[43]

According to Xinghua Fuzhi in Putian, Fujian Province, the way of making white sugar came from Quanzhou and people in Putian learned this way in the period of Zhengtong (1436-1449 AD) in Min Dynasty. People did not know the

---

42   See the book of Shanju Xinyu (Miscellaneous on Shanju) written by Yang Yu, The book of Kuixin Zashi by Mi Zhou ([Sequel to the Miscellaneous Notes in the Year of Kuixin], 1991, Shanghai Classics Publishing House.

43   Ma Jinpeng, translation work. The Journey of Ibn Battuta, p. 545.

way of making the white granulated sugar and it was impored from overseas until the end of Ming Dynasty. Song Yingxing narrated the way of making white granule sugar in his book "The Exploration of the Work of Nature" Song Yingxing wrote that the top layer, around five inch thick, is very white, so this sugar is called the foreign sugar. Song Yingxing[44] added that this sugar was famous for its pure white color. Therefore, the technology of making white sugar started spreading into the whole country. The white sugar produced in China did not only meet the demand in the domestic markets, but was also exported to other countries. When the white sugar was exported to India, the white sugar became popular among the local rich people. They no longer consumed the local brown sugar of India. Still today, the white sugar is called "cini" in Indian language—literally "cini" means something which came from China.[45]

China was the first country which possessed the rock sugar production technology. According to Book on Making Sugar by Wang Zhuo in the Southern Song Dynasty, a Buddhist, whose family name was Zou, taught the rock sugar production technology in Suining, Sichuan Province. Up to Song Dynasty, there was no rock sugar in foreign countries. However, the rock candy was one of the main export commodities of China. According to Dao Yi Zhi Lue by Wang Dayuan at the end of Yuan Dynasty, the rock sugar was exported to India.[46]

507

---

44   Song Yingxing was a Chinese scientist and encyclopedist who lived during the late Ming Dynasty (1368–died around). He was the author of Tiangong Kaiwu, an encyclopedia that covered a wide variety of technical subjects, including the use of gunpowder weapons.
45   Ji Xianlin, the Cini Question–An Example of Cultural Exchange between China and India, in Papers on A Collection of Ji Xinlin's Academic Works, Ed. 1991, Beijing Normal University Press, pp. 650-661.
46   Jin Qiupeng, "Sino-foreign Scientific and Technological Exchanges in Maritime Activities," in Papers on China and the Maritime Silk Road, pp. 13-15.

Chapter 5. The Heyday of the Maritime Silk Road

The prosperity of the Maritime Silk Road had developed on the basis of advances in the world's shipbuilding industry and the navigation technology. If we look from the perspective of the marine communication history between the East and the West of the world, we can say that compared with Chinese sea voyages to India in the Western Han Dynasty period, the voyages led by Roman ships which sailed to China across India in the Eastern Han Dynasty period were slightly more prosperous.

One of the most important representative works of navigation during the Sui and Tang Dynasties is Jia Dan's book Huang Hua Si Da Ji (Imperial Ships Travel All Directions); the representative figures of navigation in the Song and Yuan Dynasties were Yang Xiu and Wang Dayuan. The sailing level of the two periods was nearly equal to that of Dashi (Arab empire) and Persia or slightly got the upper hand, compared to the latter two. Zheng He's voyages in the early Ming Dynasty are known as the peak period of China's navigation. While, at that time, the navigation in Dashi and Persia was in a stagnant state. Europe was still in the eve of the great development of navigation. In those days, Chinese navigation technology enjoyed a remarkably dominant position among the world countries. Chinese navigation technology in the Ming Dynasty period occupied a leading position in the world navigation history, which made China become the leader of the Maritime Silk Road. World's numerous foreign cultures and civilization were introduced to China and closely interacted with the Chinese culture. At the same time, the ancient Chinese civilization was introduced to the foreign countries.

1. Zheng He's Voyages

Zheng He's voyages are important events that mark the beginning of the peak time of Chinese ancient navigation. During the Yongle and Xuande periods (1403-1435), Zheng He had led a large ocean fleet to visit Asian and African countries in total 7 voyages. It was not only an unprecedented feat in Chinese maritime history, but also a great event in the history of world navigation. During 1990 and 1991, I participated in the investigation of the Maritime Silk Road research project initiated by the UNESCO. Following the International research ship from Venice of Italy to Guang Zhou, I visited more than 10 countries by the Mediterranean Sea, the Red Sea, Bay of Bengal, the Western Pacific Ocean and in Southeast Asia, and participated 18 International Symposiums. Everywhere, I could feel the profound influence of Zheng He. When the fleet entered the Arabian Sea, nearly all scholars talked about Zheng He when introducing me their nation's marine navigation history. They all honored Zheng He as Admiral Chengho, respecting him "the commander of navy". Zheng He was indeed the great son of our motherland.

(1) The Maritime Heritage Since Song and Yuan Dynasties

Zheng He's voyages were a continuation of voyages made in the Song and Yuan Dynasties. During the 400 years of the Song and Yuan dynasties, Chinese navigation had long been in a state of prosperity. The Chinese navigators in the Tang Dynasty had opened sea routes across India Ocean. Chinese navigators during the Song and Yuan Dynasties had obvious advantages in the navigation of Western Pacific Ocean and North India Ocean. The navigation targets of China's southeast coastal ports and regions were spread to all over East Asia, Southeast Asia, South Asia, the Persian Gulf, Arabia Peninsula and East Africa. Especially after the Mongolian people established the Yuan Dynasty Empire, Chinese seafarers learned the Islam nautical knowledge, which offered another reference system to the Chinese navigation and pushed it to a new higher level. We can say that, otherwise in no way could the Chinese seafarers could alone achieve such an advanced level. After since the overseas geographical writings were produced in the Song and Yuan dynasties, many relevant books such as the Ling Wai Dai Da (by Zhou Qufei), Zhu Fan Zhi, Da De Nan Hai Zhi, Dao Yi Zhi Lue, Yi Yu Lu, and Jingshi Dadian (1329-1333) were written one after the other. It is generally accepted that Chinese people in the Song and Yuan Dynasties have been quite familiar with the geographical regions of Western Pacific Ocean to Northern India Ocean. The development of Chinese and foreign contacts has made Chinese geographers learn from the fruits of the Islam geography works, which all laid the foundation for the further development of navigation knowledge in the Ming Dynasty period.

If we look, from the perspective of navigation technology, in period of the Song and Yuan dynasties, China's navigation technology had advanced to the "quantitative navigation" stage. Chinese navy had a clear understanding of the weather, monsoon and hydrology of the Western Pacific Ocean- the North India Ocean region. Chinese navigators had mastered all-weather magnetic compass navigation technology, and formed the "compass road" through combining that with the inertia route, that is, using admiralty sailing directions and Hui Hui sea chart. Chinese sailors had already grasped the technology of celestial positioning which could make sure the latitude of the ship by determining the azimuth and height of the celestial bodies. At the same time, Chinese boatmen grasped the technology of sailing the boat by shifting the helm and sails in various wind conditions, and paid attention to the depth of the sea. Therefore, Zheng He's oceangoing voyage was a general test to Chinese navigation technology.

Meanwhile, the government in the early Ming Dynasty period was committed to eliminating of Mongolian oppression, maintaining social stability, reducing corvee labor, recruiting refugees, encouraging reclamation, constructing water conservancy, and popularizing advanced agricultural production technology. Therefore, the social productivity recovered rapidly. In the early Ming Dynasty, the porcelain represented by Jingdezhen, the textile industry in Jiangnan and the shipbuilding industry in coastal regions and regions along the Yangtze River achieved further development. The development of agriculture and handicraft industry not only made China's economic strength more and more powerful, but also boosted the business circles' demand for expanding the markets. China was a big country and the whole society was basically self-sufficient. But many countries in Asia and Africa had limited territory. Thus their countries' production was not sufficient to meet the social consumption, and they had to rely on overseas trade. Chinese tea, silk, porcelain, copper and other commodities were high in quality but cheap in price, which led to a large overseas demand. With the recovery and growth of Chinese economy, Chinese commodities became more and more abundant, and those commodities more and more attractive to overseas countries, all of which became the internal driving force for the development of overseas trade.At the same time, the recovery of socio-economy not only irritated the desire of the upper class to pursue exotic treasures, but also made the imperial court show its power to overseas countries. China feudal rulers had always believed that China was the Celestial Empire, foreign rulers should bow to the Central Plains Dynasty and pay rare tribute in their countries to the emperor. At that time, tributary system was the one used to maintain the official trade between nations. One of the main purposes of Zheng He's voyages was going abroad and exchanging wealth with overseas countries, and shipped them back for a small number of rulers to enjoy.

(2) The Family Background of Zheng He

Zheng He was a member of Hui people. His original surname was Ma, given name San Bao, or Sanbao. He was born in Hedai Village, Kunyang County, Yunnan. At present, the most reliable information about Zheng He's family background can be received from the epigraph of Zheng He's father, which was written by scholar Li Zhigang entrusted by Zheng He in the 3rd year under the reign of Emperor Yongle (1405).[1]

1   Yuan Shuwu: The Postscript on the Gravestone of Kun Yang Ma Haji, Examination of Zheng He Research Material Selections Ed. 1985, China Communications Press.

At that time, Zheng He had been promoted to an eunuch officer rank. It was just on the eve of Zheng He's first time to sailin the western oceans, so he had to trust others to take the epigraph to his hometown and stand it in front of his father's grave. In the 9th year under the reign of Emperor Yongle (1411), Zheng He went back home to worship ancestors before his fourth voyage, and engraved inscription in the shade of the epitaph, which is 1.65 meters high, 94 cm wide, and 15 cm thick, with "Epitaph for The Deceased Revered Mr. Ma" on it. According to this historical material, Zheng He's great grandfather who was named as Baiyan, the transliteration of Mongolian name Bayan, which meant richness. The surname of his great grandmother was Ms. Ma. In the Yuan Dynasty period, the Hui people belonged to Semu (color-eyed), whose position was only after the Mongolian people. The Mongolian people and the Semu people both enjoyed upper status in the society, and they contacted with each other very frequently. It was common that Hui people were given Mongolian or Turkic names. Zheng He's grandfather and father were both named Haji, which was the respected title for the people who had been to Mecca for a pilgrimage. According to the requirements of Islam, believers should go on a pilgrimage to holy Mecca in their life. It seemed that the Zheng He's family had always followed this custom. Zheng Zheng He's grandmother and mother were both surnamed Wen, who possibly were the daughters of a Hui family. Later on, Zheng He was interested in sailing, which was closely related with the sea expedition tradition of his father and grandfather. Zheng He's father was born

512 in the 4the year of the Zhizheng Period of the Yuan Dynasty, (1344), died in the 15th year of the Zhu Yuanzhang (Hongwu) reign in the Ming Dynasty period (1382). So, it should be in the transitional period of the Yuan and Ming dynasties that Zheng He's father visited Mecca. And Zheng He's grandfather's pilgrimage should be in the end of the Yuan Dynasty. His great grandfather Bayan had probably lived in the period under the reign of Emperor Chengzong of the Yuan Dynasty.

Zheng He was the second son of Mahazhi. In the 14th year of Hongwu (1381), Emperor Zhu Yuanzhang (reign title "Hongwu") sent armies led by his generals Fu Youde, Lanyu and Mu Ying to Yunnan region and defeated the army of Liang Wang, the remaining forces of Yuan Dynasty there. As the Ming Dynasty abolished the ethnic oppression policies of the Mongol Yuan Dynasty, most Hui people in Yunnan region joined Liang Wang's anti-Ming army. The war ended with the failure of Liang Wang and the Mongolian and Hui people in the Yunnan region were harshly suppressed. Zheng He, as a Hui child, was captured and castrated by the Ming army and then was assigned to the mansion of Zhu Di, the Prince Yan, as an eunuch.

Since then, Zheng He gradually earned the trust of Zhu Di. After the Ming emperor Zhu Yuanzhang died, his oldest grandson Emperor Jianwen ascended the throne. In order to consolidate his reign, he decided to remove the military leadership of the Prince Yan. Therefore, the Prince Yan raised his army to fight against Emperor Jianwen and finally seized the power. Zheng He made contribution in the war at Zhengcunba (current Dongba in Beijing), thus given the family name Zheng by Zhu Di. Zheng He loved learning since his childhood and as a Hui person, he was born with cultural links with the Arab countries in the Western Asia region. Also, he believed in Buddhism which was also the main belief for the majority of people in Southeast Asia and South Asia regions, therefore it was easier for him to communicate with them. In addition, he had good knowledge of military affairs. These advantages made him the commander of the navy forces which launched military expeditions against foreign countries. According to Records of Incense and Icon of Feihuan Hut affixed at the end of the Volume 20 of the block-printed edition of the book Popular Romance of the Treasure Voyages of Sanbao Eunuch written by Taoist priest, Zheng He died in Kuri in his 7th Treasure Voyage in the 8th year of the reign of Emperor Xuande (1433). And Kuri was the current Calicut City (Kozhikode) in the western coast of Southern India.

(3) Zheng He's Seven Treasure Voyages[2]

There are a number of different views on the number of voyages Zheng He had led. According to the records of Stories carved on the tablet in the Tianfei Temple of Liujiagang in Loudong (Tianfei lingying zhiji) found in the Changle county, Fujian, it was written that Zheng He has made seven Treasure Voyages, respectively in the 3rd year, the 5th year, the 7th year, the 11th year, the 15th year and the 19th year during the reign of Emperor Yongle and in the 6th year of the reign of Emperor Xuande.

513

However, some historical records give different descriptions. Some sources say that admiral Zheng He made a voyage to Siam in the 1st year of Yongle (1402). The Coastal Defense Planning by Zheng Ruozeng records Zheng He's voyage to Japan in the 2nd year of Yongle (1403). Also, Guoque and History of Ming describe his voyage to Vieux Port (current Palembang City in Sumatra, Indonesia). Zha Shengxing at the beginning of the Qing Dynasty pointed out that Zheng He ever took 4 voyages to Korea. If these records are reliable, Zheng He had probably led 14 expeditions rather than seven.[3]

---

2   The Chinese expeditionary fleets carried great amounts of treasures, which would served to introduce China's power and wealth to the known world.

3   Guan Jincheng, "The Ships of Zheng He's Voyages to the West Oceans" Zheng He Yanjiu bainian lunwen ji (Beijing: Beijing University Press, 2005), 1, pp. 68-71. Zhou Shide, "Assessment of the Rudder from the Treasure Shipyard and the Inference of Zheng He's Treasure Ships") in ZHYJ, pp. 72-81. See also Joseph Needham et al., Science and Civilization in China Part 3, Vol 4 (Cambridge: Cambridge University Press, 1971), pp. 480-482. "A Gold Covered Statue of Zheng He Found in the West Coast of India. People's News Agency, last modified December 13, 2004, http://tinyurl.com/ozrmndj. See also Wan Ming, "The Ming Statue of Zheng He: Revisit of the Colored Statues in Xianyin Palace, Changle, Fujian Province , Journal of the Forbidden City Museum, vol. 3 (2005). Liang Qichao, "The Biography of Zheng He, the Great Navigator of Our Homeland", originally published in 1904 in ZHYJ, 1.

Scholars have found that the records related to Zheng He's voyages to Japan and Korea are unreliable. And we have evidence that Zheng He's voyage in the 22nd year of Yongle was countermanded by Emperor Renzong. And, the scripts Carved on the Tablet found in the Tianfei Temple of Liujiagang in Loudong has been written in a book titled as the Continuation of the Highlights of Literature of Wu City authored by Qian Guo in Changzhou during the reign of Emperor Jiajing in the Ming Dynasty period. And the original tablet of Tianfei Temple still remains in the Changle county, in the Fujian province. The two monuments were built by Zheng He himself, which are the most credible evidences, that Zheng had seven voyages in his whole life. The seven "treasure voyages" were as follows:

The First Voyage

In the summer of the 3rd year of Yongle (1405), Zheng He and his fleet moved from Liu Jiahe (Liuhe in Taicang, Suzhou, Jiangsu province) to Fujian. In the winter of the same year, as North wind sprang up, they finally reached Kuri by way of Champa, Java, Vieux Port (current Palembang City in Sumatra, Indonesia), Sumatra (current Samaranga in Sumatra Island), Lambri and Ceylon. Sumatra was the main distributing center of the Southeast Asia—Bengal Bay region at that time. Zheng He's fleet came here many times to send sub-fleet toregions like Malacca, Bengalese (current Bangladesh), Ceylon and Liushan (current Maldives Islands).

514

The destination of Zheng He's first three voyages were all the Kuri city. To commemorate this, Zheng He built a monument there with inscriptions on that "My destination is now several thousand miles away from China. And like in China, this place is rich and people live a happy life here. I build this monument to commemorate this and tell the whole world that everything is good." But, the inscriptions recorded in Ying Yulan sheng—Kuri is a little bit different. According to Popular Romance of the Treasure Voyages of Sanbao Eunuch*, in their return voyage Zheng He and his fleet met with the local pirates led by Chen Zuyi who severly disturbed the merchants of Samboja. After this meeting Zheng He sent a messenger to Chen Zuyi to subjugate him. Chen Zuyi pretended to accept Zheng He's demand and continued to secretly plunder the Ming Dynasty navy and traders.[4]

But, Zheng He became aware of his trick and made full preparation and defeated Chen Zuyi and latter's 5000 troops were anhiliated.[5]

In the autumn of the 5th year of Yongle (1407), Zheng He returned to Nanjing to report on his mission to Emperor Chengzu. Together with him were the envoys which he brought with him from Sumatra, Kuri, Malacca, Quilon and Aru (today's Western region of Sumatra Island, Indonesia).

---

4 See Volume 13, Chapter 6, Shanghai Ancient Books Publishing House, 1985, p. 792.
5 This were recorded in tablet found in Tianfei Temple of Liujiagang in Loudong The Records of Emperor Chengzu (Volume 71) and also in History of Ming and Samboja.

The Second Voyage

In the winter of the 5th year of Yongle (1407), Zheng He started his second voyage. The destinations this time included peoples like Champa, Siam, Malacca, Lambri, Kaval (current southern region of India), Ceylon, Koci (currentKoci in the Western coast of India) and Kuri. And he returned in the 7th year of Yongle (1409).

In this voyage, Zheng He carved three kinds of characters including Chinese, Persian and Tamil on the stones in Ceylon island at the beginning of the 7th year of the reign of Emperor Yongle. The Chinese inscription describes the flourishing of Buddhism in Ceylon in those days and explains the reasons why Zheng He donated a large amount of money to local Buddhist temples that he believed that his safe voyage could be attributed to the bless of Buddha. The total donation included a thousand money coins, five thousand silver coins and treasures like many kinds of worsted fabrics, incense burners, vases, candlesticks, lamps, incense box, troll flowers, sesame oil and candles.[6]

The Persian inscription was divided into 22 lines but today the handwriting is seriously damaged and hard to interpret that only few characters like "The Emperor of Ming" and the list of Zheng He's donations can be recognized. The amount of the gold, silver and other items on the list is the same with that of Chinese inscription and the only difference is the Buddha in Chinese version was changed into the "Islamic Light". And Tamil inscriptions has a total of 24 lines and are well-preserved, which mentions that the donors were the Chinese envoys Cinbo and Uvincuvin, referring to Zheng He and Wang Guitong in the Chinese inscription. Line 13-22 of the inscription is the list of items which were donated by Zheng He, the same with that list in the Chinese version. In the book, naming of several artifacts are different from the current Tamil language, therefore its meaning can only be recognized by comparing with the Chinese version. These stones are now exhibited in the Colombo National Museum of Sri Lanka. At the end of 1990, when I participated the study expedition of Maritime Silk Road organized by UNESCO, I saw them in this museum.

515

The Third Voyage

In the autumn of the 7th year of reign of Emperor Yongle (1407), Zheng He and his fleet set sail from Liujiagang and stopped in Fujian to wait for the north wind. When the wind appeared, they set off in December and came to Champa in ten days and nights. Then they finally reached Ceylon via Java islands, Malacca, Siam and Sumatra. In Ceylon, the fleet was divided into two sub-fleets, one to regions like Kaval and Gamba (current Kanyakumari in the southern end of India) and the other to Quilon, Koci and Kuri led by Zheng He himself. Both sub-fleets sailed near the southern coast of India.

---

6   Book on Western Countries written by Gong Zhen, quoted by Xiang Da, Zhonghua Book Company, Ed.1982, p. 50.

When Zheng He first visited Ceylon, Vira Alakesvara, the king of Ceylon, was too arrogant and annoyed, he prepared to attack the fleet. Zheng He noticed that and left this island. Since then, the king of Ceylon continued to take advantage of Ceylon's favorable position as a transit point on the sea route from East to West and looted the vessels passing by, which had frustrated the neighboring countries. When Zheng He reached Ceylon in his second voyage, he donated abundant gifts to local temples. The reasons were not included in the inscription of the monument. However, considering that in the third voyage, the king of Ceylon asked gold and silver form Zheng He, we can estimate that the purpose of him was to ease the relationship with the Ceylon rulers.

The name of the Ceylon king as mentioned in Chinese records, i.e., "Alie Khanna," should be corrected as Alagakkonara. I should mention that according to historical records of Sri Lanka, the king of Ceylon in this period (1372-1410) was the Bhuvanekabahu V. Probably, bur since Alagonakkara had monopolized the power, in his hands, and king Bhuvanekabahu V. had become a puppet of Alagonakkara his name was not recorded as the king of Ceylon in the Chinese historical records.

Zheng He and his fleet passed via Ceylon again, the Ceylon king Alagonakkara pretended to invite them and sent his son Naye to ask for gold and silver, which was refused by Zheng He. So the king secretly sent a troop of 50,000 soldiers to hijack Chinese ships and the Chinese navy on board. Also, they cut down trees to hinder Zheng He returning to the ship. Zheng He was aware of the conspiracy of the king immediately and led his troops back to the ship, but the road was blocked by the enemy forces. The Ming Navy faced the risk of complete annihilation. Zheng He was not alarmed and told his generals that the king must look down on them because they came so far here, and the whole army of Ceylon rushed out for them so that there were few soldiers back in the central city of Ceylon. Under these conditions if Zheng He's troops could penetrate the central city of Ceylon, skillfully and quietly, they could be able to defeat the Ceylon army. After discussion, Zheng He sent a few soldiers to take the trail back to the ships and ordered those on the ships to struggle to resist the enemy ships so as to preserve the fleet. Then Zheng He led 2000 sergeants to penetrate into the capital of Ceylon kingdom. The defense of the capital city was really weak and Zheng He's troops broke the gate of the capital and captured the king of Ceylon, his family members and a number of other leaders. Getting the news, the main troops of the Ceylon army withdrew from the front line and came to rescue the king. Zheng He and his army implemented a death-life battle and finally defeated the Ceylon kingdom. Zheng He escorted the king of Ceylon back to the Ming Dynasty court. The Emperor Chengzu did not punish the Ceylon king Alagonakkara, on the contrary sent out an imperial decree to pardon him and his wife. Also, Chengzu offered food and clothing to them and ordered Ceylon to choose a qualified person from the royal family to be the new king.

The Fourth Voyage

The destinations of the first three voyages of Zheng He were mainly in Southeast Asia and South India. Emperor Cheng Zu thought that countries in these regions had already paid tribute but those farther had not done that. Therefore in the 10th year of the reign of Emperor Yongle (1411), he ordered Zheng He to set the fourth sail. Zheng He made the voyage in the winter that year. This time, the fleet berthed more regions in Southeast Asia than the first three times, including Kelantan (current Kota Bharu, the capital of Kelantan State, at the junction between Malaysia and Thailand) and Pahang (current Pekan region at the estuary of Pahang River in Pahang State of Malaysia). Then the fleet bypassed the Malay peninsula and went Westbound by way of Kaval (current southern end of India) to Kuri. After that, the fleet went Northwest with downwind and reached Hormoz in 25 days. Zheng He presented damask, colored silk, leno to the king, the queen and the chancellors. And in return, the king sent his ministers to the Ming Dynasty. The Arab ministers arrived in Beijing in the 12th year of the reign of Yongle (1414) and offered a giraffe, horses and other local expensive products as tribute.[7]

The Ceylon on the opposite side of the southern end of India and Kuri in the western coast of South India and its left regions were traditional juncture point of the traditional Arabian Sea maritime route. Any such juncture point in a maritime route was formed based on the following conditions: Firstly, seafaring in this region should be well-developed with many accessible routes. Secondly, the region should be an international trade center which will facilitate merchant ships to rest. Thirdly, the property here should be rich so that merchant ships can easily get supply and purchase and sale goods. Ceylon and regions in the Southern end of India were sailing center of the North Indian Ocean region in the history. Zheng He and his fleet stayed here to send sub-fleets to the Arab peninsula, the East Africa and Liushan in the Arabian Sea (current Maldives Islands) for many times since his fourth voyage. In the fourth voyage, Zheng He and his fleet visited Adan (current Yemen Aden) in the southwest end of the Arab peninsula, Mogadiscio (current Mogadishu in Somalia) in the East Africa, Brawa (current Barrave), Maiindi (current Elva Kissina) and Liushan in the Arabian Sea (current Maldives Islands).

Zain al-Abidin, the King of Semudera (in Northern Sumatra) was protected by Ming Emperor Chengzu. Zheng He, in his return sail towards China, coincided with the civil strife of Sumatra wherein Zain al-Abidin and Sekander, the son of his stepfather had a big conflict with each other. Since, Zheng He's fleet was weakly armed, Sugan led a big army to attack Zheng He's fleet, but was crushed by the sailors. Zheng He allied with Zain al-Abidin and defeated Sekander and captured him in Lambri[8]. In the summer of the 13th year of Yongle (1415), Zheng He sailed back to China.

---

7   History of Ming—History of Hormoz.
8   History of Ming—History of Sumatra.

The Fifth Voyage

Zheng He's fifth voyage set sail in the winter of the 15th year of Yongle. The route this year was the same with the 4th voyage. The fleet visited Champa, Java, Kelantan, Malacca, Vieux Port, Sumatra and Lambri. Then the fleet sailed along the end of South India to the Arabian Sea and reached Hormoz following the Southward wind. After that, the fleet went pass Adan in the southwest end of the Arab peninsula and finally arrived in the east of Africa. The fleet returned back home in the summer of the 19th year of the reign of Emperor Yongle (1419).

Koyil, the King of Koci (Kochi) in the west coast of India ever came to China to pay tribute in the 9th year of Yongle (1411). Later, Kochi king sent envoys to China twice to persuade the Chinese emperor to confer the king Koyili the title of "king of the lands nation and mountains." Therefore, this time, Emperor Chengzu ordered Zheng He to take the royal seal to confer the title of the king and write the Emperor Chengzu's orders as engraved on a stone. This inscription engraved on the stone was very long, saying that "Emperor Chengzu confers Koyil as the king of Koci and confers the seal to him to encourage him better run his people. And Emperor Chengzu asked the king of Koci to determine a mountain in his country as the mountain of the country and order his craftsmen to build a monument on this mountain so that the later generations of the nation know this story." This monument is not yet discovered.[9]

The Sixth Voyage

In the winter of the 19th year of Emperor Yongle (1421), Zheng He and his fleet set sail for the 6th voyage and under the order of Emperor Chengzu, they sailed together with the envoys from 16 countries such as Hormoz who also needed to go back to their motherlands. The fleet and its sub-fleets visited Hormoz, Adan, Zufar, Zeila, Brawa, Mogadiscio, Kuri, Koci, Kaval, Ceylon, Bengala, Liushan, Lambri, Aru, Malacca, Gambari and many other countries. The fleet sailed back to China in the next year.

The Seventh Voyage

In the 5th year of the reign of Emperor Xuande, during the Ming Dynasty period (1430),, Zheng He set sail for his seventh voyage. According to Qianwenji, a historical book written by Zhu Yunming, the fleet arrived in Champa in the 6th year of Xuande (1431) and stayed for a year. Then in the next year, the fleet visited Surabaya of Java (current Surabaya in Java) and then went to Vieux Port, Malacca, Sumatra, Ceylon, Beruwala, Kuri and Hormoz. At that time, it took ten months to sail from Champa to Hormoz. In the 8th year of the reign of Emperor Xuande (1433), the fleet set sail from Hormoz and arrived in Kuri in March and it is recorded that Zheng He died after arrival. The fleet returned to China in the summer of the same year. According to Zhu Yunming's book, Zheng He and his fleet stayed in these regions at least several or ten-odd days and up to several months.

---

9   History of Ming—History of Koci.

(4) Large Ocean-going Fleets

The most important feature that made his voyage quite different from other voyages both in China and world history is that his voyage was large-scale navigation activities organized by the Chinese government. During the Yuan Dynasty period, the government had ever sent its navy forces to conquer Japan, Champa and Java, whose scale exceeded that in the previous dynasties but only within the West Pacific region. The scale of Zheng He's fleet was much larger than the average number of the people in the first, the third, the fourth, and the seventh voyage exceeded 27,000 troops with nearly 300 officials. The average number of the other voyages is yet unknown but is estimated to be no less than the four voyages. Also, each voyage has probably lasted for two or three years and the fleet was known as an ocean-going fleet. The fleet crew was organized under the following departments:

Firstly, the command department of the fleet was led by Zheng He and his deputies, which can be seen as the headquarter of the fleet.

Secondly, the implementation of the sailing includes the length of each boat, responsible for geography-identification based on map, equivalent to the captain. The rest includes sailors among which the rudder workers are responsible for conn; the anchor operators responsible for landing anchor; the material makers responsible for making iron anchor, wooden rudder and other materials. The sail seamen were responsible for raising and lowering sails, arranging sculls and so on. The yin and yang officials or observers, were responsible for observing the stars and the weather.

Thirdly, the foreign affairs. This included the usher of the court of state ceremonial, responsible for the affairs of protocol. And compradors were responsible for overseas trade; interpreters were responsible for interpretation. There were several major languages were used in the regions through which Zheng He and his fleet sailed across, including Malay, which was the most important international business language in the Southeast Asia region, Tamil, was the main language in southern Indias and Sri Lanka; Persian, was widely used in Islam countries. There were many local Chinese minority people in the Southeast Asia who helped the fleet leaders and seamen to communicate with the local people. And the fleet at least included several Persian and Tamil translators. The monument found in Sri Lanka proves this point. And the authors of several existing books on Zheng He's navigation including Ma Huan, Fei Xin and Gong Zhen were all such interpreters who were included in the fleet.

Fourthly, the logistics support. This included the managers from the Board of Revenue, responsible for the fleet of grain and grain and logistics supply business. Advisers, accountants, doctors and medical officers. Fifthly, the armed forces part. This included command in chief or senior military commanders; command and Qianhu, namely middle military officer, Baihu and Qixiao, namely low-level officers. Warriors, sergeants, Lishi and Yuding were all soldiers. In addition to the wind, pirates and the sabotage of some hostile countries were also major factors threatening the fleet. Although Zheng He's navigation was different from that made by Emperor Yuanshizu in the purpose of conquering Japan, Champa and Java, but the powerful force was necessary at that time to protect the security of the fleet.

Zheng He's voyage every time had more than 200 ships in the fleet, including many different kinds of ships, known as a huge mixed fleet. The largest ship was known as the Treasure Ship, with the number of 20—30, sailing among the fleet. According to the record of Fei Xin, accompanying personnel of Zheng He, these treasure ships had 9 mast and 12 sails. Gong Zhen, another accompanying personnel said that the canopy, sail, anchor and rudder of the ship could be moved by at least two or three hundred people.[10]

The medium-sized treasure ships, which were also known as the horse ship or horse clippers, were a kind of ship which could be used for both combat and transport functions. There were grain vessels used to carry food and other necessary supplies. The ships used only for combat was called as the Zuochuan (warship). Besides, there were other kind of boats which supplied logistic support for vessels in the ports where the waters were shallow, which conveniently provided fresh water and transported this fresh water for the whole fleet.

Many scholars have sought to compare Zheng He's fleet and several famous European fleets in the Age of geographipcal discoveries. The fleet of Colombus which sailed across the Atlantic Ocean to the America in 1492, only had three light sailboats with 90 sailors, among which the flagship, i.e, the largest one "Santa Maria" had weighed 250 tons. The Portuguese fleet led by Vasco da Gama sailed around the Cape of Good Hope and arrived in India in 1497. The fleet only had four small sailboats with 160 people and its main flagship weighed just 120 tons, and was less than 25 meters in length. Also, Magellan's Spanish fleet could only carry 265 people and had 5 small sailboats, among which two were 130 tons, two were 90 tons and one was 60 tons. The scale of this fleet cannot be compared to that of Zheng He's.

Zheng He's fleet, when visiting overseas countries, sometimes sailed as an entire fleet, known as the "huge midship". During the return sail, all ships moved together. Sometimes, the fleetwas divided to several sub-fleets, known as "separated midship sailing", going to different destinations. Fleet carried limited living supplies, therefore needed to visit many countries and ports. To better arrange the voyage and meet the time schedule, Zheng He did not visit all countries and the fleet, when arriving at certain important trade centers (ports), often sent a sub-fleet to these ports to perform its missions.

Considering the huge scale of the fleet, there must be a certain means of communication to ensure the command and the contact between the flagship and other ships in order to control the speeds of the ships, moving forward or backward, lifting or lowering the sail, the distance between the ships, avoiding

---

10 The Records of Western Countries, 1982, quoted by Xiangda, Zhonghua Book Company, p. 5.

the collision, informing the direction and force of wind, measuring and observing the stars, risk dealing, scheduling and command and the order of the ships sailing into the port as well as anchor weighing and dropping. Pure shouting was the most common means of communication, but this method had its limitations. Even when the sea was calm, due to repeated shoutings, the frequency of the sound had decreased, consequently, the possibility of mis-hearing could increase. The distances between the ships were quite different. To avoid collision, the ships had to maintain a considerable distance, making it difficult to communicate. According to Voyage to the West, Shuyuzhouzilu, Ji Xiao Xin Shu and Chou Hai Tu Pian, the Ming Dynasty navy used flag signaling method to communicate among the ships in the daytime and used 20-odd five-color flags hung on a red mantle. This way was similar with that used between modern ships. The fleet used lanterns for communication in the night. The location and number of the lanterns could indicate the level and formation of different ships and other information. However, when it comes to rainy days or conditions with low visibility, the two means could not be used. In this case, the ships in the fleet contacted with each other by voice which were generated by gongs and drums.

2. Sea Routes

According to the tablet found in Tianfei Temple of Liujiagang in Loudong which was erected by Zheng He, Sumatra was the transfer center in the expedition to the countries in the Western Ocean. Some scholars have argued that the concept of "Western" Ocean used during the later period of the Ming Dynasty was different from the concept used during the reign of Emperor Wanli of the early Ming Dynasty period. In the period before the reign of Emperor Wanli— in the book Research on Eastern and Western Ocean written by Sun Guangqi— Brunei Darussalam[11] was deemed as the border line between the eastern and western oceans. The full name of this country is Negara Brunei Darussalam

Sumatra was a prominent shipping center of the Southeast Asia in that period. When the Chinese fleet sailed to the Western Ocean, generally visited Sumatra first, and further sailed to other regions. According to historical records, there were one route to Sumatra and six routes from Sumatra to other regions.[12]

Sumatra to Malacca (9 days, in the Malacca Strait, from West to East)
Sumatra to Longyanyu (westward for one day and night, at the junction between the West-end of Malacca Strait and Bengal Bay, from East to West)
Routes mentioned in Description of the Starry Raft by Fei Xin:
Sumatra to Bengala (20 days and nights following wind, from Southeast to Northwest, bypassing Bay of Bengal)
Sumatra to Ceylon (12 days and nights following wind, from East to West, cross the Bay of Bengal)

---

11 See The History of Ancient Chinese Navigation, p. 498.
12 Qian Wenji written by Zhu Yunming, Zhu Yunming's Qianwenji which recorded Zheng He's voyage.

Routes mentioned in Yingyashenglan by Ma Huan:

Sumatra to Lambri (due West for 3 days following wind, from the West-end of Malacca Strait to Bay of Bengal)

Sumatra to Liushan (from East to West, cross Bay of Bengal, then to Arabian Sea in West Indian Ocean)

Historical records have shown that Champa (current Qui Nhon in central region of Vietnam and its surrounding regions) covered two arriving routes and six sailing routes.

The routes from Champa to other destinations recorded in the Description of the Starry Raft are as follows:

Champa to Jiaolanshan (current Koh Larn Island near the southwest of Kalimantan Island of Indonesia, 10 days and nights following wind, from North to straight South.)

Champa to Siam (10 days and nights following wind, bypassing Kunlun Mountains in the South-end of the Indochina peninsula southwestward and bypassing the Gulf of Siam northwestward)

Champa to Java (20 days and nights following wind; the route was similar with Champa to Jiaolanshan in its first half and extends southward.)

Champa to Chenla (3 days and nights; the route was similar with the first half of the route form Champa to Siam.)

The routes recorded in Yingyashenglan are as follows:

Champa to Malacca (southward for 8 days following wind to Longyamen, then Westward for 2 days. The routes started from Champa, then Southwards to the top of Malay Peninsula and finally Westwards into the Malacca Strait).

The Routes Recorded in Yingyashenglan Are as Follows:

Champa to Wailuoshan Mountain (current Lishan Island in Vietnam, 2 days, alongside the West of part of the South China Sea, from the South to the North).

According to historical records, there were four arriving routes and four sailing routes in Malacca (current Malaysia Malacca).

The routes from Malacca to other destinations recorded in Description of the Starry Raft are as follows: Malacca to Aru (currently in Sumatra), 3 days and nights following the wind; in the Malacca Strait).

The routes recorded in Zheng He's Nautical Chart were as follows: Malacca to Siam (from West to East, across the Malacca Strait to the Siam Bay, then Northwestward)

The routes recorded in Description of the Starry Raft are as follows:

Malacca to Sumatra (9 days and nights following wind, from East to West in the Malacca Strait)The routes recorded in Qianwenji are as follows:

Malacca to Champa (eastward to the southern end of the Malay Peninsula and Northward when entering into the South China Sea)

Historical records show that there were three sailing routes from Longyanyu to other destinations. The routes recorded in Description of the Starry Raft are as follows:

Longyanyu to Cuilanyu (current Great Nicobar Island in the Southern end of the Andaman Sea, Northwestward for 5 days, alongside the Bay of Bengal)

The routes recorded in Zheng He's Nautical Chart are as follows:

Longyanyu to Ceylon (The route contained that from Longyanyu to Cuilanyu and then was Westward from Cuilanyu across the Bay of Bengal.)

Longyanyu to Orissa (currentKoricancha in the southern region of Cuttack of India; the route was from Southeast to Northwest, across the Bay of Bengal.)

According to historical records, there were four arriving routes and seven sailing routes in Ceylon (current Sri Lanka). The sailing routes recorded in Description of the Starry Raft are as follows:

Ceylon to Liushan (westward for 7 days and nights from Beruwala, current Beruwala in the southwest of Sri Lanka)

Ceylon to Brava (current Barawe in Somalia) 21 days and nights following the wind, from East to West, across the Arabian Sea)

Ceylon to Kuri (10 days and nights following wind; the first half included that from Ceylon to Quilon and from Ceylon to Koci and then northwards alongside the Western coast of India.)

The Routes Recorded in Yingyashenglan Are as Follows:

Ceylon to Quilon (current Quilon in the western coast of India, 8 days and nights following Northwest wind from Beruwala; the route was across the strait between India and Sri Lanka and then alongside the Western coast of India.)

The routes recorded in Zheng He's Nautical Chart are as follows:

Ceylon to Liushan (The sailing port was Qainfotang, currently Dondra Head in the southernmost point of Sri Lanka and the destination port was Guanyu, currently Male island. The route was similar with that from Ceylon to Liushan.) 523

Ceylon to Liushan (The sailing port was Gaolangwu, currently Colombo and the destination port was Jiapingnianliu, (currently Garpini island). This route was similar to the above one.)

Ceylon to Koci (The sailing port was Qianfotang and the destination port was Koci. The first half of the route was the same with that from Ceylon to Quilon and then northwards alongside the Western coast of India.) According to historical records, there were four arriving routes and six sailing routes in Kuri (current Calicut in the west coast of India).

The routes from Kuri to other destinations recorded in Description of the Starry Raft are as follows:

Kuri to Zeila (current Zeila in Yemen, 20 days and nights following wind; the route started from Southwestern coast of India and Northward across the Arabian Sea to the Red Sea through the Mandab Strait.)

Kuri to Hormoz (10 days and nights following wind, to the Persian Gulf alongside the Western coast of India)

Kuri to Adan (Aden in Yemen, 22 days and nights following wind; the route was the same with that form Kuri to Zeila.)

Kuri to Dhofar (current Salalah, the capital of Dhofar province of Oman; 20 days and nights following wind; the route started form Southwest coast of India and was Northwestward to Salalah in the middle of the southern part of the Arab peninsula.)

The routes recorded in Qianwenji[13] are as follows:

Kuri to Sumatra (27 days and nights, from the Southwestern coast of India to the Bay of Bengal and then Eastward into the Malacca Strait.)

The routes recorded in Yingyashenglan are as follows:

Kuri to Mekka (The destination port was Matouzhida of Mekka, currently Chittagong Port of Saudi Arabia. The routes were 3 days and the half part was the same with that from Kuri to Zeila and then Northward to Zeila alongside the Red Sea.)

There were two routes form Quilon to other destinations recorded in Description of the Starry Raft:

Quilon to Mogadiscio (Mogadishu-Somali) (20 days and nights following wind, Westward form Southwestern coast of India across the Arabian Sea)

The routes recorded in Yingyashenglan are as follows:

Quilon to Koci (one day and night following wind, alongside the Southwestern coast of India)

There were 6 arriving routes and 7 sailing routes in Liushan (current Maldives islands) and its surrounding islands. According to Zheng He's Nautical Chart, the routes from Liushan to other destinations are as follows:

Liushan to Ganbali (The sailing port was the official port and the destination port was in Kanyakumari in the South-end of India. The route was from Male islands Northeastward to the South-end of India)

Liushan to Quilon (The sailing port was the official port and the route was North by East to the Southwestern coast of India)

Liushan to Mogadiscio (The sailing port was the official port and the route was Westward across the Arabian Sea.)

Liushan to Koci (The sailing port was Jiapingnian Island of Liushan. The route was Northeastward to the southwestern coast of India.)

Liushan to Kuri (he sailing port was Jiapingnian Island of Liushan. The route was Northeastward to the Southwestern coast of India and similar with that to Koci, but was by North.)

Liushan to Kuri (The sailing port was Anduliliu, currently Andrott Island of the Maldives Islands. The routes was Northeastward to the Southwest coast of India.)

Liushan to Hormoz (The sailing port was Jiajialiu, currently Kavaratti island of the Maldives islands. The route was Northwestward to the Persian Gulf, across the Arabian Sea.)

There were two routes from Hormoz to other regions according to records.

The routes recorded in Description of the Starry Raft are as follows:

Hormoz to Mekka (40 days and nights, Southward from the Persian Gulf to the southeast corner of the Arab peninsula, then Westward alongside the South coast of the peninsula, then to the Red Sea through Bab el-Mandeb and northward to Zhida port (currently Jeddah Port in Middle East).

The Routes Rcorded in the Qianwenji were as Follows:

Hormoz to Kuri (23 days, Southeastward alongside the Western coast of India from the Persian Gulf)

---

13   Zhu Yunming's Qianwenji which recorded Zheng He's voyage.

According to Zheng He's Nautical Chart, there were two routes from Mangaluru to other destinations.

Mangaluru to Kuri (southeastward alongside the Southwest coast of India)

Mangaluru to Qalqat (currently the ruins of ancient city of Qalqat in the southeast end of the Arab peninsula, northwestward from the southwestern coast of India to southeastern end of the Arabpeninsula)

In fact, the actual destinations were more than that mentioned above.

The most noteworthy component part of the route network used in Zheng He's era was the navigation routes in the West Indian. During the Tang and Song dynasties periods, Chinese ships were able to sail across the Indian Ocean, but only a few routes were used with few changes in routes. It can be seen that in the Zheng He's era, there were at least seven routes used by the Chinese ships when they sail acrossed the West Indian Ocean, which included the following:

1. Ceylon (current Sri Lanka) to Brava (current Barawe in the Southwestern coast of Mogadishu, Somalia), 260 degrees in heading, 2100 nautical miles of sailing;

2. Guan Yu (current Male Island as part of the Maldives Islands) to Mogadiscio (current Mogadishu, the capital of Somalia), 262 degrees in heading, 1800 nautical miles of sailing;

3. Quilon (current Quilon in the southwest coast of India) to Mogadiscio, 258 degrees in heading, 2000 nautical miles of sailing;

4. Kuri (current Calicut in the West cosat of India) to Adan (current Aded, the capital of the Democratic People's Republic of Yemen), 267 degrees 30 minutes in heading, 1800 nautical miles of sailing;

5. Kuri to Zeila (currently in the Republic of Yemen), 300 degrees in heading, 1400 nautical miles of sailing;

6. Kuri to Dhofar (current Salalah, the capital of Dhofar province of Oman), 300 degrees in heading, 1400 nautical miles of sailing;

7. Kuri to Hormoz (current Hormuz Strait in the Persian Gulf), 305 degrees in heading, 1400 nautical miles of sailing.[14]

This gives us sufficient evidence which demonstrates that in the Zheng He's era, Chinese ships have led the shipping industry in the Indian Ocean and that they could sail to numerous regions of the world.

Zheng He's voyage covers the longest ocean-going route in the history of the ancient Silk Road. The sailing routes stretched from the east of the Western Pacific, northwest to the Arabian Sea, the Persian Gulf and the Red Sea and Southwest to East Africa, reaching Malindi (current Kilwaschia, in Tanzania) at 8°55' Southern latitude. In fact, Chinese ships sailed farther than Malindi in East Africa. Dr. Joseph Needham ever mentioned that the European cartographer Fra Mauro wrote in a note on his map in 1459 that there was an expedition of Chinese zonchi [junks or boats] that, thirty years earlier, in 1420, traveled

---

14 Sun Guangqi: The Development of China's Maritime Technology and the Evolution of the Maritime Silk Road Delivered in China and the Maritime Silk Road, p. 215.

under the southern tip of Africa from east to west. Chinese sailboat started from India, sailed across the Indian Ocean towards the direction of Man and Woman islands near the Diab island (current Madagascar island). This ship, sailed across the green islands and dark seas, sailed West and southwest for 40 days. Possibly, this ship had sailed for about 2,000 nautical miles. Later, the ship returned back due to bad whether conditions and after 70 days reached the Diab (Madagascar island port). Joseph Needham has argued that this Chinese sailboat had sailed across the Cape Agulhas which is in the southernmost tip of Africa and had entered the Atlantic Ocean, consequently.[15]

Navigation in the early Ming Dynasty arrived in countries around India, but also arrived in Europe. Paolo del Pozzo Toscanelli, a Florentine ever helped Columbus's navigation, mentioned, from 1431-1447 (the 6th year of the reign of Emperor Ming Xuanzong to the 12th year of the reign of Emperor Ming Yingzong), the Ming Dynasty ever sent envoys to Europe. These envoys have sailed northwards along the Red Sea and landed in this region, then they traveled to the Nile river and passed across the river and arrived at Italy through the Mediterranean sea. But, yet their expedition records aren't discovered.

In ancient times most Chinese conceived the place where they lived the world's center and called their homeland as Zhong Guo (meaning central country), and believed China was a great and impressive country and even used the term "Tianxia" (the world) to refer to China, and the other countries except China were barbarians and of little importance. This conservative concept seriously hindered development of geography of China. But not all Chinese people have advocated this concept. Zou Yan—the cosmologist of the Qi Dynasty during the Warring States Period, was the pioneer of a new geographical concept. Qi State was close to the sea and enjoyed the advantages of fishery and salt and had promoted overseas trade. Such geographical environment enabled the people of the Qi State to learn more about the overseas regions of the world. Zou Yan had criticized the conservative ideas of Confucianism and proposed: "The so-called China "Middle Kingdom" as conceptualized by Confucianists only accounts for 1/81 of the world... within it there are the nine provinces which were those laid out by Yü the Great[16].

But these provinces cannot be numbered among the real continents (i.e. province in its broader sense). The Middle Kingdom is only one of a total of nine continents, and these are the real Nine Chou (s). Around each of these Chou(s) there is a small encircling sea, so that men and beasts cannot pass from one to the other. But these Nine Chou(s) form only one division and make up one Great Continent. There are again such nine Great Continents, and around them is a vast Ocean, which encompasses them and stretches to the bounds where the heavens and the earth met."[17]

---

15 History of Science and Technology in China, Volume III, p. 989.

16 Yü the Great is a legendary emperor and hydraulic engineer who mastered the floods.

17 Records of the Great Historian Selected Chronicles of Mencius and Xun Qing.

Zou Yan's propositions were not just baseless estimations or imagination, but based on his enhanced overseas knowledge.

(1) Zheng He's Nautical Chart

During the early period of the Ming Dynasty the Chinese people have made great achievements in obtaining overseas geographic knowledge. Zheng He's Nautical Chart was one of the most important masterpieces. Chinese naval forces before the Ming Dynasty must use nautical charts, but no chart was passed on. The literature of the Song Dynasty had the records of "map of overseas countries", but the map was lost long time ago and it was hard to know exactly. At the end of the Yuand Dynasty, there was a "sea route guide chart" which covered only the domestic and coastal region of Northern Sea and did not include the long-distance routes to the East and West seas. Zheng He's Nautical Chart was the extant earliest nautical chart of China's naval forces. This chart was originally named Map for Route from Baochuan Shipyard to Longjiang Pass and the Foreign Countries, included in Volume 240, A Corpus of Classified Military Writings compiled by Mao Yuanyi of the Ming Dynasty and Zheng He's Nautical Chart was an abbreviated name. The original map was 24 pages, including foreword, map and star hopping chart etc. Zheng He's Nautical Chart had the following characteristics:

(1) A wide coverage of sea region. It covered an region starting from the lower reaches of the Yangtze River, East China Sea and South China Sea on the East to Java on the Southeast, the Persian Gulf, Strait of Hormuz, Jeddah city at the coast of the Red Sea of Saudi Arabia on the Northwest, East Africa and Somalia, Kenya and Tanzania coastal region on the Southwest, about 4°S Southernmost, the vast regions of East Asia, Southeast Asia, South Asia, Southwest Asia and East Africa within the waters of the West Pacific Ocean, the North Indian Ocean, and recorded more than 530 geographic names.

(2) The nautical chart did not mark longitude and latitude or scale, but recorded the place name and landscape in the vast region from left to right in the style of traditional Chinese painting by imitating the "10,000-li Yangtze River Chart". This was a kind of mapping with the moving ship as the observation base, the marks of upper, lower, left and right did not refer to the fixed geographic direction, but practical and useful for navigators.

(3) Generally, the chart was mainly the landscape painting, supplemented by text description of the shipping routes. However, there were changes because of differences of route sections. In the section from Nanjing to Taicang on the Yangtze River, the chart mainly clarified the landmarks because of the changing direction and high definition of the landmarks; from Taicang to the waters of Southeast Asia and the coastal regions of India, Zheng He's fleet normally navigated along the coast; therefore the chart described the landmarks in details, correspondingly the text navigation guide increased significantly and main routes were marked with hand positions of compass, geng (a voyage unit) number, direction change and port of destination; in the waters of Indian

Ocean, most maritime routes were long distance trans-oceanic routes and there was rare landmarks for reference, accordingly the maps only marked typical landmarks. However, in addition to text description of hand position of the route, it also recorded the astronomical fixation data of various sea points.

(4) In addition to the direction and hand positions of the compass, the route guide of the nautical chart also recorded the water depths of ports and submerged reefs etc.; on the landmark localization, it used the method of determining the arrival direction of ships with three landmarks, which is the origin of the current three-point localization method. This manual route determination was not a simple one which determined direct sailing between two points, but the track navigation method, i.e., starting from a known port, changing the hand positions when passing through known landmarks, and finally arriving the port of destination; when using the compass in the waters with the wind direction not identical to the ship heading, the corrected value under the impact of wind should be input in advance to ensure successful arrival of the port of destination. All these reflect the development of navigation technology in the Ming Dynasty.

(5) In the waters of Indian Ocean, especially the route from Sumatra to Arab peninsula through the Bengal Bay and southern tip of India, and route from East Africa and Arabian Sea Maldives Islands to west coast of India, it was one of the main reference means to ensure correct heading by observing different constellations to determine ship latitude in navigation. Zheng He's Nautical Chart clearly recorded the star hopping data of these navigation zones above mentioned and was the first in the navigation history of China.

(2) The Star Hopping Technology

The star hopping technology has been the most remarkable progress in the astronomical based navigation in this period. The so-called the "qianxing shu" (star hopping technology) was a method which helped to observe the height of stars above the sea level, i.e., thus determine the latitude position of the ship by using altitude angles. In other words, it was the marine astronomical location determination. It was a technology which was more complicated than the land referenced sea navigation. The sea navigation by using land or mountains and islands as reference points was a relatively primary navigation technology and its fatal weakness was that the ship could not sail far from the land or could not sail along the shortest sea route. The development of the star hopping technology was the result of precise cognition of the relationship between Polaris height and the South-north mileage. Nangong Yue from the Tang Dynasty used the principle of relationship between Polaris height and South-north mileage in the territorial survey in 12th year of Kaiyuan period (724). During the Song Dynasty period the star hopping method employed in navigation. When returning from Quanzhou, Fujian in the late 13th century, Macro Polo took the official ship that the Yuan government allocated for Princess Cocacin's journey to Persia. In his travel notes Macro Polo mentioned that in Java a part of the Circumpolar star could not be seen, but in Ma'abaar (Malabar)Kingdom (east coast of South India), one could see Polaris at the position of one or two elbows above the water level. In the 1st year of Yongle Period of the Ming Dynasty, Zheng He was ordered to prepare for the large-scale overseas expedition. Zheng He and his attendants used the collected compass hand position charts, star hopping maps, chart of water resources and mountains around rich water sources to make correction with true measurements.[18]

All these records reflect that Zheng He's large-scale expedition during the Ming Dynasty period was based on the mature navigation technology of the Song and Yuan dynasties.

From Zheng He's Nautical Chart we can see his fleet depended on the star hopping technology in the section of the Indian Ocean starting from Sumatra, i.e. Gong Zhen's "observing the rise and set of sun and moon to distinguish the direction and height of stars to measure the distance". For example in the section from Sumatra to Sri Lanka, the fleet did not sail along the near-shore route along Indo-China Peninsula around the Bay of Bengal and East Indian coast, but used the star hopping technology to cross the Bay of Bengal. Zheng He's Nautical Chart had two star hopping charts related to this route marking Silongliu Island with "Hua Gai five zhi (digit) two jiao (a measurement unit)". After passing by the Sri Lanka, the fleet mainly depended on the astronomic navigation and two star hopping charts were related. In the four charts, there were more than 70 star hopping data, the geographic direction of the observation place, name, height and angle of stars etc. In addition to the star hopping data, the charts also included the hand route and geng number, indicating that people also used compass and distance measurements in navigation in addition to the astronomic localization. In the section of Indian Ocean, the star hopping technology mainly used Polaris, Hua Gai (two stars in Ursa Minor), Chamaeleontis, Northwest Busi Star, Southwest Busi Star (two stars in Gemini), Denglonggu (Southern Cross), Vega, Nanmen Twin Stars (two stars in Centaurus), and two upper stars of the Big Dipper, Southwest Shuiping Star and Pleiades etc. Sometimes two stars were used simultaneously in the star hopping for cross-reference. For example the captains of that time had known the relationship between the Polaris and height of Denglonggu, i.e. knowing the sum of height of the two stars were 15.5 zhi.[19]

During the early Ming Dynasty period, the astronomic navigation technology used by Zheng He in the overseas expedition was called "Guoyang star hopping". The point that "Guoyang star hopping" was better than the predecessors lied in that it measured the height of stars above the sea level and navigated with the fixed height value. The units for measuring the star height were "zhi (digit)"

18 Voyage with a Tail Wind Foreword part, see Two Sea Route Compass Hand Treatises revised by Xiang Da. See also Ningbo Haizhou Pingyang Quarry Stream Flow Table collected by the Navigation School of Jimei University, Fujian Province.
19 Liu Nanwei, Li Qibin, Li Jing: Star Hopping Chart, contained in the Analects of Astronomic Relics in Ancient China compiled by the Institute of Archaeology of the Chinese Academy of Sciences, Ed, 1989, Cultural Relics Press, pp. 369-380.

and "jiao (angle)", and the instrument used for measurement and observe was Qianxingban (star hopping board). "Zhi" was a traditional unit in the ancient astronomic observation of China, first seen in the divination notes of the silk manuscripts of Wuxing Divination unearthed in No. 3 Tomb of Mawandui Han Tombs, which mentioned the relative position of Venus planet and the moon, "the moon meets with the star, the moon rises from south of the Taibai (Venus planet)... at the position of three digit, there is the city Youcheng, at the location position of two digits, there is..." Here "zhi" referred to the degree of about 1.9°. Moreover, Yi Si Divination and Treatises on Divination in the Kaiyuan reign period (712-756) also had records which used the measurement unit term "zhi" as the latitude goniometry measurement unit. Although these two books were written during the Tang Dynasty period, their contents were quoted from the ancient astronomer Wu Xian's star map and divination texts which he created in the Warring States Period. Therefore the unit "zhi" first appeared in the Warring States Period. "Zhi" used in the star hopping technology had certainly inherited the tradition of ancient measurement method of China. Its basic meaning was identical with that in the Warring States Period, Han and Tang dynasties. In Zheng He's "Guoyang star hopping", "zhi" referred to 1°34'-1°36' degrees.

Li Xu (1505-1592) of the Ming Dynasty mentioned "Suzhou Ma Huaide Star Hopping Board" in volume 1 of his book Ramble of Jie'an Laoren, and described its structure: 12 pieces ebony chips arranged from small to large, the largest one measured more than 7 cun, and the chips were marked from "1 zhi" to "12 zhi" respectively and detailed division. And a piece of ivory measured 2 cun, without four corners, marked with "half zhi", "half jiao", "1 jiao" and "3 jiao", opposite to each other upside down. According to this description, the Star Hopping Board was a square wooden board which consisted 12 pieces of square chips, and the largest one measured about 24 cm-long of each side (converting to 7 cun 7 fen of the ruler of the Ming Dynasty) and indicated 12 zhi, and the smallest piece measured 2cm long of each side, indicating 1 zhi.

When using the Star Hopping Board, the user stretched out one's arm and held the board with the surface vertical to the sea level, with a rope of certain length at the lower end of the board to fix the distance between the board and eyes of the observer. When observing, the lower edge of the board should be coincided with the intersecting line of the heaven and the sea, the upper edge met the celestial body to be observed, then one could get the height of the celestial body above the sea level. The unit was "zhi". Below "zhi", it was "jiao", 1 zhi = 4 jiao. The reading of jiao could be gotten from the scale of the Star Hopping Board or measured with the small ivory chip.

The Star Hopping Board must be the instrument Zheng He used in the "Guoyang Star Hopping Technology" in the overseas expedition. Its structure was identical to the one used by the Arab sefarers.[20]

---

20   See Yan Dunjie: Star Hopping Technology–A Glance at the Navigation Knowledge of the Ming Dynasty, contained in the Collected Papers on the History of Science, Science Press, 1966/9.

Star Hopping Technology was called as "kamal" in Arabic, and the unit indicating the star height was "isba" which had the same meaning with "zhi". The value of "zhi" in Zheng He's Guoyang star hopping technology was very close to "isba". Some members of Zheng He's fleet were descendants of Uyghur people who entered China with Mongolian in the period of Yuan Dynasty. Ma Huaide was possibly Uyghur too, and that was the reason why he knew the star hopping technology. Therefore, Guoyang Star Hopping Technology which was passed on from the Yuan to the Ming Dynasty was a result of combining the traditional astrology of China and Arabs.

(3) Treasured Private Copies of Nautical Charts

In addition to official nautical charts such as Zheng He's Nautical Chart, some warship forces and sea merchants held nautical books passed on from generation to generation in the Ming and Qing dynasties. For example, A Tour of Duty in the Taiwan Strait of the Qing Dynasty mentioned "boatmen" have treasured copies of records about various seas named "yang jing". Such books were the navigation guidebooks of private navigators with very high values. The existing literature of the Ming Dynasty mentioned many of such books. For example, A Glance at Japan mentioned Compass Chart, the Compass Directions mentioned Compass Hand Chart, The Study of the East and the West mentioned Navigation Compass Guide, the Catalog of the Western Tributes mentioned Chapter on Compass Hand Positions, and the Duhai Fangcheng (sea-crossing solutions), Four Sea Handbook, Secrets of Navigation, All about Navigation etc. With these books which were inherited by later generations , China's navigation industry gradually developed to a higher level.

The extant most important navigation guides were two handwritten copies of the Voyage with a Tail Wind and the Compass Directions which is kept in the Bodleian Library of Oxford University. These two books were written by common navigators, records of seamen without any exaggeration in their wording. Though the books had some color of superstition, they objectively reflected the maritime exchanges between China and "East and West oceans" in the period between the early Ming Dynasty and the middle period of the Qing Dynasty, and provided valuable materials for study of the development of the Maritime Silk Road and the East-west cultural exchanges.

(1) The Famous Book "Voyage with a Tail Wind"

This book was presented by Archbishop Laud, Archbishop of Canterbury and president of Oxford University to Bodleian Library in 1639, the 12th year of the reign of Emperor Chongzhen of the Ming Dynasty. Laud had purchased the collected books of a Jesuit University in Europe and Voyage with a Tail Wind was one of these books. It was estimated that the book was obtained by a Jesuit in China and sent to Europe and collected by the Jesuit University. Finally, the book was sent to Oxford University via Archbishop Laud.

It was estimated that the Voyage with a Tail Wind was completed during the middle Ming Dynasty period. The author said in the foreword that his works was based on Duke Zhou's Method of Direction Determination. The Method of Direction Determination was a treatise on navigation compass written under the name of Duke Zhou. The author said: "it has lasted for a long time from ancient times" and contained "both topography and water resources", but there were clerical errors in the process of circulation and drawing, thus supplements and deletions were made in the book. The Method of Direction Determination it existed in the middle period of the Ming Dynasty, and was a necessary compass usage handbook for all navigators, "When getting lost on a land expedition one could look for routes or ask for directions. But when sailing in the vast seas, it was hard to identify the right direction although there were mountains and islands. People depended on Duke Zhou's method and compass hand chart to find the right direction." But "the old copy was damaged over time" and the place names "are hard to verify". Though we do not know the specific contents of the Method of Direction Determination, the author said: "record the geng number, compass hand route, topography and water resources, the depth of bays and islands from Nanjing and Zhili to Taicang and foreign countries and seas in the book", and mentioned "treasured ship" and "to Western countries upon order in the first year of Yongle period". Obviously the Voyage with a Tail Wind was compiled by combining contents of the Method of Direction Determination and Zheng He's navigation materials.

At the beginning and the middle of the book, there were several paternosters praying Duke Zhou, Jade Emperor, Goddess Matzu and other deities to protect the sailors. Then it introduced the tideway, wind direction, time of tide rising and falling, compass hand position, and the chart introducing mountains, water resources, the water depth, soil or sand bed and reefs from Fujian to East and West seas (it defined Hormuz as the farthest sailing point which links the Persian Gulf (west) with the Gulf of Oman and the Arabian Sea (southeast), and compass hand positions of the routes from Fujian to Southeast Asia, sea routes among various ports of Southeast Asia, routes from ports of Southeast Asia to ports of South Asia, routes from ports of South Asia to ports of West Asia, routes from Fujian to ports of Penghu, Luzon (Philippines) and Ryukyu, the routes among various ports of East sea. This book was the first-hand material to learn about the navy navigation technology of the Ming Dynasty before arrival of the Western colonists and the sea routes of the Western Pacific Ocean and North Indian Ocean.

(2) The Book "Compass Directions"

This book was attached to the book the Art of War of the early Qing Dynasty and was completed at about the last years of the reign of Emperor Kangxi, i.e., the beginning of the 18th century. It was verified and revised by a man surnamed Wu from Zhangzhou county. Some intellectuals in Fujian once worked as translators/interpreters and many of them used the surname Wu. Wu must be one of them and probably a figure who travelled foreign countries. Although he proofread edited the book, he did not make substantive editing work. Therefore translation of some geographic names were inconsistent, for example Nagasaki, Malacca and Pahang. Therefore, the book basically maintained its original situation, in the main.

This book also had a foreword as in the book "Voyage with a Tail Wind", and mentioned about this book as follows: "the Methods of Direction Determination" written by Duke Zhou, contains "the information about mountains and water sources", which was probably indicating the landmark with landscape painting. However, because of "clerical errors", the "number of geng" that indicated distance was changed and showed many mistakes. The other copies were damaged and could "hardly to make comparison". There were many identical textual descriptions with the Voyage with a Tail Wind, and the foreword had a paternoster praying for protection of deities as the Voyage with a Tail Wind, with not only similar caption, but also basically identical contents. These two books must originate from the same mother edition.

However, the routes recorded by the Compass Directions had obvious differences from those in the Voyage with a Tail Wind. In addition to Fujian, this book had also ports of departures in Guangdong and Zhejiang, and more contents on the routes to East seas, and supplements of star observation methods. The routes to West seas were less than the Voyage with a Tail Wind and ended at Southeast Asia.

From the books of "Voyage with a Tail Wind" and the "Compass Directions", we can see from the early Ming Dynasty to the middle Qing Dynasty, the routes mastered by private navigators could be basically divided into the following sections: Firstly, Cambodia, Chikan and Siam region, mainly routes from the South part of Indo-China Peninsula and the Gulf of Siam to Southeast Asia. Secondly, Malay Peninsula region, mainly routes from Malay Peninsula to Southeast Asia, Indian subcontinent and Sri Lanka. Thirdly, Calicut of South India, mainly routes on Arabian Sea. Fourthly, Java region, mainly routes from Java to Southeast Asia and Japan. Fifthly, Luzon (Philippines) region, mainly routes from Luzon to Southeast Asia and Japan. Sixthly, Japan region, mainly includes the sea navigation routes from Japan to Eastern and Western seas.

3. Friendly Sino-foreign Exchanges

The Ming Dynasty witnessed frequent Sino-foreign exchanges. After the founding of the Ming dynasty, foreign countries in the Southeast Asia sent envoys to the Ming dynasty and expressed their willingness for maintaining friendly relationships with the Ming dynasty. Among the numerous envoys from various countries, which visited the Ming, there were many prominent officials and eminent personages and their escort people, and even the heads of states. They have generally admitted obedience and vassals status, besides some demanded investiture, and received honorable ranks attached to China from the Ming dynasty. In return the Ming Dynasty allowed them to pay tribute, that is, the weak countries of the Southeast Asia have served the demands of the Ming rulers in exchange for the official trade relations between the two parties. In order to facilitate the exchanges with foreign countries, the Ming court especially established a foreign language school in the Hanlin Academy to foster professionals who could speak and write foreign languages. In this period, the Han people at the Southeast coast have emigrated abroad and formed communities in the many regions of the Southeast Asia. In fact they were the forefathers of contemporary Chinese people in these countries.

(1) Tomb of the King of Borneo in Nanjing

Borneo is the current Brunei, located in the north of Borneo island, along the coast of South Sea, and had bonds with China since the ancient times. After Kublai's failed attempts, Emperor Shizu of the Yuan Dynasty, had also failed in conquering and subjugating the Majapahit Empire of Java, consequently Majapahit Empire grew stronger and Borneo kingdom became its vassal. During the early Ming Dynasty period, the King of Borneo was Sultan Muhammad Shah. In 1370, the 3rd year of the reign of Emperor Hongwu, who was the founder of the Ming Dynasty ordered envoys Zhang Jingzhi and Shen Zhi, chancery21 official of Fujian Province to visit the Borneo kingdom and inform it that the Ming dynasty had toppled the Yuan dynasty and replaced it.

The Ming envoys started from Quanzhou and requested the Borneo king to accept submission and pay tribute to the Ming dynasty. The Borneo king refused with excuses that his kingdom had become poorer with the invasion of Sulu and also said that its suzerain Java kingdom was opposing Borneo's submission to China. Zhang Jingzhi and his attendants tried to persuade King Sultan Muhammad Shah and said that Java had submitted to the Ming dynasty. Finally, the King of Borneo was persuaded and sent envoys to pay tribute to the Ming dynasty. Borneo's tribute sheet was made of gold foil and the statement was engraved on the silver foil. Emperor Taizu of the Ming Dynasty thanked Borneo's envoys and rewarded generously.

In the winter of 1405, the 3rd year of Yongle period, Sultan Abdul Majid Hassan, King of Borneo, sent envoys to pay tribute to the Ming. Emperor Chengzu sent envoys to the kingdom and conferred him King and granted seal, tally, kan he, and other tokens and silk products. The king was highly encouraged and headed a batch of relatives, including his sisters, brothers, children and retainers to the Ming. After arriving Fujian, the local officials immediately reported to the imperial court and the court sent officials to meet the Borneo guests and guided them to the capital (current Nanjing). Officials on the way all hosted banquets for the guests. In August 1408, the 6th year of Yongle period, King of Borneo arrived in the capital. After having an audience of Emperor Chengzu, Sultan Abdul Majid Hassan congratulated Emperor Chengzu on the

---

21   Chancery is a general term for a medieval writing office, responsible for the production of official documents. The title of chancellor, for the head of the office, came to be held by important ministers in a number of states.

Ming's achievement of unifying China and thanked him for conferring the honorable title. He said: after receiving the investiture the kingdom enjoyed a favorable weather and it was the blessing of the Ming. Emperor Chengzu feasted the King of Borneo at Fengtian Gate and princess consort and other guests somewhere else, and also granted the king a ceremonial mace, a folding chair and a large quantity of expensive gifts thus his entourage was also generously rewarded.

Unfortunately Sultan Abdul Majid Hassan (Manarejiana) fell ill during the stay in the capital city Nanjing and died in the guest house in October. Emperor Chengzu suspended the court for three days for mourning and sent a commissioner to hold a memorial ceremony for the king. Crown princess and princesses also sent envoys to mourn for the king. The Ming court buried the King of Borneo outside Ande Gate in Shizigang, Nanjing. The tomb had a stone tablet, a spirit way and a memorial hall beside the tomb. An immediate sacrificial ceremony was held by the Ming government. Emperor Chengzu ordered the king's son Xia Wang to succeed to his father's crown.

Before returning back to Borneo, Xia Wang (4 years old) and his uncle told Emperor Chengzu that the kingdom paid a large quantity of borneol to Majapahit Kingdom of Java. Kingdom of Borneo requested that the Ming court would ask Java to allow Borneo not to pay tribute borneol to the Majapahit but to the Ming only; and asked the Ming court to escort the Borneo envoys back home and station military forces in Borneo for a year to comfort the people of the Borneo kingdom, and clarify the tribute system. Emperor Chengzu approved all their requests and sent an envoy to Java and notified the Java kingdom that Borneo would not render tribute to Java any longer. The Ming emperor also agreed Borneo to pay tribute only in every three years and granted Xia Wang a large quantity of gold, silver and gifts and ordered Zhang Qian to escort them back to Borneo.

Sultan Abdul Majid Hassan had once asked the Ming to confer a mountain in the kingdom as the Zhengguo Mountain and Xia Wang restated his willingness before returning to his country. Emperor Chengzu thus conferred the mountain in the capital of Borneo as "Changning Zhenguo Mountain", determined the inscription in person and ordered Zhang Qian to engrave the inscription there. In 1410, the 8th year of Yongle period, king Xia Wang sent envoys to the Ming with Zhang Qian to express his appreciation. In the following year, Emperor Chengzu sent Zhang Qian to Borneo and granted a large quantity of silk to Borneo. In 1412, the 10th year of Yongle period, Xia Wang and his mother visited the Ming dynasty again and the Ming court accommodated them at Huitong State Guesthouse. Emperor Chengzu feasted them at Fengtian Gate and rewarded Xia Wang and his entourages generously. Xia Wang and his mother stayed in the capital city for several months and returned at the beginning of the next year.

The records about the accurate location of the Tomb of the King of Borneo were vague and it was not clear where the relics were located over time. During the Republic of China period some researchers once made an investigation to find this tomb in the region of Shizigang but had failed. After the founding of the People's Republic of China, a large-scale survey of the cultural relics was carried out and finally the bomb was discovered at 3km Southwest to Ande Gate, Southern foothill of Tortoise Mountain, in the west of the East Xianghua Village, Tiexin Township, Yuhua District, and Nanjing in 1958. The tomb building site originally had a burial mound, stone carvings of the spirit way, a memorial hall and other buildings. Today the mound, 15 pieces of stone carvings of seven kinds and the base of columns of the memorial hall still exist. It is a symbol of the friendly exchanges between China and Brunei which was experienced since the ancient times. The municipal government of Nanjing city and Jiangsu provincial government have restored the Tomb of the King of Borneo as the prominent site to be protected.

(2) Tomb of East King of Sulu in Dezhou

Sulu is today's Sulu Archipelago in the western edge of the Sulu Sea, in the southern Philippines. In the Yuan Dynasty period Sulu was prosperous once and occupied the neighboring region, including Borneo. At the end of the 13th century, Borneo became a vassal of the Majapahit Empire after this empire had become strong in Java. At the beginning of the Ming Dynasty, Sulu invaded Borneo and then retreated after Majapahit sent troops to support and protect Borneo.

After ascending to the throne, Emperor Chengzu sent Zheng He abroad and a squadron once arrived Sulu and the Ming dynasty enjoyed an enhanced prestige. In 1417, the 15th year of Yongle period, Eastern King Paduka Batara, and Western King Maharajah Kamal ud-Din, and Princess Paduka Patulapok and their families and chieftains, totaling more than 340 persons, visited the Ming court through the sea route and presented the gold engraved statements and treasures to Emperor Chengzu. The Ming court received guests with the standard used when receiving the king of Malacca. Emperor Chengzu conferred them the title of king and granted seal, official costume, crown, saddle and horse, ceremonial mace and so on.. The entourages were also generously rewarded. The three kings lived in Beijing for 27 days and returned back. Emperor Chengzu granted a large quantity of treasures and silk to them before their journey back home.

Kings of Sulu sailed southwards along the Grand Canal. When reaching Dezhou, Eastern King of Sulu died of an illness in the guest house. When the news came to Beijing, Emperor Chengzu sent officials to attend the funeral, bury him at Dezhou district and erect a tombstone with epitaph beside the tomb. The Ming court retained princess consort of the Eastern King and 10 attendants to keep the tomb for three years and the rest of the attendants went back home. Emperor Chengzu also sent envoys to Sulu, sent to Paduka Batara's son Rakiah

Baginda an imperial edict, and praised his father's feat of heading a delegation to pay respect to the Ming against the long distance. Rakiah was also notified the Eastern King's investiture, rewards, death and funeral. Emperor Chengzu ordered Rakiah to succeed to his father's title of Eastern King.

In 1421, the 19th year of the reign of Yongle, mother of the former Eastern King sent his brother to pay tribute to the Ming. In 1423, the 2st year of Yongle period, princess consort fulfilled the three-year tomb keeping rite and was to go back. The Ming court rewarded her generously. The princess left some of her attendants to care and maintain the tomb of Eastern King, in an orderly manner. Currently, the tomb still exists in Dezhou in a good condition and Sulu people who were ordered to care and maintain the tomb have lived in China for generations, increased and gradually formed a populous village. The story of Eastern King's visit to the Ming dynasty was narrated among them since then for long years, became a popular narration which marked the friendship between China and the Philippines.

(3) Academy of Foreign Languages (Siyi Guan) and Huitong State Guesthouse

Foreign language teaching has a long history in China. The tradition of learning foreign languages in China started with learning Buddhist scriptures. From the Southern and Northern Dynasties to the Tang Dynasty, Sanskrit education was the most important one in the foreign language studies. It was described by a Ming scholar as follows: "Translators were employed for a long time since the ancient times. But, they have only interpreted the spoken language. At that time, foreigners had no writing system. Since Buddhism was introduced to China, Indian scripts were seen in China... In the Tang and Song dynasties, although the translations were proof-read and polished in order to make them consistent and fluent. Only the Buddhist scripture translation requested the translators to master relatively comprehensive information about both China and foreign countries." (Supplement to the Exposition of the Great Learning, Volume 145) That means the Sanskrit learning was mainly a specialized practice in China.

The official language school was first established in the Yuan dynasty. After Mongol establishing the empire spanning over Europe and Asia, foreign language became an important instrument to maintain normal operation of the huge country. At that time, Mongolian, Persian and Uyghur were the most important languages in addition to Chinese language. Important departments of the Yuan court had dedicated translators for document translation and record. Emperor Shizu Kublai of the Yuan Dynasty also established "Uyghur Language School" and Mongolian School under Hanlin Academy.

Deeply worrying the lack of language talents, Emperor Chengzu of the Ming Dynasty created Siyi Academy in 1407, the 5th year of Yongle period, which was a language school. Siyi Academy had eight schools when it was opened, namely Hui, Tartar, Jurchen, Xifan, Xitian (ancient India), Baiyi, Gaochang and Myanmar. The Memoir of the Ming Dynasty (Ming Shi Lu) recorded its establishment, "Because of language difficulties when foreigners paying tributes", the Ministry of Rites was ordered to select 38 students from the Imperial College to learn foreign languages and translation under the Hanlin Academy. The treatment of the students was "a dan rice per student per month". After graduation, the students "were ordered to attend the imperial examination and translate documents in the examination. After passing the examination, they were allowed to serve as officials and the academy was located outside the Left Gate of Changan Gate."[22]

Specifically, the students enjoyed the treatment of Juren (passing the provincial examination) and "attended the examination of the Ministry of Rites and their translation was the examination content." After passing the examination of the Ministry of Rites, they could be included on the Jinshi (passing the highest imperial examination) list, and "were appointed as Wenxue (name of an official rank) to translate books as in the past." Moreover, the imperial court also "selected outstanding people" from those who mastered a foreign language and "ordered them to devote themselves to language studies. When they became proficient in a foreign language, they would have to take an examination.. Those who were able to pass the examinations would be rewarded a certain title. They would be appointed to a certain position after 3 years since the imperial court attached great importance to their selection."[23]

538

We do not have, any strong evidence about the background of teachers of Siyi Academy, when it was first established. Its students were selected from the Imperial College, and mostly came from the Han nationality.

From the eight languages which were taught, we can understand that the Siyi Academy was an Asian language school. When it was first established, the languages taught were chosen by considering the land neighbors of the Ming Dynasty. In early days only the schools teaching Xitian and Myanmar languages were related to the maritime silk routes. The Ming inherited the system of the Yuan Dynasty and used the Uyghur language, i.e., Persian as the main external communication language. Actually, not many people had mastered the Persian language in the East Asian countries, especially in those countries that did not believe in Buddhism, Uyghur language was not useful at all. In 1497, the 10th year of Hongzhi period, Siam sent envoys to pay tributes to the Ming and Siyi Academy had nobody understanding Thai language. Minister Xu Pu et al suggested Guangdong Administrative Commissioner to recruit talents who were proficient in Thai to the capital.[24]

During the Zhengde period, the Uyghur School of the Siyi Academy reported to the Ming court that "tribute documents from Champa and Siam and other countries from Siam Sea region" were translated by "Uyghur School",

22 Memoir of Emperor Taizong, Vol. 48.
23 Supplement to the Exposition of the Great Learning, Volume 145.
24 Memoir of Hongzhi Period of Emperor Xiaozong, Volume 129.

"but the languages of these countries were different from Uyghur language" and the "Uyghur School" was not competent for the job. It was interpreters of the delegations interpreting the documents and then wrote down. The edicts and reward lists were written in "Uyghur language" by the "Uyghur school". During Zhengde period, "nobody could read the golden statement" presented by King of Siam. In the past when "Babai School" was lack of teachers, the Ming court once retained the envoy Lanzhege to serve as a teacher to foster teachers. Uyghur School suggested the Ming court to use this method to retain some members from the Siam delegation to serve as teachers, and select students from children of staff members of Siyi Academy and allow the Siam teachers to go back after these students master the language. The suggestion was adopted by the Ming court.[25]

In 1577, the 5th year of Wanli period, the Ming court engaged interpreter Wowenyuan and three Siam envoys to teach Thai at Siyi Academy.[26]

In the following year, Zhang Juzheng suggested to set up Siam School at Siyi Academy and enrolled 12 students. Lyu Weiqi of the Ming Dynasty once listed name of teachers of the Siam School, and on the top of the list were these four teachers.[27]

In addition to Siyi Academy, the Ming court also had Huitong State Guesthouse which was established to receive governmental guests. People working there were also requested to master a foreign language. Siyi Academy and Huitong State Guesthouse compiled textbooks for students and these books were collectively called "Chinese-Foreign Language Translation. According to existing materials, the Huitong State Guesthouse consisted of eight divisions, "Korea", "Ryukyu", "Japan", "Annan", "Siam", "Tartar", "Uyghur" and "Malacca".28 It can be seen that the foreign languages taught at Huitong State Guesthouse had overlap and differences with Siyi Academy. Ryukyu, Japan, Siam and Malacca divisions had the most frequent overseas exchanges.

Chinese-Foreign Language Translation was spread abroad quite early. The British Museum houses six block-printed editions of the Ming Dynasty brought by J. Edkins, the Library of School of Oriental and African Studies, University of London has a hand-written copy of the Ming Dynasty, Berlin State Library houses 24 hand-written copies of the Ming Dynasty collected by F. Hirth, Toyo Bunko houses 8 kinds of hand-written copies of the Ming Dynasty (Collection and Study of Foreign Countries on the Chinese-Foreign Language Translation–Comments on Nishida Tatsuo's Studies of Chinese-Foreign Language Translation, contained in Studies of China of Foreign

25 Studies of Siyi Academy, Volume II, The Institute of Eastern Culture Publication, p. 20-21.
26 Memoir of Wanli Period of Emperor Shenzong, Vol. 81.
27 Siyi Academy Rules, Vol. 7, publication of the Department of Oriental History, College of Letters, Kyoto Imperial University, the 12th month of the 2nd year of the reign of Showa era, (early 1928).
28 Translated by Huo Yuanjie, Di Bofu compiled Chinese-Foreign Language Translation, Taiwan Wating Publishing Co. Ltd.

Countries, China Social Sciences Press, 1979). The Chinese-Foreign Language Translation was a thesaurus which included phonetic symbols of foreign languages in Chinese. It consisted of two systems, Siyi Academy and Huitong State Guesthouse systems. These two systems were complied independent with each other. The basic format of the volume of Siyi Academy was: foreign language, Chinese translation, and phonetic symbol with Chinese language. There were differences between spelling of foreign languages and Chinese phonetic symbols, indicating that the Chinese phonetic symbols were not transferred letter by letter, but transliterated by pronunciation. The volume of Huitong State Guesthouse had only the transliteration with Chinese and Chinese translation, without the original foreign language. The classification of the volumes of the Siyi Academy and the Huitong State Guesthouse was not completely identical: both of them made classification by "astronomy", "geography", "seasons", "food and drink", "human affairs", and "treasures".

Translation of Malacca Language of the Chinese-Foreign Language Translation was complied in 1549, the 28th year of the reign of Emperor Jiajing of the Ming Dynasty. The so-called "Malacca Language" was Malay, i.e. the communication language of nearly the 200 million people of current Malaysia, Indonesia and Brunei. Translation of Malacca Language was actually Malay-Chinese thesaurus and collected 482 words. This thesaurus was later than the world's first Malay dictionary which was compiled by Pigafetta in 1521, and thus was the world's second Malay dictionary. The Translation of Siam Division of the Chinese-Foreign Language Translation was completed in the late 16th century. Siyi Academy and Huitong State Guesthouse were the cradle of instutionalization of translation during the Ming Dynasty and had an important status in the history of foreign and ethnic nationalities language teaching in China.

4. Islamic Secular Culture in China

Culture can be divided as religious culture and secular culture. The religious Islamic culture and civilization is associated with the Holy Koran and Islam religion. As for the secular culture, it has a far broader meaning, including Islamic language philology, historiography, philosophy, theory of Yin and Yang, medicine, astronomy, geography, maps and Engineering Technology. The Islam culture was introduced into China and also developed into a part of Chinese culture, which went through Yuan, Ming and Qing Dynasties.

Same as Buddhism, Islam was not a native religion of China, but a foreign religion brought in by immigrants. Its holy texts and classics were not translated into Chinese, but written in Arabic and Persian. To practice their faith in China, the descendants of immigrants formed the Hui ethnic community and other Chinese Islamic communities who diligently preached Islam just like the devout Buddhists who have traveled to faraway India to reach the Scriptures, which was thousands of miles away from China. For them, the first problem faced was the education and learning of the Islam-Arabic language.

On the basis of current evidence numerous Islamic scholars—being entirely Sinophone—lived in China including Shaanxi and Gansu regions. The descendants of the Semu Muslims had after all, been living in China for as long as two centuries by the time of Hu Dengzhou- six to eight generations.[29]

From the currently available historical materials, the Islam culture dates back to the Yuan Dynasty period, and Hu Dengzhou Mosque education in the Ming Dynasty period had probably inherited and developed the Islam Chinese education of the Yuan Dynasty period. The materials of Islam Chinese education are mainly in Farsi language, which suggests that the Islam people who immigrated to China were not mainly the Arabs but people who spoke Persian or those who were influenced by the Persian culture.

(1) Hui Language and Its Literature

One of the most significant characteristics of the Yuan Dynasty that distinguishes it from other dynasties in China was its cultural diversity and tolerance. The relationship between the Central Plains and Persia was closely linked due to the conquests of Genghis Khan (famous leader of the Yuan Dynasty) and its descendants. Chinese, Mongolian and Hui were the prevalent languages in the Yuan (Mongolian) Dynasty period. There were Persian language translation institutions among the Yuan official departments. And the main institution for the cultivation of talents for translation works was the Hui Imperial College (the highest educational institution and administering organ for education). The language materials used for teaching Persian in the Yuan Dynasty no longer exists, just leaving some clues for today. It is said in the book of Shu Shi Hui Yao (by Tao Zongyi) that the Hui language had just 29 letters and written in a row, from front to back, back to front. That is to say, the Hui language was written from left to right and from one line to another line. In his book, Tao Zongyi had mentioned the 29 letters. Among them, 28 letters were in the Arabic language. The Hui alphabet used by Tao Zongyiwas probably related with the systems developed by the Hui Imperial College. The character called "Istifi" (other appellation of Arabic language in the Yuan Dynasty period) except Persian language was taught in the Hui Imperial College. Few people had mastered "Istifi" characters until 24th year of Yuan (1287). About the "Istifi" language, there is an important record in Tong Zhi Tiao Ge. (Legislative articles from the Comprehensive Regulations" is a collection of jurisdictional edicts and of laws from the Yuan period).[30]

The learning of "Istifi" language was proposed by Maisad-Din who is mentioned in the book Zhong Tang Shi Ji which was written by Wang Yun. He has narrated that only few people had learned "Istifi" language, and only one or two

541

---

29 See The evolution and textbook of Chinese Mosque education written by Pang Shiqian and the Vol.7 No.4 of Yugong Semi-monthly Magazine; and History of Islam in China (Published Date: 1982; Publisher: Ningxia People's Publishing House) written by Bai Shouyi.
30 See Tong Zhi Tiao Ge (The Administrative Law of Yuan Dynasty), 1986, Zhengjiang Classics Publishing House, p. 80.

people worked with him on this language, he himself added, "I also know little about it". Therefore, he was worried about that the offspring would no longer learn and understand this language, thus he asked the government to establish schools, to teach "Istifi" language. Finally, Kublai Khan agreed to his proposal and asked him to be responsible for this work. According to the records of the book Yuan Shi Baiguan Zhi, in the 26th year of the Yuan (1289 years), officials working in Shang Shu Sheng (a government institution in ancient China) proposed to Kublai Khan that Bachelor Ha Lu Ding from the Imperial Academy was proficient in "Istifi" language and he should be assigned for this task. And it was also suggested that Chinese school education system should be responsible for the "Istifi" education of officials and nobles. These proposals were approved by the Yuan Emperor Kublai Khan.

"Istafa" is the Persian equivalent of the word in the "Istifi" language. As a proper noun, it refers to "accounting management of property and taxes". In the Middle Ages, the majority institutions of the Islam countries in charge of the fiscal and taxation departments were called "Istifi department". Istifis another meaning is a special character sign that had specific writing rules, and the government's financial documents, clearing documents and so on were written with the Istifi script. The Hui people held many postsin the fiscal and taxation departments of the Yuan government, and they used Istifi script when writing some financial documents, this was the reason why the education of Istifi was promoted. Arabic and Persian books were introduced into China through various ways during the Yuan Dynasty period. A lot of careful examination of historical materials revealed that there were a lot of materials about Islam language and philology. For example, there was a word named Shi Ai Lishi listed in the 7th part of the book Yuan-Mishujian (The Account of the Palace Library of the Yuan Dynasty). In 1955 in Guangming Daily a prominent scholar named Ma Jian had pointed out that the word "Shi Ai Li" was the Chinese transliteration of the original Arabic word Shi'r (Şiir), which meant "poem". Ma Jian, wrote that the word Shi'r (Şiir) was used in the book "The Account of the Palace Library of the Yuan Dynasty," in the 1st part of the book. It seems that the many Hui people were good educated.

Besides, Yuan-Mishujian (The Account of the Palace Library of the Yuan Dynasty) which subtantially informed about the Hui culture, the books titled as Tian Fang Dian Li (Islamic Principles and Rites) and Tian Fang Xing Li (The Real Record for the Great Prophet Muhammad) written by Liu Zhi (a scholar during the reign of Emperor Kangxi of the Qing Dynasty period) also gave comprehensive information about the Hui culture. Scholar, Liu Zhi, in his books which we have mentioned above has given 40 and 45 references respectively. Although there are some repeated information and references in these two books, reliable references given in them still play a significant role in the research of Islam culture, which has caught the attention of many scholars at home and abroad during the 20th century. And the latest research paper on Liu Zhi has discussed the Arabic and Persian historical materials used by him, which was published in the Journal of Central Asia, Volume 26, Issue 1-2, in 1982, co-authored by two Australian scholars Leslie & Wassel. Scholars, D.D. Leslie & Wassel, on the basis of their study on Kuwata Rokuro's works, and have examined the books "A History of Arabic Literature" written by Brockelmann, and the "Persian Literature" written by Stalley, the Catalog of Persian Manuscripts preserved in the National Library of Brussels, and the "Encyclopedia of Islam".[31]

The two scholars have reviewed the studies of their predecessors, in order to find out the origins of references used by Liu Zhi. According to the paper co-written by Leslie and Wassel and considering the books used by Liu Zhi, we can see that Liu Zhi has used a lot of books which belonged to the Islam literature in his writings. The books Liu Zhi used as reference in his works include the following:

The 10th reference book, the word "Lu Ba Ya Ti" given among the references of Liu Zhi's book "Tian Fang Xing Li", is possibly from the book written in Arabic language titled as the "Ruba'iyat". The Chinese transliteration of "Ruba'iyat" is "Four Lines Poetry". Liu Zhi translated this word as "harmony of rhymes". From, Liu Zhi's translation as "Lu Ba Ya Ti" it is indeed hard to determine its original meaning, but certainly it is the same as "Shi Ai Lishi", which possibly originated from the Hui people who lived in the Western regions, and who loved literature and poems.

Another example is the 40th reference, "Miftah al' Ulum" which he used 543 in his book named as Tian Fang Xing Li. Possibly, "Miftah al Ulum" is the title of an Arabic book, (its Chinese transliteration is "the Key to learning". In these two words, the Arabic word "Miftah" means "key" and the Arabic word "Oulu Mi" (al Ulim) means "knowledge". The author of this book was a Persian scholar (Aba Ya'qfib Yusuf b. Abi Bakr al-Sakkaki Siraj al-Din), who died in the year 629 (Persian calendar) (1229 AD).

About the 44th one "Muqaddimat al Adab"(one book that was written in accordance with word meanings) listed in the references of Tian Fang Dian Li, is possibly the title of an Arabic book "Muqaddimat al Adab" (the Chinese transliteration of "the basis of knowledge"); among them, the Arabic word "Muqaddimat" means "preface or basis" and the Arabic word "Adab" means "etiquette, learning and literature". Liu Zhi translated it as "summary of meaning of words" written by Abu al-Qasim Mahmud ibn Umar al-Zamakhshari (Life 1075-1144 AD).

As for the 39th and 45th references "Sahah" listed in both the two books "Tian Fang Xing Li" and "Tian Fang Dian Li", is possibly the Chinese transliteration of "complete and correct". Liu Zhi has translated it as "correct word". According to the translation of "Sahah" and "word correctness", today we cannot determine its original meanings and its author, but it is certain that it is related to an Arabic textbook.

---

31 Published in 1983 by the publishing House Leiden, E.J. Brill.

About the 3rd reference, "Ta'lim al Muta'allim" mentioned in Tian Fang Dian Li, it should be the Chinese transliteration of "disciplines for scholars"; among them, "Ta'lim" refers to "scholars" and "Muta'allim" means "disciplines and teaching"; Liu Zhi translated it into "notes for learning" written by Burhana Din al Zarnughi in the year AD 1203. It is possibly a preliminary book if we consider its title and the literal meaning of the title. About the 2nd reference, Tafsir al Qadi referred in the both two books "Tian Fang Xing Li" and "Tian Fang Dian Li", it should be the Chinese transliteration of the first three-parts of the Koran. Liu Zhi has translated it as "The most true interpretative writings". Here the Arabic word Tafsir refers to "annotation and interpretation" and Qadi means "judge ". It is the Chinese transliteration of Arabic language, but it was usually called "Hadi" or "Hedi" in its Persian pronunciation".

According to the prominent scholar Pang Shiqian such most true interpretation was made by Al Baydawi Abd Allah Ibn Umar. Al Baydawi Abd Allah Ibn Umar has once served as a judge in Shiraz, his name included the word "judge" in Arabic which is Qadi (Kadı) He wrote a commentary on Holy Koran entitled as The Light of Revelation and The Secrets of Interpretation (Anwar al-Tanzil Asrar al-Tawil): He is considered as one of the soundest and most authoritative interpreters and commentators of Islam and Koran.

He died in 791 (1291 AD according to the Persian lunar calendar. This book belongs to the Shafi school of Sunni Islam and it has mainly focused on the interpretation issues. It was a concise book, which can help our studies on Islamic literature. From the above bibliographies, we can see that although the language learning in China was aimed at teaching, understanding and disseminate Islamic classics, the Arabic and Persian language education itself led by Hui people has been a very important stage in the history of foreign language teaching in the history of ancient China.

(2) History, Philosophy and Yin Yang Theory by the Hui Scholars

During the Tang and Song Dynasties periods, when the ancestors of the Hui (Islam) nationality came to inland China, in the first stage, they lived as immigrants. In addition to the Holy Koran, the Hui scholars have brought books of history, philosophy, Yin and Yang, astrology, and astrology, with them. To read their own Islam homeland history, can be evaluated as readings about their distant hometown, or nostalgia, Islams and Arabs inherited the philosophy of Greece, classical Roman works, and Islam together, Yin and Yang concept is a component part of ancient customs among the people of Hui nationality. At present, the materials we have about the history of Hui, about their philosophy and about the Yin Yang theory are mainly the books from the Hui nationality left from the periods of two dynasties, i.e., the Yuan and Qing. The Yuan Dynasty history is mainly recorded in "Mi Shu-jian-Zhi" ((Description of the General Secretariat) written by Wang Shidian.[32]

32 See Wang Shidian, "Mi shu jian- zhi" (Description of the general secretariat), Guang cang xue jun zong shu I. Yu Dajun, "Meng-gu Duo-er-bian shi Bu-luo shi-ji" (Studies on the activities of Bolod of the Mongolian Dörben clan), in Yuan shi lun-cong (Studies on the history of the Yuan dynasty) Vol. I, Beijing, 1982.

Also the bibliography of Hui writings in the early Qing, was mainly recorded in the two books which was written by Liu Zhi[33] titled as follows: "Tian Fang Xing Li "and "Tian Fang Dian Li" (The Rites of Islam). The book, "Tian Fang Xing Li "the Nature and Principle in the Direction of Heaven", was considered the authoritative exposition of Islamic beliefs and were re-published 25 times between 1760 and 1939, and were constantly referred to by those Islams who could write and read in Chinese.

In a book entitled Mi Shu Jian Zhi written by Wang Shidian and Shang Qiweng in the early 14th century, there is a list of so called "Hui Hui books," namely Islamic books which was prepared in 1273 (all the titles of the books collected in this list were transcribed into Chinese characters, as well as being provided with Chinese translations). The 17th book on this list is entitled "Tie Li Hei" and contains 3 chapters. The Chinese translation is given as "Histories and Names of Countries". Apparently, this "Tie Li Hei" is the Chinese transcription of the Persian or Arabic word "Tarikh", and it could be either a Persian or an Arabic historic book. Unfortunately, all these above mentioned sources were unknown to Chinese scholars of that time. Despite the fact that missionaries increasingly introduced Chinese sources to Europe from the first quarter of the 16-century onwards, when the Portuguese arrived in Southeast China, until the end of the 19th century Chinese scholars relied mainly on Chinese sources for their research. Apart from the Secret History of the Mongols, they had almost no idea about the sources written in non-Chinese languages, nor of the contributions of their foreign colleagues.

Let us overview Liu Zhi's 2 books and references in it:

The 34th and 29th ones respectively listed in the references of the two books "Tian Fang Xing Li" and "Tian Fang Dian Li" is probably the Chinese transliteration of the Persian book which is named as "Qisas-i Mi'raj". In which, the Arabic word Qisas referred to "tale, story or legend" and the Arabic word al-Ma'raj referred to "ladder and staircase". Another book in Chinese was translated as "Mohamed Deng Xiao". Liu Zhi translated it as "Deng Xiao Lu". The Persian author Mu'in al-Din al-Farahi (Mu Yin) who probably died in 907 AD (in Hicri lunar calendar as 1501-1502) had written this book. His book was a work about the early activities of Islam prophet Mohamed, the founder of Islam, including legends and which has mythological colors.

The 32nd and 25th one listed respectively in the references of the two books "Tian Fang Xing Li" and "Tian Fang Dian Li" is probably the Chinese transliteration of Arabic book named as Qisas-al-Anbiya. Liu Zhi called it "Records of All Saints" in his book "Tian Fang Xing Li" and "All saints" in "Tian Fang

---

33   Liu Zhi, a famous Chinese Hui Islam scholar, in the early 18th century published two books entitled Tian Fang Dian Li and Tian Fang Xing Li in which he cited about 70 Islamic books, mainly Arabic and Persian. Both transcribed names and translations were given. But the materials about Ming Dynasty period and literature about Huis from this period are still rare, not sufficient enough, yet to be discovered and classified.

Dian Li". If we evaluated from the book's name, we can guess that it was a book about the deeds of other prophets before the Islam prophet Mohamed which included also Jesus Christ who was recognized by Islam believers.

The 35th one listed in the references of "Tian Fang Xing Li" is probably the Chinese transliteration of Arabic book name Tadhkirat al-Auliya. In which, the Arabic word "Tadhkirat" refers to "biography and memorial" and the Arabic word "al-Auliya" (Evliya) referred to "saints". Liu Zhi translated it as "wise men". Considering the Arabic original name of the book and Liu Zhi's translation, we can guess that it was a narration about leading followers (Evliya) of the Islam prophet Mohammed.

The 35th and 36th ones respectively listed in the references of "Tian Fang Xing Li" and "Tian Fang Dian Li" should be the Chinese transliteration of Persian book name "Shajar-Nama". In which, the Persian word "Shajar" refers "tree or branch" and the Persian word "Nama" referred to "letters, notes and records". Liu Zhi translated it as "The Origin of the World Spectrum". It is probably a record about Mohamed's lineage or his descendants (the so-called the "holy or saint people").

The 36th reference listed among the references of "Tian Fang Dian Li" is possibly the Chinese transliteration of the Arabic book named as Sharh al-Madahib. In which, the Arabic word "Sharh" refers to "doctrines" and the Arabic word "Al Madahib" means "various sects, various, doctrines" Liu Zhi has translated this title as "the Source of Teaching".

As can be seen from the above materials, the Hui scholars have been quite better than the Han Scholars of the same period in regard to their knowledge about the post-Islam era in the period Western Asia regions. Most of the historical works authored by the Hui people are related to Islam. Due to the limitation of their religious ideas, their works on the Western Asian history, mainly aimed to promote the historical consciousness on Islam, which has limited the horizon of the Hui authors.

The situation of the Hui philosophy is closely related with the history of the Hui nationality and also mainly related with the study of Islam. In the sense of pure philosophy, we have few references and studies in regard to the philosophy of Hui nationality.

In the Volume 7 of the book "Mi Shu-jian-Zhi" (Description of the general secretariat) written by Wang Shidian a book called "passive flow of arguments" was mentioned.

The title "Ai Jie Ma Da" is possibly an Arabic book with the original title "Hikmat" in Arabic. Its Chinese version is from the Yuan dynasty period. The Arabic word "Hikmat" means "wisdom or philosophy", the metaphorical Chinese translation of this title can be translated as "passive flow of arguments".

This is undoubtedly a philosophical work, which is preserved in the Secretariat Office of the Yuan which consists of 12 volumes (Department). We know that, this work is quite comprehensive. It is a book that studies existence, but its details are yet unknown. Due to limitations caused by religious ideas, Islam scholars have not paid much attention to discuss the purely philosophical issues. Almost all their works which deals with purely philosophical problems were influenced by the ancient Greek philosophy to a certain extent, so the above book is probably a translated version of an ancient Greek philosophical book.

The study of Yin and Yang was a unique part of the secular culture of Hui people in the ancient times. Currently, these books are kept in the archives of Yuan Dynasty, and the Hui people (Chinese Islam people) have attach great importance to study Yin and Yang. One of the important characteristics of their study of Yin and Yang was to understand the practical life issues. The purpose of these ancient Hui scholars to study them was to use this set of theories to predict the future, especially disasters. The ancient Chinese ephemeris was similar to that of Yin and Yang understanding of the Hui scholars, which also combines natural phenomena, i.e., the movement of celestial bodies with the men's fate, which means it saw the fate as the expression of the will of the nature. Consequently, ancient Chinese ephemeris was often associated with Hui scholars' Yin and Yang (a kind of ephemeris). Thus, In the Yuan Dynasty period these Hui (ephemeris) scholars were called "Yin and Yang people".

An Islam-Arab book titled as "Akan: Deciding Disasters and Happiness", included in Volume 7 of Mi Shu Jian Zhi (Records by the Secretariat). Here, Akan was the Chinese transliteration of the Arabic word "Ahkam" which was paraphrased "ordering" or "deciding the disasters and happiness" in the Yuan Dynasty. It was not clear how many volumes were included in Mi Shu Jian Zhi which contained another book titled as "Fulasan Anthroposcopy" in its 7th volume. Fulasan was the Chinese transliteration of the Persian word "Frasa" of which the Arabic equivalent was "Farasat" which was paraphrased as "anthroposcopy" in the Yuan Dynasty. According to the Islamic Dictionary: Profession (Farasat) was annotated as "physiognomist" (the 196th word). All in all, "Fulasan Anthroposcopy" which was mentioned in the Mi Shu Jian Zhi was the paraphase naming of the book which forecasted the future based on people's palms (hands) and based on their physical looking. This book had remained in the Secretariat Office of the Yuan Dynasty. The specific contents of this book are unknown since it was later lost. It was spread to China in the Yuan Dynasty and then, in the Ming Dynasty, it was translated and some parts of it were included in the Islamic Astronomy Book (in Chinese). The title On People's Characteristics of Item 5 in the Part 3 of the Islamic Astronomy Book elaborated the following: "a person's fate, depends on the locations of the sun, the moon and the stars when he/she was born." And people's looking was classified as follows: "dark hair, honey-colored skin, hairy chest, good eyes and gentle personality", "wheat-colored skin, thin hair and body, good proportion, dark eyes and harsh personality", "white skin, lustrous, big body, good hair, good eyes, proper and enthusiastic personality" or "pale skin, lacklustre, thin, straight and dry hair, good eyes, shorter body and moderate personality" etc.

Islamic Astronomy Book, translated by Haidar, Adawuding, Mashayihi and Maham et al. This book edition was engraved in the 16th year of the Hongwu Period, and the quotations were from pages 12a-b, Volume B of Preface to the Translation of the Islamic Astronomy Book, Volume 3 of Treasure Books of Hanfenlou. The Volume 7 of Mi Shu Jian Zhi (Records by the Secretariat) also mentioned another book: 15-volume book Lanmuli Divination Methods. Lanmuli was the Chinese transliteration in the Yuan Dynasty of the Arabic book name "Raml" which was paraphrased "sand-based divination", a method that was used by Arabs who spread sand on the ground and forecasted good or bad fate based on the shape of the sand. It was a huge book with quite abundant contents.

In Volume 7 of Mi Shu Jian Zhi (Records by the Secretariat) another book was mentioned as: Matahezheng Disaster and Happiness Explanation. Matahezheng should be Matahezhi, a transliteration of Arabic Mugta which means "must". So the book's full name should be "The Must Be Read for Divination". The name Disaster and Happiness Explanation was the paraphrase used by the Chinese interpreter. Another Yin-Yang book included in the same volume 7 was the Mi'a Fengshui Identification. The word, "Mi'a" was the Chinese transliteration of the famous Arabic book name Mir'at which means "mirror". The book's full name was Mir'at al-Ghaib which literally means A Treasure Mirror for Identification and was translated as "Fengshui Identification". It was a book on divination and had two volumes collected by the Secretariat of the Yuan Court.

Islamic Astronomy Book was collected by the court during the Yuan Dynasty and not translated.[34] When the Yuan dynasty collapsed, Emperor Taizu of the Ming Dynasty (Zhu Yuanzhang) got the book. In the 15th year of the Hongwu Period (1382), Zhu ordered the Islamic Hui scholars and Chinese scholars to cooperate in the translation. The next year, the book was printed. It was an extremely important study material for the further researches about the Yin-Yang understanding of China's Hui people.

After reading the translated book, the Han scholars of the Ming Dynasty praised it as follows: "This astronomy book from the western regions arrives at the same goal with the Chinese ones despite their different research paths. We know that the principles of this science are sophisticated and universal, and will not be different due to the differences of locations and cultures." The content of this Islamic Astronomy Book is divided into 4 parts: the first part includes the general introduction; the second part is about predicting the good and bad things; the third part is the about fate of people; the fourth part is about various options and choices. The details can be briefly explained as in the following:

---

34 Islamic Astronomy Book, pages 2b-3a, Volume A of Preface to the Translation of the Islamic Astronomy Book.

The first part includes 23 chapters:

The first chapter explains the reasons for the writing of the book; the second chapter is about temperament; the third chapter is about human diseases and disasters; the 4th is about Yin and Yang idea. The 5th is about day and night; and the 6th chapter is about the distance between the sun and other stars; the 7th chapter is about the five stars rising from East to West. The 8th chapter is about the characteristics and functions of the stars; the 9thchapter is about the categories of Zodiac; the 10th chapter is about the days and nights of Zodiac; the 11th chapter explains the characteristics of Zodiac; the 12th chapter is about the positions; the 13th chapter is about the celestial Palace; the 14th chapter is about the position of temples; the 15th chapter is about the main stars; the 16th chapter is about the angle of each Palace belonging to the five stars; the 17th chapter is about each Palace which is divided into three parts; the 18th chapter is the position of each Palace; the 19th chapter is about corresponding mutual relationships among the sun, moon and the stars; the 20th chapter is about the powers and strengths of each Star; the 2st chapter is about the destiny Palace which is divided into 12 equal parts; the 22nd Chapter is about blessing and virtue; the 23rd Chapter is about the position of the main star of each Palace.

The second part includes 12 chapters to predict the good and bad things, in the future: The first chapter is about the general topics; the second chapter includes answers to inferior issues; the third chapter is about disasters and wars; the 4th chapter about diseases and illnesses; the 5th chapter explains that people can easily catch cold when it's windy and rainy. The 6th chapter is about rainy and wet days; the 7th chapter is about curious abnormal situations; the 8th is about how to predict future things; the 9th chapter is about the price of goods; the 10th chapter is about eclipse; and the 11th chapter is about explanations of the two stars combinations of partners, and relationship between the Saturn and the Jupiter; the 12th chapter is about the destiny.

The third part includes 20 chapters, which is about the fate of the people:

The first chapter deals with the general topics; the second chapter is about the events which has occur before birth; the third chapter is about the fate of people; the 4th chapter is about the effect of stars and Zodiac upon the child; the 5th chapter is about the soul of people; the 6th chapter is about whether men's life will be short or long; the 7th Chapter is about the illnesses among the people; the 8th chapter is about the wisdom of life; the 9th Chapter tells about how people catch various illnesses; the 10th chapter is about parents; the 11th chapter is about sisters and brothers; the 12th chapter is about happiness and richness; the 13th chapter is about skills; the 14th chapter is about marriages; the 15th chapter is about relations between men and women partnership; the 16th chapter is about friends and foes; the 17th chapter talks about migration issues; the 18th chapter talks about the reasons of death; the 19th chapter explains about every star controlling several years of one's life; and the 20th chapter talks about happiness and sorrow throughout a year.

The fourth part includes three chapters, which explains about all kinds of miscellaneous issues:

The first chapter talks about general choices; the second chapter talks about conditions of sub-choices; and the third chapter makes conclusive remarks and explains about how to make best use of the book.

The customs mentioned in this book are no longer preserved in the Hui culture. But there are some issues that scholars should pay more attention to in regard to the Hui ancient customs. For example, in the third chapter of the second part, the author wrote: "look into the anniversaries of your life events and four palace lives, take the palace points. If the two stars, i.e., the Mars and the Saturn are in an opposite relation, disasters and wars will occur. If the two Stars are in the four pillars of the palace, then things will be particularly urgent."

Another example is given related to the 9th chapter of the second part as follows: "look at the Syzygy[35] situation to best predict the prices goods", and "if the palace is the earth branch, it controls the grain; if the palace is the water branch, it controls all matters related to the water issues; if the palace is fire branch, it controls all that are produced in regard to mining; if the palace is wind branch, it controls the slaves and animals, etc.

About the marriage, the Hans paid more attention to the date of birth and the eight characters of a horoscope. Chinese love horoscope compatibility was analysed basing upon the pair of lovers' birth year-month-date-time information, which was called the Four Pillars of Destiny or the Eight Characters of Birth Time. According to this traditional Chinese marriage culture, it was a routine step for the matchmakers of both sides to exchange the pair's Four Pillars of Destiny dates. In the book "On Marriage", there was one sentence in the 14th part of the book, that is, "when talking about the marriage, for men people looked to the 7th house as well as its dominant. and people also looked to the Venus planet and marriage arrow as well as its dominant. For women, people looked at the 7th house and its dominant, and look at the Sun as well as marriage arrow and its ruler. All mentioned above, people saw which one was strong and which one was the dominant. If they matched, it would be a harmonious marriage and they will be a harmonious couple. If not, the relation between wife and husband would not be good. If the rulers do not match, the marriage would not be successful."

In addition, this book also talked about the astrological signs of "marriage between the famous families", "marriage between the rich families", and "marriage between the poor families". Among all the reference books listed in the book "Tian Fang Xing Li" (written by Liu Zhi), there were abundant tbooks related to the Hui Yi and Ying Yang theory. For example, the 3rd one "Mili Teerbi" should be the Chinese transliteration of Arabic book name Kamil al Ta'bir, here, Kamil means "complete" and the word Ta'bir means "explanation"

---

35 Syzygy, the nearly straight-line configuration of three celestial bodies such as the sun, moon, and earth during a solar or lunar eclipse.

and interpretation". Liu Zhi translated it into Dream Dictionary, which might be written by Abu'l-Fadl al-Husayn b. Ibrāhīm al-Mutatabbib al-Tiflisi (died in AD 1203). It was one book that explained the relation between the reality and the future, which we usually called it "oneiromancy". The 24th one listed in the references of "Tian Fang Xing Li" should be the Chinese transliteration of Arabic book name Ahkam al Kawakib, which referred to "Star determination". In which, "Ahkam al" was "determination" recorded in the 7th part of "Mi Shu Jian Zhi" and "Kawakib" is the plural form of "Kukib". Liu Zhi translated it as "Tian Jing Xing Qing" which might be the same as "All disasters can be determined" to judge disasters and predict the future based on ephemeris.

(3) The Hui Medical Science

The natural science studies by Hui originated scholars and practitioners is an important component part of the Chinese Islam culture as well as an major foreign facilitator for the development of Chinese science and technologies, only second to Indian science. The Hui medical science played an important role in the interaction of Chinese and foreign cultures.

The central plains of China established ties with the Western and overseas regions in the pre-Qin period. In the Western Han Dynasty, Zhang Qian, a diplomat and an imperial envoy, blazed a trail in the Western regions. Since then, the Chinese and Western communication entered a flourishing era, with foreign products like medicine continuously flowing into the Central Plains region. Under such circumstances, the Hui medicine gradually became popular among the Han people.

551

The Hui medicine as possibly brought to China by the Arabic and Persian merchants. However, books about the Hui medicine were only used by the Arabs and Persians living in China at first. The Islamic medicine was introduced to China around the founding of the Yuan Dynasty, when Genghis Khan and his descendants led their armies to conquer the Western Regions to the East bank of the Mediterranean.

A great number of books were brought to the Central Plains Region following the establishment of the Yuan Dynasty, which made great efforts to collect works of various ethnic nationalities at the same time. The Hui medical and pharmacy books were also in these collections. The Tibb (Tıb in Arabic), which is the 13th volume of more than 600 Hui books mentioned in the 7th volume of the book "Mishujian Zhi" (The Account of the Palace Library of the Yuan Dynasty) which is a work about the Hui medicine.

The Hui people brought the Western therapies and drugs to the Central Plains region during the Tang dynasty period. However, according to Xu Youren, a scholar of the Yuan Dynasty, the Han people in the Tang dynasty were not familiar with these therapies and medicines. But during the Yuan dynasty period, alongside increasingly closer ties with the Western regions, many Hui merchants entered the inland of China, and have brought various Western products.

Xu wrote in his Zhi Zheng Ji (Volume 31), "The Northwestern medicine boasts a great variety of excellent therapies and drugs which were effective in curing diseases. The imperial court established a special department, namely Guang Hui Si, for the management of the Hui medicine."

The introduction of Islamic medicine to China broadened the eyes of the people in the central plains and highlighted the disadvantages of the medical books written by the Han people. Kublai Khan once received treatment based on Han therapies and inquired about the Materia Medica (Ben Cao) with the Han doctors. He pointed out that the book about the Han medicine has many defects, including the lack of mentioning of medical science of other nationalities.[36]

Therefore, Kublai Khan ordered to amend the Materia Medica, especially adding the Western medicine into it. According to Su Tianjue, a scholar living in the Yuan Dynasty, famous doctors like Han Lin were summoned to the imperial palace, where Kublai Khan asked them to distinguish Western drugs from Han drugs. Su wrote in his book, "A Han man tasted a drug and said, 'It has equal effect with a Han drug.'"[37]

For more details about that mentioned above, please refer to Amendment of Materia Medica under the Order of Kublai Khan, by Gao Hua.[38]

Guang Hui Si[39] was not only an organization for the management of the Hui-hui medicine, but a hospital that provided treatment to imperial guards and immigrants coming from the Western Regions.[40]

It was established in the late period of Kublai Khan by incorporating two existing departments. In addition to imperial Hui doctors, there were also many folk doctors from the Western regions in the Yuan Dynasty. According to the ballad called "Medicine Seller", people from the Western regions sold medical plasters and other drugs in the streets.[41]

It is a story about a Western trader, who was also a proficient doctor giving treatment to people in the Southern regions. Ding Henian was a scholar from Hui ethnic origin who lived in the late Yuan Dynasty period. His ancestors were among the earliest Hui merchants who came to the central plains for trade.

---

36   Yao Sui's Collections: Volume 29: Epitaph on Medical Scientist Li Jun.
37   Su Tianjue's Collections: Vol. 22: Brief Biography of Deceased Imperial Academy of Medicine Executive Han Lin.
38   Collection on Studies on History of Yuan Dynasty and Northern Ethnic Nationalities, Ed. 1986, Vol. 10.
39   In Yuan Dynasty, an administrative organ Guang Hui Si was set up as a branch of the royal hospital to research on Hui and Arab medicines. In Yuan Shi (The History of Yuan Dynasty), it was written in the chapter of "Bai Guan Zhi" (the government system) that "officials of Guang Hui Si were the third highest ranking officials.
40   Tao Zongyi's Out of Tillage: Vol. 9: Uncommon Diseases, Zhonghua Book Company, p. 109. See also, History of Yuan Dynasty: Records of Officials.
41   Yi Bin Ji, Wang Yi, Complete Library in the Four Branches of Literature, Vol. 5.

Although the later generations of his family were accustomed to the lifestyle of the Han people, Ding was still proficient in various Hui skills and sciences, including the medicine field.[42]

The most famous book about Islam medicine in China is the book called Hui Formularies (Hui Hui Yao Fang). It consists of 36 volumes, only four of which survived till today (its copies were made in the Ming dynasty period) and are kept in Capital Library of China. These copies show different writing styles, indicating that they should be copied by different people. Most of them are in Chinese, while a few in Arabic and Persian (such as medicine names). The writing styles indicate that the copiers of texts must be good in writing Arabic and Persian, but did not understand their meaning very well, since there are abundant errors. These works are probably the copies of copies. One of the four volumes is about the Contents of the Hui Formula, which includes the list of titles of Volumes 19 to 36. The other copies are Volumes 12, 30 and 34. Each of these volumes includes the symptoms of a series of diseases as well as, their relevant therapies.

Contents I (lost)

Contents II (58 pages).

Volume 12: on stroke and related diseases; (The current copy has four pages of contents and 63 pages of text.)

Volume 19: on cough;

Volume 20: on chest diseases;

Volume 21: on intestinal diseases;

Volume 22: on diarrhea;

Volume 23: on emesis, epigastric fullness and related diseases;

Volume 24: on fever and coldness and related diseases;

Volume 25: on blood diseases, malaria and other related diseases;

Volume 26: on body;

Volume 27: on jaundice and related diseases;

Volume 28: on dermatophytosis, rectocele, anal fistula and related diseases;

Volume 29: on miscellaneous diseases;

Volume 30: also on miscellaneous diseases; (The current copy has three pages of contents and 63 pages of text.)

Volume 31: on gynecological diseases and pediatric diseases;

Volume 33: on sores and tinea;

Volume 34: on incised wound, fractures, acupuncture, scald, burn and other injuries. (The currency copy has three pages of contents and 49 pages of text.)

Volume 35: on injuries by animals;

Volume 36: on decocting methods and medical effects of vegetables and fruits.

---

42   Biography of Sages and Hermits, Jiuling Mountain Hermit's Works, Collections of Classics of Four Schools, Vol. 19.

Based on these volumes, we can estimate that the whole book included 40 volumes, with more than 2,000 pages, with more than 1.5 million characters. The current copies only account for one tenth of the whole book. The book "Hui Formularies" is a translation work translated by an unknown Islam person. The names mentioned in the book indicate that it should be a medical work in Arabic. However, the Chinese version of the book was possibly translated from the original work. Possibly, it was translated from the Persian version. The book Hui Formularies mentions a great number of sages about medicines. They were mentioned as Hui doctors by the translators. However, actually, among them were many ancient Greeks and Romans. For example, the Volume 30 mentions Iskandar, which is the Persian name of Alexander the Great from the ancient Greece, and doctor Arastatalis, which is the Persian name of Aristotle, an ancient Greek medical scientist and the instructor of Alexander the Great. There is another example in the same volume 30, namely, "the Hui doctor Jalinus". Jalinus is actually the Persian name of Galen (Galenos), who was not a Hui doctor but a medical scientist of the ancient Greece. Likewise, the volume also mentions Rufus, who was an ancient Greek doctor, and Farfuriyus, the Arabic name of Roman philosopher Porphyrios. The Volume 34 mentioned Abuqrat, the Arabic name of ancient Greek medical scientist Hippocrates.

Many names of medicinal herbs mentioned in this book are translations from Greek or Latin. For example, the Volume 30 mentions aftimun, which is the Arabic name of epithymum in Greek, referring to Cuscuta. Ustukhudus is the Arabic and Persian word for stoichas in Greek, referring to Mentha spicata (eng. spearmint). Apsinthion is also the Greek name of an herb. In Volume 12, farfiyun is originated from Latin euphorbium, referring to Euphorbia, while ghariqun is originated from agarikon in Greek, which refers to agaric (a type of mushroom). Also in the Volume 12, the word "karanb" refers to krambae (cabbage) in Greek. In Volume 30, an Aristotle's prescription includes kamadariyus, referring to a kind of Greek herb named chamaedrus. In the same volume, kamafitus, originated from chamaepitus in Greek, refers to a kind of diuretic. The book Hui Formula includes many medicine names translated from those languages other than Persian and Arabic, mostly from Greek and Latin language to Chinese. The mentioning of the ancient Greek and Roman people and medicine indicates that, the works about Islam medicine in China, including the Hui Formularies, are collections about medical science of different ethnic nationalities dwelling along the banks of Eastern Mediterranean. These works include but not limited to Persian and Arabic medical science.

(4) The Hui Astronomy (Hui Lifa[43]) and Calendar

The Hui astronomy, the most influential component part of Islamic culture in China, was brought to China by the Hui people from Central Asia in the Yuan Dynasty period (1271-1368).

---

43   Hui Lifa, can be translated as Islam System of Calendar Astronomy, it was a set of astronomical tables published throughout China from the time of the Ming Dynasty in the late 14th century through the early 18th century. The tables were based on a translation into Chinese of the Zij (Islamic astronomical tables).

The Hui Lifa, which was first only used by the Hui people, was recognized by the government of the Ming Dynasty (1368-1644) due to its precision and unique reckoning methods that could serve as a supplement and reference to the Han calendar system. Therefore, the Hui Lifa was widely spread until the Western missionaries flooded China in late Ming Dynasty period.

The Hui ephemerides served as the foundation of the Hui astronomy. Many of them were in the collections of the Yuan government's Book Collection and Edition Office (Mishujian), which was dedicated to collecting and editing books, while some were translated into the Han language in the early Ming Dynasty period. The Ming Dynasty period was much richer in regard to published and translated Hui Lifa materials compared to the Yuan Dynasty period. The 7th volume of the Records of the Book Collection and Edition Office (Mishujian Zhi) mentioned several books translated from the Arabic. These books are mainly about the Hui astronomy, calendar and theories about the motion and routes of the celestial bodies.

The Hui Book of Astronomy (Hui Tian Wen Shu), which is passed down to our generation, can be evaluated as one of the most important books about the Hui astronomy from the Ming dynasty period. It is the only book about the Yin-Yang astrology written by the Hui ethnic people as well as, one of a few books that verified the fact that books about the Hui astronomy were introduced to China during the Yuan dynasty period. It was authored by Kushyar, an Arabic scholar who lived in early 11th century, and translated by a number of Hui scholars who served the imperial court of the Ming Dynasty, such as Hai Da Er, A Da Wu Ding, Shaikh Muhammad and Ma Ha Da. The Chinese version of the book was printed in the 16th year under the reign of Emperor Hongwu of the Ming Dynasty. As mentioned in the preface, the book was taken to Nanjing city by the Ming army that invaded Khanbaliq, capital of the Yuan Dynasty, in 1368, together with tens of thousands of imperial books of the Yuan Dynasty. In 1382, Zhu Yuanzhang, first emperor of the Ming Dynasty, ordered officials to read some books of the Yuan Dynasty for him. Hence hundreds of books written with unfamiliar characters were discovered. In those days, many Han people in the Ming Dynasty knew that the astrologists in the Western regions had extremely precise astronomical calculations, especially those on latitudes, which are not seen in the Han books. However, the Hui books were strictly protected by the Yuan government which meant that the Hans had little opportunity to examine them before the Yuan Dynasty perished. Therefore the Ming emperor, who was eager to explore the unique features of the Hui books, ordered the Hui scholars mentioned above to translate the books, and the Hui Book of Astronomy was one of such books. Wu Bozong, a member of the Imperial Academy and the author of the preface, said: "The book about the Western Regions was promoted by the Yuan Dynasty for more than 100 years." Wu believed that it was fortunate that the book could studied widely in the Ming Dynasty period. The emperor ordered the Hui scholars to translate the books and the Han scholars to proof-read the translations in order to guarantee the clarity and readability of the translations. The emperor was insistent that the translations should be faithful to the originals. That is why we can make use of the reliable translations of the Hui books today.

The book, mainly about the Yin-Yang theories, is fundamentally a work about the Hui astronomy. According to the book, "Astronomical devices were used to measure the motions of the celestial body". On the other hand, it also said, "The celestials are auspicious or ominous, corresponding to things on the Earth." It shows that the Hui ephemerides are mixed with science and superstition. Another book is the one-volume Hui Calendar, which was printed in the 16th year under the reign of Emperor Hongwu of the Ming Dynasty. It is today among the collections of the Capital Library of China. It must be one of the books translated by the Hui scholars under the order of Emperor Zhu Yuanzhang. The book covers the Hui lunar and solar calendars, the conversion between the two kinds of calendars, the names of the Sun and the Moon, the intercalary months in the lunar calendar, the solar elevation, the longitude and latitude of planets, the relations between the moon and the planets, as well as the solar and lunar eclipses.

According to the book, a year was divided into 12 months—all in Persian language—as follows:

The 1st month: Farwardin
The 2nd month: Urdibihisht
The 3rd month: Khurdad
The 4th month: Tir
The 5th month: Murdad
The 6th month: Shahriwar
The 7th month: Mihr
The 8th month: Aban
The 9th month: Azar
The 10th month: Day
The 11th month: Bahman
The 12th month: Isfand

The Hui solar calendar begins on March 3rd which follows the sun's cycle, while the Hui lunar calendar is based on moon's cycles and the lunar phases. This determines the solar calendar changes relative to the lunar calendar. Therefore, the 12 months mentioned in the book actually refer to the "dynamically changing months".

The Chapter on Seven Luminaries in the book said that a week consists of seven days, with names as follows:

Yebieshan (in Chinese), Ik Shanba in Persian, refers to the third day of the week (Sunday in the Gregorian calendar). In different books and articles there are have different translations of this word, but they refer to the same day. According to the book the Records of Western Countries written by Chen Cheng: "(The customs of the Timurid Dynasty) follows a period of seven days, and Ik Shanba is the third day."

In the Hui Calendar, Ik Shanba is mentioned as Riyishu, meaning the first luminary of the seven luminaries. The Islam week starts on Friday when compared with the Gregorian calendar we use today.

Dubieshan (in Chinese), which is equivalent of Du Shanba in Persian, refers to the 4th day of the week (Monday on the Gregorian calendar), according to the Records of Western Countries, and is mentioned as "yue'ershu" in the Hui Calendar, meaning the second luminary of the Seven Luminaries.

Xiebieshan, which is equivalent of Sba Shanbain in Persian, refers to the fifth day of the week (Tuesday on the Gregorian calendar), according to the Records of Western Countries, and is mentioned as Huosanshu in the Hui Calendar, meaning the third luminary of the Seven Luminaries.

Chaerbieshan (in Chinese), which is equivalent of Chahar Shanba (Çarşamba) in Persian, refers to the 6th day of the week (Wednesday on the Gregorian calendar), and is mentioned as "Shusishu" in the Hui Calendar, meaning the fourth 4th luminary of the seven Luminaries.

Panshanbie (in Chinese), which is equivalent of Panj Shanba (Perşembe) in Persian, refers to the seventh day of the week (Thursday on the Gregorian calendar), and is mentioned as "muwushu" in the Hui Calendar, meaning the fifth luminary of the Seven Luminaries.

Adina (in Chinese), which is equivalent of Adina in Persian, refers to the first day of the week (Friday on the Gregorian calendar), and is mentioned as jin- 557 liushu in the Hui Calendar, meaning the 6th luminary of the Seven Luminaries.

Shanbie (in Chinese), which is equivalent of Shanba in Persian, refers to the second day of the week (Saturday on the Gregorian calendar), and is mentioned as "tuqishu" in the Hui Calendar, meaning the seventh luminary of the Seven Luminaries.

The Persian elements in the book mentioned above prove that the Hui Calendar was written by Persians. On the other hand, the book contains methods for conversion from the Hui calendar to the Han calendar, which must be added by the translators. Obviously, the book was not just a translation.

The Chapter on Hui Calendar in the book History of the Ming Dynasty was possibly based on the Hui Calendar mentioned above and the Hui Calendar Days were created by a Persian astronomer Jamal al-Din under the order of an Anxi based feudal lord. According to the book "History of the Ming Dynasty", "The Hui Calendar was written by Mahama, a king of a Western kingdom which was located over 8,000 li to west of Yunnan......This calendar does not include leap months. A year consists of 365 days in 12 months......There are leap days......There were several calendars used in the Western regions during the Tang and Yuan dynasties period. However, only the Hui calendar was used together with the Han calendar for a long period, namely more than 270 years. The scholars in the Ming Dynasty studied on the Hui calendar and wrote books based on it. Then, the translation was out of use. The Hui Calendar was written after consulting with related experts and making supplement to the original book."

The paragraph mentioned above gives an account of the dissemination history of the Western calendars in China. In the Tang and Yuan dynasties, the Hui calendar was mainly used by the Hui people. It became popular in the Ming Dynasty, when the government recruited scholars who were proficient in Hui calendar to teach the Han people calculation methods in the Hui calendar. For example, Liu Xin, an official at the Imperial Board of Astronomy, edited the Summary on Hui Calendar (Xi Yu Li Fa Tong Jing), which currently has 8 volumes remaining, namely, the Volumes 11, 12, 13, 14, 21, 22, 23 and 24.

Bihlam, a man who had worked for the Imperial Board of Astronomy of the Ming Dynasty in the Nanjing city, wrote the seven-volume book titled as "Seven-Star Astronomical Calculation" (Qi Zheng Tui Bu), which was made part of the Complete Works of Chinese Classics (Si Ku Quan Shu) compiled in the Qing Dynasty. The seven stars in this book refer to the Sun, Moon, Saturn, Jupiter, Mars, Venus and Mercury. The book is about astronomical calculation based on the seven stars. Bihlam, a name which is possibly a word from the Turkic language background, is supposed to belong to a Persian person. In this book "Seven-Star Astronomical Calculation" the author wrote: "In the 18th year under the reign of Emperor Hongwu of the Ming Dynasty, minority ethnic nationalities were subordinated to the rule of the Ming Dynasty and presented the Western astronomical calculation methods, which were later translated into Han language and became quite popular in China since then." This book demonstrates the inheritance of scientific knowledge from the Hui scholars, it was translated by Hai Da Er and other scholars. For example, the length of months and weeks and their names are all the same with that in the Hui Calendar, even with the same errors in transliteration. Bihlam made a supplement to the Hui Calendar based on the Western astronomical calculation methods. In addition to the book "Seven-Star Astronomical Calculation", Bihlam also wrote a book entitled as the Explanatory Examples for the Hui Calendar, which consisted of four volumes.

The Hui Calendar had its important merits. That is why it was used as a supplement to the Han calendar in the Han and Ming dynasties periods. However, it also has some defects, such as inaccurate calculation and estimation, and lacked continuous updating. That's why it was gradually cast into the shade by new sciences brought by European missionaries, such as Matteo Ricci, Sabatino de Ursis, Johann Terrenz, Emmanuel Diaz and Giacomo Rho, as well as astronomical works written by Chinese scholars, such as Li Zhizao and Xu Guangqi. However, there were still other narrations about the Hui astronomy in the works by scholars of the Qing Dynasty period, for example, in Liu Zhi's 2 famous books we have mentioned above the Tian Wen Xing Li" (The Rites of Islam) and the "Tian Fang Dian Li (the Nature and Principle in the Direction of Heaven) Although, Liu Zhi was famous scholar from the Hui ethnic people.

Liu Zhi did not have access to the new European culture that had been introduced into China at that time.

The Hui astronomical works mentioned in Liu Zhi's books include the following:

Atar al' Ulwiya (in Arabic), which means phenomena of celestial bodies, is the 25th reference for Astronomical Principles. Itis probably related with Atar al'-Ulum.

The Arabic word Af'al i Aflak, which means movements and motions of celestial bodies, is respectively the 23rd and 40th references for the Astronomical Principles and the Islamism.

The Arabic word Ahkam al Kawakib, which means astrology, is the 24th reference for the Astronomical Principles.

The Arabic word Ilm al Afaq, which means "the science about the universe", is the 21st reference for the Astronomical Principles. It includes the principles of ancient Greek astronomy.

The Arabic word Al' Ahd al-Kabir, which means great times, it is respectively the 25th and 39th references for the Astronomical Principles and the Islamism.

The Hui mathematics was an achievement of Islamic scientific exploration, which deserves appreciation and pride. It has inherited the achievements of ancient Greek mathematics and has become an independent school after being introduced to China. The Hui Book of Astronomy said: An armillary sphere[44] was used to make measurement for calculating the rules of the movements of celestial bodies."

It means to process the device measurement results using mathematical methods to learn about the operation rules of the celestial bodies.

The preface part of the Chapter on Hui Calendar in the History of the Ming Dynasty said that the Hui people in China still used their own calendar. The Hui mathematics is narrated in the Records of the Book Collection and Edition Office, which are mostly dated back to the Yuan Dynasty period, for example:

The Pargar and Ruler (Pergel and Cetvel) which is used for drawing circles and Squares is mentioned in the 7th volume of the Records of the Book Collection and Edition Office. Pargar means compass in Persian. There was one such book kept in the Book Collection and Edition Office. Ruler for Drawing Circles and Squares is the translation of the tool during the Yuan Dynasty period according to the functions of these tools.

---

44 An armillary sphere is a model of objects in the sky (on the celestial sphere), consisting of a spherical framework of rings, centred on Earth or the Sun, that represent lines of celestial longitude and latitude and other astronomically important features.

Hisabiya Algorithms is mentioned in the seventh volume of the Records of the Book Collection and Edition Office. Hisabiya means mathematics or calculation in Arabic. It is a monograph on mathematics. There were seven volumes of the book in the Book Collection and Edition Office.

Safina Algorithms is mentioned in the seventh volume of the Records of the Book Collection and Edition Office. Safina means collections. It is a collection of algorithms, covering algebra and geometry. There were 12 volumes of the book in the Book Collection and Edition Office.

Safina Handasiya Geometry is mentioned in the 7th volume of the Records of the Book Collection and Edition Office. Safina Handasiya means a collection of eludications on geometry. There have been 17 volumes of this book in the archives of Book Collection and Edition Office. It is an excellent presentation of Hui geometry and also includes ancient Greek mathematics.

Euclidean Elements of Geometry is mentioned in the 7th volume of the Records of the Book Collection and Edition Office. Euclidean Geometry refers to the ancient Greek mathematician who had written the Elements of Geometry. It is mainly about graph partition. There were 15 volumes of this book in the Book Collection and Edition Office. The Historical Records (Shi Ji) in Persian said that Emperor Xianzong of the Yuan Dynasty once did exercises on Euclidean geometry under the guidance of an Islam scholar.

560 In 1956, Shaanxi Cultural Relics Administration Committee discovered five iron plates bearing six-row and double six-column magic square (Double six magic square) with Arabic numerals at the archeological-historical site of Seignior Anxi Palace, which is located in the northeast of Xi'an. Magic square, also called "Zonghengtu" in Chinese, which is a square matrix of number of rows and columns. The first n^2 integers are arranged in the cells of the matrix in such a way that the sum of any row or column or diagonal is the same. Magic square originated from China. The Book of Changes: Seven Discussions (Zhou Yi: Xi Ci) mentioned: "Map sourced from Yellow River, while book its sources from Luo River." Here the book actually refers to a magic square with three rows and three columns, each with a sum of 15.

According to the Historical Records (Shi Ji) written in Persian, Prince Anxi, who was brought up by Hui people, embraced Islam. Therefore, the magic square[45] discovered in his palace must belong to him or his fellows or Mongolians who believed in Islam.

45　Such plates were buried in the corner of the foundation to ward off evil spirits. The belief in the magical properties of numbers is one of those beliefs that crops up in many cultures. The belief in the good and bad properties of certain numbers had been well seated before this import from the Western worlds in the Yuan Dynasty (1271 1368). During the Northern Song Dynasty, Xi'an was known as Jingzhaofu. Its name was changed to Fengyuan in 1273 under the Yuan Dynasty. In 1275 Prince Anxi, built a palace city near Xi'an. It was called Dawang Dian in Chinese and Gan Erduo in Mongolian.

In 1958, based on an in-depth study on the magic square, Li Yan, a Chinese Mathematician, pointed that the sum of any row or column or diagonal of the magic square is 111. He also found that the six-row and six-column magic square contains a four-row and four-column one, and the sum of its row or column or diagonal is the same. In 1980, the Department of Archaeology of Shanghai Museum discovered a jade tablet that bears a four-row and four-column magic square with inscribed Arabic numerals when sorting out the cultural relics excavated from the Liujiazui Tomb. The sum of each row, column or diagonal of the magic square is 34. The cultural relics mentioned above are rare and valuable witnesses of the Eastern and Western communication during the ancient times of the world.[46]

(5) Hui Geography, Engineering and Sciences

The Arab people soon accepted the concept of a spherical Earth form after the ancient Greek science was introduced to them. Then they brought this concept to China. Liu Zhi wrote in his Astronomical Principles: "The Earth......is a sphere sitting in the center of the air." In the Islamism, he quoted the Arabic theories about the Earth, saying, "The Earth is as round as a ball. It consists of water and soil. The earth emerged out of the water is called ground (soil), covering one fourth of the surface of the ball......There is an east-west straight line, with equal distance from the south and north poles. It is called the middle line of the earth (equator)." These theories were more advanced than the Chinese geography theories at that time. Liu used the Hui books as references when he was writing his books.

These books include the following:

Jami'al Bilad (in Arabic), the 27th reference for Astronomical Principles, means collected information about different countries.

Hay'at Aqalim, respectively the 28th and 43rd references for Astronomical Principles and Islamism, means the images of shapes of different countries. Liu translated it into Shapes of Seven Continents.

The "Seven Continents" refer to the landmasses divided by a number of ancient Western scholars, such as Ptolemy, the well-known Greek geographer, according to their knowledge on the Earth at their times. They cover the region in the Eastern Hemisphere from the Equator to the North Pole, currently the region north of Ethiopia in Africa and the Eurasia. The Arabs accepted such classification. Liu Zhi quoted the names of the "Seven Continents" in the Volume 2 of Astronomical Principles, including Arab, Persia, Europe, China, Syria, India and Sudan.[47]

---

46 For more details, please refer to the History of Science and Technology Development of the Mongol Ethnic Nationality of China by Li Wenzhong, Science Publishing House, 1990, pp. 15-22.
47 Manazil al-Bilad, the 28th reference for Astronomical Principles, examines stations in different countries.

The book Jahan-i Danish, the 2nd reference for Astronomical Principles, means knowledge on the world. It is probably a translation from Arabic to Persian. The books mentioned above are all works on geography. There is also a reference about topography science. It is the 38th reference for Astronomical Principles, namely Ka'aba Nama (in Persian), meaning records of square architectures, which possibly refers to the Holy Mekka.

Since the Hui geography originated from the ancient Greek geography, it was much more advanced than the Han geography. It built on the thought that the Earth is a spherical system of longitudes and latitudes. The Hui Book of Astronomy said, "The region inhabited by people and other living creatures can be divided into four regions. The latitudes extend from the equator line northwards to the 66° latitude, while the longitudes extend from the east coast to the west coast, spanning 180°. From the central point, namely longitude 33°and longitude 90°, thus this vast region is divided into four sub-regions: northwestern, southwestern, northeastern and southeastern sub-regions. All these demonstrate the knowledge of Hui scholars on Europe, Asia and Africa on the north of the equator line. There are few Han Chinese works mentioning the Hui engineering science. According to the History of Yuan Dynasty: Astronomy (Yuan Shi: Tian Wen Zhi), the Western astronomical instruments introduced by Jamal al-Din in the 3rd year of the reign of Emperor Zhiyuan. Here below are some records of Hui scholars' astronomical instrument manufacturing activities:

Techniques for Manufacturing Sand Clocks and Other Instruments, in the 7th volume of the Records of the Book Collection and Edition Office, is about the usage of scientific and mechanical (physical) principles in manufacturing devices and transporting heavy stuff. It is probably related with the ancient Greek science.

Ptolemy's Collection on Astronomy, in the 7th volume of the Records of the Book Collection and Edition Office, is a number of articles written by ancient Greek astronomer Ptolemy. There were 15 volumes of this book kept in the Book Collection and Compilation Office.

The book San'at-ı Alat, mentioned in the 7th volume of the Records of the Book Collection and Edition Office, discusses tools and techniques of manufacturing armillary sphere. There were 8 volumes of this book kept in the Book Collection and Compilation Office.

In addition, some works record jewelries from the Western regions. In the Yuan Dynasty, the merchants from the Western regions frequently presented jewelries as tributes to the imperial court to ingratiate themselves with the rulers. There is a narration about the Hui "stones" and their value in the Out of Tillage (Chuo Geng Lu). The people in the Yuan Dynasty needed knowledge on how to identify the value of Hui jewelries. That's why there is a book named Jewelry Identification Skills in the Book Collection and Edition Office. The book consists of five volumes.

Liu Zhi gave reference to the following two books as references when he was writing his books. One was Jawahir, the 11th reference for Astronomical Principles. Jawahir is an Arabic word, meaning jewelries. The other book was the Hajar Nama (in Persian), meaning records of gems. It is respectively the 38th and 37th reference for the Astronomical Principles and the Islamism. It should be a book about jewelry analysis and evaluation. The Hui chemistry was only partly scientific, it was rather part of alchemy. The word Iksir which was mentioned in the 7th volume of the Records of the Book Collection and Edition Office was one of the few works about it. In fact, there were 8 volumes of the book kept in the Book Collection and Edition Office. The Arabic word "Iksir" means "alchemy medicine", which can be evaluated as the predecessor of modern chemistry.

Chapter 6. Europeans Arriving at the East

Westerners got to know the East in the course of historical development. In the age of Ancient Greece, European got to know Persia and India through the Greco-Persian Wars and Alexander the Great's "Eastern expedition". European sailors started their journey from the Red Sea to East. Generation after generation, they finally crossed Sri Lanka and Southeast Asia and managed to Southern part of China. However, in the Middle Ages, European development fell into stagnation. The Arab Empire then emerged. Islam navigators from West Asia inherited Greek and Roman sailing tradition and formed a triangular navigation network that linked West Pacific, North Indian Ocean and Mediterranean. During the Song Dynasty period, the Christian Crusades let the European re-consider their benefit with the East. By expanding to Eastern Europe and Middle and Near East, Mongolian established a world empire that directly contact to Western Christendom. Distance between East and West was then shortened. Westerners gained more knowledge on China than ever. Hence, their interest in East soared. According to historical data, the number of European been to China during this period exceeded the total number of the past centuries. At the same time, this number also exceeded total Chinese and far Eastern people who had been to Europe, in particular. All of these have reflected a rising European economy and a huge eager for getting to know outside world. However, the main route from Europe to China was by land, and the other choice was the maritime route but with the help of Islam navigators and Chinese official and private ships.

In the late period of the reign of Emperor Xuande, Ming dynasty, massive official navigation activities suddenly came to an end. But private navigation activities have continued. I should mention that the new technologies of sea navigation had not appeared yet. On the contrary, with the development of the European economy, their needs on the Eastern luxury goods soared more than ever. While routes to the East were controlled by Arab and Ottoman Turk empires, so to find a possible new route became an inevitable pursuit, then. Traditional European astronomy had believed that the earth was spherical. With more connections to Arabs and China's compass and other navigation tools introduced to Europe, Western navigation developed a lot. European navigators believed that they would reach to India and China as long as sailing along the west African coasts tonorthwards. As the Chinese artillery was mastered, distant navigation had became safer. If we can say that compass and artillery were technologies learned from China, then we can comfortably say the invention of the spheroid earth, was unique to the traditional European science. Impact of this spheroid earth thought had greatly promoted the development of navigation. This thought when combined with advanced compass navigation and sharp artillery equipment, small fleets of the small countries like Portugal and Spain could also have the ability to navigate to distant regions and became a new drive to push navigation to new era, even though European continent was sparsely-populated. Since Portuguese came to the East, world navigation has changed a lot. The opening of direct route between Europe and Asia and global ship routes exemplified that European navigation was more developed than Asian. But this was just a beginning. As Western productivity grew by day, scientific development speeded up. So did navigation, shipbuilding and geosciences. By comparison, traditional Chinese navigation was out of date.

1. Colonial Aggression against the East

(1) Great Geographical Discoveries

(a) Bypassing the Cape of Good Hope

During the Ming Dynasty period, people called Portugal as Pudulijia, Pululia or Porduwar, the transliteration of Portugal. Sometimes, they called Portuguese and Spanish both as Feringee. Feringee is the transliteration of the word "Frank" (Frenk) in Arab or Persian languages. Franks were a branch of Germanic people who once established an empire during the Middle Ages. And in Arab and Persian language, the word Frank (Frenk) referred to Europeans. When Portuguese traveled to the East, they did not know Chinese. They had to hire Southeast Asian Islams who knew Arab or Persian language as translators. That was the history of Feringee. Before coming to China, Portuguese had occupied Malacca. In the middle period of the Ming Dynasty, Chinese people was not aware of Europe but believed that Portugal was located near Malacca.[1]

From the 27th year in Emperor Hongwu's reign (1394) to the 4th year of Emperor Tianshun's reign (1460), Henry, the Portuguese navigator built school to train sailors. In 1460, Portuguese sailors had reached to the half of West African coast. In 22nd year of Emperor Chenghua's reign (1486), Bartholomeu Diaz reached to the South of African continent and named it as Cabo Tormentoso

---

1　History of Ming Dynasty, the Legend of Feringee.

because he encountered storm. John II, the King of Portugal then ordered to re-name it as Cape of Good Hope. By the 10th year of Emperor Hongzhi's reign of Ming dynasty (1496), Vasco da Gama, Portuguese explorer, bypassed the Cape of Good Hope to East and reached the East coast of Africa. Then with the help of a Arab seafarers, he sailed across the Arabian Sea and arrived at Malabar, i.e., the western coast of India. This important geographical discovery changed the East-west expedition routes. The goods that Vasco da Gama brought from the East were worth more than 60 times of navigation costs. The huge profits brought more adventure seeking traders to the East. The great traveler Vasco da Gama's maritime expedition was about 70 years later than Zheng He's.

Taking Cochin, the south of Calicut (a city in the state of Kerala in Southern India on the Malabar Coast), India as a stronghold, Portuguese occupied Goa and founded a colony in 1510, then started to invade Eastern Indian coastal regions and Sri Lanka. Malacca has been the most important navigation hub in the Southeast Asia. Earlier in 1509, Diogo Lopes de Sequera had already led a fleet to Malacca for trade relation. With the permission of the king of Malacca, he was preparing to start trade at coastal regions but was faced with great troubles due to resistance by the local people. Thus, Diogo Lopes de Sequera and his men were forced to retreat, and some of his men were ar-rested. Then Portuguese navy commander, Alfonso d'Albuquerque, suggested the Portuguese King to deploy more military ships so as to force Malacca allow free trade in this country. Consequently, Alfonso led 8 ships which started from India and reached to Malacca in June, 1511. After, Alfonso led captured Sultan Mahmud, they also occupied Malaca in August. In 1513, Portuguese forces came to China's Guangdong Province and have planned to occupy the Macao island in 1557. Then traditional maritime Silk Road that linked Southern China, the South China Sea, Southeast Asia and Indian Ocean was replaced by Macao-Malaca-Gua-Lisbon route after Portuguese coming to East and the connection to the Atlantic Ocean.

(b) The Discovery of America and the Sea Expeditions around the Globe

Spain was called as Ganxila, transliterated as Castile in Chinese (later a province of Spain) as recorded in the books of the Ming Dynasty period. When Portuguese sailors are busy with coming to East through Africa, the Italian navigator Columbus believed sailing to West also reaching to India and China. At first, he turned to the King of Portugal with no answer, then to the King of Spain, Ferdinand and his queen Isabel. With the support of the Spanish royal family, Columbus started his journey in 1492 (the 5th year of the reign of Emperor Hongzhi of the Ming Dynasty) and reached to the West Indies of Caribbean, America. After making some investigations, he went back to Europe. To divide the world colonies among them, Portugal and Spain have made Tordesillas Agreement in 1494. According to this agreement, the merid-ian near Cape Verde, center of the Atlantic Ocean was the boundary. East part was the Portugal sea sailing regions and the sea sailing regions in the West re-gions of the world belonged to Spain. Hereafter, Columbus has been to America in 1493, 1498 and 1502 respectively. Apart from Brazil which was colonized by Portugal, the rest of America was colonized by the Spanish colonists.

Spanish colonists found that neither Columbus nor his successor did reach to China or India. It was believed that they had benefited from American colony less than Portuguese from controlling Asian spice trade. So they had to find a new route to the East through America. In 1519 (the 14th year in the Emperor Zhengde's reign), Magellan, the Portuguese navigator started his global journey from Spain under the help of Spanish royal family. By 1520, he entered the Pacific Ocean from the southern end of Africa and then arrived at Luzon (Philippines) in 1521. Even though Magellan was killed by local dwellers, his crew led by Del Cano returned to Spain through Cape of Good Hope in 1522. This was the first global voyage which lasted 33 months. Consequently, Europeans acquired abundant knowledge about the world geography. Asian spice carried by Del Cano was more valuable than the efforts he had paid for them. According to Spanish history, after ascending to throne, King Philip ordered Mexican governor to send troops to Philippines islands. Later, Andres de Urdaneta, (the Christian missionary) and the Spaniard Miguel Lopez de Legazpi, the military officer with 5 ships, 400 persons were dispatched to Philippines. They departed from Mexico in 1564, and invaded the Southern islands of Philippines in the next year. Legazpi sent his grandson Juan Salcedo to carry on invading Philippines and finally succeeded.[2]

In history, Philippines did not have a unified state. Dwellers of many islands in the region of Philippines had established their own kingdoms. When Magellan first arrived at Philippines, he named it as San Lazarro, because he discovered these islands on that specific day. Then other navigators renamed these islands as Islas del Poniente. In the memory of Philip, son of Felipe II, Spanish called these Luzon islands as Phillippines in 1542 which currently possesses the same name. In 1565 Spanish colonists established colonial rule upon Philippines at Cebu. Spanish colonists were not satisfied by conquering Philippines. They worked on piracy at coastal regions of Fujian and Guangdong and soon found trade potentials among Southeast coast of China, Philippines islands and Japan. Soon they occupied Taiwan but still are not satisfied to the range of its global colonial empire and even wanted to invade China. Fortunately, King Felipe II and some officials have kept a cool mind. After realizing the splendor of China, they snapped at Spanish controlled Philippines's desperate hope of invading China and pursued friendly relationships with China. To maintain a large colonial empire, Spanish kingdom promoted the development of the global maritime expedition routes, i.e., Spain-South America-Manila-Spain. The direct routes from continent to continent were established by these navigations. Traditional Maritime Silk Road from Far East to the Red Sea was expanded East to America to world. Asia was linked to Europe from East and West. Hence distance between parts and countries of the world were shortened,

---

2   Zhang Minghua, Legends about Four European Countries in Qing History, Ed 1982, Shanghai Guji Press, p. 62.

international economic relation was closer than ever and world market started to take shape. Britain, France and Russia began to join competition for Asian market with renowned Portugal, Spain and Netherland.

(c) Portuguese Settlements

According to Chinese history, the time when Portuguese came to China was as follow:

(1) In the 12th year of Emperor Zhengde's reign (1517), recorded by Eastern and Western Study, Chouhai Pictures, historical geography on countries, Mountain and Sea maps and so on.

(2) In the 13th year of Emperor Zhu Houzhao's reign, recorded by Mingshan History, Xianhui Record, Xiangxu Record, Guangdong Tongzhi compiled by Jin Zuguang, Guangdong Tongzhi edited and compiled by Hao Yulin, the Ming History and so on.

(3) In the 14th year, recorded by Shuyuzhou Record.

People of Ming Dynasty did not only hold different about the Portuguese traders who came to China but they had differences on the location of Portugal. They thought Portugal was near Malacca which was mentioned in the book "Ming History-The Feringee Legend". The reason was that the most Portuguese who came to China had sailed from Malacca.

According to Portuguese historical materials, some merchants first came to Southeast coastal regions of China in the 8th year of the reign og Emperor Zhu Houzhao (Zhengde) (1513). Jorge Alvares arrived at Tunmen, Guangdong in 1514. Rafael Perestrello then came to China between 1515 and 1516. Thome Pires, envoy of the King of Feringee (Portugal) first the first time visited China in 1517 (the 12th year of the reign of the Emperor Zhu Houzhao of the Ming Dynasty period). Thome Pires' ship sailed directly to Guangzhou through Humen. By bribing, Thome Pires finally reached Beijing in 1520 and met Emperor Zhu Houzhao (Zhengde). In the end of 1520, king of Malacca, a vassal of the Ming Dynasty presented letters which recorded about the Portuguese invasion of Malacca and asked for help. Portuguese in China robbed travelers and set fences arbitrarily. Local officials started to change their attitude towards the Portuguese traders. In 1520, He Ao, a procurator presented a suggestion of expelling foreigners to the Ming court. In the next year, the government of Ming Dynasty imprisoned Thome Pires. The first war between Ming Dynasty and Portugal occurred in 1522 (the 1st year of the reign of Emperor Jiajing's reign) and the victor was the Ming Dynasty.[3]

After defeating the Portuguese forces, local government in Guangdong once banned the entrance of foreign merchants into China, including not only Portuguese but merchants of traditional foreign trade partner such as Southeast Asia and others. The close-door policy had decreased Guangdong's customs

---

3   See Mingshan History and Ming Record.

revenues. Both public and private became anxious. In 1529, local government of Guangdong abolished maritime trade ban and allowed foreigners to do business at Langbai'ao. But, Langbai'ao was far from Guangzhou and inconvenient for business. Soon, by bribing local officers, foreign traders were allowed to do business at Haojing, at entrance of the Pearl River in 1535. Defeated by the Ming Dynasty, Portuguese rushed to the coastal regions of Fujian and Zhejiang for harassment and robbery and was stroked by Ming's navy. Leonel de Sousa finally realized Ming Dynasty's power and made his mind to open its gate for trade by a peaceful way. He told the prince of Portugal in his letter that he stopped those Portuguese at China cost resisting local government. In the negotiation, he claimed themselves as Portugal not Feringee and expressed his willingness to pay taxes like Thai merchants. By bribing officers in Guangdong, Portuguese merchants gained the approval for trading in all ports of Guangdong. His story was then testified by the 69th volume of Guangdong Tongzhi, edited and compiled by Guo Fei. After the establishment of bilateral trade relationship, most Portuguese were staying at Langbai'ao. They increasingly moved to Haojing after 1562. "Portuguese built rooms for trading. And the number has increased to hundreds within few years and now we can say there are thousands of them. Possibly, "several ten thousands of Portuguese people have lived here".[4]

Consequently, in those days, Jinghao became far-east Portuguese residence. In Chinese historical data, Haojing'ao referred to current Macao and was belonged to Xiangshan County. In the Macao Jilie Map, a place was named as Niangmajiao which in fact referred to Macao.[5]

(2) The Competition among the European Colonists in Asia

People in the Ming Dynasty period have named Netherland (Dutch) as Helan or Hongmaofan. They did not know much about this country. And information about Netherland was quite rare in the books published during the Ming Dynasty period but in Zheng He's maritime expeditions to the West in the Ming History, there is some information about it. Schloars in the Ming Dynasty period did not quite understand the significance of Zheng He's maritime expeditions, because they had not sailed beyond the borders of traditional China and had experienced little overseas communication. Consequently, they were quite doubtful about the new nautical knowledge and experience enjoyed by Zheng He. Dutch fleets came to the East later than Portuguese and Spanish. Netherland is located at the coastal region of European North Sea with a strong tradition of marine navigation and sea trade. It was the most important maritime country at the North Sea and the Baltic Sea. After purchasing goods from Far East, Portuguese traders sold them to Dutch for wholesale trade. In 1580, Portugal was conquered by Spain. Since Netherlands had conflicts with Spain, Dutch merchant ships were no longer able to enter the Lisbon port of the Portuguese.

---

4   Recorded in the Vol. 1 of Pang Shangpeng's Baiketing Zhaigao (Selected Texts of Baiketing or Excerpts from the Baike Pagoda.
5   Fei Chengkang, Four Hundred Years in Macao, Shanghai People Press, 1988.

As a result transit trade had ceased. Dutch started to explore new sea routes to the East. Horsman led 4 ships starting his journey from Netherland in 1595. A year later, he arrived at Banten port of current Indonesia. However, he had attempted piracy and robbed Java's merchant ships which triggered Java kingdom and people to fight back. Then he had to sail back.

Dutch did not benefit much from this voyage, but discovered the rich Southeast Asia. Hence, they poured in. Dutch organized 14 long-distant sailing fleets successively within 4 years (1590-1601) to Indonesia for capturing trade. As trade profits were lucrative, more and more Dutch ships came to the East. And main rivals of for Dutch were Portuguese and Spanish. To beat them and intensify colonial predation, Dutch merchants united all shipping companies at the East together and set up the United East India Company. The company was a modern joint stock company. Each of its shares was valued as 3000 Dutch guldens, and the total capital was 6.5 million guldens. Since the piracy activities of the Dutch fleets in the Far East was supported by the Dutch government just from the beginning. The United East India Company was even authorized by the government with the sole trading right between the Cape of Good Hope of Africa and the Strait of Magellan of America. The company occupied territories, built armies, issued currency, appointed officers and even could sign treaties with the foreign countries. Actually, it severed as the representative of Dutch government on abroad colonist activities. By implementing battles against the Portuguese and British colonists, Dutch forces occupied Indonesia, renamed the Djakarta region as Batavia and set up a colonial government there.

Before and after the establishment of the United East India Company, Dutch vigorously continued its activities of conquering regions in the the East part of the world, including southeastern coastal regions of China. Early as 1584, Dutch sailors had reached Macao by Portuguese trade ship.[6]

The book Yuejian Story has recorded the first visit of the Dutch to China. It mentioned that in September, 1601, two foreign ships arrived to Xiangshan'ao. Foreigners in these ships were tall with red hair and round eyes. Their ships looked like a big copper leaf. To avoid trade conflict, local government sent troops to expel them. Then these two ships headed to the Pacific Ocean and a naked eye could not see them anymore. Zhang Xie from Ming Dynasty once recorded that 'those guys with red hair called themselves as Dutch, a country which is not far from Portugal, with no connection to China. Observing that Portugal occupied Philippines and were trading at Xiangshan'ao, Dutch was so envious that they sailed between Java and Borneo and built a safe hidden base there. Since, China was distant and a military attack would be too risky, consequently Dutch aimed to find a convenient stepping stone to attack China. They tried to invade Luzon but failed, then attempted to conquer Xiangshan'ao, failed again.' These words were related to Dutch threatening China in the 29th year of Emperor Wanli's reign (1601) after Dutch occupied

---

6   Zhuang Guotu, Leonard Blusse, A study on Dutch Envoy's First Visit to China, 1989, Xiamen University Press, pp. 27-28.

Java and Borneo. After controlling Java, Dutch reached to the West Pacific Ocean in the early 17th century. Then they established a trade center on the Hirado Island, Japan. Then Japan-Dutch bilateral relationship developed rapidly. Many, new European technologies were introduced into Japan through bilateral trade. Japanese called this Western learning as Orchidology. Dutch accelerated its plans to control the Southeast Asia in 17th century. Before occupying Djakarta, Dutch had already fought against Britain, to grab Thailand from it, and defeated Britain. By 1641, Dutch defeated Portuguese to occupy Malaca and took the control of maritime routes to Southeast Asia.

Dutch was eager to break Portuguese's trade monopoly on China by building beachheads. The Dutch Wijbrant van Warwijck led a fleet to coastal regions of Macao in 1604. Because of typhoon sea storms, he had to sail to Penghu and built castle for long-term residency and aimed to check the fleets sailing towards Japan as well. However, Dutch forces were hindered by the local Chinese forces of Fujian (China) and their food supply was cut, consequently Dutch forces had to return to Pattani in October. After a failed attack against Macao island, Dutch occupied Penghu Island and established a base there. The navy of Ming Dynasty retrieved Penghu in 1624. Later, the Dutch forces invaded and occupied Taiwan, and the Dutch built a defensive fort to act as a base of operations. This was built on the sandy peninsula of Tayouan (now part of mainland Taiwan, in current-day Anping District). This temporary fort was replaced four years later by the more substantial Fort Zeelandia. Maritime merchants of Fujian transported silk and china material from China's coastal regions to Taiwan and traded them with the Dutch who then would transport these goods to other regions. However Dutch was not satisfied to this trading way and hoped to control trade between China coastal regions and Taiwan, and also aimed to control the prices of goods. This period was the rising period of Manchu forces and the decline period of the Ming Dynasty. In 1644, the Battle of Shanhai Pass, occurred at Shanhai Pass (Shanhaiguan) at the eastern end of the Great Wall of China, was a decisive battle leading to the formation of the Qing dynasty in China. Zheng Chenggong who claimed to be loyal to Ming Dynasty, had benefited a lot from the Ming trade with Dutch via Taiwan. He used these profits to support the Ming Dynasty against the rise of Manchu forces.

After the Manchu army (the army of the newly established Qing Dynasty) had occupied Guangzhou in 1653, Dutch merchants went there from Taiwan for trade. Shang Kexi, (the prince of Pingnan) and Geng Jimao, (the prince of Jingnan) both wrote a letter to Nicolaas Verburgh, the Dutch governor in Taiwan and expressed their hopes on promoting bilateral trade relationships between the Netherlands and Qing Dynasty. After evaluating this demand, Dutch East India Company decided to send a delegation to China. In 1654, a Dutch task commission was formed, which was ordered to write down a detailed report of the Dutch visit to China. There was also a painter in this commission to paint China's mountains and towns. In the summer of 1655, Peter de Goyer and Jacob de Keyzer, Dutch envoy, started from Djakarta with their attendants and reached to Guangzhou a month later. They spent half a year in Guangzhou. In the next spring, they were allowed to visit Beijing, the capital of the Qing Dynasty. Peter de Goyer and Jacob de Keyzer had sailed along the traditional tribute road, as long as 2400 km. in the South China sea, which was used by the envoys of vassal countries who visited Chinese emperors. They crossed Guangdong along Beijiang River, climbed over Dayuling Mountain to reach Jiangxi on horse, reached to Yangtze River along the Ganjiang River, then entered the Grand Canal through Anqing, Nanjing and Yangzhou, and finally arrived at Beijing in summer. After staying in Beijing for 3 months, the Dutch envoy went back taking the same route with a letter written by the Emperor Shunzhi. On the last year of the Emperor Qianlong's reign, the Dutch had dispatched 6 envoys to China. In 1494, Spain and Portugal, with the encouragement of the Pope, divided the world's oceans between them along a line in the mid-Atlantic, West of Cape Verde Islands as the division point. Other maritime powers followed suit.

Portugal and Spain had reached the Treaty of Tordesillas in 1494. The West part would belong to Spain and the East to Portugal. By promoting the global maritime expedition routes,, Spanish colonists carried back abundant spice from Molucca Islands which resulted in a disagreement between these two countries on the eastern border. Portuguese believed Molucca Islands (The Maluku Islands or the Moluccas are an archipelago within Banda Sea, Indonesia) belonged to their exclusive sea navigation zone, so they deemed Spanish activities in these seas as an offence. However, Spanish forces thought that not only Molucca islands, but also China and Malacca belonged to their exclusive control regions. In 1529, Charles V, the King of Spain acknowledged the dominant status of the Portuguese kingdom in Molucca, but intensified the Spanish efforts on invading Luzon (Philippines) islands at the same time. In Ming Dynasty period, silver was official currency. While gold was the currency for Japan which was even though abundant silver resources. Hence in terms of exchange between silver and gold, China was in disadvantage. Besides, there was a strong complementary in the bilateral trade. In the meantime, the rapid development of Japanese economy had become the inner drive to invade Korean peninsula and piracy. Japan had an increasingly close trade relationship with the Southeast Asia regions. Before Western colonialism expanded to the East, lots of maritime merchants from Guangdong, Fujian and Zhejiang had ran Sino-Japan people to people trade and the trade between Japan and Southeast Asia. In the books of Shunfeng Xiangsong (a nautical reference book in Ming Dynasty) and Zhinan Zhengfa (another nautical reference book), included many route descriptions from China to Japan, and from Japan to Southeast Asia.

In their early days, after they have arrived at Macao, Portuguese became aware of the lucrative benefits of trading in the East. Due to Japanese pirates' continuous harassment around China's Southeast coastal regions and since

573

Japan had then launched the invasion of Korea, Sino-Japan relationships began to frustrate. This was an opportunity for Portuguese who then took the whole control of Sino-Japan trade. By taking advantage of price differences between these two currencies, Portuguese purchased amounts of raw silk and silk, then sold them to Japan at high price and finally changed the profit into silver. By keeping doing this on and on, they earn huge profit. At the same time, silk and china from Japan and china were popular on European market.

After settling down in Macao, Portuguese established a far-east trade network center in Macao and called fleet working on China-Japan trade as China-Japan fleet. This fleet left with Indian ivory, pepper and spice, and American silver from Goa, India which was then belonged to Portugal, to Macao. Then it would rest in Macao till early of the next summer and export theses goods and purchase Chinese local products such as silk, gold, lead, tin, mercury, musk and so on. Soon as the Southeast monsoon started, the fleet sailed to Japan. Nagasaki had become Japan's stationary foreign trade port since 1570s. After closing all trade deals in Japan, the fleet would sail back to Macao by utilizing the north wind. With silver currency earned in Japan, merchants of the fleet purchased large amount of local products from China and went back to Goa by utilizing the north wind in the next autumn. Apart from a bunch of taxes paid to Portuguese customs in Malaca and Goa, they still could earn lucratively. The value of these products would often soar once they were transported back to Europe.

Macao was one of the starting points of the route China- Philippines -Island-Mexico-Peru. When the news that Portuguese had arrived in the East was spread in Europe, the major marine powers of Europe followed their footsteps. Spanish colonist maritime forces occupied Luzon (Philippines) Islands in order to intervene in the oriental trade and realize the Far East -America-Europe trade. Portuguese regarded the arrival of Spanish people as a threat and encouraged residents of Philippines to fight against Spanish forces in 1565. After Spanish forces occupied Philippines, Portuguese insisted on their trade monopoly upon China and calumniated Spanish envoys from time to time in front of the officials of the Qing dynasty in fear of Spanish establishing a direct contact with Chinese authorities. In 1576, Portuguese urged Vatican to set up Macao parish which included China and Japan, according to this demand Portuguese King would be the protectorate of the Christian missionaries working in Chinese territories. The purpose of this agreement was to prevent Spanish missionaries entering China.

The situation in Europe had changed in 1580. Spanish invaded Portugal and annexed it in the next year. Philip II, the King of Spain, served as the King of Portugal concurrently. However, the fights and severe competition between the Portuguese and Spanish kingdoms did not cease. Initially, the Portuguese parliament and King of Spain reached a consensus to ban the trade between colonies of the two countries, and the trade between Southeast coast of China and Philippines Islands was mainly monopolized by the Chinese merchants. After the 1620s, the Netherland (Dutch) became stronger in the Far East, forcing the Portuguese and Spanish in the Far East to join hands to resist the Dutch forces. Thus the control of trade between China and Philippines had passed from Chinese traders to Portuguese traders of Macao. Spanish occupied Taiwan in order to control the trade in the Far East. After 1635 the Far East trade was controlled by Spanish. The King of Spain dispatched Ouvidor to Macao island to concurrently arrange trade relations with Japan. The profits of this trade poured to the treasury of the King of Spain in addition some trade fees should be paid to Spanish governor of the Macao island and soldiers' salary and rations of the Spanish garrison in Macao had to be funded with the very trade profits.

In the early 17th Century, the Dutch forces established several strongholds in Southeast Asia, controlled spice resources of South Seas Islands and set up a commercial firm in Japan. In their scheme, they could sell goods from Europe, India and Southeast Asia to China and trade silk and ceramics from China to Japan against silver, thus pay their purchases of spice they supplied from Southeast Asia. In this way the Dutch did not need to bring capital from Europe and could maintain their colonial activities in the East solely relying on the earnings from the trading. In 1601 the Dutch colonists reached Macao to explore the seaway and were captured by Portuguese in Macao. In order to exclusively monopolize the trade with China, they killed those Dutch sailors. In revenge the Dutch colonists cut off the Malacca seaway in the next year, intercepted the Portuguese fleet from Macao to Goa and robbed Portuguese merchant ships to Japan at the coastal waters of Macao. Within 10 years, the command of the seas of the Far East fell in the hands of the Dutch colonists. The British also joined the fight with Portuguese in the Far East. The fight among European powers in the Far East was a part of the war for trading right of the overseas colonies among colonial powers across the world.

(3) European Colonists in the Eyes of Chinese People

China held different traditional partition principles distinct from the West in regard to world geography. Traditionally the Chinese termed the regions in the west of China as the Western Regions, the countries South to China and accessible through the sea route as the South Sea; Italian Matteo Ricci arrived in the Ming Dynasty and introduced the Western geographic knowledge to China. He said China was located in Asia, and there was a continent called Europe where there were more than 70 countries and Italy was one of them. Most of the Chinese official scholars did not believe him and evaluated his remarks as "ridiculous and untenable ". But after seeing more and more European people arriving in China, they thought that "there should be such a land and it could not be an illusion or false" and held a skeptical attitude. Matteo Ricci called himself as the "Great Atlantic Man". The Ministry of Rites of the Ming Dynasty referred to the official archive the Code of the Great Ming Dynasty and found there was a name "Sir Lanca (Sri Lanka) in the Western ocean" in the record after Zheng He's expedition and thus concluded the authenticity could not be confirmed. In short, though China had established contacts with

European countries earlier, frequent contacts started in the Ming Dynasty. The historical materials available in the period of Ming Dynasty included abundant facts and evaluations about European foreigners, which reflected the views of the Chinese people, below we will give a brief description on these views:

(1) Portuguese ate children

According to the History of Ming Dynasty, in the 13th year of the reign of Zhengde (1518) during the Ming dynasty period, "a Portuguese envoy led by Ghabdan Captain and his attendants arrived and they offered tribute ". Here the word "Ghabdan" refers to the Portuguese ship owner "Capitan Moor".[7]

The part "offered tribute" in the above sentence was in fact, meant that Portuguese sold goods in China. The Emperor Zhengde "ordered the Portugueseto immediately leave after selling their goods", but the Portuguese "stayed in China for a long time and robbed travelers and even plundered children as food."[8]

The narration that Portuguese "bought or kidnapped Chinese children and ate them" was widely narrated among the people in the late Ming Dynasty period. According to Gu Yanwu's quotation from Yueshan Essays, Portuguese "loved to eat children and they said that their country only boys were eaten". Yueshan Essays also mentioned that Portuguese asked officials at various levels for help, but were strictly refused. Then they "secretly purchased children to eat" and each child was priced at 100 wen (cents) and "the villains in Guangdong competed to plunder children and numerous children were eaten." It was narrated the eating method was as follows: putting the child in the boiling boiler and steam him/her till sweating, and the skin was stripped off. Till that moment the child was still "alive", then when the child is dead his intestines and stomach were detached than further steamed before served for eating. It was said in several years in Guangdong "a number of children were robbed and the neighbors dwelling in this city had greatly suffered from this plunder."[9]

Although there were detailed records about the Portuguese men (Feringee) "eating children", these records don't seem credible, possibly they were based on hearsay. Such texts reflected the brutal impression of Portuguese by the eyes of the Chinese people when they first arrived in China.

(2) Asking for a land lot as big as a cowhide sheath

The historical materials from the Ming Dynasty period also recorded some stories about the European colonists getting land plots by cheating. Zhang Xie said: "A Portuguese said he came from Castile (near Spain) West and traded

7 See the book by Zhang Weihua, Annotations of the Biography of Four Countries of Europe, the History of the Ming Dynasty, 1982, Shanghai Ancient Books Publishing House, p. 5.
8 Biography of Portugal, the History of the Ming Dynasty.
9 Merits and Drawbacks of Provinces and Counties in China, Volume 19, Fuwen Court Treasure Edition, p. 54; in You Xitang's Biography of Portuguese (Feringee), the Biography of Foreign Countries of the History of Ming, Shanghai Ancient Books Publishing House, p. 177.

with Philippines. The chief once told him secretly: "you can replace the King"..
Then, he presented gold to King of Luzon (Philippines) as a birthday gift and
asked for a land lot as large as a cowhide sheath to build a house. King of
Philippines believed him and agreed. Portuguese then cut the cowhide into
string and connected the string to encircle a land and said that it was the land
he asked for. King of Philippines felt embarrassed, but was also afraid of refusing foreigners and granted them the land. Portuguese obtained land plots,
built barracks there and heavily equipped with blunderbuss, knife and shield.
After a long time, Portuguese besieged Philippines, killed the King and expelled the local people into mountains. Thus Philippines was occupied by the
Portuguese. Then King of Castile[10] sent commanders to the military garrison in
the Philippines and changed them every several years."

Zhang Xie recorded the process of the Portuguese occupying Philippines.
According to him, some European people said that they came from Castile
Kingdom located near Spain, i.e. the far West. On the occasion of celebrating
the birthday of King of Philippines, the Portuguese presented gold material
as a gift and asked for a land as large as a cowhide sheath to build a house.
The King of Philippines (Luzon) approved. Then the Spaniards cut the cowhide into string and made the string into a rope to encircle a land. Although
discontent, the King of Philippines honored his words and agreed to grant the
requested land lot. The Spaniards built a town and settled there. Later they
killed the King of Philippines and conquered the region. The story of Spaniards
encircling a land plot with cowhide rope was also included in the History of
the Ming Dynasty. It was recorded that the Portuguese realized that Philippines
"was weak and could be easily occupied, and then presented gifts to the King
of Philippines and asked for a land plot as large as a cowhide sheath. The
King of Philippines could not catch the trick and agreed. The Portuguese cut
the cowhide and made a long fence of rope all around the land plot and asked
the king to honor his words. The King of Philippines was shocked, but had to
agree."[11]

Moreover, some other historical materials from the Ming Dynasty period
have also narrated this story, for example the Mingshan Cang, Records of
Foreign Countries and Ethnic Nationalities.[12]

The Chinese historical materials from the Qing Dynasty period also have
descriptions about the Dutch forces occupying Taiwan. Yu Wenyi recorded in
his "Taiwan Prefecture Annals" that the red-haired Dutch colonists drifted to
Taiwan by the hurricane and wanted to borrow a land lot from the local tribe

577

---

10   The Kingdom of Castile was a large and powerful state on the Iberian Peninsula during
the Middle Ages. Its name comes from the host of castles constructed in the region. It began
in the 9th century as the County of Castile, an eastern frontier lordship of the Kingdom of
León. The Study of the East and the West, Ed. 1981, Zhonghua Book Company, p. 89.
11   Biography of Luzon (Philippines), the History of the Ming Dynasty.
12   See The chapter related to Luzon (Philippines), Wang Tingshi's Outspoken Suggestions
on Expelling Foreigners.

chief. The local residents did not permit and the Dutch then cheated: "Just a land lot as large as a cowhide sheath at any price you can charge." Then the chief agreed. The red-haired "cut the cowhide into string" and encircled a land plot to "build the fortress called Port Zeelandia and settle there", later built Saccam opposite to Taiwan City. Xiaotian Annals of the Qing Dynasty has various records which narrate that the Japanese forces had occupied Taiwan first and the red-haired Dutch colonists reached Taiwan since they were hit by a sea hurricane. The Dutch asked for a land plot, but the Japanese did not agree. Then the Dutch colonists lied: "we want a land plot as large as a cowhide sheath at any expense" and were permitted. The Dutch colonists then "cut the cowhide into string and encircled a land plot and settle down", but the Dutch forces finally expelled Japan and occupied Taiwan. These records seem groundless and probably hearsay among Chinese merchants who travelled among Fujian, Philippines and Taiwan. But this hearsay reflected the colonists' efforts of gaining benefits through various fraudulent means and have left deep impressions over the people living in the coastal regions.

(3) Strong Ships and Powerful Cannons

European people depended on their ships and cannons when seeking fortunes in the East. The cannon was invented in China and introduced to the Western Regions of China in the 13th century. In the contacts with Islam countries West to and South to the Mediterranean sea, the European people soon discovered the new type hot weapons which could perform much better the traditional knives, sword and other cold weapons. They mastered the technology of the rifle weapon and rapidly developed it. After a century and a half, the European's technology of making cannons was much better than the inventor Chinese people when they came to the East. At the beginning of relationship with Portuguese, the Ming people discovered that the Portuguese mastered advanced cannon technologies. The Ming called this Western cannon "Portuguese Gun". According to Chen Shouqi's General Annals of Fujian, in the autumn of 1510 (the 5th year of the Zhengde Period of the Ming Dynasty), vagrants of Ding and Zhang prefectures intruded into Xianyou County, and the local officials attacked the vagrants with more than 100 Portuguese cannons. At that time Portuguese had not entered the Southeast coast of China. If the record was reliable, the Portuguese cannons were purchased by maritime merchants of Fujian from South Sea and brought back China. We know that in 1519, the 14th year of the reign of Emperor Zhengde during the period of Ming Dynasty, Lin Jiansu cast Portuguese cannon with tin mould and copied the gunpowder formula of Portuguese army to suppress the Chenghao Rebellion.[13]

In 1520, the 20th year of the reign of Emperor Zhengde, Censor He Ao reported to the imperial court as follows: "The Portuguese are very cruel and cunning, and more proficient in weaponary than the other foreigners. The year

13   Wang Shouren: Incidents Related to Portuguese, Collected Works of Wang Wencheng, Vol. 24, photocopy of the Four Categories of Books Series, Shanghai Hanfenlou Bookstore.

before last year they steered big ships to intrude in Huicheng, Guangdong, their artillery made thunderous sound." During the Emperor Zhengde Period, He Ru, patrol commissioner of Guangdong, inquired Yang San, Dai Ming and other Chinese employees of the Portuguese about the Western shipbuilding and cannon cast technology. After mastering the Western firearm manufacturing technology, the Ming army used the technology to subdue the Westerners. In 1522, the first year of the reign of Emperor Jiajing, the Ming army defeated the Portuguese with imitated firearm in Guangdong, and captured two military ships and more than 20 firearms from the Portuguese. The small cannon weighed less than 10kg, but could fire 600 steps far. The Ming officers presented the captured weapons to the imperial court and reported, "the Portuguese were fierce because of the firearms and the ships. Their cannons are so powerful that no weapons in history could vie with them", and suggested to equip China's boreder defense forces with such weapons.[14]

In 1620 and 1628, Xu Guangqi and Li Zhizao chaired the cannon procurement from Portuguese in Macao. Jesuit Joao Rodrigues imparted the cannon operation and shell cast technology to the Ming army. In 1624 the first batch of Portuguese cannons were transported to Beijing. But during the testing of the cannons an explosion had occurred. The Portuguese officer named Jean Correa was killed in the explosion. In 1940 his tomb was discovered at Qinglongqiao, Beijing, and the epigraph was written in Chinese and Portuguese. In 1626, General Yuan Chongghuan of the Ming Dynasty, when his army was in a difficult situation in a key battle around the Ningyuan City, General Yuan had employed dozens of Portuguese gunners which were invited from Macao. By using these cannons General Yuan were able to defeat the Qing army.

579

After evaluating its utility a cannon was allocated and delivered to "Homeland Safeguarding Liaodong Suppression and Pacifying Headquarter". In 1629 Joao Rodrigues and Portuguese gunner Gonçalves Texeira Correa defended the Zhuozhou city with 10 cannons and the Qing army fled away upon learning about the capability of this new weaponry. Soon, the destructive power of the western cannons was widely acknowledged. Emperor Chongzhen ordered Johann Adam to supervise the cannon casting works for the army. The Chinese craftsmen who had worked at the Macao cannon factory were recruited by the Ming imperial court and became the technical backbone of the new firearm factory administrated by the Ming army. The Qing aristocracy soon noticed the efforts of the Ming government to improve military equipment and weopanry and began to imitated this policy and promoted the casting of western cannons.

The Ming people were deeply impressed by the strong ships and powerful cannons of the Dutch colonists. Zhang Xie wrote: "it is said that the Dutch are especially good at shipbuilding and cannon manufacturing. The ship measures 30 zhang long and 5-6 zhang wide, and the board is more than 2 chi thick; it has five masts. The ship uses iron nets and is polished with paint and horse

---

14   Biography of Feringee (Portuguese), History of the Ming Dynasty.

oil, shiny and smooth." The Dutch were not only good at making five-mast ships, but installed various kinds of weaponry on these ship. The ship has three floors, cannons are arranged along the "walls" on either side of the ship, facing outwards. When a battle begins, the cannons are rolled forward so that their muzzles protrude through small square or round openings in the ship's hull known as "gun ports". These can be clearly visible on larger warships: rows and rows of holes on its side.. When firing, the blunderbuss would open the window and retreat after firing, needing no manpower. Below the masts, large cannons would be established, which measured more than 2 zhang, with the center hollow as a 4-chi wheel. It was said the cannon could break the strong city wall and make thunderous noise which spread to miles away. When the enemy was near to capture the ship, the cannons were often used to sink the ship, thus prevent it from being captured." This kind of military ship which had numerous cannons arranged along the "walls" on either side of the ship and a main cannon placed on the deck was commonly used in Northern Europe in the 16th century. Moreover, "there is a copper disc behind the rudder, with its diameter measuring several chi, and it is named Zhaohai (sea detecting) mirror and could help sailors when they have lost their route in the sea."[15]

Probably, the Zhaohai mirror was a kind of compass. When the Southeast Navy of the Ming Dynasty battled against the Dutch navy for the first time, the Ming navy did not know the advantages of the enemy and attacked the enemy with common firearm from a long distance. The Dutch colonists responded with the cannons on their ships and caused heavy casualties to the Ming navy.[16]

In 1622, the 2nd year of the reign of Emperor Tianqi, the Ministry of War of the Ming Dynasty had commented on the Dutch navy and said that the Dutch ships were equipped with big cannons on their four sides of the ships which possessed a firing range of several miles. Any solid target would be certainly destroyed upon being hit.[17]

The public during the Ming Dynasty period called the Dutch cannons as "Hongyi (red-haired foreigner) cannons". When the Ming navy met with the red-haired ships (i.e. the Dutch ships) on the sea, they found the ships were as large as five times of the Ming's ships.[18]

The Ming people also discovered the weaknesses of the Dutch ships, "the ship is too large to change direction and easily get stranded in the shallow waters."[19]

---

15 The Study of the East and the West, Ed. 1981, Zhonghua Book Company, p. 89.
16 An Unofficial History, Vol. 30.
17 Shen Guoyuan: Records of Historical Events of Two Regions, Vol. 16, Chongzhen edition, p. 7.
18 Shi Cheng et al: Annals of Guangzhou Prefecture, Vol. 120, Biography of Cui Qiguan, Yuexiu Academy edition published during the reign of Emperor Guangxu of the Qing Dynasty.
19 Biography of the Netherlands, the History of the Ming Dynasty.

Many Italian missionaries came to China in the late Ming Dynasty period and the History of the Ming Dynasty recorded the Italia was good at making cannons bigger than Portuguese cannons. The Chinese people imitated these cannons, but could not reach the desired quality and effect.[20]

In the second half of the Ming Dynasty, the Ming people learned the Portuguese cannons from the Portuguese, Philippines cannons from the Spaniards, Hongyi cannons from the Dutch and Italian cannons from Italia. But China was in the late feudal period, and the emerging bourgeoisie had not become a leading force in the society. Therefore the new type of ordnance industry was not formed. In the war with the late Jin Dynasty, the Ming army was defeated in Liaodong and cannons were captured by the Later Jin. Since 1631, the late Jin armies "carried the Hongyi General Cannons wherever they marched".[21] Finally the Ming dynasty suffered a fatal defeat and perished.

2. A New Era of East-West Trade

(1) Export goods of the Ming and Qing Dynasties and the World Market

In the initial period the European explorers came to the East as pirates. Their expeditions was accompanied by bloody massacres and plundering, but their eastward expansion for the purpose of trading and the global colonial activities have significantly enhanced the world trade. The international economic contacts following the opening of the new sea routes implied the preliminary stage of the world market. However, from this stage the Chinese goods were marketed to the Southeast Asia, American and European markets in large volumes.

(1) Silk exports

Since the late Ming Dynasty, the imperial court had forbidden the private overseas trade and the Sino-foreign silk trade was mainly the tributary trade. As a traditional export product of China, silk was not only an important gift the Chinese government gave to foreigners, but also a settlement instrument of tributary trade. During Hongzhi period of the Ming Dynasty (1488-1505), it was stipulated that a bolt of ramie silk converted to 500 strings (a string equals to 1,000 coins), a bolt of thin satin valued 100 strings, and one could exchange the converted silk with converted tributary goods.[22]

The two mutual parties of the tributary trade were the Chinese and foreign governments. The silk exported from China in this context was mainly for kings and nobles of the foreign countries and the common people did not have access, to such kind of trade. By the age of geographical discoveries, the Chinese silk was exported to the regions America and Europe in an unprecedentedly scale. In the traditional trade regions of Asia, silk trade grew significantly. A world-scale silk market took shape.

20　Biography of Italy, the History of the Ming Dynasty.
21　Chronicles of the Emperor Gaozong of the Qing Dynasty, Vol. 10, photocopy of Taiwan Huawen Publishing House, p. 6.
22　The Great Ming Dynasty Code, Vol. 113.

Japan was a traditional market of Chinese silk. As early as in the Song Dynasty, Japan had developed the silkworm breeding and silk industry. However, silkworm was hard to survive in Japan because of the significant changes of temperature and Japan still needed import silk from China. Since the 1570s, Japan gradually ended the internal turmoil and was reunited with social and economic recovery. In the late 16th century, Japan's silver ore mining reached a peak and the silver output accounted for a quarter of the world's total.[23]

With improving purchasing power, the demand on silk was on the daily increase. Therefore in the Ming and Qing dynasties, Japan imported raw silk and silk products in a large volume. Xu Guangqi once mentioned that Japan "purchased various kinds of goods from China, the highest quality silk.... The whole country uses silk and is never tired of it."[24]

China's refined silk products enjoyed a large market in Japan. Each year Japan imported a large volume of plain or embroidered velvet, satin, chiffon and various kinds of dressing cloth and related goods which were demanded hotly in Japan.[25]

According to studies of Japanese scholars, for Japan, raw silk and silk products accounted for 70% of the total value of goods imported from China.[26] In the early Tokugawa Shogunate period, Japan imported hundreds of thousands of jin raw silk each year and most purchased from China.[27] According to investigation of L. Camps, director of the commercial firm of the Dutch colonists in Hiroda city in early 1616, Japan imported about 3,000 dan, or about 180 tons of raw silk each year. The Portuguese controlled half of the total imports, and the rest half was imported to Japan by the Japanese merchants from Chinese merchants in Tonkin, Vietnam and Taiwan etc.. The high import could not meet the market demand of Japan.[28]

After the arrival of European traders in the East, the non-governmental economic contacts between China and Southeast Asia were still very active. China's raw silk enjoyed a very large market in Southeast Asia, and Tonki, Java, Malacca and regions along the Indian Ocean were still the main destination of

582

23   Leonard Blusse and Jaap de Moor ((Netherland): Nederlanders Overzee, 1983, Franeker, p. 186.
24   Xu Guangqi's Collected Works, Vol. 1, A Collection of Writings about Coastal Defence.
25   See Zhuang Guotu: On Overseas Chinese Silk Trade in the Late Ming Dynasty Period (1567-1643), contained in China and Maritime Silk Road, pp. 36-45.
26   Kimura Yasuhiko, History of Sino-Japanese Cultural Interaction, Commercial Press, 1980, p. 664.
27   Wei Nengtao: Sino-Japanese Nagasaki Merchant Ship Trade in the Ming and Qing Dynasties, contained in the Journal of Chinese Historical Studies, Issue 2, 1986.
28   Leonard Blusse (Netherland): Tribuut aan China, p. 41) (Zhuang Guotu: On Overseas Chinese Silk Trade in the Late Ming Dynasty (1567-1643), contained in China and Maritime Silk Road, pp. 36-45.

Chinese silk in the late Ming Dynasty. According to estimation of Dutch historian Van Ruhel, in the 17th century 2,000-3,000 dan of China's raw silk was sold each year in Southeast Asia, excluding the Philippines. Among the goods marketed by Chinese merchants to Philippines, silk was the bulk goods and the Chinese traders market in Manila (Philippines) was also called "the Raw Silk Market".[29]

Colonists from the West soon discovered the popularity of Chinese silk in the Asian market. With the advanced navigation technology and the large overseas colony network, they muscled in the Asian silk trade. European merchants purchased a large quantity Chinese silk from the Southeast coastal region of China, but did not ship all the silk to Europe. Quite a part was sold to other Asian countries for profits to maintain their control over colonies in the East. According to L. Camps's investigation in 1616, Japan needed to import a large quantity of China's raw silk. Though the Portuguese and Japanese merchants monopolized import, there was a gap of 2.5 million guilders. If the Dutch East India Company could grasp this part of market share, it could gain more than 2 million guilders. The profits could be used sufficiently as expenses of the company in Asia and other regions.[30]

During the late Ming Dynasty period, ships regularly transported silk to Taiwan wherein Japanese merchants were active. In 1624, the Dutch colonists invaded Taiwan and established Zeelandia as their base of pirate activities and trade in the Far East. The Dutch merchants tried to squeeze the Japanese merchants out and Taiwan became the most important stronghold of Dutch merchants to acquire Chinese silk. The Dutch traders exported Chinese silk first to Japan to compete with the Portuguese. Meanwhile, the Dutch East India Company tried to lure Chinese merchants to Batavia, Malacca, Siam and other regions where Dutch firms had.

European Markets

Before the Age of geographical discoveries, Chinese silk was already marketed in Europe, but but the consumption of Chinese silk in European region was quite limited due to low level of purchasing power which was in turn constrained by the level of development of productive forces. After the 15th century, the major European forces expanded overseas, and began to make colonial fortune, especially silver from America, continuously flew into Europe. In the 16th century, the stock of precious metals in Europe increased by 10 times, which caused skyrocketing of commodity prices in the European markets and significant improvement in the purchasing power of a part of European people. In the late Ming Dynasty and early Qing Dynasty period, there were two sea routes from China to Europe, the Indian Ocean sea route which was controlled by the Portuguese and the Manila-Mexico-Europe route developed

---

29 Chen Ching-ho, Overseas Chinese in the Philippines during the 16th Century, 1963, Hong Kong, Southeast Asia Studies Section, New Asia Research Institute, p. 58.
30 The History of Sino-Dutch Intercourse, Translated Into Chinese by Zhuang Guotu: 1989, Originally published in Netherlands, 1989, p. 41.

by the Spaniards. Chinese silk in the European market was mainly supplied by the Portuguese and Spanish merchants through these two sea routes. The Portuguese's trade bases in the East mainly included Goa, India, Malacca, Macao and Nagasaki, Japan. Macao was the silk trade hub. The trade procedure was generally like this: the Portuguese merchants purchased silk in Macao and Guangzhou and sold the silk to Japan for silver, and then shipped the silver to Macao to purchase silk and other goods, and then add local products of the South Seas in Malacca before departure to Europe. Lisbon, capital of Portugal, was the largest distribution center of Europe and a large quantity of Chinese silk was distributed to various regions of Europe from there.

"Asia Protugeza", which was published in late 17th century, quoted from a newspaper that in the late 16th century, the Portuguese imported 5,300 containers of silk from China each year, and each container held 250 bolts of silk. But some scholars estimated 1,300 containers.[31]

According to estimation of some scholars in the Chinese mainland, China exported several thousand dan of silk to Portugal each year, for example 6,000 dan in the year 1635.[32]

The quantity of silk transported to Europe by the Spanish merchants was not small-scale either. During the late Ming Dynasty period, each year about 25-30 Chinese ships from Macao, Fujian and Ningbo shipped silk and other goods to Manila. The Spaniards then transshipped the goods to Port Acapulo on the West coast of Mexico after crossing the Pacific Ocean. Most of Chinese silk imported from Manila was shipped to Vera Cruz at Mexico Bay through the land route and then transshipped to Europe, except for a part that was left for consumption or processing in Mexico, Peru and other American colonies owned by Spain.[33]

In the beginning of the 17th century, Dutch East Asia Company gradually occupied an important position in the European markets with marketing of the Chinese silk. The Dutch colonists and the British joined hands to break monopoly of the Portuguese and the Spaniards over Chinese silk trade by force. In late July 1603, the Dutch colonist Wijbrant van Waerwijk led 2 Dutch military ships to attack the Portuguese merchant ships which were sailing to Japan at the open seas of Macao and robbed the Portuguese ships. The captured goods included 2,800 packs of raw silk, each pack with a value of 500 guilders.[34]

---

31   Zhuang Guotu: On Overseas Chinese Silk Trade in the Late Ming Dynasty Period (1567-1643), contained in China and Maritime Silk Road, p. 38.

32   See Huang Qichen, Deng Kaisong: Macao's Foreign Trade During the Period between the Reign of Emperor Jiajing and Reign of Emperor Chongzhen of the Ming Dynasty, contained in Journal of Sun Yat-sen University, Issue, 1984/3.

33   C.G.F. Simkin: The Traditional Trade of Asia, London, 1968, Oxford University Press; First Edition, p. 188.

34   Robert Fruin: Verspreide Geschriften (Scattered Writings), Vol. 3, Den Haag, 1900-1905. p. 398.

In 1606, the Board of Directors of the Dutch East India Company decided to price the raw silk at 12-16.2 Dutch guilder per pound. Before 1620, the Dutch colonists sold about 72,000 pounds of raw Chinese silk to the European market. Later, after the Dutch colonists opened the supply channel of Persian raw silk, Chinese silk purchased from the Far East was mainly traded with Japan, and the shipment to Europe reduced gradually to 10,000 pounds in 1631. After the reign of Emperor Qianlong of the Qing Dynasty, the annual raw silk export in Guangzhou reached more than 350 gross tons.[35]

The annual raw silk export to the British East Asia Company valued 200,000 tael to 500,000 tael on average from the reign of Emperor Qianlong to the reign of Emperor Daoguang of the Qing Dynasty.[36]

The European merchants not only imported a large quantity of Chinese silk products, but also developed their own silk industry. Italian cities and Spain used the raw silk from the East as the raw materials to establish a developed silk industry. Before the 1620s, China was the main supplier of raw silk of the European market. With development of the raw silk industry of Persia, the Persian raw silk flew into Europe in a large quantity. Though European merchants still purchased Chinese silk, most was transshipped to other Asian countries for profits. Therefore the sales of Persian raw silk gradually exceeded China's raw silk in the European market. In the middle 17th century, cheaper Bangladeshi raw silk entered the European Market and its quantity exceeded China's raw silk too. The price of raw silk from China was higher, but it was still worth trading because of the high quality. The local silk industry of Europe could not restrict sales of Chinese silk products because China's products boasted high quality, lower price and unique patterns, compared with the local products. Therefore the profit of trading Chinese silk was still as high as 100%.[37]

585

After the 17th century, Chinese silk producers followed changes of the consumers' market and designed silk products with patterns of European styles according to aesthetics of European, for example the silk products with double-head eagle patterns to cater to Habsburg aristocracy who ruled Austria and Spain in the 16th and 17th centuries, and embroidered curtains with European styles to cater to the Portuguese.[38]

The large quantity export of Chinese silk made the silk industry of Europe to face serious crisis. In the late 17th century and early 18th century, the silk factory owners of the UK and France urged the governments to take protective measures to prevent entrance of Chinese silk with legislative measures. But because

35 Huang Qichen, Guangdong's Foreign Trade in Early Qing Dynasty Period, contained in Journal of Researches on Chinese Economic History, 1988/4.
36 Yao Xianhao: Materials of the History of Foreign Trade of China in the Modern Times, ed. 1962, Volume I, Zhonghua Book Company, pp. 275, 279).
37 G. F. Hudson: Europe & China: A Survey of Their relations From the Earliest Times to 1800, London, 1931, p. 259).
38 Royal Antarion Museum, ed.: Silk Roads and Chinese Ships, Toronto.1983. p. 9, p. 24.

Chinese silk was highly favored by the aristocracy and the rich class, Chinese silk products were still shipped to the European market without interruption.

The American market

Since the 16th century, Mexico and Peru saw exploitation of silver mines, especially Peru which contributed to 60% of the world's silver output in the 16th century. In the late 16th century, the Spaniards opened the route from Mexico to Manila and shipped silver from America to the Philippines to trade in Chinese silk. Therefore, in addition to meeting demand of the local consumers, quite a part of China's raw silk and silk products shipped to Manila market were transshipped to America and Spain by the Spaniards. The silk market of America was first monopolized by the Spaniards. At the beginning of the inauguration of Port Manila, only several sailboats reached Manila from China each year. From the 1580s to the late Ming Dynasty, about 25-30 sailboats reached Manila each year. After 1583, the Portuguese merchant ships were permitted do business in Manila by the King of Spain. Each year several Portuguese ships traded silk products in Manila. Before 1636, the big sailboats registered about 300-500 containers of various kinds of silk products, and even up to 1,200 containers, and each container could hold several bolts of silk.[39]

In the early period only the Spaniards who occupied Philippines marketed silk from Luzon to America, and later the Spanish merchants in Mexico and Peru also purchased Chinese silk from Manila. The elegant and soft Chinese silk not only was characterized by rich colors and a variety of designs, but also lower price and strong competitiveness. The American people soon became familiar with the silk cloth. Not only Spanish colonists in Spanish American made clothes with silk, but quite a number of black slaves and Indians in the silver producing regions could afford the silk clothes.[40]

586

Based on the quantity of American silver which poured into China from Manila, it can be estimated that at least 1.1 million Spanish Peseta worth of Chinese silk was shipped to America per year in the late Ming Dynasty period.

The raw silk material produced in China has supported the development of the silk cloth production industry in many parts of the world. Chinese raw silk was long been the main raw material for the silk weaving (cloth) industry across the world. Many factories in Japan and Europe used the Chinese raw silk to produce cloth and other silk products, so did America. Spanish colonists in the Spanish America established many silk weaving mills. According to the report of Mofacton, a Spanish prosecutor of the Philippines, Mexico alone had 14,000 people living on weaving with exported Chinese raw silk in the 1630s.[41]

---

39   Quan Hansheng: Chinese Silk Trade in Spanish America from the Late Ming Dynasty to the Middle Ming Dynasty, contained in the Journal of Chinese Studies of the Chinese University of Hong Kong, Volume 4, Issue 2.
40   E.H. Blair & J. A. Robertson, ed.: The Philippe Islands 1493-1893, Volume 12, p. 63.
41   See The Manila Galleon by William Lytle Schurz, Dutton; First American Edition edition (1939) New York, 1939.

Spain's silk industry was once seriously frustrated since the China began selling silk to the Latin American markets. After this event the Spanish silk industry and trade sector had a long debate on this issue. Those Spanish merchants engaged in the Chinese silk trade could gain lucrative profits nearly 400%, and even 1000% in some years during the 16th-17th centuries. The silk trade between Lima and Manila generated profits of two times of the investment amount. The high profits stimulated the Spaniards to flock to the trade and were unwilling to stop the silk trade with China. The silk-silver trade among China –the Philippines– Spanish America had been prosperous till the middle Qing Dynasty. North America was also an important market for Chinese raw silk and silk products. After gaining its political independence, the United States gradually developed silk trade with China. In some years, the volume of raw silk and silk products exported to the United States had even gratly surpassed to that exported to the UK, the largest trading partner of China since the middle Qing Dynasty. For example, in 1832 the British merchants purchased about 50,000 bolts of Chinese silk; in contrast, the merchants from the United States purchased more than 210,000 bolts from Guangzhou.

(2) The Porcelain Trade

Though the quantity of Chinese silk exported to Southeast Asia increased slightly, it did not mean the local people could afford such goods. For example the Ryukyuan market had higher demand on Chinese porcelain and iron boiler than silk.[42]

The Chinese merchants "carry only porcelain and iron boilers" to the Philippines (Biography of Shayao and Binahui), the History of the Ming Dynasty). Wenlang and Mashen and other regions "trade with Chinese people and gradually use porcelain, and especially love porcelain jar with dragon patterns".[43]

According to study of archaeologists of the porcelain of the Ming and Qing dynasties unearthed in the East Africa, China-East Africa porcelain trade in the Ming and Qing dynasties could be divided in three stages: early Ming Dynasty, middle and late Ming Dynasty and early Qing Dynasty. The quantity of porcelain discovered in the east of Africa, which belonged to the middle and late Ming Dynasty period has been the highest quantity, followed by that of the early Ming Dynasty period, the least quantity belongs to the early Qing Dynasty period. The porcelain of the early Ming Dynasty in East Africa was related to Zheng He's expedition. From Yongle period to Xuande period of the Ming Dynasty, the official fleets of China had visited East Africa for several times for large-scale trade. In this period, there was a number of private merchants shipped Chinese porcelain to East Africa. After arriving ports along coast of East Africa, the Chinese porcelain was marketed to various regions by dealers. After the middle Ming Dynasty, Malacca was controlled by the Portuguese and the Dutch successively and the number of Chinese merchants to the Persian Gulf and East Africa decreased gradually. Indian and Turkic

---

42 Biography of Ryukyu, the History of the Ming Dynasty.
43 Biography of Wenlang and Mashen, the History of the Ming Dynasty.

merchants who were active in Southeast Asia became main dealers of Chinese porcelain. Portuguese Tome Pires[44] in his book wrote: "between 1512-1515, we could see active merchants from India, Persia, Kilwa, Malindi, Mogadiscio and Mombasa of East Africa purchasing a large quantity of goods in Malacca; and in 1511, we could see active merchants from Cairo and Adam (current Aden) in India's Cambay who purchased local products and goods were shipped from Malacca, to East Africa and Arabia. Quite a part of porcelain produced during the middle Ming Dynasty period were exported to East African regions in exchange for local products."

After taking a foothold in Asia, the European forces soon discovered and established the profitable Asia-Africa bilateral trade network and made adjustments to join in. In 1602, the Dutch robbed the Portuguese merchant ship "San Tiago" which carried 28 packs of porcelain plates and 14 packs of porcelain bowls which was purchased from China. In 1604, the Dutch captured the Portuguese ship "Santa Catarina" at Dani (current Pattani, the south of Thailand), which carried about 100,000 pieces of decorative porcelain goods produced in the Emperor Wanli (China) period, which weighed 60 tons. The Portuguese ships only accounted for a small part of the Portuguese commercial fleets shuttling between the Far East and Europe. The main destination of the Chinese porcelain was Europe. Meanwhile, the Portuguese had many strongholds in East Africa, for example Malindi, Mombasa, Kilwa and Mozambique etc. The Portuguese ships often berthed at these ports when returning from Asia to Europe. The Portuguese distributed Chinese porcelain to the inland regions of Africa through these big central cities.

The Portuguese merchants not only purchased porcelain from China, but also from the Southeast Asia and South Asia. In 1563, Venice merchant Friedrich's visited Joel Port, South to Bombay and saw a large quantity of porcelain and other goods in the port. The destination of the porcelain was East Africa. Diu Island, oppose to Kathiawar Peninsula, India, was a base of the Portuguese, where merchants often went to Macca and Adam (Aden) in the Arabpeninsula and Mogadiscio (Mogadishi- Somali), Malindi, Brava, Mombasa of East Africa to sell porcelain from China and Malacca. The Dutch traders actively participated in the East-West porcelain trade, but they didn't not directly ship to East Africa, but distributed the porcelain to East Africa with Mokha, in the Arab peninsula being their base. For example, when the Dutch ships arrived to Mokha in 1614, the merchant ships from Mozambique and Malindi of East Africa traded with the Dutch. Mokha port was a quite large porcelain transit shipment port. In 1643, the Dutch traders shipped nearly 110,000 pieces of porcelain from India, and the quantity had increased to nearly 200,000 pieces in 1645.[45]

44 The "Suma Oriental" was written in 1518 by Tomé Pires. The work was written for the king, Manuel I, and it is a report that focuses on the different economies within the Portuguese empire.
45 Meng Fanren, Ma Wenkuan: Unearthed Ancient Chinese Porcelain Ware in Africa, Forbidden City Press, 1987, p. 126.

Since the Tang and Song dynasties, a large quantity of Chinese porcelain were shipped to East Asia and distributed to regions around the Mediterranean sea by Islam merchants and the royal family of the Ottoman Empire was the most ardent collector of Chinese porcelain. Meanwhile many Chinese types of porcelain flew to Europe. Since the Middle Ages, the Chinese porcelain has been cherished by the European and till today their enthusiasm has not diminish. The most renowned artistic work highlighting the beauty and technique of the Chinese porcelain is the "Feast of the Gods" created by the renowned artist Giovanni Bellini from Venice, Italy, which is collected by the National Gallery of Art, Washington. This detail of Mercury (God) shows the earliest known depiction of Chinese porcelain in European painting.

The bowls with fruits and soup in the center of the painting are authentic blue and white porcelain from the Ming Dynasty period. One bowl carries fresh fruits before the gods, and the rest two, one is carried by one male god on his head and the other by a female god in her hands. According to experts' textual research, these three bowls are obviously the style of Xuande and Chenghua period of the Ming Dynasty in terms of their shape and patterns. The painting was created in 1514, meaning such porcelain as in the painting must have been shipped to Europe before the Age of Discovery.[46]

The word "porcelain" in many contemporary European languages originated from the Portuguese. They discovered a pure white conch in East India when they first arrived in the East and called the conch "porzella", meaning "piglet". Later the Portuguese found porcelain in China sharing similar texture and color with the conch and thus named it porcelain. This word was later adopted by different languages in Europe. In 1435, Duke of Kazinbogen of the Hesse family of Germany has bought and collected a blue and white porcelain bowl produced during the middle Ming Dynasty period, and treasured the bowl as precious as a large jade and embedded it with a silver stand. It has been cherished as the family treasure for several hundred years.

589

The strong fashion of possessing Chinese porcelain and the high price of Chinese porcelain drove development of the porcelain manufacturing industry of Europe. In 1540, the Venetian people made a kind of porcelain named Medici, which looked similar to the Chinese porcelain, but crudely made with sordid yellow color. After a century, the porcelain making technique was introduced to Netherlands, and the porcelain produced there was named Delft. Later the technique was introduced to France and Germany. The most popular Chinese porcelain in France was the decorative porcelain with flowers and bird figures on a white background. In the 18th century, porcelain was very popular in France. It was German Johann Friedrich Boettger et al. who discovered the secret of porcelain making technology. Boettger was a hermetic believer and established a laboratory with support from Augustus, King of

---

46   Zhu Longhua: From Silk Road to Marco Polo–Cultural Exchanges between China and Italy, contained in the History of Sino-Foreign Cultural Exchanges, pp. 282-283.

Saxony (Germany). He successfully produced red porcelain in 1708. In 1710, he established a workshop in Messin, near Dresden and used Kaolin as the raw material to make hard porcelain under high temperature. That was the beginning of porcelain industry in Europe. In the early stage the European porcelain production Chinese porcelain production was imitated in regard to shape and decorative patterns, but used obviously different European technology.[47]

Chinese Artwork and Chinese Art Introduced to Europe

After colonists have become active in the East, the artworks of China were introduced to Europe. In 1698, the first French ship "Amphrityite" arrived in China and in 1701 it reached the East again. The ship transported a large quantity of artwork from China, including lacquer ware. The exquisite lacquer ware from China was popular among the European people and in French it was called Amphrityite. Immediately it became fashionable to wear silk clothes and use Chinese porcelain and lacquer ware in France. Soon the European started to imitate lacquer ware. In the 17th the French could imitate quite exquisite lacquer ware. Madame de Pompadour was a renowned lacquer ware lover. In 1752, she ordered a large batch of lacquer paintings for Bellevue. Martin family of France was famous for making lacquer ware in Europe. Voltaire once praised highly of their lacquer works with a poem, "Martin brothers' lacquer cabinet is better than China's art". After the middle 18th century, the fashion lacquer ware was also introduced to Germany. German artist Johann Heirieh Stobwasser developed sell lacquer ware and established a factory in Braunschweig. Factory output included furniture—tables, chests, desks—and trays, snuff bottles, decorative plates and a variety of boxes. Even a lacquered carriage might be ordered for a special occasion. Many products were decorated with Chinese figures and landscape scenes.

In the scenes painted on the small lacquer pieces by German craftsmen, landscapes, portraits, erotic scenes and non-figurative decorations predominated. Russian merchant Korobov acquired a quantity of lacquer and paint from Stobwasser and invited several craftsmen to join him in Russia. That year, 1795, the merchant founded his own "lakir" factory in a wooden building in tiny Danilovkovo and began production. Chinese sedan chair was introduced to Europe in the 17th century. Princess and dukes of Europe learned the system of distinguishing ranks from the color and shape of sedan chairs from China. In 1727 Vienna saw the patrol ceremony with sedan chairs arranged by rank for the first time. The Emperor of Germany took an extraordinary sedan chair at the first of the queue, followed by sedan chairs of the imperial court and the Privy Council. The fashion of possessing sedan chairs by high ranked nobles and senior officials continued till the middle of the 19th century.[48]

47 Ding Jianhong: Sino-German Cultural Exchange in the Frame of East and West Communications, contained in the History of Sino-Foreign Cultural Exchanges.
48 Ibid.

The gardening arts was one of the Chinese arts that have greatly influenced Europe. French missionary Attiret send a letter to his friend to describe the Yuanmingyuan of Beijing, China in 1743. He pointed out that the man-made river in the garden was not arranged in symmetry, but as natural as that in the wild, and decorated with rockeries on banks, and flowers growing from crevices in rocks. In the 18th century the French society was tired of the rigid symmetrical classical architecture in the period of Louis XIV and the architectural style of Chinese garden aroused their great interests. In 1744, a duplicate of Forty Views of the Yuanmingyuan, a color silk scroll created by the Chinese artists Tang Dai and Shen Yuan, was sent to France by Wang Zhicheng. Some nobles in France imitated the Chinese gardening styles and built bridges and brooks, pavilions, pagodas and rockeries in their private gardens, and even planted flowers of the Yuanmingyuan.[49]

(2) Import of Silver

During the early and middle period of the Ming Dynasty, the overseas trade was mainly tributary trade, basically exchanging overseas spice and treasures with gold, silver, copper coins, lead, tin, porcelain and silk products. The balance between revenue and expenses of gold and silver was not high in the tribute and rewards. In the early days when the European traders arrived in the East, their products were not competitive in the Far East. Silver from the Spanish America flew to Europe in an endless flow, enabling the European colonist and merchants to pay with silver when purchasing in the East. The Portuguese used most Spanish peseta shipped from Europe to the Far East to pay the Chinese silk purchased in Macao and transported the silk to Japan for profits. It was estimated that during the trade booming period between Macao and Japan from 1569 to 1636, the Portuguese paid about 33.50 million Spanish pesetas to China in total for the silk and vessel taxes.[50]

In the early 17th century, the Dutch purchased the Chinese silk in exchange with silver from Taiwan and various regions of South Sea and shipped to Japan. It is generally acknowledged that in more than a half century from the late 16th century to the late Ming Dynasty period, about 3 million to 5 million Spanish pesetas flew from Spanish America to Manila, Philippines each year, and up to 12 million in 1579. Most of the silver was used to purchase the Chinese silk products. Zhang Xie of the Ming Dynasty said: "There is no other product to purchase from Philippines, and the foreigners use silver to purchase goods. Therefore the ships had little to transport except sliver, and other goods were in small quantity, if any."[51]

49　Zhang Zhilian: Sino-French Cultural Exchange, contained in the History of Sino-Foreign Cultural Exchanges.
50　Zhuang Guotu: On Overseas Chinese Silk Trade in the Late Ming Dynasty Period (1567-1643), contained in China and Maritime Silk Road.
51　The Study of the East and the West, Vol. 7, p. 132.

This resulted in a high foreign trade surplus for China in this period and alarge quantity of silver flew into China. It is generally acknowledged that before the late Ming Dynasty period, silver that flew into China from Philippines was above 75 million.[52]

Zhang Xie has described the silver outflow from Philippines as follows: the large coin weighs 7 qian 5 fen, foreign name "huangbishi", the secondary large coin weighs 3 qian 6 fen, foreign name "tuchun", the tertiary large coin weighs 1 qian 8 fen, namely "luoliaoxia", and the smallest coin weighs 9 fen, namely "huangliaoxia".[53]

In basically the same period, the amount of silver flowing from Japan to China was even much higher. Silver flowing from Japan to China through different channels, all related to silk trade. In the early 17th century, the Japanese merchants controlled a half of the Japanese silk market and their payment was transferred to China through Chinese merchants. Moreover, the Portuguese marketed Chinese silk from Macao to Japan. It was estimated the annual sales was up to 2.35 million silver tael (or 3.29 Spanish Pesetas). The Portuguese merchants transported the earned money to Macao to purchase the Chinese silk. In the period from 1569 to 1636, more than 200 million Spanish peseta worth silver flowing to China from Japan through the Portuguese merchants. Moreover, the Dutch merchants were also active in the silk trade with Japan with Taiwan as the base. The money they earned in Japan flew to the Chinese mainland in the form of silk payment indirectly. The total amount of silver flowing from Europe, America and Japan to China must be more than 350 million.[54]

That reason why silver became a common means of exchange in China during the Ming Dynasty was possibly related with the significant increase of silver inventory.

3. Jesuits and East-West Cultural Exchange

After the Yuan Dynasty perished in 1368, the East-west land transportation declined and contacts between China and Europe plumbed. After a century and a half, when the Portuguese arrived in the East, both China and Europe experienced great changes. The Mongol Yuan Dynasty was overthrown in China while Europe entered a new era because of Renaissance and the Age of Discovery. In the middle 16th century, the Portuguese occupied Macao and since then the contacts between China and Europe became more frequent. In order to expand the church power, the Vatican sent batches of missionaries to China. Many Jesuits earnestly learned the Chinese culture while introduced advanced science and technology of the West to China. These contacts opened a new chapter of East-West cultural exchange.

52 Zhuang Guotu: On Overseas Chinese Silk Trade in the Late Ming Dynasty Period (1567-1643), contained in the book titled as China and Maritime Silk Road.
53 The Study of the East and the West, Vol. 5, p. 94.
54 He Guotu: On Overseas Chinese Silk Trade in the Late Ming Dynasty Period (1567-1643), contained in China and Maritime Silk Road.

(1) Matteo Ricci and Xu Guangqi

Among the Jesuits implementing their careers in China, Matteo Ricci was the most renowned one. He was born in 1552, Macerata, Italy. He once lived in India before arriving in China and reached Zhaoqing, Guangdong in 1583. Before Matteo Ricci, Michele Ruggieri arrived in Macao in 1579, studied Chinese language there and arrived in the Ming in 1581. The local government of Guangdong approved him to do missionary work in Zhaoqing. Ricci lived with Ruggieri for nearly 10 years in China and learned Chinese. Ricci's most important contribution was opening a window for China to learn about the world and introducing China to Europe.

Matteo Ricci was well educated before coming to China, mastered the new knowledge of main disciplines of Europe since Renaissance and carried astronomical instruments, chime clock, map, optical glasses and books with him when he came to China. He introduced the Western sciences to China, compiled the Measurement Principles and Map of All Countries and other works. Of the scientific works he introduced, Elements of Geometry was the most important. The Elements of Geometry was not the translation of Euclides' works, but lecture notes of Euclides' teacher Clavius. Clavius means "nail" in Latin (in Chinese "ding") and therefore Ricci translated as Mr. Ding. He dictated the lecture notes and Xu Guangqi translated it into Chinese. The book was published in the 3rd year of Wanli period in Beijing and reprinted for many times.

Matteo Ricci's arrival attracted high importance from the advanced intellectuals of China. He preached his religion by means of mastering the Chinese learning and imparting the Western learning. In contacts with Ricci, some Chinese intellectuals received baptism, for example Xu Guangqi, Li Zhizao, Qu Taisu, Feng Yingjing, Zhang Tao et al. Therefore they had more chances to learn advanced elements of European science and brought new impetus for the scientific development of China.

Of the Chinese intellectuals converted to Christianity, Xu Guangqi was the most renowned. Xu was born in Shanghai and studied hard since he was a child. In 1597, the 25th year of the Wanli period, he ranked first in the provincial examination. He scored achievements in academia before knowing Matteo Ricci. He compiled Calculation in River Engineering Works and Method of Topographic Measurements with the traditional mathematical knowledge of China as the basis. After passing the highest imperial examination in 1604, he worked at the National Academy for four years and got acquaint with Matteo Ricci. The contacts of these two scholars who mastered sciences of the East and the West respectively was an important chapter in China's history of science. Xu and Ricci cooperated with each other in introducing Western sciences. With Ricci making dictation and Xu Guangqi the translation, they translated the classical works of European Elements of Geometry. They also co-compiled the works Measurement Principles (Ce Liang Fa Yi) and the Pythagorean Theorem (Gou Gu Yi) etc. After Ricci passed away, Xu cooperated with other missionaries in China. Xu Guangqi compiled Taixi Water Law with Italian Sabathinus de Ursis (1575-1640), and the Complete Works on Agriculture and Agricultural Administration (Nong Zheng Quan Shu) from 1621 to 1628. He chaired the amendment work of the calendar from 1629 to 1632. Italian missionaries Giacomo Rho (1590-1638) and Nicolaus Longobardi (1559-1654) and Switzer Joannes Terrenz (1576-1630, arrived in the Ming China in 1621 and died in Beijing) and had cooperated with Xu Guangqi. In 1631, the 4th year of the reign of Emperor Chongzhen, Xu Guangqi presented the scientific translations that he had chaired to the imperial court of the Ming, including the Solar Equation Treatise and the two volume book of Solar Equation Table of Giacomo Rho, two volume book of the Measurement of Universe, two volume book of the Great Measurements, which were co-authored by Giacomo Rho and Johann Adam Schall von Bell, one volume book (someone researcher said it was two volumes) of the Table of Distance between Ecliptic and Equator, a six volume book of Table of Trigonometric Functions written by Joannes Terrenz, a seven volume book of Ecliptic Degrees, one volume book of the Table of Tonglyu etc. In the winter of the same year, he submitted the book Four Methods of Astronomical and Meteorological Observation. In the late Ming Dynasty, when Liaodong was in a great danger and Xu Guangqi was ordered to cast Western cannons to resist the Qing rebellion, but had resigned due to a disagreement with head of the Ministry of War.

Ricci lived in Beijing for 10 years and had a wide circle of acquaintances. In addition to Xu Guangqi, he also cooperated with Li Zhizao. At that time most Chinese scholars attached importance to Confucianism and regarded science as an insignificant skill. In contrast, Li Zhizao had great interests in astronomy, geography, mathematics, fine arts, music and engineering. Ricci once said after arriving in China, that he saw only Xu Guangqi and Li Zhizao wise, reasonable and sensible. Li co-worked with Ricci to translate Tongwen Suanzhi, Illustrated Description of Astrolabe, Qiankun Tiyi (Treatise of Universe) and Yuanrong Jiaoyi (Treatise on Circle in Geometry) etc. These books were published in the Yuan Dynasty. In the books on mathematics he put a note: "if compared with the same topic in the old books, my current translation is better than them, if there are differences from the former books, you can understand that this new content was not included in the old works."

Li was a comprehensive scholar who was enthusiastic to learning from the West. After Ricci died, he worked with Portuguese Jesuit Franciscus Eurtado to translate the works of Aristotle, and completed 6 volumes of Huanyouquan (Explanation of Cosmology) and 10 volumes of Minglitan (An Introduction to Aristotle's Dialectics). When a department was established to amend the calendar in early reign of Emperor Chongzhen, Li was the assistant of Xu Guangqi and organized Nicolaus Longobardi and others to join in. Li passed away before completion of the 100 volumes of their new work New Mathematics (Xinfa Suanshu). Before his death, he was preparing to publish the book Complete Works of Astronomy (Tianxue Chuhan) which would have 20 volumes. What

Xu and Li had achieved in comparison to their predecessors was that they were based on the Chinese traditional learning and absorbed the modern sciences and technology of the West. They were the true founders of the modern sciences of China.

Ricci was famous for his rich knowledge and experience. He had contacts with many Chinese scholars and kept up regular correspondence with them. His reading notes were compiled into the History of the Spread of Christianity in China by French Jesuit Nicholas Trigault after his death. This book was widely spread in the 17th century. Ricci's introduction to China in his notes was more detailed than Marco Polo. He wrote about science and technology, structure of Chinese characters and humanities and introduced Confucius and Confucianism to the West.

Ricci died in Beijing in 1610. According to Jesuit Giulio Alenio's book[55] "The Life of Mr. Matteo Ricci", the local government of the Ming reported to Emperor Wanli and said that: "Ricci is diligent, sensible and his works are rich in content" and asked the Emperor to grant him a special graveyard.

This petition was approved by Emperor Wanli. But some ministers disapproved, and questioned: "there has never been such a case of granting a graveyard to a foreigner. Why should we treat Matteo Ricci so generously?" Premier Ye Wenzhong refuted, "of all foreigners since ancient times", no one can be compared with Matteo Ricci in terms of "morality and learning", "no to mention anything else, the merits of translating the Elements of Geometry was enough to get a graveyard." From this we can see the high evaluation to him. His tomb is still in Erligou, Fuchengmenwai, Beijing, in the campus of the Party School of the CPC Beijing Municipal Committee.

595

(2) Missionaries Introducing the Western Learning

In addition to Matteo Ricci, some other European missionaries also contributed to the East-West cultural exchanges, below are some prominent ones: Sicilian Nicolaus Longobardi (arrived in China during the Ming period in 1597 and died in Beijing), Chinese name Long Huamin, who wrote the Study of Earthquake and First Aids. The Study of Earthquake was published in 1626,

---

55 The life and works of Giulio Aleni are the subject of several conferences in 1994 and 2010. Two of his books, Life of Matteo Ricci, Xitai of the West and Holy images of the Heavenly Lord have been presented to the public by Fondazione Civiltà Bresciana in two separate occasions, on 13 and 25 October 2010. He published works in Chinese on a variety of topics, his cosmography, Wanwu Zhenyuan (The True Origin of the Ten-thousand Things), was translated into Manchu language during the reign of Kang-he as Wylie: Tumen chakai unengki sekiyen, Möllendorff: Tumen jakai unengki sekiyen. A copy was sent from Beijing to Paris in 1789, he completed the work of earlier Jesuit scholars to produce the Zhifang waiji, China's first global geography. Among his most important religious works are a controversial treatise on the Catholic Faith, in which are refuted what he saw as the principal errors of the Chinese; and The Life of God, the Saviour, from the Four Gospels (Peking, 1635-1637, 8 vols.; often reprinted, e.g. in 1887 in 3 vols) and was used even by Protestant missionaries.

the 6th year of the reign of Emperor Tianqi period, and republished in 1679, the 18th year of the reign of the Emperor Qianlong. This book introduces causes, earthquake magnitude division and omens of earthquake etc.

Italian Sabathinus de Ursis (arriving in the Ming in 1606, died in 1620, Macao), used the Chinese name Xiong Sanba. In early years of the reign of Emperor Chongzhen, some scholars of the Imperial Board of Astronomy did not correctly forecast the solar eclipse, and Emperor Chongzhen was to punish the concerned. Xu Guangqi pointed out that the Imperial Board of Astronomy was based on the calendar of Guo Shoujing of the Yuan Dynasty. In the Yuan Dynasty, the Shoushi Calendar had cases of not correctly forecasting the solar eclipse. It was better to amend the calendar than to punish the officials. Therefore he commented as follows: "foreigners from the Atlantic Ocean Didacus de Pantoya and Sabathinus de Ursis et al. are proficient in calendar calculation and the calendar they have introduced carry valuable contents which our calendar does not have. It is suggested to order them to translate the calendar for us to use"; meanwhile, officials of the Ministry of Rites requested the Ming government to allow Didacus de Pantoya and Sabathinus de Ursis et al. to observe astronomical phenomena with scholars of the Imperial Board of Astronomy, like establishing the "Hui Department" during the early years of Hongwu period. The request was approved.[56]

Therefore Ursis and Xu Guangqi translated and compiled the Datong Calendar. Moreover, he co-worked with Xu Guangqi to compile An Introduction to Astrolabe.Giulio Aleni (1582-1649, arrived in the Ming dynasty in 1613 and died in Fuzhou) he was from Brescia, Italy, and enjoyed the Chinese name Ai Rulue, courtesy name Siji. He first visited Beijing, and then was ushered to Shanghai by Xu Guangqi, and then to Zhejiang and Fujian. In addition to Zhifang Waiji (Records of Foreign Lands), he also wrote An Introduction to the Western Learning, which introduces disciplines of universities of Europe, for example Rhetofica (liberal arts), Philosophia (i.e. philosophy), Medicina, Leges (law), Canones (ecclesiastical law), and Theologia (theology). Another famous work which introduced Europe was Questions and Answers on the West. The book was published in 1637, the 10th year of the reign of Emperor Chongzhen. In two volumes, the book consists of "Territory", "Distance", "Maritime Ships", "Marine Risks", "Manufacturing", "Western Learning", "Civil Officials", "Medicine", "Armament", "Map", "Calendar", "Solar and Lunar Eclipses", "Constellation", "Time", "Beginning of the Year" etc. Moreover, he also wrote Essentials of Geometry and Treatise on Geographic Maps etc.

Giacomo Rho (who arrived in the Ming dynasty in 1622, died in Beijing, also was known as Yage in Chinese) he was from Milan, Italy and enjoyed the Chinese name Luo Yagu, and used the courtesy name Maishao. Giacomo Rho was proficient in ephemeris calculation. With growing deviation in Datong

---

56 Biography of Italy, the History of the Ming Dynasty.

Calendar in the reign of Emperor Chongzhen, Xu Guangqi proposed to the emperor to invite Giacomo Rho and Johann Adam "to refer to their new calendar and amend our calendar". The calendar designated the first year of the reign of Emperor Chongzhen as the first year of the calendar, and thus named "Chongzhen Calendrical Science". In the 4th year of the reign of Emperor Chongzhen, he cooperated with Xu Guangqi and Johann Adam to write the New Book of Western Calendar, totaling 36 volumes. He wrote many works in his life, including Complete Treatise on Measurements (10 volumes), Explanation of Proportional Compasses (one volume), Table of Five Planets (10 volumes), Treatise on Five-Planet Calendar (nine volumes), Lunar Eclipse (four volumes), Table of Moon Motion (four volumes), Solar Equation Calendar (one volume), Table of Solar Equation (two volumes), Ecliptic and Equator Sphere (one volume), Rod Calculus (one volume), Calender Introduction (one volume), Solar Equation Survey and Day and Night Division etc.

Adam Schall von Bell (1591-1666), with the Chinese name Tang Ruowang, from Cologne, Germany, was the first missionary who had close contacts with the Chinese imperial court. He was a mathematician and astronomer and came to China under influence of Matteo Ricci. He arrived in Macao in 1619, the 47th year of Wanli period of the Ming Dynasty, and arrived in Beijing in 1623, the third year of Tianqi period. He exhibited instruments and books he took, and correctly forecast the lunar eclipses in October 1623 and September 1624. Therefore he was appreciated by Emperor Chongzhen and some officials. In 1630 he joined in the calendar amendment recommended by Xu Guangqi, and completed Chongzhen Calendrical Science in 1634, the 7th year of the reign of Emperor Chongzhen. After demise of the Ming Dynasty, he was still highly evaluated by the Qing rulers. He revised the Chongzhen Calendrical Science and renamed it Calendrical Science Based on New Western Method and presented the book to the Qing government. Emperor Shunzhi approved and named it "Shixian Calendar". This is the lunar calendar we still use today. He was appointed director of the Imperial Board of Astronomy to take charge of the national observatory works. In 1665, the 4th year of the reign of Emperor Kangxi, he was accused of "10 crimes" by the former Chinese director of the Imperial Board of Astronomy and was put into the condemned ward. He got out of jail for merits and died in the following year. He was vindicated in 1669, in the 8th year of the reign of Emperor Kangxi.

Adam Schall fostered numerous famous Chinese students. Xu Guangqi learned astronomy, calendar, mathematics, measurement and water conservancy knowledge from him. He also designed astronomic, optical and mechanics apparatuses, and made cannon and musical instruments. He wrote 28 books when he was in China, and compiled A Study of Ancient and Today's Solar Eclipse, Theory of the Eclipse Calculation, On Stars, On Armillary Sphere, Essentials of Geometry, New Calendar Calculation and other astronomical and mathematics works. His works Zhuzhi Qunzheng deciphered the nature, animals and plants, and even functions of internal organs of man and man's blood, which highly caught the attention of medical circles in China. Records of his lectures was published in the book Essentials of Firearm which introduced the structure, manufacturing technology and usage of of cannons; the book Theory of Telescope introduced the modern optical knowledge and theories, manufacturing, use and maintenance knowledge for telescopes. Adam Schall von Bell has made important contributions to the scientific and technological progress of China. Ludovius Buglio (1606-1684, arrived in the Ming dynasty in 1637, and died in Beijing), used the Chinese name Li Leisi, and co-operated with Ferdinand Verbiest (Nan Huairen) to write Essentials of the West for the Imperial Reading. Philippus Marie Grimaldi (1639-1712, arrived in China in 1669), used the Chinese name Min Mingwo, once served as director of the Imperial Board of Astronomy of the Qing Dynasty, and wrote the Illustrated Explanation of Astronomy.

(3) Missionary Jean Francois Gerbillon: His Map Surveying and Mapping

The Western missionaries have successfully penetrated in the upper class of China in the late Ming and early Qing Dynasty periods. They were trusted and appreciated by rulers of the Ming and Qing dynasties. The commonly used academic language was Latin among European countries and Latin was the re-quired course in the schools of Europe. In the early years of the Qing Dynasty, China and Russia had frequent interactions. The two countries did not know each other's language in the early days of their contacts, and and the Latin lan-guage that was fluently spoken by the European missionaries in China became the main language which was used in the China- Russia diplomatic relations.

Some of the missionaries served in Beijing in the early Qing Dynasty. French missionary Jean Francois Gerbillon (Chinese name Zhang Cheng) lectured to Emperor Kangxi on geometry and philosophy and had close contact with the emperor. He quickly learned the Chinese and Manchu language and became the most important interpreter of the Qing government in communications with the Western countries. In the middle 17th century, Russia expanded Eastward by the opportunity of the Qing entering the region of Shanhai Pass, causing armed conflicts on the Sino-Russia borders. After the Jiangnan kingdom was pacified, the Qing government concentrated its forces and sent troops to the Heilong River drainage region to confront Tsarist Russia. Jean Francois Gerbillon served as interpreter for the Qing government. In 1689, China and Russia started nego-tiations by the city of Nerchinsk. Gerbillion took part in the negotiations in the capacity of rank three official, and he left detailed records about these nego-tiations, which are valuable historical materials for the study of Sino-Russian relationships in this period. On September 7 of the same year, China and Russia signed the Treaty of Merchinsk, which determined theborders between the two countries. The treaty was in duplicate in Latin, one copy in Manchu language and Chinese language respectively. The Latin version was translated by Gerbillion.

When the delegation led by Evart Isbrand Ides came to China from Russia in 1693, Gerbillion also served as interpreter. In 1720, when Russian delegation led by Ismailoff came to China, French missionary Dominique Parrenin had served as the interpreter.

Since ancient times, China had the science of mapping. But constrained by the theory of round heaven and square ground, China's maps could not correctly reflect the geographic positions and distances. Gerbillion presented a map of Asia to Emperor Kangxi during Merchinsk negotiations. He accompanied Emperor Kangxi in tours of inspection and surveyed longitude and latitude in the tours. Emperor Kangxi approved his suggestion and organized a nation-wide survey, on this issue. From 1707 to 1717, missionaries Jean-Baptiste Régis (Chinese name Lei Xiaosi), Joachim Bouvet (Chinese name Bai Jin) and Pierre Jartoux (Chinese name Du Demei) surveyed the Great Wall, Northeast China, North Korea, North China, Northwest, Jiangnan, South central China, Yunnan and Guizhou upon the imperial order. Dbus-Gtsang and the other regions of Korea were surveyed by others and audited by Jean-Baptiste Régis and Pierre Jartoux. During the survey, missionaries discovered the differences of the longitude length between the North and the South, proving that earth was in the shape of oblateness. In 1718, the survey was completed and titled as A Complete Map of China in the Reign of Emperor Kangxi. Joseph Terence Montgomery Needham (Chinese name Li Yuese) had commented: "this map has been the best of all maps produced in Asia up today time, but also better than all existing maps of Europe, and more precise."[57]

599

In 1718, A Complete Map of China in the Reign of Emperor Kangxi was made into copperplate in Europe and was reprinted for many times, and included in Jean-Baptiste Du Halde's book A Description of the Empire of China. In the middle 18th century, the Qing defeated Junggar and the Qing government ordered Antoine Gaubil (Chinese name Song Junrong) and Benoist Michel (Chinese name Jiang Youren) to mainly survey the Western territory that was newly included in the Qing. Based on the survey, the Copper Plate Map of the Imperial Storehouse of Emperor Qianlong was completed in 1761, which not only included the current Xinjiang, but also Central Asian and the neighborhood regions that was occupied by the Tsarist Russia.

4. Eastward Transmission of European Sciences and Westward Transmission of Chinese Learning

During the Ming Dynasty period, many developed regions of China had obvious buds of capitalism which pushed and vigorated the development of productive forces, science and technology. In the same period, Europe saw a strong capitalist development momentum which consequently led to industrial revolution and emergence of modern sciences. As a result, the social, economic

---

57 Zhang Zhilian, Sino-French Cultural Exchange, contained in the History of Sino-Foreign Cultural Exchange, pp. 57-58.

and scientific development of Europe surpassed China which still remained in the traditional track. Some of the first Western missionaries who came to China possessed certain level of scientific knowledge. The scientific knowledge and instruments, tools and products they brought to China aroused great attention and interest in the Ming imperial court and intellectuals of China. Among the scientific knowledge, introduced to China, the Western mathematics and calendrical study attracted the highest importance. From the Emperor Wanli period of the Ming Dynasty to the Opium War, the Imperial Board of Astronomy of the Ming and Qing dynasties was the arena of the missionaries. The introduction of Western sciences drove development of the science and technology of China.

(1) Introduction of Western Sciences to China

a) Optics

Eye glasses and the principle of refraction

Eye glasses was introduced to China in about the Yuan and Ming dynasties. Before the early Ming Dynasty, it had three Chinese name, and one was "aidai" which must be the transliteration of Arabic "ainak". Zhang Ning of the Ming Dynasty recorded in Miscellaneous Notes of Zhang Fangzhou that he saw in Commander Hu's in the capital city "a gift of Lord Zongbo granted by Emperor Xuande. It has two parts as large as the coin with color identical to mycalex, and looks like glass, very thin, with gold frame and handles. It has a lock at the end. When closing, it becomes one piece and when opening, it becomes two parts, like a medium-sized case in the market. If an old person has blurred eyesight and cannot read small characters, people can wear this over their eyes. With this glass one can see the characters much more clearly and the size of the characters are larger." Later the author mentioned "I saw such an instrument at Sun Jingzhang Administrator's Office and tried it. It is really ideal and satisfactory." Sun Jingzhang said: "I traded in this with a good horse from the Western Regions, and I heard its name was like 'youdai'." "Gift granted by Emperor Xuande" in Commander Hu's in the capital city must be one of the Western treasures Zheng He took from the West in the Xiande period and granted by Emperor Xuande to his minister. The 'youdai" he saw in Sun's was another name of "aidai". Some Chinese learned about the eye glasses from the Hui merchants and thus uses the name given by the Hui merchants in Hui language.

Another name for the eyeglasses was "danzhao". In Wumen Biaoyin (Supplement to Suzhou Annals), Gu Zhentao, the Qing Dynasty, recorded, "In the Ming Dynasty, there was danzhao which was used by carrying with hand." Suzhou Annals in the reign of Emperor Daoguang mentioned, "There was danzhao in the Ming Dynasty and it was said a technique of the West." It was probably an old-style hand-held eye glasses. This name perished after the hand-held eye glasses were no more consumed. Another name was the modern name "yanjing" (eye glasses). Eye glasses have assumed this name in the Ming Dynasty. In Mao Ruizheng's work Translation of the Hui Division of Chinese-Foreign Language Translation, "Division of Instruments and Tools (No. 1360 words) "wonaike, eye glasses", proves that the word "yanjing" had appeared in the Ming Dynasty period. "Wonaike" was the equivalent sound of the Arabic word "aink", another version of the same name as "youdai" which I have mentioned above. In Yuexiaoji (Notes on Guangdong) which was completed in 1818 by Huang Zhi, the Qing Dynasty, said "eye glasses came from the West and made of glass, named "aidai". It was brought to Guangdong in the late Ming Dynasty. The domestic merchants imitated the style and replaced glass with crystal, which was named yanjing. Consequently, it became popular all across China.[58]

The import of eye glasses from the West has enhanced development of the optometry industry of China and fostered a batch of lens making technicians. Sun Yunqiu was the most renowned. He was born in about 1630 and died in about 1662. His teacher was a student of Matteo Ricci.[59]

He could make concave and convex lens with crystal and he had learned the method of "making lens according to eyesight" and achieve that the degrees of the lens match agree with the wearers' eye sights. Sun could also manufacture telescope. He once erected a telescope on the Tiger Hill, where one could see the buildings, pagodas and pavilions in Suzhou and Taiping and Lingyan Mountains with it. Thus he was praised highly for his "magic technique". Sun has manufactured up to 70 kinds of optical instruments, for example "Cunmu lens" (magnifying lens), "Chawei lens" (microscope), "Wanhua lens", "polygonal lens", "night lens", "huanrong lens", "yuanjing lens", and all were "incredibly ingenious". Sun wrote the History of Lens, which enabled the introduced of the knowledge of lens grinding and optical instrument. It is a pity that the book does not exist any more.[60]

The systematic introduction of the Western optical knowledge has direct relation with Jesuits. Italian Jesuit Michele Ruggieri (Chinese name Luo Mingjian, who arrived in Macao in 1579) and other foreign merchants who were active at the coastal regions of China had brought the triple prism to China to demonstrate the light synthesis principle, arousing curiosity of witnesses. Italian Jesuit Matteo Ricci who entered China earlier included a triple prism in his gifts to the emperor in 1601. He used the prism to demonstrate the optical dispersion principle. Among, the optical knowledge introduced to China in this period, the lens principle was the most important. In the works of Western missionaries, Ferdinand Verbiest (Chinese name Nan Huairen) wrote the Light Direction Verification and Inference, but the book was not passed on. Volume 4 of the Lingtai Yixiang Zhi (Observatory Planetarium and Astronomical Phenomena) which Ferdinand Verbiest worked as the chief editor introduced the optical

---

58   See Miscellaneous Notes of Five Directions.
59   See Annals of Hufu (Barbarian clothes), Vol. 6, edition during the reign of Emperor Qianlong.
60   Wang Jinguang, Hong Zhenhuan, History of Optics of China, Hunan Education Publishing House, 1986, pp. 157-159.

knowledge, for example light dispersion and refraction. He divided the light propagation media into "object easy for light transmission" and "object hard for light transmission", which are today's "optically thin medium" and "optically thick medium". He also introduced the concept of "apical line", i.e. normal. His purpose of explaining the refraction principle was to calculate the atmospheric refraction correction value of the aster position. He pointed out, "if the light of the sun, moon and starts enters the object hard for light transmission from the object easy for light transmission, the transmission light must be away from the apical line and divergent." In Chongzhen Calendrical Science, he introduced the correction value. Based on the method in Chongzhen Calendrical Science, he listed the "table of differences" from 1 to 90 degrees, and the actual position of asters and actually surveyed differences of altitude angle. Lingtai Yixiang Zhi also includes the "table of deviation differences" of light entering water and glass from air and from water to glass. But the book did not offer any formula of refraction law, and data in the "table of deviation differences" were approximate value obtained through empirical measurement instead of calculation.

Telescope and microscope

Telescope, which is made based on the refraction principle, was among the most important optical instruments which was introduced to China in the Ming and Qing dynasties. In 1615, the Portuguese missionary Emmanuel Diaz (1574-1659) wrote Tian Wen Lue (Explicatio Sphaerae Coelestis). At the end of the book, he introduced "a celebrity in the West who was good at calendar invented an instrument" for the celestial observation. He did not mention the name of the "celebrity", or what was the "instrument", or the making principle. But scholars who study the history of science know the "celebrity" was Galileo and the "instrument" for celestial observation was telescope. The reference in the book was only six years after Galileo's invention of telescope. Obviously after the Age of Discovery, the information spread speed in regard to science and technology was quite rapid..

Among the extant works of Western missionaries, German Jesuit Johann Adam wrote the Treatise on Telescope in 1626, which was the first introducing the making and use of Galileo's telescope, together with simple drawings, to China, and exploded views of Cancer and Orion nebula. The book also attached importance to use of telescopes in the wars. The first part "Use" introduced looking-up and looking-down views of telescope and the basic principle of imaging of convex lens and concave lens. The second part "Basis" introduced the light refraction phenomena, together with the optical lines diagram, the principle of using convex and concave lens in combination, and pointed out that "these two kinds of lens complement each other and with it one can see objects larger and clearer." The third part explained how to use the two kinds of lens together, i.e. using convex lens as "cone end lens", i.e., objective lens, and concave lens as "kaoyanjing", i.e. ocular lens, and several sections of the lens cones were nested for extendable when use. This book was of enlightenment for the development of optical knowledge and manufacturing of telescope in

China. But the vague description, especially mistake in the optical path, had adverse impact on the later generations.

The Western optical knowledge introduced by missionaries had shocked the scientific community of China of that time. Liu Dong and Yu Yizheng of the Ming Dynasty recorded the introduction of folding telescope in A Brief Introduction to Scenery and Objects of Capital, "Jesuit Matteo Ricci reached China from Europe after sailing hundred of thousand miles. Emperor Shenzong ordered to offer grants and a house to him... Ricci's country was good at making instruments... telescope, looks like a one-chi long bamboo shoot, and can pull out. When stretching, it measured about five chi, and each section was embedded with glass. With it, one could see something small, much larger and objects in the far distance as in the near." Surprised by the technique of the West, the Chinese scientists and craftsmen started to imitate the optical instruments that were based on the Western scientific knowledge. In 1629, Xu Guangqi applied to the emperor for materials to make 3 telescopes. In only 22 years after Galileo used his telescope to observe the celestial phenomena, Xu Guangqi also used the telescope to observe the solar eclipse in 1631. It was not known whether he used the home-made telescope or the telescope brought by missionaries. Following Xu Guangqi, the Calendar Bureau, headed by Li Tianjing, also made some telescopes. In addition to imitation of Western optical instruments supported by the Ming government, many scientists and craftsmen also engaged in the telescope development in the Ming and Qing dynasties. In 1631, Bo Yu from Wujiang, Suzhou, installed the telescope on the home-made copper cannon. This was the world's first artillery telescope.

603

The telescope introduced above were the refraction type. In 1668 Newton made the world's first reflecting telescope. This new type of telescope was introduced to China rather late, in the early Qing Dynasty there was an imitation of it named "Sheguang Qianli Lens". The Scheme of Ritual Vessels of the Imperial Court which was completed in 1759 described this China made telescope, "Sheguang Qianli Lens made in this dynasty has a cone measuring 1 chi and 3 fen, a copper tube 2 cun and 6 fen. It has four lenses and a small hole on the end of the tube. Inside it installs a microscope and glass lenses at the conjunction. All lenses protrude outward. A large bronze lens is installed with the concave facing outward to take images. Within the lens there is a small hole. At the near end a small bronze lens is stalled with concave facing inward. Light is allowed in through crevices to the large lens and contain its shape. The sections of cone are nested. When stretching the cone, one can see the far distance. With a column stand of 3 chi long, it measures one chi, one cun and five fen tall." Optic specialist Zheng Fuguang carefully studied principle and structure of lens introduced in the Treatise on Telescope and wrote a book Addict of Lens. This book introduced three kinds of telescopes: "Kuitong Telescope", "Guanxiang Telescope" and "Sightseeing Telescope", and expounded on the structure, principle, use and maintenance of telescope, and made annotation to each article of the "lens use" in the Treatise on Telescope and introduced the reflecting telescope.

Microscope was introduced to China probably at the same time of telescope. Zhang Rulin and Yin Guangren wrote the Short Account of Macao, in the chapter of Foreigners in Macao it was narrated as follows: "There is an instrument called microscope, with which one can see clearly the stamen and several seeds on it, and fly louse that has dark hairs of about one cun long and can be counted easily one by one." Chinese craftsman Sun Yunqiu once made the "cunmu lens" which was said to "magnify 100 times and no tiny object could be missed " when used. He also made "chawei lens". We are not certain whether these two kinds of instruments with lens were microscopes due to lack of strong evidence. A Chinese optician basically from the same period of Sun Yunqiu has made a "microscope". According to the Addict of Lens, there was a "photic microscope" which consisted of a plane mirror and a convex lens and could be used for seeking to reduce eyesight problems.

Astronomy and Geographical Knowledge

There is a star chart from the late Ming Dynasty contained in the First Historical Archives of China, which was prepared by Xu Guangqi as the director. It has 8 sections: 3 sections included the Southern and Northern equator star charts respectively, one section includes Xu Guangqi's Foreword to the General Star Chart of Southern and Northern Equators, and one section includes German Jesuit missionary Johann Adam's Introduction to the General Star Chart of Southern and Northern Equators. This is the earliest extant star chart of China and a large-scale general star chart including Antarctic region. It has inherited the contents of the ancient star charts of China and absorbed the latest achievements of the European astronomy. It was the harbinger of star charts made in the period the Qing Dynasty, which indicated the epoch-making progress in the history of star charts of China.

In July 1629, the 2nd year of the reign of Emperor Chongzhen, Xu Guangqi was ordered to revise the calendar. In September of the same year, the calendar commission was set up. Its members included some members of the Imperial Board of Astronomy and also some missionaries. Johann Adam was one of them. In the revision work of the calendar, Xu Guangqi organized missionaries to translate and introduce the astronomic knowledge from Europe and compiled 137 volumes of books. Li Tianjing, the successor of Xu Guangqi, selected essentials to compile another astronomy book titled as the Chongzhen Calendrical Science. Li Tianjing's book was published at the end of the Ming Dynasty period. Johann Adam revised it in the early Qing Dynasty period and renamed it as the Calendrical Science Based on New Western Method. His work was the basis of Shixian Calendar that the Qing Dynasty had used for more than 200 years. We can learn from Xu Guangqi's foreword that he drew several star charts before, but the size was too small and the drawings were was not quiet identical with the star images and was not convenient for reference. By the guidance of German Jesuit missionary Johann Adam, Xu Guangqi he redrew them. The Calendrical Science Based on New Western Method mentioned that in 1631, the 4th year of the reign of Emperor Chongzhen, Xu Guangqi presented the General Chart of

Stars and the Star Ephemeris, which must be the small-sized star charts he drew earlier. The drawing of the General Star Chart of Southern and Northern Equators started after the 4th year of the reign of Emperor Chongzhen. In the 7th year of the reign of Emperor Chongzhen, Li Tianjing Xu Guangqi's successor presented a "star chart" to the imperial court. This "star chart " was probably the star chart drawn by the guidance of Xu Guangqi. Therefore this star chart was probably completed in the 7th year of the reign of Emperor Chongzhen.

At the center of the Northern and Southern equator star chart, there was a small circle with a diameter of about 2cm marked with "Chi Ji" note, i.e. the Southern celestial pole and the Southern celestial pole. There was a wide white belt on both charts, which was the Milky Way. In addition to stars in the belts, there were even black dots, indicating that the Milky Way consisted of abundant number of stars. The constellations in China were connected with yellow line, marked with name of asterism, basically identical with the ephemerides and star charts of China in the ancient times, with slight differences. The constellations in the Northern equator out of China were not connected, and they were given no names either. There was no record about constellations in the Southern equator in ancient China. Therefore the star charts marked the constellation complexes and have translated the name of the Western constellations. The size of stars indicated the brightness of them which were divided into six grades. The Ephemeris of the Calendrical Science Based on New Western Method contained 1365 stars in it, on the other side, this chart included 1812 stars, 477 stars more than the Calendrical Science Based on New Western Method. Johann Adam has mentioned in the introduction of his book that some newly detected stars were included in the chart map, which were not included in the Ephemeris in the Calendrical Science Based on New Western Method. Although these newly detected stars were included in the map, their locations were not given by their coordinate.

It is noteworthy that the Ephemeris in the Calendrical Science Based on New Western Method had omitted about 460 stars and some constellations that were already named traditionally in China. Part of the omitted stars was supplemented in the Ephemeris in the Calendrical Science Based on New Western Method. This reflects that, Xu Guangqi and Johann Adam, when drawing the star charts, stars and their coordinates in the Calendrical Science Based on New Western Method they did not do this work according to the new Western method, but drawn according to some ephemeris brought forward by the missionaries. Actually Johann Adam et al. have referred to Tycho Catalogue which was published in 1602 in Denmark and Prague. Of course the Tycho Catalogue was not the only material Johann Adam had referred to. As the Tycho Catalogue has only 768 stars, 597 stars less than the Calendrical Science Based on New Western Method. What other sources that Johann Adam had referred to needs further exploration.[61]

---

61   Lu Yang, Bo Shuren, Liu Jinyi, Wang Jianmin, A Brief Introduction to the General Star Chart of Southern and Northern Equators of the Ming Dynasty, contained in the Analects of Astronomic Relics in Ancient China compiled by the Institute of Archaeology attached to the CASS, Cultural Relics Press, 1989, pp. 401-408.

This map completed by domestic and foreign astronomers together opened a new stage characterized by absorbing Western astronomic achievements in the 17th century. In all the star maps after the Ming Dynasty, we can see influence of the General Star Chart of Southern and Northern Equators, for example, Tianhou Temple Ephemeris in Putian, Fujian, and the stone carving astronomic map in Mongol language in Hohhot Monastery in the Inner Mongolia. The Chongzhen Calendrical Science had used the Tycho system in the universe theory statement, i.e. planets revolving around the sun, sun, moon and stars revolving around the earth. In respect to calculation, it used the Ptolemy's epicycle and deferent system. These theories were outdated in Europe and Ptolemy's methods were proven wrong, but it enabled the Chinese scientists to learn from the Western scientific system, especially the concept that the earth is spheric and the sphere surface was delineated by longitudes and latitudes, and introduced the star chart of the Southern celestial pole, and adopted the system of 360 degrees and the Sexagesimal (base 60) system. These achievements have enabled the Chinese astronomy surpass its isolation in the history of the world astronomy, thus it has embarked on a path that merged with the Western astronomy.

The frequent travels of missionaries between Europe and the East accelerated the speed of the new scientific knowledge spreading from Europe to China. French Jesuit Michel Benoist (Chinese name Jiang Youren) wrote the

Draft of Illustrated Geographic Map which mentioned Copernicus's revolutionary discovery as follows: "Copernicus's theory on stars had argued that the sun is static while the earth revolved around the sun". "People who, for the first time, heard such a theory normally regarded it as a heresy because, if you only depend to eyewitness with your naked eyes, one could think that the sun is only several times bigger than the moon, but if you examine and deduce by the science of natural laws, we can know the sun's diameter must be hundred times bigger than the earth's while the moon's diameter is only one fourth of the earth's." Based on the observation by the naked eyes of people it seemed that the sun was moving while the earth was static, today Copernicus assumes that the earth is revolving while the sun is static, the research shows that it is reasonable and also compatible with the theory."[62]

Benoist's book was edited by He Guozong and Qian Daxin and was soon published.[63]

There are wide differences between the geographical concepts held by the Westerners and Chinese. Tazi people inherited the scientific traditions of Greece and divided the world into seven continents. This theory was later introduced into China in the Yuan Dynasty. However, it was only spread among Hui people and was seldom known by Chinese. After the great geographical discovery, Europeans arrived in the East and brought new geographical knowledge with

62   Fang Hao: History of East-West Communications, 1977 (IV), Taipei, p. 213.
63   Illustrated Handbook of the Earth–Attached to the General Geographic Map, extant copy of the Qing Dynasty.

them. The most important figures that introduced world geographical knowledge to China were Australian Matteo Ricci and his brother Julius Aleni. As was described by Ricci himself, he arrived in Guangdong in the 10th year of the reign of Emperor Wanli (1582) and local residents invited him to depict those nations that he saw along his travel route to China. Back then, Matteo Ricci knew very little Chinese. Although he brought brochures and notes of the past years with him, all his conversations depended on translation, which made errors inevitable. According to The Traveling Logs of Mr. Great Sealy, Aleni settled in Duanzhou in the 11th year of the reign of Emperor Wanli (1583). Together with another Italian named Michele Ruggieri, he constructed the armillary sphere, the celestial sphere, the globe and chime clocks. Meanwhile, he drew the Great Universal Geographic Map (which is also referred to as Map of Mountains and Seas, Yudi Comprehensive Map and Kunyu Comprehensive Map of All Countries), which included and listed all continents in the world. In the early 15th century, Europeans divided the world into five continents: Asia, Europe, Africa, North America and Magallanica (currently the south of the Magellan Strait).

In the short period of 24 years from the 12th year (1584) to the 36th year during the reign of Emperor Wanli (1608), this map was reprinted for 12 times in Guangdong, Zhaoqing, Nanchang, Suzhou, Nanjing, Beijing and Guizhou.[64]

This shows the new geographical knowledge introduced to China by Matteo Ricci exerted a huge impact on the traditional Chinese geographical thinking which had assumed that the earth was square and the heaven was round. This map uniquely demonstrated that China was only a part of Asia, which was located in the east of Asia, thus it challenged the traditional thinking that China was the center of the world. Back then, quite few advanced, progressive Chinese intellectuals believed in this new thought. However, most Chinese literati and officialdom of feudal China did not believe in or were doubtful towards this approach. Zhifang Waiji (Chronicle of Foreign Land) was another treatise in the Ming Dynasty that introduced the world geography. It was written by Aleni in the third year during the reign of Emperor Tianqi (the year of 1623). After Matteo Ricci drew the Great Universal Geographic Map and Records and Maps of All Nations, the Spanish missionary named Diego de Pantoja was entrusted to translate these two books into Chinese. Based on the translation, Aleni made further complement and compiled them into books.

Zhifang Waiji (Chronicle About Foreign Lands) is divided into five volumes. The preface introduces the relations between the heaven and the sky as follows: "The sky is a giant globe and earth is the globe's center. The earth is also a globe. The four directions of North, South, East and West are not defined, but are just determined according to people's residential districts. There are Northern and Southern poles, which are the axis of movement. Corresponding, there exist the North Pole and the South Pole, which are used to divide the longitudes

---

64   Hao Fang: The Stories of Chinese Catholics, Ed. 1988, Zhonghua Book Company, p. 79.

and latitudes." The first volume introduces Asia and says China is the largest country in Asia, followed by Tartars (which extends from Northern Ming Dynasty to East Europe), Hui (namely Islam countries in the central Asia), India (Southern India), Mughal (namely the Mughal Kingdom that was established by Tamerlane's (Timur Khan) descendants to rule the northern India), Persia, Duerge (the Turkic Ottoman Empire, which also includes Arab lands) and Rudeya (the Jewish region, currently the eastern Mediterranean region).

The second volume introduces Europe, which was mentioned as the second largest continent in the world. It has over 70 countries, which mainly includes Spain, France, Italy, Germany, Boronia (currently Bologna in Italy), Hungary, Denmark, Sweden, Norway, Greek, Grand Duchy of Moscow, Ireland and England. When introducing the colonization efforts of the Spanish Kingdom, Aleni said: "The territory of Spain covers many other countries. Regarded as the largest country in the world, China is the crown rank for its unitary territory, however, Spain is the crown for its scattered territories." Aleni also introduced European academics and suggested that the Chinese academics should "learn the science of logic, which can be defined as the method of telling right from wrong", namely the current science of logic. Chinese academics should also learn "physics, which is defined as delving into the way of things", namely the current physics. These science branches are all under the term of philosophy. Besides, philosophy also includes mathematics, which "especially researches the measurement of materials' sizes and numbers". Aleni also especially introduced the public library and hospital system of Europe, saying "most capital cities of European countries" have set up public libraries that collect books. Such libraries are opened twice a day to allow scholars to enter for copying and reading. However, readers are not allowed to take books out of libraries". "There are also public hospitals. In large cities, often there are many hospitals, which are divided into lower and medium-level class hospitals that serve the people in the lower social classes and the upper-level hospitals which serve the aristocrats and noblemen. Hospitals are set up by Kings and the masses of people. These hospitals are also established by joint efforts of all citizens living in a city. One aristocrat is assigned to be in charge of hospitals' affairs on a monthly rotational basis."

The third volume, has introduced Africa, which mainly included knowledge about Egypt, Morocco, Libya and Ethiopia.

The fourth volume has introduced America. The author mainly discussed the process of discovering America and mentioned Columbus was a knowledgeable figure and an expert in navigation who had "skills in exploring principles and making the practice of traveling on the sea"; Aleni also introduced the role played by other navigators in discovering America, such as Amerigo. He naoted that: "the main countries located in America include Peru, Brazil, Mexico and California".

The fifth volume has introduced the Oceans, including a part titled as "an overview on four oceans", "names of oceans", "islands", "maritime species", "maritime products", "maritime situations", "maritime navigation" and "maritime routes". The section of "maritime routes" mainly introduced the routes joining Europe and China. After the global navigation route was opened, there had been two maritime routes for Europeans to sail to China: the Eastern maritime route and the Western maritime route. The Western route was the route for Portuguese to leave from the East: Europeans started from their own countries to the coastal regions and sailed North via the Atlantic Ocean. After passing the Northern Regression Line, the Equator, the Southern Regression Line, the Southern Africa, Europeans then sailed towards the North. Next, they respectively passed the Southern Regression Line, the equator line, the Arabian Seas and the Goa in Southern India, which took about a year. After that, Europeans shifted to take medium size ships and started to sail towards North in the spring season, during which they passed Ceylon, the Bangal Bay, Sumatra, Malacca, Singapore Straight, Siam, Champa and eventually arrived in Guangzhou. The Eastern maritime route was the navigation route adopted by Magellan, who started his expedition towards the West from the Mediterranean Sea or Spain to the American continent, then passed the Panama Strait to enter the Pacific Ocean and arrived in Guangzhou via Philippines Island in the West Pacific Ocean.

Chinese individuals who contacted European cultures

The cultures and customs brought by Europeans who entered China on a large scale inevitably attracted social attention from people. When Xianzu Tang, a Ming Dynasty dramatist, was demoted in Xvwen, he made a detour to Macau to know the local customs and practices. He wrote Listen to the Translator of the Fragrant Hill, Examine and Verification of the Gathered Slogans of Fragrant Hill, Meet Portuguese Merchants in Macau and other poetry. These poems described that Portuguese "were not engaged in agriculture or planting, but wore elegant clothes and walked down from the sailing ships". He also described Portuguese women as: "having flowery beauty that surpassed 15 peoples and enjoying rosy make-up". In The Peony Pavilion, Tang also introduced some overseas situations of Macau (current Macao in PRC) and inserted the plot that the protagonist Mengmei Liu dreamed of traveling in Macau. After the craftsmen of Guangdong's Xinhui learned the techniques of the weaving industry in Macau (Macao), they were also capable of weaving velvet, whose quality could match with the imported goods. In the early 17th century, Tianyu Liu who had traveled in Macau introduced the music, arts and food of local Portuguese. Meanwhile, the European styled sculptures had left deep impression on him. Tianyu Liu wrote: "After seeing the sculptures, I wished to speak yet hesitated several times. I did not stop watching them, until I became familiar with them." After a large number of European missionaries entered China, some Chinese also believed in Catholicism after these missionaries' preaches. Guangqi Xv and Zhizao Li, which we have mentioned above, were the most prominent figures. Meanwhile, some upper-class noblemen has also converted to Catholicism. There was an exchange of letters between the officials of Chinese Ming Dynasty and the Pope. At present, the imperial letters written by the Southern Ming Dynasty to the Pope in the Holy See is well-preserved and collected by the national Museum of Vatican. Back then, the Qing Dynasty's army has seized the majority of Chinese territory. The imperial court of the Southern Ming Dynasty was located in Wuzhou, Guangxi. A German missionary named Andre Xavier Koffler stayed in the imperial court of Emperor Yongli for three years. Back in Beijing, the eunuch named Tianshou Pang had been converted into Catholicism. He then persuaded the Empress Dowager Wang, who was the imperial concubine of King Gui and the "renowned" mother of Emperor Yongli, Empress Dowager Ma who was the biological mother of Emperor Yongli, Emperor Yongli's Empress Wang and Emperor Yongli's son Ci Huan to be converted to Catholicism under the leadership of Shawei Zhao. However, Emperor Yongli failed to be baptized for having too many imperial concubines. Due to the endangered national situation, Empress Dowager Wang sent messengers to the Saint Peter's Square in Rome and St Paul (namely current Saint Peter's Square in Vatican and the Saint Paul Cathedral) to invite the Pope Innocent and the bishop of the Society of Jesus to pray for the Ming Dynasty. In the 4th year of the reign of Emperor Yongli (1650), they sent Michael Boym, a Polish missionary, to the imperial court. The Empress Dowager Wang invited Michael Boym to convey two state letters written by the pope and the president of the Society of Jesus. The eunuch named Tianshou Pang also sent a letter to the pope. Michael Boym first went to Macau and sailed to Goa in India. After four years' shipping, Michael Boym eventually arrived in Rome. The new pope Alexander VII sent a letter to Emperor Yongli and ordered Michael Boym to visit the Southern Ming Dynasty's imperial court again. In 1656, Michael Boym arrived in China when the Empress Dowager Wang was dead and Emperor Yongli receded to Yunnan. It seemed that the response letter of Alexander VII did not reach Emperor Yongli's hands.

610

As is demonstrated by the original letter by Empress Dowager Wang that is kept in the Vatican Museum, Empress Dowager Wang named herself Helene after being converted to Catholicism; Empress Dowager Ma, who was the birth mother of Emperor Yongli, named herself Maria; Empress Yongli named herself Anna; the son of Emperor Yongle named himself Constantine; the eunuch Tianshou Pang named himself Achilleus Christian. There were as many as 540 persons in the Southern Ming Dynasty that had converted to Catholicism. As increasing number of Jesuits entered into China, many Chinese people wanted to travel to Europe. Manuo Zheng, a Macaonese from Guangdong's Xiangshan, was one of early Chinese who traveled in Europe. Manuo Zheng's style name was Tuixin and received overseas study in Italy's Rome at the age of 20 when Qing Dynasty was set up. "Learning the doctrine of everything, the study of reason, the language and words of Western countries and the study of phonetics", Manuo Zheng tried to learn everything about the West. In the 10th year of the reign of Emperor Kangxi (1671), Manuo Zheng returned to Beijing and had started to live there ever since.[65]

Among the Chinese individuals who went to Europe in the early Qing Dynasty period, the person most worthy of mentioning is Shouyi Fan. Shouyi Fan was born in Shanxi's Pingyang and was a Catholic. In 1707, Shouyi Fan was entrusted by the Qing imperial court to visit Europe with missionary P. Joseph Antoine Provana after passing the Cape of Good Hope and taking a detour of Brazil in Southern America. After passing Portugal, Shouyi Fan arrived in Genoa in Italy in 1909. Since then, Shouyi Fan had studied in Turin and Rome for 10 years and traveled in Italy. From 1719, Shouyi Fan returned to China from Portugal and arrived in Guangzhou in 1720. After returning to China, he was summoned by Emperor Kangxi and was "questioned and consulted for a while". Later, he wrote down his personal experience into one article named Record of Personal Experience, which was the earliest European traveling log written by Chinese.

Shouyi Fan first arrived in Italy's Genoa and then went to Laiatico's Livorno. Taking the land route from Pisa and Sinai to Rome, Shouyi Fan traveled in Naples in the South and visited Florence, Bolognese, Poland and Turin in the North of Italy when he stayed in Italy. Shouyi Fan said that Genoa has "grand aristocratic families, high buildings, gold, silver and treasures which are appreciated by people. In the Western world, Genoa of Italy is reputed as the crown. The "shell" is brilliant, palaces are beautiful; talents are numerous; aristocratic families are rich, which are very hard to be described, fully. The city is close to the sea, where there is a port hosting more than one hundred foreign ships. A tower is constructed at the entrance of the sea, which offers light to faraway ships in the evening." The "shell" mentioned by Shouyi Fan refers to the church's vault. Such architectural forms that did not exist in China were extremely interesting for him..

When talking about Florence, Shouyi Fan said: "The palaces, balconies, halls, schools and Monastic orders are nearly the same as those in Rome". He also said: "there is a church, namely the Florence Church. After being constructed for over 200 years, it is still under construction. Its stability and exquisiteness cannot be described by words." This church's dome was an outstanding work of the Renaissance period. However, the entrance of the church was constructed in the mid-19th century. At that time when Shouyi Fan had visited there, the construction of church was still ongoing. As for Turin, there were two "rare objects" that deeply impressed him, namely the hydraulically-driven spinner and saw bench. Fan described the spinner as: "It has a huge framework and takes a giant wood column as the axis of the water wheel. There are several other wheels on the pillars, which are driven by water and do not consume man power. These wheels rotate automatically to weave threads. With two

65 Xingniang Zhang: Historical Materials of Chinese and Western Transportation, Vol.1, 1977, Zhonghua Book Company, p. 392.

workers standing beside to monitor it, this machine is equal to five or six hundred people's manpower." The hydraulically-driven saw bench is used in this way: "To saw a giant wood into wood plates, people needn't saw it themselves but should put it in the water. Then the saw can pull and push the wood. There is a rope that can make wood stretch and draw closer to become plates." This hydraulically-driven machinery represents the industrial level of Europe before the European modern engine that worked with steam power was invented.

Shouyi Fan said: "Rome has been the capital city of Italy since ancient times, with city walls covering a hundred miles and the bishop living inside"; "In aristocratic families, people hang up embroidered cloth on the walls as decorations and inlaid golden flowers on stools. In the house, there are priceless vessels and exquisitely laid bed coverlets that are extremely valuable. When traveling, people use carriages, which are extremely grand. The employed servants wear different clothes and hats that display their specific duties. Shouyi Fan was familiar with Roman relics and mentioned: "There is an artificially constructed high beam, which is as long as 45 km. It carries the spring waters from high mountains into the city." This was the ancient catchment channel in ancient Rome. Meanwhile, Shouyi Fan mentioned: "There is a building that is neither a palace nor hall. It resembles a tower and has a round shape. It has five floors in all, with over ten thousand rooms. These rooms have windows and people can watch from each window through the glass. It was used to rear lions in the ancient times. However, over half of its structure has been ruined." This building is the Colosseum from the ancient Rome. When recalling the Baroque-style sculptures and foundations at the garden in the city's center, Shouyi said: "The cross street piles stones into a small hill and carve humans out of the hill. Water springs up from four directions. The street is paved with stones and there are water fountains in every house."

Shouyi Fan offered his highest praises for the St Peters Cathedral and mentioned: "There is a square in front of the cathedral, where there erect high and giant Egyptian monuments. There is a stone column corridor near the square." When describing this world-famous cathedral, Shouyi Fan said: "Its hall is grand and majestic. Its column is of six armful's length. Its column bases are extremely huge. The canopy is over 33 meters in height and the empty ball on it can hold 20 people. Standing on the cathedral, one can see the scenery that is 50 km. away." This canopy of an empty ball shape is the arch design of the Saint Peters' Cathedral. The cathedral is so huge that adult men are as short as little children in the hall. The Vatican library that was located besides had left a deep impression on him. Shouyi Fan said: "There is a huge warehouse of books, where there stand huge bookshelves. The books are so numerous that cannot be counted even by counting the bookshelves and boxes. The historical books of all peoples are stored here, which were written since the occurrence of the world."[66]

---

66   Hualong Zhu: From Silk Road to Marco Polo.

When Shouyi Fan was traveling in Europe, China was still a traditional agricultural country with stagnant growth and development. However, the occurrence of new productive forces in Europe had greatly accelerated the speed of social wealth accumulation. The differences between China and foreign countries had inevitably left a huge impact on his mind.

(2) Further Introduction of Foreign Agricultural Crops

The great geographical discoveries have closely connected America and the old continent. When staying in America, European settlers have discovered that native Indians were planting some plants which they didn't acknowledge yet. They learned to plant them and as the first step introduced these plants into their other colonies across the world. Next, they introduced them to China, which has greatly enriched the Chinese agricultural crop species.

(1) Sweet potato and potato

Sweet potato is a root plant, which has numerous sub-species. Botanically, it belongs to the Convolvulaceae family and is in the same category of morning glory and water spinach. Sweet potato had originated from America. Archaeologists have excavated the sweet potato roots that were dated back to 8,000 years ago which were discovered in ancient Peruvian tombs. The biggest excavated sweet potato root is 7.5 cm in length, huge in the center and it was an artificially cultivated sub-species. Scholars have argued that sweet potato was introduced from America to the Pacific Ocean's Polynesian islands in the prehistoric era. After the great geographical discovery, Europeans brought sweet potatoes to all over the world.[67]

As is recorded by Guangqi Xu's (1562-1633) Complete Works on Agricultural Administration, there are two types of "Shu": The first type is Shanshu (yam), which exists in Fujian and Guangdong. The other type is called sweet potato, which was promoted by local residents. In recent years, people introduced this species from foreign countries. Foreign countries had also banned its export and prohibited people from taking outside the country. A Chinese people secretly got its stems and hided it among ropes that were buried in water. In this way, it was exported out of the country, divided into several strains and was generally spread across Fujian and Guangdong. These two types of stems are greatly similar. However, Shanshu (yam) grows by climbing over other plants, while sweet potato grows by crawling all over the ground; yam is huge, while sweet potato is round and long. Regarding the taste, sweet potato is sweeter, while yam's taste is a bit sour. In conclusion, the term of "Shu" referred to in all books in the central plain discusses the "yam". "The book Records of Dongguan County wrote: "In the 8th year during the reign of Emperor Wanli (1580), Yi Chen, a person from Guangdong's Dongguan county went to Vietnam and locals served him sweet potatoes. Yi Chen got sweet potatoes' stems from the servants of the chief and brought them back to China. As

---

67   Tong Pingya: History of Agricultural Crops, 1979, China Youth Press.

sweet potatoes stems were acquired through hardship, they were first planted in a flower bed and yielded sweet potato lumps, which were named Fanshu (sweet potato). Later, it was promoted and became the main grain crop in the Dongguan county.

In 1961, Chinese antiquarians found the rare edition of Collection of Planting Golden Shu in Fujian and published it in 1765. The book's author mentioned that his ancestor, a man named Zhenlong Chen from Fujian's Changle county, migrated to live in Luzon (Philippines). After finding out "a local plant which is as big as a man's fist; has dark red skins, a juicy core and edible raw skin, which could be cultivated widely in summer and harvested in autumn, is tolerant to barren land; has a high yield and gives a good taste", he decided to introduce it into China. Back then, Philippines was ruled by Spain and Spain strictly prohibited the sales of sweet potato tubers (stems) to foreign countries. Before returning to China in 1593, Zhenlong Chen secretly wrapped the sweet potato stems on a rope and covered them with mud. After sailing for seven days, he arrived in Fujian. In June 1593, Zhenlong Chen ordered his son Jinglun Chen to offer sweet potato stems to Fujian's governor and introduced its usage and planting methods. Soon, sweet potato was planted in Fujian successfully. In summer, typhoon constantly occurred in Fujian and Guangdong. However, sweet potato has a strong adaptation and a high yield, which make people soon realize its values. To remember the achievements made by Zhenlong Chen and his son in spreading the stems of sweet potatoes, people of future generations have set up the Ancestor Potato Exhibition Hall for them.[68]

There are some other records that mentioned the introduction of sweet potatoes from Southeastern Asia into China in the Ming Dynasty, such as Notes on Fujian and Record of Fuzhou Mansion. This shows that the introduction of sweet potatoes was completed through various occasions and via multiple channels, rather than being introduced once through one channel.

In the late Ming Dynasty, sweet potatoes were introduced to Northern China. In the 17th century, Guangqi Xv tried to plant it beside his house. Later, Shiyuan Chen, the descendant of Zhenlong Chen, introduced and planted it in Northeastern plain. However, it wasn't promoted. Northeast China has plenty of barren sandy land. In April and May when plants are supposed to grow prosperously, there is nearly no rain fall. However, the plants which were planted and grown near the rivers or in the regions wherein wells could be drilled, farming could benefit from irrigation systems. But the farming in the other regions faced irregularities and problems. Back then, the eunuch official, whose native home was in Northern China and was born in Jiangnan, had noticed that nearly half of food in the tables of poor farmers in Fujiana and Zhejiang Provinces were sweet potatoes. For this reason, the officials decided to introduce sweet potatoes. As of the 23rd year of the reign of Emperor Qianlong (1758), the Qing government had realized the value of sweet potatoes farming.

614

---

68   Tong Pingya: History of Agricultural Crops, 1979, China Youth Press.

Since then, many farmers began to plant sweet potatoes regularly which has benefited them greatly."[69]

During the Qing Dynasty period, the farmers in Shandong and Hebei Province constantly sought ways ro promote irrigation systems to cultivate barren land and introduced the methods of planting sweet potatoes in the Northeastern China. At present, sweet potatoes can be planted in high-altitude and cold regions of the Changbai Mountain, the river banks of Liao River and the banks of Songhuajiang River. The capacity of producing sweet potatoes has reached over 5,000 kilos/acre, making it one of the crops with the highest seasonal yield in the Northeastern China regions. Potato was originated from America and was introduced into China in the reign of Emperor Wanli of the Ming Dynasty period. In the minds of common people, potato was planted in the European countries much earlier than in China. As of the late 18th century, potato had been popular and much appreciated. Grand Records of Jifu: The Record of Agricultural Products once mentioned: "Tuyu is also called potato. After being steamed, potato tastes like sweet potato." In around 1750, the book Record of Qizhou: Record of Products also mentioned potatoes. This means Chinese people has realized the value of potatoes for the people's livelihood earlier than Europeans. There were two routes of introducing potatoes: The first route was from Southeast Asia into Fujian and Macau located in Northeastern coastal regions of China. The second route was direct from foreign countries into Beijing-Tianjin regions of China.[70]

615

(2) Corn

According to the researches of Western scholars, corn was originally planted in America. In the tombs in Mexico, Peru and Chile, archaeologists have excavated many corn plants and other grains. In Mexico, archaeologists also found the ruins of ancient corn plants that were dated back to more than 7,000 years ago, which were probably the wild ancestors of the corn. In fact, corns was planted for thousands of years in the American continent. In 1492 when Columbus discovered the new continent, he was attracted by the wild corn in the fields. On November 15th, 1492, Columbus mentioned in his writings: "There is a type of cereal named Maize. It is sweet and delicious. After being dried, it can be ground to achieve powder form." After the mid-16th century, corn planting was spread across the world.[71]

However, corn was originally planted in America. Although Columbus introduced it to Europe, it does not mean that there was no corn in the old continent before the great discovery of America by Columbus. In the history, corn

69   Qianxiang Zuo: History of Introduction of Sweet Potatoes and Potatoes to Northeastern China, a book published in a series book "Agricultural Science and Technology in Ancient China"; 1980, Agricultural Publishing House, pp. 237-248.
70   Kunxiang Zhai: The History of Introducing Sweet Potatoes and Sweet Potatoes into the Northeastern Plain, published on Chinese Ancient Agricultural Scientific Technology, 1980, Agricultural Publishing House, pp. 237-248.
71   Tongping Dong: History of Agricultural Crops, 1979, China Youth Press, pp. 37-42.

was also called "foreign wheat" and "imperial wheat". As was recorded by Records of Laian County During the Reign of Emperor Yongzheng, Emperor Huizong of the Song Dynasty (1101-1125) tasted corns. Since then, this cereal has been enjoying the title of "imperial wheat". During the Yuan Dynasty period, there was a type of food named Chongluo Noodles which was enjoyed by the masses. The third chapter's lyrics of Hanqin Guan's Bao Zheng Investigated Thrice in the Dream of Butterflies described: "In the beggar's leftover food, there are some Chongluo Noodles." In the Daily Notes on Carved Bamboo Strips·Imperial Wheat written by Yiheng Tian in the Ming Dynasty period, Yiheng Tian had predicted as follows: "the Chongluo Noodles which are kept and exhibited in the Korean imperial dietary bureau is probably the current foreign wheat which is planted" and this was in fact the corn. In the Yuan Dynasty, Gao Li wrote in his Classics on Dietary Herbs: "Corn is a cereal planted in Sichuan, middle China. It is a type of rice and has a sweet taste, with no toxicity. It mainly regulates and stimulates one's appetite. Its root is used to cure dribbling urination. If the patient is unable to tolerate his pains, he can boil the root and drink the soup of it." He also noted about other types of corn under the name of Sichuan corn: "Jade sorghum is produced in the Western world. Its seedling's leaves resemble those of Sichuan cereals, they are fat and short. It also looks like Job's tears (Coix lacryma-jobi).[72]

Corn's seedlings are three or four feet in height and its flowers often blossom in June or July, with the shape of immature wheat. In the center of each seedling, there is a bud in the shape of brown fish. On the bud, there are white whiskers hanging downward. As time passes, closely arranged grains appear once the husk is ripped off. The ears of corns are also as big as Zhongzi and are yellowish white, which can be fried and eaten. After being fried, corn grains become white and resemble the shape of fried sticky rice." As is shown by the above paragraph, it describes certain types of corns. This paragraph was later compiled and completed by Shizhen Li, who was born later. However, we need further research to determine its author. When mentioning about the jade sorghum, Compendium of Materia Medica has basically quoted the latter paragraph. During the Ming Dynasty period, Heng Yi described corn's monoecism, the part of flowers and scions, the shapes of spike bud and its main differences from Sichuan cereals and Job's tears in the book titled Daily Notes on Carved Bamboo Strips·Imperial Wheat: "Imperial wheat is originated from the Western world and its name is foreign wheat. It used to be sent to the imperial court and consequently was called the "imperial wheat". Its dry leaves are like millet; its flowers resemble the ears of rice; its cob is as big and long as a fist; its whiskers look like Job's tears; its grains are huge and white. Flowers are born at the top, while fruits are born on cobs."

---

72 Job's tears grow all across Asia, and have been consumed there in various forms for centuries. In China, people boil the grains in sweetened water to make a cloudy, wheaty-tasting tea, often throwing out the grains themselves.

All of the literature shows the history of how Maize was introduced in Asia is still a mystery to be solved. Although Maize was planted in ancient China, it did not become the main agricultural crop. After Europeans came to the East, they brought with them the American maize species. At present, corn has become the main agricultural crop in many dry regions of China, which is related with the introduction of new corn species into China.

(3) Peanuts

As an annual leguminous herb, peanuts had originated from America. In Brazil, over a decade of wild peanut species were discovered. In the ancient tombs of Ancon, a town in the northern Peru, these nearly totally carbonized peanut findings that dated back to over 2000 years ago were excavated. In 1492, Europeans brought peanut seedlings to Europe after discovering America. In about the late 15th century or the early 16th century, peanuts were introduced into China from Southeast Asia. In 1695, Lu Zhang's Drug Classics Based on Shen Nong's Herbal Classic recorded: "The fruit of longevity was originated from northern Fujian and it blossoms after its flowers wither and fall on the land. It did not exist in the ancient times and planted only in the recent years." During the early Qing Dynasty, Fengjiu Wang has recorded in Hui Shui (Collected Book): "There is a plant named Luo Huasheng, whose stems and leaves resemble those of beans. Its flowers also look like bean flowers and are yellow. The fruits do not grow on stems. After flowers fall on the ground, fruits start to grow underground. It is rather a rare plant."

The domestication of peanuts is not unitary and China is also one of the   617
countries wherein it originated. In 1962, archaeologists excavated four carbonized peanuts in the ancient ruins in Jiangxi Province's Xiushui County, which were huge in size and had an oval shapes, 11 mm. long, 8 mm wide and 6 mm thick. This shows China has been growing peanuts for at least 4,000 years.[73]

Chinese ancient treatises have also kept the records about peanuts before the discovery of the new continent. In Miscellaneous Morsels from Youyang, Renduan Tang recorded one plant named Xiangyu—"Xiangyu is sprawling and the planter peasant should set up small fences to allow it to sprawl. After flowers fall on the land following the blossom, it bears fruits that resemble Xiangyu and is also called peanut." Meanwhile, the third volume of Classics on Edible Herbs, which was written by Gao Chen in the Yuan Dynasty period, narrated as follows: "Luohuasheng and yam are of the same category. It has sprawls and leaves that resemble lentils. After flowers are in blossom and fall on the ground, it starts to bear fruits under the ground."Although corn has been planted in China since the ancient times, it has never become the main oil crop. After the great geographical discoveries, Europeans brought the peanut species of America to Northeast Asia and then to China. At present, peanut has become the main oil crop in many dry regions of China, which is related to the introduction of the new peanut species into China.

---

73   Tong Pingya: Historical Narration of Agricultural Products, China Youth Publishing House, 1979, pp. 110-112.

(4) Tobacco

Tobacco was originally planted in America and domesticated by the Maya people, who smoke tobacco during the religious ceremonies. After Columbus arrived in the West Indian Isles, he discovered that local Indians rolled up some dry tobacco leaves and then put them into their mouths after lighting them. Later, Columbus brought such leaves to Europe, which then introduced tobacco leaves to Europe. Classified Anecdotes of Qing Minor Officials wrote: "Since its first arrival in Philippines State, tobacco has been called Danbagu and started to be brought to the inland China since the Ming Dynasty period". As recorded in the book "Quotes from Yin'an", "Tobacco originated from the central Fujian Province and was banned in the 8th year during the reign of Emperor Chongzhen." These two records prove that tobacco had been introduced into Chinese coastal regions before the reign of Emperor Chongzhen in the Ming Dynasty. Whole Collection of Zhang Jinyue, which was written by Jingjie Zhang in the Ming Dynasty, described as follows: "This has never been heard of since the ancient times", which proves tobacco was indeed an introduced foreign species. In 1668, Yizhi Fang wrote in his Minor Knowledge on Physics as follows: "In the late years of the reign of Emperor Wanli, a person whose family name was Ma carried it to Zhangquan, processed it and called it Danba Fruit. Since then, it has been introduced to Jiubian."

(5) Sunflowers

Sunflower is a plant of the composite family. Botanists have argued that the sunflower had originated from America and spread to all over the world after the great geographical discoveries. Sunflower started to be taken as one viewing plant species in the botanic garden of Madrid of Spain in 1510. Around the 17th century, sunflower was introduced to China from Southeast Asia. As recorded by the book Collection of Flowers, sunflower was called as the western chrysanthemum or Zhang chrysanthemum. Flower Mirror described: "There is one flower on every plant, with yellow petals and a huge round heart. It revolves around the sun. If the sun rises in the East, the flower leans towards the East. If the sun is located in the middle of the sky, the flower is leans to the middle. If the sun sets in the west, the flower leans towards the east and bears many seeds."

As early as the early Qin Dynasty period, China had already known the plant of Kui (herbaceous plants with big flowers). As recorded in the 17th year of the reign of Emperor Cheng in The Commentary of Zuo, Confucius had said that Zhuangzi Bao's knowledge about the Kui plant was not deep, this plant which can shade its feet." There were quite a few records about the Kui plant from the past dynasties. The Family Instructions of Master Yan asked: "Does Kui plant exist in Jiangnan?" Meanwhile, Chinese also noticed the heliotropism of Kui plant years ago. Huainanzi Shuolinxun mentioned as follows: "Sages treat the doctrine as the sunflower treats the sun. Although they cannot be with the doctrine all the time, they are sincere towards the doctrine." The book also recorded: "Flint makes fire from the sun; magnets attract iron... Sunflower turns towards the sun." The History of the Three Kingdoms The Record of Wei The Legend of Chen Si and Wang Zhi also mentioned: "If the leaves of sunflowers and pulse plants turn towards the sun, they do not reflect the sun. Instead, they are paying their sincerity towards the heaven."

Ancient people also ate the seeds of sunflowers. General Record Brief Introduction to Insects and Herbs·Vegetables said: "Sunflowers' seeds look like beans. Raw seeds are green, yet dry seeds are black, which then turn purple after being pressed." The book "Record of Flowers" mentioned: "Western sunflowers' stems are like bamboos, which are several feet high. Their leaves are as big as Sichuan flowers. The flower is 66.6 cm or 99.9 cm in diameter, it is as flat as a lotus seed pot. Its flower is yellow, yet its seeds are flat and look like the castor beans." The sunflower grown in the ancient China was different from the sunflower species grown in the contemporary times. Although sunflower was planted in the ancient China, it did not become the main crop species. Only after the great geographical discovery that the sunflower become on of the main crop species in China.

3. Spread of Chinese Learning to the West

(1) Han learning treaties translated and written by Jesuits

Europeans learned about China by reading various books written by missionaries who wrote abundantly about the cultures in China. Among the treaties that introduce Chinese language and character study, the most important book was A Help to Western Scholars, which was written by French missionary Nicolas Trigault in 1626. It was the world's earliest Chinese dictionary which was written with Latin language and included phonetics. Nicolas Trigault visited the Ming Dynasty in 1610 and got to know Chinese scholar Yun Han during his preaching in the Shanxi region. Later, Nicolas Trigault got to know Zheng Wang. Based on the Han phonetic notation formulated by Matteo Ricci, Nicolas Trigault formulated this book with the help of Weiqi Lv and other officials of the Ming Dynasty's Foreign Language Translation Bureau. The book named An Audio and Visual Guide for Foreign Scholars, which was formulated by Zheng Wang and Nicolas Trigault, included the following parts and contents.

This book is divided into three parts: The first part describes the formulation process and aims of the book. It also introduces basic knowledge related to the Chinese phonology. The second part is called Listed Phonetic Ortho-spectrum, namely the current indexing system by phonetic order. After the Wei and Jin Dynasties, the Chinese phonology scholars were influenced by the Indian phonology and started to research the initial and the final of a syllable. With the aim of making it convenient for writing poems and articles, the rhyme category indexing method was created, which became the source of the phonetic indexing method. The biggest advantage of the phonetic indexing method lies in helping users to refer to the characters with known phonetics and unknown character formation. The third part is the side-listing ortho-spectrum, namely indexing through Chinese character components and the most ancient method of compiling dictionary through characters. The method of indexing through character components is mainly used in the situation with known character formation and unknown phonetics. By combining these two methods, the speed of indexing characters was greatly accelerated. Modern Chinese dictionaries have also used these two methods.

Nicolas Trigault matched five self-sounding letters (vowels: a, e, i, o, u), 20 synchronized sound letters (consonants) and tone signs to write in Chinese, which was the first in defining Chinese phonetics. Since then, other Jesuits had also written Chinese dictionaries. For example, Joachim Bouvet, a Frenchman who arrived in China in 1687, formulated Petit Dictionnaire Francais-Chinois (French-Chinese). Besides learning Chinese, some missionaries worked hard to study the Manchu language alphabet. The French Amiot once formulated a Manchu-French dictionary and Five Integrated Language Essentials. The latter was compiled in Sanskrit, Tibetan, Chinese, Manchu script and French. Pere de la Charme wrote dictionaries in French, Chinese and Manchu scripts. In the mid-18th century, Florian Bahr, a German Jesuit missionary, compiled the Chinese—German dictionary and collected over 2,200 Chinese words in all, making it the earliest Chinese—German dictionary in the world.

Jesuits have contributed greatly to introduce the Chinese history to Europe. The early history of the Qing Dynasty period was the priority of missionaries' research. In 1688, French priest Pere d'Orleans published The History of Two Tartar (Manchurian) Conquerors of China. Joachim Bouvet published the biography of Emperor Kangxi in 1697. This book caused attention from Gottfried Wilhelm Leibniz, a famous German scholar, who later translated it into Latin. Antoine Gaubil was a missionary that made outstanding contributions to the Chinese history and compiled Officials of Tang Dynasty. Antoine Gaubil had a huge interest in Mongolian history and published Genghis Khan and History of Mongolia in French language in 1739. For the first time, he researched the history of Mongolia by combining and cross checking Chinese historical materials with the Islam historical materials. The most important treatise in French which introduced the general history of China was the book called Crale de China written by Moyriac de Mailla, major materials of the book were drawn from Zhu Xi's Tongjian Gangmu (Outline and Explantion of Comprehensive mirror for Aid in Government). Moyriac de Mailla also wrote about the history of the Qing and Ming Dynasties and published the book in 13 volumes between 1777 and 1783. It has been the world's first historical treatise published in Western characters. Besides the Chinese history, missionaries have also paid great efforts in the research of the Confucian classics.

(2) Influences of Confucianism on Leibniz

Missionaries carried abundant information and news about China to Europe, which provoked the interest of Europeans in regard to China to an unprecedented level. In the 18th century, the most important thinkers who noticed China was Voltaire (1694-1778), Charles Louis de Secondat Montesquieu (1689-1755) and German philosopher and scholar Gottfried Wilhelm Leibniz (1646-1716). Leibnitz was a famous German scholar, philosopher and natural scientist. Leibnitz and Newton were jointly called the founders of calculus and the forerunners of symbolic logic. Before 1687, Leibnitz contacted the works related to Chinese Confucian, Taoist and Buddhist thinking and the works written by Confucius and Laozi through missionaries' reports. In 1689, Leibnitz met Grimaldi in Rome, who was the director of Qing Dynasty's Imperial Board of Astronomy. After Grimaldi returned to China, he kept intermittent connections with Leibnitz. Those who exerted huge influences on him included Chinese Philosopher—Confucius, which was translated by Philippe Couplet, a Jesuit of Belgium and was published in Paris. This book translated The Great Learning and The Doctrine of the Mean into Latin and enclosed them with the explanations to The Book of Changes.

Leibnitz held the opinion that culture was universal. In 1697, Leibnitz edited and published an important book titled New Theory on China, which has argued that there were many similarities between Confucianism and Christiantenets and took China and Europe as two major cultural sources. Leibnitz argued that Western natural science, speculative philosophy and logic offered revelations to the Eastern world, while Chinese practical philosophy and ethnics were attractive to the Western world. In a memorandum to the King of Prussia, he mentioned that some ancient Chinese mathematic signs contain new keys to mathematics. Leibnitz's New Theory on China was praised by French missionaries in China. He advised Leibnitz to research the mathematical principles in The Book of Changes. After Leibnitz researched the mathematical sequence of the images of trigrams, Leibnitz eventually found out the binary system in The Book of Changes.

(3) Debates between Voltaire and Montesquieu

Although the politicians and thinkers of French Enlightenment era did not visit China, they knew about China indirectly from the treatises, traveling logs and from the reports of religion missionaries. Due to different positions, the opinions of these politicians and thinkers towards the Chinese system varied and even debates have occurred among them. Both Voltaire and Montesquieu have strictly criticized the autocratic system. However, their views on China varied greatly. Montesquieu rather emphasized the theoretical aspects and devoted himself to the research of the essential aspects of things, consequently he didn't focus on the criticism of any country's political system. But, Voltaire favored the Chinese political, moral, religious systems, and argued that these systems were more practical than Europe and suggested to absorb beneficial components of the Chinese despotism. Neither Voltaire nor Montesquieu were independent individuals, instead their ideas generally reflected the ideas of European intellectual thinking circles, in those days. Targeting at some missionaries' endless praises for China, Montesquieu showed his oppositions and chatted with the Chinese living in Paris personally, thereby he tried to prove his opinions on China, he wrote:" there are two types of despotism, legal and illegal or arbitrary, and the despotism in China belongs to the former meaning that the Chinese emperor was limited by "the constitution founded upon wise and irrevocable laws.", Montesquieu also wrote a treatise named The Spirit of Laws that thought: Although China had no constitution, it had strong moral institutions. For example, sons are supposed to behave with filial piety; fathers should behave with paternity; subjects should serve kings with loyalty; kings should treat subjects with royalty. In the ancient times, China had a large population, who lived with low living standards. The society would be turned into turmoil once natural and human-made disasters occur. In this context, emperors had to promote farming and weaving, promoting hydraulics, implementing imperial examinations and setting imperial censors. Although such measures have restricted rulers' rights, they failed to change the Chinese society as autocratic. Knowing that there existed famines, tortures, abandonment of babies and other bad phenomena in China, Montesquieu thought China was undoubtedly an autocratic country; Chinese emperors implemented autocratic and terrorist rule across the whole country according to their individual will and had the right of depriving any one's life and even exterminating the whole family; back then, people had no freedom at all.

Although Denis Diderot, a representative figure of the Encyclopedia School, thought Chinese culture enjoys a long history, he pointed out that China had remained standstill in the contemporary era and ran the opposite direction to the historical progress trend. The radical bourgeois thinker Rousseau has argued: "China is ruled by minorities, yet its peoples have no rebellious spirit. No matter how advanced its culture is or how many scholars it possesses, China will achieve nothing." Voltaire once wrote three articles to criticize Montesquieu, which argued that China did not implement absolutism. For him, this was because emperors' power had been restricted by imperial censors and advisers, while death penalties sentences for local officials in China had to be approved by the Grand Court of Revision. Voltaire praised the Confucian ethics of China, i.e, "do not do unto others what you would not do unto yourself" and have argued that Chinese people emphasized tolerance and wisdom. He advocated that France can learn pottery making from China and it should also learn from the advantages of Chinese ethics and administration system. Although such debates by French thinkers over Chinese issues have noticed some part of the truth in regard to China, their many arguments have discussed a part of the issues instead of offering a holistic comprehensive view, and all the debaters have believed that they had a complete cognition about China, which seems an exaggeration. In conclusion, the Montesquieu school's criticism of China included harsh critique and seemed to be more comprehensive. Conversely, Voltaire's opinions seem to be superficial. However, this debate over Chinese systems reflects such a basic fact, namely the influences exerted by China had greatly enhanced due to the great geographical discoveries.

Conclusions

Before navigation was developed, the oceans used to be an obstacle that hindered the exchanges among men from various regions. With the development of humans' navigating science, however, the ocean gradually became a channel for people. Before the Western colonists marched towards the East, the maritime Silk Road used to be a peaceful expedition route and the main channel for people in Asian countries to conduct communications with the Western world. No large-scale maritime conflicts had occurred both among the Asian countries and between the Asian and African countries in the past history of 2,000 years, except the wars launched by Mongolian rulers (Yuan dynasty period[74]) in the 20 years between the 1270s and the 1280s to conquer Japan, Champa and Java, secondly a series of maritime wars had occurred between the Ming Dynasty and Korean Dynasty and Japanese dynasty in the mid-Ming Dynasty period[75] (1368-1644).

People in various countries have carried out trade, communications, traveled, spread cultures and preached religions via various maritime routes. In the ancient world, China was reputed as the country of civilization. Due to the far distance from other civilization centers of the world, China has been the center of civilization in the Far East region and has developed quite independently. Within nearly 2,000 years beginning with the Han Dynasty till the Qing Dynasty, China has played the role as the main country which has delivered civilizational and cultural output to the other countries of the world. However, it will be a mistake to think that China has only delivered civilizational and cultural output without receiving inputs throughout the history. Cultural communications and material exchanges have never been one-way, but always been bi-directional and multi-directional. Since the ancient times, China has been a country that has been good at learning. After learning Buddhism from India, Chinese people pleasantly allowed Buddhism flourishing on the Chinese land, thus it has become a dispensable component of the Chinese culture. Besides, China has also absorbed a large number of worldly cultures and scientific technology that were introduced into China along with Buddhism. At present, Buddhism has disappeared in India, consequently today only about 7.5 million

---

74 The Yuan Dynasty (1279-1368) was China's first foreign-led dynasty, in between the Chinese Song and Ming dynasties. It was established by Kublai Khan, leader of the vast Mongol Empire, and fell into internal rebellion after it lost touch with its Mongol roots.
75 In the Ming dynasty period between 1550-1570 attacks from Japanese pirates along the south-eastern coast caused widespread destruction, with the cities of Hangzhou and Ningbo set to the torch. When Japan invaded Korea in 1593, China stepped in to defend Korea and repulse the Japanese attack.

people practice this religion in India. However, it has been preserved and maintained in China and by many other countries of the East Asia and Southeast Asia. In the communications with foreign nations, Chinese have also learned how to use spices. When we see smoke curl up over temples, we can hardly think that it is a custom that originated from a foreign country.

Before the Europeans came to the East, Chinese have long played a dominating role in the exchanges between the East and the West and between China and foreign countries. After the great geographical discoveries, colonial rule, plunder and suppression came along the way, which has weakened the role played by China in the communications between the East and West. However, the Maritime Silk Road did not stop. Europeans "discovered" the Eastern world and Eastern products flourished into the world market in a large scale, such as silk, tea leaves and porcelain. Meanwhile, European industrial products were exported to the east world on a large scale. In this context, the opening up of the world navigation routes makes the communications between the East and the West enjoy rapid development. After the 1980s, China's development has entered a completely new era. The rapid growth of Chinese economy has enabled China occupy an increasingly important position in the global trade. Meanwhile, Chinese cultures and values have begun to exert increasingly stronger influences on the peoples of other countries. The exchanges between China and foreign countries in the new era are the continuation of communications between China and foreign countries in the past history. The Maritime Silk Road is not only a historical witness of friendly communications between people in Asian and African countries and between the East and the West, but also a channel for people in various peoples of the world to communicate with each other. In the past history, this path of friendly communications used to benefit the people living in many different countries. Thus we have good reasons to believe that it will be wider, more comprehensive and smoother in the future.

www.ingramcontent.com/pod-product-compliance
Lightning Source LLC
Chambersburg PA
CBHW020426130626
46549CB00001B/7